AND BOOK TRAINING PACKAGE AVAILABLE

ExamSim

Experience realistic, simulated exams on your own computer with The Osborne Media Group's interactive ExamSim software. This computer-based test engine offers both standard and adaptive test modes, knowledge, scenario-based, and product simulation questions like those found on the real exams. ExamSim also features review tools that help you verify your performance, assess what you know, and identify difficult exam topics—the exam also allows you to mark difficult or unanswered questions for further review.

Knowledge-based questions and case study-based questions present challenging material in a multiple-choice format. Answer treatments not only explain why the correct options are right, they also tell you why the incorrect answers were wrong.

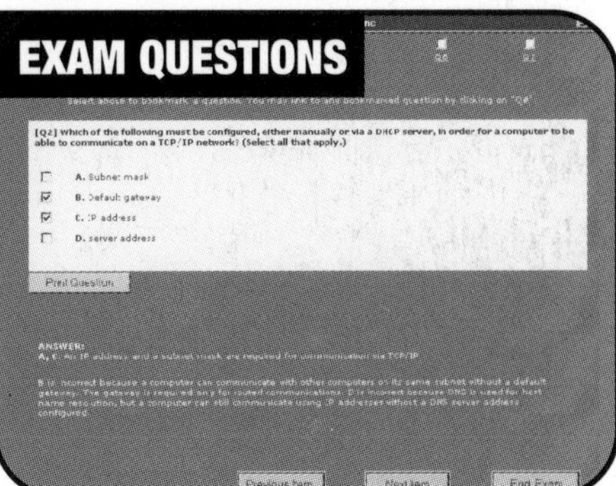

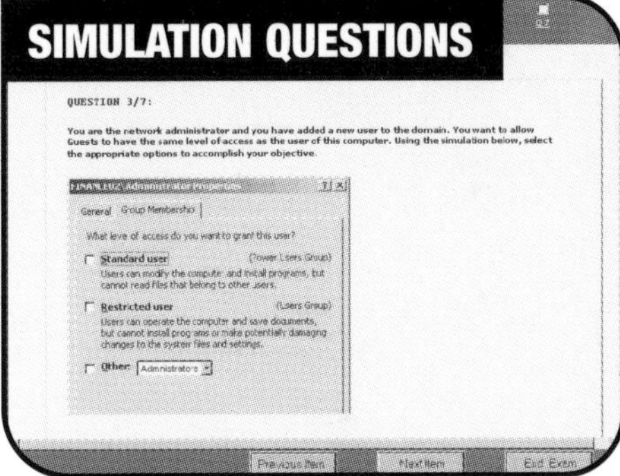

Realistic Windows 2000 product **simulation questions** test the skills you need to pass the exam—these questions look and feel like the simulation questions on the actual exam.

Additional CD-ROM Features

- Complete hyperlinked **e-book** for easy information access and self-paced study.

- **Bonus Self-Test Section**—over 330 knowledge, scenario, and lab-based exam questions in printable form.

System Requirements:

A PC running Microsoft® Internet Explorer version 5 or higher.

The **Score Report** provides an overall assessment of your exam performance as well as performance history.

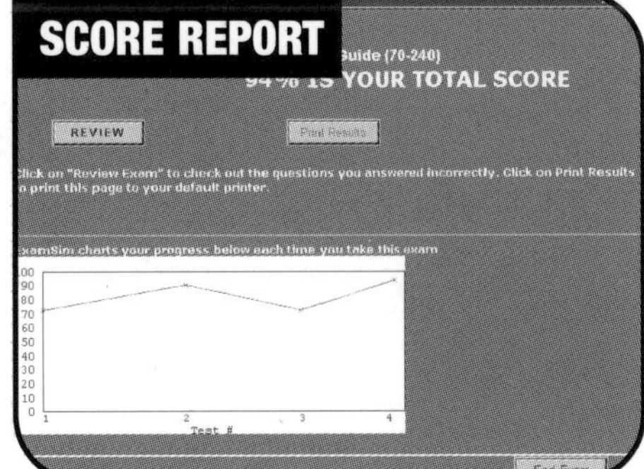

MCSE Windows® 2000 Accelerated Study Guide

(Exam 70-240)

Syngress Media, Inc.

Osborne McGraw-Hill

Berkeley New York St. Louis San Francisco Auckland Bogotá Hamburg London Madrid Mexico City Milan Montreal New Delhi Panama City Paris São Paulo Singapore Sydney Tokyo Toronto

Osborne/McGraw-Hill
2600 Tenth Street
Berkeley, California 94710
U.S.A.

For information on translations or book distributors outside the U.S.A., or to arrange bulk purchase discounts for sales promotions, premiums, or fund-raisers, please contact Osborne/**McGraw-Hill** at the above address.

MCSE Windows® 2000 Accelerated Study Guide (Exam 70-240)

1234567890 DOC DOC 0198765432109

Book p/n 0-07-212500-4 and CD p/n 0-07-212499-7
parts of ISBN 0-07-212500-4

Publisher
Brandon A. Nordin

Associate Publisher and Editor-in-Chief
Scott Rogers

Acquisitions Editor
Gareth Hancock

Associate Acquisitions Editor
Timothy Green

Project Editors
Jennifer Malnick
Julie Smalley

Editorial Assistant
Jessica Wilson

VP, Worldwide Business Development / Global Knowledge
Richard Kristof

Series Editors
Dr. Thomas W. Shinder
Debra Littlejohn Shinder

Technical Editors
Neil Ruston
Dr. Thomas W. Shinder
Ryan Sokolowski
James Truscott

Copy Editors
Beth Roberts
Adaya Henis
Darlene Bordwell

Proofreader
Susie Elkind

Indexer
Jack Lewis

Computer Designers
Lucie Erickson
Roberta Steele

Illustrators
Lyssa Sieben-Wald

Series Design
Roberta Steele

Cover Design
Greg Scott

Editorial Management
Syngress Media, Inc.

This book was published with Corel VENTURA™ Publisher.

FOREWORD

From Global Knowledge

At Global Knowledge we strive to support the multiplicity of learning styles required by our students to achieve success as technical professionals. In this series of books, it is our intention to offer the reader a valuable tool for successful completion of the MCSE Windows 2000 Certification exams.

As the world's largest IT training company, Global Knowledge is uniquely positioned to offer these books. The expertise gained each year from providing instructor-led training to hundreds of thousands of students worldwide has been captured in book form to enhance your learning experience. We hope that the quality of these books demonstrates our commitment to your lifelong learning success. Whether you choose to learn through the written word, computer-based training, Web delivery, or instructor-led training, Global Knowledge is committed to providing you the very best in each of those categories. For those of you who know Global Knowledge, or those of you who have just found us for the first time, our goal is to be your lifelong competency partner.

Thank you for the opportunity to serve you. We look forward to serving your needs again in the future.

Warmest regards,

Duncan Anderson

Duncan Anderson
President and Chief Operating Officer, Global Knowledge

The Global Knowledge Advantage

Global Knowledge has a global delivery system for its products and services. The company has 28 subsidiaries, and offers its programs through a total of 60+ locations. No other vendor can provide consistent services across a geographic area this large. Global Knowledge is the largest independent information technology education provider, offering programs on a variety of platforms. This enables our multi-platform and multi-national customers to obtain all of their programs from a single vendor. The company has developed the unique Competus™ Framework software tool and methodology which can quickly reconfigure courseware to the proficiency level of a student on an interactive basis. Combined with self-paced and on-line programs, this technology can reduce the time required for training by prescribing content in only the deficient skills areas. The company has fully automated every aspect of the education process, from registration and follow-up, to "just-in-time" production of courseware. Global Knowledge Network through its Enterprise Services Consultancy, can customize programs and products to suit the needs of an individual customer.

Global Knowledge Classroom Education Programs

The backbone of our delivery options is classroom-based education. Our modern, well-equipped facilities staffed with the finest instructors offer programs in a wide variety of information technology topics, many of which lead to professional certifications.

Custom Learning Solutions

This delivery option has been created for companies and governments that value customized learning solutions. For them, our consultancy-based approach of developing targeted education solutions is most effective at helping them meet specific objectives.

Self-Paced and Multimedia Products

This delivery option offers self-paced program titles in interactive CD-ROM, videotape and audio tape programs. In addition, we offer custom development of interactive multimedia courseware to customers and partners. Call us at 1-888-427-4228.

Electronic Delivery of Training

Our network-based training service delivers efficient competency-based, interactive training via the World Wide Web and organizational intranets. This leading-edge delivery option provides a custom learning path and "just-in-time" training for maximum convenience to students.

ARG

American Research Group (ARG), a wholly-owned subsidiary of Global Knowledge, one of the largest worldwide training partners of Cisco Systems, offers a wide range of internetworking, LAN/WAN, Bay Networks, FORE Systems, IBM, and UNIX courses. ARG offers hands on network training in both instructor-led classes and self-paced PC-based training.

Global Knowledge Courses Available

Network Fundamentals

- Understanding Computer Networks
- Telecommunications Fundamentals I
- Telecommunications Fundamentals II
- Understanding Networking Fundamentals
- Implementing Computer Telephony Integration
- Introduction to Voice Over IP
- Introduction to Wide Area Networking
- Cabling Voice and Data Networks
- Introduction to LAN/WAN protocols
- Virtual Private Networks
- ATM Essentials

Network Security & Management

- Troubleshooting TCP/IP Networks
- Network Management
- Network Troubleshooting
- IP Address Management
- Network Security Administration
- Web Security
- Implementing UNIX Security
- Managing Cisco Network Security
- Windows NT 4.0 Security

IT Professional Skills

- Project Management for IT Professionals
- Advanced Project Management for IT Professionals
- Survival Skills for the New IT Manager
- Making IT Teams Work

LAN/WAN Internetworking

- Frame Relay Internetworking
- Implementing T1/T3 Services
- Understanding Digital Subscriber Line (xDSL)
- Internetworking with Routers and Switches
- Advanced Routing and Switching
- Multi-Layer Switching and Wire-Speed Routing
- Internetworking with TCP/IP
- ATM Internetworking
- OSPF Design and Configuration
- Border Gateway Protocol (BGP) Configuration

Authorized Vendor Training

Cisco Systems

- Introduction to Cisco Router Configuration
- Advanced Cisco Router Configuration
- Installation and Maintenance of Cisco Routers
- Cisco Internetwork Troubleshooting
- Cisco Internetwork Design
- Cisco Routers and LAN Switches
- Catalyst 5000 Series Configuration
- Cisco LAN Switch Configuration
- Managing Cisco Switched Internetworks
- Configuring, Monitoring, and Troubleshooting Dial-Up Services
- Cisco AS5200 Installation and Configuration
- Cisco Campus ATM Solutions

Bay Networks

- Bay Networks Accelerated Router Configuration
- Bay Networks Advanced IP Routing
- Bay Networks Hub Connectivity
- Bay Networks Accelar 1xxx Installation and Basic Configuration
- Bay Networks Centillion Switching

FORE Systems

- FORE ATM Enterprise Core Products
- FORE ATM Enterprise Edge Products
- FORE ATM Theory
- FORE LAN Certification

Operating Systems & Programming

Microsoft

- Introduction to Windows NT
- Microsoft Networking Essentials
- Windows NT 4.0 Workstation
- Windows NT 4.0 Server
- Advanced Windows NT 4.0 Server
- Windows NT Networking with TCP/IP
- Introduction to Microsoft Web Tools
- Windows NT Troubleshooting
- Windows Registry Configuration

UNIX

- UNIX Level I
- UNIX Level II
- Essentials of UNIX and NT Integration

Programming

- Introduction to JavaScript
- Java Programming
- PERL Programming
- Advanced PERL with CGI for the Web

Web Site Management & Development

- Building a Web Site
- Web Site Management and Performance
- Web Development Fundamentals

High Speed Networking

- Essentials of Wide Area Networking
- Integrating ISDN
- Fiber Optic Network Design
- Fiber Optic Network Installation
- Migrating to High Performance Ethernet

DIGITAL UNIX

- UNIX Utilities and Commands
- DIGITAL UNIX v4.0 System Administration
- DIGITAL UNIX v4.0 (TCP/IP) Network Management
- AdvFS, LSM, and RAID Configuration and Management
- DIGITAL UNIX TruCluster Software Configuration and Management
- UNIX Shell Programming Featuring Kornshell
- DIGITAL UNIX v4.0 Security Management
- DIGITAL UNIX v4.0 Performance Management
- DIGITAL UNIX v4.0 Intervals Overview

DIGITAL OpenVMS

- OpenVMS Skills for Users
- OpenVMS System and Network Node Management I
- OpenVMS System and Network Node Management II
- OpenVMS System and Network Node Management III
- OpenVMS System and Network Node Operations
- OpenVMS for Programmers
- OpenVMS System Troubleshooting for Systems Managers
- Configuring and Managing Complex VMScluster Systems
- Utilizing OpenVMS Features from C
- OpenVMS Performance Management
- Managing DEC TCP/IP Services for OpenVMS
- Programming in C

Hardware Courses

- AlphaServer 1000/1000A Installation, Configuration and Maintenance
- AlphaServer 2100 Server Maintenance
- AlphaServer 4100, Troubleshooting Techniques and Problem Solving

ABOUT THE CONTRIBUTORS

About Syngress Media

Syngress Media creates books and software for Information Technology professionals seeking skill enhancement and career advancement. Its products are designed to comply with vendor and industry standard course curricula, and are optimized for certification exam preparation. You can contact Syngress via the Web at www.syngress.com.

Contributors

Carol Bailey (MCSE+I). Based in London, the UK, Carol has over ten years of experience in networking, and more than a dozen Microsoft exams to her name. She is a Senior Technical Consultant working for Metascybe Systems Ltd., a company that specializes in PC software communications, offering their own connectivity products in addition to project work and consultancy for a diverse customer base. Working for a Microsoft Solutions Provider has provided Carol with a wide range of technical opportunities. Her work includes supporting the in-house networking services as well as all aspects of external customer support and consultancy.

Pawan K. Bhardwaj (MCSE, MCP+I, CCNA) has spent 13 years in the IT industry working at various systems and network support levels. He has been involved in designing and implementing LAN and WAN solutions for several small and medium sized companies. He has also taught MCSE classes for a year in India before coming to the US.

He is currently working as a Windows NT Consultant with a turnkey solution provider in New Jersey. He can be reached at pawan_bhardwaj@hotmail.com.

Chris O. Broomes (MCSE, MCP+I, MCT, CCDA). A 1995 graduate of Temple University, Chris has more than 7 years of networking experience. He started his career as a consultant at Temple University and has worked with organizations such as Morgan, Lewis & Bockius, Temple University Dental School, and Dynamic Technologies, Inc. Currently, Chris is a Network Administrator in Philadelphia, PA, at EXE Technologies, Inc., a global provider of business-to-business e-fulfillment solutions. Chris resides in Lansdowne, PA with his wife, Keisha, and son, Jared Christopher.

Brian K. Doré (MCSE, MCT) is the Coordinator of the Microsoft Authorized Academic Training Program (AATP) at the University of Louisiana at Lafayette. In addition to managing the program, he also teaches Windows 2000 certification courses at the University. Prior to his current position, he worked nine years for the University Computing Support Services Department supporting a wide variety of computer systems. Brian had also spent five years as a software developer at a privately held company. Brian and his wife, Jennifer, live in Carencro, LA. He can be reached via e-mail at bkd@louisiana.edu.

Adam M. Doxtater (MCP, MCSE) is a computer consultant for RHI Consulting in Las Vegas, Nevada. Prior to RHI, he was employed as a Network Administrator/Senior Technician at Data Connections in Simi Valley, California. With extensive experience in both hardware and software, his expertise is well rounded and diverse. He can be reached for questions or comments at adoxtater@earthlink.net. Adam dedicates his writing to his loving wife and best friend, Cristy.

Jocelyn Fowke (MCSE, MCP+I) is a Technology Solutions Associate for Clarica Life Insurance Company. Her background includes experience as a network administrator and software developer. She recently joined the Internet Strategy Team at the Clarica Corporate Head Office in Waterloo, Ontario. Jocelyn enjoys the challenges and potentials available in the IT industry. Outside of IT she enjoys traveling, hiking, music, reading, and her new-found love, scuba diving! Jocelyn lives in Mississauga, Ontario, with her partner, Jason Tratch, who is employed as a Strategic Consultant for an Internet/E-Commerce company.

Damon Merchant (CCDP, CCNP, CCNA, CCDA, MCSE, MCP, CNE, and CNA) is the President of Corbus Systems, Inc., an information technology firm in Detroit, Michigan. He has about ten years experience in networking. Not only is he a network engineering guru, he is also a seasoned software developer. His most recent application, Touch-Tone Administrator for NT, allows network administrators to manage their Windows NT networks from a telephone. Damon also provides training and technical workshops for IT professionals. In his spare time, Damon enjoys playing basketball, ping pong, video games, weight lifting, and candlelight dinners with his wife, Lortensia.

More information about Damon Merchant and his software products can be found at his company's Web site, www.corbus-systems.com. Damon can be e-mailed at damon@corbus-systems.com.

Eriq Oliver Neale is a systems architect and technology strategist, consulting with IT organizations to plan and implement computing infrastructures based on current and forthcoming technologies. Eriq spends some of his spare time writing on topics such as Windows 2000, Macintosh, internet and music technologies, computer education, and anti-virus issues. He also enjoys writing music for guitar and keyboard. Eriq maintains a home in North Texas with his wife, seven cats, two dogs, and dozens of fish.

Chris Thi Nguyen is a research analyst with Killer Apps, Inc. and Assistant News Editor for *Windows 2000 Magazine*. His specialty areas are user interfaces, knowledge management applications, collaboration applications, and emergent networking technologies. He has written for *Windows 2000 Magazine* on real-time community applications, Total Cost of Ownership studies, and new network-based storage solutions. He received a bachelor's degree in Philosophy from Harvard University and is currently writing technology white papers for a variety of enterprises.

Robert A. Patton (MCDBA, MCSD, MCSE+I, MCP+I) is a software engineer specializing in Microsoft Windows DNA applications utilizing Interdev and Visual Basic with Windows 2000 and SQL Server. He is currently a Senior Applications Developer at PurchasingFirst.com in Dublin, Ohio and has done work for First Union National Bank, Corporate Strategic Services, the Midland Life Insurance Company and Sykes Enterprises. He attended the University of Chicago, where he studied Public Policy and played varsity football. Robert earned his Bachelor of Science degree in Software Engineering from The Ohio State University and is an avid fan of Buckeye athletics. He lives in Dublin, Ohio, with his wife, Jenny, and their sons, Michael and Alex.

Mary Robinson (MCP) is a Network Administrator at the University of Victoria in Victoria, British Columbia. Along with her colleagues, she has recently been spending much of her time with Windows 2000 Server and Professional in order to upgrade her organization's Windows NT network in the near future. Mary also works with Exchange 5.5 and BackOffice 4.5, and she has a Bachelor of Arts degree in Liberal Studies.

Michael Seamans (MCSE, MCP) is a Networking Consultant for Long and Associates in Rochester, NY, where he is currently contracting with the Eastman Kodak Company supporting their Digital Camera division. He has been a Microsoft Certified System Engineer for over three years and he has over ten years of IT management experience with the White House, United States Army, National Reconnaissance Office, and the Eastman Kodak Company. During his career, Michael has worked on many extensive and diverse projects involving the deployment of Windows NT and Windows 2000 networks, along with projects involving other technologies such as Lotus Notes and Microsoft Systems Management Server.

Michael lives with his wife, Denelle, and their four children, Joshua, Brittany, Mikaela, and Tyler. He can be reached at mseamans@rochester.rr.com, mseamans@kodak.com, or through his Web site at http://home.rochester.rr.com/seamans.

Debra Littlejohn Shinder (MCSE, MCP+I, MCT) is an instructor in the AATP program at Eastfield College, Dallas County Community College District, where she has taught since 1992. She is Webmaster for the cities of Seagoville and Sunnyvale, Texas, as well as the family Web site at www.shinder.net. She and her husband, Dr. Thomas W. Shinder, provide consulting and technical support services to Dallas area organizations. She is also the proud mom of a daughter, Kristen, who is currently serving in the U.S. Navy in Italy, and a son, Kris, who is a high school chess champion. Deb has been a writer for most her life and has published numerous articles in both technical and nontechnical fields. She can be contacted at deb@shinder.net.

Thomas W. Shinder, M.D. (MCSE, MCP+I, MCT) is a technology trainer and consultant in the Dallas-Ft. Worth metroplex. Dr. Shinder has consulted with major firms, including Xerox, Lucent Technologies, and FINA Oil, assisting in the development and implementation of IP-based communications strategies. Dr. Shinder attended medical school at the University of Illinois in Chicago, and trained in neurology at the Oregon Health Sciences Center in Portland, Oregon. His fascination with interneuronal communication ultimately melded with his interest in internetworking and led him to focus on systems engineering. Tom works passionately with his beloved wife, Deb Shinder, to design elegant and cost-efficient solutions for small and medium-sized businesses based on Windows NT/2000 platforms.

Holly C. Simard (MCSE, MCP+I, A+) is the Lab Network Administrator for the University of Victoria, Division of Continuing Studies. In addition to her work at UVIC and co-authoring technical books, Holly also delivers online instruction and enjoys learning new technologies. Holly loves hiking, running, playing the piano, and spending time with her "little sister." Holly lives in Victoria, British Columbia, with her husband, Hervey, who is a multimedia web designer, dogs Hubert and Hailey, and cats Daisy and Marigold.

Amy Thomson (A+, MOUS) is a Technical Writer for Core Networks, located in Halifax, Nova Scotia. The flagship product of Core Networks is CoreOS, a system designed to provide cable ISPs with tools to manage data-over-cable services. Amy also has a long history as an instructor in both computer software and A+ certification. She has more than 10 years of experience in dealing with computer hardware and applications and holds an Honors B.Sc. in Psychology. Amy lives in Bedford, Nova Scotia, with her husband, Jeff.

Cameron Wakefield (MCSD, MCP) a Senior Software Engineer and has passed 10 Microsoft Certification exams. He works at Computer Science Innovations, Inc. (http://www.csihq.com) in Melbourne, Florida, where he develops custom software solutions ranging from Satellite Communications to data mining applications. His development work spans a broad spectrum including Visual C++, Visual Basic, COM, ADO, ASP, Delphi, CORBA, UNIX and others. He does some work through his own business developing software for a Brazilian Hematology company and developing Business-to-Business Web applications. He also teaches Microsoft Certification courses for Herzing College (AATP) where he teaches in the MCSE and MCSD programs. His formal education was in Computer Science with a minor in Math at Rollins College. He lives in Rockledge, Florida, with his wife, Lorraine, and daughter, Rachel. He also plays racquetball competitively in central Florida. He can be contacted at cwakefield@csihq.com.

Martin Wuesthoff (MCSE, MCT, CNE, A+, N+) is a Certified Technical Trainer for New Horizons Computer Learning Center in Trumbull, Connecticut. He currently teaches the entire Windows 2000 track as well as the NT 4.0 track and A+ certification courses. A lifelong teacher, Martin's philosophy is that all of the knowledge in the world is of no use in the classroom if a teacher cannot clearly transfer it from his head to the students.

Martin and his wife Michelle are the proud parents of three children: Erik, 7, their biological son, and Noel, 2 and Emilee, 6 months, two beautiful girls adopted from Korea. He would like to dedicate his portion of this book to the girls' birth mothers, wherever they are, for having the courage and strength to give their daughters a better life and for blessing his family as a result.

Technical Editors

Stace Cunningham (CMISS, CCNA, MCSE, CLSE, COS/2E, CLSI, COS/2I, CLSA, MCPS, A+) operates SDC Consulting in Biloxi, MS. He has assisted several clients, including a casino, in the development and implementation of their networks, which range in size from 20 nodes to over 12,000 nodes. Stace has been heavily involved in technology for more than 14 years. During that time he has participated as a Technical Contributor for the IIS 3.0 exam, SMS 1.2 exam, Proxy Server 1.0 exam, Exchange Server 5.0 and 5.5 exams, Proxy Server 2.0 exam, IIS 4.0 exam, IEAK exam, and the revised Windows 95 exam. Stace was an active contributor to The SANS Institute booklet "Windows NT Security Step by Step." In addition, he has co-authored 18 books published by Osborne/McGraw-Hill, Microsoft Press, and Syngress Media. He has also performed as technical editor for 8 books published by Osborne/McGraw-Hill, Microsoft Press, and Syngress Media. Recently, an article written by Stace appeared in Internet Security Advisor magazine. His wife, Martha, and daughter, Marissa, are very supportive of the time he spends with the computers, routers, and firewalls in his "lab." Without their love and support he would not be able to accomplish the goals he has set for himself.

Brian M. Collins (MCNE, MCSE, MCT, CTT) is a Technical Trainer for Network Appliance, Inc., in Sunnyvale, CA. A Technology Industry veteran of 20 years, his employment background includes US Navy Electronics, Semiconductor Industry Robotics, Software Development in several languages, and System Administration. Brian's hobbies include hiking, operating systems, and coding. When not traveling the world training for NetApp, Brian can be found in the Santa Cruz Mountains of California, 30 miles from the center of Silicon Valley.

Neil Ruston (MCSE, CNE) is currently working for Perot Systems at a large Swiss bank, in London, UK. Originally, Neil designed and implemented Netware systems, but more recently, has focused on Windows NT and Windows 2000 network design. Neil participated in the Microsoft sponsored Joint Deployment Programme (JDP), which involved the design and implementation of a large, global Active Directory. He dedicates this book to his wife, who regularly endured his late nights at the PC.

Thomas W. Shinder, M.D. (MCSE, MCP+I, MCT) is a technology trainer and consultant in the Dallas-Ft. Worth metroplex. Dr. Shinder has consulted with major firms, including Xerox, Lucent Technologies, and FINA Oil, assisting in the development and implementation of IP-based communications strategies. Dr. Shinder attended medical school at the University of Illinois in Chicago, and trained in neurology at the Oregon Health Sciences Center in Portland, Oregon. His fascination with interneuronal communication ultimately melded with his interest in internetworking and led him to focus on systems engineering. Tom works passionately with his beloved wife, Deb Shinder, to design elegant and cost-efficient solutions for small and medium-sized businesses based on Windows NT/2000 platforms.

Ryan Neil Sokolowski (MCSE, CCNA, CCDA, CNE, CNA, VCE) is currently a Senior Technical Analyst in the Design and Engineering group at a Fortune 100 company in Minneapolis, MN. He also operates Onyx Consulting, an independent consulting company. Sokolowski is a participant in the Internet Engineering Task Force (IETF) and a member of the Institute of Electrical and Electronics Engineers (IEEE), the SANS Institute, the Association of Windows NT Systems Professionals and NetWare Users International. With a true love of technology and a strong background in design, implementation, engineering and consulting services, Sokolowski's specialties include network operating systems, directory services and Cisco networking environments. He dedicates this book to his parents, who taught him everything they knew…and how to learn the rest for himself.

James Truscott (MCSE, MCP+I) is an instructor in the MCSE program at Eastfield College and the Dallas County Community College District. He is also Senior Instructor for the Cowell Corporation and, is teaching the Windows 2000 track for CLC Corporation in Dallas, Texas.

He is the Webmaster for Cowell Corporation in Richardson, Texas, and does consulting services for several Dallas-based businesses. His passion for computers started back in the 1960's when he was a programmer for Bell Telephone. One of his current projects includes developing Web sites for his students.

Series Editors

Thomas W. Shinder, M.D. (MCSE, MCP+I, MCT) is a technology trainer and consultant in the Dallas-Ft. Worth metroplex. Dr. Shinder has consulted with major firms, including Xerox, Lucent Technologies, and FINA Oil, assisting in the development and implementation of IP-based communications strategies. Dr. Shinder attended medical school at the University of Illinois in Chicago, and trained in neurology at the Oregon Health Sciences Center in Portland, Oregon. His fascination with interneuronal communication ultimately melded with his interest in internetworking and led him to focus on systems engineering. Tom works passionately with his beloved wife, Deb Shinder, to design elegant and cost-efficient solutions for small and medium-sized businesses based on Windows NT/2000 platforms.

Debra Littlejohn Shinder (MCSE, MCP+I, MCT) is an instructor in the AATP program at Eastfield College, Dallas County Community College District, where she has taught since 1992. She is Webmaster for the cities of Seagoville and Sunnyvale, Texas, as well as the family Web site at www.shinder.net. She and her husband, Dr. Thomas W. Shinder, provide consulting and technical support services to Dallas area organizations. She is also the proud mom of a daughter, Kristen, who is currently serving in the U.S. Navy in Italy, and a son, Kris, who is a high school chess champion. Deb has been a writer for most her life, and has published numerous articles in both technical and nontechnical fields. She can be contacted at deb@shinder.net.

ACKNOWLEDGMENTS

We would like to thank the following people:

- Richard Kristof of Global Knowledge for championing the series and providing access to some great people and information.
- All the incredibly hard-working folks at Osborne/McGraw-Hill: Brandon Nordin, Scott Rogers, Gareth Hancock, and Tim Green for their help in launching a great series and being solid team players. In addition, Tara Davis and Jenny Malnick for their help in fine-tuning the book.
- Monica Kilwine at Microsoft Corp., for being patient and diligent in answering all our questions.

CONTENTS

Custom Corporate Network Training

Train on Cutting Edge Technology We can bring the best in skill-based training to your facility to create a real-world hands-on training experience. Global Knowledge has invested millions of dollars in network hardware and software to train our students on the same equipment they will work with on the job. Our relationships with vendors allow us to incorporate the latest equipment and platforms into your on-site labs.

Maximize Your Training Budget Global Knowledge provides experienced instructors, comprehensive course materials, and all the networking equipment needed to deliver high quality training. You provide the students; we provide the knowledge.

Avoid Travel Expenses On-site courses allow you to schedule technical training at your convenience, saving time, expense, and the opportunity cost of travel away from the workplace.

Discuss Confidential Topics Private on-site training permits the open discussion of sensitive issues such as security, access, and network design. We can work with your existing network's proprietary files while demonstrating the latest technologies.

Customize Course Content Global Knowledge can tailor your courses to include the technologies and the topics which have the greatest impact on your business. We can complement your internal training efforts or provide a total solution to your training needs.

Corporate Pass The Corporate Pass Discount Program rewards our best network training customers with preferred pricing on public courses, discounts on multimedia training packages, and an array of career planning services.

Global Knowledge Training Lifecycle Supporting the Dynamic and Specialized Training Requirements of Information Technology Professionals

- Define Profile
- Assess Skills
- Design Training
- Deliver Training
- Test Knowledge
- Update Profile
- Use New Skills

College Credit Recommendation Program The American Council on Education's CREDIT program recommends 53 Global Knowledge courses for college credit. Now our network training can help you earn your college degree while you learn the technical skills needed for your job. When you attend an ACE-certified Global Knowledge course and pass the associated exam, you earn college credit recommendations for that course. Global Knowledge can establish a transcript record for you with ACE, which you can use to gain credit at a college or as a written record of your professional training that you can attach to your resume.

Registration Information

COURSE FEE: The fee covers course tuition, refreshments, and all course materials. Any parking expenses that may be incurred are not included. Payment or government training form must be received six business days prior to the course date. We will also accept Visa/ MasterCard and American Express. For non-U.S. credit card users, charges will be in U.S. funds and will be converted by your credit card company. Checks drawn on Canadian banks in Canadian funds are acceptable.

COURSE SCHEDULE: Registration is at 8:00 a.m. on the first day. The program begins at 8:30 a.m. and concludes at 4:30 p.m. each day.

CANCELLATION POLICY: Cancellation and full refund will be allowed if written cancellation is received in our office at least six business days prior to the course start date. Registrants who do not attend the course or do not cancel more than six business days in advance are responsible for the full registration fee; you may transfer to a later date provided the course fee has been paid in full. Substitutions may be made at any time. If Global Knowledge must cancel a course for any reason, liability is limited to the registration fee only.

GLOBAL KNOWLEDGE: Global Knowledge programs are developed and presented by industry professionals with "real-world" experience. Designed to help professionals meet today's interconnectivity and interoperability challenges, most of our programs feature hands-on labs that incorporate state-of-the-art communication components and equipment.

ON-SITE TEAM TRAINING: Bring Global Knowledge's powerful training programs to your company. At Global Knowledge, we will custom design courses to meet your specific network requirements. Call 1 (919) 461-8686 for more information.

YOUR GUARANTEE: Global Knowledge believes its courses offer the best possible training in this field. If during the first day you are not satisfied and wish to withdraw from the course, simply notify the instructor, return all course materials, and receive a 100% refund.

In the US:

CALL: 1 (888) 762-4442

FAX: 1 (919) 469-7070

VISIT OUR WEBSITE:

www.globalknowledge.com

MAIL CHECK AND THIS FORM TO:

Global Knowledge
Suite 200
114 Edinburgh South
P.O. Box 1187
Cary, NC 27512

In Canada:

CALL: 1 (800) 465-2226

FAX: 1 (613) 567-3899

VISIT OUR WEBSITE:

www.globalknowledge.com.ca

MAIL CHECK AND THIS FORM TO:

Global Knowledge
Suite 1601
393 University Ave.
Toronto, ON M5G 1E6

REGISTRATION INFORMATION:

Course title ______________________________

Course location ____________________ Course date __________

Name/title ____________________ Company __________

Name/title ____________________ Company __________

Name/title ____________________ Company __________

Address ____________ Telephone ________ Fax __________

City ____________ State/Province ________ Zip/Postal Code __________

Credit card ________ Card # ____________ Expiration date __________

Signature ______________________________

PREFACE

This book's primary objective is to help you prepare for the MCSE Windows 2000 Accelerated exam under the new Windows 2000 certification track. As the Microsoft program transitions from Windows NT 4.0, it will become increasingly important that current and aspiring IT professionals have multiple resources available to assist them in increasing their knowledge and building their skills.

At the time of publication, all the exam objectives have been posted on the Microsoft Web site (see each of the Core Four exam requirements) and the beta exam process has been completed. Microsoft has announced its commitment to measuring real-world skills. This book is designed with that premise in mind; its authors have practical experience in the field, using the Windows 2000 operating systems in hands-on situations and have followed the development of the product since early beta versions.

Because the focus of the exams is on application and understanding, as opposed to memorization of facts, no book by itself can fully prepare you to obtain a passing score. It is essential that you work with the software to enhance your proficiency. Toward that end, this book includes many practical step-by-step exercises in each chapter that are designed to give you hands-on practice as well as guide you in truly learning Microsoft Windows 2000, not just learning *about* it.

In This Book

This book is organized in such a way as to serve as an in-depth review for the MCSE Windows 2000 Accelerated exam for experienced Windows NT professionals. Each chapter covers a major aspect of the exam, with an emphasis on the "why" as well as the "how to" of working with and supporting Windows 2000 as a network administrator or engineer.

On the CD

The CD-ROM contains the CertTrainer software. CertTrainer comes complete with ExamSim, Skill Assessment tests, CertCam movie clips, and the e-book (electronic version of the book). CertTrainer is easy to install on any Windows 98/NT/2000 computer and must be installed to access these features. You may, however, browse the e-book direct from the CD without installation. For more information on the CD-ROM, please see Appendix A.

In Every Chapter

We've created a set of chapter components that call your attention to important items, reinforce important points, and provide helpful exam-taking hints. Take a look at what you'll find in every chapter:

- Every chapter begins with the **Certification Objectives**—what you need to know in order to pass the section on the exam dealing with the chapter topic. The Objective headings identify the objectives within the chapter, so you'll always know an objective when you see it!

- **Exam Watch** notes call attention to information about, and potential pitfalls in, the exam. These helpful hints are written by authors who have taken the exams and received their certification—who better to tell you what to worry about? They know what you're about to go through!
- **Practice Exercises** are interspersed throughout the chapters. These are step-by-step exercises that allow you to get the hands-on experience you need in order to pass the exams. They help you master skills that are likely to be an area of focus on the exam. Don't just read through the exercises; they are hands-on practice that you should be comfortable completing. Learning by doing is an effective way to increase your competency with a product. The practical exercises will be very helpful for any simulation exercises you may encounter on the MCSE Windows 2000 Accelerated exam.

- The **CertCam** icon that appears in many of the exercises indicates that the exercise is presented in .avi format on the accompanying CD-ROM. These .avi clips walk you step-by-step through various system configurations and are narrated by Thomas W. Shinder, M.D., MCSE.
- **On The Job** notes describe the issues that come up most often in real-world settings. They provide a valuable perspective on certification- and product-related topics. They point out common mistakes and address questions that have arisen from on the job discussions and experience.
- **From The Classroom** sidebars describe the issues that come up most often in the training classroom setting. These sidebars highlight some of the most common and confusing problems that students encounter when taking a live Windows 2000 training course. You can get a leg up on those difficult to understand subjects by focusing extra attention on these sidebars.
- **Scenario and Solutions** sections lay out potential problems and solutions in a quick-to-read format:
- The **Certification Summary** is a succinct review of the chapter and a restatement of salient points regarding the exam.
- ✓ The **Two-Minute Drill** at the end of every chapter is a checklist of the main points of the chapter. It can be used for last-minute review.

SCENARIO & SOLUTION	
Is Active Directory scalable?	Yes! Unlike the Windows NT security database, which is limited to approximately 40,000 objects, Active Directory supports literally millions of objects.
Is Active Directory compatible with other LDAP directory services?	Yes! Active Directory can share information with other directory services that support LDAP versions 2 and 3, such as Novell's NDS.

The Global Knowledge Web Site

Check out the Web site. Global Knowledge invites you to become an active member of the Access Global Web site. This site is an online mall and an information repository that you'll find invaluable. You can access many types of products to assist you in your preparation for the exams, and you'll be able to participate in forums, online discussions, and threaded discussions. No other book brings you unlimited access to such a resource. You'll find more information about this site in Appendix B.

Some Pointers

Once you've finished reading this book, set aside some time to do a thorough review. You might want to return to the book several times and make use of all the methods it offers for reviewing the material:

1. *Re-read all the Two-Minute Drills*, or have someone quiz you. You also can use the drills as a way to do a quick cram before the exam. You might want to make some flash cards out of 3 x 5 index cards that have the Two-Minute Drill material on them.
2. *Reread all the Exam Watch notes.* Remember that these notes are written by authors who have taken the exam and passed. They know what you should expect—and what you should be on the lookout for.
3. *Review all the S&S sections* for quick problem solving.
4. *Review the Multiple-Choice Questions on the CD-ROM.* Reviewing the questions on the CD-ROM right after you've read each chapter is a good idea, because the questions help reinforce what you've just learned. However, it's an even better idea to go back later and do all the questions in one sitting. Pretend that you're taking the live exam. (When you go through the questions the first time, you should mark your answers

on a separate piece of paper. That way, you can run through the questions as many times as you need to until you feel comfortable with the material.)

5. *Complete the Exercises.* Did you do the exercises when you read through each chapter? If not, do them! These exercises are designed to cover exam topics, and there's no better way to get to know this material than by practicing. Be sure you understand why you are performing each step in each exercise. If there is something you are not clear on, re-read that section in the chapter.

INTRODUCTION

MCSE Certification

This book is designed to help you pass the MCSE Windows 2000 Accelerated exam. We wrote this book to give you a complete and incisive review of all the important topics that are targeted for the exam. The information contained here will provide you with the required foundation of knowledge that will not only allow you to succeed in passing the MCSE Windows 2000 Accelerated exam, but will also make you a better Microsoft Certified Systems Engineer.

The nature of the Information Technology industry is changing rapidly, and the requirements and specifications for certification can change just as quickly without notice. Microsoft expects you to regularly visit their Website at **http://www.microsoft.com/mcp/certstep/mcse.htm** to get the most up to date information on the entire MCSE program.

Windows 2000 Certification Track

Core Exams		
Candidates Who Have Not Already Passed Windows NT 4.0 Exams **All 4 of the Following Core Exams Required:**	**OR**	**Candidates Who Have Passed 3 Windows NT 4.0 Exams (Exams 70-067, 70-068, and 70-073)** **Instead of the 4 Core Exams on Left, You May Take:**
Exam 70-210: Installing, Configuring and Administering Microsoft® Windows® 2000 Professional		**Exam 70-240**: Microsoft® Windows® 2000 Accelerated Exam for MCPs Certified on Microsoft® Windows NT® 4.0. The accelerated exam will be available until December 31, 2001. It covers the core competencies of exams **70-210, 70-215, 70-216, and 70-217.**
Exam 70-215: Installing, Configuring and Administering Microsoft® Windows® 2000 Server		
Exam 70-216: Implementing and Administering a Microsoft® Windows® 2000 Network Infrastructure		

Exam 70-217: Implementing and Administering a Microsoft® Windows® 2000 Directory Services Infrastructure
PLUS – All Candidates – 1 of the Following Core Exams Required:
***Exam 70-219**: Designing a Microsoft® Windows® 2000 Directory Services Infrastructure
***Exam 70-220**: Designing Security for a Microsoft® Windows® 2000 Network
***Exam 70-221**: Designing a Microsoft® Windows® 2000 Network Infrastructure
PLUS – All Candidates – 2 Elective Exams Required:
Any current MCSE electives when the Windows 2000 exams listed above are released in their live versions. **Electives scheduled for retirement will not be considered current.** Selected third-party certifications that focus on interoperability will be accepted as an alternative to one elective exam.
***Exam 70-219**: Designing a Microsoft® Windows® 2000 Directory Services Infrastructure
***Exam 70-220**: Designing Security for a Microsoft® Windows® 2000 Network
***Exam 70-221**: Designing a Microsoft® Windows® 2000 Network Infrastructure
Exam 70-222: Upgrading from Microsoft® Windows® NT 4.0 to Microsoft® Windows® 2000
*Note that some of the Windows 2000 core exams can be used as elective exams as well. An exam that is used to meet the design requirement cannot also count as an elective. Each exam can only be counted once in the Windows 2000 Certification.

Let's look at two scenarios. The first applies to the person who has already taken the Windows NT 4.0 Server (70-067), Windows NT 4.0 Workstation (70-073), and Windows NT 4.0 Server in the Enterprise (70-068) exams. The second scenario covers the situation of the person who has not completed those Windows NT 4.0 exams and would like to concentrate ONLY on Windows 2000.

In the first scenario, you have the option of taking all four Windows 2000 core exams, or you can take the Windows 2000 Accelerated Exam for MCPs if you have already passed exams 70-067, 70-068, and 70-073. (Note that you must have passed those specific exams to qualify for the Accelerated Exam; if you have fulfilled your NT 4.0 MCSE requirements by passing the Windows 95 or Windows 98 exam as your client operating system option, and did not take the NT Workstation Exam, you don't qualify.)

After completing the core requirements, either by passing the four core exams or the one Accelerated exam, you must pass a "design" exam. The design exams include Designing a Microsoft Windows 2000 Directory Services Infrastructure (70-219), Designing Security for Microsoft Windows 2000 Network (70-220), and Designing a Microsoft Windows 2000 Network Infrastructure (70-221). One design exam is REQUIRED.

You also must pass two exams from the list of electives. However, you cannot use the design exam that you took as an elective. Each exam can only count once toward certification. This includes any of the MCSE electives that are current when the Windows 2000 exams are released. In summary, you would take a total of at least two more exams, the upgrade exam and the design exam. Any additional exams would be dependent on which electives the candidate may have already completed.

In the second scenario, if you have not completed, and do not plan to complete the Core Windows NT 4.0 exams, you must pass the four core Windows 2000 exams, one design exam, and two elective exams. Again, no exam can be counted twice. In this case, you must pass a total of seven exams to obtain the Windows 2000 MCSE certification.

How to Take a Microsoft Certification Exam

If you have taken a Microsoft Certification exam before, we have some good news and some bad news. The good news is that the new testing formats will be a true measure of your ability and knowledge. Microsoft has "raised the bar" for its Windows 2000 certification exams. If you are an expert in the Windows 2000 operating system, and can troubleshoot and engineer efficient, cost effective solutions using Windows 2000, you will have no difficulty with the new exams.

The bad news is that if you have used resources such as "brain-dumps," boot-camps, or exam specific practice tests as your only method of test preparation, you will undoubtedly fail your Windows 2000 exams. The new Windows 2000 MCSE exams will test your knowledge, and your ability to apply that knowledge in more sophisticated and accurate ways than was expected for the MCSE exams for Windows NT 4.0.

In the Windows 2000 exams, Microsoft will use a variety of testing formats which include product simulations, adaptive testing, drag-and-drop matching, and possibly even "fill in the blank" questions (also called "free response" questions). The test-taking process will measure the examinee's fundamental knowledge of the Windows 2000 operating system rather than the ability to memorize a few facts and then answer a few simple multiple-choice questions.

In addition, the "pool" of questions for each exam will significantly increase. The greater number of questions combined with the adaptive testing techniques will enhance the validity and security of the certification process.

We will begin by looking at the purpose, focus, and structure of Microsoft certification tests, and examine the effect that these factors have on the kinds of questions you will face on your certification exams. We will define the structure of exam questions and investigate some common formats. Next, we will present a strategy for answering these questions. Finally, we will give some specific guidelines on what you should do on the day of your test.

Why Vendor Certification?

The Microsoft Certified Professional program, like the certification programs from Cisco, Novell, Oracle, and other software vendors, is maintained for the ultimate purpose of increasing the corporation's profits. A successful vendor certification program accomplishes this goal by helping to create a pool of experts in a company's software and by "branding" these experts so companies using the software can identify them.

We know that vendor certification has become increasingly popular in the last few years because it helps employers find qualified workers and because it helps software vendors like Microsoft sell their products. But why vendor certification rather than a more traditional approach like a college degree in computer science? A college education is a broadening and enriching experience, but a degree in computer science does not prepare students for most jobs in the IT industry.

A common truism in our business states, "If you are out of the IT industry for three years and want to return, you have to start over." The problem, of course, is *timeliness*; if a first-year student learns about a specific computer program, it probably will no longer be in wide use when he or she graduates. Although some colleges are trying to integrate Microsoft certification into their curriculum, the problem is not really a flaw in higher education, but a characteristic of the IT industry. Computer software is changing so rapidly that a four-year college just can't keep up.

A marked characteristic of the Microsoft certification program is an emphasis on performing specific job tasks rather than merely gathering knowledge. It may come as a shock, but most potential employers do not care how much you know about the theory of operating systems, networking, or database design. As one IT manager put it, "I don't really care what my employees know about the theory of our network. We don't need someone to sit at a desk and think about it. We need people who can actually do something to make it work better."

You should not think that this attitude is some kind of anti-intellectual revolt against "book learning." Knowledge is a necessary prerequisite, but it is not enough. More than one company has hired a computer science graduate as a network administrator, only to learn that the new employee has no idea how to add users, assign permissions, or perform the other day-to-day tasks necessary to maintain a network. This brings us to the second major characteristic of Microsoft certification that affects the questions you must be prepared to answer. In addition to timeliness, Microsoft certification is also job-task oriented.

The timeliness of Microsoft's certification program is obvious and is inherent in the fact that you will be tested on current versions of software in wide use today. The job task orientation of Microsoft certification is almost as obvious, but testing real-world job skills using a computer-based test is not easy.

Computerized Testing

Considering the popularity of Microsoft certification, and the fact that certification candidates are spread around the world, the only practical way to administer tests for the certification program is through Sylvan Prometric or Vue testing centers, which operate internationally. Sylvan Prometric and Vue provide proctor testing services for Microsoft, Oracle, Novell, Lotus, and the A+ computer technician certification. Although the IT industry accounts for much of Sylvan's revenue, the company provides services for a number of other businesses and organizations, such as FAA pre-flight pilot tests. Historically, several hundred questions were developed for a new Microsoft certification exam. The Windows 2000 MCSE exam pool is expected to contain hundreds of new questions. Microsoft is aware that many new MCSE candidates have been able to access information on test questions via the Internet or other resources. The company is very concerned about maintaining the MCSE as a "premium" certification. The significant increase in the number of test questions, together with stronger enforcement of the NDA (Non-disclosure agreement) will ensure that a higher standard for certification is attained.

Microsoft treats the test-building process very seriously. Test questions are first reviewed by a number of subject matter experts for technical accuracy and then are presented in a beta test. Taking the beta test may require several hours, due to the large number of questions. After a few weeks, Microsoft Certification uses the statistical feedback from Sylvan to check the performance of the beta questions. The beta test group for the Windows 2000 certification series included MCTs, MCSEs, and members of Microsoft's rapid deployment partners groups. Because the exams will be normalized based on this population, you can be sure that the passing scores will be difficult to achieve without detailed product knowledge.

Questions are discarded if most test takers get them right (too easy) or wrong (too difficult), and a number of other statistical measures are taken of each question. Although the scope of our discussion precludes a rigorous treatment of question analysis, you should be aware that Microsoft and other vendors spend a great deal of time and effort making sure their exam questions are valid.

The questions that survive statistical analysis form the pool of questions for the final certification exam.

Test Structure

The questions in a Microsoft form test will not be equally weighted. From what we can tell at the present time, different questions are given a value based on the level of difficulty. You will get more credit for getting a difficult question correct, than if you got an easy one correct. Because the questions are weighted differently, and because the exams will likely use the adapter method of testing, your score will not bear any relationship to how many questions you answered correctly.

Microsoft has implemented *adaptive* testing. When an adaptive test begins, the candidate is first given a level three question. If it is answered correctly, a question from the next higher level is presented, and an incorrect response results in a question from the next lower level. When 15 to 20 questions have been answered in this manner, the scoring algorithm is able to predict, with a high degree of statistical certainty, whether the candidate would pass or fail if all the questions in the form were answered. When the required degree of certainty is attained, the test ends and the candidate receives a pass/fail grade.

Adaptive testing has some definite advantages for everyone involved in the certification process. Adaptive tests allow Sylvan Prometric or Vue to deliver more tests with the same resources, as certification candidates often are in and out in 30 minutes or less. For candidates, the "fatigue factor" is reduced due to the shortened testing time. For Microsoft, adaptive testing means that fewer test questions are exposed to each candidate, and this can enhance the security, and therefore the overall validity, of certification tests.

One possible problem you may have with adaptive testing is that you are not allowed to mark and revisit questions. Since the adaptive algorithm is interactive, and all questions but the first are selected on the basis of your response to the previous question, it is not possible to skip a particular question or change an answer.

Question Types

Computerized test questions can be presented in a number of ways. Some of the possible formats are used on Microsoft certification exam and some are not.

True/False

We are all familiar with True/False questions, but because of the inherent 50 percent chance of guessing the correct answer, you will not see questions of this type on Microsoft certification exams.

Multiple Choice

The majority of Microsoft certification questions are in the multiple-choice format, with either a single correct answer or multiple correct answers. One interesting variation on multiple-choice questions with multiple correct answers is whether or not the candidate is told how many answers are correct.

EXAMPLE:

Which two files can be altered to configure the MS-DOS environment? (Choose two.)

Or

Which files can be altered to configure the MS-DOS environment? (Choose all that apply.)

You may see both variations on Microsoft certification exams, but the trend seems to be toward the first type, where candidates are told explicitly how many answers are correct. Questions of the "choose all that apply" variety are more difficult and can be merely confusing.

Graphical Questions

One or more graphical elements are sometimes used as exhibits to help present or clarify an exam question. These elements may take the form of a network diagram, pictures of networking components, or screen shots from the software on which you are being tested. It is often easier to present the concepts required for a complex performance-based scenario with a graphic than with words.

Test questions known as *hotspots* actually incorporate graphics as part of the answer. These questions ask the certification candidate to click on a location or graphical element to answer the question. For example, you might be shown the diagram of a network and asked to click on an appropriate location for a router. The answer is correct if the candidate clicks within the *hotspot* that defines the correct location.

Free Response Questions

Another kind of question you sometimes see on Microsoft certification exams requires a *free response* or type-in answer. An example of this type of question might present a TCP/IP network scenario and ask the candidate to calculate and enter the correct subnet mask in dotted decimal notation.

Simulation Questions

Simulation questions provide a method for Microsoft to test how familiar the test taker is with the actual product interface and the candidate's ability to quickly implement a task using the interface. These questions will present an actual Windows 2000 interface that you must work with to solve a problem or implement a solution. If you are familiar with the product, you will be able to answer these questions quickly, and they will be the easiest questions on the exam. However, if you are not accustomed to working with Windows 2000, these questions will be difficult for you to answer. This is why actual hands-on practice with Windows 2000 is so important!

Knowledge-Based and Performance-Based Questions

Microsoft Certification develops a blueprint for each Microsoft certification exam with input from subject matter experts. This blueprint defines the content areas and objectives for each test, and each test question is created to test a specific objective. The basic information from the examination blueprint can be found on Microsoft's Web site in the Exam Prep Guide for each test.

Psychometricians (psychologists who specialize in designing and analyzing tests) categorize test questions as knowledge-based or performance-based. As the names imply, knowledge-based questions are designed to test knowledge, while performance-based questions are designed to test performance.

Some objectives demand a knowledge-based question. For example, objectives that use verbs like *list* and *identify* tend to test only what you know, not what you can do.

EXAMPLE:

Objective: Identify the MS-DOS configuration files.

Which two files can be altered to configure the MS-DOS environment? (Choose two.)

A. COMMAND.COM

B. AUTOEXEC.BAT

C. IO.SYS

D. CONFIG.SYS

Correct answers: B, D

Other objectives use action verbs like *install*, *configure*, and *troubleshoot* to define job tasks. These objectives can often be tested with either a knowledge-based question or a performance-based question.

EXAMPLE:

Objective: Configure an MS-DOS installation appropriately using the PATH statement in AUTOEXEC.BAT.

Knowledge-based question:

What is the correct syntax to set a path to the D: directory in AUTOEXEC.BAT?

A. SET PATH EQUAL TO D:

B. PATH D:

C. SETPATH D:

D. D:EQUALS PATH

Correct answer: B

Performance-based question:

Your company uses several DOS accounting applications that access a group of common utility programs. What is the best strategy for configuring the computers in the accounting department so that the accounting applications will always be able to access the utility programs?

A. Store all the utilities on a single floppy disk and make a copy of the disk for each computer in the accounting department.

B. Copy all the utilities to a directory on the C: drive of each computer in the accounting department and add a PATH statement pointing to this directory in the AUTOEXEC.BAT files.

C. Copy all the utilities to all application directories on each computer in the accounting department.

D. Place all the utilities in the C: directory on each computer, because the C: directory is automatically included in the PATH statement when AUTOEXEC.BAT is executed.

Correct answer: B

Even in this simple example, the superiority of the performance-based question is obvious. Whereas the knowledge-based question asks for a single fact, the performance-based question presents a real-life situation and requires that you make a decision based on this scenario. Thus, performance-based questions give more bang (validity) for the test author's buck (individual question).

Testing Job Performance

We have said that Microsoft certification focuses on timeliness and the ability to perform job tasks. We have also introduced the concept of performance-based questions, but even performance-based multiple-choice questions do not really measure performance. Another strategy is needed to test job skills.

Given unlimited resources, it is not difficult to test job skills. In an ideal world, Microsoft would fly MCP candidates to Redmond, place them in a controlled environment with a team of experts, and ask them to plan, install, maintain, and troubleshoot a Windows network. In a few days at most, the experts could reach a valid decision as to whether each candidate should or should not be granted MCDBA or MCSE status. Needless to say, this is not likely to happen.

Closer to reality, another way to test performance is by using the actual software and creating a testing program to present tasks and automatically grade a candidate's performance when the tasks are completed. This *cooperative* approach would be practical in some testing situations, but the same test that is presented to MCP candidates in Boston must also be available in Bahrain and Botswana. The most workable solution for measuring performance in today's testing environment is a *simulation* program. When the program is launched during a test, the candidate sees a simulation of the actual software that looks, and behaves, just like the real thing. When the testing software presents a task, the simulation program is launched and the candidate performs the required task. The testing software then grades the candidate's performance on the required task and moves to the next question. Microsoft has introduced simulation questions on the certification exam for Internet Information Server 4.0. Simulation questions provide many advantages over other testing methodologies, and simulations are expected to become increasingly important in the Microsoft certification program. For example, studies have shown that there is a very high correlation between the ability to perform simulated tasks on a computer-based test and the ability to perform the actual job tasks. Thus, simulations enhance the validity of the certification process.

Another truly wonderful benefit of simulations is in the area of test security. It is just not possible to cheat on a simulation question. In fact, you will be told exactly what tasks you are expected to perform on the test. How can a certification candidate cheat? By learning to perform the tasks? What a concept!

Study Strategies

There are appropriate ways to study for the different types of questions you will see on a Microsoft certification exam.

Knowledge-Based Questions

Knowledge-based questions require that you memorize facts. There are hundreds of facts inherent in every content area of every Microsoft certification exam. There are several keys to memorizing facts:

- **Repetition** The more times your brain is exposed to a fact, the more likely you are to remember it.
- **Association** Connecting facts within a logical framework makes them easier to remember.
- **Motor Association** It is often easier to remember something if you write it down or perform some other physical act, like clicking on a practice test answer.

We have said that the emphasis of Microsoft certification is job performance, and that there are very few knowledge-based questions on Microsoft certification exams. Why should you waste a lot of time learning filenames, IP address formulas, and other minutiae? Read on.

Performance-Based Questions

Most of the questions you will face on a Microsoft certification exam are performance-based scenario questions. We have discussed the superiority of these questions over simple knowledge-based questions, but you should remember that the job task orientation of Microsoft certification extends the knowledge you need to pass the exams; it does not replace this knowledge. Therefore, the first step in preparing for scenario questions is to absorb as many facts relating to the exam content areas as you can. In other words, go back to the previous section and follow the steps to prepare for an exam composed of knowledge-based questions.

The second step is to familiarize yourself with the format of the questions you are likely to see on the exam. You can do this by answering the questions in this study guide, by using Microsoft assessment tests, or by using practice tests on the included CD-ROM. The day of your test is not the time to be surprised by the construction of Microsoft exam questions.

At best, performance-based scenario questions really do test certification candidates at a higher cognitive level than knowledge-based questions. At worst, these questions can test your reading comprehension and test-taking ability rather than your ability to use Microsoft products. Be sure to get in the habit of reading the question carefully to determine what is being asked.

The third step in preparing for Microsoft scenario questions is to adopt the following attitude: Multiple-choice questions aren't really performance-based. It is all a cruel lie. These scenario questions are just knowledge-based questions with a story wrapped around them.

To answer a scenario question, you have to sift through the story to the underlying facts of the situation and apply your knowledge to determine the correct answer. This may sound silly at first, but the process we go through in solving real-life problems is quite similar. The key concept is that every scenario question (and every real-life problem) has a fact at its center, and if we can identify that fact, we can answer the question.

Simulations

Simulation questions really do measure your ability to perform job tasks. You must be able to perform the specified tasks. There are two ways to prepare for simulation questions:

1. Get experience with the actual software. If you have the resources, this is a great way to prepare for simulation questions.
2. Use the practice test on this book's accompanying CD-ROM, as it contains simulation questions similar to those you will find on the Microsoft exam. This approach has the added advantage of grading your efforts. You can find additional practice tests at www.syngress.com and www.osborne.com.

Signing Up

Signing up to take a Microsoft certification exam is easy. Sylvan Prometric or Vue operators in each country can schedule tests at any testing center. There are, however, a few things you should know:

1. If you call Sylvan Prometric or Vue during a busy time, get a cup of coffee first, because you may be in for a long wait. The exam providers do an excellent job, but everyone in the world seems to want to sign up for a test on Monday morning.
2. You will need your social security number or some other unique identifier to sign up for a test, so have it at hand.
3. Pay for your test by credit card if at all possible. This makes things easier, and you can even schedule tests for the same day you call, if space is available at your local testing center.

4. Know the number and title of the test you want to take before you call. This is not essential, and the Sylvan operators will help you if they can. Having this information in advance, however, speeds up and improves the accuracy of the registration process.

Taking the Test

Teachers have always told you not to try to cram for exams because it does no good. If you are faced with a knowledge-based test requiring only that you regurgitate facts, cramming can mean the difference between passing and failing. This is not the case, however, with Microsoft certification exams. If you don't know it the night before, don't bother to stay up and cram.

Instead, create a schedule and stick to it. Plan your study time carefully, and do not schedule your test until you think you are ready to succeed. Follow these guidelines on the day of your exam:

1. Get a good night's sleep. The scenario questions you will face on a Microsoft certification exam require a clear head.
2. Remember to take two forms of identification—at least one with a picture. A driver's license with your picture and social security or credit card is acceptable.
3. Leave home in time to arrive at your testing center a few minutes early. It is not a good idea to feel rushed as you begin your exam.
4. Do not spend too much time on any one question. You cannot mark and revisit questions on an adaptive test, so you must do your best on each question as you go.
5. If you do not know the answer to a question, try to eliminate the obviously wrong answers and guess from the rest. If you can eliminate two out of four options, you have a 50 percent chance of guessing the correct answer.
6. For scenario questions, follow the steps we outlined earlier. Read the question carefully and try to identify the facts at the center of the story.

Finally, we would advise anyone attempting to earn Microsoft MCDBA and MCSE certification to adopt a philosophical attitude. The Windows 2000 MCSE will be the most difficult MCSE ever to be offered. The questions will be at a higher cognitive level than seen on all previous MCSE exams. Therefore, even if you are the kind of person who never fails a test, you are likely to fail at least one Windows 2000 certification test somewhere along the way. Do not get discouraged. Microsoft wants to ensure the value of your certification. Moreover, it will attempt to so by keeping the standard as high as possible. If Microsoft certification were easy to obtain, more people would have it, and it would not be so respected and so valuable to your future in the IT industry.

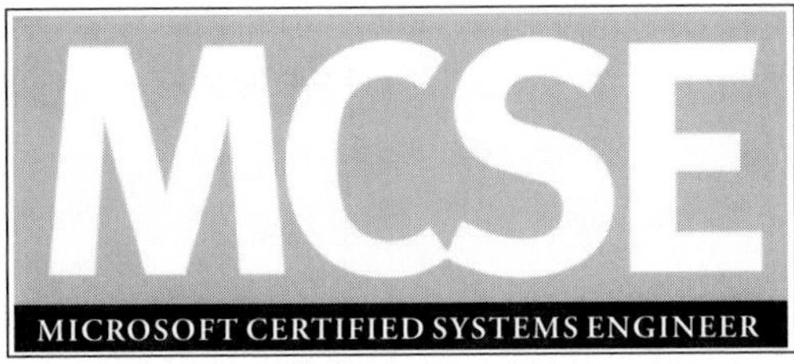

Part I

Active Directory

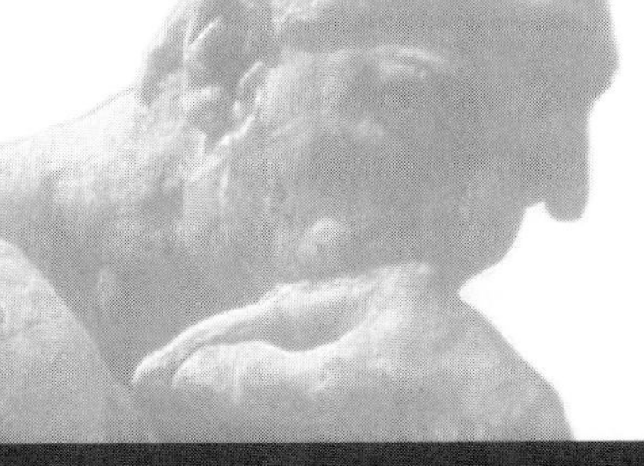

CHAPTERS

MCSE
MICROSOFT CERTIFIED SYSTEMS ENGINEER

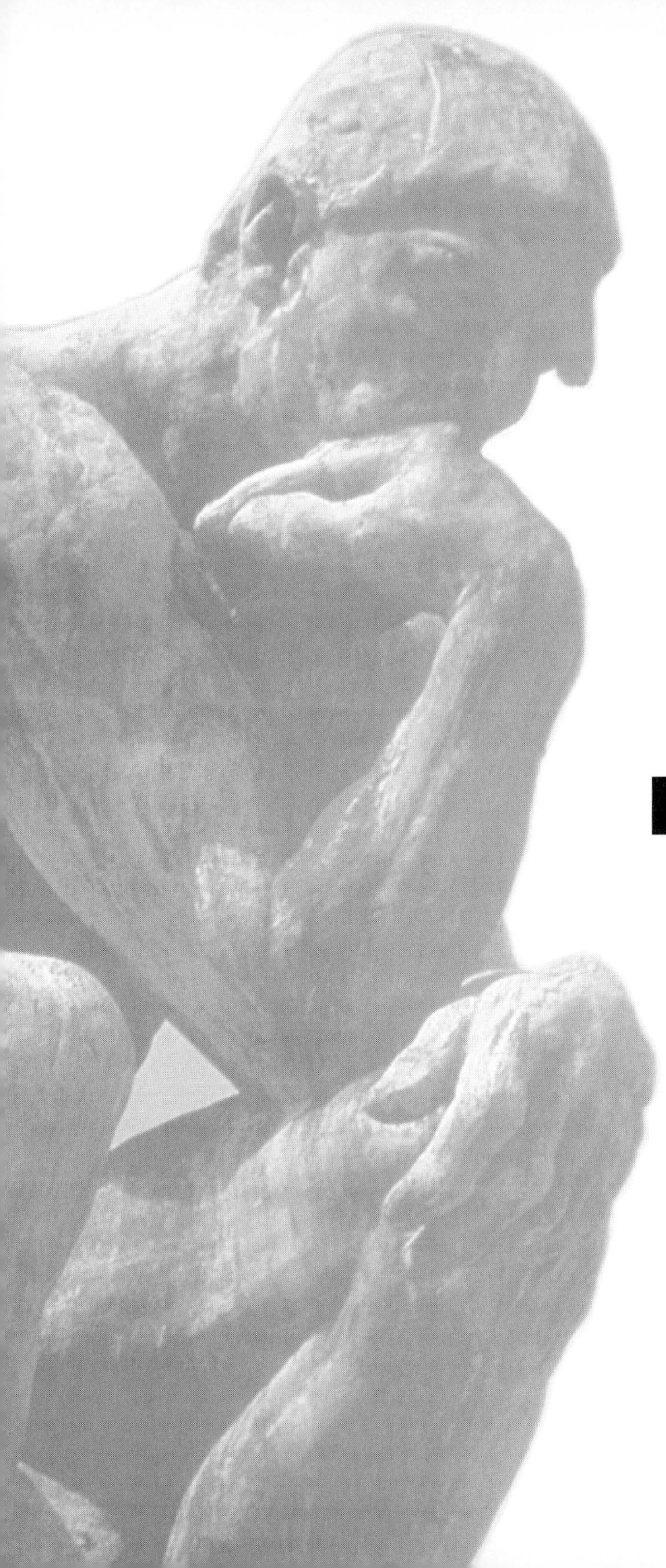

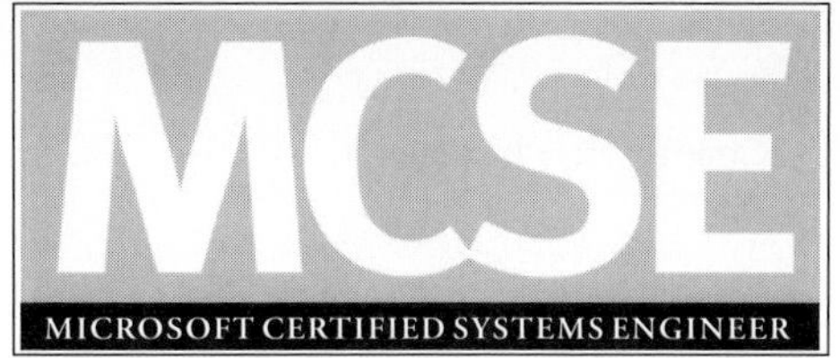

1

Installing the Active Directory

CERTIFICATION OBJECTIVES

1.01	Installing Active Directory
1.02	Creating Sites
1.03	Creating Subnets
1.04	Creating Site Links
1.05	Assigning Bridgehead Servers
1.06	Creating Site Link Bridges
1.07	Creating Connection Objects
1.08	Creating Global Catalog Servers
✓	Two-Minute Drill

Although installing AD is relatively easy (as is shown later in this chapter), tailoring AD to your specific domain needs is much more complex. You must examine and address many intricate details in your network design before starting to lay out and install your domain.

Such details as sites, site links, connection objects, and global catalogs are only a few of the details you need to think about before jumping into creating a network design. All these details, when properly planned and organized, will provide a very fast, reliable, and trouble-free environment for AD and your network overall.

If you have not realized it by now, Windows 2000 is a totally new concept, different from Windows NT 3.51 and 4.0. It requires much more planning and design than did Windows NT 3.51 and 4.0. This is primarily due to the addition of Domain Name System (DNS) and AD to Windows 2000. Although it requires more planning and design, Windows 2000 will show the fruits of your labor by providing you with a high-performance network capable of meeting all your enterprise needs.

CERTIFICATION OBJECTIVE 1.01

Installing Active Directory

Before sitting down and building your domain, you need to have completed your homework. First, you must have thoroughly researched your network needs. This process includes not only looking at what you are currently doing on your network, but also assessing what Windows 2000 can do for your network in the future.

Next, you should plan how to design your network based on the information gathered through your research. Here is where you will decide on such matters as how many domains you need in your network, how many servers you need to act as domain controllers, where to place domain controllers, and placement of global catalog servers. The last step is the fun one: installing your domain controllers and configuring AD.

Although we've presented a very high-level view of the planning stage to the implementation stage, this is a logical path you should take to the end result, which is a fully functional Windows 2000 network that is capable of handling the most stressful of situations your network can throw at it.

Data Collation

One of the most important things you can do to ensure a successful deployment of Windows 2000 is to thoroughly research your current network. You must dig deep and examine everything you are doing inside your network. Some of the things on which you should concentrate your efforts are:

- Number of domains in your enterprise. Determine whether they are still needed and whether a restructuring of your domain could be useful or required.
- Special domain-specific services such as Directory Replication for logon scripts, policies, and roaming profiles.
- Management of specific maintenance tasks such as account management, delegation of authority, and group policy management throughout your enterprise. These are only a few of the tasks that may need to be managed by individuals on a full-time basis, depending on the size of your network.

At the same time you are analyzing your current network, you need to keep in mind the new technologies that Windows 2000 brings to your network. These new technologies may have such a direct, positive impact that it might make sense to not only migrate to Windows 2000 but also to change your network infrastructure to use these new technologies to your company's benefit. Some of the new technologies that could directly impact your network are:

- **Transitive trusts.** With Windows 2000, all domains within your enterprise tree have implicit *transitive trust relationships* with each other. This means that anywhere in your domain structure, you can access another domain's resources, if you have the proper permissions to access that resource. For example, in Windows 2000, if Domain A trusts Domain B, and Domain B trusts Domain C, then Domain A trusts Domain C, and vice versa. In Windows NT models, by contrast, there are no implicit transitive trusts. For Domain A to trust Domain C, as in the Windows 2000 example, you must *explicitly* create a two-way trust relationship between Domain A and Domain C. This requirement creates an administrative nightmare when many domains enter the picture. Windows 2000 eliminates this problem.
- **Active Directory sites.** Using the concept of *sites* within AD allows administrators to define resource "boundaries" for domain clients. Clients within a site use only those resources located within the site and can use

resources outside the site only in certain circumstances. This setup eliminates such problems as remote site systems authenticating over slow wide area network (WAN) links to main office systems. A good example is a client in a remote office in London being authenticated by a domain controller in the New York headquarters office over a 128K Integrated Services Digital Network (ISDN) link. This authentication could be quite expensive, not to mention a huge performance hit for the client. Using sites within Windows 2000 allows administrators to control clients' use of resources.

- **Virtual Private Networking (VPN).** With improved VPN functionality and the addition of Layer 2 Tunneling Protocol (L2TP) and IPSec to Windows 2000, companies can rethink their strategies of providing remote access service to employees. Companies that provide RAS to employees for business use usually incur the considerable costs of long distance connections. Using a VPN can eliminate this expense. Employees can dial into the Internet locally and tunnel to a VPN server provided by the company. Using L2TP to provide the tunnel, and IPSec to encrypt the data, you can use the Internet as your RAS backbone and eliminate the company's added RAS expense.

These are only a few of the technologies that could affect the way you currently do business in your company. You must make sure that you look at all angles—past, present, and future—to make the most of your upgrade or migration to Windows 2000.

Prerequisites

Once you have analyzed all your network needs and designed your network topology and Active Directory, covering special needs such as multiple domains to support remote sites, AD schema modifications to support enterprise applications, and location of global catalogs, you can start to move to the next phase of your migration, which is resource planning. You need to decide what resources you need and where to deploy them. One of the largest factors in choosing your resources is the prerequisite for Windows 2000 and Active Directory.

Although hardware requirements can vary with each network, dependent on network load, users, and resources such as storage and memory, it is safe to assume that the vast number of IT offices around the world will not implement

Windows 2000 on systems that Microsoft specifies as the minimum requirements. According to Microsoft, you can install Windows 2000 Server/Advanced Server on a Pentium 166MHz system with 64MB of memory. If you want Windows 2000 to do more than just sit on your network, however, you require a system that is a little more robust than this one. Recommended minimums are more realistic, which are in the neighborhood of a Pentium II 400MHz system with at least 128MB of memory.

As for the prerequisites for Active Directory, you need two things:

- **A DNS server installed on your network.** This DNS server must be at least BIND 8.1.2 compliant, which supports the requirement for service resource records (SRV RRs) per RFC 2052. SRV RRs are required to support services within Windows 2000 such as Kerberos and global catalog. Using Microsoft's implementation of DNS is *not* required (Dynamic DNS is also *not* required) but is *strongly* encouraged. As you will see later when installing Active Directory via the DCPROMO process, you can install AD without using Microsoft's DNS, but doing so becomes much more cumbersome and labor intensive (which Windows 2000 strives to eliminate).
- **One disk with at least 250MB of storage.** It is preferred, as you will see later, that the AD database and logs be stored on separate disks. The AD database requires a minimum of 200MB; the AD log requires a minimum of 50MB. The AD database and log files do not require an NT File System (NTFS) partition, but it is recommended, not only for its fault tolerance but also due to its transactional logging of all disk activity. These features of NTFS make it perfect to use for AD (Note: it is recommended that you have at least 1 GB of disk space to install Server; the 250 MB is in addition to that).

Once you have all your prerequisites filled and your design is finalized, the next step is to put a CD in a drive and start installing!

exam Watch

Make sure you understand the requirements for the Active Directory database and log files and for installing the Shared System Folder (SYSVOL). The requirements for these two parts of AD are commonly confused with one another. Individually, the AD database and log files do not require NTFS, but AD as a concept does require NTFS, because the SYSVOL folder must have an NTFS 5.0 partition.

DCPROMO

Once you have installed and configured your first Windows 2000 server, your next step is to promote it to create your domain structure. Initially, your first Windows 2000 domain controller is your most important server, the one you will use to create your whole AD structure and root domain, and, most likely, the one that will house your DNS server, if you choose to use Microsoft's DNS.

Using DCPROMO

Starting the DCPROMO process is quite easy. To start your journey, choose Start | Run. In the text box, type **DCPROMO** and click OK. The Active Directory Installation Wizard window signals the beginning of the AD installation on your system. Before starting this process, we should probably look at the various scenarios you might run across when you use DCPROMO.

DCPROMO Scenarios

When starting the DCPROMO process to install Active Directory, you are faced with your first decision: to create a new domain or to create a domain controller in an existing domain (see Figure 1-1). First-time installations require you to select the option to install a domain controller for a new domain.

FIGURE 1-1

Installing a new domain or adding to an existing domain

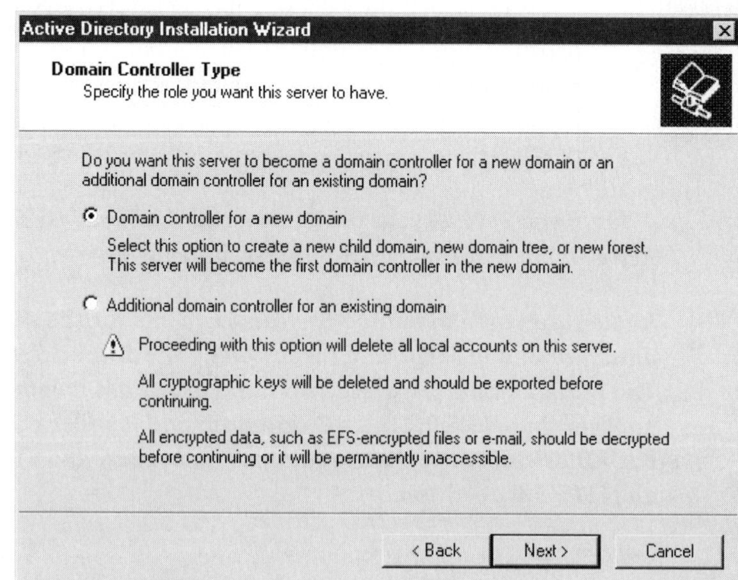

on the Job

One of the shortcomings of Windows NT 4.0 was the inability to demote and promote primary domain controllers (PDCs) to backup domain controllers (BDCs) to member servers, and vice versa. With DCPROMO, you can promote and demote member servers to domain controllers with ease. The only caveat to this capability (and it is a big one) is that you must remember that if you demote your last domain controller to a member server, you will lose your Active Directory, because your last domain controller contains the last copy of your domain's Active Directory.

Selecting the option to install a new domain brings up another window in which you have to choose to create your own domain tree or add your domain to an existing tree (see Figure 1-2). Again, first-time domain installations must choose to create a new domain tree. Choosing to create a new domain tree results in a third, and last, choice, which asks whether you want to create a new forest of domain trees or connect this tree to an existing forest (see Figure 1-3).

Creating your own forest results in establishing your own root domain from which all other trees or child domains will attach (e.g., MICROSOFT.COM, INTEL.COM, etc.). Selecting this option makes your domain controller the top level of your domain tree. Once you select this option, Windows 2000 prompts you for the fully qualified

FIGURE 1-2

Creating a new domain tree or child domain

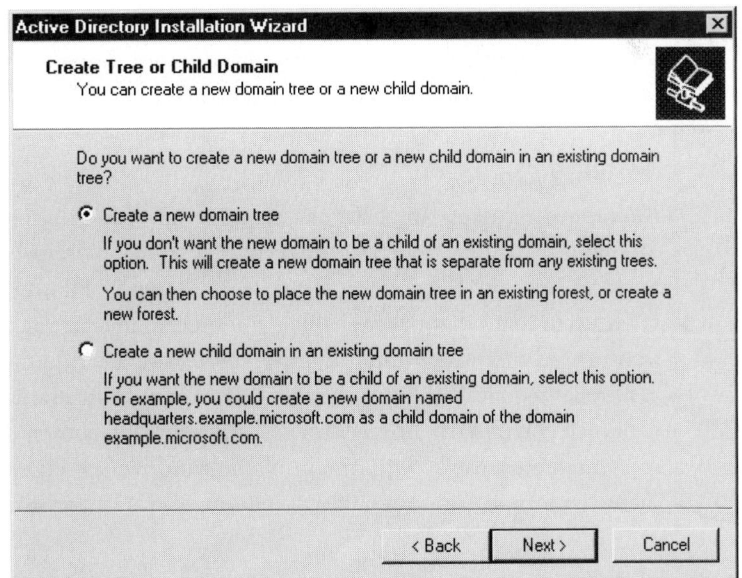

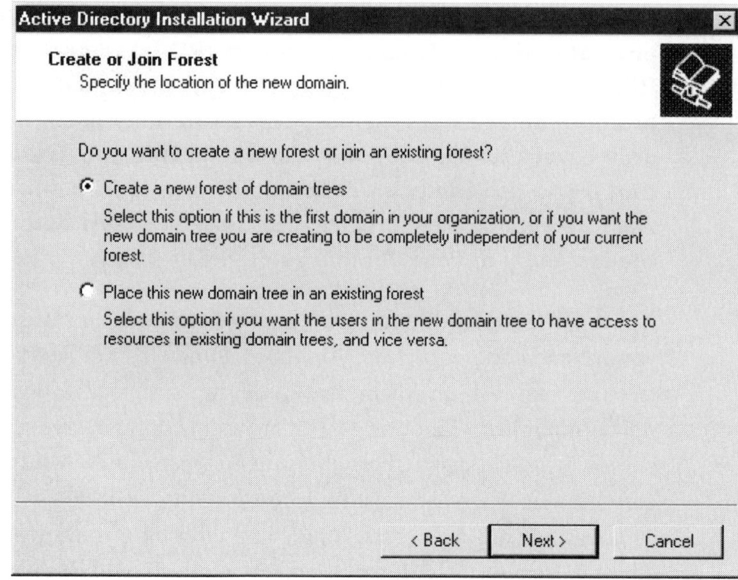

FIGURE 1-3 Creating your own forest or joining an existing forest

domain name (FQDN) of the domain you are installing. This information is used to register this domain controller in DNS and start the process of installing AD.

Selecting the second option, placing the domain tree into an existing forest, establishes a transitive trust with the root domain to which you attach. Selecting this option prompts you for Enterprise Administrator-equivalent credentials in order to establish a transitive trust with the root domain of the tree to which you are attaching (see Figure 1-4).

Moving On

Before you progress any further, you must have chosen how you will install your domain controller. Selecting the second option shown in Figures 1-1, 1-2, or 1-3 yields a Network Credentials window, as shown in Figure 1-4.

Keep in mind that the credentials you use to add or create a new forest or domain must have Enterprise Administrator-equivalent rights. Adding or creating a new domain controller requires either Enterprise or Domain Administrator-equivalent rights.

Once you enter your credentials, or if you have chosen different options, you are presented with the New Domain Name window (see Figure 1-5). This is where you name your new Windows 2000 domain by its DNS domain name (e.g., W2K.NET).

FIGURE 1-4

The Network Credentials window

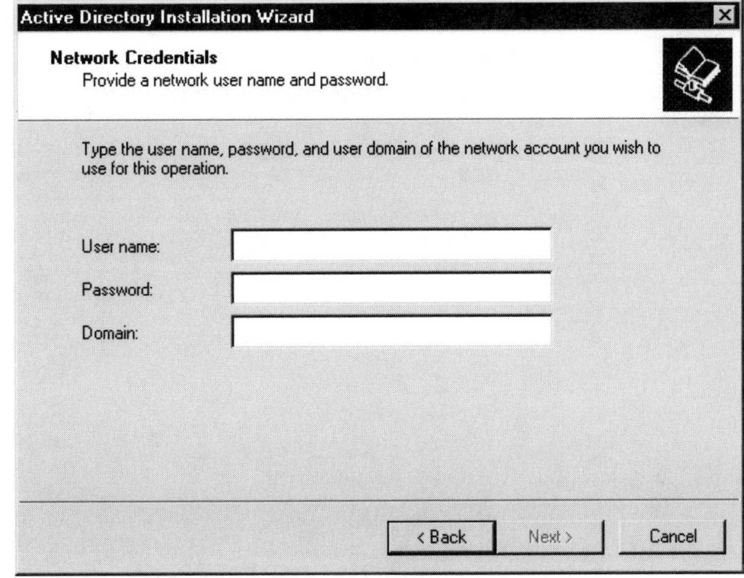

FIGURE 1-5

Entering your new domain's DNS name

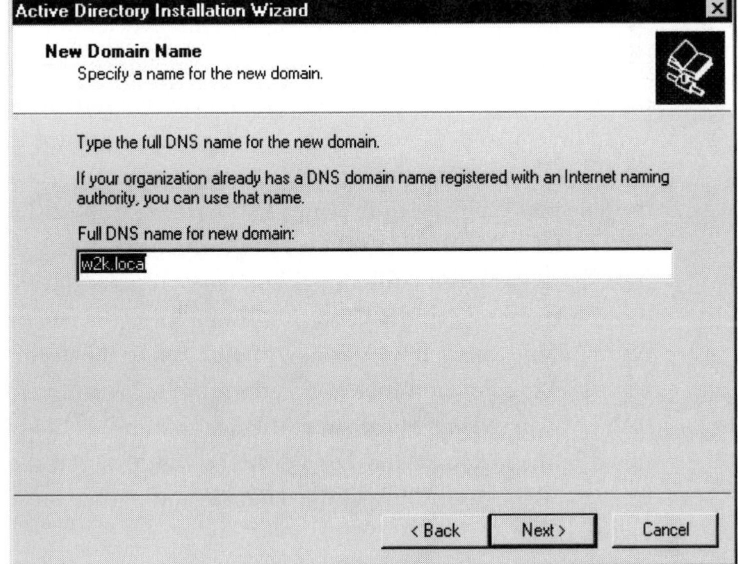

FIGURE 1-6

Assigning a NetBIOS name for legacy systems

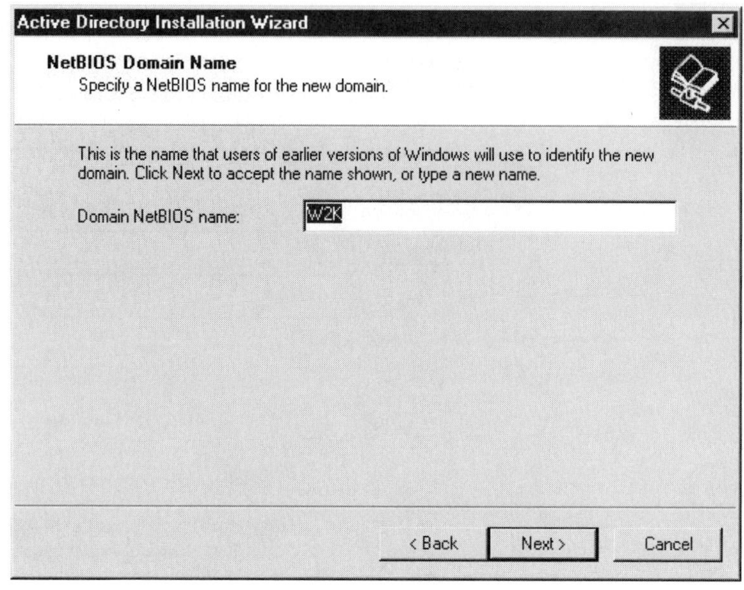

exam Watch

You do not enter the name of a domain controller in the DNS domain name; however, you will see later that the last name provided in the DNS name is used as the NetBIOS name for the domain (see Figure 1-6).

After you enter your domain's name, the next window in the Active Directory installation process is the NetBIOS Domain Name window. Here, you specify the NetBIOS domain name to be used by legacy systems such as Windows 95, Windows 98, and Windows NT 4.0. It is recommended that, as pointed out earlier in the chapter, the NetBIOS name assigned to the domain be taken from the left-most name listed in your DNS name (e.g., W2K assigned from the domain W2K.NET). Windows 2000 uses this format to assign a default NetBIOS domain (refer back to Figure 1-6). Unless you have an urgent need to name your DNS domain and your NetBIOS domain differently, it is recommended that you use the default name assigned by Windows 2000. Using this format, you also help eliminate any possible confusion that could arise from using different naming conventions.

Next, you specify where your AD database and AD log files will be installed. As stated in the Database and Log Locations window, you should, for performance and recoverability reasons, install the database and log file on separate partitions (see Figure 1-7).

FIGURE 1-7

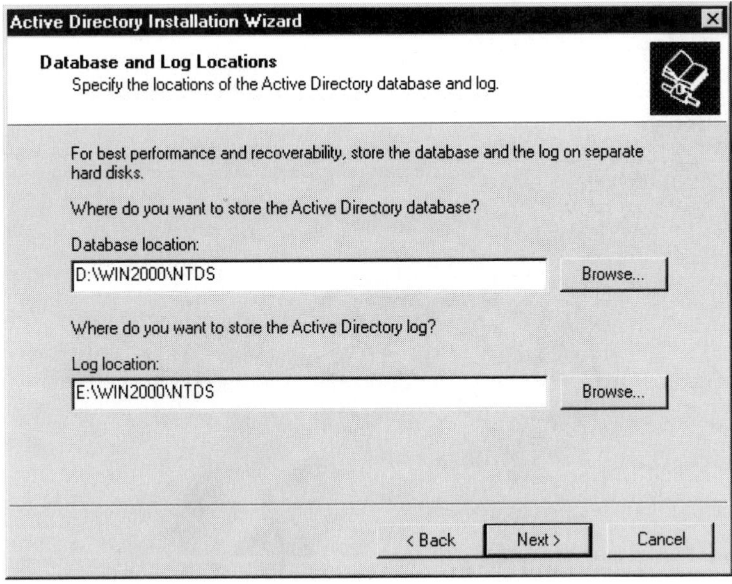

Installing your Active Directory database and log files

When installing your domain controllers, format two drives for AD using NTFS. Format one with a 4K-cluster size and use it for your Active Directory database, because the database uses 4K pages. Next, format the second drive for your AD log file and use an 8K-cluster size. The AD log file uses 8K pages. This procedure sets your AD files to optimal size and helps reduce fragmentation problems.

Next, you must specify where your SYSVOL folder will be installed. The SYSVOL folder is where all your public files reside (see Figure 1-8).

Files such as logon scripts and policies that need to be replicated to all other domain controllers in the domain are placed in SYSVOL. Note that your SYSVOL folder needs to be placed on a NTFS 5.0 partition, so you need to plan for at least one NTFS 5.0 partition on your domain controller(s).

Once you have specified the location for your SYSVOL folder, Windows 2000 tries to contact DNS to determine whether it supports dynamic updates. If it cannot find a DNS server that is authoritative in the domain, a notification window appears, stating that Windows 2000 cannot find a DNS server (see Figure 1-9).

FIGURE 1-8

Specifying the location for the SYSVOL folder

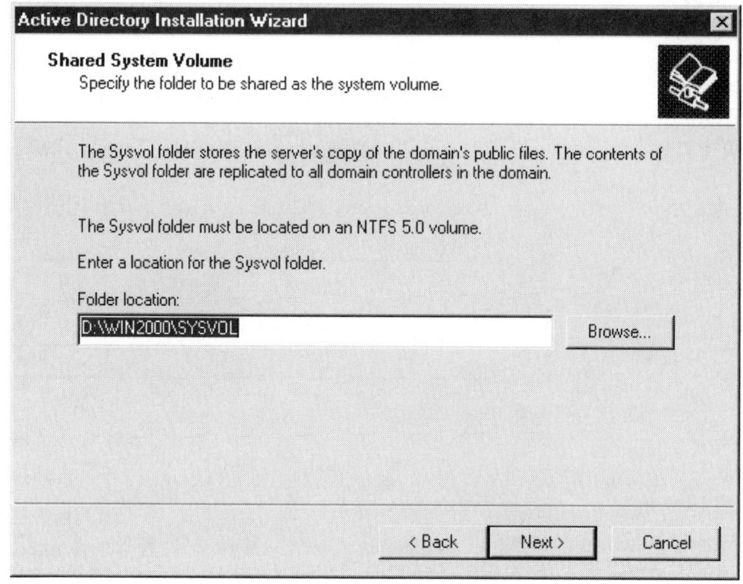

Once you click OK, another window appears, stating that DNS is not installed. You must select whether you want Windows 2000 to install DNS on your current system or to install DNS on another system (see Figure 1-10). This is one of your biggest decisions when installing Windows 2000, especially if you are installing your first domain controller, because once you start installing more domain controllers, it becomes increasingly hard to reverse your decision and use a different DNS solution. Make sure that you have carefully planned your DNS solution *before* installing your domain controllers!

Regardless of your DNS selection, once you click Next, you are asked about setting default permissions for User and Group objects (see Figure 1-11).

FIGURE 1-9

The window indicating Windows 2000 is unable to contact a DNS server

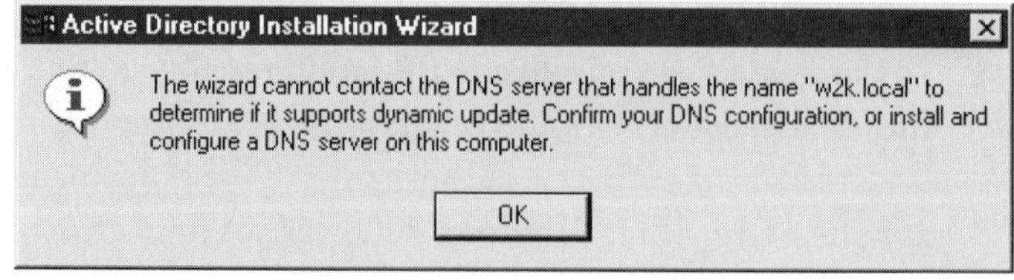

FIGURE 1-10

Deciding to install DNS or configure DNS separately

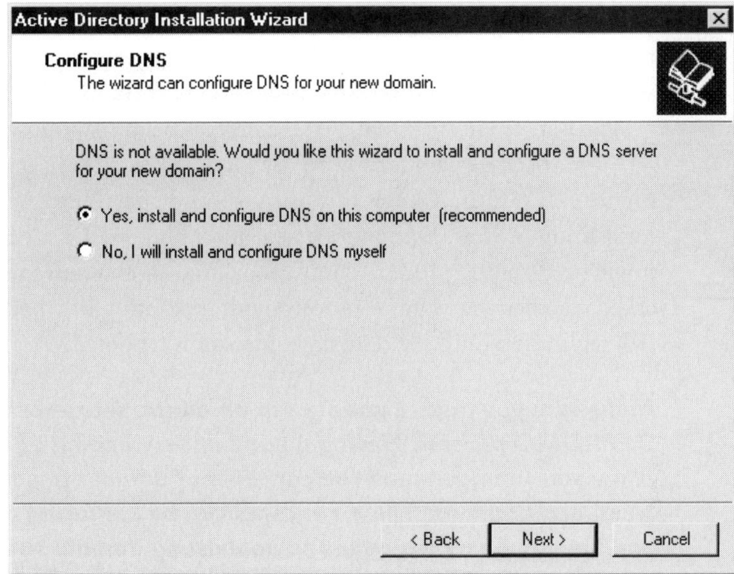

FIGURE 1-11

The default Permissions window

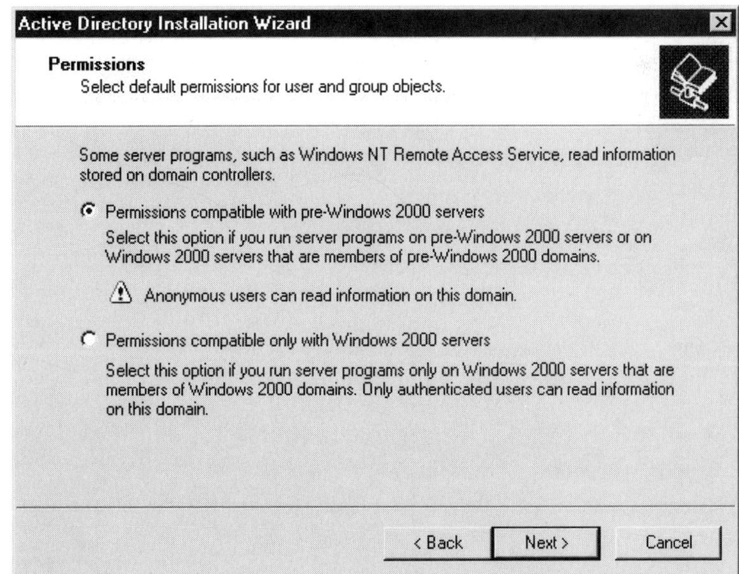

As shown in Figure 1-11, if you have any pre-Windows 2000 servers, it is recommended that you select the Permissions Compatible with pre-Windows 2000 servers option to avoid possible problems with these systems later.

The last step in the DCPROMO process before Windows 2000 starts configuring AD is to specify a password to be used for Directory Services Restore Mode (see Figure 1-12). Once you set this password and click Next, Active Directory begins the installation process. During the installation process, if DCPROMO determines that it will be a lengthy process to replicate all the objects currently stored in AD, you are asked whether you want to proceed with replication or whether you want to defer AD replication until the domain controller is rebooted.

exam Watch

Make sure you have a good grasp on all the setup scenarios involved with the DCPROMO process. Having a good understanding of this process will, in turn, allow you to understand the concepts of domain structures such as forests, trees, and domains. These concepts can be confusing at times. These concepts and how domains are added to an existing domain structure will definitely be covered in the certification tests.

FIGURE 1-12

Specifying the Directory Services Restore Mode password

Active Directory Installation Wizard
Directory Services Restore Mode Administrator Password
Specify an Administrator password to use when starting the computer in Directory Services Restore Mode.
Type and confirm the password you want to assign to this server's Administrator account, to be used when the computer is started in Directory Services Restore Mode.
Password:
Confirm password:
< Back
Next >
Cancel

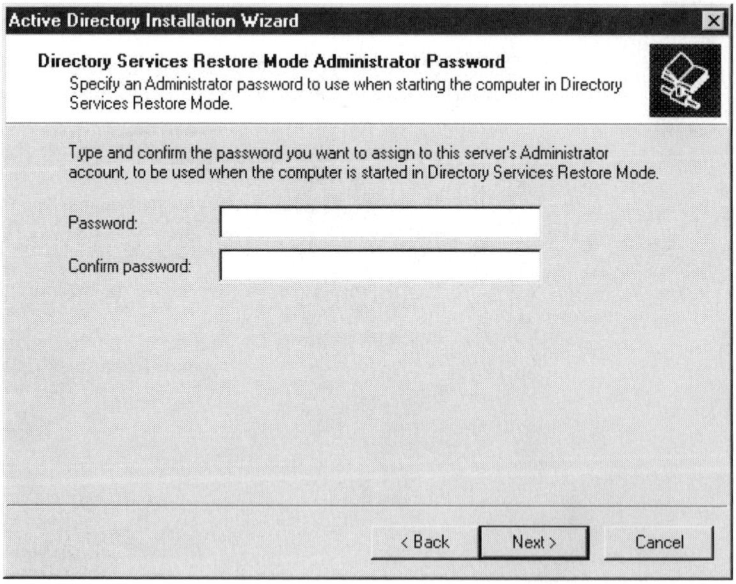

Verifying Successful Installation

After you successfully complete the installation of AD, the Active Directory Installation Wizard reports that it has successfully installed AD (see Figure 1-13).

To further verify that AD has been installed correctly, check your DNS server to see if the correct DNS entries have been made. When you install AD on a domain controller, approximately 15 DNS entries are made for the server in question, if your DNS solution supports Dynamic DNS.

If you do not have the Active Directory Installation Wizard automatically install your domain controller in DNS, Windows 2000 generates all the DNS entries necessary for you to register your domain controller manually in DNS. Windows 2000 places these DNS entries in a file named NETLOGON.DNS under the %SystemRoot%\System32\config directory. All the entries in this file must be made on your DNS server(s) if you choose to install DNS separately or if your DNS servers do not support Dynamic DNS. Figure 1-14 shows an example of the NETLOGON.DNS file.

If your DNS server(s) are configured for zone transfers, you might need to enter the required DNS entries on only one of your DNS servers.

FIGURE 1-13

Completing the Active Directory installation

FIGURE 1-14 Example of a NETLOGON.DNS file

```
; w2k.local. 600 IN A 192.168.1.1
; _ldap._tcp.w2k.local. 600 IN SRV 0 100 389 excalibur.w2k.local.
; _ldap._tcp.pdc._msdcs.w2k.local. 600 IN SRV 0 100 389 excalibur.w2k.local.
; _ldap._tcp.gc._msdcs.w2k.local. 600 IN SRV 0 100 3268 excalibur.w2k.local.
; _ldap._tcp.26e4eec0-bffc-4aaf-a635-9839c512c149.domains._msdcs.w2k.local. 600 IN SRV 0 100 389 excalibur.w2k.local.
; gc._msdcs.w2k.local. 600 IN A 192.168.1.1
; 72552f1f-ebc2-49ef-8811-ed04add14317._msdcs.w2k.local. 600 IN CNAME excalibur.w2k.local.
; _kerberos._tcp.dc._msdcs.w2k.local. 600 IN SRV 0 100 88 excalibur.w2k.local.
; _ldap._tcp.dc._msdcs.w2k.local. 600 IN SRV 0 100 389 excalibur.w2k.local.
; _kerberos._tcp.w2k.local. 600 IN SRV 0 100 88 excalibur.w2k.local.
; _gc._tcp.w2k.local. 600 IN SRV 0 100 3268 excalibur.w2k.local.
; _kerberos._udp.w2k.local. 600 IN SRV 0 100 88 excalibur.w2k.local.
; _kpasswd._tcp.w2k.local. 600 IN SRV 0 100 464 excalibur.w2k.local.
; _kpasswd._udp.w2k.local. 600 IN SRV 0 100 464 excalibur.w2k.local.
```

Along with checking DNS to make sure that the appropriate DNS entries have been made (whether in DNS or the NETLOGON.DNS file), you should check several other things to make sure AD has been completed successfully:

1. Check the SYSVOL share to make sure that it contains:
   A. The SYSVOL share
   B. The NETLOGON share
   C. Policy and Script folders
2. Check the Active Directory Users and Computers snap-in to ensure that your domain controller has been placed in the Domain Controllers container for the AD domain that you specified.
3. Check the Directory Services Restore Mode boot option to make sure that not only does this option work, but it works with the password you provided. When your Directory Service has problems, it is not the time to find out that your recovery option does not work.

EXERCISE 1-1

Installing and Uninstalling Active Directory

In this exercise, we install Active Directory on a Windows 2000 server. The exercise covers two scenarios: how to install Windows 2000 using Microsoft DNS via Dynamic DNS and how to install AD using a non-Microsoft DNS solution.

For this exercise, you need a single system installed with either Windows 2000 Server or Advanced Server. Do not use any other domain controllers in this exercise. In addition, make sure you have at least one NTFS drive to allow for the installation of the SYSVOL folder.

To fully complete this exercise, it is recommended that you follow the exercise from the beginning instead of starting in the middle, because the first part of the exercise sets up the environment for later sections of the exercise.

First, install AD using Microsoft DNS:

1. To start installing Active Directory, choose Start | Run. Type in **DCPROMO** and click OK.
2. The Active Directory Installation Wizard appears to start the installation of Active Directory. Click Next to start installing AD.
3. The first window to appear is the Domain Controller Type. Because you are working with a single server, make sure you select the Domain Controller for a New Domain option. This option lets Windows 2000 know that you are installing a root domain controller for a new domain. This root serves as the parent domain for all other domains added to it.
4. Next, the Create Tree or Child Domain window appears. You must select whether this domain will join an existing domain (become a child domain) or will be a stand-alone domain. Select the Create a New Domain Tree to make a stand-alone domain. We use this option because we are not connecting our domain to any existing domains. Click Next.
5. In the Create or Join Forest window, you have the choice of joining your new domain to an existing forest or creating your own forest. Although you are installing only one domain controller, you are actually installing the root for a new domain, tree, and forest with your single domain controller. Select the Create a New Forest of Domain Trees option to create your new forest. Click Next.

6. At the New Domain window, you must type in the name of the new domain. Remember, this is the DNS domain name and *not* the Windows NT NetBIOS domain name. For this exercise, use the DNS domain name **W2K.LOCAL**.When you have entered the DNS domain name, click Next.
7. In the NetBIOS domain name window, enter the NetBIOS name you want to use for this domain. This NetBIOS domain name is used by legacy systems to identify the domain. It is recommended that you use the last section of the DNS domain name as the NetBIOS name. Given our DNS name of W2K.LOCAL, we would use W2K as the NetBIOS name. Enter **W2K** as the NetBIOS name and click Next.
8. At the Database and Log Locations window, you must specify where the Active Directory database and log will be located. As covered earlier in the chapter, it is recommended, but not required, to install AD files not only on separate drives but also on NTFS drives for better performance and fault tolerance. Specify the locations for your database and log files and click Next.
9. When the Shared System Volume window appears, you must specify where your SYSVOL folder will be installed. As the window states, it must be on an NTFS 5.0 volume. Place the SYSVOL folder on your NTFS drive and click Next to continue the installation process.
10. At this point, you are presented with an information window stating that the Installation Wizard cannot contact a DNS server that handles the name W2K.LOCAL to determine whether it supports Dynamic DNS. Click OK and you will continue the installation by moving to the Configure DNS window.
11. For this exercise, select the Windows 2000 Install and Configure DNS on This Computer option. Later in this exercise, you will select the option to install and configure DNS yourself. Click Next.
12. In the Permissions window (refer back to Figure 1-11), you must select the default permissions to be applied to this domain controller. Since we are using only one Windows 2000 server, select Permissions Compatible Only with Windows 2000 Servers. Click Next.

13. The last window the Active Directory Wizard shows is the Directory Services Restore Mode Administrator Password window. Here you must specify the password to be used for the Directory Services Restore Mode boot menu option in Windows 2000. This boot option is used to help troubleshoot problems in the AD. Once you specify the password, click Next.
14. The Active Directory Wizard Summary window appears, with all your selections listed. Review this window carefully before proceeding, because once you click Next, Windows 2000 starts installing AD and there is no Back or Cancel button to allow you to change your installation settings.
15. Once AD has completed its installation, the wizard opens a notification window. Click Finish to complete the installation process. Once you click Finish, you are prompted to reboot to have your changes take place.

Now, let's uninstall AD on a server:

1. To start uninstalling AD, choose Start | Run. Type **DCPROMO** and click OK.
2. The Active Directory Installation Wizard appears, ready to start the removal of AD. Click Next to start the removal process.
3. If the server you are demoting is a global catalog server, you receive an information window stating such. The window also reminds you to make sure that there are other global catalog servers available to users before removing AD from the system on which you are working.
4. Next, the Remove Active Directory window appears with a message warning about the consequences of removing AD from this system. *Before* you click Next to proceed, *carefully read* the warning messages provided! Failure to read these warnings can have a huge impact on your network operations. If this is the last domain controller in your domain, check the "This server is the last domain controller in the domain" check box before clicking Next.
5. After clicking Next, you must authenticate with Enterprise Administrator credentials. This is a security safeguard to prevent accidental or intentional removal of AD from domain controllers. Enter the appropriate credentials and click Next.

6. Because this system will be demoted to a member server, Windows 2000 prompts you to enter a local Administrator password. Enter a password for the server to use and click Next.
7. The Active Directory Wizard now has all the information it needs to remove AD. Note that the wizard has summarized all your selections and has specified all the consequences of those actions. To start removing AD from this system, click Next.
8. Windows 2000 starts the demotion process. There is no Cancel or Back button available once you reach this step, so make *absolutely sure* that you want to proceed.
9. When the process has completed, a window appears, stating that Windows 2000 has finished removing Active Directory. Click Finish and another window appears, stating that the system must be rebooted for the changes to take effect. Click Restart to finish the removal process.

Now we'll install Active Directory using non-Microsoft DNS servers:

1. Follow Steps 1–10 for installing Active Directory using Microsoft DNS.
2. In the Configure DNS window, select the No option to install and configure DNS yourself.
3. Continue to follow Steps 12–15 for installing Active Directory using Microsoft DNS.
4. Once Active Directory has finished installing, open Explorer and navigate to the `%SystemRoot%\System32\config` folder. Find and open the NETLOGON.DNS file. You will notice that Windows has made all the DNS entries you need to manually install your domain controller in DNS. This file can now be e-mailed to your DNS administrator(s) to be added to DNS.

CERTIFICATION OBJECTIVE 1.02

Creating Sites

Once you have successfully installed AD on your domain controllers, it is time to start modifying it to fit your domain. One of the first things you need to do is start defining your network's logical layout by planning your network's sites within Active Directory. Using the information gathered through researching your networks, you list your sites in AD to help define how physical boundaries should be laid out in your network. Sites, as you will see, help define how domain controllers should replicate and how workstations use resources. Sites help you cut down unnecessary WAN traffic and help make Windows 2000 and AD perform more efficiently.

Sites help partition and group your network in a way that makes logical sense. A good example is a company located in a large metropolitan area. The company has an east-side site and a west-side site. You do not want east-side systems authenticating or using services over your WAN connection to your west-side site.

What Is a Site?

By definition, a *site* is a collection of subnets and domain controllers that are well connected. The definition of *well connected* can vary from network to network, so you must use care when planning. Basically, *well connected* means a collection of subnets and domain controllers that are connected by some sort of high-speed medium, such as a 10MB Ethernet network. Several of these subnets grouped together make a site.

Site boundaries are usually determined where there are slower media, such as a 56K dial-up connection or even possibly an ISDN connection. In these locations, a site usually terminates each end of the slow medium.

In general, WAN links should be considered a good dividing line for sites. Including domain controllers in a site that crosses a WAN link could be disastrous, because replication traffic and service requests could easily consume all the WAN's bandwidth, resulting in very slow performance for the network overall.

When you install your first domain controller, the site object named Default First-Site-Name is created in the Sites object container, and your domain controller is placed there. As recommended throughout this chapter, you should give all your objects meaningful names; sites are no exception. It is a good idea to rename the Default First-Site-Name to a name that is meaningful within your network.

When you have all your sites created, each domain controller will exist as a certain site. If you properly set up your sites and subnets beforehand, all your domain controllers will be *automatically* placed in their correct sites when they are installed.

How to Create a Site

To create a site, you must use the Active Directory Sites and Services Microsoft Management Console (MMC) snap-in and create a new site by right-clicking the Sites folder and selecting New | Site (see Figure 1-15).

After you elect to create a new site, a new Site window appears (see Figure 1-16) to create a new site and assign a site link to it. Note that if you want a different site link, you can either create a new site link before creating your site, or you can assign a different site link after the site is created. One of the Catch-22 situations with site links is that you cannot create one without having at least two sites created, but you cannot create a site without first assigning a site link. How do you get out of this loop? Windows 2000 provides DEFAULTIPSITELINK as the default site link. When you create a new site, your site is placed in DEFAULTIPSITELINK by default, unless you place it in another available site link. Once you have at least two sites created in DEFAULTIPSITELINK, you can create other site links using the sites within DEFAULTIPSITELINK.

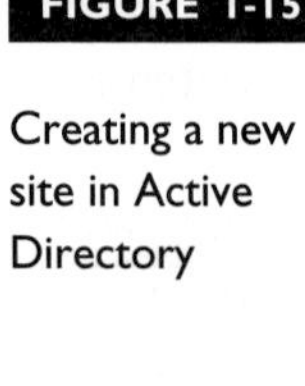

FIGURE 1-15

Creating a new site in Active Directory

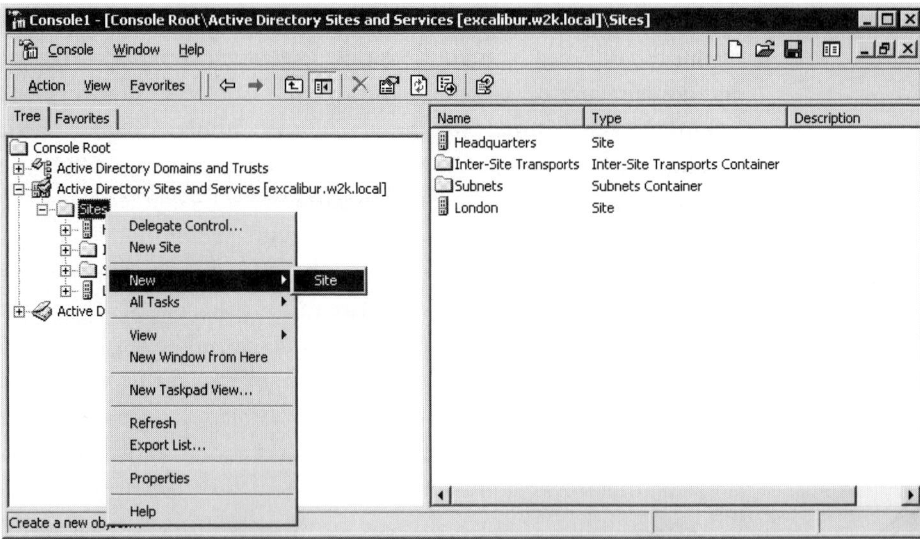

FIGURE 1-16

The New Object–Site window

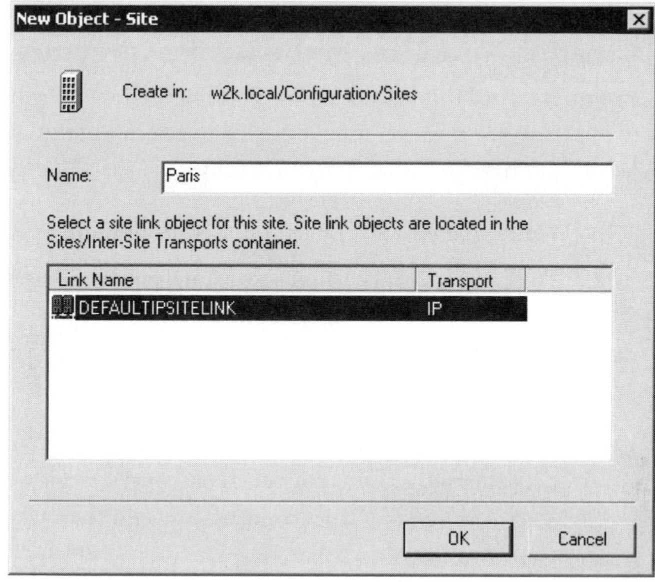

Site links, as you see later in the chapter, are a means of linking two or more sites for replication purposes. Site links help specify preferred replication paths as well as specifying the frequency with which sites should replicate with each other. Each site in Active Directory has at least one associated site link.

Once you create a new site by clicking OK, a notification window appears (see Figure 1-17) reminding you that there might be several other housekeeping items that you must complete before you can use the new site.

Linking the new site to other sites, as appropriate, adding necessary subnets, and installing or moving domain controllers into this new site are among the tasks you need to make sure are completed before your site is finished.

FIGURE 1-17

New site object notification window

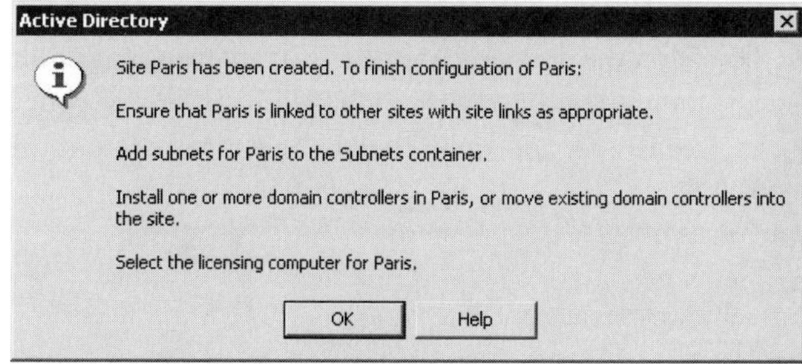

EXERCISE 1-2

Creating New Sites in the Active Directory

In this exercise, you learn how to create new sites and move servers from one site to another. For this exercise, you need to use Windows 2000 Server or Advanced Server and have installed Active Directory via the DCPROMO process.

1. Verify that you are logged on to your domain as Administrator.
2. To open an empty Microsoft Management Console, choose Start | Run. Type **MMC** in the text box and click OK.
3. Click the Console menu item and select the Add/Remove snap-in pop-up menu item.
4. From the Stand-alone tab, click Add. From the Add Stand-alone snap-in, click the Active Directory Sites and Services snap-in and then click Add. After adding the snap-in, click Close and then click OK to close the Add snap-in window.
5. Expand the Active Directory Sites and Services snap-in by double-clicking the snap-in. A Sites object appears underneath the Active Directory Sites and Services entry. If you double-click the Sites object, you see the Inter-Site Transports, Default-First-Site, and Subnets objects. You work with these objects in later exercises.
6. To create a site, right-click Sites and select New Site from the pop-up context menu.
7. In the New Object–Site window, type the name of your new site.
8. Select a site link to assign to this site and click OK. Click OK in the Active Directory information window. Practice creating sites by repeating Steps 6–8 until you understand the concept. Try creating a site that already exists. What happens?
9. Find the domain controller you are using (most likely under Default-First-Site, unless you have already moved it) in one of your sites. Select this domain controller and right-click it. Select Move from the pop-up context menu.

10. In the Move Server window, select the site you want to move the server into and click OK. Open the destination site to find the server you moved. Repeat Steps 9 and 10 to move the server back to its original position.
11. Delete all the sites you created except two, because you will use them for future exercises. Delete sites by right-clicking the site and selecting Delete from the pop-up context menu. Try deleting the site that contains your server. What happens?

CERTIFICATION OBJECTIVE 1.03

Creating Subnets

As explained previously in this chapter, subnets play a vital role in determining where domain controllers and services, such as DNS, are located. If subnets are not defined within Active Directory, sites and services cannot be accurately reflected in your domain structure, leading to uncontrolled and inefficient directory replication and resource usage.

What Is a Subnet?

Subnets are the means by which network traffic is routed through a network. Dependent on the subnet mask, each IP address is divided into two separate sections: a network address and a host address. Think of an IP address as directions on how to reach a friend's house. Your friend gives you the address, and you break the address down, first by the name of the street (the network address of the IP address), and then, once you find the street, by the house number (the host address of the IP address).

Subnets work much the same way. First, a message is routed to a remote destination using the network ID portion of the IP address. Once the message arrives at the correct subnet, the packet is broadcast to all systems on that subnet. The system with the correct destination IP address is the one that responds. All others ignore the packet.

Consider another example. Your friend told you what street he lived on, but he forgot to tell you the house number. If you knocked on all the doors on the street that he lived on, eventually you would find his house. IP addresses work in the same fashion, but much faster.

Using subnets in Active Directory allows you to group a series of subnets together to form a site. Subnets are the building blocks of sites.

How to Create a Subnet

Subnets are easy to create within Active Directory. From the Active Directory Sites and Services snap-in, open Sites, right-click Subnets, and select New | Subnet to create a new subnet, as shown in Figure 1-18.

FIGURE 1-18 Creating a new subnet in Active Directory

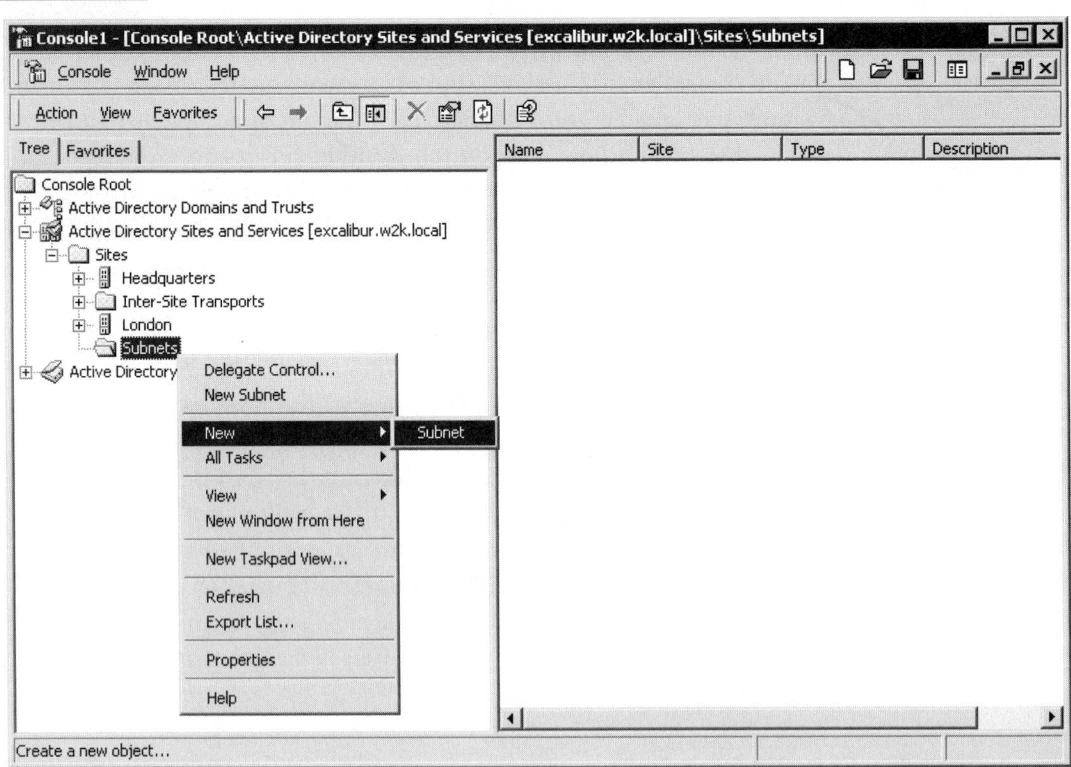

Once you elect to create a new subnet, you need to enter the information for a new subnet along with its corresponding subnet mask. After entering this information, you need to assign the subnet to a specific site. In Figure 1-19, the Default-First-Site has been renamed Headquarters, and a London site has been created. Also in Figure 1-19, you can see that subnet 192.168.1.0 will be assigned to the Headquarters site. A subnet can be assigned to only one site, so you must remember that you cannot split a subnet into two different sites.

Also note that underneath the address and mask is the subnet name, which in this case is 192.168.1.0/24. The */24* represents the number of subnet mask bits used for the subnet mask. It is an acceptable representation of the subnet mask, instead of using 192.168.1.0/255.255.255.0.

Finally, Windows 2000 does not allow subnet masks that do not have *contiguous* bit masks. Examples such as /20, 255.255.240.0 and /26, 255.255.255.192 are valid, but a subnet mask such as 255.255.255.193 is not because this mask cannot be represented using this type of subnet annotation.

Once you have created all your sites and subnets, you are ready to link the sites together for an efficient replication topology for AD.

FIGURE 1-19

Assigning a subnet to a site

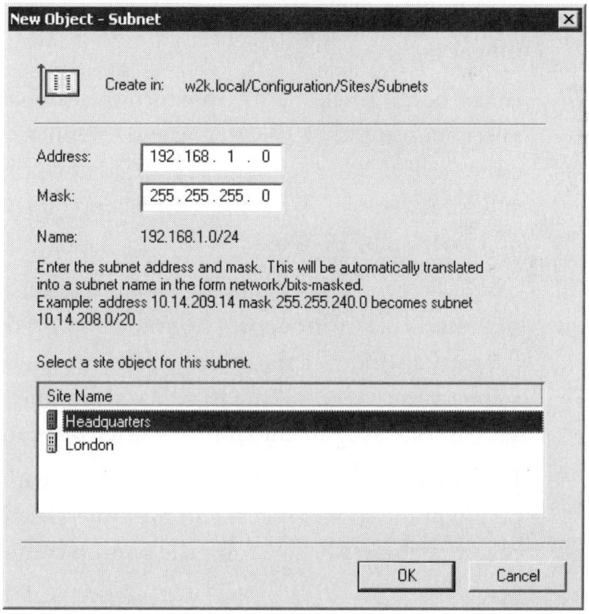

EXERCISE 1-3

Creating Subnets in Active Directory

In this exercise, we create subnets and assign them to different sites in Active Directory:

1. Verify that you are logged on to your domain as Administrator.
2. Open the MMC, click the Console menu item and select the Add/Remove snap-in pop-up menu item.
3. From the Stand-alone tab, click Add. From the Add Stand-alone snap-in, click the Active Directory Sites and Services snap-in and click Add. After adding the snap-in, click Close and then click OK to close the Add snap-in window.
4. Expand the Active Directory Sites and Services snap-in by double-clicking the snap-in. A Sites object appears underneath the Active Directory Sites and Services entry. Double-clicking the Sites object shows the Subnets object.
5. To create a new subnet, right-click the Subnet object and select New Subnet from the pop-up context menu.
6. In the New Object–Subnet window, enter the new subnet address and subnet mask that you want to create. Notice that as you enter each octet of the subnet mask, the subnet's actual name starts to appear underneath the subnet mask entry.
7. At the bottom, select a site to which this subnet will be assigned. Once you select your site, click OK to create the subnet object. Repeat Steps 5–7 to create several other subnets. Try different combinations of subnet addresses and subnet masks. What happens when you try to use a subnet mask of 255.192.255.0? Why?
8. Once you have created all your subnets, select a subnet. Right-click the subnet and select Properties from the pop-up context menu. A subnet Properties window appears, in which you can enter a description for the subnet and change the site to which this subnet is assigned. Change the subnet's site assignment and click OK. Does anything happen?
9. Delete all your subnet objects, with the exception of two. To delete, either highlight the subnet object and press the Delete key, or right-click the subnet object and select Delete from the pop-up context menu.

CERTIFICATION OBJECTIVE 1.04

Creating Site Links

Once your sites and subnets have been placed in the Active Directory, the next step is to link your sites together. Site links allow you to communicate to the *Knowledge Consistency Checker (KCC)* what *cost* links are, how frequently they should replicate, and when they should replicate.

The KCC is a built-in process that runs on all domain controllers. Although the KCC can, and will, build the replication topology for the whole forest or domain, it also uses the site links you designate to replicate between sites. Creating links between domain controllers in the same site is not necessary, because the KCC assumes that there is a well-connected network between all domains and domain controllers in the site. Therefore, the KCC creates the most favorable connections to all domain controllers for replication purposes.

What Is a Site Link?

As stated earlier, site links are a method of defining how sites replicate traffic between each other. Because some WAN links (for example, an overseas ISDN connection) might be slower or more costly than others, you can set link costs appropriately so these links are used only as a last resort. Not only does this procedure cut operational costs, but it also guarantees efficient use of WAN links and the best speed of service for your network. Without site links, all WAN links would be treated the same, which could result in degraded service and higher operational costs for your network.

How to Create a Site Link

All site links are created in the Active Directory Sites and Services MMC snap-in under the Sites object. Underneath the Sites object, you will find an object called Inter-Site Transports (see Figure 1-20). This object is where you will create all site links.

As you can tell from Figure 1-20, there are two objects beneath the Inter-Site Transports object. These are the IP and SMTP site link objects. Any link created

FIGURE 1-20 Locating Inter-Site Transports to create a new site link

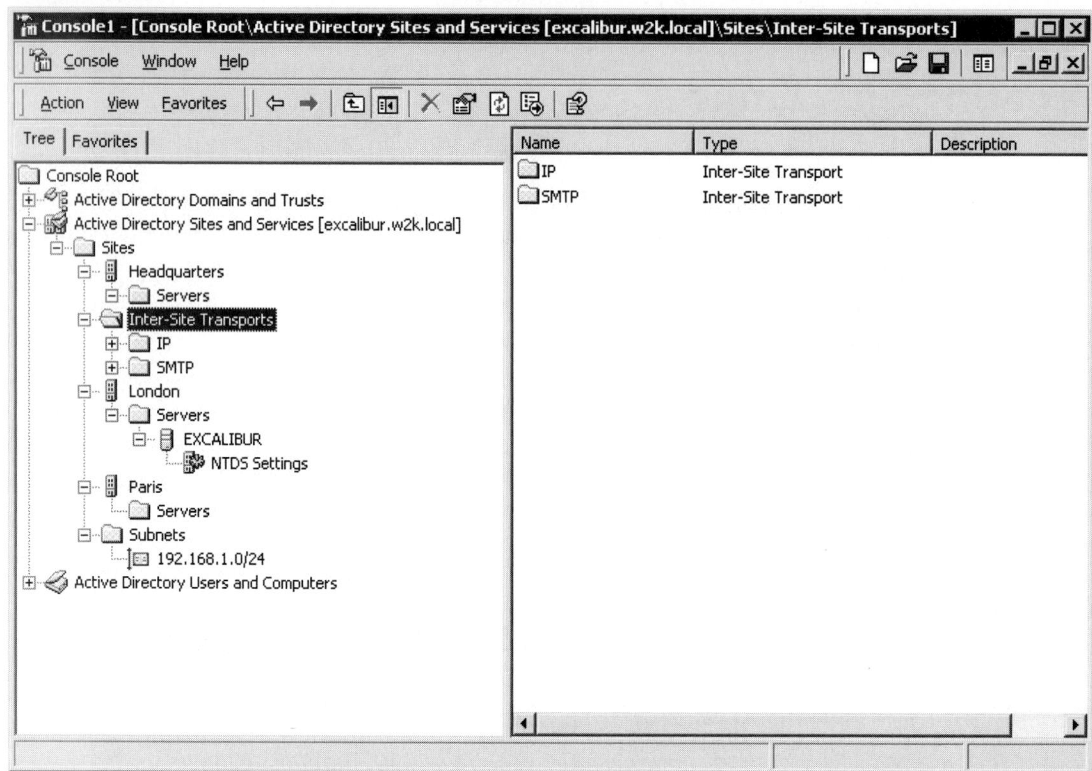

under IP uses IP as its transport protocol; and any link created under SMTP uses SMTP as its transport protocol.

What is the difference between IP and SMTP, you ask? *Simple Mail Transfer Protocol (SMTP) site links* are used when low-speed, *asynchronous* replication is necessary between sites. SMTP site links take advantage of the fact that because they are asynchronous, they can process several replication transactions at the same time. *Internet Protocol (IP) site links* must communicate *synchronously*, which requires each replication transaction to complete before another transaction can start. SMTP site links take into consideration the possibility that it may not be desirable to have synchronous IP site link replication over slow links.

exam
Watch

You should be aware of the terms used with site links. Although you might see IP and remote procedure call (RPC)-based communications referred to or implied as being separate, they are, in fact, one and the same. RPC is used when discussing replication within a domain or site, whereas IP is used when discussing replication between sites. In fact, the two are equal, because they are actually RPC over IP (much in the same way NetBIOS is carried over IP).

To create a site link, open the Active Directory Sites and Services MMC snap-in and navigate to Sites | Inter-Site Transports. From here, right-click either IP or SMTP for your site link transport and select New Site Link from the context menu. A new site link object window appears (see Figure 1-21) so that you can link the proper sites together.

Note that in Figure 1-21, the site link is named HQ-London because the site link contains the sites Headquarters and London. As stated earlier in the chapter, it is recommended that you name your objects appropriately so that they are not confusing to others who view them. Using location names for such objects as sites and site links helps describe them and their purpose.

FIGURE 1-21

Creating a new site link object

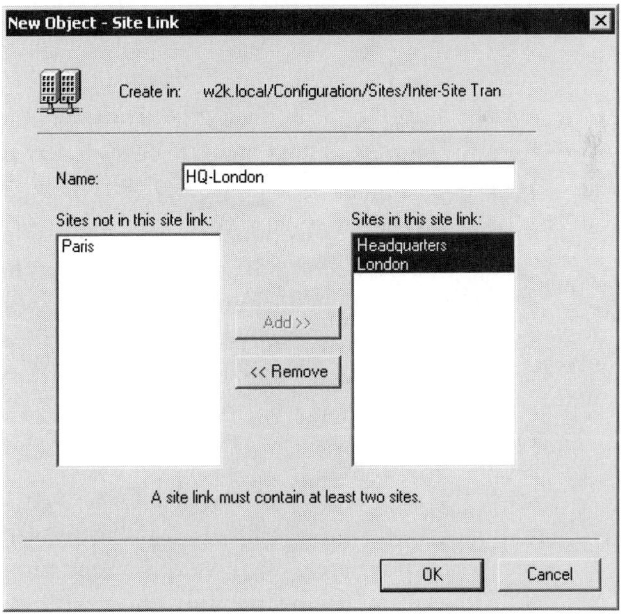

New Object - Site Link

Create in: w2k.local/Configuration/Sites/Inter-Site Tran

Name: HQ-London

Sites not in this site link: Paris

Sites in this site link: Headquarters, London

Add >>

<< Remove

A site link must contain at least two sites.

OK Cancel

EXERCISE 1-4

Creating Site Links in Active Directory

In this exercise, you create site links for sites within Active Directory. You also modify existing site links by varying link costs and replication schedules.

1. Verify that you are logged on to your domain as Administrator.
2. Open the MMC, click the Console menu item and select the Add/Remove snap-in pop-up menu item.
3. From the Stand-alone tab, click Add. From the Add Stand-alone snap-in, click the Active Directory Sites and Services snap-in and click Add. After adding the snap-in, click Close and then click OK to close the Add snap-in window.
4. Expand the Active Directory Sites and Services snap-in by double-clicking the snap-in. A Sites object appears underneath the Active Directory Sites and Services entry. Double-clicking the Sites object shows the Inter-Site Transports object.
5. Underneath Inter-Site Transports, you will find both the IP and SMTP objects. For this exercise, you may create Site link objects in either the IP or SMTP object, but keep in mind that when you do use either IP or SMTP, you are actually selecting the *replication protocol* that the site link will use. Select either IP or SMTP and right-click the object. Select New Site Link from the pop-up context menu to create a new site link.
6. In the New Object–Site Link window, you must enter the name of the site link before the OK button becomes available. Next, select at least two sites to which this link will connect. Once you have made your selections, click OK to create the site link object. Create several site links until you are comfortable with this process. *Do not edit any site links until you are instructed to do so.* Try to create a site link with exactly the same name under the IP object. What happens? Try to create the exact same site link under the SMTP object. What happens? Why?
7. Once you have created all your site links, select a site link and double-click it to edit. The site link's Properties window appears. Notice in the bottom-left corner that there are Cost and Replication settings along with a Change Schedule button for this site link. Link costs can be incremented or decremented by factors of 1, while replication times can be incremented or decremented by factors of 15 minutes. If you click the Change Schedule

button, a window appears that allows you to tell Windows 2000 when this link is available to pass replication traffic.

8. Work with the open site link and change its costs, replication frequency, and replication schedule to familiarize yourself with how each setting works for the site link. Try to set the replication frequency to 0. What happens? Try to modify a site link so that it only has one site. What happens?

CERTIFICATION OBJECTIVE 1.05

Assigning Bridgehead Servers

Once you have designed the layout of your network, it is time to start thinking about load balancing your network traffic, specifically your Active Directory replication. Keep in mind that not only do you have to contend with replication traffic consuming precious bandwidth, but you also need to remember that there is a server receiving all this replication traffic that needs to be processed quickly. Using bridgehead servers allows you to partially load-balance your replication traffic by assigning certain servers to receive replication traffic from other sites.

What Is a Bridgehead Server?

Bridgehead servers are much like connection objects. Bridgehead servers are inbound-only connections that specify which server(s) in a site receive replication traffic from other sites. They act as the "bridge" into the site for replication traffic; once the replication traffic is received over the bridgehead server, it then replicates all the AD changes from other sites to all the domain controllers within its own site. This designated bridgehead server acts as a shield for all other domain controllers in the site because it takes on the extra responsibility of receiving AD replication from other sites and then replicates those changes to all other domain controllers in its own site.

As you can imagine, this places an extra burden on the bridgehead server, which not only has to keep up with bridgehead replication but also has to keep up with replication within its own site. This is why you should only specify high-end servers as bridgehead servers within your sites. Assigning a low-end server as a bridgehead server, especially with several sites, will crush it.

As you will see later, the KCC handles all replication connections such as connection objects and bridgehead servers. The KCC can automatically assign bridgehead servers, but if you have very few high-end servers and many average to low-end servers, it may beneficial to assign your own bridgehead servers instead of allowing the KCC to assign them. You can create your own bridgehead servers, but you have to use care when assigning them, because the KCC cannot automatically select an alternative bridgehead server if a preferred one is unavailable. Allowing the KCC to manage all bridgehead servers makes for more efficient management of replication connections, but it also has the potential of placing the replication burden on systems on which you do not desire to have this burden placed.

How to Create a Bridgehead Server

Creating a bridgehead is relatively simple. All you need to do is select the server to become the bridgehead server and decide what replication transport you will allow it to use. In the Active Directory Sites and Services MMC snap-in, navigate to Sites | *<Site name>* | Servers | *<Server name>* (see Figure 1-22).

FIGURE 1-22 Selecting a server to become a bridgehead server

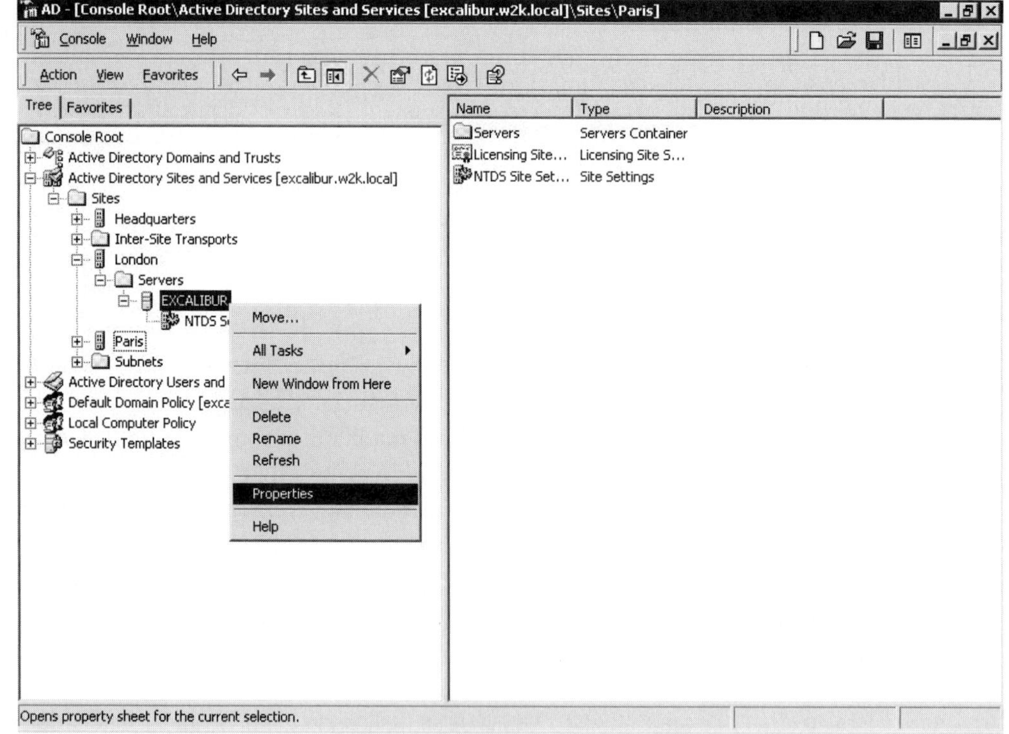

FIGURE 1-23

Designating a server to be a bridgehead server

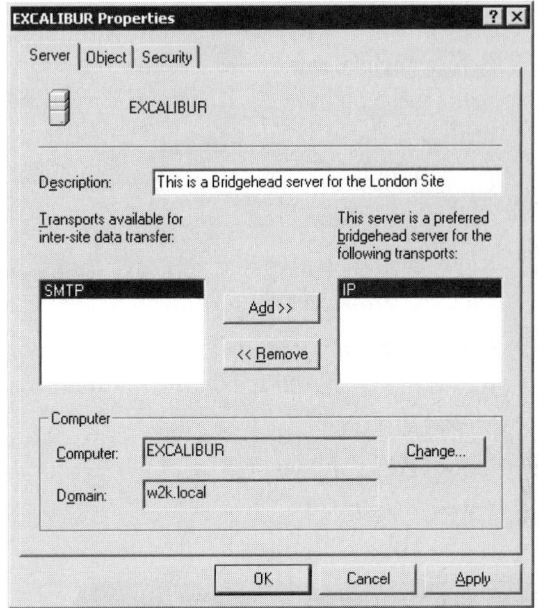

Right-click the server and select Properties from the pop-up context menu. The server Properties window appears, as shown in Figure 1-23.

From here you can select the transport on which the bridgehead server will receive replication traffic from other sites. Click OK, and you have created your Bridgehead server.

EXERCISE 1-5

Designating a Server as a Bridgehead Server

In this exercise, you designate your Active Directory server as a bridgehead server. Your server must have AD already installed to complete this exercise.

1. Verify that you are logged on to your domain as Administrator.
2. Open the MMC, click the Console menu item and select the Add/Remove snap-in pop-up menu item.
3. From the Stand-alone tab, click Add. From the Add Stand-alone snap-in, click the Active Directory Sites and Services snap-in and click Add. After adding the snap-in, click Close and then click OK to close the Add snap-in window.

4. Before navigating down the Active Directory Sites and Services snap-in, make sure you have chosen the server you want to designate as a bridgehead server.
5. Expand the Active Directory Sites and Services snap-in by double-clicking the snap-in. Navigate to Sites | *<Site name>* | Servers | *<Server name>*.
6. Right-click the server that you have chosen to be a bridgehead server and click the Properties context menu item.
7. In the Properties window, select the transport that will accept replication traffic and click Add to add the transport to the list of preferred bridgehead servers.
8. Click OK to save your changes.

CERTIFICATION OBJECTIVE 1.06

Creating Site Link Bridges

If your network has several sites, you can model the routing of your network by creating site link bridges, which also allows you to efficiently distribute AD replication so that backup links are used when they are needed. This technique allows companies to cut costs and ensure efficient use of resources when they are needed. In Figure 1-24, you can see how the use of site link bridges allows the employment of faster, more efficient WAN connections and how backup connections can be used only when needed.

What Is a Site Link Bridge?

A *site link bridge* allows network administrators to "tell" Windows 2000 networks how to route replication traffic from one site to another. Using site link bridges allows administrators to route replication traffic to best fit their networks and build efficient routing of AD replication. Without the use of site link bridges, replication traffic might have to use slower, less efficient, and possibly more costly WAN

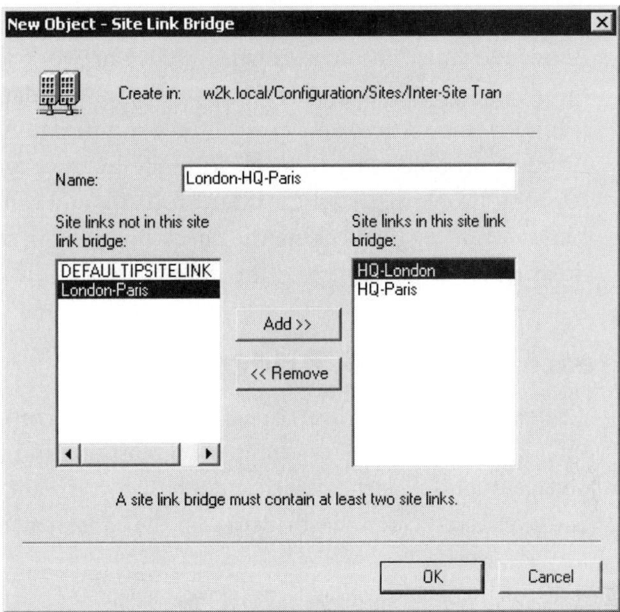

FIGURE 1-24 Effective use of a site link bridge

connections. As a network administrator, you want to ensure that your company uses its resources efficiently.

Site link bridges are a way of connecting or linking sites with one another without creating massive numbers of site links. Think of a large corporation with 20 satellite offices around the country. Creating the large number of site links needed to link all these sites is not practical and can possibly become a performance bottleneck. Creating one site link bridge that consists of the minimum number of site links needed to link all your sites guarantees that your sites replicate correctly. All links within a site link bridge are considered transitive; therefore, if Site A is linked to Site B, and Site B is linked to Site C, then Site A is connected to Site C.

Looking at Figure 1-24, you could remove the London-Paris site link and use a London-HQ-Paris site link bridge, which would allow you to:

- Route your replication traffic exclusively from London through HQ to Paris, thereby using a more efficient replication route (as specified by the low link costs for the site links HQ-London and HQ-Paris)
- Remove one unnecessary site link because the site link bridge London-HQ-Paris serves the same function as a London-Paris site link

One other point to keep in mind is that if your network is fully IP routable, Active Directory automatically links your network without any assistance, which means that you do not have to create site link bridges to link site objects. If this feature is not desired, you must disable the Bridge All Site Links option for the IP transport object. By right-clicking the IP Inter-Site transport object and selecting Properties from the context menu, you can disable the Bridge All Site Links option by unchecking the check box. Doing so allows you to create site link bridges as you desire.

How to Create a Site Link Bridge

To create a site link bridge, open the Active Directory Sites and Services MMC snap-in. Navigate to Sites | Inter-site Transports and find both the IP and SMTP objects. Right-click the object under which you want to create the site link bridge, and select New Site Link Bridge from the context menu (see Figure 1-25).

FIGURE 1-25 Creating a new site link bridge

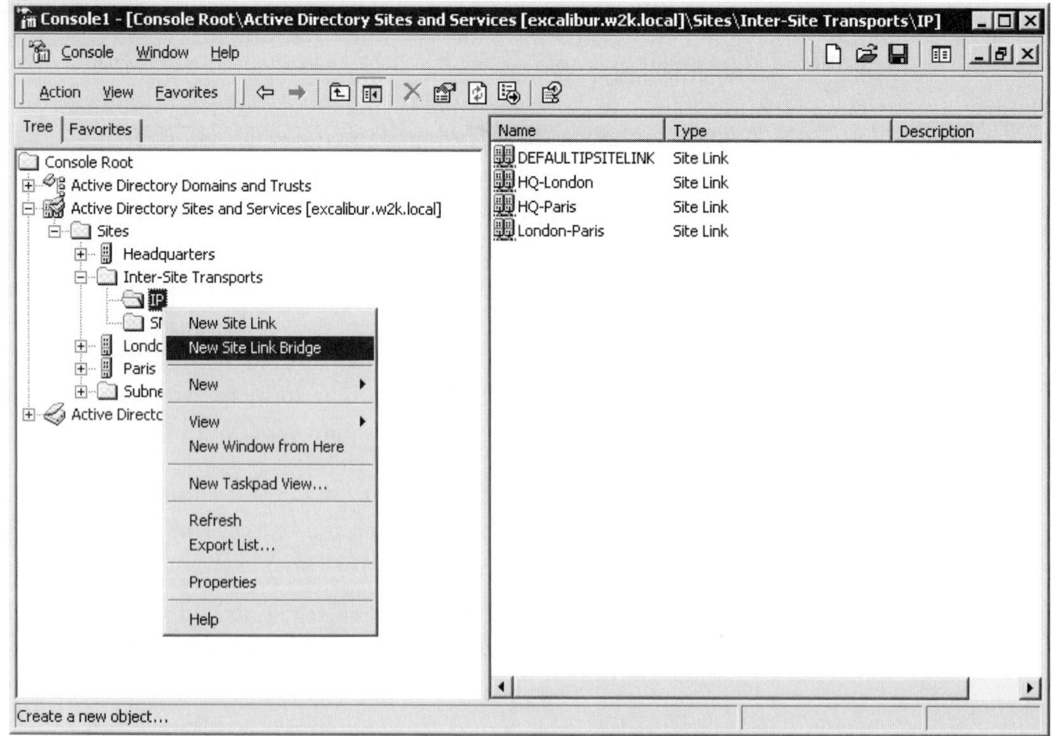

Once you select the New Site Link Bridge context menu, a New Object–Site Link Bridge window appears (see Figure 1-26). You must select at least two site links to create a new site link bridge.

Again, the general recommendation is that you create or name your site link bridges in much the same manner as your site links, which is to use the names of the sites that you are linking. Looking at Figure 1-26, you can see that two site links, HQ-London and HQ-Paris, are both selected, making the site link bridge London-HQ-Paris. Once you have created your site link bridge, you can double-click it to add comments, add or delete site links, and so on (see Figure 1-27).

Note that when you create your site link bridge, it does not have a *link cost* assigned to it. The link cost is computed by adding the link costs of all the site links that make up the site link bridge. Care must be taken when creating site link bridges so that Active Directory properly uses them and that backup links are used when the site link bridge loses a link.

exam Watch

Make sure you are careful about the difference between site links and site link bridges. Remember that site links contain link costs and replication times, whereas site link bridges are a set of site links grouped together to form a site link bridge. Site link bridges have no link cost, because their link cost is a dynamic cost dependent on the links included in the site link bridge.

FIGURE 1-26

Creating a new site link bridge

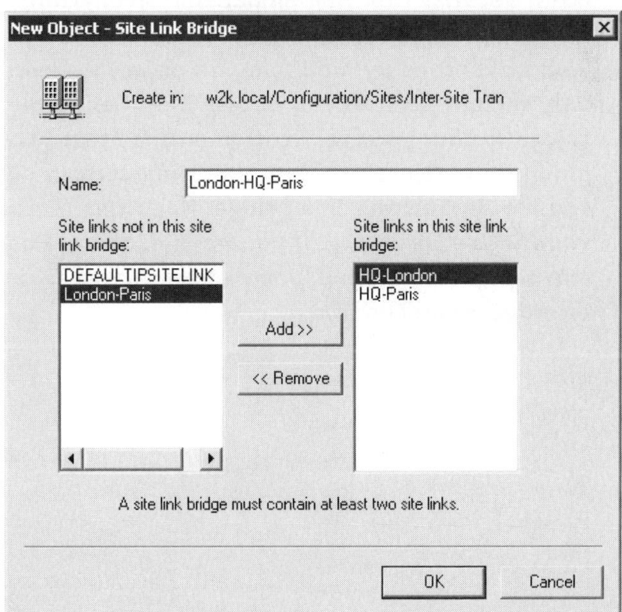

FIGURE 1-27

Editing the site link bridge properties

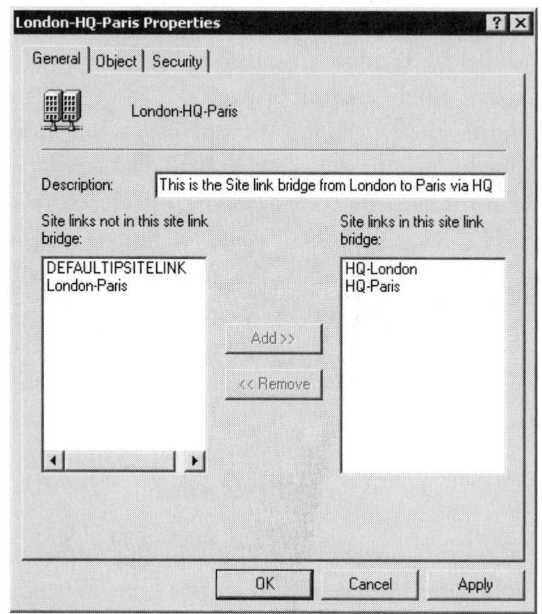

Looking at Figure 1-27, you will notice that this site link bridge object has a Security tab. Remember that everything you create is an object and is therefore stored in the Active Directory. You can use this fact to your advantage by modifying an object's access control list (ACL) so that only certain persons can access it. For example, if you create a site link bridge so that your replication traffic must take a certain route, you can modify the object's ACL so that only certain person(s) and/or group(s) can modify this site link bridge. Keep this feature in mind when modifying your Active Directory. If you have dedicated administrative duties, you can delegate certain aspects of the Active Directory to an individual or group of individuals.

FROM THE CLASSROOM

Getting a Good Grasp

After reading more than half this chapter, you should be starting to get a good idea of how Active Directory handles replication through the placement of domain controllers, subnet assignments, and the use of sites, site links, and site link bridges. This is by far the hardest concept to understand in using and administering Windows 2000, because there is so much complexity involved with AD replication.

AD replication is much like a set of nesting dolls. First, domain controllers within each domain replicate between each other. Second, you can have several domains (such as ABC.COM and 123.COM) that are in the same site. Not only do a domain's domain controllers replicate with each other within their own domain, but each domain replicates Active Directory and schema data with each other because of the use of global catalogs. Third, domain controllers from different sites must replicate with one another, so site links and site link bridges provide the mechanisms to replicate between sites. Before moving on in the chapter, make sure that you really understand the concepts already covered; as in some subjects, such as mathematics, these concepts build on one another. If you do not have a good grasp of one concept, it can affect how you understand future concepts. Make sure you know all the mechanisms involved with Active Directory because the certification tests expect that you know this information by heart.

—Michael Seamans, MCSE

Since we have covered sites and all the objects associated with them (site links, subnets, bridgehead servers, and site link bridges), here are some scenarios and solutions to keep in mind.

SCENARIO & SOLUTION	
You want to route replication traffic through your high-speed backbone and use your backup links only when needed. How do you go about this?	Make sure you use site link bridges to route your replication traffic as desired. Using site link bridges allows you to specify which site links to use to get from Site A to Site B.
Sites are too confusing. Can't you just put all of your domain controllers into one site?	You might be able to put all of your domain controllers into a single site, but you must remember the golden rule with sites: Domain controllers that are linked via slow connections need to be placed in separate sites and connected via site links. Failing to do so will result in poor Active Directory and network performance.
You've got domain controllers on the same subnet, but they are in different buildings. You want to put domain controllers in a site for each building. Should you keep all of them in the same site, or should you put them in their own separate sites?	If you have domain controllers on the same subnet, the assumption is that they are "well connected" by some means (such as a 10MB LAN). If this is the case, there is no need to create separate sites, unless your AD structure requires that you create sites for each building. If this is the case, you need to put the domain controllers on different subnets to accommodate the different sites.
You've got a remote site that uses a 56K connection. What type of site link should you use?	Typically, you would use an SMTP site link, because that type takes advantage of the fact that the link is slower and allows the link to use asynchronous replication. A replication then becomes more efficient because you can now have several replication transactions without having to wait for a response.
You've got a high-speed connection between my headquarters and overseas sites. Unfortunately, the connection can be unreliable at times. How should you configure your site link(s)?	First, you should use an SMTP site link due to the fact that the link can be unreliable. An SMTP site link can have outstanding replication transactions and still work, whereas an IP site link must wait for its replication transaction to complete before starting another. Also, if you have other ways to connect to your overseas site, you might want to configure your site links and site link bridges to use this link only when necessary. Setting a high link cost for this site link allows you to use this link only when necessary.

EXERCISE 1-6

Creating Site Link Bridges in Active Directory

In this exercise, you learn how to create site link bridges in Active Directory.

1. Verify that you are logged on to your domain as Administrator.
2. Open the MMC, click the Console menu item and select the Add/Remove snap-in pop-up menu item.
3. From the Stand-alone tab, click Add. From the Add Stand-alone snap-in, click the Active Directory Sites and Services snap-in and click Add. After adding the snap-in, click Close and then click OK to close the Add snap-in window.
4. Expand the Active Directory Sites and Services snap-in by double-clicking the snap-in. A Sites object appears underneath the Active Directory Sites and Services entry. Double-clicking the Sites object shows the Inter-Site Transport object.
5. Double-click the Inter-Site Transport object to show the IP and SMTP objects. As in Site links, you can create site link bridges using either IP or SMTP as the transport. The only stipulation is that you must use site links from the same protocol object (in other words, an IP site link bridge may use only site links from the IP protocol object).
6. Right-click either the IP or SMTP object and select New Site Link Bridge from the pop-up context menu. The New Object–Site Link Bridge window appears. In this window, you must specify a name for the site link bridge and select at least two site links to create the site link bridge. Once you have selected these, click OK to save the object.
7. Repeat Steps 5 and 6 to create several more site link bridges until you understand the process. Try to create a new site link bridge under a protocol object that does not have at least two site links in it. What happens? Try to create a site link bridge with the same name as a current site link bridge. What happens?

CERTIFICATION OBJECTIVE 1.07

Create Connection Objects

Connection objects are aptly named because they are exactly what their name implies. Connection objects enable inbound connections to every domain controller in your network. The KCC, as discussed earlier, automatically handles the creation and management of all connection objects as well as establishing a replication topology between all domain controllers.

What Are Connection Objects?

Connection objects are *inbound-only* connections to domain controllers. The KCC cannot create outbound connection objects. As stated, the KCC manages all connection objects and creates a replication topology automatically, without administrators needing to configure their own topologies. Some of the reasons that you might want to create manual connection objects include these:

- **Changing the replication scheduling for connection objects.** When the KCC creates a connection object automatically, it sets the replication schedule for the connection object. The only way to change the replication schedule is to take ownership of the connection object. Taking ownership of the connection allows you to change the replication schedule, but it also makes the connection object a manual object instead of an automatically created object made and managed by the KCC. This becomes important when deciding to depend on the KCC for replication or making your own connection objects and planning your own replication topology.
- **Creating your own replication topology.** You might need to create your own replication topology, based on your network topology.

How to Create Connection Objects

To create a connection object, open the Active Directory Sites and Services MMC snap-in and navigate to the site in question. Once you reach your site, navigate to Server | <*Server name*> | NTDS settings. At the NTDS settings object, right-click to create a New Active Directory Connection (see Figure 1-28).

FIGURE 1-28 Creating a new connection object

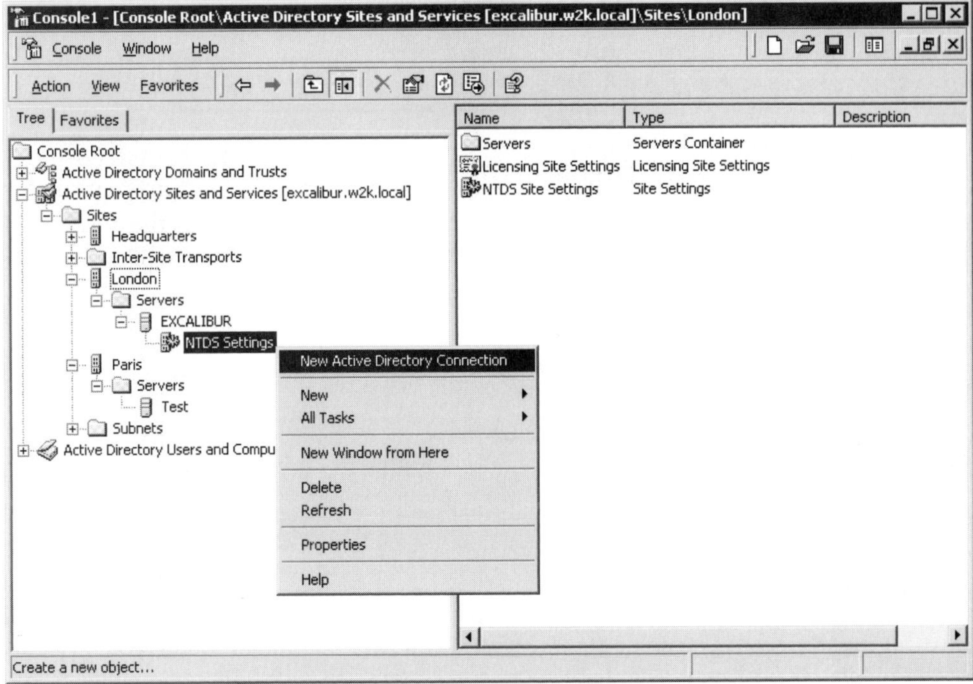

When you select the New Active Directory Connection context menu option, a connection object Properties window appears for you to select the domain controller with which this connection object will be associated. Select your domain controller and click OK.

Next, you must name your connection object. As recommended in the past, name your connection object with both domain controller names. This makes it obvious which two domain controllers this connection object is connecting. Once you name your connection object, it appears as a connection object in your NTDS settings. Double-click to edit and modify the object (see Figure 1-29).

Looking at Figure 1-29, you can see that not only can you select the transport method (IP, RPC, or SMTP), you can also change the scheduling of replication by clicking Change Schedule.

Earlier in the chapter, we clarified the difference between RPC, IP, and SMTP connections. Basically, RPC and IP connections are one and the same, although the terms are used to describe replication connections at different levels. RPC is used at the domain controller level, whereas IP is used at the sites level of replication.

FIGURE 1-29

Editing the connection object

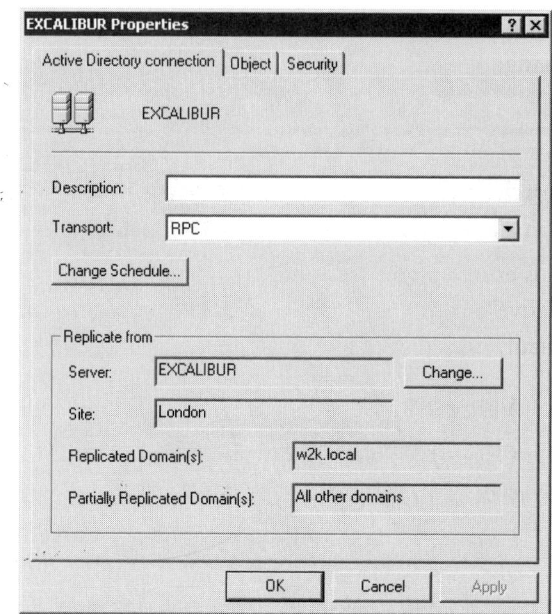

Another point to keep in mind is that RPC replication (mostly used for intrasite replication) does not compress replication data, because it assumes that connections are using well-connected media, whereas IP replication (mostly used for intersite replication) does compress replication data for efficient use of bandwidth.

RPC and IP connections use synchronous communications, which require each replication transaction to be acknowledged before the next transaction can take place. SMTP connections use asynchronous communications, which allow several replication transactions to be unacknowledged while still allowing communications to continue.

When looking at these protocols, we normally associate RPC and IP connections with faster network connectivity because they are more efficient yet less tolerant of network problems than SMTP connections. SMTP connections are more tolerant of network problems, such as noisy lines, and perform well with lower-speed network connections. That is why they are sometimes favored over IP connections when administrators create site links. When you create connections that require you to choose among RPC, IP, and SMTP protocols, look at exactly where you will be applying these connections; that will help you determine what protocol to use.

Remember that you can change the replication schedule only on connection objects that you manually create. You can change the scheduling of replication on automatically generated objects, but for these changes to be permanent, you must change these objects from automatically generated connections to manual ones.

EXERCISE 1-7

Creating Connection Objects for Active Directory Domain Controllers

In this exercise, you create manual connection objects for domain controllers in Active Directory. You also learn how to change the replication frequency for manually created connection objects.

1. Verify that you are logged on to your domain as Administrator.
2. Open the MMC, click the Console menu item and select the Add/Remove snap-in pop-up menu item.
3. From the Stand-alone tab, click Add. From the Add Stand-alone snap-in, click the Active Directory Sites and Services snap-in and click Add. After adding the snap-in, click Close and then click OK to close the Add snap-in window.
4. Expand the Active Directory Sites and Services snap-in by double-clicking the snap-in. To create a new Active Directory connection, select which domain controller you would like to make the connection. Navigate to Sites | *<Site name>* | Servers | *<Server name>* | NTDS Settings. Right-click NTDS setting from the context menu and select the New Active Directory Connection menu item.
5. Next, select a domain controller from the Find Domain Controllers window and click OK. This is the domain controller that will replicate to the domain controller that you are using. The New Object–Connection window appears so that you can name the connection. Name the connection object and click OK. You will find the object located under NTDS Settings for the selected server. To familiarize yourself with creating connection objects, repeat Steps 4 and 5 to create more connection objects.
6. To edit a connection object, select a connection object and double-click. A Properties window for the connection object opens, showing several settings for the object, including its transport, the domain that the connection object is replicating from, and a Change Schedule button to allow changes in

replication scheduling. First, change the transport for the connection object by clicking the drop-down box for Transports. Select a different transport.

7. You can change the replicating server that uses this manual connection object by clicking Change next to the Replicate From Server entry. A Find Domain Controllers window appears. Select the domain controller to which you want to reassign this connection object and click OK. The new domain controller selected now replicates with the domain controller with which you are currently working.
8. Finally, click Change Schedule to work with the replication schedule for this manual connection. The replication schedule shows several settings for replications per hour. You can specify replication to occur once, twice, or four times per hour. You can also specify that no replication occur during certain hours. This option is useful to limit the amount of replication during your network's peak operational hours. To change replication times, select the time frame that you want to modify, then click one of the replication frequencies to change the replication schedule. Once you have modified the replication schedule, click OK to save the changes. Try modifying the replication schedule so that there is no replication at all and save the configuration. What happens? Do you think that Active Directory would allow this choice? Why or why not?

CERTIFICATION OBJECTIVE 1.08

Creating Global Catalog Servers

To finish the configuration of your Windows 2000 network, you need to consider the placement of *global catalog servers* within your network. Global catalog servers must be strategically placed and, as you have seen from all the other objects you created in this chapter, creating too many of any one global catalog can lead to unwanted replication and resource usage. When creating global catalog servers, keep the following in mind:

- Each global catalog server has to bear the burden of extra replication and must have enough storage capacity to hold partial replicas of all objects from other domains in the network.

- Global catalog servers are required for the logon process; therefore, placement of global catalog servers is crucial to performance on your network. Inefficient placement of a global catalog server can translate to poor performance for a segment of your network. As a general guideline, it is recommended that you have at least one global catalog server in each site to provide adequate resources for your network. The drawback is, as explained previously, increased replication traffic on your network. If your network can handle the traffic, having a global catalog server in each site may be beneficial.

on the job

The only exception to the rule that a global catalog server must be available on the network to fulfill logon requests is the Administrator account. The Administrator account is allowed to log on to the network by default, because the Administrator needs to access the network in order to fix any problems.

What Is a Global Catalog Server?

A *global catalog server* holds both a full copy of the local Active Directory as well as a partial replica of all objects from all other domains in the network. Many objects from other domains are not stored in the global catalog because some of this information is not critical enough to be replicated through AD. This storage scheme not only cuts down on replication, but it also relieves some processing pressure on global catalog servers to keep up with replication of non-essential AD information.

How to Create a Global Catalog Server

Creating a global catalog server is very simple (much simpler than making the decision to designate a domain controller as a global catalog). Using the Active Directory Sites and Services MMC snap-in, drill down to the server that you want to make a global catalog server by navigating to Sites | <*Site name*> | Servers | <*Server name*> | NTDS Settings. Right-click the NTDS Settings object and select Properties from the context menu. The NTDS Settings Properties window appears, as shown in Figure 1-30.

Creating a global catalog server is as easy as checking the global catalog check box, as shown in Figure 1-30. Once you check this box and click OK, the server in question becomes a global catalog server. Remember that the *first domain controller* you install automatically becomes a global catalog server, because a global catalog server is necessary for logons to occur.

FIGURE 1-30

The NTDS Settings window

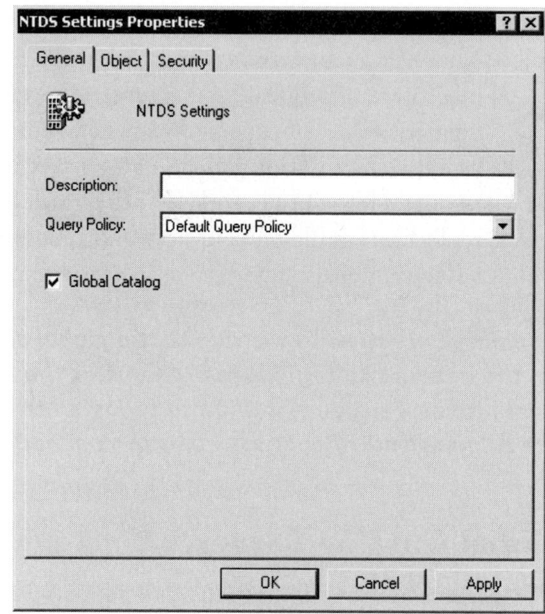

EXERCISE 1-8

Defining Global Catalog Servers in Active Directory

In this exercise, you learn how to set domain controllers as global catalog servers.

1. Verify that you are logged on to your domain as Administrator.
2. Open the MMC, click the Console menu item and select the Add/Remove snap-in pop-up menu item.
3. From the Stand-alone tab, click Add. From the Add Stand-alone snap-in, click the Active Directory Sites and Services snap-in and click Add. After adding the snap-in, click Close and then click OK to close the Add snap-in window.
4. Expand the Active Directory Sites and Services snap-in by double-clicking the snap-in. To set a domain controller as a global catalog server, navigate to Sites | *<Site name>* | Servers | *<Server name>* | NTDS Settings. Right-click the NTDS Settings object and select Properties from the pop-up context menu. The NTDS Settings Properties window appears. On the General tab, the last item on the tab is a Global Catalog check box. To set the selected server as a global catalog, click the Global Catalog check box and click OK.

Here are a few scenarios and solutions to keep in mind relating to connection objects and global catalog servers.

SCENARIO & SOLUTION	
You need to have your domain controllers updated as quickly as possible. Can you manually adjust their replication times?	You can manually adjust replication times by adjusting the frequency at which controllers replicate. This is done through the NTDS Settings for a server object. You can only adjust replication from once per hour to four times per hour.
You want to create your own replication topology so that you know how your domain controllers are replicating at all times and that they are replicating to the nearest domain controller. Can this be done?	The short answer is "Yes." Keep one *very* important thing in mind, however: When you create manual connection objects, the KCC uses these over automatically generated ones. If a connection between two domain controllers has only one manually created connection object and it fails, the KCC will not compensate for that failure. You must make sure that your replication topology is solid before deciding to make an all-manual replication topology.
Do you need to have a global catalog server? You have only a single domain.	Even though you have only one domain, you still must have at least one global catalog server. Fortunately, when you install your first domain controller, it is automatically installed as a global catalog server.
Your company is very large, and your network will have a forest with several domains. What is the impact of having several domains and using global catalog servers?	Each global catalog server keeps a listing of its local domain as well as a partial listing of important objects from all other domains. Having a network with several domains places an additional replication burden on your domain controllers that serve as global catalog servers. This burden is multiplied by the number of global catalog servers you have throughout your network, again because of replication. You must carefully choose how many global catalog servers you will have and scale them appropriately.

CERTIFICATION SUMMARY

In this chapter, we covered the necessary steps to install, configure, and optimize Active Directory for any given network.

First, we covered the DCPROMO process and the various scenarios that one could face when installing a domain controller. Next, we covered the concept of sites and subnets. Subnets are groups of systems located locally on a network that, when combined with other subnets in a local geographic area, form a site. Sites are a collection of "well-connected" subnets and domain controllers. Sites form a logical partition of network systems which, when used by clients, allows for efficient use of resources and Active Directory replication.

We then covered site links and site link bridges, which allow for connecting separate sites for Active Directory replication and resources. Site links allow sites to replicate with one another; site link bridges allow the ability to route AD replication according to your existing network topology. Site link bridges can be configured to use more favorable, and faster, network links over those that are more costly and slower.

Last, we looked at connection objects and global catalog servers. Connection objects are inbound-only connections to domain controllers that allow Active Directory replication. We discussed global catalog server placement, and it was discovered that the placement of too many global catalog servers could dramatically increase network traffic.

TWO-MINUTE DRILL

Installing Active Directory

- ❑ When using a non-Microsoft DNS solution, you must use a version of DNS that is BIND version 8.1.2 or higher. This version supports service resource records (SRV RRs), which are a requirement for Windows 2000.
- ❑ Active Directory requires at least one NTFS partition.
- ❑ The SYSVOL folder stores all your public files and contains the NETLOGON share, from which all file replication takes place. The SYSVOL folder must be installed on an NTFS 5.0 partition.
- ❑ When you choose to install DNS separately, Windows 2000 automatically generates all the DNS entries required for Active Directory and places them in the NETLOGON.DNS file under the %SystemRoot%\System32\config directory.

Creating Sites

- ❑ Sites help partition your Active Directory into logical groups based primarily on location. Sites allow clients to use local resources and replicate AD traffic efficiently.
- ❑ Sites, by definition, are a group of subnets and domain controllers that are well connected. The definition of *well connected* can vary from network to network, but in most cases the term is defined as a local area network-equivalent connection.
- ❑ Slow network connections usually create site boundaries, and they usually connect two sites.

Creating Subnets

- ❑ Subnets help map domain controllers to Active Directory sites. If all your subnets and sites are properly defined before installing the remaining domain controllers in your network, they will be properly placed in the correct site when they are added to the Active Directory via DCPROMO.

- Subnets are annotated in the form of 0.0.0.0/24. The first number is the IP subnet address; the second number is the subnet bit mask. With this type of subnet annotation, you cannot use subnet masks such as 255.255.129.0 or 255.255.255.127. The subnet bit mask assumes that the mask is a set of contiguous masking bits.
- When creating a subnet, you may associate the subnet with only one site. This requirement makes it impossible to split a subnet between two different sites.

Creating Site Links

- Site links tell AD how to connect sites within your network.
- Site links tell AD the links that are most favorable for AD replication.
- Site links control the frequency of AD replication between sites.
- Site links can use either IP or SMTP as their transport. IP uses synchronous communications for higher-speed and higher-quality connections; SMTP uses asynchronous communications for lower-speed and lower-quality connections.

Assigning Bridgehead Servers

- A bridgehead server acts as a "bridge" into a site by being a receiving point for Active Directory replication from other sites. When other sites use this bridgehead server, the bridgehead server then replicates the changes received to all other domain controllers in the site.
- Bridgehead servers receive a larger amount of replication traffic because they must receive replication traffic from all other sites as well as keeping up with replication traffic within their own sites.
- The Knowledge Consistency Checker (KCC) can, and does, create its own bridgehead server topology, but you can override this topology by designating your own bridgehead servers. Be aware that the KCC cannot automatically select alternate bridgehead servers if you have designated a bridgehead server manually. If you choose to manually assign a bridgehead server, make sure that you designate several bridgehead servers to compensate for any lost servers.

Creating Site Link Bridges

- ❑ Site link bridges are much like site links, but they allow you to model AD replication to your network topology. You can build site link bridges that allow you to route replication traffic over the most favorable, high-speed connections in your network.
- ❑ Site link bridges must consist of at least two site links.
- ❑ Site link bridges do not have assigned link costs; rather, they have a cost assigned to them by adding together all the costs of the site links that make up the site link bridge.

Creating Connection Objects

- ❑ The KCC creates and manages all connection objects between all domain controllers.
- ❑ The KCC can adjust the replication topology for domain controllers using automatically generated connection objects; it cannot automatically adjust manual connection objects.
- ❑ You can change the replication schedule for connection objects, but if they are automatically generated objects, you must take ownership of the connection object which, in turn, makes the connection object a manual object.

Creating Global Catalog Servers

- ❑ Global catalog servers are required for the logon process.
- ❑ Global catalog servers hold a full replica of the local AD and a partial replica of all other domains.
- ❑ Placement of too many global catalog servers on your network can dramatically increase network traffic.

MCSE

MICROSOFT CERTIFIED SYSTEMS ENGINEER

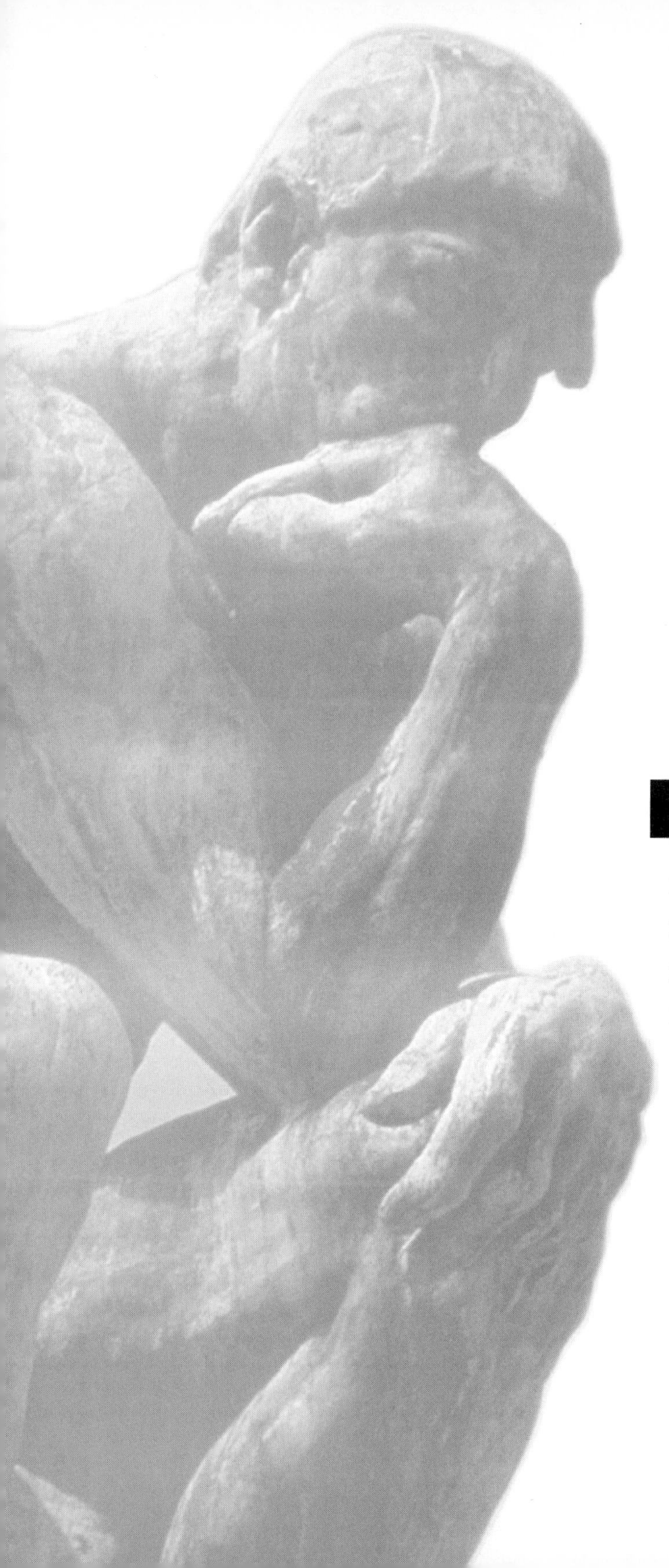

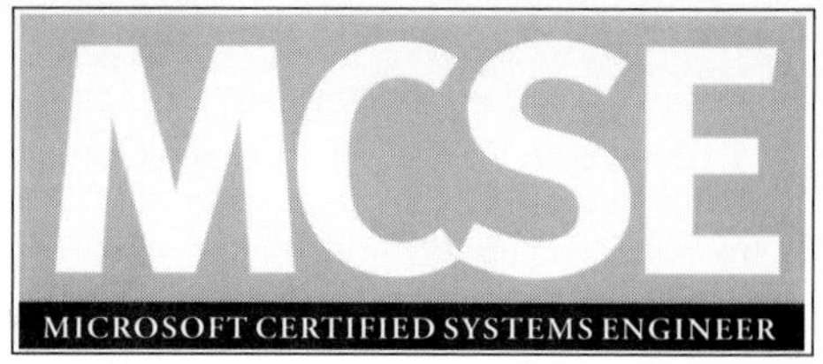

2

Active Directory Configuration

CERTIFICATION OBJECTIVES

2.01	Verifying Active Directory Installation
2.02	Moving Server Objects Between Sites
2.03	Transferring Operations Master Roles
2.04	Implementing an Organizational Unit Structure
✓	Two-Minute Drill

In the previous chapter, you learned about installation of Active Directory on a Windows 2000 Server. AD components must be configured in order to get benefits from this new feature of the Windows 2000 Server operating system. The topics that we discuss in this chapter include verification of AD installation, creating and moving server objects between sites, transferring operations master roles, and implementing an organizational unit (OU) structure.

Once the Active Directory is installed and you have verified the domain controller and the Domain Name System (DNS) server, you need to decide on the operations master roles for various domain controller computers in the network. You also need to create OUs in the Active Directory that will be the containers for AD objects. Depending on the requirements of your organization, a careful plan has to be chalked out before implementing an OU structure.

CERTIFICATION OBJECTIVE 2.01

Verifying Active Directory Installation

The first thing you should do after installation of Active Directory is to check whether it has been installed properly and is functioning in the desired way. When you start a Windows 2000 Server domain controller computer, the Configure Your Server dialog box appears by default if you have not cleared the "Show this screen at startup" check box. If you click the Active Directory option in the list on the left-hand side, you will notice that the screen that appears next tells you that Active Directory is installed (see Figure 2-1).

The addition of Active Directory management snap-ins in the Administrative tools is another indication that the installation is complete. However, this is merely an indication of the installation. This section discusses the methods of more detailed verification of Active Directory installation.

FIGURE 2-1

The Configure Your Server dialog box after Active Directory installation

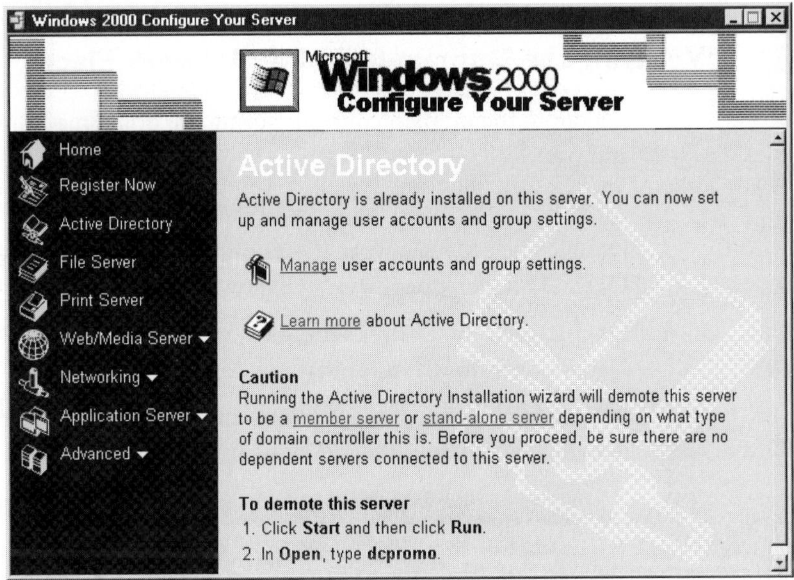

Verifying the Domain Controller

Active Directory is installed on a member server to promote it to a domain controller. You may want to check whether the domain controller that you recently upgraded from a member server is available on the network. There are several different ways to accomplish this check, but the two methods described here are the ones that give you immediate verification information. Exercises 2-1 and 2-2 will help you verify the domain controller from My Network Places and from Active Directory Users and Computers.

EXERCISE 2-1

Verifying the Domain from My Network Places

1. Log on to the domain controller using the domain administrator username and password.
2. Close the Windows 2000 Configure Your Server Wizard that appears.
3. Double-click My Network Places on the desktop or right-click and select Open. This step opens the My Network Places window.
4. Double-click the Entire Network icon. This opens the Microsoft Windows Network window. Notice that the domain icon appears.
5. Double-click the name of the domain. This displays the newly installed domain, as shown in the following illustration.

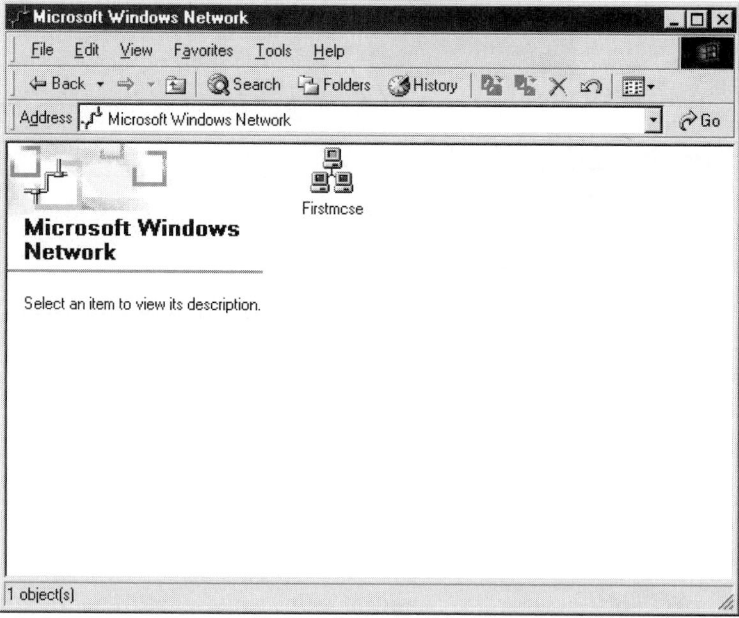

6. The display of the domain name verifies that the Active Directory installation was successful. Close the Microsoft Windows Network window.

EXERCISE 2-2

Verifying the Domain Controller from Active Directory Users and Computers

1. Log on to the domain controller with a domain username and password.
2. Click Start | Programs | Administrative Tools and select Active Directory Users and Computers. This step opens the Active Directory Users and Computers console.
3. Click the plus (+) sign before the name of the domain to expand it. Click the Domain Controllers icon.
4. Notice that the name of the domain controller appears on the right-hand pane, as shown in the following illustration.

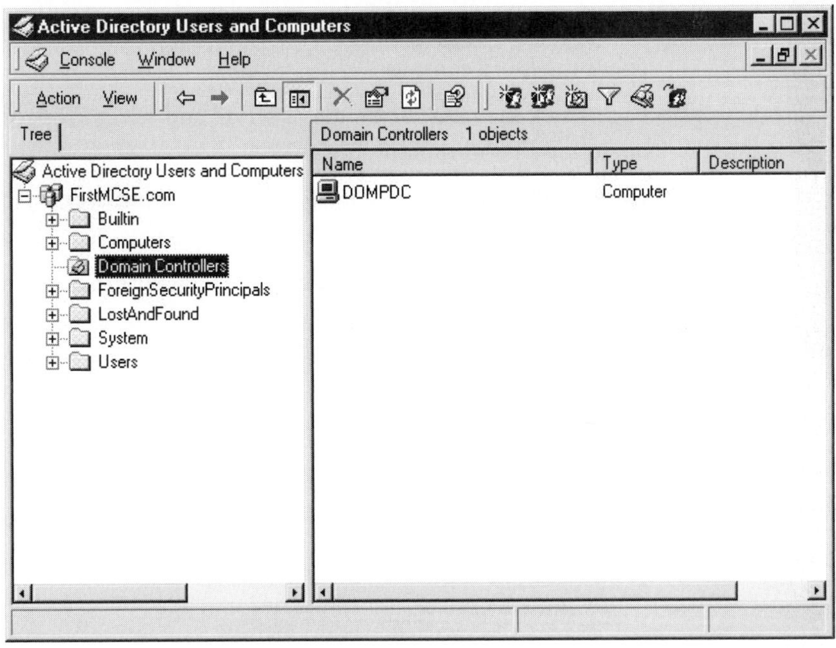

Verifying the DNS Server

When the DNS server is installed, a DNS management tool is added to the Administration tools. In Exercise 2-3, we verify that the DNS server works correctly by performing a test from the DNS server properties.

CertCam 2-3

EXERCISE 2-3

Verifying the DNS Server

1. Log on to the domain controller as an administrator.
2. Click Start | Programs | Administrative Tools and select DNS. This step opens the DNS console.
3. Right-click the name of the DNS server and select Properties. This step opens the DNS Properties sheet.
4. Click the Monitoring tab. Look for "Select a test type." Notice there are two types of test options.
5. Select both test options: "A simple query against this DNS server" and "A recursive query to other DNS servers," as shown in the following illustration.

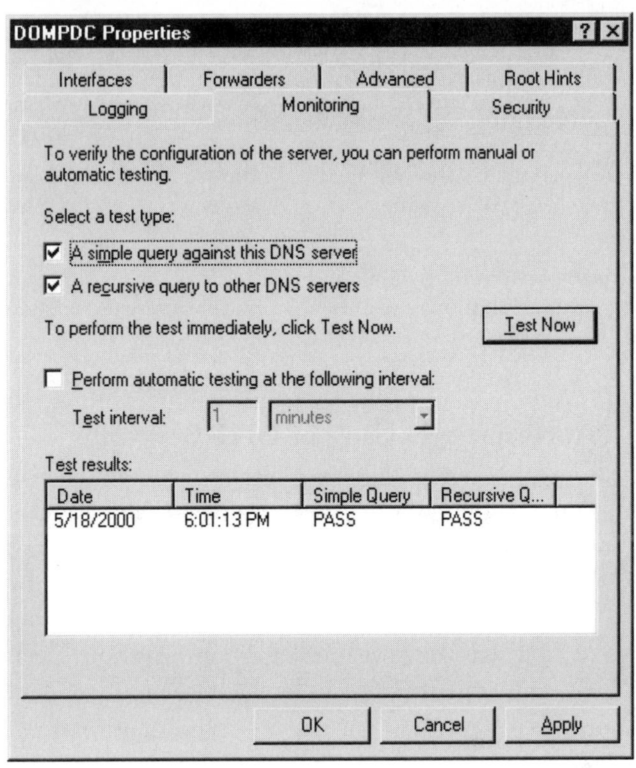

6. Click the Test Now button to start the test immediately. It takes only a moment or two for the test to complete.
7. Notice that the Test Results portion of the dialog box shows PASS for both simple and recursive query tests.
8. This completes the DNS server verification. Close the DNS properties dialog box. Close the DNS console.

SCENARIO & SOLUTION	
You know you have installed Active Directory. Why is there a need for verification?	It is necessary to verify that AD was installed properly .
How do you verify that the DCPROMO has upgraded your member server to domain controller?	Browse the domain from My Network Places. If your server was upgraded, you will find it listed as one of the domain controllers.
What is the purpose of performing simple and recursive queries in the Monitoring tab of DNS server properties?	These queries ensure that the DNS is working properly and the present configuration has no problems.

Automatic Testing of DNS Server

The DNS configuration can also be tested automatically at specified time intervals. You might notice from step 5 in the previous exercise that the "Perform automatic testing at the following interval" option allows you to specify time intervals in minutes. If selected, this option performs automatic testing at specified intervals. If you want to perform periodic tests, fill in the interval time and click Apply.

Now that you have learned about the various methods of verifying the Active Directory installation, let's look at some real-world scenarios.

CERTIFICATION OBJECTIVE 2.02

Moving Server Objects Between Sites

Several tasks are necessary to maintain Active Directory sites. These tasks include maintenance of server settings. Performing one or more of the site maintenance activities might be required on a regular basis in order to get the best benefits of the

Active Directory services of Windows 2000. This section explains how to perform the following maintenance processes:

- Creating a Server object in a site
- Moving Server objects between sites
- Removing a Server object from a site

Creating a Server Object in a Site

In order to help you understand the procedure, we first create a dummy Server object in Active Directory Sites and Services. When this process is complete, you perform exercises that explain how to move and remove this Server object. This procedure holds true for creating member servers and domain controllers in the site. Exercise 2-4 shows the procedure to create a Server object.

EXERCISE 2-4

Creating a Server Object in a Site

1. Log on to the domain controller as a domain administrator.
2. Click Start | Programs | Administrative Tools and select Active Directory Sites and Services. This choice opens the Active Directory Sites and Services console.
3. Click the plus (+) sign before the site in which you want to create the Server object to expand it. Notice that the existing Server objects are listed in the Servers folder.
4. Right-click the Server folder and select New. Click Server, as shown in the following illustration.

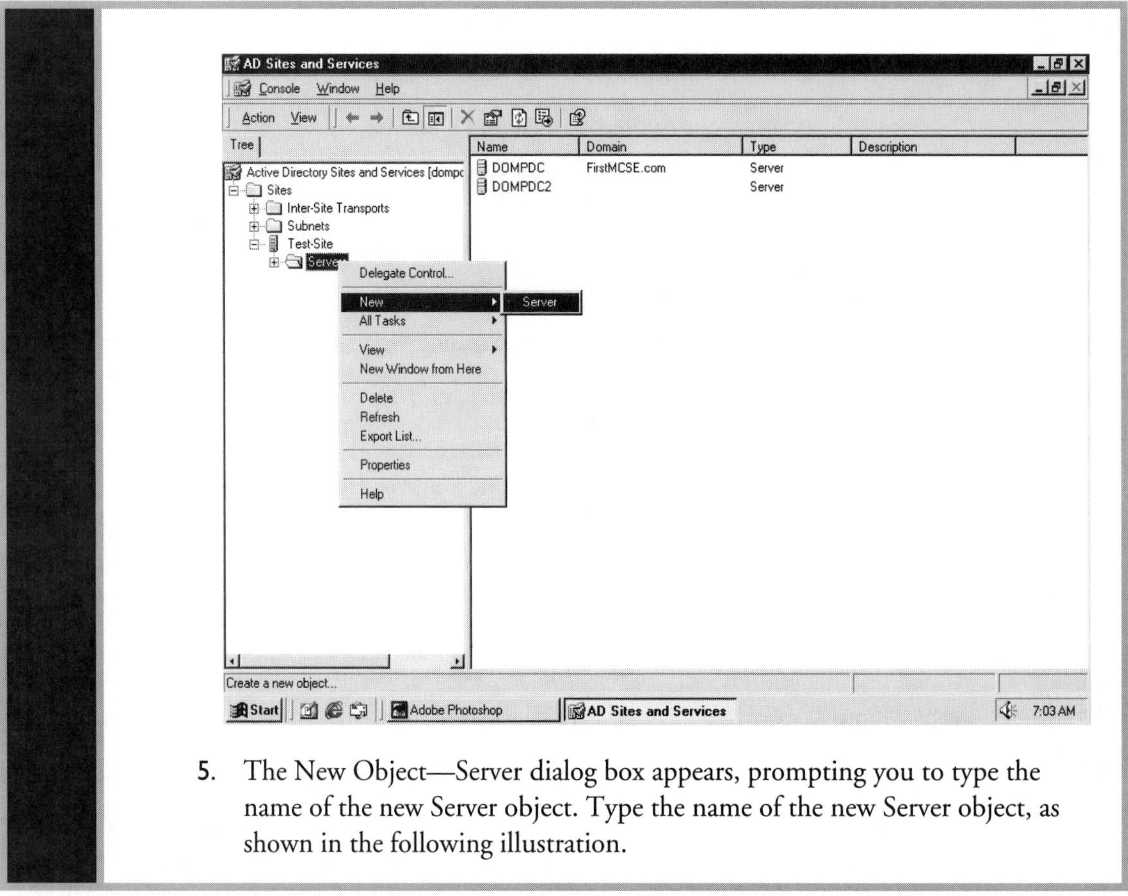

5. The New Object—Server dialog box appears, prompting you to type the name of the new Server object. Type the name of the new Server object, as shown in the following illustration.

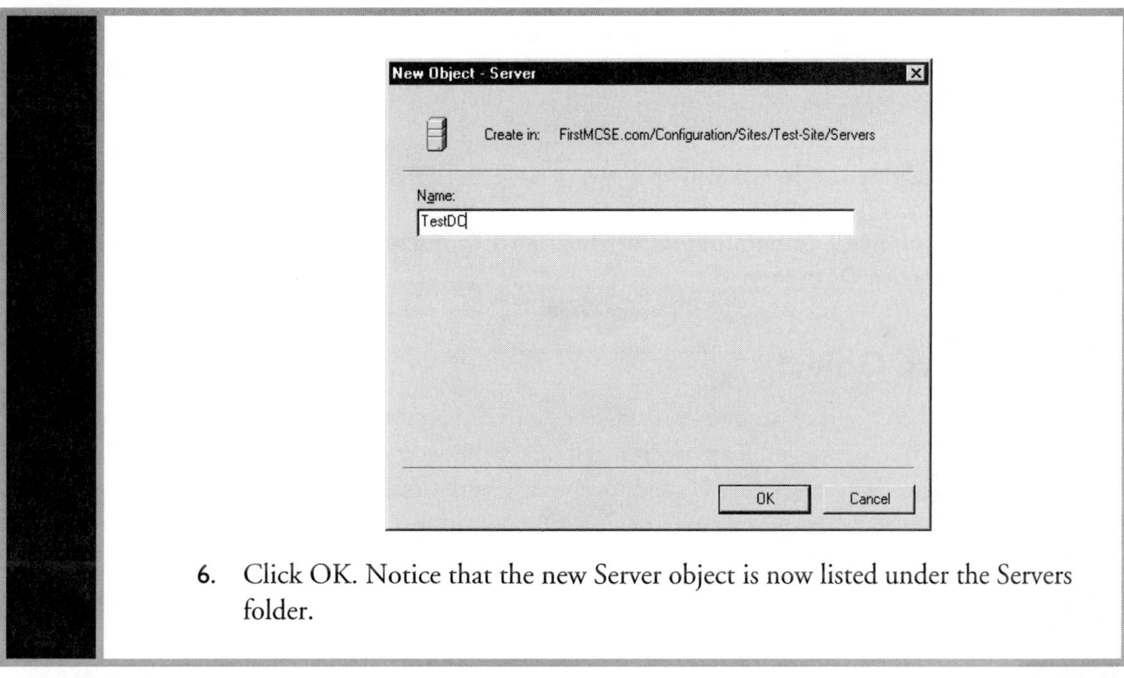

6. Click OK. Notice that the new Server object is now listed under the Servers folder.

exam Watch

The procedure for creating a domain controller Server object in a site is not a substitute for installing a domain controller in a site. The domain controller must first be installed using the Active Directory Installation Wizard. Once it is installed, the Domain Controller object will be moved automatically to the Domain Controllers container in the Active Directory in the Sites and Services console.

When to Move Objects

Requirements of any organization change from time to time, with a changing competitive landscape or through mergers or acquisitions, for example. The Active Directory Server objects that you designed and created at the time of deployment of Windows 2000 might no longer be suitable to fulfill the needs of your organization after some time. This situation calls for regular maintenance of Active Directory objects. Server objects are ones that you might need to move from one site to another in order to attain seamless network performance.

In today's competitive business scenario, sometimes small and medium-sized companies merge their operations to form a bigger organization. If both the constituent companies have Windows 2000-based domains, they might need to restructure the Active Directory components. Creating new site containers and moving site objects will be a part of such an Active Directory restructuring.

exam Watch

You need domain administrator rights to move or remove Server objects from Active Directory.

How to Move Objects

Server objects are moved using the Active Directory Sites and Services console. Exercise 2-5 will help you understand the process of moving Server objects between sites. The procedure is good for moving both domain controllers and member servers from one site to another. You need at least two domain controllers in order to complete this exercise.

EXERCISE 2-5

Moving Server Objects from One Site to Another

1. Log on to the domain controller as a domain administrator.
2. Click Start | Programs | Administrative Tools and select Active Directory Sites and Services. This choice opens the Active Directory Sites and Services console.
3. Click the + sign before the site from which you want to move the Server object in order to expand it. Select the Server object you want to move to a different site.
4. Right-click the Server object and select Move, as shown in the following illustration.

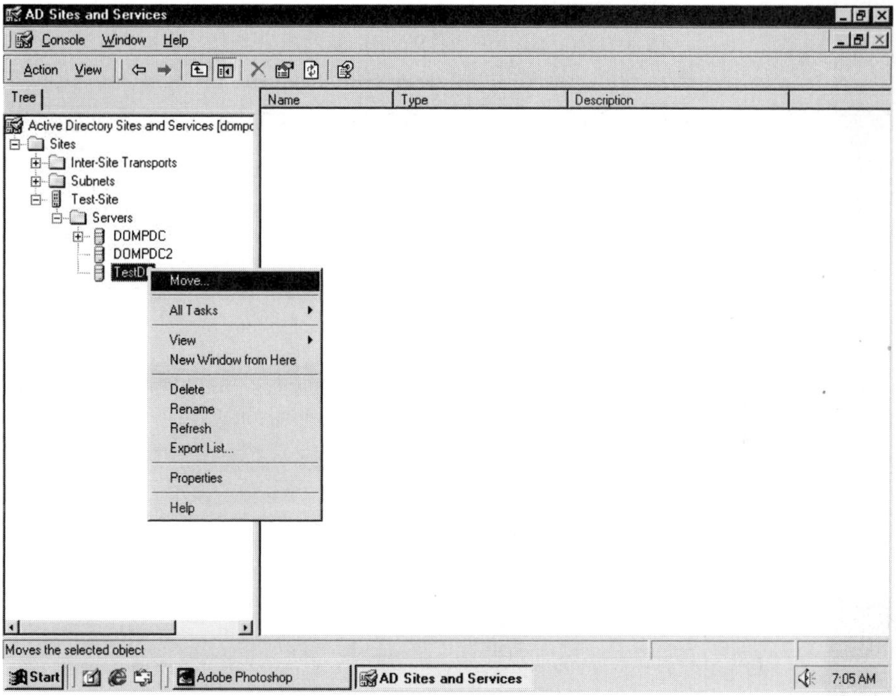

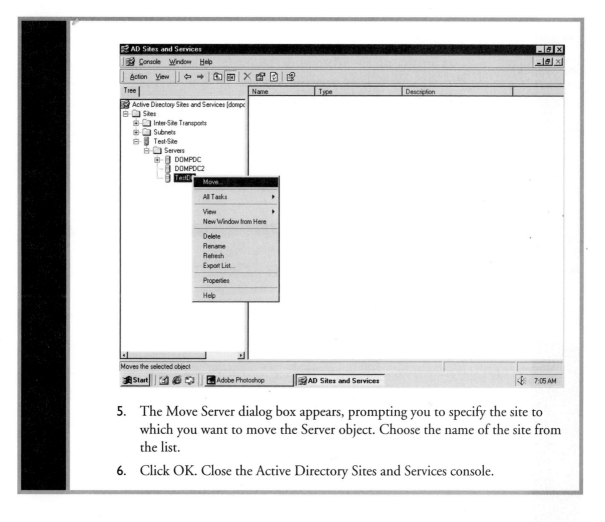

5. The Move Server dialog box appears, prompting you to specify the site to which you want to move the Server object. Choose the name of the site from the list.
6. Click OK. Close the Active Directory Sites and Services console.

Another important part of this discussion is removal of Server objects from the sites that are no longer in use. This procedure is detailed in Exercise 2-6.

EXERCISE 2-6

Removing a Server Object from a Site

1. Log on to the domain controller as a domain administrator.
2. Click Start | Settings | Administrative Tools and select Active Directory Sites and Services. This step opens the Active Directory Sites and Services console.
3. Select the Server object that is no longer required and that you want to remove from the site.
4. Right-click the Server object and select Delete, as shown in the following illustration.

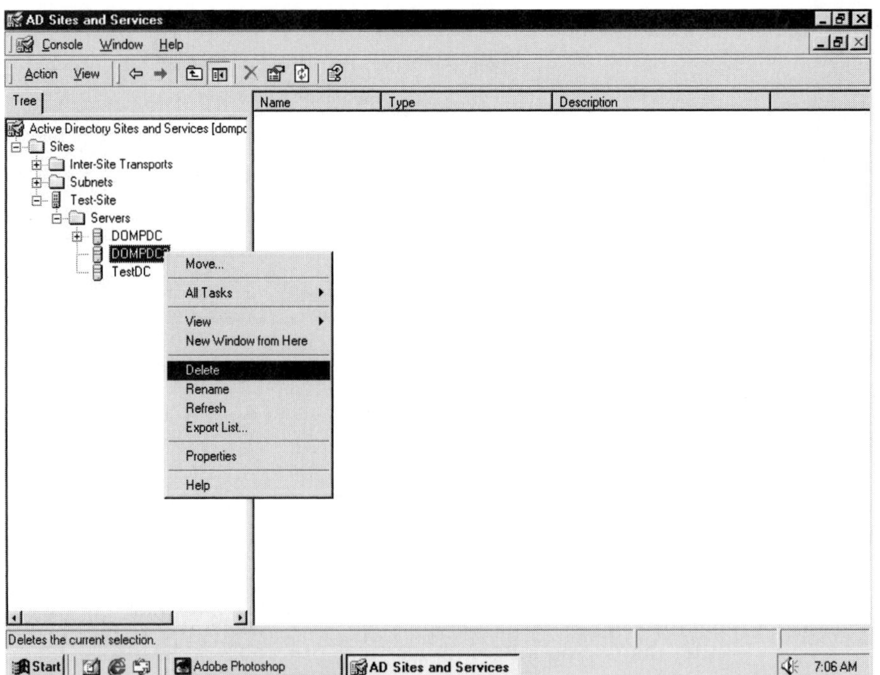

5. Notice that a warning message appears on the screen, as shown in the following illustration.

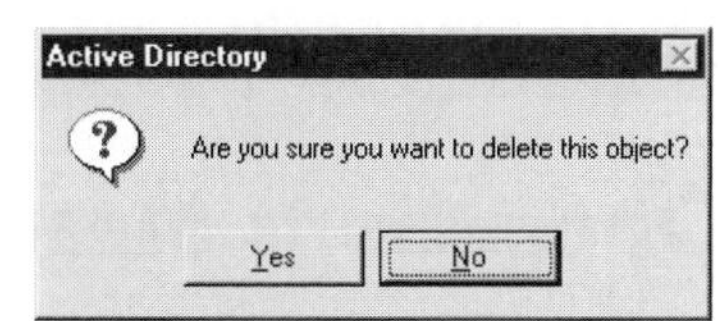

6. As a built-in safety feature against accidental removal of an object, No is the default selection in this warning dialog box. Click Yes to remove the Server object.
7. Notice that the Server object no longer appears under the tree. Close the Active Directory Sites and Services console.

Usually, you remove a Server object from a site only when it is no longer required or has been inoperative for a long time. If you want to remove the object only temporarily, remove the NTDS Settings objects for the server instead. This option allows you to reactivate the server any time you need it again.

When you bring the server online later, the Active Directory creates a new NTDS Settings object for the server. To be on the safer side, even if you will not need the Server object again, it is best to first delete the NTDS Settings object for that server and remove the Server object at a later date.

Now let's check some scenarios that could arise when you work with Active Directory.

SCENARIO & SOLUTION

Scenario	Solution
Which of the Active Directory consoles is used to manage server objects?	The Active Directory Sites and Services is used to create, remove, and move server objects between sites.
Why should there be a need to move server objects once they have been created for one site?	It is necessary to move server objects as the needs of a company change.
Can you use the New Server option from Active Directory Sites and Services to promote a member server to domain controller?	No. Member servers are promoted to domain controllers using the DCPROMO command. Creating servers in Active Directory is altogether a different operation.

CERTIFICATION OBJECTIVE 2.03

Transferring Operations Master Roles

Domain controllers are assigned various roles, depending on their location in the domain forest or domain tree. The *operations master roles* are assigned to enable single-master replication instead of multimaster replication. *Single-master replication* ensures that no two domain controllers are assigned the same operations master role in the domain. One domain controller holds the master copy of a particular component of Active Directory, and others act as its backups. In this section, we discuss various operations master roles, their significance in the domain forest or domain tree, and methods to transfer roles among domain controllers.

To start, we take a closer look at the term *operations master roles* and the purpose for which these roles are meant.

What Are the Operations Master Roles?

When you have more than one domain controller in your network, the *File Replication System* keeps the domain controllers synchronized. Each domain controller participates in the replication system to keep its database up to date. This *multimaster replication* is a built-in feature of Active Directory.

In some situations, this multimaster replication does not allow you to make changes to the domain. Making changes calls for assigning some operations to one or more domain controllers that are single master. This way you can prevent other domain controllers from performing the same operations at the same time. These specified domain controllers then perform single-master operations when assigned operations master roles. The single-master role ensures that only one domain controller keeps the specific AD data, and others remain as backups.

There are five types of operations master roles in an AD forest. These roles must be assigned to one or more domain controllers for proper functioning of the replication in the network. It is necessary to understand various operations master roles in order to maintain the domain controllers.

There are two primary types of operations master roles, each having its particular significance:

- Forestwide operations master roles
- Domainwide operations master roles

Forestwide Operations Master Roles

The *forestwide operations master roles* must be unique to a particular domain forest. There are two roles, both of which are unique—in other words, you cannot have more than one schema master role or domain-naming master role in a single domain forest. The following are the two types of forestwide operations master roles:

Schema Master Role There can be only one *schema master* in a domain forest. The domain controller assigned this role is in charge of all changes and modifications to the forest schema.

Domain-Naming Master Role As with the schema master, there can be only one domain controller having the *domain-naming master role.* This domain controller is in charge of any additions or deletions of domains in the forest.

exam Watch

It is important to note that the forestwide operations master roles are unique in the forest. You cannot have more than one domain controller with the same forest-wide operations master role.

Domainwide Operations Master Roles

The *domainwide operations master roles* are relative ID (RID) master, primary domain controller (PDC) emulator, and infrastructure master. These roles are also unique to the domain.

Relative ID Master *Role* The domain controller holding this role is responsible for generating a security ID for each object created in the domain. When you create a user, group, or computer object, it is assigned a security ID that consists of two parts: a domain security ID and a relative ID (RID). The *domain security ID* is the same for all objects created in the domain. The *relative ID* of the object is unique to the object. No two objects can have an identical relative ID. Whenever you want to move an object across domains, you must do it from the domain controller that has the RID master role.

Primary Domain Controller Emulator Role As its name suggests, the domain controller assigned the PDC emulator role acts as a Windows NT primary domain controller when there are non-Windows 2000 computers in the network or when some Windows NT backup domain controllers (BDCs) still exist on the network. The domain controller acting as PDC emulator actually behaves as a PDC to all BDCs. This role is also unique to the domain and can be assigned to only one domain controller. This feature is very useful in Windows 2000 networks working in mixed mode.

Even if a Windows 2000 network is running in native mode, meaning that there are no Windows NT domain controllers, the domain controller that has the PDC emulator role gets replication information on password changes from other domain controllers.

Users on a network keep changing their passwords for secrecy and data security. In a Windows 2000 network that has several domain controllers, a password change at one domain controller might take time to replicate to other domain controllers. However, if a user changes a password and the change has not been passed on to all domain controllers, there is no need to worry. The logon request is first sent to the domain controller acting as PDC emulator before refusing to log the user on. Hence, it is incorrect to say that the PDC emulator role is useful only in mixed-mode environments.

Infrastructure Master Role As with other domainwide master roles, only one domain controller can be assigned the infrastructure master role in a domain. The domain controller hosting this role is connected to the global catalog and takes care of updating information when there are changes in group memberships. When a member of a group is moved from one domain to another, that group might not reflect the member's presence in the group for a while. The domain controller that has the infrastructure master role takes care of the new location of the member.

When to Transfer Roles, and Why

If your network is very small and has only one domain controller computer, all the operations master roles are assigned to it by default. However, for reasons of providing redundancy, it is never a good decision to keep a single computer as domain controller. There should be at least two domain controllers, even if the network is very small: one that acts as an operations master domain controller and the other that acts as a standby operations master domain controller. These domain controllers must be direct replication partners for normal operation. This ensures that if for some reason one of the domain controllers fails, the other is ready to take over.

When the network is large, you must assign the domainwide operations master roles first. When this is done, the forestwide operations master roles can be assigned. Usually, when you install the first domain controller in the forest, both schema master and domain-naming master roles are assigned to the same domain controller. Usually, when you install the first domain controller, it will host all the operations master roles.

The question is, why change operations master roles? One thing is certain: The schema master and the domain-naming master roles should be assigned to the same domain controller. The only roles that are changed among domain controllers are the domainwide operations master roles. The following are some of the reasons for transferring operations master roles:

- **Load balancing.** Transfer of roles among domain controllers enables you to balance the load among various domain controllers.
- **Changes in the network.** When the network is growing at a fast pace and changes take place very frequently, you might need to transfer operations master roles from one domain controller to another for the network to run smoothly.
- **Maintenance and hardware upgrades.** Another reason for transferring operations master roles is maintenance. When a domain controller is taken offline for repairs, the role that this domain controller was performing must be transferred to another domain controller within the same domain.

Due to rapid changes in technology and the needs of organizations, server hardware needs to be upgraded occasionally. New hardware replaces old servers.

So, you need to transfer to another domain controller the particular operations master role to which the obsolete server is assigned.

How to Transfer Roles

Let's look at how to transfer these roles from one domain controller to another. The exercises that follow will be helpful in explaining the procedures required to accomplish the job of transferring roles. In practice, you transfer only the domainwide operations master roles, although you can transfer any of the forestwide roles, too. The transfer operations take place only in a single domain.

Identifying and Transferring Forestwide Operations Master Roles

The forestwide schema master role can be viewed and transferred using the Active Directory Schema snap-in. The Active Directory Schema snap-in is not installed to any domain controller by default. You need to install it from the Control Panel using Add/Remove Programs and install all the Administrative tools. Once this is done, follow the steps in Exercise 2-7 to check which domain controller is responsible for this role. This procedure also explains how the schema master role can be transferred.

EXERCISE 2-7

Transferring the Schema Master Role

1. Log on to the domain controller as a domain administrator.
2. Click Start | Run and type **mmc** in the open box. Click OK. This step opens a blank MMC.
3. Click Console and select Add/Remove snap-in from the drop-down menu. Another dialog box appears. Select Active Directory Schema. Click Add. Notice that Active Directory Schema now appears in the left-hand side of the console.
4. Right-click Active Directory Schema and select Change Domain Controller from the menu. This step opens the Change Domain Controller dialog box, as shown in the following illustration.

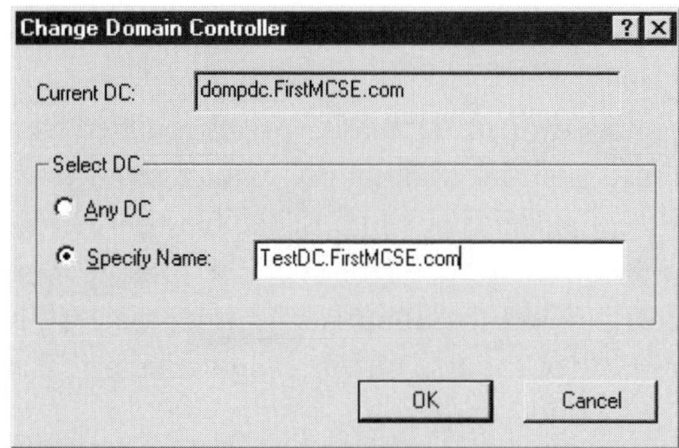

5. The Change Domain Controller dialog box gives you two options to change the schema master role, as shown in the previous illustration. The Any DC option lets Active Directory select a domain controller for the purpose. The Specify Name option enables you to specify the name of the domain controller yourself.
6. Type the name of the new domain controller and click OK. This step closes the Change Domain Controller dialog box.
7. Right-click Active Directory Schema again and select Operations Master. This choice brings up the Change Operations Master Role dialog box, as shown in the following illustration.

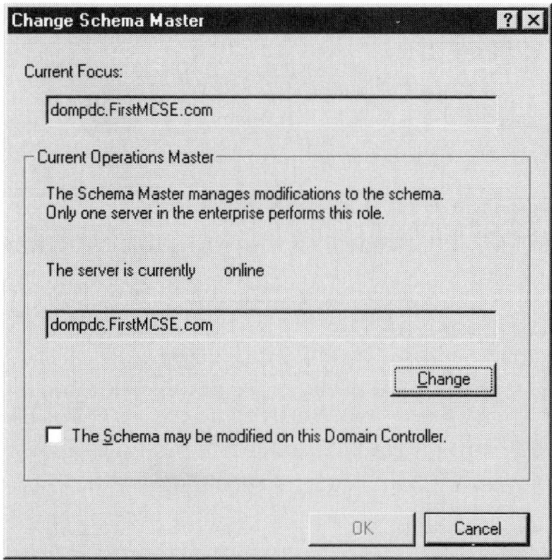

8. To transfer the schema master role, click the Change button.

The domain-naming master role is changed from the Active Directory Domains and Trusts snap-in. Making this change requires that you first connect to the domain controller that will host the new domain-naming master role. This is done from the console root. Right-click the console root, and select Change Domain Controller. Select the domain controller that will host the role. Follow these steps to view or change the assignment of this role:

1. Open the Active Directory Domains and Trusts console.
2. Right-click Active Directory Domains and Trusts, and select Operations Master.
3. The Change Operations Master dialog box appears, as shown in the following illustration. The dialog box shows the name of the domain controller that is responsible for this role.

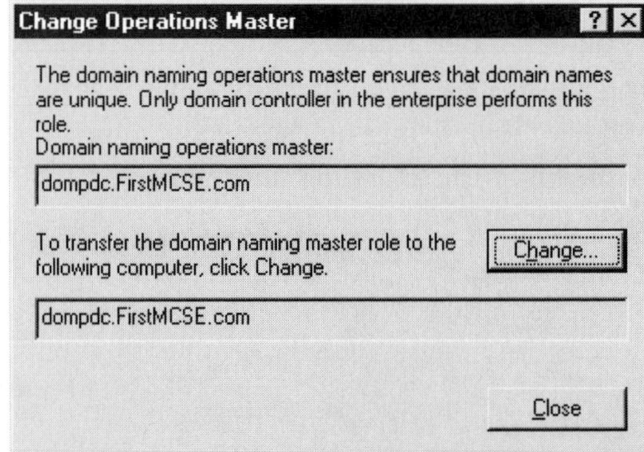

4. Click Change to transfer this role to another domain controller.
5. Click Close to close the dialog box. Close the Active Directory Domains and Trusts console.

exam Watch

The MCSE exams have several questions based on simulations. It is important to note that the two forestwide operations master roles are viewed and changed from two different AD snap-ins. The schema role is changed from the Active Directory Schema snap-in; the domain-naming role is changed from Active Directory Domains and Trusts.

Identifying the Current Assignment of Domainwide Operations Masters Role

In order to transfer the domainwide operations master roles in a domain from one server to another, it is necessary to know what role is currently assigned to various domain controllers. Exercise 2-8 explains how to get this information.

In order to get complete information on domain controllers that hold various operations master roles, you need to connect to them using the "Connect to" option from the Active Directory Users and Computers drop-down menu.

Transfer of domainwide operations master role assignments can be performed for any of the roles following the steps given in Exercise 2-9.

EXERCISE 2-8

Identifying the Present Assignment of Roles

1. Log on to a domain controller as an administrator.
2. Click Start | Programs | Administrative Tools and select Active Directory Users and Computers. This step opens the Active Directory Users and Computers console.
3. Right-click the Active Directory Users and Computers node from the Console tree and select Operations Master, as shown in the following illustration.

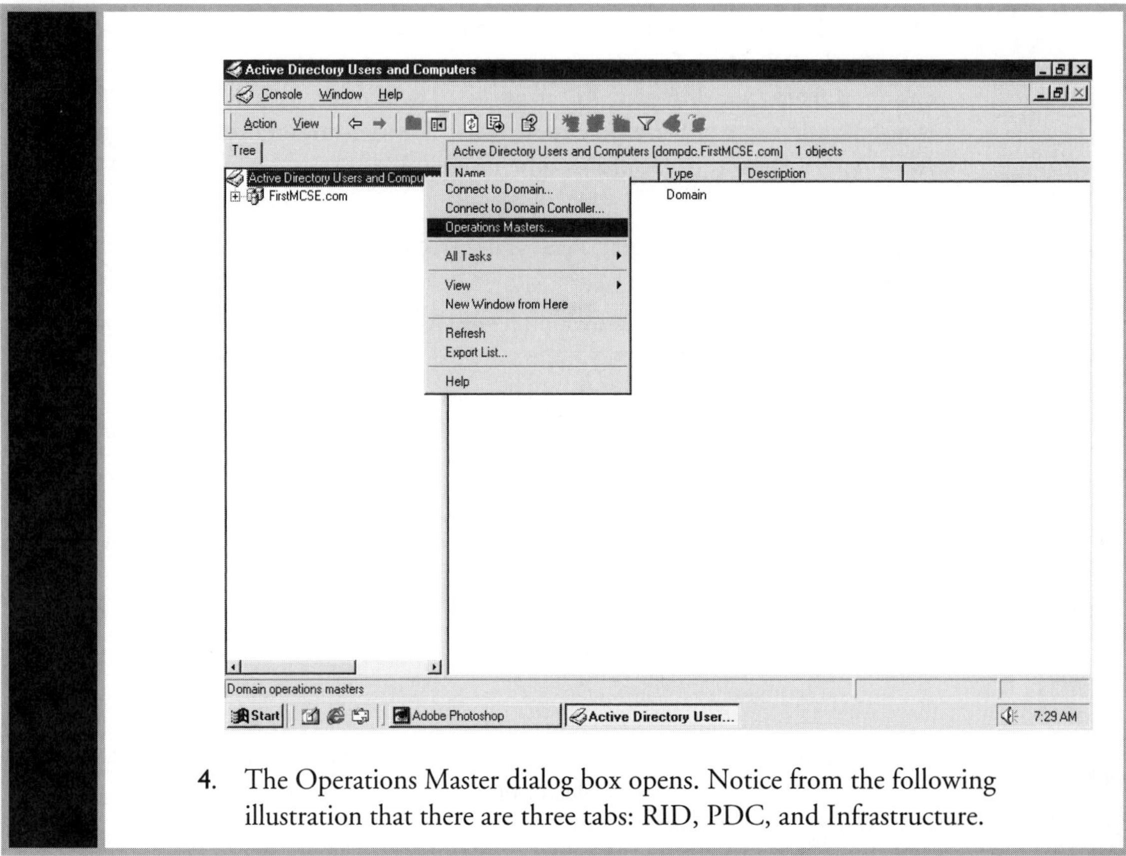

4. The Operations Master dialog box opens. Notice from the following illustration that there are three tabs: RID, PDC, and Infrastructure.

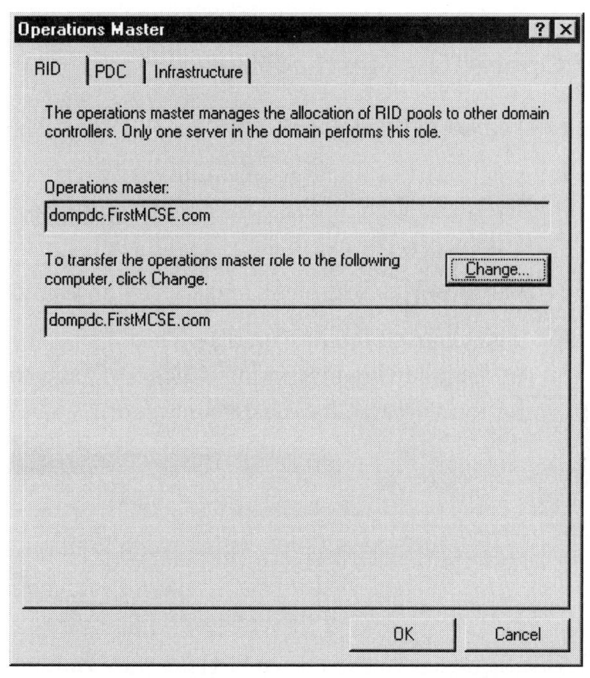

5. The RID tab is the default view that shows the name of the relative ID master in the Operations Master box.
6. Click the PDC or Infrastructure tab to view the name of the appropriate domain controller that holds the respective operations master role.
7. Click Cancel to close the Operations Master dialog box.

EXERCISE 2-9

Transferring Domainwide Assignment of Operations Master Roles

1. Log on to the domain controller as a domain administrator.
2. Click Start | Programs | Administrative Tools and select Active Directory Users and Computers. This choice opens the Active Directory Users and Computers console.
3. Click the Console menu and select Connect to Domain.
4. The Connect to Domain dialog box opens. Type the domain name as shown in the following illustration. Click OK. You could also click the Browse button to search for the domain name.

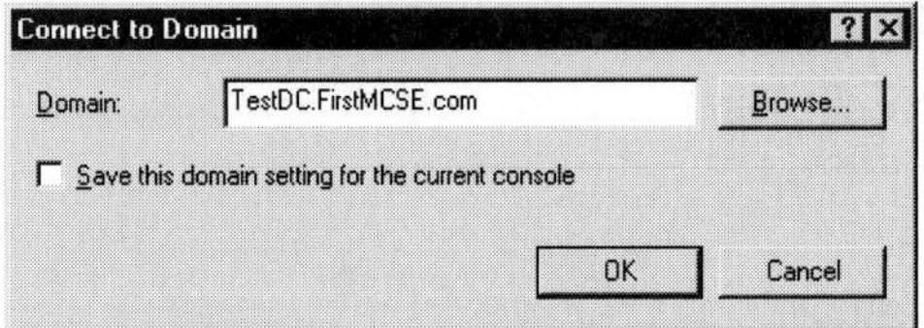

5. Right-click Active Directory Users and Computers in the console tree and select Operations Master. This choice opens the Operations Master dialog box.
6. To change any of the roles, select the RID, PDC, or Infrastructure tab. Click Change. For example, if you need to transfer the PDC role to the new domain controller, click the PDC tab and click Change.
7. Click OK to confirm and close the Operations Master dialog box.

Seizing an Operations Master Role

Computer hardware and networking issues can often either bring down servers or cause connectivity problems. When the server is a domain controller and assigned to one or more operations master roles, it is necessary to either transfer the role to another domain controller or, under certain circumstances, *seize* the role.

If the server will be offline for long or cannot be brought up again, you might want to seize the role and assign it to another domain controller. Seizing the role is done as a last resort step to keep the AD-based functions running properly in the network. Seizure of a role is also called *forceful transfer of an operations master role.* In any case, you must first determine the length of time the failed domain controller will remain offline. If the server that is experiencing problems will be available online again, you must wait. It is notable that domain controllers for which schema, domain-naming, or RID roles have been seized must never be brought online again. If you still want to use the same server as a domain controller, reformat its hard drive and reinstall Windows 2000 Server OS on it.

Operations master roles are seized using the NTDSUTIL command-line tool that is a part of the Windows 2000 Server Resource Kit and is included in the setup CD-ROM. This utility is used for several other administrative tasks for AD maintenance.

The following sections briefly discuss the impact of the failure of domain controllers that are assigned various operations master roles.

Seizing Schema Master If the domain controller assigned the role of schema master is offline for very short periods, it will not make much difference. Even domain administrators are not able to notice such short durations unless they try to make some changes in the schema. You must seize the role only if the server will be permanently offline.

Seizing Domain-Naming Master Failure of a domain controller assigned the role of domain-naming master is also not visible if the failure duration is very short. However, if the domain administrator is trying to add or remove domains in the forest, the operation will not be successful. You must seize the role only if the server will be permanently offline.

Seizing RID Operations Master The failure for short periods of a domain controller that performs the role of RID master has no immediate effect on the network. The effect is visible only if the domain administrator tries to add or delete any objects during the period when the RID operations master domain controller is offline. This is because the RID domain controller assigns RIDs and the administrator is not able to get a RID for the new object. You must seize the role only if the server will be permanently offline.

Seizing PDC Emulator Operations Master Failure of a domain controller holding this role affects network users. If you have even one Windows NT backup domain controller in the network or you have some clients that are not running Windows 2000, this role must be seized immediately and assigned to another domain controller. The role can be reassigned to the original domain controller when it is back online.

Seizing Infrastructure Operations Master The failure of domain controller assigned the infrastructure operations master role also does not make any immediate impact on the network. The domain administrator feels its absence only if he or she is trying to move or rename user or group accounts during the period when this particular domain controller is not available. The domain controller hosting the infrastructure role is connected to the global catalog, and if you want to transfer this role to another domain controller, you must ensure that it has a good connection to the global catalog.

exam Watch

When the schema, domain-naming master, or RID roles have been seized from a domain controller, they must not be brought online again without first reformatting the hard drive and then reinstalling Windows 2000 Server. Other roles such as PDC emulator and infrastructure can be seized and reassigned to the original domain controllers when they are back online.

Table 2-1 summarizes various operations master roles, their scopes, and the Active Directory snap-in that is used to manage each of them.

TABLE 2-1

Summary of Operations Master Roles

Operations Master Role	Scope	Description	Managed from Which Snap-in?
Schema	Forest	Controls updates and modifications to the schema	Active Directory Schema snap-in
Domain Naming	Forest	Controls addition or deletion of domains in the forest	Active Directory Domains and Trusts snap-in
Relative ID	Domain	Controls allocation of domain security IDs and object security IDs to objects	Active Directory Users and Computers snap-in

TABLE 2-1 Summary of Operations Master Roles *(continued)*

PDC emulator	Domain	Processes password changes and acts as PDC for Windows NT BDCs	Active Directory Users and Computers snap-in
Infrastructure	Domain	Controls renaming or groups and keeps track of changes in membership	Active Directory Users and Computers snap-in

Now that you have a fairly good idea of operations master roles, let's check some real-world scenarios.

SCENARIO & SOLUTION

Your domain has 10 domain controllers that are working fine. Why should there be a need for transferring operations master roles?	There may be one or more reasons for transferring these roles. Hardware failures, maintenance, or upgrades are the most important reasons.
You want all domain controllers in the domain to take one or more operations master roles. How do you accomplish this?	The operations master roles can be distributed among one or more domain controllers, but one role cannot be given to more than one domain controller.
Which Active Directory console is used to transfer operations master roles within a domain?	Use Active Directory Users and Computers to manage domainwide operations master roles.
One of the domain controllers holding the PDC emulator master role has gone down. What should you do?	Seize the role immediately and assign it to another domain controller.
You seized the domain-naming role from a domain controller when it was down. Can you put it back on the network after repairs?	No. A domain controller whose domain-naming master role has been seized must not be put back in the network without first reformatting its hard drive and reinstalling Windows 2000 Server on it.

CERTIFICATION OBJECTIVE 2.04

Implementing an Organizational Unit Structure

Organizational units (OUs) are created based on the needs and functions of your organization. Your organization might be a small one with only a single domain, or it might be a large organization spread around the globe and consisting of several domains. You need to address many factors while planning and implementing the OU structure. In a large organization, all the domains might not have similar requirements, but at the same time the business goals remain the same.

The most important thing to remember in implementing an OU structure is that there must always be room for the future growth of the organization and its business needs. The discussion that follows will help you understand the various factors that you must take care of while designing and implementing an organizational structure.

OU Design Overview

OUs are containers in Active Directory that reflect the hierarchy of your organization. The OU structure must be designed to fulfill the current business needs, at the same time leaving room for growth. The structure should be designed in such a way that the administration burdens are manageable. When working for a large, globally dispersed organization, you must design the OU structure in a flexible manner so that local administrators can implement the designs in their own way.

Some of the important design considerations for the OUs are as follows:

- **Organization structure.** Keep in mind the structure of the organization. This structure should be reflected in the domain. Keep different departments or different locations in separate OUs.
- **Ease of administration.** When designing an OU for a multidomain, multilocation organization, you must consider delegation of administrative authorities to lower-level administrators. The top-level administrators should be made responsible for delegating administrative responsibilities.

- **Room for change and growth.** Keep in mind that the business needs of a company keeps changing to accommodate itself due to changes in the market or competition. You must design the OU structure in such a way that there is scope for change and future growth.
- **Group policies.** To control the working environment for users and user groups within your domain, you must plan group policies for them. These group policies must be placed below their respective administrative areas so that the lower-level administrators are able to manage them. Objects such as users, computers, and network resources must be grouped so that they are easy to locate in Active Directory.
- **Restricted access.** Create an environment for the users that gives them access to only the resources they are supposed to view and use. Other resources can be restricted from them. User accounts, computers, printers, and other Active Directory objects must have proper access set for them. Care must be taken that even after setting the most restrictive access permissions, users should have no difficulty performing their jobs.

Besides these considerations, the Active Directory allows you to perform the following actions on the OUs:

- Objects created in one OU can be moved to another OU.
- OUs can be created, removed, or moved from one domain to another.
- Changes in OUs do not create any significant load on current network traffic.
- Organizational properties can be changed at any time.

There are three main hierarchy models from which you can choose. These are:

- **Function based.** This model can be designed and implemented based on the functions of various units or departments and divisions of the organization. For example, you can have an administration unit, a marketing unit, and a research unit.
- **Location based.** This model is suitable for organizations that have divisions located in different parts of the country or the globe. Each location is considered an OU. For example, the company can create three OUs based

on its operations in the East Coast, the central United States, and the West Coast. The office in New York can be in charge of operations in New York, Boston, and Washington, D.C., making one OU. The office in Dallas can be in charge of operations in Dallas and Chicago, making a second OU. The third OU can consist of offices in Seattle and Los Angeles.

- **Function and location based.** This mixed model is based on requirements in regard to both functions and locations of the organization.

With careful consideration of all factors, you can achieve a good plan for your OU structure. While planning, you must be careful to ensure that the structure you design suits the business needs of the company and allows for future growth. You should not change it time and again.

Creating the OU Structure

OUs are created using the Active Directory Users and Computers snap-in. Each OU represents an important part of the organization's hierarchy. You must plan the OUs and document your plans before starting the creation process. The OUs should fulfill the business requirements of your organization. If the organization consists of more than one domain, each domain can create its own OUs following the guidelines set by the parent domain.

Two parts of this section describe the following important processes necessary to implement the OU structure:

- Creating an organizational unit
- Creating objects in a domain

Each of these processes is explained with the help of step-by-step exercises. Exercise 2-10 explains the steps necessary to create an OU in a domain. When you have designed and documented the complete OU structure, you can follow the same procedure to create other OUs.

exam Watch

The exam could contain simulation-based questions from the design part of an OU. Therefore, it is important to understand the important points of planning an organizational structure.

EXERCISE 2-10

Creating an Organizational Unit

1. Log on to the domain controller as a domain administrator.
2. Click Start | Programs | Administrative Tools and select Active Directory Users and Computers. This choice opens the Active Directory Users and Computers console.
3. Locate the domain in which you want to create the OU. If you are creating the OU under an existing OU, locate it and click the plus (+) sign to expand it. Otherwise, you need not expand the domain tree.
4. Select the container in which you want to create the OU. Right-click the container and select New, then click Organization Unit from the drop-down menu. This process is shown in the following illustration. You can also click the Action menu, then select New, and click Organization Unit from there.

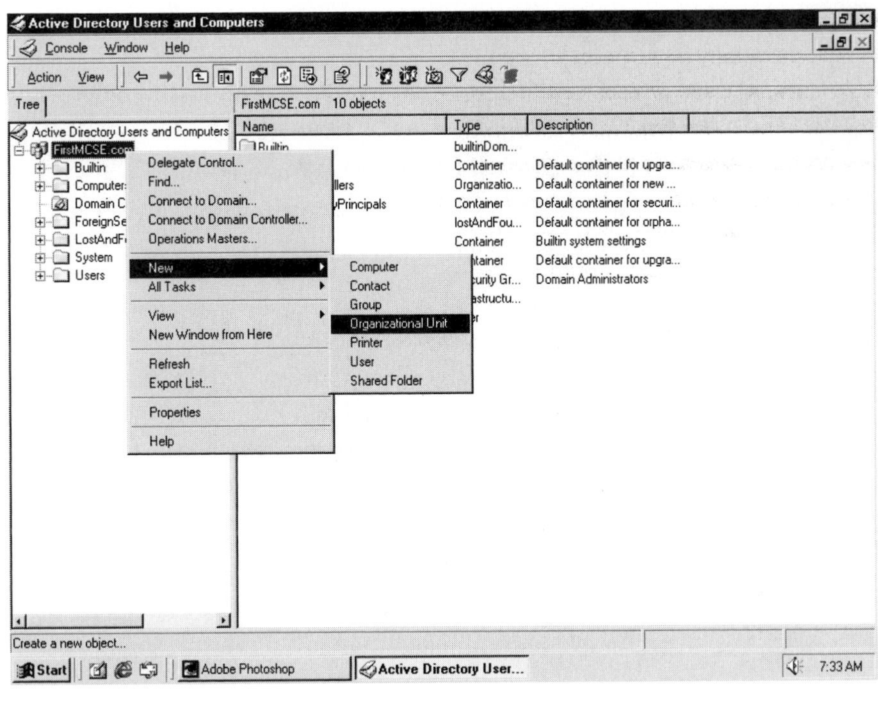

5. The New Object—Organization Unit dialog box appears. Type the name of an organization unit, as shown in the following illustration. Click OK.

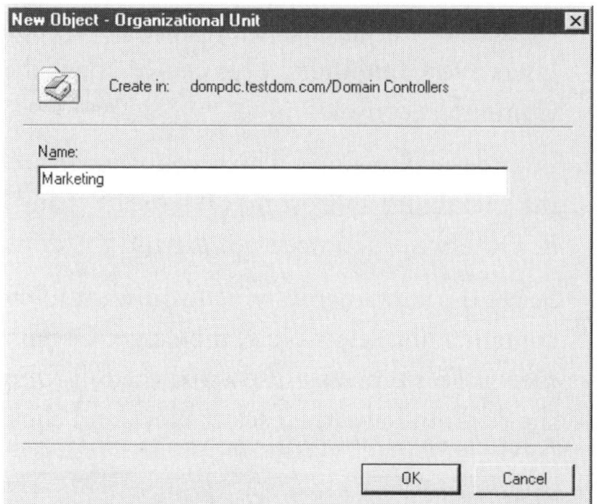

6. Notice that the newly created Organization Unit object is now displayed in Active Directory Users and Computers.
7. To create additional OUs under this new object, expand the new container and repeat Steps 4 and 5. You can create as many OUs as required.

Setting OU Properties

Once you have created an OU, you might want to set its properties. Each OU has a set of properties that are assigned to it by default when it is created. Additional properties can be set from the Properties sheet of the OU. Figure 2-2 shows the Properties sheet for the OU we created in Exercise 2-10. This illustration shows the Object and Security tabs that are visible when you enable the Advanced View by clicking View from the MMC menu and selecting Advanced features.

FIGURE 2-2

The organizational unit Properties sheet

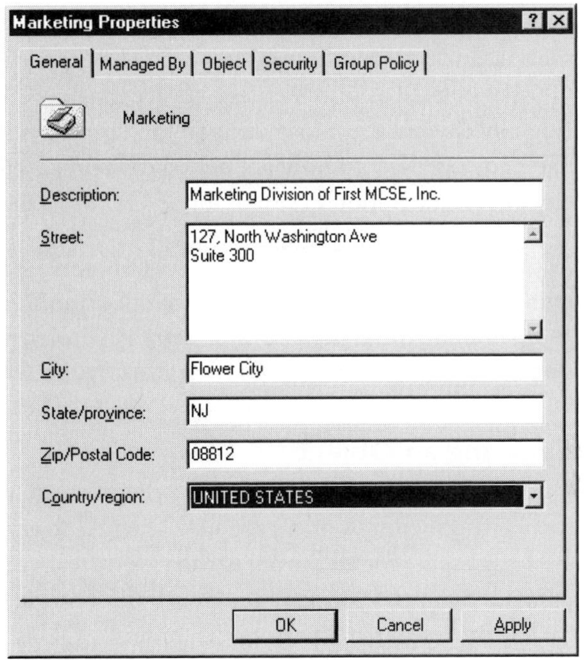

The tabs in the OU Properties sheet are as follows:

- **General.** This tab gives the description and location details of the OU, such as its street address, city, state, ZIP or postal code, and country.
- **Managed By.** This tab describes the name of the OU manager, location of the office, and other address details.
- **Object.** This tab gives details of the object.
- **Security.** This tab gives details of the security parameters currently applicable to the OU.
- **Group Policy.** This tab gives details of the group policy applied to the OU.

Any of these properties can be changed for an OU by opening the OU's Properties sheet and selecting an appropriate tab. The properties you define or set on an OU can be used as search criteria for locating an OU. In other words, if you have carefully entered the information in the Properties sheet, it could be helpful at a later date. For example, a newly appointed domain administrator can use the name of the city or the description to search for an OU or its other details.

on the Job

In practice, you will create OUs and objects under an OU after a careful study of all the aspects of your organizational requirements. It is a good idea to document the design so that even if you leave the organization, the document remains as a reference for anyone who replaces you.

Creating an Object

Once you have created an OU, you need to create various objects under that unit, such as users, groups, or computers. The OU that you created works as a container or storage space for all the objects that you create under the unit. These objects are the ones that need your day-to-day administration.

The process for creating objects under an OU is more or less similar to creating an OU itself. For practice, let's create a user account. Exercise 2-11 explains the procedure.

EXERCISE 2-11

Creating an Object

1. Log on to the domain controller as a domain administrator.
2. Click Start | Programs | Administrative Tools and select Active Directory Users and Computers. This choice opens the Active Directory Users and Computers console.
3. Select the OU under which you want to create the new object. Right-click the OU and click New. Select User from the drop-down menu that appears. This choice opens the New Object—User dialog box.
4. Type the first, middle initial, and last name of the user. Also type the user logon name, as shown in the following illustration. Notice that the Full Name and the Pre-Windows 2000 User Logon Name boxes are automatically filled.

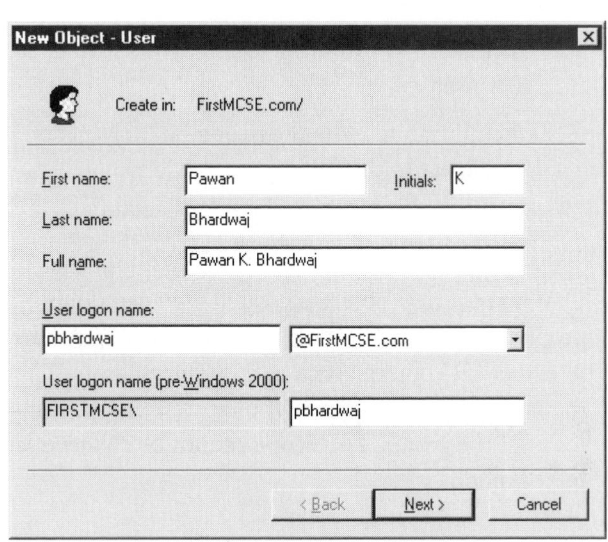

5. Click Next. The dialog box that appears prompts you to specify a password and password settings for the user. Type an initial password for the user and check the "User must change password at next logon" check box, shown in the following illustration. It is a good practice to let the user choose his or her own password.

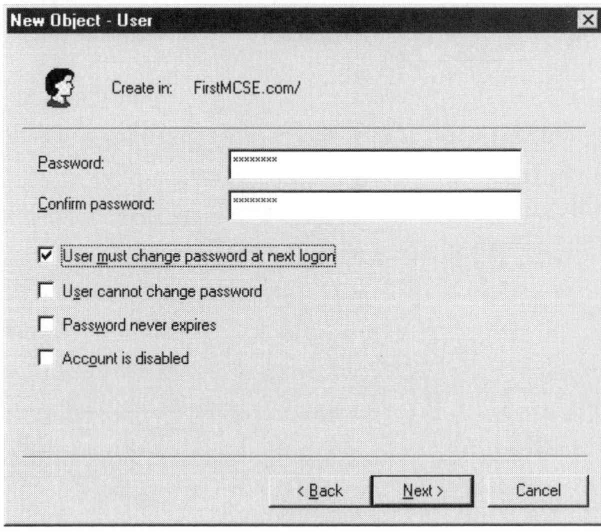

6. Click Next. A summary screen shows various settings you made for the new user.
7. Click Finish to close the dialog box. This completes the creation of a new user object in the OU.

When the new object is created, you can double-click it to see or change its properties. Figure 2-3 shows the membership properties of a user.

Other OU objects, such as computers, groups, and printers, can be created using the same procedure. When you create a group, you are given a choice to select the scope of the group. This scope cannot be changed later if the domain is working in mixed mode.

FIGURE 2-3

User membership properties

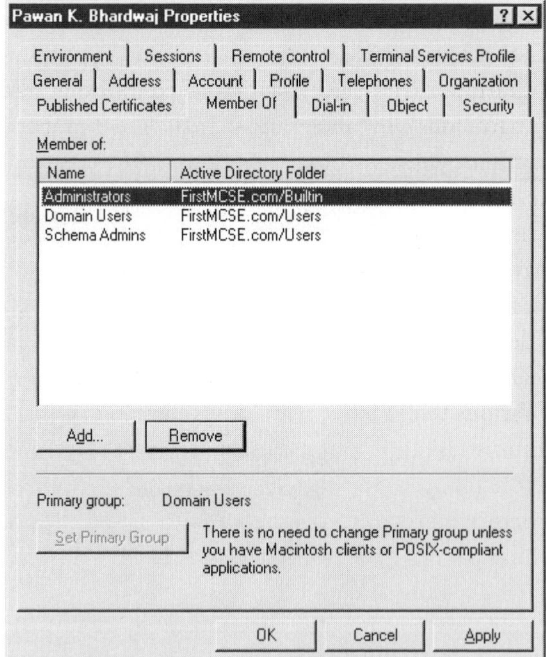

CERTIFICATION SUMMARY

After the installation of Active Directory on a Windows 2000 Server to promote it to become a domain controller, it is necessary to verify that the AD components are working well. If the newly promoted domain controller is listed in the Active Directory Users and Computers console under the Domain Controllers container, it is verified that the installation is successful. Another way to verify the new domain controller is from My Network Places. The DNS server is verified from the Administrative tools DNS option, which again opens the Active Directory Users and Computers console. The simple and recursive queries from the Monitoring tab must show a Pass result.

Server objects are moved between sites for many purposes, including maintenance, performance, and change in needs of an organization. The Active Directory Sites and Services console can be used to move Server objects or remove an inoperative Server object. An inoperative server is removed from the same console. A preferred way of removing a Server object from the Active Directory is to remove the NTDS settings object for that server. This gives you the option of bringing the server online again. When the server is no longer required, it can be removed permanently.

Operations master roles are assigned to specific domain controller computers to configure single-master replication. The schema master role and the domain-naming master role are forestwide operations master roles. RID master, PDC emulator master, and infrastructure master are domainwide operations master roles. These roles can be transferred from one domain controller to another when some domain controller is unavailable on the network for maintenance purposes. It is not advisable to seize any role from any domain controller except the PDC emulator master role unless it is evident that a particular domain controller will never be online again.

Design of an organizational unit in Active Directory calls for a careful study of various requirements of the organization. In addition, organization structure, administration, future growth of the company, and group policies are some other factors that must be considered while you are designing an OU. An organizational structure is created from the Active Directory Users and Computers console. A similar procedure is adopted for creating objects under the OU container.

FROM THE CLASSROOM

Designing an OU Structure

Design of an OU is a huge responsibility; it is unlikely that you will be the only person assigned this job. If the organization you work for is small, you will probably have no problems designing an excellent working model. But if the company is large and has multiple locations, you might well be a member of a design and implementation team. A good knowledge of design factors will help you perform your job with excellence.

Active Directory is new to everyone working in the Windows NT environment. AD and its benefits are one of the main features of Windows 2000 for upgrading your domain to this new platform. In most cases, organizations have predefined group policies in effect. If you are responsible for the structural design for AD, keep the following important things in mind:

1. Study the organizational structure in detail. Grab every piece of document that you can lay your hands on for details on the current setup.
2. Consult each person that is affected by the new design. Keep notes of your meetings.
3. Keep future growth of the organization in mind. Use a model that is most flexible and will not need changes very frequently.
4. Do not rush to implement things that you have designed. Prepare a test lab and conduct experiments first to get a feel for how the new design will take shape.
5. Make one change at a time. Keep a slow pace so that you can go back in case there are problems.

And finally, as I insist in all my writings, documentation must not be ignored at any cost. You might not be a member of the organization tomorrow. Documentation will help the person who replaces you in continuing to work successfully in the environment you create.

—Pawan K. Bhardwaj, MCSE, MCP+I, CCNA

TWO-MINUTE DRILL

Verifying Active Directory Installation

- If the Active Directory tab in the Configure Your Server dialog box shows that Active Directory is installed in your computer, this is the first indication that the installation is successful. You can also browse the network to see that the domain controller is installed.
- Open the Active Directory Users and Computers and click Domain Controllers to verify that the domain controller is present.

Moving Server Objects Between Sites

- The Active Directory Sites and Services console is used to create, remove, and move Server objects.
- Expand the Servers objects under the name of the site. Select the Server object you want to move and right-click it. Select Move. Specify the site name to which you want to move the Server object.

Transferring Operations Master Roles

- Relative ID master, PDC emulator master, and infrastructure master roles are domainwide operations master roles and are unique to the domain. Only one instance of these master roles is to be defined in each domain, although a single domain controller can perform more than one of these roles.
- Transfer of roles is done for the reasons of load balancing, maintenance, network changes, and hardware upgrades. Except for the domain controller that is assigned the role of PDC emulator master, the domain controllers can be taken offline for short periods without having to transfer the role to another domain controller.

Implementing an Organizational Unit Structure

- ❑ The OU design must reflect the structure of an organization and should be easy to administer. There must be enough scope for growth and changes in the organizational structure.
- ❑ The three models that can be adapted for designing OUs are function based, location based, and function and location based.

3

Planning an Active Directory Implementation

CERTIFICATION OBJECTIVES

- 3.01 Establishing the Scope of Active Directory
- 3.02 Designing the Namespace
- 3.03 Planning the DNS Strategy
- 3.04 Naming Conventions
- ✓ Two-Minute Drill

Throughout this chapter, we will discuss Active Directory (AD) naming strategies as they apply to the unique needs of individual networks. Installing and configuring Active Directory services for Windows 2000 should not be both your initial step and your final step; it takes time and effort to create a seamless, well-balanced infrastructure. The following are a few of the questions that should come to mind when planning an Active Directory naming scheme:

- What will be the purpose, or scope, of the Active Directory?
- What existing domains are there, and can they be logically grouped?
- What domain, whether existing or planned, will be considered the root domain in the forest?
- How are the domains separated, physically or logically? And how will it affect the approach to the architecture of your Active Directory implementation.

We will cover these concerns and many other aspects of the possible naming conventions using Windows 2000 Active Directory. Live, breathe, and sleep this material… know it cold, as Microsoft will surely be emphasizing this component on its exams for some time to come.

CERTIFICATION OBJECTIVE 3.01

Establishing the Scope of Active Directory

When we speak of the Active Directory scope, we are referring to the specific use of the component. Will it be used for your central employee database, or perhaps a location to which current databases will be replicated? This is a very important consideration, as it will determine the use of the directory, and leave room to expand upon it in the future. In the following sections, we will review these scenarios.

AD as your central Employee Database

Using Active Directory as a central employee database has apparent benefits to a mid- to large-sized company which either does a lot of hiring and firing, or has many temporary employees filtering in and out of the company. These types of employees require extensive amounts of administrative effort to maintain. This includes user accounts, Exchange mailboxes, and other databases that the Human Resources (HR) department may keep pertaining to their staff.

Active Directory can eliminate this overhead when working in conjunction with applications from companies such as PeopleSoft or SAP. In a nutshell, what these applications do is simple: manage people. They handle everything from hiring and firing, to promotions, salary, training, and retirement. When integrated with Active Directory services, the power of these applications grows. Active Directory will synchronize changes with all databases relational to the update being made. For instance, when an employee is fired, the application will call to the Active Directory structure to mark the employee as terminated. Active Directory will remove all records in connected databases pertaining to that individual. Attributes such as salary, phone number, e-mail address, and so on can also be replicated throughout the Active Directory structure. These are just two examples of directories in an organization that store information about your employees, but the Active Directory scope can be molded to match any organization's needs.

exam Watch

Objects that have been marked for deletion are not deleted immediately. They are marked as a "tombstone." A tombstone is similar to deleting an item and sending it to the Recycle Bin. The object is not actually eliminated until it is purged from the Recycle Bin. All tombstones are purged at a set interval known as garbage collection, which occurs every 12 hours by default. Also note that tombstones are invisible to Lightweight Directory Access Protocol (LDAP) searches of the directory, just as objects in the recycle bin are invisible to searches of the local hard drive.

Replicating with *Existing Databases Using AD*

In July 1999, Microsoft bought the Zoom IT Corporation, a company well known for its innovative metadirectory services. Through the acquisition of this technology, Microsoft was able to integrate it into the Windows Directory Services structure. The metadirectory can contain detailed information about the entire enterprise, including not only physical items, but virtual items as well. These include the following object categories:

- **Physical** Including workstations, servers, and users.
- **Conceptual** Including departments, organizations, and groups.

- **Digital** Including documents, spreadsheets, and images.
- **Geographic** Including locations in the same city, separate cities, or countries.

Like the Active Directory, the metadirectory must be organized in a hierarchical fashion. This is the equivalent of the forest structure in AD. For example, the metadirectory would contain a document on a computer located in Sacramento, California, USA.

Dissection of the Metadirectory Namespace

The figure that follows is a dissection of the metadirectory namespace, of which there are two distinct parts: the *metaverse* and the *connector space.* We will now list each component and explain its purpose to the metadirectory as a whole. Figure 3-1 presents a graphical representation of the metadirectory.

- **Metaverse** The part of the directory that represents all joined objects, whether they are from connected directories or are unique objects with no connection to external directories.
- **Connector Space** The connector space is the location into which directories are initially imported. Each directory will maintain its own area in the connector space.

SCENARIO & SOLUTION	
You are asked to construct a metadirectory for your company. In which object category would you place each of the following items: Human Resources PDF File Los Angeles, California Windows 2000 Advanced Server	Human Resources: Conceptual PDF File: Digital Los Angeles, California: Geographic Windows 2000 Advanced Server: Physical

FIGURE 3-1

Dissection of the Microsoft metaverse

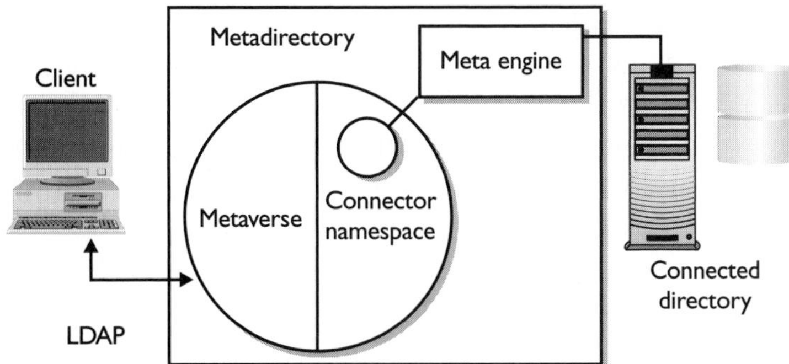

The Active Directory Connector and Exchange 5.5

In Windows 2000, the Active Directory Connector (ADC) is the component that allows communication and synchronization between the Active Directory and the Microsoft Exchange Server 5.5 Directory Service. By utilizing LDAP (Lightweight Directory Access Protocol), the ADC automatically keeps information between the Exchange Server and Active Directory consistent. Natively, Exchange will not communicate with Active Directory. Therefore, without the ADC, new data or changes would have to be inputted manually into both directories. Another key feature of the ADC is the ability to automate administrative tasks such as creating a new mailbox when a new user is created, tracking its changes, and removing the mailbox if the user is ever removed from the system.

The following list exemplifies the functions and benefits of the Active Directory Connector.

- **Bi-directional Synchronization** Changes in either directory service will be reflected in the other. This allows the administrator to update information in either directory, and both directories will remain consistent and current.
- **Selective Attribute Synchronization** You may selectively synchronize specific attributes within the directory, while avoiding synchronization of others.
- **Change Synchronization** Method in which Windows 2000 will synchronize changes only at the object level. For instance, if you were to update 100 objects for 10,000 users, Windows will update only those 100 objects. These changes would, by default, be reflected onto each user, eliminating excessive bandwidth and time consumption.

- **Attribute Level Changes** When Windows 2000 attempts to synchronize two objects, the ADC will compare the attributes and determine which will need to be a part of the synchronization. For instance, if a user's home address has changed in his or her Exchange mailbox properties, only that particular information would be synchronized. This allows the synchronization to be more effective, and eliminates excess bandwidth usage transferring large amounts of data over the network.

exam Watch

In order for Exchange data to be synchronized to the Active Directory, it requires the Active Directory Connector (ADC).

Figure 3-2 represents a domain using Active Directory to synchronize information with an Exchange Server 5.5 using the Active Directory Connector.

FIGURE 3-2

Synchronization of the Exchange 5.5 directory service with the Windows 2000 Active Directory using the Active Directory Connector

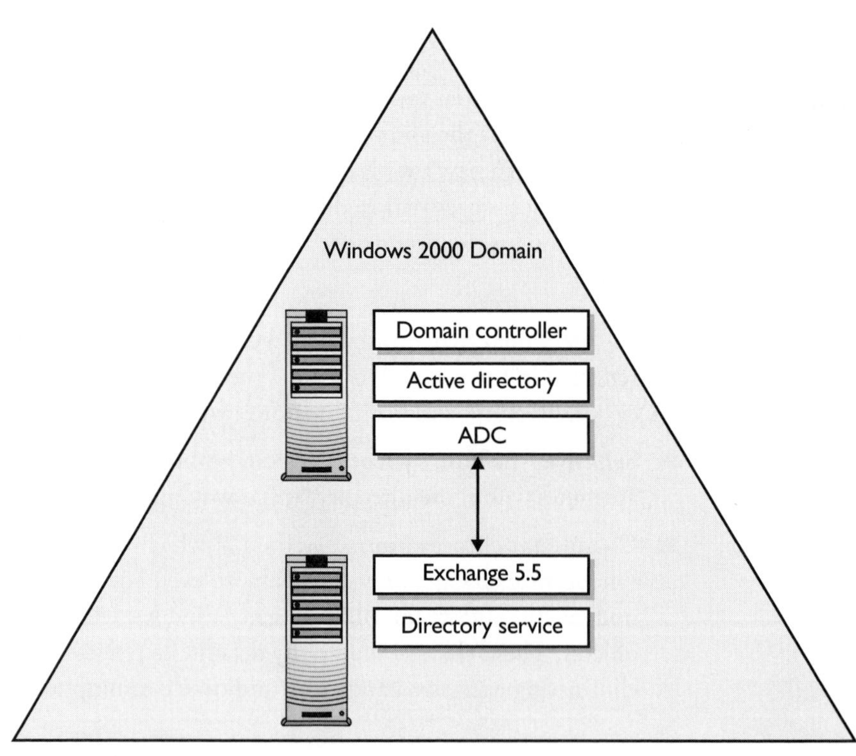

EXERCISE 3-1

When Should You Extend Your Schema?

In this exercise, you will decide what information should be added to your directory schema and which is better left on other applications.

Scenario: You work for a shoe manufacturer that is just moving to Windows 2000. Your CIO would like to store a number of different items in Active Directory and is looking to you for guidance. The following is a list of fields that the CIO would like to add to Active Directory.

Field	Description
Shoe Size	Because we are a shoe company, employees are frequently given free shoes. The CIO says it would be much easier to keep one database with employee shoe sizes.
Salary	Your manager feels that since everybody gets paid, AD is a perfect place to store this information. After all, AD has excellent security, doesn't it?
Employee Number	When an employee is hired, the first thing that happens is that HR gives him or her an Employee Number. This information is used by all systems that work with employees.
Introduction Video	The CIO would love to have every employee "star" in a five-minute introduction video so employees can see their co-workers in different departments.

Points to consider:

1. Any changes to Active Directory cannot be deleted, and thus will form a permanent part of your schema.
2. Although Active Directory has an efficient and schedulable replication system, it was not designed for large amounts of data.
3. Active Directory is a secure place to store data, but is it as secure as your payroll system?

Solution:

Your answers to these questions may vary; what is important here is the decision process.

Field	Decision
Shoe Size	In a shoe company, adding shoe size to the Active Directory might be an excellent idea. Keep in mind that you will have to create your own user interface because the Windows 2000 tools do not automatically add new fields to each administration program.
Salary	Although adding salary to AD is very easy technically, including providing security, it is generally not recommended for a number of reasons: Why have an extra copy of confidential data? It only increases the risk of the data falling into the wrong hands. Although AD is secure, Windows 2000 administrators could potentially view and change this data. Some employees may not have AD accounts—would one be created just to store their salary information?
Employee Number	This is the best example of a field to add. If you have a unique employee number, this number can be used to easily synchronize information with other systems such as HR.
Introduction Video	It is clear that your CEO has attended one too many Microsoft presentations. Although technically this can be done (AD can store binary data), and would be very cool, your directory would become very large and hard to replicate, back up, and restore. A better alternative would be to store your videos on your Web server and insert a HTTP link in AD.

CERTIFICATION OBJECTIVE 3.02

Designing the Namespace

When designing the Active Directory namespace, you must first decide the hierarchy of the forest. Initially, you must designate which domain will be the root domain and assign its Domain Name System (DNS) name. For each additional domain, decide whether it will be a child or subdomain of the root or a new tree root, then assign the names for each new domain respectively. Here are a few points to take into consideration when designing the namespace:

- *Use trees sparingly.* Too many trees can get confusing to end users as well as the system administrators of that organization. Try to organize your domain model in such a way that resources are easily found. It will also lead to less names being entered in the proxy client exclusion suffixes listing.
- *Keep domain names short enough to remember in the future.* You will have enough to keep you busy without the burden of long nonsensical domain names such as MSTS40LA41.
- *Use unique domain names.* Never duplicate domain names, even if those domains are not physically connected. For instance, if your company has a domain on the internal network that is named ourcompany.com and also has a domain outside of the local area network (LAN) named ourcompany.com that is hosting the company Web site, it will surely cause problems with name resolution for those individuals within the company that have Internet access. In this scenario, a client machine would select the domain that answered first to its locator request. Internal DNS servers must be configured to address this.
- *Use standard Internet character sets.* Designing namespaces in this fashion will ensure compatibility with third-party software and legacy systems. RFC (Request for Comments) 1123 defines this as follows:
  - Any letters from A to Z (or a to z respectively).
  - Any numbers between 0 and 9.
  - The hyphen character (-).
- *Use names that are descriptive and distinct.* This means using names that will stand out from the others and give a clear understanding as to the resources it offers.
- *Keep the first part of the domain name the same as the NetBIOS name.* This is a handy little trick when Windows 9*x* legacy systems or software that is not AD-aware are involved.

exam Watch

Be prepared for domain naming questions such as this one: "Which is the better domain name to use for Company A: ourcompany.com or mfg.local.ca.com?" What they are getting at is using a simple name, not necessarily a description of the company's physical location.

FROM THE CLASSROOM

What Is RFC?

RFC, or the Request for Comments, is a compilation of documents, originally started in 1969, concerning the Internet (which was called the ARPANET at that time). These documents outline the standards of communication between computers.

Request for Comments are formed in the following manner. The document is published by its author as an *Internet Draft* (ID) where it can be read and commented on by other authors. Once the document has been posted as an Internet Draft, the author contacts the RFC Editor and requests that it be considered for an Informational or Experimental RFC. At that point, the RFC Editor will request the Internet Engineering Steering Group (a body of the Internet Engineering Task Force, or IETF) to review the document and add comments. When the document is in this stage it is referred to as being in the RFC Queue. If the document is approved by the IESG, it will be edited and published. If it is rejected, the author will be notified through e-mail of the rejection and the reasons behind the decision. If and when the document is ready for publishing, the author will be given 48 hours to review and edit the material. If the situation arises in which the IETF is already working on a similar document, the author will be asked by them to collaborate on it.

The RFC Editor's Web site can be found at http://www.rfc-editor.org. You may search the contents of the RFC index here.

—Adam M. Doxtater, MCP, MCSE

Active Directory Replication

Another point to consider when designing the namespace is replication of the Active Directory. Replication simply means that changes made on any specific domain controller are reflected on other domain controllers in the domain or forest of which it is a member.

Now that you have a solid understanding of namespace design, let's run through a quick pop quiz.

When working with naming in the real world, it is a good practice to document, or diagram, the current network as it is (if it has not already been done by a previous administrator). This includes both physical and logical layout, and in some cases, both methods will need to be approached. You will find it much easier to approach a naming strategy when you have a bird's eye view of the entire network structure.

SCENARIO & SOLUTION	
Which domain names in this list are compatible with the RFC 1123 standard? Company1.com Main_Street_Cafe.com Harveys-FiveAndDime.com	All of them are compliant, with the exception of Main_Street_Cafe.com. The underscore (_) is not an acceptable character to use. The hyphen (-) is acceptable, as is the use of capital letters and numbers throughout the name.
In the following listing of domain names, choose the domain with the best namespace usage: NTsvr1local.Company1.com FileServer.Company1.com	FileServer.Company.com is the logical choice. Even though the first choice is more descriptive as to what the server is (to an administrator, maybe), the latter is using the most efficient naming scheme.

EXERCISE 3-2

Deciding on Your Domain Names

You have designed Active Directory Domains; all that remains is to decide what names to give them.

Scenario: Your company is a large international company with a two strong Internet sites representing your two lines of business (books and wax). Your internal organization matches that of your lines of business and thus you have decided to have two separate domains, one for books and one for wax.

Points to consider:

- All domain names used should either be real Internet names, or names that will never exist on the Internet.
- You need to have both a NETBIOS and a DNS name for your domain.
- Do you want your internal hosts exposed as names in the Internet?

Solution:

Because your company already has a strong Internet presence, you should consider using different external and internal domain names. In this manor you would have to manually enter any server that is exposed internally and externally in DNS—thus ensuring that your internal file server was not listed in the external DNS.

Because both businesses work very independently, having separate domain trees would also seem like a logical decision.

Domain	DNS Name	NetBIOS Name
Books	Books.Local	Books
Car Wax	Wax.Local	Wax

In both cases, if you are able to register a second DNS name like BOOKSSYNGRESS.COM and WAXSYNGRESS.COM, you will have a valid DNS name that will never be used by another organization.

CERTIFICATION OBJECTIVE 3.03

Planning the DNS Strategy

In this portion of the chapter, we will discus the pros and cons of the Windows 2000 DNS. DNS is a distributed database that provides host to Internet Protocol (IP) address resolution. Windows 2000 DNS is comprised of three parts: domains, zones, and DNS servers. Domains are top-level DNS names such as mcse2000.com and contain child domains such as exams.mcse.com or study.mcse2000.com. Zones are sections of DNS replication managed by Windows 2000 DNS servers.

Some key features of the Windows 2000 DNS implementation are:

- Server configuration can be loaded directly from the Actve Directory.
- Dynamic updates (covered later in this section).
- Incremental zone transfers (IXFRs), which permit only updates to the zone table to be synchronized.
- Zones can be stored in Active Directory.
- Notification of zone changes. This allows for the authoritative DNS server to notify secondary DNS servers that a change has been made to the zone, which the secondary server will replicate.

We will cover all aspects and configurations including integrated DNS, stand-alone, legacy, and separate external DNS servers. It is important to understand the Windows DNS, as it is the method by which Windows 2000 locates other machines on an IP-based network. Every Windows 2000 domain has a DNS name, such as mcse2000.com, and every Windows 2000 machine has its own DNS name, such as win2k.mcse2000.com. When dealing with DNS, there are two distinct parts of the name to remember:

- DNS host name
- Primary DNS suffix

The end result of these two parts is the *fully qualified computer name.* The following table gives you an idea of how a full computer name is developed. Note that the full computer name will inherit the subdomain in which the computer resides, if it applies.

DNS Host Name	+	Primary DNS Suffix	=	Full Computer Name
CEO		SYNGRESS.COM		CEO. SYNGRESS.COM
LARRY		ACC.SYNGRESS.COM		LARRY.ACC. SYNGRESS.COM

Integrated DNS

Windows 2000 DNS is included with Windows 2000 Server, and is the most attractive method of name resolution when used in a homogeneous Windows 2000 network. The benefits of Active Directory-integrated DNS are evident immediately. It allows for storage and replication of DNS zone databases, wherein zone data is stored as an Active Directory object and is replicated as such. Windows 2000 naïve DNS also supports the *Dynamic Update* protocol, which is the standard (RFC 2136) that allows hosts in a domain to automatically, or dynamically, register their names into the DNS database. One thing to note is that the server will not perform a dynamic update for the client unless it has authenticated it in Active Directory, and it has the proper permissions to perform the dynamic update.

exam Watch

The server will not perform a dynamic update for the client unless it has authenticated it in Active Directory, and it has the proper permissions to perform the dynamic update.

Stand-alone DNS

A stand-alone DNS server will most likely be found, or placed, in a domain that only has one zone to maintain. This type of network would most probably belong to a small to mid-sized company that would not require multiple domains and locations. The benefit of this setup is ease of administration. If the domain were to

EXERCISE 3-3

Planning Your DNS Strategy

If your organization does not have existing DNS servers, or you only use them to browse the Internet, your DNS strategy will be simple—use Windows 2000 DNS. For this exercise we will concentrate on a company that has a significant implementation of UNIX DNS servers.

Scenario: Your organization uses DNS extensively internally and externally to provide access to both UNIX workstations and UNIX servers. Your CIO says that you cannot replace your existing UNIX DNS servers with Windows 2000.

Points to consider:

- DNS servers that support RFC 2782 "DNS SRV Resource Records" can work with Windows 2000.

Solution:

You talk to the existing DNS administrators in your firm to find out if their version of DNS supports RFC 2782. They inform you that it *does not* and say that they have no plans to upgrade *their* system.

You meet with the CIO and suggest that since the existing DNS does not support RFC 2782, you should just replace it with Windows 2000 DNS. The answer is a very firm "No."

- Given the firm "No" from your organization, you decide to set up your DNS as follows:
- Create a new sub-DNS name such as Books.Syngress.com.
- Set up your Windows 2000 server to forward all non-local requests to the corporate UNIX DNS servers for resolution or further forwarding to the Internet.
- Create an *A* record for the Windows 2000 server that will host the Windows 2000 DNS server in your UNIX DNS (such as Windows2000. Books.Syngress.com).
- Create an *NS* record for Books.Syngress.Com in your UNIX DNS database.

grow in size, taking on new domains and zones, it might call for the addition of more DNS servers. Figure 3-3 illustrates this for you.

Working with Non-Windows 2000 DNS Servers

In a heterogeneous, or mixed, Windows network, you will need to devise a strategy on working with pre-Windows 2000 DNS servers, such as Windows NT DNS server. Natively, this kind of DNS server will not support Active Directory; it must be configured to do so.

If you are working with non-Windows 2000 DNS servers, it is most probably due to an existing domain that contains pre-Windows 2000 domain controllers or DNS servers. The primary DNS server for that particular domain must support the Service Location Resource Record, or SRV RR (RFC 2782), to be compatible with Active Directory. SRV RR is defined in the IETF Internet-draft as "A DNS RR for specifying the location of services (DNS SRV)." If it does not support DNS SRV RR, it must coexist with a Windows 2000-based DNS server. The Windows 2000 DNS server must be made the primary server that is authoritative over all the DNS names that will be registered by the domain controller.

When working with non-Windows 2000 DNS servers that need to have authoritative information changed, the administrator must edit the zone file manually. The Windows NT DNS implementation was designed to feed from a static database. This was essentially a design flaw. Even though changes in the database were expected to be made, these changes were anticipated to happen very

FIGURE 3-3

Stand-alone DNS server in a single domain model

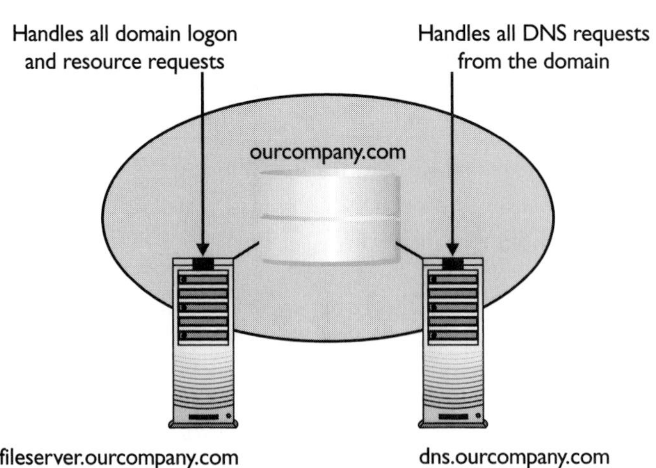

infrequently and were to be made manually by the administrators. With the advent of Windows 2000 DNS, this issue has been addressed by Microsoft and fixed with Dynamic Update integration.

As seen in Figure 3-4, even though the Windows 2000 DNS server is not located within the same domain as the non-Windows 2000 DNS server, it maintains the records through the Active Directory structure. It has been delegated to keep records for that zone.

exam Watch ***In order for a DNS server to be compatible with Active Directory services, it must support the SRV Resource Record.***

FIGURE 3-4

Windows 2000 DNS server coexisting with a legacy Windows NT DNS server

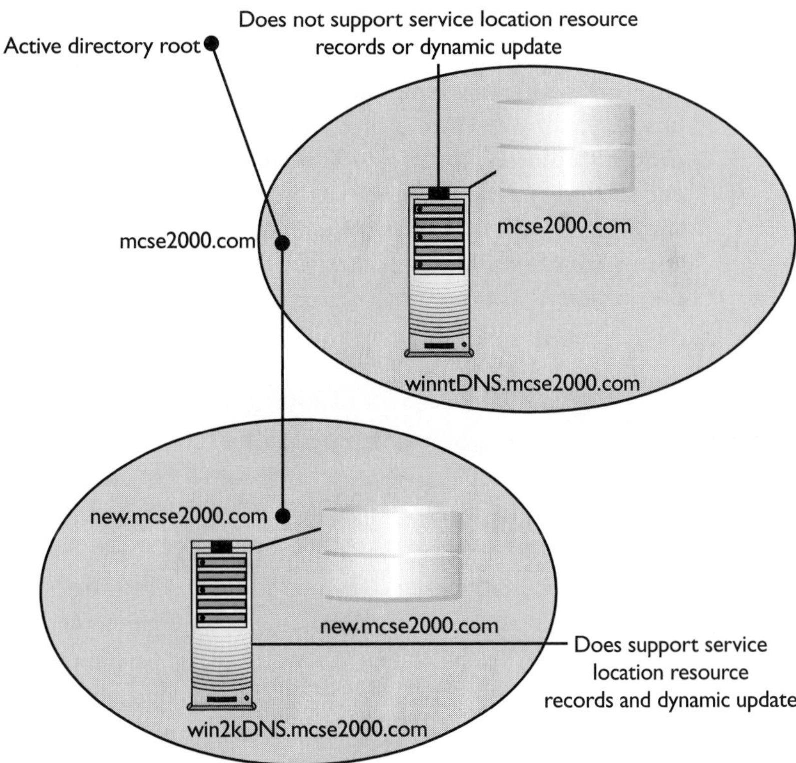

Separate External DNS Servers

Using external DNS servers independent of the internal network would most likely come into play when you have two domains that use identical names. For example, you have an internal domain name of MCSE2000.COM, and an external Internet domain named MCSE2000.COM. This scenario would pose problems without separate internal and external DNS servers, as client machines would attempt to authenticate with whichever domain answered the request first. This would lead to either logon failures or a lack of proper resources, depending on the network configuration.

The only logical way to avoid this scenario would be to implement two DNS servers, one on the internal network and one externally. The internally installed DNS server would essentially point to the IP address of the internal domain. The externally installed DNS server would do the same, except that it would handle all internal requests for external resources.

on the job

Even though it may seem a brilliant idea to replicate everything everywhere within the Active Directory structure, this is not always a smart thing to do. Network traffic is a real issue in day-to-day administration, and if not handled properly, can turn into a nightmare. I would recommend only replicating data that is absolutely necessary. The main purpose of a network is for users to access the information they need to perform their duties, and believe me, they like to access it in an expedient manner. Using too much of your network's available bandwidth for data replication will result in poor performance of other network applications.

CERTIFICATION OBJECTIVE 3.04

Naming Conventions

When speaking of naming conventions, we are referring to the logical structuring of domain names and forests within a Windows 2000 network. The physical structure of the domains involved may or may not play a part in this convention. The key here is to make the whole Active Directory experience as effortless as possible. For instance, if you were employed by a school district that had a domain root named allofourteachers.com and two sub-domains labeled busyard.com and cafeteria.com, these subdomains and their resources would not be found easily.

Forest Name

Put simply, a forest is a collection of Active Directory domains. Forests offer a way to group domains of like nature to simplify administration. For example, if you are working for a large corporation that has multiple domains in place, forests would be an excellent way to group them. As outlined in the figure that follows, you will notice that all domains associated with accounting are in the Accounting forest. Likewise, all of the domains associated with sales would be located within the Sales forest. Also note that the domains within a forest do not have to have the same root DNS address. For example, domain.com and its tree (which might possibly contain sub1.domain.com and sub2.domain.com) can reside in the same forest as win2k.com and its subdomains. Figure 3-5 illustrates the usage of root and child domains with different DNS roots.

Forests should be used in this manner. That way, if a user is trying to access the Accounts Receivable domain, he or she will not have to wade through endless domains in search of it.

FIGURE 3-5

Forests can contain domains with disparate DNS names

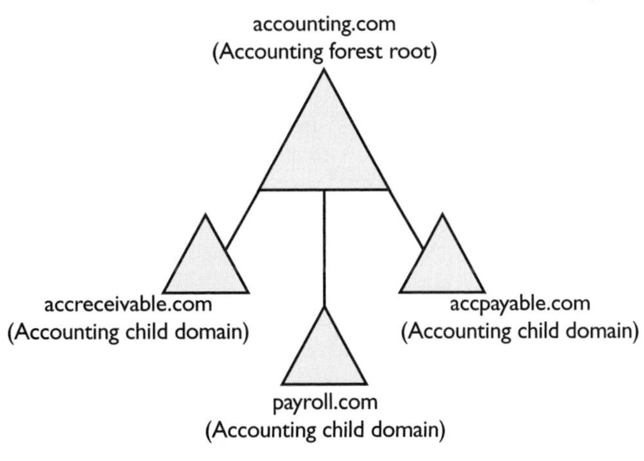

Domain Names

Domain names are at the heart and soul of any Active Directory implementation, and any naming scheme you choose to follow should be designed with this in mind. Domain names should be kept simple and to the point, leaving no question to end users as to what the resources of that domain will be. The grouping of domains and their subdomains should be considered as well, meaning that their resources should all be of like nature. Physical location should not be the determining factor when grouping domains.

Logically, both locations can be associated with the same root domain, and if servers were placed at both locations providing network authentication, it would alleviate a lot of the wide area traffic. Figure 3-6 illustrates this scenario using a single root domain and forest. Please note that this diagram is not the best illustration of a naming scheme. It is only being used to demonstrate that there are no physical boundaries to a single domain model.

You may also take the wide area network (WAN) scenario and apply a naming scheme to it. A basic scheme may look something like Figure 3-7.

FIGURE 3-6

Illustration of a forest containing two geographically different locations

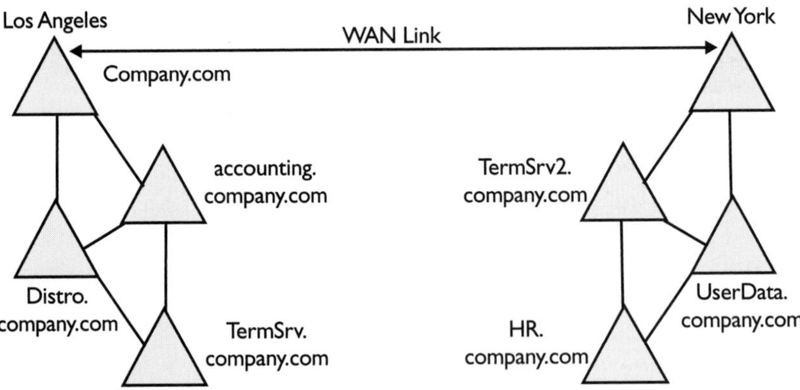

FIGURE 3-7

Logical naming scheme applied to a forest located in two geographical locations

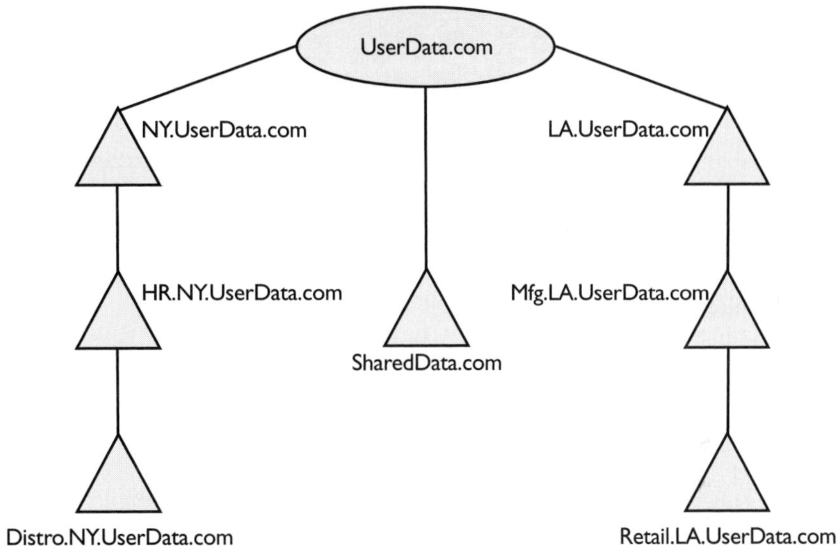

In the preceding figure, you should note the following points:

- UserData.com is the forest root domain, as well as the tree root domain.
- SharedData.com is also a tree root domain. We will assume that this domain is used for shared data between locations, and is not physically located between the two sites. It may be in New York or Los Angeles.
- Domain names are logically and physically arranged in the root domain. Each department is easily found by end users.

on the Job

In the preceding example, the domains are arranged by physical location and logical location. By logical, we are speaking of how the information contained in the domains would be applied to the overall structure. In the real world, this situation may not apply. In many cases you will be forced to design the structure strictly in accordance with physical location, or vice versa.

Now that you have a better understanding of naming conventions as they apply to forests and domains, answer the following scenario questions.

SCENARIO & SOLUTION	
From the following list, choose the domains that could be child domains in the mcse2000.com domain: Study.mcse2000.com New.Exams.mcse2000.com TestingSite.com Host.Exams.mcse2000.com New_domain.mcse2000.com	Okay, so I threw a curve in there. New_domain.mcse2000.com is unacceptable, as it has an underscore in the name. Everything else here is an acceptable child domain in the mcse2000.com domain.

OUs

An organizational unit (OU) is essentially a container used to maintain logical structure within a domain model. OUs will not directly affect the end user, and should not be designed with the end user in mind. They should be grouped appropriately to ease administration. When creating the structure of the domain, consider the following points:

- Organizational units can be nested. Like root domains and their child domains, organizational units can contain other OUs, allowing for creation of a logical structuring inside of a domain.
- End users will not navigate through an OU.
- OUs can be used to control access to objects in the directory. If OUs are used in combination with ACLs (Access Control Lists), you can grant rights to certain objects, while restricting rights to others. For instance, you may provide a group of users the ability to grant permissions to individual users, but not add or remove users or groups.

- OUs can be associated with Group Policies. Applying a Group Policy to an OU will allow for different security policies within the same domain.
- OUs are not to be mistaken for security models. OUs cannot be made members of a security group. You also cannot grant user permissions to resources because they reside in the OU structure.

The Organizational Unit Planning Process

The steps used in planning a successful OU structure are outlined in the following list:

1. Create OUs to delegate administration.
2. Create OUs to hide objects.
3. Create OUs for Group Policy.
4. Understand the impact of changing OU structures after deployment.

It is critical that you follow these steps during deployment in their exact order. Each design, you will notice, will take on a different structure completely. For instance, an OU designed for Group Policy will be different from an OU designed strictly for delegating administration. Designing an OU structure for Group Policies can be done in many different ways. There is only one way to delegate administration, so the OUs for delegation of administration should be done first. Note that OUs can become complex very quickly, so it would be a good practice to document every reason for adding the OU when it is done so that administrators that may follow in your footsteps will be able to understand the logic behind its creation. In the following exercise, we will cover the steps necessary in designing a logical Active Directory structure.

EXERCISE 3-4

Defining Object Naming Standards in Windows 2000

In this exercise, we will set up standards for a naming convention for various objects in Windows 2000. This is meant to be an example; in your organization you will need to define your own standards.

Scenario:

Your organization, Syngress Media Inc., has decided to move to Windows 2000 and has asked you to produce naming standards for all major object types in Windows 2000. Syngress is a multibillion dollar organization with offices in 15 countries and 10,000 employees.

Points to consider:

- Naming conventions have a tendency of dividing people into "religious" debates. It is important to understand where standards are very important, or just look good, and spend your energy on the important ones.
- Although Microsoft Windows 2000 DNS supports a wide variety of characters, many DNS servers only support A-Z, a-z, 0-9, and "-". Unless there is a very important reason to use special characters, it is best to keep it simple.

Solution:

Object Type	Recommendation
Forest	A forest does not have a name.
Domain	Domains have two names, DNS and NetBIOS. In most companies, domains will rarely be created so they can be handled on an individual basis. In general, you should keep your names short and not use special characters. For Syngress, it was decided that domains would be regionally based thus: NA.Syngress.com Europe.Syngress.com Asia.Syngress.com

Organizational Units	The naming of OUs will depend on how you plan to use them. If an OU is used to store your users, then you would generally call it “Users.” Syngress OUs are used to store each type of object as follows: Printers Users Desktops Servers
Users	The important thing to remember is that standards will make it easier to find the data you are looking for. For Syngress, the following rules are proposed: First Name Last Name In cases where the preceding creates a duplicate, the user is asked for the name that they would like to use.
Servers	Most companies are going with names that are based on location and function. For Syngress, this is a seven digit code as follows: First three characters of the office name “-” First three characters of server function, such as SQL or MSX
Workstations	The workstation-naming standard is very much like that of servers. Because workstations are a shared resource and not assigned to an individual, the servers are named based on their asset code number as follows: First three characters of the office name “-” Asset Code Number

CERTIFICATION SUMMARY

Now that we have concluded this chapter, you should have a better understanding of the structuring of Windows 2000 Active Directory. For this reason, I suggest gaining a solid understanding of the technologies used on Windows NT platforms, as it will help you to better understand where Windows 2000 has its roots. The world of computers is an ever-changing world; so quick sometimes that it seems to happen overnight. A better understanding of technology as it is today and as it was yesterday will give you the ground on which to stand tomorrow.

TWO-MINUTE DRILL

Establishing the Scope of Active Directory

- ❑ The Active Directory Connector (ADC) is required to replicate information between the Active Directory and Exchange Server 5.5.
- ❑ Active Directory can be used as a central location to keep employee records and track their respective changes and updates.
- ❑ Deleted objects are marked as a tombstone.

Designing the Namespace

- ❑ Replication means that changes made on any specific domain controller are reflected on other domain controllers in the domain or forest of which it is a member.
- ❑ Use trees sparingly to avoid confusion when expanding on the directory.
- ❑ Use simple, descriptive names when creating the domains, as their resources will be easily located in the future.

Planning the DNS Strategy

- ❑ In order for a DNS server to be compatible with Active Directory, it must support the Service Location Resource Record (SRV RR).
- ❑ The server will not perform a dynamic update for the client unless it has authenticated it in Active Directory, and it has the proper permissions to perform the dynamic update.
- ❑ Incremental zone transfer (IXFR) permits only updates to the zone table to be synchronized.
- ❑ In order for a legacy DNS server to work with Active Directory, it must coexist with a Windows 2000 DNS server that is authoritative over the domain.

Naming Conventions

- ❑ A *forest* is a collection of Active Directory-enabled domains.
- ❑ Domains within a forest do not have to maintain the same root DNS address.
- ❑ An organizational unit (OU) is a container used to maintain the logical structure within a domain model.

4

Planning an Active Directory Replication

CERTIFICATION OBJECTIVES

4.01	Managing and Troubleshooting Active Directory Replication
4.02	Managing and Troubleshooting Domain Name System Replication
✓	Two-Minute Drill

Windows 2000 Active Directory was designed to meet the scalability needs of the large enterprise through the concept of a domain forest. AD spans the entire forest, regardless of whether the forest contains a single domain or a multitude of domains. The forest is also the boundary to AD; it cannot span multiple-domain forests. AD "lives" on domain controllers, which are often distributed throughout the enterprise network to provide high availability and redundancy. Windows 2000 uses an advanced topology that allows changes to objects in a domain to be performed by any domain controller that belongs to that domain. This means that it is possible for domain controllers within a domain to have a different or even conflicting view of the domain data at any given time. *Replication* is the process that migrates these changes between domain controllers and resolves conflicts when they occur.

Replication in Windows 2000 is managed automatically by default, but the feature allows for administrative intervention to customize or optimize the replication process. A thorough understanding of how replication works is needed to grasp the capabilities and impact of manual configuration of replication.

Windows 2000 relies heavily on Domain Name System (DNS) service for proper domain operation, and the same issues of high availability and redundancy that apply to domain controllers apply to DNS servers. Microsoft provides a DNS server as part of the Windows 2000 Server operating systems but also supports the use of non-Microsoft DNS servers. Many organizations have an existing DNS infrastructure and want to leverage their existing equipment and expertise. To provide interoperability with these other DNS servers, Microsoft has provided Windows 2000 with the capability to replicate and interoperate with any Request For Comments (RFC)-compliant DNS server but added new features unique to Windows 2000 DNS, such as the ability to store DNS records in Active Directory. DNS information stored in AD is replicated between domain controllers using the AD replication model and inherits the replication efficiency and scalability that AD provides.

CERTIFICATION OBJECTIVE 4.01

Managing and Troubleshooting Active Directory Replication

AD replication is highly automated in Windows 2000 to minimize administration. The default settings have been designed to work well in most network environments. Replication is a very important part of maintaining a properly functioning and secure AD installation, and a good understanding of how the replication process functions is vital to troubleshooting and correcting problems with replication. This section assumes that the reader is familiar with general AD concepts such as domains, forests, and organizational units (OUs).

What Is Active Directory Replication?

Replication is the process of keeping data stored in Active Directory synchronized on all domain controllers. Each domain controller in a Windows 2000 domain is able to function independently and therefore must contain a complete copy of the domain information for which it is responsible. AD is not static, and entries change with use. When a change is made, it is written to the directory by a single domain controller. Changes made on each domain controller must be distributed to other domain controllers. The replication process efficiently distributes these changes to the other domain controllers in the forest that maintain the same information, and it resolves any conflicts that occur.

In a Windows 2000 domain forest, there are many reasons for choosing to deploy multiple domain controllers. A small office network configured as a single Windows 2000 domain requires only one domain controller to establish the domain. The resulting domain is fully functional but has no redundancy. If the domain controller fails, network operations are interrupted until it is repaired or replaced. In this scenario, additional domain controllers are often used for fault tolerance. If one domain controller fails, others are available to keep the network running. Of course, each additional domain in the forest requires at least one additional domain controller to establish the new domain.

Performance is often another reason to add additional domain controllers. When the number of accesses to Active Directory increases to a point where the existing domain controllers are overwhelmed, additional controllers can be added to distribute the load. Because all domain controllers operate independently, a client can contact any one with the required information to perform a query or submit a change to the directory.

When a network becomes distributed over a wide area, the network links between those areas are typically expensive and provide limited bandwidth. If we place a domain controller on each side of a wide area network (WAN) link, client traffic for directory access can utilize the local domain controller over the local area network (LAN), increasing client performance. It is generally much more efficient to add a domain controller to a LAN rather than have all client traffic cross a slow WAN link to access a domain controller. Client accesses to the directory are often interactive, and the time it takes for a user to log on or get a response to a query is an important part of a network's performance.

The goal of AD replication is to maintain a *loose consistency* of the database information on all domain controllers by utilizing a minimum of domain resources. Loose consistency means that there might be a period of time after a change is made during which other domain controllers will not have the updated data immediately available. Network bandwidth is the most critical resource to replication because it provides the path for the replicated data to travel. In order to reduce the amount of bandwidth required by replication, Windows 2000 makes use of data compression and replication when possible. In addition, Windows 2000 uses store-and-forward technology, which avoids duplicate replication when possible, and ensures that only the minimum amount of information needed to make the change is transmitted across the network.

Active Directory contains objects of many types. A Container object such as an organizational unit or domain can contain other objects such as User or Computer objects. All objects have properties, or *attributes,* that specify information such as the name of the object and describe properties of the object. A User object, as shown in Figure 4-1, has the attributes display name, e-mail address, and telephone number, to name a few. Active Directory is able to replicate changes at the attribute level. If only the e-mail address of a user is changed in AD, only the change in that attribute, not the entire User object, needs to be replicated to other domain controllers. This significantly reduces the amount of bandwidth used in replication.

Naming Contexts

The data that makes up AD is divided into multiple partitions, or *naming contexts.* These containers are logical partitions; all AD information on a domain controller is physically stored in a file named NTDS.DIT. Two naming contexts are shared among all domain controllers in the forest: the *schema* naming context, which is essentially a blueprint for all containers, objects, and attributes that make up Active Directory, and the *configuration* naming context, which contains information that describes the physical layout of the enterprise network. Each domain in the forest also has its own naming context that is a Parent object for all the Child objects that exist in that domain. Replication for each naming context is performed separately; information in the naming context for a domain is replicated only between domain controllers responsible for that domain. However, both the schema and the configuration container must be replicated to every domain controller in the forest, regardless of the domain to which they belong. A complete copy of a naming context stored on a domain controller is called a *full replica* of the information.

FIGURE 4-1 User objects and their many attributes

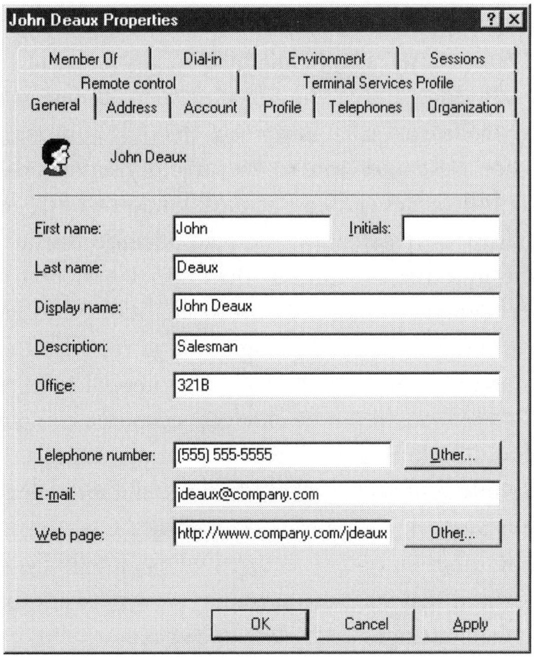

Global catalog servers participate in the replication process for their own domain and can also replicate with domain controllers from other domains and/or other global catalog servers to maintain the global catalog. Since the data used by the global catalog is read only and contains only a small subset of attributes, the global catalog information is considered a *partial replica.* A partial replica cannot be used to update a full replica, but it can be used to update a partial replica on another global catalog server. Table 4-1 summarizes the replication scopes for the various naming contexts.

exam Watch

The global catalog contains information about objects from all domains in the forest and can replicate information in the domain naming context with domain controllers from domains other than its own.

TABLE 4-1 Naming Contexts and Their Replication Scopes

Naming Context	Replication Scope
Configuration	All domain controllers in the forest.
Schema	All domain controllers in the forest.
Domain (one for each domain)	Only domain controllers within the domain and global catalog servers within the forest.

Single-Master and Multimaster Replication

Microsoft used a *single-master directory model* in versions of Windows NT prior to Windows 2000. The single master was designated as the Primary Domain Controller, or PDC, and it was the only computer in the domain that was able to both read and write to the directory services database. Additional domain controllers, designated Backup Domain Controllers, or BDCs, could be deployed to assist with validation and read operations from clients, but changes had to be written to the directory by the PDC. Changes made to the directory on the PDC were eventually passed down to the BDCs through the process of replication.

One weakness of the single-master model is the existence of a single point of failure. Should the PDC fail, no writes could be made to the directory database; passwords could not be changed, accounts could not be added or deleted. A single PDC also limited the availability of write access to the database. Since the PDC was the only system that allowed writes, the number of changes and updates that could be made at one time were limited by the performance of that system.

Another limitation recurred when large NT 4 domains spanned several physical locations that were connected by slow network links. With a single PDC in a domain, changes that originated at remote sites had to cross these slow links to be made on the PDC. If BDCs were located at these sites, the changes made on the PDC then had to be replicated back over the link, once for each BDC. These were limitations that needed to be overcome to improve scalability and acceptance of Windows in large enterprise environments.

With Windows 2000, Microsoft implemented a *multimaster directory model.* In a multimaster configuration, all domain controllers hold a copy of the directory database information for which they are responsible and are allowed to perform both reads and writes to their databases. Whereas this solves many of the scalability problems with previous versions of Windows NT, the process of replication, in which changes are propagated to all the other domain controllers in the enterprise, becomes more complex.

Store and Forward

Windows NT replication was further limited by the fact that the PDC was a single point for updates. Every BDC, regardless of its location, had to receive updates to the database directly from the PDC. In the case in which four NT 4 BDCs were located across a slow WAN link from the PDC, a single change on the PDC resulted in that change being replicated over the WAN link four times, once to each BDC.

AD replication in Windows 2000 is transitive and uses a *store-and-forward model* in which a domain controller that learns about changes from one domain controller is able to pass the learned changes to other domain controllers. In a properly configured Windows 2000 network, a change made on a domain controller on one side of a WAN link is replicated across the link to a single domain controller on the other side. That domain controller then distributes the changes to all the other domain controllers at that site. This results in much lower utilization of the WAN link for directory replication.

How Domain Controllers Track Changes

In order to provide the most efficient replication possible, domain controllers must keep track of each change made to Active Directory and differentiate between changes made by themselves as opposed to changes they have learned about through replication with other domain controllers.

Update Sequence Numbers

Each domain controller maintains a counter for each naming context that is used to assign a unique numeric identifier to every change made to the replica stored on that particular domain controller. These numbers are known as *update sequence numbers (USNs).* When a write occurs (either an originating write or one due to replication), the USN counter is incremented and the new value is attached to the objects or attributes that were changed as a result of the write. If the write operation fails for any reason, those changes are not made to the database, and that USN goes unused. It is important to realize that each domain controller maintains its own USN counters for changes written to its own replica of the directory. The USN counters for other domain controllers in the domain will very likely be different.

High-Watermark Vector

The *high-watermark vector* is used to determine whether changes are available to be replicated. Each domain controller maintains a high-watermark vector for each naming context. This is a two-column table (shown in Table 4-2) that contains the globally unique identifier (GUID) of each domain controller to which it has a Connection object in one column and the highest USN seen from those systems. During replication, the domain controller receiving updates passes the high-watermark vector to the domain controller providing updates as part of the pull

TABLE 4-2

A High-Watermark Vector

Server Globally Unique Identifier	Highest USN Seen from Server
362BEB43-0433-4B2F-9CF7-A0981865AF49	6284
2324C2A1-B41C-4BED-A4AA-Cce3E27A145B	4976

request. By examining the high-watermark vector, the domain controller providing updates is able to determine which information the receiving domain controller already knows about. Any updates with a USN greater than the one in the high-watermark vector of the receiving computer are potential candidates for replication.

There is, however, the possibility that both the receiving systems have already received some or all of the updated information through replication with another domain controller. If this is the case, some of the information planned for replication might not have to be replicated. The up-to-dateness vector is what further allows replication traffic to be reduced.

Up-to-Dateness Vector

In addition to the high-watermark vector, each domain controller also maintains an *up-to-dateness vector* for each naming context. Like the high-watermark vector, it is a two-column table (shown in Table 4-3) with the GUID of a domain controller on the left side and a USN on the right side. The difference is that the up-to-dateness vector tracks *originating updates.* Originating updates are those that are accepted from a user or program and written to the directory for the first time on a particular domain controller. The up-to-dateness vector for a naming context on a domain controller has an entry for every system that it knows has made an originating write. The USN entry is the highest USN seen for an originating write from that particular domain controller.

TABLE 4-3

An Up-to-Dateness Vector

Server Globally Unique Identifier	Highest Originating Write Seen from Server
362BEB43-0433-4B2F-9CF7-A0981865AF49	6280
A2AA5A76-E8D5-4D8C-8868-02E445D460E9	3201
2324C2A1-B41C-4BED-A4AA-CCE3E27A145B	4976

As before, the up-to-dateness vector is passed to the sending computer when the receiving computer initiates pull replication. The sending computer uses this information to further reduce the list of updates sent to the receiving computer. If a change marked for replication has an originating USN of 2033 and the up-to-dateness vector shows that the destination computer has already seen a USN of 2033 from the computer that performed the originating write, the change does not have to be replicated.

Making Changes to Active Directory

When a domain controller writes changes to the Active Directory, those changes can be classified into one of four types: addition, change, move, or deletion. A domain controller further distinguishes these changes into *originating updates*, or *replicated updates*. Originating updates are those that are accepted from a user or program and written to the directory for the first time on a particular domain controller; replicated updates are those that originate on other domain controllers and are learned through the replication process.

When a new object is created on a domain controller by a user or process (other than by replication), it is marked as an originating update and is assigned a version number of one, as well as a time stamp and the GUID of the originating domain controller. There are two USN entries for the object and every attribute of that object, one to track when the object was initially created and another to track the last change to the object. Both are set to the same USN during object creation. Each subsequent change to the object increases the version number by one in order to determine the most current version of the object, and the USN entry that tracks changes is updated. Moving an object works in the same way as a change, because a move is essentially a change to the name attribute of the object.

Of the possible changes to AD, deletions are by far the most problematic in replication. In order to remove an object from AD and update the removal to other domain controllers, a special kind of change operation is used. Instead of actually deleting an object, a special attribute is set to mark the object as a tombstone or deleted object. Most of the nonessential attributes of the object are changed to null values to reduce the amount of space the object takes up in the directory. This Tombstone object can be replicated to all other domain controllers.

Tombstone objects continue to take up space in AD, and a method for removing them must be implemented to prevent AD from continuously increasing in size over time. After a certain age, tombstones are permanently deleted from AD through a process known as *garbage collection.* A garbage collection process runs by default every 12 hours on each individual domain controller, checks for tombstones that have expired, and deletes them. The garbage collection process is also responsible for removing unused log files and the defragmentation of the database.

By default, tombstones have a lifetime of 60 days. Tombstone lifetime can have some serious consequences for restoring a domain controller from backup. Backups of AD that are older than the tombstone lifetime can no longer be used for nonauthoritative restores. If such a backup restored an object that had been deleted, such as a user account, and the Tombstone object no longer existed in the database, there would be no replication conflict and the deleted object would become fully restored. Tombstone lifetime must be set to a period that is longer than the time it takes for AD to replicate completely. If set to too short an interval, garbage collection could remove tombstones on domain controllers before they were replicated to other domain controllers, leaving AD in an inconsistent state.

Conflict Resolution

Since it is possible that a conflicting change to the same object could be made on two different domain controllers at the same time, the resulting replication forces the domain controller that receives the updates to resolve these conflicts. Each domain controller is able to follow a simple consistent set of rules to resolve these conflicts without having to query or otherwise discuss the conflict with any other domain controllers.

In order to implement this process, an originating write tags an object with a version number, a time stamp, and the GUID of the domain controller that originated the write. This information is replicated with the object. Each object has its own version number, which starts at one when it is created. These version numbers are replicated with the objects. Every time the object is changed or updated, the version number is increased by one, and the time stamp and originating domain controller GUID are refreshed. When conflicts occur, the object or attribute with the highest version number is written, and others are discarded. If two conflicting attributes have the same version number, the time stamps of the changes are compared and the most recent change is written. In the very unlikely event that the changes occurred at the exact same time, the GUID of the originating domain controller is used to break the tie.

The significance of the version number is that time alone does not dictate the changes that are made to the directory. If time was the primary deciding factor for resolving a conflict, differences in time between domain controllers could cause serious problems. For example, suppose a change is made and time stamped 1:59 AM. At 2:00 AM, daylight savings time ends and the clocks are all rolled back to 1:00 AM. Any changes made during the next hour would be immediately overwritten by the change time stamped at 1:59 AM. Imagine what could happen if the date was inadvertently set forward 10 years on a domain controller and objects were written. Once the correct time was restored, those objects with origination dates in the future would override any new updates or deletions! By making the version number the primary decision maker, you avoid a dependence on time synchronization.

In order to delete a container from AD, it cannot contain any Child object; but consider what happens when an empty OU that has replicated to multiple domain controllers is part of a conflicting change. On one domain controller, an administrator adds a user to the empty OU. On another domain controller, an administrator deletes the empty OU. When changes replicate, the Tombstone object for the OU replicates and the new User object remains without a parent container. A special container called "lost and found" exists in Active Directory for this reason, and the orphaned User object is relocated there.

Network and Knowledge Consistency Checker Topology

In most cases, Windows 2000 handles replication automatically. The *Knowledge Consistency Checker (KCC)* generates the virtual replication topology within a site. The KCC runs on all domain controllers every 15 minutes by default. It examines the information in the Active Directory configuration container to generate the replication topology. To provide a level of fault tolerance to the replication process within a site, a bidirectional ring configuration is used. This configuration allows for multiple replication paths to any domain controller in the ring, and if a domain controller fails, replication can still occur to all the other domain controllers in the ring. In fact, the KCC maintains the ring such that any domain controller is no more than three hops from any other domain controller in the domain.

The KCC on each domain controller uses the unique GUIDs of all the domain controllers installed at a site to sort them into an ordered list and virtually connects the first domain controller in the list to the last domain controller in the list to create the bidirectional ring. Each domain controller determines the replication topology independently, and since they are operating under the same rules with the same data, all can come to the same conclusion without any network traffic being sent. A separate bidirectional ring is created for each naming context in the forest. A forest with a single domain has three naming contexts and thus three replication rings, one for the domain naming context, one for the configuration naming context, and a third for the schema naming context. Each additional domain in the forest introduces a new naming context and a new replication path. Since both the schema naming context and the configuration naming context replicate to all domain controllers in a forest, they share the same replication path, regardless of the number of domains in the forest.

After creating the virtual topology for AD replication, the KCC creates *Connection objects.* A Connection object is a unidirectional path along which replication can take place. Connection objects are created between domain controllers that the KCC has determined to be neighbors in the virtual topology. The Connection objects on a domain controller point to other domain controllers that can be the source for replicated data. Because Connection objects are one-way, a domain controller can use a Connection object to obtain information from another domain controller. Each domain controller creates connection objects to its neighbors in order to receive updates from other domain controllers. The KCC automatically regenerates the site topology and creates and removes Connection objects if domain controllers fail or if they are added or removed from the forest. A Connection object is not tied to a particular naming context and can be used by multiple naming contexts.

Administrators can create their own Connection objects in addition to the ones created by the KCC. Connection objects are owned by the user or process that creates them. The KCC does not manipulate any Connection objects that it did not create. If an administrator modifies a KCC-created Connection object, that object is no longer owned by the KCC and it no longer maintains it. Figure 4-2 shows an example of using the Active Directory Sites and Services snap-in to view the KCC-generated Connection objects.

Overview of Sites, Subnets, Links, and Replication

A *Site object* in Active Directory represents a group of computers networked together with a reliable high-speed network. Logically, a site is a Container object with attributes that is stored in the configuration container. Most sites contain one or more domain controllers, but that is not a requirement for a site. Sites are required to use TCP/IP as their network protocol, and a site can contain multiple TCP/IP subnets. Subnets cannot span sites, however. When you define multiple sites in AD, there must be some type of network link to interconnect the sites so that replication

FIGURE 4-2

Three domain controllers have a Connection object to each of its ring neighbors, DC2 and DC3

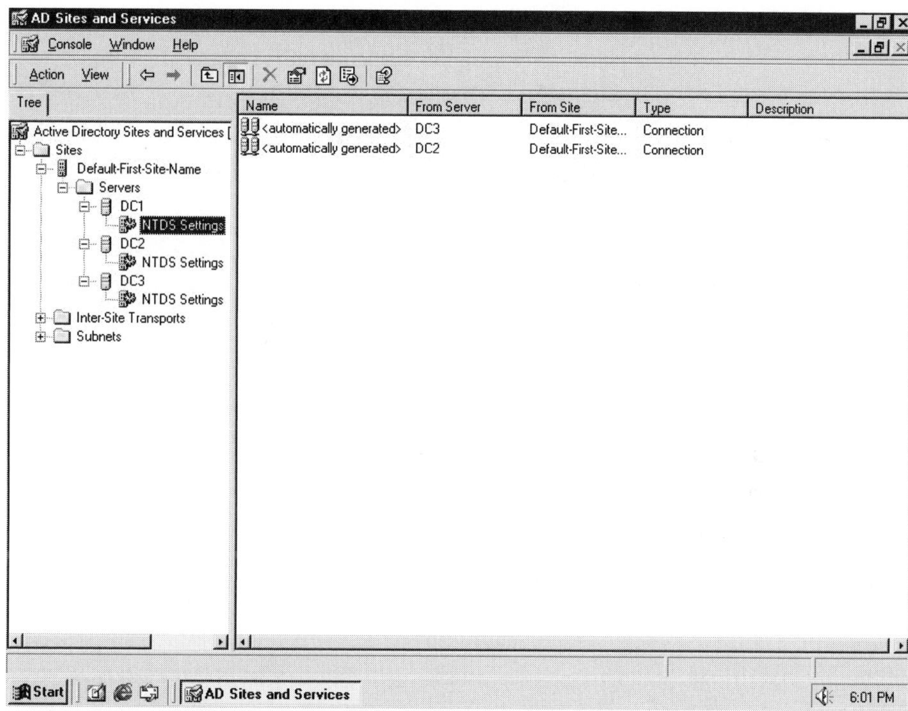

traffic can be passed. These network links are represented in AD by a site link or site link bridge object.

In order to utilize network bandwidth efficiently, Windows 2000 differentiates between two types of connectivity, within a site (or intrasite) and between sites (or intersite). When you install the first domain controller in a forest, an initial default site is created. In addition, a Server object is created for your domain controller and placed in that site. This Server object should not be confused with the Computer object created in the Domain Controllers OU. The Computer object is part of the domain naming context. The Server object is created within a site, which is part of the configuration naming context for the forest. The site is called Default-First-Site-Name, which can, of course, be renamed. If you don't plan on configuring any additional sites, Windows 2000 assumes that you have good network connectivity and will configure and perform intrasite replication between all domain controllers in the forest, regardless of where they are physically located.

FROM THE CLASSROOM

Physical and Logical Sites

There is a big difference between physical sites and the logical sites that are configured in Active Directory. Some physical network designs map to the logical idea of sites very well. A company with an office in New York and an office in Los Angeles that has a T1 line connecting the 100MBps Ethernet network at each office is a textbook example of where you could create two sites and a site link in Active Directory. On the other hand, if the company has a lot of available bandwidth on its T1 connection, makes few changes to AD, and needs low latency for those updates, using a single logical site is a reasonable option. Alternatively, an office that shares two floors of a building could have a 155MBps ATM link between the floors, but due to high utilization of the bandwidth, large numbers of changes to AD that can easily wait a day to propagate to the other floor, and a need to schedule replication between floors after business hours, each floor of its office is configured as a logical site to meet employees' requirements.

—Brian K. Doré, MCSE, MCT

Sites are configured by using the Active Directory Sites and Services snap-in. Figure 4-3 shows the configuration for a single domain forest within a single site. Domain controllers DC1 and DC2 have Server objects that have been created in the site named Default-First-Site-Name. Company.com has two domain controllers in the domain located within a single site. The Server objects for DC1 and DC2 are shown in the Servers container for the site Default-First-Site-Name. Notice the Connection object for DC1 points to DC2 as a source for directory updates.

Creating New Sites

When a site is created, it must have a *site link*. A site link defines a connection to another site or sites. A site link is a logical representation of the physical network that connects sites. A site link named DEFAULTIPSITELINK is created along with the default site when a forest is created, as shown in Figure 4-4. Site links have two important attributes that can be used to manipulate replication: cost and replication schedule.

FIGURE 4-3

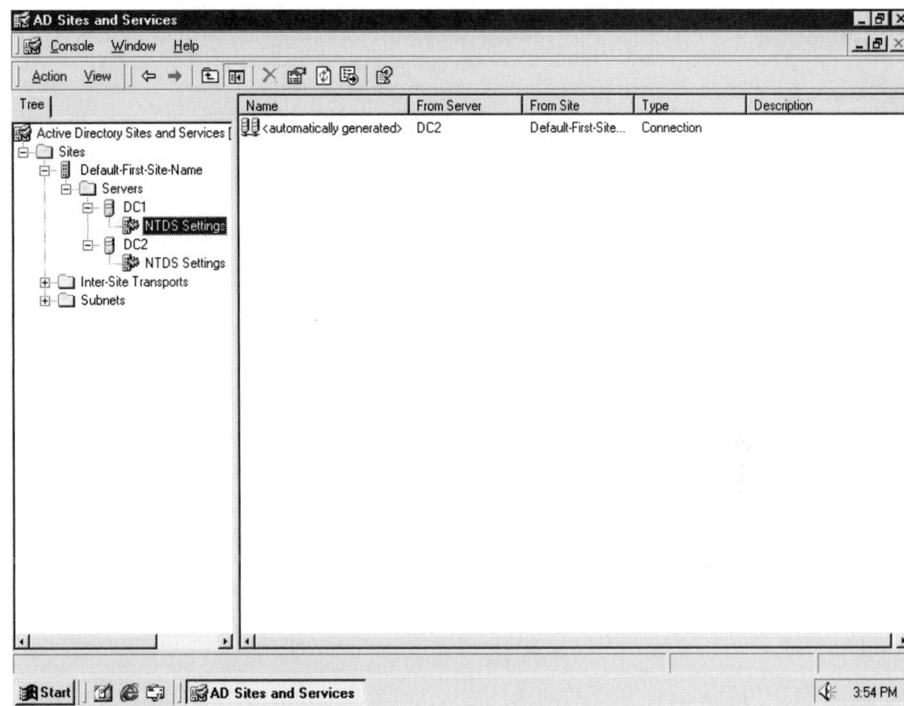

The Active Directory Sites and Services snap-in

Cost is expressed by assigning a value to a site link. If there are multiple paths between sites, the intersite topology generator configures replication to occur on the path with the lowest cost. In general, slow links are configured with a higher cost than fast links.

The times that replication is allowed to occur over a link are determined by the replication schedule, which is set on the site link Properties sheet. Clicking the Change Schedule button opens the window shown in Figure 4-5. By default, links are available seven days a week, 24 hours a day. Notice that the scheduling is limited to allowing or disallowing replication in one-hour blocks.

You can also create subnet objects within the Active Directory Sites and Services snap-in and assign these subnets to sites. Multiple subnets can be assigned to the same site. Assigning subnets to sites is important for placing new domain controllers in the correct site when they are first installed as well as for clients to locate resources in their own sites.

FIGURE 4-4

The Default IP site link

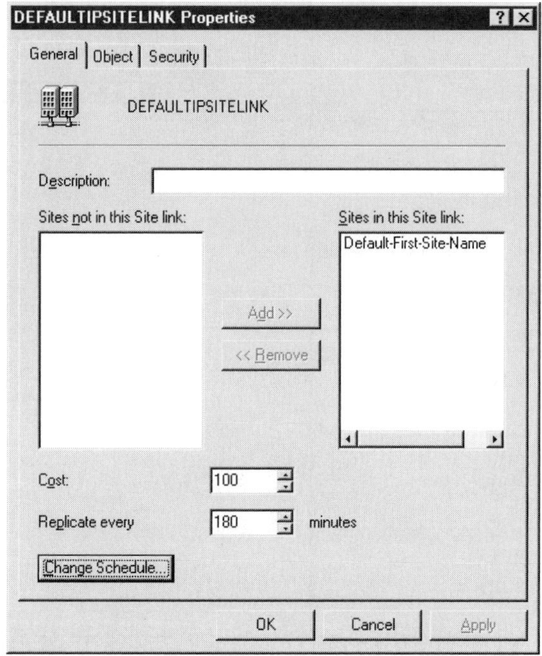

FIGURE 4-5

Site link schedules can be set to allow replication only at certain times and only on certain days of the week

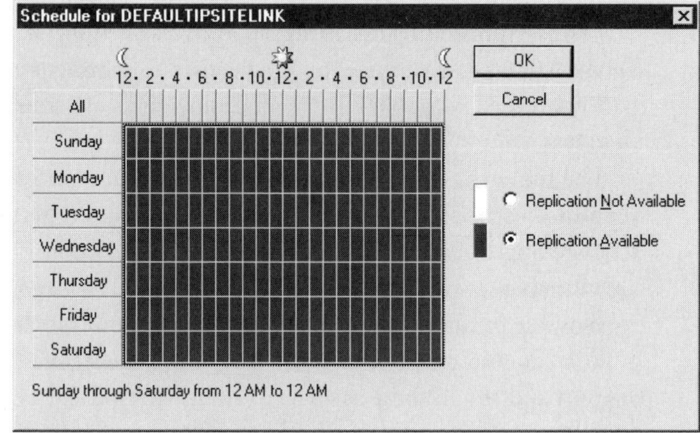

Site link bridges form the basis for very advanced network topologies. These objects can be used to describe a connection between site links. Site links are transitive by default, but this state can be turned off via the site link Properties sheet. Once transitivity is disabled, site link bridges can be used to create a replication through multiple site links. Like site links, site link bridges have cost and replication schedule attributes.

Managing Intrasite Replication

Network connectivity within a site is assumed to be fast and reliable. This high bandwidth allows for frequent replication, which results in low latency within the site. When replicating within a site, domain controllers do not use compression to save bandwidth.

Replication within sites occurs when a domain controller performs a write to Active Directory and needs to inform other domain controllers that changes have been made. The domain controller waits for five minutes before announcing that updates are available. The five-minute wait allows time for additional changes to be made to the database before replication starts so that a group of changes made close together can be replicated together in one efficient cycle. When the replication partners receive notification of an update, they initiate the pull replication sequence by sending their high-watermark and up-to-dateness vectors, the maximum number of updates they will accept at a time, and other information. After determining the data that needs to be replicated, the source domain controller sends the data.

For domain controllers within a site, the KCC attempts to create Connection objects so that replication needs to travel through no more than three domain controllers to replicate to all points in the network. When a small number of domain controllers are present in a site, simply creating Connection objects to neighboring domain controllers in the ring is sufficient, but when more than seven domain controllers are present, the KCC creates additional Connection objects in order to keep the replication path between any two domain controllers to three hops or fewer. Since the default replication period within a site is 5 minutes, this means that any change made on a domain controller should fully replicate to all other domain controllers in a site within 15 minutes.

As a backup procedure, a domain controller also attempts to replicate on schedule. By default, this replication is scheduled to occur every hour. This system helps reduce replication latency in conditions where update notifications were missed due to network or system outages.

Urgent Replication

Some changes to Active Directory, such as account lockouts, are critical in nature and must be replicated to all domain controllers immediately. Otherwise, if an administrator locked a user's account, it could take up to 15 minutes for that change to replicate to all domain controllers through normal replication and could result in a major security problem. Urgent replication immediately replicates an account lockout to the PDC emulator and then to all domain controllers within a site. By default, site links do not pass change notifications but can be configured to do so. If site links are configured to allow change notifications to cross them, the changes propagate to domain controllers within those connected sites as well. Sites connected by links that do not support change notification receive the lockout through normal intersite replication.

Managing Intersite Replication

When you are replicating data between sites, it is important to use as little bandwidth as possible. Replication between sites is heavily compressed before it is sent and must be uncompressed at the destination. The trade-off for this reduction in bandwidth utilization is higher CPU utilization on both domain controllers while the compression or decompression is taking place.

Replication Protocols

When Active Directory information is replicating between sites, the Remote Procedure Call (RPC) protocol used for intrasite replication is normally used. Windows 2000 also provides the ability to use Simple Mail Transfer Protocol (SMTP) to transfer replication information in certain circumstances. SMTP replication requires an SMTP service configured such as the one included with IIS 5.0 on the Windows 2000 Server CD. It also requires a Certificate Authority (CA) configured to verify the authenticity of SMTP replication messages. SMTP requires more network bandwidth than RPC replication because the protocol uses message headers that cannot be compressed. SMTP is valuable in that it supports very slow connections, intermittent connections, and intrasite connections that might not be based on the IP protocol but can pass SMTP messages.

For optimal replication performance, use RPC as your replication protocol whenever possible.

Unlike replication within a site, update notifications are not sent across intersite links. Instead, replication between sites is scheduled to occur on a periodic basis. These schedules can be controlled further by limiting replication between sites to occur only during certain times of the day. This method allows an administrator to schedule updates between sites to occur during periods of low network utilization. For redundancy, it is common that sites are connected by multiple paths. A cost factor can be applied to these links individually to set a preferential path for replication. By default, intersite replication occurs every 15 minutes, 24 hours a day.

The replication topology between sites is the responsibility of the *Intersite Topology Generator.* Each site has one domain controller that is responsible for examining the WAN connections between sites and determining the replication path.

A *bridgehead server* is the domain controller at a site that is responsible for replication with the bridgehead servers at other sites. The Intersite Topology Generator designates a single bridgehead server in a site automatically. A single domain controller can be the bridgehead server for multiple protocols, or a separate bridgehead server can be chosen for each protocol. Should the automatically determined bridgehead server fail, the Intersite Topology Generator recovers and chooses another one.

Administrators have the ability to designate *preferred bridgehead servers,* as shown in Figure 4-6. This allows the administrator to choose a domain controller that has the extra capacity to handle intersite traffic. Since all intersite traffic must be compressed before it is sent and uncompressed when it is received, bridgehead servers experience higher CPU utilization due to replication. Multiple domain controllers can be designated as preferred bridgeheads, but only one is used at any given time. If a preferred bridgehead server fails, another preferred bridgehead server is selected to replace it. If a preferred bridgehead server fails and no other preferred bridgehead servers are available in that site, intersite replication ceases.

exam Watch

Bridgehead servers are selected and maintained automatically by default. An administrator can intervene in this process by designating one or more preferred bridgehead servers. Once a preferred bridgehead server is designated, only domain controllers that are marked as preferred bridgehead servers can become bridgehead servers.

FIGURE 4-6

The Server Properties sheet for the domain controller DC2 from the Active Directory Sites and Services snap-in

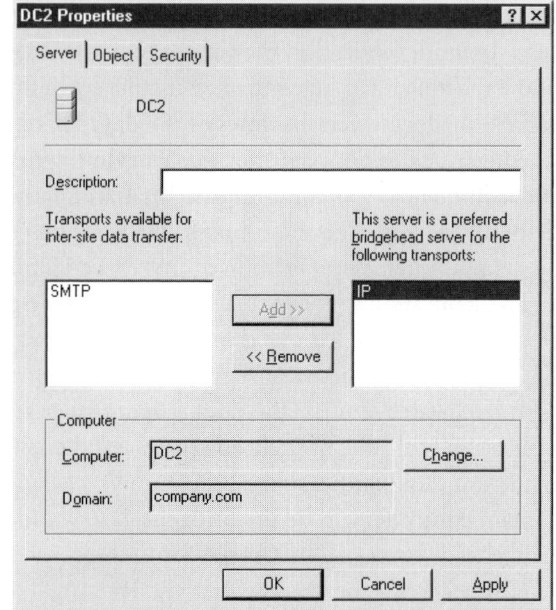

Replication with NT 4.0 Backup Domain Controllers

There are some operations critical to domain operation that, when implemented as multimaster operations, could cause complicated conflicts that could not be easily resolved. For these special cases, Microsoft has resorted to using single-master operations. Domain controllers devoted to these operations are known as *operations masters.* Operations masters are not covered in depth here, but a specific operations master, the PDC emulator, is of particular interest to replication.

Windows 2000 domains can operate in two modes: Mixed Mode or Native Mode. The primary purpose of Mixed Mode is to provide backward compatibility with Windows NT 4.0 BDCs. Domains in Mixed Mode cannot use features of Windows 2000 such as nested groups that could not be replicated to an NT 4.0 BDC. Conversion to Native Mode is a one-way operation because, once a domain is operating in Native Mode, it is a difficult operation to remove all objects from the domain that are not backward compatible with NT 4.0.

Windows NT 4 BDCs are designed to exist in a single-master domain and therefore look for a PDC to provide directory updates. NT 4 BDCs can replicate with a single Windows 2000 domain controller. The PDC emulator is the domain controller responsible for replication. All Windows NT 4.0 BDCs in a domain receive their updates from the PDC emulator, regardless of which site they are in.

The NT 4.0 Security Accounts Manager (SAM) database is stored in the registry, and due to maximum size limitations on the NT registry, the SAM database is limited to approximately 30,000 objects. It is important that domains operating in Mixed Mode and replicating to NT 4 BDCs keep the number of Domain objects below this number to avoid replication problems.

Password Changes

Password changes within a Windows 2000 domain are immediately replicated to the PDC emulator for the domain, regardless of which domain controller originated the change and regardless of in which site the PDC emulator is located. Other domain controllers in the domain obtain these changes through normal replication.

The reason for replicating password changes to the PDC emulator immediately is that pre-Windows 2000 clients that are not able to access the Active Directory Services always contact the PDC emulator for authentication. When a domain controller gets a logon request from a Windows 2000 or other Active Directory-aware client, it first attempts to validate that client using the data stored in its replica of the domain information. If the logon fails, the domain controller contacts the PDC emulator for the domain to make another attempt to validate the logon in case the password was recently changed and the change had not yet replicated.

Domain Controller and Global Catalog Placement

The decision of whether to place a domain controller or global catalog server at a site is determined by a number of issues, including the speed and reliability of network connectivity to that site, the number of clients that access the directory at that location, and the size and number of changes made to the enterprise directory as a whole. A primary design goal is to choose the approach that minimizes the amount of directory traffic sent over the WAN during times when users are working, freeing that bandwidth for use by applications. Since Active Directory replication traffic can be scheduled to occur outside normal working hours, whereas logons and queries are interactive, it is not a simple situation of choosing which approach uses the least amount of bandwidth.

In most cases, the need for low response times for client logons and queries means that you should have at least one global catalog server in a site. One situation in which it is better not to place a domain controller or global catalog server at a site is a small site, operating 24 hours a day, seven days a week, that is part of a large enterprise forest. Suppose this site had 5 or 10 users who made minimal accesses to the directory, perhaps a logon and a couple of queries per user per day, but used the WAN link heavily for application traffic. Furthermore, at other sites the enterprise directory for this large organization is very dynamic, with thousands of additions and changes made to the directory daily. In this situation, the replication traffic that occurs to a domain controller or global catalog server located at the small, remote site is significantly higher than the bandwidth required by the client logon, query operations, and group policy application traffic.

Troubleshooting Active Directory Replication

When Active Directory replication fails to occur, inconsistencies in the database usually manifest themselves as inconsistent behavior. Different domain controllers in a domain have different information, and depending on the domain controller used for a particular operation, the results can vary. Replication is dependent on reliable network connectivity, which should be the first thing checked in the case of Active Directory replication failures. Network connectivity and TCP/IP configuration can be verified using the PING command-line utility between the domain controllers that are not replicating data. After verifying connectivity, use the Active Directory Sites and Services tool on each domain controller and verify that each has proper site configuration and that Connection objects exist between the domain controllers. Several tools are included in the Support Tools folder of the Windows 2000 Server CD-ROM that can further assist in troubleshooting replication issues such as REPLMON, which is described in an upcoming section.

Event Logs

Replication events are logged in to the Directory Services log and can be monitored using Event Viewer. An administrator should monitor these logs regularly to spot potential problems with replication or other aspects of Active Directory.

Many normal informational messages are logged regularly. For example, event IDs 700 and 701 are logged every 12 hours when the garbage collection process defragments the directory. Some other common events and their descriptions are:

- **1009.** The KCC is updating the replication topology for this domain controller.
- **1013.** The KCC has completed updating the replication topology.
- **1265.** Replication with a specific replication partner failed.
- **1404.** The server has assumed the role of the intersite topology generator.

Monitoring Replication

Active Directory replication can be monitored through the use of the Windows 2000 System Performance Monitor, which includes counters for replication traffic under the NTDS object. Counters are available to measure total bytes of inbound and outbound replication traffic, the number of bytes replicated per second, and counters that differentiate between compressed (inter-site) and uncompressed (intra-site) replication traffic. System Performance Monitor can be a useful tool in spotting problems, but it is very important to monitor normal operation of the system to establish a baseline value. In other words you must know what normal performance is for your system in order to determine if activity captured by System Performance Monitor is indicative of a problem. AD is periodic and replication performance will vary greatly depending on performance of the domain controller, the network, and the number of changes made to the directory.

Windows 2000 Server also includes an Active Directory replication monitor tool in the support tools folder on the CD that can be used to monitor and verify the replication process. Exercise 4-1 will introduce this tool and give an overview of the capabilities.

EXERCISE 4-1

Using the Active Directory Replication Monitor

The Active Directory Replication Monitor is a tool provided on the Windows 2000 Server CD in the Support Tools folder. It provides an interface to monitor the replication processes on individual or multiple domain controllers. In order to complete this exercise, you must have at least two domain controllers in the same domain and have installed on one of them the Replication Monitor from the Support Tools folder on the Windows 2000 Server CD.

1. Log in to one domain controller as Administrator.
2. Start the Active Directory Replication Monitor. Click Start | Programs | Windows 2000 Support Tools | Tools | Active Directory Replication Monitor.
3. In the left pane, right-click Monitored Servers and choose Add Monitored Server from the context-sensitive menu. The Add Monitored Server Wizard starts.
4. Choose "Add server explicitly by name" and click Next.
5. Type the name of the server you are logged on to as the server you want to monitor. Click Finish. You can add additional servers, as shown in the following illustration.

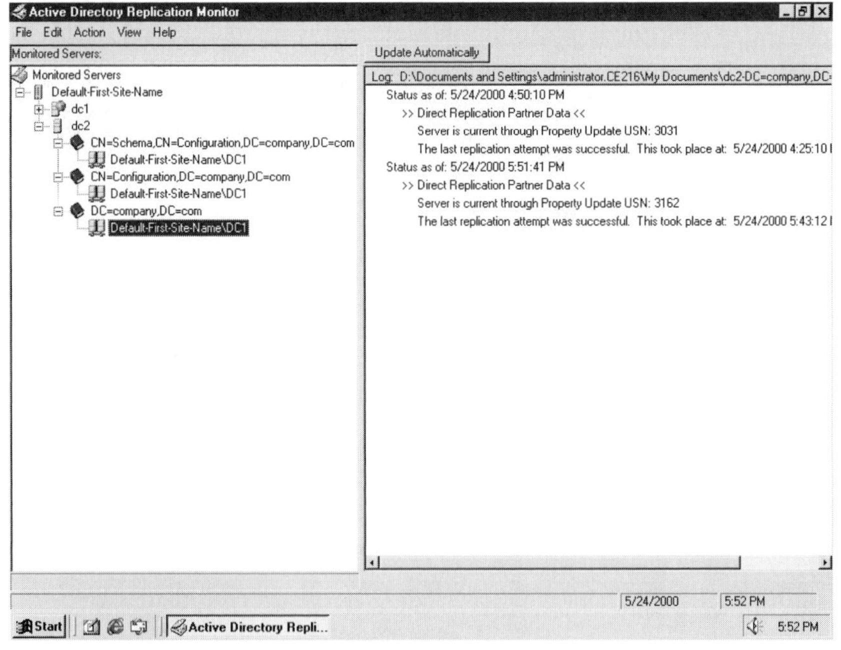

6. Your server should now be added to the left pane. If the pane is not already expanded, click the plus sign (+) next to your server to expose the naming contexts for which it is responsible.
7. Right-click the Server object and choose Check Replication Topology from the context-sensitive menu, as shown in the following illustration. This choice forces the KCC to run. Click OK in the resulting dialog box.

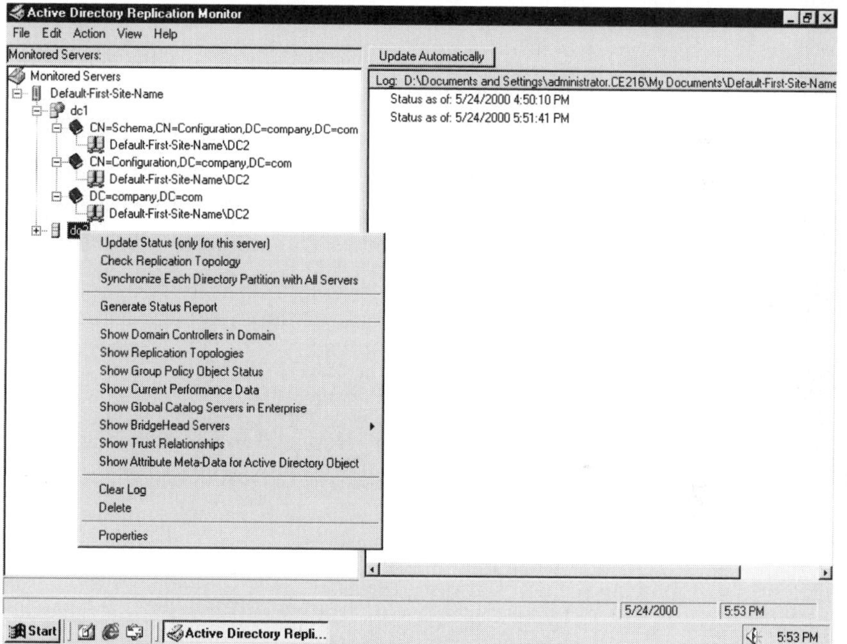

8. Expand the schema naming context. This step exposes the Connection objects, as shown in the following illustration.
9. Right-click a Connection object. Choose "Synchronize this with replication partner" to force replication to occur immediately.
10. Spend some time exploring the features and capabilities of the Active Directory Replication Monitor. For example, choose "Show replication topologies" from the context-sensitive menu of a Domain Controller object to view a graphical layout of the replication topology.

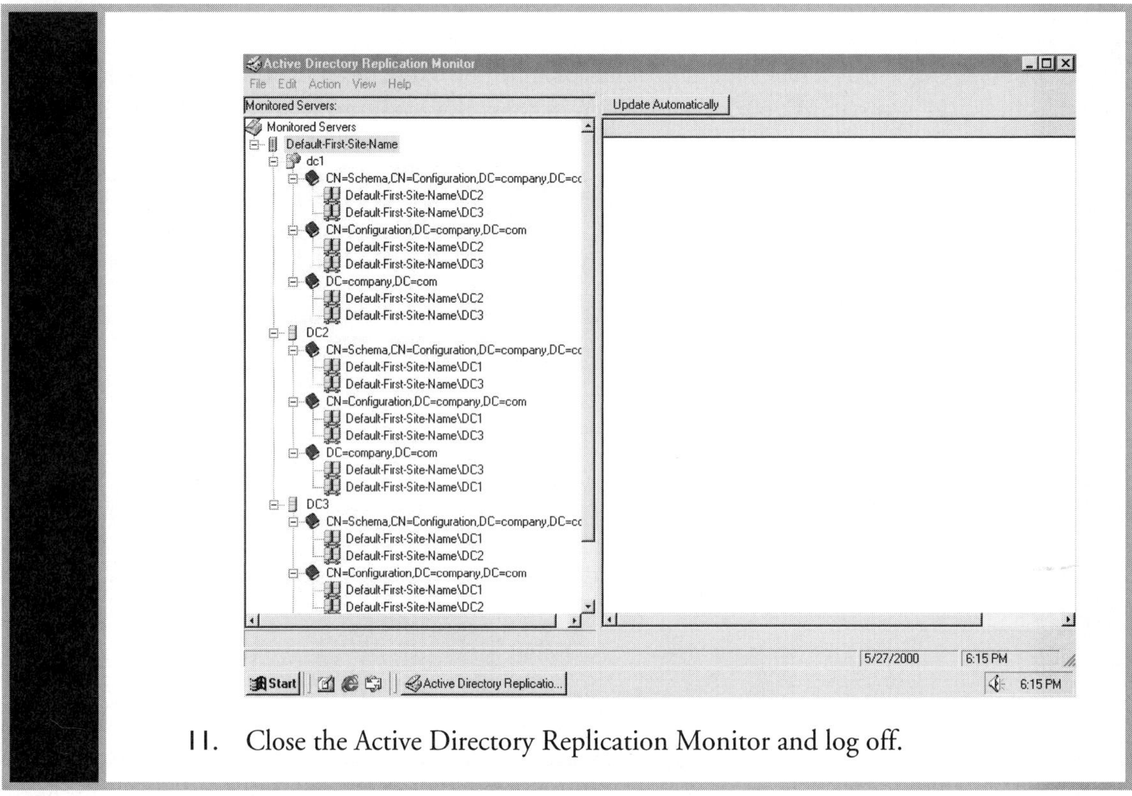

11. Close the Active Directory Replication Monitor and log off.

Test your comprehension of Active Directory Replication Concepts with the following scenarios and solutions.

SCENARIO & SOLUTION

What tool would you use to change the replication schedule between sites?	The AD Sites and Services snap-in.
How is replication bandwidth between sites minimized?	Intersite replication is compressed to save bandwidth, and replication traffic can be scheduled to occur at off-peak times.
What is a tombstone?	A tombstone is a deleted object in the Active Directory. Tombstones must replicate to other domain controllers for the object to be fully deleted. Tombstone objects are eventually removed from Active Directory through the process of garbage collection.

SCENARIO & SOLUTION

In a meeting, your boss instructs your team to change information about a user. Both you and your co-worker change this information at the same time on different domain controllers. Which change will take effect?	The change with the highest version number will take effect. If both users started with a fully replicated directory and made only a single change, the two changes will likely have the same version number and the change with the later time stamp will take effect. If by some chance the time stamps are exactly the same, the change made on the domain controller with the higher GUID will take effect.

CERTIFICATION OBJECTIVE 4.02

Managing and Troubleshooting Domain Name System Replication

Domain Name Service (DNS) is an Internet Directory System that allows mapping of IP addresses to host names. DNS is designed as a distributed system and is based on a single-master model. DNS is an Internet standard protocol that is part of the TCP/IP protocol stack and is defined by RFCs. Like most Internet protocols, it has been changed and extended over time to provide new functionality. Windows 2000 DNS provides an implementation of DNS that is fully interoperable with any Internet-standard compliant name servers yet provides new functionalities that have been submitted as draft standards.

exam Watch

A common UNIX-based DNS server is BIND, which is an acronym for Berkley Internet Naming Daemon.

The basic unit of DNS storage is a *zone.* A DNS zone contains resource records for the zone. DNS zones can be either forward lookup zones or reverse lookup zones. A *forward lookup zone* is used to resolve a host name to an IP address; a *reverse lookup zone* is used to retrieve a host name from an IP address. Windows 2000 DNS zones are configured and managed through the DNS snap-in shown in Figure 4-7.

FIGURE 4-7

The DNS snap-in can be used to administer DNS servers

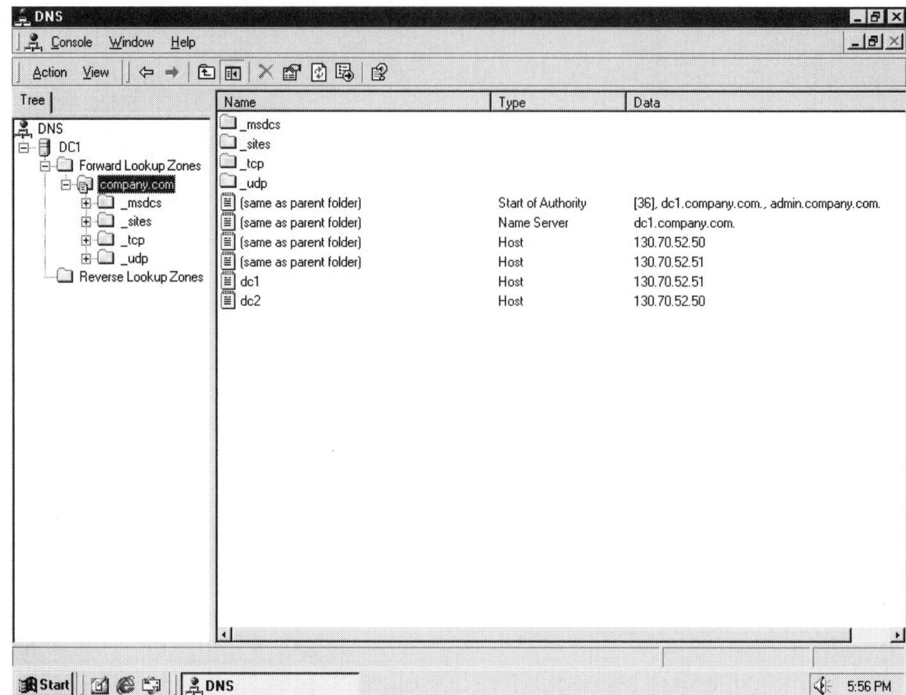

Windows 2000 DNS Features

Traditional DNS servers use a single-master configuration in which one DNS server is designated as the *primary* DNS server for a zone. The primary DNS server is the only system that can add or change resource records in the zone. All changes and updates are made on the primary DNS server. For redundancy and load balancing, DNS provides for *secondary* DNS servers that maintain a read-only copy of the zone files and can answer queries against the database. A DNS server that provides zone information to a secondary DNS server is called a *master DNS server.* Either a primary or secondary DNS server can be a master DNS server and provide records to a secondary server. The process of replicating DNS data from a master name server to a secondary name server is called a *zone transfer.*

A single DNS server can host multiple zone files. The DNS server can serve as the primary or secondary server for any combination of zones. Within the DNS snap-in, Standard Primary, Standard Secondary, or Active Directory-integrated zones can be created using the New Zone Wizard, which is shown in Figure 4-8.

FIGURE 4-8

New DNS zones can be created with the New Zone Wizard

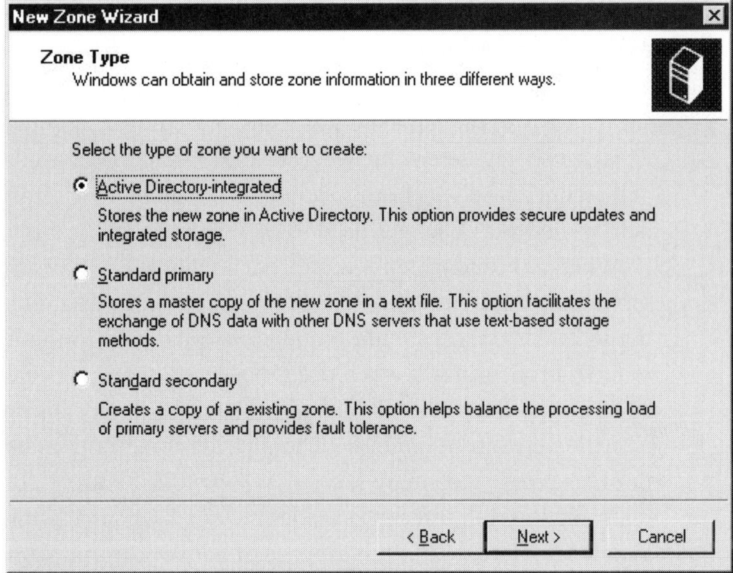

Windows 2000 DNS is fully interoperable with the "traditional" DNS server and can store the DNS zone information in standard files and participate in zone transfers. Windows 2000 also allows Active Directory-integrated zones, which store the DNS records in Active Directory. There are several benefits to this method, including support for secure dynamic updates, aging, and scavenging of the zone records. By integrating the DNS zone into Active Directory, DNS is able to take advantage of the multimaster nature of AD and dynamic updates to DNS can be made by any domain controller. DNS records stored in an AD-integrated zone replicate automatically to all domain controllers within the domain according to existing replication rules and schedules.

Replication of Non-Active Directory-Integrated Zones

Early DNS standards specified that a zone transfer from a master to a secondary DNS server would be done by moving the entire zone database. These full zone transfers were initially limited to transmitting one record per packet, but later the system was improved to allow multiple records per packet. As zone files got larger, the inefficiency of transferring the entire zone was realized, and improvements defined in RFC 1995 defined an *incremental zone transfer,* in which only the changed records are transferred during a zone transfer. In order to implement incremental zone transfers, both the master and the secondary server must support them.

A master DNS server uses a *serial number,* as shown in Figure 4-9, which is part of the Start of Authority (SOA) record to track changes to the DNS database. When a zone transfer is initiated, the secondary DNS server sends a copy of the SOA record for the copy of the database it is using. By comparing serial numbers, the master DNS server can determine whether there are updates available. If both the master and secondary servers both support incremental zone transfers, the master can also determine which changes need to be replicated to the secondary.

When a secondary zone is created, a reference is provided to the master name server that is providing the zone records, and a refresh interval indicates how often the secondary server should request a zone transfer. Secondary name servers first request a zone transfer when the DNS server is started, and then again regularly at each refresh interval. By default, the refresh interval is set to 15 minutes. Master name servers can be configured to provide zone transfers to any secondary server or only specific secondary servers, as shown in Figure 4-10.

A small refresh interval provides for quick updates from the master zones to the secondary zones, but at the expense of network traffic. Longer refresh intervals can be used to reduce the replication, but changes take longer to propagate. RFC 1996 defined a method of update notification in which a master name server could inform a secondary server that changes were available. The notification provided another situation in which the secondary server initiates a zone transfer.

FIGURE 4-9

The DNS serial number and refresh interval are part of the SOA record in a DNS zone

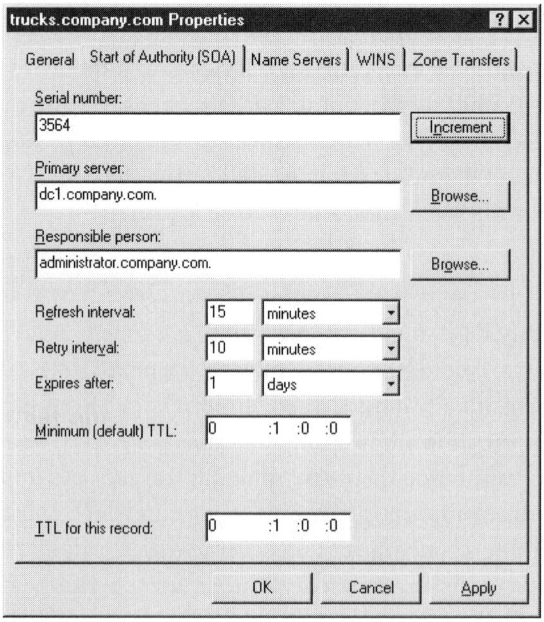

FIGURE 4-10

The Properties sheet for an Active Directory-integrated zone

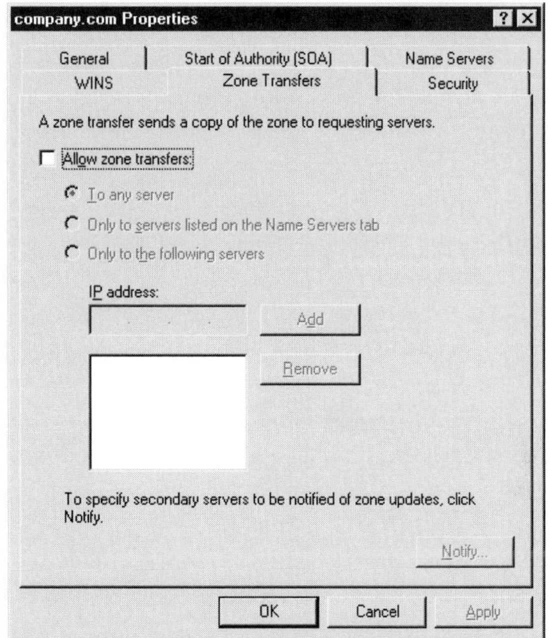

Replication of Active Directory–Integrated Zones

DNS zones that are stored in Active Directory replicate to all domain controllers in a domain through normal Active Directory replication. An Active Directory-integrated zone can be used to provide DNS records to a standard secondary name server through full or incremental zone transfers. Figure 4-11 shows the objects in an Active Directory-integrated zone viewed with the Active Directory Users and Computers snap-in. It is important to notice that Active Directory–integrated DNS zone information is stored in the domain naming context. Active Directory–integrated zone information is replicated only within a domain using Active Directory replication. You must select the Advanced Features option on the View menu to expose the System Container.

on the Job

Windows 2000 DNS supports notification of secondary servers when DNS records are changed. You can enable this feature on the Transfer tab of the Zone Properties sheet. This feature can reduce latency in DNS update replication and can be used to reduce network traffic by allowing the refresh interval to be raised.

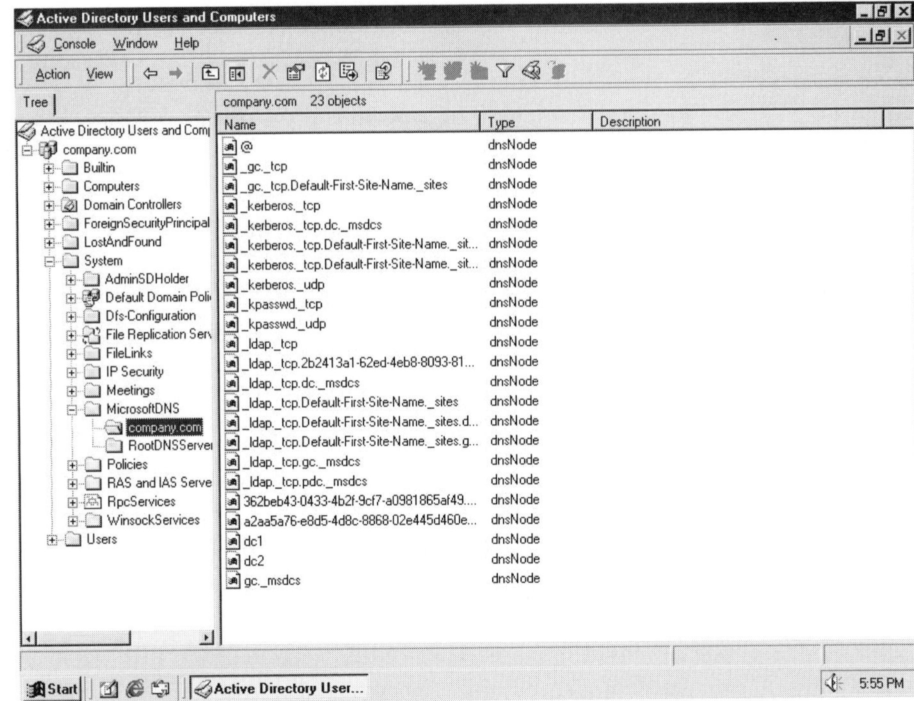

FIGURE 4-11 Viewing AD-integrated zones using Active Directory Users and Computers

Here are some scenario questions and answers to test your knowledge about Windows 2000 DNS.

SCENARIO & SOLUTION

Scenario	Solution
What types of DNS zones does Windows 2000 DNS support?	Primary, secondary, and Active Directory integrated.
What is the term that describes a server that provides information to a secondary?	Master name server.
Which types of DNS zones can a secondary name server receive data from through a zone transfer?	A secondary DNS server can receive data from a Standard Primary, Standard Secondary, or Active Directory–integrated zone through a zone transfer.

Troubleshooting Domain Name System Replication

Replication failure in an Active Directory–integrated zone can be identified by the same symptoms as Active Directory replication failure—the process used to replicate them is the same. Troubleshooting and resolution of replication failures with Active Directory–integrated zones is therefore also the same as general Active Directory replication troubleshooting, described in the previous section. With standard DNS zones, the failure of a primary DNS server might not be noticed until the expiration interval defined in the SOA records has passed. At this point, secondary DNS servers no longer maintain their DNS records, and clients configured to use those DNS servers fail to resolve queries.

DNS replication problems can occur for a variety of reasons. Failure of network connectivity between the master and secondary servers is a common source of replication problems. When troubleshooting DNS replication problems, begin by ensuring TCP/IP connectivity between the master and secondary zone servers using the PING or TRACERT TCP/IP utilities. Ensure that TCP/IP connectivity exists between the master and secondary servers. If connectivity is found to be satisfactory, you should check the DNS server logs for errors using the Event Viewer.

Verify the configuration of both the primary server and secondary server. On the secondary, ensure that the IP address of the master name server is correct. On the master name server, ensure that zone transfers are allowed and that the secondary is allowed to retrieve the zone data by checking the zone transfers tab on the zone Properties sheet. If the master name server is also a secondary name server for the zone, verify that replication is occurring from the primary name server. When using secondary servers that are not running Windows 2000, verify that they are able to accept the records you are providing. Some BIND servers, for example, might not accept Windows Internet Naming Service (WINS) resource records or Unicode DNS names.

Finally, verify that the DNS server service is operating properly on both the master and secondary servers. You can use the NSLOOKUP command from the Windows 2000 command prompt to perform DNS queries against both the master and secondary servers to see if they are responding and to verify the records have replicated properly. If the service does not respond, attempt to stop and restart the service. In cases in which the DNS service fails regularly, you can configure it to

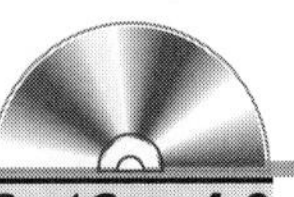

EXERCISE 4-2

Creating Primary and Secondary DNS Zones

In this exercise, you create primary and secondary DNS zones and force a zone transfer to occur. You need two networked Windows 2000 servers (we refer to them as Server1 and Server2, but their computer names are not important for this exercise) running the Windows 2000 DNS. You should complete these exercises while logged in as an Administrator.

First, create the primary zone on Server1.

1. Start the DNS Administrative Console from the Administrative tools menu.
2. Expand Server1 in the left pane (click the + next to it). Select Forward Lookup Zones in the left pane. Right-click Forward Lookup Zones and choose New Zone from the context-sensitive menu.
3. The New Zone Wizard appears. After reading the introductory information, click Next.
4. On the Zone Type Panel, select the radio button used to create a Standard Primary Zone. (This screen was shown in Figure 4-11.) Click Next.
5. Name your new zone **school.edu** and click Next.
6. Accept the default name for the zone file (school.edu.dns) and click Next.
7. Click Finish. You have successfully created a new zone file for SCHOOL.EDU. Now you add a new host record and configure the refresh interval for your new zone.
8. In the left pane, expand the list of forward lookup zones. Right-click SCHOOL.EDU in the left pane and choose New Host from the context-sensitive menu.
9. In the new host dialog box, enter **www** for the host name and **10.0.0.1** as the IP address for the new record. Choose not to create a reverse lookup record by making sure the check box is not marked. Use the default TTL. Click the Add Host button to create the record.
10. Click OK in the confirmation dialog box. Click Done to close the New Host dialog box.

11. Right-click the SCHOOL.DNS zone in the left pane. Choose Properties from the context-sensitive menu.
12. Choose the Start of Authority (SOA) tab. Change the refresh interval to 1 minute. Click OK.

Next we configure a secondary zone on Server2.

13. On Server2, start the DNS Administrative Console from the Administrative Tools menu.
14. Expand Server2. Select Forward Lookup Zones. Right-click Forward Lookup Zones and choose New Zone from the context-sensitive menu.
15. The New Zone Wizard appears. Click Next.
16. On the Zone Type Panel, choose to create a Standard Secondary Zone. Click Next.
17. Enter **school.edu** as the name for your secondary zone and click Next.
18. Add the IP address of your first DNS server as the IP address of the master name server and click Next.
19. Click Finish to create your secondary zone.
20. Expand the Forward Lookup Zones entry in the left pane.
21. Right-click on the SCHOOL.EDU secondary zone and choose Transfer from Master to initiate a zone transfer.
22. Select the SCHOOL.EDU zone in the left pane and verify that the host record for **www** has transferred from the master to the secondary server by looking for it in the results (right) pane.

The exercise is now complete. You may want to experiment further by making changes to the primary zone and waiting for them to replicate to the secondary. Because the refresh interval was set to 1 minute in Step 12, your changes should be available on the secondary zone in about a minute without forcing a manual zone transfer.

automatically restart using the Recovery tab on the DNS Properties sheet accessed through the Services snap-in.

CERTIFICATION SUMMARY

Multimaster replication in Active Directory provides the foundation for large-scale deployment of Windows 2000 domains. With no single point of failure as in single-master domain models, the Active Directory forest is more reliable. The ability to allow writes to any domain controller increases performance, especially for enterprises that span multiple sites.

Whereas traditional DNS is single master and uses inefficient zone transfers, Windows 2000 DNS supports storing DNS records in Active Directory, which provides for multimaster update capability, efficient replication for DNS records through the Active Directory replication process, secure dynamic updates, and support for aging and scavenging of DNS records.

TWO-MINUTE DRILL

Managing and Troubleshooting Active Directory Replication

- ❑ Use the Active Directory Sites and Services snap-in to create sites, site links (including site link bridges), and subnets.
- ❑ The KCC runs on each domain controller and generates the replication topology automatically.
- ❑ Replication traffic within a site uses the RPC protocol and is uncompressed.
- ❑ Replication between sites is compressed. RPC is used for all replication traffic within a domain naming context. In some cases, SMTP can be used to replicate the global catalog, schema, or configuration naming contexts.
- ❑ A high-watermark vector and the up-to-dateness vector are maintained individually by each domain controller to identify updates they have received through replication.
- ❑ A bridgehead server is a domain controller in a site that can replicate with other sites.
- ❑ Replication to NT 4.0 BDCs is possible only in Mixed Mode.

Managing and Troubleshooting Domain Name System Replication

- ❑ A zone transfer is the process of replicating a standard DNS zone.
- ❑ A single Windows 2000 DNS server can host multiple zones, which can be any combination of primary, secondary, or Active Directory-integrated zones.
- ❑ Active Directory-integrated zones can exist only on Windows 2000 domain controllers.
- ❑ Standard DNS zones are single master, whereby only one DNS server has write access to the zone file.
- ❑ A secondary DNS server holds a read-only copy of the DNS zone file and can be used to resolve queries and provide a copy of the zone file to other secondary servers.

- A master name server is a replication source for a zone. Either a primary or a secondary server can be a master DNS server.
- Windows 2000 Active Directory–integrated zones take advantage of multimaster updates and replication.
- DNS information stored in Active Directory replicates to all domain controllers in the domain, regardless of whether they are running the DNS server or not.
- Active Directory–integrated zones are stored in the domain naming context and replicate only to domain controllers in that domain.

5

Active Directory Security Solutions

CERTIFICATION OBJECTIVES

5.01 Configuring and Troubleshooting Security in a Directory Services Infrastructure

5.02 Monitoring and Analyzing Security Events

✓ Two-Minute Drill

By this time you must be quite familiar with Active Directory, configuration of sites, group policies, replication, and DNS integration with Active Directory. This chapter deals with options included with the Windows 2000 operating system to configure security for domain controllers and server computers.

Security is important for every organization. Windows 2000 offers more options for configuring security than its previous counterpart, Windows NT. The built-in features, which include group policies, the Security Configuration and Analysis tool, and auditing, make it easy for the administrator to implement organizationwide security. The Event Viewer gives you a detailed look at the security events when auditing is enabled.

CERTIFICATION OBJECTIVE 5.01

Configuring and Troubleshooting Security in a Directory Services Infrastructure

Security is one of the most important aspects of any operating system, and Windows 2000 is no exception. The built-in security features of Windows 2000 include several tools to keep the network secure from undesired actions of users. Security is not only applied to data files but is also applicable to user actions, such as misuse of the rights assigned to them.

Using group policies, you can apply required security policies at the local level, site level, domain level, or OU level. This section discusses how to implement useful and manageable security policies in a Windows 2000 network.

Applying Security Policies Using Group Policy

In Windows 2000, group policies are defined using the Group Policy snap-in and its extensions. Group policies are used to restrict users' rights and control what actions users can perform. Active Directory enables Group Policy and Group Policy objects (GPOs) to store policy information. Group Policy has built-in features for setting policies. The data created by Group Policy is stored in a GPO and is replicated to all domain controllers in the domain.

The following security areas can be configured using the Group Policy snap-in:

- **Account Policies.** This area includes Password Policy, Account Lockout Policy, and Kerberos Policy.
- **Local Policies.** These policies affect the local computer only. These policies include Audit Policy, User Rights Assignment, and Security Options.
- **Event Log.** The Event Log area defines such settings for event log files as maximum log file size, rights given to users on each log file, and the like.
- **Restricted Groups.** The Restricted Group area defines policies for built-in user groups such as power users, backup operators, and domain administrators.
- **System Services.** These policies are used to define startup types for system services and user rights on these services.
- **Registry.** These policies define user rights on registry keys.
- **File System.** The File System policies are used to configure security on files and folders.
- **Public Key Policies.** These policies are used to define encrypted data recovery agents and trusted certificate authorities.
- **IP Security Policies.** These policies are used to define network Internet Protocol Security (IPSec).

Figure 5-1 shows, for example, the User Rights assignment policies for a particular domain controller computer. You might notice that the policy set to back up files and folders is set for server operators, backup operators, and administrators.

There are three basic parts of Group Policy:

- **Group Policy objects.** GPOs contain configuration settings for Group Policy. A group policy is applied to an entire site or domain or an entire OU.
- **Group Policy containers.** The Group Policy container (GPC) is the Active Directory object and contains Group Policy object properties.
- **Group Policy templates.** Group Policy information that changes frequently is stored in a Group Policy template (GPT). Templates are stored in the SYSVOL folder.

FIGURE 5-1

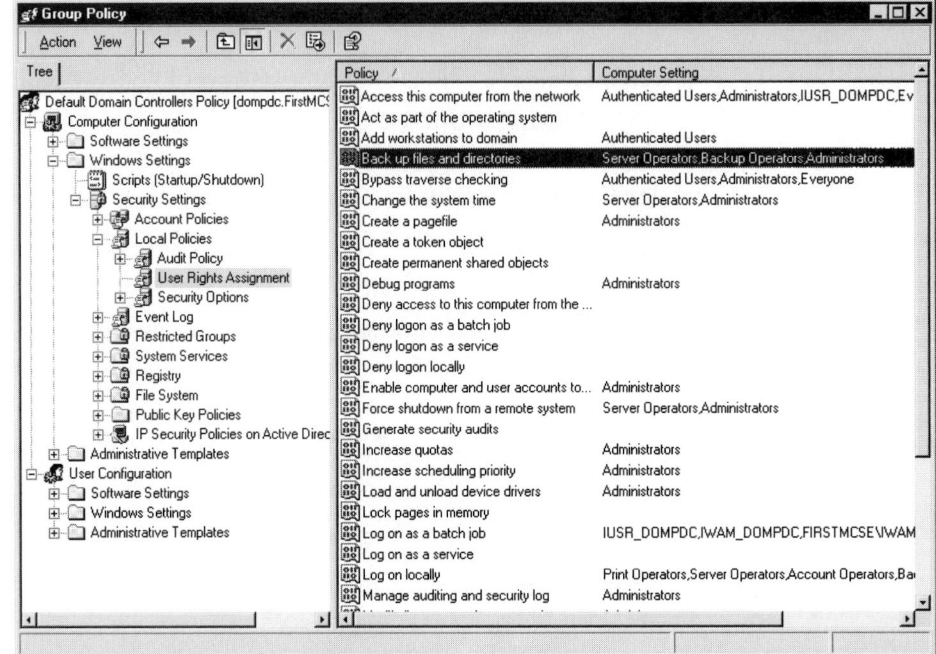

Group Policy for security settings

When to Use Security Policies

The security policies in a Windows 2000 domain can be set at the domain level, site level, or OU level. If the network is small and has only one or two domain controllers, planning security might not be a big issue. When you are responsible for implementing security policies for larger networks, it is important to understand when and how to use the security policies of Windows 2000.

The local security policies are effective only on the local computer. These policies include the audit policy, which determines the events that are written to the security logs. User policies determine the assignment of user rights and privileges on the computer and become effective only after a user logs in. As the name implies, these policies are local to the computer. The policies must be imported to a GPO in Active Directory. Computer policies are effective whether or not a user is logged on to the computer and are executed when the computer starts.

Security policies are used when you want to have a set of standard policies throughout the organization. These policies allow you to configure security at a centralized place in the network; you do not have to manually configure every server. The policies defined at the root of the domain become applicable automatically to all domain controllers and member servers in the network. This functionality greatly reduces administrative efforts and time required to implement security. Once defined and configured, these policies are your primary tool for controlling the network.

exam Watch

Windows 2000 allows you to have only one account policy throughout the domain, and that account policy is applied to the root of the domain.

How to Create Security Policies

Security policies are created using the Group Policy editor. In Exercise 5-1, you create a Group Policy object and then configure its settings.

EXERCISE 5-1

Creating a New Group Policy Object

1. Log on to the domain controller with Administrative privileges.
2. To create a GPO in a domain or an OU, choose Start | Programs | Administrative Tools and select Active Directory Users and Computers. This sequence opens the Active Directory Users and Computers Console. To create a GPO that is linked to a site, open the Active Directory Sites and Services Console.
3. From the View menu, click Advanced View. Select the AD object for which you want to create a GPO. Right-click the selected object and click Properties. Click the Group Policy tab from the Properties window.

4. Click New and type a name for the GPO. The new GPO is linked to the selected object by default. See the following illustration.

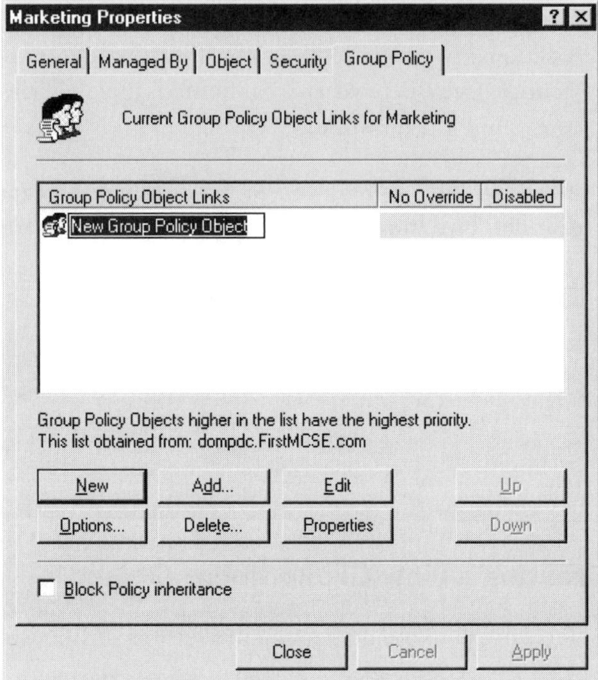

5. Click Close. Close the Active Directory Users and Computers Console.

When a new GPO is created, all security settings for this GPO are undefined until configuration is complete. Assignment of security settings is accomplished using the Group Policy Editor. Exercise 5-2 explains the necessary steps. This exercise serves as an example for setting all or most security policies.

EXERCISE 5-2

Using Group Policy Editor to Change Security Settings

1. Log on to the domain controller with Administrative privileges.
2. Choose Start | Programs | Administrative Tools and select Active Directory Users and Computers. This choice opens the Active Directory Users and Computers Console.
3. Right-click the OU for which you created the new GPO in the previous exercise and select Properties from the drop-down menu.
4. The Properties sheet appears. From the View menu, click Advanced View. Click the Group Policy tab. Notice that New Group Policy Object (or the name you might have given to the GPO) appears in the Group Policy Object Links list, as shown in the following illustration.

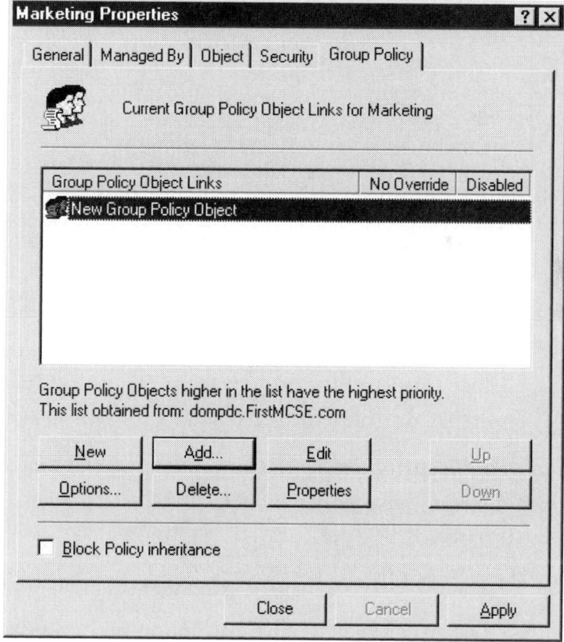

5. Click New Group Policy Object. Click Edit. This step opens the Group Policy Console.

6. Double-click Computer Configuration, double-click Windows Settings, double-click Security Settings, and double-click Local Policies.
7. Click User Rights Assignments. Notice that a list of user rights is displayed as Not Defined in the results pane, as shown in the following illustration.

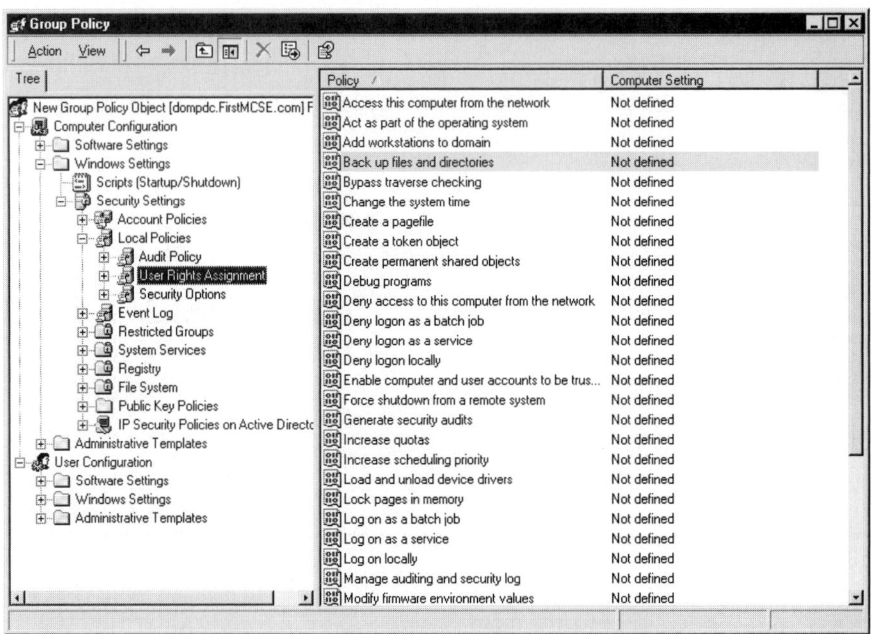

8. Select a user right that you want to configure. For the purpose of this exercise, double-click "Back-up files and directories."
9. The Security Policy Setting dialog box appears. Click the check box for "Define these policy settings." This choice enables the Add and Remove buttons. Click Add.
10. The Add User or Group box appears next. Click Browse.
11. The Select Users or Groups dialog box appears. Select Everyone (or any other user or group appropriate to your requirements), as shown in the following illustration.

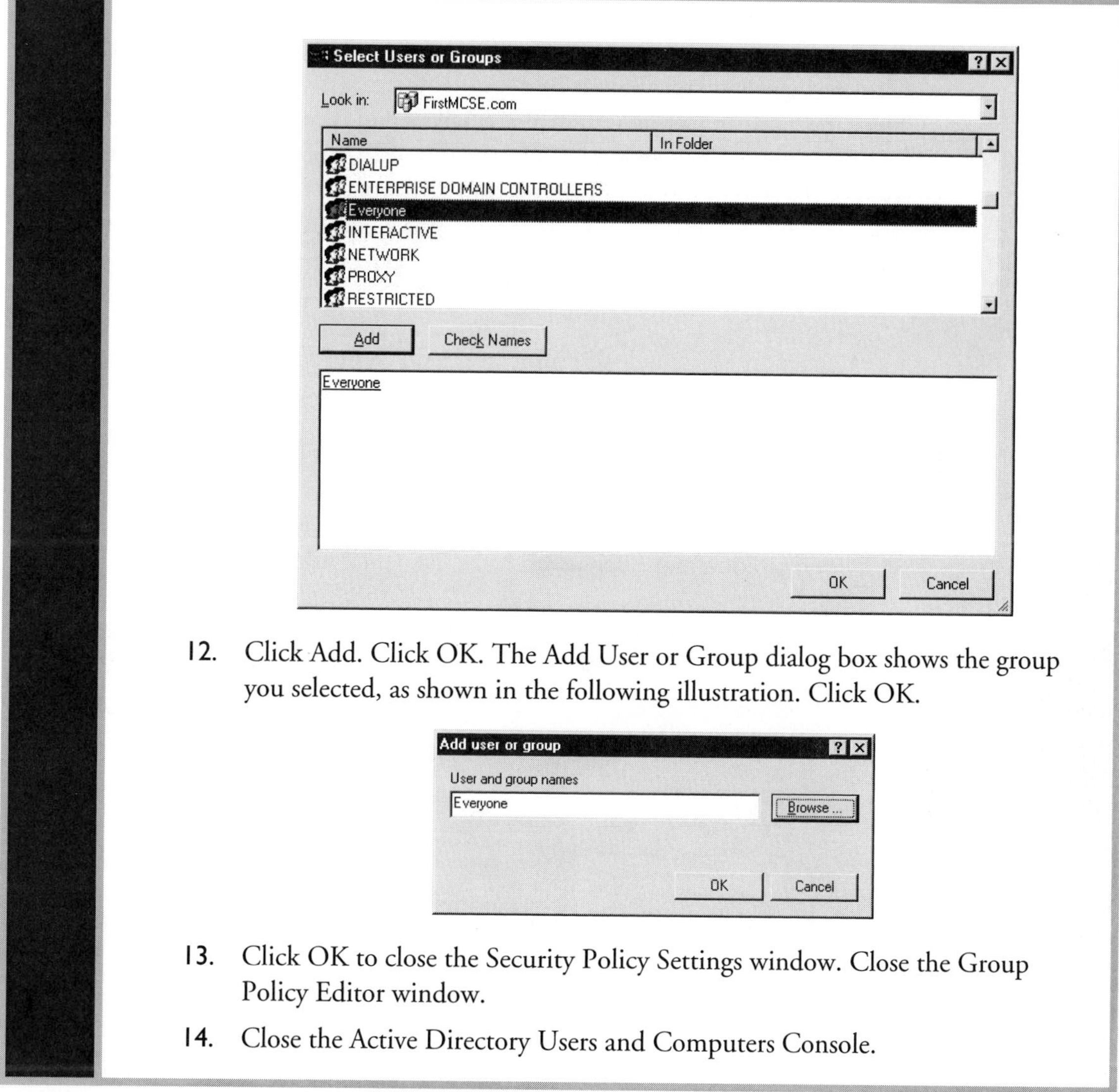

12. Click Add. Click OK. The Add User or Group dialog box shows the group you selected, as shown in the following illustration. Click OK.

13. Click OK to close the Security Policy Settings window. Close the Group Policy Editor window.
14. Close the Active Directory Users and Computers Console.

Security Configuration and Analysis

Windows 2000 includes a powerful tool to manage security in a domain. The Security Configuration and Analysis tool helps you configure security, analyze the results, and resolve any problems that concern system and resource security. This tool uses a database to perform these functions. This database is computer specific and allows you to use personalized databases, import and export templates, and create new security templates that suit your requirements.

Since the Security Configuration and Analysis tool is computer specific, you can collect and analyze data on a local computer only. This tool allows you to make quick analysis of the system security. The tool also gives you its recommendations based on your settings in comparison to what is proposed by the operating system.

The Security Configuration and Analysis tool can be installed using the following steps:

1. Click Start | Run and type **mmc** in the Open box. This step opens an empty console.
2. From the Console menu, click Add/Remove Snap-in. The Add/Remove Snap-in dialog box appears. Click Add.
3. The Add Standalone Snap-in dialog box appears. Select Security Configuration and Analysis from the list. Click Add. (See Figure 5-2.)

FIGURE 5-2

Adding a security snap-ins to the MMC

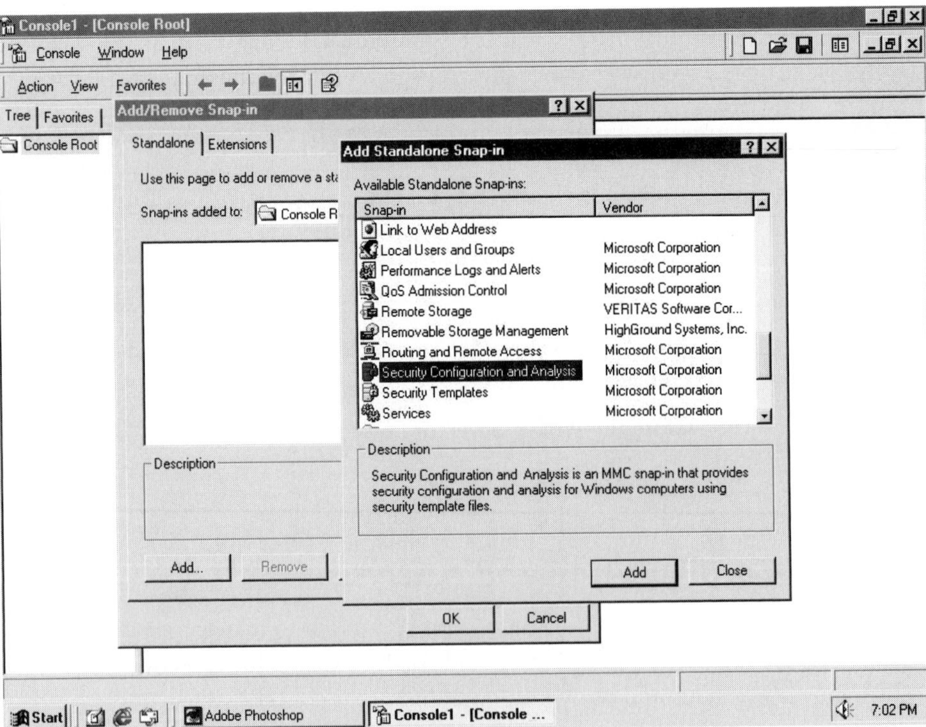

4. Select Security Templates and click Add. Click Close.
5. Click OK in the Add/Remove Snap-in dialog box. The selected snap-ins are now added to the console. When you open the console for the first time, it looks like the one shown in Figure 5-3.
6. Click Save As from the Console menu. Notice that the path shown in the Save As dialog box defaults to Administrative Tools. Type **Security Configuration and Analysis** in the File Name box and click Save. You can open this console later from the Administrative Tools menu.

Security Templates

The Security Templates Console allows you to set up security templates for one or more of the following areas:

- **Account policies.** These policies include local account policies such as minimum password length, account lockout duration, and Kerberos settings. For example, you can set a minimum password length of ten characters to discourage "crackers."

FIGURE 5-3

Initial Security Configuration and Analysis Console

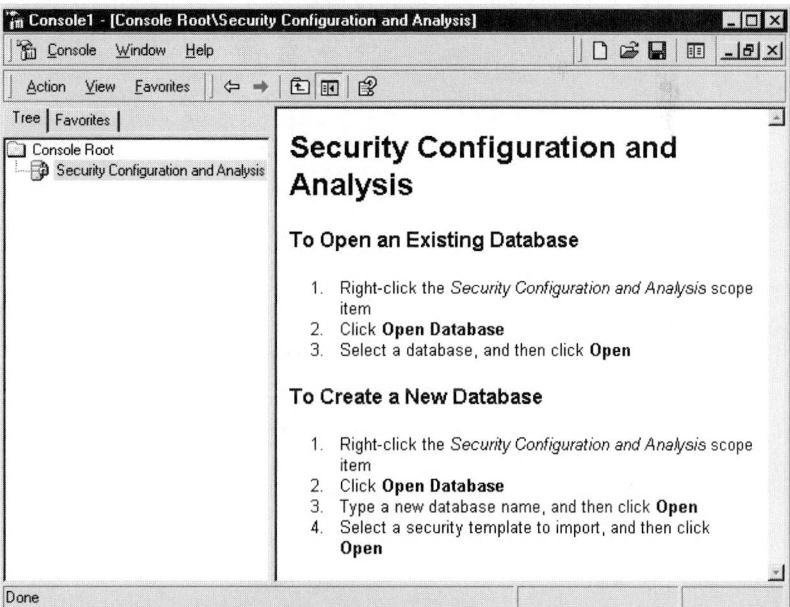

- **Local policies.** These policies include audit policy, user rights, and other policies that affect the local system.
- **Event log.** The security settings include configuration of log files for the system, applications, and security. You can set the minimum size of log files, overriding the default size of 512KB.
- **Restricted groups.** These groups are predefined user groups in Windows 2000.
- **System services.** The system services include a list of services on the local system. Some of these are file and print services and network and telephony services.
- **Registry.** You can configure security descriptors on the system registry from these templates.
- **File system.** This template allows you to access the hard drive partitions as a single tree and apply security settings for files and folders.

Figure 5-4 shows the Security Templates Console.

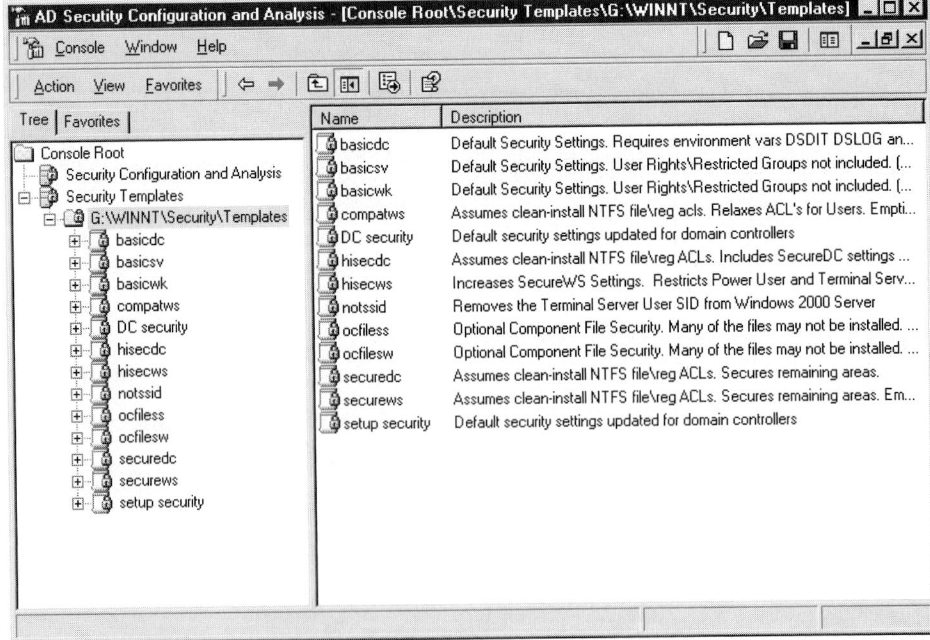

FIGURE 5-4

The Security Templates Console

Any of the security templates can be imported into the Security Configurations and Analysis Console. Some predefined security template files are included with the operating system, as outlined in the following list. These files are stored in the \Systemroot\Security\Templates folder:

- **BASICWK.INF.** Default workstation.
- **BASICSV.INF.** Default server.
- **BASICDC.INF.** Default domain controller.
- **COMPATSWS.INF.** Compatible workstation or server.
- **SECUREWS.INF.** Secure workstation or server.
- **HISECWS.INF.** Highly secure workstation or server.
- **DCSECURITY.INF.** Default security settings updated for domain controller.
- **SECUREDC.INF.** Secure domain controller.
- **HISECDC.INF.** Highly secure domain controller.
- **OCFILESS.INF.** Optional component file security for servers.
- **OCFILESW.INF.** Optional component file security for workstations.
- **SETUP SECURITY.** Default security settings for domain controllers.
- **NOTSSID.** Removes Terminal Server security ID from Windows 2000 Server.

These templates can be grouped in categories; for example: basic, compatible, secure, highly secure, optional and so forth.

Microsoft does not recommend using the Security Configuration and Analysis tool to analyze security of domain-based clients, because you would then have to visit each client computer individually. A solution to this problem is to modify the Security Template from the Security Templates Console and reapply it to the GPO.

Why Perform Security Analysis? The security templates included with Windows 2000 enable systems administrators to perform a quick inspection of security settings for a Windows 2000 computer by comparing configured security against settings recommended by Microsoft. After the security analysis is performed, the administrator is informed of any discrepancies in the configured security settings compared with the settings proposed by the system.

By regular security analysis, individual Windows 2000 computers can be tuned to an acceptable level of security. The security analysis tool also allows administrators to reset the security settings so that they conform to the recommended level. This is a great help in overcoming any flaws that might creep into a system over time.

Setting Rights on System Services

The System Configuration and Analysis Console allows you to set user rights and privileges on system services. These services include file and print services, network services, and telephony services. Figure 5-5 shows system services when no settings are defined.

Setting Rights on a File System

The Security Configuration and Analysis Console allows you to set security policies for the local file system. The procedure is similar to setting security for system services. Exercise 5-3 explains the steps to configure file system security.

FIGURE 5-5

The system services in the Security Configuration and Analysis Console

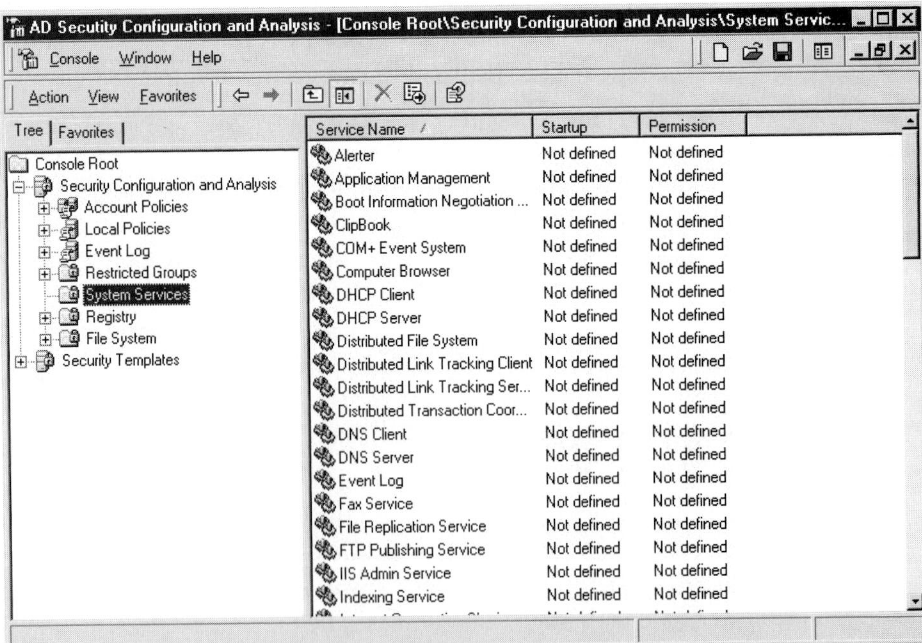

EXERCISE 5-3

Setting Security on a File System

1. Click Start | Programs | Administrative Tools and select Security Configuration and Analysis. This choice opens the Security Configuration and Analysis Console.
2. Double-click Security Configuration and Analysis to expand the node. Double-click File Systems to expand the node.
3. A list of existing drives is displayed. Double-click the drive to view a list of folders.
4. Right-click a folder for which you want to set up security. Click Security from the menu, as shown in the following illustration.

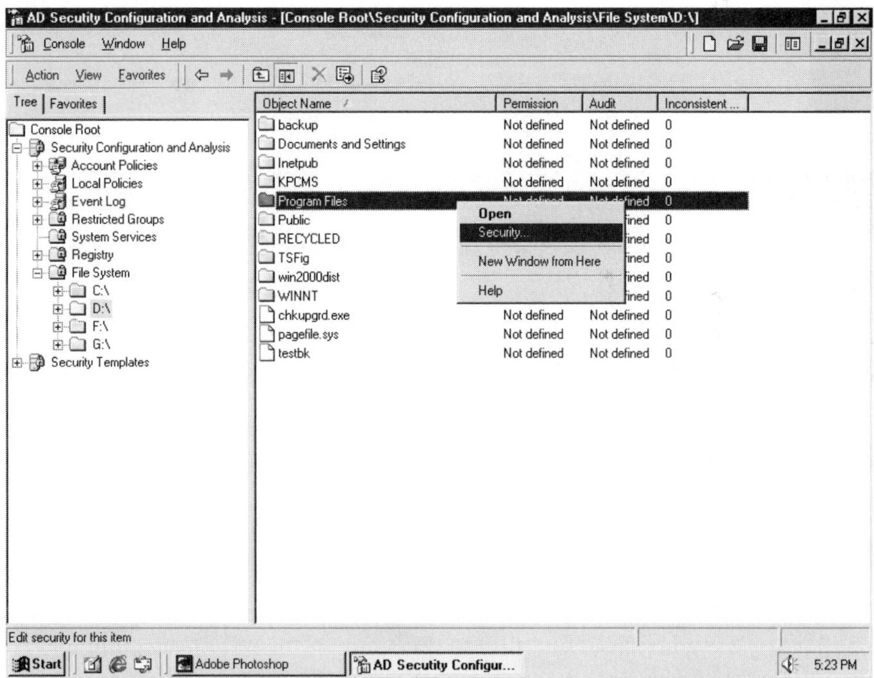

5. The Analyzed Security Policy Setting dialog box appears. Notice that by default the computer setting is not defined. Click the "Define this policy in the database" check box, as shown in the following illustration.

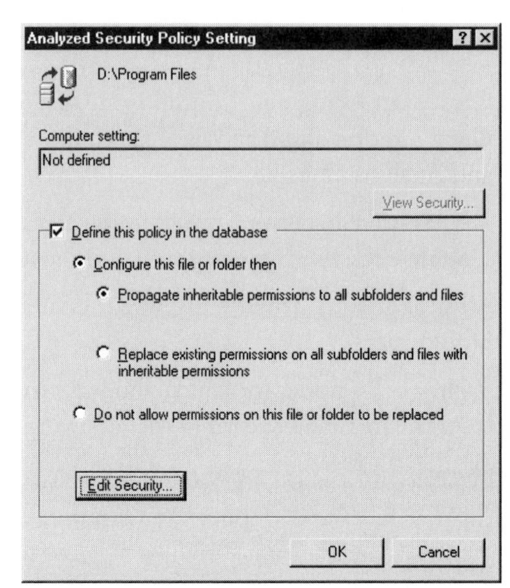

6. Click Edit Security button to configure policies for users and computers. This step opens the database security dialog box for the selected folder.
7. Click OK. Close the Security Configuration and Analysis Console.

Implementing an Audit Policy

Auditing user and system activities in a Windows 2000 computer involves recording events that happen to log files on the system. These logs help you analyze various events that happen on local systems and on domain resources. Auditing is an efficient tool to track user activities that concern security.

Once you have completed setting up permissions on network resources, it is important to keep track of access to these resources by setting up audit policies. Auditing can be set up to track user logon and logoff, computer startup and shutdown, and changes made to Active Directory objects. Attempts to access secure company data files and folders can also be logged.

The events that occur on a Windows 2000 domain are recorded on the domain controller computers, except those for which auditing is set up locally. The recorded events are read using the security log of the Event Viewer.

Why Audit Events?

As a systems administrator, it is your responsibility to secure network resources. You must have some solid plans to minimize the risk of unauthorized access to the secure data. Network resources include network components and data. These resources are equally important. *Network resources* include domain controllers, system services, shared printers, and shared data files. Each resource is vital in keeping the organization working smoothly. Unless you have some means of determining who is using what resources and how these resources are accessed, there is no way to track what is going on with the secure data or resources.

Security configuration in Windows 2000 helps you secure data and resources; auditing helps you find out what kind of activities are being performed on these resources. In order to keep a check on user and system activities, it is necessary to log the events to log files. Logging helps in tracking authorized or unauthorized access attempts to network resources. Examples of such events are logon attempts of users to restricted computers or attempts to read, delete, or modify secure data. Auditing helps you track information by recording events in the system security log files. These events include the action that was initiated, the user who initiated the action, and whether the attempt succeeded or failed.

Auditing configuration tools allow you to specify which events must be written to the security event logs. With careful planning, you can secure the system and network resources in the domain by implementing domainwide audit policies.

By default, auditing is disabled on all Windows 2000 computers. Without using audit policies, however, it is very difficult to track network security events.

How to Implement an Audit Policy

Audit policies can be set only on those resources that reside on NTFS drives. The person setting up audit policies must have administrative rights in the domain. Another right that allows auditing is Manage Auditing and Security Log. The Administrators group on each machine has this auditing right, by default. The following are important points to remember:

- Auditing is disabled by default. A domain administrator must enable auditing.
- The administrator must specify the resources and events that should be audited.
- The events that occur on a Windows 2000 computer are logged to the security log files.
- The recorded events must be scanned and interpreted on a regular basis to get the results of auditing.

There are several types of objects on which you can set up auditing. Auditing each and every event and access to each and every shared resource would result in the collection of large amounts of data. A decision must be taken to specify the computers on which auditing will be set up. In addition, it is also important to decide which events will be audited.

Configuring Auditing Configuration of auditing is a two-step process. First, you must set up the audit policy. Second, the auditing must be enabled on specified computers on events that you need to track. These events can be related to files, folders, network printers, and other Active Directory objects. You must select the categories of events that should be audited. The size of the security log file is limited, so you must take care that unnecessary events are not logged.

The events audited in Windows 2000 computers are classified into the following categories:

- **Account logon events.** Logon requests received by the domain controller.
- **Account management.** Actions that concern attempts to create, remove, or modify user and group accounts.
- **Directory Service access.** Attempts to access objects in the Active Directory.
- **Logon events.** Attempts to log on and log off in the domain.
- **Object access.** Attempts to access files, folders, or printers.
- **Policy change.** Attempts to change user security options, user rights, or audit policies.
- **Privilege use:** Attempts to exercise privileges given to a user.
- **Process tracking.** Attempts by program files to perform an action.
- **System events.** Shutdown/startup of computer or events that affect system security.

If you want to set audit policy on a stand-alone server that is not a part of the domain, you need to access the Local Security Policy from Administrative Tools. Exercise 5-4 explains how to set up audit policy on such a computer.

EXERCISE 5-4

Setting Up Audit Policies on a Stand-Alone Computer

1. Log on to the computer as Administrator.
2. Click Start | Programs | Administrative Tools and select Local Security Policy. This step opens the Local Security Policy Console.
3. Click the plus (+) sign before Local Policies to expand it. Double-click Audit Policy.
4. Right-click the event that you want to audit from the right-side pane. Click Security. This choice opens the Local Security Policy Settings dialog box. Notice that No Auditing is the effective policy setting by default.
5. Click Success or Failure, as required. The following illustration shows the Local Security Policy Setting dialog box for the account logon events.

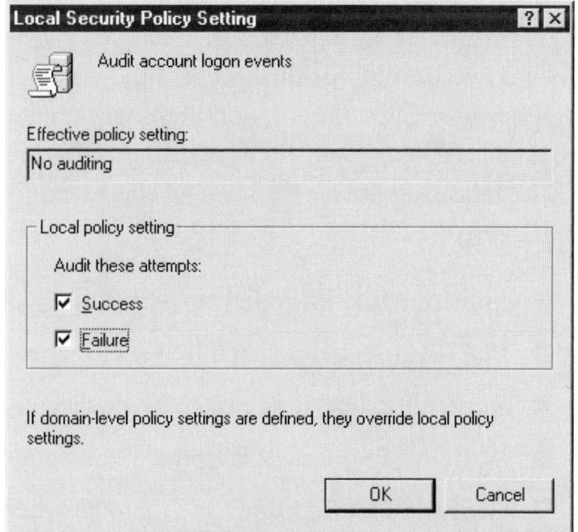

6. Click OK.

Making the Security Policy Changes Effective The changes you make to the security policies do not take effect immediately but wait for the policies to propagate. The automatic propagation of policies occurs every eight hours by default. If you cannot wait for such a long duration, there are two ways to immediately make the policy changes effective:

- Restart the computer. However, this action is not recommended when the computer is active in the domain.
- Type **secedit /refreshpolicy machine_policy** at the command prompt and press Enter. This option does not require restarting.

To force the changed security policies, you must select an appropriate method for your environment.

Auditing Active Directory Objects Auditing access to Active Directory objects is also a two-step process. First, you have to configure the audit policy and then set up auditing for the specific objects. These objects can be users, groups, computers, or OUs. This action helps you track events that concern authorized or unauthorized access and changes made to the Active Directory objects.

The following list details some of the auditing event entries and when they are triggered.

- **Full Control.** Triggered by performing any type of access to the object.
- **List Contents.** Triggered by viewing the objects.
- **Read All Properties.** Triggered by viewing object attributes.
- **Write All Properties.** Triggered by making some change to the object attributes.
- **Create All Child Objects.** Triggered when a child object is created within the audited object.
- **Delete All Child Objects.** Triggered when a child object is deleted within the audited object.
- **Modify Permissions.** Triggered when the permissions of the audited object are changed.
- **Modify Owner.** Triggered when someone takes ownership of the audited object.

It might not be necessary to enable auditing for all events. Since auditing degrades system performance, you must study your requirements carefully and decide what events you need to audit to maintain an acceptable balance between security and performance.

Auditing Files, Folders, and Printers Access to files, folders, and printers can be set up following the procedure given in the exercises. You must take care that you audit only those events that are absolutely necessary to track. Enabling auditing for a large number of events not only fills up log files quickly, but it also affects the performance of computers on which the events are being recorded. You might recall that auditing can be enabled on only those files and folders that reside on NTFS volumes.

Exercise 5-5 explains the steps necessary to audit file and folder access.

EXERCISE 5-5

Auditing Access to Files and Folders

1. Click Start | Programs | Accessories and select Windows Explorer.
2. In Windows Explorer, right-click the file or folder for which you want to enable auditing and select Properties.
3. Click the Security tab from the Properties dialog box. Click Advanced. This step opens the Access Control Settings dialog box for the selected file or folder.
4. Click the Auditing tab. Click Add, and from the next dialog box, select the users or groups for whom auditing of the selected file or folder access is required. Click OK.
5. The Auditing Entry dialog box now appears. Check the Failure or Success boxes for the events that you want to audit. Refer to the list of event details following this exercise.
6. In the Apply Onto list, you can specify where the objects are audited. The default is "This folder, subfolders, and files." Click OK.
7. If you want to prevent the audit settings from the parent folder of the selected file or folder to propagate to this file or folder, clear the "Allow inheritable auditing entry from parent folder to propagate to this object" check box.
8. Click OK.

The following list explains some of the events that you can audit for file and folder access and what triggers them:

- **Traverse Folder/Execute File.** This event is triggered when some user tries to move through folders to find a particular file or tries to execute a file even though the user does not have permission for such an action.
- **List Folder/Read Data.** This event is triggered when a user tries to list folder contents or read data from a file.
- **Read Attributes and Read Extended Attributes.** This event is triggered when the attributes of a file or folder are displayed.
- **Create Files/Write Data.** This event is triggered when a file is created within a folder or the contents of a file are changed.
- **Create Folders/Append Data.** This event is triggered when a folder is created within the audited folder or data is appended to the audited file. This does not apply to deleting or changing the data in a file.
- **Write Attributes and Write Extended Attributes.** This event is triggered when the attributes are changed.
- **Delete Subfolders and Files.** This event is triggered when a subfolder or a file within a folder is deleted.
- **Change Permissions.** This event is triggered when file or folder permissions are changed.
- **Take Ownership.** This event is triggered when a user takes ownership of the audited file or folder.

Best Practices Implementation of audit policies is effective when you make a concrete plan as to how to implement and which events to record in the event logs. The following points will help you implement the audit policies effectively:

- Logon and Logoff failure audits help you track who is attempting to log on to the domain but is not granted access.
- Auditing success events for user and group management, system shutdown and restart, and changes in security policies help you track misuse of privileges.

- Success or failure of access to files, folders, and read/write access helps track suspected users who attempt to access secure data.
- Success/failure audits for printer management help track attempts to change network printers.
- Auditing success/failure of process tracking events helps track attacks from virus programs.

exam Watch

In order to track access to a particular object by any person on the network, you need to audit the Everyone group. The Everyone group contains all users and groups in the network.

CERTIFICATION OBJECTIVE 5.02

Monitoring and Analyzing Security Events

Configuration of Windows 2000 security, such as auditing of events, is only half the job of making your network secure. To exercise complete control of system and data security, you must monitor and analyze data collected by security configuration. You must check security events on a regular basis. The previous section of the chapter detailed how to configure security of Active Directory objects. This section details how to monitor and analyze the events that are recorded in the security log files.

Events to Monitor

It is not possible to view and interpret each and every event in the security log files. When you are looking at the events to monitor system and data security, you must have a clear idea of what types of events should be monitored. Viewing all events is not only undesirable, it is also a time-consuming job.

The decision of which events to monitor largely depends on what type of network environment you have and what type of security breaches you fear from outside or within the organization. Data is always valuable. The importance of a single file lost, altered, or viewed by undesired personnel can cause unpredictable loss. Depending on your network environment and the business needs of the company, you might find these suggestions helpful for monitoring security events:

- **Logon attempts.** You must monitor users' unsuccessful attempts to log on to secure systems. If any such attempts are found in the security logs, the responsible users must be warned.
- **Access to confidential files and folders.** Files and folders that contain confidential business data must be monitored regularly. Any users found attempting to view, alter, or delete data must be warned of legal consequences of his or her action. You must ensure proper access rights to these confidential files and folders from the beginning.
- **Undesired use of user rights and privileges.** You might have delegated some of your responsibilities to some users to lessen your administrative burdens. You must ensure that the delegated privileges are being exercised in the desired way. You must keep a check on user and group management. This check also ensures that company policies are followed properly.

The Security Event Log

The Event Viewer in Windows 2000 Administrative Tools is your ultimate tool for tracking the events occurring on the system and the network. The Event Viewer displays events depending on the configuration of a Windows 2000 computer. The computer acting as a domain controller essentially has the Directory Services, DNS server, and file replication logs in addition to application, system, and security logs that are standard in any Windows 2000 computer. Only administrators can view the security logs. All other users can view the application and system logs.

In order for you to monitor security events on a Windows 2000 computer, auditing of files, folders, and other Active Directory objects must be enabled. Group policies must be configured to ensure that the system and data security is maintained at all times. Figure 5-6 shows the security log of the Event Viewer, with no events. This is because auditing has not been configured; hence, no security events have been written to the security log files.

exam Watch

By default, only administrators have the right to view security events. The application and system logs are available to all users.

FIGURE 5-6

The empty security log when no auditing is enabled

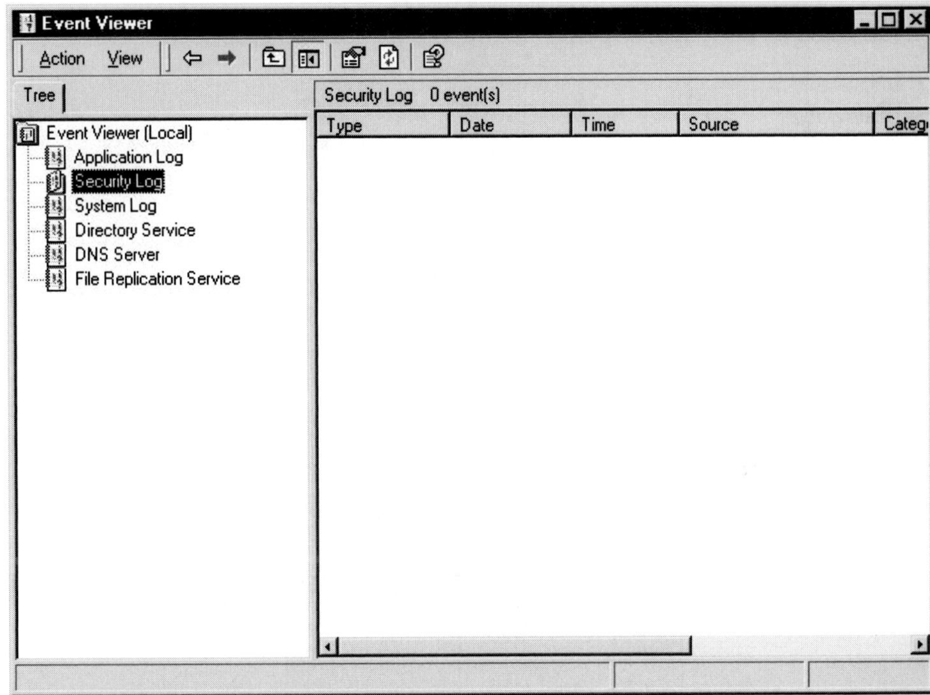

Locating Events in the Security Log When a large number of events are in the security snap-in, it becomes difficult to look for a particular event. To search for a particular event, click the Find option in the View menu of the security log. The Find in Local Security Log dialog box appears.

As shown in Figure 5-7, the Find dialog box has the following options:

- **Event types.** You can find only audit events in the security log.
- **Event source.** The source of the event, either a software or driver component.
- **Category.** Category of the event.
- **Event ID.** An event ID number.
- **User.** The name of the user who is logged on.
- **Computer.** The name of the computer.
- **Description.** Detailed text of the event.
- **Search direction.** To search the log in an up or down direction.

FIGURE 5-7

Locating events in the security log

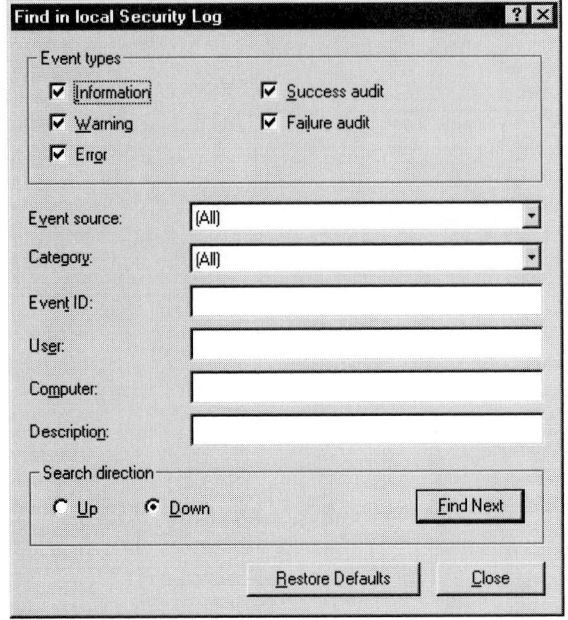

Filtering Events The Filter option in the Event Viewer enables you to specify how the events are displayed. Via filtering, you do not have to look at all the events. To filter the event display, click Filter in the View menu. This opens the Filter tab of the Security Log Properties sheet, as shown in Figure 5-8.

As with the Find option, the Filter option can be configured on the basis of event type, event source, event ID, and so on to display only those events that fulfill the conditions set in the Filter option. You can also specify the start and end dates of the events.

Security Log Settings It is essential to configure the security logs in order to ensure that important information is not missed due to full security log files or overwritten events. When you have configured auditing, the next step is to configure the security log settings so that these do not become constrained by security event monitoring. It is important to note that when the security log file is full, further security events are not recorded. In this case, an error is written to the application log. To avoid this situation, you must configure the security log options. Exercise 5-6 explains the steps to configure a security log.

FIGURE 5-8

Event Viewer display filtering

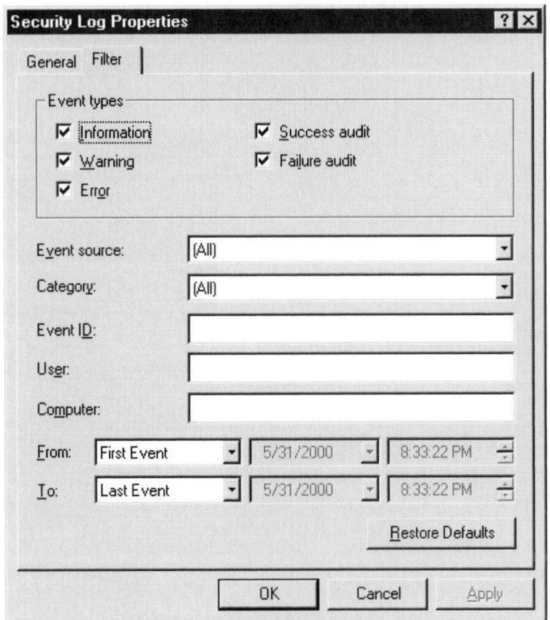

EXERCISE 5-6

Configuring a Security Log

1. Log on to the computer as Administrator.
2. Click Start | Programs | Administrative Tools and select Event Viewer. This step opens the Event Viewer.
3. Click Security Log on the left-side pane. The security logs are displayed on the right-side results pane.
4. Right-click Security Log and select Properties. This sequence opens the Properties sheet of the security log, as shown in the following illustration. Notice that the name of the security log file is SecEvent.Evt and it is stored in the \Systemrooot\System32\Config folder.

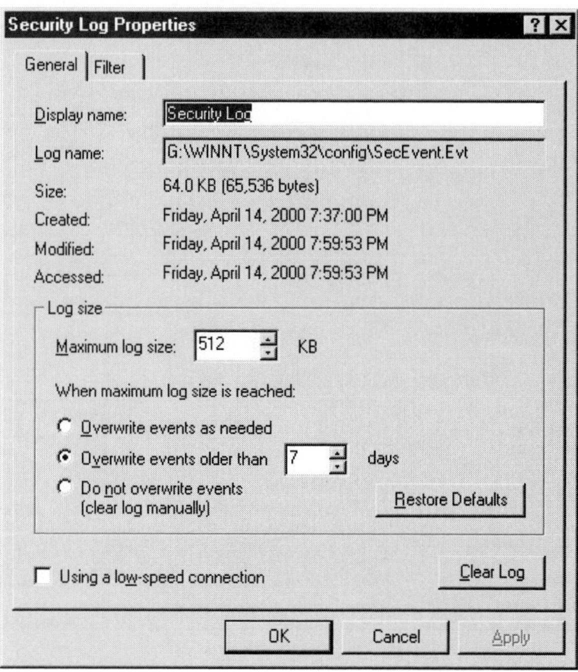

5. In the "Maximum log size" box, either select one of the file size options or type in the required size of the file. The log file size must be a multiple of 64KB. If you reduce the size of the log file, the new size takes effect only after the log has been cleared. The log file size can vary from 64KB (minimum) to 4,194,240KB or 4GB (maximum).
6. Select one of the following options from the "When maximum log size is reached" section:
   - "Overwrite events as needed" allows the system to delete the older events in favor of the newer ones when the log file is full.
   - Specify the number of days to keep the events in the log file in "Overwrite events older than" box. Default is seven days.
   - Select "Do not overwrite events" if you want to clear the events manually. Select "Using a low-speed connection" if the log is located on a computer connected by a slow link, such as a modem.
7. Click Apply. Close the Security Log Properties sheet.

Archiving Security Logs

Security logs can be archived in the Event Viewer for later viewing. This allows you to maintain a history of security-related events. The logs can be archived in log-file format (*.EVT file) that retains the binary format. If the logs are saved in text format, you can use a word processor to view the events later. Furthermore, the log can be saved in comma-separated format; that way, a spreadsheet can then be used to view and manipulate the saved log file. Some organizations have a policy to archive security logs for a specified period.

To archive a security log, follow these steps:

1. Open the Event Viewer from the Administrative Tools menu.
2. Right-click Security Log and select Save Log File As.
3. Type a name for the log file in the File Name box.
4. Select a format for the file. Click Save.

In order to view an archived file, follow these steps:

1. Open the Event Viewer from the Administrative Tools menu.
2. Right-click Security Log and click Open Log File.
3. Select the file you want to open. Click Security from the Log Type list.
4. Type a display name for the log file in the Display Name box. Click Open.

The archived log files are usually kept for a certain period of time that is decided by company policies. After the specified time period expires, these files can be deleted.

Clearing Security Logs

You might have noticed a Clear Log button in the Security Log Properties sheet. When you select "Do not overwrite events," you can click the Clear Log button to clear the security log manually. You are given a warning before clearing the log. The cleared logs are permanently removed from the system.

You can also clear the security logs from the console tree in the Event Viewer. Follow these steps to manually clear the security log:

1. Open the Event Viewer from the Administrative Tools menu.
2. Right-click the Security Log and select Clear All Events.

3. A message dialog box appears. Click Yes if you want to archive the security logs before clearing. Click No if you want to clear the events without archiving.
4. If you click Yes from the message box, you are prompted to type a filename for the archive file. You can also select a format for the archive log file. After typing a name and selecting a format, click Save.
5. If you select No from the message box, the security logs are deleted permanently.

Interpreting Security Events

As described earlier in this chapter, the security-related events are not written to the security log files unless audit policies are configured and auditing is enabled on the selected objects. The events that are monitored by the system after auditing is enabled are recorded in the security log files. The events are displayed in the Security Events category in the Event Viewer.

Follow these steps to view the security log on a computer:

1. Log on to the Windows 2000 computer as administrator, or a user with the user right to Manage Auditing and Security Logs.
2. Click Start | Programs | Administrative Tools and select Event Viewer. This step opens the Event Viewer.
3. Click the Security Log. Notice that the security events are displayed in the results pane on the right side.

The display depends on how the Event Viewer is configured. The security events that should be of interest to you are especially those that indicate violation of the organizationwide security policies. Examples of such events are:

- Logon attempts by unauthorized users
- Logon attempts by authorized users in off hours when access is restricted
- Attempts by users to access confidential files or folders
- Misuse of administrative privileges, such as opening of undesired user accounts or giving rights to undesired users
- Attempts to alter security settings on Active Directory objects, such as changing attributes of an object

Tracking security events can lead you to find solutions to security problems, even before they happen. In order to understand the severity of an event, you must first interpret the event. Each event listed in the security log has plenty of information that can be helpful in complete interpretation of what actually happened.

The events listed in the security log display only summary information of the event, such as event ID, event type, date, and time. When you double-click a particular event, the details of the event are displayed in a separate box.

Events with Similar IDs

It is important to note that many events get a common event ID and might look similar, but in fact, they are not. Microsoft recommends that you read the details of the event to completely understand it. For example, when a user logs on interactively or from the network, the events generated get the same event ID in both instances.

In any case, the events that you ignore at first view, considering that they have similar event IDs, might in fact be distinct ones. Another example of such events is a user connecting to a shared resource. The event ID is generated when the user first connects to the resource, but the ID does not explain how the resource was accessed.

CERTIFICATION SUMMARY

In this chapter, you studied various tools included with the Windows 2000 operating system for configuration and analysis of security. Security is important for every organization. Security in Windows 2000 is applied using group policies. Group Policy enables you to configure security for account policies, local policies, event logs, system services, registry, and many other areas. Security policies are usually defined at the domain level. The three constituents of Group Policy are Group Policy objects, Group Policy containers, and Group Policy templates.

The Security Configuration and Analysis tool is used to manage security via the security database files. Several template data files are included with Windows 2000, and a suitable template can be imported to set up a working security database that meets your requirements. The Security Configuration and Analysis tool allows you to immediately analyze your security settings by comparing them with the predefined settings.

Audit policies are used to monitor usage of network resources and maintain applied security policies. In order to view security events happening on the network, auditing must be enabled. Auditing helps you track authorized or unauthorized access to resources, which helps ensure that user rights and privileges are not misused.

The security-related events are written to security log files. The events can be viewed from the security log of the Event Viewer. It is important to check the security logs at regular intervals. The logs contain detailed information on all events. You must check events related to logon attempts, access to confidential folders, and undesired use of user rights. The Event Viewer allows you to filter events and save log files. The log settings can be configured to strike a balance between disk space and recording of all required events.

TWO-MINUTE DRILL

Configuring and Troubleshooting Security in a Directory Services Infrastructure

- ❑ Using group policies, you can implement a manageable security policy in Windows 2000 networks. The data created by Group Policy is stored in Group Policy objects.
- ❑ The three elements of Group Policy are GPOs, GPCs, and GPTs. The GPTs are stored in the SYSVOL folder.
- ❑ The Security Configuration and Analysis tool is used to manage security on a computer. By default, this tool is not installed. You can add this snap-in to an empty MMC using the Add/Remove Snap-in option.
- ❑ Security templates are included with Windows 2000 and contain predefined security settings stored in database files. Any template file can be imported to the Security Configuration and Analysis tool. Changes can be made to the template file to set up a working security database.
- ❑ Auditing is disabled by default. Configuring auditing enables you to specify which security events must be monitored to maintain security. You must be an administrator to have the user right to Manage Auditing and Security Logs.

Monitoring and Analyzing Security Events

- ❑ Security events happening in a Windows 2000 network must be monitored in order to maintain security. The most important events that must be monitored are logon attempts, access to confidential folders, and misuse of user rights.
- ❑ It is necessary to configure audit policies and enable auditing on resources in order to log security events to log files. The security logs must be checked regularly.

- ❑ The displayed events in the security logs can be filtered to view only desired events, such as events classified by category or originating from a particular source.
- ❑ The security log files can be configured with regard to its size and whether or not to overwrite events when the file is full. You can also clear the log files manually if you do not want the system to overwrite events automatically.

6

Optimizing Active Directory Components

CERTIFICATION OBJECTIVES

So far you have learned about such various aspects of Active Directory as installation of domain controllers, configuration of sites and services, and DNS. Any running network needs regular monitoring and maintenance; a Windows 2000-based network is no exception. Several administrative tasks in Windows 2000 Active Directory require administrative effort to keep the system running and performing seamlessly.

Windows 2000 comes with many utilities that help you in monitoring the network performance and resolving problems related to Active Directory. The built-in management features of Windows 2000 Server make many otherwise complex jobs easier for you. Active Directory consoles such as Schema, Users and Computers, Sites and Services, and Domains and Trusts provide interactive interfaces to handle day-to-day maintenance functions. Active Directory performance is monitored using the Performance console. The Event Viewer console now includes additional event logs such as Directory Service, DNS Server, and File Replication Service.

CERTIFICATION OBJECTIVE 6.01

Managing Active Directory Objects

Each of the components of Active Directory is known as an *object.* Different objects can be spread across physically diverse locations on the network. Management of Active Directory objects includes creating, publishing, moving, and removing objects in the AD database. The AD consoles enable administrators to manage various objects efficiently and effectively. This results in reduced administrative efforts and minimized total cost of ownership (TCO). In addition, AD makes it easy for users to locate and use network resources regardless of their physical location. At the same time, administrators can enforce group policies throughout the organization without having to manage each network resource from its individual computer.

The AD design that you implement in your organization today is most likely based on the organization's current requirements. These requirements can change with time and due to changes in organizational hierarchy. Growth of the company or its diversification into other business areas can also contribute to changes in Active Directory structure.

Moving Active Directory Objects

Active Directory objects include users, groups, computers, shared folders, printers, and other network services that need regular maintenance. Moving objects from one OU to another is a common administrative function required to keep the AD database in synchronization with organizational changes.

Why Move Objects?

When some changes take place at the organization level, you might have to make corresponding changes in the network setup. An organization that is using AD definitely must incorporate the changes at different levels of AD setup. Moving AD objects contributes to such changes. The objects you create today might not be suitable to the needs of the organization after six months. Hardware upgrades, failures of network components, and regular maintenance could also require movement of objects.

The movement of objects can take place within the domain or between different domains, depending on the size of the organization. The following are some of the reasons for moving AD objects:

- Changes or growth in company hierarchy
- Creation of new domains
- Movement of users from one location to another
- Hardware upgrades
- Network maintenance

Depending on the reason for the movement of objects, you might have to move only one user from one group to another or a whole group to become part of a larger group at another location of the company. The basic methods for moving objects, however, remain the same. The next section describes various methods to implement movement of AD objects.

How to Move Objects

Moving objects from one container in the AD to another is an easy process. Two methods can be employed to move AD objects. The choice of a method to move objects depends on whether you want to move an object within a domain or from one domain to another. Certain restrictions apply to object movement in AD. These restrictions are discussed in the following sections.

Moving Objects Within a Domain You can move one or more objects at a time from one OU to another within the domain. Depending on the situation, you might have to move a user's account when he or she is shifted to a different department or office location, or you might need to move a computer account when the computer is reconfigured for a different function. When you move objects within a domain, you must remember the following points:

- Any original permissions that were set directly for the objects do not change. You need not apply a new set of permissions after moving the object. This feature reduces your administrative burden.
- When you move an object from one OU to another, the permissions set for the destination OU apply. The inherited permissions from the old OU are lost. Make sure that when you move objects from one OU to another that the network functions are not affected.

Exercise 6-1 illustrates the steps to move user objects from one OU container to another OU container within a domain.

Moving Objects Across Domains The process described to move objects works when objects are moved within a domain. To move objects across domains, use the *MOVETREE* and *NETDOM* utilities. These utilities are located in the \Support\Tools folder on the Windows 2000 Server setup CD-ROM. You can use these utilities to move objects such as users, computers, and OUs from one domain to another. Member servers and workstations are moved across domains using the NETDOM command-line utility.

EXERCISE 6-1

Moving User Accounts Within a Domain

1. Log on to the domain controller with domain administrative privileges.
2. Choose Start | Programs | Administrative Tools and select Active Directory Users and Computers. This choice opens the Active Directory Users and Computers console.
3. Click Users from the console tree on the left-side pane. Notice that a list of users is displayed on the results pane in the right side.
4. Select the Users that you want to move from this OU. Right-click and select Move from the drop-down menu, as shown in the following illustration. You can also click Move from the Action menu.

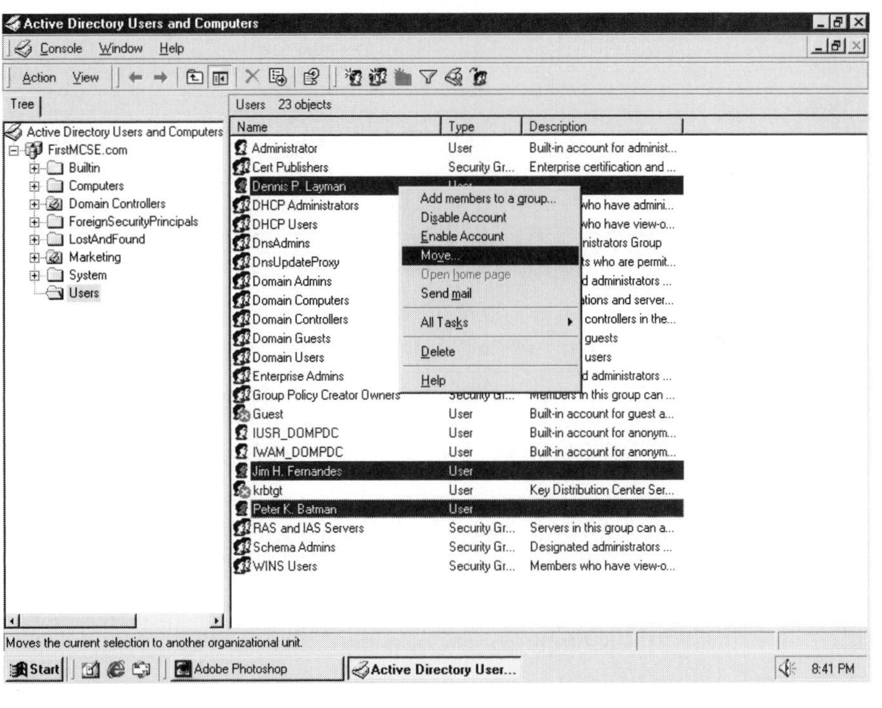

5. A Move dialog box appears. Select the container to which you want to move the User objects, as shown in the following illustration.

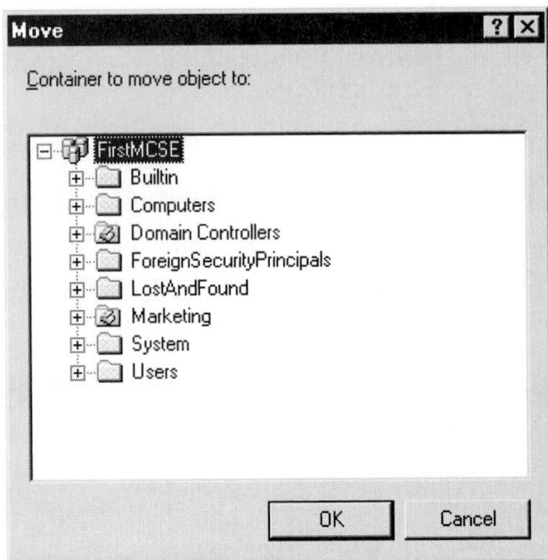

6. Select OK to close the Move dialog box. Notice that the users you moved are no longer displayed in the Users container.
7. To verify the Move operation, open the container to which you moved the users. The users are now listed there.
8. Close the Active Directory Users and Computers console.

A similar procedure can be followed to move other objects such as computers or printers within the same domain. Printers do not normally appear as Active Directory objects in the same way as users or computers do. However, in essence, any object visible from the snap-in can be moved in a similar way. Printer objects appear within computer objects and can be viewed only by selecting View | Users, Groups and Computers as Containers.

Users and groups have a security ID (SID) that is unique in the domain. When you move any users from one domain to another, the SID changes. The SIDHistory feature of Windows 2000 preserves security settings that enable users to enjoy their original privileges. This option is available only when the network is functioning in Windows 2000 native mode.

You must be familiar with certain important points before you can use the MOVETREE tool effectively. The following conditions and restrictions apply for moving objects between domains using the MOVETREE command:

- MOVETREE can move only objects between domains in the same forest. If this condition is not met, the move operation will not succeed.
- Locked objects cannot be moved. If a folder is locked by a user, you cannot move it without first unlocking it.
- Replication delays can cause a move operation to fail. For example, if a printer is deleted from the source domain but is still shown in the source domain, and the destination domain has updated its records to show the printer as deleted, you will not be able to move it.
- If there are capacity problems at the destination domain, such as hard disk space limitations, the MOVETREE command will not work.

Besides these restrictions, the following operations are not supported when you use the MOVETREE command to move objects between domains:

- Global groups that reside at the domain level and have member user accounts cannot be moved. Similarly, local groups with members cannot be moved.
- The group policies associated with an object do not move with the object. You might have to apply new policies after the move operation. This caveat holds true for users, groups, and computers.
- System objects cannot be moved using the MOVETREE command.
- You cannot move objects that reside in the special-purpose containers such as LostAndFound, Built-in, ForeignSecurityPrincipals, and System.

- You cannot move an object that has a namesake at the destination domain. Two objects with an identical name cannot co-exist.
- Domain controllers and objects whose parent is a domain controller cannot be moved.
- Users with global group membership cannot be moved. If a user is moved, its object attributes/properties must meet the criteria imposed by the destination domain (for example, password length).

Using MOVETREE to Move an Organizational Unit from One Domain to Another The MOVETREE command is used from the DOS prompt or can be run from the Start menu. If you are good at scripting, you can also choose to write a batch file to run this command. Figure 6-1 displays the syntax of the MOVETREE command.

Exercise 6-2 explains how an OU can be moved from one domain to another using the MOVETREE command. In this exercise, we move an OU named Onlinesales from Server1 in the Marketing domain to Server2 in the Support domain and rename the new OU *Records.*

FIGURE 6-1 MOVETREE command syntax

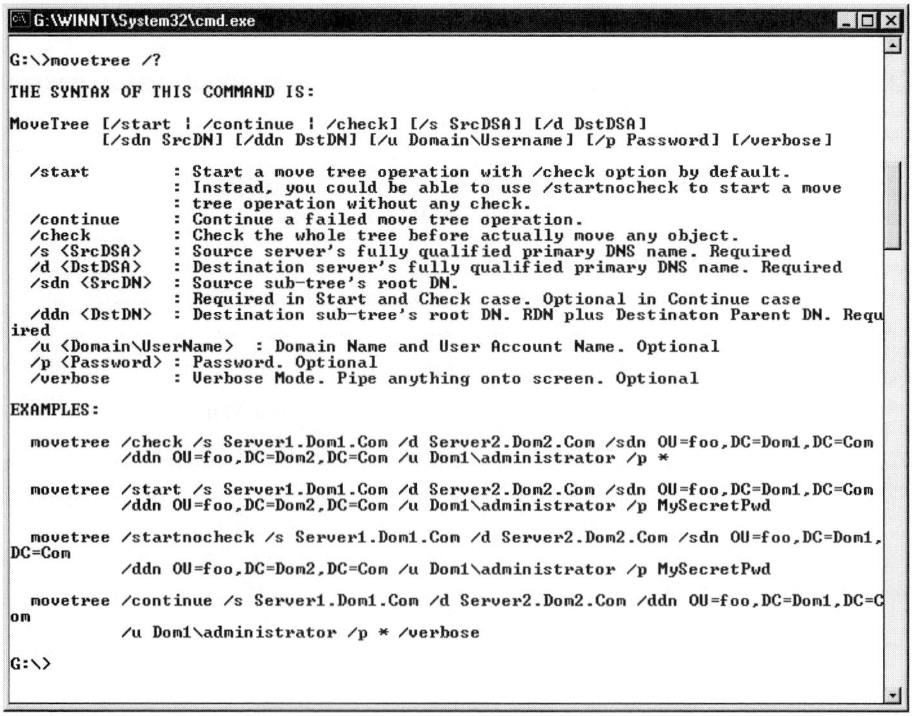

```
G:\WINNT\System32\cmd.exe

G:\>movetree /?

THE SYNTAX OF THIS COMMAND IS:

MoveTree [/start | /continue | /check] [/s SrcDSA] [/d DstDSA]
         [/sdn SrcDN] [/ddn DstDN] [/u Domain\Username] [/p Password] [/verbose]

  /start          : Start a move tree operation with /check option by default.
                  : Instead, you could be able to use /startnocheck to start a move
                  : tree operation without any check.
  /continue       : Continue a failed move tree operation.
  /check          : Check the whole tree before actually move any object.
  /s <SrcDSA>     : Source server's fully qualified primary DNS name. Required
  /d <DstDSA>     : Destination server's fully qualified primary DNS name. Required
  /sdn <SrcDN>    : Source sub-tree's root DN.
                  : Required in Start and Check case. Optional in Continue case
  /ddn <DstDN>    : Destination sub-tree's root DN. RDN plus Destinaton Parent DN. Requ
ired
  /u <Domain\UserName>   : Domain Name and User Account Name. Optional
  /p <Password> : Password. Optional
  /verbose        : Verbose Mode. Pipe anything onto screen. Optional

EXAMPLES:

  movetree /check /s Server1.Dom1.Com /d Server2.Dom2.Com /sdn OU=foo,DC=Dom1,DC=Com
           /ddn OU=foo,DC=Dom2,DC=Com /u Dom1\administrator /p *

  movetree /start /s Server1.Dom1.Com /d Server2.Dom2.Com /sdn OU=foo,DC=Dom1,DC=Com
           /ddn OU=foo,DC=Dom2,DC=Com /u Dom1\administrator /p MySecretPwd

  movetree /startnocheck /s Server1.Dom1.Com /d Server2.Dom2.Com /sdn OU=foo,DC=Dom1,
DC=Com
           /ddn OU=foo,DC=Dom2,DC=Com /u Dom1\administrator /p MySecretPwd

  movetree /continue /s Server1.Dom1.Com /d Server2.Dom2.Com /ddn OU=foo,DC=Dom1,DC=C
om
           /u Dom1\administrator /p * /verbose

G:\>
```

EXERCISE 6-2

Moving an Organizational Unit from One Domain to Another

1. Log on to the domain controller with domain administrative privileges.
2. Choose Start | Run and type **cmd** in the Open box. This command opens the MS-DOS window.
3. Type the following command at the prompt:

   ```
   Movetree /check /start /s:Server1.Marketing.Firstmcse.com
   /d:Server2.Support.Firstmcse.com /sdn:OU=Onlinesales,DC=
   Marketing,DC=Firstmcse,DC=com
   /ddn:OU=Records,DC=Support,DC=Firstmcse,DC=com
   ```

4. The given command includes the /check switch, which performs a test run without moving any object. If the test does not encounter any errors, the command is executed.
5. If you are sure that everything is fine with the move operation, you can add the /startnocheck switch in place of the /start switch. Using this switch completes the move operation without performing any check. Make sure that you use only one switch because it is not possible to use both /start and /startnocheck in a single MOVETREE command.

When the MOVETREE command completes the move operation, it creates three log files. These files are very useful for verifying details of the move operation. These log files are named MOVETREE.ERR, MOVETREE.LOG, and MOVETREE.CHK and are located in the same directory from which you run the MOVETREE command.

The NETDOM Utility *NETDOM* is a Windows 2000 domain manager support utility that is used to move member servers and workstations from one domain to another. NETDOM is also a command-line tool. As we saw, a limitation of the MOVETREE command is that it cannot be used to move member servers and workstations between domains. The reason is that the MOVETREE command cannot disjoin a computer object from the original source domain and join it with the destination domain. We use NETDOM for these tasks instead.

The following is a simple example of a NETDOM command:

```
netdom move /d:destination_domain server1 /ud:sourcedomain\admin
/pd:password
```

This command moves a member server named Server1 to the specified destination domain. The /ud switch is used to specify the user who is performing the move operation. The /pd specifies the password of the user.

You can use the NETDOM /? command to view a list of syntax and switch options for this command. The full syntax for the NETDOM command is as follows:

```
netdom move /D:domain [/OU:ou_path] [/Ud:User /Pd:{password|*}] [/Uo:User
/Po:{password|*}] [/Reboot:[time_in_seconds]]
```

where:

- **/domain** is the name of the destination domain to which the member server or workstation is being moved.
- **/OU:ou_path** is the name of the destination organizational unit in the domain specified by the /domain argument.
- **/Ud:User** is the user account used to connect to the destination domain specified in the /domain argument. If no user account is specified, the current user account is used.
- **/Pd:{password|*}** is the password of the user account specified in the /Ud argument. When the asterisk (*)is used, the user is prompted for the password.
- **/Uo:User** is the user account that will make a connection to the object on which the move action is being performed. If the account is not specified, the current user account is used.
- **/Po:{password|*}** is the password of the user account specified in the /Uo argument. If the asterisk (*)is used, the user is prompted for the password.
- **/Reboot:**[**time_in_seconds**] specifies that the computer being moved should be shut down and restarted after the move operation is complete. If the time is not specified, a default time of 20 seconds is used.

Publishing Resources in Active Directory

Active Directory provides a centralized database for all network resources. This setup makes administration and maintenance easy for network administrators. In addition, network users can easily look for a desired resource such as shared folder or printer from a single search engine. Resources on the network such as users, computers, printers, and network services need to be published in AD so that network users can easily locate them. Many of the network resources on Windows 2000 computers are published automatically when installed.

Active Directory allows you to publish these resources and set appropriate security attributes to these resources. AD also enables you to set various administrative controls on the published resources so that you can ensure that users gain access to only those resources that they need to perform their job functions. AD also ensures that the data security is not at stake at any time. The published resources can be made available to network users irrespective of their physical location.

What Are Published Resources?

The network resources that can be searched in AD are known as *published resources.* The network users can use AD search tools to find any published resource. Access to these resources is provided to users based on their credentials and security settings for each user or group. The following are the examples of some of the resources that can be published in AD:

- Users and groups
- Shared folders
- Shared printers
- Computers
- Network services

The next section discusses various methods that can be employed to publish resources in Active Directory.

How to Publish a Resource

Users, groups, and computer accounts are published in Active Directory when they are created. Similarly, Windows 2000 printers are published automatically when installed and shared using the Add Printer Wizard. A List in the Directory check box is enabled by default in the Sharing tab of the Printer Properties dialog box. Non-Windows 2000 printers such as those on Windows NT computers need to be published manually.

The Active Directory Users and Computers console is the centralized place to view and create published network resources. The creation of AD objects can also be scripted using the Active Directory Services Interface (ADSI) application programming interfaces (APIs). This is a nice alternative to user interfaces. Later in this chapter we discuss creation of user accounts using the scripting method.

Publishing Users, Groups, and Computers When you use the Active Directory Users and Computers console to create a user or a user group, it is published in the directory automatically. Similarly, computers, including servers and domain controllers, need not be published manually. The Active Directory database makes it easy for users to search for other users on the network. AD ensures that only the information that is relevant to the user is displayed. For example, a malicious user trying to change security credentials of another user or trying to create a bogus user account cannot succeed in doing so.

Publishing a Shared Folder Publishing shared folders in AD is done from the Active Directory Users and Computers console. Once published, the AD-enabled clients can search for these shared folders using the Find option. The shared folders that are published in AD basically reside in their original locations. AD maintains a link to these folders so that users do not have to search for the share anywhere else on the network.

Exercise 6-3 explains the steps to publish a shared folder in Active Directory. Before you proceed, you must ensure that the folder you want to publish is shared on the network.

Publishing a Shared Printer Printers that are shared on the network can be published in Active Directory from the Users and Computers console. The printers installed on non-Windows 2000 computers such as Windows NT printers must

EXERCISE 6-3

Publishing a Shared Folder in Active Directory

1. Log on to the domain controller with domain administrative privileges.
2. Choose Start | Programs | Administrative Tools and select Active Directory Users and Computers. This choice opens the Active Directory Users and Computers console.
3. Click the Domain container from the console tree on the left-side pane. The existing OU containers are displayed on the results pane in the right side.
4. Select the container to which you want to publish the shared folder. Right-click the container, click New, and select Shared Folder.
5. The New Object-Shared Folder appears. Type the share name of the folder.
6. Type the location of the shared folder in the Path box, as shown in the following illustration. Ensure that you follow the Universal Naming Convention (UNC)—that is, \\server_name\share_name.

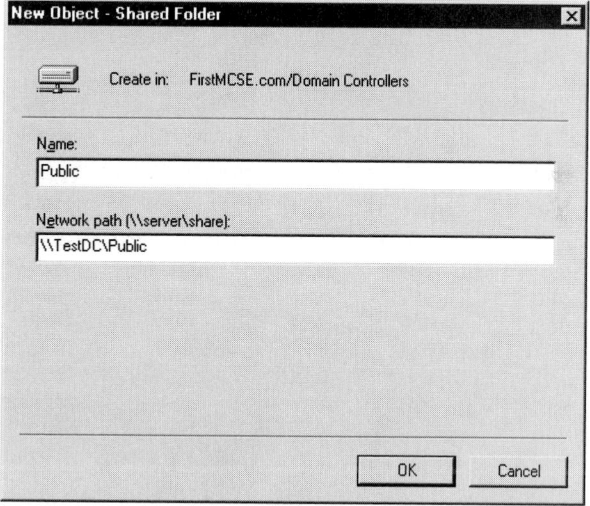

7. Click OK to close the dialog box. Notice that the new Shared Folder object is now listed in the container that you selected.
8. Close the Active Directory Users and Computers console.

be installed manually. Windows 2000 allows you to publish printers automatically when they are created and shared using the Add Printer Wizard. The Sharing tab of the Windows 2000 Printer Properties dialog box has a List in the Directory check box that is selected by default. This can be verified from the Printer Properties sheet, as shown in Figure 6-2. When this check box is checked for a shared Windows 2000 Printer, it is automatically published in the Active Directory. You have to uncheck this box if you do not want to publish the printer.

Exercise 6-4 explains the steps to publish a non-Windows 2000 printer in Active Directory.

exam Watch

Only those printers that are on non-Windows 2000 servers need to be published in Active Directory. Windows 2000 printers are published automatically when they are created and shared. The Sharing tab of the Windows 2000 Properties dialog box has a List in the Directory check box that is selected by default. Clear this check box if you do not want to publish the shared printer in Active Directory.

FIGURE 6-2

Windows 2000 printers are published automatically in Active Directory

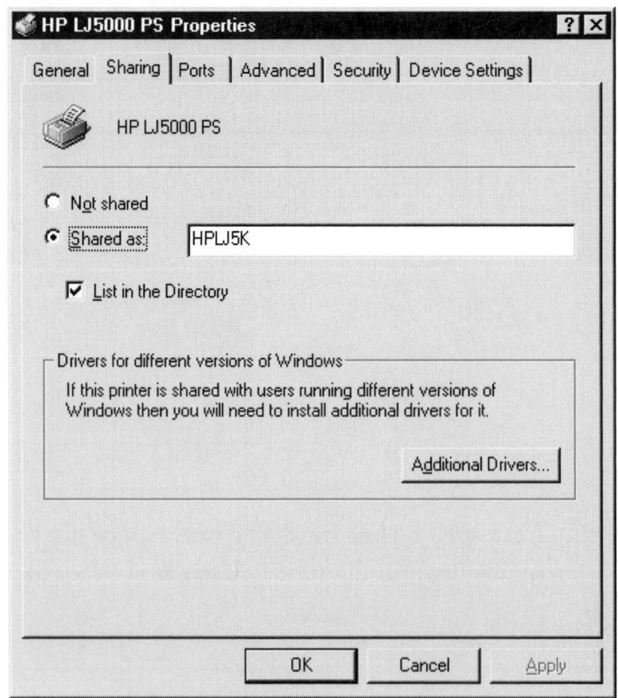

EXERCISE 6-4

Publishing a Non-Windows Printer in Active Directory

1. Log on to the domain controller with domain administrative privileges.
2. Choose Start | Programs | Administrative Tools and select Active Directory Users and Computers. This step opens the Active Directory Users and Computers console.
3. Right-click the Computers object and click New. Select Printer from the drop-down menu that appears.
4. Type the share name and UNC path of the printer, as shown in the following illustration. Ensure that you type the printer name in UNC convention, \\Printserver_name\Printer_name.

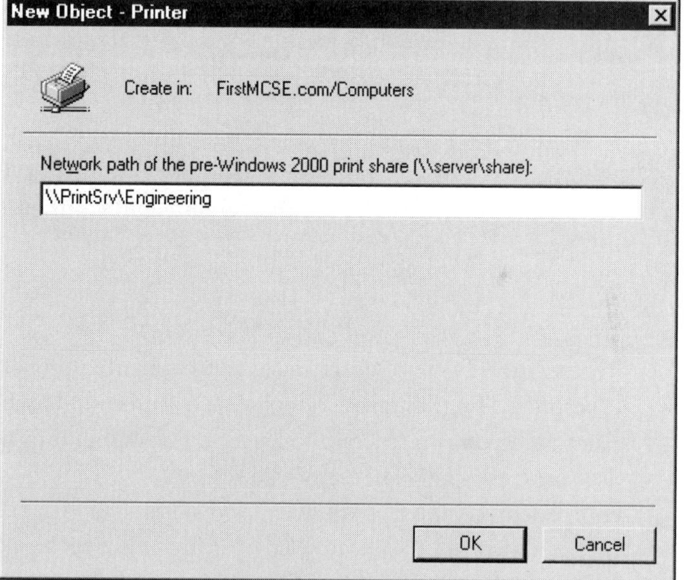

5. Click OK to close the New Object—Printer dialog box. Notice that the printer is listed in the Computers OU.
6. Close the Active Directory Users and Computers console.

Publishing Network Services When published in Active Directory, network services can easily be managed from a centralized location by administrators, rather than from individual computers. In Windows NT, it was rather a tedious job to check the status information or to start and stop services on a particular server. Active Directory can be used as a single location for all these network maintenance activities. You need not use any third-party software or bother about the physical location of the server.

The Active Directory Sites and Services console is used to publish and manage network services. This somewhat advanced operation requires experience and knowledge. The following are some of the services that can be published:

- **Binding information.** Allows client desktops to automatically establish connections to services.
- **Configuration information.** Allows administrators to distribute configuration information for a particular application to all network clients.

Exercise 6-5 explains how to view a published service.

Other types of network services can be published in Active Directory, but most frequently you deal with only the Binding and Configuration information.

Locating Objects in Active Directory

When Active Directory is installed and configured properly in a large organization, it becomes a huge database of network resources and useful information. This database becomes a centralized location for finding information on the resources, users, and computers in the organization. As we've seen, each Active Directory component is known as an *object.* Active Directory enables users to find objects on the network without knowledge of the object's location.

EXERCISE 6-5

Viewing Published Network Services in Active Directory

1. Log on to the domain controller with domain administrative privileges.
2. Choose Start | Programs | Administrative Tools and select Active Directory Sites and Services. This step opens the Active Directory Sites and Services console.
3. Click Show Services Node from the View menu. Click Active Directory Sites and Services.
4. Click Services from the Console menu. Expand each service tree. The published services look like the ones shown in the following illustration.

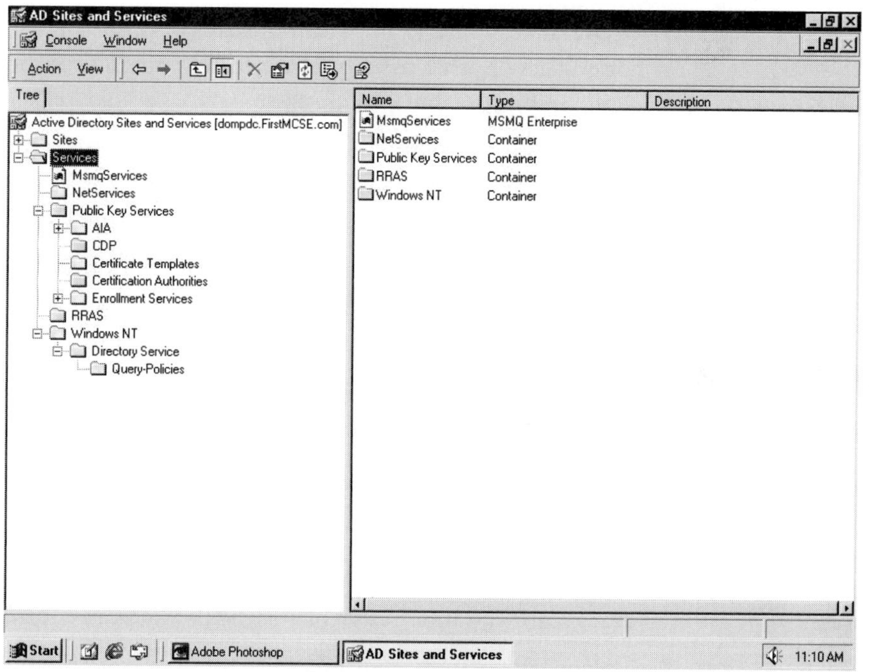

5. Close the Active Directory Sites and Services console.

What Is Stored in Active Directory?

Active Directory contains information on all the network objects in a centralized database. The Find option in Active Directory allows you to search for the following objects:

- **User accounts.** Active Directory stores information on all users created on the domain. This information includes user logon name, first name, last name, and other information such as the user's contact telephone number and e-mail address. You can also store the home-page address of the user.
- **Contacts.** Information on anyone who has business connections with the organization can be listed in Active Directory. This information can include name, address, telephone number, and e-mail address.
- **User and computer groups.** Groups are collections of user accounts, computers, or other user groups. Information on user and computer groups is important for administrative purposes.
- **Shared folders.** Information on shared folders that are published in Active Directory includes the actual location of the folder; the server name and share name tell you on which server the folder is actually located.
- **Printers.** This object contains information on printers that are published in the Active Directory either automatically or manually. (Only non-Windows 2000 printers need to be published manually.)
- **Computers.** Any computer that is a member of domain is listed in the Active Directory database. You can search for a particular computer using its host name.
- **Domain controllers.** Information on Windows 2000 domain controllers includes its host name, its DNS name, its pre-Windows 2000 name, the OS version used, and its location, as well as other information such as the person who is in charge of a particular domain controller.
- **Organizational units.** Organizational units are basic Active Directory components that store other OUs. However, an OU doesn't have to contain other OUs. OUs can also store users, groups, shared folders, and more. Active Directory stores information about all the OUs in the domain.

When you create new objects in Active Directory, they either become a part of the existing containers or they can form a new OU. You must be careful to include every piece of important information about the object that you create so that finding an object is easy at a later date.

Searching Active Directory

Searching for network resources or looking for particular users or computers was never as easy as it is with Active Directory. When you are looking for an object on the network, the Active Directory Users and Computers console is the right place to search, provided the object is published and listed in AD. Figure 6-3 shows the objects that you can search for using the Find option.

The Find option is used to locate objects in the Active Directory database. This is a powerful command that has many advanced search options. You can search for an object using any of the search criteria, and you can use a condition list to limit your search. If the number of objects is very large and you have found a particular object you are looking for, you can terminate the search using the Stop tab at any time during the search process. The Clear All button is used to clear previously specified search criteria so that you can start a new search.

Exercise 6-6 explains the steps to search for a shared folder on the network.

FIGURE 6-3

Using the Find option in Active Directory Users and Computers

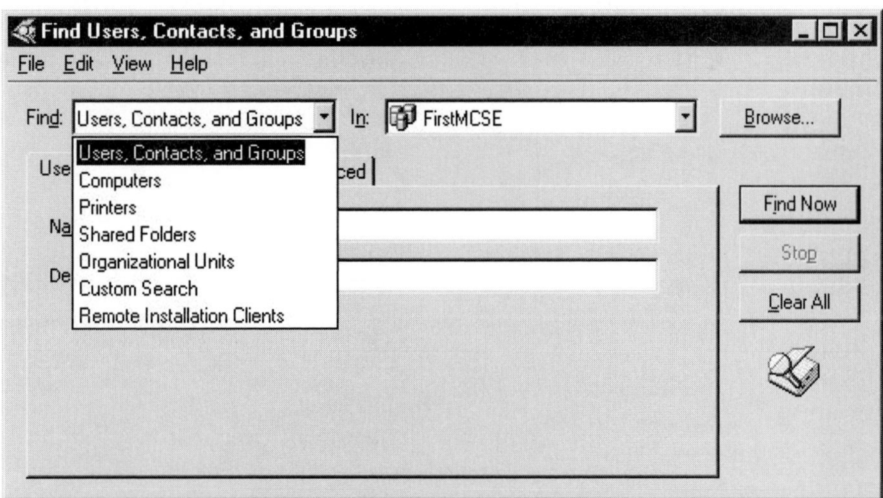

EXERCISE 6-6

Searching for a Shared Folder in Active Directory

1. Log on to the domain controller with domain administrative privileges.
2. Choose Start | Programs | Administrative Tools and select Active Directory Users and Computers. This choice opens the Active Directory Users and Computers console.
3. Right-click the domain on which you want to search for the shared folder. Select Find from the menu that appears. The Find dialog box appears.
4. Select Shared Folders from the Find drop-down menu. Type the share name of the folder in the Named box.
5. Click Find Now. Notice that a new section opens in the dialog box and lists the search results, as shown in the following illustration.

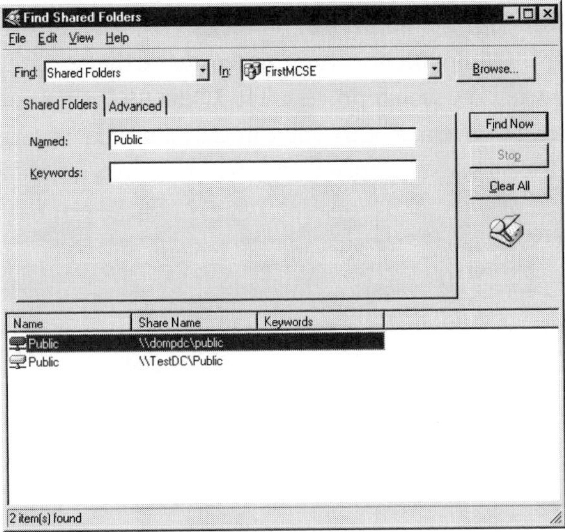

6. In the results, look for the folder for which you are searching. If you are successful in locating the folder, click Clear All. This choice closes the search results section of the dialog box.
7. Select a different name for another shared folder. Click the Advanced tab to specify advanced search criteria.
8. When you are done, close the Find dialog box from the File menu.
9. Close the Active Directory Users and Computers console.

Using the same procedure, you can locate any network resource, such as users, groups, computers, domain controllers, or printers. You can use any of the object properties as your search criteria. For example, if you know only the last name of a user, you can get a list of all users who have similar last names. You can use conditions such as "5th floor" to limit your search to those users who have the same last name and whose offices are located on the fifth floor.

on the job

When you try to locate objects in Active Directory based on some search criteria, the same criteria must have been previously included in the Object properties. For example, if you are looking for a printer on the 11th floor and enter "11th floor" as a search criterion, the Find command is able to locate it only if the printer properties contain "11th floor" in their description.

Creating and Managing Accounts Manually or by Scripting

When you create new OUs in Active Directory, the next important job is to create accounts for users. You will probably create user groups first and then create user accounts in those groups. Creating a user account is a simple process that can be done manually or by writing scripts. The next section details the process of creating user accounts in a domain.

Manual Creation vs. Scripting

Creation of user or group accounts can be handled either manually or by writing scripts that run as batch files. When you use the Active Directory Users and Computers console to create accounts, the process is manual. This process does not require very expert skill, but the person creating accounts must have sufficient rights to create accounts in the domain.

Scripting the creation of user accounts, on the other hand, requires you to be familiar with at least one scripting language such as VBScript or Jscript. If you know how to write scripts and know various parameters of the account that you will create, scripting is a fast process. It does not involve interaction with any of the interfaces, and you need not provide each and every answer to the Windows 2000 wizards manually. All answers are included in the script file.

Creating an Account Manually

User and group accounts are created manually using the Active Directory Users and Computers console. When you have made plans regarding user groups and users that will become members of each group, you are ready to proceed.

The process is straightforward. As a domain administrator, you can create the accounts yourself, as can any other person to whom you have delegated control of the specific Active Directory container and can create new objects. All accounts created using Active Directory are domain accounts.

Exercise 6-7 explains the procedure of creating a user account.

EXERCISE 6-7

Creating User Accounts in a Domain

1. Log on to the domain controller with domain administrative privileges.
2. Choose Start | Programs | Administrative Tools and select Active Directory Users and Computers. This step opens the Active Directory Users and Computers console.
3. Select the container in which you want to create the account. Right-click it, select click New, and select User. This is shown in the following illustration.

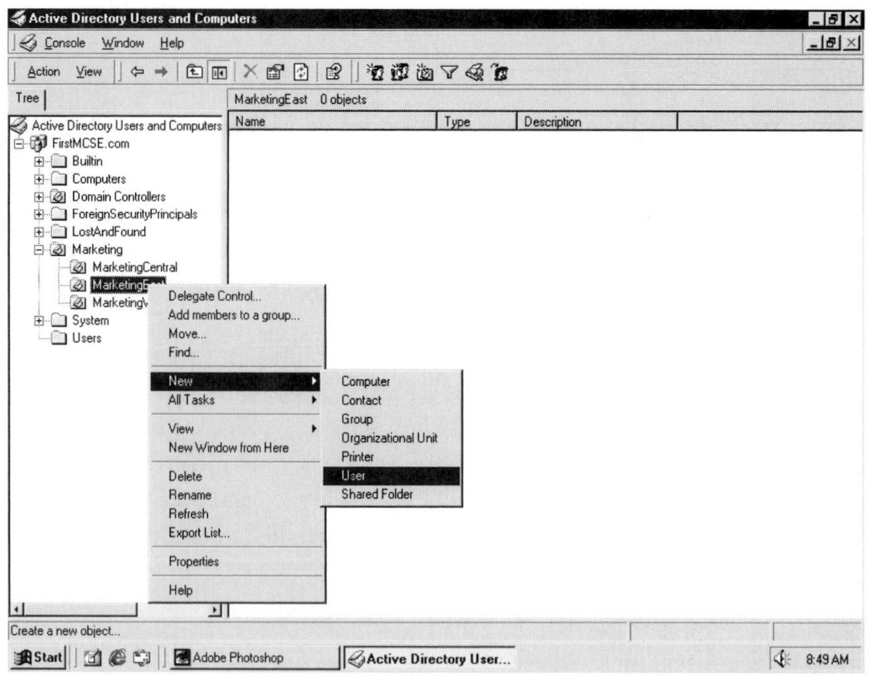

4. The New Object—User dialog box appears. Type the user's first, middle, and last names in the appropriate boxes. Type a logon name in the User Logon Name box. Notice that a pre-Windows 2000 logon name is automatically created, as shown in the following illustration. Click Next.

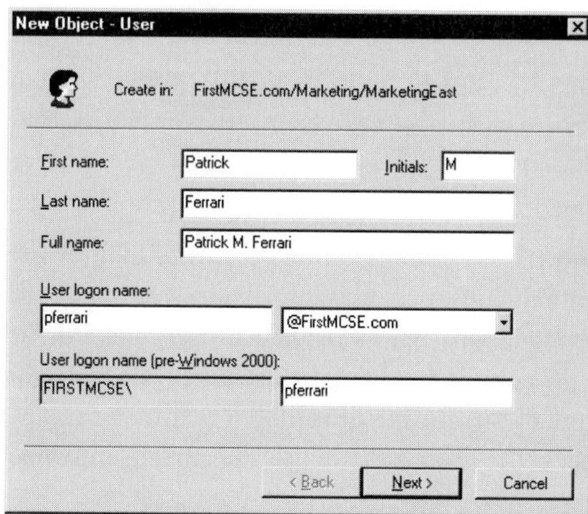

5. The next screen prompts for the user's initial password. Type a password in the Password box and retype it in the Confirm Password box. Click "User must change password at next logon," as shown in the following illustration. Click Next.

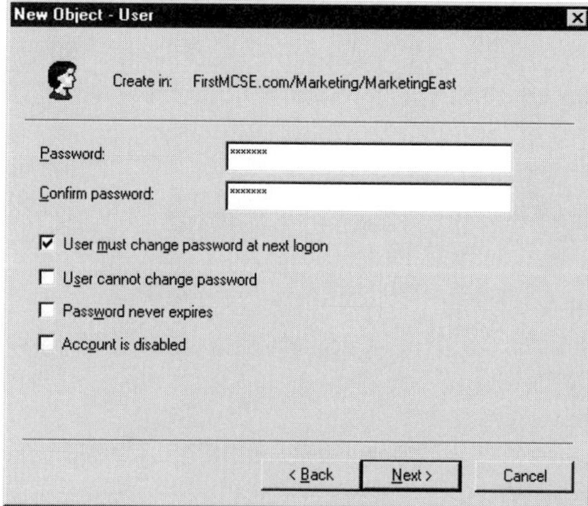

6. The next screen displays a summary of parameters that you entered for the new user account. If everything is fine, click Finish.
7. This completes the process for creating a user account manually. Notice that the new account appears in the right-side pane of the container where you created the account. Repeat Steps 3–6 for creating more user accounts.

When the creation of the user account is complete, the next step is to set properties for the account. Properties include user's account properties, group memberships, personal information, a user profile, and dial-in properties. To view or set properties for a particular user, select the user account from the right-side pane of the container where the account resides. Right-click the account name and select Properties from the drop-down menu. A Properties sheet for the selected account opens; the sheet contains all the current information for the user. Figure 6-4 shows

FIGURE 6-4

Account properties for the selected user

Account properties for a user account. The properties shown also contain Advanced properties that can be enabled from the View menu by selecting Advanced View.

You can select any required tab from the Properties dialog box and set other user account properties. Whenever you want to view or change any user properties, you access this dialog box and view or make necessary changes to the account.

Scripting the Creation of Accounts

Scripting of user account creation is a fast process that needs no interaction with Windows 2000 account creation interfaces. This process is also faster than manually creating accounts. The script file can be run from the command line.

To write a script, you need to collect the following information regarding a user account:

- Name of OU
- Fully qualified domain name (FQDN)
- User's full name
- Account name
- Initial password

You also need additional, optional information such as the user's telephone number, his or her title, and the name of the department. When you have collected all this information, you are ready to write a script.

Windows 2000 Active Directory Services Interface (ADSI) comes with a set of interfaces that are called by the scripts written in Windows Scripting Host, VBScript, Jscript, and the like. You can use any other scripting language in which you are proficient, but if the network is running in Windows 2000 native mode only, Windows Scripting Host, VBScript, and Jscript languages are supported.

The following script is an example of script that can be modified to suit your requirements:

```
'----The following script creates a user account for Peter Ferrari in the
Marketing East object in Marketing OU. The domain name is FirstMCSE.com----------

Set ou = GetObject("LDAP://OU=Marketing,OU=MerketingEast,
DC=dompdc,DC=FirstMCSE,DC=com")
```

```
Set usr = ou.Create("user", "CN=Patrick Ferrari")

'--- The following line must be included. It is mandatory.----
usr.Put "samAccountName", "pferrari"

'---- The following steps are optional and can be skipped----
usr.Put "sn", "Ferrari"
usr.Put "givenName", "Patrick"
usr.Put "userPrincipalName", "pferrari@firstmcse.com"
usr.Put "telephoneNumber", "(732) 424 8974"
usr.Put "title", "Marketing Supervisor, New York"
usr.SetInfo
'—This completes account creation. The next lines reset the password and enable it.
usr.SetPassword "pass321"
usr.AccountDisabled = False
usr.SetInfo
```

Various functions used in the given script are as follows:

- **GetObject.** The specific OU is bound to the Lightweight Directory Access Protocol (LDAP) using the GetObject function.
- **Create.** The Create function is used to create the new user object in the OU.
- **Object type (user) and canonical name (CN).** These are parameters of the Create Function.
- **SamAccountName.** This is a mandatory property of the account and must be specified. Other properties are specified using the Put function.
- **SetPassword.** This function specifies the initial password of the user.
- **SetInfo.** This function is used to save the settings in the OU.

exam Watch

When you use the scripting method to create new accounts in an Active Directory container, it is important to note that the user running the script must have sufficient rights to create new objects in the OU.

Now that you have read in detail about moving Active Directory objects and publishing and locating resources in Active Directory, let's look at some real-world scenarios and solutions.

Controlling Access to Active Directory Objects

You might be familiar with *access control lists (ACLs)* in Windows NT, which are used to define how a user or a group can get access to the network and existing resources. The same ACLs are used in Windows 2000 to describe permissions of users to various objects in Active Directory. Every object in AD has attached to it an ACL that defines which users or groups have access to it and what level of access is granted.

SCENARIO & SOLUTION	
You want to move two servers from this location to another location of the company within the same domain. Should you delete the servers in Active Directory and create them again in a different container?	No. You can move the servers from one container to another.
You are not sure about the syntax of the MOVETREE command. Do you have to consult the Resource Kit?	No. Use the MOVETREE /? command. This command lists the command syntax and the switches available for the command.
You installed a printer on a Windows 2000 server last week, but it does not show up in Active Directory. What could be the reason?	Check the Sharing properties of the printer. Make sure that the List in the Directory check box is enabled.
You are installing several servers in my company, which is spread over four floors of our building. How do you make sure that you are able to know the location of a particular server in Active Directory at a later date?	Fill in the server information in detail when you set its properties. Use location details so that you can find it in Active Directory later.

AD permissions enable you to control access to objects. The objects can be computers, printers, and other network resources such as shared folders. You can define a user or group level of access to a particular object. The discussion that follows details various aspects of controlling access to AD objects.

Degrees of Granularity

The *degree of granularity* that you want to achieve by assigning permissions to AD objects depends basically on the needs of your organization and policies that have been set for the entire corporation. Many companies prefer to limit administrative access to senior people in the company and give only as much access to general users as is required for them to perform their job functions. This strategy has several benefits, including ease of administration and security of sensitive data.

AD permissions allow you to go as far as possible to secure access to objects. Careful planning is required in deciding the permissions that you assign to users or groups. You must remember that many users are members of multiple groups, which can change their effective permissions on some objects.

Object and Attribute Permissions

As described earlier, AD object permissions work in the same way as the usual NTFS permissions. Each object in the AD database has an associated ACL. If a user is a member of multiple groups, his or her effective permissions are the combination of permissions for all the groups. However, this assignment is subject to whether or not any group of which the user is a member has Deny permission, which overrides all other permissions.

For example, if John is a member of one group that gives him Read permissions on a folder and a member of another group that gives him Modify permissions on the same folder, his effective permissions on the folder are Modify. Certain permissions cannot be assigned to specific objects. Obviously, you cannot assign Reset Password permission for a printer object.

Besides Standard and Special Active Directory permissions, there are two other main sets of permissions. These are Allow and Deny. The Deny permission always overrides all other individual or combined permissions of a user. You should use the Deny permission only in certain cases. Otherwise, use the most restrictive permissions that still allow users to perform their job functions.

Standard Active Directory Permissions The following are the standard Active Directory object permissions that can be set to Allow or Deny:

- **Full Control.** This permission allows users to take ownership of the AD object, change its permissions, and perform all actions permitted by other permissions.
- **Read.** Allows users to view only the objects and associated attributes.
- **Write.** The Write permission allows specified users to change object attributes.
- **Create All Child Objects.** This permission allows users to create child objects in an existing OU.
- **Delete All Child Objects.** Users given this permission can delete objects from the OU.

Special Active Directory Permissions In practice, you will find the standard permissions sufficient to control access to Active Directory objects. However, when these permissions are not enough and you want to achieve finer control on some objects, you can use the *special permissions.* The special permissions are viewed and set from the Advanced tab of the Security properties of an object.

Inheritance of Active Directory Object Permissions The AD object permissions inheritance works in the same way as standard NTFS permission inheritance. While setting permissions on an object, you can uncheck the "Allow inheritable permissions from parent to propagate to this object" check box.

Exercise 6-8 explains the procedure to set permissions on Active Directory objects.

exam Watch

The permissions on Active Directory objects are automatically inherited from the parent container to the child container. You must clear the "Allow inheritable permissions from parent to propagate to this object" check box to disable the propagation of inheritance.

EXERCISE 6-8

Setting Permissions on Active Directory Objects

1. Log on to the domain controller with domain administrative privileges.
2. Choose Start | Programs | Administrative Tools and select Active Directory Users and Computers. This choice opens the Active Directory Users and Computers console.
3. Select the object for which you want to set permissions. Right-click and select Properties. This choice opens the Properties window for the selected object.
4. Click Security tab. The standard security properties are displayed, as shown in the following illustration.

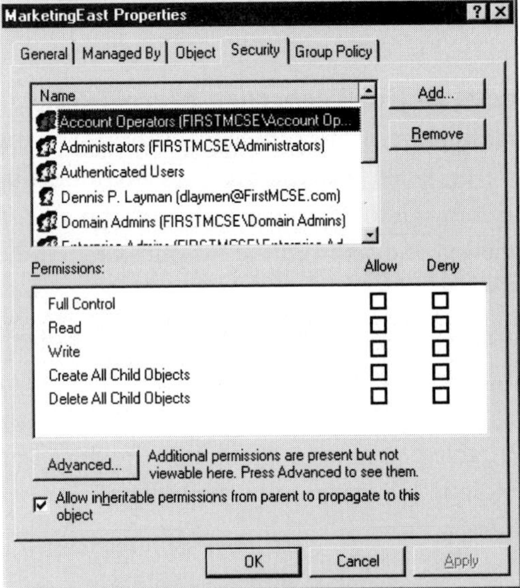

5. From the list in the upper portion of the dialog box, select the users to which you want to give access. Select the access type you want to assign from the lower portion of the dialog box.
6. If you want to set Access special permissions, click the Advanced tab. The Advanced Security permissions are displayed, as shown in the following illustration.

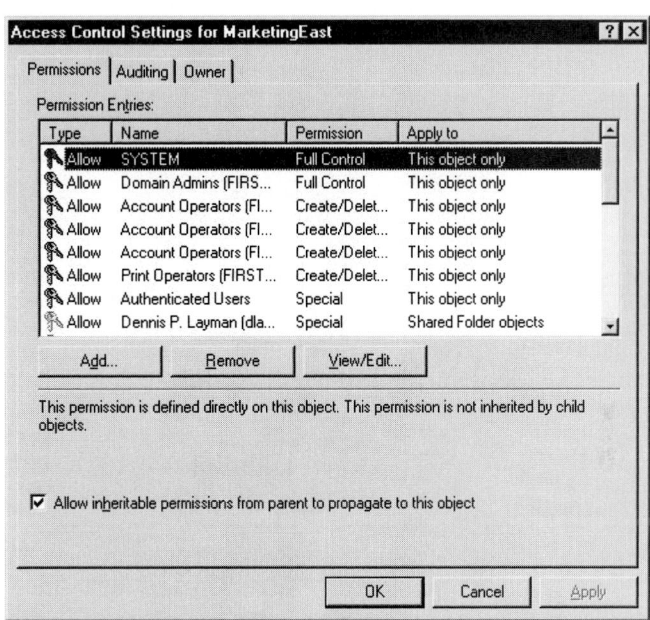

7. To add a user, click Add. The next screen is Select User, Computer, or Group, as shown in the following illustration.

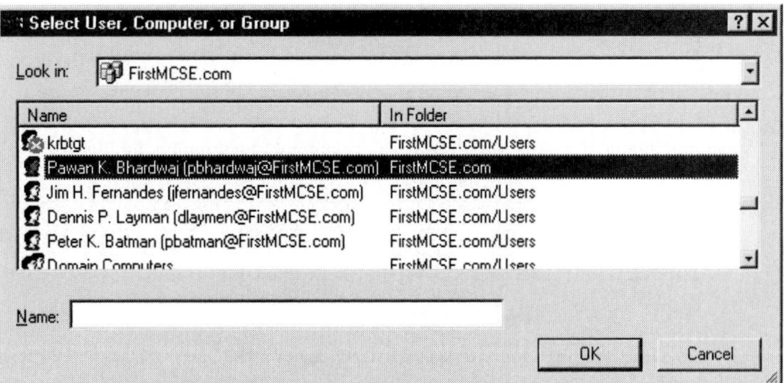

8. Select a user from the list and click OK. This action opens the Permission Entry screen for the selected object, as shown in the following illustration. Select the appropriate object from the "Apply onto" the drop-down box. The default is "This object and all child objects."

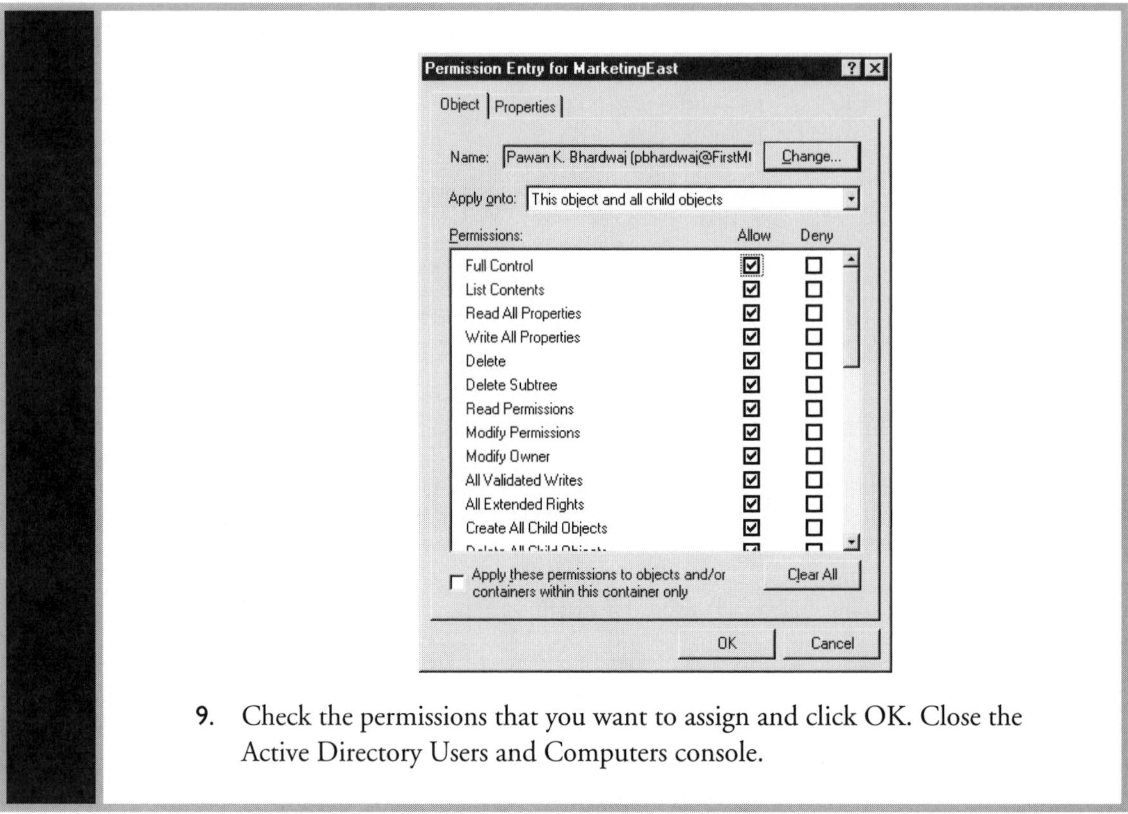

9. Check the permissions that you want to assign and click OK. Close the Active Directory Users and Computers console.

Delegating Administrative Control of Objects in Active Directory

If the organization is small, you can handle the administrative responsibilities yourself, without any help from anyone. But when the network is an enterprise-level network spread across various parts of the country or the globe, you will definitely want to share the administrative tasks among other administrators. Giving permissions to other users or departmental administrators on AD objects is known as *delegation of control*. Delegating control helps you offload some of your administrative tasks so that the administration functions run smoothly.

Why Delegate Control?

Many factors call for delegation of control; size of the organization is first among them. A single network administrator cannot handle all network-related functions.

These tasks must be divided among many other administrators or users, depending on the policies of the organization.

For example, if your organization has 12 branches across the country, one person cannot look after the maintenance needs of all locations single-handedly. There must be local administrators with full or limited privileges to handle day-to-day administrative tasks. If you are at the top of the network administrator hierarchy, you are responsible for delegation of administrative tasks. Even when the network is at a single location, you may want to delegate control of many network resources to selected users.

This stands true for AD components, too. The organizations that use Windows 2000 Active Directory are using this wonderful feature to manage network resources effectively. Delegation of control is required for Active Directory components such as OUs and specific containers to distribute administrative functions. The following discussion helps you understand the process of delegating control of AD components.

How to Delegate Control

Administrative control of Active Directory is delegated by assigning permissions to objects so that other administrators, users, or groups of users can handle their functions more effectively and according to their needs. This delegation helps achieve more granular control of function-based OUs. You could also call it *decentralization of administration* at various levels of the organization, which lessens the centralized administrative burden.

Delegation of control of AD objects works equally well at both the OU level and the container level. This again depends on the organization's hierarchy and how you want to distribute various administrative functions. This method of delegation ensures that you are able to track permissions in a better way than tracking permissions on an individual object level. You can also easily maintain documentation of permission assignments.

The Delegation of Control Wizard is the best way of assigning permissions. This wizard is helpful in simplifying the delegation process. Figure 6-5 shows the Delegation of Control Wizard welcome screen.

Once you have decided about the users or groups that will be assigned permissions to handle AD objects, you are all set to use the Active Directory Delegation of Control Wizard to complete the job. Exercise 6-9 explains the steps that will help you understand the procedure.

FIGURE 6-5

Delegation of Control Wizard Welcome screen

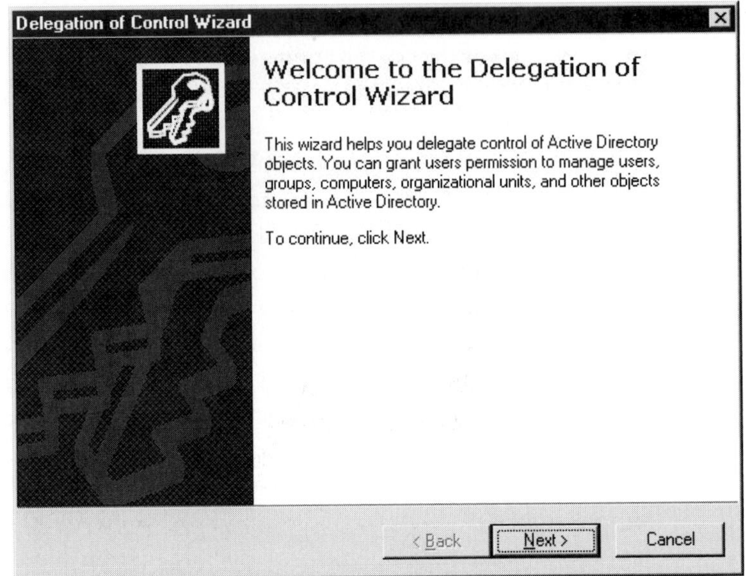

EXERCISE 6-9

Delegating Control of Active Directory Objects

1. Log on to the domain controller with domain administrative privileges.
2. Choose Start | Programs | Administrative Tools and select Active Directory Users and Computers. This choice opens the Active Directory Users and Computers console.
3. Select the OU object of which you want to delegate control. Right-click and select Delegate Control from the menu that appears. The Delegation of Control Wizard Welcome screen appears.

4. Click Next, then click Add. The Select Users, Computers, or Groups screen appears, as shown in the following illustration.

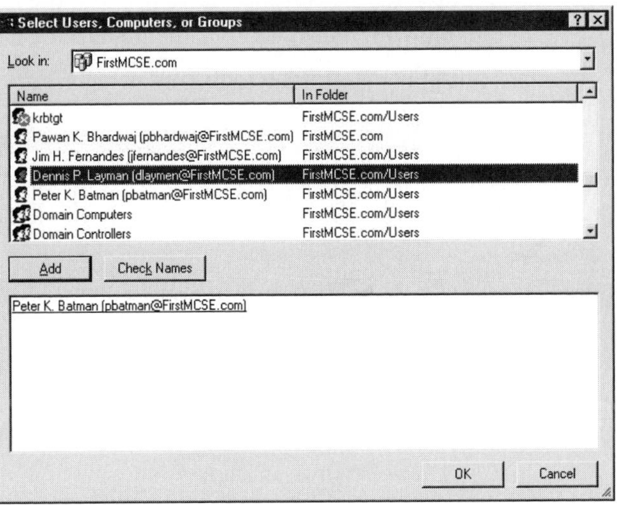

5. Select the user(s) and/or group(s) to which you want to delegate control of the previously selected object. The "Look in" drop-down list allows you to select a user or group from any domain in the forest. Click Add. Click OK.
6. Click Next. The next screen that appears is Tasks to Delegate. The common list of tasks is displayed, as shown in the following illustration.

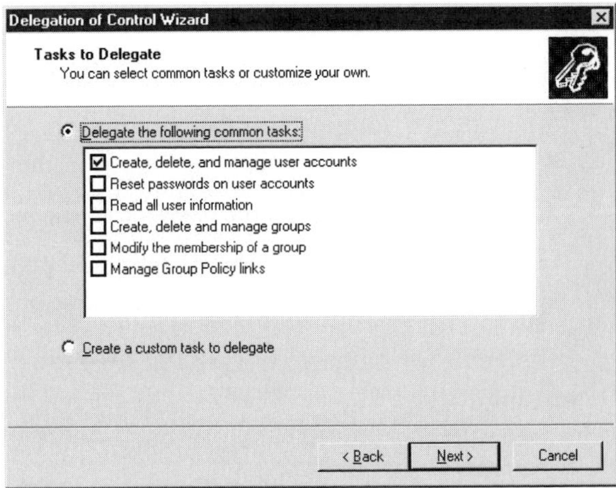

7. If you want to delegate custom tasks that include Active Directory-related tasks, click the radio button for "Create a Custom task to delegate." This action disables the common tasks list, and the next screen appears as shown in the following illustration. If the uppermost radio button is selected, along with appropriate check boxes, click Next and skip to Step 12.

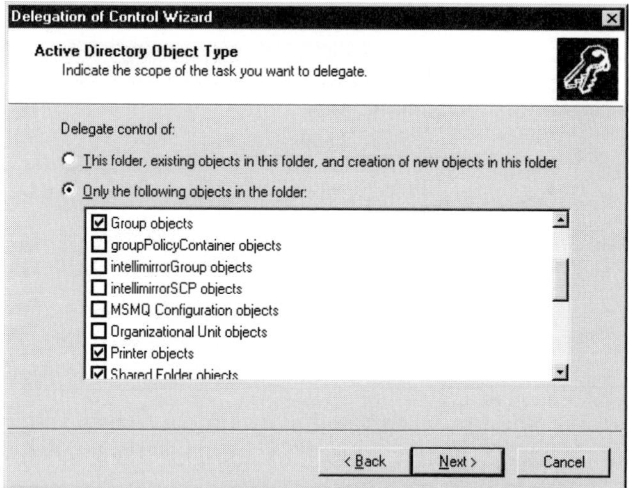

8. In this screen, you can select one of the following options:
   - This folder, existing objects in this folder, and creation of new objects in this folder
   - Only the following objects in this folder

   The latter choice gives you the option to check objects from a given list. Choose the "Only the following objects in this folder" option.
9. Check each object you want to select. Click Next.
10. The Permissions screen appears. Select the permissions that you want to delegate, as shown in the following illustration.

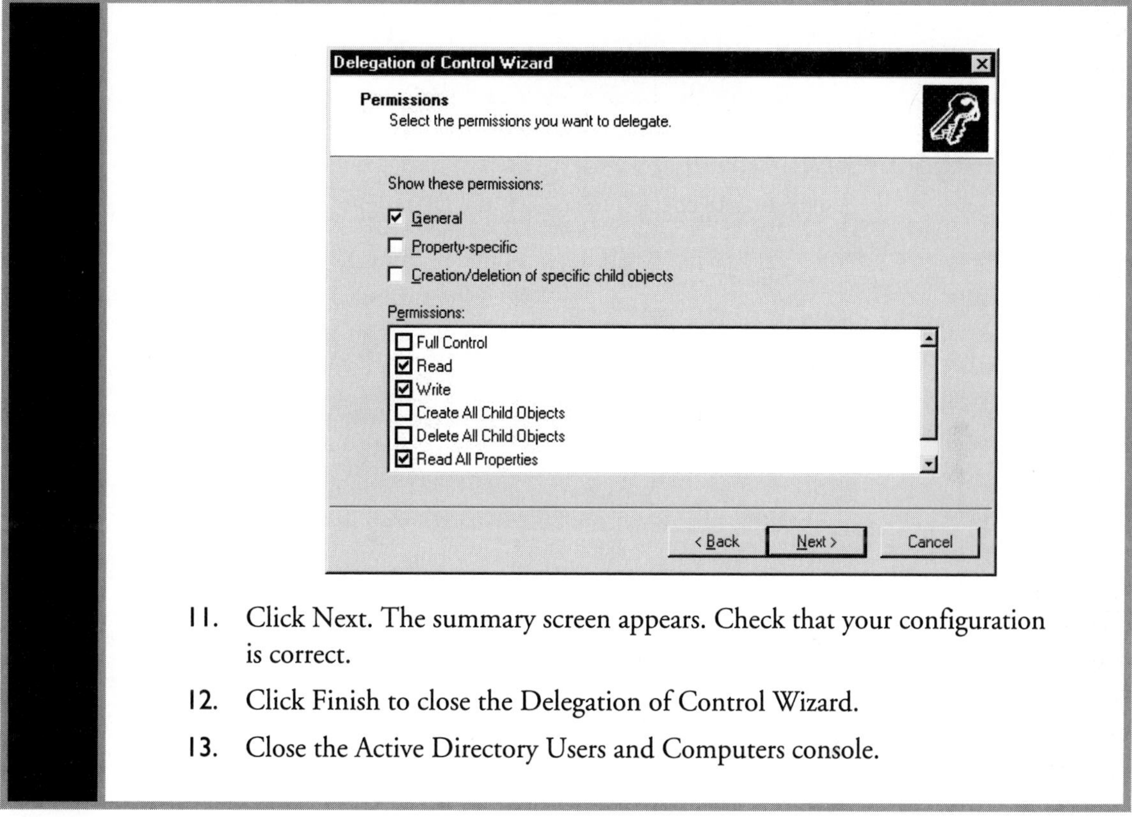

11. Click Next. The summary screen appears. Check that your configuration is correct.
12. Click Finish to close the Delegation of Control Wizard.
13. Close the Active Directory Users and Computers console.

exam watch

When configuring the Delegation of Control Wizard, you must select the "Create a Custom Task to Delegate" option in order to customize the list of tasks for which you want to delegate control for Active Directory maintenance.

FROM THE CLASSROOM

A Word About Active Directory Administration

Delegation of control and controlling access to AD objects are very important functions of Active Directory administration. Delegation of control helps you offload many of your administrative responsibilities. When working in a large organization, it is not possible to handle all network functions alone. Even if a team of administrators is involved in network activities, some of the functions are distributed among users to help reduce administrative burdens. Controlling access to AD objects is necessary to secure configuration and AD data. The following are some guidelines for delegating control of AD objects:

- Wherever possible, delegate control on containers instead of individual objects.
- Consult other people involved in administrative activities to understand their requirements. In addition, follow the policies of your organization.
- Delegation of control requires that the users whom you select for delegation are familiar with Active Directory and its functions. If necessary, arrange training for users.
- When controlling access of AD objects, do not forget that at least one person must have Full Control permissions.
- Use the Deny permission with caution. Be as restrictive as possible, but ensure that you do not prevent users from performing their duties.
- When you are done with configuration of distributing control activities, never forget to track the assignment of permissions. Tracking assignments requires a bit of extra work, but it helps you keep tighter control on AD objects.

Finally, do not forget documentation. Documenting your AD object control decisions not only helps your fellow administrators understand the configuration, but it also could help you at a later date. Sometimes you will forget the configuration parameters yourself, so do keep notes.

—Pawan K. Bhardwaj, MCSE, MCP+I, CCNA

CERTIFICATION OBJECTIVE 6.02

Managing Active Directory Performance

Performance monitoring and optimization are important aspects of Active Directory administration. As an administrator, you must have an idea of various performance-monitoring tools that are included with Windows 2000 Server. The Performance console and Event Viewer are the tools administrators most frequently use to find performance bottlenecks. These tools help you resolve many performance- related problems. This section discusses how to monitor the performance of domain controllers with regard to Active Directory.

Monitoring, Maintaining, and Troubleshooting Domain Controller Performance

Active Directory administrative functions include monitoring, maintaining, and troubleshooting domain controllers that are basic storage places for its components. The Event Viewer console gives you a view of various events that happen in separate sections of the domain controller. The Performance console gives a real-time display of the system performance based on the counters that you select for monitoring. Both of these utilities allow you to save your data so that you can analyze it at a later time.

Event Logs

Most of the domain controllers activities are recorded in the event logs. You can access the event log files from the Administrative Tools Event Viewer console. The event logs are helpful in locating information on various system and application problems that are running on the domain controller. The Event Viewer on a domain controller has the following types of logs:

- **Application logs.** These event logs display information generated by applications.
- **Security logs.** Security events are recorded only if the administrator sets some auditing on security events, such as success or failure of logon or access to shared resources.

- **System logs.** These events display information on services that are used by the Windows 2000 operating system.
- **Directory service logs.** These events relate to Active Directory services.
- **DNS server logs.** The Domain Name Service (DNS) server generates these events.
- **File Replication Service logs.** The File Replication Service events are displayed in this section.

Each of the given event types contain information, warnings, and error messages. The event logs that should concern you while you track problems in Active Directory are the Directory Service logs. These logs are the first place to check for any problems or bottlenecks with Active Directory. Figure 6-6 shows the Event Viewer console with Directory Services events in the results pane. You can double-click any event to get detailed information on it.

FIGURE 6-6

Directory Service events in the Event Viewer

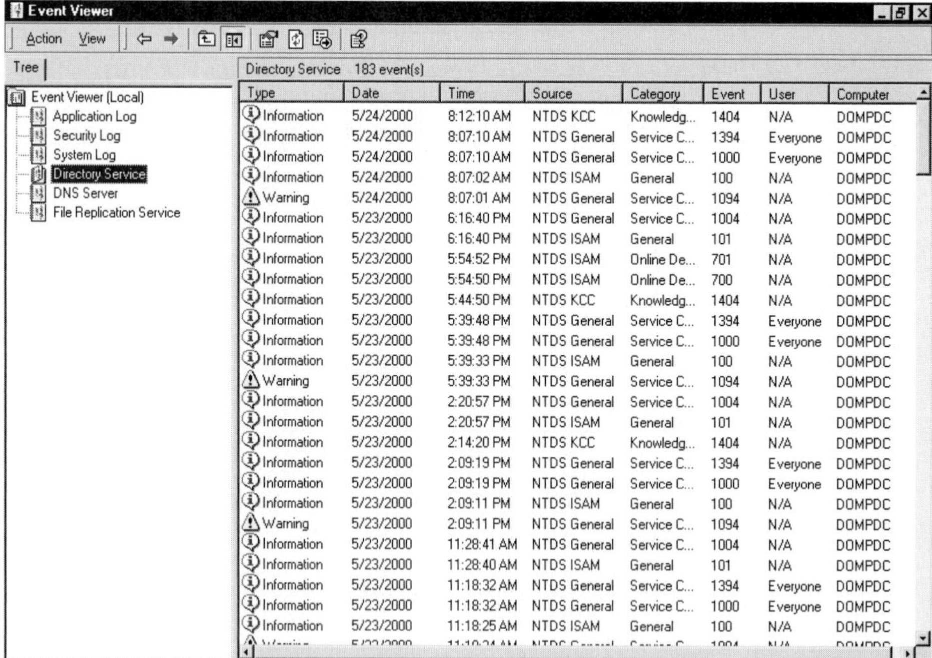

If you have more than one domain controller on the network, each participating in Active Directory data replication, the File Replication System logs give you details of events that occur during replication. The event logs enable you to understand each event as it happens on the domain controller and help you diagnose the problems quickly.

Performance Counters

The Performance console gives a real-time analysis of domain controller performance. You can configure the Performance console by adding only those counters that you want to monitor. You can also monitor performance of the remote domain controllers.

There are two snap-ins within the Performance console. These are System Monitor and Performance Logs and Alerts. The System Monitor snap-in is used to monitor system performance by adding counters for specific objects. The Performance Logs and Alerts snap-in allows you to create counter logs, trace logs, and system alerts.

The monitored events can be saved in log files. For example, you can configure some Active Directory counters to monitor a particular domain controller, set the intervals for monitoring events, and configure the System Monitor to save the results in a file. You can analyze this file later to find any problems with the Active Directory services.

System Monitor The System Monitor snap-in enables you to view, collect, and print real-time performance data on selected performance counters. You can view performance for local as well as remote domain controllers. The formats available for viewing data are graph, histogram, or report. A previously saved performance log file can also be viewed. The Active Directory performance counters are included in the System Monitor snap-in. Figure 6-7 shows the System Monitor with counters selected from NTDS, which refer to Active Directory and Processor objects.

You can configure the System Monitor to display Active Directory data by selecting the performance objects and counters available for that object. The source of data can be the local or any remote domain controller on the network. The System Monitor enables you to collect samples of data by specifying time intervals. The System Monitor view can also be configured to display any specified colors, fonts, or characteristics.

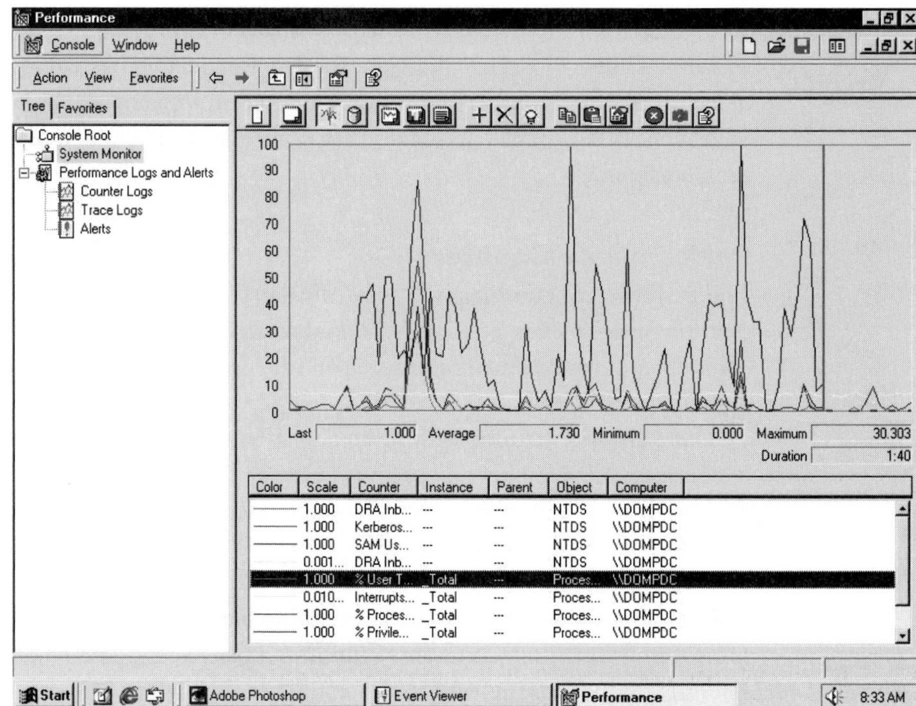

FIGURE 6-7 The System Monitor snap-in of the Performance console

When you open the Performance console from the Administrative Tools menu, by default no objects or counters are selected. You must select objects and specific counters for that object that have to be monitored. The Active Directory object that concerns us while monitoring a domain controller is NTDS. Before you can get any useful statistics from the System Monitor, you must decide on what objects and counters to monitor.

Under any specified object are three types of counters of importance:

- **Statistics counters.** These counters show the totals per second for the specific counter.
- **Ratio counters.** These counters show the percentage of the total.
- **Accumulative counters.** These counters show the accumulated total since Active Directory was last started.

As discussed earlier, the NTDS object contains counters for monitoring Active Directory performance. The counters of special interest are those that start with DRA Inbound and DRA Outbound names. Other counters are those with DS, LDAP, NTLM, and XDS client sessions. You can add the counters that you want to monitor from the System Monitor snap-in. In addition to NTDS object counters, the DNS and Processor object counters must also be monitored to keep watch on overall performance.

Exercise 6-10 will help you understand the Active Directory performance-monitoring procedure.

exam watch

If you want to monitor Active Directory performance on a remote computer, ensure that you have administrative privileges on that computer.

EXERCISE 6-10

Monitoring Active Directory Performance

1. Log on to the domain controller with administrative privileges.
2. Choose Start | Programs | Administrative Tools and select Performance. This action opens an empty Performance console
3. Click System Monitor. Notice that the right-side pane of the console shows nothing.
4. Right-click the free area in the right-side results pane. Select Add Counters from the menu that appears.
5. The Add Counters dialog box appears. Select the computer from which you want to collect performance data. You can choose the local computer or a remote computer.
6. Select NTDS in the Performance Objects box. Click the Explain button to open another box that explains the purpose of the selected counter. The

counters for NTDS objects are displayed in the "Select counters from list" box, as shown in the following illustrations.

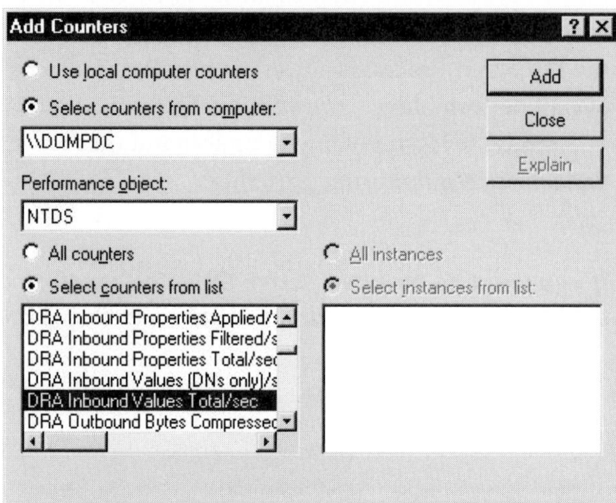

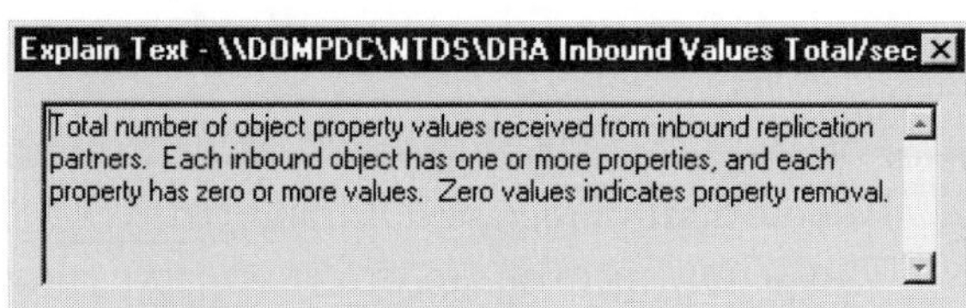

7. You can click the Select All Counters button if you want to monitor all counters from the NTDS object. Otherwise, skip to the next step.
8. Click Add. You can add as many counters as you want. Click Close to close the Add Counters dialog box.
9. Notice that the console has started collecting and displaying a graph of the data for the selected counters. The selected counters appear in the box on the bottom of the console. Refer back to Figure 6-7 for a view of the console after adding counters.
10. Close the Performance console.

Performance Logs and Alerts The Performance Logs and Alerts snap-in is used to create counter logs, trace logs, and system alerts. You must have Full Control permissions on the following registry key for creating or modifying these logs:

```
HKEY_LOCAL_MACHINE\System\CurrentControlSet\Services\SysmonLog\Log Queries
```

The Security menu from the registry editor can be used to grant these permissions to other users. Administrators have these rights by default.

Counter logs enable you to specify counters that you want to collect and save to a file. These logs can also be exported to a spreadsheet or a database application. The database program can read these logs because they are written in tab-separated format. Interpreting the data collected by trace logs requires special tools.

With both counter and trace logs, you can set the start and stop times, name of the file, file size, and other parameters for creation of logs. The logging can also be scheduled for a specific time slot. The logs can be viewed during the time the data is collected or after the data collection is complete. Figure 6-8 shows the Log Files tab of the Counter Log dialog box of the counters log. You can schedule the log data collection from the Schedule tab.

FIGURE 6-8

The Log Files tab of the counter log

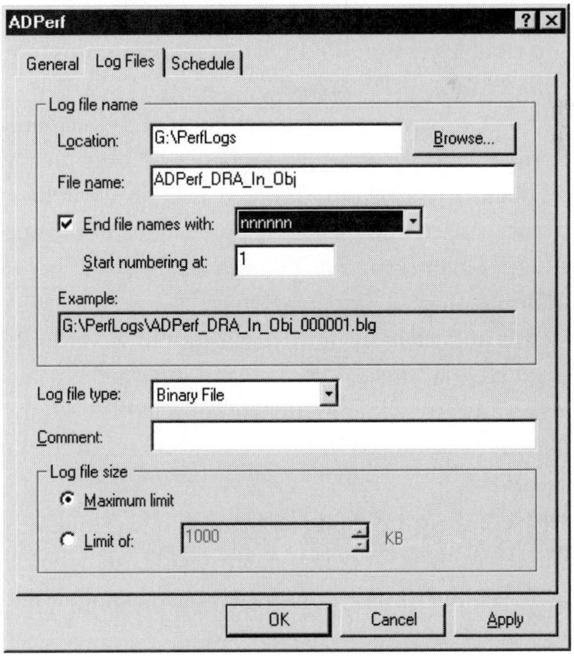

Performance alerts enable you to monitor hardware and system services for specified periods of time. Alerts use the performance objects and counters to scan the collected data. When a specified performance threshold, such as percentage processor time, is reached, an alert can be sent to a designated computer on the network and an event is written to the application event log. Alert scans can either be run manually or configured to run automatically.

Monitoring, Maintaining, and Troubleshooting Active Directory Components

Some Active Directory components need consistent monitoring of performance and error messages generated by them. This section of the chapter deals with monitoring, maintaining, and troubleshooting services such as DNS service and schema.

Domain Name Service

DNS is one of the most important components of Active Directory. All domain-related functions are dependent on proper configuration and maintenance of DNS. Windows 2000 Server comes with built-in tools for monitoring, maintaining, and troubleshooting DNS. As an administrator, you should be familiar with all maintenance tools available.

The DNS events are written to the DNS server log, which is stored separately from other applications and services running on a Windows 2000 server. You might recall that these logs are classified as DNS server logs under the Event Viewer console. Events written in these logs are predefined in the operating system. Figure 6-9 shows a DNS server event log. You can double-click any event log name to get detailed information on a particular event.

It is important to note that the DNS server in the Event Viewer keeps a history of only DNS server-related events. The client-related DNS events go to the system logs, and these client events are collected from only Windows 2000 clients. The DNS logs are stored in the file DNS.LOG in the \Systemroot\System32\Dns folder.

DNS Debug Logging Options There are several logging options for a Windows 2000 DNS server. By default, all debug logging options are disabled for reasons of DNS server performance. Enabling all debug logging options puts a significant load on the DNS server.

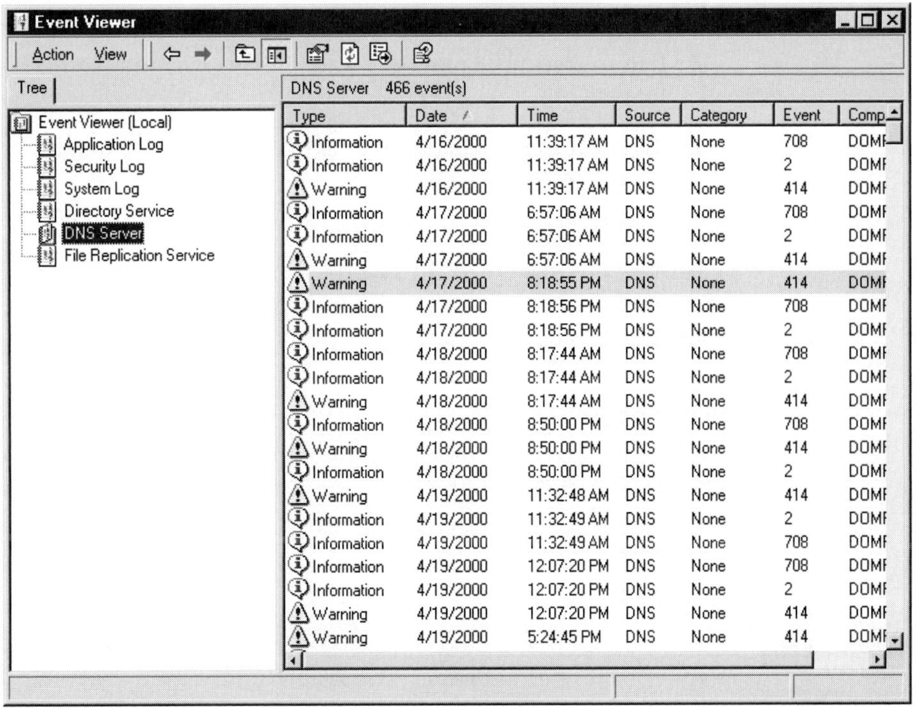

FIGURE 6-9 DNS server events in the Event Viewer

You can set any number of debug logging options from the DNS console. Open the DNS console from the Administrative Tools menu, select the DNS server from the console root, and open its Properties sheet. Click the Logging tab and select the debug options, as shown in Figure 6-10. Click OK.

The following is the description of the debug logging options:

- **Query.** The queries sent by the clients to the DNS server.
- **Notify.** Notification received by the DNS server from other servers.
- **Update.** A record of DNS updates received from other servers.
- **Questions.** Contents of the questions section of a DNS query.
- **Answers.** Contents of the answers section of a DNS query.
- **Send.** The number of DNS query messages sent by the DNS server.
- **Receive.** The number of DNS query messages received by the DNS server.
- **UDP.** The number of DNS requests received on the UDP port.

- **TCP.** The number of DNS requests received on the TCP port.
- **Full packets.** The number of full packets sent and received by the DNS server.
- **Write-through.** The number of packets written through by the DNS server back to the DNS zone.

Troubleshooting Domain Name Service You could experience problems in the DNS if the DNS on the master or secondary servers is stopped. There might be problems if the DNS zone is paused on any of these servers. Network connectivity among DNS servers can also cause DNS update problems. You can use the PING command to verify connectivity.

Whenever you experience problems with DNS, the first thing you should check is the DNS server logs in the Event Viewer. Any warning or error entry in the log must be examined carefully so that you can discover the cause of the problem and

FIGURE 6-10

Selecting DNS debug logging options

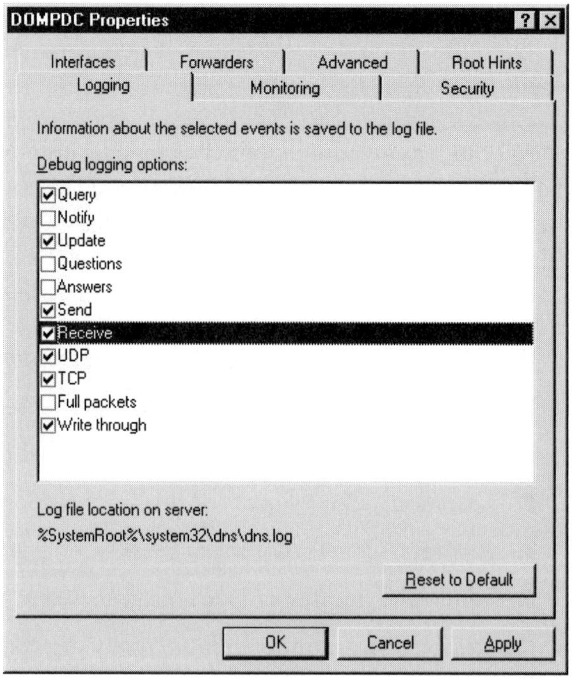

find a resolution. In case the Event Viewer console is not helpful in diagnosing the DNS server problem, you could monitor DNS counters in the Performance console.

Schema

Schema reside at the center of Active Directory. Schema store information about the types of objects that you can create in Active Directory and their location. There is only a single schema in one forest. *Classes* and *attributes* are two types of schema subsets. Several classes and attributes are included in schema by default. Maintenance of schema requires you to make modifications to schema classes and attributes.

The domain controller hosting the schema operations master role keeps the master copy of schema. All modifications are made on this domain controller. There are at least two copies of schema in the forest. The domain controller that hosts the schema master replicates the changes in schema to other domain controllers after a default five-minute interval.

Modifications in schema allow you to extend the types of objects and the information that can be stored for each object in the directory. By default, the schema console is not included in the Active Directory administration tools.

Note that once an attribute has been added, it can never be deleted. You can, however, disable the attribute. The disabled attribute cannot be added to any class. The same rule applies to classes; once a class is created, it cannot be deleted, but it can be disabled. A disabled class is replicated in the domain. Hence, proper planning is a must for any modifications in schema.

We must also mention here that if you ever need to merge two forests, both of them must have identical schema. Forest mergers are seldom required, but due to business expansion, companies do merge to form a larger organization. This change might require modifications in the existing schema.

Adding and Modifying Attributes A new attribute is required when you need to extend the attributes used by an existing class. A new attribute is also needed when you want to add a new class. Before you extend the Active Directory schema, however, you must have a unique object ID (OID) for each object you want to create.

Schema attributes can be added from the Active Directory Schema console. Exercise 6-11 explains the steps.

EXERCISE 6-11

Adding a New Schema Attribute

1. Log on to the domain controller with domain administrative privileges.
2. Choose Start | Programs | Administrative Tools and select Active Directory Schema.
3. Right-click Attributes in the left-side pane and select Create Attribute.
4. A warning message is displayed, telling you that if you add a new attribute, you will not be able to delete it. Click Continue.
5. The Create New Attribute dialog box appears, as shown in the following illustration.

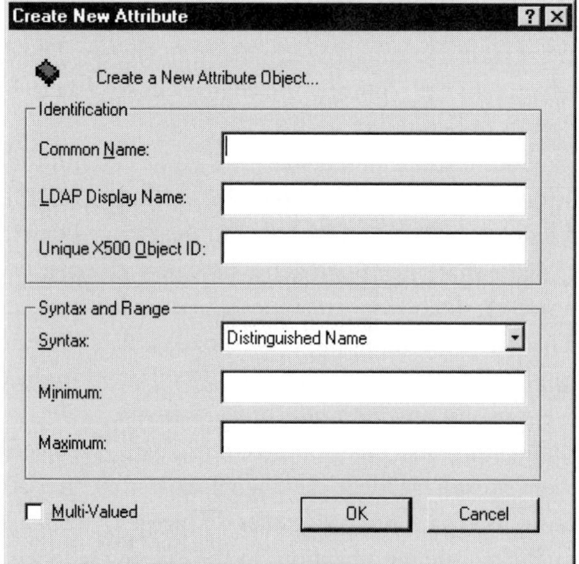

6. Fill in the required information—Common Name, LDAP Directory, Unique X500 Object ID—and set the minimum and maximum range values.
7. Click OK. Close the Active Directory Schema console.

Modifications in schema attributes are required when you have to change the syntax and range, for indexing the attribute, to include the attribute in the global catalog, or to change the description of an object. To modify an existing attribute, open the Active Directory Schema console and select the attribute you want to modify. Right-click the attribute and select Properties. Here you can make any changes that are required.

Adding and Modifying Classes Every object in Active Directory is an instance of *class*. Several classes are included in the schema by default. Each class is defined by the set of attributes used by that class. A new class is added when no existing class meets your requirements. An existing class can also be modified.

The addition and modification of schema classes is done from the Active Directory Schema console. Exercise 6-12 explains how to add a new class.

Modifications in an existing class are required when you need to add one or more mandatory or optional attributes to the class. You can add an existing attribute in the class or remove any existing attribute. An attribute or class that you create in Active Directory Schema can never be deleted, but it can be deactivated. A *deactivated class* is no longer replicated to other domain controllers. It is not possible to create new objects in a class that has been deactivated. Similarly, a deactivated attribute cannot be added to any class. A class that has been deactivated can be activated again at any time.

exam Watch

Once you add an attribute or a class to the schema, it can never be deleted. You can, however, deactivate it. A deactivated class is never replicated to other domain controllers. A deactivated attribute cannot be added to a class.

Additional Tools for Active Directory Support

The Windows 2000 Server CD-ROM contains several tools that can help you monitor, manage, and maintain Active Directory. These tools are optional and are not installed by default. To install these tools, run SETUP.EXE file from the \Support\Tools folder of the Windows 2000 Server CD-ROM. This installation adds a Resource Kit folder in the \Systemroot\Program Files directory.

EXERCISE 6-12

Adding a New Schema Class

1. Log on to the domain controller with domain administrative privileges.
2. Choose Start | Programs | Administrative Tools and select Active Directory Schema.
3. Right-click Classes in the left-side pane and select Create Class.
4. A warning message is displayed, telling you that if you add a new class, you will not be able to delete it. Click Continue.
5. The Create New Schema Class dialog box appears, as shown in the following illustration.

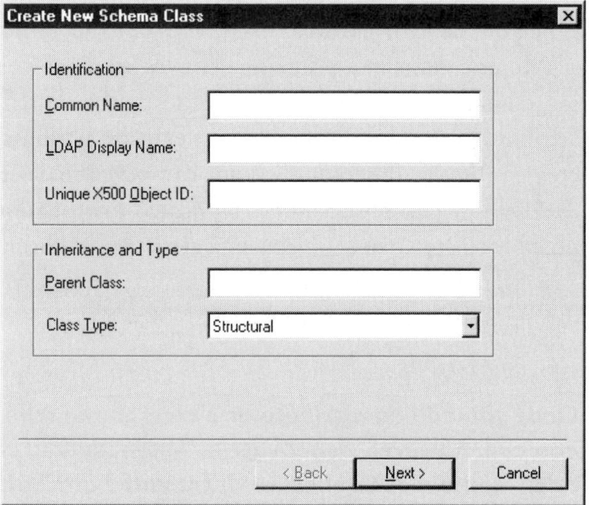

6. Fill in the required information, including Common Name, LDAP Display, Unique X500 Object ID, and Parent Class. Select Class type.
7. Click Next. The Attributes window appears. Click Add in the Mandatory section.
8. Highlight the displayed attribute in the list. Click OK.
9. Notice that an OID for the new class is listed. Click Finish.
10. Close the Active Directory Schema console.

The following tools are installed; they can be helpful in maintaining Active Directory components:

- **LDP.** This is the Active Directory Administration tool that is helpful in carrying out Lightweight Active Directory Protocol (LDAP) operations.
- **REPLMON.** This tool is used to monitor replication of Active Directory. It can also force a synchronization between various domain controllers on the network
- **REPADMIN.** This tool is used to diagnose replication problems in Windows 2000 domain controllers. REPADMIN is a command-line tool.
- **DSASTAT:** DSASAT is another command-line tool; it is used to compare and detect differences between naming contexts on domain controllers.
- **SDCHECK:** This command-line tool shows the security descriptor for any selected object in Active Directory. In other words, this tool shows the ACL for the selected object.
- **NLTEST.** NLTEST is a command-line tool that tests and forces synchronization of trust relationships. It can also be used to force shutdown of a Windows 2000 domain controller.
- **ACLDIAG.** ACLDIAG is used to diagnose problems with permissions set on Active Directory objects.
- **DSACLS.** DSACLS is used to view and change security permissions on AD objects (command line only.)

on the Job

The additional Active Directory tools discussed here are advanced-level tools and must be used with caution. Microsoft has included these tools on the Windows 2000 setup CD-ROM for use by its support personnel and experienced administrators.

CERTIFICATION SUMMARY

The built-in management features of Windows 2000 Active Directory enable administrators to efficiently maintain a Windows 2000 network. Active Directory maintenance includes tasks such as creating, configuring, monitoring, and troubleshooting its components. The Active Directory administrative consoles provide the administrator a centralized location to perform these functions.

Active Directory objects such as servers, users, and computers can be moved within a domain or across domains. Movement of objects can be required due to changes in the organization or network maintenance. The MOVETREE command is used to move objects from one domain to another, with certain restrictions. Users, computers, shared folders, and printers are published in Active Directory from the Users and Computers console. The network resources that are published in Active Directory can be located using the Find option.

Accounts are created in Active Directory manually using the Users and Computers console. Scripts can also be written to create accounts; this method requires knowledge of a scripting language. Access to AD objects is configured by setting permissions, which work like standard NTFS permissions. The Delegation of Control Wizard is used to delegate control of objects to other users to reduce administrative burdens.

Active Directory performance is monitored from the Performance console. Performance Monitor has two snap-ins: System Monitor and Performance Logs and Alerts. Counters related to AD are located under the NTDS object in the System Monitor. Network performance can be monitored on a real-time basis, or you can create a schedule to record performance events to a log file. The Event Viewer console is used to trace events on the domain controller. It contains logs for applications, security, system, directory service, DNS, and file replication. DNS server events are recorded in a DNS.LOG file that is separate from other system and application logs. DNS.LOG is the place to check DNS server-related events in case of a problem.

Schema modifications are done from the Active Directory Schema console. New classes and attributes can be added but cannot be deleted. Classes and attributes can be modified and deactivated. Deactivated classes are not replicated to other domain controllers. Deactivated attributes cannot be added to any class.

TWO-MINUTE DRILL

Managing AD Objects

- Managing Active Directory includes tasks such as creating, moving, and removing objects as well as troubleshooting problems with AD components.
- Active Directory objects can be moved from one container to another within and across domains. Users or computers need to be moved within or between domains due to changing requirements of an organization.
- The MOVETREE command is used to move objects from one domain to another. When moving objects between domains, you must have sufficient permissions to complete the move operation.
- Network resources such as users, computers, shared folders, and printers are published in AD using the Users and Computers console. Only non-Windows 2000 printers need to be published.

Managing Active Directory Performance

- The Performance console is used to monitor domain controller performance. It has two snap-ins: System Monitor and Performance Logs and Alerts. You can monitor performance on a local or a remote computer.
- Active Directory performance counters are located under the NTDS object in the System Monitor snap-in of the Performance console. You can perform real-time monitoring of Active Directory performance or schedule it and save the results in a log file.
- Care must be taken while running the Performance console because it can put a significant load on system resources. You should add only counters that are absolutely necessary.
- The DNS server has debug logging options that are disabled by default. To troubleshoot a DNS server, use the DNS console to enable debug counters. The log file is named DNS.LOG.

MCSE

MICROSOFT CERTIFIED SYSTEMS ENGINEER

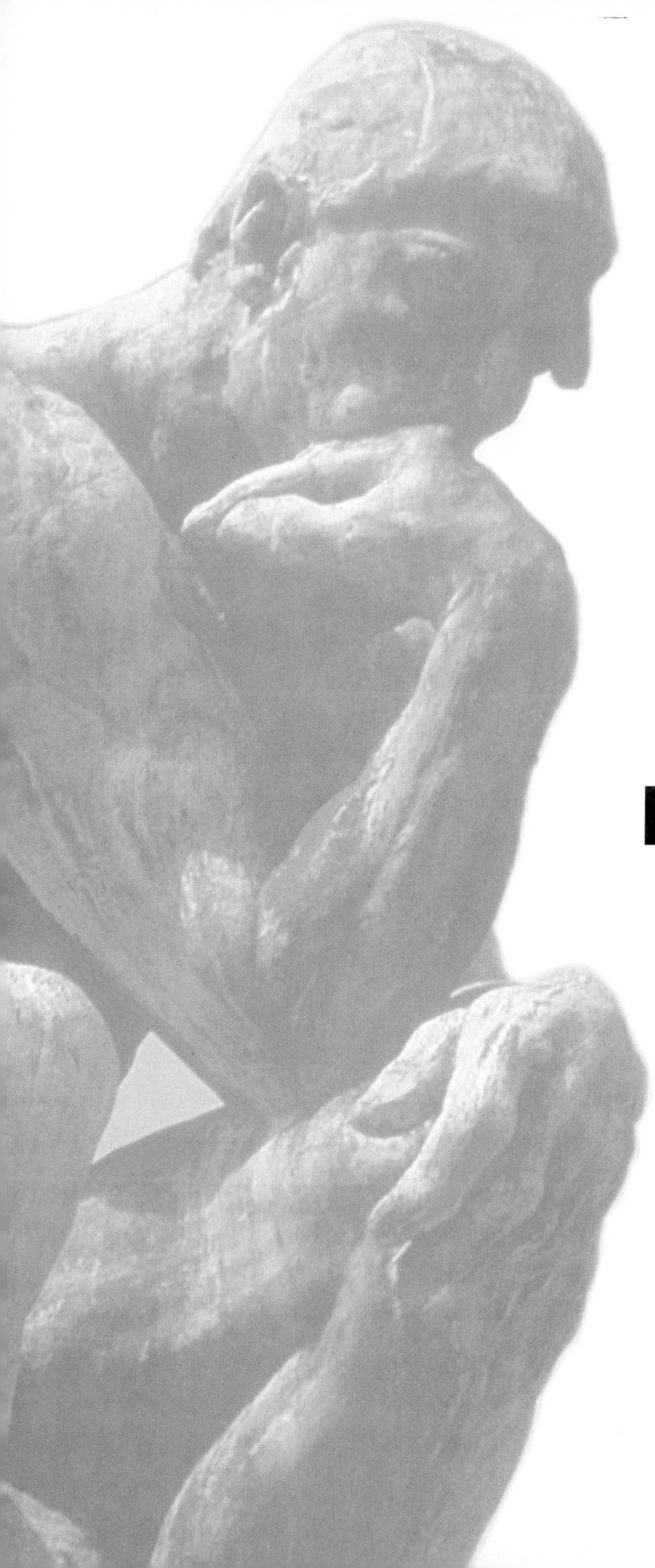

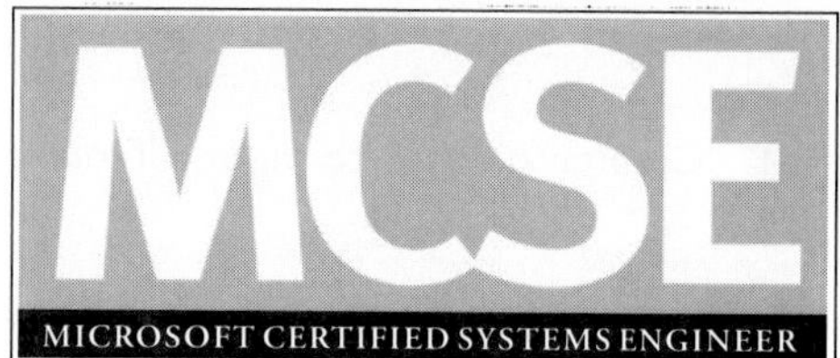

7

Monitoring and Troubleshooting Active Directory

CERTIFICATION OBJECTIVES

7.01 Backing Up and Restoring Active Directory

✓ Two-Minute Drill

This chapter explains the backup and restore procedures for Active Directory. This important chapter introduces you to the Backup Wizard and the Restore Wizard. You will learn about NTBACKUP options and the NTDSUTIL utility. This chapter also introduces you to the components that make up Active Directory (AD).

CERTIFICATION OBJECTIVE 7.01

Backing Up and Restoring Active Directory

One of the most important tasks of a Windows 2000 network administrator is performing system backups. Unfortunately, this task is underrated and sometimes overlooked by many network administrators. Priority is usually given to other, more visible activities such as upgrades to software that impacts end users. Backup solutions and backup problems are postponed until higher-priority activities are complete. This is not smart administration! Nobody cares about backups until they need a restore. So, if you value your job, perform regular backups, do a restore to save the day, and be a hero in the eyes of upper management. Otherwise, the only hero you will be is the guy flipping burgers for satisfied customers.

Components and Files that Make Up AD

One of the most important backups you can perform in a Windows 2000 environment is a backup of Active Directory. The importance of AD stems from the abundance of network resources stored within it. These resources, or *objects,* consist of user data, groups, servers, databases, printers, services, computers, and security policies. If AD became corrupt, users might not be able to log on and gain access to printers, servers, and other network resources.

Architecture

Active Directory uses a layered architecture to provide directory services to client applications. The AD architecture consists of three primary services layers and the data store. Above the three services layers are the protocols and application programming interfaces (APIs) that allow clients to interface with directory services. Figure 7-1 shows the Active Directory architecture.

FIGURE 7-1

Active Directory architecture

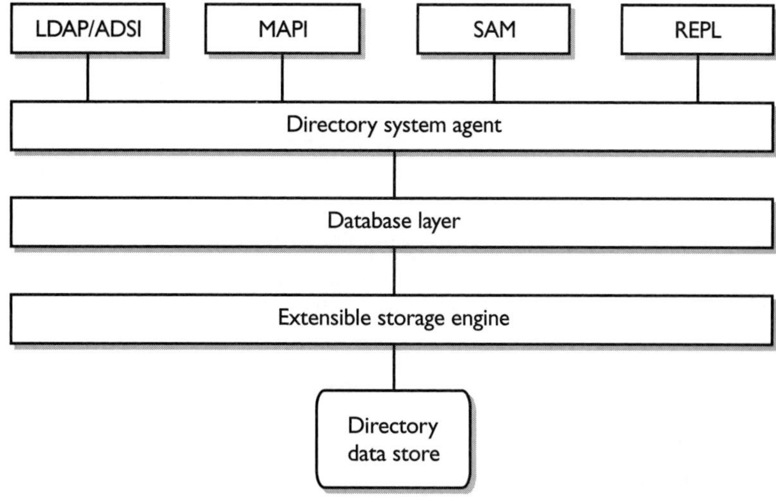

The three primary service layers are as follows:

- Directory System Agent (DSA)
- Database Layer
- Extensible Storage Engine (ESE)

The protocols and APIs for client directory services are:

- LDAP/ADSI
- Messaging API (MAPI)
- Security Accounts Manager (SAM)
- Replication (REPL)

Directory System Agent The *DSA service layer* builds a hierarchical structure from the parent/child relationships stored in the directory. This layer provides the APIs necessary for directory access calls. Without this layer, for example, clients using LDAP would not be able to gain access to directory services.

Database Layer The *database layer* provides an interface between client applications and the directory database. This layer prevents client applications from directly accessing the directory database. All application calls must first pass through the database layer. This system prevents bad application calls from adversely impacting the directory database.

Extensible Storage Engine (ESE) The *Extensible Storage Engine (ESE)* sits between the database layer and the directory data store. It directly accesses individual records in the directory data store based on the relative distinguished name attribute of the object. This is the only layer that directly manipulates the directory data store. The directory data store is located in the \<systemroot>\NTDS folder in a file called NTDS.DIT. This file can be administered with the NTDSUTIL tool on the domain controller. (The NTDSUTIL tool is discussed later in this chapter.) A file named ESENT.DLL is the dynamic link library (DLL) file that controls the ESE. Each request to the DSA is treated as an individual transaction and is recorded to log files associated with the NTDS.DIT file on the domain controller. This means that whenever a user, printer, or server object is added, deleted, or modified, ESE appends an entry to a log file.

LDAP/ADSI Clients that support LDAP use it to gain access to the DSA. Windows 2000 clients use LDAP, as do Windows 98 and Windows 95 clients with the Active Directory client installed. *LDAP*, or *Lightweight Directory Access Protocol,* is the primary directory access protocol for manipulation of Active Directory information. It defines how directory clients can access a directory server, perform directory operations, and share directory data. The LDAP protocol is used to add, modify, and delete Active Directory information. LDAP is also used to request and retrieve data from Active Directory. Versions 2 and 3 of LDAP are supported by Windows 2000 Active Directory. You can find more information about the two LDAP versions in RFC 1777 for LDAP version 2 and RFC 2251 for LDAP version 3.

ADSI, or *Active Directory Service Interface,* is an API that can be used to access information in Active Directory. The ADSI API set is accessed with programming environments such as Microsoft Visual Basic and Microsoft Visual C++. ADSI allows programmers to design applications that manipulate objects in Active Directory.

Messaging API (MAPI) *Messaging API,* or *MAPI,* is an API set that is used by applications such as Microsoft Outlook and Microsoft Exchange to send and receive e-mail. MAPI clients connect to the DSA using the MAPI remote procedure call (RPC) address book provider interface. Similar to ADSI, the MAPI API set can be used with programming environments such as Microsoft Visual Basic and Microsoft Visual C++. This flexibility allows programmers to design applications that integrate messaging services with Active Directory objects such as users and groups, for example.

Security Accounts Manager (SAM) The *SAM*, or *Security Accounts Manager*, is used to authenticate users during login. The SAM is used only by Windows NT 4.0 and earlier clients to gain access to the DSA. In comparison, Windows 2000 clients use LDAP to gain access to the DSA. Additionally, SAM is also used to replicate to and from Windows NT domain controllers in a mixed-mode Active Directory.

Replication (REPL) *REPL*, or *replication*, is the process that replicates DSA data between domain controllers. When replication occurs, Active Directory DSAs connect to one another using a proprietary RPC. This RPC is the replication transport between DSAs on domain controllers.

Components

Active Directory allows company resources to be accessible from a central and logical location, regardless of physical location. The logical components that make up AD are:

- Domains
- Organizational units (OUs)
- Trees
- Forests

These components relate to each other in a hierarchical manner.

Domains Administrators of previous Windows operating systems such as Windows NT 4.0 will be familiar with the concept of *domains*. In Active Directory, the domain is the core unit of logical structure. A domain can store literally millions of directory objects, including users, printers, documents, and other network resources. A domain contains only information about objects within it. A domain does not contain information about objects within other domains.

Organizational Units *Organizational units,* or *OUs,* provide a method for subdividing domains into smaller, more manageable pieces. This manageability is achieved by organizing directory objects within a domain into logical groups that are parallel to the functional or business structure of your organization.

Objects that can be contained in an OU are users, groups, printers, file shares, computers, and even other OUs from the same domain. OUs are helpful when you want to delegate administrative responsibility to specific areas of Active Directory. For example, the sales department of your organization might have its own network administrator. Let's assume that the user accounts and sales resources are located in an OU named SALES. The enterprise network administrator could assign administrative authority to the sales network administrator for the SALES OU. This means the sales network administrator would only have administrative control over directory objects for which he or she was responsible.

Trees *Trees* further organize AD by grouping Windows 2000 domains together. To better organize trees, Windows 2000 domains use DNS as the naming system to facilitate a true domain hierarchy. The logical structure of a tree is actually an upside-down tree. In other words, the root is at the top, with the leaves at the bottom. The first domain created is normally the *root,* or *parent domain,* of the tree. For example, corbus-systems.com is the parent domain of Corbus Systems, Inc. Additional domains underneath the root are considered *leaves,* or *child domains.* An example of a child domain at Corbus Systems, Inc., is detroit.corbus-systems.com. Notice that the parent domain name is appended at the end of the child domain name. However, the relative domain name of the child domain is simply detroit. All child domains append the parent domain name to their relative domain name.

All domains within a specific tree share the following:

- **Common schema.** Define object types that can be stored within Active Directory.
- **Global catalog.** Central repository of object information in the Active Directory tree.

Forests *Forests* further organize AD by grouping Windows 2000 trees together. Forests can contain multiple AD trees. This is helpful when multiple parent domains need to be created or a company merger takes place. Let's say Corbus Systems, Inc., merged with ACME Corporation. Before the merger, the root of Corbus Systems, Inc., was corbus-systems.com, and the root of ACME Corporation was acme.com. Since the root, or parent, domains of the two merging companies are not contiguous, meaning they do not share a common parent domain, they cannot be added to the same tree. In this case, they both retain their individual tree structure and are added as trees to a common forest within Active Directory.

All trees within a forest share the following:

- Common schema
- Common global catalog

exam watch ***Two trees can be merged only if they share a common schema before the merge begins.***

Backing Up Active Directory Components

As you know by now, backing up Active Directory is a very important task. The objects contained within the domains, OUs, trees, and forests are the critical components that must be backed up to ensure recovery in case of Active Directory failure. But before we can attempt a backup, the following tasks must be performed:

- Make sure all files to be backed up are closed.
- Verify that your backup device is on the Windows 2000 Hardware Compatibility List (HCL).
- The backup device should be configured and powered on.
- The proper backup media are inserted properly in the backup device.
- The Task Scheduler service should be running if scheduled backups are to be performed. Otherwise, this is not necessary for backups that will run immediately.

After the preliminary tasks are performed, you can use one of the following two methods for backup:

- Backup Wizard
- NTBACKUP

In addition to the backup tools that ship with Windows 2000, third-party backup utilities such as Veritas Backup Exec 8 can be used to back up Active Directory. More third-party backup utilities will be on the market soon. Third-party utilities are usually more robust than the tools that ship with an operating system.

As companies become increasingly dependent on electronic filing, the need for solid backup procedures becomes imperative. The Windows 2000 backup system is the answer to this growing need.

The NTBACKUP command invokes the very same Backup Wizard dialog box that you get when you access it via Start | Programs | Accessories | Systems | System Tools.

The Backup Wizard

Windows 2000 improves on previous versions of Windows NT by providing a GUI-based *Backup Wizard* to simplify the backup process. This section steps you through using the Windows 2000 Backup Wizard. The next section covers the command-line backup utility NTBACKUP.

Perform the following steps when performing a backup using the Backup Wizard:

1. Log on to the appropriate domain as a user with administrative rights or in the Backup Operators group, preferably Administrator.
2. Start the Backup program by choosing Start | Programs | Accessories | System Tools | Backup.
3. At the Welcome screen, click the button that corresponds to the Backup Wizard. See Figure 7-2.
4. At the Backup Wizard Welcome screen, click Next.
5. At the What to Back Up screen (see Figure 7-3), click "Only back up the System State data." This backs up Active Directory if the server is a domain controller. In addition to AD, the system state data includes the following:
   - SYSVOL directory
   - Windows 2000 registry
   - System boot files
   - Certificate Services database
   - COM+ Class Registration database

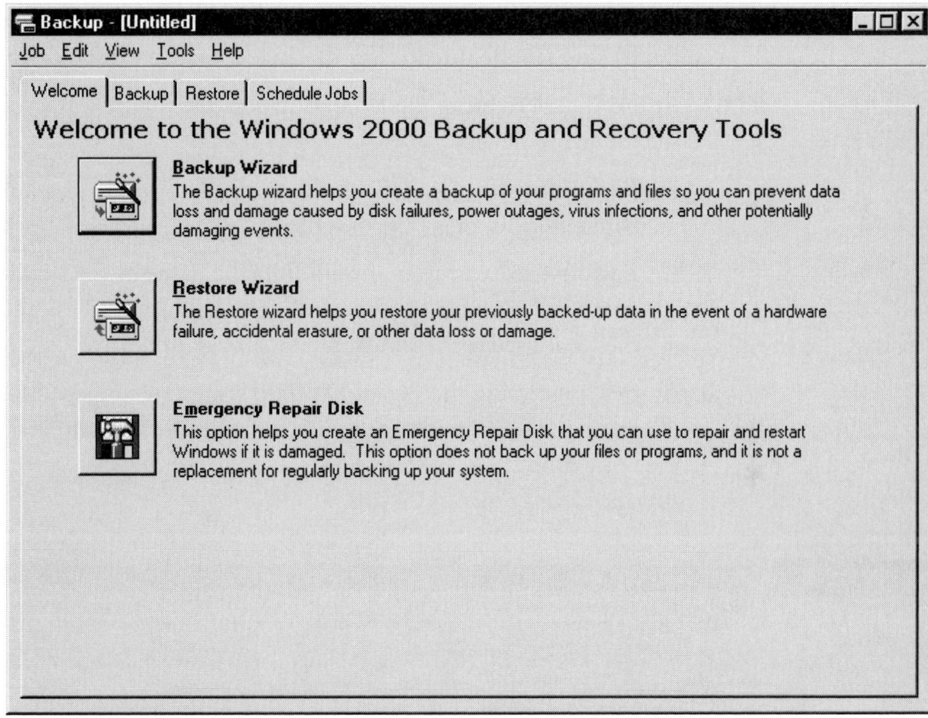

FIGURE 7-2

The Backup Wizard's main Welcome screen

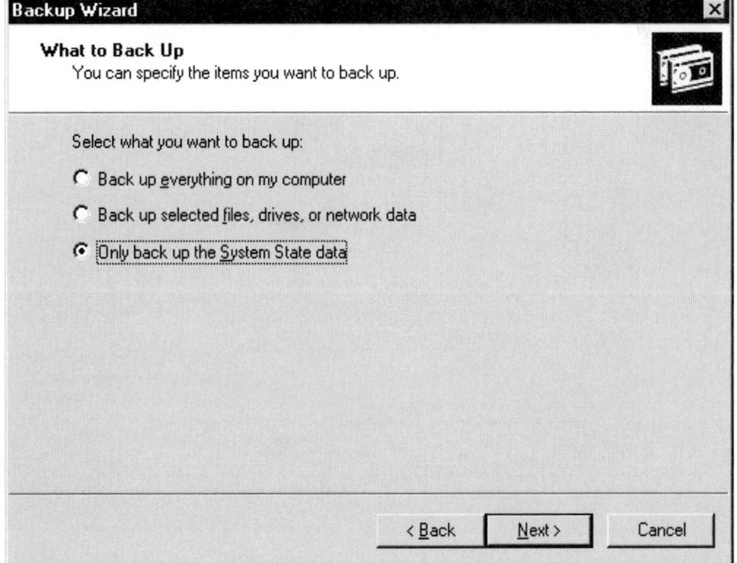

FIGURE 7-3

The What to Back Up screen

6. You also have the option of manually making your backup selections by clicking the Backup tab. Be sure to click the System State check box. See Figure 7-4.
7. At the Where to Store the Backup screen (see Figure 7-5), you must complete the following fields:
   - **Backup media type.** This is the media type of the target device. This parameter can be a tape or a file.
   - **Backup media or filename.** This is the name of the backup media or the name and path of the target backup file. Backup files can be located on the local hard disk, removable disk, or shared drive.
8. At the Completing the Backup Wizard screen (see Figure 7-6), click Finish to complete the backup job configuration with the default parameters and skip the remaining steps. If you want to change the default parameters, click Advanced and proceed to Step 9.

FIGURE 7-4

The manual backup selection screen

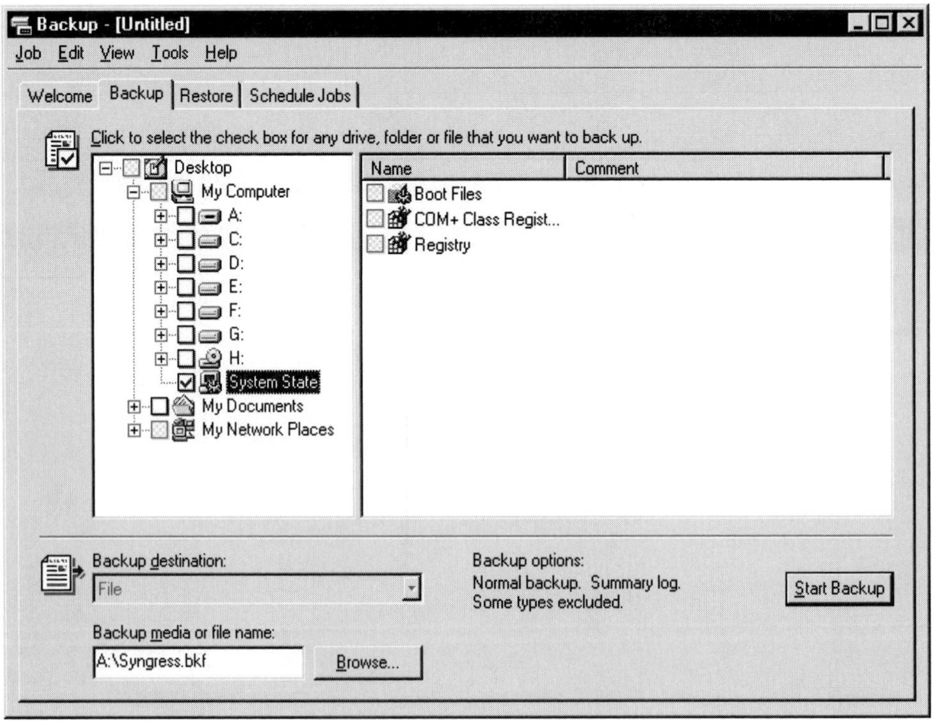

FIGURE 7-5

Where to Store the Backup screen

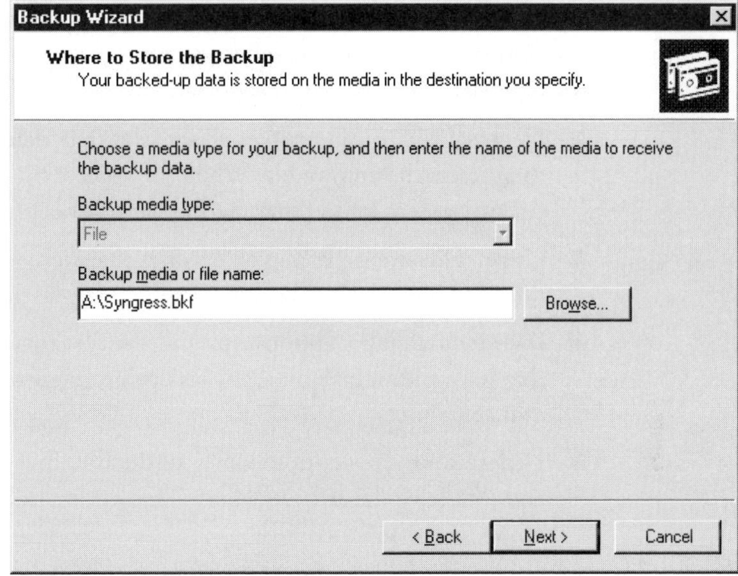

FIGURE 7-6

The Completing the Backup Wizard screen

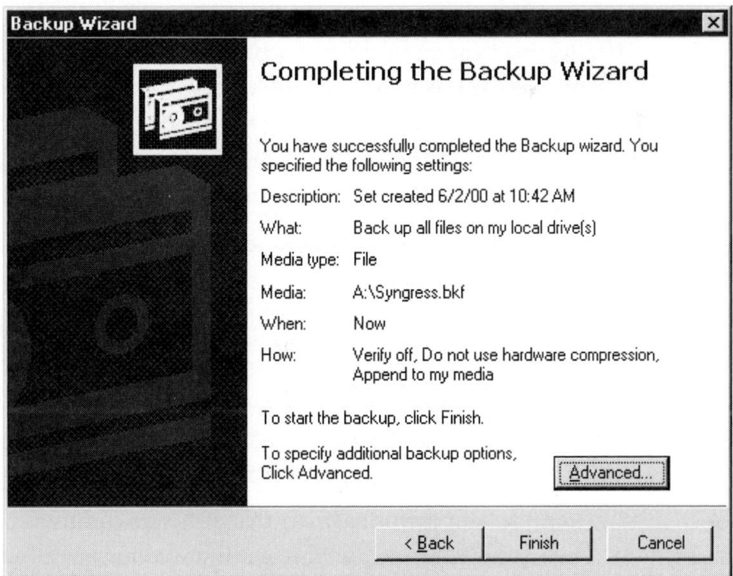

9. At the Type of Backup screen, select the type of backup operation to be performed for the job. The following list defines the backup types available for selection:
   - **Normal.** This option copies all the files that were selected for backup and then resets the archive bit. When the archive bit of a file has been set, the backup system knows that the file has just been created or modified.
   - **Copy.** This option copies all the files that were selected for backup but does not reset the archive bit.
   - **Incremental.** This option copies all the files that were selected for backup that have the archive bit set. This option resets the archive bit of the files that get copied.
   - **Differential.** This option copies all the files that were selected for backup and that have the archive bit set. This option does *not* reset the archive bit of the files that get copied.
   - **Daily.** This option copies all the files that were selected for backup and that were modified on the day the backup was performed. The archive bit is *not* reset.
10. At the Type of Backup screen (see Figure 7-7), you also have the option of backing up the contents of files that have migrated to remote storage. This option is selected by clicking the "Backup migrated Remote Storage data" check box. The Remote Storage Service allows infrequently used files to be archived to remote storage, thus saving valuable disk space.
11. Click Next and proceed to the How to Backup screen.
12. At the How to Backup screen, click the "Verify data after backup" check box to allow the backup system to verify the backed-up data. This option almost doubles the overall backup time. You should not select this option if you do not have a large enough backup window.
13. At the How to Back Up screen (see Figure 7-8), you can also configure the backup system to use hardware compression, if it is available. As a rule, hardware compression performs better than software compression. This option can be selected by clicking the "Use hardware compression" check box.
14. Click Next to proceed to the Media Options screen.

FIGURE 7-7

The Type of Backup screen

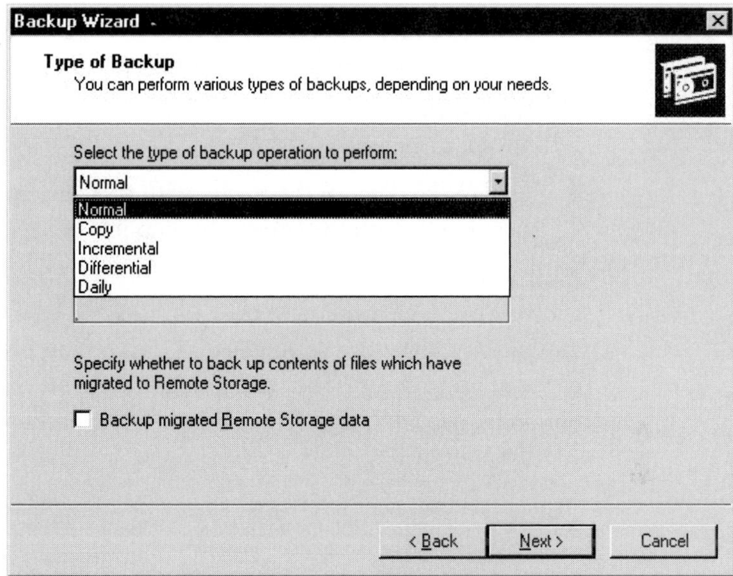

FIGURE 7-8

The How to Back Up screen

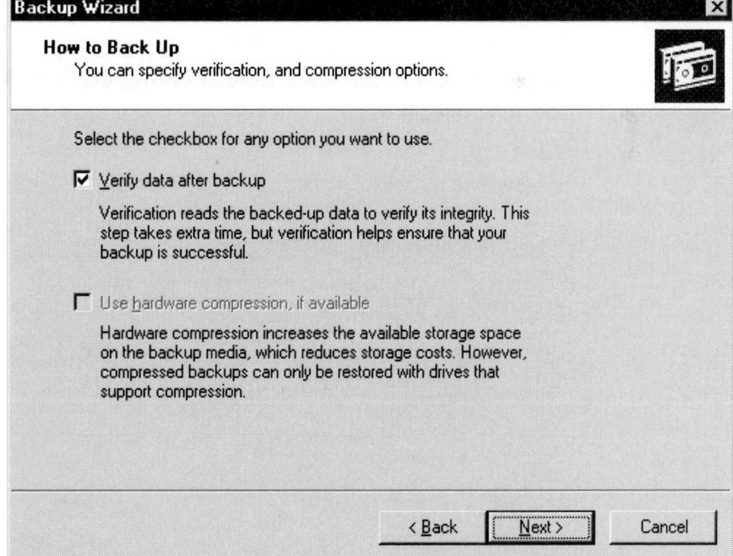

15. At the Media Options screen, you can instruct the backup system to perform one of the following actions if the archive media already contains backups:
    - **Append this backup to the media.** Allows you to have multiple backup jobs on a single tape.
    - **Replace the data on the media with this backup.** Overwrites all previous backup jobs with the current backup job.
16. Also, at the Media Options screen (see Figure 7-9), you have the option of allowing only the owner and the administrator access to the backup data and any backups appended to the media. This option is selected by clicking the corresponding check box. This option is available only when the Replace option is selected. It should be selected if the backup contains a copy of the AD/system state.
17. At the Backup Label screen (see Figure 7-10), you can provide a name for the following labels:
    - **Backup label.** Relate to individual backup jobs on a tape. There can be one or more backup labels per tape.
    - **Media label.** Relate to a whole tape. There is only one media label per tape.

FIGURE 7-9

The Media Options screen

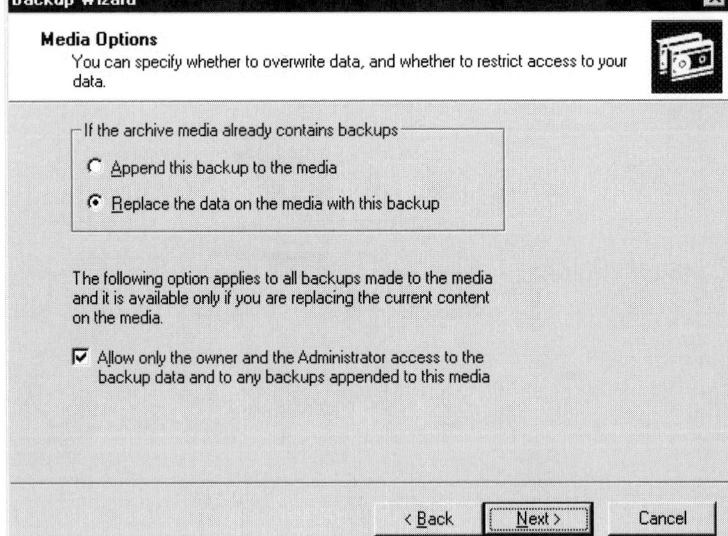

FIGURE 7-10

The Backup Label screen

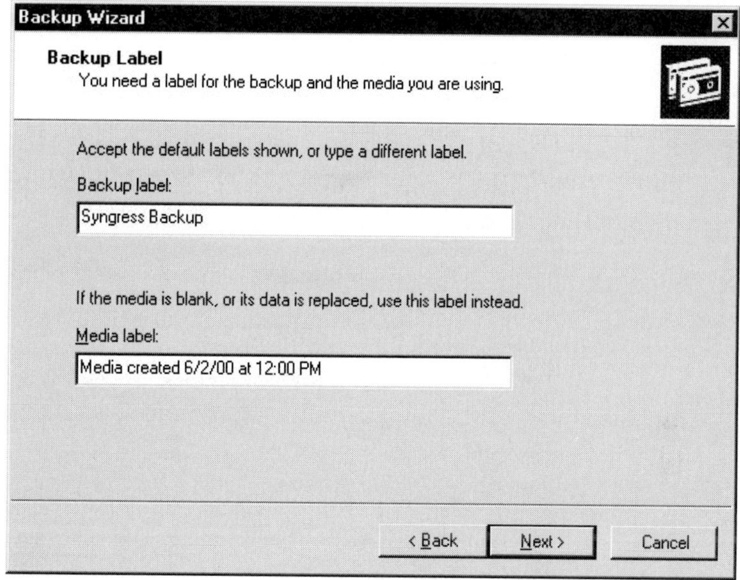

18. At the When to Back Up screen (see Figure 7-11), you are given the option to run the backup job now or schedule it to run later. To run the backup job now, select the Now option. To schedule a time for the backup job to run later, select the Later option. You are then able to configure a name and start date for the job. Click the Set Schedule button to configure the days and times for the backup job to run.
19. Finally, you are returned to the Completing the Backup Wizard screen (see Figure 7-12). If you are satisfied with the options you selected for your backup job, click Finish. If your backup job was configured to run now, it will start immediately. Otherwise, it will start when scheduled.

NTBACKUP

NTBACKUP is the command-line version of the backup system. It invokes the same (GUI) Wizard dialog box that you get when you access it via Start | Programs | Accessories | System Tools. The NTBACKUP utility has many parameters of which you should be aware. To effectively use this utility, you must review these

FIGURE 7-11

The When to Back Up screen

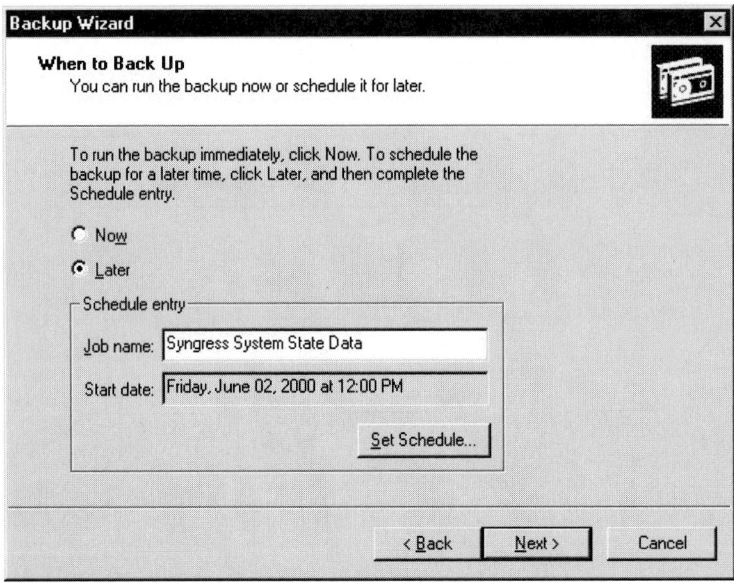

FIGURE 7-12

The final options of the Completing the Backup Wizard screen

parameters. With a good understanding of NTBACKUP, you can make powerful backup scripts using any text editor. NTBACKUP is strictly for backups. It cannot perform restores of any kind. The NTBACKUP syntax follows:

```
ntbackup backup [systemstate] "bks file name" /J {"job name"} [/P
{"pool name"}] [/G {"guid name"}] [/T { "tape name"}] [/N {"media
name"}] [/F {"file name"}] [/D {"set description"}] [/DS {"server
name"}] [/IS {"server name"}] [/A] [/V:{yes|no}] [/R:{yes|no}]
[/L:{f|s|n}] [/M {backup type}] [/RS:{yes|no}] [/HC:{on|off}]
```

Table 7-1 describes the NTBACKUP parameters.

TABLE 7-1 NTBACKUP Parameters

Parameter	Description
systemstate	Backs up the system state data.
bks file name	Specifies the name of the selection information file.
/J {"*job name*"}	Specifies the name of the backup job.
/P {"*pool name*"}	Specifies the media pool from which you want to use media. The following switches cannot be used with this option: /A /G /F /T.
/G {"*guid name*"}	Specifies the name of the tape that this job will overwrite or append to. Do not use with /P.
/T {"*tape name*"}	Specifies the name of the tape that this job will overwrite or append to. Do not use with /P.
/N {"*media name*"}	Specifies the new name of the tape. Do not use with /A.
/F {"*file name*"}	Specifies the logical disk path and filename of the file to which the backup will be copied. The following switches cannot be used with this option: /P /G /T.
/D {"*set description*"}	Specifies the label name for each backup set.
/DS {"*server name*"}	Backs up the Directory Service file of the specified Microsoft Exchange Server.
/IS {"*server name*"}	Backs up the Information Store file of the specified Microsoft Exchange Server.
/A	Instructs the backup system to perform an append operation. Either /G or /T must be used with this option. Do not use /P with this option.

TABLE 7-1

NTBACKUP Parameters *(continued)*

/V:{yes|no}	Instructs the backup system to verify files on backup media after backup.
/R:{yes|no}	Access to this backup is limited to the owner or members of the Administrators group.
/L:{f|s|n}	Specifies the type of log file to be created during the backup: f: Full (logs every copied file, errors, and other backup events) s: Summary (logs errors and important backup events) n: None (no log file is created)
/M {*backup type*}	Specifies the backup type as one of the following: Normal Copy Differential Incremental Daily
/RS:{yes|no}	Instructs the backup system to back up the removable storage database.
/HC:{on|off}	Instructs the backup system to use hardware compression.
/UM	Finds the first available medium, formats it, and uses it for the current backup operation. The following media pools are searched: Free pool, Import pool, Unrecognized pool, and Backup pool. /P must be used with this option. Not applicable to tape loaders, only stand-alone tape devices.

The following scenario questions and solutions will help you understand when to use one backup method over another.

SCENARIO & SOLUTION	
You need to create a backup job to run immediately. How do you do that?	Use the Backup Wizard.
How do you run a backup job from a script?	Use NTBACKUP.

EXERCISE 7-1

Backing Up Active Directory

The following exercise creates a Windows 2000 backup job that backs up Active Directory. The job starts immediately and stores the backup file onto the local hard drive. This exercise should not be done on a production server.

1. Log on to the domain controller as Administrator.
2. Start the backup from the Start menu.
3. At the Welcome screen, select the Backup Wizard.
4. At the Backup Wizard Welcome screen, click Next.
5. At the What to Back Up screen, click "Only back up the System State data" option.
6. At the Where to Store the Backup screen, select File as the backup media type and give it the filename **Exercise1** on the local hard drive.
7. At the Completing the Backup Wizard screen, click Finish and watch your backup job in progress.

Restoring Active Directory Components

Backups would be meaningless if you were not able to perform a restore from the backed-up data. It is a good practice to periodically perform a restore from backed-up data to verify that your data is being backed up properly. The "Verify after backup" option does not catch everything. For example, if your backup selections do not include all the data you want to be backed up, the backup system still runs without error. Remember, it is better to be safe than sorry! So perform that periodic restore and have some peace of mind.

Performing a Restore of Active Directory

Windows 2000 introduces two restore methods: authoritative and non-authoritative. These two methods will be covered shortly. Before we can perform the actual restore, we must perform the following tasks:

- Log on to the Windows 2000 domain as a member of the Backup Operators or Administrator groups.
- Verify that you can access all shares and file locations that require files to be restored.
- Verify that the medium containing the data you want restored is in the backup device.
- Verify that the Remote Storage Manager is running. This is necessary only if you are restoring from a media pool.

exam Watch

Be sure you know the difference between an authoritative restore and a non-authoritative restore.

What Is a Non-authoritative Restore?

When system state data changes on a domain controller participating in replication, it is given a higher update sequence number than the system state data of other domain controllers. Since the replicating controller's system state data has a higher update sequence number, the other domain controllers in the replication system know that it has the most up-to-date data. The system state data with the highest update sequence number in the Active Directory replication system gets replicated to the other domain controllers participating in replication.

When a non-authoritative restore is performed, the system state data that is restored maintains the same update sequence number it had when it was last backed up. In other words, the domain controller will be restored to its last backup state. So, if your backup is five days old, odds are that other domain controllers have more current system state data with higher update sequence numbers. Once entered back into the replication topology, the domain controller receives any updates made since that backup. This means that your restored data can potentially be overwritten with another domain controller's system state data. This is not an issue when there is only one domain controller, because there are no other domain controllers from which to receive replication updates.

What Is an Authoritative Restore?

What happens if Active Directory becomes corrupt? What happens if, for example, a disgruntled employee deletes an entire Active Directory tree? In such a case, the AD replication system replicates both the corrupt data and the sabotaged data. The quickest way to resolve this problem is to perform a restore. Unfortunately, a non-authoritative restore is overwritten by the unwanted system state data of other domain controllers. The solution is to perform an authoritative restore. An authoritative restore is similar to a non-authoritative restore. The main difference is that an authoritative restore modifies the update sequence number of the restored system state data to have the highest number in the Active Directory replication system. This means that the restored system state data is replicated to all the other domain controllers in the Active Directory replication system. As a result, the corruption of Active Directory is removed from domain controllers receiving the replica.

Performing a Restore

To perform an authoritative restore, you must first perform a non-authoritative restore as follows:

1. Reboot the domain controller that will have its system state data restored. System state data can be restored only on the local computer. Currently, there is no method for performing remote system state data restores.
2. At the screen that allows you to select your operating system, press the F8 key (see Figure 7-13). This brings up the Windows 2000 Advanced Options Menu.

FIGURE 7-13

The operating system selection screen

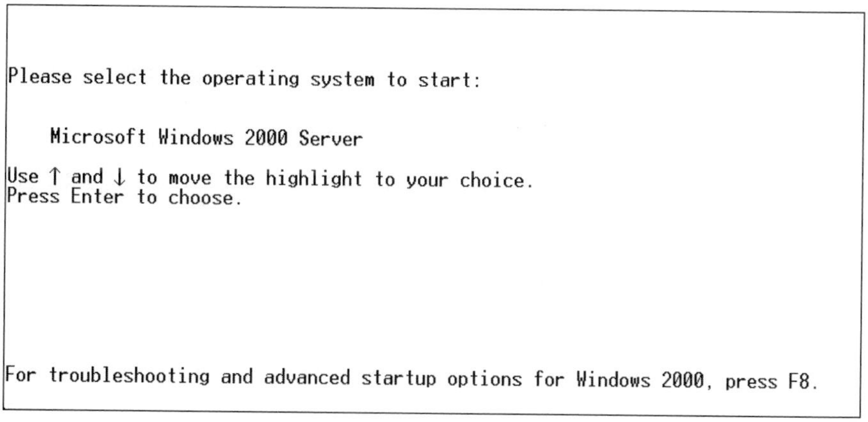

```
Please select the operating system to start:

    Microsoft Windows 2000 Server

Use ↑ and ↓ to move the highlight to your choice.
Press Enter to choose.

For troubleshooting and advanced startup options for Windows 2000, press F8.
```

3. Select Directory Services Restore Mode from the Windows 2000 Advanced Options menu. This choice prevents the domain controller from connecting to the network during the restore process. See Figure 7-14.
4. Select Microsoft Windows 2000 Server from the operating system selection screen.
5. Log on to the server as Administrator. Use the password specified during the promotion of the server to DC status, not the domain administrator password.
6. A pop-up box informs you that you are running in Safe mode. Click OK and continue.
7. Select Programs | Accessories | System Tools | Backup from the Windows 2000 Start menu.
8. Select the Restore Wizard from the Welcome to the Windows 2000 Backup and Recovery Tools screen.
9. Click Next at the Welcome to the Restore Wizard screen.
10. At the What to Restore screen (see Figure 7-15), select the media and files you want to restore and click Next.
11. Review the settings you have selected and click Advanced to modify advanced restore parameters. See Figure 7-16.

FIGURE 7-14

The Windows 2000 Advanced Options menu

```
Windows 2000 Advanced Options Menu
Please select an option:

    Safe Mode
    Safe Mode with Networking
    Safe Mode with Command Prompt

    Enable Boot Logging
    Enable VGA Mode
    Last Known Good Configuration
    Directory Services Restore Mode (Windows 2000 domain controllers only)
    Debugging Mode

Use ↑ and ↓ to move the highlight to your choice.
Press Enter to choose.


Press ESCAPE to disable safeboot and boot normally.
```

FIGURE 7-15

The What to Restore screen

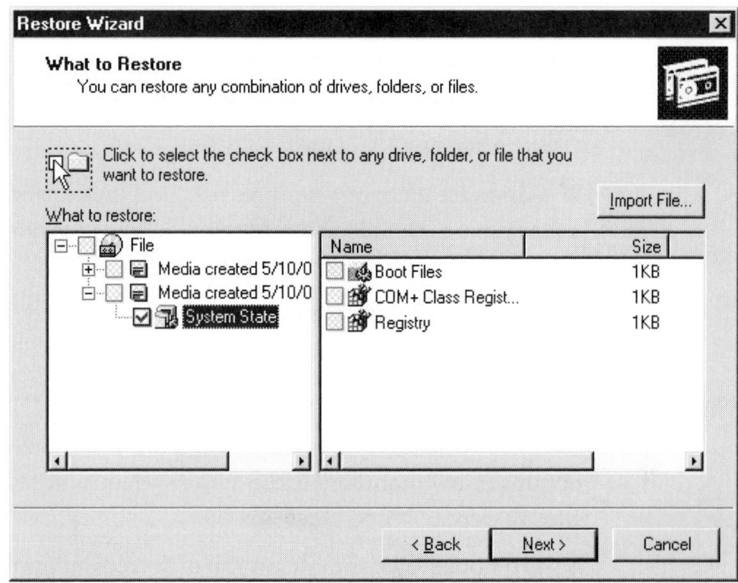

FIGURE 7-16

The Completing the Restore Wizard screen

12. At the Where to Restore screen (see Figure 7-17), select one of the following locations for the restored data:
    - **Original location.** Restores files to their original location, thus replacing corrupted or lost data.
    - **Alternate location.** Restores files to a location other than the original. Maintains the file and folder hierarchy. This option requires that a path be specified.
    - **Single folder.** Restores all files to a single folder without maintaining the file and folder hierarchy. This option requires that a path be specified.
13. Click Next and proceed to the How to Restore screen.
14. At the How to Restore screen (see Figure 7-18), select one of the following options to instruct the Backup system what to do when restoring files that already exist:
    - **Do not replace the file on my disk (recommended).** Restores any lost directory components, such as organizational units and leaf objects.
    - **Replace the file on disk only if it is older than the backup copy.** Ensures that the most recent copy of the file exists on the computer.

FIGURE 7-17

The Where to Restore screen

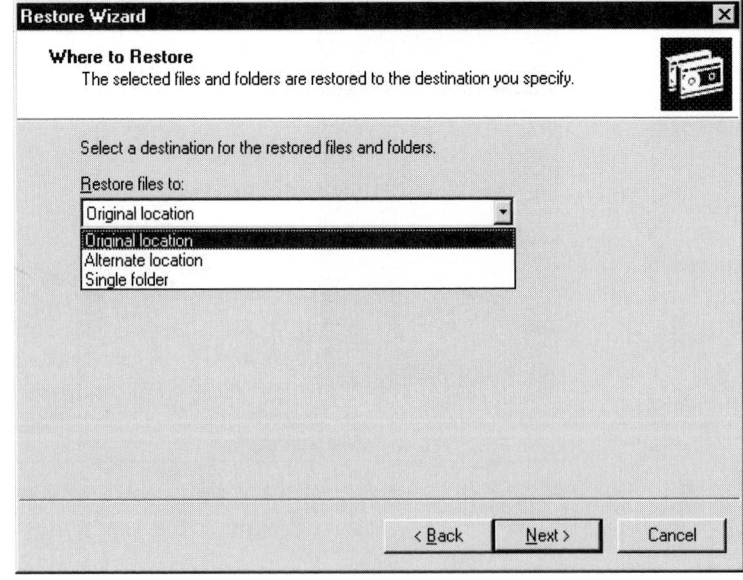

FIGURE 7-18

The How to Restore screen

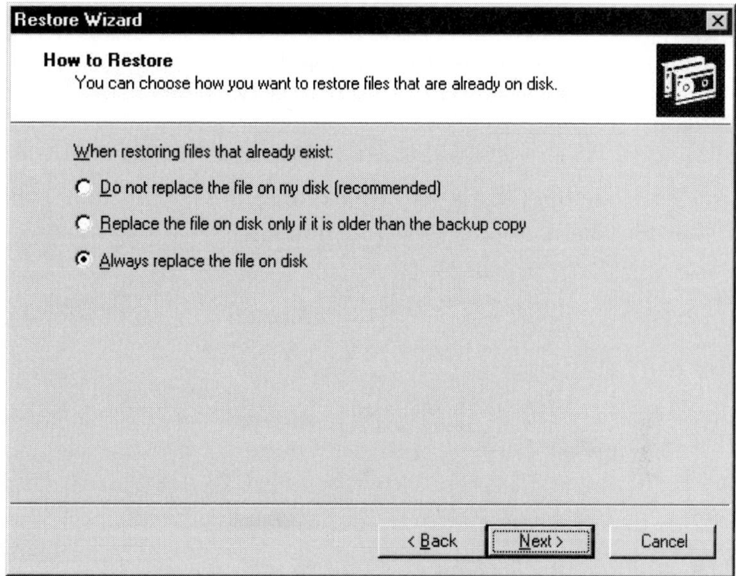

- **Always replace the file on disk.** Replaces files on disk with restored files, even if the files on disk are newer.

15. Click Next and proceed to the Advanced Restore Options screen.
16. At the Advanced Restore Options screen (see Figure 7-19), select from the following restore options you want to use:
    - **Restore security.** Applies the original security settings to the files being restored. This option is available only if you are restoring data originally from NTFS to an NTFS partition.
    - **Restore Removable Storage Management database.** Restores the media pools and RSM database located in *systemroot*\system32\Ntmsdata.
    - **Restore junction points, not the folders and file data they reference.** Restores the junction points needed if drives were mounted in the partition being restored.
17. Click Next and proceed to the Completing the Restore Wizard screen.
18. At the Completing the Restore Wizard screen (see Figure 7-20), verify your restore settings and click Finish to start the restore.

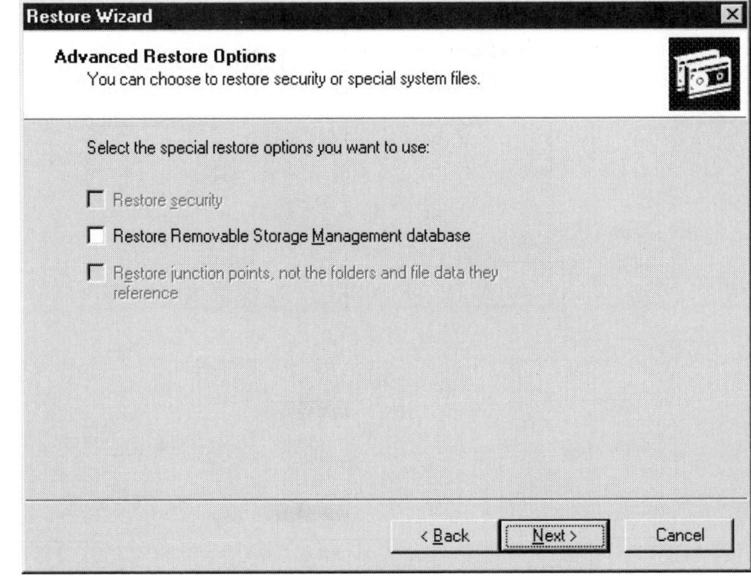

FIGURE 7-19

The Advanced Restore Options screen

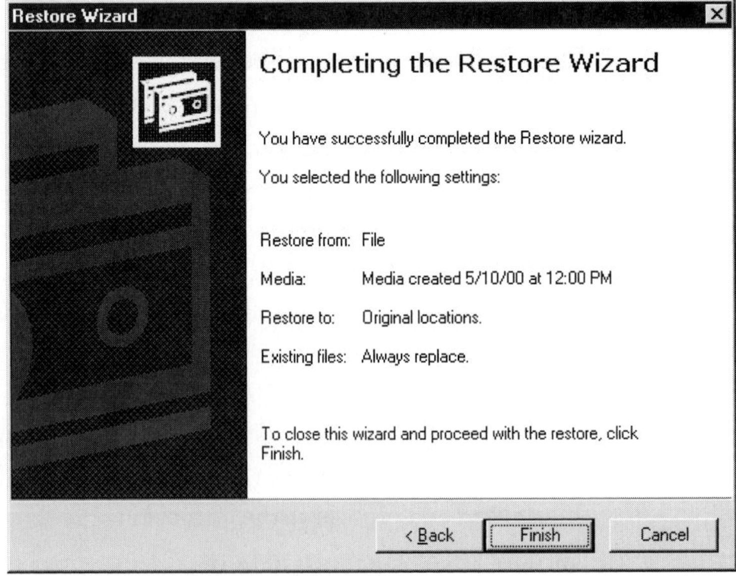

FIGURE 7-20

The final options of the Completing the Restore Wizard screen

To this point, we have been performing a standard non-authoritative restore. The following steps extend the non-authoritative restore and perform an authoritative restore.

19. After the non-authoritative restore (Steps 1–18) completes, reboot your computer and press F8 at the operating system selection screen.
20. Select Directory Services Restore Mode from the Windows 2000 Advanced Startup Options menu.
21. Select Windows 2000 Server from the operating system selection screen and log on as Administrator. Use the password specified during the promotion of the server to DC status, not the domain administrator password.
22. Click OK on the Safe Mode pop-up box.
23. Open a command prompt by selecting Programs | Accessories | Command Prompt from the Start menu.
24. Type **ntdsutil** at the command prompt and press Enter.
25. Type **authoritative restore** at the ntdsutil prompt.

    At this point, the following four commands are available to you for performing an authoritative restore:

    - **RESTORE DATABASE.** Authoritatively restores the entire database.
    - **RESTORE DATABASE VERINC** *<version increase>*. Authoritatively restores the entire directory and overrides the version increase.
    - **RESTORE SUBTREE** *<subtree distinguished name>*. Restores a select portion or subtree of the directory.
    - **RESTORE SUBTREE** *<subtree distinguished name>***VERINC** *<version increase>*. Authoritatively restores directory subtree and overrides the version increase.

    The *VERINC option* should be used in situations that require more control over the authoritative restore process. When the VERINC option is not used, the version increase is automatically calculated.

26. Type **quit** to exit Authoritative Restore Mode.
27. Type **quit** again to exit the NTDSUTIL utility.

28. At this point, restart the computer in Normal Mode with the computer connected to the network.
29. This final step ensures the integrity of the computer's group policy. If you are performing an authoritative restore of the entire directory:
    - Copy the SYSVOL directory from the alternate location over the existing SYSVOL directory *after* the SYSVOL share has been published.

    If you are performing an authoritative restore of a portion of the directory:
    - Copy the policies folder corresponding to the restored objects from the alternate location *after* the SYSVOL share is published to the existing policies location.

Make sure you know what NTDSUTIL is used for and how to use it. Know the commands associated with this utility.

Recovering from a System Failure

Total system failure has a way of happening at the most inconvenient time. We could put the blame on Murphy's Law: If anything can go wrong, it will. In other words, if there is a possibility of your production Windows 2000 server crashing while you are on vacation, it will crash. Since you are the network administrator, in this scenario you would be called in from your vacation to get the production server up and running. For this reason, you should always know your options for disaster recovery and have some type of plan or policy in place to ensure that you or your backup can be successful. Some potential causes of system failure are:

- Hard drive failure
- Power failure
- Systems software failure
- Negligent use of deletion or modification commands
- Damaging viruses
- Sabotage
- Natural disaster

FROM THE CLASSROOM

An Introduction to NTDSUTIL

Like NTBACKUP, NTDSUTIL is a command-line utility for the Windows 2000 Active Directory. In addition to allowing authoritative restores to be performed, NTDSUTIL performs the following functions:

- Database maintenance of the Active Directory store
- Management and control of the flexible single master operations (FSMO)
- Cleaning up metadata left behind by domain controllers that were removed from the network without being properly uninstalled.

The NTDSUTIL utility supports the following menu modes:

- Authoritative restore
- Domain management
- Files
- Metadata cleanup
- Roles
- IPDeny List
- LDAP policies
- Pop-ups
- Security Account Management
- Semanntic database analysis
- Help
- Quit

Each of these menu modes contains submenus and commands that facilitate the management of Active Directory. A solid foundation of the NTDSUTIL commands allows you to design powerful scripts that can manipulate the Windows 2000 environment.

—*Damon Merchant, MCSE, CNE, CCDP, CCNP*

Restoring from Backup Media

Restoring from backup media is a common method of recovering from system failure. The key to success, though, is to perform regular backups *before* system failure. In the event of system failure, perform the appropriate restore using the most recent media.

Restoring Via a Replica

Another method of recovering from system failure is to let the other domain controllers replicate their data to the failed system. This method assumes that data on other domain controllers is current and accurate.

CERTIFICATION SUMMARY

This chapter was designed to help you understand the importance of being prepared for disaster and actually recovering from disaster. Backups were explained for disaster preparation; restores were explained for disaster recovery. This chapter also identified the main components of Active Directory.

You learned about various backup options available for Windows 2000. You learned how to back up Active Directory using the Windows 2000 Backup Wizard. You were also introduced to the NTBACKUP scripting utility.

Restoring AD was also covered in this chapter. You learned how to perform a restore using the Windows 2000 Restore Wizard. You also learned about authoritative restores, which are created by performing a non-authoritative restore and then using the NTDSUTIL utility.

TWO-MINUTE DRILL

Backing Up and Restoring Active Directory

- ❑ DSA provides APIs for directory access calls.
- ❑ The database layer provides an interface between client applications and the directory database.
- ❑ ESE sits between the database layer and the directory data store.
- ❑ LDAP/ADSI is used to gain directory access.
- ❑ MAPI is used to send and receive e-mail.
- ❑ SAM authenticates users during login.
- ❑ Logical components of Active Directory consist of domains, organizational units, trees, and forests.
- ❑ An Incremental backup copies all selected files that have the archive bit set, and it does reset the archive bit.
- ❑ A Differential backup copies all selected files that have the archive bit set, but it does not reset the archive bit.
- ❑ The "Verify data after backup" option instructs the backup system to check the files on the media after the backup is complete.
- ❑ A non-authoritative restore retains the original update sequence numbers of restored data.
- ❑ Data can be restored to its original location, an alternate location, or to a single folder.
- ❑ The NTDSUTIL utility allows you to perform an authoritative restore.

Part II

Change and Configuration Managements

CHAPTERS

MCSE

MICROSOFT CERTIFIED SYSTEMS ENGINEER

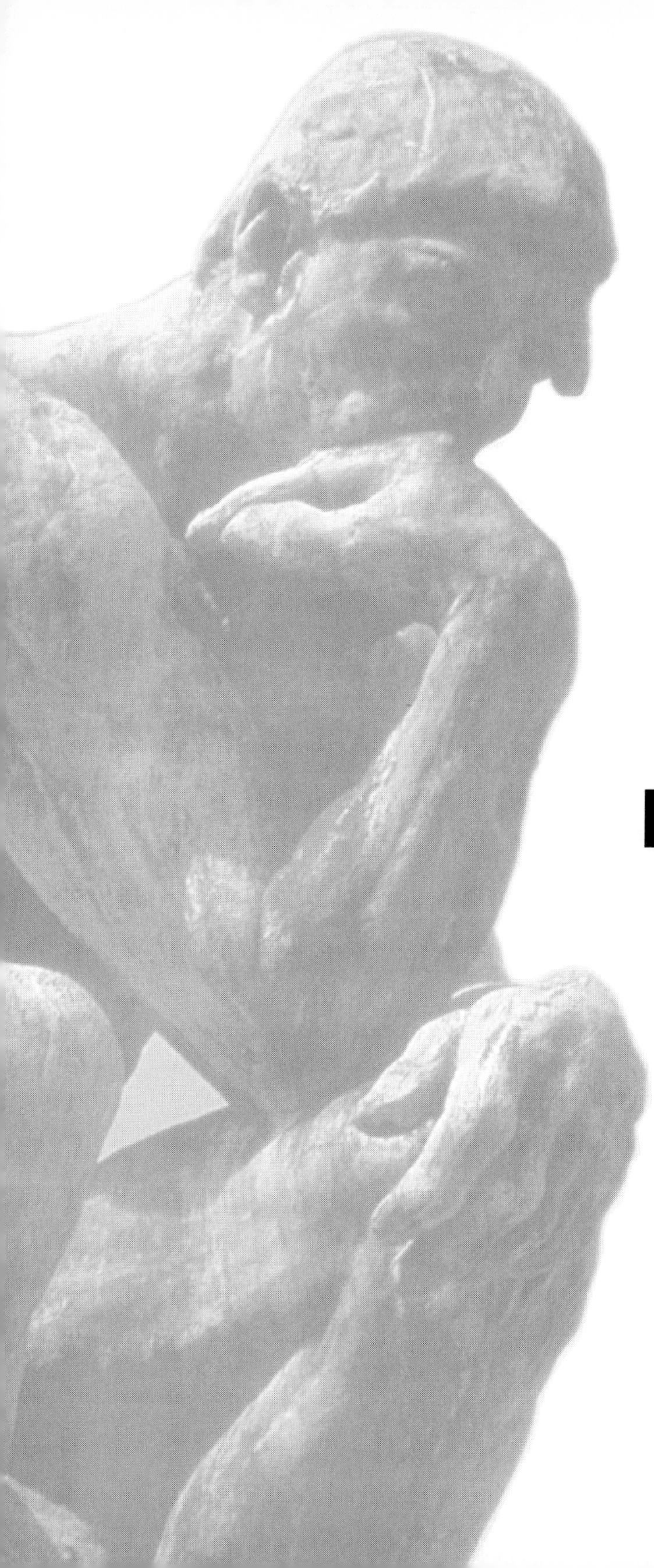

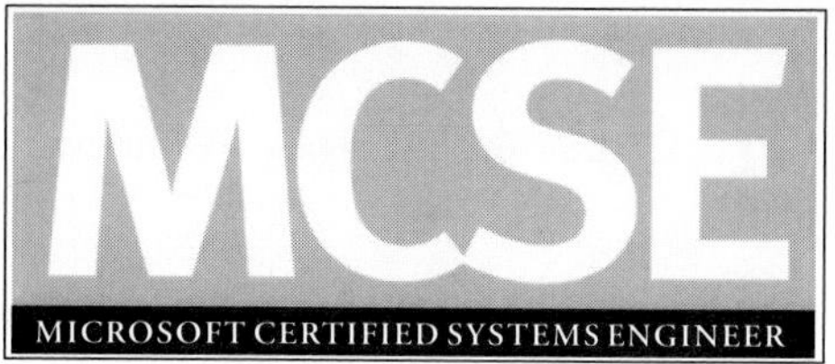

8

Managing a Windows 2000 Network with Group Policy

CERTIFICATION OBJECTIVES

8.01 Creating a Group Policy Object

8.02 Linking an Existing Group Policy Object

8.03 Delegating Administrative Control of Group Policy

8.04 Modifying Group Policy Inheritance

8.05 Filtering Group Policy Settings

8.06 Modifying Group Policy

8.07 Controlling User Environments Using Administrative Templates

8.08 Assigning Script Policies to Users and Computers

✓ Two-Minute Drill

This chapter discusses Group Policy objects (GPOs) in-depth, covering all aspects of GPOs, from creation, delegation, and modification of GPOs to assigning, filtering, and controlling users and computers. As you will see, GPOs allow you to control just about anything—from desktop settings to installation of new software.

GPOs are descendants of the System Policy Editor in Windows NT 4.0. In NT 4.0, you could create system policies that were enforceable when a user logged on to your domain. If you were smart enough, you could also tailor system policies by scripting your own custom policy. By adding the elements that you could not find in standard policies, you could control just about anything with policies in the Windows NT environment.

Today, GPOs have evolved. They have been modified, expanded, and integrated into Windows 2000 to allow a tighter, more flexible means of easily managing Windows 2000 users and computers on your network. As you see later in the chapter, GPOs greatly simplify the management of Windows 2000 systems.

CERTIFICATION OBJECTIVE 8.01

Creating a Group Policy Object

One of the biggest problems you face as an administrator is the management of users and computers. Settings such as user interface options (background colors, wallpaper), running logon scripts, location of user home directories, and the like are only a fraction of the items that need to be managed on a daily basis. You need a tool to help configure and manage these systems. Group Policy is that tool.

What Are GPOs?

What are Group Policy objects, anyway? GPOs are collections of common configurations that can be applied to a single user or computer or a group of users or computers. GPOs consist of Software Settings, Windows Settings, and an Administrative Templates section for both computers and users (see Figure 8-1).

Using these settings, you can dynamically control the computers and users on your network. Software settings allow you to distribute packaged software to target

FIGURE 8-1

The Default Domain Policy GPO

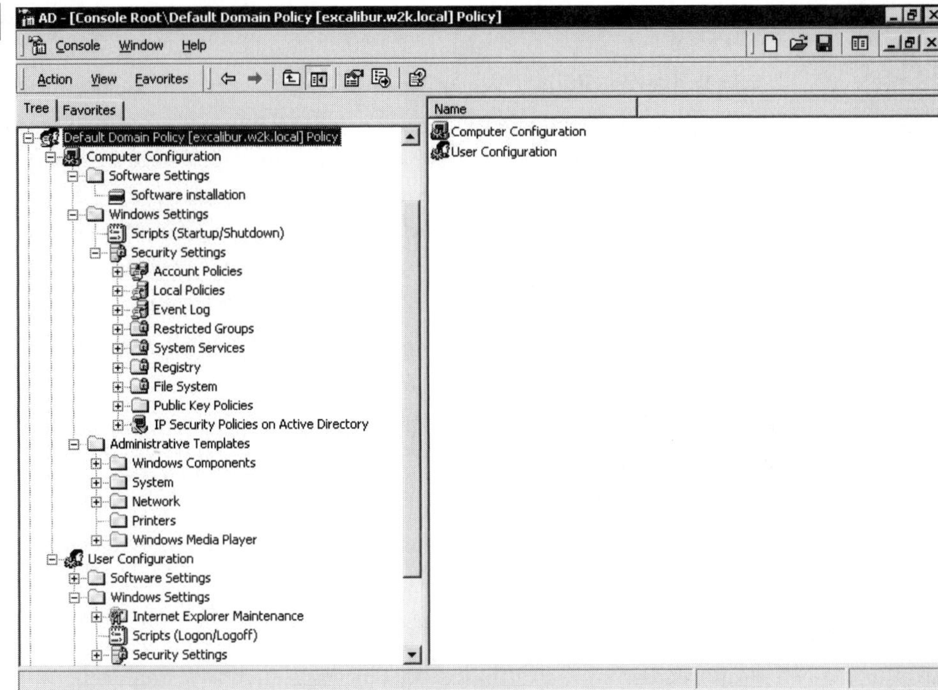

users and computers. Imagine the ability to install a set of applications on a new system without ever having to touch the keyboard! Just turn on the system and the applications are installed automatically.

Windows settings are probably the most powerful in a GPO. With Windows settings, you can add or modify key parts of Windows 2000, such as:

- Restricted user groups
- Enforce startup/shutdown scripts
- System services
- Registry settings
- Public key policies (such as Encrypting File System recovery agents)
- IP Security (IPSec) policies
- Other local security settings (such as Event Log settings, audit and account policies, and user right assignments)

Windows settings are what really make GPOs so powerful in Windows 2000.

Finally, there are the Administrative Templates. Administrative Templates give GPOs their flexibility. Administrative Templates are very close to what System Policies are in Windows NT 4.0. Basically, Administrative Templates are registry settings that can further control a user or computer and are grouped together in folders (such as Network, System, Printers). Administrative Templates can control users and computers, whereas other parts of a GPO cannot. By creating your own templates and importing them into Administrative Templates, you can modify your users and computers beyond what can be managed by the default templates provided with Windows 2000. The rule of thumb here is if it has a registry setting, it can be modified.

Deciding Where to Apply a Group Policy Object in the Organizational Unit Structure

Deciding where to apply your GPO(s) can be hard. Many factors must play a role in the decision as to where to apply your GPOs. As you see later in this chapter, you can selectively apply your GPOs in several different ways:

- Assigning GPOs based on a location such as a site, domain, or OU
- Filtering the assignment of GPOs using security groups
- Modifying the inheritance of a GPO by using the Block Inheritance and No Override switches for group policies

Although there are many ways to apply GPOs within Windows 2000, it is a good idea to select a method in which you apply the majority of your GPOs. You might not be able to apply all your GPOs with the method you choose, but at least you have a *default* method. This helps your organization eliminate some confusion that is bound to arise when there is doubt as to what GPO has been applied to a user or computer.

How to Create the Policy

Creating group policies within Windows 2000 is pretty simple. Open the Microsoft Management Console (MMC) by clicking Start | Run and typing **MMC**. Click OK, and the MMC console appears. To work with Group Policy, click Console | Add/Remove snap-in. In the Add/Remove snap-in window, click the Add button, and select Group Policy from the Add Standalone snap-in window (see Figure 8-2).

Click the Add button again, and the Select Group Policy Object window appears (see Figure 8-3). Here you must select the group policy you want to put in the MMC. By default, the Group Policy snap-in selects the Local Computer GPO, but you can select another GPO by clicking the Browse button.

Clicking the Browse button creates a Browse for Group Policy Object window, as shown in Figure 8-4. Here you can browse for a GPO that is stored in Active Directory, or you can create a new object by right-clicking in the Browse for Group Policy Object window (see Figure 8-4). Notice that you have a broad range from which to select, or you can create a new GPO. You can browse any domain, OU, or site or select a local computer GPO from another computer.

Once you have either selected or created your GPO, click OK, close the Add Standalone snap-in window, and click OK in the Add/Remove snap-in window to add the selected or created GPOs to the MMC.

FIGURE 8-2

Selecting the Group Policy snap-in

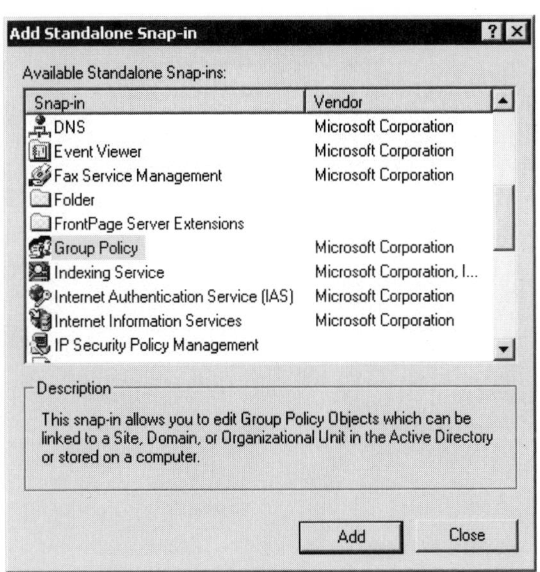

FIGURE 8-3

Selecting the Group Policy object

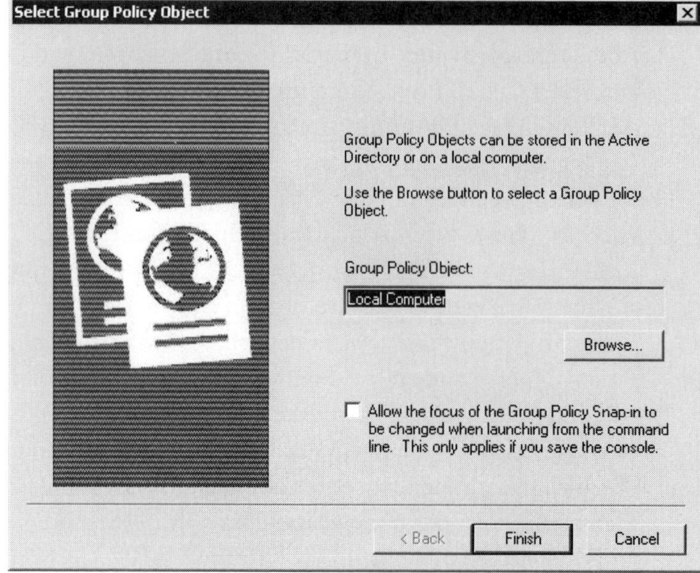

FIGURE 8-4

Browsing for a Group Policy object

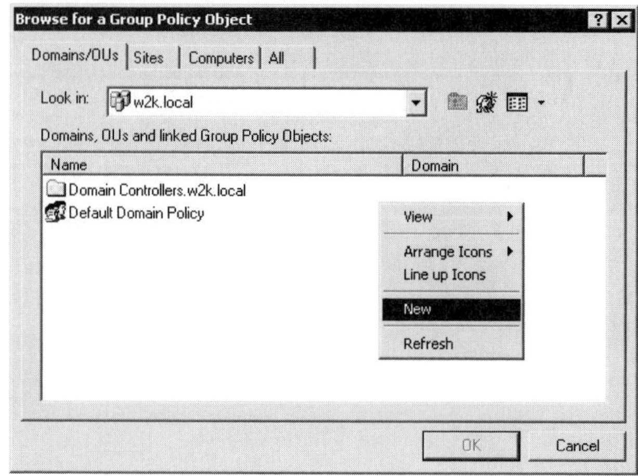

EXERCISE 8-1

Creating a Group Policy Object

For this exercise, you need Active Directory installed through the DCPROMO process. To create a group policy, we use the domain name that was used to install Active Directory.

1. Verify that you are logged on as Administrator.
2. Open the Group Policy MMC snap-in by clicking Start | Run. Type **MMC.** Click OK to run the MMC.
3. To add the Group Policy snap-in, click Console | Add/Remove snap-ins.
4. In the Add/Remove snap-in window, click the Standalone tab and then click the Add button.
5. In the Add Standalone snap-in window, select the Group Policy snap-in and click Add.
6. When the Select Group Policy Object window appears (refer back to Figure 8-3), click Browse.
7. When the Browse for a Group Policy Object window appears (refer back to Figure 8-4), select either the Domain/OUs or Sites tabs shown in Figure 8-4, right-click the tab, and select New from the pop-up context menu. This series of actions creates a new GPO in the tab. Name the new GPO **ABCFUTURES**. You will use this GPO in later exercises.
8. Click OK and then click on the Finish button to add the ABCFUTURES GPO to the list of snap-ins to be included in the MMC.
9. Click Close to close the Add Standalone snap-in window.
10. Click OK to add the new GPO to the MMC console.

Note that this GPO is stored in the object in which you created it. In other words, if you created a new GPO in the Sites tab, the GPO is stored in the Sites object.

CERTIFICATION OBJECTIVE 8.02

Linking an Existing Group Policy Object

Linking an existing GPO to a site, domain, or OU is the way to assign a GPO in order to apply the selected policies within the GPO. By linking the GPO to the site, domain, or OU, you make it possible to apply the policies within the GPO to all or part of the group that exists within the Domain or OU. Later in the chapter, you will see that just because you assign a GPO to a Domain or OU, that does not actually mean that all the computers or users within the Domain or OU have the GPO applied to it. You see later in the chapter how to selectively apply GPOs to computers and users.

An Overview of Group Policy Object Location in Active Directory

When GPOs are created, they exist in the container in which they were created. In another words, when you create a GPO in a site, the GPO can be found in that site by browsing for GPOs in Active Directory. To browse for GPOs, open the MMC and select the Group Policy snap-in. When the Select Group Policy Objects window appears, click the Browse button. In the Browse for a Group Policy Object window, you can see that GPOs can be found in Domains, OUs, and local computers (see Figure 8-5).

Once the browsing window is open, select the GPO from the proper container. If you do not find the appropriate existing GPO, you can create your own GPOs in any container (Domains or OUs), just by right-clicking in the window and selecting the New context menu item. This action creates a new GPO in the container with which you are working.

Although you can browse for GPOs, you can also see what GPOs are assigned to a specific container (i.e., Domain or OU). By viewing a container's properties and selecting the container's Group Policy tab, you can see exactly what GPOs are assigned to that container.

FIGURE 8-5

Browsing for GPOs in Active Directory

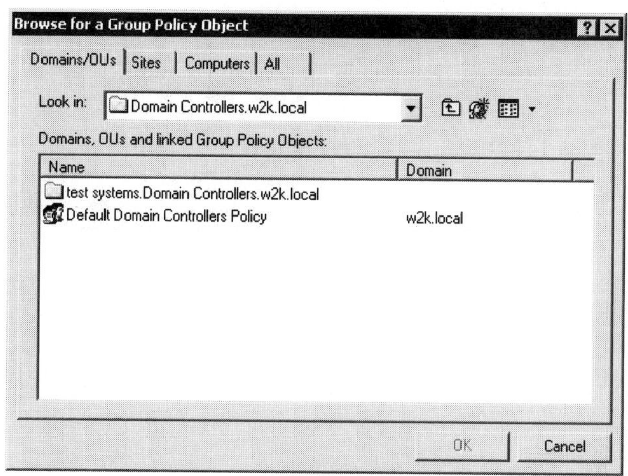

Finally, although GPOs are logically located in the container in which they are created, they physically reside in one location on all domain controllers in the %SystemRoot%\SYSVOL\sysvol\<domain name>\Policies folder.

How to Link a Group Policy Object, and Why

Once you have your GPOs created, you will want to link them to the appropriate containers to start managing users and computers in your network. To link a GPO to a container (site, domain, or OU), right-click the receiving container, and click the Properties context menu item. The Properties window for the container object appears. Click the Group Policy tab, and you will see the list of currently assigned GPOs for the container object (see Figure 8-6).

To create a new GPO, you can click the New button. When creating a new GPO, you have to modify the GPO according to the policies you want to apply. To add an existing GPO, click Add. Once all GPOs have been created or added to the container object, click Apply and then click OK to apply all the changes.

One thing to keep in mind is that once a GPO is created, it can be applied again to any other container object in Active Directory. By clicking the Add button, as shown in Figure 8-6, you can apply a GPO that has already been created to any

FIGURE 8-6

Viewing GPOs assigned to a container object

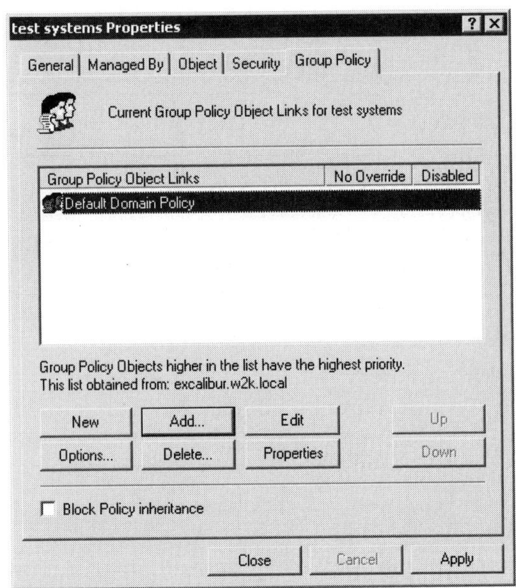

container object. GPOs can be applied any number of times, since they are not solely dedicated to the container object to which they are applied.

Once GPOs are linked to a container object, you will want to assign the proper security groups to the GPO in order to correctly apply the GPO settings to all the desired computers and users in the container object. Later in the chapter, we discuss the need to assign the proper security groups for filtering GPOs in container objects.

EXERCISE 8-2

Linking a Group Policy Object

For this exercise, you need to have Active Directory installed through the DCPROMO process. To link a GPO to an object, we use the Domain object that was created when Active Directory was installed. We also use the ABCFUTURES GPO that you created in the previous exercise and link it to the Domain object.

1. Verify that you are logged on as Administrator.
2. Open the Control Panel by clicking Start | Settings | Control Panel. Open the Administrative Tools applet and click the Active Directory Users and Computers administrative tool.
3. When the Active Directory Users and Computers tool opens, it shows the domain name of your network. Right-click the domain name and select Properties from the pop-up context menu.
4. When the <domain name> Properties window appears, click the Group Policy tab. Your window will be the same as the one shown in Figure 8-6, with the exception that you will find the ABCFUTURES GPO already added to the Domain object. Select the ABCFUTURES GPO and click the Delete button to remove the link from the list. Make sure that you select the option to remove the GPO from the list only; do not delete the GPO from Active Directory! Click OK and the ABCFUTURES GPO is removed from the list.
5. To link the ABCFUTURES GPO to the Domain object, click Add. In the Add a Group Policy Object Link window, select the All tab and make sure the Look In drop-down window has your domain selected. The ABCFUTURES GPO is listed here.
6. Click the ABCFUTURES GPO and click OK. The ABCFUTURES GPO is added to the Domain object. The ABCFUTURES GPO is now linked to the Domain object. Leave the ABCFUTURES GPO linked; we use this linked GPO for exercises later in the chapter.

CERTIFICATION OBJECTIVE 8.03

Delegating Administrative Control of Group Policy

One of the first observations you will make regarding Windows 2000 is that it is complex. One of the features that makes Windows 2000 complex is Group Policy. The nature of Group Policy and its flexibility, which allows easy configuration of computers and users, also makes it extremely hard for only one person to manage all the configurations. You will find that Group Policy, along with several other tasks, needs to be broken into pieces and managed by a few select individuals for each task. Breaking up the burden not only allows administrators to approach management of Windows 2000 with a "divide and conquer" attitude with respect to the amount of work, but it also allows administrators to delegate parts of Windows 2000 to certain administrators and be able to secure the assigned part of Windows 2000 so that only those assigned to work with a specific section are allowed to do so.

Why Delegate Control?

Why delegate control of Group Policy? The answer to that question is easy to see when you open a default group policy, such as the Default Domain Policy. By browsing through this policy, you can get a feel for just how powerful group policies are. Delegating control of group policies allows administrators to control exactly who enforces and modifies a group policy. Strict control of *all* group policies is necessary for a large enterprise network because a poorly configured group policy, placed on the wrong Active Directory object, can spell disaster for your network.

How to Delegate Control of Group Policy Objects

Delegating control over GPOs is a little complicated, so we take it step by step. First, open the Active Directory Sites and Services snap-in and navigate to the Sites object. From the Sites object, expand the object and select a site. In Figure 8-7, we selected the London site to use as our example, but keep in mind that any Active Directory container object (such as a site or OU) could be used. When you right-click London

FIGURE 8-7

Selecting the London site to view its Properties page

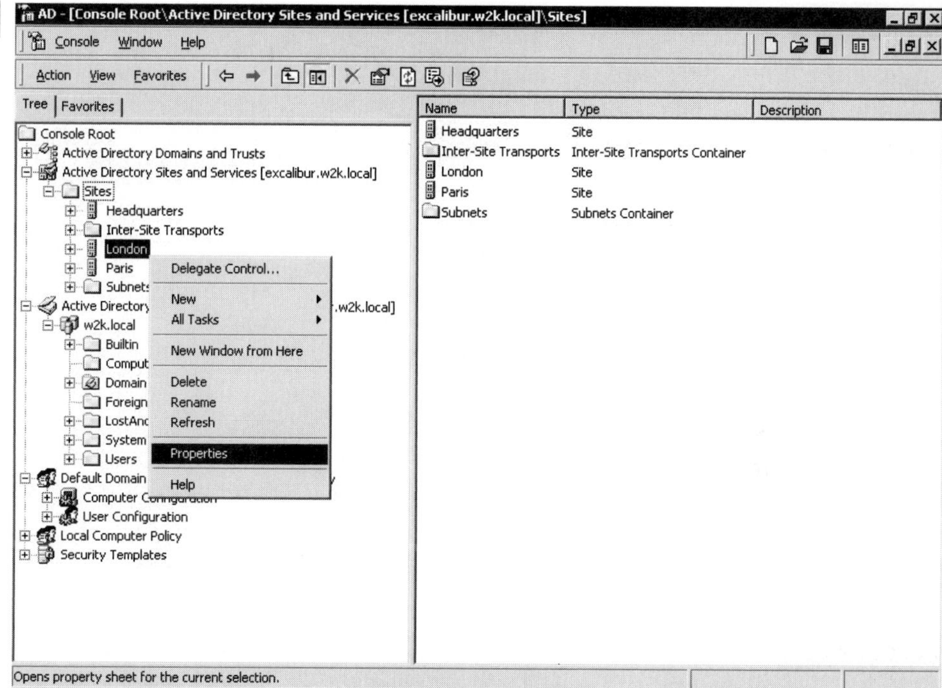

and select Properties, a London Properties window appears, as shown in Figure 8-8. Do *not* select the Delegate Control context menu item by mistake. This menu item controls the delegation of control over the London object, not the GPOs for London.

In the London Properties window, click the New button, which creates a new GPO. A newly created GPO is initially named New Group Policy Object, but as shown in Figure 8-8, we renamed the GPO *GPO Control*.

Continuing on, click the Properties button, which opens the GPO control Properties window. By clicking on the Security tab, as shown in Figure 8-9, you can view the access control list (ACL) for Control GPO. This ACL is where you delegate the control over any GPO. Clicking each access control entry (ACE) reveals its permissions in the Permissions text box. Notice that Authenticated Users has only Read and Apply Group Policy permissions—just enough permission to allow any authenticated user to read and apply the GPO in question.

FIGURE 8-8

London Properties window and the new group policy, GPO Control

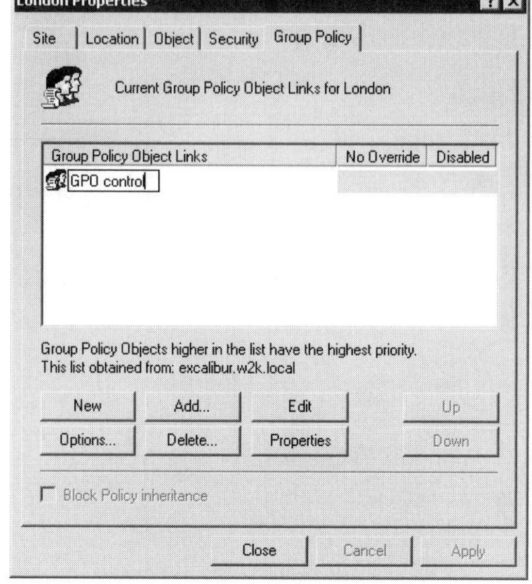

FIGURE 8-9

Viewing the ACL for GPO Control

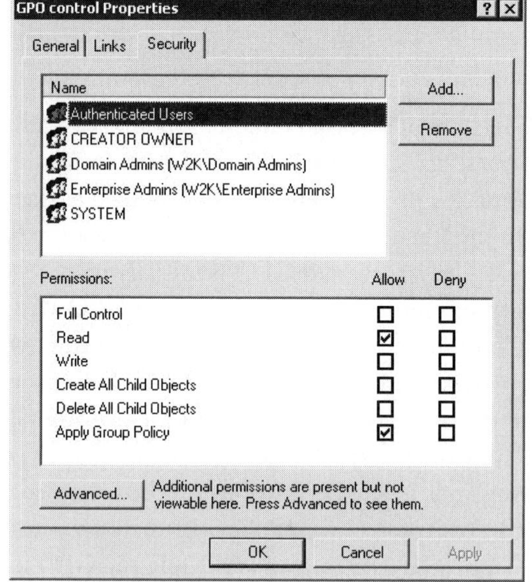

To delegate new users or groups to work with this GPO, click Add to add the necessary users or groups. Once all users and/or groups have been delegated, remember to assign the necessary permissions for each user and group and click OK to save your changes. These permissions are:

- **Full Control.** Allows assigned users or groups to have full control over the object specified. Users or groups have all permissions that are listed below.
- **Read.** Users or groups are only allowed to open and read the specified object. They are not allowed to write to the object, nor are they permitted to apply the object.
- **Write.** Users or groups are only allowed to write to the specified object. They cannot read the object, nor are they permitted to apply the object.
- **Create All Child Objects.** Users or groups can create objects that are children to the object in question.
- **Delete All Child Objects.** Users or groups can delete objects that are children to the object in question.
- **Apply Group Policy.** Allows users or groups to apply the GPO that is linked to the Active Directory container. This permission is always assigned along with the Read permission because users or groups must be able to read the GPO in order to apply it.

EXERCISE 8-3

Delegating Control of a Group Policy Object

In this exercise, you create a security group, ABCFUTURES-ADMIN, and delegate control of the GPO, ABCFUTURES, to this security group.

1. Verify that you are logged on as Administrator.
2. Open the Control Panel by clicking Start | Settings | Control Panel. Open the Administrative Tools applet and click the Active Directory Users and Computers administrative tool.
3. When the Active Directory Users and Computers tool opens, it shows the domain name of your network. Right-click the domain name and select Properties from the pop-up context menu.
4. When the <domain name> Properties window appears, click the Group Policy tab. The ABCFUTURES GPO is listed as the only GPO linked to this domain object.
5. Click the ABCFUTURES GPO and then click the Properties button. The ABCFUTURES Properties window appears. Click the Security tab to view all the groups linked to this GPO.
6. To delegate exclusive control over this GPO, remove the Domain Admins, Enterprise Admins, and Creator Owner security groups. This leaves the Authenticated Users and SYSTEM security groups only. Authenticated Users remains so that they can apply the GPO once it is finished. *Note:* Make positively sure that the administrator account that you are using is a member of the ABCFUTURES-ADMIN security group. If it is not, you will *not* be able to access the GPO for later exercises!
7. Add the ABCFUTURES-ADMIN security group and give this group Full Control access to the GPO. Click OK to make your changes effective.

Make sure you keep the ABCFUTURES-ADMIN security group and the ABCFUTURES GPO because we use them for later exercises.

CERTIFICATION OBJECTIVE 8.04

Modifying Group Policy Inheritance

One of the most important concepts that you need to clearly understand is the concept of GPO inheritance. *Inheritance* is the acceptance of GPO settings as designated by group policies assigned higher in the chain of Group Policy processing.

Group policies, as stated earlier in the chapter, can be assigned to local computers, sites, domains, and OUs. Processing of group policies occurs in this order while, at the same time, multiple GPOs for objects are applied in order from *bottom to top*. As shown in Figure 8-10, it is stated below the GPO links that GPOs higher in the GPO list have the highest priority.

Looking even deeper into how GPOs are applied, once a GPO is selected to be applied, it applies all sections within the Computer configuration section first, including the execution of any startup scripts, followed by the application of all sections within the User Configuration section. Again, all sections are applied, including any logon scripts. One thing to keep in mind is that if there are computer and user policies that specify contradictory settings and/or behavior, the computer policy generally wins out over the user policy.

Looking at Figure 8-10, you can see that for the W2K.LOCAL domain object, several GPOs are assigned. Note that the Default Domain Controllers Policy GPO is highlighted, and the Up and Down buttons are enabled to allow the GPO to be moved up or down the list of GPOs in order to change its processing order.

What Is Inheritance?

Inheritance, as explained previously, is the acceptance of GPO settings that were applied by a previous GPO. Take the example of desktop settings. The ABC Company decides that it wants to place its logo as the wallpaper for all company workstations and change the mouse pointer to an animated mouse. The GPO for this policy is placed in the ABC Company's only site, ABC. The ABC Company has a marketing organization that deals with external kiosks and cannot have the company's logo for wallpaper, but the staff like the animated mouse for marketing purposes. They create a GPO that changes the wallpaper to a blue background, but they leave the animated mouse pointer. They assign this new GPO to the OU that

FIGURE 8-10

Multiple GPOs assigned to the W2K.LOCAL domain object

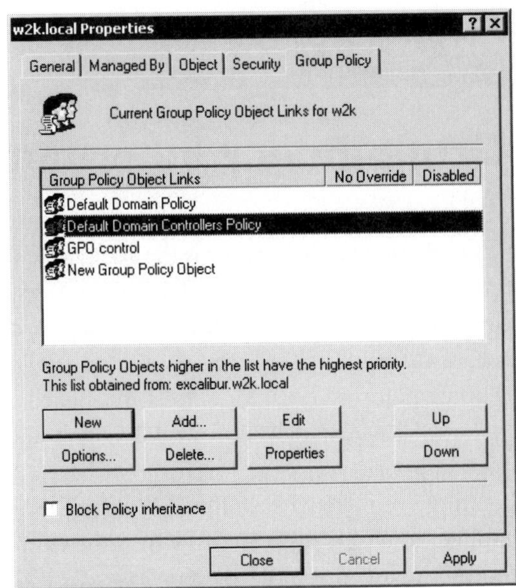

handles marketing. When the marketing systems are rebooted, the Sites GPO is processed first, which assigns the wallpaper logo and the animated mouse pointer. Next, the marketing GPO is applied and, because there is a new configuration for the wallpaper, the wallpaper is set to a blue background. Since there is no new configuration for the mouse pointer, the workstation inherits the GPO setting that was last applied to the workstation. In this case, the last applied mouse pointer setting was the animated mouse pointer.

Managing Inheritance

There are several methods of modifying the inheritance of GPO changes in order to apply the settings you need to the right computers or users. You can:

- **Block Policy Inheritance.** By checking the Block Policy Inheritance check box at the bottom of the Group Policy tab for any Domain or Organizational Unit object, you can block the inheritance of any group policies for this object. Instead of inheriting policies applied higher in the GPO processing order, the object that has this check box selected ignores all policies. This option can be selected without specifying any GPOs for an object (such as a Domain or Organizational Unit object).

- **No Override.** This option works much like the Block Policy Inheritance option in that it blocks the inheritance of any group policies for a container object, but this option applies only to a specific GPO. Not only that, but this option is considered the "king" of options because it specifies that all settings within the GPO cannot be overridden by any other GPO during the processing of group policies. Any policy assigned the No Override option assigns its GPO settings regardless of any other settings found later in the processing of GPOs, including any Block Policy Inheritance settings. To select the No Override option, you must click the GPO in question, and then click the Options button (refer back to Figure 8-10). Once you click Options, you can select the No Override check box, as shown in Figure 8-11.

How to Change the Group Policy Object Inheritance

To change the GPO inheritance, you first must open a GPO. Open the Active Directory Users and Computers snap-in and navigate to the <domain name> | Domain Controllers Organizational Unit object. Right-click the Domain Controllers object, and select the Properties context menu item. A Domain Controllers Properties window appears. Click the Group Policy tab. To block policy inheritance, click the Block Policy Inheritance check box at the bottom of the tab (refer back to Figure 8-10). Again, any other Active Directory container object could be used, but for this example, we have chosen to use the Domain container object.

Next, click the New button to create a new Group Policy object. Once the object has been created, click the object and then click the Options button. In the Options window that appears (refer back to Figure 8-11), select the No Override check box and click OK. You will be able to see that New Group Policy Object now has a check in the No Override column.

FIGURE 8-11

Modifying the inheritance of GPOs

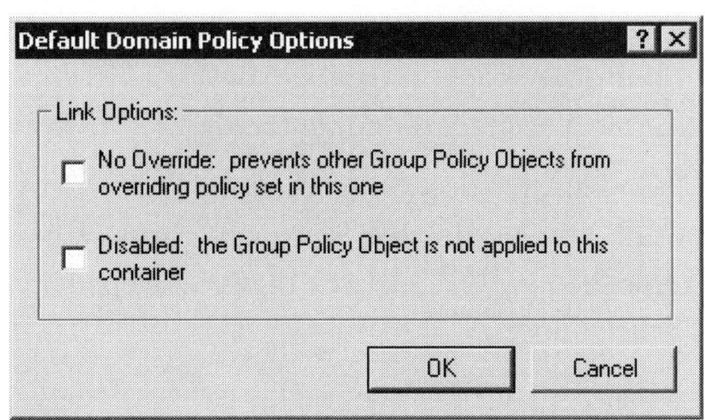

EXERCISE 8-4

Modifying Group Policy Inheritance

In this exercise, you learn how modifying inheritance can affect GPO processing.

1. Verify that you are logged on as Administrator.
2. Open the Control Panel by clicking Start | Settings | Control Panel. Open the Administrative Tools applet and click the Active Directory Users and Computers administrative tool.
3. When Active Directory Users and Computers opens, it shows the domain name of your network. Right-click the domain name and select Properties from the pop-up context menu.
4. When the <domain name> Properties window appears, click the Group Policy tab. The ABCFUTURES GPO is listed as the only GPO linked to this Domain object.
5. Click New to add another GPO to the Domain object. You can name this GPO anything you want. Ensure that the new GPO was created and placed second in the list of policies for the domain.
6. Modify both GPOs with the following User Configuration setting: Administrative Templates/Desktop | Hide all icons on Desktop. Configure the ABCFUTURES GPO as Enabled and the new GPO with Disabled. Make no other modifications. Save your settings and log off.
7. Log on to your system. What happened? Was it what you expected? What should have happened was that the desktop icons were hidden on your desktop. This is because GPOs are applied in order, and since you specifically enabled and disabled the policy Hide all Icons on Desktop for both GPOs, the policy was applied in both GPOs. Since the new GPO was created and placed second in the list, its policy was applied first (remember, bottom to top). Since the ABCFUTURES GPOs policy was set to Enabled, it has the effect of hiding the desktop icons, since it was applied last.
8. Go back to the <domain name> Properties window and modify the new GPO by clicking the Options button. When the Options window appears for the new GPO, check the No Override check box, click OK, and then click Close.

9. Log off the system and then log on again. What happened? Was it what you expected?
   What should have happened was that the desktop icons became visible on your desktop. Since the No Override option was enabled on the new GPO, no other GPO policies could be inherited. The new GPO policy stated that the Hide all Icons on Desktop was disabled. Since no other GPO policy could be inherited, this policy remained disabled through the processing of all GPOs, which, in turn, allowed the desktop icons to remain visible.
10. Go back to the <domain name> Properties window and delete the new GPO. Change the ABCFUTURES GPO back to its original state by resetting the User Configuration at Administrative Templates/Desktop | Hide all icons on Desktop.

CERTIFICATION OBJECTIVE 8.05

Filtering Group Policy Settings

You can filter group policies using various Active Directory objects, but it is very difficult to do this when you have a large enterprise. A finer granularity is needed when dealing with smaller groups that must have certain settings. Using Active Directory objects then becomes impractical. Using security groups with group policies, you can achieve a finer granularity by applying a GPO only to those computers or users that require it, even though these computers or users might belong to a larger group within an OU or domain.

Why Filter a Group Policy Object?

Why filter GPOs? As stated previously, you might need to apply unique computer or user GPO settings to a small group within a company. This need could grow with the size of your company. The larger the company, the greater the possibility that you will need to treat certain groups of computers or users uniquely. This is where you can filter the application of GPOs to certain groups of computers and users through the use of security groups.

Take, for example, a small company of 100 people. All computers and users are in the same site because of the size of the company. The human resources (HR) department, however, needs to have several policies enforced on both their computers and for each user, along with having a couple of HR-specific applications installed to their computers. We call the GPO needed for the HR group HRTWEAKS. No other group in the company needs this configuration. Once the HRTWEAKS GPO is linked to the company's site, an administrator can create a security group called HR and place all the computers and users from HR within this group.

on the Job

Remember, with Windows 2000 you can use computers as well as users within security groups. In Windows NT, you only had the ability to use users within security groups. Windows 2000 has been expanded to allow administrators to place computers into security groups, mostly to allow the filtering of GPOs.

Once the HRTWEAKS GPO is linked to the site, the administrator applies the HR security group to the GPO and sets the Read and Apply Group Policy permissions to allow all the computers and users within this security group to apply the HRTWEAKS GPO (see Figure 8-12). The Authenticated Users group must also be removed to correctly apply the GPO. Remember that this GPO is in a site, so not only are there users in the HR group in this site, but there are also the rest of the domain users in this site. Without removing the Authenticated Users group, you apply the GPO to all users in this site.

When the HR computers are rebooted and HR users log on, the settings within the HRTWEAKS GPO are applied.

How to Apply a Filter to a Group Policy Object

Applying a filter to a GPO is relatively simple. If you have applied security permissions to files or folders on NTFS drives, you will be able to apply filters to a GPO because the two are very similar procedures.

As a simple example, we apply a new GPO to the W2K.LOCAL domain and apply the previously used HR security group to the new GPO.

First, for our example, the Active Directory Users and Computers MMC snap-in must be opened. Underneath Active Directory Users and Computers, the Windows

FIGURE 8-12

Applying the security group HR to the HRTWEAKS GPO

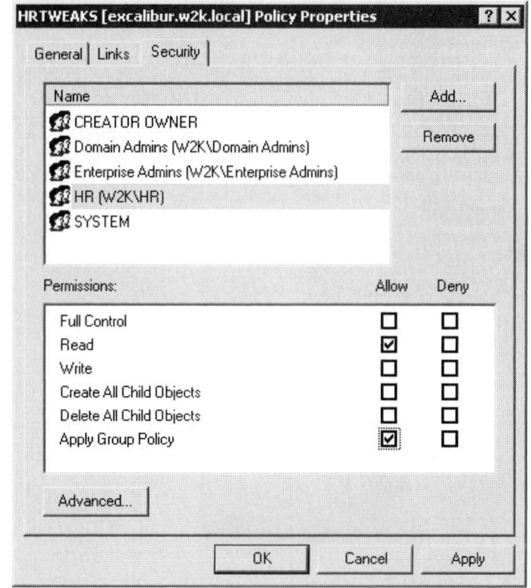

2000 domain can be found. For our example, we use the W2K.LOCAL domain, as shown in Figure 8-13. When you right-click the W2K.LOCAL domain and select the Properties context menu item, the W2K.LOCAL Properties windows appears. To apply a GPO and filter, click the Group Policy tab to show all the GPOs currently assigned to the W2K.LOCAL Domain object. For this example, we use the GPO control GPO, as shown in Figure 8-14.

By clicking the Control GPO and then clicking the Properties button, we can view the security groups assigned to the GPO by clicking the Security tab in the GPO Control Properties window, as shown in Figure 8-15. To add the HR security group, click Add, scroll down the W2K.LOCAL list, select the HR security group, and click OK.

Once the HR security group is added to the GPO Control object, click HR to be able to modify the permissions for the HR security group. As shown in Figure 8-15, you want to assign Read and Apply Group Policy permissions to the HR security group. This assignment gives the minimum amount of permission in order for the HR security group to apply the GPO correctly. Again, note that the Authenticated Users group has been removed because the GPO is being applied to a specific set of users. Once you have applied permissions to the security group, you have successfully applied a GPO filter using security groups.

FIGURE 8-13

Selecting the W2K.LOCAL domain in order to apply a GPO

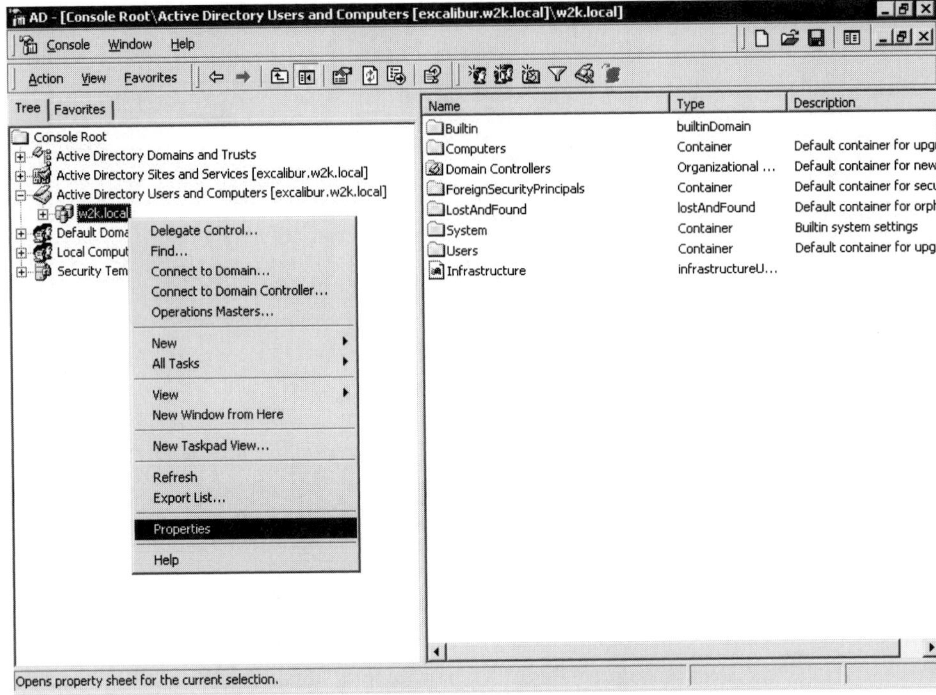

FIGURE 8-14

List of GPOs assigned to the W2K.LOCAL Domain object

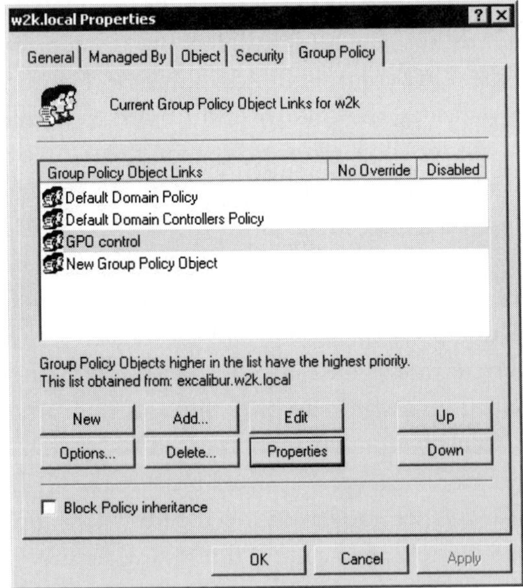

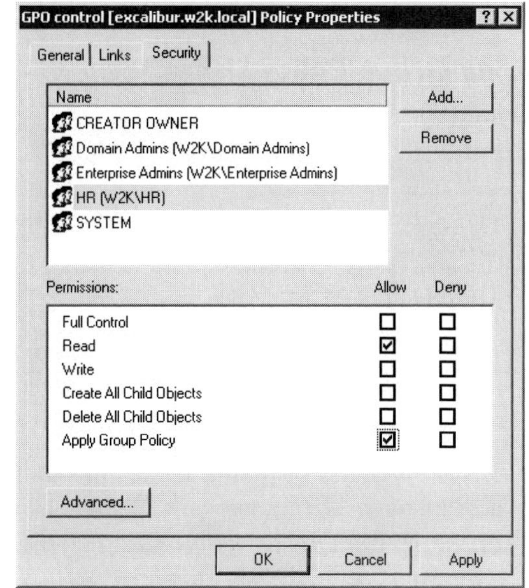

FIGURE 8-15

Applying the HR security group to the GPO Control GPO

EXERCISE 8-5

Filtering Group Policy Using Security Groups

In this exercise, you learn how to apply GPOs through the use of security groups. You use the security group ABCFUTURES-ADMIN to filter GPOs.

1. Verify that you are logged on as Administrator.
2. Create a new user account, **TEST1**, and place it in the global group ABCFUTURES-ADMIN.
3. Open the Control Panel by clicking Start | Settings | Control Panel. Open the Administrative Tools applet and click the Active Directory Users and Computers administrative tool.
4. When the Active Directory Users and Computers tool opens, it shows the domain name of your network. Right-click the domain name and select Properties from the pop-up context menu.
5. When the <domain name> Properties window appears, click the Group Policy tab. The ABCFUTURES GPO is listed as the only GPO linked to this domain object.
6. Click the ABCFUTURES GPO and then click the Properties button.
7. In the ABCFUTURES Properties window, modify permissions for ABCFUTURES by adding Domain Admins and Enterprise Admins as Full Control, remove Authenticated Users, and modify the ABCFUTURES-ADMIN security group so that it has only Read and Apply Group Policy permissions.
8. Next, click ABCFUTURES and then click Edit. In the Group Policy window, navigate to the User Configuration/Administrative Templates/ Desktop | Hide all icons on Desktop entry. Modify the entry from Not Configured to Enabled. Click OK to save the modification.
9. Close the GPO windows and log off. Log back on to the system with the TEST1 account. What happens? Was this expected? Why or why not? What should have happened is that all desktop icons were removed from the desktop. Because TEST1 is a member of the ABCFUTURES-ADMIN security group and this group was given Read and Apply Group Policy permissions, TEST1 was able to apply the Hide all icons on Desktop policy.

10. Log off and log on with the Administrator account. Remove TEST1 from the ABCFUTURES-ADMIN security group.
11. Log off the system and log on with TEST1. What happens? Was this expected? Why or why not?
    What should have happened is that all desktop icons became visible on the desktop. Since TEST1 was removed as a member of the ABCFUTURES-ADMIN security group, it could not apply the ABCFUTURES GPO.

CERTIFICATION OBJECTIVE 8.06

Modifying Group Policy

So far in this chapter, we have talked about what GPOs are, linking GPOs to objects, and even how GPOs work, but we have not yet closely looked at or talked about GPOs in detail. In this section, we do just that.

GPOs consist of two main sections, the Computer Configuration section and the User Configuration section. Within these two sections is another set of three main folders: Software Settings, Windows Settings, and Administrative Templates (see Figure 8-16). These folders contain settings for such items as software installation(s), security configurations (such as account policy, event log, and IP Security policy settings), and registry settings to control the configuration of Windows 2000 systems.

Digging even deeper into GPOs, you will find many hidden gems via which to control and manage your Windows 2000 system.

on the job

You are strongly encouraged to open a default GPO and examine the contents that lie within. Only by exploring, analyzing, and understanding GPOs will you be able to get a feel for exactly how they work and how they can be applied. This exploration is extremely valuable in conjunction with the study of any Windows 2000 textbook.

FIGURE 8-16

A view of the Default Domain GPO, showing the various settings sections

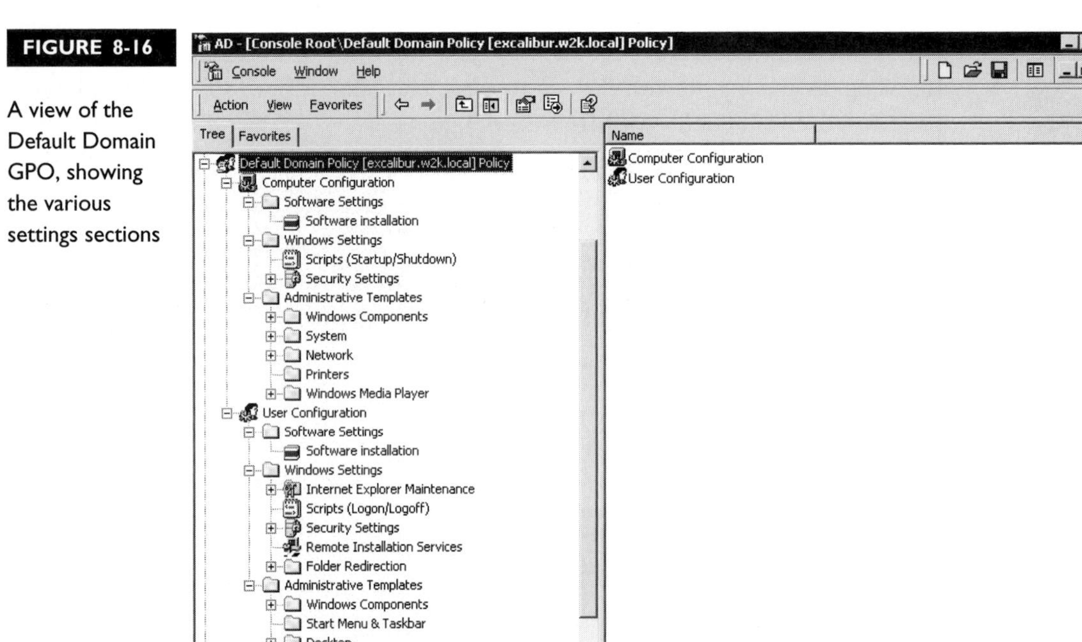

Changing the Policy

Changing a policy is relatively easy. Using the MMC, you can add any group policy by clicking Console | Add/Remove snap-in in the MMC and adding the Group Policy snap-in. You are prompted to select a group policy, which was shown in Figure 8-3; by clicking Browse, you can select any Group Policy in the Active Directory, or you can create a new policy, which was shown in Figure 8-4.

Once you have your group policy selected, you can open and modify it as needed. Remember that there is no saving mechanism, so any changes you make are applied immediately. Anyone rebooting a computer or a user logging on to the network that uses the group policy you are modifying will receive these changes.

When changing a policy, you must pay close attention to how each setting is configured. Leaving a setting Not Defined or Not Configured is basically akin to instructing Group Policy to ignore the setting and to use the last setting that was applied. (This is where the concept of inheritance comes into play; however, inheritance applies to all objects, whether they are configured or not.) Group Policy using the last applied setting might or might not be what you want. Having policies set as Not Defined or Not Configured allows GPOs to be processed faster. This is true because the system can see that each individual policy is not configured, so it can move onto the next individual policy. If there is an individual policy that is configured as Enabled or Disabled, there is extra processing time involved with making the correct configurations to enforce this individual policy setting.

You must understand both of these settings in order to correctly set up group policies, because these settings can affect not only how a group policy is applied to a computer or user, but how fast group policies are processed on a system. For example, look at Figure 8-17, which is a policy that defines the Slow Network Connection Timeout for User Profiles. As shown, the policy is Not Defined. This individual policy will be ignored when the group policy is processed.

Another way of changing a GPO is to disable some of its parts. If you are not using either the User or Computer Configurations within a GPO, you can disable them in order to speed GPO processing in Windows 2000. You can also disable a whole GPO by selecting the Disabled check box in the Options window (refer back to Figure 8-11). You usually disable GPOs in order to help troubleshoot their application.

When you disable Computer or User Configuration settings, you are asked to confirm that you want to disable that part of the GPO that you have selected.

FIGURE 8-17

Policy defining slow network timeout for user profile processing

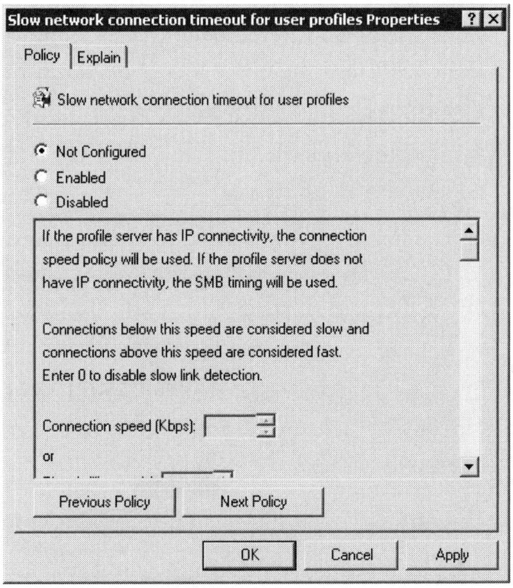

EXERCISE 8-6

Deleting a Group Policy

In this exercise, we look at deleting GPOs from Active Directory. We also look at the options to remove a GPO from a container object and to actually delete a GPO from the Active Directory.

1. Verify that you are logged on as Administrator.
2. Open the Control Panel by clicking Start | Settings | Control Panel. Open the Administrative Tools applet and click the Active Directory Users and Computers administrative tool.
3. When the Active Directory Users and Computers tool opens, it shows the domain name of your network. Right-click the domain name and select Properties from the pop-up context menu.
4. When the <domain name> Properties window appears, click the Group Policy tab. The ABCFUTURES GPO is listed as one of the GPOs linked to this Domain object.
5. Click the ABCFUTURES GPO and then click the Delete button. A Delete window appears, asking whether you want to remove the GPO link from the list of linked GPOs or if you want to remove the GPO link from the list and delete the GPO permanently from Active Directory. Make sure that you select the option to remove the GPO link from the list of linked GPOs, and click OK. The GPO link is removed from the domain container.
6. Add the ABCFUTURES GPO back to the domain object by clicking the Add button and selecting the ABCFUTURES GPO. You need to use this GPO for later exercises.
7. Next, click the New button to create a new GPO. Name this new GPO **ABC123**. To confirm that the GPO has been created and that it exists in Active Directory, click Add. You should be able to see the ABC123 GPO by looking in either the Domains/OUs or All tabs.
8. Once you have verified that the ABC123 GPO exists in the Active Directory, click the Cancel button to return to the <domain name> Properties window.

9. Click the ABC123 GPO and then click Delete. When the Delete window appears, select the option to remove the GPO link and permanently delete the GPO from Active Directory. Click OK.
10. A Delete Group Policy Object window appears, asking you to confirm that you want to delete the GPO. Click Yes.
11. To confirm that the ABC123 GPO has not only been removed from the GPO list but has also been deleted from Active Directory, click Add.
12. If you look under the Domains/OUs or All tabs, you will not find the ABC123 GPO, which confirms that it was deleted from Active Directory.
13. Click Cancel to close the Add a Group Policy Object Link window. Click Close button to close the <domain name> Properties window

CERTIFICATION OBJECTIVE 8.07

Controlling User Environments Using Administrative Templates

Although each part of Group Policy (Software Settings, Windows Settings, and Administrative Templates) is very powerful, only one, Administrative Templates, can be modified through the addition or deletion of templates. Software Settings and Windows Settings are dependent on modifications to change (through modified settings), and you cannot actually add to either part, whereas Administrative Templates allows administrators to add to the section for adding templates. These templates consist of new registry settings that allow administrators to control certain computer or user settings, depending on which section the template focuses.

Although Windows 2000 includes several default templates, administrators can create their own custom templates and import these templates into group policies, to be applied as needed. This feature makes Group Policy an even more powerful management tool because it gives administrators more flexibility to manage Windows 2000.

What Can the Administrator Control?

What can the administrator control? With all the talk about creating custom administrative templates, what can you really control with the Administrative Templates feature?

Administrative templates are templates that can modify registry settings for a computer or user. For a computer, the Administrative Templates component can only modify registry settings within the HKEY_LOCAL_MACHINE (HKLM) registry hive. For a user, Administrative Templates can only modify registry settings within the HKEY_CURRENT_USER (HKCU) registry hive. Although these limitations might seem restrictive, think about exactly what is covered within these two hives. All software configurations (HKLM\Software) and all aspects of desktop settings for users (HKCU\Control Panel) are a couple of broad examples of the functions covered within these registry hives.

How to Create and Import Templates

As previously discussed, you can create your own custom administrative templates to use in group policies. Once created, custom administrative templates should be saved with the .ADM file extension and saved to the %SystemRoot%\INF folder. This is the target/default folder for all template files. Although this is the default folder for storing administrative templates, when you add custom templates to a GPO, the custom template is copied to the GPO's ADM folder in the SYSVOL folder (i.e.%SystemRoot%\SYSVOL\Sysvol\<domain name>\Policies\<GPO GUID>\ADM). The reason for this difference is that the GPO is replicated to all other domain controllers in the domain, and this custom template must also be replicated to all domain controllers in order to properly apply it.

To import templates, simply navigate to either Computer Configuration | Administrative Templates or User Configuration | Administrative Templates in the target GPO, right-click Administrative Templates, and select Add/Remove Templates from the pop-up context menu (see Figure 8-18). Make sure that if your template has both User and Computer policies, you select both Computer Configuration and User Configuration to import the appropriate policies. If your template has both User and Computer policies and you import from only one configuration (such as the User configuration), you will not import the other section's policies. You *must* import the policy in both User and Computer configurations.

Once you have clicked Add/Remove Templates, the Add/Remove Templates window appears with a list of currently installed templates in the Administrative Templates section of your GPO (see Figure 8-19).

FIGURE 8-18

Adding a template to the Administrative Templates section of a GPO

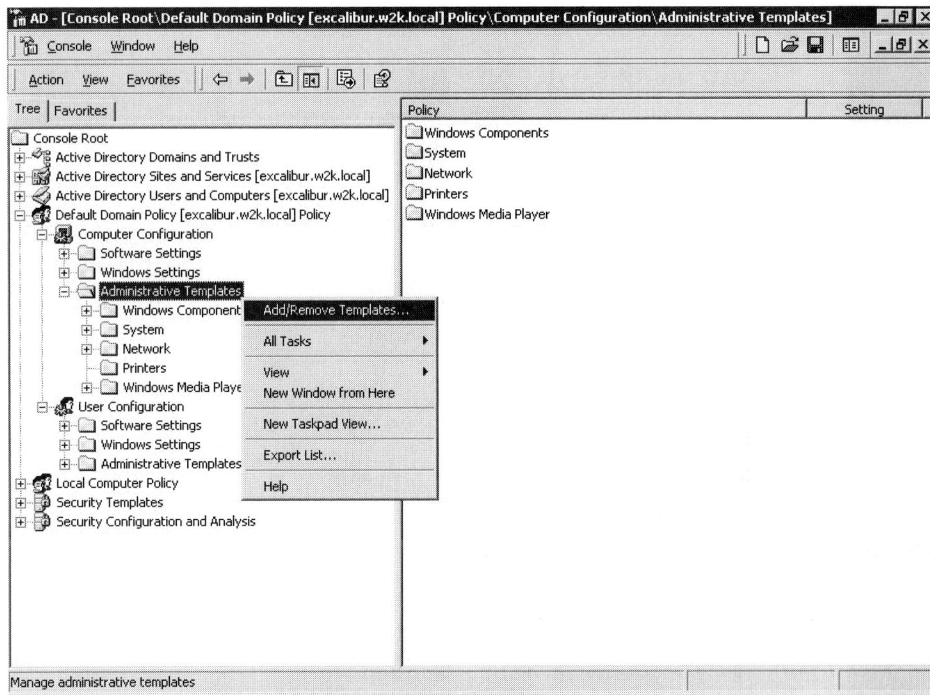

To add a template, click Add. A window appears to select a template to add to the current list of templates. Select a template file and click Open to add it to the list of installed templates. Once you are finished, click Close. Once you click Close, all new templates are checked for syntax and, if no errors are found, they are added to the correct Computer or User Configuration section of Administrative Templates.

FIGURE 8-19

Current list of templates installed in Administrative Templates

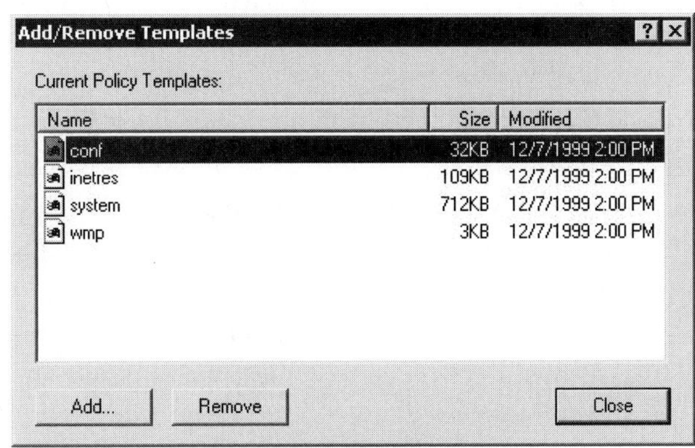

EXERCISE 8-7

Controlling Environments with Administrative Templates

In this exercise, you learn how to change the desktop environment by importing and configuring templates in Administrative Templates.

1. Verify that you are logged on as Administrator.
2. Open the Control Panel by clicking Start | Settings | Control Panel. Open the Administrative Tools applet and click the Active Directory Users and Computers administrative tool.
3. When the Active Directory Users and Computers tool opens, it shows the domain name of your network. Right-click the domain name and select Properties from the pop-up context menu.
4. When the <domain name> Properties window appears, click the Group Policy tab. The ABCFUTURES GPO is listed as the only GPO linked to this Domain object.
5. Click the ABCFUTURES GPO and then click Edit. When the Group Policy window appears, navigate to the User Configuration/Administrative Templates of the GPO.
6. Right-click the Administrative Templates section and select Add/Remove Templates from the pop-up context menu.
7. In the Add/Remove Templates window, click Add to add a new template to the list of imported templates already in the GPO.
8. Search the %SystemRoot%\INF folder for Administrative Templates (look for .ADM extension files). Once all these files are found, select the WMP.ADM template (the Windows Media Player template) and click Open to import this template.
9. Once the template is imported, click Close to return to the Group Policy window.
10. The GPO then takes the template, scans the template for syntax and other errors, and, if no problems are detected, the template is added to the GPO. You will see a Windows Media Player entry added beneath the Administrative Templates section.

11. Navigate to the Windows Media Player/Windows Media Player Configurations section. Double-click the Customize the Windows Media Player entry to modify the entry.
12. In the Customize the Windows Media Player window, click the Policy tab, click the Enabled radio button to enable this entry, and then type **This is the Windows Media Player** in the text box for the Title Bar for the Windows Media Player. Click OK to accept the changes.
13. Modify the ABCFUTURES GPO security groups by adding the Authenticated Users group back and giving the group Read and Apply Group Policy permissions.
14. Log off and log on again. Start the Windows Media Player and check the Title Bar. You will see that it has changed.

CERTIFICATION OBJECTIVE 8.08

Assigning Script Policies to Users and Computers

Another new feature of Windows 2000 that is implemented in Group Policy is the ability to assign scripts, not only to users but also to computers. Furthermore, you can also assign the scripts to run during computer startup or shutdown or user logon or logoff.

As for the order of processing, when a computer boots, the Computer Configuration section of a Group Policy is processed first, which includes any startup scripts, followed by the processing of the User Configuration section within any group policies, when a user logs on. This includes the execution of any logon scripts found in the GPO. On shutdown, however, the reverse is true. First, all user configurations in group policies are processed, including logoff scripts, followed by the processing of all Computer Configuration sections, including shutdown scripts.

With the inclusion of startup or shutdown scripts for computers, along with logoff scripts for users, Windows 2000 makes workstation and user configurations much more flexible.

User vs. Computer Scripts

What is the difference between user and computer scripts? The main difference between the two, as explained previously, is that user scripts are processed at logon and logoff, whereas computer scripts are processed only at startup or shutdown. Computer scripts are not processed every time a user logs on or off a computer. Looking at Figures 8-20 and 8-21, you can see the difference between user scripts and computer scripts.

FIGURE 8-20

User scripts (Logon/Logoff) in the Default Domain Policy GPO

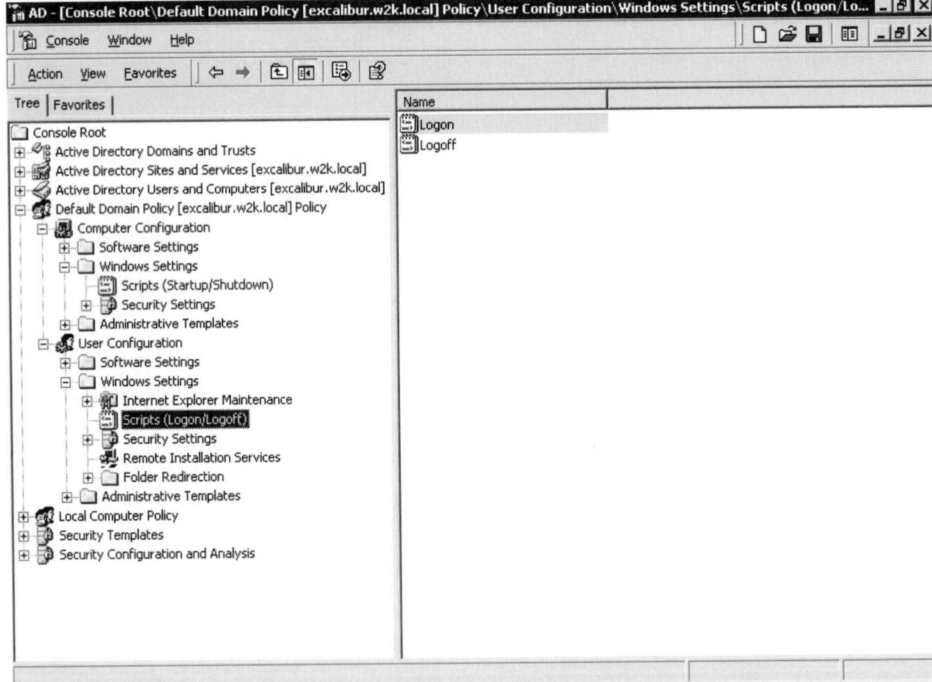

FIGURE 8-21

Computer scripts (Startup/Shutdown) in the Default Domain Policy GPO

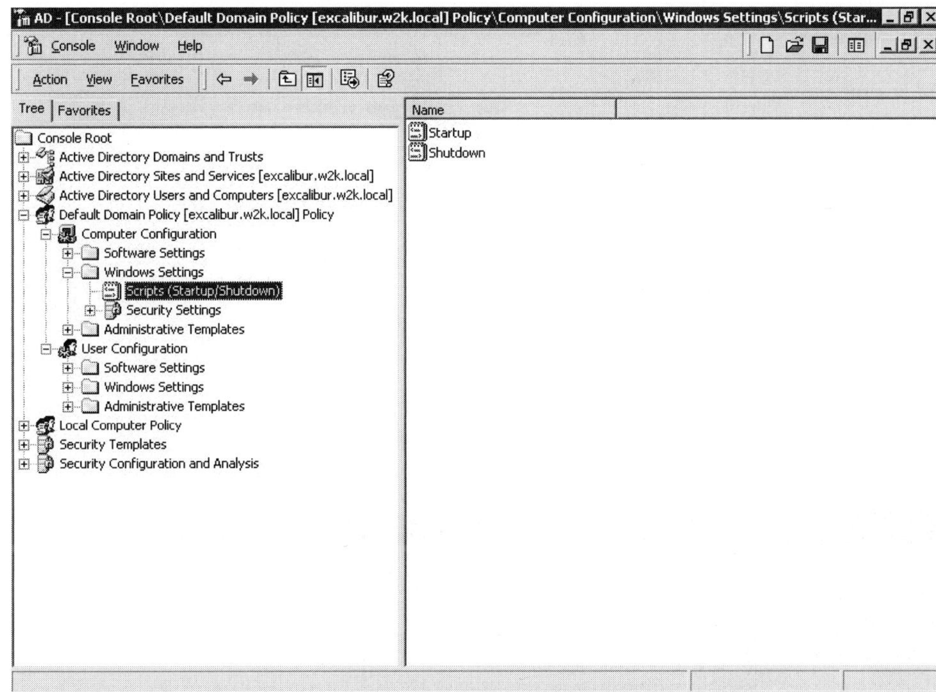

To have a script processed in either section, you must place it in the spot where you want it processed. Take the example of a logon script that needs to be processed by all employees within a company. This script assigns three drive letters, one each for a home directory (H:), an application directory (R:), and a projects directory (P:). Without these drives, users cannot use applications, store their personal data, or work on company projects. To assign these drives, you must place the logon script in a group policy so that all users run the script when they log on. The script, LOGON.BAT, must be placed in the User Configuration section of Group Policy.

To set up the script correctly, an administrator must navigate to the User Configuration | Windows Settings | Scripts (Logon/Logoff) section of the GPO. Once there, double-click the Logon section, and a Logon Properties window appears, as shown in Figure 8-22.

FIGURE 8-22

Adding the script LOGON.BAT to the Logon section of Scripts

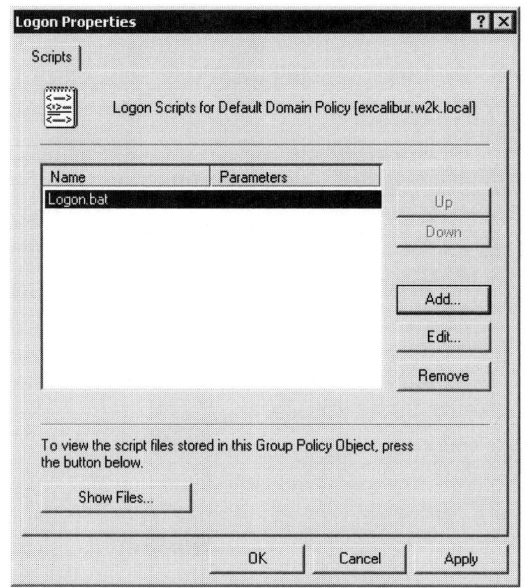

To add a script, click Add and add the script(s) needed. In our example, we need to add only one script, LOGON.BAT, to the Logon section. Once the script is added, click OK to accept all the additions. Note that in Figure 8-22 there are Up and Down buttons, which allow you to change the processing of logon scripts. Remember that scripts are processed in order from top to bottom.

EXERCISE 8-8

Assigning Script Policies

In this exercise, you learn how to assign scripts through the use of GPOs.

1. Verify that you are logged on as Administrator.
2. Create a sample logon script called LOGON.BAT. The only line of text should be NET SEND ADMINISTRATOR "HELLO". Save the script under the %SystemRoot%\SYSVOL\<domain name>\SCRIPTS\ folder. Saving the script here not only places the script in a place to be used by other GPOs, it also allows the script to be replicated to all other domain controllers and makes it available to down-level clients (i.e., Windows NT 4.0 clients) so that they can run the logon script(s), since this folder is the NETLOGON share for all domain controllers. You can place the script anywhere, but remember that the script needs to be placed in the same location on all domain controllers. For example, if you choose to place scripts in a folder called SCRIPTS on your D: drive, you need to place this folder on each of your domain controllers. If you do not, your scripts will fail because the script is pulled from the domain controller that authenticates you.
3. Open the Control Panel by clicking Start | Settings | Control Panel. Open the Administrative Tools applet and click the Active Directory Users and Computers administrative tool.
4. When the Active Directory Users and Computers tool opens, it shows the domain name of your network. Right-click the domain name and select Properties from the pop-up context menu.
5. When the <domain name> Properties window appears, click the Group Policy tab. The ABCFUTURES GPO is listed as the only GPO linked to this Domain object.
6. Click the ABCFUTURES GPO and then click Edit. When the Group Policy window appears, navigate to User Configuration/Windows Settings/Scripts (Logon/Logoff).

7. Double-click Logon, and in the Logon Properties window, click Add to add the LOGON.BAT file. Click OK to exit.
8. Log off and log on again with the Administrator account. Once your logon is complete, you get a pop-up window that states HELLO. This message signifies that the sample logon script ran. *Note:* You need to use the Administrator account in order to see the notification when you log on.

CERTIFICATION SUMMARY

In the first two objectives, we talked about creating and linking GPOs. We covered what GPOs are, the value they give to administrators for management purposes, and how to link GPOs to Site, Domain, and Organizational Unit objects within Active Directory.

Next we covered how to manipulate GPOs by delegating control, modifying inheritance of Group Policy, and filtering the application of GPOs through the use of security groups. We talked about delegating control of GPOs to individuals because of the complexity and power of group policies. Because GPOs are so powerful and complex, they need to be strictly controlled by only a select group of individuals. Furthermore, we covered the need to manipulate how group policies are applied. Modifying the application of GPOs through the use of the Block Inheritance and No Override fields, along with filtering the application of GPOs through the use of security groups, proved that GPOs could be applied in almost any type of situation without problems.

Lastly, we talked about modifying group policies, along with discussing specific sections within Group Policy: Administrative Templates and assigning script policies to computers and users. We covered how to modify GPOs, what Not Defined or Not Configured meant when processing GPOs, and, along with learning how to add and remove templates to GPOs in order to more easily manage computers and users, we learned about adding scripts within GPOs for computers and users to run during startup and shutdown as well as logon and logoff.

TWO-MINUTE DRILL

Creating a Group Policy Object

- ❑ Group Policy is highly flexible; it allows the configuration and management of just about any computer or user setting.

Linking an Existing Group Policy Object

- ❑ When GPOs are created, they can be assigned only to a Local Computer, Domain or Organizational Unit object. They cannot be assigned to an object such as the built-in folders in Active Directory.

Delegating Administrative Control of Group Policy

- ❑ Delegating control of group policies allows administrators to divide the task of managing group policies into an IT support group that manages only Group Policy or assignment of GPOs to specific individuals for security purposes.
- ❑ Delegating control of GPOs is different from delegating authority to objects in Active Directory; delegation is very much like assigning permissions to a folder within NTFS.

Modifying Group Policy Inheritance

- ❑ Remember that group policies follow the inheritance path of Local Computer | Sites | Domains | Organizational Units (OUs).
- ❑ Remember that GPOs are processed from the bottom to the top due to the fact that the top of a GPO link list has higher priority when enforcing individual policy settings.

Filtering Group Policy Settings

- ❑ Filtering GPOs should always be performed using security groups and not using Active Directory objects such as OUs.
- ❑ Filtering GPOs gives administrators the flexibility to apply GPO settings to a subset of computers or users within a Domain or Organizational Unit.

Modifying Group Policy

- GPOs consist of two main sections, Computer Configuration and User Configuration. Each section has three subsections: Software Settings, Windows Settings, and Administrative Templates. Remember not to confuse settings between Computer and User Configurations, which could lead to improper application of GPOs.
- Most policies have either an Enabled/Disabled/Not Configured setting or a Not Defined/Not Configured setting. These settings are used to let Windows 2000 ignore the processing of individual policy settings in order to speed the processing of GPOs. Make sure you know the impact of using or not using these settings.

Controlling User Environments Using Administrative Templates

- Administrative Templates is the only section in a GPO that can be added to or removed from a GPO. The Software and Windows Settings sections can be modified, but not through the addition or removal of templates such as administrative templates.
- Administrative Templates can be expanded through the use of customized templates.
- The only parts of the registry that Administrative Templates can modify through customized or default templates are the HKEY_LOCAL_MACHINE (for computer) and HKEY_CURRENT_USER (for user) registry hives.

Assigning Script Policies to Users and Computers

- Scripts can now be assigned to computers along with users.
- Users have scripts applied at logon and logoff; computers have scripts applied at startup and shutdown.

9

Managing the Windows 2000 Application Environment

CERTIFICATION OBJECTIVES

9.01 Deploying Software Using Group Policy

9.02 Maintaining Software Using Group Policy

9.03 Configuring Deployment Options

9.04 Troubleshooting During Software Deployment

9.05 Managing Network Configuration Using Group Policy

✓ Two-Minute Drill

In this chapter, you learn how you can use Group Policy to automatically distribute, maintain, and remove software throughout your organization. You also see how to remotely administer change to many of the resources throughout your network.

Microsoft Windows 2000 includes several technologies under the blanket name *IntelliMirror;* these technologies are intended to decrease total cost of ownership (TCO) of the product by providing the ability to remotely implement change throughout an enterprise. Among the IntelliMirror features we inspect in this chapter are the *Windows Installer service,* which allows automated, hands-off installation of self-repairing software packages, and the *Software Installation and Maintenance technology,* which uses Group Policy Objects (GPOs) to deploy and administer these software packages. We also look at *Folder Redirection,* which allows us to automatically send files in user folders such as My Documents to a central location for backup and security.

CERTIFICATION OBJECTIVE 9.01

Deploying Software Using Group Policy

It used to be that deployment of software to a few, several hundred, or several thousand machines meant that an administrator had to visit each and every desktop at various points throughout the life cycle of an application. Since ordinary users did not (and probably should not) have the ability to install software on their own workstations by default, an administrator had to visit each individual desktop whenever any of the following occurred:

- Initial software deployment
- Upgrades to software, such as service packs
- Corruption of software
- Unknown file types encountered by user
- Removal of software

By using Software Installation and Maintenance in conjunction with Windows Installer and Group Policy, the entire process is now automated and performed remotely from an administrator's desktop, resulting in a great savings of time, effort, and money.

The software deployment process essentially consists of two steps: preparation or acquisition of a Microsoft Windows Installer (.MSI) package and, optionally, the construction of a MSI transform file (.MST), as well as the publication or assignment of that package through a GPO. To fully understand the deployment process, we must first take a look at what is being deployed.

Windows Installer and .MSI Files

The *Windows Installer Service*, available for Windows 95, 98, 2000, and NT 4.0, is a local service on each workstation that allows for the automated installation of software through the use of *Microsoft Software Installation* (*.MSI*) files. Windows Installer and .MSI files replace the traditional SETUP.EXE file that required a good deal of user input during the installation process. With Windows Installer, an application is installed and configured on a test computer and then repackaged into an .MSI file by a third-party application. Once an .MSI is created, a user needs only to find and invoke the application in order to install it, possibly without answering any configuration questions during the installation. Additionally, a user needs no sort of administrative privileges in order to install software using an .MSI file. This is in contrast to the old SETUP.EXE file, for which a user needed to have administrative privileges on his or her own machine in order to run the setup program. Using .MSI files, it is very easy for the administrator to deploy a preconfigured application and ensure that it appears and behaves the same for all users.

There are essentially two ways to acquire a package. *Native packages* usually come packaged with the software. Office 2000, for example, contains .MSI packages for various operating systems. If no native package exists, you can *repackage* the application to create a package. We first take a brief look at the repackaging process, and then we look at one example of how a third-party repackaging tool works to create and modify Microsoft Installer packages.

The Repackaging Process

If you do not have a native .MSI file available with the software, or if you decide you need to create a custom package to meet your organization's needs, you need to use third-party repackaging software. Fortunately, Windows 2000 Server includes such software on its CD. The program, called Veritas WinINSTALL LE, is located in %CDROOT%\VALUEADD\MGMT\WINSTLE. Once you have WinINSTALL or your software loaded and placed into a shared folder, it is a four-step process to create a package:

1. You need a clean computer with only Windows 2000 Professional installed. From that machine, you connect to the share with your repackaging software and run the program, taking a "before" snapshot, per your application's instructions.
2. You then install and configure the application for which you want to create an installation package.
3. You need to reconnect to the repackaging software and take an "after" snapshot. This creates a package based on the differences your test computer found between the before and after snapshots.
4. Finally, you need to test and tweak the application as necessary before full-scale deployment.

CertCam 9-1

EXERCISE 9-1

Creating an .MSI Package Using WinINSTALL LE

1. From the Windows 2000 Professional, Server, or Advanced Server compact disc, run \VALUADD\3RDPARTY\MGMT\WINSTLE\SWIADMLE.MSI and follow any prompts. This installs WinINSTALL LE.
2. Share C:\PROGRAMFILES\VERITAS SOFTWARE\WINSTALL with its default settings (or giving only administrators full control).
3. Install Windows 2000 Professional on a source machine.
4. Choose Start | Run, then type *servername*\winstall\discoz.exe and click Next.
5. Type a name for the application to be packaged and a location in which it will be stored. This location should be a Universal Naming Convention (UNC) path to a server (see the next illustration).

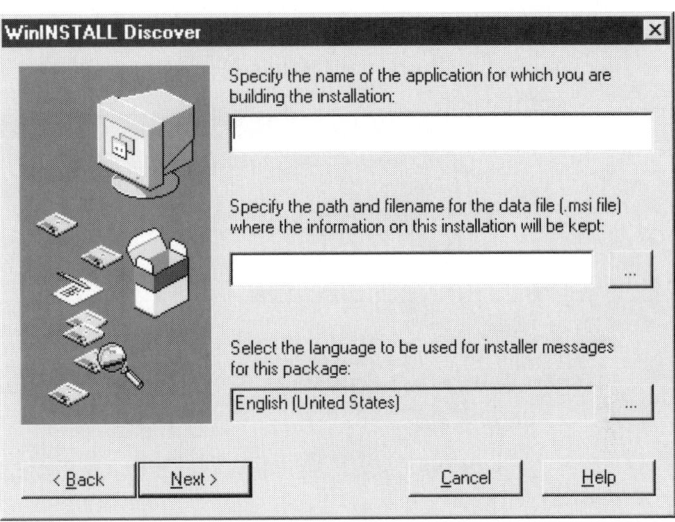

6. Click Next to accept the default temporary file drive letter.
7. Choose the source computer drive or drives to scan while making the "before" snapshot. Choose any drives that might be affected by the installation (see the following illustration). Click Next.

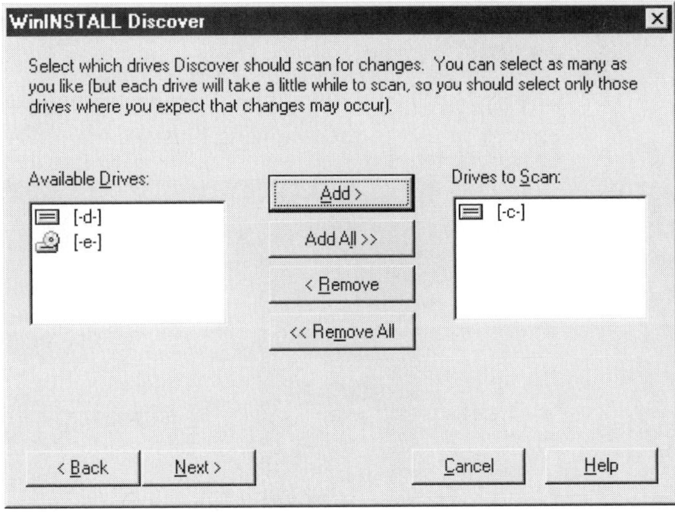

8. Choose any files or types of files to be left out of the directory (see the following illustration). Click Next.

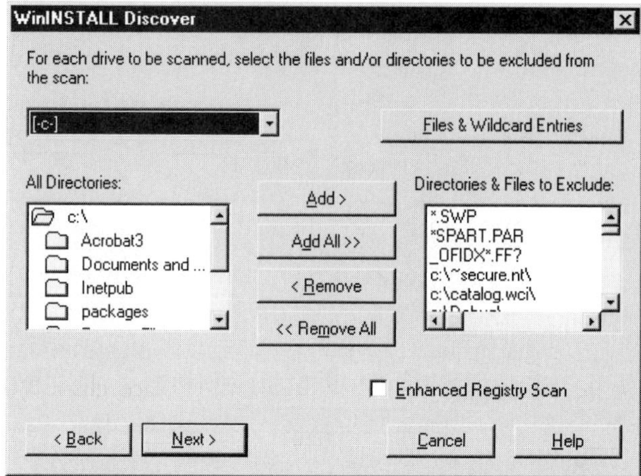

9. When Discover indicates it is through taking the "before" snapshot, click OK.
10. Discover asks you to launch a setup program. Choose the program for which you want to create a package, and click OK.
11. Install and configure the application on the source computer. *Do not reboot if prompted.*
12. Choose Start | Run, then type ***servername*\winstall\discoz.exe**. You will see a screen similar to the following illustration.

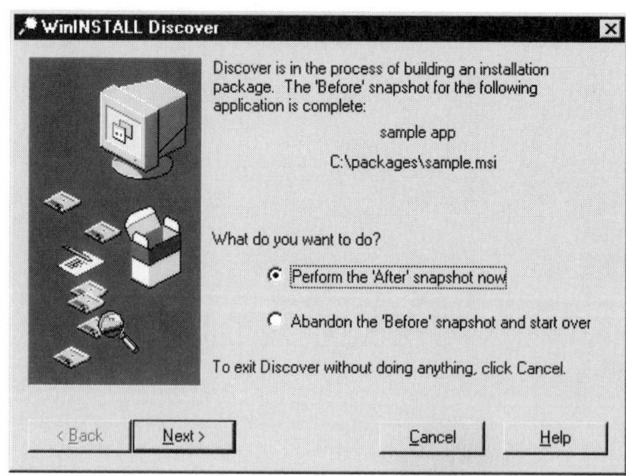

13. Click Next to choose the default, "Perform the 'After' snapshot now."
14. Discover takes an "after" snapshot and create an .MSI file. Place it and any other support files created into a shared folder.

Modifying Packages

Once a package has been created, it can be opened up and modified at any time using the Veritas Software Console (see Figure 9-1). With this utility, you have the ability to view and edit all aspects of the package that was created. You can add or remove files, create new shortcuts, determine exactly how different portions of the registry will be affected by the package, configure how services and .INI files will be changed, and configure the advertising attributes of the package. All of this can be done after the actual creation of the package takes place, eliminating the need to redo the "before" and "after" snapshots, should a change need to be made after the fact. (For more information regarding changing the characteristics of a package, refer to the Veritas help files or the help files that came with your third-party repackaging software.)

FIGURE 9-1

Veritas Software Console

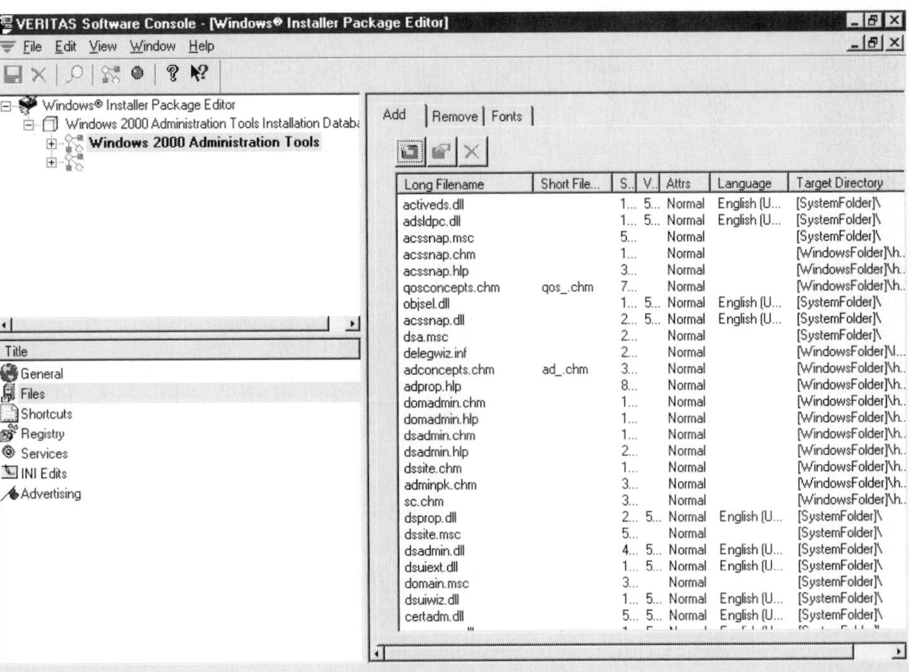

When to Use GPOs to Deploy Software, and Why

Now that we have created or acquired our Microsoft Software Installer package, we need to look at how to get this package to the user. With their dynamic nature and ease of administration, Active Directory and Group Policy Objects make the distribution of packages simple and flexible. Whenever we need to be sure that a software package is available to a large number of users or computers, we use Group Policy to distribute the package. The following is a review of some of the key benefits of Group Policy and a look at how it can aid in the distribution of software:

- GPOs can be placed in any organizational unit (OU) and through the use of filtering applied to any user, group, or computer you want.
- Because they can be placed in any OU, the administration of GPOs can be delegated to a user or group without giving that user or group full-fledged administrative privileges.
- When a package is applied with a GPO, you have several options regarding how to distribute it, such as whether to make it mandatory or optional for the user.
- As is usually the case with Group Policy, if a policy can be assigned, it can easily be unassigned, although with software distribution, the process is slightly different than in most other cases.
- When software is distributed as .MSI files through the use of GPOs, users do not need to have administrative control of their own machines. They need to have only that particular package assigned or published to them.

Applying the Package to an Organizational Unit

Once we have our package ready to go, we need to associate it with one or more GPOs at the site, domain, or OU level. This is usually done through Active Directory Users and Computers. Any existing GPO can be modified to include a software distribution package, but you might want to create a separate one for the sake of clarity.

Once inside the GPO, you need to decide whether to associate the software package to a computer or a user. If you assign it to a computer, you work with the Software Settings under the Computer Configuration section of the policy. If you associate with a user, you again work with Software Settings, but this time under the User Configuration section.

Either way, the actual association is very simple. After opening the appropriate Software Settings section under either User or Computer Configuration, you see an icon labeled Software Packages. Right-click this icon and choose New | Packages, browse to find the package, specify whether it will be assigned or published, and you're done. The real trick lies in understanding the differences between assigning and publishing software and assigning it to users as opposed to assigning it to computers.

Assigning Packages to Computers

If you need to make sure that every computer in a certain department has access to an application, assigning that package to a group of computers is the most foolproof way to do it. When you *assign* a package to a computer, that package is automatically installed the next time the machine reboots, regardless of who is sitting at that machine. This method is useful if, for example, all your accountants needs to have Excel 2000 on their desktops.

When a package is assigned in this way, it is installed as a *self-repairing* application. Every time the computer is restarted and the policy is applied, the package is checked to see if it has been run on that machine. If any files are missing from the original installation, they are replaced. Likewise, future changes to the original package are very easy to distribute.

To assign a package to a computer or group of computers, apply the package under Software Settings in the Computer Configuration section of the GPO. When asked whether you want the package published or assigned, choose Assigned (see Figure 9-2). You are not able to choose Published in this case. Assuming you have not filtered out the rights of any computers in this OU to receive the GPO, the software is automatically installed the next time the computer boots up.

FIGURE 9-2

Choosing Assigned rather than Published in the Deploy Software screen

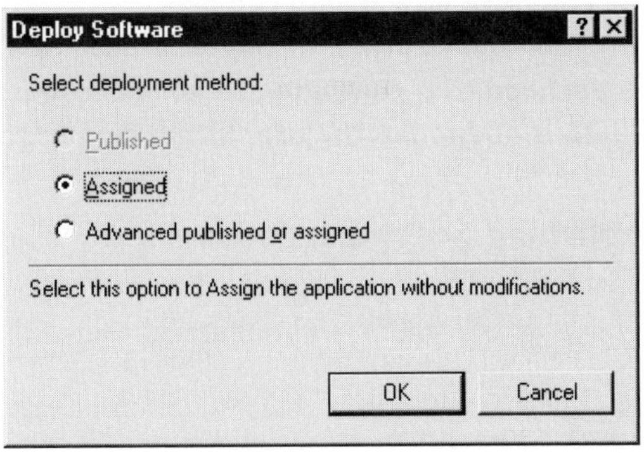

Assigning Packages to Users

When you assign a package to users, you are essentially advertising to the users that the package is there for them when they need it. A package that has been deployed in this way appears to the user as though it has been installed, but in reality it is installed only when the user calls on the application in one way or another.

When you assign a package to a user or group of users, the GPO that contains that package assigns that package when the user logs on. At that time, the application appears on the user's Start menu, but it is not actually installed. In addition, any files that were of a previously unknown type but that now have extensions associated with the assigned application now show the application's icon instead of the "flying window" for the unknown file type.

The first time a user calls on an application, either by choosing it from the Start menu or through *document invocation* (double-clicking a file of that type), it is installed automatically on the user's computer. If the user logs on to a different machine, the same process occurs on that machine as well.

This method of software deployment is useful when you have a group of users, most of whom need to use an application but some of whom might not. Via this method, the application is readily available to the users who need it but does not take up precious disk space on the machines of the users who do not need it. As is the case when you assign a package to a computer, software is self-repairing when you assign it to a user. Each time the user calls on that application, the package is checked for changes or missing files.

To assign a package to users, associate the package with the User Configuration side of the GPO and, when asked, assign the software instead of publishing it.

on the Job

Take care when assigning large packages to users. Imagine innocently clicking on an e-mail attachment, thinking you have Word installed, only to realize that you have now begun the process of dumping the entire Office 2000 suite onto your workstation! In this situation, it is probably better to either assign the package to a computer, in which case it would install on startup, or publish it and make the user intentionally go find it if he or she wants it.

Publishing Software to Users

When you *publish* a package to a user or group of users, you give the user or group permission to install it, without actually advertising its presence. On the surface, a package deployed in this way does not appear to the user at all. It is only when the user goes to Add/Remove Programs that he or she discovers its availability.

When a user logs on after a package has been published to that user, the package is not installed, nor is it placed on the Start menu, nor do any icons change. Instead, it simply appears in Add/Remove Programs as a program that is available to the user. Choosing the program from here starts the appropriate .MSI file, and automated installation occurs.

Document invocation also installs a published package. When a user double-clicks on a file of an unknown type, Active Directory is searched for a published package that will open files of that type. If any exist, the associated GPOs are checked for the necessary permissions. If the package has been published to the user, it is installed. (Incidentally, this makes for some interesting trivia for your next slow cocktail party. The reason it takes a few seconds longer for the Open With dialog box to appear than it did in NT 4.0 is that all of Active Directory is being searched for published software first.)

To publish a package to users, associate the package with the User Configuration side of the GPO and, when asked, publish the software instead of assigning it. Note that packages can be published only to users, not to computers.

CERTIFICATION OBJECTIVE 9.02

Maintaining Software Using Group Policy

Just as Group Policy in conjunction with Software Installation and Maintenance allowed us to easily and automatically deploy software to users and computers, it also provides us flexibility and simplicity when it is time to upgrade, change, or remove the software. When we want to upgrade version 1 to version 2, for example, we can decide whether we want that upgrade to happen automatically to all users of version 1 or whether we want the user of the software in question to be able to decide whether or not he or she wants the upgrade. If version 2 is installed, we also have options regarding what to do with version 1. Likewise, when we want to remove a package, we can decide whether we want current users to be able to continue to use the software or whether it should be removed from their machines.

Software Upgrades

There are two types of software upgrades we can deploy: mandatory and optional. With a *mandatory upgrade*, the new version of the software is automatically installed the next time the user calls the application. With an *optional upgrade*, the user has the option of going to Add/Remove Programs to get the new software.

Mandatory Upgrades

A mandatory upgrade automatically installs the new version of the software and optionally removes the old version. This is useful if you want to roll out the new version of the software fairly quickly and universally. It is important to be sure that the new version is completely compatible with everyone's hardware, existing software, and current needs. If there are users whose productivity could be hampered by the installation of the new software, or if you just don't feel comfortable running the latest and greatest version of your graphics software on some of your less powerful machines, this might not be the proper option for you.

A mandatory upgrade is a very simple process. You need to come up with an .MSI for the new version of the software, and share it out. You then publish it or assign it in a GPO. You can pull up a property sheet for the new package by right-clicking it in the GPO. When you do this and click the Upgrades tab, you see a sheet like Figure 9-3.

In the Add Upgrade Package dialog box, click Add and find version 1 of the software. You can also decide at this point whether to remove the first package or upgrade over it. Checking the "Required upgrade for existing packages" box makes this a mandatory upgrade.

Incidentally, if versions 1 and 2 of the software are both *native* .MSI packages—that is, if they were both provided by the manufacturer with the software—you do not need to specify which package you are upgrading. The new package automatically finds and replaces the old. When the user runs the application the next time, it replaces version 1 with version 2.

on the Job

It is interesting to note that *any* ***package can be used to "update" any other package. The two packages do not necessarily need to be related. This feature comes in handy if you want to replace one vendor's word processor with that of another vendor. For that matter, you could replace your accounting department's spreadsheets with a game if you wanted to really send them into a tizzy.***

FIGURE 9-3

The Upgrades tab in a package's Properties sheet

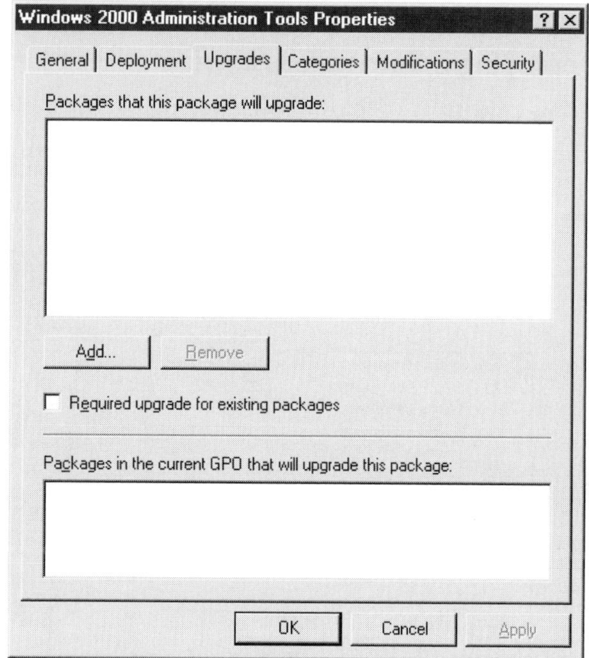

Optional Upgrades

With an optional upgrade, you give users the choice of whether to install the new package or leave the old one intact, giving users more flexibility over the packages they think they need.

Optional upgrades are done in almost the same manner as mandatory ones. You create the new package, share it, deploy it using Group Policy, and go to the Properties sheet for that package in the GPO. This time, you simply clear the "Required upgrade for existing packages" box.

If a user already has version 1 of an application, version 2 is installed automatically if the user opens a file that requires the new version of the software. If this does not happen, the user must go to Add/Remove Programs to apply the upgrade.

EXERCISE 9-2

Deploying a Software Upgrade

In this exercise, we deploy a software upgrade via the following steps:

1. Acquire or create a new Windows Installer package and deploy it through Group Policy, as you did before (see the following illustration).

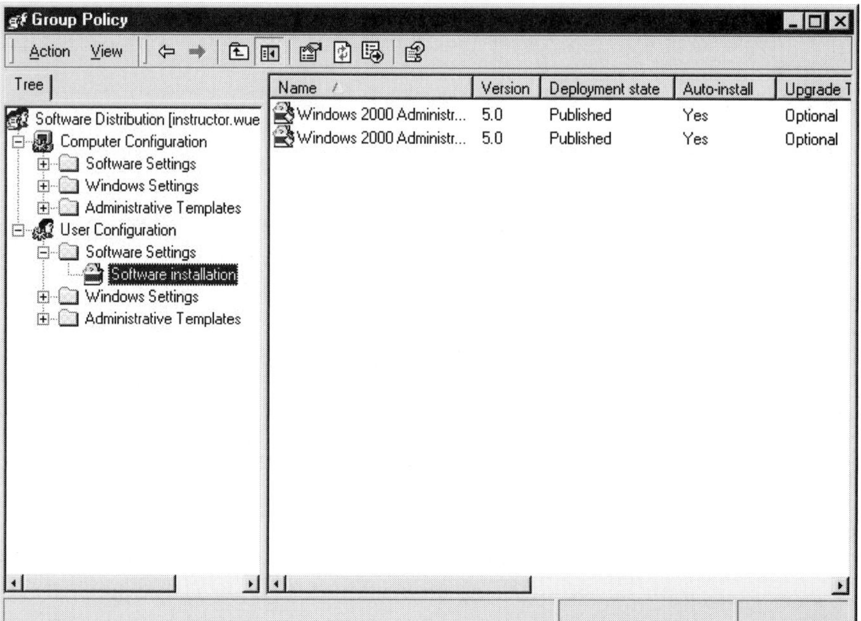

2. Right-click on the new package, and choose Properties.
3. Click the Upgrades tab.
4. Find the package you want to upgrade, and decide whether to have it remove the old package or install over it (see the following illustration).

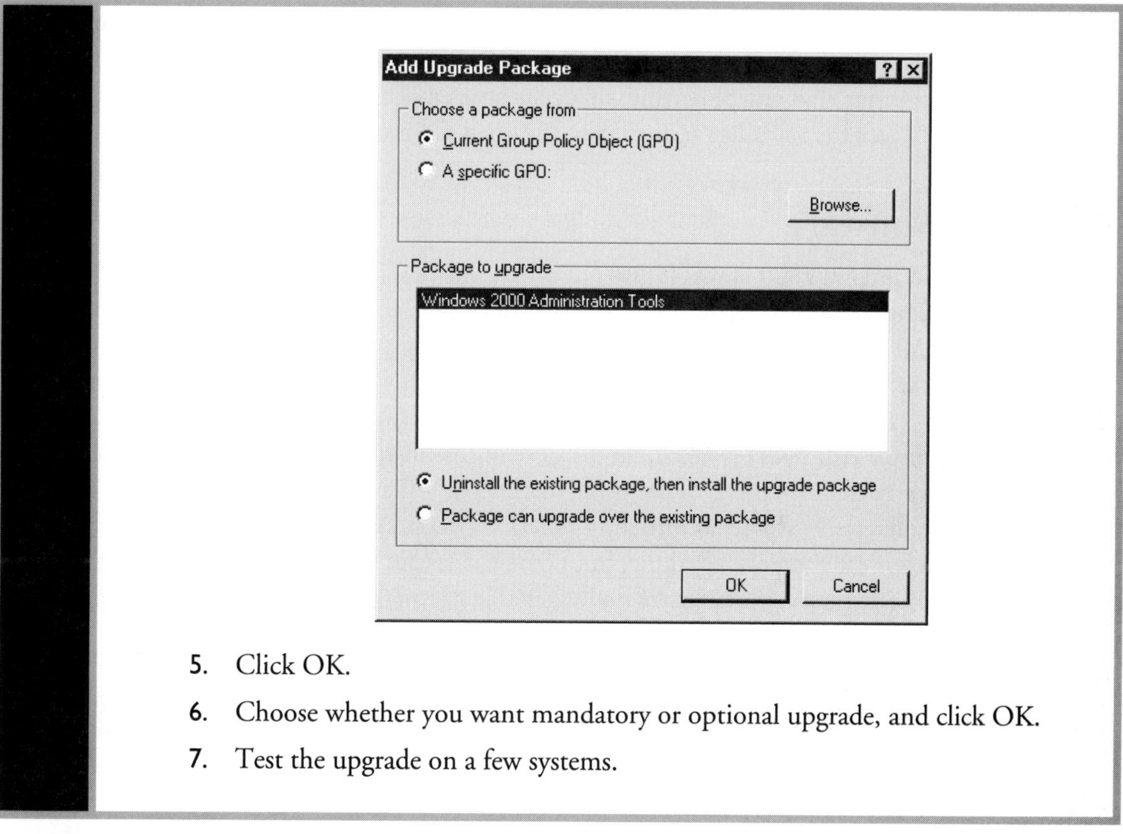

5. Click OK.
6. Choose whether you want mandatory or optional upgrade, and click OK.
7. Test the upgrade on a few systems.

Redeploying Software

Software Installation and Maintenance allows you to easily redeploy software to users when there are a few changes to be made to the installation. Perhaps you want to install a service pack onto everyone's installation of Microsoft Office, or maybe everyone in your marketing department suddenly decided to start speaking Swahili, so they now need new dictionaries for their word processors. These changes can be easily deployed throughout your network, assuming that the original installation was done using Group Policy.

To redeploy, simply include the new files with the original package, go to the package in the GPO, right-click, and choose All Tasks | Redeploy. You get a warning that redeployment will occur on all machines that already have the package. Bypass the warning, and you have finished the process.

Removing Software

Windows 2000 makes it just as easy to remove software that was originally installed through a GPO. You simply need to right-click the package in the GPO, and choose All Tasks | Remove. You get a dialog box asking you to choose a removal method (see Figure 9-4).

If you choose "Immediately uninstall the software from users and computers," also called *forced removal*, the GPO sends the instruction to physically remove the software from users' desktops. If you choose "Allow user to continue to use the software, but prevent further installations," also called *optional removal*, it does not physically remove anything, but no new users get the software distributed to them. Furthermore, the users are no longer able to install the software from Add/Remove Programs.

exam Watch

There is one bothersome quirk in the removal process. If you choose an optional removal, the package disappears because it is no longer needed. However, if you later decide you want to forcibly remove the package from users' desktops, you have no way to go back and change the removal status. In that case, you need to visit each workstation individually to remove the software. You could also redeploy the application to everyone, wait until it has had a chance to be applied, and then force removal.

FIGURE 9-4

Software removal options

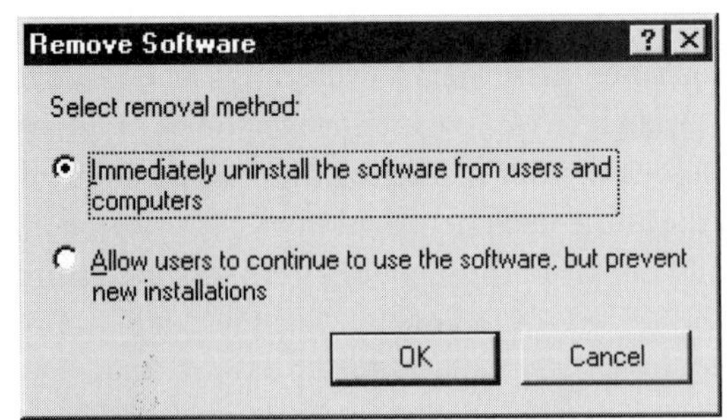

FROM THE CLASSROOM

Uninstalling Packages

Be sure you understand that the process to "undo" a software installation is very different than the process to undo most Group Policy Object effects. Usually, you simply need to remove or disable a Group Policy Object in order to undo it. Here, that will not do the trick. You must physically tell the package to uninstall itself.

If you were to delete a Group Policy Object that had been used to distribute a software package, you would make it impossible to use Group Policy to automatically uninstall the package. In this case, you would physically have to visit each machine and manually uninstall the software. As with many other aspects of Windows 2000, you are far better off spending a few extra moments contemplating the results of an action before performing the action.

—Martin Wuesthoff, MCSE, MCT, CNE, A+, N+

If an order to uninstall has been received by a computer, it checks an information cache on the local machine. If software was installed through Group Policy, uninstall directions are listed in the cache. If no such directions are found, the software is not installed. This feature prevents you from inadvertently uninstalling software from machines that had it manually installed.

CERTIFICATION OBJECTIVE 9.03

Configuring Deployment Options

We have looked at how to distribute, upgrade, redeploy, and uninstall a package to all the users or computers in an OU. Sometimes, however, you do not want the same action performed on all members of an OU. In this section we review the process of filtering GPOs so that only specific users or computers receive a policy. We also look at some other options that are available for tweaking the deployment process. Finally, we look at transforms, which allow us to create customized packages for groups of users with slightly different needs.

Filtering the Package

If you have your OUs set up so perfectly that everyone in each OU should receive exactly the same software all the time, more power to you. Most of us, however, need to pick and choose to whom certain software is distributed. *Filtering* is the process of determining exactly who will and who will not receive policy.

Filtering is done on the Security tab of the Properties sheet of a GPO (see Figure 9-5). If we want to prohibit some users or computers in the OU from receiving the software distribution, we need to remove the Apply Group Policy permission from the Authenticated Users group and explicitly grant it to whomever we want to have it.

FIGURE 9-5

Group policy object Security settings

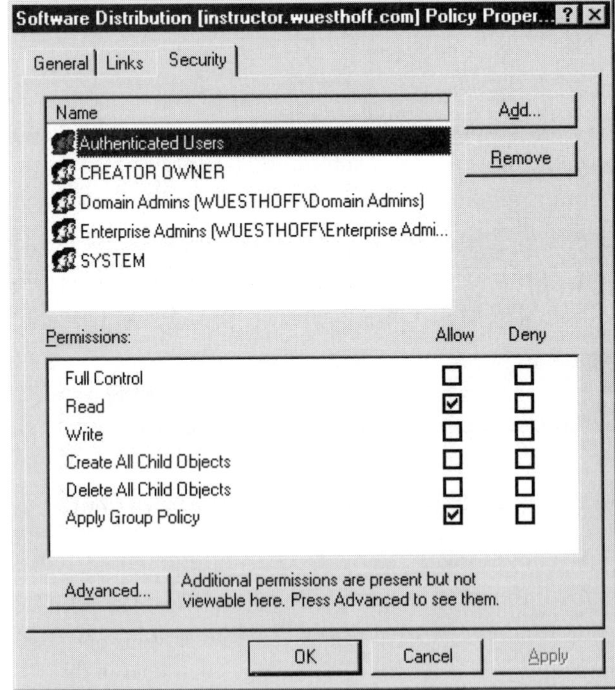

It is also important to remember that the package is stored in a shared folder. Users need read permission to access the folder where the package is shared.

Remember, too, that you can choose how you want permissions to flow from site to domain, domain to OU, and parent OU to child OU. If you click the Advanced button in the Security sheet, you have the ability to determine whether permissions should be propagated to child containers and whether to allow parent container permissions to propagate onto this one.

Miscellaneous Deployment Options

We can choose from among several other options when we deploy our package; these options affect naming, deployment, and how the package is displayed to the user. These options are reached by choosing Properties of the software package from within the GPO. For these examples, you see a standard deployment of the Administrative Tools package that is available automatically when you install Windows 2000 Server.

In the General tab (see Figure 9-6), you can change the display name of the application. This option changes the way the application name is displayed in the GPO as well as the way it is displayed to users in Add/Remove Programs. The other information either comes with a native package or can be placed in a package when the package is being created.

SCENARIO & SOLUTION	
Propagation	Allows the permissions from one OU to flow down onto another OU.
Block Permission Inheritance	Check this option if you want to prevent permissions from flowing onto a child OU.
User and Group Permissions	Keep in mind that this is a separate topic from parent/child inheritance. Users get permissions from the groups they are in, regardless of any OU properties.
No Override	Prevents one GPO from overriding the settings of another in the same OU.

FIGURE 9-6

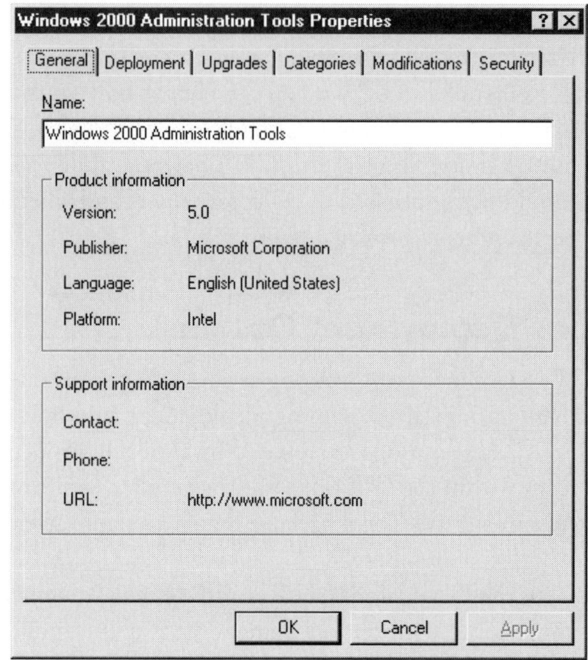

Changing the name of the package

The Deployment tab (see Figure 9-7) contains three sections. The "Deployment type" section simply allows you to switch between a published and an assigned package. In the "Deployment options" section are three options from which to choose. "Auto-install this application by file extension activation" (selected by default and not available if Assigned) indicates whether you want document invocation to be used to call a package. If this option is not selected, users must call the application through the Start menu or Add/Remove Programs, for example. "Uninstall this application when it falls out of the scope of management" indicates whether you want an application to be removed when a user or computer moves out of the group or OU to which it is assigned. For example, if only accountants in your company need your spreadsheet program, you can select this box. Then, when Betty moves from the accounting department to sales, the application is automatically removed from her machine. "Do not display this package in the Add/Remove Programs control panel" (not available if Assigned) means just that. "Installation user interface options" specifies whether a user sees installation screens, messages,

FIGURE 9-7

Changing deployment options

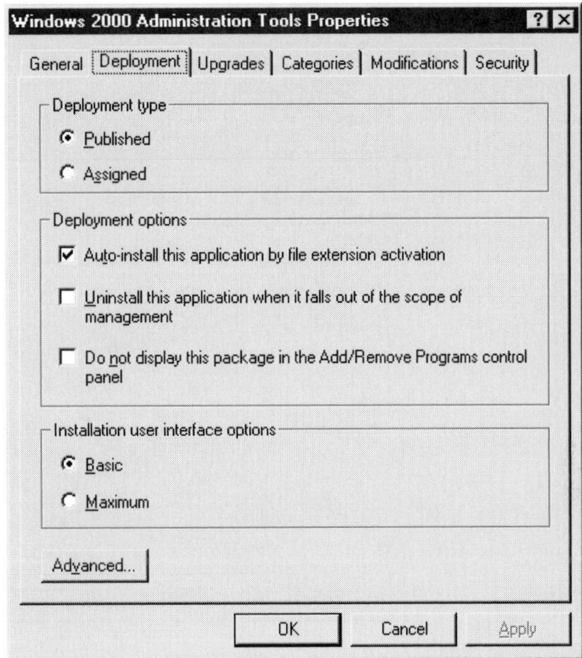

and settings when the program is being installed (Maximum) or simply a basic message that the application is being installed (Basic).

Clicking the Advanced button displays two other options (see Figure 9-8). "Ignore language when deploying this package" allows you to deploy a package, even if its language conflicts with the language of the machine. "Remove previous installs of this product for users, if the product was not installed by Group Policy-based Software Installation" allows you to deploy the package to users, even if they already have the software installed on their machines. This option allows you to control users' installation through Group Policy when the time comes to upgrade or remove the software.

The Categories tab of Administration Tools Properties allows you to place packages into categories in Add/Remove Programs. This option helps users identify the software that is available to them and might help prevent them from installing more software than they actually need.

FIGURE 9-8

The Advanced Deployment Options screen

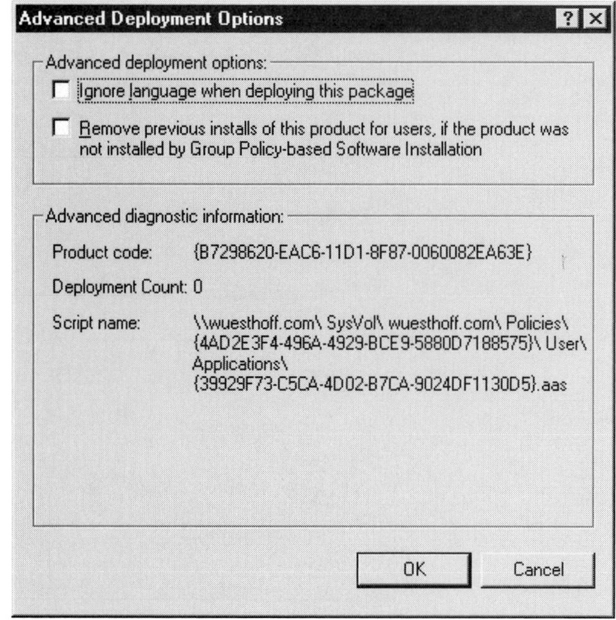

EXERCISE 9-3

Changing Categories

Now let's take a look at the process of changing categories.

1. Open Active Directory Users and Computers.
2. Right-click your domain name, and choose Properties.
3. On the Group Policy tab, double-click your Default Domain Policy.
4. Under Computer Configuration, expand Software Settings.
5. Right-click Software Installation, and choose Properties (see the following illustration).

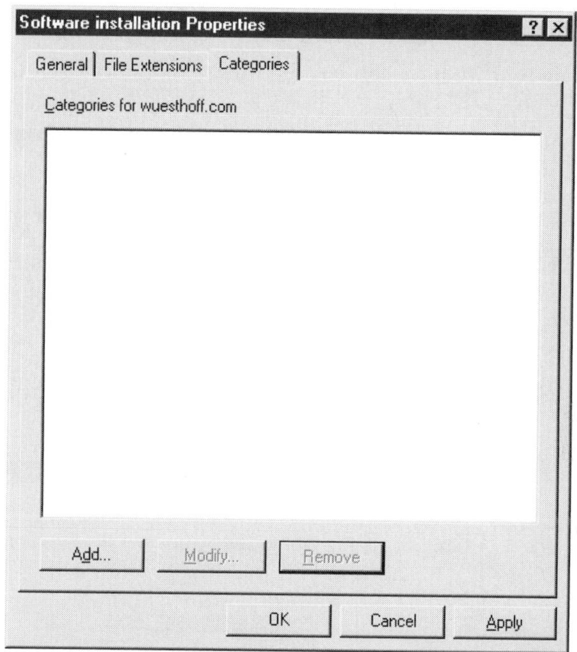

6. On the Categories tab, click Add.
7. Type the name of a category that you want to appear in Add/Remove Programs (see the following illustration).

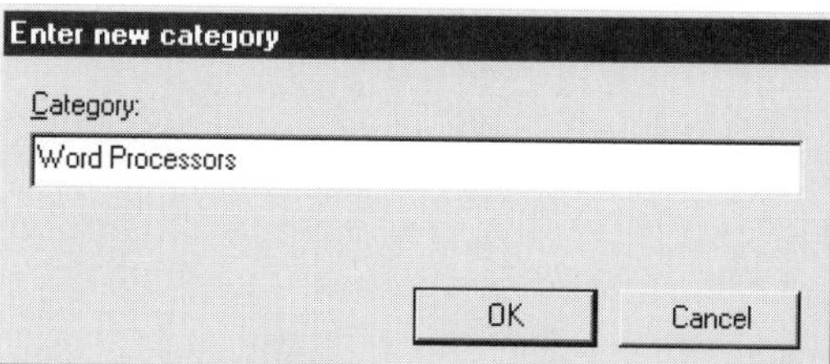

8. Repeat Steps 6 and 7 for all categories you want to add. (I added Spreadsheets, Games, and Graphics.)
9. Click OK to close Software Installation Properties, and close the Group Policy window.

EXERCISE 9-4

Categorizing Packages

Now that we have some categories, let's categorize our packages for users.

1. In Active Directory Users and Computers, right-click the OU that contains your GPO with your package.
2. On the Group Policy tab, double-click your software Installation GPO.
3. Under Computer Configuration or User Configuration (wherever your package lives), expand Software Settings and click Software Installation to view your packages.
4. Double-click a package and choose the Categories tab (see the following illustration).

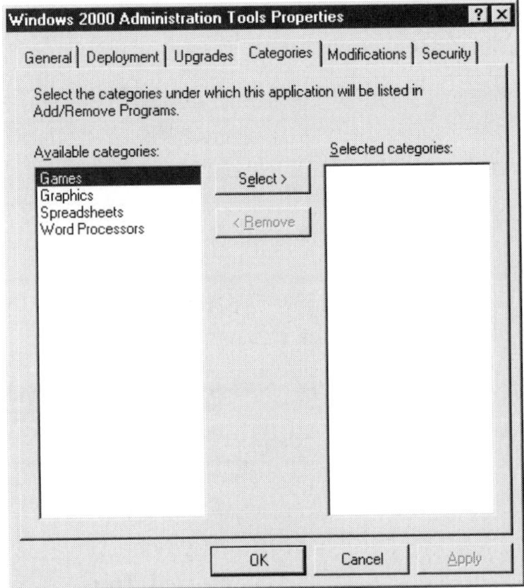

5. Select the Category under which you want the package to appear, and click Select. Repeat this step if you want the package to appear in more than one category.

The published package now appears in users' Add/Remove Programs under the appropriate categories.

Using Transforms

As more software companies begin including Windows Installer packages with their applications, the same companies might also include tools that allow you to customize the package for different groups of users. Office 2000 already includes such a tool, which you could use to include different language dictionaries to groups of users in an international or multilingual corporation. These customizations are stored as .MST files (the T stands for *Transform*) and are associated with the main package.

A transform can be added to the package only before it is actually deployed; the transform is done from the Modifications tab of the package's Properties sheet. You can add multiple modifications to a package, but they must all be added at the same time.

To assign different modifications to different groups of users, you must assign the package multiple times and add a different modification to each instance of the package. For example, suppose you have an Austria OU and a Brazil OU. In the former, you would add the German dictionary as a modification to the Word 2000 package in that OU's GPO. For the latter, you would create a GPO in the Brazil OU with the Word 2000 package and add an .MST that installs the Portuguese dictionary.

CERTIFICATION OBJECTIVE 9.04

Troubleshooting During Software Deployment

Even though Software Installation and Maintenance greatly simplifies the process of deploying software throughout your organization, there are still times when things do not work exactly as you planned. In this section, we look at a few of the most common problems that could occur. We also take a quick look at using the Event Viewer snap-in to help diagnose software installation problems.

Common Deployment Problems

Most deployment problems fall into one of three categories: packages that do not install at all on a machine or for a user, packages that install with unexpected or unintended results (such as the incorrect files), or packages that are deployed in an improper way.

Package Fails to Install

If you expect a package to be installed on a machine, advertised for a user, or appear in Add/Remove Programs and it does not, the problem most likely lies somewhere within Group Policy. Remember that for Group Policy to be assigned to a user, the user must be given the Read and Apply Group Policy permissions (see Figure 9-9). By default, these permissions are assigned to Authenticated Users in the OU. However, if the user or any group of which the user is a member has the Deny box checked for either of those permissions, the software overrides the default policy, and the Group Policy, in this case the package distribution, does not apply. In this case, you do not receive any warning message to tell you the process did not complete correctly.

If you get a message like “The Network Path could not be found…,” you probably have some sort of connectivity issue (incorrect protocol, address conflict, or the like) or you have shared the package to an invalid share name. Make sure the two machines can “see” each other, the package has been installed and shared on the network, the path to the object in the GPO has been entered correctly, and the user or computer has read access to the shared folder and files.

FIGURE 9-9

The Security tab of a group policy object

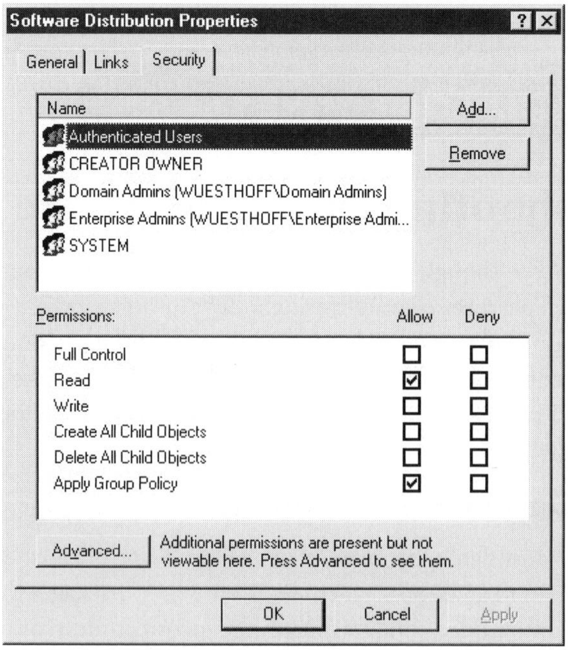

The Package Installs Incompletely or with Unexpected Results

A message telling you that the package installed incompletely or with unexpected results usually indicates a problem in the initial repackaging process. Remember the example of creating a package to install Excel on a source computer that already contains the Word files? The package would not be enough to install Excel on many machines. It would have no files that are shared between the two applications. Likewise, if something else other than software installation was done on the source computer between snapshots, the extra changes are reflected in the package.

The Package Does Not Install Itself But Appears on the Add/Remove Programs Control Panel

If the package fails to install but appears on the Add/Remove Programs Control Panel, you are not deploying the package in the correct manner. If you definitely want to install software, assign it. Published software is not automatically installed or even advertised except through Add/Remove Programs. Check the Deployment tab of the package's Properties sheet to make sure you have chosen the proper method.

If the package fails to install upon document invocation, be sure you have selected Auto-install on the same Deployment tab. Auto-install turns on or off a user's ability to double-click a document's icon to install the related package.

on the job

The Windows 2000 Server Resource Kit contains an extensive list of possible package installation errors and their solutions.

Event Viewer

Whenever a new package is installed, whether successfully or not, it is logged as an event in Event Viewer. You find this information in the application log of Event Viewer. In most cases, if there was an error, enough information is given inside the log entry to help you begin an investigation as to why the installation failed. For example, if you see an entry that indicates that the desired package or some of its files could not be found, you need to check the network placement of the package as well as connectivity issues.

To view these events, open Event Viewer from Administrative Tools or type **EVENTVWR** at a Run command. You are looking for two types of entries under Source: Application Management or MSInstaller. Application Management shows events related to Software Installation and Maintenance. MSInstaller shows the status of package installation—in other words, the success or failure of .MSI files to properly install.

exam Watch

Remember, the software installation events are logged to the application log, not the system log.

CERTIFICATION OBJECTIVE 9.05

Managing Network Configuration Using Group Policy

A handful of software-related settings can be configured using Group Policy but do not fit neatly into the category of Software Installation and Maintenance. In this next section, we look at how to deploy configuration changes to Internet Explorer. We also inspect how GPOs can be used to configure login scripts, printers, offline files, and network and dial-up connections.

Configuring Internet Explorer

Using Group Policy, you can remotely configure Internet Explorer on desktops throughout your organization. You can determine everything from what will appear in users' Favorites folders to what type of content they are able to view on the Internet and what logo you want to appear in the upper-right corner of their browsers. To do this, go to Windows Settings in the GPO for a site, domain, or OU. Here we look at the five categories of settings you can change in this manner: browser user interface, connection, URL, security, and programs.

Browser User Interface

In the Browser User Interface section of Windows Settings, you can customize the look of the browser. For example, you can create your own logo to replace the standard Internet Explorer logo or change the text on the title bar (see Figure 9-10). If you are deploying these changes throughout a network, be sure to save the logos and images to a network path rather than a local one.

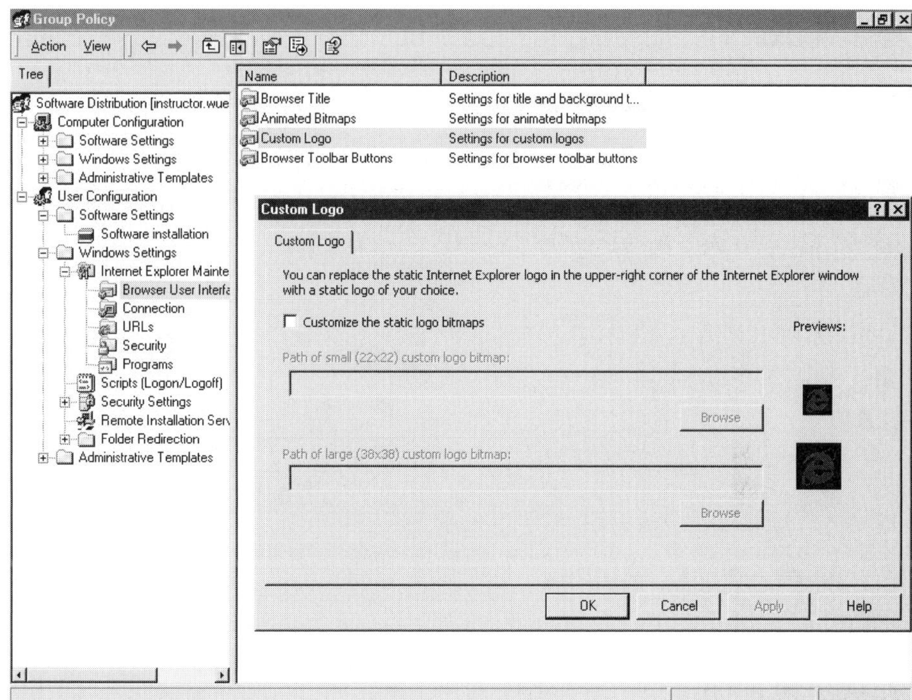

FIGURE 9-10 Choosing a custom logo

Connection

Here you can configure Internet connectivity settings for computers in your network. You have the ability to set proxy servers, specify a shared file to automatically set browser configuration, import connection settings, and set a custom string of data to be appended to the browser's identification of itself on the Internet (see Figure 9-11).

URLs

In the Important URLs section, you have the ability to set certain pages as favorites, define important sites such as a home URL, and define channels (see Figure 9-12). The Favorites and Links setting allows you define an entire hierarchy of favorite

FIGURE 9-11

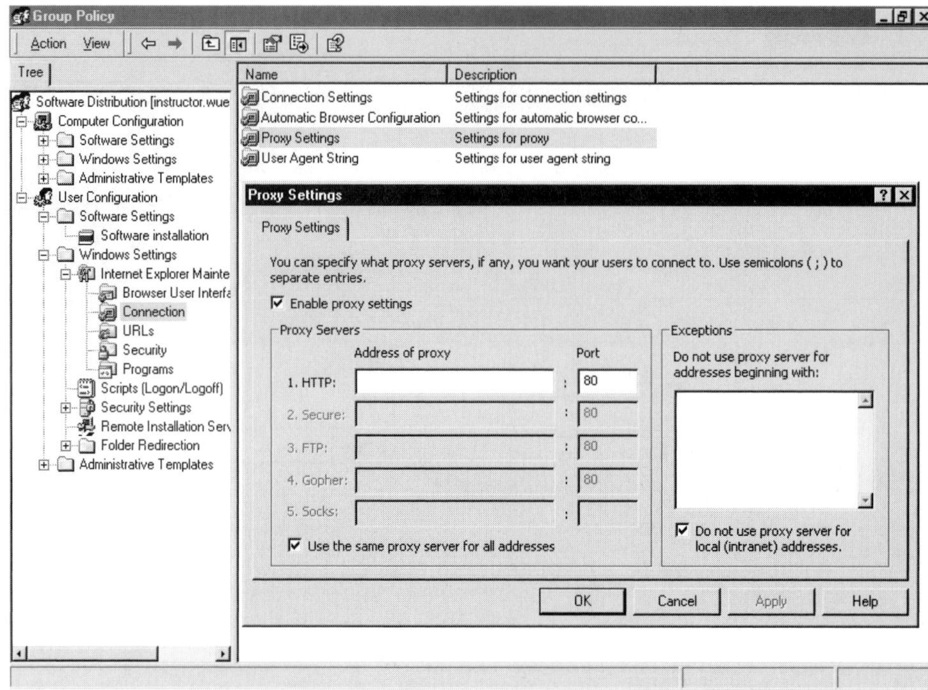

Setting proxy servers

pages and links, as well as allowing you to keep or delete existing favorites and links. The section allows you to set a home page, define a search URL, and direct users to a URL when they choose Help | Support in the browser. Channels allows you to define channels and categories, as well as to remove existing channels.

Security

Here you can define the kind of content you want to allow users to see on their browsers, as well as what publishers you want to have browsers trust (see Figure 9-13). Security Zones and Content Ratings options allow you to determine the types of content users can view, the specific sites they may or may not display, and

FIGURE 9-12

Setting a home page

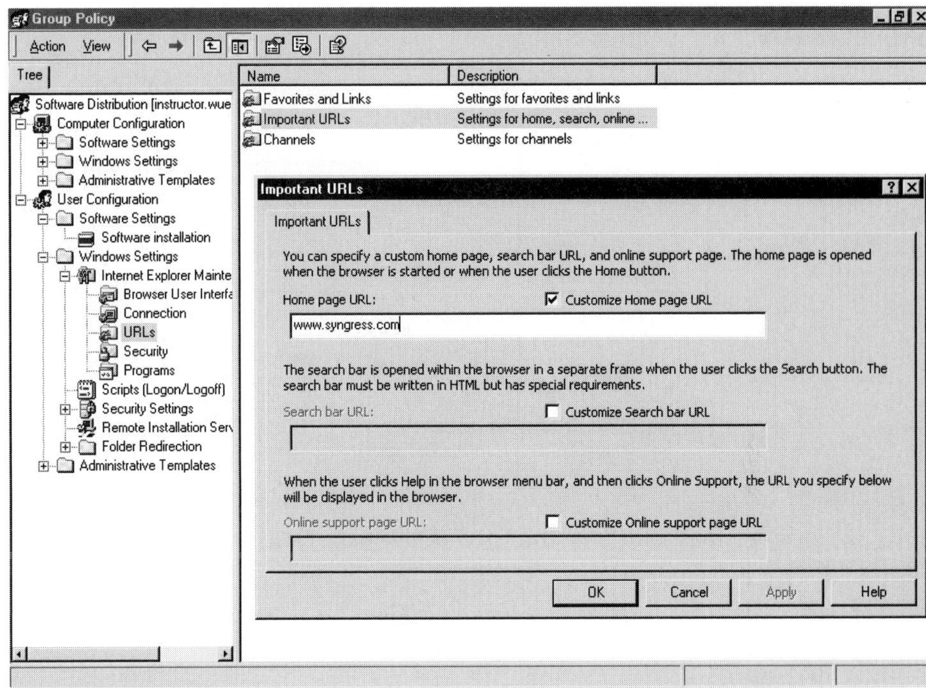

the types of ratings system you use. You can also set an administrator password to prevent others from changing their individual settings. The Authenticode Settings option allows you to determine a list of publishers and certificate agencies that you want to be identified as trustworthy by your browsers.

Programs

Under Programs, you can define the applications that automatically open when you invoke certain tasks. For example, if you use GroupWise instead of Outlook for your company's e-mail, you can set up that choice here (see Figure 9-14).

Other Configurable Options

A handful of other software options can be configured with Group Policy. They are found in various locations in the GPOs. Let's take a look at them now.

FIGURE 9-13

Approving and disapproving sites

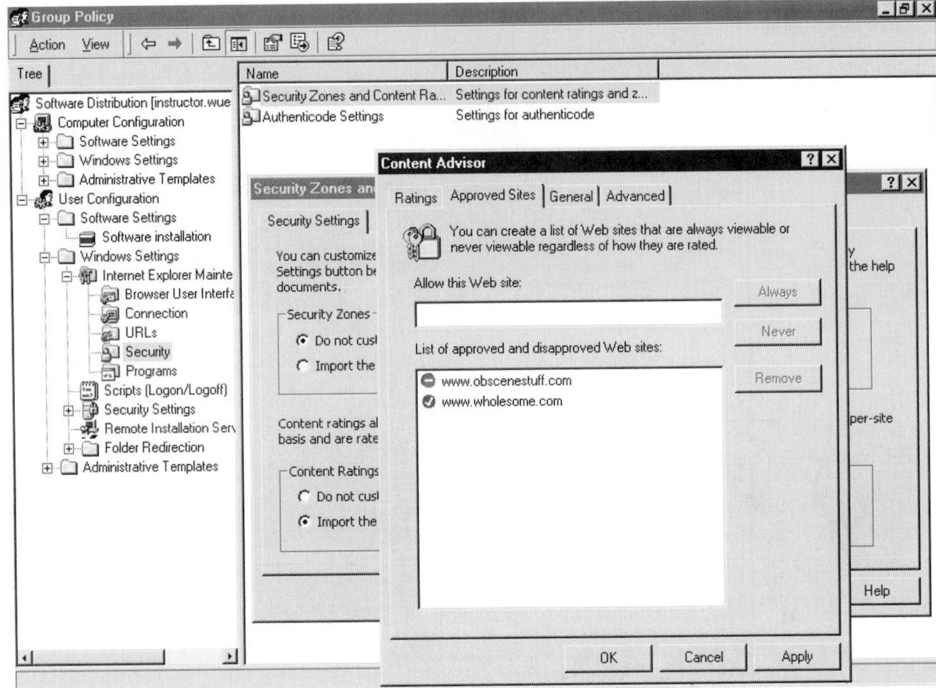

Logon Scripts

With Windows 2000, we have the ability to run four types of scripts. Under the Computer Management section of the GPO, you have the ability to set startup and shutdown scripts. As the names imply, these scripts can be written in a variety of scripting languages and perform some sort of configuration or tasks on the machine when it boots up or shuts down. Logon and logoff scripts are set up under User Management and run when the user logs on or off.

To set these scripts, go to Windows Settings under the appropriate section of the GPO, choose Scripts, and double-click the type of script you want to set. Click Add, and type or browse to the network location for the script (see Figure 9-15).

FIGURE 9-14

Changing default programs

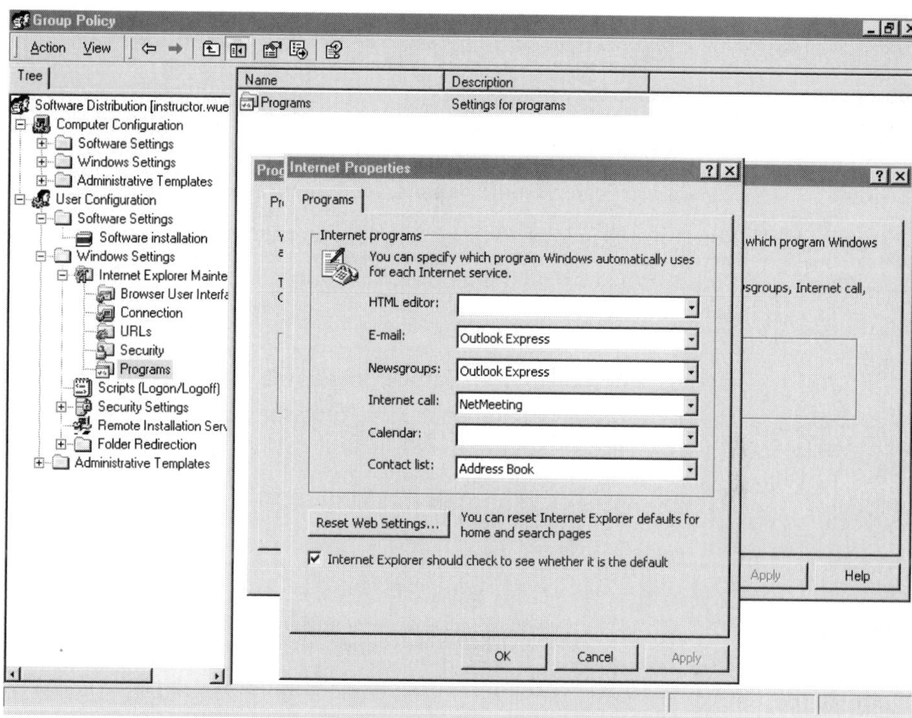

If you have scripts in different GPOs, they run in the same order as the GPOs. That is, any scripts on the site level run first, followed by those on the domain level and then those at the OU level. If you have nested OUs, the GPOs in the children run after those in the parent, thus taking precedence. If there are two or more scripts

FIGURE 9-15

Adding a shutdown script

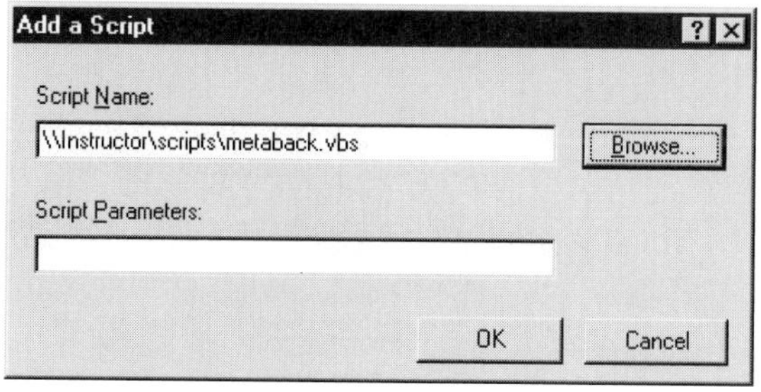

Add a Script

Script Name:

\\Instructor\scripts\metaback.vbs

Browse...

Script Parameters:

OK Cancel

SCENARIO & SOLUTION	
Logon	Runs at each user logon. Can be used to map drives, attach to printers, and so on.
Logoff	Runs at user logoff. Could be used, for example, to generate a report of the user's activities.
Startup	Runs when Windows 2000 starts. Could be used for virus checking or diagnostics.
Shutdown	Runs at Windows 2000 shutdown. Could send warning message to connected users or back up certain files.

of one kind in one GPO, you can configure which script takes precedence by moving it to the bottom of the list, thus running it last (see Figure 9-16).

FIGURE 9-16

Changing script execution order

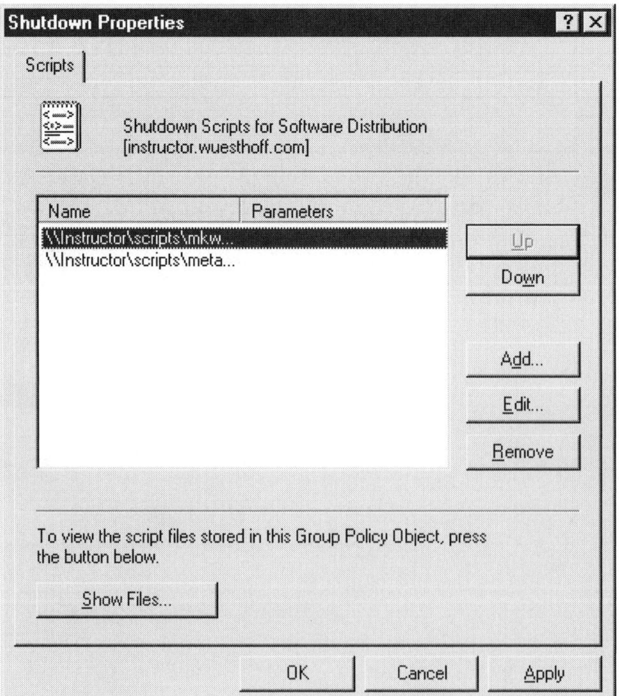

Printers

With Group Policy, you are able to set how users can search for and install printers. For example, you can allow or disallow users to add, remove, or browse the network to find printers. You can additionally configure where users will default to when they search Active Directory for printers, and you can automatically direct them to a Web site for printer support and installation (see Figure 9-17). These settings are under Administrative Templates | Control Panel | Printers in the GPO.

FIGURE 9-17

Directing users to a URL for printer support

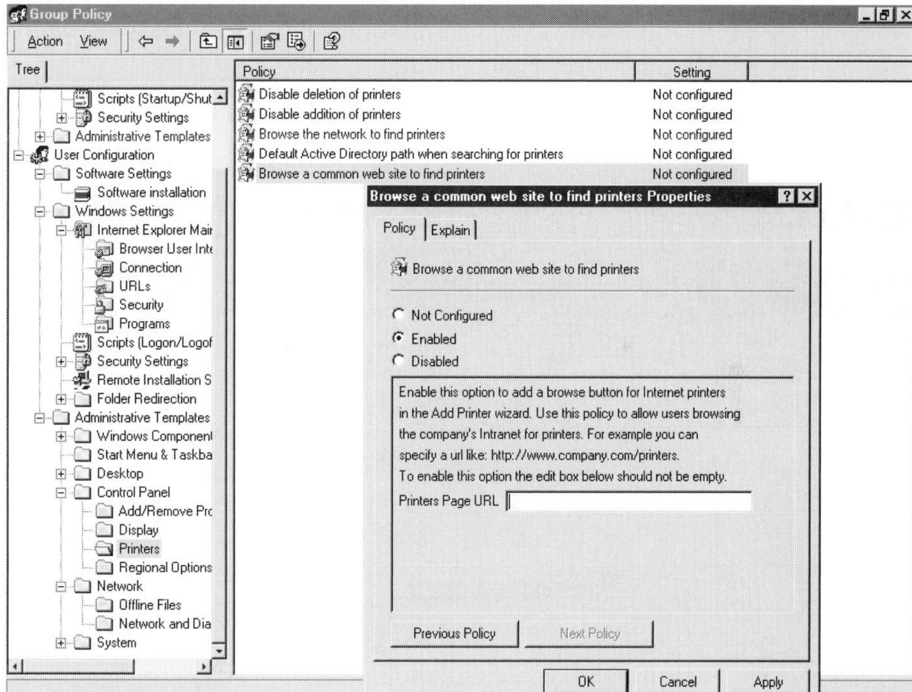

Offline Files

The ability to use offline files is set up at the shared folder itself, but we can configure the way users are able to use them in Group Policy. We can configure synchronization, reminder balloons, server actions, and logging options. These options are available under Administrative Templates | Network | Offline Files.

Network and Dial-up Connections

In the same Network portion of the GPO, where we found the Offline Files options, we can find some options for configuring network and dial-up connections. Again, we give permission to use RAS and dial-up in another place, but here we can configure how it behaves and what users can do in a RAS context (see Figure 9-18).

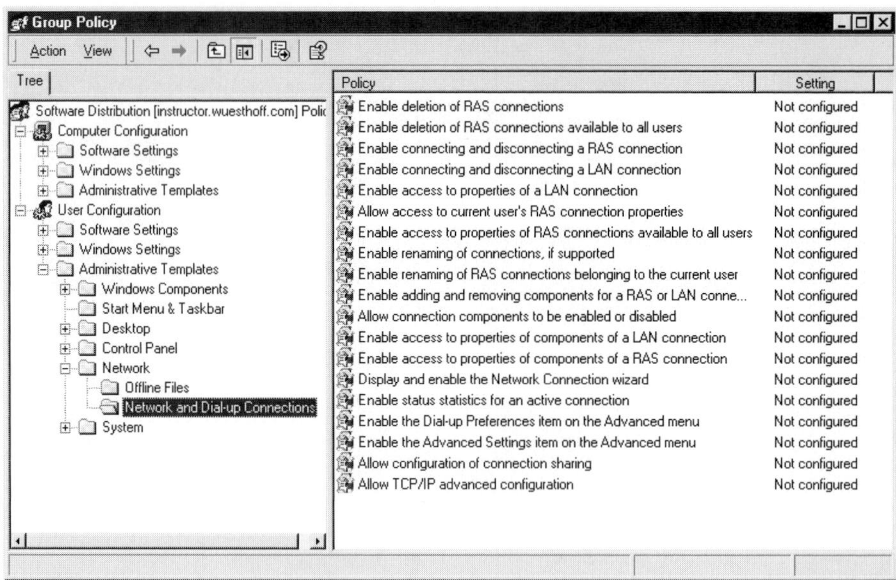

FIGURE 9-18 Network and dial-up options

CERTIFICATION SUMMARY

In this chapter, we looked at some of the new software deployment and installation features present in Windows 2000. Most of our discussion revolved around Group Policy and how it can be used to deploy and maintain applications.

We inspected the Windows Installer Service, which is used to ease the installation of software through the use of a new file type, the .MSI package. We then looked at how we could assign these packages to users or computers or publish them to users and how we could modify them or remove them through Group Policy.

Troubleshooting is mostly going to involve inspecting the assignment of GPOs as well as making sure our packages are created properly. With the Event Viewer, we can start to diagnose troubles as they appear.

Finally, we looked at some miscellaneous software settings that could be controlled through the use of Group Policy, such as Internet Explorer configuration, printer installation issues, offline file settings, and network and dial-up configurations.

TWO-MINUTE DRILL

Deploying Software Using Group Policy

- ❑ Windows Installer Service allows you to use .MSI files to automate and simplify the software installation process.
- ❑ Windows Installer Service is available for Windows 95, 98, NT, and 2000.
- ❑ Repackaging an application involves taking a "before" snapshot of a clean machine, installing software, and taking an "after" snapshot to create a package of differences.
- ❑ Software Installation and Maintenance is a new technology that allows for the automated deployment of software through the use of Group Policy.
- ❑ Packages can be assigned to users or computers or published to users.

Maintaining Software Using Group Policy

- ❑ When you upgrade a package, it replaces an existing one.
- ❑ A mandatory upgrade replaces the package the next time a user uses it or the computer reboots.
- ❑ With an optional upgrade, a user can decide whether to upgrade or keep his or her existing package.

Configuring Deployment Options

- ❑ A user needs Read and Apply Group Policy permissions for a GPO to be applied to that user.
- ❑ Clear the "Auto-install this application by file extension activation" option to disable document invocation installation.

Troubleshooting During Software Deployment

- ❑ The first thing to check in any troubleshooting situation is the application of Group Policy.
- ❑ The Event Viewer can be used to help diagnose installation and distribution problems.
- ❑ Be sure to place a package in a shared network location, accessible to users.

Managing Network Configuration Using Group Policy

- ❑ Internet Explorer configuration options can be set in Group Policy.
- ❑ Scripts run in the following order: site, domain, parent OU, child OU.

MCSE

MICROSOFT CERTIFIED SYSTEMS ENGINEER

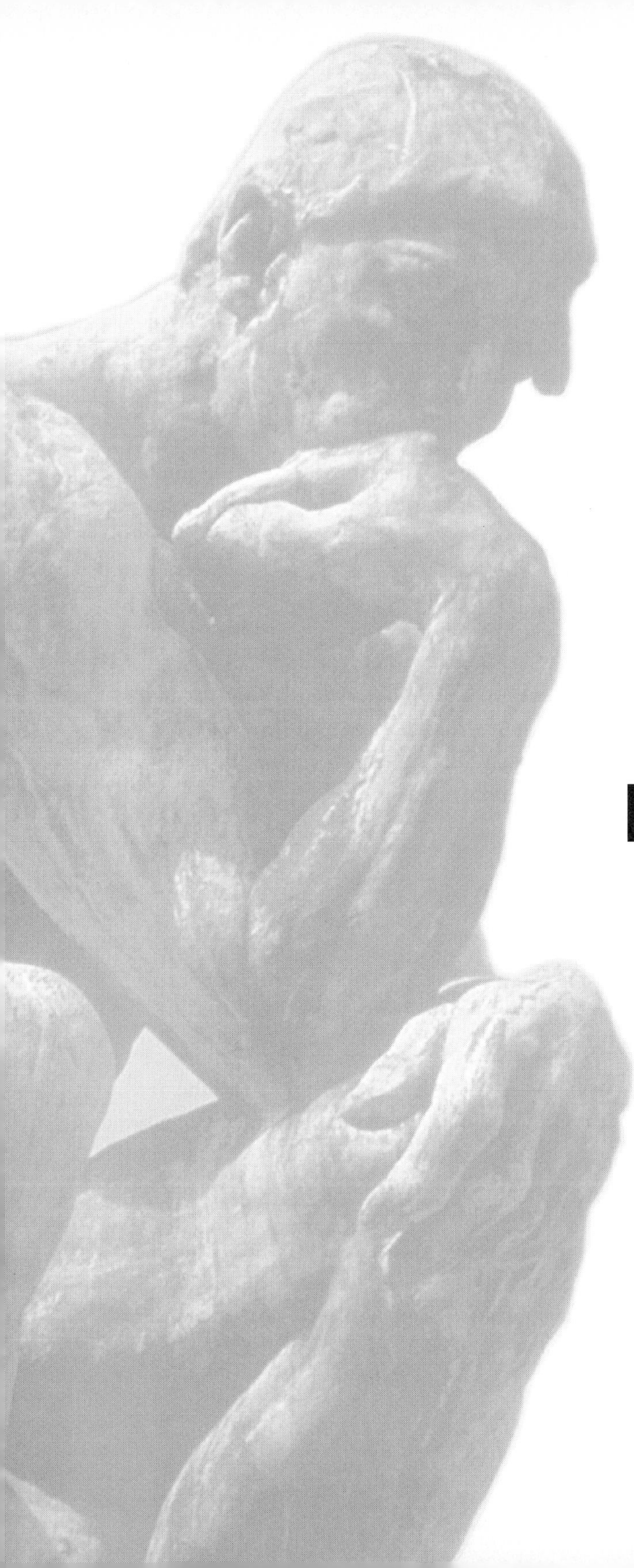

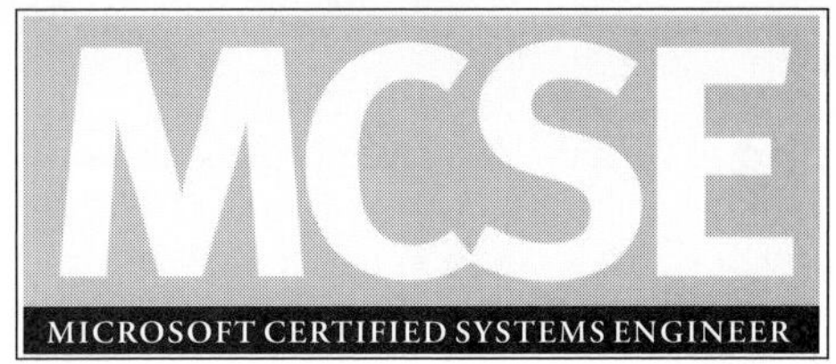

10

Remote Installation Services

CERTIFICATION OBJECTIVES

10.01	What is Remote Installation Service?
10.02	Creating a RIS Server
10.03	Authorizing a RIS Server
10.04	Configuring a RIS Server
10.05	Troubleshooting RIS
10.06	Preparing to use RIS to Install the Client Machine
10.07	Installing an Image to a Client Machine
10.08	Troubleshooting the Use of RIS to Install the Client Machine
✓	Two-Minute Drill

With Remote Installation Services (RIS), we have the ability to deploy an automated and virtually foolproof installation of an operating system, applications, and profile information. If we plan well, we can send a user who needs a new computer back to her workstation with a floppy disk if needed, tell her to boot from the floppy, press a couple of keys, go to lunch, and enjoy her completely configured and personalized computer when she returns.

This chapter discusses the details of installing a desktop operating system using RIS. We start with preparation and discuss the various requirements for using RIS once it has been installed and configured on a Windows 2000 server. We then move on to a variety of scenarios in which this service can be best utilized. We also examine the Remote Installation Preparation (RIPrep) utility, which is used to prepare an image of a fully configured desktop machine.

RIS requires a proper setup and a favorable network environment. If any of the components are not running or not responding when you start client installations, you could very well encounter one or more problems. Later in this chapter, we discuss some of the common problems you can face while running RIS installations, as well as their possible causes and resolutions.

CERTIFICATION OBJECTIVE 10.01

What is Remote Installation Service?

Remote Installation Services, or *RIS,* is an optional component that runs as a service on the Windows 2000 server operating system. RIS takes advantage of the new Pre-Boot Execution Environment (PXE) based remote-boot technology to allow a user to boot his or her workstation and have it automatically find and connect to a RIS server to download a fully configured Windows 2000 Professional image, complete with user profile and applications.

Once the operating system and basic applications have been installed through RIS, various IntelliMirror technologies can be used to further customize the desktop for the user. For example, Software Installation and Maintenance can be used to deploy additional, customized applications to individual users. Group Policy Objects can be put into place that can implement Folder Redirection, Offline Files, and Logon Scripts. In short, RIS and Window 2000 IntelliMirror technologies, when used together, can make for a completely automated installation and configuration of a new or replacement machine, saving administrative time and providing for a reduced Total Cost of Ownership (TCO).

PXE and Supported Hardware

In order for a client machine to be able to get an image from a RIS server, it must have one of the two following options:

- PXE-based remote boot ROM version .99c or later
- Peripheral Component Interconnect (PCI)–based network card that is supported by the RIS remote boot disk

In a nutshell, your client machine needs to be able to boot up either from the Read Only Memory (ROM) or the RIS boot disk, obtain an address from a Dynamic Host Configuration Protocol (DHCP) server, find a RIS server, ask it for an image, and receive it from the RIS server. Computers that are designated to be PC98 compliant should have PXE Remote Boot ROM. In addition, Net PCs will have a bootable ROM, as most of them do not have a disk drive to boot from.

If you do not have machines with PXE bootable ROM, you need to supply a boot disk to kick off the process. Windows 2000 RIS Server includes a utility called the Remote Boot Disk Generator, or RBFG.EXE (the "f" stands for "floppy"…the display name of the application was changed, but they left the actual command alone). This utility creates a single floppy that can be used to start the Remote Operating System Installation on any machines with a supported drive. The good point is that one floppy can be used for all of your supported machines, so you don't need to carry around a pocketful of boot floppies if you have different network adapters—one disk fits all (or, more accurately, "one disk fits all who are invited"). You see, as of this writing, only 25 network adapters are supported by RBFG.EXE. If yours isn't on the list, you are out of luck. Fortunately, the 25 adapters are 25 of the most popular adapters on the market.

There is also the chance that the floppy may work with your adapters even if they are not on the list. The only way to find out for sure is to try it out on one. Do not, however, expect Microsoft to support your decision to use a nonsanctioned network card.

In Exercise 10-1, you will install the Remote Boot Disk Generator and use it to check to see if your network cards are supported. You will then create a boot floppy. This exercise is included here in the text to coincide with the discussion of supported cards. It assumes that you have RIS installed on the D drive. If you do not, perform Exercise 10-1 after Exercise 10-2.

EXERCISE 10-1

Installing RBFG.EXE and Checking Network Card Compatibility

1. Click Start | Run and type **D:\RemoteInstall\Admin\i386\rbfg.exe**. Press ENTER (see the following illustration).

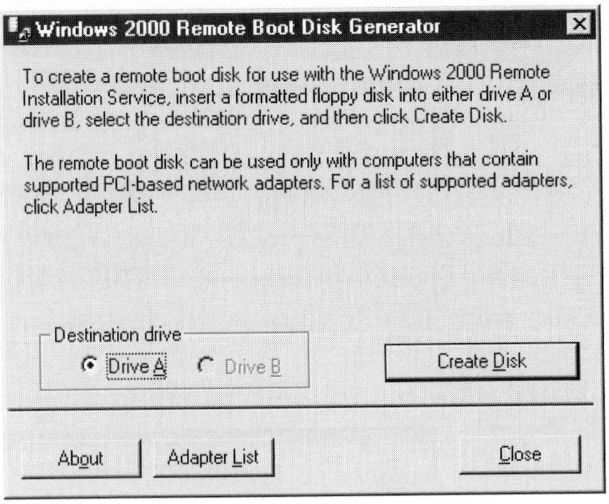

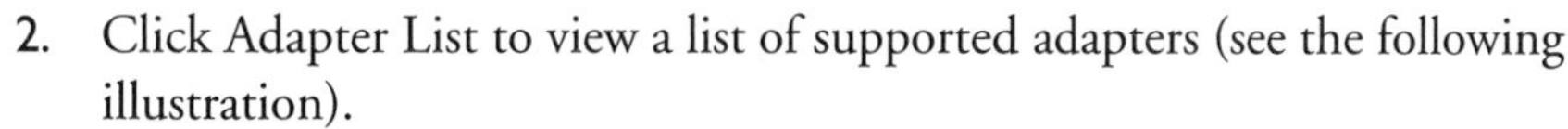

2. Click Adapter List to view a list of supported adapters (see the following illustration).

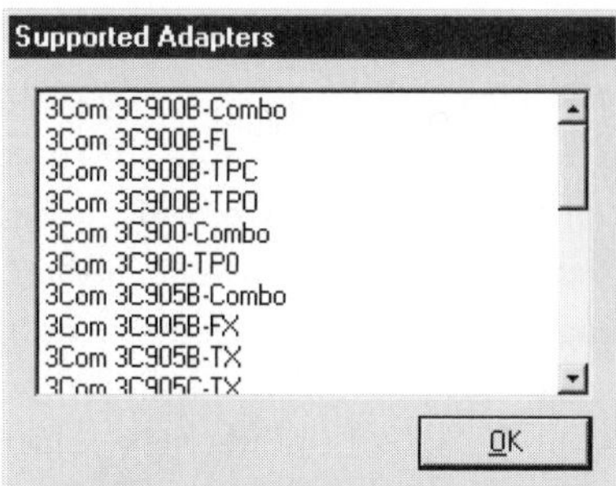

3. Click OK to close the list and click Create Disk to make the floppy.
4. Close RBFG.

The Remote Boot Floppy will only work with Plug-and-Play PCI cards. This means that they will not work will laptop machines, with the exception of certain docked machines. Even a docked machine will only work if the docking station has a supported PCI network card.

How RIS Works

When a potential RIS client boots up, either through the use of a RIS boot disk or straight from the boot ROM, a DHCP discover packet (with PXE client extension tags) is sent to get an IP address from a DHCP server and to find the address of a RIS server. In addition, the client at that time sends its Globally Unique Identifier, or GUID. A GUID is a 32-digit hexadecimal number that all PXE devices have assigned to them. After a DHCP server has sent an address (with PXE server extension tags) and a RIS server has identified itself, a message is displayed to the user to press the F12 key in order to initiate the Remote Installation.

The RIS server checks Active Directory to see if the client computer's GUID has been prestaged for any RIS servers. If so, that particular RIS server would take over the process. This is done using the Boot Information Negotiation Layer, or BINL, service. This service was added to the server upon RIS installation and is responsible for most of the communications in the RIS process.

After the RIS server knows whether there is a prestaged client account, it sends the client a small application called the Client Installation Wizard, or CIW. This asks for the user's name and password, which is then checked against Active Directory. The user's account is verified, and the RIS policy settings are checked to determine which images and options are available to the user. If there is more than one installation available, it will present a list to choose from. If only one installation is available to the user, and no options are available, the choices will not be offered. Rather, the user will be asked to confirm the installation and the reformatting of his or her hard drive.

After the user has selected or confirmed an installation, his or her account will be checked for permissions to create a new computer account, if the client machine was not prestaged. The computer will be assigned a name from the RIS server, and the transfer of files begins. From this point, the process is completely hands-off to the user.

RIS Components

To fully understand the RIS process and how to configure it for use, we need a basic understanding of the different components that work together to complete the RIS picture. We will look at five components, which require at least three computers to execute fully.

Remote Installation Services Setup, or RISetup.exe, prepares a RIS server for use by preparing a partition for installation storage and creating the initial CD-based image. One important feature of RIS involves the Single Instance Store, or SIS. If two or more images are stored on the same RIS server, there are obviously going to be many files shared among the images. Rather than having each image store its own copy of each file, SIS will inspect a new image for files that have already been stored with a different image, and will replace the second instance of the file with a pointer to the initial instance of the file. This method will dramatically reduce the amount of drive space taken up by multiple images.

When RIS is installed on a server, that server will have a Remote Install tab added to its Properties sheet in Active Directory Users and Computers. This tab gives administrators the ability to configure what images to hand out, naming schemes and placement of new computer accounts, and the ability to prestage computers. Administrators also have the ability to control what RIS servers are allowed to hand out images on the network by authorizing them in Active Directory. This all falls under the scope of Remote Installation Services Administration and Configuration Options.

The Remote Installation Preparation wizard, or RIPrep.exe, is used to create RIPrep images. It is run from a *source computer,* or a computer from which an image will be generated. After Windows 2000 Professional has been installed, and all applications that are to be a part of the image have also been installed and configured, the source computer will connect to the RIS server and run RIPrep. This will dump the contents of the C drive of the source computer onto the RIS server as a RIPrep image. This image will not contain any user-specific settings.

The Remote Boot Disk Generator, or RBFG.exe, creates boot floppies for any machines without PXE enabled BIOS but with RIS supported network cards. Unlike the boot floppies of the past, one Remote Boot Floppy will work for any of the currently 25 supported network cards.

The Client Installation wizard, or OSChooser.exe, is sent to the client machine from the RIS server. It allows the user to interact with the RIS server by giving logon name and password, choosing an installation if more than one is available, and displaying installation options if appropriate for that user.

Now that we've discussed the RIS components, here is a quick reference to help you keep these programs straight:

SCENARIO & SOLUTION	
RISetup.exe	Claims a drive for RIS, creates the first image, and sets up the Single Instance Store.
Active Directory Users and Computers	Configures the RIS server for client requests.
RIPrep.exe	Creates RIPrep images.
Rbfg.exe	Creates the boot floppy.
Oschooser.exe	Sent to client computer to allow a user to choose an image to download.

CERTIFICATION OBJECTIVE 10.02

Creating a RIS Server

Setting up a RIS server is a simple process. First, Remote Installation Services needs to be installed. The server must then be authorized in Active Directory. RISetup must be run to create an initial image. RIS must be set up to allow users to create accounts in Active Directory. Additional images may also be created and placed on the RIS server for distribution. These steps are discussed in more detail later in this chapter.

Prerequisites

A number of things must be present on your network in order for the RIS process to be able to distribute an image to a client machine. First, a client machine is going to need an IP address in order to communicate on the network and find the RIS server. The idea behind RIS is that a user should be able to get an image without any special knowledge or skills, other than the ability to press F12 and type in a username and password. Configuring IP would definitely be considered a special skill. Thus, we have the need for a DHCP server somewhere on the network, accessible to the client machine.

A user will need to be granted permission to create a computer account. This permission is given out in Active Directory. Thus, we need an Active Directory server available. Of course, in order to find an Active Directory server, the client machine needs to ask Domain Name System (DNS). So, our third service that must be available is DNS.

Here are scenario questions and answers relating to the software prerequisites and their purposes:

SCENARIO & SOLUTION	
Why do you need a DHCP server somewhere on the network?	The DHCP server gives the client computer an IP address so it can communicate with the RIS server.
Why do you need DNS?	DNS allows the RIS server to find and use Active Directory.
Why do you need Active Directory?	Active Directory allows a RIS server to determine user rights and permissions.

There is one server-specific requirement that must be met as well. In order to store images on the server, you must have a partition with at least 2GB of space dedicated to the RIS process. It will not allow you to install images on your system or boot partition. The partition used must be formatted with NTFS.

Installing RIS

Once we have an established DHCP, DNS, and Active Directory server in place on our network, we need to install the Remote Installation Services. This is done through Add/Remove Programs. When you are there, choose Add/Remove Windows Components. Select Remote Installation Services, follow prompts, and RIS is installed. We discuss installation in Exercise 10-2.

Installing RIS

1. Click Start | Settings | Control Panel.
2. Double-click Change/Remove Programs (see the following illustration).

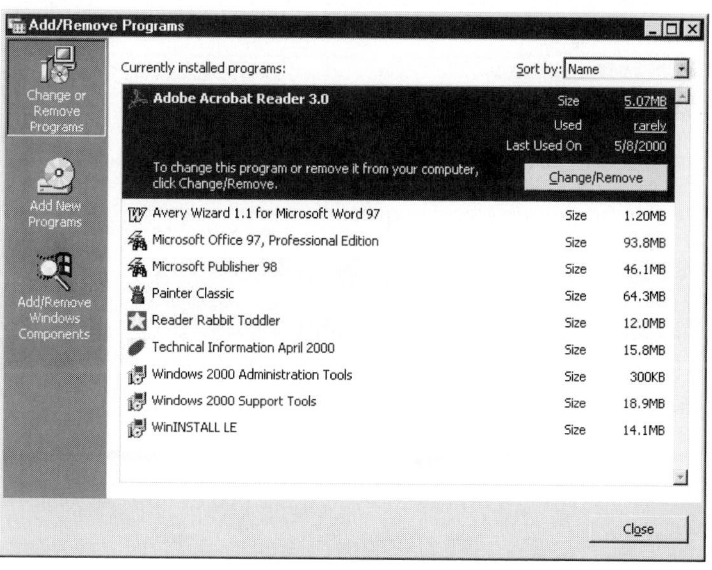

3. Click Add/Remove Windows Components.
4. Check Remote Installation Services and click Next (see the following illustration).

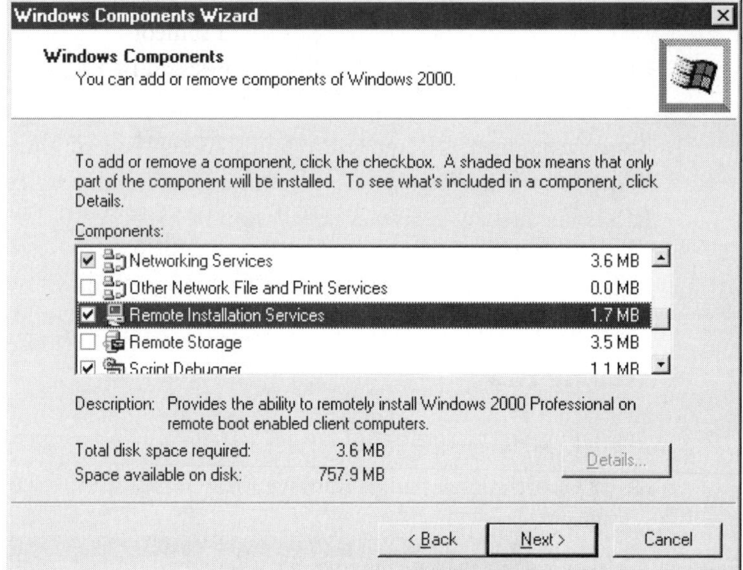

5. Click Finish and reboot when prompted.

CERTIFICATION OBJECTIVE 10.03

Authorizing a RIS Server

Before a RIS server can deploy images, it must be *authorized* in Active Directory. The authorization process is described in more detail next.

Why Authorize a RIS Server?

A DHCP server needs to be authorized in Active Directory before it starts handing out IP addresses. This helps to prevent someone from setting up another server with either duplicate or invalid addresses on your network, potentially causing you a great deal of headaches trying to troubleshoot all of the new bad addresses that start popping up. Likewise, it would be relatively simple for someone to install Windows 2000 Server on a machine, set it up as a RIS server with some bad images (possibly virus-ridden images?), and start letting it serve. Unless you were prestaging computers, you would have no guarantee that a user would get his or her image from your RIS server rather than the imposter's. For this reason, we need to have a way to guarantee that we approve of all RIS servers that are handing out images. This guarantee is the *authorization process.*

Only a user with Enterprise Administrator privileges can authorize a machine in Active Directory. A RIS server will not give out images unless it is authorized in Active Directory. As a result, only a user with Enterprise Administrator privileges has the ability to start deploying RIS images.

The Authorization Process

The funny thing about the authorization process is that you have to pretend that your RIS server is a DHCP server, even if it is not. There is no interface to authorize a server from within RIS, so we "borrow" the interface from DHCP.

exam Watch

If your intended RIS server is already an authorized DHCP server, you do not need to do this step. Read exam questions regarding authorization very carefully. If you are asked what the requirements are for a RIS server, one of them is that it must be authorized in Active Directory. However, if you are asked what the steps are to prepare a RIS server, you may not need to authorize it if it is already a DHCP server.

To authorize your RIS server, you need to make sure you are logged on under an account with Enterprise Administrator privilege.

EXERCISE 10-3

Authorizing a RIS Server

1. Click Start | Programs | Administrative Tools | DHCP (see the following illustration).

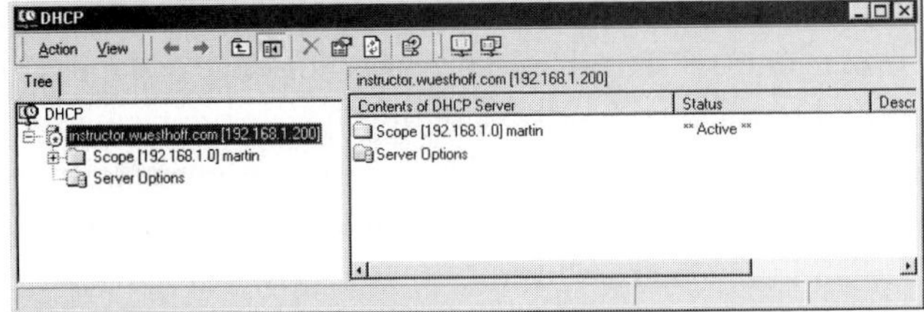

2. Right-click DHCP and choose Manage Authorized Servers.
3. Click Authorize (see the following illustration).

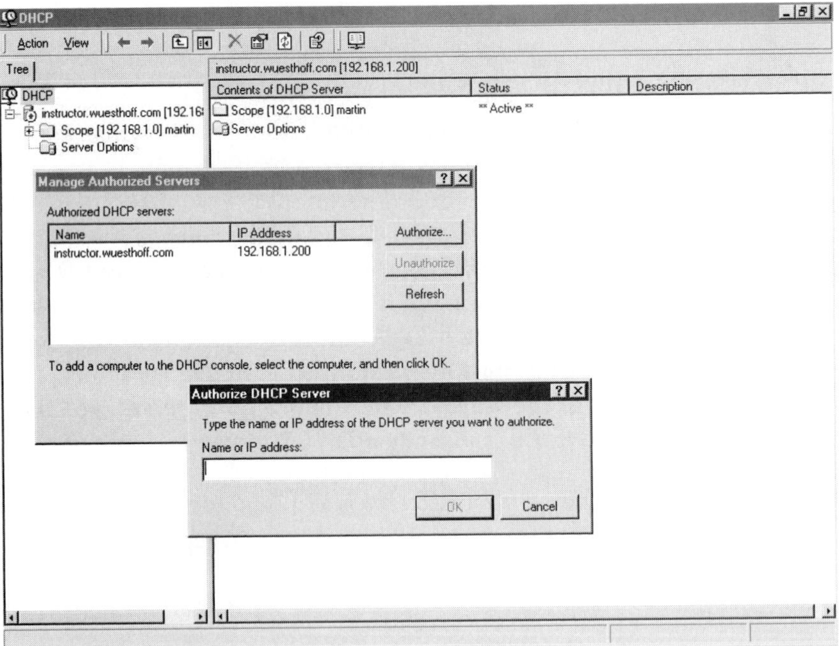

4. Type the IP address or server name of the RIS server. Click OK, then Yes, then OK again.
5. Exit DHCP.

CERTIFICATION OBJECTIVE 10.04

Configuring a RIS Server

Now that we have our prerequisites taken care of and we have installed and authorized our RIS server, it is time to get down to the process of creating images, and then making sure users can get them from the server when needed. Before we can create images, we need to have an understanding of the types of images we can create.

Types of Images

There are two types of images we can deploy: CD-based and RIPrep images. A *CD-based image* is simply a copy of the i386 folder off the Windows 2000 Professional CD-ROM, associated with an answer file. When you create your first CD-based image using RISetup, it creates a standard answer file called RIStandard.sif. This answer file will allow you to install a bare-bones default operating system. You can create your own answer files, which will allow for more customized installation. This is the simplest method to set up and administer, although it is certainly not the fastest method to deploy or the most powerful.

If you want to deploy applications with the operating system, or you want to get the image onto target machines in the quickest method possible, you will want to create a *RIPrep image*. This image is derived by copying a preconfigured computer. It will allow you to deploy applications along with the operating system.

Here is a review of the two types of images:

- **CD-Based** Uses answer files to customize an installation. Contains the Windows 2000 Professional source files.
- **RIPrep** Contains a complete image of a computer, including applications and configuration.

RISetup and CD-Based Images

Before you can install any other images, you must run the RISetup program, which will claim a drive for RIS, set up the Single Instance Store, and create the first image with a default answer file.

Running RISetup

Before you run RISetup to set up RIS and install your first image, there are a few things you need to do:

- Make sure you have a nonsystem drive with at least 2GB of disk space formatted with NTFS.
- Put your Windows 2000 Professional CD in the CD-ROM drive.
- Decide on a name and description for your first image.

exam Watch

Make sure you know that the images must be copied to an NTFS partition. Real world says that you will get an error message if you try to put them on a FAT partition (Figure 10-1), but you don't get to see that message when you're in the exam room!

Once these steps are completed, running RISetup is a simple process of starting the program, following the prompts, and waiting. The only thing you need to be aware of is that you might want to wait until all of your images have been created and your configuration is done before allowing your server to respond to client requests.

FIGURE 10-1

Non-NTFS error message

EXERCISE 10-4

Running RISetup

1. Click Start | Run, type **risetup**, and press Enter (see the following illustration).

2. Click Next. RIS will scan your drives and suggest a location for its Installation Folder (see the following illustration).

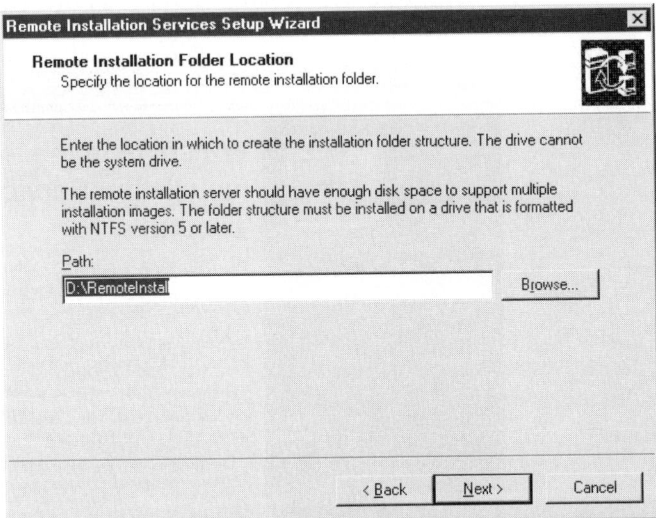

3. Choose a location or click Next to choose the default. RIS will ask if you want to start responding to client requests (see the following illustration).

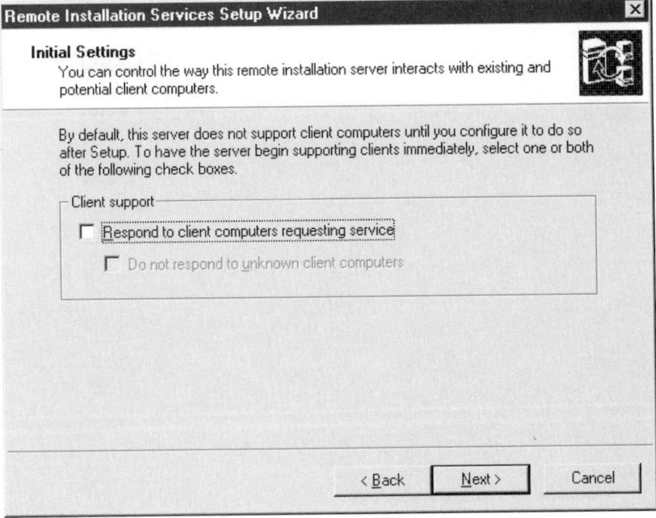

4. You do not want to respond to clients until you have created your images, so leave this unchecked and click Next. RIS will ask for the location of the Source Files (see the following illustration).

Remote Installation Services Setup Wizard
Installation Source Files Location
Specify the location of the Windows installation files.
Enter the path to the CD or network location of the Windows installation files.
Path:
E:\i386
Browse...
< Back
Next >
Cancel

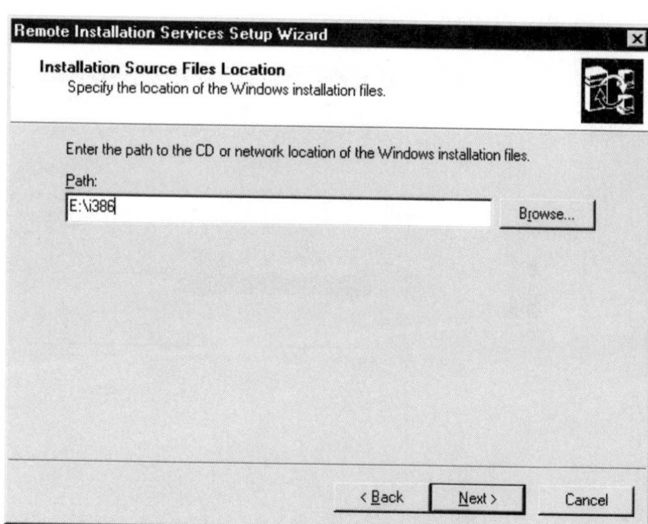

5. Type *%cdroot%*\i386 and click Next. You will be asked for a folder name for the initial image (see the following illustration).

Remote Installation Services Setup Wizard
Windows Installation Image Folder Name
Provide a name for the Windows installation image folder.
Type a name for the folder to which the Windows files will be copied on this remote installation server.
Folder name:
win2000.pro
< Back
Next >
Cancel

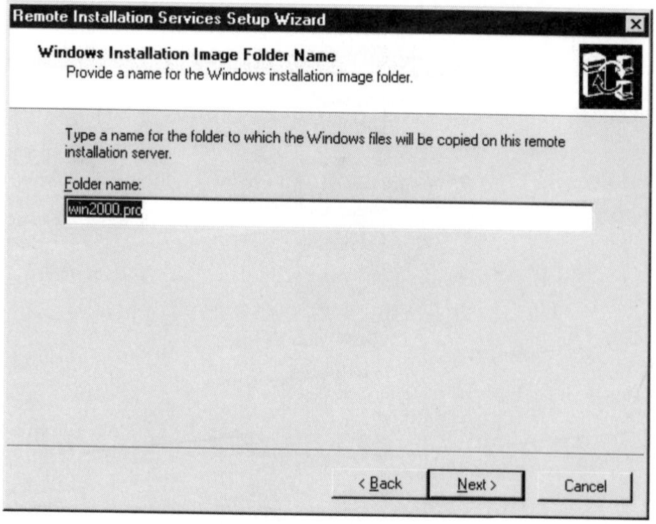

6. Accept the default name and click Next. You will be asked to type a friendly description and help text for the installation (see the following illustration). These will appear to users as they boot to a RIS server and try to choose an installation.

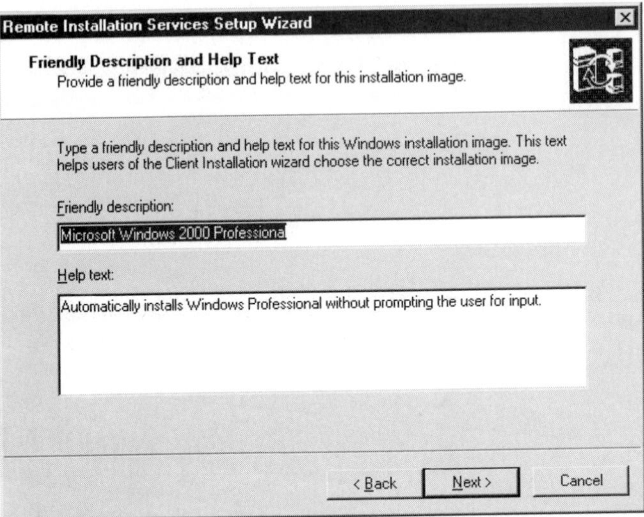

7. Type the appropriate text and click Next. You will be asked to confirm your choices (see the following illustration).

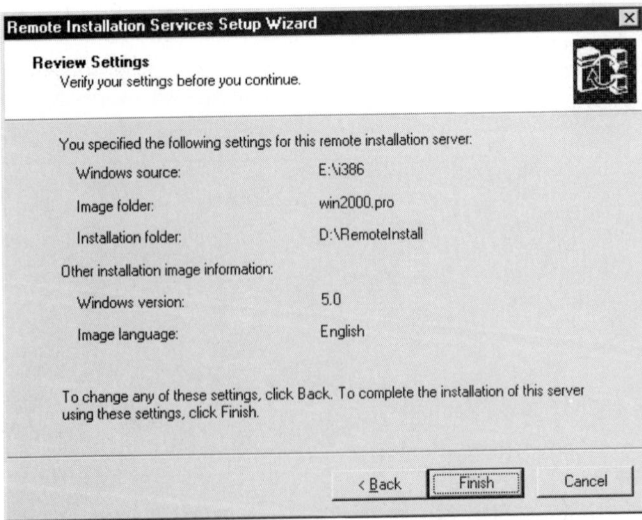

8. Click Finish. You will see a progress indicator (see the following illustration). Get a cup of coffee; this will take 10–20 minutes or so. When it is finished, your first image is ready.

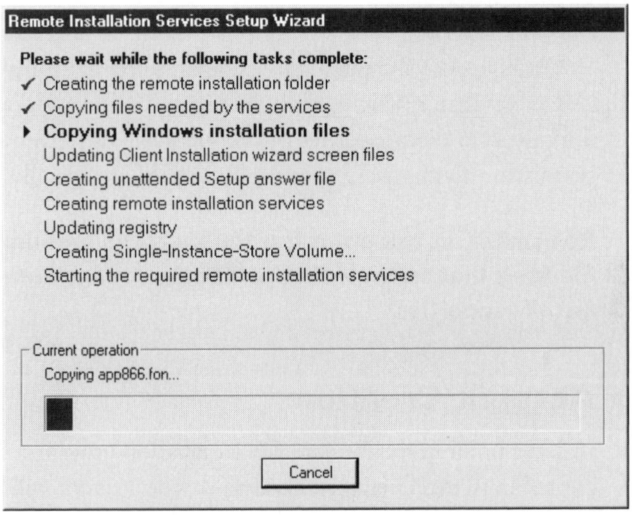

Remote Installation Services Setup Wizard

Please wait while the following tasks complete:
✓ Creating the remote installation folder
✓ Copying files needed by the services
▶ **Copying Windows installation files**
Updating Client Installation wizard screen files
Creating unattended Setup answer file
Creating remote installation services
Updating registry
Creating Single-Instance-Store Volume...
Starting the required remote installation services

Current operation
Copying app866.fon...

Cancel

Remember that this initial image is required on the RIS server, even if you have no intention of ever using it.

Modifying CD-Based Images

Once you have created the default image, you will probably want to customize it through the use of answer files. An *answer file* is a text file that pre-answers some or all of the information a user would normally provide during installation. Answer files can be created manually or by using the Windows 2000 Server's Setup Manager Wizard. Once you have an answer file created, the process of applying it involves going to the RIS server's properties in Active Directory Users and Computers and installing a new image from the Remote Install tab. You will have the option of using your own text file, or taking one of the samples that is included with RIS. One sample file instructs RIS to not automatically repartition the client's drives.

exam Watch

By default, RIS will wipe out all existing partitions on a client machine and reformat everything as one large drive with NTFS. If you do not want this to happen, you need to include a parameter in your answer file. Under the [RemoteInstall] section of the file, add a parameter that reads "repartition=no." RIS will then read the answer file to see how to partition the drives.

Once you have created and associated the new answer file with your CD-based image, you can restrict who is able to use it through ordinary NTFS permissions. Simply go to the properties of the file itself and give Read and Read & Execute permission to the users who should be able to install the image.

exam Watch

Remember, at this point it is simply NTFS permissions applied to the answer file itself that restricts this installation. It has nothing to do with the Remote Install properties.

Computer Account Creation

At some point in the Remote OS Installation process, a computer account needs to be created in Active Directory. By default, the account will be created upon installation, and a computer name will be generated by the RIS server, following parameters that were preconfigured by the administrator. In order for this method to work, the user who is starting the RIS process needs to have the appropriate permissions to create a computer account. This may not always be desirable. For this reason, and to give more control to the administrators over computer names, there is another option called *prestaging* computer accounts. In this method, you use a number that is unique to each piece of hardware, a Globally Unique ID, or GUID, and you tell Active Directory to create a computer account with a specific name when a request comes from that particular machine. In this section, we will compare the two methods.

Default Installation and Computer Naming

If you do not wish to prestage client computers, you need to decide on a naming convention and choose where in Active Directory new computer accounts will be placed. You then need to be sure to give the user who is going to start the RIS process on a client machine permission to create a computer account in the appropriate Organizational Unit. The former is done in Active Directory Users and Computers on the Remote Install tab of the RIS server's Properties sheet. The latter is done through Group Policy.

In the Advanced section of the Remote Install tab, you have the option of choosing a predefined naming scheme or developing a custom scheme of your own. These schemes involve either the user's name or the Media Access Control (MAC) address of the client computer. From the same place, you can also define a single OU for new computer accounts to be created,
or specify that the account will be created in the user's OU.

Assigning Permissions to Users

If you are not going to prestage client computers, you need to make sure that the user who is going to begin the client installation process has the right to add computers to the Organizational Unit that the new account will be placed in. This can be done through the Delegation of Control Wizard.

Prestaging Client Computers

As an alternative to giving users the right to add computer accounts and choosing a default naming scheme, you can set up computer accounts ahead of time and designate them as RIS accounts. *Prestaging* is the process of creating an account ahead of time and associating it with a particular machine's network card or BIOS. Besides eliminating the need to give users permissions we may not wish to hand out and giving us control of computer names, prestaging computers will also allow us to distribute the load across multiple RIS servers if we wish.

Before you can prestage a computer, you need to know its Globally Unique ID, or GUID. A *GUID* is a 32-digit hex number that is given to all PXE-based devices. It is usually located on a sticker somewhere on the computer or inside the case. For non-PXE machines, the GUID is 20 zeros followed by the computer's MAC address.

on the job

If you are having difficulty determining a computer's GUID, the following suggestions may help. For a non-PXE machine, type ipconfig /all from a command prompt. You will find the computer's MAC address. Add 20 zeros to the beginning and you have a functional GUID. For a PXE-based machine, the process is a little more difficult if you can't find the number printed on the case or in the machine somewhere. One method is to run a network sniffer such as Network Monitor and issue an ipconfig /renew command. If you look inside the captured DHCP Discover packet, you will find the client's GUID.

To prestage a computer, you must first create the account in Active Directory Users and Computers. Right-click the Organizational Unit into which you wish to place the new account and choose New | Computer. Give the account a name as usual and click Next. You will be asked whether this is a managed computer or not. Indicate that it is and type in the GUID for the computer that will receive the account (Figure 10-2).

When you click Next, you will have the opportunity to designate a particular RIS server to service this machine if you wish. This will allow you to spread the work across multiple RIS servers (Figure 10-3).

Clicking Next will allow you to review your choices. Review, press Finish, and you have a prestaged computer (Figure 10-4).

FIGURE 10-2

Prestaging a computer

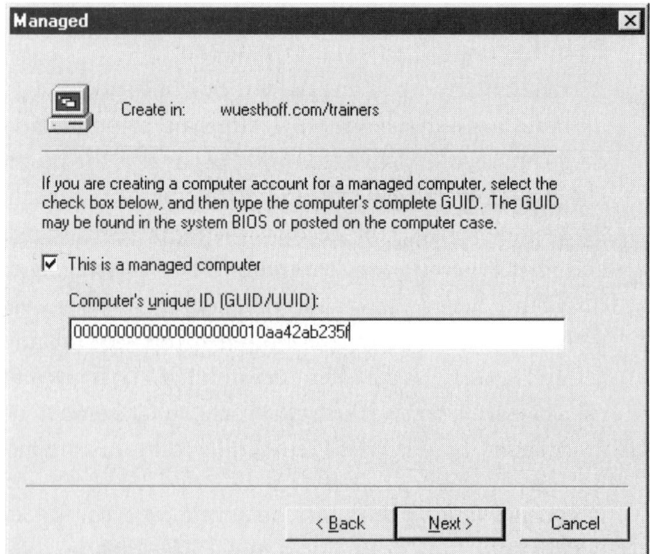

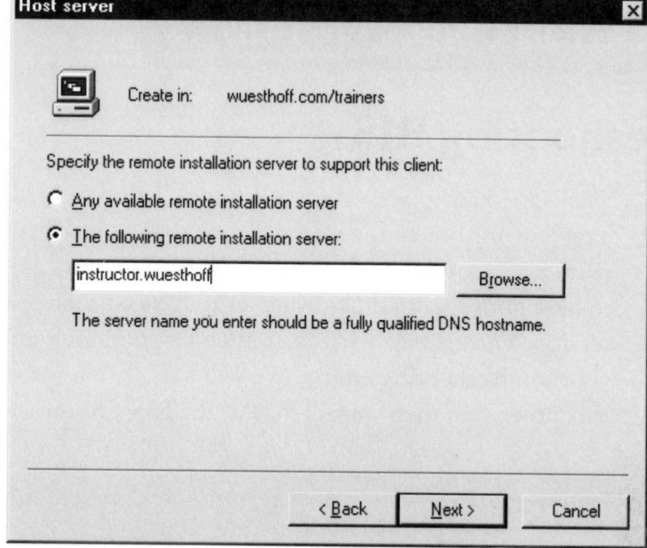

FIGURE 10-3

Designating a RIS server

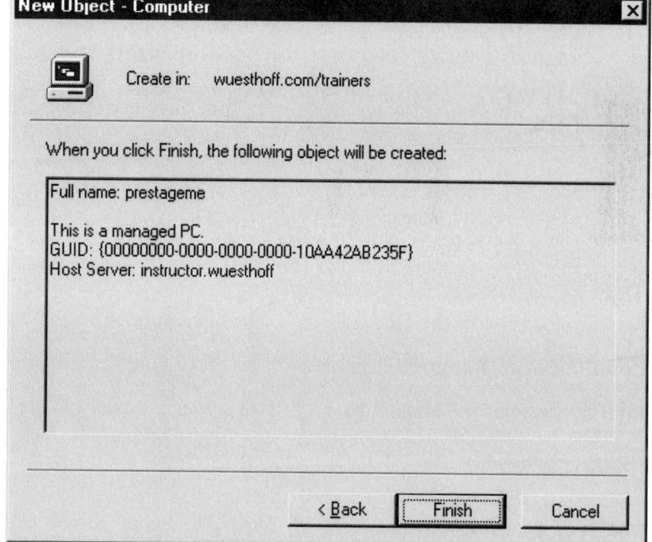

FIGURE 10-4

Confirming the prestaging

CERTIFICATION OBJECTIVE 10.05

Troubleshooting RIS

There are many places where a RIS installation can fail. At the simplest level, a typo in any one of the many dialog boxes can lead to a failed installation. This is particularly common when typing GUIDs to prestage computers. It is also common to have nonsupported hardware, or to have a problem with one of the network services. Fortunately, Microsoft provides good tools and documentation to aid your troubleshooting efforts. We will look first at some common errors you will encounter, and then we will look at the RIS Troubleshooter.

Common Errors

There are different points in the boot process where the RIS installation might fail. By inspecting how far you are able to get in the process before an error, you can get some idea of what problem you might be having.

Here is a quick reference for possible errors you might encounter and their causes:

SCENARIO & SOLUTION	
Client computers cannot boot to the RIS server.	The client may not be on the list of supported adapters.
Clients get a BootP message, but go no further.	The DHCP server is likely unavailable.
Clients get a DHCP message and then stop.	RIS server is either offline or not authorized.
Clients get a BINL message and then stop.	The BINLSVC service on the RIS server may be stalled. Try stopping and restarting the service on the RIS server.
Installation options or images not available to user.	Most likely a permissions problem somewhere, or an incorrectly set Group Policy Object.

The Troubleshooter

Windows 2000 Help includes many troubleshooters to assist you when you run into trouble. There is a troubleshooter for the Remote Installation Services as well. The troubleshooters are presented in a problem /solution format. Common problems are listed, and when you select a proble, a discussion on solutions appears. Many of the solutions have hyperlinks to bring you to the tools that you will need to perform a task. Some of the troubleshooters present error messages you may encounter. As with all other Windows 2000 errors, details of all error messages will be stored in the Event Log, which you can access using the Event Viewer. Most of the RIS-based errors will be found in the Application or System logs.

Make use of the troubleshooters in Windows 2000. They are more useful and more in depth than they have been in the past.

EXERCISE 10-5

CertCam 10-5

Accessing the RIS Troubleshooter

1. Select Start | Help (see the following illustration).

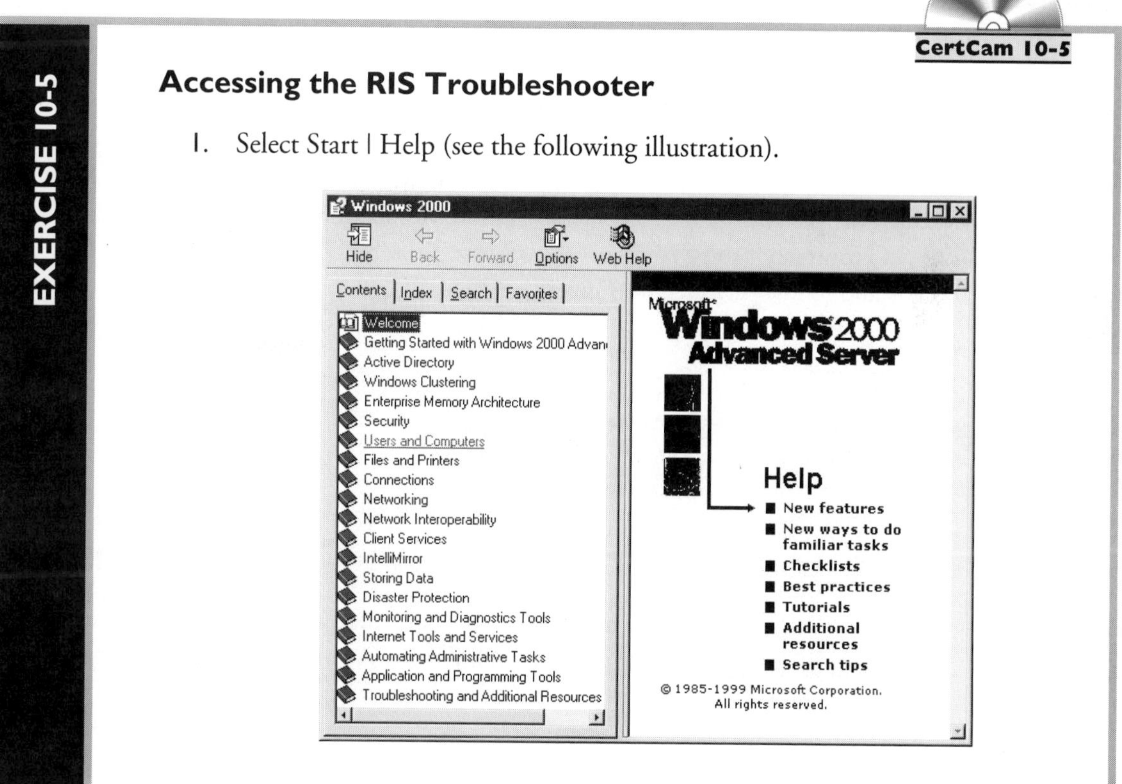

2. Choose Intellimirror | Remote installation services (see the following illustration).

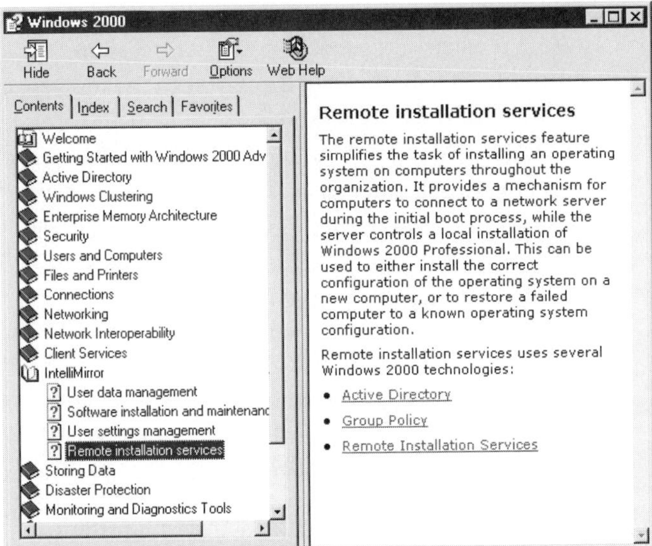

3. On the right-hand side, choose Remote Installation Services and then Troubleshooting. You will see a number of topics on the right. Choose one and follow the directions given.

CERTIFICATION OBJECTIVE 10.06

Preparing to Use RIS to Install the Client Machine

Utilizing RIS for large-scale deployment of the Windows 2000 Professional operating system on a desktop needs careful planning and preparation. In order to gather full benefits from RIS, you must consider certain planning issues and make some important decisions in advance. For example, you need to check your client hardware, check the RIS server configuration, check network adapters, plan which images to install, and decide who will perform RIS installations.

Check Hardware Check whether or not the hardware of the client machines meets the minimum requirements for using RIS. It is not recommended that you stick to the minimum requirements. For example, if the documents say that you need a minimum of 32MB RAM, you should use 64MB or more RAM so that you get the best results. The next section details the minimum hardware requirements for client desktop machines.

Check RIS Server Configuration Before you start installing a client machine, you must check that the RIS server is up and running. In addition, the Domain Name System (DNS) and the Dynamic Host Configuration Protocol (DHCP) services must be running. There must be a scope created and activated on the DHCP server so that client computers can get IP addresses. The DHCP must be authorized in Active Directory. You must also ensure that if there are routers being used in the network for segmentation, they are not blocking any BootP broadcasts. The client machines depend on BootP protocol to get an IP address from the DHCP server.

Check Network Adapters Make a thorough check of all the desktop machines that will use RIS for installation to ensure they have supported network adapters or a PXE-based Boot ROM. In order to use RIS, a machine with a PXE boot ROM must be configured to boot from this ROM. If the desktops have supported PCI adapters, you need to create remote installation boot disks, a process that is discussed later in this chapter.

Plan Which Images to Install If you are using prepared images to install the operating system and application software, you must decide in advance which desktop will receive which image. For example, a desktop in the accounting department might not have the same image as that of a desktop in the marketing department.

Decide Who Will Perform RIS Installations It is important to decide who will perform installations. In most large organizations, the help desk staff is responsible for desktop installations. If that is the case in your organization, you need to give the members of the help desk group proper rights in the domain so that they can do their jobs without running into problems. If you decide to let users perform the installations, you must configure the RIS server in such a way that a user does not pick up a wrong image to install.

With proper planning, you can achieve a trouble-free deployment of Windows 2000 Professional in your organization. At the same time, you can implement organizationwide desktop policies. Make sure that you document each and every aspect of planning and implementation for your installation.

Supported Hardware

This section gives you a brief idea of client hardware requirements so that clients are able to utilize RIS for quick and hassle-free installation of operating system and applications. RIS is different from several disk-imaging utilities available in the marketplace today in that it does not require that all the desktop machines be identical in each and every hardware configuration. This flexibility frees your company's staff involved in purchasing hardware from depending on a single vendor.

Even so, certain requirements must be met before you start using RIS. The client computers requesting RIS must have the following minimum hardware:

- A Pentium processor of 166MHz or faster
- A minimum of 32MB RAM; 64MB is recommended
- A hard disk with a minimum capacity of 800MB
- A PCI plug-and-play adapter supported by RIS or a PXE-based remote boot ROM version .99 or later; desktops that are Net PC compliant can also be RIS clients

There are certain other requirements for Net PC-compliant desktops. These are as follows:

- The Net PC BIOS must be configured such that the network adapter is the primary boot device.

- The user account that is used to run the remote installation must be given "Logon as batch job" rights.
- Users must have sufficient privileges to create computer accounts in the domain.

For desktops that do not have either a PXE-based boot ROM or are not Net PC compliant, RIS includes a *Remote Installation Boot Disk Generator utility, RBFG.EXE*. This utility can create a remote boot disk that supports a number of PCI plug-and-play network adapters. When you create a boot disk using the RBFG.EXE utility, as discussed later in this section, you are able to view a list of the supported network adapters.

exam watch

For running RIS-based installation on a Net PC, you must ensure that the user account used during the installation has "Logon as batch job" rights. These rights must be given even if the administrator's account is used for this purpose, because the administrator's group does not have these rights by default.

Unsupported Hardware

The RBFG.EXE utility does not support any Industry Standard Architecture (ISA), Extended Industry Standard Architecture (EISA), or Token Ring network cards. It is also not possible to add support for additional network adapters because the included drivers are hard coded in the RGBF.EXE utility. Laptops usually have PC Cards or Personal Computer Memory Card International Association (PCMCIA) cards and are not supported as RIS clients. One exception is laptop computers in their docking stations that have a supported network adapter.

Group Policy Settings

When you have a large network with hundreds of computers and many images, you need to restrict access to the options that are presented to users when the Client Installation Wizard runs. You can actually restrict clients from choosing an incorrect installation option by applying a group policy for the RIS server. This restriction is accomplished via the Active Directory Users and Computers snap-in.

EXERCISE 10-6

Restricting Client Installation Options

1. Log on to the RIS server as a domain administrator.
2. Choose Start | Programs | Administrative Tools | Active Directory Users and Computers.
3. Select the container for the RIS policy settings. By default, these settings are at the domain container level, in the Default Domain Group Policy.
4. In the left pane, right-click the domain name and click Properties. Click the Group Policy tab in the Properties window.
5. Click the Default Domain Policy and click Edit. Double-click the User Configuration. Double-click the Windows Settings.
6. Click Remote Installation Services. An icon for Choice Options appears on the right-side pane.
7. Double-click the Choice Options icon. Three choice options are displayed, as shown in the following illustration.

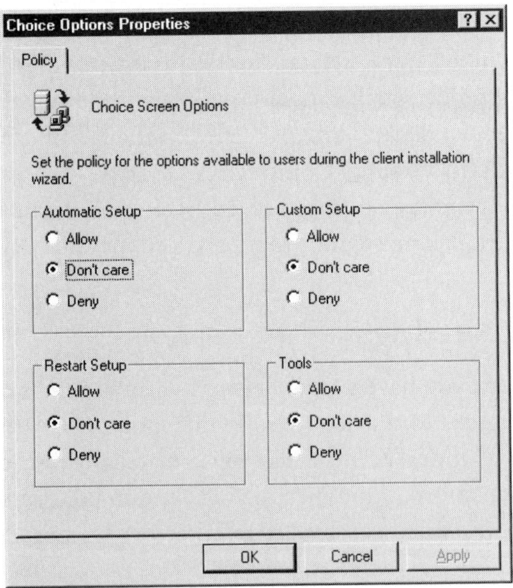

- **Allow** This option allows users to choose an installation option.
- **Don't care** In this option, the predefined group policy is applied to all users. This is the default setting for all choice options.
- **Deny** When selected, this option does not allow users to access a particular installation option.

8. After making a selection, click OK. Close all the windows. Close the Active Directory window as well.

exam Watch

The don't-care option is the default setting for all four types of Client Installation Wizard choice options.

Restricting the Operating System Image Options

The next step is to specify which client or user will use which image. This is an important step to ensure that each user installs a correct operating system image. If this step is not done, the client could choose a wrong image, and all the efforts for saving time on unattended installations would be wasted. By applying user or group security policies, we can specify which image the user can see and install. You can either choose to show all the images to the user or you can restrict the user from seeing any images that are available on the RIS server but not meant for him or her.

Now that you have read about various requirements for RIS-based client installations, take a look at some real-life questions.

SCENARIO & SOLUTION	
Your network has a mix of desktop computers supplied by different vendors. Can you use RIS for installing Windows 2000 Professional?	Yes. RIS-based installations can be performed, provided the desktops meet the minimum hardware requirements.
You have already implemented NTFS security on all the servers. Why do you need separate Group Policies for the RIS images?	The Group Policy settings are different from NTFS security. These policies ensure that users choose a correct image to install.
Some of the managers in your office use laptops in the office and at home. Can you use RIS to install Windows 2000 Professional on these laptops?	Yes and no—yes because you can use RIS if the laptops are used in docking stations and these docking stations have supported network adapters; no because, unless the said condition is met, laptops are not supported as RIS clients.

CERTIFICATION OBJECTIVE 10.07

Installing an Image to a Client Machine

Installation of an operating system image to client computers requires significant planning and preparation, as discussed earlier in this chapter. This preparation effort can include setting up and configuring a RIS server, creating and activating a DHCP scope for client computers on the DHCP server, and configuration of group policies that affect the behavior of RIS server. When the client computers are not Net PC compliant or do not have PXE-based boot ROMs, another task is added to the list: creation of a remote boot disk so that all such clients that have supported PCI network adapters are able to boot from the RIS server.

The following sections describe the creation of a remote boot disk and cover various installation scenarios.

Creating the RIS Boot Disk

When the client computer starts, it needs to contact the RIS server. There are two ways to accomplish this contact. One, the client must have a PXE-based boot ROM on the network adapter. Alernatively, the client must boot using a remote installation boot disk. The *remote installation boot disk* simulates the PXE boot process, helping the client get an IP address from any DHCP server on the network. Once the client gets a IP address, it can communicate with other computers on the network.

For the client computers that do not have a PXE boot ROM, the RIS includes a boot disk generator utility, as mentioned earlier. This RGBF.EXE disk can be used to initiate the remote installation process.

The Remote Installation Boot Disk Generator currently supports only a limited number of PCI-based network adapters. Because many of the popular adapters are supported, there is no need to purchase new adapters for hundreds of client computers. The RGBF.EXE utility can be run from any of the following computers:

- The RIS server
- A client computer that has a connection to the RIS server
- Any client connected to the RIS server on which the Windows 2000 Server Administrative Tools are installed

exam watch

The Remote Installation Boot Disk Generator program supports only PCI plug-and-play network adapters. ISA, EISA, or Token Ring network adapters are not supported. It also does not support PC Cards and PCMCIA cards that are used in laptop computers.

EXERCISE 10-7

Creating a Remote Installation Boot Disk

1. Ensure that the RIS server is up and running. Log on as an administrator.
2. Click Start | Run and type in RGBF.EXE. Click OK. If you are running this command from another computer, type the following command and click OK:

   \\RISServer_name\RemoteInstall\Admin\i386\RGBF.exe
3. The Windows 2000 Remote Installation Boot Disk Generator window opens, as shown in the following illustration.

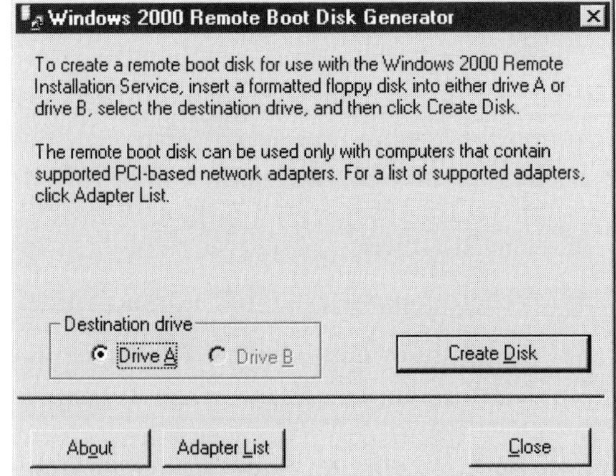

4. Check the path of the destination disk. It is usually drive A. The Drive B radio button remains disabled if a second floppy disk drive is not found on the computer. Insert a blank, formatted 3.5-inch high-density floppy disk in drive A.

5. To see a list of supported adapters, click the Adapter List button. Make sure that the adapters you have are in the list. See the following illustration.

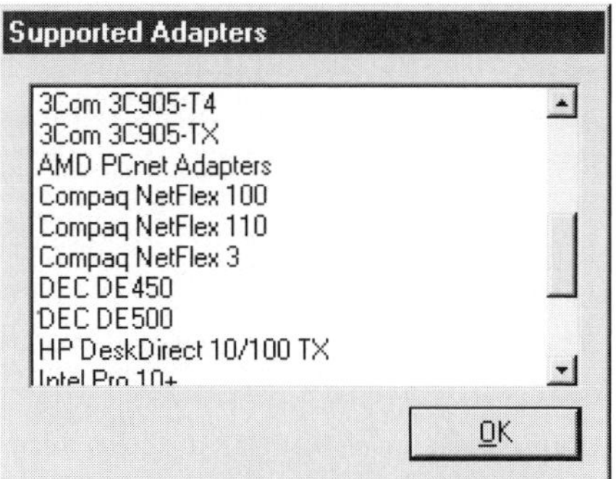

6. Click Create Disk. Doing so creates a remote installation boot disk. Remove the disk and close the Windows 2000 Remote Boot Disk Generator window.

Installation Scenarios

Depending on the requirements of a particular organization, a number of methods can be employed for installation of a desktop operating system throughout the organization. Many factors affect the selection of a deployment method. The simplest method for an organization that has 5–10 desktops is to perform a manual installation using the setup disks or a network file server. However, this method can be an expensive choice if the number of desktops is large. The following alternative methods can be used for deploying a desktop operating system:

- **Attended installation.** This is the simplest method when you have only a few desktop machines. You can use the setup CD-ROM for this installation and answer every question that the setup programs prompts. This method should not be used for multiple installations due to the time consumed and the cost involved in terms of person-hours.
- **Unattended installation.** This method involves creation of setup scripts for automated or unattended installation. This script is also known as an *answer file*. This script contains answers to all or most of the setup queries that otherwise have to be answered by the user. A network file server can be employed to distribute the setup files. This method is, again, an expensive one because it requires good technical expertise.
- **Imaging utilities.** A number of disk-imaging utilities are available in the marketplace today. All of them have their own advantages and limitations. These utilities save deployment time and involved costs. One of the factors that does not go in favor of many such utilities is that they require the source and destination computers to be identical in all respects.

When you decide to use Windows 2000 Remote Installation Service for deployment of Windows 2000 Professional in your organization, it saves you from many troubles such as time spent on deployment, costs incurred, and buying a third-party imaging utility. RIS includes the RIPrep utility, which can be used to prepare the disk image of a fully configured computer. In addition, the source and destination computers need not have identical hardware. The next section describes how RIS can be employed for desktop installations.

Fresh Installations

RIS can be employed for installation of a fresh operating system on desktop computers. The RIS client computers can be desktops that are already running operating systems, or they can be newly purchased desktops. All desktops that have either network adapters supported by RIS or network adapters with PXE-based boot ROMs can utilize RIS for a fresh installation. RIS can be used to create a remote boot disk for supported network adapters using the RGBF.EXE utility.

Many desktop hardware vendors supply computers with preinstalled operating systems. This operating system might or might not meet the requirements of a particular organization. Sometimes the bundled operating system and any applications do not fall within the standards of an organization and need to be removed. This can be a cumbersome process. RIS can help administrators save time and costs in installing fresh Windows 2000 Professional operating systems on these desktops.

You can also use the included imaging RIPrep utility, which can further help in duplicating and distributing disk images. The only limitation of RIPrep is that it can be used on single disks and single partitions. However, because most desktops do not have multiple disk partitions, this RIPrep limitation does not outweigh its advantages. A source desktop machine is first installed with the base Windows 2000 Professional. Any required application software is installed on this desktop and thoroughly tested in all respects. RIPrep is run on this desktop to prepare an image of the hard disk, which is stored on the RIS server. Other desktops run the Client Installation Wizard to select and install an image. The RIS-based installation reformats the destination computer's hard disk and installs a fresh operating system. This process is discussed in more detail later in this chapter.

OS Recovery

One of the best features of RIS is that it can be used to recover even desktops in which the hard drive fails. In a very short time, you can replace the hard drive of a failed desktop and use an existing operating system image from the RIS server to rebuild the desktop. This method works in conjunction with the IntelliMirror technology that can be used to recover the user-specific settings and data from the network.

When a desktop reports a failed hard drive problem, you can replace the disk and boot the desktop using the remote boot disk. The Client Installation Wizard gives you an option of selecting an image from the available OS images on the RIS server. You can select the required image so that the basic operating system and application software is installed on the desktop. After this installation is complete, other user-specific settings, such as user profile and user data in the My Documents folder, can be made available to the user from the network when he or she logs on for the first time after installation. This feature saves you the trouble of reinstalling the operating system and each application separately and performing a number of other user-specific configuration operations.

Preinstall vs. Prestage

Preinstall and *prestage* are altogether different terms. Most of the hardware vendors supply desktop computers with an operating system that is bundled with the hardware. Often, the desktop also has other unwanted software packages installed that might not be required at all. The installed operating system either might be totally useless for your organization or, if required, might not be in accordance with the desktop standards that you have implemented in the organization.

In some cases, the hardware vendor installs the operating system and the applications specified by you when an order is placed. This is known as *preinstalled* software. Preinstalled software saves you time that you might otherwise spend installing the OS and the applications on each desktop. In large organizations that have thousands of desktops already in place, new desktops usually number in the hundreds, and installations on these new entrants can be a costly process. Once the vendor has done a base preinstallation, you might need to perform minimal further configuration so as to utilize Windows 2000 features, such as specifying computer names and configuring Active Directory.

Prestaging a computer is a term that is used in the context of RIS. Prestaging a computer in RIS is the process of creating computer accounts in the Active Directory before an attempt is made to use RIS. This process ensures that only those computers that have been prestaged can use the RIS server for installation. You might recall that the RIS server can be configured not to respond to unknown client computers. If you have a very large network with more than one RIS server, prestaging also allows you to specify which RIS server will respond to a particular client requesting the service.

on the job

Two practical issues relate to prestaging of client computers in the RIS server:

If more than one RIS server exists on the network, prestaging ensures that clients get a response from only the RIS server that is configured to respond to that particular client.

If you have multiple images spread across multiple RIS servers, prestaging ensures that a client does not get a wrong image.

Using RIPrep

Remote Installation Preparation (RIPrep) is a disk duplication tool included with Windows 2000 Server. It is an ideal tool for creating images of fully prepared client computers. Having fully prepared clients helps in fast deployment of the operating system and applications on a large number of client computers using the RIS of a Windows 2000 Server. It is notable that RIPrep can only prepare the images of fully configured client computers that are running the Windows 2000 Professional operating system. The deployment of images created by RIPrep does not need the client computer hardware to be identical, but the *Hardware Abstraction Layer (HAL)* on both the source and destination computers must be identical.

RIPrep requires that RIS and its associated services are configured and running on one or more servers on the network The client computers are first configured with an operating system and all standard or custom-built business applications. The Remote Installation Preparation Wizard is run on the client computer to create an image of the computer. This image is uploaded to a Windows 2000 server running RIS for further distribution to other client computers. During the RIPrep process, the client computer loses all its user-specific settings, such as security IDs. This loss allows computers with different hardware configurations to use the same image.

Advantages and Disadvantages of RIPrep RIPrep is another method of preparing images of computers running Windows 2000 Professional. The following advantages and disadvantages are important to study before deciding to use RIPrep.

Some of the advantages of using RIPrep are as follows:

- The RIPrep utility is bundled with Windows 2000 Server, and no third-party tool is required for creation or delivery of images.
- RIPrep uses Single-Instance Store (SIS), a feature that saves a good deal of hard drive space by eliminating duplicate copies of setup files.
- RIPrep is independent of hardware configuration.
- RIPrep helps in standardizing a Windows 2000 Professional-based desktop environment in an organization.

The following points highlight some disadvantages of using RIPrep:

- RIPrep incurs high administrative costs because it requires trained professionals to implement.
- RIPrep is dependent on several other services, such as RIS, Active Directory, DNS, and DHCP. These must be running on the network.
- RIPrep can be used for clean installations only. Upgrades are not supported.

- RIPrep can be used to prepare images of Windows 2000 Professional only.
- RIPrep can duplicate images of a single hard drive consisting of a single partition only.
- Only a limited number of PCI-based network adapters or PXE-ROM version .99 or later are supported for booting the remote client.

exam Watch

RIS can be used only to deliver the Windows 2000 Professional operating system. RIPrep runs only on computers that have the Windows 2000 Professional operating system installed.

Preparations for Using RIPrep To use the RIPrep utility, you must select one of the desktop computers that will be treated as a source computer for preparing the image. Windows 2000 Professional is installed on this desktop using RIS. Any standard application software such as Office 2000 or custom-built software that you want to use is installed on this desktop. The source desktop is tested in all respects of functionality. It might be necessary to configure more than one source computer to prepare multiple images, depending on the requirements of the organization's departments. The RIPrep utility is run on this desktop to prepare an image of the hard disk that is uploaded to the RIS server. This image can then be distributed to other desktops that are to be configured with a similar image.

When you decide to use RIPrep, you must test the source computer thoroughly. Any configuration you skip will result in replication of the same to all the destination desktops that receive the image. Testing is very important because failing to do so could cause you a great deal of work later. You must also ensure that you are not violating any software agreement while distributing images of the operating system or any application software.

Now that you have studied the details of using the RIPrep utility and the RBFG.EXE tool to create a remote installation boot disk, let's take a quick look at some practical questions.

SCENARIO & SOLUTION	
How do you know which of the network adapters are supported by RIS?	Run the RBFG.EXE utility and click the Adapter List tab to view the supported adapters.
The desktop that you want to use as a source computer has two hard disk partitions. Will there be any problems using RIPrep on this desktop for creating an image?	Yes. RIPrep supports images of only a single partition.
You have desktop hardware that is supplied by two different vendors. Can you use the RIPrep image created on one for duplicating on the other?	Yes. So long as the desktops supplied by the two vendors have an identical HAL, you can use the image created on one to duplicate on the other.
Can you configure the RIS server not to respond to any curious users who might try to use RIS just to see how it works?	Yes. Prestage the client computers that need RIS installations. Configure the RIS server to "Do not respond to unknown client computers."

Installation Options

It's time now to turn to the client side. When a client computer boots using either the remote boot disk or the PXE-based boot ROM, it tries to establish a connection to the DHCP server. A BootP message is displayed on the client computer during this time. If the DHCP server is preconfigured to service the RIS clients, it allocates an IP address from the DHCP scope. Once the client is successful in getting an IP address, it tries to connect to the RIS server. At that time, the BootP message changes to DHCP. This is because the client uses the DHCP broadcasts to connect to the RIS server.

Once the RIS server is contacted, the client computer shows a Boot Installation Negotiation Layer (BINL) message. It might also prompt the user to press the F12 key to proceed. The BINL message indicates that the client is waiting for the RIS server to download the initial boot files, which include the Client Installation Wizard (CIW). The RIS server uses the Trivial File Transfer Protocol (TFTP) to download initial boot files to the client. On some machines, the BINL or TFTP message might not be noticed because it flashes very quickly.

The Client Installation Wizard

The *Client Installation Wizard* has four installation options. The options that are presented to the user depend on the group policy set in the Active Directory. Starting an automatic setup, a user might get all four options or might not get any of the options. The four installation options are as follows:

- Automatic Setup
- Custom Setup
- Restart a Previous Setup Attempt
- Maintenance and Troubleshooting

Each of these options is discussed in the following sections.

Automatic Setup

Automatic Setup is the default option. This is also the easiest installation method that is available to all users. The various configuration parameters are predetermined. The automatic installation option can be configured in such a way that the user is not prompted for even a single question during the installation process.

You might also configure the Automatic Setup option in such a way that users are given an option to select an image from the available images on the RIS server. Because each RIS image has an attached friendly help and description section, the users can select the appropriate image. It is recommended, however, that when you have multiple images on the RIS server, you must restrict users from choosing an incorrect image. This is particularly helpful when you have images relevant to the requirements of various departments in the organization.

The following are the main points to consider when using the Automatic Setup method:

- Users are able to see only those images that have been configured in Group Policy. If only one image exists, a user is not given an option to select the image. In this case, the installation starts as soon as the user logs on.

- You must ensure that in case of multiple images, the user is shown only the relevant images in order to avoid the user selecting an incorrect image.
- Permissions set on images should preferably be based on user groups instead of individual users. This policy helps reduce administrative efforts.
- Use security options on the Templates folder instead of individual .SIF files.

Custom Setup

Custom Setup is a more flexible option that allows the user to override the process of automatically naming a computer. It also allows users to select a location in Active Directory where the computer account will be created. This option requires significant administrative efforts because almost every aspect of the installation can be customized. The following are the main points to remember when using this option:

- This option is usually helpful when the help desk staff is involved in the deployment process. Using Custom Setup, you can prestage a client computer. This ensures that only those computers can request the RIS service that has been predetermined.
- The Custom Setup option is usually selected when end users are not involved in the setup process. This is a flexible setup option and can be utilized in the best way by either the help desk staff of the administrators. Custom Setup also allows you to override the default naming format.

Restart a Previous Setup Attempt

As its name suggests, the Restart a Previous Setup Attempt option enables the user to restart a failed setup attempt. The user is not prompted for any input that he has already entered. This option is particularly useful when for some reason the user loses connection to the RIS server during setup or in case there is accidental shutdown of the client computer.

If the remote installation on a desktop computer fails for some reason, this option gives users the ability to restart the installation. The following are the main points to remember while using this option:

- The Restart a Previous Setup Attempt option does not restart installation from the point where the installation aborted. It starts from the beginning but does not prompt the user for any questions that have already been answered.

- This option is best utilized in an unstable network that frequently has networking problems. Another scenario in which it is helpful is when unstable power sources cause frequent failures.
- This option should not be given to end users. Rather, keep this option for the help desk staff or for yourself.
- If the previous setup was aborted due to some problem with the client hardware, it cannot be fixed using this option. You might have to contact the hardware vendor for assistance resolving specific hardware problems.

Maintenance and Troubleshooting

The Maintenance and Troubleshooting option provides access to any third-party maintenance tools that you may want to use before the installation starts. Because this option is not meant for every user, the administrator can restrict access to it in the Group Policy set in the Active Directory.

The tools that can be used range from updating Basic Input/Output System (BIOS) to memory virus scanners. By default, RIS does not install any maintenance tools. The following are the main points to keep in mind when using this option:

- This is an advanced option and preferably should not be available to end users performing remote installations. You might, however, want to delegate the help desk staff to use these tools, if a need arises.
- By default, RIS does not install any maintenance tools. You might have to contact hardware vendors to acquire Windows 2000-compatible maintenance tools.

After making a selection from among these options, the user sees a displayed list of available image options. When a selection has been made, the user is presented with a summary screen. The installation begins immediately afterward.

exam watch

If the domain administrator has authorized a user for only one image, the user is not prompted for image selection and the installation starts as soon as the user selects the Automatic Setup option.

CERTIFICATION OBJECTIVE 10.08

Troubleshooting the Use of RIS to Install the Client Machine

RIS is dependent on a number of other network services, such as AD, DNS, and DHCP. It also requires that the RIS server and the desktops meet the specified hardware requirements in terms of hard drive space and network adapters. Failure of any network service while starting to perform an RIS-based installation or anytime during the installation process can result in many problems. A careful study of various problems that can occur can help reduce the chances of failed installations.

The following sections describe various issues that can cause trouble during RIS-based installations. If any step is missed or any requirement is overlooked, you might end up in an endless loop of trouble. The flip side of this is that if all issues are taken care of before you start RIS-based installations, you might actually enjoy the job assigned to you.

Before you actually start an RIS-based installation, you must ensure the following:

- The RIS server is up and running.
- The RIS server has been configured in the Active Directory to service remote clients requesting the service.
- A scope has been created in the DHCP server for the remote clients, and the scope is active. Ensure that the DHCP service is running.
- The user accounts exist for performing remote installations, and each user is assigned rights to create computer accounts in the domain.

The other issues related to network and hardware are discussed in the next section.

Network Errors

It is important to have a look at the sequence of processes that take place on the network when a client computer starts using the remote installation boot disk.

RIS, AD, DNS, and the DHCP server all team up to provide a workable operating system to the desktop machine. This sequence of events is more or less similar in all desktops, regardless of the fact that the desktop is a Net PC or has a network adapter with PXE-based boot ROM. The sequence holds true for those desktops that start using the remote boot disk generated by the RBFG.EXE utility.

Sequence of Events When the Client Computer Starts

When the client computer is started using the remote boot disk, it displays a DHCP message. This message indicates that the client is trying to contact the DHCP server to get an IP address. The message stays there, even when the client has received the IP address and is trying to connect to the RIS server.

Step 1: DHCP If the client does not move further and keeps displaying the DHCP message, this could mean there is a problem. Either the client is not able to get an IP address or the RIS server is not responding. The RIS server service that is relevant here is BINL. Perform the following checks:

1. The DHCP server is available.
2. The DHCP scope is activated, and it has an IP address available for the client.
3. If there is a router between the client and the DHCP server, it is configured to forward BootP broadcasts.
4. Other clients on the same segment of the network are getting IPs from the DHCP server.
5. You might also want to have a look at the system event logs on the DHCP server.

Step 2: BINL When the client has received an IP address successfully, the client computer message changes to BINL. This indicates that the client is trying to connect to the RIS server. If no RIS server is available or there are some network connectivity problems between the RIS server and the client, the BINL times out and the following error message is displayed: "No Boot File received from DHCP, BINL, or BootP."

To get around this problem, perform the following checks:

1. Ensure that there is no connectivity problem between the client computer and the RIS server.
2. Ensure that the BINL service is running. This problem is also caused if the RIS server is not authorized in Active Directory.
3. Ensure that the RIS and DHCP servers are authorized in Active Directory.
4. Check to see whether the other RIS clients are facing the same problem. If the problem is with this client only, check that the client has a supported network adapter.
5. If there is a router on the network, check that it is not blocking any BootP broadcasts.
6. You can also check the system event log to find any DHCP, BINL, or AD-related errors or warnings.

on the job

When you get some error message during an RIS-based installation on one client computer, you must check one or two other clients to see whether or not they are exhibiting similar behavior. This check helps pinpoint the source of the problem. For example, if the remote boot disk works well with one computer but causes a DHCP error on the other, the possible cause could be an unsupported network adapter.

Step 3: TFTP When the client computer is successful in connecting to the RIS server, the message on the client screen changes from BINL to TFTP. This is the *Trivial File Transfer Protocol,* which is used to download initial boot files to the client computer. At this time, the user is prompted to press the F12 function key. The TFTP message indicates that the client is waiting for the initial files to be downloaded. These files start the Client Installation Wizard on the client. If the process is successful, you might not be able to see this message because it flashes too quickly on some fast computers.

Continuous display of TFTP messages could again mean a problem. No response from the RIS server causes these messages. If you run into this problem, perform the following checks:

1. Stop and restart the BINL service on the RIS server. This can be done from the command prompt. Start the command prompt on the RIS server and type the following commands:

   ```
   net stop BINLSVC
   net start BINLSVC
   ```

   If the problem is due to a misbehaving BINL service on the RIS server, these commands will hopefully resolve it.
2. Ensure that the RIS server is configured to "Respond to Known Client Computers." Also clear the "Do Not Respond to Unknown Client Computers" check box if it is checked. If the latter option is checked, make sure that the client computer on which installation is being performed is prestaged in the Active Directory.
3. You might also want to check the system log for any error or warning messages concerning the DHCP, DNS, or BINL and AD.

exam Watch

The correct sequence of events is DHCP, BINL, and TFTP. Make sure you do not forget this sequence; you could get exam questions based on it.

Step 4: CIW Welcome Screen When the client computer gets through all the stages discussed, the Client Installation Wizard is downloaded to the client machine. A welcome screen is shown to the user; here, he or she can select an installation option and start the installation process.

Stopping and restarting the BINL service, or any other service, from the command prompt is a quick method used by many network administrators. It requires that you know the correct name of the service as it should appear in the command. The BINL service is written as BINLSVC, and you can use the following two commands from the command prompt to stop and start the service, respectively:

```
net stop BINLSVC
net start BINLSVC
```

It is not mandatory to write BINLSVC in all capital letters, because the command is not case sensitive.

Hardware Issues

RIS-based desktop installations require certain minimum hardware, as described earlier in this chapter. The RIS-based installation process can be an enjoyable project to work on when the present desktops or the newly purchased ones have specified recommended hardware. The following issues are very important to consider while installing RIS-based operating system images.

Check Hardware Requirements

Before you start any RIS-based installation, make sure you have all hardware specified as the minimum recommended. For example, the hard drive must have a capacity of 800MB for receiving an RIS image.

Using RIPrep Images

For an image created by RIPrep, the capacity of the hard disk on destination computers must be either equal to or larger than that of the computer on which the image is created. Distributing RIPrep images also requires that at least the HAL of the source and destination computers must be identical. Again, there must not be any partitions on the hard disk; the RIPrep utility can be used for only single-drive and single-partition computers. An attempt to install a RIPrep image of a client that has a different HAL from the source will not be successful.

Network Adapters

Requirements for the network adapters were discussed in detail earlier in this chapter. As a reminder: The client computer must be either a Net PC-compliant computer or have a network adapter with PXE-based Boot ROM. The network adapter must be configured in the computer BIOS to boot from the network. Otherwise, the client must have one of the supported PCI plug-and-play adapters. Failure of the client computer to comply with these network adapter requirements can lead to installation troubles. The computer will not be able to connect to the network and will display a DHCP message indefinitely.

Laptop Computer Considerations

Laptop computers usually have PC Cards or PCMCIA cards. These are not supported by RIS. An exception is laptops that are in docking stations that have a supported network adapter.

PXE Boot ROM Version

RIS supports PXE Boot ROM version .99 or later. Any version prior to .99 can cause problems in using RIS. To check which version is used by your network adapter boot ROM, read the messages that appear on the client screen when the client starts booting up.

After a detailed study of various troubleshooting scenarios, let's take a quick look at some practical problems.

SCENARIO & SOLUTION

You are getting the same DHCP error from all client computers when you try to start them using the remote boot disk. Is the floppy disk corrupted?	Yes, that might be a problem. However, if the error persists with a second good remote boot disk, look for other reasons.
When you installed Windows 2000 Professional on my desktop, you were not given any option to select an image. What could be the problem?	This is not a problem. RIS is configured for an automatic installation when your user account is used.
You created an image using RIPrep on a desktop with a 6.4GB hard disk. You are unable to distribute the image to other desktops that have 4.3GB hard drives. Why?	You made a mistake. The hard disk on the destination computers must be either equal to or larger than the source computer where the image is created. The solution is to recreate the image, keeping that specification in mind.
Are there any event logs for RIS?	Yes. Check the system log for any error or warning messages regarding AD, DHCP, DNS, or BINL services.

FROM THE CLASSROOM

Getting Ready for Remote Installations

The details of employing RIS for rolling out Windows 2000 Professional and using RIPrep to prepare Windows 2000 Professional-based disk images have been discussed in this chapter. The brief discussion here is on some of the best practices that you can adopt while implementing your RIS-based deployment plans. Consider the following practical points, which are generally overlooked:

1. The hardware required is the minimum recommended for the RIS server and the clients. Most of the present-day servers

FROM THE CLASSROOM

and desktops meet these requirements. The only thing you must be very careful about is the disk space requirement. On the server side, make sure you have a separate partition dedicated to RIS images of large capacity. This must be an NTFS partition.

2. When using RIPrep, make sure the source and the destination computers have identical HALs. Disk space on the destination computers must be either equal to or larger than that of the source computer.
3. When planning for RIS-based or any other imaging solution, you must ensure that you have a sufficient number of licenses for the operating system and the application software. Remember, because you are the one in charge of deployment, you will be the first to be questioned if there are any license agreement violations.
4. Document each and every aspect of RIS configuration. Doing so helps ensure that you are not going wrong at any time. If you are delegating the deployment responsibilities to help desk personnel, create a detailed document explaining how to use RIS. Make sure you also include some of the common troubleshooting scenarios so that help desk staff do not keep calling you for every little problem.
5. The RIS-based deployment option needs careful planning, so make a thorough study of the requirements of your organization. This is particularly important if you were hired recently and are not familiar with the desktop policies or standards of the organization.

—Pawan K. Bhardwaj, MCSE, MCP+I, CCNA

CERTIFICATION SUMMARY

Remote Installation Services gives us the ability to automate the installation of Windows 2000 Professional on client computers. Using RIS, we are able to allow an average user to do his or her own installation without fear of getting any configuration options incorrect.

We began this chapter by looking at RIS, inspecting cases where it may be useful, and studying the RIS process. Next, we looked at how to set up and install a RIS server. We discussed the network prerequisites and the fact that you need to have DNS, DHCP, and Active Directory running on your network before you can set up RIS. We saw that a RIS server needs to be authorized in Active Directory, whether or not it is already a DHCP server.

In the next section, we discussed how to configure the RIS server, particularly how to create images for deployment. We learned the difference between CD-based images and RIPrep images. We looked at how to create computer accounts for your RIS installed clients, and whether to prestage client machines or not. Then, we looked at the Troubleshooter, a tool you can turn to when RIS installations do not work.

Remote Installation Service (RIS) can be employed for large-scale deployment of the Windows 2000 Professional operating system in the organization. The RIS-based deployment calls for careful planning, keeping in mind all the requirements of this service and the requirements of a particular organization. You must check hardware compatibility and various factors regarding RIS server configuration and decide on the users or user groups that will be responsible for installations. Accordingly, group policies must be set so that a trouble-free installation can take place.

RIS supports desktop clients that are Net PC compliant; these machines have the network adapter configured to boot from the network. Desktops that have network adapters with a PXE-based boot ROM can also be RIS clients. For other desktops, RIS provides the RGFG.EXE utility that can create a remote installation boot disk. This disk contains drivers for several popular PCI-based network adapters.

When a client computer boots using the remote boot disk or using the PXE-based boot ROM, it looks for the DHCP server for getting an IP address. After getting the IP address, it requests the RIS server to download startup files. The startup files start the Client Installation Wizard (CIW) on the client machine, giving four different installation options, depending on the Group Policy set for the user who is performing the installation. The administrator could set client choice options, and Group Policy is a method by which the user does not have to intervene in the installation process. Otherwise, the administrator can also choose to show some or all the image options. RIPrep is used on a fully configured client computer to prepare an image of the disk. This image can be distributed to other clients that have an identical Hardware Abstraction Layer (HAL).

With proper planning and careful inspection of various requirements of RIS-based installations, many problems can be eliminated. Most of the problems occur during the time when the client computer boots. The problems related to DHCP, BINL, and TFTP services display self-explanatory error messages on the client machine. You can also check the system logs for any errors related to AD, DHCP, DNS, and BINL services to find a resolution to a problem.

TWO-MINUTE DRILL

What Is Remote Installation Service?

- Remote Installation Service allows you to deploy images from a RIS server to compatible client machines.
- RIS can only deploy images based on Windows 2000 Professional.
- A RIS image contains the preconfigured OS, plus any applications that may need to go on all client machines.

Creating a RIS Server

- DHCP, DNS, and Active Directory must be running and available somewhere on your network for RIS to work.
- A RIS server must have a partition other than the system and boot partitions to store images. The partition should have 2GB of free space and be formatted with the NTFS file system.

Authorizing a RIS Server

- A RIS server will not respond to client requests unless it has received permission to do so. That permission is granted by authorizing the server in Active Directory.
- The server must be authorized in the DHCP manager as an authorized DHCP server, even if we have no intention of ever running DHCP on this machine.

Configuring a RIS Server

- There are two types of images: CD based and RIPrep.
- CD-based images are derived from a simple copy of the Windows 2000 Professional files from the CD, and use answer files for customization purposes.
- RIPrep images are snapshots of an entire source machine's configuration. With these issues, you can deploy applications along with a fully configured OS.

Troubleshooting RIS

- ❑ Troubleshooting involves two main tools: Event logs and the Troubleshooter.
- ❑ The Event log will help us to track down the reasons for RIS failure by keeping track of and recording all error messages.

Preparing to Use RIS to Install the Client Machine

- ❑ RIS-based installations can be performed on any client machines that meet the minimum hardware requirements. At a minimum, the client machines must have a Pentium 166MHz processor, 32MB RAM, and hard disk capacity of 800MB.
- ❑ Because laptops use either PC Cards or PCMCIA cards, they are not supported as RIS clients. An exception is laptops in their docking stations that have a supported network adapter.

Installing an Image to a Client Machine

- ❑ The RBFG.EXE utility does not support ISA, EISA, or Token Ring cards. Furthermore, you cannot add support for any additional adapters because the drivers are hard-coded in the RBFG.EXE utility.
- ❑ Prestaging of client computers is done to create computer accounts in the domain and to ensure that client computers are serviced by a predetermined RIS server. This also ensures that client machines obtain a correct image.

Troubleshooting the Use of RIS to Install the Client Machine

- ❑ To avoid any possible problems during RIS installations, you must ensure that the RIS server is up and running and a DHCP scope is active for the RIS clients.
- ❑ User accounts must exist for users who will perform RIS installations. To make sure the installation process runs smoothly, these users must have rights to create computer accounts in the domain.
- ❑ If there is a router between the client computer and the RIS and DHCP servers, it must be configured to forward BootP messages. This configuration ensures that the client computer receives an IP address.

Part III

Installing Windows 2000

MCSE
MICROSOFT CERTIFIED SYSTEMS ENGINEER

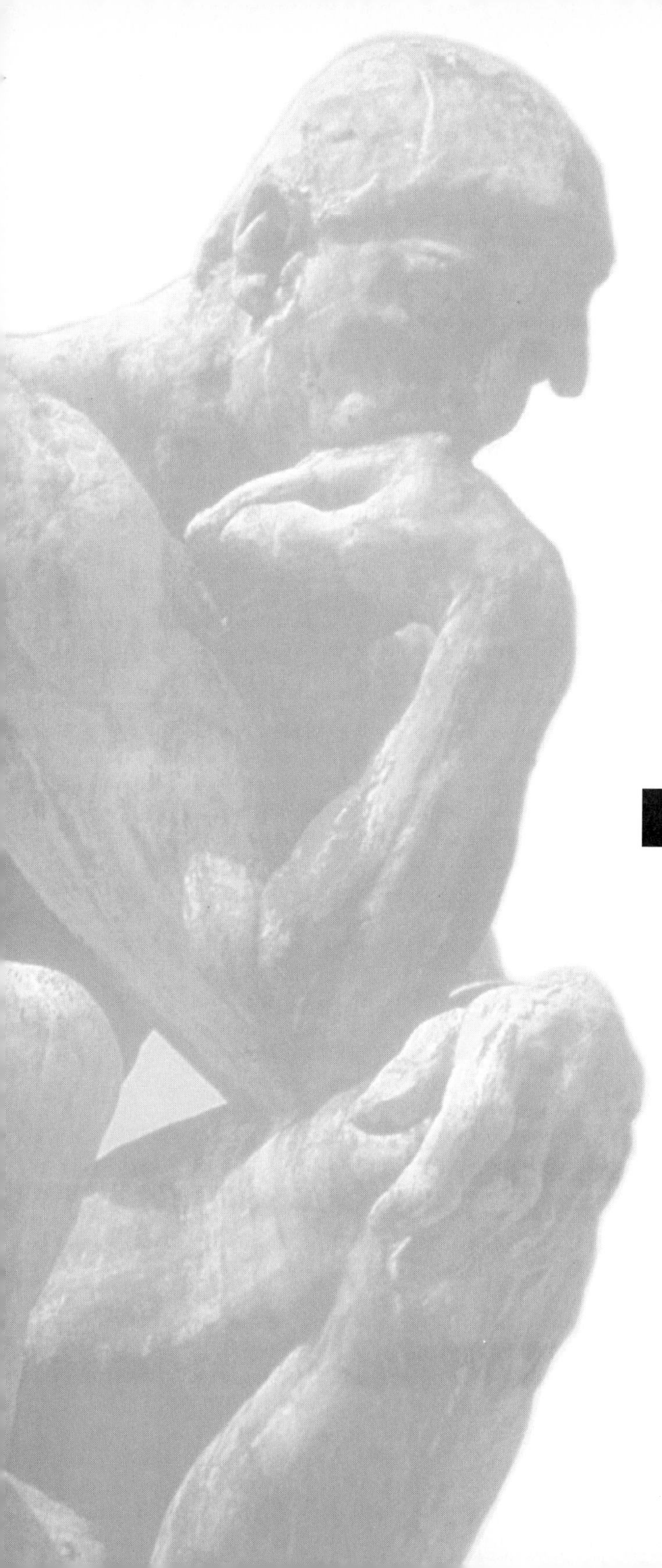

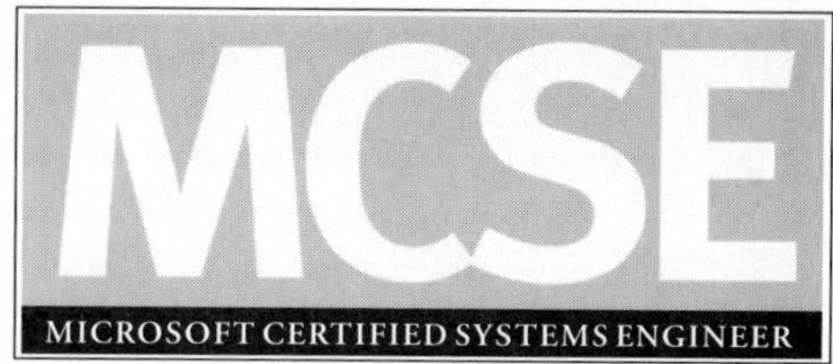

11

Windows 2000 Attended Installation

CERTIFICATION OBJECTIVES

11.01 Performing an Attended Installation of Windows 2000

✓ Two-Minute Drill

In this chapter, we will discuss how to perform an attended installation of Windows 2000 Server and Windows 2000 Professional. In Windows 2000, installation has been made easier than it was in Windows NT 4.0, and some additional features have been added. Before actually starting the installation process, you should plan ahead.

You should prepare for installation before you start. You need to determine whether your computer meets the minimum hardware requirements. You will need to decide how to partition your hard drive and what file system to use. During installation of Windows 2000 Server, you will have to choose a licensing mode, so you should determine ahead of time which one is best for your situation. You also have to decide whether to join a domain or a workgroup. Also during installation, you need to choose which optional components to install and how to configure the computer to operate on the network.

You can perform an attended installation of Windows 2000 Server or Professional from a CD-ROM or across the network from a distribution server. When you install over the network, you have many options for customizing the installation process. It is important to understand these options.

Periodically, Microsoft releases fixes to its operating systems known as *service packs*. Service packs contain bug and security fixes. Normally, you want to have your computers running the latest service pack that is available. However, you should test the service packs for your environment prior to deploying them.

On occasion, the installation of Windows 2000 will fail. When it does, you need to be prepared to solve the problem. You should know the common problems that can occur, and understand that Setup creates log files that can be used to help with troubleshooting.

CERTIFICATION OBJECTIVE 11.01

Performing an Attended Installation of Windows 2000

When you perform an attended installation of Windows 2000 Professional or Server, you will have to make many choices. By planning for installation ahead of time, you will be prepared to make these choices. You should make sure that you meet the hardware requirements, determine how to partition the hard disk, select the file system and licensing mode to use, decide whether to join a domain or workgroup, and decide which components to install. For attended installation, you can install from the CD-ROM or across the network.

Preparing for Installation

There are some options that you will be required to choose from during installation, and things will go more smoothly if you determine which choices to make ahead of time. You will need to ensure that your computer has the minimum required hardware, determine how to partition your hard disk, choose a file system, choose a licensing mode, and decide whether to join a domain or a workgroup.

Hardware Requirements

Before starting installation, you need to check to make sure that your hardware meets the minimum requirements and that it is compatible with Windows 2000. See the list below for the minimum requirements for running Windows 2000.

- 133 MHz Pentium or higher CPU.
- Up to four CPUs supported by Server, and Professional supports up to two processors.
- 64MB of RAM required, with 128MB of RAM recommended as the minimum. 4GB of RAM is the maximum.

To install Windows 2000 Server, the Setup process needs approximately 1GB of free space. You need a minimum of 671MB (650 MB for Professional) of free space with 2GB recommended on the partition on which Windows 2000 Server is to be installed. Once Setup is complete, the temporary files will be deleted and less free space is then required by Windows 2000. You might need more than the minimum space required depending on your configuration and options. See the following list for cases in which more disk space is needed:

- You will need additional space for each additional component you install.
- If you use the FAT file system, you will need an additional 100–200MB of free space.

- If you install across the network, you will need as much as 100–200MB of additional free space to store driver files required for the network installation.
- If you are upgrading Server, you will need additional space to import the existing user account database.

exam watch

There are usually some questions pertaining to the hardware requirements. Make sure you know what they are and how to determine whether an existing computer meets the requirements.

Keep in mind that your computer will be severely limited if it just meets the minimum hardware requirements. You should always perform some analysis and testing to determine what hardware is needed for your computer. You will need to take into account the applications that will be run, and how much network traffic your server will handle.

You also need to make sure your hardware and BIOS are compatible with Windows 2000. Before installation, verify that all of your hardware is on the Hardware Compatibility List (HCL). The HCL is a listing of all the hardware that has passed the Hardware Compatibility Tests (HCTs) and the devices that are supported by Windows 2000. This testing is performed by Windows Hardware Quality Labs (WHQL) and by hardware vendors to prove compatibility with Windows 2000. If your hardware is not on the HCL, your computer may not work correctly after Windows 2000 is installed. The HCL can be found on the Windows 2000 CD-ROM in the Support directory, or you can access the latest version of the HCL on the Microsoft Web site.

It is also important to ensure that your BIOS is compatible. If it is not compatible, you might not be able to use the advanced power management or Plug and Play features of Windows 2000, or your computer may not work correctly. If your hardware is not found on the HCL, contact the hardware vendor to see whether it has any updates to make the hardware compliant with Windows 2000.

To help with determining the compatibility, you can use the Windows 2000 Compatibility Tool to generate a hardware and software compatibility report. This tool is run during Setup, but you should run it before running Setup so you can fix any potential problems ahead of time. There are two ways to use the Compatibility Tool. First, you can run **Winnt32 /checkupgradeonly**. This will start Setup to generate a compatibility report without starting installation of Windows 2000. This will generate a report named Winnt32.log in the *<systemroot>* folder. Second, you can run the Windows 2000 Readiness Analyzer. This will generate the report without running Setup. This tool can be downloaded from Microsoft at www.microsoft.com/windows2000/upgrade/compat. The Readiness analyzer will not work if you have a dual-boot configuration with Windows 95, Windows 98, and Windows NT. The report will provide a listing of the hardware and software that is incompatible with Windows 2000.

Partitioning the Hard Disk

When you perform a new installation, you need to decide how to configure your hard disk. The hard disk contains one or more partitions. A primary partition can be seen as a logical drive, whereas an extended partition can contain multiple logical drives. Each partition can be assigned a drive letter such as C: or D: and can use a different file system such as FAT, FAT32, or NTFS. You can create partitions prior to installation, during the setup process, or after Windows 2000 is installed. During setup, you should create and size only the partition you are installing the operating system on. You can use the Disk Management tool to configure other partitions after installation. The partition that you installed the Windows 2000 operating system files on is called the boot partition. It contains all the files you need to run Windows 2000. When the computer boots, the active partition (normally the C:\ drive) searches for the files needed to load Windows 2000 (Ntldr, Ntdetect.com, Boot.ini). These files load the Windows 2000 operating system from the system partition. If Windows 2000 is installed on the boot partition, this partition is both the system partition and the boot partition.

It is important to remember that if you delete an existing partition, you cannot access the information that was previously stored on that partition. Before deleting a partition, if there is any data that you need on that partition, make sure you back up the data. Actually, it is recommended that you back up all of your data before changing your partition configuration.

When you create a partition to install Windows 2000 on, you need to make sure the partition is large enough for the operating system, applications, and data that will be stored on the partition. To install Windows 2000, Setup needs at least 1GB of free disk space with 671MB (650 MB for Professional) of free space on the partition where Windows 2000 will be installed. If you are going to configure your computer for multiple operating systems, you need to install Windows 2000 on its own partition. This prevents setup from overwriting files needed by other operating systems.

Choosing a File System

Once you have decided how to partition your hard disk and which partition to install Windows 2000 on, you need to decide which file system to use for the partition. Windows 2000 supports the NTFS, FAT, and FAT32 file systems. In most configurations, the NTFS file system is the best choice. The only reason to use FAT or FAT32 is for a dual-boot configuration in which you have more than one operating system. Microsoft does not recommend using the dual-boot configuration on a server. During setup, you can convert an existing FAT or FAT32 partition to the new NTFS. This allows you to keep your existing data on the partition. If you do not need to keep the existing data on the partition, it is recommended that you format the drive with NTFS rather than converting it. This will erase all existing data on the partition, but the partition will have less fragmentation and thus better performance.

exam Watch

The only reason to use the FAT or FAT32 file system is for dual-booting configurations. Microsoft recommends NTFS and does not recommend dual-boot configurations for servers.

NTFS The NTFS file system provides these features:

- **Security at the file and folder level** This allows you to control access down to the file level.
- **File compression** This allows you to compress folders, subfolders, and files to increase the amount of file storage, but slow down access to the files.
- **Disk quotas** This allows you to limit the amount of disk space used by each user.
- **File encryption** Folders, subfolders, and files can be encrypted and decrypted automatically by the operating system.
- **Active Directory** This allows domain-based security.

With Windows 2000 using NTFS, you can use remote storage, dynamic volumes, and mount volumes to folders. These features will be discussed later in the book. Partitions that use the NTFS file system can be accessed only by Windows NT and Windows 2000. However, if you use any of the new NTFS features provided by

Windows 2000, you will not be able to access it from Windows NT. NTFS is the best choice when security is an issue.

You can use important features such as Active Directory and domain-based security only by choosing NTFS as your file system.

FAT and FAT32 FAT (or FAT16) allows access from multiple operating systems, including Windows 2000, Windows NT, Windows 95/98, MS-DOS, and OS/2. It is a less efficient file system with fewer features than NTFS and does not offer any built-in security. FAT32 enhances the FAT file system by allowing larger partition sizes and smaller cluster sizes. FAT partitions are limited to 4GB. With hard disks commonly larger than 8GB, FAT32 was introduced in Windows 98 to extend the partition sizes. FAT32 is compatible with Windows 95b (OSR2), Windows 98, and Windows 2000. Windows NT cannot use FAT32 partitions.

So how do you choose which file system to use on partitions? It depends on how your computer will be configured. Microsoft recommends the NTFS partition with single boot operating system for servers. NTFS is the only file system that supports the new Active Directory introduced with Windows 2000. If you want to dual-boot with Windows 2000 and Windows 95/98, you will need to choose the FAT or FAT32 file system. Also, some new features have been added to NTFS by Windows 2000. For example, if you used the new encryption feature on a file, that file would not be readable when you booted up into Windows NT. For configuring a computer for dual-booting between Windows 2000 and Windows NT 4.0, Microsoft recommends using a FAT partition (not FAT32. because Windows NT 4.0 does not recognize it). This ensures that when the computer is booted up into Windows NT 4.0, it will have access to all of the files on the computer. Windows NT 4.0 with Service Pack 4.0 or later can access NTFS 5.0 volumes. However, it cannot access files that have been encrypted or use volumes that use NTFS 5.0 compression and other specific features.

Multiboot Configurations

With many versions of the Windows operating system now available, some users will need to have multiple operating systems installed on the same computer. The user can choose which operating system to load. During installation, you can upgrade an existing Windows operating system to Windows 2000, but when you do, you

FROM THE CLASSROOM

Installing Windows 2000

The installation process for Windows 2000 is much improved over Windows NT. Microsoft integrated some of the features used in the Windows 98 Setup program to enhance installation. Windows 2000 Setup Plug-and-Play technology allows your devices to automatically be detected and configured as in Windows 98. One of the most common Setup problems has to do with hardware problems. This is why checking your hardware for compatibility with Windows 2000 is one of the most important steps in the installation process. Specifically, many people find that their serial ports do not work after installing Windows 2000. Windows 2000 uses serial ports differently than it did in Windows NT. The fix for this is to upgrade the computer's BIOS with a version that is compatible with Windows 2000.

Other types of problems have to do with understanding the installation process, and the settings and options that are available and how to choose them. Another question often asked is why FAT32 cannot be selected for a partition's file system during Setup. This is not a problem, per se, but a feature. Setup will choose between FAT (sometimes called FAT16) and FAT32 for you based on the partition's size. If a partition is smaller than 2GB, then it automatically uses FAT. If the partition is larger than or equal to 2GB, then it uses the FAT32 file system.

When entering the computer name, some users complain that the name originally contained an underscore (_) that was replaced by a dash (-). This is also a feature, not a problem. Active Directory is based on DNS, and some DNS servers do not allow the underscore character (Microsoft DNS servers do). If you wish, you can change the name to use the underscore after installation. Setup does allow you to enter other characters that are not compliant with DNS, and you are given a warning when you do. It is recommended that you do not use any characters that are not compliant with DNS in a Windows 2000 network (including those that were previously allowed under NetBIOS naming conventions) because of the move to DNS for name resolution.

These are just a few of the problems that may arise during Setup. Remember to check your hardware and software for compatibility and make sure you understand the Setup processes. Determine ahead of time the options you will choose. It is also important to understand the differences between Windows 2000 and Windows NT.

—Cameron Wakefield, MCSD, MCP

cannot load the preexisting operating system. When you configure your computer for multiboot operations, consider the following things:

- To upgrade an existing Windows operating system to Windows 2000, you must install Windows 2000 in the same directory. To dual-boot with the existing Windows operating system and Windows 2000, you must install Windows 2000 in a different directory so it doesn't overwrite the existing files.
- When dual-booting Windows 2000 with MS-DOS or Windows 95/98, install Windows 2000 last, because older operating systems overwrite the Master Boot Record and you won't be able to boot into Windows 2000.
- You cannot install Windows 2000 in a compressed drive that is not compressed with NTFS.
- All applications must be reinstalled on Windows 2000 when you do not upgrade from the existing operating system. To save disk space, you can install most applications to the same directory that they are currently installed in.
- With Windows NT 4.0 Service Pack 4 and later, NT 4 is able to read data on NTFS partitions, but it cannot read files encrypted in Windows 2000.

Now that we have discussed the different file systems available for Windows 2000, let's test what you have learned so far.

SCENARIO & SOLUTION

What type of file system should you use if you are dual-booting between MS-DOS and Windows 2000?	FAT is the only file system that MS-DOS recognizes.
What types of file systems should you use if you are dual-booting between Windows 98 and Windows 2000?	FAT and FAT32 are the only file systems that you can use with Windows 98. FAT32 is a better choice if your partition is greater than 2GB.
What types of file system should you use if you are dual-booting between Windows NT 4 and Windows 2000?	FAT or NTFS. Windows NT 4 does not recognize FAT32. You should be concerned about the new NTFS 5, since some features in the new version of NTFS, such as file and folder encryption, won't function correctly in version 4.
What types of file system should you use if you are dual-booting between Windows 95 and Windows 2000?	FAT or FAT32 are the only file systems that you can use with Windows 95. FAT32 is only available on Windows 95 OSR2. FAT32 is a better choice if you are running OSR2.*x* and your partition is greater than 2GB.

Choose Licensing Mode for Windows 2000 Server

When you install Windows 2000 Server, you will have to choose a licensing mode. This determines where the Client Access License (CAL) will reside. The CAL allows clients to access the Windows 2000 Server's network services, shared folders, and printers. The licensing modes are the same as under Windows NT 4.0. It important to understand the difference between the two modes: Per Seat and Per Server. When you use the Per Seat mode, each computer that accesses the server must have a CAL. The Per Server mode requires a CAL for each connection to the server. This is a subtle but significant difference.

The difference is in where the license resides. When you use the Per Seat mode, a client can access multiple Windows 2000 Servers with the same license. This mode is the most common when a network has more than one Windows 2000 server. Use this mode when clients need to access more than one server. When the Per Server mode is used, each concurrent connection requires a license on the server. That means there is a limit on how many simultaneous connections a Windows 2000 Server can have. For example, if you are using the Per Server mode with five concurrent connections, five computers can simultaneously access the server without additional licenses on the client. Once the number of concurrent connections reaches the maximum, Windows 2000 will reject any further access attempts until the number of concurrent connections goes below the maximum. This is the preferred mode if there is only one server on the network or for Internet/RAS computers when clients don't need to be licensed. If you are not sure which mode to use, choose the Per Server mode, because you can change to the Per Seat mode at no cost. However, you cannot change from the Per Seat mode to the Per Server mode.

on the Job

If you are not sure which type of licensing mode to use, choose the Per Server mode. When you choose Per Server, you can convert to Per Seat later if needed. You cannot convert from the Per Seat to the Per Server mode.

Domain or Workgroup Membership

A *domain* is a collection of accounts and network resources that are grouped together using a single domain name and security boundary. All user accounts, permissions, and other network details are all stored in a centralized database on the domain controllers. A single login gives the users access to all resources they have permissions for. Domains are recommended for all networks with more than ten computers or for networks that are expected to grow to larger than ten computers in the near future. There are a few requirements for joining a domain. You will need to know the domain name. You must have a computer account for the computer you are installing Windows 2000 on. This account can be created either by the administrator before installing Windows 2000 or during setup with the username and password of an account with the permissions to create a computer account. You will also need at least one domain controller and Domain Name Server (DNS) online when you install Windows 2000 Professional. If you are installing Server, you can add the server as a member server or as a domain controller. A member server is a member that does not have a copy of the Active Directory. A member server does not perform security functionality for the domain.

A workgroup is a logical grouping of resources on a network. It is generally used in peer-to-peer networks. This means that each computer is responsible for access to its resources. Each computer has its own account database and is administered separately. Security is not shared between computers, and administration is more difficult than in a centralized domain. It is intended only as a convenience to help find resources. When you browse the network, the resources in your same workgroup are grouped together. It does not provide any security. In a workgroup, you might have to remember a different password for every resource you want to access. To join a workgroup during installation, all you need is a workgroup name. This can be the name of an existing workgroup or a new one. You must join a workgroup or a domain during installation, but you can change these memberships later as needed.

Server Optional Components

When you install Windows 2000 Server, there are some optional components you can install. You need to determine how your server will be utilized so you can decide which optional components to install. These optional components extend the functionality of Windows 2000 Server. If you do not install a component that you determine a need for later, you can add any optional components later, after installation, through the Add/Remove Programs application in Control Panel. The more components you install, the more functionality your server will have. However, do not install components you know you will not need, as they will just take up disk space and possibly use system resources unnecessarily. Table 11-1 shows the available optional components.

TABLE 11-1 Optional Components for Windows 2000 Server

Option	Description
Accessories and Utilities	Includes desktop accessories such as Wordpad, Paint, Calculator, and CD Player, as well as games such as Solitaire. To select individual items, click Details and select from the list.
Certificate Services	Provides security and authentication support, including secure e-mail, Web-based authentication, and smart card authentication.
Indexing Services	Provides indexing functions for documents stored on disk, allowing users to search for specific document text or properties.
Internet Information Services (IIS)	Provides support for Web site creation, configuration, and management, along with Network News Transfer Protocol (NNTP), File Transfer Protocol (FTP), and Simple Mail Transfer Protocol (SMTP).
Management and Monitoring Tools	Provides tools for communications administration, monitoring, and management, including programs that support development of customized client dialers for remote users and implementation of phone books that can be automatically updated from a central server. In addition, includes the Simple Network Management Protocol (SNMP).
Message Queuing Services	Provides a communication infrastructure and a development tool for creating distributed messaging applications. Such applications can communicate across heterogeneous networks and with computers that might be offline. Message Queuing provides guaranteed message delivery, efficient routing, security, transactional support, and priority-based messaging.
Networking Services	Provides important support for networking, including the items in the following list. For information about network monitoring, see "Management and Monitoring Tools" in this table. For background information about IP addresses and name resolution, see Networking: TCP/IP, IP addresses, and name resolution. **COM Internet Services Proxy** Supports distributed applications that use HTTP to communicate through Internet Information Services. **Domain Name System (DNS)** Provides name resolution for clients running Windows 2000. With name resolution, users can access servers by name, instead of having to use IP addresses that are difficult to recognize and remember. **Dynamic Host Configuration Protocol (DHCP)** Gives a server the capability of assigning IP addresses dynamically to network devices. These devices typically include server and workstation computers, but can also include other devices such as printers and scanners. With DHCP, you do not need to set and maintain static IP addresses on any of these devices, except for intranet servers providing DHCP, DNS, and/or WINS service.

TABLE 11-1 Optional Components for Windows 2000 Server *(continued)*

Option	Description
Networking Services	**Internet Authentication Service (IAS)** Performs authentication, authorization, and accounting of dial-up and VPN users. IAS supports the RADIUS protocol. **QoS Admission Control.** Allows you to control how applications are allotted network bandwidth. You can give important applications more bandwidth, less important applications less bandwidth. **Simple TCP/IP Services** Supports Character Generator, Daytime Discard, Echo, and Quote of the Day. **Site Server ILS Service** Supports IP telephony applications. Publishes IP multicast conferences on a network, and can also publish user IP address mappings for H.323 IP telephony. Telephony applications, such as NetMeeting and Phone Dialer in Windows Accessories, use Site Server ILS Service to display user names and conferences with published addresses. Site Server ILS Service depends on Internet Information Services (IIS). **Windows Internet Name Service (WINS)** Provides NetBIOS name resolution for clients running Windows NT and earlier versions of Microsoft operating systems. With name resolution, users can access servers by name, instead of having to use IP addresses that are difficult to recognize and remember.
Other Network File and Print Services	Provides file and print services for the Macintosh operating system, as well as print services for UNIX.
Remote Installation Services	Provides services that you can use to set up new client computers remotely, without the need to visit each machine. The target clients either must support remote startup with the Pre-Boot eXecution Environment (PXE) ROM, or must be started with a remote-start floppy disk. On the server, you will need a separate partition for Remote Installation Services. For more information, see Planning disk partitions for new installations.
Remote Storage	Provides an extension to your disk space by making removable media such as tapes more accessible. Infrequently used data can automatically be transferred to tape and retrieved when needed.
Script Debugger	Provides support for script development.

TABLE 11-1 Optional Components for Windows 2000 Server *(continued)*

Option	Description
Terminal Services	Offers two modes: remote administration mode or application server mode. In application server mode, Terminal Services provides the ability to run client applications on the server, while "thin client" software acts as a terminal emulator on the client. Each user sees an individual session, displayed as a Windows 2000 desktop, and each session is managed by the server, independent of any other client session. If you install Terminal Services as an application server, you must also install Terminal Services Licensing (not necessarily on the same computer). However, temporary licenses can be issued for clients that allow you to use Terminal servers for up to 90 days. In remote administration mode, you can use Terminal Services to remotely log on and manage Windows 2000 systems from virtually anywhere on your network (instead of being limited to working locally on a server). Remote administration mode allows for two concurrent connections from a given server and minimizes impact on server performance. Remote administration mode does not require you to install Terminal Services Licensing.
Windows Media Services	Provides multimedia support, allowing you to deliver content using Advanced Streaming Format over an internetwork or the Internet.

Networking Components

Most of the time, a Windows 2000 Server will need just the TCP/IP network protocol. This is the protocol used on the Internet. Prior to installation, you need to determine whether you will use the automatic settings for TCP/IP. If you need to manually configure TCP/IP, you should determine the settings before starting installation. The TCP/IP settings can be changed after installation. If you are going to be using a different protocol, you need to know how to configure it and the settings you will be using.

Windows 2000 Application Compatibility

In addition to determining if your hardware is compatible with Windows 2000, you should also verify that your software is compatible with Windows 2000. Most applications that were compatible with Windows NT 3.51 and 4.0 will be compatible with Windows 2000. Since Windows 95 and 98 were compatible with MS-DOS applications, some applications that ran on Windows 95 and 98 will not be compatible with Windows 2000. This is especially true for older programs that accessed the hardware directly. Windows 2000 does not allow the hardware to be accessed directly; it must be accessed through the operating system. This was also true in Windows NT. Prior to upgrading to Windows 2000, you should remove the following types of applications:

- Any third-party Plug and Play tools. These are no longer needed, since Windows 2000 is now Plug and Play compatible.
- All third-party network protocols and client software. However, you can look on the CD-ROM in the i386\winntupg folder to see if there is an update for your networking software. If there is, then you can leave your software installed.
- Antivirus software and any third-party disk quota software because of the changes to NTFS. It needs to be compatible with NTFS 5.
- Third-party power management software, you should remove it, because Windows 2000 has changed its power management support.

Installing from the Windows 2000 CD-ROM

When installing Windows 2000 from a CD-ROM, you will need to boot the computer from either the CD-ROM or from floppy disks. During installation, you will use setup wizards to guide you through the process. This process is similar to the installation of Windows NT 4.0. The installation of Windows 2000 has four basic steps:

1. Running the setup program.
2. Running the Setup Wizard.
3. Installing networking.
4. Completing installation.

You have several options to start the installation. On the Windows 2000 CD-ROM, you can run Setup.exe to launch the installation. Setup will then run either Winnt.exe or Winnt32.exe, depending on which operating system you are currently running. If you are running MS-DOS or Windows 3.*x*, Setup will run Winnt.exe. If you are running Windows 95/98 or Windows NT, Setup will run Winnt32.exe. You can also run Winnt.exe or Winnt32.exe directly. The Winnt.exe and Winnt32.exe files are located in the I386 directory on the CD-ROM. You can also start installation by booting from the Windows 2000 CD-ROM or from the Setup boot disks.

Step 1: Run the Setup Program

The first step for installing Windows 2000 is the text-mode portion of Setup, which is very similar to the Windows NT 4.0 text-mode portion of Setup. This portion of Setup copies the minimum version of Windows 2000 to memory to begin the setup. You will have the option to run Setup, repair an existing Windows 2000 installation, or exit Setup. Then you will have to agree to the terms of the license agreement in order to continue with Setup. The next step is to select a partition on which to install Windows 2000. You can choose an existing partition, create a new partition from free space, or delete a partition to create free space. When deleting partitions, keep in mind that you will lose all the data on that partition. After you have selected a partition to install to, you will have to decide whether to use the FAT or NTFS file system. Setup will copy files to the hard disk and reboot the computer. Exercise 11-1 walks you through the steps for this phase of Setup.

EXERCISE 11-1

Starting the Installation for Windows 2000

In the following four exercises, we will walk through installing Windows 2000 Professional. Let's get started installing Windows 2000 Professional and perform the text-mode portion of Setup.

1. To start installation from the CD-ROM, you can boot from the Windows 2000 Professional CD-ROM. Place the CD-ROM in the drive and reboot the computer. Make sure your BIOS is set up to boot from the CD-ROM drive. When you boot from the CD-ROM, Setup will copy the minimum version of Windows 2000 Professional to memory and start the text-mode portion of Setup. If you have any Small Computer System Interface (SCSI) or Redundant Array of Independent Disks (RAID) devices on the computer, press F6 to install the drivers for these devices.
2. You will come to the Welcome to Setup screen (the following illustration). You have three options from which to choose:
   A. You can run Windows 2000 Setup. Press ENTER for this option.
   B. Repair an existing Windows 2000 installation. Press R for this option.
   C. Exit Setup without installing Windows 2000. Press F3 for this option.

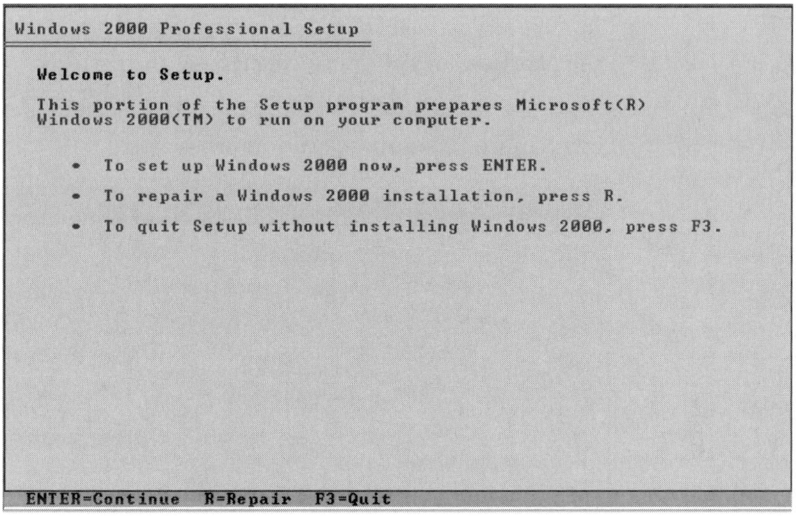

```
Windows 2000 Professional Setup

  Welcome to Setup.

  This portion of the Setup program prepares Microsoft(R)
  Windows 2000(TM) to run on your computer.

      •  To set up Windows 2000 now, press ENTER.

      •  To repair a Windows 2000 installation, press R.

      •  To quit Setup without installing Windows 2000, press F3.

 ENTER=Continue   R=Repair   F3=Quit
```

3. If the hard disk contains an operating system that is not compatible with Windows 2000, a screen will appear, notifying you that you could lose data if you continue with Setup. You have two options at this point:

   A. Continue Setup. Press C for this option.

   B. Quit Setup. Press F3.

4. Now you will have to read the license agreement and then choose to agree or to not agree with it. If you do not agree to the terms, then you will not be able to continue with Setup. You can use PAGE DOWN to read the entire agreement. To accept the conditions of the agreement, press F8. If you do not accept the terms of the agreement, press Esc key. Setup will quit.

5. The next screen will show you the existing free space and/or existing partitions on the hard disk (the following illustration). You will have three options:

   A. To set up Windows 2000 Professional on the selected partition, press ENTER.

   B. To create a new partition in the unpartitioned space, press C. When you select this option, you will have the option of how large to make that partition, or to go back to the previous screen without creating a new partition. Either accept the default size of all remaining free space or type in the size you want for the new partition. Then press ENTER to create the partition, or ESC to cancel creating the partition.

C. To delete the selected partition, press D. Be careful deleting any partitions; any files stored on that partition will be lost.

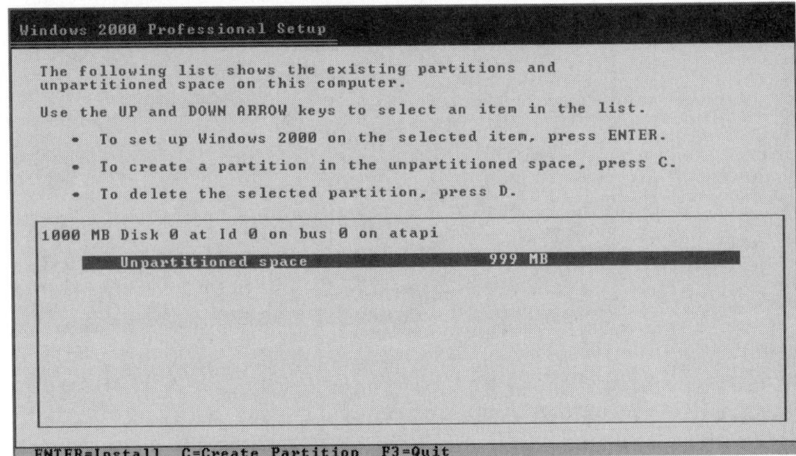
Windows 2000 Professional Setup
The following list shows the existing partitions and unpartitioned space on this computer.
Use the UP and DOWN ARROW keys to select an item in the list.
• To set up Windows 2000 on the selected item, press ENTER.
• To create a partition in the unpartitioned space, press C.
• To delete the selected partition, press D.
1000 MB Disk 0 at Id 0 on bus 0 on atapi
Unpartitioned space 999 MB
ENTER=Install C=Create Partition F3=Quit

6. After you press ENTER to install Windows 2000 Professional on the selected partition, you will come to the screen for formatting the partition. You can choose from NTFS or FAT—NTFS is the default. (Note: If the partition size is larger than 2GB, then it will automatically use the FAT32 file system.) Choose the file system for the partition, and press ENTER. Since you are

installing Windows 2000 Professional, you should always choose NTFS (see the following illustration).

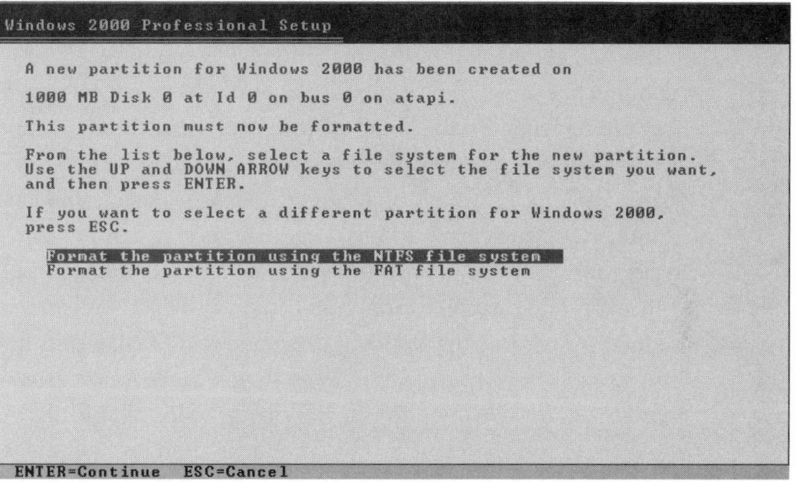

7. A screen will appear, showing the progress of formatting the partition. When the formatting is complete, it will start copying files to the Windows 2000 Professional installation folder without user interaction.
8. Setup will then initialize your Windows 2000 configuration and copy the necessary files to the hard disk for the next phase of setup.
9. The last step for this phase is to reboot your computer. A screen will appear, telling you to remove any floppy disks from your drive, and to press ENTER to restart the computer. If you don't respond in 15 seconds, it will automatically restart the computer.
10. When the computer boots up, there will be a progress bar at the bottom that says "Starting Windows….". You can press F8 for troubleshooting options. When the computer boots up, you will be in the Setup Wizard phase of the Windows 2000 Professional installation.

Step 2: Run the Setup Wizard

The second step for installing Windows 2000 uses the Setup Wizard. This begins the Windows or GUI portion of Setup. You will have to provide some information for setting up Windows 2000. Setup will perform some initial hardware detection and allow you to customize your keyboard and locale configuration. Then you will need to enter name and company information. This allows you to personalize the software on the computer. You will need a product key in order to continue with Setup. The product key can be found on the Windows 2000 CD-ROM case. A unique computer name needs to be entered, as well as a password for the Administrator account. The computer name is a NetBIOS name that can be up to 15 characters in length. Setup will automatically generate a 15-character computer name for you. You can either accept this name or enter your own. The NetBIOS name must be different from other computer names, workgroup names, and domain names on the network. The Administrator account password can be up to 127 characters in length. Although it is strongly recommended not to do it, you can leave the password blank. Then you need to choose which optional components to install. Finally, you need to set up the date, time, and time zone for the computer. Exercise 11-2 walks you through the steps for this phase of Setup.

CertCam 11-2

EXERCISE 11-2

Running the Setup Wizard

Now we will perform the GUI portion of Setup and enter some information needed by the Setup program.

1. After completing the text-mode portion of the installation, your computer will reboot. After reboot, the first screen will welcome you to the Windows 2000 Setup wizard. Click Next to continue.
2. The Setup wizard will detect and configure some of the devices on your computer, such as the keyboard and mouse (the following illustration).

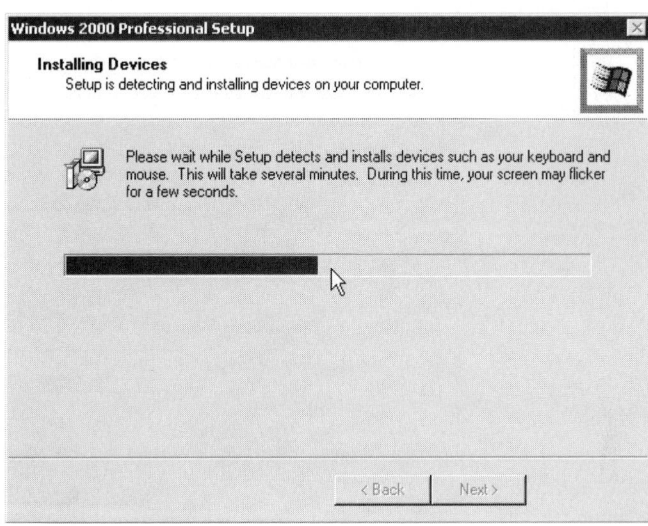

3. Next you will need to select your Regional settings. You can customize your locale and keyboard settings. Either customize the settings or accept the default, and click Next to continue.
4. This screen allows you to personalize your software by entering your name and organization information. After you have entered your information, click Next to continue.
5. Next you need to enter your product key. This key can be found on the Windows 2000 CD-ROM case. Enter the number, and click Next to continue.
6. This screen allows you to enter a name for your computer and the password for the Administrator account. The computer name will need to be unique on the network. You will have to enter the Administrator password twice (the following illustration). When you have entered this information, click Next to continue.

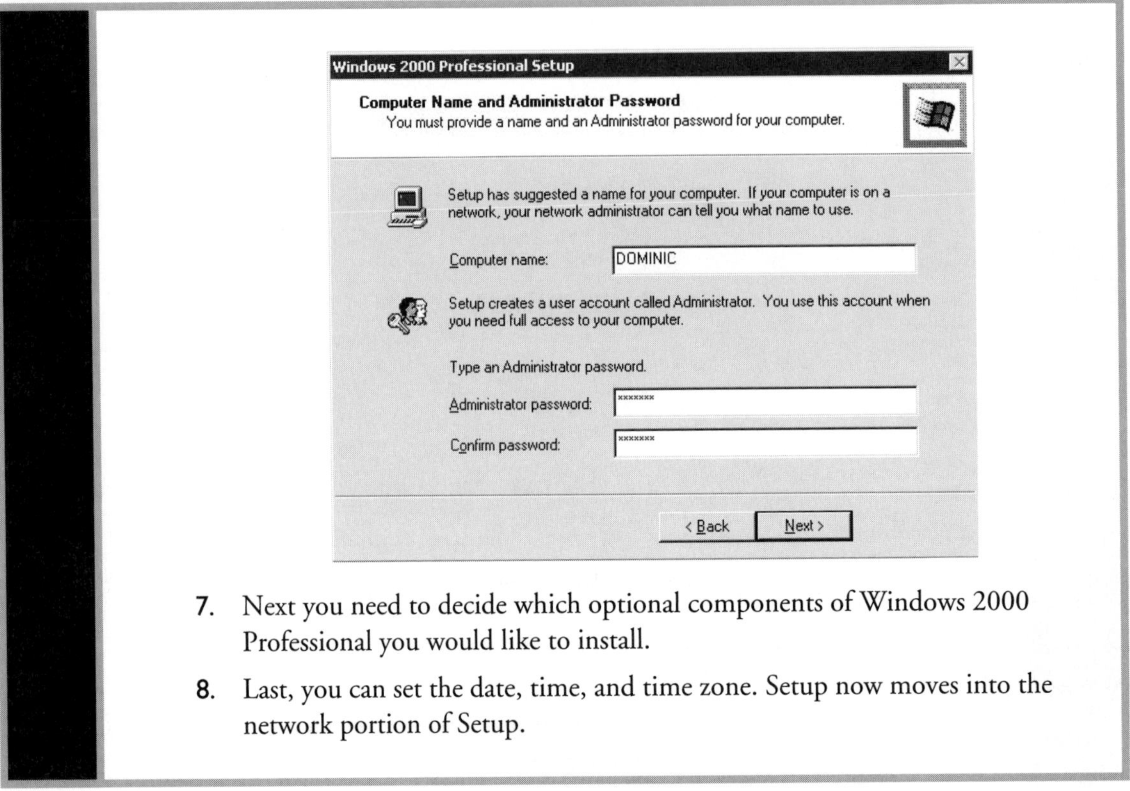

7. Next you need to decide which optional components of Windows 2000 Professional you would like to install.
8. Last, you can set the date, time, and time zone. Setup now moves into the network portion of Setup.

Step 3: Install Windows 2000 Networking

Now that Setup has finished gathering information about your computer, it is time to install the Windows 2000 networking components. You will need to decide which networking components to install. By default, Setup will install the following components:

- Client for Microsoft Networks
- File and Print Sharing for Microsoft Networks
- TCP/IP with automatic addressing

You can install other components if you need them. In this phase, you will also join a domain or workgroup. If you join a domain, you will need to have a computer account on the domain. If you don't already have an account for your computer, you can add one from Setup (you will need administrative privileges for the domain to do so). Exercise 11-3 walks you through the steps for this phase of Setup.

EXERCISE 11-3

Installing the Networking Components

1. The Network Settings screen allows you to either choose the typical settings or customize the settings (see the following illustration). The Typical settings option will install Client for Microsoft Networks, File and Print Sharing for Microsoft Networks, and TCP/IP with automatic addressing. The Customize settings option allows you to install and configure the networking components to your requirements, such as specifying TCP/IP addresses and choosing other components to install.

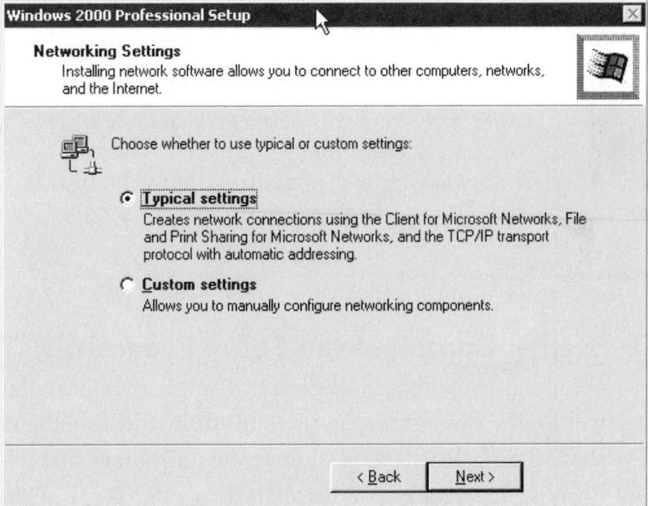

2. The Workgroup or Computer Domain screen allows you choose between joining either a workgroup or a domain. To join a workgroup, select "No," and enter the workgroup name. To join a domain, select "Yes," and enter the name of the domain you want to join.

3. The Join Computer to Domain dialog box allows you to enter the username and password of an account that has the proper permissions to join the computer to the domain (see the following illustration).

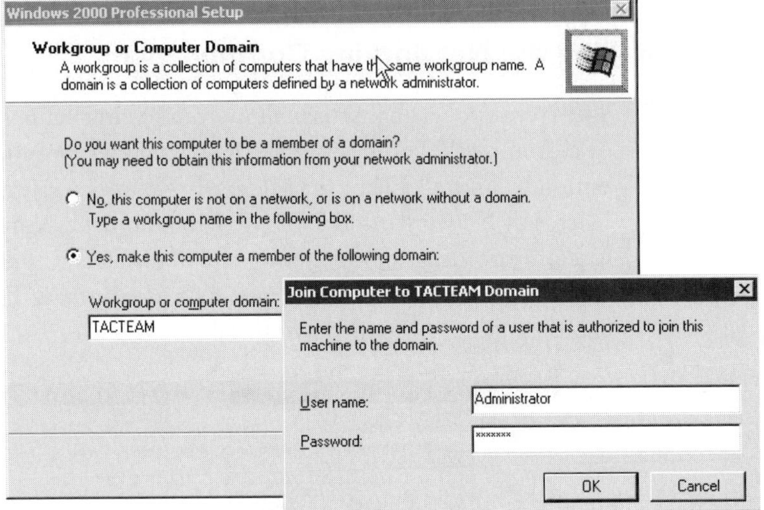

4. The networking components will now be installed. The networking portion of Setup is now complete.

Step 4: Complete the Setup Program

Setup has a few more tasks left to complete the installation of Windows 2000. It will finish copying files to the hard disk, and save the configuration you have chosen to hard disk. It will then remove the temporary files and restart the computer. Exercise 11-4 walks you through the steps for this phase of setup.

EXERCISE 11-4

Completing the Setup Program

1. Setup will now complete the installation. It will set up the Start menu shortcuts and register components.
2. Setup will then finish copying files to the computer, such as accessories and bitmaps.
3. Then Setup will apply and save the configuration settings you entered earlier.
4. Finally, Setup will remove the temporary setup files and restart the computer.
5. Windows 2000 Professional is now installed on your computer.

Installing over the Network

Installing Windows 2000 over the network is similar to installing it from the CD-ROM, except the source location is different and the process will be slower since the files have to be transferred across the network. When Windows 2000 is installed on multiple computers, installing over the network is easier and more efficient than installing each one separately from a CD-ROM. The installation can be performed on identical computers or computers with different configurations. The setup program will be run from a shared folder on the network. The setup program will then copy the needed files to the client computer to start installation. The installation can be customized by using different setup options available from command-line switches.

Distribution Server

The first requirement for network installation is a distribution server that contains the installation files. The distribution server can be any computer on the network that the clients have access to. To set up the distribution server, create a shared folder to hold the setup files. For Intel-based installations, copy the /I386 directory from the Windows 2000 Professional or Server CD-ROM to the shared folder.

Second, the computer that Windows 2000 is to be installed on needs to have a 850MB (or more as necessary) partition. In Windows NT 4.0, network installations required a FAT partition. In Windows 2000, you can perform a network installation to either a FAT or a NTFS partition.

Third, the client computer that you are installing to needs networking software and hardware that allows it to connect to the distribution server. If the client has an existing operating system with a network client, you can connect to the distribution server and start the installation from it. Otherwise, you need to create a boot disk that includes a network client that can connect to the distribution server.

Exercise 11-5 shows the basic steps for installing Windows 2000 using a network installation.

EXERCISE 11-5

Network Installation of Windows 2000

Let's look at the basic steps used to install Windows 2000 over the network.

1. Boot from the network client on the target computer.
2. Connect to the shared folder on the distribution server.
3. Run Winnt.exe from the shared folder on the distribution server. Setup starts and creates a temporary folder named Win_nt.~bs on the system partition, and copies the Setup boot files to the folder.
4. Setup then creates a temporary folder named Win_nt.~ls and copies the installation files from the distribution folder to this folder. Setup does not create the Setup floppy disks as it did in Windows NT 4.0.
5. You will then be prompted to restart the computer. When the computer restarts, you can proceed with the installation as described earlier.
6. Setup restarts the client computer and starts the Windows 2000 installation.

Modifying Setup Using WINNT.EXE

You can customize the network installation process for Windows 2000 by changing how the setup program runs. This can be accomplished by using command-line switches when you run the Winnt.exe program. The Winnt.exe program is used for network installations that use an MS-DOS network client.

Enumerate the Switches The options available for customizing setup can be seen in Table 11-2. It lists the available options for running Winnt.exe. Notice that there aren't any switches for creating Setup disks. To create the Setup disks, you must use the Makeboot.exe program located on the Bootdisk folder of the Windows 2000 installation CD-ROM. To create the Setup disks using floppy drive A, just run makeboot a:.

TABLE 11-2 The Winnt.exe Switches

Switch	Description
/a	Enables the accessibility option.
/e[:command]	Executes a command before the final phase of setup.
/I:[:inf_file]	The filename of the setup information file (without the path). The default filename is DOSNET.INF.
/r[:folder]	Creates an additional folder within the system root folder (where the Windows 2000 system files are located).
/rx[:folder]	Also creates an additional folder within the system root folder, but Setup deletes the files after installation is completed.
/s[:sourcepath]	Specifies the location of the Windows 2000 installation files. It must contain the full path using drive letter (i.e., f:\path) or UNC (\\server\shared_folder\path).
/t[:tempdrive]	The drive that contains the temporary setup files. If you do not use this switch, Setup will decide for you by using the partition with the most available space.
/u[:answer_file]	Performs an unattended installation by using an optional answer file. When you use the unattended installation option, you are required to use the /s switch.

TABLE 11-2

The Winnt.exe Switches *(continued)*

Switch	Description
/udf:id[,*UDF_file*]	Indicates an identifier (*id*) that Setup uses to specify how a Uniqueness Database File (UDF) modifies an answer file (see the /u entry above). The UDF overrides values in the answer file, and the identifier determines which values in the UDF file are used. For example, /udf:RAS_user,Our_company.udf overrides settings specified for the identifier RAS_user in the Our_company.udf file. If no *UDF_file* is specified, Setup prompts the user to insert a disk that contains the $Unique$.udf file.

exam Watch

It is important to know the command-line switches for Winnt.exe to pass the exam.

Modifying Setup Using WINNT32.EXE

The Winnt32.exe program is used to customize the process for upgrading existing installations. The Winnt32.exe program is used for installing Windows 2000 from a computer that is currently running Windows 95/98 or Windows NT. As with the Winnt.exe program, you can use command-line switches to customize the setup process. The options available for Winnt32.exe are listed in Table 11-3.

TABLE 11-3

The Winnt32.exe Switches

Switch	Description
/copydir[:folder_name]	Creates an additional folder within the system root folder (where the Windows 2000 system files are located).
/copysource[:folder_name]	Also creates an additional folder within the system root folder, but Setup deletes the files after installation is completed.
/cmd[:command_line]	Executes a command before the final phase of setup.
/cmdcons	Installs additional files to the hard disk that are necessary to load a command-line interface for repair and recovery purposes.
/debug[level][:file_name]	Creates a debug log at the level specified. By default, it creates C:\Winnt32.log at level 2(the warning level).

TABLE 11-3 The Winnt32.exe Switches *(continued)*

Switch	Description
/s[:source_path]	Specifies the location of the Windows 2000 installation files. It must contain the full path using drive letter (i.e., f:\path) or UNC (\\server\shared_folder\path). To simultaneously copy files from multiple paths, use a separate /s switch for each source path.
/syspart[:drive_letter]	Copies Setup start files to a hard disk and marks the partition as active. You can then install the hard disk in another computer. When you start that computer, Setup starts at the next phase. Use of this switch requires the /tempdrive switch.
/tempdrive[:drive_letter]	Places temporary files on the specified drive and installs Windows 2000 on that drive.
/unattend[number] [:answer_file]	Performs an unattended installation. The answer file provides the custom specifications to Setup. If you do not specify an answer file, all user settings are taken from the previous installation.
/udf:id[,udf_file]	Indicates an identifier (*id*) that Setup uses to specify how a Uniqueness Database File (UDF) modifies an answer file (see the /u entry, above). The UDF overrides values in the answer file, and the identifier determines which values in the UDF file are used. For example, /udf:RAS_user,Our_company.udf overrides settings specified for the identifier RAS_user in the Our_company.udf file. If no *UDF_file* is specified, Setup prompts the user to insert a disk that contains the $Unique$.udf file.

exam Watch

It is important to know the difference between command-line switches for Winnt.exe and Winnt32.exe. Most of the switches have similar functionality with a different syntax. Make sure that you know the different syntaxes for each.

Now that we have discussed the Winnt command-line switches, let's answer a couple of questions.

SCENARIO & SOLUTION	
To specify which drive to use to store the temporary files during setup, which Winnt command-line switch should you use?	The /t switch allows you to specify the drive to use to store the temporary files during Setup.
To specify an unattended installation of Windows 2000 Server and answer file to use, which Winnt command-line switch should you use?	The /u[:answer_file] performs an unattended installation using the specified answer file.

Upgrading to Windows 2000 Professional

When you have existing Windows computers on your network, you have to decide whether to upgrade them or install Windows 2000 Professional as a new installation for dual-booting. In this section, we are going to talk about upgrading an existing Windows computer to Windows 2000 Professional. When you upgrade an existing operating system, you install it in the same partition and folder in which the existing operating system is installed. When you select to perform an upgrade, Windows 2000 will automatically install in the same folder as the existing operating system. When upgrading from Windows, you can upgrade from the following versions: Windows NT 3.51 and 4.0 Workstation, Windows 95, and Windows 98. If you are running Windows NT 3.1 or 3.5, you must first upgrade to Windows NT 3.51 or 4.0, and then upgrade to Windows 2000.

on the Job

You can upgrade Windows NT 3.51 or 4.0 Workstation from any service pack that has been released. You don't have to upgrade to the latest service pack first.

Networking Requirements for Windows 2000 Professional

When determining the network requirements for Windows 2000, some areas to consider are the network protocol requirements and name resolution. When using TCP/IP as the network protocol, you should decide whether to provide automatic or manual assignment of IP addresses. For name resolution, you need to determine your DNS requirements and whether you need to use WINS.

TCP/IP Requirements The TCP/IP network protocol is the protocol used across the Internet. The Windows 2000 Setup program makes it easier to configure TCP/IP. Each Windows 2000 Professional workstation should be given an IP address. This IP address can be assigned dynamically through a DHCP Server or manually by assigning a static IP address. If there are a small number of computers on a workgroup (i.e., five or less), then you can allow the computers to automatically assign themselves IP addresses to the computer using Automatic Private IP Addressing (APIPA). For larger networks, especially networks with more than one subnet, you should dynamically assign IP addresses using DHCP. The DHCP server must be assigned a static IP address so other computers can locate it, and the DHCP server will assign other computers an IP address dynamically.

DNS Services Now that your workstation has an IP address, we need to discuss name resolution. Since an IP address is a group of numbers (e.g., 192.168.1.1), you need to provide a way for users to use names to access computers rather than IP addresses. Name resolution allows users to use a name that is easier to remember than an IP address to access a computer on the network or Internet. One of the types of name resolution is the Domain Name System (DNS). DNS maps a domain name to an IP address. Windows 2000 uses DNS as the primary name resolution method. DNS services are required for Internet e-mail, Web browsing, and support for clients running Windows 2000 and Active Directory Services.

WINS Services If your network will be supporting clients that are running Windows NT or Windows 95/98, then you should use the Windows Internet Name Service (WINS) to support them. WINS is used to map NetBIOS computer names and services to IP addresses. This allows users to access other computers on the network by their computer names. WINS servers should be assigned a static IP address. This allows clients to be able to find the WINS server by its IP address. It cannot find the WINS server by name, because it needs to know where the WINS server is to translate the name into an IP address.

Upgrading with a Compact Disc To upgrade an existing version of Windows to Windows 2000 Professional, insert the Windows 2000 Professional

CD-ROM in the CD-ROM drive, and if Autorun is on, it will automatically start Setup. Or, you can run Winnt32.exe from the I386 folder on the CD-ROM. You cannot upgrade using the boot disks or when booting from the CD-ROM. You must upgrade by starting Setup from Winnt32 or using Autorun on the CD-ROM. When you start using Autorun, you will see a window which asks if you would like to upgrade to Windows 2000.

When you click Yes to upgrade to Windows 2000 Professional, Windows 2000 Setup will check to see if you can upgrade. For example, if you are running Windows 3.1, you cannot upgrade to Windows 2000 Professional. If you try, you will get the message box notifying you that you cannot upgrade from the existing operating system. If you click on OK, it will bring you to the Setup screen, but the only option available will be to perform a clean install (Figure 11-1).

If your computer can be upgraded, you can choose the upgrade option and run Setup to upgrade your computer to Windows 2000 Professional.

Upgrading from a Network Distribution Upgrading to Windows 2000 Professional is basically the same as from the CD-ROM, except you will start the installation by running the Winnt32.exe program from a distribution server. You will still have the same limitations and requirements as with the CD-ROM

FIGURE 11-1

Upgrade or clean install option screen

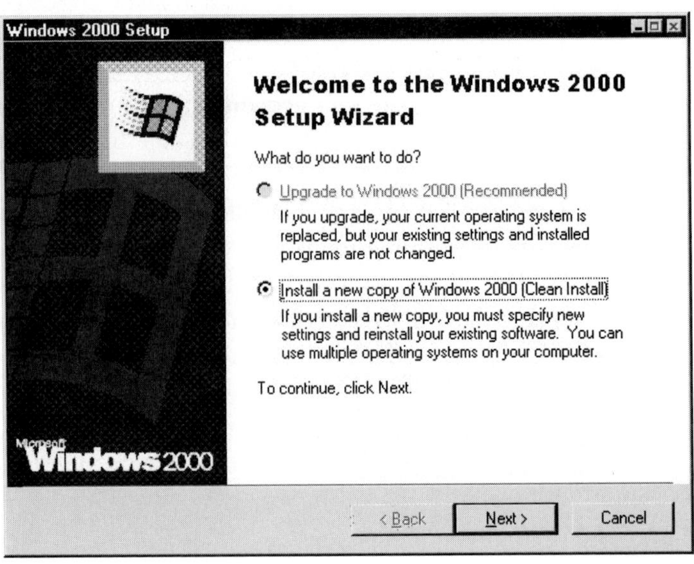

installation, plus you will have to be able to access the shared folder where the Setup files are located.

Upgrading Using unattend.txt You can also upgrade to Windows 2000 Professional with an unattended installation. Instead of prompting the user, Setup will retrieve answers to the questions from an answer file called unattend.txt. You can use the Winnt.exe and Winnt32.exe programs to perform an unattended installation of Windows 2000 Professional. Following is an example of using the Winnt.exe program. The example assumes the X:\ drive is mapped to the distribution folder. The /s switch specifies the location of the source files; the X:\i386 folder in the example. The /u switch specifies an unattended installation using the X:\unattend.txt file as the answer file. The /t switch specifies the destination drive for the source files.

```
Winnt /s:X:\i386 /u:Z:\unattend.txt /t:c
```

The syntax for using the Winnt32.exe program to perform an unattended installation is shown next. The /s switch is used to specify where the source files are located; the X:\i386 folder is used in the example. The Winnt32.exe program uses the /unattend switch rather than the /u switch to specify an unattended installation. The number after the /unattend switch specifies how long to wait to reboot the computer after copying the source files. The number is ignored when run from Windows 95 or 98. The Winnt32.exe program uses the /tempdrive switch rather than the /t switch to specify the drive where the temporary files are to be stored.

```
Winnt32 /s:X:\i386 /unattend 10:X:\unattend.txt /tempdrive:C
```

Applying Update Packs to Installed Software Applications

Update packs (also called upgrade packs) are used to update applications to make them compatible with Windows 2000. During the upgrade process to Windows 2000, you will be given the opportunity to apply any update packs. The software vendor provides these update packs. You should contact your software vendors for your software's compatibility with Windows 2000 and see if they have any update packs available. These update packs can move registry keys, and update files to resolve incompatibility problems. This is performed by a migration DLL that is used by Setup to update an application.

Deploying Service Packs

Periodically, Microsoft releases service packs for its operating systems. A service pack typically contains bug fixes, security fixes, system administration tools, drivers, and additional components. Microsoft recommends installing the latest service packs as they are released. Also, new in Windows 2000, you do not have to reinstall components after installing a service pack as you did in Windows NT. You can also see what service pack is currently installed on the computer by running the winver utility program. Winver opens the About Windows dialog box, which will display the version of Windows you are running and the version of the service pack.

To install a service pack, you use the Update.exe program. When a service pack is applied, Windows 2000 tracks which service pack was installed and which files were added and/or replaced. This way, when a component or service is added or removed, if any of the required files were included in the service pack, the operating system will automatically retrieve those files from the service pack. This prevents you from having to reinstall the service pack.

Testing Service Packs

Prior to deploying them to the enterprise, you should perform some testing first. Some applications have problems running after new service packs are installed. To test new service packs, you should create test environments for each computer configuration in your enterprise. Make sure the test computers have the same hardware, are running the same software, and are performing the same operations as the computers in the enterprise. This allows you to find potential errors prior to deploying a service pack throughout your enterprise.

Integrating Service Packs with Distribution Images

You can include service packs with a distribution image. This is called service pack *slipstreaming*. Using slipstreaming, you can install Windows 2000 with the service pack already applied to the installation files on a CD-ROM or distribution folder. You will not have to apply the service pack after installation of Windows 2000. To apply a service pack to distribution files, you use the Update.exe file with the /slip switch. This will overwrite the existing distribution files with the service pack files.

Troubleshooting Failed Installations

Once in a while, you will have some problems when trying to install Windows 2000. Problems can also occur after installation is complete and you are restarting the computer for the first time. You need to be able to solve these problems when they occur.

Resolving Common Problems

If the CD-ROM you are installing from has media errors on it, you will not be able to install from it—you will have to get another CD-ROM. If you don't have an additional copy, contact Microsoft or your vendor. Windows 2000 does not support some CD-ROM drives. If this is the case, you will have to either replace the CD-ROM drive with a drive that is supported, or choose a different installation method such as a network installation. When you install Windows 2000, you have to ensure that you have enough free disk space. If you don't, the Setup program can create a new partition if there is any unpartitioned space on the hard disk. If not, you can delete and create partitions as needed so that you can create a partition large enough to install Windows 2000 on. You can also add another hard disk or delete some files that are not being used to free up some space.

When installing Windows 2000, you can sometimes get an error when trying to locate the domain controller. Check that you entered the correct domain name and that a domain controller is running on the network. Also verify that the DNS server is running. If you cannot locate a domain controller, join a workgroup and then later, after installation, when you can locate a domain controller, join the domain.

Sometimes problems show up after installation is complete and you are starting Windows 2000 for the first time. If Windows 2000 fails to start, verify that all of the hardware is on the HCL, and that all of the hardware is being detected. Sometimes a dependency service will fail to start. If this occurs, verify that the correct network adapter was detected, and check the configuration settings (e.g., transceiver setting). Also verify that you have installed the correct protocol and that the computer name is unique on the network.

Setup Logs

During the GUI phase of Setup, log files are created. These log files are located in the directory in which Windows 2000 is being installed. The following are four of the log files that are created:

- **Setupact.log** The Action log file contains details about the files that are copied during Setup.
- **Setuperr.log** The Error log file contains details about errors that occurred during Setup.
- **Setupapi.log** This log file contains details about the device driver files that were copied during Setup, and can be used to facilitate troubleshooting device installations. This file contains errors and warnings, along with a timestamp for each issue.
- **Setuplog.txt** This log file contains details additional information about the device driver files that were copied during Setup.

Here are a couple of questions to test what we covered in this section.

SCENARIO & SOLUTION	
You have a distribution server that clients use to upgrade to Windows 2000. After they upgrade, they install a service pack from another network location. What can you do to simplify this process?	Service packs can be integrated or slipstreamed into a distribution image using the Service Pack Update.exe program. This will install the service pack files during Setup.
You are trying to install Windows 2000 with a dual-boot configuration. The partition you want to install to is not big enough, but you have 2GB of unpartitioned disk space. What can you do to make the partition large enough?	During Setup, you can delete the partition that is not large enough and then create it again, using the unpartitioned space of the hard disk to increase the size.

CERTIFICATION SUMMARY

Installing Windows 2000 is easier than it was in Windows NT 4.0. Some of the administrative overhead that was required in Windows NT 4.0 has been removed. Before starting the installation process, there is some preparation you should do first. Make sure the computer meets the minimum hardware requirements. Check that all of the hardware is on the Hardware Compatibility List. You must decide how to partition the hard disk and which file system to use. You should decide whether to join a workgroup or a domain, and whether to configure the computer for single or multiboot operations. When installing Server, you must decide which licensing mode to use.

Windows 2000 is most commonly installed from the CD-ROM. The CD-ROM installation has four basic stages: running the setup program, running the Setup Wizard, installing networking, and completing installation. Phase one, running the setup program, is the text mode portion of Setup. You will choose the partition for installing to and choose which file system to use. Then Setup will copy files to the hard disk and reboot the computer. Phase two, running the Setup Wizard, will configure the licensing mode. You can choose Per Seat or Per Server. If you choose Per Server, you must enter the maximum number of concurrent connections. You must enter a unique computer name and password for the Administrator account. Then, choose the optional components to install. Phase three, installing networking, configures the computer to use the network. It installs the protocols and networking services. If you join a domain, your computer must have an account on the domain. Phase four, completing installation, finishes copying files to the hard disk, saves the settings to hard disk, removes temporary files, and restarts the computer.

Installing Windows 2000 from the network is much like installing from the CD-ROM, except that the source is located in a different place. When installing Windows 2000 to a large amount of computers, installing over the network is more efficient. For network installations, a distribution server must be used. A distribution server is a computer on the network that can be accessed by the client computers. It needs a shared folder that contains the /I386 folder from the Windows 2000

Professional or Server CD-ROM. You can customize the installation using command-line switches.

There are a variety of methods you can use when upgrading your Windows computer to Windows 2000 Professional. You can use the Windows 2000 Professional CD-ROM, install across the network, and even perform unattended installations. One crucial aspect of upgrading is verifying that your hardware is compatible with Windows 2000. You should check the HCL for compatibility.

Windows 2000 has made using service packs easier. You can use slipstreaming to integrate service packs with a Windows 2000 distribution image. Another new feature is that you don't have to reinstall a service pack after adding components or installing applications; Windows 2000 automatically uses the existing service pack files.

On the rare occasion that a Windows 2000 installation should fail, you should understand the common causes of failure and how to solve the problems. In the event of more complicated failures, you can use the Setup log files to assist you in troubleshooting.

Performing an Attended Installation of Windows 2000

- ❑ You should check your existing hardware against the Hardware Compatibility List (HCL).
- ❑ The hard disk can be partitioned before, during, or after installation.
- ❑ Windows 2000 can be installed on a FAT, FAT32, or NTFS partition.
- ❑ To create the Setup floppy disks, you must use the Makeboot.exe program.
- ❑ A Windows 2000 computer must join either a workgroup or a domain.
- ❑ In Windows 2000, you can perform a network installation to a client with a FAT or NTFS partition. In Windows NT 4.0, you could only perform a network install to a client with a FAT partition.
- ❑ Only Windows NT 3.51 and 4.0 Workstations, Windows 95, and Windows 98 can be upgraded to Windows 2000 Professional.
- ❑ Microsoft periodically releases updates to Windows operating systems.
- ❑ These updates contain bug and security fixes called service packs.
- ❑ Service packs are installed using the Update.exe program.
- ❑ You don't have to reinstall service packs after adding or deleting components or services.
- ❑ The Setupact.log contains details about the files that are copied during Setup.
- ❑ The Setuperr.log contains details about errors that occurred during Setup.
- ❑ The Setupapi.log contains details about the device driver files that were copied during Setup.
- ❑ The Setuplog.txt contains details additional information about the device driver files that were copied during Setup.

MCSE

MICROSOFT CERTIFIED SYSTEMS ENGINEER

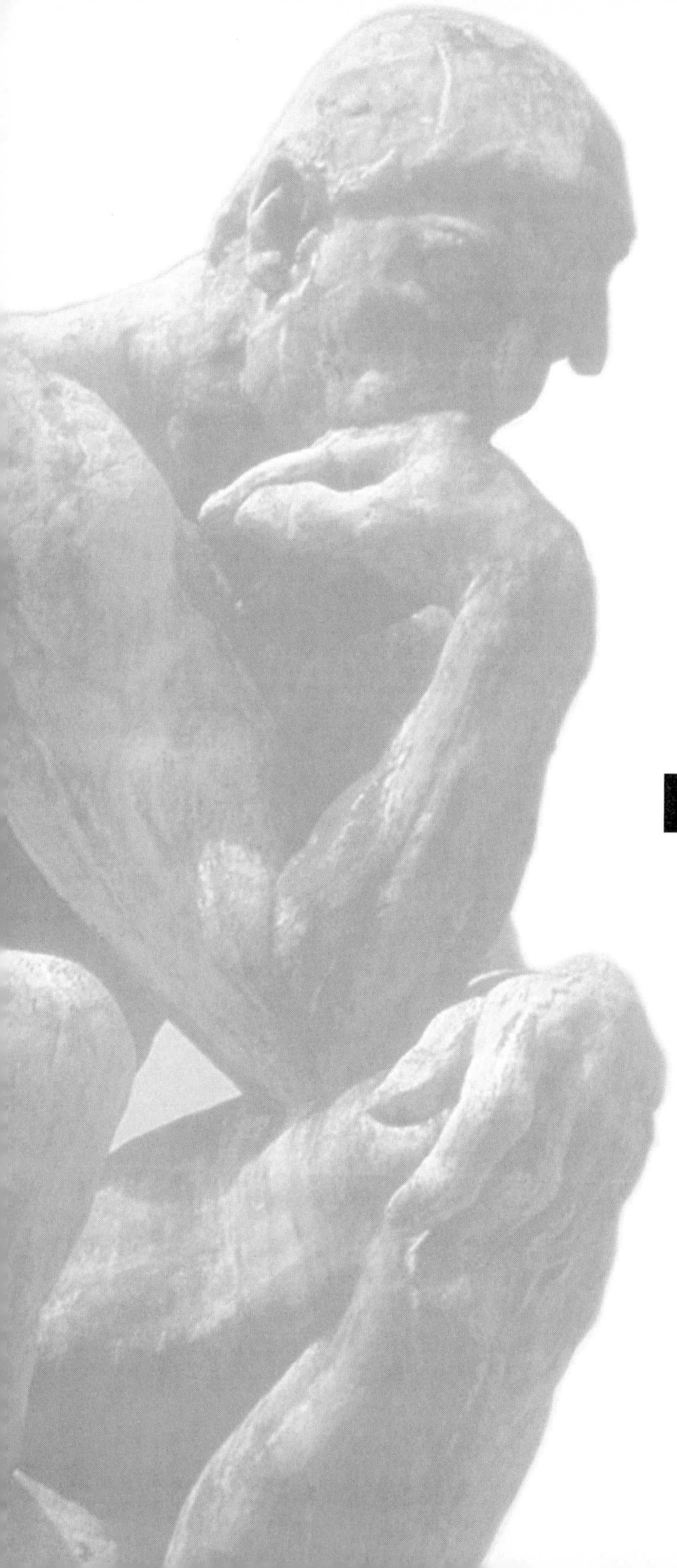

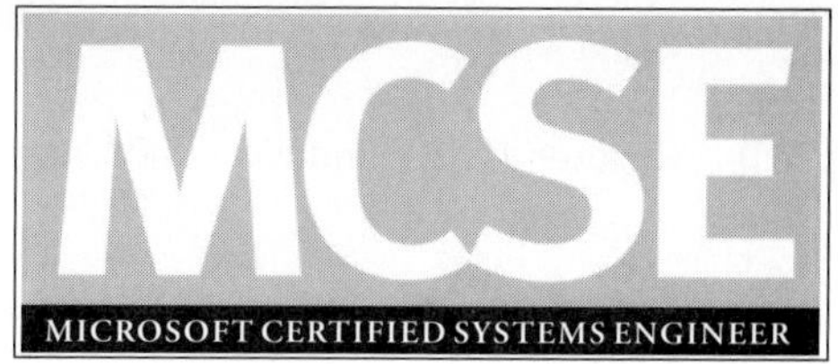

12

Windows 2000 Unattended Installation

CERTIFICATION OBJECTIVES

12.01	Disk Duplication Methods
12.02	The Scripted Method
12.03	Performing an Unattended Installation of Windows 2000 Professional
12.04	Understanding the Difference Between Unattended Installations and Prepared Images
12.05	Understanding Remote Installation Services (RIS)
12.06	Performing an Unattended Installation of Windows 2000 Server
✓	Two-Minute Drill

The attended installation methods for Windows 2000 consume a significant amount of time, and the administrator must answer a lot of setup questions. In a large organization with hundreds of computers, it is neither a desired method of installation nor it is it recommended to perform attended installations. Attended installations can cost the organization a significant amount of time and money and can delay projects. Windows 2000 comes with some tools and utilities that help you automate the installation process, thereby reducing the time and deployment costs for implementation. These methods also help in standardizing the server configurations throughout the organization.

You might be familiar with the unattended installation of Windows NT Workstation 4.0 using the Setup Manager. While the improved Setup Manager still remains an excellent choice for generating custom answer files in Windows 2000 for unattended installations, we now have other deployment tools such as the System Preparation tool (Sysprep) and the Remote Installation Service (RIS). We will learn how the automated and customized installations can be performed on computers with similar or different hardware configurations using these tools.

This chapter describes how the automated and customized installations can be performed on computers with similar or different hardware configurations using these tools. This chapter also discusses the installation and configuration of Remote Installation Services for deployment of Windows 2000 Professional.

CERTIFICATION OBJECTIVE 12.01

Disk Duplication Methods

The deployment of a new operating system is one of the most challenging and time-consuming tasks that a network administrator has to perform. The disk duplication methods are particularly useful when you need to deploy Windows 2000 Professional on a large number of computers. This is also known as *disk imaging* or *cloning*. These tools make the rollout fast and easy. The installations using disk duplication become more easy and efficient when all the computers have identical hardware. The disk duplication tools that we will be discussing here are the System Preparation (Sysprep) and Remote Installation Preparation (RIPrep).

Which Duplication Tool to Use, and When

Given that we have two excellent disk duplicating or imaging tools, it becomes necessary to decide on what tool to use and where. The first condition is that both Sysprep and RIPrep tools are meant for clean installations and cannot be used for upgrading the computers from any previous operating system. While images created using Sysprep can be distributed with any third-party utilities, RIPrep requires that you distribute the image using the Remote Installation Service only. Both methods have their own merits and demerits, and some basic requirements that must be met.

Where to Find Sysprep and RIPrep?

Before we can use any of the tools, we need to find out where these tools are located in the Windows 2000 Professional CD. The RIPrep tool comes with Windows 2000 Server. You will find the Sysprep tool and the Setup Manager in the Deploy.cab file of the Support\Tools folder on your Windows 2000 Professional CD (with the exception of the Remote Installation Preparation [RIPrep] tool, which comes with Windows 2000 server). Writing installation scripts or answer files using the Setup Manager is discussed later in this chapter.

Sysprep

Sysprep provides an excellent means of saving installation time and reducing installation costs. It is also helpful in standardizing the desktop environment throughout the organization. Since one Sysprep image cannot be used on computers that have different hardware and software applications, you can create multiple images when you have more than one standard. It is still the best option where the number of computers is in hundreds or thousands and you wish to implement uniform policies in the organization.

After configuring one computer with the operating system and all the applications, Sysprep is run to create an image of the hard disk. This computer serves as the master or model computer that will have the complete setup of the operating system, application software, and any service packs. The image is called the *master image* and is copied to a CD or put on a network share for distribution to many computers. Any third-party disk-imaging tool can then be used to replicate the image to other identical computers. Some of the images copying tools are DriveImage from PowerQuest and Norton Ghost from Symantec.

The Sysprep tool can be used only for clean installations. It cannot be used for upgrading a previous operating system.

Requirements for Running Sysprep

As we observed earlier, the Sysprep tool is an ideal imaging solution for computers that have identical hardware configurations. The following points describe in the various requirements that must be met in order to use Sysprep.

- The master computer where the image is to be created must be identical to all the computers that will receive the image. The administrator can use disk duplication to conduct a fast, easy deployment on systems that aren't identical using the same image on different hardware configurations (as long as they are compatible with the copied image). For example, you cannot use the image created on a single-processor unit on a computer with two processors. The Hardware Abstraction Layer (HAL) must be similar.
- The master and the destination computers must have identical hard drives and controllers. The hard drive capacity required on the destination computers has to be at least equal to or higher than the hard drive capacity on the master computer. For example, Sysprep will not help if the master computer has an IDE hard drive and the destination computer has a SCSI hard drive, even if the capacity of both hard drives is the same.
- There is an exception for Plug and Play devices. These Plug and Play devices need not necessarily be identical. Examples of such are video cards, network adapters, sound cards, and modems. The Sysprep master image automatically runs a full Plug and Play device detection on the destination computer.
- The Sysprep tool only creates the master image. You will need some third-party utility to distribute the master image. There is no limit on the number of master images that you can create. For example, if your company has five different hardware configurations, you can create five master images.
- You need to have administrative privileges on the master computer where you wish to run Sysprep. It is also advisable that you test the applications thoroughly and apply all necessary service packs before creating a master image.
- The most important and mandatory requirement for running Sysprep is that you must have a volume licensing agreement.

Components of Sysprep

The Sysprep utility has the four components associated with it: sysprep.exe, sysprep.inf, setupcl.exe, and the Mini-Setup Wizard. The following sections describe the function of each of these components.

Sysprep.exe This is the main Sysprep executable file. This command has the following syntax:

```
Sysprep.exe [/quiet] [/nosidgen] [/pnp] [/reboot]
```

- **/quiet** This option runs SysPrep in a quiet mode and does not generate any messages on the screen.
- **/nosidgen** Runs SysPrep without generating any security ID. This allows the user to customize the computer. This is particularly useful when you do not wish to clone the master computer where SysPrep is being run.
- **/pnp** This option forces a full Plug and Play detection on the destination computer.
- **/reboot** This forces a reboot of the master computer after the image has been created.

Sysprep.inf Sysprep.inf is an answer file that must be used when you wish to automate the Mini-Setup Wizard. This file needs to be placed in the %Systemroot%/sysprep folder. When the Mini-Setup Wizard is run on the computer where the image is being distributed, it takes answers from the Sysprep.inf file without prompting the user for any input.

Setupcl.exe The function of this file is to run the Mini-Setup Wizard and to regenerate the security IDs on the master and destination computers. The Mini-Setup Wizard starts on the master computer when it is booted for the first time after running Sysprep.

Mini-Setup Wizard The purpose of this wizard is to add some user-specific parameters on the destination computer. These parameters include the following information:

- End user license agreement (EULA)
- Product key (serial number)

- Username, company name, and administrator password
- Network configuration
- Domain or workgroup name
- Date and time zone selection

The preceding information in the Mini-Setup Wizard can be automated using the Sysprep.inf file. The syntax and structure of the Sysprep.inf file is similar to the answer file created by Setup Manager. You may also use the Setup Manager to create an answer file for the Mini-Setup Wizard.

The Sysprep Process—Creating a Master Image

Let's look at the process of creating a master image using Sysprep to better understand the various steps involved.

1. Select a computer that has hardware identical to all or many of the other computers. Install Windows 2000 Professional on this computer. It is recommended that you do not make the computer a member of any domain. Also, keep the local administrator password blank.
2. When the Windows 2000 Professional setup is complete, log on to the computer as administrator. Make necessary changes to the Windows configuration that you wish to standardize throughout your organization. Install any custom or business applications on this computer. Apply service packs, if any.
3. Test all the components of operating system and the applications on the master computer for reliability. When you are finished, delete any unwanted files, such as setup and audit logs.
4. Prepare the master image by running the Sysprep utility. When the image has been created, the system either shuts down automatically or prompts you that it is safe to shut down. When you restart the computer, a Mini-Setup Wizard starts running on the master computer. This happens because the Sysprep process takes off the security ID of the computer, and this needs to be restored.
5. The next step is image distribution. This can be accomplished by using any third-party utility. When the destination computer is started for the first time, a Mini-Setup Wizard is run. Sysprep adds this wizard to the master image.

EXERCISE 12-1

Running Sysprep from the Command Prompt

This method of running Sysprep gives you the option of using any or all of the optional switches associated with Sysprep. In this exercise, we will use the /reboot switch.

1. Log on to the master computer as an administrator.
2. Select Start | Run and type **cmd**. The DOS prompt window opens.
3. Change to the system root by typing **cd \\.** Create a directory named Sysprep by typing **md Sysprep.**
4. Change to the Sysprep folder by typing **cd Sysprep**.
5. Copy the sysprep.exe and the setupcl.exe files from the DepTools folder to this folder. Use the following two commands:

```
copy c:\deptools\sysprep.exe
copy c:\deptools\setupcl.exe
```

6. Run Sysprep from the c:\Sysprep directory by typing the following command:

```
Sysprep /reboot
```

7. A warning message appears on the screen, as shown in the following illustration, saying that the execution of Sysprep may change some security settings of this computer. Click OK.

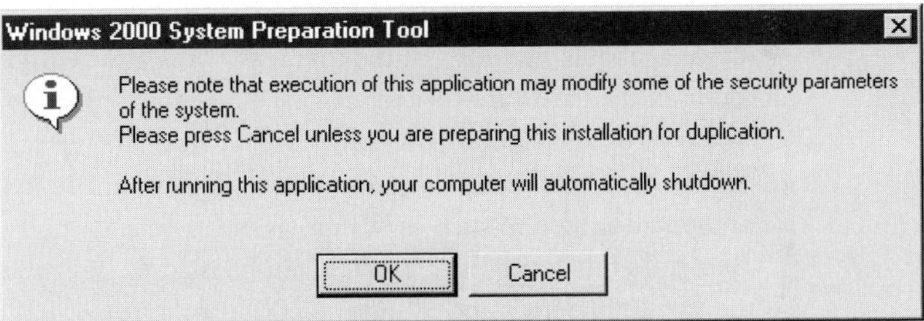

8. Since we used the /reboot option with Sysprep.exe, the master computer prepares the image and restarts automatically.

What Is RIPrep?

Remote Installation Preparation (RIPrep) is a disk duplication tool included with Windows 2000 Server. It is an ideal tool for creating images of fully prepared client computers. RIPrep helps in fast deployment of the operating system and applications on a large number of client computers using the RIS of a Windows 2000 Server. It is notable that the RIPrep can only prepare the images of fully configured client computers that are running Windows 2000 Professional operating system. The deployment of images created by RIPrep does not need the client computer hardware to be identical.

RIPrep requires that the RIS and its associated services be configured and running on one or more servers on the network The client computers are first configured with an operating system and all standard or custom-built business applications. The RIPrep wizard is run on the client computer to create an image of the computer. This image is uploaded to a Windows 2000 Server running the RIS for further distribution to other client computers.

Preparing and Deploying Images Using SysPrep and RIPrep

As we have observed, SysPrep and RIPrep are utilities that prepare master images of fully configured computers. SysPrep only prepares a master computer for creating an image; RIPrep works with the RIS to complete the image creation and distribution job. The preparation and distribution of operating system images need a careful study of available methods of deployment. This also requires that you take into account all the hardware-related factors. The choice of an imaging method depends on the type of installation you need. SysPrep and RIPrep can be used only for clean installations. These methods will not work if you want to upgrade a previous version of an operating system such as Windows NT 4.0.

Remember that although SysPrep can be used for preparing images of both Windows 2000 Server and Windows 2000 Professional, RIPrep can be used only for Windows 2000 Professional. Again, neither of these tools can be used for upgrading any previously installed operating system.

The Remote Installation Preparation Wizard

The RIS supports two types of images: CD-ROM-based images and those prepared using the RIPrep wizard. The CD-ROM-based image is similar to installing Windows 2000 Professional from the setup CD-ROM. The only difference is that the installation files are stored on the RIS server.

The RIPrep wizard enables the network administrator to distribute to a large number of client computers a standard desktop configuration that includes the operating system and the applications. This not only helps in maintaining a uniform standard across the enterprise; it also cuts the costs and time involved in a large-scale rollout of Windows 2000 Professional.

The limitation of RIPrep is that it can replicate images of only a single disk with a single partition. But the flip side is that the client computers need not have identical hardware configurations. The RIPrep utility automatically detects the difference between the source and destination hardware configurations using the plug-and-play support.

How does RIPrep work? First you need to install Windows 2000 Professional on a client computer that is chosen to act as a model. This installation is performed as a remote installation using an existing RIS server on the network. Next, all the required applications as defined in the enterprise standards are installed locally on this computer. The operating system and the applications are tested for reliability in all respects. The RIPrep is then run on this computer to create an image of the operating system and the applications. This image is uploaded to the RIS server for further distribution to the clients that need a similar configuration. When RIS is installed on a Windows 2000 Server, the Single-Instance Store (SIS) service is also added to the server. This service is utilized to reduce the hard disk space requirements for the volumes that hold the RIS images. The SIS service keeps a check on any duplicate files; if duplicates are found, SIS replaces them with a link. This practice helps save disk space.

The image preparation and replication to the RIS server takes a few minutes. Once the image is copied to the RIS server, any remote boot client can use the image for installation.

EXERCISE 12-2

Running the Remote Installation Preparation Wizard

Follow these steps to run the Remote Installation Preparation Wizard.

1. Select a client computer as a model and install the Windows 2000 Professional operating system from an existing RIS server on the network.
2. Install any applications on this computer that meet the requirements of your desktop standards. Configure the operating system and the applications. Test all aspects of the client computer for reliability.
3. Connect to the RIS server for running the RIPrep Wizard. Click Start | Run and type in the correct path of the RIPrep.exe file as follows:

   ```
   \\RISserver_name\RemoteInstallshare_name\Admin\i386\RIPrep.exe
   ```
4. The Remote Installation Preparation Wizard starts with a welcome screen. Click Next.
5. When prompted, type in the name of the RIS server where the image is intended to be copied. By default, the same RIS server is chosen that is running the RIPrep Wizard. Click Next.
6. Next, you are prompted for the name of the directory where the image is to be copied. Type in the name and click Next.
7. The Friendly Description and Help Text prompts appear. In case you plan to create more than one image, it is recommended that you type in the correct name and description of the image. This is helpful for identifying an image when the other clients are presented with image selection options.
8. The next window displays a summary of the selections that you have made. In case you need to change any settings, click Back and review the settings.
9. If everything seems fine, click Next.

The image preparation and replication to the RIS server takes a few minutes. Once the image is copied to the RIS server, any remote boot client can use the image for installation.

Advantages and Disadvantages of SysPrep

Any new feature in an operating system comes with added benefits to the user. Automating the Windows 2000 installation using SysPrep has associated with it certain advantages and disadvantages.

Advantages of SysPrep The following are the advantages of SysPrep:

- SysPrep is the quickest way to prepare the image.
- SysPrep is ideal for clean installations.
- SysPrep requires low administrative overheads.
- SysPrep saves installation time and money.
- SysPrep works for Windows 2000 Server as well as Windows 2000 Professional.

Disadvantages of SysPrep The following points outline the disadvantages of SysPrep:

- The master and destination computers need to be identical in the hardware, except plug-and-play devices.
- SysPrep cannot be used for upgrading a previously installed operating system.
- A third-party tool is required for creating and delivering images, accruing additional deployment costs.
- The computer on which the image is created must be reconfigured using the Mini-Setup wizard.

Advantages and Disadvantages of RIPrep

RIPrep is another method of preparing images for computers running Windows 2000 Professional. The following advantages and disadvantages are important to study before deciding to use RIPrep.

Advantages of RIPrep Some of the advantages of using RIPrep are:

- The RIPrep utility is bundled with Windows 2000 Server, and no third-party tool is required for creation or delivery of images.
- RIPrep's Single-Instance Store (SIS) saves a good deal of hard drive space, eliminating duplicate copies of setup files.

- RIPrep is independent of hardware configuration.
- RIPrep helps standardize the Windows 2000 Professional-based desktop environment in an organization.

Disadvantages of RIPrep The following points highlight some disadvantages of using RIPrep:

- RIPrep accumulates high administrative costs and needs trained professionals to implement.
- RIPrep is dependent on several other services, such as RIS, Active Directory, DNS, and DHCP. These must be running on the network.
- RIPrep can be used for clean installations only. Upgrades are not supported.
- RIPrep can be used to prepare images of Windows 2000 Professional only.
- RIPrep can duplicate images of a single hard drive consisting of a single partition only.
- Only some PCI network adapters or PXE-ROM version .99 or later are supported for booting the remote client.

Now that you have some idea of automating Windows 2000 Server operating system, let's consider some real-life scenarios.

SCENARIO & SOLUTION

Three different vendors have supplied the server hardware in my office. Can you use SysPrep to create one standard image for these servers?	No, SysPrep requires the hardware to be identical for all servers.
You are already running Windows NT 4.0 on seven servers. What is the best way to upgrade in unattended mode?	Use the scripted method. Create custom answer files using Setup Manager.
Can you use Remote Installation Service to deploy Windows 2000 Server in your organization?	No, RIS can deliver only Windows 2000 Professional.
Is it necessary for the hardware to be identical if you want to use RIPrep for creating images of your Windows 2000 Professional computers?	No. RIPrep is independent of hardware.

CERTIFICATION OBJECTIVE 12.02

The Scripted Method

This method for Windows 2000 Professional installation uses an answer file to specify various configuration parameters. This is used to eliminate user interaction during installation, thereby automating the installation process. Answers to most of the questions asked by the setup process are specified in the answer file. Besides this, the scripted method can be used for clean installations and upgrades.

Windows 2000 Professional CD-ROM includes a sample answer file unattend.txt located in the \i386 folder. This file can be edited and customized for individual installation needs. The Setup Manager Wizard can be used to quickly create a customized answer file. This minimizes the chances of committing syntax-related errors. Once the answer file is ready, the Windows 2000 installation can be started in an unattended mode by using the winnt or winnt32 command with /u switch.

The following is the command syntax for unattended installation using a script file:

```
Winnt32 /b /s:d:\i386 /u:d:\i386\unattend.txt
```

The /b switch tells the setup that it is a floppyless install, /s specifies the source path for the installation files as d:\i386, and the /u switch tells that it is an unattended install and specifies the location of the answer file as d:\i386\unattend.txt.

When to Use UNATTEND.TXT Instead of SysPrep or RIPrep

The decision of using a particular method of automating installation for an operating system largely depends on the host organization's requirements. A number of factors must be taken into account. All deployment methods have certain requirements as well as their own advantages and disadvantages.

The creation of customized UNATTEND.TXT answer files is the simplest form of providing answers to setup queries and unattended installation of Windows 2000. This can either be done using the Setup Manager or by editing the sample UNATTEND.TXT file using Notepad or the MS-DOS text editor. The UNATTEND.TXT file does not provide any means of creating an image of the computer. This method works for both Server and Professional versions of Windows 2000. It is independent of the computer hardware and can be used for clean installations as well as upgrades.

The SysPrep and RIPrep methods of disk duplication require considerable planning and preparation before you can create and distribute system images. SysPrep works on both Windows 2000 Server and Professional and can be used only for clean installations, when all the computers have nearly identical hardware. The prepared images must be distributed using a third-party utility. On the other hand, using RIPrep requires a fully configured RIS server and its associated services such as Active Directory, DNS, and DHCP to be functional on the network. RIPrep can deliver only Windows 2000 Professional images and does not support the use of third-party disk imaging tools.

Table 12-1 will help you understand and decide on the method of unattended installation of Windows 2000 that's right for you.

TABLE 12-1 Comparison of Automated Installation Methods

Installation Requirements	UNATTEND.TXT	SysPrep	RIPrep
Clean installation	Yes	Yes	Yes
Upgrade	Yes	No	No
Similar hardware	Yes	Yes	Yes
Dissimilar hardware	Yes	No	Yes
Windows 2000 Server	Yes	Yes	No
Windows 2000 Professional	Yes	Yes	Yes

CERTIFICATION OBJECTIVE 12.03

Performing an Unattended Installation of Windows 2000 Professional

Unattended installations are the desired way to deploy Windows 2000 Professional when it is not feasible to install the operating system manually on a large number of computers. Windows 2000 can be installed in an unattended mode by creating custom script files. These script files provide answers to the setup questions that would otherwise have to be typed in by the person who is installing the operating system.

This section deals with creating custom answer files using Setup Manager. We will learn how to set up a network share for distribution of Windows 2000 Professional installation files, and how to use the Setup Manager to create customized installation scripts.

Setting Up a Network Share

A network share is a centralized shared folder on the network usually located on a file server where the installation files are stored. This folder also holds the necessary service packs or upgrades for the applications. Creation of a network share is a recommended method of distributing installation files for many reasons. Many of the computers on the network may not have a CD-ROM drive. In order to run the installation on a large number of computers simultaneously, it is necessary to have setup files on one or more of the file servers. The winnt32 setup command permits use of up to eight source file locations when we use the /s switch.

EXERCISE 12-3

Creating a Network Share

Perform the following steps to create a Network Share.

1. Log on to a server that has been selected to act as a distribution server.
2. In Windows Explorer, create a folder named Win2kPro.
3. Share the folder with the share name "Installs."
4. Insert the Windows 2000 Professional CD-ROM in the CD-ROM drive. Copy the entire i386 folder to the Installs folder.
5. Create another folder named OEM under the Win2Kpro folder. Copy any driver files you may need during setup. The Windows 2000 setup automatically copies the contents of this folder to a temporary folder during the text mode of setup.

Using Setup Manager to Automate the Installation Process

The Setup Manager is an interactive graphical wizard that makes it easy to create or modify customized answer files for unattended setup of Windows 2000. It provides you with the option of either creating a fresh answer file or modifying an existing file. You can also choose to copy the configuration of the computer on which you are running the Setup Manager. This wizard makes it easy to indicate the computer- and user-specific information in the answer files and create a distribution folder. When you create answer files using the Setup Manager, the following three files are created:

- UNATTEND.TXT This is the actual answer file.
- UNATTEND.BAT This file is used to run the UNATTEND.TXT file.
- UNATTEND.UDF This file is the Uniqueness Database File, which provides customized settings for each computer using the automated installation.

Answer files help automate the installation process as all the queries presented to you during installation are answered by the answer files. With careful planning, you can prepare answers that eliminate the possibility of incorrect answers typed in by the person performing the installation, thus reducing the chances of setup failure. The Setup Manager wizard can be used to quickly create a customized answer file.

This technique minimizes the chances of committing syntax-related errors while manually creating or editing the sample answer files.

When you need to customize automated installation of each computer, you can use the Uniqueness Database Files. These files have a .UDB extension. A UDF file allows the automated installation with unique settings contained in the UDF file. The data contained in the UDF file is merged into the answer file during setup.

EXERCISE 12-4

Using Setup Manager to Create Answer Files

Perform the following to utilize Setup Manager to create answer files.

1. Log on as administrator on a computer running the Windows 2000 Professional operating system. In Windows Explorer, change to the folder where the deployment tools are located.
2. Double-click on the setupmgr.exe file. The Windows 2000 Setup Manager welcome screen opens. Click Next to continue.
3. You are prompted to select the type of answer file. Click the radio button for the option "Create a new answer file," as shown in the following illustration. This opens another screen where you are prompted to select an operating system.

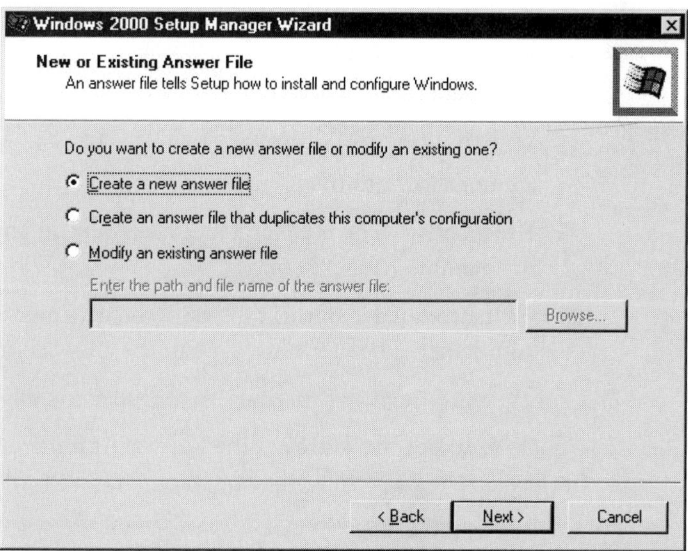

4. Select Windows 2000 Unattended Installation, as shown in the following illustration. Click Next. In the next screen, select Windows 2000 Professional.

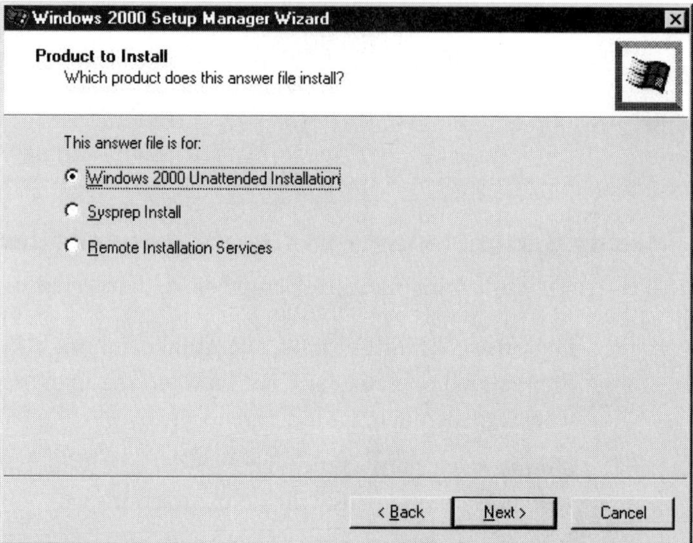

5. The User Interaction Level screen appears next. You are presented with the following five options:
   - **Provide Defaults** To accept or modify the default answers.
   - **Fully Automated** The setup is fully automated. The user is not allowed to change any answers.
   - **Hide Pages** The pages for which the answers are supplied by the script are not shown to the user.
   - **Read Only** The user can see the answers on any unhidden setup pages, but cannot change them.
   - **GUI Attended** In this case, only the text-mode phase of the setup is automated. The user must type in the answers in the graphics phase
6. For the purpose of this exercise, we will select "Fully automated" option.
7. Click "I Accept the Terms of the License Agreement." Click Next. This brings up the Customize the Software screen.

8. Type in your name and the name of your organization. Click Next.

The next screen is for the Computer Names. You may select to create answer files for one computer or for many computers. In this exercise, we will create two answer files for use with two computers. Here you may either type in the names yourself or give the name of a text file that contains the various computer names. This is useful when you have a large number of computers that will use this answer file. The Setup Manager can also generate the computer names automatically.

9. Type **TestComp1** and click Add. Type **TestComp2** and click Add. As shown in the following illustration, these names are added in a separate box that shows the names of the computers to be installed. Click Next.

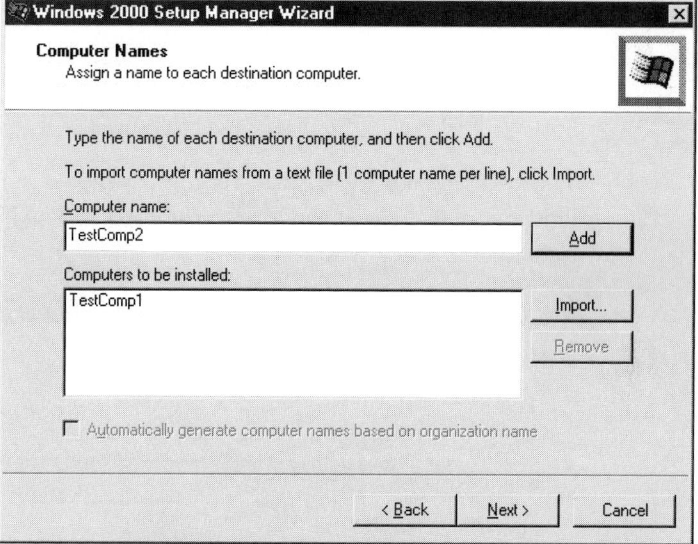

10. The next window is for supplying the Administrator Password. There are two options: "Prompt the user to supply a password" and "Use the following Administrator password." You will notice in the following illustration that the first option is grayed out because we selected a Fully Automated installation earlier. Leave the password blank in this exercise.

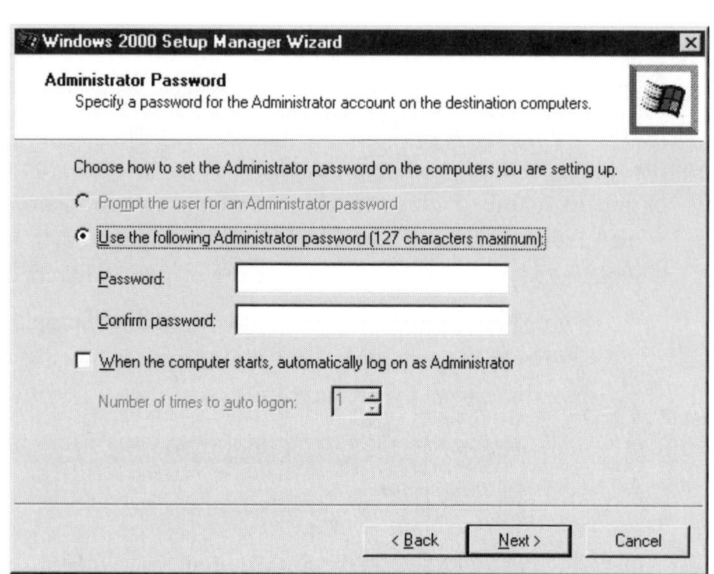

11. The next screen is for Display Settings, as shown in the following illustration. We have changed the colors to 256 and Screen Area to 800×600. Click Next.

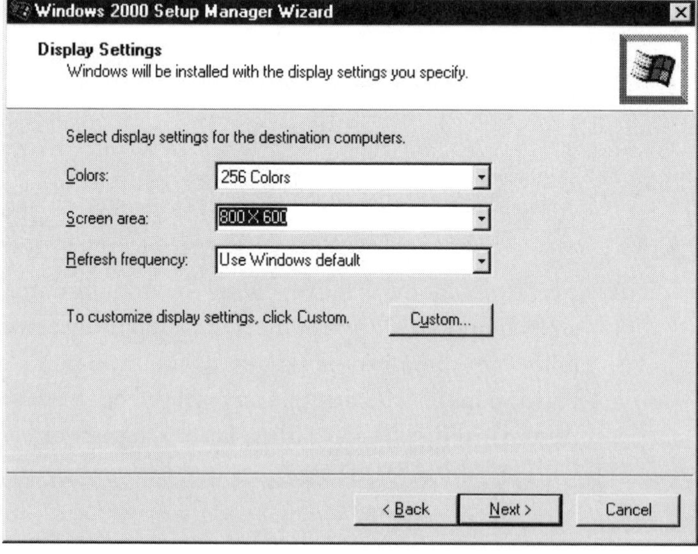

12. Next comes the Network Settings window. If you select the Typical Settings, the TCP/IP protocol is installed, DHCP is enabled, and the Client for Microsoft Networks protocol is installed. Click Custom because we will not use DHCP in this exercise.
13. Select One Network Adapter in the next screen, which is the default. Select Internet Protocol (TCP/IP) and click Properties. Click Cancel because TCP/IP properties can be configured during the installation.
14. Accept the default Workgroup option in the next screen, as shown in the following illustration.

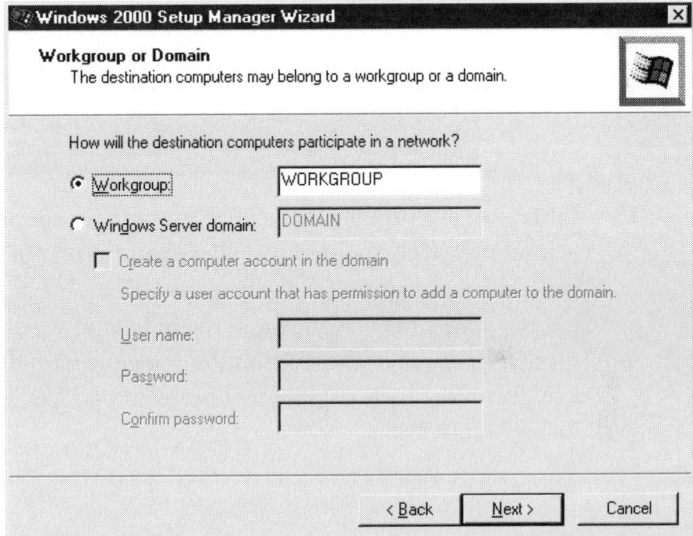

15. The next screen prompts you to select the Time Zone. Select the appropriate time zone and click Next.
16. The Additional Settings screen appears next. Select the defaults in the next few screens that prompt you for answers on Telephony, Regional Settings, Languages, and the Browser and Shell Settings. Click Next.
17. The following illustration shows the Installation Folder window. Type in the folder name where you wish to install Windows 2000 Professional.

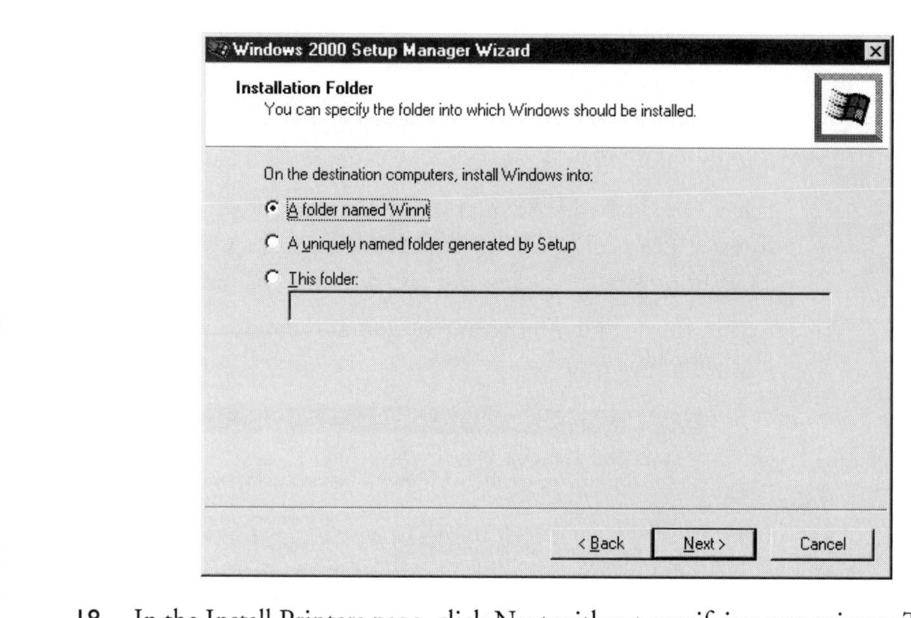

18. In the Install Printers page, click Next without specifying any printer. The Run Once screen appears that allows you to run one or more commands when the user logs on for the first time. Click Next. The Distribution Folder screen appears next, as shown in the following illustration. You can either specify the name of the distribution folder or have the Setup Manager create a folder on the local computer. The default is "Yes, create a new distribution folder." Click Next.

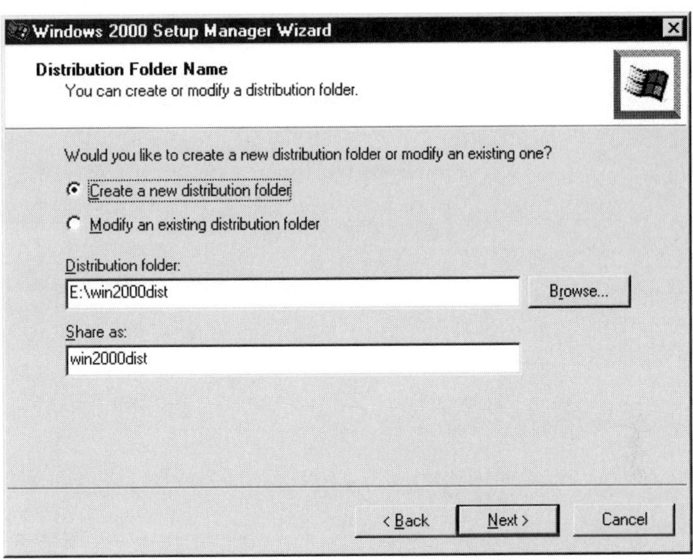

19. The next few screens prompt you for Additional Mass Storage Devices, Hardware Abstraction Layer, running any Additional Commands, and OEM Branding. Accept defaults and click Next.
20. The Answer File Name window is next, as shown in the following illustration. Type in the name of the folder where you wish to save the answer file. Click Next. In the next screen, you are prompted to specify the location of the setup files. Click Next to accept the default location as CD-ROM drive.

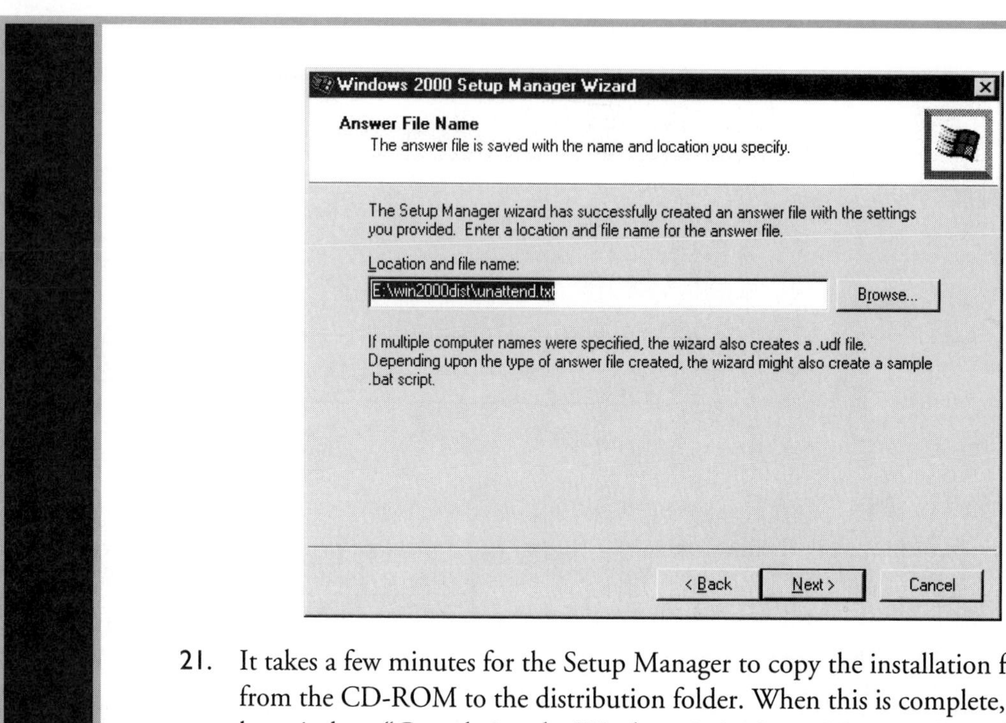

21. It takes a few minutes for the Setup Manager to copy the installation files from the CD-ROM to the distribution folder. When this is complete, the last window, "Completing the Windows 2000 Setup Manager Wizard," appears, as shown in the following illustration. Notice that Setup Manager has creates two files in the distribution folder: unattend.txt and unattend.bat.

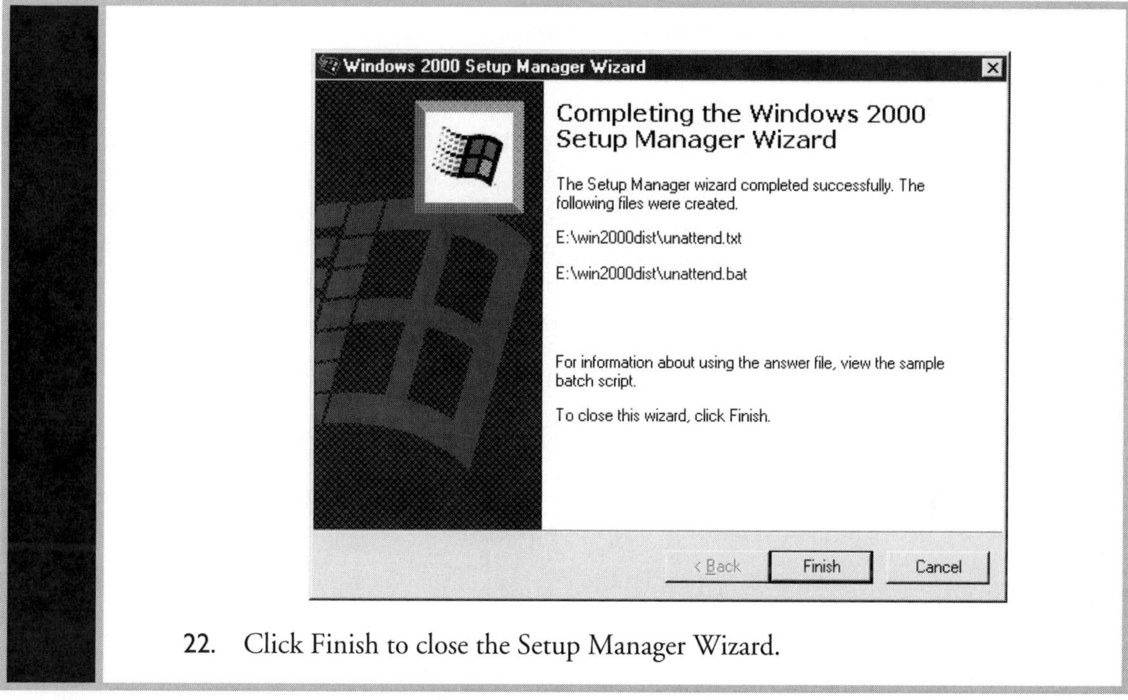

22. Click Finish to close the Setup Manager Wizard.

Using an Unattend.txt Script

In Exercise 12-4, we created an unattended answer file named unattend.txt. Once the file is created, it is recommended that you print a copy of this file to check for any irregularities. If you find anything wrong, you may use Notepad or any text editor program to make necessary corrections in this file; otherwise, leave the file intact.

Note that the scripted method of installation can be used for clean installations as well as for upgrades. In order to use the answer file or the script file for automatic setup, we use it with winnt or winnt32. The following is the syntax for this setup command:

```
Winnt32 /b /s:d:\i386 /u:c:\install\unattend.txt
```

The various switches used in the preceding command are as follows:

- **/b** Tells the setup that this is a floppyless installation. The user is not prompted to insert any floppy disks.
- **/s: d:\i386** Specifies the location of the Windows 2000 Professional setup files, which in this case is the \i386 folder on the D drive. Change it to the correct letter of your CD-ROM drive.
- **/u: c:\ install\unattend.txt** Specifies that this is an unattended installation and the unattend.txt answer file is located in the \install folder on the C drive.

Check the syntax of the command and press ENTER. You are done!

FROM THE CLASSROOM

Using Setup Manager for Unattended Installations

In practice, when you choose to use Setup Manager for unattended installations, there is a lot of planning that has to be done beforehand. Installation needs vary from one network environment to another. Here are some general guidelines that are helpful while using Setup Manager:

1. Know the present setup, including computer hardware and installed applications. Make a list of the computer names. Decide whether you need to upgrade or do a clean install.
2. Make a note of all network-related information, such as TCP/IP addressing scheme, name of the domain controller, DHCP server, DNS server, etc.
3. Arrange for any service packs or application upgrades to address any compatibility issues with Windows 2000 Professional.
4. Document each piece of information that you collect.
5. When you create scripts for unattended answer files, test one or two installations using your script files before applying them to mass setup. It is recommended that you take a hard copy of some scripts and check for any irregularities.

In practice, it is a bit difficult to have a complete automated installation process that does not ask for any user intervention. Setup Manager helps you automate it to an extent wherein very little user intervention is needed.

—Pawan K. Bhardwaj MCSE, MCP+I, CCNA

CERTIFICATION OBJECTIVE 12.04

Understanding the Difference Between Unattended Installations and Prepared Images

The unattended installation of any operating system is the preferred method of installation when you have a large number of computers. Disk imaging systems have become popular because they save the network administrator from a number of hardships while rolling out any operating system. These installation methods drastically reduce the costs incurred and time spent in deployment.

But before you decide on some method of automated deployment of an operating system, it is necessary that you understand all the ups and downs of using a particular method. Windows 2000 Server includes some tools to automate the installation process. The Setup Manager is one such interactive graphical wizard that helps you create custom answer files. To create such answer files, you need not be an expert in writing long scripts.

The basic difference between unattended installations and prepared images lies in the requirements of each method and its usage. The imaging methods discussed later in this chapter are the System Preparation (SysPrep) tool and the Remote Installation Preparation (RIPrep) wizard. These can be part of your completely automated installation plans. The method that you use for automating the Windows Server installations depends on the results that you want to get when the installation process is over. The following methods can be used to perform unattended installations:

- The WINNT32.EXE command used with the /unattend switch specifying an answer file
- The bootable CD-ROM method, which requires a prepared answer file that is to be stored on a floppy disk
- Installations using the Systems Management Server (SMS)

The imaging tools that can be used are as follows:

- The System Preparation (SysPrep) tool
- The WINNT32.EXE command used with the /syspart switch

- The Remote Installation Preparation (RIPrep) utility, which uses the Remote Installation Services (RIS); this method can be used for installing Windows 2000 Professional only

The details of each of these methods are given in the following sections.

Creating Answer Files for Unattended Installation

Answer files can be created by any of the following methods:

- By writing a fresh script using the correct syntax required using the Notepad or the MS-DOS editor program
- By editing the sample answer file that is located in the i386 folder of the Windows 2000 Server Setup CD-ROM
- By using the Setup Manager wizard; this is the fastest and most accurate method and can also create a distribution folder

The unattended method for Windows 2000 Server installation uses the answer file to specify various configuration parameters. This method eliminates user interaction during installation, thereby automating the installation process and reducing the chances of input errors. Answers to most of the questions asked by the setup process are specified in the answer file. In addition, the scripted method can be used for clean installations and upgrades.

The Windows 2000 Server CD-ROM includes a sample answer file, UNATTEND.TXT, which is located in the \i386 folder. This file can be edited and customized for individual installation needs. Once the answer file is ready, the Windows 2000 Server installation can be started in unattended mode using the WINNT.EXE or WINNT32.EXE command with /u switch.

Creating a Custom Answer File

The UNATTEND.TXT answer file included in the Windows 2000 Server CD-ROM may not be suitable for all unattended installations. You can create custom answer files by either using the Notepad or modifying the UNATTEND.TXT file. In case you decide to use Notepad, be careful to follow the correct syntax. It is also not mandatory to name the answer file *UNATTEND.TXT.* If you want to create several answer files, you can name the files as suits your requirements. The other option is to use the Setup Manager to create a customized answer file.

The following is an edited version of the UNATTEND.TXT file that comes with Windows 2000 Server CD-ROM:

```
; This file contains information about how to automate the installation
; or upgrade of Windows 2000 Professional and Windows 2000 Server so the
; Setup program runs without requiring user input.
 [Unattended]
Unattendmode = FullUnattended
OemPreinstall = NO
TargetPath = WINNT
Filesystem = LeaveAlone

 [UserData]
FullName = "PBHARDWAJ"
OrgName = "First MCSE, Inc."
ComputerName = "TestComp"

 [GuiUnattended]
; Sets the Timezone to the Pacific Northwest
; Sets the Admin Password to NULL
; Turn AutoLogon ON and login once
TimeZone = "004"
AdminPassword = pass
AutoLogon = No
AutoLogonCount = 15
 [GuiRunOnce]
; List the programs that you want to launch when the machine is logged into for
the first time

 [Display]
BitsPerPel = 8
XResolution = 800
YResolution = 600
VRefresh = 70

 [Networking]
; When set to YES, setup will install default-networking components. The
components to be set are
; TCP/IP, File and Print Sharing, and the Client for Microsoft Networks.
InstallDefaultComponents = YES

 [Identification]
JoinWorkgroup = Workgroup
; In order to join a domain, delete the line above and add the following lines
; JoinDomain = DomainName
```

```
; CreateComputerAccountInDomain = Yes
; DomainAdmin = Administrator
; DomainAdminPassword = AdminPassword
```

After the study of scripted installation methods, you must be able to understand the utility of customized answer files and ways to create or edit them.

exam Watch

If a Fully Automated installation mode is selected in the Setup Manager wizard, the user is not prompted for an administrator password.

Creating and Using UDFs for Multiple Users

When you use the WINNT32.EXE command with the /unattend option, you can also specify a Unique Database File (UDF), which has a .UDB extension. This file forces Setup to use certain values from the UDF file, thus overriding the values given

SCENARIO & SOLUTION	
If an answer file comes with Windows 2000 Professional, why can't you use it for all installations?	The answer file included with Windows 2000 Professional is basically intended to help administrators understand the program's use and syntax and is in its most generalized form using many default parameters. Many setup parameters in this file might not suit your requirements. The file has to be edited before you can use it.
Why do you need to create a network share when you can use the CD-ROM for installations?	You need a network share when you want to install Windows 2000 Professional or any other operating system simultaneously on many computers. If you have many computers running Setup and notice that the server holding the network share is very slow, you might need to create more network shares.
You hate using Notepad or Word Pad and typing the tough syntax for editing or creating a custom answer file. Is there any other option that can help you create an answer file?	Yes. Use the Windows 2000 Setup Manager wizard. This graphical tool helps you create custom answer files or scripts for many computers at a time without much effort.

in the answer file. This is particularly useful when you want to specify multiple users during the setup. The syntax for using an UDF with WINNT32.EXE is as follows:

```
/udf:ID[,UDB_File]
```

An identifier (ID) in this switch tells Setup how to modify the values given in the answer file. When you use the /udf option without specifying the .UDB file, Setup prompts you to insert a disk that contains such a file.

CERTIFICATION OBJECTIVE 12.05

Understanding Remote Installation Service (RIS)

The *Remote Installation Service (RIS)* is a part of the Windows 2000 Server operating system. It is installed as an optional service on the Windows 2000 Server and facilitates installation of Windows 2000 Professional remotely on a large number of computers with similar or dissimilar hardware configurations. This not only reduces the installation time but also helps keep the deployment costs low. The Remote Installation Preparation (RIPrep) utility is used to create a master image of a fully configured client computer running Windows 2000 Professional. This image that is independent of the client hardware is uploaded to the RIS server for distribution to other client computers.

While RIS is an excellent utility provided by Microsoft, it requires careful study and planning before it can be used. RIS needs services like Active Directory, DNS, and DHCP to be running on the network. The client computers need to have either one of the 25 supported network adapters or a PXE-based Boot ROM that supports booting from the network.

How Does RIS Work?

To gain an understanding of the remote installation process, consider that a client computer boots using either the Remote Boot Disk prepared by a RIS server or a compatible Boot ROM on the network interface card. While a *BootP* message is displayed on the client, it connects to the DHCP server that is preconfigured to allocate an IP address to this client. The Boot Information Negotiation Layer (BINL) extensions on the DHCP server redirect the client computer to the RIS server on the network.

A Client Installation wizard (CIW) is downloaded to the client. This utility prompts the user to log on. Once the user has successfully logged on, the RIS server contacts the Active Directory to determine what options of the CIW are to be displayed to the user. It also checks with the Active Directory to find out what images the user is authorized to select. Active Directory uses Trivial File Transfer Protocol (TFTP) to transfer the first few required files to the client. The DNS server plays its role in locating the Active Directory server on the network. Once the user selects an image, Setup starts running on the client computer. It is evident that the sequence of protocol activities is DHCP, BINL, and TFTP.

The image that is to be distributed to the client can be prepared by any of the disk duplication methods. The *Remote Installation Preparation (RIPrep)* is one such wizard that is more or less similar to the SysPrep tool. The difference is that RIPrep removes not only the security ID from the master computer; it also removes all the hardware-specific settings. This makes the image independent of the hardware configuration. RIS is a useful utility aimed at reducing deployment time, administrative efforts, and costs.

exam Watch

RIS can be used only to distribute Windows 2000 Professional operating system images. You cannot use it to deploy any version of Windows 2000 Server or any other operating system.

Components of the Remote Installation Service

Let's see what components make up the RIS service. Primarily, there are five parts of the RIS service:

- **RIS on the server running Windows 2000 Server operating system** The RISETUP.EXE file is run from the Start menu.
- **Administration of RIS**
- **Client Installation wizard** The executable file is OSCHOOSER.EXE.
- **Remote Installation Preparation wizard** RIPREP.EXE is the executable for this wizard and has to be run from the RIS server.
- **Remote Installation Boot Disk** This disk is used to boot the client and connect to the RIS server to get an initial IP address from the DHCP server. This disk also starts the Client Installation wizard.

The Single-Instance Store Volume

As we observed earlier while discussing RIPrep, RIS creates a Single-Instance Store (SIS) volume. What is the SIS for? When you have more than one image on the RIS server, each holding Windows 2000 Professional setup files, there will definitely be duplicate copies of hundreds of files. This duplication can consume significant hard drive space on the RIS server. To overcome this problem, Microsoft introduced a new feature, the SIS, which works on NTFS partitions. The SIS helps eliminate duplicate files, thus saving hard drive space.

Installing the Remote Installation Server

Now that you are familiar with the RIS service and the various components that make it up, let's see how can we set up the RIS server. First, we need to know the requirements that must be met in order to set up the RIS server.

RIS needs the following additional network services running on the RIS server or elsewhere on the network:

- **Domain Name Service (DNS)** RIS is dependent on the DNS for locating the directory services and the machine accounts for the client computers.
- **Dynamic Host Configuration Protocol (DHCP)** The DHCP services are used to provide initial IP addresses to the client computers when they start up. An IP address is necessary to continue participating in a TCP/IP network.
- **Active Directory Service** This service provides the means for locating the RIS servers and the client computers on the network. The RIS server must have access to the Active Directory.

EXERCISE 12-5

Installing the Remote Installation Service

Select the Windows 2000 Server (in case you have many servers running on the network) and log on as an administrator.

Insert the Windows 2000 Server CD-ROM in the CD-ROM drive. Close the dialog box that pops up after inserting the CD-ROM. Then do the following:

1. Click Start | Settings | Control Panel. The Control Panel Window opens.
2. Click Add/Remove Programs. The Add/Remove Programs Window opens.
3. Click the Windows Components tab. It takes a while for this window to open.
4. Click the Remote Installation Service checkbox. Click Next.
5. At this point, the Remote Installation Service is installed. Click Finish to complete the installation.
6. A dialog box appears that says that the systems settings have changed and that you must restart your computer. Remove the Windows 2000 Server CD-ROM from the CD-ROM drive.
7. Click Yes to restart.

In Exercise 12-5, you simply clicked Yes to reboot the server. In practice, you must be very careful while rebooting any server that is live on the network. If you are performing this exercise on a live server or you are not the network administrator, you must ask the network administrator whether it is safe to reboot the server. At a minimum, you must send a message to all the connected users that the server will be rebooted in the next five minutes or so and that they must save their work.

Once the RIS service has been installed on a Windows 2000 Server, it needs to be configured. In the following exercise, we learn how to configure this service.

EXERCISE 12-6

Configuring the Remote Installation Service

1. Click Start | Run and type **RISetup.exe**. Press Enter. This starts the Remote Installation Services Setup wizard. A welcome screen appears.
2. In the Remote Installation Folder Location window, you are prompted to type the path name of the volume that will hold the remote installation images. Type the correct path of the folder. (You could also click the Browse button to locate the folder). Click Next.
3. The Initial Settings window opens. In this window you can specify how the RIS server will respond to the clients. By default, the RIS server will not respond to the clients until it is configured to do so. Here you may choose for the RIS server to respond or not to respond to the unknown clients requesting the RIS service. For the purpose of this exercise, click the checkbox opposite "Respond to client computers requesting service." Click Next.
4. The Installation Source Files Location window appears. You are prompted to specify the location of Windows 2000 Professional files. These files are located in the i386 folder of the CD-ROM drive. Check for the correct drive letter of the CD-ROM drive and type the path name. If you are unsure about the CD-ROM drive letter, click the Browse button to locate the correct path. We are using F:\i386 in this exercise. Make sure that the Windows 2000 Professional CD-ROM is inserted in the CD-ROM drive.
5. The next window prompts you to enter the name of the folder in which the Windows 2000 Professional image(s) are to be stored. The default folder name is WIN2000.PRO. This folder resides under the folder we selected in step 2 earlier in this exercise.
6. The Friendly Description and Help Text window is the next to appear on your screen. You can give a description to the image so that users can identify the image when the Client Installation wizard runs. The default friendly description of the image is "Microsoft Windows 2000 Professional" and the default help text is "Automatically installs Windows 2000 Professional without prompting the user for input." You can type in any custom friendly description and help text that suits the requirements of your organization. This is particularly useful when you have more than one image meant for various departments in your company. If there is only one image, it is best to keep the defaults.

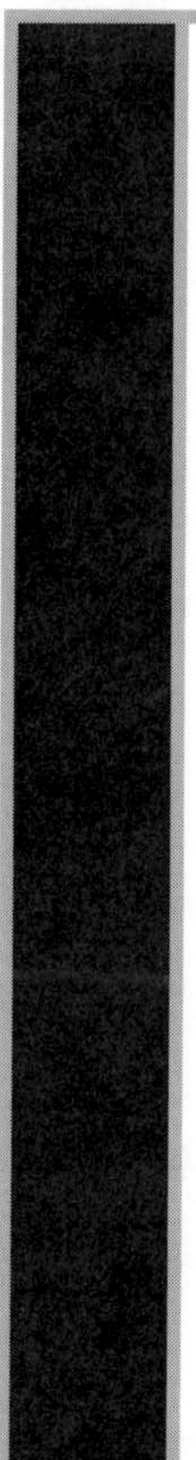

7. The Review Settings window appears next in the RIS configuration wizard. The Review Settings screen shows the various settings you have chosen. If you see anything that is incorrect, click the Back button and make necessary corrections. Otherwise, click Finish.
8. It takes a while for the wizard to install the settings of the RIS that you have selected. When it's finished, a window appears that shows each of the services. The following tasks are shown as they are completed:
   - A remote installation folder is created.
   - The necessary files needed by the service are copied into the above folder.
   - The Windows installation files are copied to the WIN2000.PRO folder.
   - The screen files for the Client Installation wizard are updated.
   - An unattended Setup answer file is created.
   - The remote installation services are created.
   - The registry of the RIS server is updated with new and/or modified entries.
   - A Single-Instance Store volume is created.
   - The required RIS is started.
9. This finishes the initial configuration for RIS. A check mark appears before each of the tasks when it is complete. You are prompted to click the Done button. Why wait? Click it and you are finished! The server does not reboot after this configuration.

Authorizing the RIS Server

The next step in establishing the RIS server is to authorize it in the Active Directory in order for the RIS server to serve the client computers. If this step is skipped, the RIS clients will not be able to get a response from the RIS server. In Exercise 12-7, we authorize the RIS server in the Active Directory to respond to the requesting RIS clients and provide IP addresses. This authorization is done from the DHCP Manager MMC snap-in on a server that is running the DHCP service. By default, this service is disabled.

EXERCISE 12-7

Authorizing the RIS Server

1. Log on to the server as a domain administrator where the DHCP services are running. This may or may not be the same server as the RIS server.
2. Click Start | Programs | Administrative Tools | DHCP.
3. The DHCP Manager window opens. Right-click DHCP in the left pane and click Add Server.
4. The Add Server dialog box appears. Type in the IP address of the RIS server and click OK.
5. Right-click DHCP again and click Manage Authorize Servers.
6. Select the RIS server and click Authorize. Click OK.

exam Watch

In order to authorize the RIS server in the Active Directory, you must have domain administrator rights.

Restricting Client Installation Options with Group Policy

When you have a large network with hundreds of computers and many images, you need to restrict access to the options that are presented to the users when the Client Installation Wizard runs. We can actually restrict the clients from choosing an incorrect installation option by applying a group policy for the RIS server. This is accomplished from the Active Directory Users and Computers MMC snap-in.

EXERCISE 12-8

Restricting Client Installation Options

To follow is the method to restrict client installation options.

1. Log on to the RIS server as domain administrator.
2. Click Start | Programs | Administrative Tools | Active Directory | Users and Computers.
3. Select the container for the RIS policy settings. By default, these are set within the Default Domain Policy Object.
4. In the left pane, right-click on the domain name and click Properties. Click on the Group Policy tab in the Properties window.
5. Click the Default Domain Policy and click Edit. Double-click on the User Configuration. Double-click on the Windows Settings.
6. Click on the Remote Installation Services. An icon for Choice Options appears in the right pane.
7. Double-click the Choice Options. The following three choice options are displayed:
   - **Allow** This option allows the users to choose an installation option.
   - **Don't Care** In this option, the predefined group policy is applied to all users.
   - **Deny** This does not allow the users to access a particular installation option.
8. After making a selection, close all the windows. Close the Active Directory window as well.

Restricting the Operating System Image Options

The next step is to specify which client or user will use which image. This is an important step to ensure that the user installs a correct operating system image. If this is not done, the client may choose a wrong image, and all the efforts for saving time on unattended installations would be wasted. By applying user or group security policies, we can specify which image the user can see and install. You may either choose to show all the images to the user, or you can restrict the user from seeing any of the images available on the RIS server that are not meant for him.

EXERCISE 12-9

Restricting the Operating System Image Options

Perform the following steps to restrict the image options.

1. Log on to the RIS server as a domain administrator.
2. Click Start | Programs | Accessories | Windows Explorer.
3. Locate the win2000.pro folder and double-click on it to expand. Double-click on the i386 folder.
4. Right-click on the Templates subfolder and click Properties. The Properties window for the templates opens.
5. Click on the Security tab. This is where you can set permissions on users and groups. Select the Everyone group in the upper part of the dialog box and click Remove.
6. To add a particular user or group that will have access to this image, click Add. Select the user or the group and click OK. It is recommended that you set permissions for groups rather than individual users.
7. To add another group that will have access to this image, repeat step 6. Click OK to exit. Close all windows.

To ensure that the users pick up a correct image, the following steps are recommended:
1. Determine the client requirements and make groups of users with identical requirements.
2. Prepare images based on the group requirements.
3. Set permissions on images based on the user groups. Do not allow all user groups access to all images.

Hardware Requirements for RIS

In order to use RIS for automating the deployment of Windows 2000 Professional in your organization, you need to fulfill certain hardware requirements for the RIS server and the RIS client. These requirements are described in this section.

Hardware Requirements for the RIS Server

The server that is selected to host RIS must have the following minimum hardware components:

- A Pentium 166MHz processor. It is recommended that you use a 200MHz. Pentium II or a later processor with higher speed.
- A minimum of 64MB RAM if RIS is the only service hosted by the server. If the server is hosting any additional services such as Active Directory, DNS, or DHCP, a minimum of 128MB RAM is required.
- Free hard drive space of 2GB, which should be dedicated to the RIS directory. The partition chosen for RIS must not be the boot partition of the server.
- A network adapter with 10Mbps data transfer speed. A 100Mbps adapter is recommended.

Hardware Requirements for the RIS Client

The client computers requesting RIS must have the following minimum hardware components:

- A Pentium processor, 166MHz or faster
- A minimum of 32MB RAM minimum, 64MB recommended

- A hard disk with a minimum capacity of 800MB
- A PCI plug-and-play adapter supported by RIS or a PXE-based Remote Boot ROM version .99 or later

When you create a boot disk using the Remote Boot Disk Generator utility, as discussed later in this section, you are able to view a list of the supported network adapters.

PXE-Capable BIOS

The *Preboot Execution Environment (PXE)* is a new DHCP-based technology used to help client computers boot from the network. The Windows 2000 RIS uses the PXE technology along with the existing TCP/IP network infrastructure to implement the RIS-based deployment of Windows 2000 Professional. The client computer that has the PXE-based ROM uses its BIOS to contact an existing RIS server and get an IP address from the DHCP server running on the network. The RIS server then initializes the installation process on the client computer.

PXE-Capable Network Interface Cards

Any computer with a network interface card that has a PXE-based ROM can use RIS for initializing the installation process. When such a computer starts, the PXE ROM contacts an existing RIS server and requests an IP address using the normal DHCP process. The RIS server that is preconfigured to respond to client computers in the Active Directory responds and provides an IP address to the client.

A *boot ROM* is a chip on the network adapter that helps the computer boot from the network. Such a computer need not have a previously installed operating system. The BIOS of the computer that has a PXE-based boot ROM must be configured to boot from the network. Windows 2000 Server RIS supports PXE ROM versions .99 or later.

NetPC

A computer that meets NetPC specifications is another kind of computer that can be a RIS client. The following are some additional requirements for computers with NetPC configuration:

- The network adapter must be configured as the primary boot device.

- The user account for performing the installation must have rights to log on as a batch job.
- The users who will use NetPC computers must have permission to create computer accounts in the domain.

How do you know which PXE ROM version you are running? This is a typical question that arises when we talk about the PXE ROMs. There are two methods to find out the correct version of the PXE ROM:

- **Check the documentation.** This is the best method; it will tell you which version of PXE ROM is run by your system. Windows 2000 supports only version .99 or later.
- **From the startup messages.** When the PXE ROM-based computer starts, a PXE ROM boot sequence is run. The PXE ROM code messages displayed on the screen will tell you the version of PXE ROM you are running.

RIS Support for Laptops

RIS with Windows 2000 Professional is not supported on laptop computers that have PC Cards or PCMCIA network cards. Some laptop computers can be addressed by RIS when used in docking stations that use supported network adapters. Since the number of laptops and docking stations tested by Microsoft is very limited, you must check the documentation of such computers before attempting to install Windows 2000 remotely.

The Remote Installation Boot Disk

When the client computer starts, it needs to contact the RIS server. It can accomplish this task in two ways. One, the client must have a PXE-based boot ROM on the network adapter. Second, the client must boot using a remote installation boot disk. The remote installation boot disk simulates the PXE boot process. This helps the client get an IP address from any DHCP server on the network. Once the client gets the IP address, it can communicate with other computers on the network.

For client computers that do not have a PXE boot ROM, RIS includes a boot disk generator utility. This disk can be used to initiate the remote installation process.

Creating a Boot Disk

The boot disk generator utility RBGF.EXE currently supports only 25 PCI-based network adapters. Many of the popular adapters are supported, so there's no need to purchase new adapters for hundreds of client computers. The RBGF.EXE utility can be run from any of the following computers:

- The RIS server
- A client computer that has a connection to the RIS server
- Any client connected to the RIS server on which the Windows 2000 Server Administrative Tools are installed

exam Watch

The Remote Boot Disk generator program supports only PCI Ethernet adapters. PCMCIA, ISA, EISA, MCA, and Token Ring network adapters are not supported.

EXERCISE 12-10

Creating a Remote Installation Boot Disk

1. Ensure that the RIS server is up and running. Log on as an administrator.
2. Click Start | Run and type in RBGF.EXE. Click OK. If you are running this command from another computer, type in the following command and click OK:

   ```
   \\RISServer_name\RemoteInstall\Admin\i386\RBGF.exe
   ```
3. The Windows 2000 Remote Installation Boot Disk Generator window opens.
4. Check the path of the destination disk. It is usually drive A:. Insert a blank formatted floppy disk into drive A:.
5. To see a list of supported adapters, click the Adapter List button. Make sure that the adapters you have are on the list.
6. Click Create Disk. This creates a remote installation boot disk. Remove the disk and close the Windows 2000 Remote Boot Disk Generator window.

Deploying Windows 2000 Using Remote Installation Service

As observed earlier in this chapter, RIS can be used only for deployment of the Windows 2000 Professional operating system. This service requires that other services such as Active Directory, DNS, and DHCP are also running on the network. These services may reside on the same server that is hosting the RIS service or any other server that is part of the domain. Once the RIS server is fully configured, you can start the Client Installation wizard on any of the client computers. The remote boot disk can be used to boot and start the network services on the client computer.

The Client Installation Wizard

It's time now to turn to the client side. When a client computer boots using either the Remote Boot Disk or the PXE-based Boot ROM, it tries to establish a connection to the RIS server. If the RIS server is preconfigured to service the RIS clients, it helps the client get an IP address from the DHCP service. The Client Installation wizard is then downloaded from the RIS server. This wizard has four installation options. The options that are presented to the user depend on the group policy set in the Active Directory. In starting an automatic setup, a user might get all four options or none of the options. The four installation options are as follows:

- **Automatic Setup** Automatic Setup is the default option. This is also the easiest installation method. It allows the user to select the operating system image. No more questions are asked of the user. The various configuration parameters are predetermined.
- **Custom Setup** This option is a bit more flexible, allowing the user to override the process of automatically naming a computer. This option also allows the user to select a location in the Active Directory where the computer account will be created. This option requires significant administrative effort because almost every aspect of the installation can be customized.
- **Restart a Previous Setup Attempt** As its name suggests, this option enables the user to restart a failed setup attempt. The user is not prompted for any input that he or she has already entered. This option is particularly useful when for some reason the user loses connection to the RIS server during setup or in case there is accidental shutdown of the client computer.

- **Maintenance and Troubleshooting** This option provides access to any third-party maintenance tools that you may want to use before the installation starts. Since this option is not meant for every other user, the administrator can restrict access to this option in the group policy set in the Active Directory.

After making a selection from the above options, a list of available image options is displayed to the user. When a selection has been made, the user is presented with a summary screen. The installation begins immediately after this screen appears.

Troubleshooting Using Remote Installation Service

RIS is dependent on many other services running on the network. The complete RIS setup itself is not an easy operation for any network administrator. To have a fully functional RIS system, you must ensure the following:

1. The RIS server is up and running.
2. The DHCP server is authorized to service RIS clients in the Active Directory.
3. An IP address scope has been created in the DHCP server for RIS clients and has been activated.
4. If there is a router on the network between the RIS server and the clients, configure it to forward BootP broadcasts.

We have discussed the Remote Installation Service in detail. Let's have a quick look at some of the important questions that you could face on the job.

SCENARIO & SOLUTION	
You want to use the RIS service. Is it necessary that the Active Directory, DNS, and DHCP are installed on the same server?	No. The Active Directory, DNS, and DHCP may reside anywhere on the network, but these should be functional before you configure RIS.
You need to install Windows 2000 on 50 computers. How do you ensure that the distribution server is not overloaded when simultaneous installations are running?	Create more than one distribution folder to balance the load.

SCENARIO & SOLUTION	
Is there any way to know online that the Remote Installation Service supports the network adapters in the client computers?	Yes. When you run the RBGF.EXE utility, you can click the Adapter List tab to view a list of supported adapters.
When you were running the Client Installation wizard, someone pulled the wire and the setup aborted. What should you do?	Run the Client Installation wizard again and, when prompted, choose the "Restart a previous setup attempt" option.

CERTIFICATION OBJECTIVE 12.06

Performing an Unattended Installation of Windows 2000 Server

An automated or unattended installation of any software product means that the person performing the job does not have to answer any questions that the setup programs generally ask. Answer files, also known as *installation script files*, usually provide the answers automatically. Disk duplication methods provide another way to automate the installation.

The simplest form of performing the unattended installation is by using the WINNT32.EXE setup command with the /unattend switch. This method uses the answer file that you already have created. The WINNT.EXE command uses the /u switch.

WINNT32 or WINNT?

Two different commands can be used from the command prompt for initializing the setup process of Windows 2000 Server, depending on the previously installed operating system on the computer:

- The command WINNT.EXE is used for starting the setup from a computer running MS-DOS or Windows 3.x. This command cannot be used for upgrading the previous operating system to Windows 2000.
- The WINNT32.EXE command is used to start the setup from a computer running Windows 95, Windows 98, or Windows NT.

Remember that direct upgrade to Windows 2000 Server of any Windows NT Server prior to version 3.51 is not supported. In case you still want to install on such a computer, you must either do a clean installation or first upgrade it to Windows NT 3.51 or 4.0.

The setup can be run from either a local CD-ROM drive or the network. In order to run the unattended installation on a computer running MS-DOS or Windows 3.x from the network, you must first connect to the network share containing the Windows 2000 Server installation files. You can choose to use the share created on the distribution server.

Running Unattended Setup with the WINNT.EXE Command

The WINNT.EXE command has the following syntax:

```
Winnt  /s:x:\i386 /u:x:\i386\unattend.txt /t:c
```

- /s specifies the location of the source containing the installation files; in this case, *x* points to the drive that contains the i386 folder
- /u tells the setup that this is an unattended installation and specifies x:\i386 as the location of the custom answer file UNATTEND.TXT
- /t is used to specify a folder for storing any temporary files used during the setup process

Running an Unattended Setup with the WINNT32.EXE Command

When you are running the setup from within Windows 9x or Windows NT, the WINNT32.EXE command is used. The following is the syntax of this command:

```
Winnt32 /s:x:\i386 /unattend 5:X:\i386\unattend.txt /tempdrive:c
```

This command is different from the WINNT.EXE command in only minor ways. You might have noted that this time we are using the /unattend switch instead of /U. Furthermore, we used a number 5, which specifies the time that the computer will wait before rebooting when the file copy phase is over. This wait time works only on computers running Windows NT and Windows 2000 but is ignored in Windows 9x. All other switches and their syntax are similar to those used in WINNT.EXE command.

EXERCISE 12-11

Running an Unattended Installation Using the WINNT32.EXE Command

This exercise assumes that you have already created a custom answer file called UNATTEND.TXT. The Windows 2000 Server setup files are on a network file server share named Installs. The UNATEND.EXE and the UNATTEND.BAT files are placed in the \i386 folder of the Installs share. This exercise needs a running network and you must be able to connect to the network file server. Now do the following:

1. From the Start menu, click Run | cmd. Click OK. The MS-DOS window opens.
2. Connect to the file server using the following command:

   ```
   net use x: \\server name\installs
   ```
3. You will notice that a message is displayed on the screen saying that the command completed successfully. This means that the x: drive is now connected to the Installs share on the file server.
4. Change to the x: drive by typing the following at the command prompt:

   ```
   cd x:
   ```
5. Type the following command again at the prompt to initiate the setup:

   ```
   winnt32 /s:x:\i386 /unattend:X:\i386\unattend.txt
   /tempdrive:c
   ```
6. The installation starts. Very little or no interaction is needed from you during the setup, depending on the parameters specified in the answer file.
7. If a fully automated method has been selected for installation when using the Setup Manager, you will not be able to select the local administrator password.

Installing Optional Programs

Unattended setup can be used to install optional application programs during the GUI phase of the setup. The CMDLINES.TXT file can be used for such an installation. The CMDLINES.TXT file can have some commands that run the files with an .INF extension. In order to use this feature, you need to copy the application in the OEM subfolder in the distribution folder.

Multiple commands can be used in the [Command] section of the UNATTEND.TXT file. The following is the syntax for using CMDLINES.TXT:

```
 [Commands]
 "command_1"
 "command_2"
....
 "command_3"
```

You need to place all the commands in double quotation marks. This feature has certain limitations:

- You must place the applications in the distribution folder.
- The installation must run in fully unattended mode. Any interaction by the user will stop the execution of the command.
- The CMDLINES.TXT runs as a service rather than using any user account.

Unattended Installation Using a Bootable CD-ROM

This method of unattended installation can be used on computers with BIOS that support booting from a CD-ROM. You must create an answer file and store it on a floppy disk before starting the setup program. The following are the requirements for running such an installation:

- The BIOS of the computer should support the El Torito Bootable CD-ROM (no emulation mode) format.
- The previously created answer file must be named WINNT.SIF and stored on a floppy disk.
- The answer file must include a [Data] section that contains the required keys.

When you are sure that you have the Windows 2000 Server CD-ROM and the floppy containing the customized answer file named WINNT.SIF ready, you can start the setup process as explained in the following exercise.

EXERCISE 12-12

Running Unattended Installation from a CD-ROM

1. Insert the Windows 2000 Server CD-ROM in the CD-ROM drive and recycle the computer power.
2. As soon as the blue-colored text-mode screen appears, insert the floppy disk.
3. You will notice that the computer reads the answer file from the floppy disk. The floppy disk indicator remains lit during this time.
4. When the computer has loaded the WINNT.SIF answer file from the floppy disk, the floppy disk indicator goes off. Remove the floppy disk at this point.
5. The installation continues from the CD-ROM in an unattended mode and all the answers are read from the loaded WINNT.SIF file.

The bootable CD-ROM method can be used for clean installations only. It is not possible to perform an upgrade installation using this method. It is also not possible to specify any UDF files with this method.

CERTIFICATION SUMMARY

Windows 2000 ships with many utilities that facilitate unattended installations of the operating system. The unattended installations make the rollout fast and reduce the cost in medium and large organizations. These are also helpful in standardizing the desktop environment throughout the organization. Disk duplication tools like the System Preparation tool (Sysprep) and the Remote Installation Preparation Wizard are used to prepare replicas of a completely configured Windows 2000 Professional computer. The Remote Installation Service (RIS) is included with the Windows 2000 Server and is quite useful in delivery of the Windows 2000 Professional operating system. The Setup Manager Wizard is used to create custom answer files for unattended setup.

The system images prepared by Sysprep have to be distributed to other computers using some third-party imaging utilities. This utility also requires that all the destination computers have hardware identical to the master computer. When an image of the system is created using Sysprep, it rips off the master computer from its user-specific settings. A Mini-Setup Wizard that runs on the next reboot can help restore all these settings. It is recommended that the master computer be tested in all respects before running Sysprep to create an image.

The image prepared by the RIPrep utility is independent of the hardware of the destination computers. You do not need a third-party utility to distribute the prepared image; the RIS server handles the job of distribution. RIS service requires fully functional Active Directory services, DHCP services, and the DNS services running on the network. The client computers need to have a PXE-based Boot ROM, or must boot from the Remote Boot Disk prepared using RBGF.exe utility. This Remote Boot Disk starts the Client Installation Wizard on the destination computers. The administrator can control access to the Client Installation Wizard options and the images that a user can select.

The unattended installations use an answer file that supplies answers to various questions prompted by the setup wizard. The sample answer file unattend.txt file can be edited using Notepad. The Setup Manager Wizard helps in creating customized answer files for one or many of the computers for fully automated installations. Once the answer file is ready, the installation can be started in an unattended mode using the winnt or winnt32 command using the /u switch and specifying the location of the installation files and the answer file. Unattended mode can be used either for a clean install or for an upgrade.

TWO-MINUTE DRILL

Disk Duplication Methods

- The disk duplication methods that come with the Windows 2000 operating system reduce the rollout, save costs incurred on deployment, and help standardize the desktop environment throughout the organization.
- The disk duplication methods can be used only for clean installs. These methods do not support upgrading from a previous operating system.
- System Preparation (Sysprep) is used to prepare an image of a computer fully configured with the operating system and the applications.
- Sysprep requires that the source master computer and all the destination computers have identical hardware, but Plug and Play devices are exempted from this condition. The image distribution job is handled by a third-party utility.
- The Remote Installation Service is included with the Windows 2000 Server operating system for remote installation of Windows 2000 Professional. This service is dependent on Active Directory service, DHCP service, and the DNS service running on the network.
- The RIS service can deliver images prepared by the Remote Installation Preparation (RIPrep) Wizard. The image is stored in the RIS server.
- The Client Installation Wizard runs on the RIS client computer when booted using a PXE-based Boot ROM or a Remote Boot Disk that is prepared using the RBGF.exe utility. This utility supports only 25 PCI-based network adapters.

The Scripted Method

- Windows 2000 Professional installation can be automated using scripted answer files that provide the answers to many or all of the setup questions.
- The unattend.txt is the default answer file that comes with Windows 2000. This file can be modified to suit individual installation needs using Notepad.
- The Setup Manager Wizard is used to create custom answer files that provide various configuration parameters. To start Setup Manager Wizard, run setupmgr.exe file.

- The Setup Manager can create a new answer file or modify an existing file. It can also create an answer file that duplicates the configuration of the computer where the wizard is being run.
- The Setup Manager can create answer files for one or all of the computers that need unattended installations. The installation can be fully automated wherein the user is not prompted for any input.

Performing an Unattended Installation of Windows 2000 Professional

- The unattended installation of Windows 2000 Professional is done using the winnt or winnt32 command with the /u switch and specifying the location of the installation files and the answer file.
- The user wishing to do an unattended setup may modify the default answer file using Notepad, or create a custom answer file using the Setup Manager Wizard.
- The unattended installation method can be used either for a clean install or to upgrade a previously installed operating system.
- If a Fully Automated installation mode is selected in the answer file, the user is not prompted for an administrator password.

Understanding the Difference Between Unattended Installations and Prepared Images

- Windows 2000 Server installation can be automated using scripted answer files that provide the answers to many or all the setup questions. The unattended installation method can be used for a clean installation or to upgrade a previously installed operating system.
- The disk duplication methods that come with Windows 2000 operating system reduce the rollout time and save costs incurred on deployment as well as helping to standardize the desktop environment throughout the organization.
- It is important that you understand the requirements, advantages, and disadvantages of each method of unattended installation before making a final decision on which type is right for you.

Understanding Remote Installation Services

- ❑ The Remote Installation Service (RIS) is included with Windows 2000 Server for remote installation of Windows 2000 Professional. This service is dependent on Active Directory, DHCP, and DNS running on the network.
- ❑ RIS can deliver images prepared by the Remote Installation Preparation (RIPrep) wizard. The image is stored in the RIS server.
- ❑ The Client Installation wizard runs on the RIS client computer when booted using a PXE-based boot ROM or a remote boot disk that is prepared using the RBGF.EXE utility. This utility supports many PCI-based network adapters.

Performing an Unattended Installation of Windows 2000 Server

- ❑ The unattended installation of Windows 2000 Server is done using the WINNT or WINNT32 command with the /u switch and specifying the location of the installation files and the answer file.
- ❑ The user who wants to do an unattended setup can modify the default answer file using Notepad or create a custom answer file using the Setup Manager wizard.
- ❑ If a fully automated installation mode is selected in the answer file, the user is not prompted for an administrator password.

13

Upgrading to Windows 2000 from Windows NT

CERTIFICATION OBJECTIVES

13.01	Planning a Network Upgrade to Windows 2000
13.02	Upgrading a Server from Windows NT
13.03	Deploying Service Packs
13.04	Troubleshooting Failed Installations
✓	Two-Minute Drill

In this chapter, we discuss upgrading your network from Windows NT to Windows 2000. There are many tasks involved in this upgrade. The most important task is your plan to upgrade. You need to determine your networking requirements and how to handle IP addressing and name resolution. Then you should design a strategy for upgrading your Windows NT domains to Windows 2000 domains. Will you leave them as they are, merge multiple domains into one, or split up domains?

When upgrading your Windows NT servers to Windows 2000, you need to determine the role each of them will serve in the Windows 2000 network. In Windows 2000, a server can act as a domain controller, member server, or stand-alone server. Unlike roles for Windows NT servers, roles for Windows 2000 servers can be changed after installation, so your decision doesn't have to be permanent. There are several ways to upgrade your server; you need to choose the best method for your enterprise. You should also develop a rollback plan in case of problems during the upgrade.

Periodically, Microsoft releases fixes to its operating systems; these fixes are known as *service packs.* Service packs contain bug and security fixes. Normally, you want to have your computers running the latest service pack that is available. However, you should test the service packs for your environment prior to deploying them.

On occasion, the installation of Windows 2000 Server will fail. When it does fail, you need to be prepared to solve the problems causing the failure. You should know the common problems that can occur and understand that Setup creates log files that can be used to help with troubleshooting.

CERTIFICATION OBJECTIVE 13.01

Planning a Network Upgrade to Windows 2000

As with just about anything you do, you should plan ahead. This includes upgrading your network to Windows 2000. You need to determine your network requirements and map out how you will fulfill those requirements using Windows 2000. You should determine how to configure Transmission Control Protocol/Internet Protocol (TCP/IP), how to provide IP addresses (dynamically or statically), and how to implement name resolution. You should determine how you will structure your domains using the new features of Windows 2000 such as forests and trees. In addition, decide what role each of your Windows NT servers play in the Windows 2000 environment. You should figure these things out before you start the upgrade.

Networking Requirements

When you are determining the network requirements for Windows 2000, some areas to consider are the network protocol requirements and name resolution. When you use TCP/IP as the network protocol, decide whether to provide automatic or manual assignment of IP addresses. For name resolution, determine your DNS requirements and whether you need to use Windows Internet Name Service (WINS).

TCP/IP Requirements

The TCP/IP network protocol is the protocol used across the Internet. The Windows 2000 Setup program makes it easier to configure TCP/IP. Each Windows 2000 server should be given an IP address. This IP address can be assigned dynamically through Dynamic Host Configuration Protocol (DHCP), automatically by Windows 2000 Server, or manually by assigning a static IP address. If you have a small number of computers (five or fewer) on a small network, you can allow Windows 2000 Server to automatically obtain IP addresses to the server using Automatic Private IP Addressing (APIPA). For larger networks, especially networks with more than one subnet, you should dynamically assign IP addresses using DHCP for workstations. The DHCP server must be assigned a static IP address so that other computers can locate it and so that other servers will be assigned an IP address dynamically by the DHCP server.

If a Windows 2000 Server is to be accessed directly across the Internet, it should have a static IP address. A static IP address allows users to use a domain name that can be translated into an IP address. The static IP address allows the server to always have the same IP address, so the host name always translates to the correct IP address. If the address were assigned dynamically and it occasionally changed, users might not be able to access the host across the Internet using its name.

In Exercise 13-1, we take a look at your current TCP/IP configuration. This exercise should be performed using Windows NT 4.0. However, most of the exercise will also work on Windows 95 or 98.

EXERCISE 13-1

Determining the Current TCP/IP Configuration

1. On the desktop, right-click the Network Neighborhood icon and select Properties from the context menu to bring up the Network dialog box.
2. By default, the Identification tab is displayed. This tab shows your current computer name and domain name. Click the Protocols tab. The Protocols screen is shown in the following illustration.

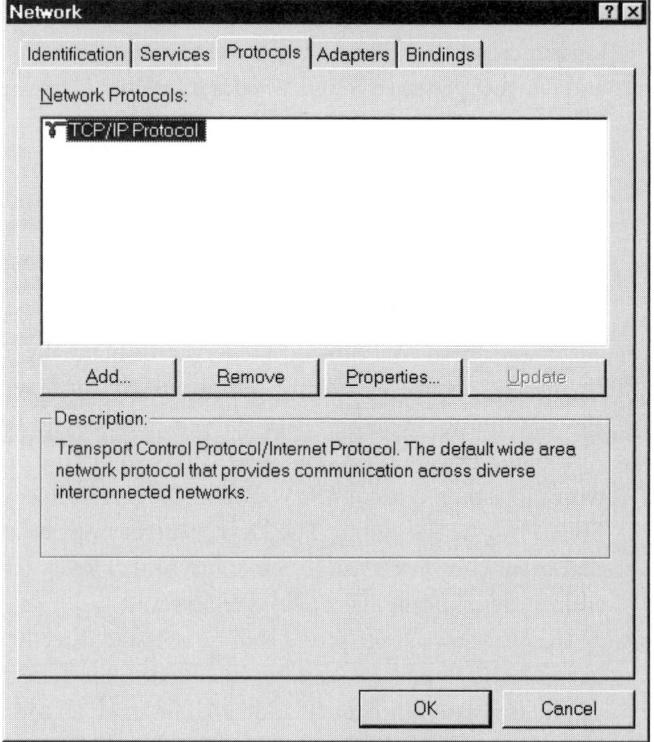

3. Select TCP/IP Protocol and click the Properties button. This brings up the Microsoft TCP/IP Properties dialog box.

4. By default, the IP Address tab is selected, as shown in the following illustration.

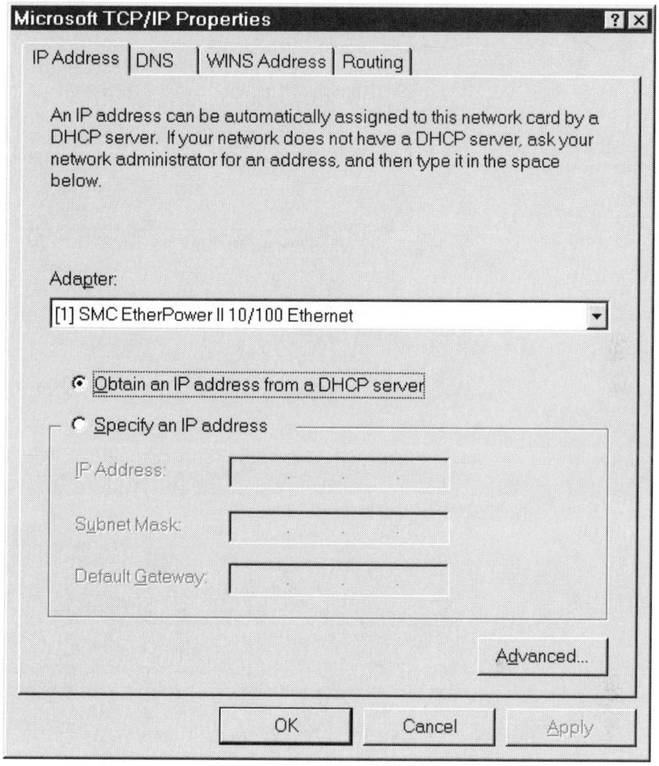

5. In the previous illustration, notice that the option for "Obtain an IP address from a DHCP server" is selected. This means it is configured for automatic IP addressing using DHCP. With the "Specify an IP address" selection, you can manually configure your IP address, as shown in the following illustration.

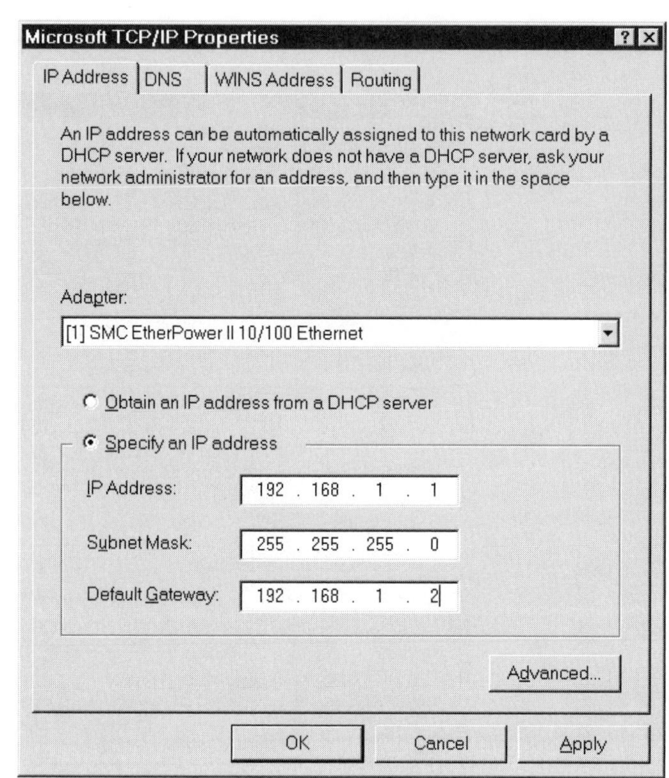

6. Click the DNS tab. Doing so displays your DNS settings, as shown in the following illustration. Since we used DHCP here, most of the settings are left blank. If your computer is manually configured, you should document the current settings.

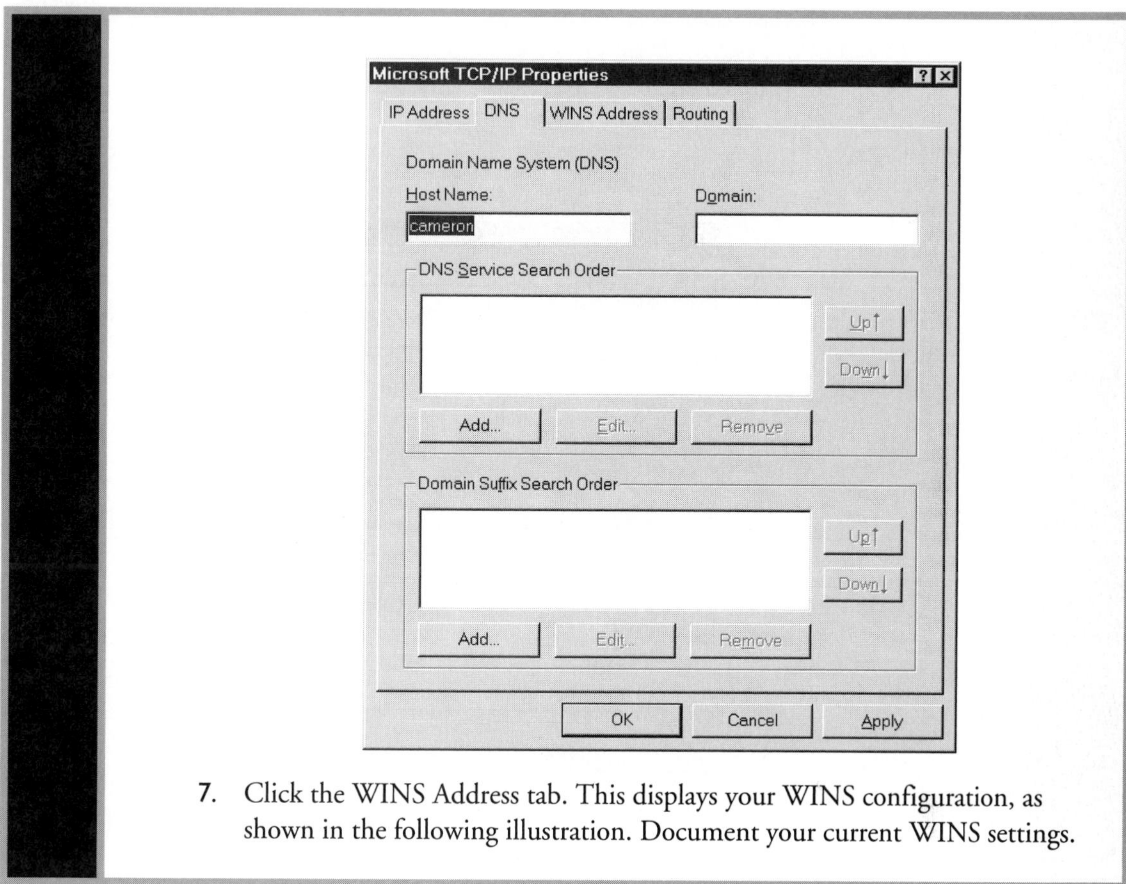

7. Click the WINS Address tab. This displays your WINS configuration, as shown in the following illustration. Document your current WINS settings.

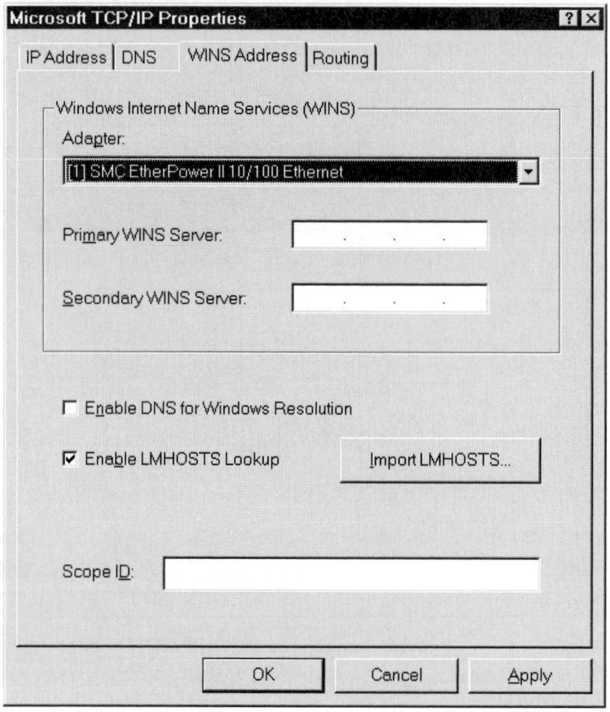

8. Once you have documented your current TCP/IP configuration, click the OK button to close the dialog box.

Domain Name System

Now that your computer has an IP address, we need to discuss name resolution. Since an IP address is a group of numbers (e.g., 192.168.1.1), you need to provide a way for users to use names rather than IP addresses to access computers. Name resolution allows users to use a name that is easier to remember than an IP address to access a computer on a network or the Internet.

One type of name resolution is the *Domain Name System (DNS).* DNS maps a domain name to an IP address. Windows 2000 uses DNS as the primary name resolution method. DNS is part of the TCP/IP protocol suite and comes with Windows 2000 Server. DNS services are required for Internet e-mail, Web browsing, and support for clients running Windows 2000 and Active Directory Services. When you install Windows 2000 Server as a domain controller or when you promote a member to a domain controller, DNS is installed automatically. DNS can also be installed during or after setup for member servers. DNS servers should be assigned a static IP address. This allows clients to be able to find the DNS server by its IP address. A client cannot find the DNS server by name because it needs to know where the DNS server is in order to translate the name into an IP address.

Windows Internet Name Service

If your network will support clients that are running Windows NT or Windows 95 or 98, you should install the *Windows Internet Name Service (WINS)* to support them. WINS is used to map NetBIOS computer names to IP addresses. WINS servers should be assigned a static IP address, which allows clients to be able to find the WINS servers. Clients cannot find a WINS server by name because they need to know where the WINS server is in order to translate the name into an IP address.

Creating a Naming Strategy

When you are planning names for your computers and domains, it is important to use names that are descriptive. Use names that are immediately indicative to whom the computer or domain belongs. Using computer names such as Comp1, Comp2, and so on is not very descriptive. With such a naming scheme, each time the network administrator (i.e., you) needed to find the computer, you would have to look up where it was and to whom it belonged—that is, of course, assuming you have documentation available.

A common approach to naming is to use the department name, title, and user's name. For example, say John Smith is the vice president of engineering. Rather than using a name such as Comp1 for Smith's computer, use *EngVPjsmith.*

The computer name is a NetBIOS name. A NetBIOS name can be up to 15 characters long. The name must contain only legal characters. You can use letters, numbers, and extended characters. Do not use spaces in your computer name. Although a name containing spaces might appear to work initially, it can cause problems with browsing in some versions of Windows.

However, ultimately, the use of extended characters can cause problems when you move away from NetBIOS names to a true DNS-compliant environment. Therefore, it is best to stick with the characters A to Z, a to z, 0 to 9, and the hyphen (-).

SCENARIO & SOLUTION	
You are upgrading a server that will be a Web server running IIS. Should the IP address be dynamic or static?	Any server that will be accessed across the Internet should be configured with a static IP address. A Web site has a domain name that is registered to an IP address, so the IP address cannot be changed.
You are upgrading your servers to Windows 2000. Many of your clients will still be running Windows NT and Windows 98. Should you use WINS?	Although Windows 2000 does not need WINS because it has been replaced in the DNS server, legacy operating systems could still require WINS. Therefore, you should install WINS if you have clients that are not running Windows 2000.

Domain Upgrade Strategy

Upgrading a domain is accomplished by upgrading your Windows NT primary and backup domain controllers to Windows 2000 Server. By upgrading your existing domain, the settings and configuration of the existing domain are preserved. You should plan the upgrade of the domain prior to starting any upgrade process.

A domain consists of a logical grouping of accounts and resources within a security boundary. As with Windows NT, a domain is needed to provide domain user accounts and domain security. Part of upgrading your Windows NT servers to Windows 2000 Server is determining the role the servers will perform. Windows 2000 servers can have one of three roles: domain controller, member server, and stand-alone server. A *domain controller* provides user login authentication and security functions via Active Directory (AD) for the domain. A *member server* belongs to the domain but doesn't contain a copy of the AD database or provide login authentication or security for the domain. A *stand-alone server* is not part of a domain but is part of a workgroup.

In order to have a domain, you must have at least one domain controller. Additional domain controllers can be added to provide fault tolerance and load balancing for the AD.

You should plan the role of your servers prior to upgrading them. However, unlike Windows NT, the role of the server can be changed without reinstalling Windows 2000 Server. Table 13-1 contains a list of the upgrade paths that are available for the Windows 2000 Server roles.

TABLE 13-1

Windows 2000 Server Upgrade Paths

Role in Windows NT Domain	Role in Windows 2000 Server Domain
Primary domain controller	Domain controller
Backup domain controller	Domain controller or member server
Member server	Member server or stand-alone server
Stand-alone server	Member server or stand-alone server

When upgrading a Windows NT domain to Windows 2000, you don't have to upgrade all the servers at the same time. Windows 2000 domain controllers can operate in Mixed Mode, which allows them to be backward compatible with Windows NT backup domain controllers. This structure allows you to upgrade the domain incrementally and test the functionality at each step, solving problems as they come along. When you upgrade the domain, the existing functionality will be preserved and some of the new features available in Windows 2000 will be available. (Mixed mode is discussed later in the chapter.)

When upgrading a Windows NT domain to a Windows 2000 domain, you should perform the upgrade in steps:

1. Plan the upgrade from Windows NT to Windows 2000.
2. Start preparing for the upgrade from Windows NT to Windows 2000.
3. Upgrade the primary domain controller.
4. Upgrade the backup domain controllers.
5. Upgrade the member servers.

There are several areas you should consider when planning the upgrade from Windows NT to Windows 2000. You need to develop a plan for the DNS domain name structure, develop a plan for consolidating existing domain structures, and determine the location of user and machine accounts in Windows 2000.

The next step is to prepare for the upgrade. The first thing you should do is back up all hard disks of the servers that will be upgraded. You should also synchronize the domain, then take one of the backup domain controllers offline in case of an upgrade failure. This way, you can always bring the backup domain controller back online, if necessary, to revert back to the Windows NT domain. Prepare a test environment or pilot. In the test environment, test the following: user and group policies, user profiles, and logon scripts. When setting up the test environment, create scenarios that are easy to verify. Create users and groups similar to the existing Windows NT domain.

The last steps involve upgrading the servers in the domain. The primary domain controller needs to be upgraded first. Then upgrade the backup domain controllers. Finally, upgrade the member servers in the domain. When these steps are complete, you can put the domain controllers in a mode (native mode) that makes it purely a Windows 2000 domain. (Native mode is discussed later in the chapter.)

Importance of the Root Domain of the Forest

When organizing your current enterprise, you need to decide how to organize the Active Directory. The Active Directory comprises components that allow you to

FROM THE CLASSROOM

Changing the Role of the Server

One of the common questions asked is, how do you decide to make a Windows 2000 server a domain controller or a member server? Fortunately, in Windows 2000 Server, you can change the role of the server after installation. In Windows NT, you must reinstall the operating system in order to change the role of the server. Now, with Windows 2000, you can make a server a member server if you don't think you need it to act as a domain controller. Then, if your domain's load changes and you need another domain controller, you can simply promote one of your member servers to a domain controller. You no longer have to plan for this possibility far in advance. If your network appears to be operating nominally, you should make any new servers member servers, and as your load on the domain controllers increases, simply promote the appropriate servers.

With Windows 2000, you no longer have to make the decision as to which domain controller will be the primary domain controller. Windows 2000 does not make a distinction between primary and backup domain controllers. They are considered basically equal with an updatable copy of the Active Directory.

—Cameron Wakefield, MCSD, MCP

structure the AD so that it is logical and intuitive to users and administrators. The components are domains, organizational units (OUs), trees, forests, and schema.

Organizational units, or OUs, are used to organize objects within a domain. These objects can include user accounts, groups, computers, printers, and even other OUs. The hierarchy of OUs is independent of other domains. Each domain can have its own OU structure. This gives you the flexibility to organize each domain to match the purpose of the domain instead of a general structure to be used by all domains.

A *tree* is a grouping of one or more domains. It allows you to create a hierarchical grouping of domains that share a common contiguous namespace. This hierarchy allows global sharing of resources among domains in the tree.

All the domains in a tree share information and resources with a single directory. There is only one directory per tree. However, each domain manages its own subset of the directory that contains the user accounts for that domain. So, when a user logs into a domain, the user has access to all resources that are part of the tree, providing the user has the proper permissions.

The tree allows the domains to share a namespace as well as a hierarchical naming structure. When you add a domain to a tree that already exists, it becomes a *child* domain of one of the existing *parent* domains, to give you a *tree* structure. For example, if you have a tree that consists of one root domain named *syngress.com.,* when you add a new domain named *author, author* would become a child domain of the existing domain *syngress.com.*

The naming structure follows the DNS standards so that the domain name for the child domain uses a relative path name. So, in our example, the *author* domain would be accessed using *author.syngress.com.* When creating the tree, the domain tree name should map to your Internet domain name if it is to be accessed across the Internet.

As you might guess, a *forest* is a grouping of one or more trees. This group of trees does not share a common namespace; in fact, it forms a noncontiguous (or *discontiguous*) namespace. However, the trees in a forest share a common configuration, global catalog, and directory schema. All trees within a forest have a two-way transitive trust between the root remains. A trust allows all the trees to share resources and have common administrative functions. Such sharing capability allows the trees to operate independently of each other, with separate namespaces, yet still be able to communicate and share resources through trusts.

When you upgrade to Windows 2000, the first domain controller that is upgraded becomes the root domain of the forest. This domain contains the configuration and schema for the entire forest. This structure is normally created when you install the Active Directory services.

The root domain of the forest is the top of the hierarchical namespace. Once the forest root domain is created, it cannot be deleted, changed, or renamed without completely restarting your Active Directory structure. The root domain of the forest contains the Enterprise Administrators and Schema Administrators groups. These groups are forestwide and reside in the forest's root domain. The decision as to which domain will be the root domain should be considered carefully. In an extreme case in which all the domain controllers for the root domain crashed and could not be restored, the Enterprise Administrators and Schema Administrators group would be lost, and you would not be able to reinstall the forest root domain.

You have two basic options for choosing the root domain. You can either use an existing domain or create a new domain that serves only as the forest root. If you choose to use an existing domain, select the most critical domain in your enterprise, because that should be the domain with the highest level of fault tolerance. If it isn't, choose as your root domain the domain that does have the highest level of fault tolerance.

Choosing to create a new domain for the root domain of the forest has some advantages and disadvantages. The most obvious disadvantage is the overhead costs associated with a domain. In some cases, the advantages outweigh the overhead costs. Since the Enterprise Administrators and Schema Administrators groups reside in this domain, the domain administrators will be able to change the membership of these groups. If you have domain administrators who you do not want to have access to these groups, you should consider a separate domain.

Another reason for choosing to create a new domain is obsolescence. If you choose an existing domain and you later decide to remove the domain, you will not be able to completely remove it. Furthermore, is since the domain will be small, it will not take a large amount of resources to replicate it on the network, even across slow links in your enterprise. So, if you have a catastrophe in one location, the domain would still be available in the location to which it was replicated.

Restructuring Domains: Merging or Splitting

When you upgrade your Windows NT domain to Windows 2000, as much of your current domain configuration and settings are preserved as possible . *Domain restructure,* also referred to as *domain consolidation,* is the method of changing the structure of your domains. Restructuring your domains can allow you to take advantage of the new features of Windows 2000, such as greater scalability. Windows 2000 does not have the same limitation as the SAM account database in Windows NT. Without this limitation, you can merge domains into one larger domain. Using Windows 2000 OUs, you have finer granularity in delegating administrative tasks.

Administration in Windows 2000 is also easier than in Windows NT. Using OUs and domains with trusts, you can simplify the administration of the domains. Domain restructure could mean anything from changing the logical structure and/or hierarchy of your domains to merging and/or splitting existing domains. In Windows NT, you must use third-party tools to restructure your domains.

The two basic functions you can perform in Windows 2000 are moving user accounts from one domain to another while still maintaining access to the same resources you had prior to the move and moving domain controllers from one domain to another without reinstalling the operating system. Now, with Windows 2000, you can restructure your domains from within Windows. You need to decide if you want to leave the domain structure as it is or restructure it. So, when do you need to restructure? If you want to change some or all of your structure or if you cannot migrate to Windows 2000 without impacting your enterprise too much, you should probably consider restructuring your domains.

The next question is, when should you restructure your domains? If you can migrate the domains as they are, you should go ahead and migrate to Windows 2000 and then restructure the domains after the upgrade. If you cannot migrate the domains as they are or if the impact from migrating is too great on your enterprise, you should restructure the domains during the migration to Windows 2000. This allows you to create a new domain structure without any latency problems. Restructuring your domains is not an easy task and should be planned carefully. You can also restructure your domains later, after migration is complete. This option allows you to change the structure as your organization changes.

When you decide to restructure your domains, one of the important decisions will be whether or not to merge or split existing domains. In Windows 2000, there is no simple operation to split a domain. You must first create a new, empty domain and move the objects from the domain you want to split into the new domain. When moving a user from one domain to another, you must create a temporary password for the user in the new domain because user passwords are not preserved when they are moved. The user can change the password back to the original password, if desired. To create a new domain, you can either promote a Windows 2000 member server to a domain controller or upgrade a Windows NT 3.51 or 4.0 primary domain controller to a Windows 2000 Server domain controller.

Merging domains is similar to splitting domains in that you are moving user, group, and computer accounts to another domain. Merging domains allows easier administration by decreasing the number of trusts that must be created and can reduce the number of domain controllers required. Windows 2000 domains can contain significantly more user, group, and computer accounts. To merge domains, you simply move all the objects from one domain to another.

Windows 2000 facilitates domain restructuring by providing the following capabilities:

- User and group accounts can be moved from one domain to another with their security identity preserved.
- You can move a domain controller to another domain by first demoting it to a member server.
- Remote administration tools (MOVETREE, SIDWALK, NETDOM, etc.) are available to move computers from one domain to another.

CERTIFICATION OBJECTIVE 13.02

Upgrading a Server from Windows NT

When you have existing Windows NT servers on your network, you have to decide whether to upgrade the servers or install Windows 2000 Server as a new installation for dual-booting. In this section, we talk about upgrading an existing Windows NT server to Windows 2000 Server. When you upgrade an existing operating system, you install it in the same partition and folder in which the existing operating system is installed. When you perform an upgrade, Windows 2000 automatically installs in the same folder as the existing operating system. When upgrading from Windows NT, you can upgrade from the following versions: Windows NT 3.51, Windows NT 4.0, and Windows NT 4.0 Terminal Server.

exam Watch

If you have an existing Windows NT 4.0 Server Enterprise Edition, you cannot upgrade to Windows 2000 Server; you must upgrade it to Windows 2000 Advanced Server or Windows 2000 Datacenter Server.

Prior to any type of installation, you should verify that the computer hardware meets the minimum requirements and is on the HCL. You also need to verify that the software you are using is compatible. To help determine the compatibility, you can use the Windows 2000 Compatibility Tool to generate a hardware and software compatibility report. This tool is run during setup, but you should run it before running Setup so you can fix any potential problems ahead of time.

There are two ways to use the Compatibility Tool. First, you can type **Winnt32 /checkupgradeonly**. This will start Setup to generate a compatibility report without starting installation of Windows 2000. This command generates a report named WINNT32.LOG in the <systemroot> folder. Or you can run the Windows 2000 Readiness Analyzer, which generates the report without running Setup. This tool can be downloaded from Microsoft at www.microsoft.com/windows2000/upgrade/compat. The report provides a listing of the hardware and software that is found to be incompatible with Windows 2000. However, the Readiness Analyzer will not work if you have a dual-boot configuration with Windows 95, Windows 98, and Windows NT.

Upgrade Paths

When upgrading a Windows NT server, you have several options as to how to perform the upgrade. You can upgrade from the Windows 2000 Server CD-ROM, from a distribution server on the network, or by using the UNATTEND.TXT answer file. Remember, only Windows NT 3.51 Server, Windows NT 4.0 Server, and earlier (beta) versions of Windows 2000 Server can be upgraded to Windows 2000 Server or Advanced Server.

Upgrading with a Compact Disc

To upgrade an existing version of Windows NT to Windows 2000 Server, insert the Windows 2000 Server CD-ROM in the CD-ROM drive and, if Autorun is on, it will automatically start Setup. Alternatively, you can run WINNT32.EXE from the i386 folder on the CD-ROM. You cannot upgrade using the boot disks or when booting from the CD-ROM. You must upgrade by starting Setup from Winnt32 or using Autorun on the CD-ROM. When you start using Autorun, you will see the window shown in Figure 13-1.

When you click the Yes button to upgrade to Windows 2000 Server, the program will check to see if you can upgrade. For example, if you are running Windows 98,

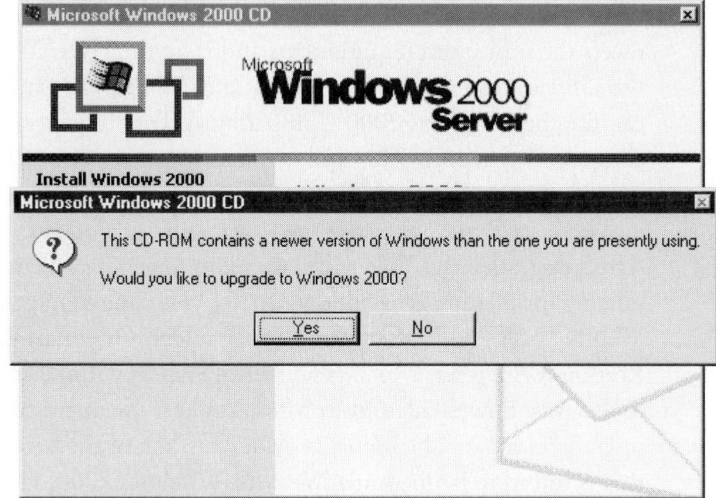

FIGURE 13-1 Upgrading to Windows 2000 Server

you cannot upgrade to Windows 2000 Server. If you try, you will get the message box shown in Figure 13-2.

If you click OK, Windows will bring you to the Setup screen, but the only option available will be to perform a clean installation, as shown on the screen in Figure 13-3.

If your computer can be upgraded, you can choose the upgrade option and run Setup to upgrade your computer to Windows 2000 Server.

Upgrading from a Network Distribution

Upgrading to Windows 2000 Server is basically the same as from the CD-ROM, except you start the installation by running the WINNT32.EXE program from a distribution server. You still have the same limitations and requirements as with the CD-ROM installation, plus you have to be able to access the shared folder where the Setup files are located.

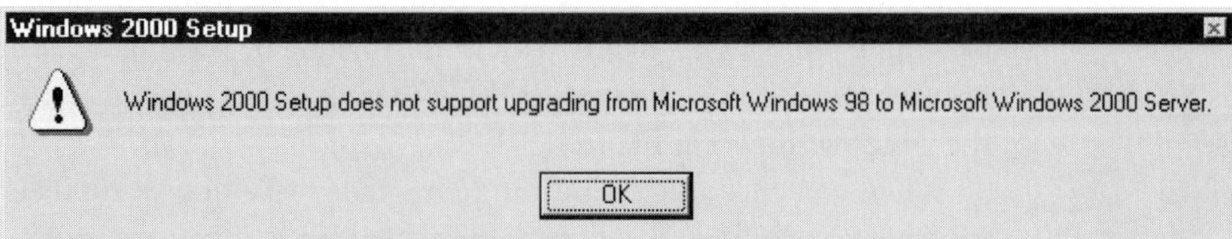

FIGURE 13-2 The message that you cannot upgrade from Windows 98

FIGURE 13-3

The screen giving you the ability to install a new copy of Windows 2000

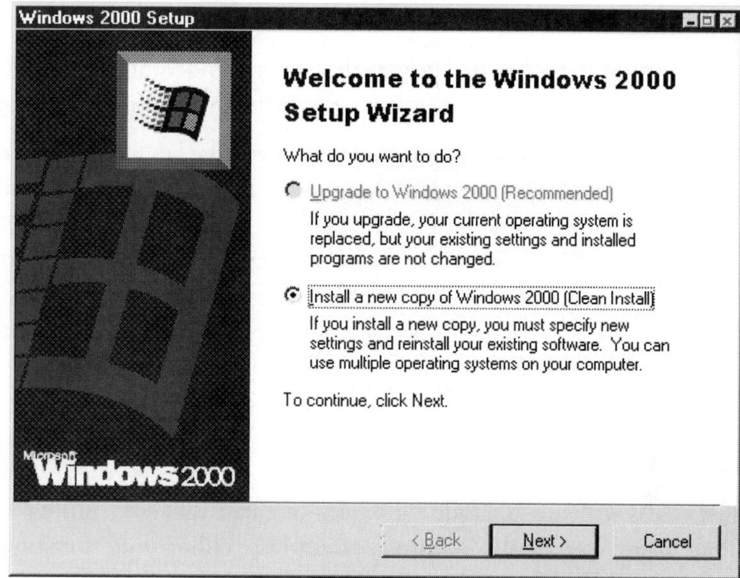

Upgrading Using UNATTEND.TXT

You can also upgrade to Windows 2000 Server with an unattended installation. Instead of prompting the user, Setup retrieves answers to the questions from an answer file called UNATTEND.TXT. You can use the WINNT.EXE and WINNT32.EXE programs to perform an unattended installation of Windows 2000 Server, as detailed in Chapter 12.

Minimum Hardware Requirements

The hardware requirements for upgrading to Windows 2000 Server are basically the same as for performing a clean installation of Windows 2000 Server. The primary difference is that if you are upgrading a Windows NT domain controller, you have to allow additional hard disk space for upgrading the domain. How much space is needed depends on the size of the domain you are upgrading. You should also ensure that the hardware is on the Hardware Compatibility List (HCL). The following is a list of the basic hardware requirements for upgrading to Windows 2000 Server.

- A 133MHz Pentium or higher CPU.

- Only up to four CPUs are supported.
- 256 MB of RAM is the recommended minimum; 4GB of RAM is the maximum; 128 MB of RAM is the minimum supported.
- To install Windows 2000 Server, the Setup process needs approximately 1GB of free space. You need a minimum of 671MB of free space, with 2GB recommended on the partition on which Windows 2000 Server will be installed. Once Setup is complete, the temporary files are deleted and less free space is then required by Windows 2000 Server. Remember to allow additional disk space for upgrading the domain user account database and any additional components you install.

Rollback Strategy

As with any upgrade, problems can arise that sometimes require going back to the previous state. This also applies to upgrading your domain to Windows 2000. You need to create a plan to roll back your network to its previous state if the upgrade to Windows 2000 fails.

When upgrading the domain controllers, do not upgrade the backup domain controller (BDC) that has the current directory database. Make sure the BDC is synchronized with the primary domain controller (PDC), and then take it offline. Leave the BDC as is until the upgrade is successful. If you run into problems during the upgrade, you can bring the BDC back online, promote it to the PDC, and recover the Windows NT state. If the upgrade is successful, you can upgrade the BDC to Windows 2000.

Determining a Strategy and Performing Upgrades of Domain Controllers to Windows 2000

Prior to upgrading a domain controller to Windows 2000, you should prepare for the upgrade. If you have any third-party network services or virus programs, remove them prior to the upgrade. If you have an uninterruptible power supply (UPS) connected to the computer, remove the serial cable prior to the upgrade, because the detection process can have adverse affects on some UPS devices. Finally, set up your BIOS. If you have any ISA bus devices that are not plug-and-play compliant, reserve their IRQs in the BIOS prior to upgrading. If you don't, you will sometimes get IRQ conflicts.

Prior to upgrading the domain controllers, you need to perform the following tasks: If the WINS service is running, disable it so that the WINS database can be converted to Windows 2000. If the DHCP service is running, disable it so that the DHCP database can be converted to Windows 2000.

In Windows 2000 networks, there is no distinction between primary and backup domain controllers. All domain controllers have equal status. In Windows NT, only the primary domain controller has a domain database that can be updated. The backup domain controllers have only a copy of the domain database. In Windows 2000, all the domain controllers have a writable domain database that can be updated. Furthermore, in Windows 2000, all domain controllers should use the NTFS file system.

on the job

If the server has any partitions that are using the FAT or FAT32 file system, it will not be able to use many security features available in Windows 2000. You will not be able to use file-level security or prevent local access to files. It is recommended that you convert all partitions to NTFS.

Upgrading Primary Domain Controllers

When upgrading your domain to Windows 2000, the PDC must be upgraded first. It is also recommended that you synchronize all the BDCs prior to upgrading the PDCs. When the PDC is upgraded, the Active Directory will be installed. Part of installing the AD is choosing between creating the first tree in a forest or creating a new tree in an existing forest. You must also choose between creating a new domain or a child domain. Also during the upgrade, you have the option to select where three critical files are located. These files are the database that contains the user accounts, the log file, and the system volume, or SYSVOL. The user account database and the log file should be stored on a partition using the NTFS file system. The system volume must be stored on a partition with NTFS.

When the PDC is upgraded to Windows 2000 Server, it is backward compatible with other servers and clients that are not running Windows 2000. It emulates the Windows NT 4.0 PDC for these computers and acts as a Windows 2000 domain controller for Windows 2000 servers and clients. The contents of the Windows NT account database and Security Account Manager (SAM) are copied into the AD during the upgrade. Even if you made changes to user accounts or groups, these changes are replicated to any existing Windows NT BDCs that still exist in the domain.

exam Watch

When upgrading your domain from Windows NT to Windows 2000, you must upgrade the PDC first.

Upgrading Backup Domain Controllers

Upgrading BDCs to Windows 2000 is the same process you used for the PDC. You do not have to upgrade all the BDCs at the same time. You can upgrade them incrementally, as needed. Make sure you back up the server prior to upgrading. When you upgrade, make sure the PDC that was upgraded is running and available on the network. This server is used as a template to copy for the BDCs when they are upgraded. After upgrading each BDC, make sure it is working correctly before upgrading the next BDC.

Switching from Mixed to Native Mode

Windows 2000 domains can operate in two modes: Mixed Mode or Native Mode. *Mixed Mode* allows Windows NT domain controllers to still operate in a Windows 2000 domain. The Windows NT domain controllers can be version 3.51 or version 4.0. The PDC has to be upgraded first when you are upgrading to Windows 2000 Server. Mixed Mode allows the remaining BDCs to still operate as domain controllers. The PDC uses the AD but exposes the data as a flat store, as in Windows NT.

When in Mixed Mode, the domain still uses master replication with a Windows 2000 PDC. The Windows NT BDCs replicate from the Windows 2000 server, as did the Windows NT PDC. When you are operating in Mixed Mode, some Windows 2000 functionality will not be available. You will not be able to use group nesting. You can still use transitive trusts; however, NT domain controllers will not be able to use Kerberos authentication. It will only be available between Windows 2000 computers. (These topics are covered later in the book.) Mixed Mode is the default mode.

Native Mode allows only Windows 2000 domain controllers to operate in the domain. When all domain controllers for the domain are upgraded to Windows 2000 Server, you can switch to Native Mode. This allows you to use transitive trusts and the group-nesting features of Windows 2000. When switching to Native Mode, ensure you no longer need to operate in Mixed Mode, because you cannot switch back to Mixed Mode once you are in Native Mode.

The Mixed and Native Modes refer only to the domain controllers. When you switch to Native Mode, clients that are not running a Windows 2000 operating system can still be part of the domain. When you switch to Native Mode, the domain uses Active Directory exclusively. This means you are not able to add Windows NT backup domain controllers to the network. You are only able to add

Windows 2000 Server domain controllers. Now all domain controllers have a master replicated copy of Active Directory. This means that there is no longer a PDC. All the domain controllers are able to update the directory.

exam Watch

Once you switch to Native Mode, you cannot switch back to Mixed Mode.

There may be situations in which you cannot switch to Native Mode. There may be cases when a BDC cannot be upgraded. Such an instance could be caused by an application that has to run on a domain controller but that is not compatible with Windows 2000 domain controllers. Another possible reason is physical security. Say a BDC is stored in a location that could be subject to attack. A Windows NT BDC has a read-only copy of the user account database and SAM. In Windows 2000, all controllers have a master copy of the Active Directory and therefore can be updated. If you determine this situation is an unnecessary security risk, you could leave the domain controllers in Mixed Mode. However, you should consider moving the computer to a more secure location.

Switching to Native Mode is a manual operation performed by the administrator. You perform it via the Active Directory Domains and Trusts dialog box. See Exercise 13-2 on how to switch mode.

EXERCISE 13-2

Switching from Mixed Mode to Native Mode

1. From the Start menu, select Programs | Administrative Tools | Active Directory Domains and Trusts.
2. Right-click the domain and select Properties. This will bring up the Properties dialog box.
3. Click the General tab to open it.
4. Click the Change Mode button. You are given a warning that when you change to Native Mode, you cannot switch back to Mixed Mode.
5. Click the Yes button on the warning message box.
6. Click the OK button to close the Properties dialog box.

Upgrade and Promote Member Servers to Windows 2000

When you are upgrading an existing domain to Windows 2000, you can upgrade existing Windows NT member servers before, during, or after the domain upgrade process. To upgrade, you must be currently running the Windows NT 3.51 or 4.0 Server operating system. If the computer has a dual-boot configuration, you must be running the operating system that you want to upgrade when you begin installation.

To start installation, insert the Windows 2000 Server CD-ROM. When prompted, click "upgrade to Windows 2000" and follow the instructions to upgrade the existing server. When you have finished the upgrade, the member server will still be a member of the domain or workgroup of which it was previously a member. The local user and group accounts are stored in the registry of the server and are not moved to the Active Directory. In the final phase of setup, all applications and operating system configuration settings from Windows NT will be available in Windows 2000.

on the Job

If the member server you are upgrading is a DHCP server, you must authorize the DHCP Server service in Active Directory or the service will not start. Authorization is not automatically granted when you upgrade to Windows 2000.

Once a member server has been upgraded to Windows 2000 Server, it can be promoted to a domain controller. To promote it, use the Active Directory Installation Wizard (DCPROMO.EXE). When you have promoted the server to a domain controller, all the local user and group accounts are then added to the Active Directory while maintaining permissions to local resources. In Windows NT, you had to reinstall the operating system to "promote" a member server to a domain controller. Exercise 13-3 walks you through upgrading a member server to a domain controller. This exercise demonstrates how to create a new domain from an existing member server.

EXERCISE 13-3

Upgrading a Member Server to a Domain Controller

1. From the Start menu, select Run.
2. In the Run dialog box, type **dcpromo,** as shown in the following illustration, and click the OK button.

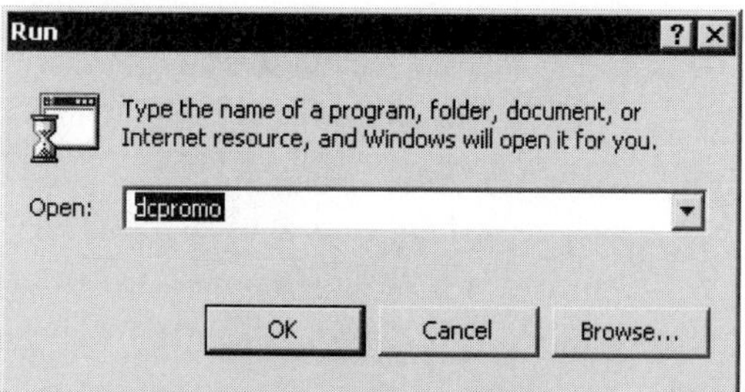

3. When the Welcome to the Active Directory Installation Wizard screen appears, as shown in the following illustration, click Next.

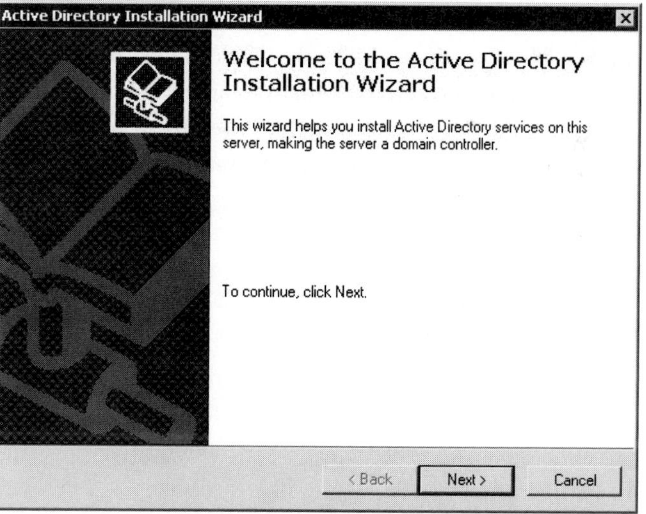

4. Now you will decide whether to make the server a domain controller for a new domain or make it a domain controller for an existing domain. For this

we will create a new domain. Select "Domain controller for a new domain," as shown in the following illustration, and click Next.

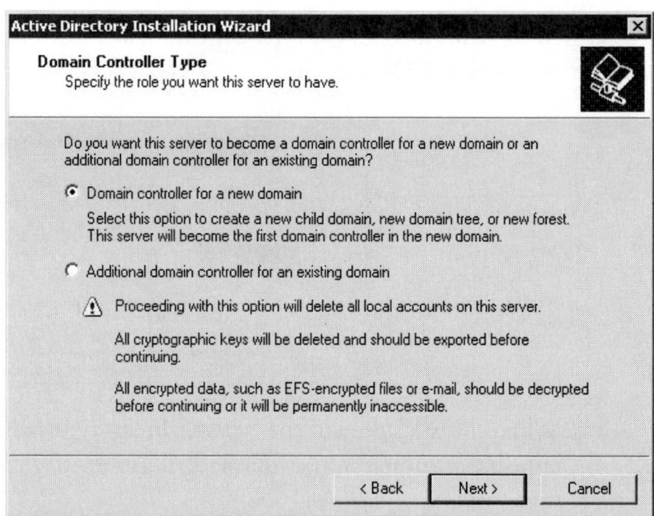

5. Next you have to choose between creating a new tree or adding the new domain as a child domain to an existing tree. In this exercise, we will create a new tree. Make sure the "Create a new domain tree" option is selected, as shown in the following illustration, and click Next .

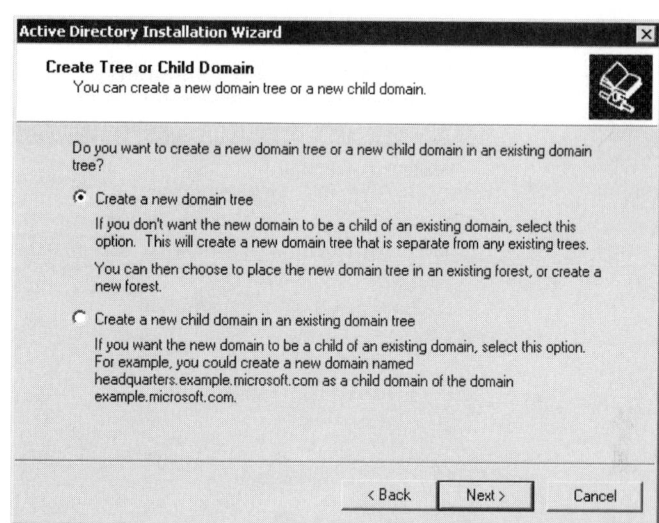

6. You can either create a new forest or add the new tree to an existing forest. For this exercise, we will create a new forest. Make sure the "Create a new forest of domain trees" option is selected, as shown in the following illustration, and click Next .

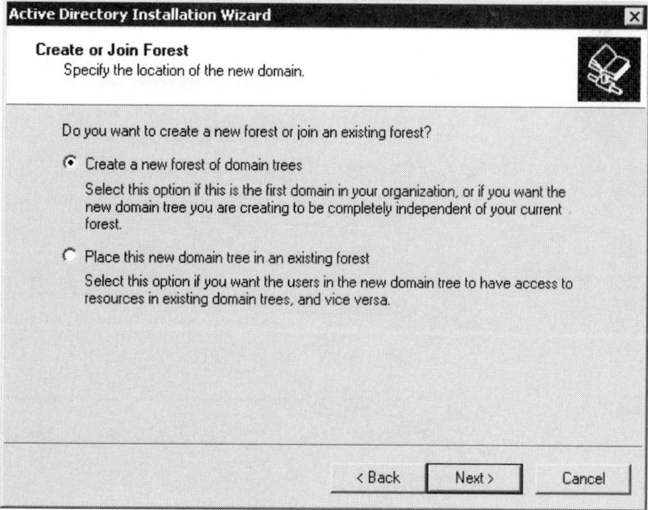

7. Now enter the NetBIOS name for the domain. Enter **CAMERON**, as shown in the following illustration, and click Next.

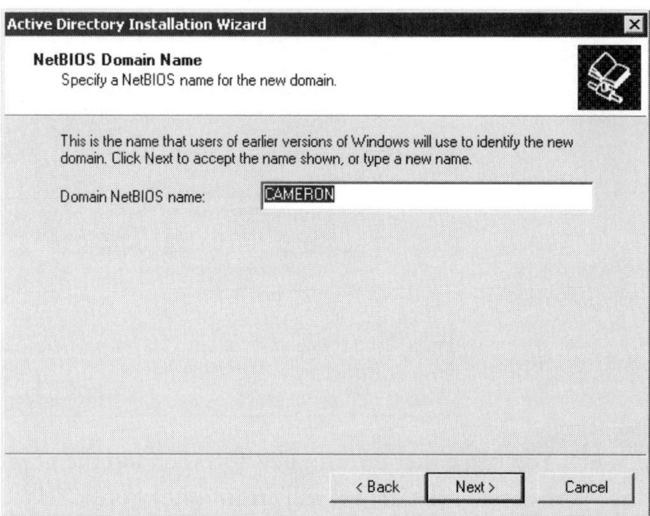

8. The next screen allows you to choose where to store the database and log. These can be stored on any partition. Accept the defaults, as shown in the following illustration, and click Next.

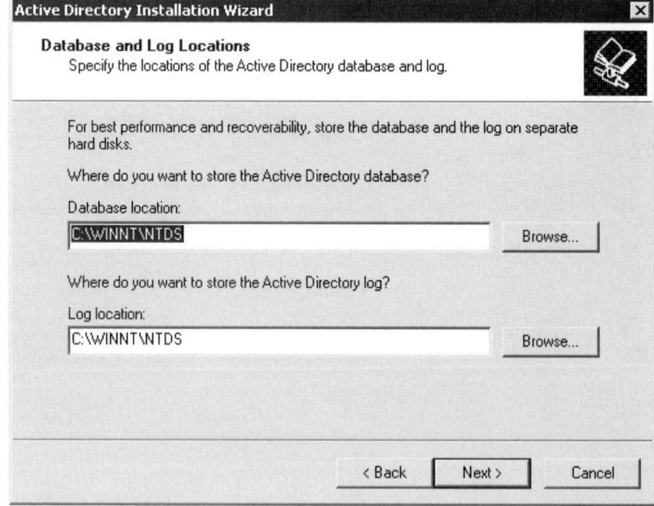

9. The Sysvol folder contains the domain's public files. It can be stored only on a partition formatted with NTFS 5.0. Ensure that the path shown is on an NTFS partition, as shown in the following illustration, and click Next .

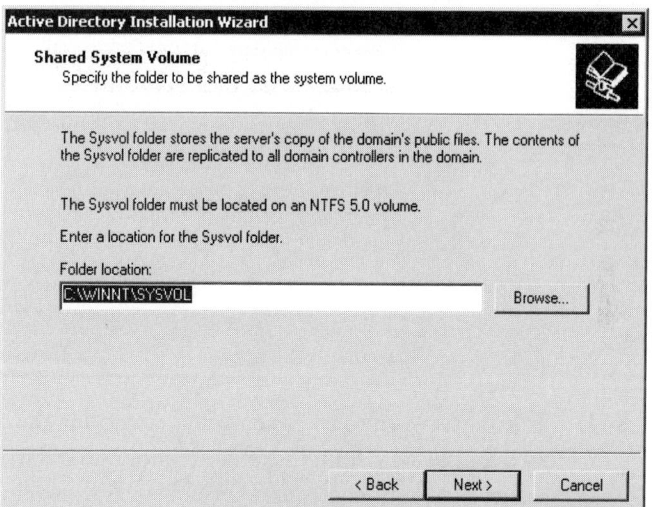

10. Now you must choose whether or not you want the permissions to be backward compatible. Make sure the "Permissions compatible with pre-Windows 2000 servers" option is selected, as shown in the following illustration, and click Next.

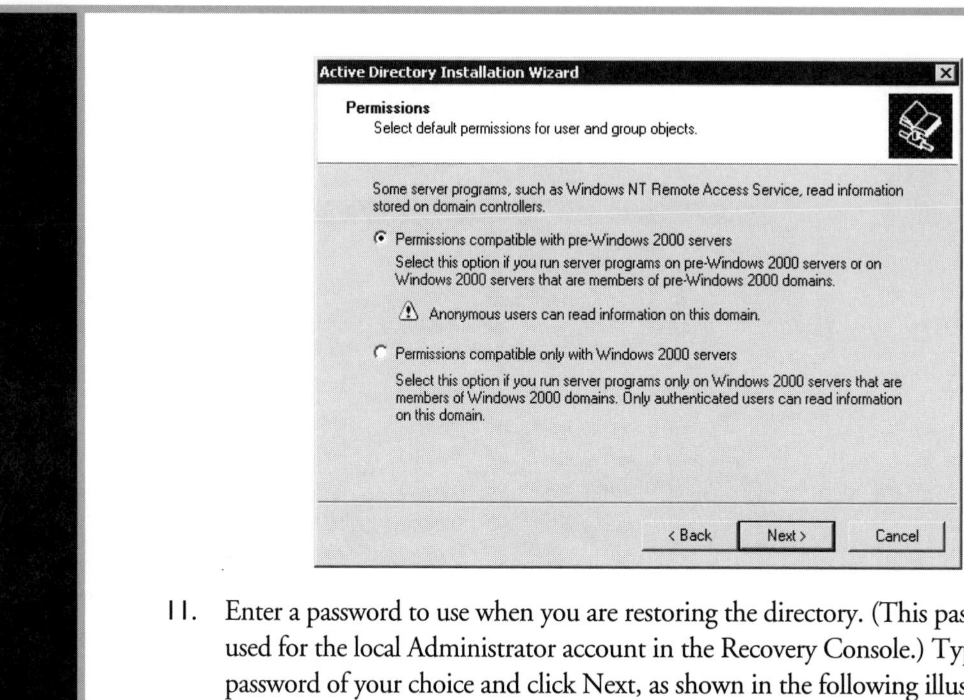

11. Enter a password to use when you are restoring the directory. (This password is used for the local Administrator account in the Recovery Console.) Type in a password of your choice and click Next, as shown in the following illustration.

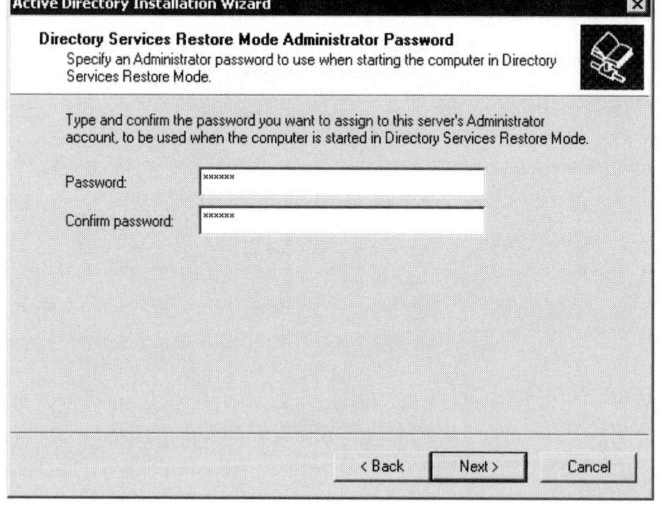

12. A summary of your choices is displayed. Review the options, as shown in the following illustration, and click Next.

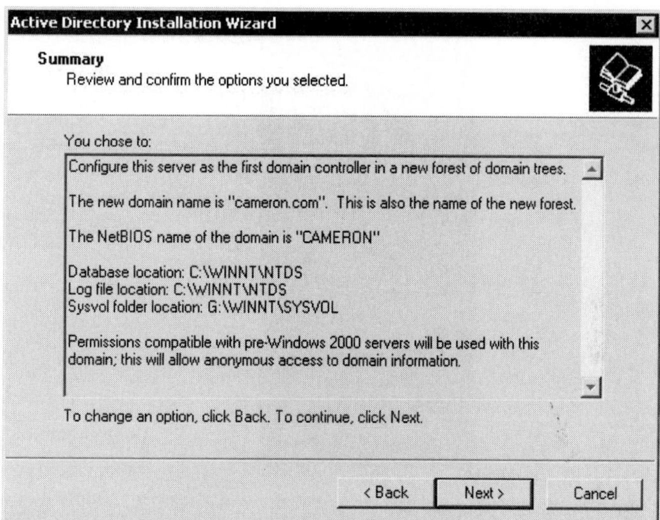

13. A splash screen is displayed while the Active Directory is installed, as shown in the following illustration.

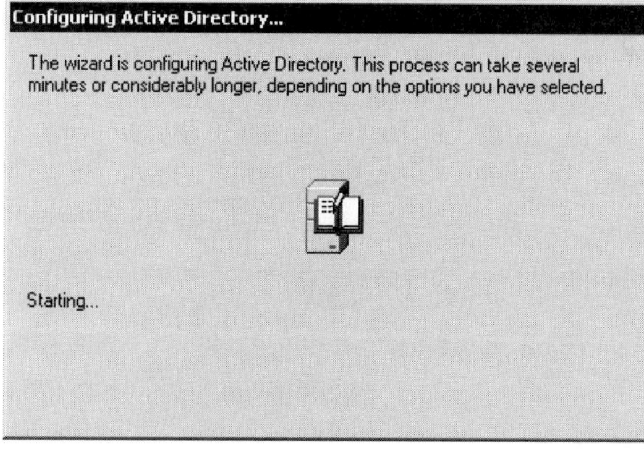

14. When the installation is complete, the Completing the Active Directory Installation screen appears, as shown in the following illustration. Click Finish.

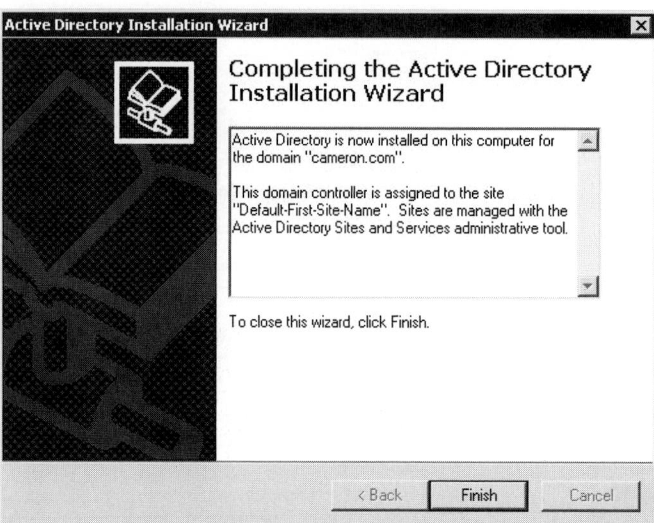

15. The last step is to restart the computer. Click Restart Now, as shown in the following illustration.

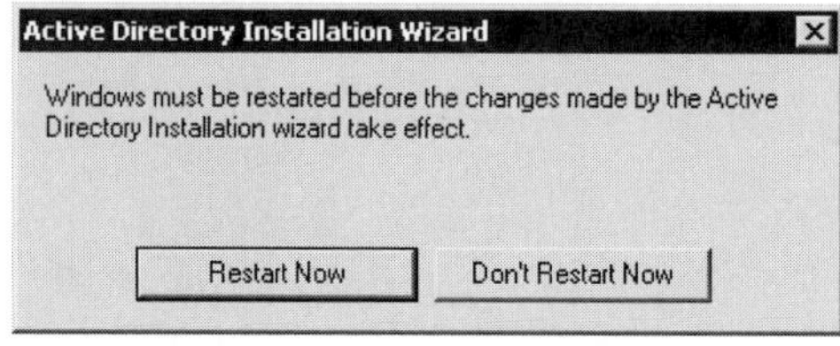

SCENARIO & SOLUTION	
You have a domain that you upgraded to Windows 2000 that has users from two different departments. You decide to split up the domain. How can you accomplish this?	First, create a new domain. Once the domain is created, you can move users to the new domain, and they will still have their security IDs.
You are preparing to install Windows 2000 and you want to determine if your computer is compatible with Windows 2000. How can you do this?	You can run the WINNT32.EXE program with the /checkupgradeonly switch. This starts Setup to generate a compatibility report without starting installation of Windows 2000. It generates a report named WINNT32.LOG in the <systemroot> folder.

CERTIFICATION OBJECTIVE 13.03

Deploying Service Packs

Periodically, Microsoft releases service packs for its operating systems. A service pack typically contains bug fixes, security fixes, systems administration tools, drivers, and additional components. Microsoft recommends installing the latest service packs as they are released. In addition, as a new feature in Windows 2000, you do not have to reinstall components after installing a service pack, as you did with Windows NT. You can also see what service pack is currently installed on a computer by running the WINVER utility program. WINVER brings up the About Windows dialog box. It displays the version of Windows and the version of the service pack you are running.

To install a service pack, use the UPDATE.EXE program. When a service pack is applied, Windows 2000 tracks which service pack was installed and which files were added and/or replaced. This way, when a component or service is added or removed, if any of the required files were included in the service pack, the operating system automatically retrieves those files from the service pack. This feature prevents you from having to reinstall the service pack.

Testing Service Packs

Prior to deploying service packs to the enterprise, you first should perform some testing. Some applications have problems running after new service packs are installed.

To test new service packs, create test environments for each computer configuration in your enterprise. Make sure the test computers have the same hardware and are running the same software and performing the same operations as the computers in the enterprise. Testing a service pack this way allows you to find potential errors prior to deploying a service pack throughout your enterprise.

Integrating Service Packs with Distribution Images

You can include service packs with a distribution image. This feature is called *service pack slipstreaming*. Using slipstreaming, you can install Windows 2000 with the service pack already applied to the installation files on a CD-ROM or distribution folder. You do not have to apply the service pack after installation of Windows 2000 Server. To apply a service pack to distribution files, use the UPDATE.EXE file with the /slip switch. This combination overwrites the existing distribution files with the service pack files.

CERTIFICATION OBJECTIVE 13.04

Troubleshooting Failed Installations

Once in a while, you will have some problems trying to install Windows 2000 Server. Problems can also occur when you are restarting the computer for the first time after installation is complete. When these problems occur, you need to be able to detect and solve them.

Resolving Common Problems

If the CD-ROM you are installing from has errors on it, you will not be able to install from it. You must obtain another CD-ROM. If you don't have an additional copy, contact Microsoft or your vendor. Some CD-ROM drives are not supported by Windows 2000 Server. If this is the case, you must either replace the CD-ROM drive with a drive that is supported or choose a different installation method, such as a network installation. When you install Windows 2000 Server, you must ensure that you have enough free disk space. If you don't, the Setup program can create a new partition if there is any space on the hard disk. If there is no space, you can delete and create partitions as needed to so that you can create a partition large enough to install Windows 2000 Server. To free some space, you can also add another hard drive or delete some applications that are not being used.

When installing Windows 2000 Server, you can sometimes get an error message when trying to locate the domain controller. Check that you entered the correct domain name and that a domain controller is running on the network. In addition, verify that the DNS server is running. If you cannot locate a domain controller, join a workgroup and then later, after installation, when you can locate a domain controller, join the domain.

Sometimes problems show up after installation is complete and you are starting Windows 2000 Server for the first time. If Windows 2000 Server fails to start, verify that all the hardware is on the HCL and that all hardware is being detected. Sometimes a dependency service fails to start. If this occurs, verify that the correct network adapter is being installed and check the configuration settings (e.g., the transceiver setting). In addition, verify that you have installed the correct protocol and that the computer name is unique on the network.

Setup Logs

During the GUI phase of setup, log files are created. These log files are located in the directory to which Windows 2000 is being installed. Four log files are created:

- **SETUPACT.LOG.** The Action log file contains details about the files that are copied during setup.
- **SETUPERR.LOG.** The Error log file contains details about errors that occurred during setup.

- **SETUPAPI.LOG.** This log file contains details about the device driver files that were copied during setup. This log can be used to facilitate troubleshooting device installations. The file contains errors and warnings along with a time stamp for each issue.
- **SETUPLOG.TXT.** This log file contains additional information about the device driver files that were copied during setup.

Let's take a look at the contents of your setup logs in Exercise 13-4.

EXERCISE 13-4

Looking at the Setup Logs

1. Open My Computer.
2. Open the C: drive. (If you installed Windows 2000 Server on a different drive, open that drive instead. The rest of the exercise assumes you're using drive C:. As you read, replace references to drive C: with the appropriate drive as necessary.)
3. Open the Winnt folder. (Again, this exercise assumes you used Winnt as the installation folder name. You can replace it if you installed to another folder name.)
4. Open the SETUPACT.LOG file for review. An example of the first few lines of the log file follows. When you double-click the log files, the log file is opened in Notepad by default:

```
GUI mode Setup has started.
C:\WINNT\Driver Cache\i386\driver.cab was copied to
C:\WINNT\System32\storprop.dll.
C:\$WIN_NT$.~LS\i386\SPOOLSV.EX_ was copied to
C:\WINNT\System32\SPOOLSV.EXE.
```

5. Close SETUPACT.LOG.

6. Open the SETUPAPI.LOG file for review. The following is an example of the first few lines of the log file:

```
[2000/02/21 13:25:25 324.12]
Munged cmdline: setup -newsetup
EXE name: C:\WINNT\system32\setup.exe
Installing Device Class:
{6BDD1FC1-810F-11D0-BEC7-08002BE2092F} 1394.
Class install completed with no errors.
[2000/02/21 13:25:26 324.15]
Installing Device Class:
{72631e54-78a4-11d0-bcf7-00aa00b7b32a} Battery.
Class install completed with no errors.
[2000/02/21 13:25:26 324.20]
Installing Device Class:
{4D36E965-E325-11CE-BFC1-08002BE10318} CDROM.
Class install completed with no errors.
```

7. Close SETUPAPI.LOG.
8. Open the SETUPERR.LOG file for review. If there weren't any errors during setup, this file is empty.
9. Close SETUPERR.LOG.
10. Open the SETUPLOG.TXT file for review. The following is an example of the first few lines of the log file:

```
13:24:58.559 syssetup.c @ 1214 Setup: (non-critical error):
Failed load of ismif32.dll.
13:24:59.510 ctls.c @ 807 SETUP: Enter RegisterOleControls
13:24:59.520 ctls.c @ 860 SETUP: back from OleInitialize
13:24:59.520 ctls.c @ 879 SETUP: filename for file to
register is rsabase.dll
13:24:59.520 ctls.c @ 433 SETUP: loading dll...
13:24:59.560 ctls.c @ 504 SETUP: ...dll loaded
13:24:59.560 ctls.c @ 533 SETUP: registering...
13:24:59.560 ctls.c @ 581 SETUP: ...registered
```

11. Close SETUPLOG.TXT.

CERTIFICATION SUMMARY

In this chapter, we talked about upgrading your existing Windows NT network to Windows 2000. The most important task in upgrading your network is planning ahead. Plan your networking requirements such as your network protocol and naming services. You also need to make sure you understand the new features available in Windows 2000 so that you can decide how to structure your domains. You need to decide on a root domain and whether or not to restructure your domains.

When upgrading your Windows NT Server to Windows 2000 Server, you can use a variety of methods: the Windows 2000 Server CD-ROM, install across the network, and even perform unattended installations. One crucial aspect of upgrading is verifying that your hardware is compatible with Windows 2000. You should check the HCL for compatibility. Prior to starting your upgrade, create a rollback plan in case of a failure while upgrading.

When upgrading your domain controllers, you must upgrade the primary domain controller (PDC) first. Once the PDC is successfully upgraded, you can upgrade your backup domain controllers (BDCs). You don't have to upgrade them all at once. Windows 2000 Server domain controllers can operate in Mixed Mode to allow Windows NT BDCs to still operate in the domain. Once all your Windows NT domain controllers are upgraded to Windows 2000, you should switch to Native Mode, which allows you to utilize all the features of Windows 2000. In addition, you can promote and demote Windows 2000 Server between the member server role and domain controller role using the DCPROMO.EXE command-line utility.

Windows 2000 has made using service packs easier. You can use slipstreaming to integrate service packs with Windows 2000 distribution images. Another new feature is that you don't have to reinstall a service pack after adding components or installing applications. Windows 2000 automatically uses the existing service packs files.

On the rare occasion that a Windows 2000 installation fails, you should understand the common causes of failure and how to solve the problems. In the event of more complicated failures, you can use the Setup log files to assist you in troubleshooting.

✓ TWO-MINUTE DRILL

Planning a Network Upgrade to Windows 2000

- ❑ Plan your upgrade in detail prior to starting.
- ❑ Determine your DHCP and WINS requirements.
- ❑ You can provide a dynamic IP address using either DHCP or APIPA.
- ❑ DNS provides name resolution to IP addresses.
- ❑ DNS allows users to remember names rather than IP addresses.
- ❑ You should provide WINS when you are supporting clients not running Windows 2000.

Upgrading a Server from Windows NT

- ❑ Only Windows NT 3.51 and 4.0 Servers can be upgraded to Windows 2000 Server.
- ❑ The System volume (SYSVOL) must be stored on an NTFS 5.0 partition.
- ❑ The BDCs can be upgraded incrementally. You do not have to upgrade them all at once.
- ❑ Mixed Mode makes your domain backward compatible with Windows NT BDCs.
- ❑ Native Mode allows you to use all the features of Windows 2000 domains and supports only Windows 2000 domain controllers.
- ❑ You can switch from Mixed Mode to Native Mode, but you cannot switch from Native Mode to Mixed Mode.

Deploying Service Packs

- Microsoft periodically releases updates to Windows operating systems.
- These updates, called *service packs,* contain bug and security fixes.
- Service packs are installed using the UPDATE.EXE program.
- You don't have to reinstall service packs after adding or deleting components or services.
- You should test your service pack for software compatibility prior to deploying it.
- You can include a service pack in a distribution image.

Troubleshooting Failed Installations

- If the installation CD-ROM is damaged, you have to replace it.
- Verify that the DNS server is running.
- SETUPACT.LOG contains details about the files that are copied during setup.
- SETUPERR.LOG contains details about errors that occurred during setup.
- SETUPAPI.LOG contains details about the device driver files that were copied during setup.
- SETUPLOG.TXT contains details additional information about the device driver files that were copied during setup.

Part IV

Windows 2000 Network Administration

CHAPTERS

14

Administering Shared Resources

CERTIFICATION OBJECTIVES

14.01 Monitoring, Configuring, Troubleshooting, and Controlling Access to Files, Folders, and Shared Folders

14.02 Monitoring, Configuring, Troubleshooting, and Controlling Access to Dfs Resources

14.03 Monitoring, Configuring, Troubleshooting, and Controlling Access to Printers

✓ Two-Minute Drill

Providing access to file and print resources is an essential function of a network. This chapter will introduce you to or reacquaint you with basic file and folder sharing, setting up a Dfs sharing tree, and print resource sharing and configuration. While the focus of this chapter is on Windows 2000 Server, some of these functions can be performed on Windows 2000 Professional as well, and there may be appropriate times to do so.

Windows 2000 provides all the necessary tools to configure and maintain these services. No third-party tools are necessary for administering these resources, even though some third-party tools may make management of these resources easier. This chapter will focus solely on the default tools provided with Windows 2000 Server to help you prepare for certification.

CERTIFICATION OBJECTIVE 14.01

Monitoring, Configuring, Troubleshooting, and Controlling Access to Files, Folders, and Shared Folders

Windows 2000 provides a greater file system security model than has been available in most other Microsoft operating systems. Many of the security features in Windows 2000 were introduced in Windows NT, but these features are more mature in Windows 2000, and new features have been added to further solidify the security model.

Windows 2000 file security is available only on volumes that have been formatted as NTFS volumes. Even though Windows 2000 can access FAT16 and FAT 32 volumes, only NTFS partitions provide any security features. This section of the chapter will cover the use of NTFS permissions for local folder and shared folder security.

Local Security on Files and Folders

Even though Windows 2000 provides different profile settings for each user who logs on to a Windows 2000 computer, file system security is not contained within the profile. In other words, unless specific NTFS permissions have been set for local folders on a Windows 2000 workstation, any user who logs in on the workstation can access the entire file system on the computer. Windows 2000 does provide some protection for the WINNT folder on the system volume so that non-administrator logins cannot modify certain system files.

NTFS Folder Permissions

NTFS folder permissions define a user's access to a folder and its contents. Table 14-1 lists the various NTFS folder permissions and their functions.

NTFS File Permissions

NTFS file permissions are applied to individual files within a folder and can be more restrictive or more lenient than the permissions set on the parent folder. Table 14-2 lists the various NTFS file permissions and their functions.

TABLE 14-1 NTFS Folder Permissions

Permission	Function
Read	Read file/folder contents Read attributes and extended attributes on files and folders Read permissions on files and folders
Write	Create, write to, and append to files Create new folders Write attributes and extended attributes on files and folders Read permissions on files and folders
List Folder Contents	Same as Read Traverse folders
Read & Execute	Same as List Folder Contents Execute applications
Modify	Same as Read & Execute All permissions for Write Delete files
Full Control	Same as Modify Delete subfolders and files Change permissions Take ownership

TABLE 14-2 NTFS File Permissions

Permission	Function
Read	Read file contents Read attributes and extended attributes on files Read permissions on files
Write	Create, write to, and append to files Write attributes and extended attributes on files Read permissions on files
Read & Execute	Same as Read Execute applications
Modify	Same as Read & Execute All permissions for Write Delete files
Full Control	Same as Modify Change permissions Take ownership

Assigning NTFS Permissions

NTFS permissions can be applied at the user or group level. Generally, it is best to use group memberships to assign NTFS permissions, but that does not preclude setting individual user permissions on a file or folder. When a user is a member of multiple groups that have different NTFS permissions on a file or folder, the effective permissions are cumulative. For instance, if a user is a member of one group that has Read permissions on a folder and is also a member of another group that has Write permissions to the same folder, the user has both Read and Write permissions to that folder.

NTFS permissions are assigned in the Security tab of the Properties window for a file or folder. Figure 14-1 shows the permissions on the Author Files folder. In this example, the Everyone Group has Read permission on the folder, but no others. Thus, anyone who logs in on this computer would be able to view the contents of the files in this folder but would not be able to save changes to any existing files, create any new files or folders, or modify any attributes or permissions on any of the files. However, members of the Administrators Group have all permissions in this folder, and since the permissions are cumulative, the members of the Administrators Group, who are members of the Everyone Group by default, have all permissions to the folder and are not limited to just the Read permission.

FIGURE 14-1

Folder permissions

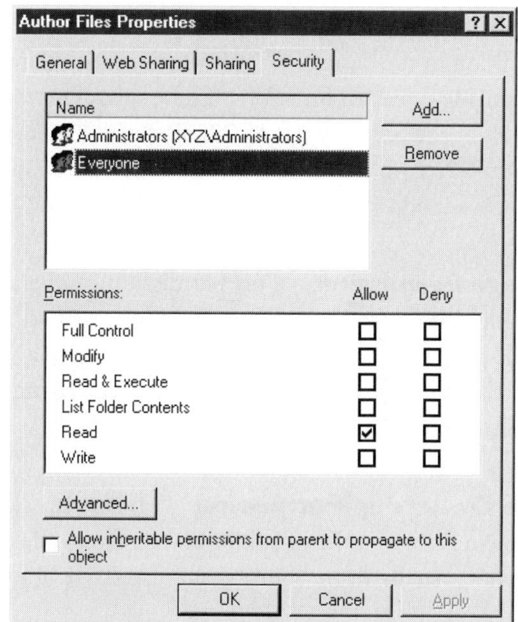

Permissions in a folder can be changed by clicking the appropriate check box in the Allow column to turn the permission on or off. Additional group permissions can be added by clicking the Add… button and selecting a group to add to the permissions list. When the permissions are set correctly, click Apply, then OK to enable the permissions configuration and close the window.

Deny Permissions Unlike the Allow permission, the Deny permission overrides all other permissions set for a file or folder. If a user is a member of one group that has the Deny Write permission for a folder and is a member of another group that has the Allow Full Control permission, the user will be unable to perform any of the tasks the Write permission allows, because it has been Denied. The Deny permission should be used with extreme caution, as it can actually lock out all users, even administrators, from a file or folder. The proper way to remove a permission from a user or group on a file or folder is to uncheck the Allow permission for that user or group, not to check the Deny permission.

NTFS Special Access Permissions

In addition to the basic NTFS permissions, there are several special access permissions that provide extended functions. These special permissions are found in the Advanced window of the Security tab of the file or folder Properties window, as shown in Figure 14-2. Two important special access permissions, Change Permission and Take Ownership Permission, are described below.

Change Permission This permission can be used to allow users the ability to change permissions on files and folders without giving them the Full Control permission. This permission can be used to give a user or group access to modify permissions on file or folder objects without giving them the ability to have complete control over the object.

Take Ownership Permission This permission can be given to allow a user to take ownership of a file or folder object. Every file and folder on an NTFS drive has an owner, usually the account that created the object. However, there are times

FIGURE 14-2 Access Control Settings for a folder

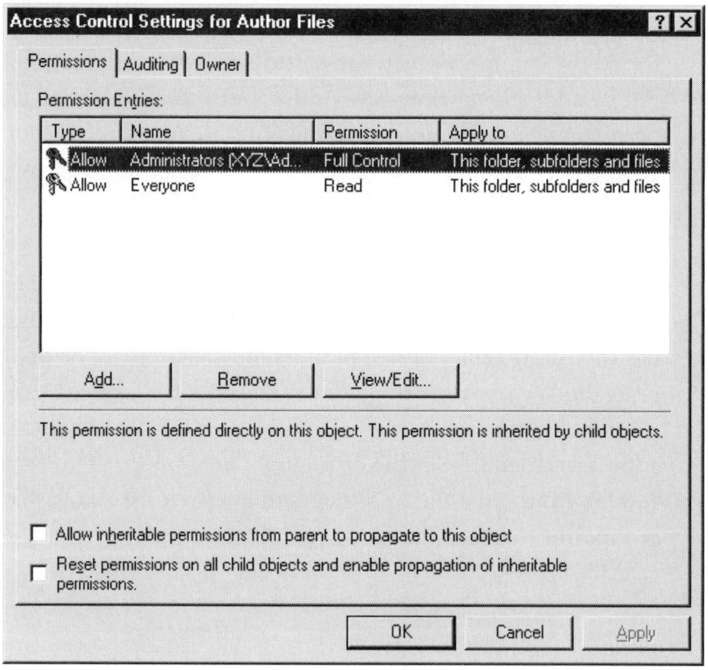

when ownership of a file needs to be changed, perhaps because of a change in team membership or a set of new responsibilities for a user.

Object ownership in Windows 2000 cannot be explicitly assigned. Ownership can be changed only when a user object takes ownership of a file or folder object. By default, only administrators can take ownership of a file or folder object, but the Take Ownership permission can be assigned to a user for a file or folder so that the user can independently take ownership and become the owner of the file or folder object. When an administrator takes ownership of an object, the Administrators Group becomes the owner of the object so that anyone in the Administrators Group can access the object as owner.

Other Special Permissions Table 14-3 describes the remaining special access permissions. In many cases, use of these special access permissions can more effectively control access to file system objects and should at least be considered when file system security is planned.

NTFS Permissions Inheritance

By default, all permissions set for a folder are inherited by the files in the folder, the subfolders in the folder, and the contents of the subfolders. When the permissions on a folder are viewed in the Security tab of the file or folder Permissions window, inherited permissions are indicated with a gray check box, as shown in Figure 14-3.

TABLE 14-3 Special Access Permissions

Special Access Permission	Function
Traverse Folder/Execute File	Browse folder contents or execute an application
List Folder/Read Data	View the contents of a file or folder
Read Attributes	View the attributes of a file or folder
Read Extended Attributes	View the extended attributes of a file or folder
Create Files/Write Data	Create a new file
Create Folders/Append Data	Create a new subfolder or append data to a file
Write Attributes	Set the attributes of a folder or file
Write Extended Attributes	Set the extended attributes of a folder or file
Delete Subfolders and Files	Remove files or subfolders from a folder
Read Permissions	View permissions of a file or folder

FIGURE 14-3

Folder with inherited permissions

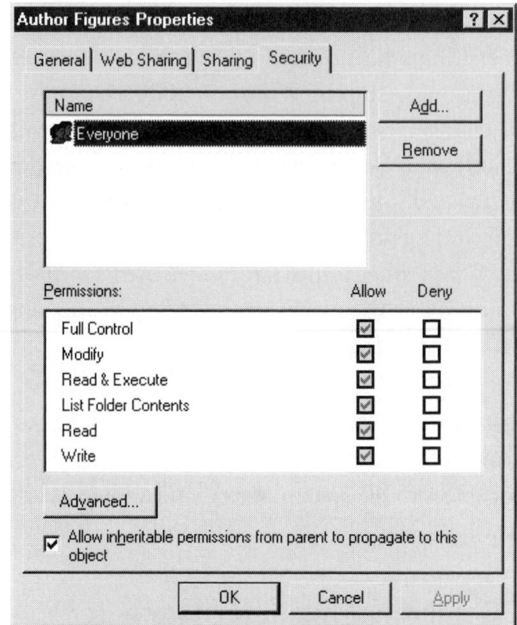

Allowing Permissions Inheritance To ensure that an object will inherit permissions from its parent object, turn on the Allow inheritable permissions from parent to propagate to this object check box in the Security tab of the object's Properties dialog. This setting is on by default unless it has been previously removed. This check box is also visible in the Access Control Settings window of the object, which can be opened by clicking the Advanced… button in the Security tab.

Preventing Permissions Inheritance There may be times when you want to assign a new set of permissions for an object and prevent any permissions from a parent object from being inherited. To "start over" with a new set of permissions for a file or folder, turn off the Allow inheritable permissions from parent to propagate to this object check box in the Security tab. When you do so, you will be prompted to choose how to assign new permissions for the object. You can either copy the inherited permissions to the object, or you can remove the permissions altogether and start clean. Either way, at the end of the task, you will be able to set specific permissions for the object, regardless of the permissions of the parent object.

exam Watch

Conflicting file and folder permissions are not only a common problem in a real-world environment; they are a favorite topic in exam questions. Be sure you understand how conflicting file and folder permissions are resolved.

Copying or Moving Files and Folders

NTFS permissions assigned to a file or folder are not necessarily kept intact when the file or folder is moved or copied to a new location. When files and folders are moved or copied from an NTFS volume to a FAT16 or FAT32 volume, all permissions are lost, as FAT16 and FAT 32 volumes do not support NTFS permissions. It is important to know the results of moving or copying files and folders to other NTFS volumes.

Copying Files and Folders In order for a user account to copy files and folders to NTFS volumes, the user account must have permissions to write to the destination location. When the file or folder is copied, it is created as a new file in the destination, and the user copying the file or folder becomes the owner of the newly created items.

NTFS permissions assigned to the new objects depend on the destination where the objects are created. Table 14-4 describes the results.

Moving Files and Folders Before a user account can move files and folders from one location to another, the user must have permissions to create objects at the new location, and must also have permission to delete the objects from the original location. When moving files and folders, the original objects will be deleted after they have been successfully created in the destination location. The user account moving the objects will become the owner of the objects in the new location.

NTFS permissions assigned to the new objects depend on the destination where the objects are created. Table 14-5 describes the results.

TABLE 14-4 NTFS Permissions Applied to Copied Files and Folders

Destination	Permissions
Objects copied within the same NTFS volume	Objects inherit the permissions of the new location
Objects copied to a different NTFS volume	Objects inherit the permissions of the new location

TABLE 14-5

NTFS Permissions Applied to Moved Files and Folders

Destination	Permissions
Objects moved within the same NTFS volume	Objects retain their original NTFS permissions in the new location
Objects moved to a different NTFS volume	Objects inherit the permissions of the new location

Access to Files and Folders in a Shared Folder

Shared folders present an additional level of security to the files and folders within the share. In addition to needing permissions to access the files and folders on the NTFS volume, users must also have permissions to access the share on the network.

Shared Folder Permissions

As only folders, not files, can be shared, shared folder permissions are a small subset of standard NTFS permissions for a folder. However, securing access to a folder through share permissions can be more restrictive or more liberal than standard NTFS folder permissions. Table 14-6 describes the permissions that apply to shared folders.

TABLE 14-6

Shared Folder Permissions

Permission	Description
Read	Users can: View file names and folder names View file contents and attributes Execute program files Traverse folders within the shared folder
Change	Users can: Create folders Add files to folders Change content of files Change file attributes Delete folders and files Perform tasks allowed with Read permission
Full Control	Users can: Change file permissions Take ownership of files Perform tasks allowed with Change permission

Shared folder permissions are applied in the same manner as NTFS permissions. Permissions can be allowed or denied to groups or individual users, although denied permissions override any allow permissions applied. Shared folder permissions are cumulative when multiple permissions are applied. If a user is a member of two groups, one that has Read permission on a shared folder and another that has Change permission on the same folder, then the user has Change permissions to that folder.

There are some significant differences between shared folder permissions and NTFS permissions:

- Shared folder permissions apply only when the folder is accessed through the share. If the shared folder exists on the local computer, only the NTFS permissions will apply to the folder if it is accessed locally. The folder must be accessed through the share before the share permissions will apply.
- Shared folder permissions are the only way to provide security to folders on FAT16 or FAT32 volumes. The protection applies only through the share.
- When both Share permissions and NTFS permissions are applied to a folder, the more restrictive permission will determine access to the contents of the folder. In other words, if a user has Full Control NTFS permissions on a folder but only Read permissions on the share, that user has read-only access to the contents of the folder when it is accessed through the share. However, if the user has only the NTFS Read permission on a folder but has Full Control on the share, that user still has only Read access to the contents of the folder.
- The default permission applied to new shares is Full Control, which is assigned to the Everyone Group.

on the Job

I've been caught more than once not setting share and NTFS folder permissions correctly. Several times I have needed to share out some space on my server to an individual for temporary storage or backup. Knowing that I wanted that person only to see the share, I removed all permissions from the Everyone Group on the share and gave the individual's account Change permission on the share so the individual could read and write to the contents of the share. Then, when I needed to access the share from a remote location to verify the contents or perform maintenance on the contents, I was unable to access the share because I had forgotten to give share permissions to my account. How embarrassing!

Copying or Moving Shared Folders When a shared folder is copied to a new location, the original folder remains shared, but the new folder is not shared. When a shared folder is moved, it is no longer shared.

Sharing Folders in the Active Directory

Folders can be shared from a Windows 2000 workstation or server, and they can also be created in the Active Directory. The advantage of sharing a folder in the Active Directory is that users can search the Active Directory for a particular share as opposed to needing the name of the server hosting the share in order to open it. Instructions for sharing a folder through Active Directory are contained in Exercise 14-1.

EXERCISE 14-1

Creating a Shared Folder in the Active Directory

In this exercise, you will go through the steps of creating a folder, setting permissions on the folder, sharing the folder, setting permissions on the share, and placing the share in the Active Directory.

1. Create a new folder in the root of the system volume called Public.
2. Right-click the folder and select Sharing from the pop-up menu. This opens the Properties dialog to the Sharing tab, as shown in the following illustration. Click the Share this folder radio button and type **Public** in the Share name: text field. Type a description in the Comment: text field.

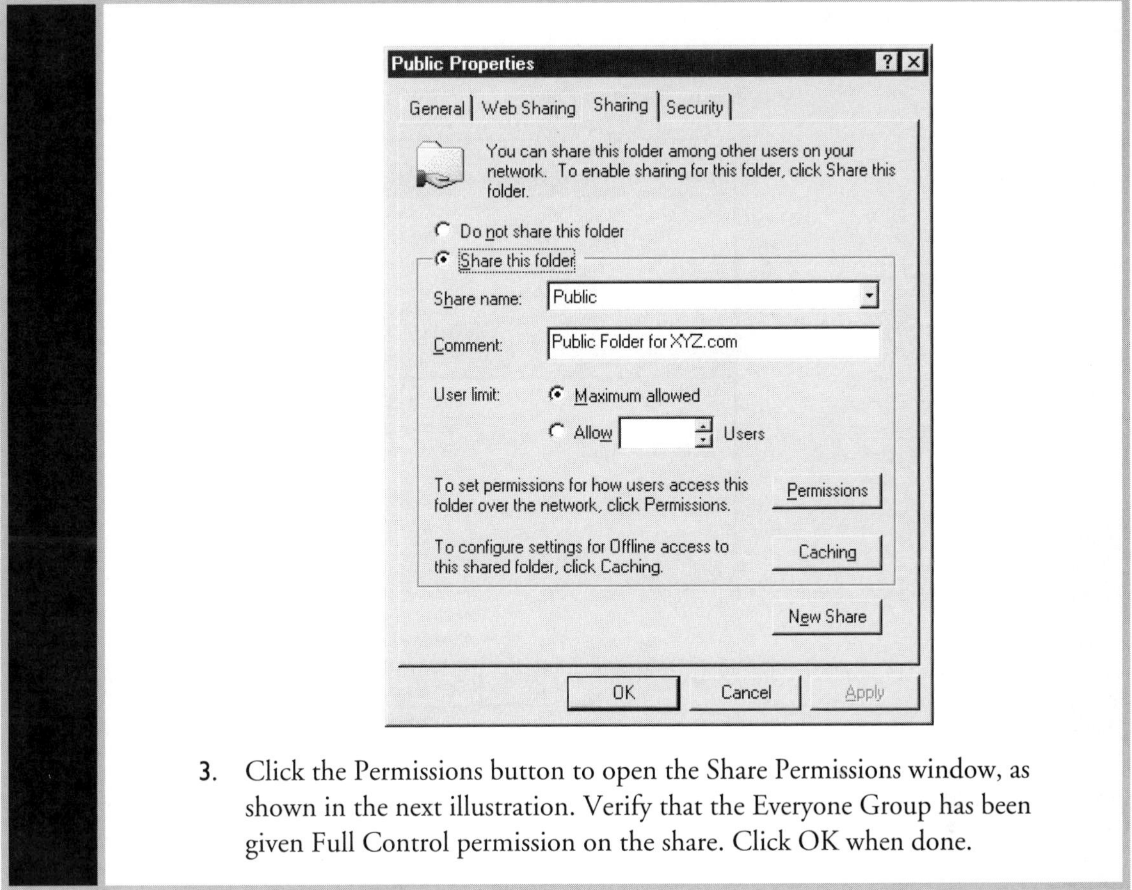

3. Click the Permissions button to open the Share Permissions window, as shown in the next illustration. Verify that the Everyone Group has been given Full Control permission on the share. Click OK when done.

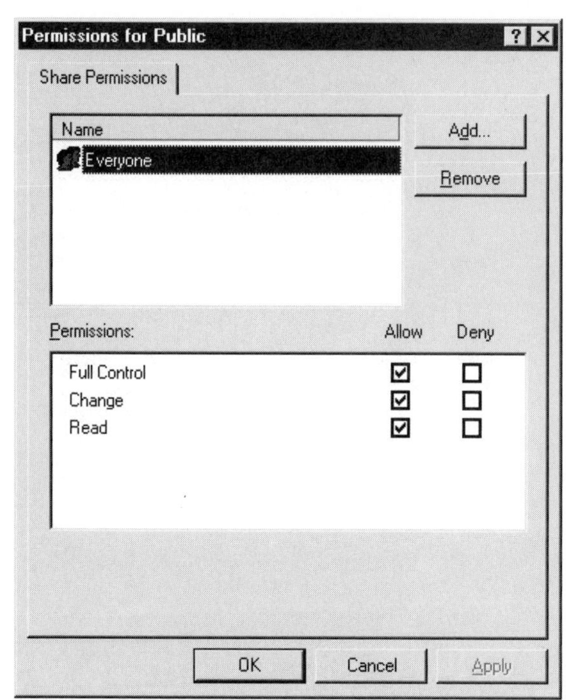

4. Click the Security tab in the Properties dialog for the Public folder. This will bring up the NTFS configuration settings window. Turn off the Allow inheritable permissions check box. This will generate the notification window shown in the following illustration. Click Copy to copy the current permissions settings to the object.

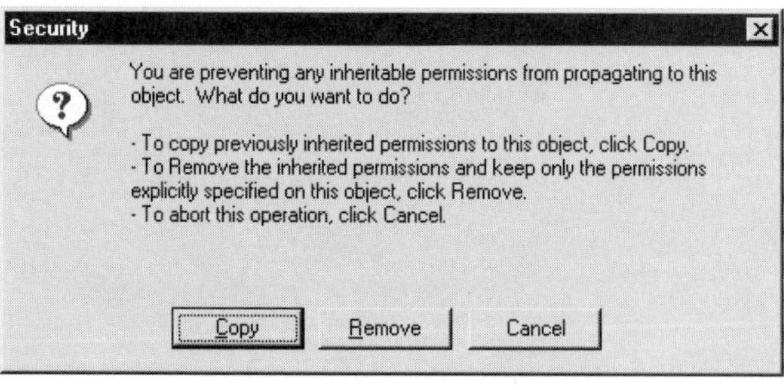

5. Assign permissions to the Everyone Group, as illustrated next. Users accessing this folder will be able to read the contents of any files in the folder, execute applications in the folder, but will not make any changes to any of the contents of the folder.

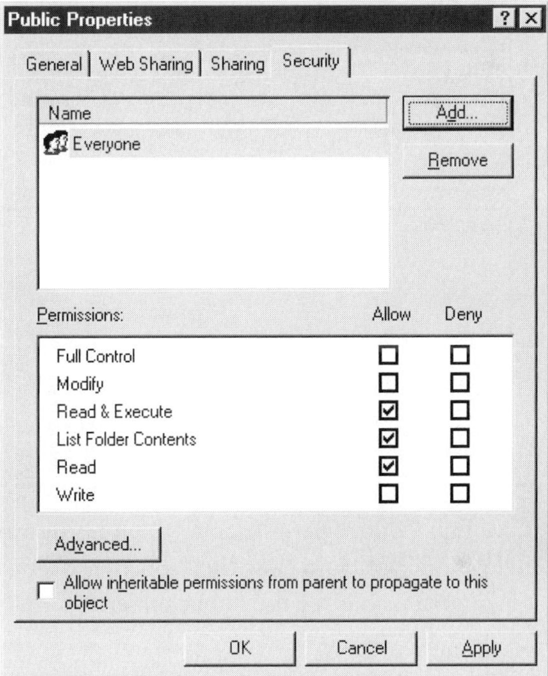

6. Add access permissions for the Administrators Group to this folder by clicking the Add... button. This will open the Select Users, Computers, or Groups window shown in the following illustration. Select the Administrators Group from the group list in the top window and click Add. The Administrators Group is added to the bottom window. Click OK.

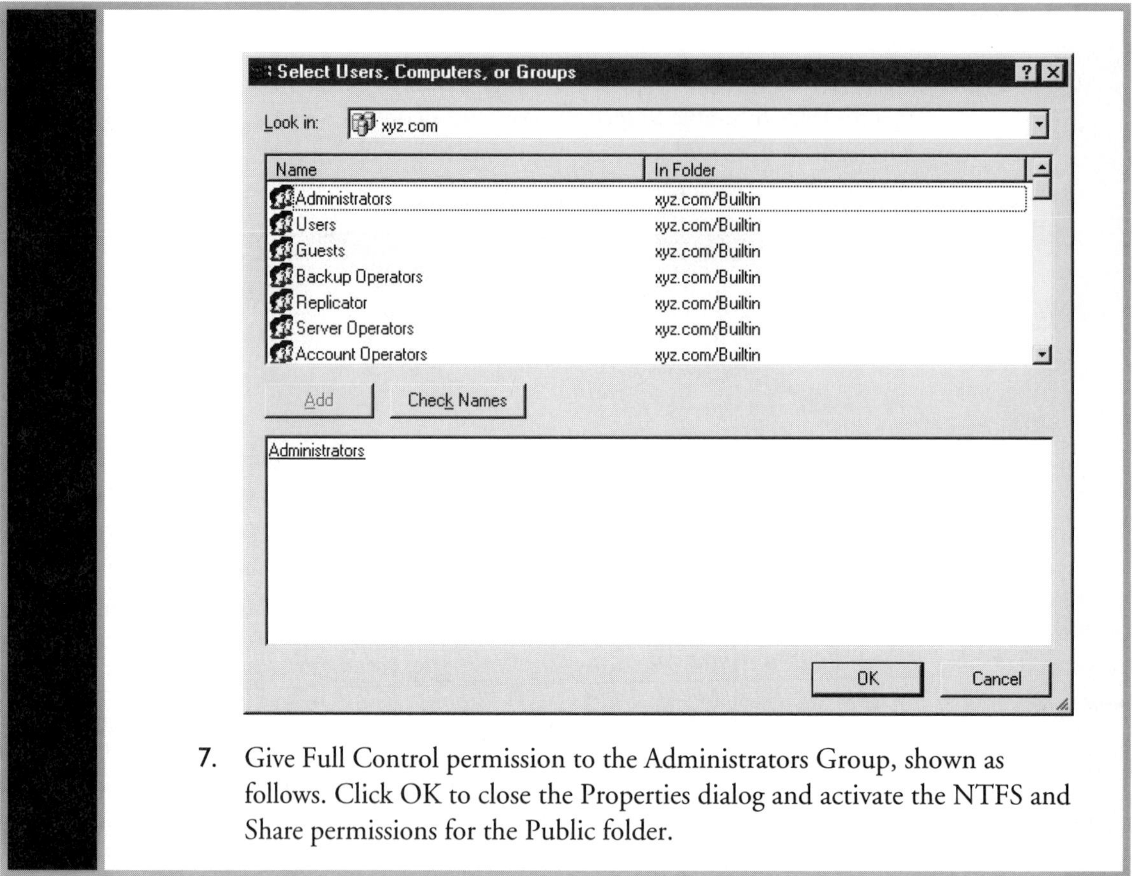

7. Give Full Control permission to the Administrators Group, shown as follows. Click OK to close the Properties dialog and activate the NTFS and Share permissions for the Public folder.

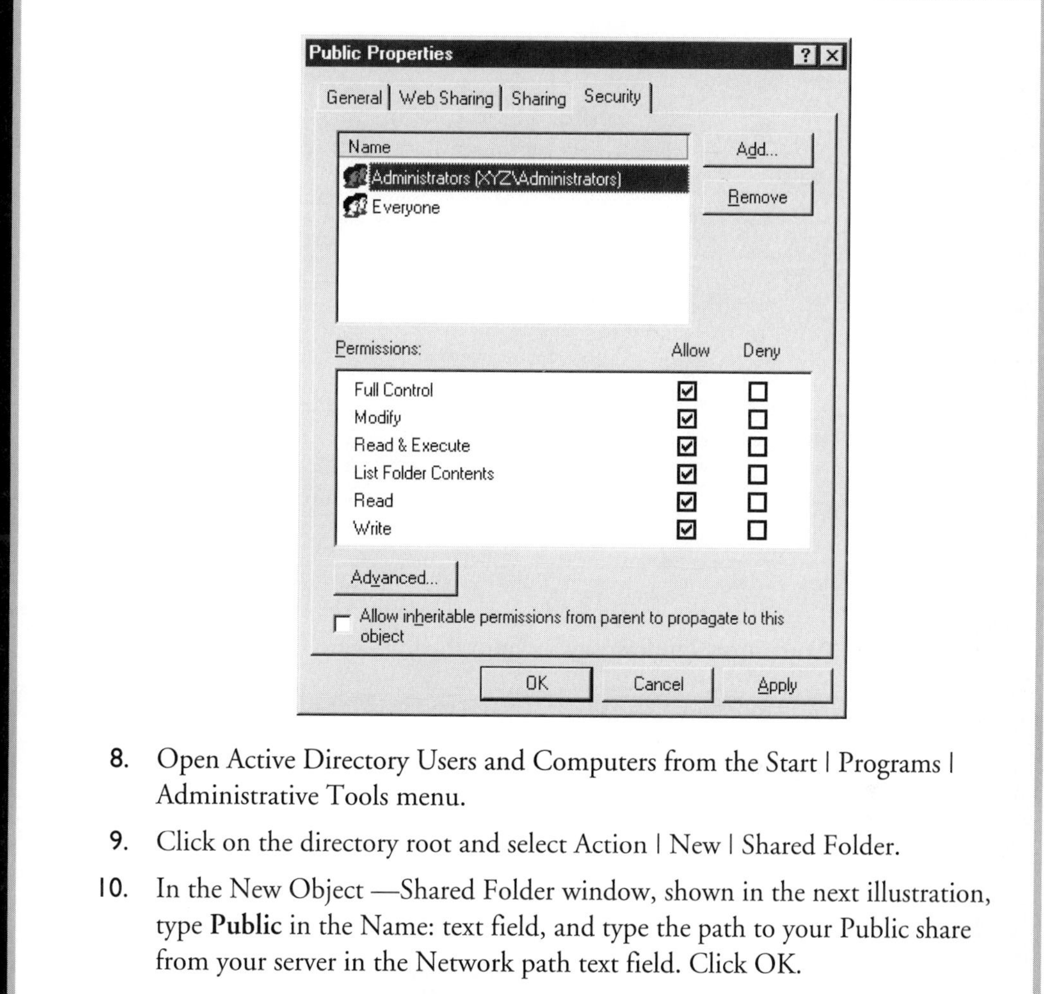

8. Open Active Directory Users and Computers from the Start | Programs | Administrative Tools menu.
9. Click on the directory root and select Action | New | Shared Folder.
10. In the New Object —Shared Folder window, shown in the next illustration, type **Public** in the Name: text field, and type the path to your Public share from your server in the Network path text field. Click OK.

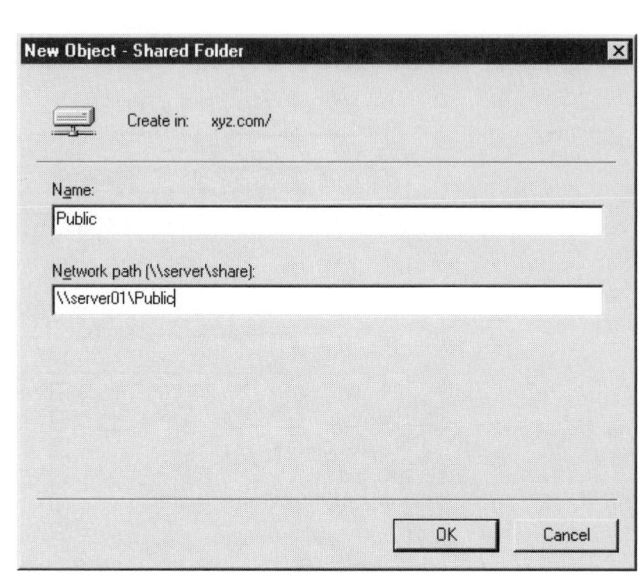

11. Verify that the shared folder now displays in the Active Directory Users and Computers window, as shown in the following illustration.

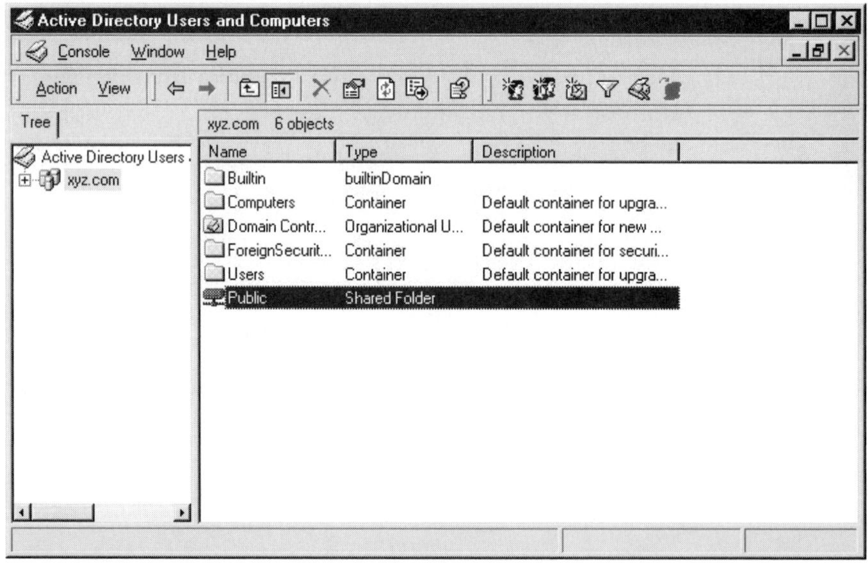

12. Open the Properties window for the share by double-clicking or right-clicking and choosing Properties… . Type a description for the share in the Description: text field, as shown next. Click OK and close Active Directory Users and Computers when finished.

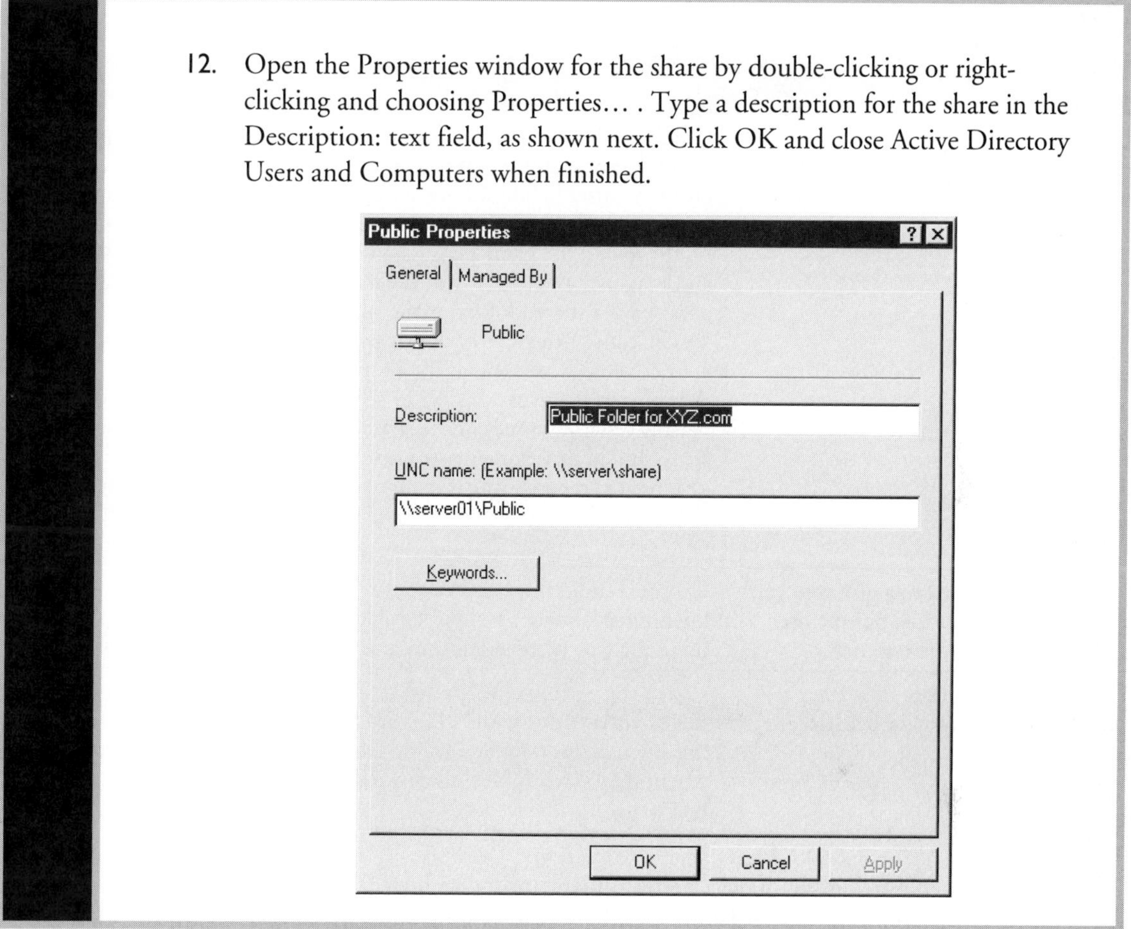

Troubleshooting Access to Shared Folders

Table 14-7 describes some common problems you may encounter with user access to folders and folder shares.

TABLE 14-7 Common Shared Folder Access Problems

Problem	Solution
User cannot access a file or folder	Check the NTFS permissions on the folder. The user needs to be a member of a group that has permission to access the folder, or a group the user belongs to must be given permission to access the folder. See whether a group has been given the Deny permission on the folder; the Deny permission overrides all other permissions and may lock the user out of the resource. If the folder being accessed is a shared folder, make sure the share permissions are set correctly. When a folder is accessed through a share, the more restrictive of the share and NTFS permissions are applied to the user object. If the user has Read access to the share but needs to be able to write to files in the share, the user's permissions on the share should be Change instead. It is almost always advisable to give the Everyone Group Change or Full Control permission on a share and configure access to the folder contents with NTFS permissions to make sure the correct permissions are being applied.
User has been added to a group to gain access to a folder or file, but the user still cannot access the resource.	Group memberships and related access rights are assigned at login time. The user will not be able to access resources dependent upon the new permissions until the user logs out and logs back in.
Users are able to delete files, even though they do not have permissions to delete the files.	Check the permissions applied to the user at the folder level. If the user's effective permissions are Full Control, consider having more restrictive permissions for the folder. To prevent users from deleting files in a folder, all permissions except Full Control can be granted for the folder.

Now that you have a better understanding of how Windows 2000 handles NTFS file and folder permissions and share permissions, here are some real-world and exam scenarios that you may encounter.

SCENARIO & SOLUTION

When a user accesses one of your folders through the network share, the user can access the contents only in the way that you want. However, when the user logs in on the machine locally, the account has full access to the folder. What's wrong?	One of two things may be happening here. First, the folder may not have the correct NTFS permissions set locally. Remember that share permissions override NTFS permissions only when the folder is accessed through the share. Second, the folder being shared may be on a FAT or FAT32 volume, which cannot have NTFS permissions set, so when users access the folder locally, they effectively have full control over the folder and its contents.

SCENARIO & SOLUTION

You have a share that you want only a certain group to access. You turned off the permissions for the Everyone Group, and now no one can access the share, not even you. What's wrong?	In all likelihood, you selected the Deny permissions for the Everyone Group instead of just removing the Allow permissions for the share. Fortunately, you can access the share locally and reset the permissions, making sure that the Everyone Group does not have any permissions assigned, Allow or Deny.
You needed to free up some disk space on one of your volumes and you moved several folders to another volume that has ample free space. Now users are complaining that they cannot access certain shares and folders anymore. What's wrong?	Remember that when you move files and folders to a new volume, the files and folders take the default permissions of the destination folder. You will need to reset the permissions on the files and folders in their new location to match the settings you had before the move. If any of the folders were shared, you will need to re-create the share as well.

CERTIFICATION OBJECTIVE 14.02

Monitoring, Configuring, Troubleshooting, and Controlling Access to Dfs Resources

The Distributed File System (Dfs) allows system administrators to logically manage a collection of network resources and present those resources to the user community as a single, hierarchical structure. Instead of forcing your users to remember that the retirement planning forms are stored on the Human Resources server, the direct deposit forms are on the Payroll server, the latest product presentations are on the Marketing server, and the latest Netscape installer is on one of the central application servers somewhere, you can configure these resources in a logical tree with Dfs. Not only can this simplify the location of resources for the user community, it can also ease your administration of these resources, allowing you to move resources around among various servers without affecting user access to the resources.

There are a number of advantages to using Dfs:

- **Resource administration** If a server fails, a network link becomes temporarily unavailable, a resource needs to be moved or replaced, or there is any other reason that access to a resource would be interrupted in a traditional network environment, the network link in the Dfs tree can be modified to point to a replacement resource without interruption to user access. The Dfs link to the resource can be remapped to the equivalent resource while the map of the Dfs tree is maintained. Users continue to access the resource with the same Dfs path as before.

- **Drive mappings** Drive mappings can be all but eliminated with a Dfs structure in place. Instead of mapping a drive letter to a shared resource on each server, the user accesses multiple resources through a single Dfs tree.
- **Fault tolerance and load balancing** Since Dfs can be configured to have multiple providers for a specific resource, the load on any single resource provider is not higher than the load on any other provider, as Dfs randomly selects from the list of providers when a resource is accessed. In this same way, if a resource provider becomes unavailable, user access to the resource is handled through the alternates, ensuring that the resource is always available.
- **Network permissions** Dfs makes use of existing network permissions for shared resources. No additional security configuration is required to access a resource through Dfs.
- **Integration with Internet Information Services (IIS)** IIS can be configured to use file resources through a Dfs tree. In the same way resource administration is provided to users, IIS directories and links can benefit from the load balancing, fault tolerance, and high reliability of access with Dfs.

Sharing Folders Using Dfs

Dfs services are automatically installed with Windows 2000. While the service can be started, stopped, and suspended on the server, it cannot be removed. Access to the Dfs services is provided through a Dfs root. The Dfs root contains nodes that point to shared resources on the network.

There are two types of Dfs roots: stand-alone and fault-tolerant.

Stand-alone Distributed File System (Dfs) Root

Stand-alone Dfs roots have the following characteristics:

- Stand-alone Dfs information is stored in the registry of the server hosting the Dfs root.
- Stand-alone Dfs roots are limited to a single level of Dfs nodes.

- Stand-alone Dfs roots are not fault-tolerant, as they are a single point of failure in the network. These roots have no replication or backup services.

Installing Dfs on a Single System A stand-alone Dfs root is created with the New Dfs Root Wizard. The wizard can be started with the Distributed File System snap-in. Here are the steps to complete the wizard.

- At the Select the Dfs Root Type screen, select the Create a stand-alone Dfs root radio button.
- At the Specify the Host Server for the Dfs Root screen, specify the network connection for the resources in the Dfs tree. Any Windows 2000 server can host a Dfs root.
- At the Specify the Dfs Share screen, select an existing share from the root server or create a new share in a new or existing folder.
- At the Name the Dfs Root screen, modify the name of the Dfs tree, if necessary, and type a description of the share in the Comment text box.
- At the Completing the New Root Wizard screen, verify that the information presented about the share is correct. Click Back to make changes to the configuration, or click Finish to complete the wizard.

Fault-Tolerant (Domain-Based) Distributed File System Root (Dfs)

Fault-tolerant (domain-based) Dfs roots have the following characteristics:

- Fault-tolerant Dfs roots exist in the Active Directory and rely on multiple servers to respond to requests for Dfs resources.
- Changes to a Dfs tree are automatically synchronized and published with Active Directory services, which ensures that a Dfs root structure can be recovered in the event of a catastrophic failure.
- Fault-tolerant Dfs roots must reside on an NTFS 5.0 disk partition and must be hosted on a Windows 2000 domain controller.

exam Watch

Make sure you understand the difference between a stand-alone Dfs server and a fault-tolerant Dfs server.

Dfs Child Nodes

Dfs child nodes are the links that connect the user browsing the Dfs tree to the shared resource elsewhere on the network. Each node appears as a folder within the Dfs tree, but opening the node in the tree actually makes the network connection to the remote resource. The location of the actual resource cannot be determined from the Dfs hierarchy; all open resources maintain their Dfs path when path information is requested or displayed.

Designing a Dfs Shared Folder System

Designing an efficient Dfs system requires planning on your part and input from your user community. First, identify resources that will be accessed by a majority of clients in your user community. Specifically target geographically distributed common information shares, such as Human Resources documentation that is stored on multiple servers that are positioned physically and logically close to large groups of clients. If possible, you may want to set up servers centrally located near large clusters of users solely for the purpose of providing Dfs shares. Next, poll your user community to learn what shared resources they access frequently. Include these resources in your Dfs plan as well. Finally, request that your user community provide you with regular updates for resources they use. Including these resources in the Dfs system will make them easier for your users to access, and getting feedback from your user community helps you to be aware of their needs and activities.

In a small computing environment, you can set up a stand-alone Dfs root on a server in your network and create all Dfs nodes on that server. You will need to make sure this server is available during all times that your user community would be using it to access Dfs resources. Depending on your environment, you may not need multiple levels of Dfs links or the added reliability of a domain-based Dfs root.

In a larger environment, specifically one that is geographically dispersed, you would set up a domain-based Dfs root. This would store the Dfs root information in the Active Directory, meaning that users could locate the Dfs root quickly no matter what part of the network they are on. Also, since the Dfs information is stored in the Active Directory and not on a specific server, when a Directory server goes down, the Dfs information is not lost.

FROM THE CLASSROOM

The Ideal Dfs System

Let's examine a fictitious organization that has set up an ideal Dfs system. This organization, the XYZ Company, has offices in New York, Chicago, and Los Angeles. Its Dfs system is set up as a domain-based root, storing the root information in the Active Directory, so it is replicated to Directory servers in each of the cities. In addition, information that is important to all employees of the company is stored on a set of servers, one set in New York, one set in Chicago, and one set in Los Angeles. These servers are replicating their file systems so that when Human Resources in New York changes a document on the server in New York, that change is automatically replicated to the servers in Chicago and Los Angeles. The Dfs links for Human Resources are set up to point to the shares for the servers in New York, Chicago, and Los Angeles so that when an employee in New York tries to access a document, it is served to him off a New York server. Should that New York server go down, however, the request would be serviced by either the Chicago or Los Angeles servers, and the employee would not be aware of any problems. In addition, local resources specific to each of the offices can be grouped under Dfs links specific to that area. The real advantage to this is when an executive from the New York office is in the Los Angeles office for a week, she uses the same Dfs tree to access resources back in her home office. Any companywide resources she may access are delivered to her off the local servers, cutting down on network traffic across the wide-area links. Also, any specific resources she needs to access from her home office are still available and presented to her as usual.

—Eriq Oliver Neale

How Clients Access and Use Dfs Shared Folders

Dfs resources can be accessed by a number of Microsoft client platforms. Table 14-8 lists the supported platforms and the way in which the appropriate client software is obtained.

TABLE 14-8 Dfs Client Availability for Microsoft Platforms

Platform	Dfs Client
DOS, Windows 3.*x*, Windows for Workgroups, NetWare server	No Dfs client available.
Windows 95	Client version 4.*x* and 5.0 can be downloaded.
Windows 98	Includes 4.*x* and 5.0 client for stand-alone Dfs roots. Client version 5.0 for domain-based roots can be downloaded.
Windows NT 4.0 with Service Pack 3 or later	Client version 4.*x* and 5.0 included for stand-alone Dfs roots. Cannot access domain-based Dfs roots.
Windows 2000	Client version 5.0 included.

Dfs roots can be served off of Windows NT servers as well, but these roots can only be stand-alone roots, as Windows NT 4.0 does not participate in the Active Directory model. Windows 2000 servers can host stand-alone or domain-based Dfs roots.

Clients access the resources in the Dfs tree by accessing the Dfs root via the Universal Naming Convention (UNC) path to the root or by mapping a drive to the Dfs root share. Either way, the client sees the Dfs resources as folders in the share and is not necessarily aware that the folder contents being used are not on the Dfs root server.

EXERCISE 14-2

Creating and Publishing a Dfs Root

This exercise will lead you through the steps of setting up a domain-based Dfs root on a server and adding Dfs links to the root. The exercise will use the shared folder created in Exercise 14-1 as the root for the Dfs tree, so you will need to complete the steps in Exercise 14-1 now if you have not already done so.

1. Open the Dfs snap-in from Start | Programs | Administrative Tools | Distributed File System.

2. Highlight Distributed File System in the left window, then select Action | New Dfs Root.
3. Select the Create a domain Dfs root radio button, as shown next.

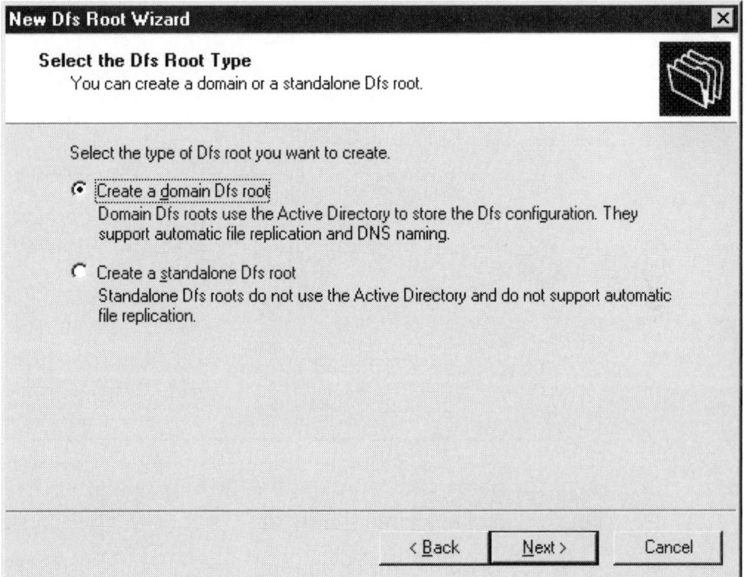

4. Select the host domain for the Dfs root. Accept the default domain selected (xyz.com in these figures).
5. Type the name of the host server for the Dfs root, **server01.xyz.com** for this exercise. You can click the Browse… button to search the network for the server to use.
6. Click the Use an existing share: radio button and select Public from the pop-up menu, as shown in the following illustration. You can also create a new share on the server in this window.

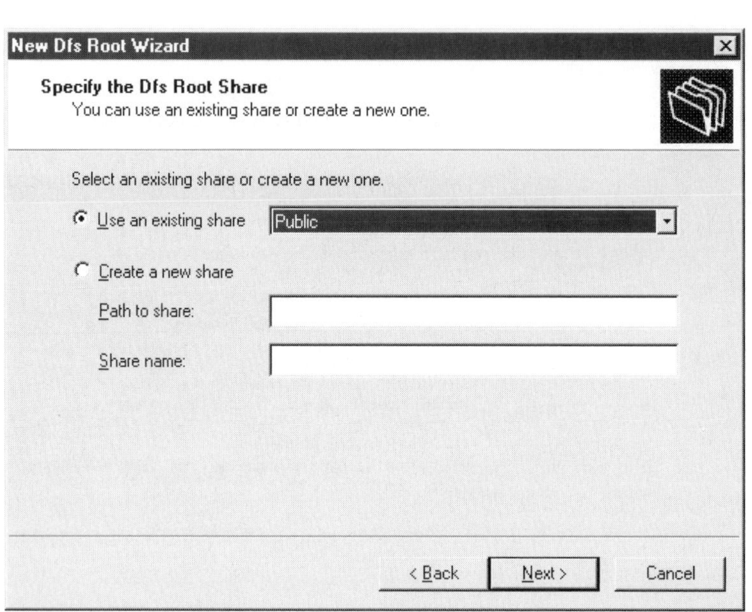

7. Type the name and comment for the Dfs root, as shown in the following illustration. This name is how the Dfs root will be accessed on the network. The UNC path for the Dfs root is displayed in the top portion of the window.

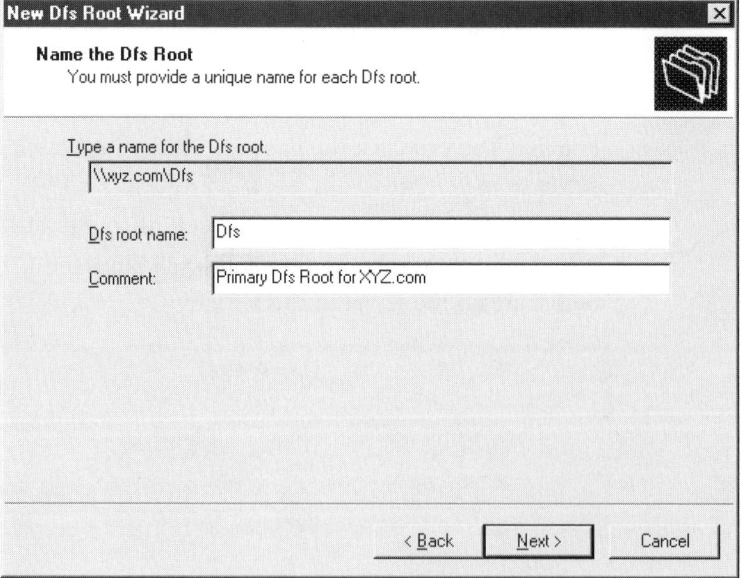

8. Verify the information in the wizard is correct before finishing the process. The next illustration shows that the Dfs root Dfs will be created in the xyz.com domain using the Public share off the server01.xyz.com server.

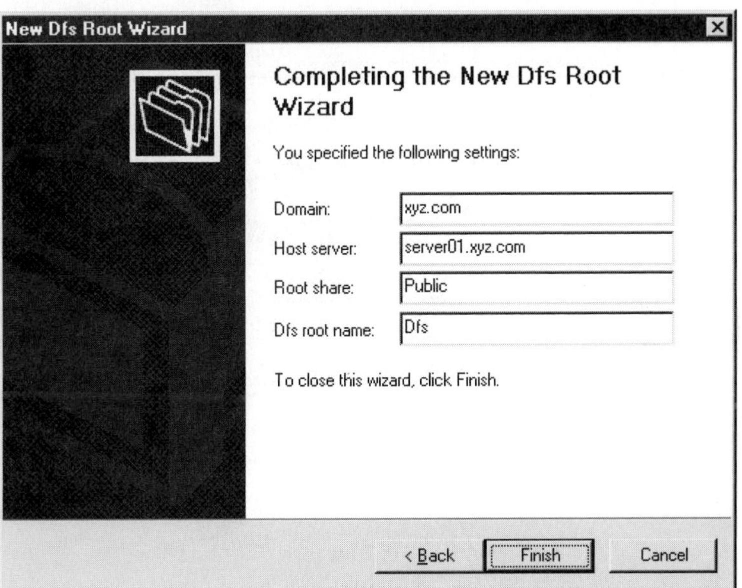

9. The new Dfs root is now visible in the Distributed File System snap-in display, as seen in the following illustration. The Dfs contents can now be accessed with the UNC path \\xyz.com\Dfs. In addition, accessing the \\Server01\Public share will also navigate the Dfs tree.

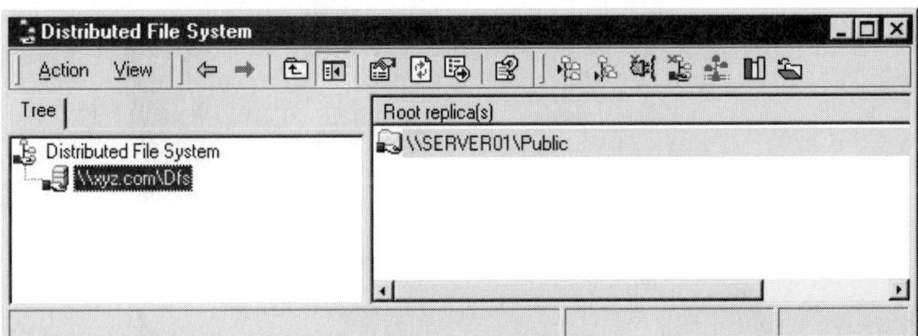

10. Create three additional shares on your server according to Table 14-9.

Share Name	Description
HR	Human Resources
MKTG	Marketing
R&D	Research & Development

11. Highlight the Dfs root entry and select Action | New Dfs Link… .
12. Create a link for the HR share, shown as follows.

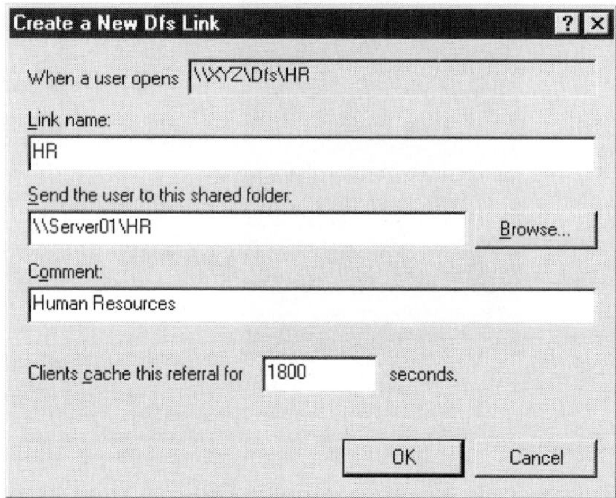

13. Repeat steps 11 and 12 for the MKTG and R&D shares.
14. When all the links are complete, the Distributed File System snap-in window should look like the following illustration with the R&D link selected.

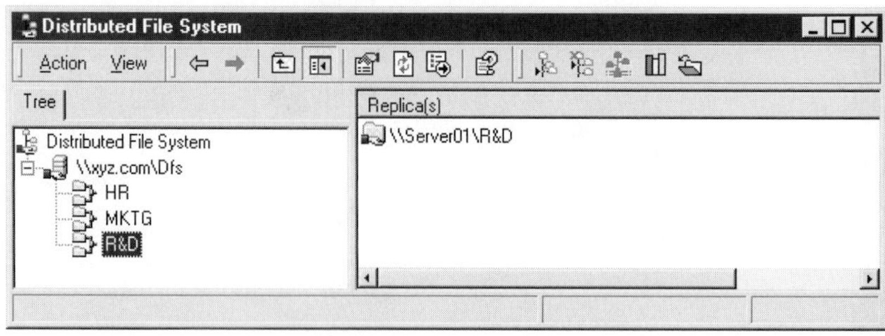

15. Open the Run… window and type *domain_name**dfs_root* (**\\xyz.com\Dfs** in this example) to open the Dfs root. Your window should look similar to the next illustration.

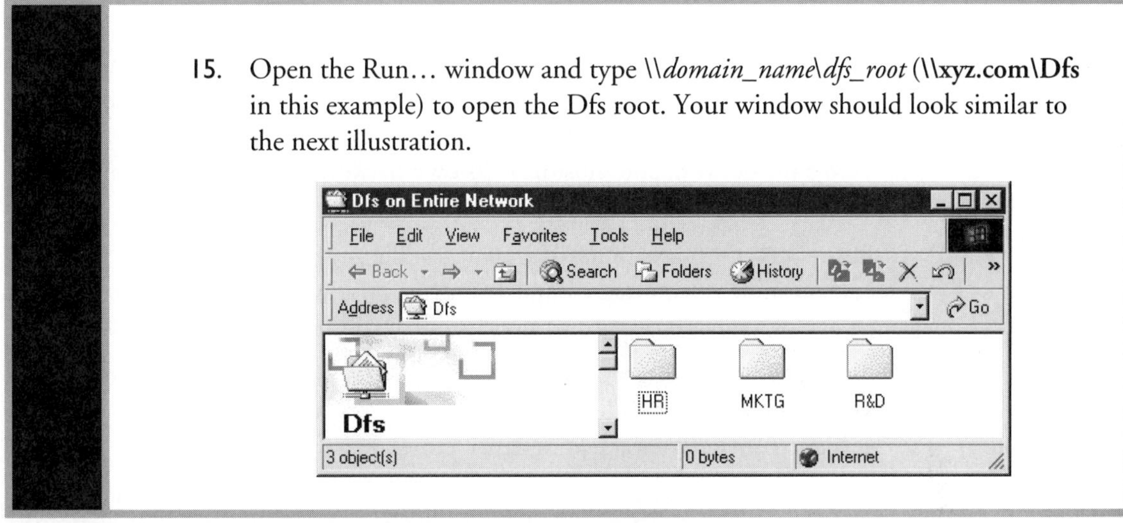

CERTIFICATION OBJECTIVE 14.03

Monitoring, Configuring, Troubleshooting, and Controlling Access to Printers

Microsoft Windows 2000 Server provides network printing services for a variety of computer platforms, not just Windows 2000 clients. The server routes print jobs from client computers to printers connected directly to the server through a serial or parallel port, or to printers connected through a network interface. Either way, the services and utilities provided with Windows 2000 Server ease administration of large numbers of printers in a network environment. This section of the chapter will introduce you to the printing terminology used with Windows 2000, show you how to set up and configure a variety of printer devices on a Windows 2000 server, and introduce you to tools and techniques for monitoring and troubleshooting printer issues.

Windows 2000 Printing Terminology

In order to work efficiently with the Windows 2000 printing environment, you must first understand the terminology used to describe the printing process. Here are a few key terms that will be used extensively in this section.

- **Print Device** The hardware that actually does the printing. A print device is one of two types as defined in Windows 2000: local or network-interface. A local print device connects directly to the print server with a serial or parallel interface. A network-interface print device connects to the printer across the network and must have its own network interface or be connected to an external network adapter.
- **Print Server** A computer that manages printing on the network. A print server can be a dedicated computer hosting multiple printers, or it can run as one of many processes on a nondedicated computer.
- **Print Driver** A software program used by Windows 2000 and other computer programs to connect with printers and plotters. It translates information sent to it into commands that the print device can understand.
- **Printer** The software interface between the document and the print device. The logical interface between the user and the print device allows the user to specify a print job's destination, the time it will be printed, and how other aspects of the process will be handled by the print server.

Network Printing Environment

Configuring the ideal printing environment can be almost as complicated as planning the ideal network environment for client computers. Here are a few issues you will need to consider in planning the printing environment.

Dedicated and Nondedicated Servers

A dedicated print server is a Windows 2000 Server whose only role is to provide printing services. The server does not provide directory space for users other than storage for spooled print jobs. It does not provide authentication services, does not host database services, does not act as a DNS server, and so on. A dedicated print server can host several hundred printers and print queues, however. Though it may not be obvious, the printing process does have an impact on the performance of the server providing the printing services. Spooling several dozen large print files to network printers can affect the performance of other tasks running on a print server, and those other tasks can slow down the printing process in turn as well. An environment with a large number of printers or print jobs should strongly consider using at least one dedicated print server.

A nondedicated print server is a Windows 2000 Server that hosts printing services in addition to other services. A domain controller, database server, or DNS server can provide printing services as well, but should be used only for a smaller number of printers or for printers that are not heavily used. Anyone setting up a nondedicated print server should monitor the performance of the printing process and the other tasks running on the server and be prepared to modify the server configuration if the performance drops below acceptable levels.

A Windows 2000 Professional workstation could also be used as a nondedicated print server. This solution can be used if a user has a local printer that he or she would like to share with other nearby users. Due to the limitation of the number of connections supported by Windows 2000 Professional and the other types of applications running on a Windows 2000 Professional workstation, printing performance will not be very efficient. In addition, only DOS, Windows, and some UNIX computers can print to printers served by Windows 2000 Professional. Configuring other types of printers requires Windows 2000 Server.

Network Printing Configurations

A number of different printing configurations are possible with Windows 2000 Server and local and network printers. Four basic configurations will serve most printing needs.

- **Local Printer** A print device that is directly attached, via a parallel or serial cable, to the computer that is providing the printing services (see Figure 14-4). For a Windows 2000 Professional workstation, a local printer is one that is connected to the workstation. For a Windows 2000 Server, a local printer is one that is connected to the server. Drivers for the print device must reside on the computer that connects to the printer.
- **Network Printer** A print device that has a built-in network interface or connects directly to a dedicated network interface (see Figure 14-5). Both workstations and servers can be configured to print directly to the network printer, and the network printer controls its own printer queue, determining which jobs from which clients will print in which order. Printing clients have no direct control over the printer queue and cannot see other print jobs being submitted to the printer. Administration of a network printer is difficult. Drivers for the print device must reside on the computer that connects to the printer.

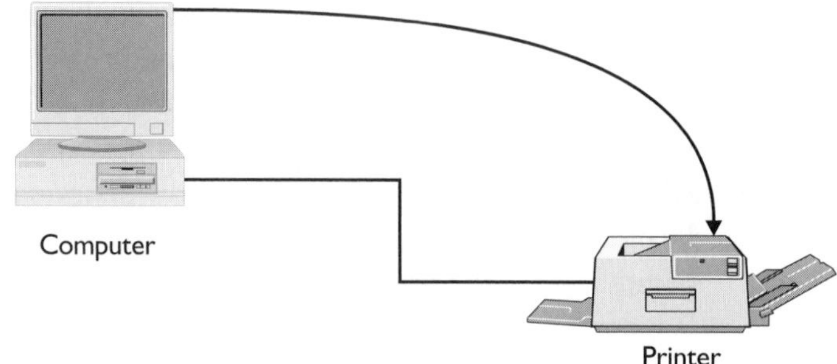

FIGURE 14-4

Local printer connection

- **Remote Local Printer** A print device connected directly to a print server but accessed by another print server or by workstations (see Figure 14-6). The queue for the print device exists on the server, and the print server controls job priority, print order, and queue administration. Client computers submit print jobs to the server and can observe the queue to monitor the printing process on the server. Drivers for the print device are loaded onto the client computer from the print server.

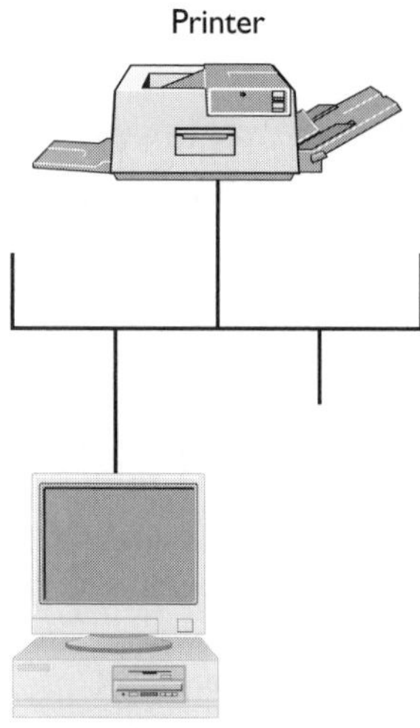

FIGURE 14-5

Network printer connection

FIGURE 14-6 Remote local printer connection

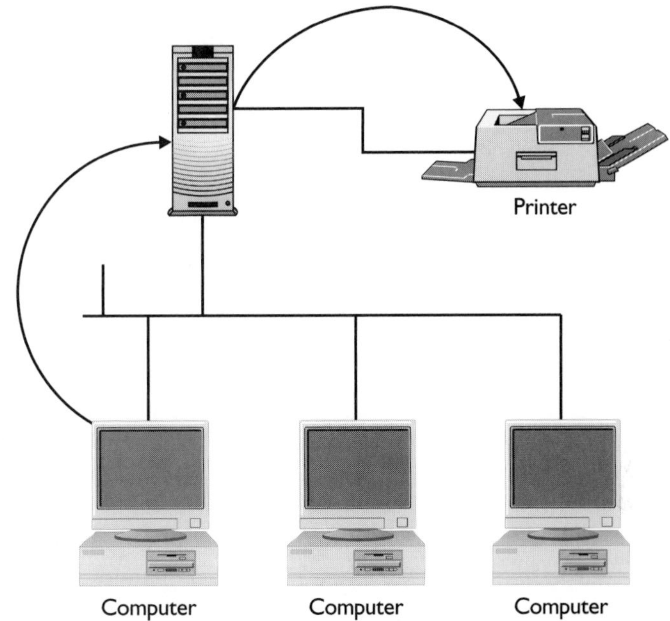

- **Remote Network Printer** A network printer connected to a print server that is accessed by client workstations or other print servers (see Figure 14-7). Like the remote local printer, the printer queue is controlled by the print server, meaning that the client computers submit their print jobs to the print server, rather than to the print device directly. This allows for server administration and monitoring of the printer queues. Drivers for the print device are loaded onto the client computers from the print server.

In most cases when print servers are used, client computers will see the printers as remote local printers or remote network printers, giving network administrators better control over the printing environment.

exam Watch

Even though Microsoft's terminology relating to the printing process can be confusing, it is a common topic on exams. Be sure you are comfortable with the terminology before taking the exam.

FIGURE 14-7

Remote network printer connection

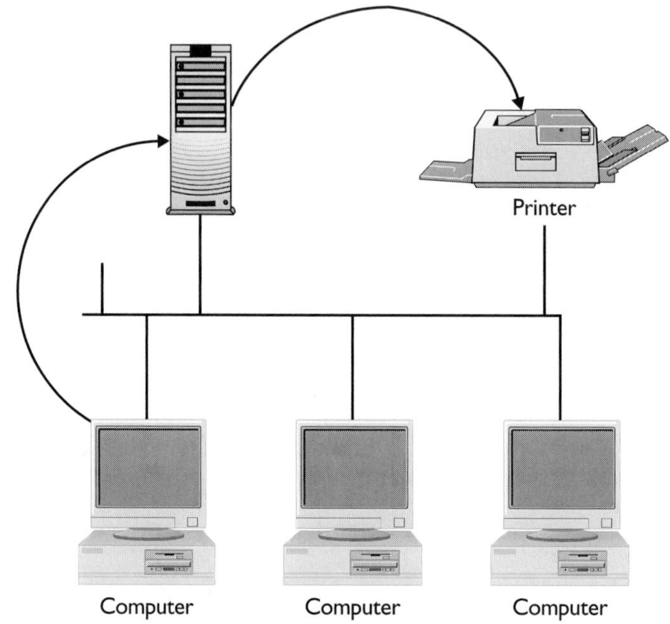

Installing and Sharing Printers

Printers must be installed and shared on a server before other clients can access the print device. The Add Printer Wizard is used to create local and network print objects on a server, which can then be shared out to the network.

Installing a Local Printer

Local printers are the easiest types of printers to set up on a Windows 2000 Professional workstation or Windows 2000 Server. To install a local printer, start the Add Printer Wizard, and select Local Printer rather than Network Printer in the wizard (see Figure 14-8). Then follow the instructions in the wizard to select the local port used to connect the printer. Most modern printers can be detected and configured automatically by Windows 2000. If your printer is not automatically detected, you will be asked to provide drivers for the printer before configuration can continue. Once the printer is configured, print a test page to verify proper communication between the computer and the printer.

FIGURE 14-8

Select Local or Network Printer

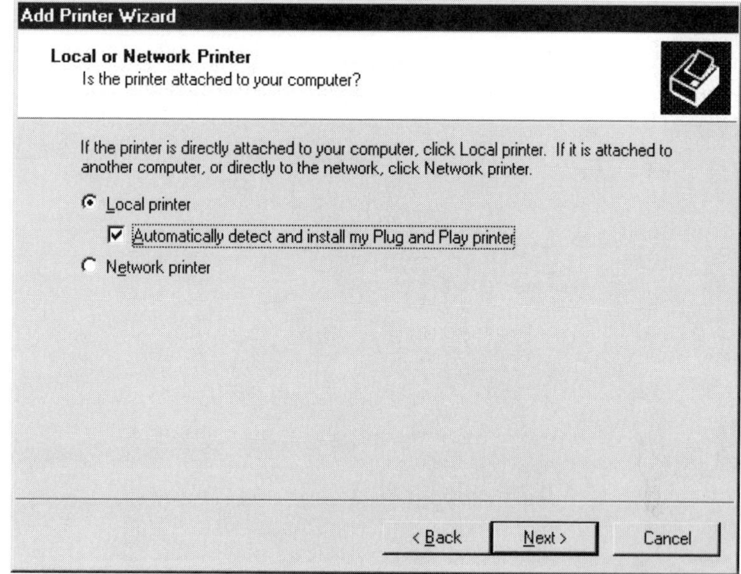

Installing a Network Printer

Network printers are more common in larger computing environments and generally perform better than local printers. Setting up network printers is more involved than setting up a local printer in that there are many types of network interfaces that can be used to communicate with the printer.

TCP/IP Printer Ports Many modern large-capacity printers provide a network interface that uses TCP/IP for communication. One popular printer manufacturer that does this is Hewlett-Packard with its LaserJet series printers and the JetDirect network cards. These devices must be configured to communicate with the TCP/IP network just like the client computers.

To set up a TCP/IP port connection for a printer, you will still define the printer as a local printer in the Add Printer Wizard. Instead of selecting one of the hardware ports, however, you will select the Create a new port: button and choose the Standard TCP/IP Port option from the Type: pop-up menu, as shown in Figure 14-9. Hewlett-Packard, Lexmark, and other printer vendors will provide additional TCP/IP interface drivers for communicating with their network devices. When those drivers are installed on the server, the network device will appear in the pop-up menu in addition to the Standard TCP/IP Port option. If you are creating an interface to a Hewlett-Packard printer with a JetDirect interface, use the JetDirect port option instead of the Standard TCP/IP Port

FIGURE 14-9

Select Standard TCP/IP Port

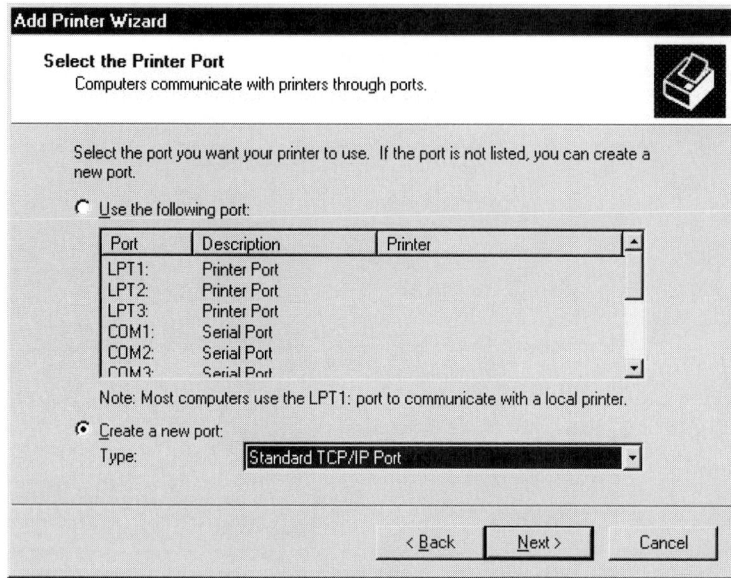

option in the Type: pop-up menu, and likewise for other printer vendors. Next, you will specify the IP address of the printer; then Windows 2000 should autodetect the type of printer and autoconfigure the settings for it. Otherwise, you will be prompted to provide drivers for the printer to proceed with the configuration. Once the printer is configured, print a test page to ensure that the communication between the computer and the printer is correct.

It is important to note that if the print server can create a TCP/IP printing connection to the print device, so can other TCP/IP clients. Having multiple clients print directly to the print device negates the management of the printer queue centrally and adds unneeded complexity to the troubleshooting process. In a large printing environment, it is best to make printing through the print server the easiest way of getting printing services; otherwise knowledgeable users will bypass the print server and print directly to the print device, increasing problems for all users and administrators.

LPR/LPD Printer Port One type of remote printing that may be encountered in a cross-platform computing environment is the UNIX LPR/LPD printing service. LPR (line printer remote) is a process that spools a print job to a remote print spool that is advertised by LPD. LPD (line printer daemon) is the server process that advertises printer queues and accepts incoming print submissions, which are then routed to the print device.

Microsoft Windows 2000 can use LPR/LPD to print to an existing UNIX LPD server or act as an LPD server for incoming UNIX print jobs. If an existing UNIX print server is already in place, it is preferable to create a printer that points to the LPD server, allowing Windows clients to print to the existing server, rather than re-create the printer configuration and have Windows 2000 act as the LPD server for the UNIX clients. The implementations of LPR vary widely among UNIX vendors, and a given LPR system on a UNIX client is not guaranteed to communicate correctly with the LPD service on a Windows 2000 Server.

To set up an LPD printer on a Windows 2000 Server, open the Add Printer Wizard, click the Local Printer radio button, and uncheck the Automatically detect and install my Plug and Play printer check box, then click Next. In the next window, click the Create a new port radio button and select LPR Port under the Type: pop-up menu. In the next window you will specify the name or IP address of the LPD host and the name of the print queue for the print device on that host. After the connection is verified, you will follow the remainder of the standard printer installation process.

AppleTalk Printing Devices Another type of remote printer is the AppleTalk printing device. Like a TCP/IP printer, an AppleTalk printer can be connected directly to an AppleTalk network or shared across the network through an AppleShare print server. Like the TCP/IP printers, a large number of modern, high-capacity PostScript printers can be configured to communicate with an AppleTalk network as well as a TCP/IP network. In fact, many Hewlett-Packard LaserJet printers have JetDirect cards that will speak TCP/IP and AppleTalk at the same time.

The advantage of having native support for AppleTalk printing devices in Windows 2000 is that printing services can be established in a multiplatform environment with a single printing interface. In other words, a single print queue can be established that will support both Windows clients and AppleTalk clients so that all users of the printer can monitor all activity to the printer from one location. Administration and maintenance of the printer queue is also simplified by having one printer interface support multiple client platforms.

Setting up AppleTalk print services requires that the AppleTalk protocol be installed and configured on the server. This installation does not occur by default when the server is installed, so the protocol usually must be added after the server is up and running. The process is the same as for TCP/IP printing in the Add Printer

Wizard. After selecting a Local Printer install, create a new port using the AppleTalk printer port, as shown in Figure 14-10. You will then have to browse your AppleTalk network to locate the printer. Once the printer is selected, you have the option to "capture" the printer on the AppleTalk network. Capturing an AppleTalk printer means that only the Windows 2000 print server can speak directly to the printer. The captured printer advertises itself only to the print server and not to any other clients on the AppleTalk network, rendering it "invisible" to other AppleTalk devices. All AppleTalk clients would have to submit print jobs to the print server, because that would be the only printing device advertised on the network. This has the advantage that all printing to the AppleTalk printer is routed through the print server, meaning that all print queue management can take place on the server. The disadvantage is that if the print server goes down, the AppleTalk printer begins advertising itself on the network again, and AppleTalk clients can, and usually will, create new printer interfaces to the printer directly, leading to mass confusion if and when print server problems are encountered. In a stable printing environment, though, this occurs very rarely.

FIGURE 14-10

Creating an AppleTalk printer port

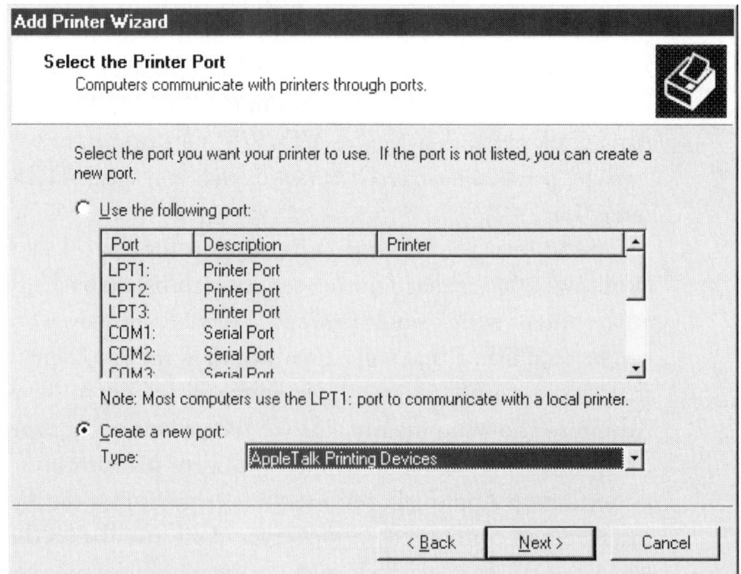

Sharing Printers

Once a printer has been created on a print server, it must be shared before any clients can use the service. Sharing a printer is very similar to sharing a folder on a server, and many of the same permissions concepts apply to both printer shares and folder shares. Printer shares can be set up during the printer installation process, which is detailed in Exercise 14-3. Otherwise, all printers share creation, and maintenance is performed in the Share tab of the printer's Properties dialog.

There are four elements in the Share tab of a printer's Properties dialog. The Not shared: button, when enabled, deactivates all sharing features for the printer. The Shared as: button, when enabled, turns on sharing for the printer and allows you to specify the share name for the printer in the adjacent text field. When a share name is specified for a printer, the name should be descriptive enough that a user can easily identify the location of the printer by the name, but it should be short enough that it can be found by all flavors of the Windows OS. Windows 95 and Windows 98 cannot see printer shares that have very long names or contain spaces within the share name.

When the Shared as: button is enabled, the List in the Directory check box becomes active. Turning on this check box will advertise the printer in the Active Directory, making it easier for users to locate the printer when they know the printer name. Otherwise, users must search for the printer name by searching through the print server's shares to locate the desired printer.

The Additional Drivers button opens a dialog where print drivers for additional Windows operating systems can be loaded on the server. In an environment with multiple versions of the Windows OS accessing printing services, it is best to load the print drivers for those OSs on the server so the client can automatically download the appropriate driver when installing a printer for the first time. If the driver for a printer is not loaded on the server, the client will have to locate and install the driver manually before being able to print to the printer on the server. Windows 2000 clients do not load printer drivers locally when connecting to server shares. Like earlier Windows NT clients, the Windows 2000 workstation client uses the print drivers on the server instead of downloading the drivers locally.

In addition to setting up the share name for the printer, the printer can be given specific network permissions to allow or prevent printing for users or groups of users on the network. Additional information about the specific printer security permissions is detailed in Managing Printers and Print Servers section later in the chapter.

EXERCISE 14-3

Installing and Sharing a TCP/IP Network Printer

In this exercise, you will set up a local printer connected via a TCP/IP port that will then be shared out on the network. This exercise will use the Standard TCP/IP port to identify the network printer.

1. Open the Printers folder and double-click the Add Printer icon.
2. Click the Local Printer radio button and turn off the Automatically detect my printer check box. Click Next.
3. Click the Create a new port radio button and select Standard TCP/IP Port from the Type: pop-up menu. Click Next.
4. The Add Standard TCP/IP Port Wizard starts. In the Printer Name or IP Address: field, type the IP address of the printer as **10.1.1.101.** The Port Name: field will automatically adjust its value to IP_10.1.1.101, as shown in the following illustration. Click Next.

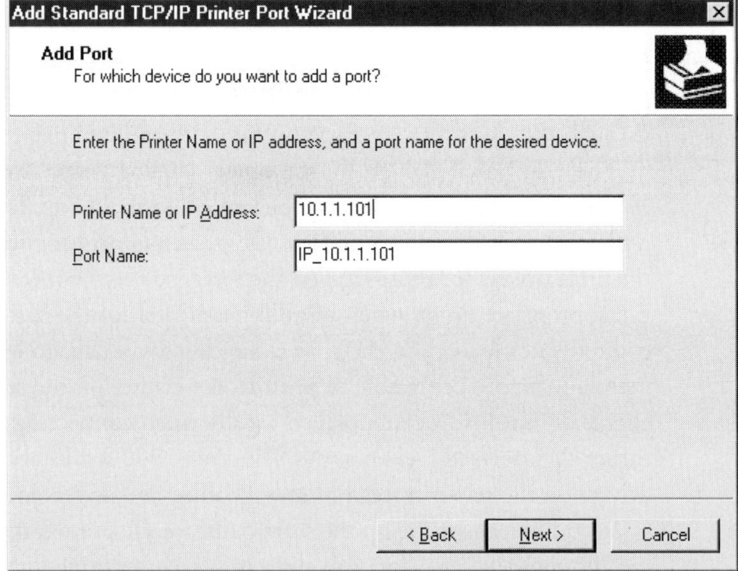

5. At this point, you will get an error that the wizard cannot connect to the printer, because the IP address specified does not exist. Click Next. Now you will see the summary page of the Add Standard TCP/IP Port Wizard, shown as follows. Click Finish.

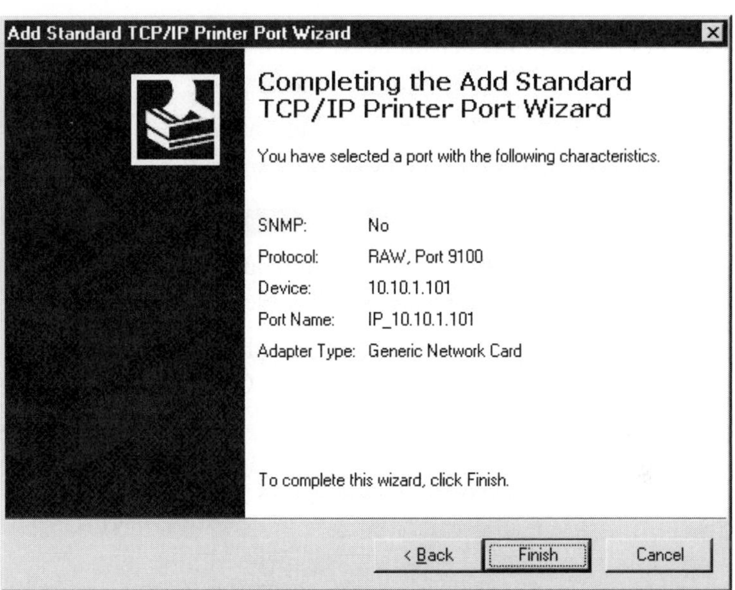

6. Select the printer manufacturer as HP under Manufacturers: and the printer type as HP LaserJet 4000 Series PCL under Printers: as shown in the following illustration. Click Next.

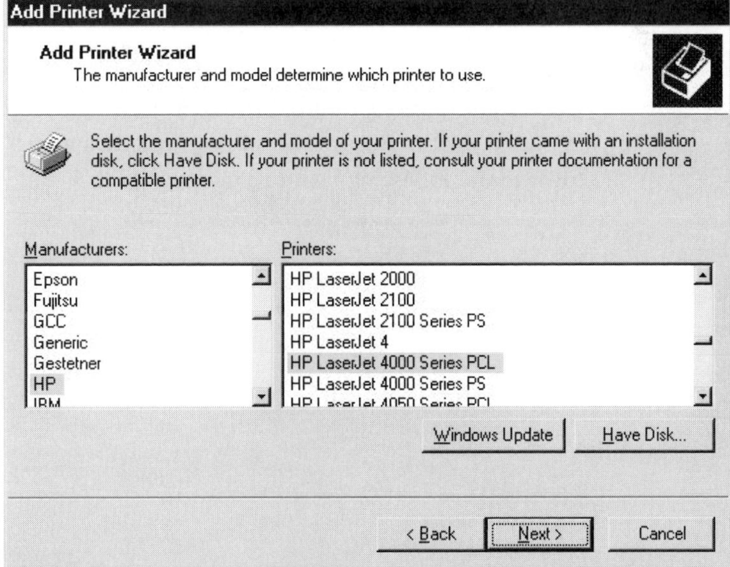

7. Accept the default name of the printer as *HP LaserJet 4000 Series PCL* in the Printer Name: field. Click Next.
8. Click the Share as: radio button and specify the share name of the printer as **HPLJ4000** in the field, as shown in the following illustration. Click Next.

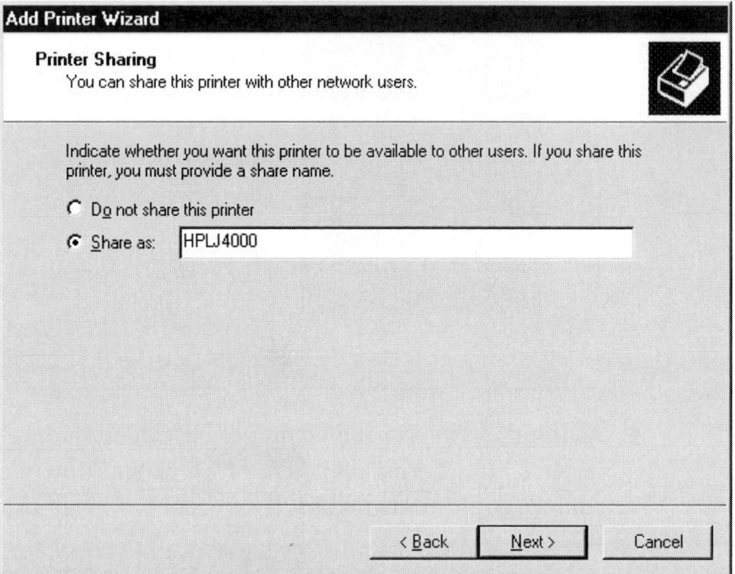

9. In the Location text box, type text that describes the location of the printer, such as **Second Floor Public Printer Area.** In the Comment text box, type text that describes the printer, such as **Second Floor Public Laser Printer,** as shown in the following illustration. Click Next.

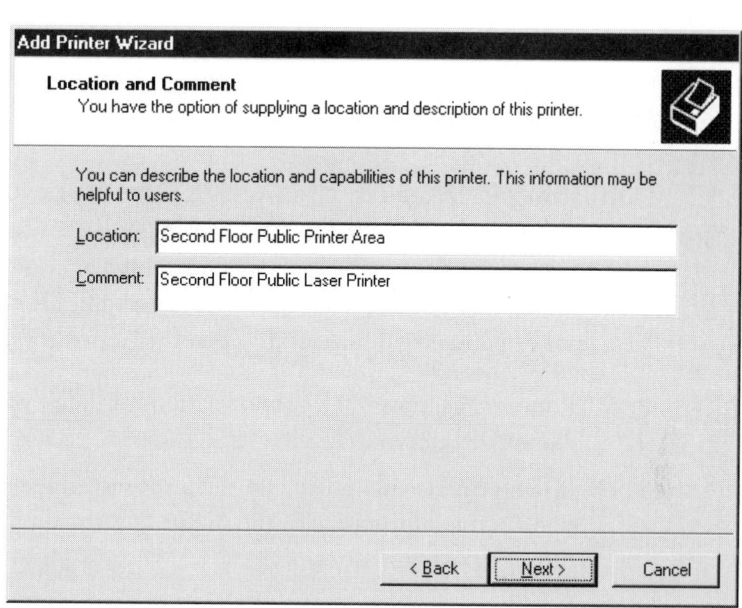

10. Click the No radio button in the Print Test Page window and click Next.
11. Review the information displayed in the Completing the Add Printer Wizard window, shown as follows, and click Finish.

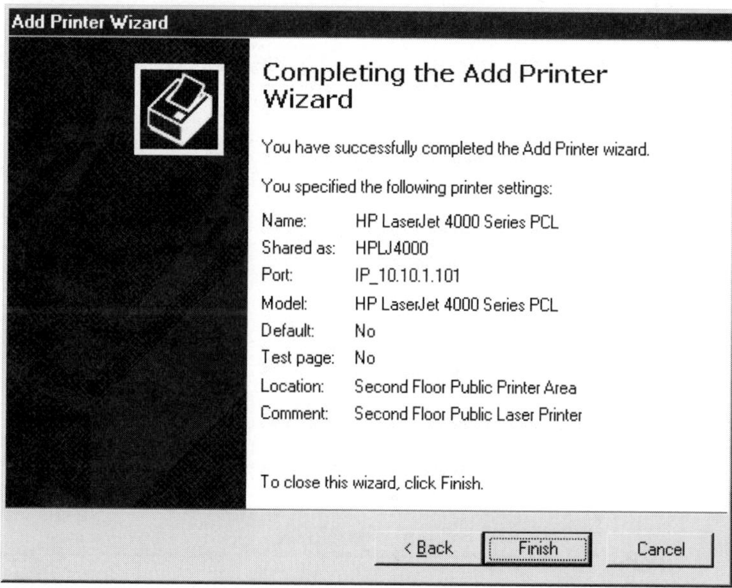

Now you will see a printer icon named HP LaserJet 4000 in the Printers window, similar to Figure 14-11. The icon will have a hand beneath the printer, indicating that the printer is shared. Other clients on the network will see the printer shared as HPLJ4000.

Publishing Printers in the Active Directory

Advertising printers in the Active Directory makes it easier for clients to locate printers on the network. A well-planned printing environment will be very easy for clients to browse and easily locate printers geographically close to them for use. Here are a few key points regarding printers and the Active Directory.

- Print servers must publish information for their own printers in the Active Directory.
- When printers are updated on the print server, the print server automatically updates the information in the Active Directory and those changes propagate through the entire directory.
- Printers are entered into the Active Directory as printQueue objects.
- By default, any printer shared by a print server is advertised in the Active Directory.

FIGURE 14-11

Printers window after new printer is added

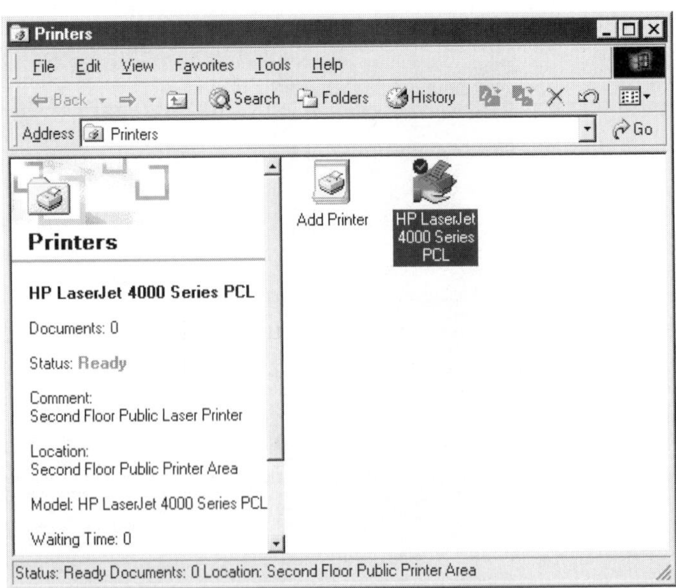

- The printQueue object is located in the print server's computer object in the Active Directory.
- When a print server disappears from the network, its printers are removed from the Active Directory.

When printers are shared with the Add Printer Wizard, the shared printer is listed in the Active Directory by default. In order to remove a printer listing from the Active Directory, turn off the List in the Directory check box in the Sharing tab of the printer's Properties dialog box.

How Clients Locate Published Printers

Once a printer has been shared by a print server, it must be set up on the client before the client can print. This process involves locating the printer on the network, setting up the logical printer interface on the client, and installing printer drivers on the client. For Microsoft clients, these processes are straightforward and, for the most part, automatic. Other steps must be performed to set up printers on non-Microsoft clients.

There are several ways to locate a printer to set up on the client workstation.

Add Printer Wizard All clients running a version of the Windows operating system (Windows 2000, Windows NT, Windows 98, and Windows 95) can use the Add Printer Wizard to create a printer entry on the client. This is the same Add Printer Wizard described earlier to create and share a printer on a print server. The Windows 2000 version of the Add Printer Wizard has more options than the wizard in other versions of Windows, but many of the same methods can be used to get the printer set up on the client.

To create a printer with the Add Printer Wizard, you will start the wizard and select the Network Printer radio button in the Local or Network Printer window of the wizard. You will then choose how to locate the printer on the network. (The three search options are shown in Figure 14-12.) You can search the Active Directory for the printer object, or you can type the UNC name or Uniform Resource Locator (URL) for the printer, if known. Once you have found the printer on the network, the printer object will be created locally and any necessary printer drivers will be downloaded to the client. As with printer installation on a print server, you will have the option of printing a test page to confirm the successful creation of the printer object.

FIGURE 14-12

Three methods for locating a printer in the Add Printer Wizard

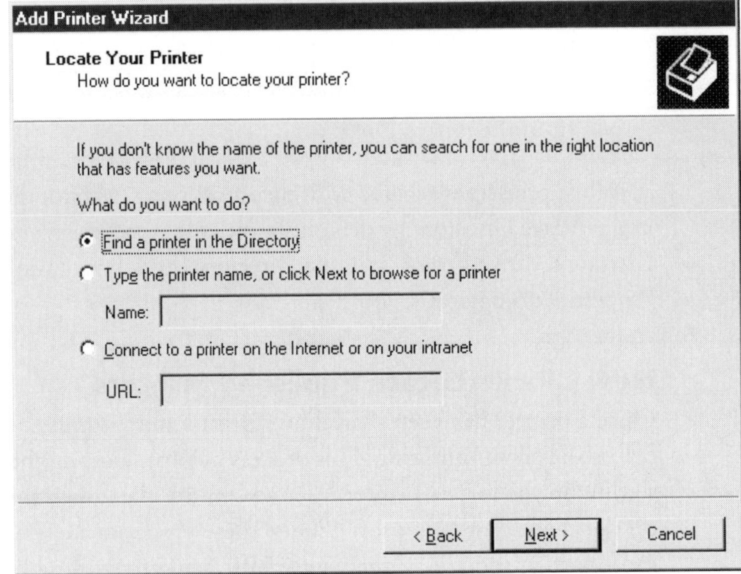

Searching the Active Directory In addition to using the Add Printer Wizard, you can locate the printer object on the network yourself and install the printer directly. If you know the name of the printer in the Active Directory, you can search for it using the Start | Search | For Printers interface in Windows 2000. Only Windows 2000 clients can search the Active Directory for printers. In addition to searching for a printer by name, you can also search on printer location or capabilities. Once the printer is located, you can right-click the printer and select Install from the pop-up menu.

UNC Name If you know the full network path to the printer, you can connect to the printer using the Run command on the Start menu from any Windows 95 or newer client. Type the UNC name of the printer in the Open box and click OK. If the printer has not already been installed on your system, you will see a note that the printer must be set up before it can be accessed. Clicking OK in the note window will proceed to install the printer on the client.

If you know only the UNC name of the print server hosting the printer, you can open the server the same way as was described earlier. This will open a window listing all the public shares on the server, if any, and all the shared printers. Once you locate the correct printer in the window, you can double-click it, which will have the same result as typing the full UNC name in the Run command, or you can right-click the printer icon and select Install from the pop-up menu. Either method will install the printer, but the latter choice will yield one less warning window.

Browsing the Network Another method for installing a printer is to browse through My Network Places. You can navigate through the network map to locate the print server, then open the server to choose from the printer shares listed. This method for locating and installing a printer can be helpful if you do not already know what server a printer is on. Otherwise, it makes more sense to use one of the more direct methods for locating a printer.

Using a Web Browser Clients running Windows 2000 can use a Web browser to locate and install printers off the print server. Type the URL for the print server as **http://<servername>/printers** to see a list of all printers supported by the print server, similar to the list shown in Figure 14-13. You can also use the share name of the printer in the URL, such as **http://<servername>/<printername>** to open the browser directly to the printer. Click the Connect link in the browser window to install the printer connection. In either case, you must have permission to use the printer in order to view and install the printer via the Web interface, as the Web browser will use your network authentication to determine your access to the printer.

The print server must be configured to accept printer requests via the Web interface. If the printer is served on a Windows 2000 Server, the server must have

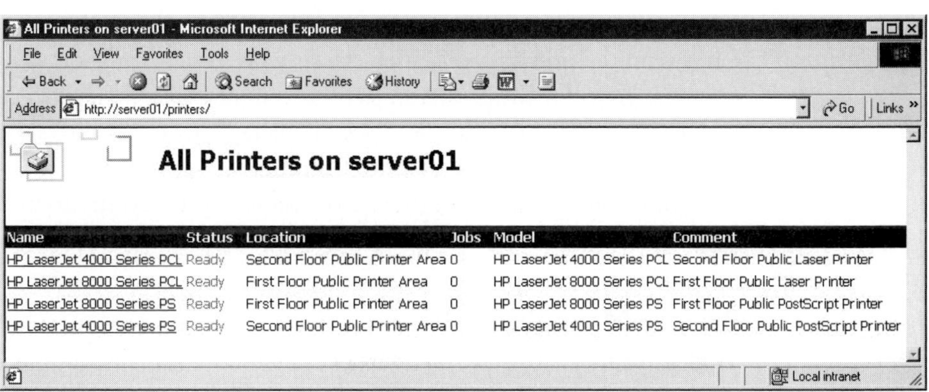

FIGURE 14-13 Viewing available printers through a Web interface

Microsoft Internet Information Services (IIS) installed and running. If the printer is served on a Windows 2000 Professional workstation, the workstation must be running Microsoft Peer Web Services (PWS).

Managing Printers and Print Servers

Managing printing services is more than just creating printer objects on a server and establishing printer shares. For a variety of reasons, access to certain printers may need to be limited to certain groups or individuals. In may be necessary to redirect print jobs to different printers when printer or server maintenance is performed. You may also be called upon to clear hung jobs from a printer queue when other users are unable to print as a result.

Printer Permissions

Printer permissions are established through the Security tab in the printer's Properties dialog. The security settings for printer objects are similar to the security settings for folder shares. The default permissions for a printer are shown in Figure 14-14.

The Everyone Group is given Print permissions by default, meaning that all users can submit print jobs to the printer. In addition, the Creator Owner Group has the Manage Documents permission, meaning that the account that submitted a job to the print queue can modify the settings on the job while it is still in the queue. However, no other users can modify document settings for print jobs they did not submit themselves. The exception to this is the Administrators Group, which is given the Manage Documents permission as well. In addition, the Administrators Group has the Manage Printers permission, which allows administrators to change settings on the printer object itself. Users who have permission to use the printer can see the settings for the printer object but cannot make changes to the configuration.

Administrators may want to delegate management of printers to additional groups of users by creating a Printer Administrators Group, adding those users to that group, and giving that group permissions on the printer to manage the printer and the documents in the queue.

Printer Management

Modern printers are quite complex devices and have many options that can be configured. The majority of the configuration and management of a printer takes place in the Device Settings tab of the printer's Properties dialog, as shown in Figure 14-15.

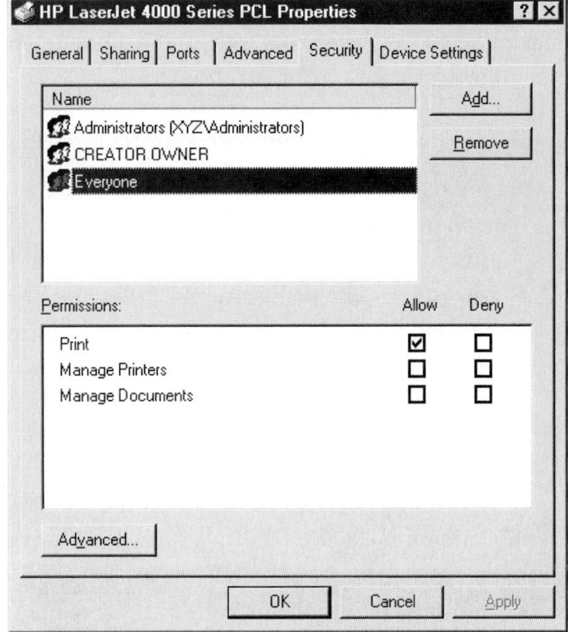

FIGURE 14-14 Default printer security settings

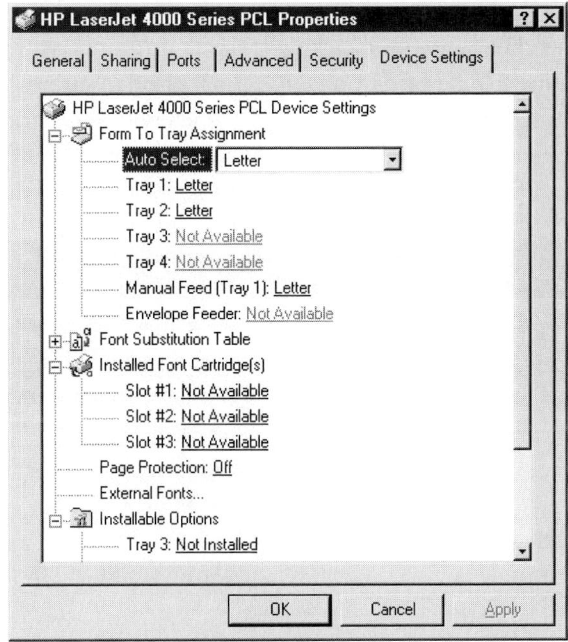

FIGURE 14-15 Print device options in the Device Settings tab

One important printing feature, configuring separator pages, is not located in the Device Settings tab. A separator page is a document that contains commands sent to the print device for one of two reasons:

- Separating print jobs and identifying the owner of the job
- Switching between printing modes. Many modern printers support at least two printer languages, usually PostScript and the vendor's printer language (such as PCL). The separator page can send instructions to the printer telling the printer what language the following print job uses if the printer cannot automatically detect the language used in the print job.

Windows 2000 comes bundled with four separator page files, stored in the %systemroot%\System32 folder. The files and their functions are described in Table 14-9.

Printers do not have to be set up on the server so that only one queue points to only one print device. Multiple queues can point to the same print device, and multiple print devices can service the same queue. Depending on your printing needs, you may set up one or both of these configurations in your environment. The first scenario is useful to help establish multiple priority queues for a single print device (see Figure 14-16). If a print device is shared by a VP, regular employees, and workers who produce large volume printouts, you may set up three queues. The first queue could be set up with normal priority settings and would be usable by everyone. A second queue could be established with high priority settings so that only the VP and his or her delegates could submit jobs to that queue. A third queue could be configured as very low priority and the only one that accepts large document

TABLE 14-9 Description of Bundled Separator Pages

Separator Page File	Description
Pcl.sep	Switches the printer to PCL printing mode and prints a page preceding each document.
Pscript.sep	Switches the printer to PostScript printing mode and prints a page preceding each document.
Sysprint.sep	Prints a PostScript-compatible page preceding each document.
Sysprtjp.sep	Prints a PostScript-compatible page preceding each document using Japanese characters.

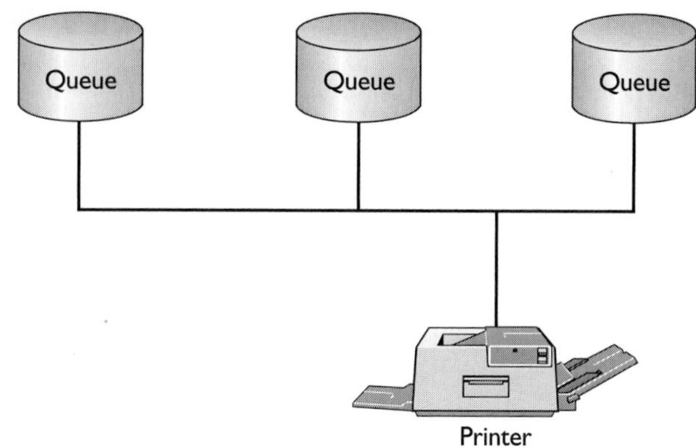

FIGURE 14-16

Priority queues printing to a single print device

submissions. In this configuration, everyone in the area would have the regular queue set up as the default printer on their computers. If the VP needed to generate a print document quickly and there were a large number of print jobs already in the queue, the document would be placed in the high-priority queue and would begin printing on the print device immediately following the current document. A large job would be printed in the low-priority queue, which would keep it from printing until all other jobs in the normal and high-priority queue finished.

To set the priority on a print queue, open the printer's Properties dialog and click the Advanced tab. This will display the information shown in Figure 14-17. The Priority: picklist contains values from 1 to 99, with 1 being the lowest priority. The queue set up for long print jobs would have a low priority, probably 1. The queue set up for the VP would have a high priority, probably 99. The regular queue would have a priority somewhere between the two values, possibly around 50.

The second scenario is called printer pooling and is ideal for high-volume printing environments. There is no default designation of priorities in this scenario other than that all print jobs need to be printed as quickly as possible. To set up a printer pool, you would need several identical printers and configure them to service the same print queue, which is illustrated in Figure 14-18. When several jobs are submitted to the queue, the first job goes to one of the printers. The next job, seeing that one of the printers is already in use, starts printing on the next printer in the pool, and so on. Ideally, you would set up at least two or three high-speed print devices in the same physical location to support this type of print scenario.

To create a printer pool, open the printer's Properties dialog and click the Ports tab, as shown in Figure 14-19. Normally, only one port can be selected in this dialog

FIGURE 14-17

Printer Properties Advanced tab Priority setting

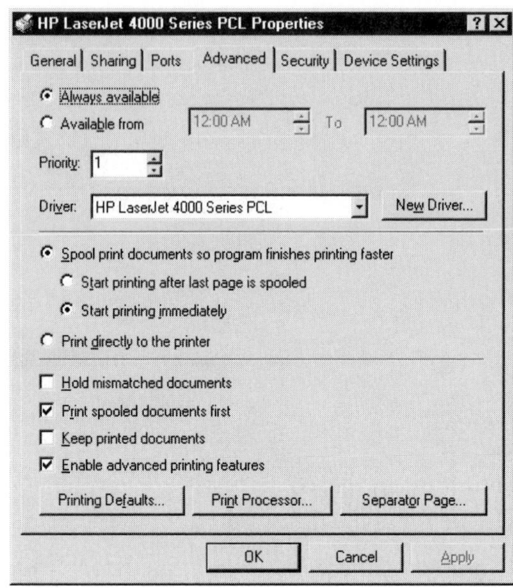

for each printer. However, turning on the Enable printer pooling check box will let you select multiple ports, and therefore multiple print devices, for a single queue. The print queue will then automatically redirect print devices through all the selected ports, spreading the print load among the print devices connected. Identical print devices must be used, however, as only one print driver can be loaded for the queue, and all the settings for the queue will be applied to all connected print

FIGURE 14-18

Printer pooling from a single queue

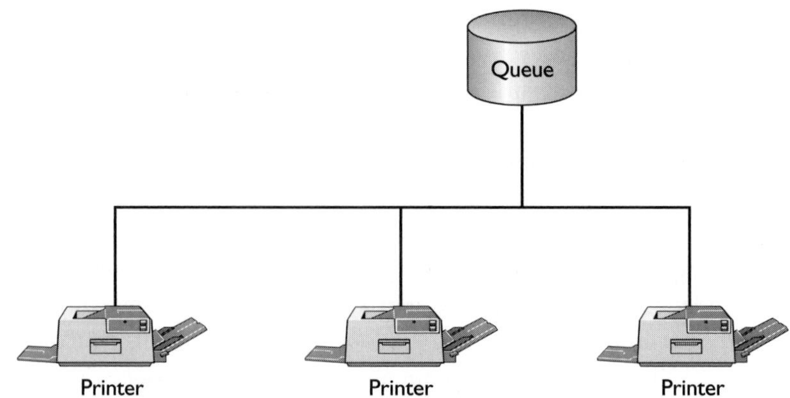

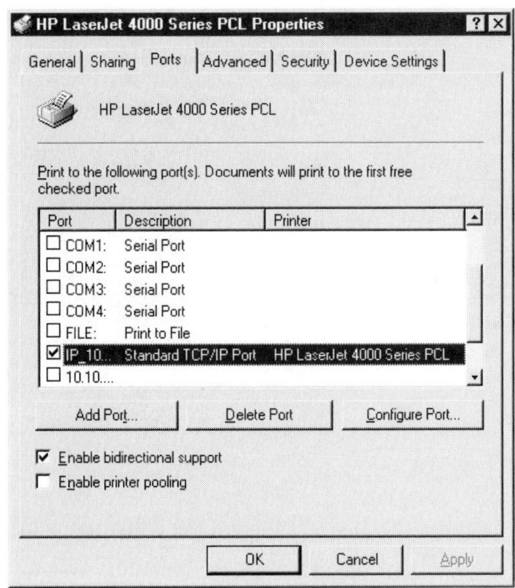

FIGURE 14-19

Printer Properties Ports tab with Enable printer pooling check box

devices. For instance, if one printer does not have a duplexing unit installed but the driver is configured to print duplex by default, any jobs sent to that printer will not print in duplex, and the owner of the job may get understandably upset.

Document Management

Providing printer support is more than connecting the print devices to the network and making them available through printer shares on the print server. In most cases, printer administrators must manage documents in the print queues as well. There may be times when a large job is preventing other users from printing documents, or a document is hung in the queue waiting for a particular form to be loaded at the printer. For these and other reasons, you may need to manipulate the documents in the queue directly.

Managing Documents from Windows 2000 There are several ways to manage print jobs in the queues. The first is to open the printer object on the server and manipulate the jobs in the queue directly. Within the print queue window, you can double-click a print job and modify settings on that job, as shown in Figure 14-20. In this window, you can modify the priority of the specific print job, change the account to be notified when the job has printed, and specify a time restriction

FIGURE 14-20

Print Job Properties General tab

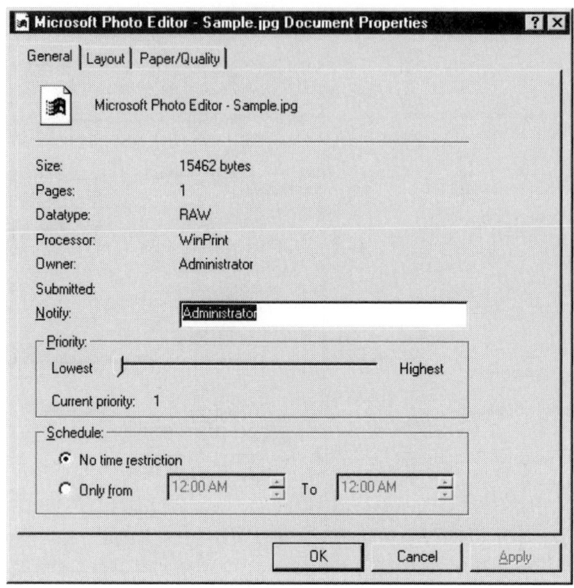

on the job. In the Layout and Paper/Quality tabs, you can modify the settings particular to the print device being used.

In addition to modifying the properties on the print job, you can also Pause, Resume, and Cancel the print job from the Document menu in the print queue window. Pausing the job will place the job "on hold," allowing other jobs in the queue to print ahead of it. You can take the job "off hold" by Resuming the job. Canceling the job deletes it from the queue, and the job will not be printed.

Managing Documents with a Web Browser From a Windows 2000 workstation or server, a Web browser can also be used to manage documents in a Windows 2000 print queue. When you are logged in to the Windows 2000 network with an account that has permissions to manage the print queue, you can point your Web browser to the print server's printer URL, usually http://<servername>/printers. Then you can click the print queue name to list the jobs active in the queue, as shown in Figure 14-21. Selecting a job in the queue will activate the Pause, Resume, and Cancel links in the Document Actions area of the browser window. These actions have the same effect as the actions just described.

FIGURE 14-21

Windows 2000 Web interface to print job management

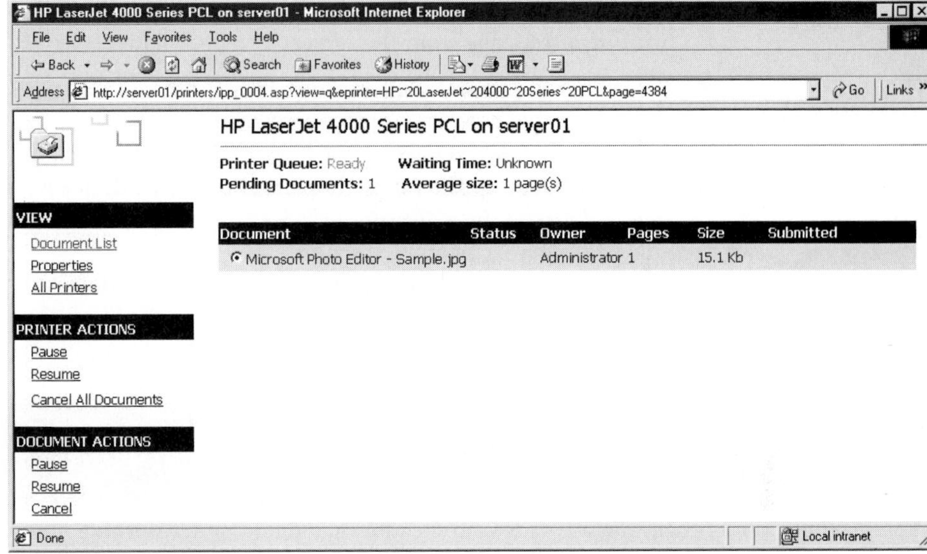

Troubleshooting Printing Problems

There are a number of problems that you can encounter in the printing environment, but most of them are minor in nature and can be resolved easily. The first class of problems deals with the print device itself and will not be detailed here. Essentially, if the printer is unable to perform its own self-checks correctly, it will need to be serviced before any troubleshooting can occur for other related printing problems on the server.

Here are some guidelines for identifying other problems with the printing process.

- Verify that the print device is plugged in and powered on, and that the network connection, if any, to the printer is active.
- Print from a different document or application to rule out issues with the document or program. Problems with a document or application generally revolve around driver conflict or incompatibilities.
- Print to the print device from a different user account to rule out problems with the user account. Problems with the user account generally revolve around permissions.
- Verify that the correct driver is loaded on the server and workstation for the print device. Incorrect drivers can generate garbled printouts or no printouts at all, especially when a PCL driver is used to print to a PostScript printer.

- Verify that the print server can communicate with the print device by printing a test page from the server.
- Verify that the Print Spooler service is enabled and active on the print server.
- Verify that there is enough disk space on the server for print jobs to spool.
- If a print queue appears to be hung and the print device is working properly, stop and restart the print spooler service.

Now that you have a better understanding of how Windows 2000 manages the printing process, here are some real-world and exam scenarios you may encounter.

SCENARIO & SOLUTION	
You've set up priority queues for a print device so that a VP and his admin can print high-priority documents ahead of other users. Sometimes jobs printed to the priority queue come out before other documents; sometimes they do not. What's happening?	Several situations could lead to this scenario. First, make sure that each queue does have a different priority set. The high priority queue should have a priority of 99, and the other queue should have a priority of 50 or less (1 being the lowest priority). If the priorities on the queues are the same, the spooler will alternate between the queues, meaning some jobs in the "low" priority queue would print before jobs in the other queue. Another possibility is that the high-priority queue has not been restricted so that only the VP and his admin can print to it. If the queue is unrestricted, other users could find the queue, realize it is a high priority queue, and print their nonpriority jobs to it if they didn't want to wait. Check the permissions on the queues as well as the priority settings to make sure the configuration matches your desired behavior.
A VP asked you to set up a color printer to be shared off his admin's computer so that only he and his staff can print to it. It is an expensive printer to maintain, and they don't want everyone in the company printing to it. You set up the share on the admin's workstation, and everything was working fine for several weeks. Then people outside his department started printing to the printer, and now he's angry with you. What happened?	Again, this is probably a permissions problem. Just because the printer has been shared off a workstation and not a server does not mean that it is hidden from the rest of the company. To ensure that only the desired people can print to the printer, you will need to set up a group on the workstation with the accounts who should have access to the printer and then restrict the printer to that group only. Users outside that group may still locate the printer, but with the appropriate permissions applied they won't be able to print to it. Connecting the printer to the admin's workstation and not to the network was a good idea, though, as it will prevent anyone else from creating a print object that connects with the printer directly across the network.

CERTIFICATION SUMMARY

Windows 2000 provides many default tools for managing shared resources such as file folders, Dfs, and printers. Files and folders on NTFS volumes can be protected by NTFS file and folder permissions. Folders that are shared out on the network can be further protected by share permissions. Management of file and folder permissions can be performed with several tools, most often Windows 2000 Explorer or the Microsoft Management Console.

Commonly used folder shares can be collected into a Distributed File System (Dfs) tree for easy access by all network users. The Dfs tree is a collection of Dfs nodes that point to network shares on multiple servers. Users see the shares as part of one file system tree and may not be aware that file resources are being served off multiple servers. Configuring multiple network shares to point to the same Dfs node can provide fault-tolerant and load-balanced access to those resources.

Printing resources can be shared off Windows 2000 servers or workstations. Print server shares can be advertised in the Active Directory, making it easier for users to find and use network printers. Printers can be set up to connect to print devices with a number of different network connection protocols. Printer configurations and queued documents can be managed through a Web browser if the print server has Internet Information Services or Peer Web Services configured and active.

TWO-MINUTE DRILL

Monitoring, Configuring, Troubleshooting, and Controlling Access to Files, Folders, and Shared Folders

- Files and folders on NTFS volumes can be protected with NTFS file and folder permissions. The permissions are Read, Write, Read & Execute, Modify, and Full Control. NTFS folder permissions have an additional permission, List Folder Contents.
- Folder shares are protected with share permissions. The permissions are Read, Change, and Full Control.
- NTFS and Share permissions are cumulative. If a user has Read permission from one group and Write permission from another, the effective permissions are Read and Write.
- The more restrictive permission is the effective permission when Share and NTFS permissions are combined. If a user has Read permission on a share but Full Control on the NTFS folder, the effective permissions are Read.
- Share permissions protect folders shared from any volume type (FAT, FAT32, NTFS), but NTFS permissions apply only to NTFS volumes.

Monitoring, Configuring, Troubleshooting, and Controlling Access to Dfs Resources

- Distributed File System (Dfs) provides access to a variety of network shares on multiple servers from a single, logical tree structure on the network. Users accessing resources via Dfs are not aware that resources from one Dfs node may be stored on a different server than resources from another Dfs node.
- Dfs provides fault tolerance and load balancing for network resources. A Dfs node can point to multiple shares that contain the same information. When the source for one share becomes unavailable because it is offline or busy, users are automatically redirected to another source.

- Dfs stand-alone roots are entirely stored on a single server. Information about the Dfs tree is stored in that server's registry, and if the server goes offline, the Dfs tree becomes unavailable.
- Dfs fault-tolerant roots make use of the Active Directory. Information about the root is stored in the Active Directory and remains available when the host server goes offline.
- Dfs resources are managed with the Distributed File System snap-in.

Monitoring, Configuring, Troubleshooting, and Controlling Access to Printers

- The four types of printer configurations are local printer, whereby the printer is connected directly to the computer; network printer, whereby the printer is connected via the network; remote local printer, whereby the printer is directly connected to a remote print server; and remote network printer, whereby the printer is connected via the network to a remote print server.
- Remote printers can be connected in a number of ways, including TCP/IP, LPR/LPD, JetDirect, NWLink, and AppleTalk.
- Windows 2000 stores print drivers on the print server. Windows 2000 print clients do not have to download and install print drivers locally when they print through a print server. Windows 2000 print servers can store print drivers for other clients that the clients must download and install locally before printing to the Windows 2000 print server.
- Windows 2000 print servers can advertise printers to Windows 2000 clients through the Active Directory. Windows 2000 clients can search the Active Directory for shared printers so users do not need to know the name of the print server hosting the printer.
- Windows 2000 print services can be administered through a Web interface if IIS or Peer Web Services are installed on the server or workstation sharing the printers.

MCSE

MICROSOFT CERTIFIED SYSTEMS ENGINEER

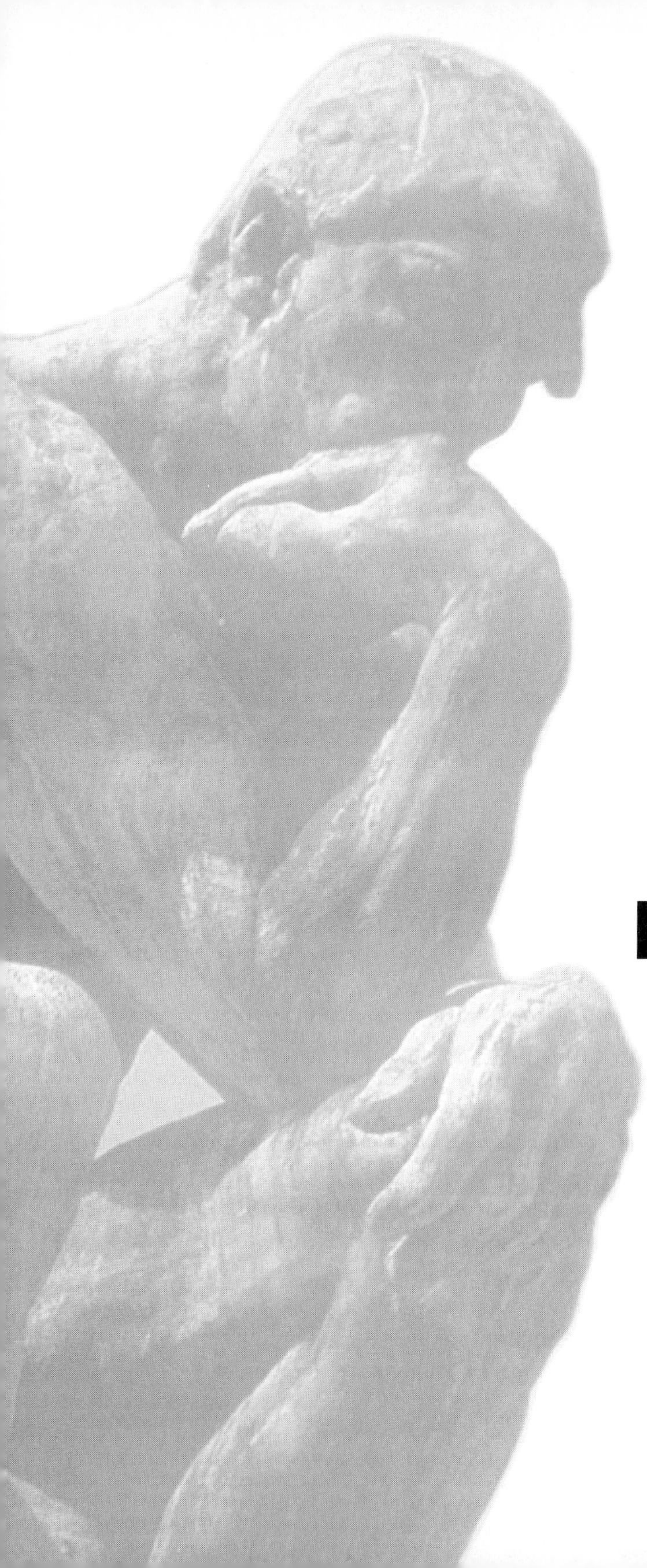

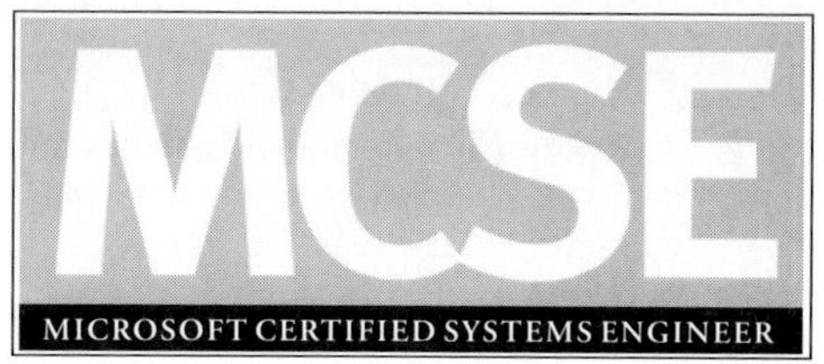

15

Terminal Services and Internet Information Services

CERTIFICATION OBJECTIVES

15.01	Understanding Terminal Services
15.02	Installing and Configuring Terminal Services
15.03	Monitoring and Troubleshooting Terminal Services
15.04	Understanding Internet Information Services
✓	Two-Minute Drill

Not so long ago, "thin was in." It was speculated that *thin clients*—computers or devices that rely on "fat" servers to get the job done—would overtake the personal computer-centric world. Consequently, a great deal of energy was channeled toward producing thin clients. In subsequent years, personal computer prices plummeted dramatically, and the excitement surrounding the thin-client movement died down. However, many companies, including Microsoft, continued to work on their thin-client initiatives.

By no means is Microsoft trying to replace the personal computer with its thin-client initiatives. It is trying to supplement the personal computer by incorporating the power of thin clients into the PC with Terminal Services and Internet Information Services. Terminal Services and Internet Information Services allow clients to do all their application processing on a server computer, greatly reducing the resources needed by the client computers. This ability allows the client to do processing with software that is installed on the server but not on the client. As a consequence, the lifetime and usefulness of client computers are greatly extended.

Terminal Services were available in a special edition of Windows NT 4.0, but Microsoft has improved it a great deal and made it an integral part of the entire Windows 2000 Server family. It comes with and can be installed on any Windows 2000 Server using one of the following modes:

- Application server mode
- Remote administration mode

Application server mode was the only mode in which Terminal Services was implemented in Windows NT 4.0. It allows clients to simultaneously access Windows-based applications that run on the server. When installed on the server, they can be available to all clients who connect to the server and can run with all the resources that the server has to offer. Generally speaking, the applications that run on a terminal server must be modified to some extent in order to function optimally when Terminal Services is in application server mode.

Being able to use Terminal Services in *remote administration mode* is new to Windows 2000. It should prove a very powerful and pervasive tool to administer the Windows 2000 Server family. Remote administration mode provides administrators with secure remote graphical administration of the Windows 2000 Server family. With Terminal Services in remote administration mode, an administrator can connect, monitor, and troubleshoot servers from almost any location.

Internet Information Services (IIS) provides interfaces that can understand HyperText Transfer Protocol (HTTP) and File Transfer Protocol (FTP) to interact with clients around the world. Whereas Terminal Services brings the Windows 2000 interface to client computers, IIS typically delivers an HyperText Markup Language (HTML) interface to client computers. Once again, this ability allows client computers to offload resource-intensive processing to a server and allows clients to do processing with software that exists on the server.

CERTIFICATION OBJECTIVE 15.01

Understanding Terminal Services

Terminal Services provides the Windows 2000 graphical user interface (GUI) to any device that can run a Terminal Services client locally. Microsoft produces client software for the following operating systems:

- Windows CE-based terminals and handheld professional devices
- 16-bit Windows-based PCs running Windows for Workgroups 3.11 with MS TCP/IP-32
- 32-bit Windows-based PCs running Windows 95, Windows 98
- Windows NT 3.51, Windows NT 4.0, or Windows 2000 Professional

Terminal Services is designed to allow a client to do all its application processing on a server, giving existing computers additional functionality provided by terminal servers. As long as the client is able to use Terminal Services, it can do almost anything that the server can do. For instance, a Windows for Workgroups 3.11 client connecting to Terminal Services has access to the Windows 2000 look and feel and all the 32-bit software that would not run on the older operating system. In this way, the older client can run the modern software without having to upgrade the client's hardware. The potential longevity of the client is greatly extended with this approach.

Terminal Services is able to support such a large variety of clients because it is built on two industry-standard protocols:

- Transmission Control Protocol/Internet Protocol (TCP/IP)
- Remote Desktop Protocol (RDP)

Terminal Services uses *Transmission Control Protocol/Internet Protocol (TCP/IP)* as the transport protocol between the client and the server for Terminal Services. This protocol allows sessions to exist over a local area network (LAN), a wide area network (WAN), the Internet, or any other method in which TCP/IP is used. Microsoft provides only support for TCP/IP communication, which allows Terminal Services connections to be implemented through any sort of network that supports TCP/IP, including virtual private networks (VPN) and wireless networks.

Remote Desktop Protocol (RDP) is the application protocol between the client and the server. It informs the server of the keystrokes and mouse movement of the client and returns to the client the Windows 2000 graphical display from the server. Microsoft RDP 5.0 is based on the International Telecommunications Union (ITU) T.120 protocol, a multichannel, standard protocol that provides various levels of compression so that it can adapt to different connection speeds and encryption levels from 40 bits to 128 bits. TCP/IP is the courier that carries the messages, and RDP is the language in which the messages are written. Both are needed to use Microsoft's implementation of Terminal Services.

Now that you have an understanding of Terminal Services, let's look at some possible scenario questions and their answers.

exam Watch ***In addition to the graphical interface, it is possible to return audio to the client.***

SCENARIO & SOLUTION	
In what modes can Terminal Services be run on a Windows 2000 Server?	Terminal Services can be run in either application server mode or remote administration mode.
What network protocol is needed for the Microsoft client to use Terminal Services?	TCP/IP is required to run Terminal Services with the Microsoft client. Third-party vendors do sell add-ons that allow other network protocols to be used.
What information is transmitted to the Terminal Services server from the client?	The keystrokes and mouse movements are sent from the client to the server, and the Windows 2000 GUI is returned from the server to the client.

EXERCISE 15-1

Connecting to a Terminal Server with Terminal Services Client

1. From the Start menu, go to Programs | Terminal Services Client | Terminal Services Client.
2. Choose the server that you want to connect to and the screen resolution. You can either type in the name of the terminal server and then click Connect, or you can double-click a server name from the available servers list.
3. Provide your login and password in the Terminal Services window.
4. From the Start menu in the Terminal Services client window, go to Log Off. It is important that you log off your Terminal Services session; *clicking the control box on the Terminal Services window will not close your session.*
5. Close Terminal Services Client.

Remote Administration vs. Application Server

When Terminal Services is configured to run in remote administration mode, it is designed to carry a very small footprint. It installs only the needed components and uses them only when they are required, leaving out components and scripts that optimize Windows applications for the Terminal Services environment. If no one is connected to Terminal Services, Terminal Services consumes a minuscule amount of resources on the server. Because running Terminal Services in remote administration mode does not consume resources from critical servers, there is no real penalty to using Terminal Services to administer all the Windows 2000 servers. Microsoft allows the use of remote administration mode with Terminal Services with no additional licenses or fees, but you are limited to two concurrent remote administration sessions.

Application server mode consumes a great deal more overhead, in both installation and in operation. This mode allows Terminal Services to run applications remotely for many users, letting the Terminal Services server do all the application processing. Application server mode has a much larger footprint and is intended to be run as an application server. Most applications, including Microsoft Word and Excel, require special installation scripts to perform well in Terminal Services. These scripts are provided and should be installed when Terminal Services is installed in application server mode but not in remote administration mode.

exam Watch

A Windows 2000 Server must be in either application server or remote administration mode; it cannot be in both.

Remote Control vs. Remote Access

Remote access is the common way of using Terminal Services. An individual uses a Terminal Services client to connect to a server and conduct application processing on it instead of on his or her local device. All the client keystrokes and mouse movements within the Terminal Services client are sent to the server, and the graphical Windows 2000 display that is a result of the client actions on the server is passed back to the client.

Remote control is a way to monitor an existing session. With remote control, a user can connect to an existing session, see everything that the client sees, and send keystrokes and mouse movements to that session. In order to initiate remote control of a session, a user with full control must log in to the server using the Terminal Services client and then use the Terminal Services Manager to take remote control of a session. It is important to understand that you cannot use the Terminal Services Manager outside a Terminal Services client session to join a session; in order to join a session, you must be connected to the Terminal Services server using a Terminal Services client. When you are about to join the session, the user is notified that his or her session is about to be remotely controlled when you join, unless you disable the warning in the RDP-TCP properties dialog box, as shown Figure 15-1.

CERTIFICATION OBJECTIVE 15.02

Installing and Configuring Terminal Services

As mentioned earlier, Terminal Services must be installed in either application server mode or remote administration mode. It cannot be in both at one time. Microsoft has

FIGURE 15-1

Setting whether you can join a user session with or without permission

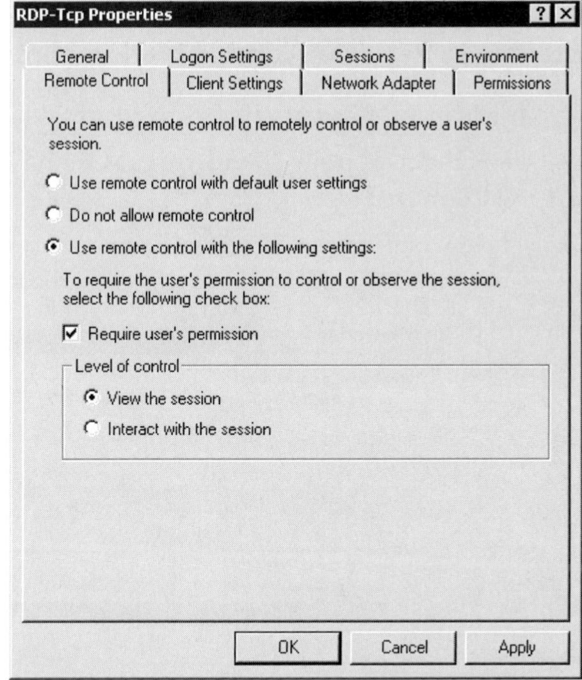

decided to make Terminal Services a core part of Windows 2000, so can you install Terminal Services using the Windows Components wizard in the Add/Remove Programs application in the Control Panel. If you are installing Terminal Services in application server mode, you need to install Terminal Services Licensing if it is not already installed (we'll do this in Exercise 15-3).

EXERCISE 15-2

Installing in Remote Administration Mode

1. Log in to the Windows 2000 Server as an administrator.
2. From the Start menu, go to Settings | Control Panel and choose Add/Remove Programs.
3. Choose Add/Remove Windows Components, and the Windows Components wizard appears, as shown in the following illustration.

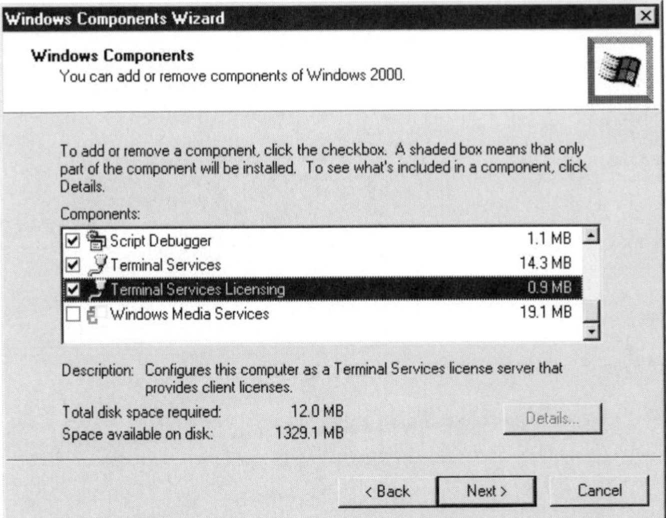

4. Select Terminal Services and click Next.
5. Choose to run Terminal Services in remote administration mode, as shown in the following illustration, and then click Next.

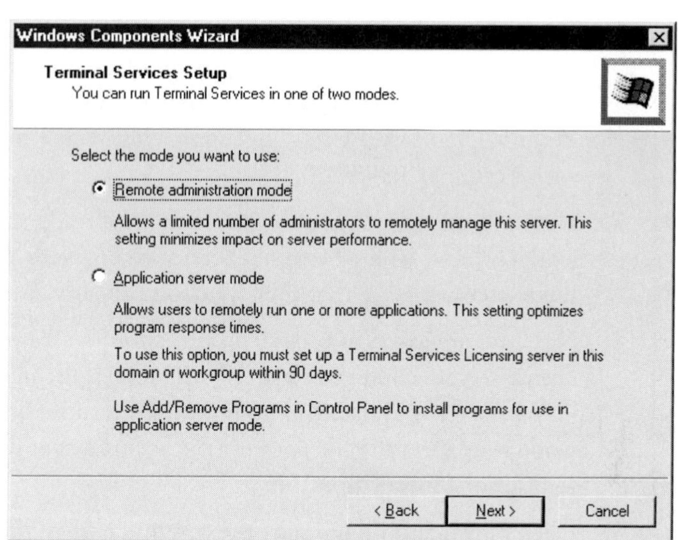

6. Click Finish and then restart the computer when prompted.

EXERCISE 15-3

Installing in Application Server Mode

1. Log in to the Windows 2000 Server as an administrator.
2. From the Start menu, go to Settings | Control Panel and choose Add/Remove Programs.
3. Choose Add/Remove Windows Components, and the Windows Components wizard appears, as was shown in Exercise 15-2.
4. Select Terminal Services and Terminal Services Licensing.
5. Choose to run Terminal Services in application server mode and then click Next.

6. The next screen prompts you to select default permissions for application compatibility. You can choose "Permissions compatible with Windows 2000 Users" to run in the most secure mode or "Permissions compatible with Terminal Server 4.0 Users" to run in a less secure mode that is compatible with Terminal Server 4.0.
7. Next you see a list of applications that are already installed and might not work correctly when Terminal Services is enabled. You will have to reinstall them later to ensure that they function properly.
8. Next you are asked to provide information to set up the computer as a license server. You need to specify the role of the license server (whether the license server is available to your entire enterprise or just your domain or workgroup) and the file path for the license server database. Click Next to begin the installation.
9. Click Finish and then restart the computer when prompted.

After you have completed your installation of Terminal Services, a number of applications are available to you inside the Administrative Tools menu:

- Terminal Services Licensing
- Terminal Services Manager
- Terminal Services Client Creator
- Terminal Services Configuration

With *Terminal Services Configuration,* you can change most of the choices that you made during installation. For instance, you can change Terminal Services from application server mode to remote access mode and permission compatibility mode. In addition, you can configure other server settings as follows:

- Delete temporary folders on exit
- Use temporary folders per session
- Use Internet connector licensing
- Use Active Directory

You can also create, modify, and delete connection properties such as encryption level, remote access, and client settings.

Terminal Services Manager, shown in Figure 15-2, allows you to monitor, kill, and join sessions. Terminal Services Licensing communicates with a licensing server that holds all the Terminal Services Client Access Licenses (TS CAL).

Terminal Services Client Creator, shown in Figure 15-3, allows you to create a floppy disk installation program for:

- 16-bit Windows
- 32-bit Windows on x86

In addition to being able to install the Terminal Services client from floppy disk, you can also install Terminal Services over the network. The network installations are stored in:

```
\\%systemroot%\\system32\clients\tsclient\net\
```

You need to establish a unique home directory for each user who will connect to the server using Terminal Services. If no home directory is specified for a user, the profile directory will be \Documents and Settings\Username.

FIGURE 15-2

Terminal Services Manager allows you to monitor and manage all the available terminal servers

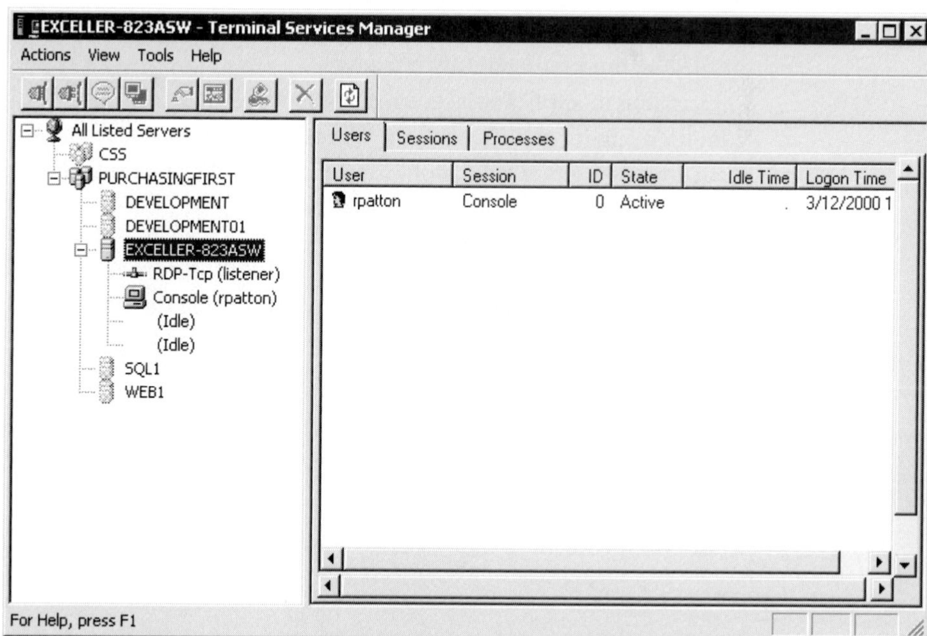

FIGURE 15-3

Terminal Services Client Creator allows you to create installation floppy disks

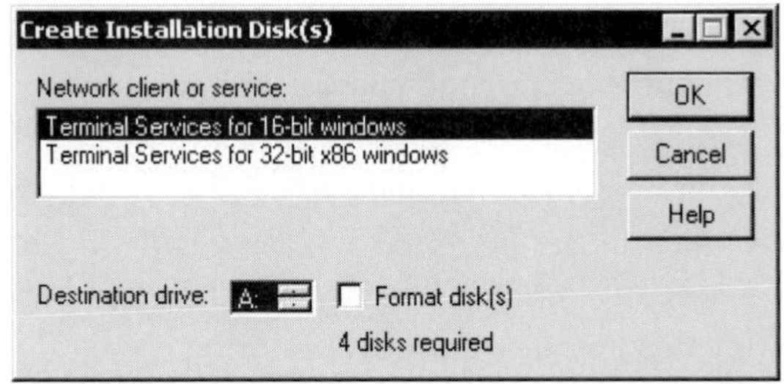

All Microsoft Terminal Services clients must be running a 32-bit version of TCP-IP and have at least a 33MHz 386 processor, 4MB or RAM, and 500KB of disk space. If you want to use the bitmap caching feature, you need more available disk space. Like most applications, the Terminal Services Client runs better if the client computer has more RAM.

Terminal Services Licensing

In the past, licensing for Terminal Services was not easily understood, and this is still fairly true with Terminal Services in Windows 2000. You do not need licenses for Terminal Services when it is in remote administration mode. Remote administration mode can—and most of the time should—be used for every Windows 2000 Server that is not in application server mode. Remote administration mode is free and, as detailed before, tremendously effective.

Licensing in application server mode is somewhat confusing because it is separate from licensing for the clients for a Windows 2000 Server. Licenses, which are needed when a server is in application server mode, are available in several types:

- Terminal Services Client Access License (TS CAL) is a purchased license for a device that does not have Windows 2000 Professional installed. When a client tries to connect to a terminal server for the first time, a license is issued to the client device.
- The licensing server issues temporary TS CALs to client devices that are trying to connect when there are no licenses available. A client is able to receive a Temporary Terminal Services Client Access License only once, and the license is valid for 90 days.
- Each copy of Windows 2000 Professional has a valid license to be a Terminal Services client.

- The Internet Connector License permits up to 200 anonymous Internet concurrent user connections. This license can be useful for demonstrating Windows-based applications to groups of Internet users for short periods; it cannot be used by employees of your company.

Licenses are stored locally on a licensing server. A single server can contain the licenses for many servers running Terminal Services in application server mode.

Microsoft Clearinghouse is the organization that can activate a licensing server and issue terminal server client licenses to licensing servers. Microsoft Clearinghouse can be accessed using the Terminal Services Licensing wizard, directly through TCP-IP. If that cannot be done, the clearinghouse can also be accessed through a Web page, by telephone, or by fax machine.

Remotely Administering Servers Using Terminal Services

You can perform almost any administrative task on a server using Terminal Services. You can defragment the hard drives, edit the registry, add COM+ components, administer print sharing, and even conduct tasks that require a reboot. However, you should not reboot an important server unless you can gain physical access to the server in case a problem occurs during rebooting, such as a floppy disk being left in the disk drive.

One of the nice features of Terminal Services is that you can transfer information using the Windows Clipboard. You can seamlessly copy information from a document on the client and paste it in the server, or vice versa. This feature is called *clipboard redirection.* However, clipboard redirection does not work with files. If you want to exchange files between the client and server, you must use either a shared network device or the file-copy utilities available in the Windows 2000 Server Resource Kit.

Configuring Terminal Services for Application Sharing

Terminal Services requires a Pentium or higher processor and a minimum of 128MB RAM. Additional RAM must be added to support each concurrent user on the server. The *Windows 2000 Terminal Services Capacity and Scaling* white paper suggests an additional 3.4MB RAM for each light user and up to 9MB RAM for each power user. Other sources recommend greater amounts of RAM per user type, and for the most part, having more RAM on a server is not a bad thing.

Configuring Applications for Use with Terminal Services

After Terminal Services is installed in application mode on the server, you need to install the applications that will be used by the clients via Terminal Services. The best way to handle application installation is through the Add/Remove Programs application in the Control Panel. If applications are installed this way, Terminal Services will be able to replicate the needed registry entries or configuration files for each user per program. The Add/Remove Programs application in the Control Panel is the recommended way to install the applications, but you could achieve a similar result by installing the applications with the CHANGE USER /INSTALL command from the command line. You put the server in install mode through the command line by typing **change user /install**, perform your installation, and exit install mode from the command line by typing **change user /execute**.

Most applications need to have additional application compatibility scripts to be run after their installation is complete. It is important to run the scripts after the programs are installed but before any client session is initiated. The scripts alter the way that the applications function so that they better coexist under Terminal Services.

on the Job

Some applications do not complete installation until after the Terminal Services server is rebooted. Once the server is rebooted, log on with the same administrator logon with which you performed the installation and let the installation finish.

In order for Terminal Services to replicate the necessary registry entries or .INI files for each user, the user must install the application in install mode. This installation is accomplished using Add/Remove Programs in the Control Panel.

Terminal Services can automatically connect local client printers at logon. When the client logs on to the server, the local printer is detected and the appropriate printer driver is installed on the terminal server. If multiple printers are connected, you can also default all print jobs to the main client printer. You can also specify an initial application through Terminal Services Configuration, but this application will be the only application available to all users.

on the Job

If you decide to disable Terminal Services while in application server mode, the applications that you installed and configured to run on a terminal server will not run when you enable Terminal Services again. You will have to configure or install the applications again in order for them to function correctly.

CERTIFICATION OBJECTIVE 15.03

Monitoring and Troubleshooting Terminal Services

Through Terminal Services Manager, an administrator can monitor all the user sessions, their processes, and all processes on the machine. With Terminal Services Manager, you can see all the processes running on a server or look at just the process for a single session. In addition to seeing the user sessions and processes, an administrator can disconnect user sessions and kill processes, providing a powerful mechanism to find and terminate a user who is consuming too many resources.

If a user is having problems, an administrator can join a session with Terminal Services Manager to help the user. In this mode, the administrator sees what the user sees and is able to send his or her own keystrokes and mouse movements to the session. In addition, administrators can send messages to users in sessions using the Terminal Services Manager.

In the event that a terminal server needs to be rebooted remotely, it is best to do it via the TSSHUTDN command. This is a special command built to provide the most graceful shutdown possible. You could simply tell a server to reboot with the Start menu REBOOT command, but some complexities in the multisession environment might not be accounted for with the traditional REBOOT command.

An administrator is not limited to the functionality of Terminal Services Manager to inspect and correct problems; an administrator can use any of the ordinary tools, even in application server mode.

FROM THE CLASSROOM

Shutting Down the Terminal Services Server

Shutting down a Terminal Services Server through Terminal Services can be done from the Start menu, just as you would do with an ordinary workstation, but it shouldn't be handled this way. The multisession Terminal Services environment is a little more complicated than running applications from your local console. It would not be

FROM THE CLASSROOM

good practice to have it appear to users that the terminal server simply disappears from time to time.

The preferred way to shut down a Terminal Services server in a controlled manner is with the TSSHUTDN command from the command line. The easy way to remember this command is TS (Terminal Services) SHUT DN (down). Using TSSHUTDN notifies users who are connected through Terminal Services that the machine will be shut down. With this command come a few switches:

- WAIT_TIME
- /SERVER:*servername*
- /REBOOT
- /POWERDOWN
- /DELAY
- /V

When you use TSSHUTDN, all connected users, whether they are at the console or in a Terminal Services session, receive a message telling them that the Terminal Services server will shut down in *X* seconds. The default is 60 seconds, but that number can be tweaked with the WAIT_TIME parameter. This time period allows users to save their work and, if necessary, you to cancel the shutdown. The /DELAY parameter is the amount of time between the point when all users are logged off and the shutdown starts.

The most important switch to remember is the /REBOOT switch. Without it, the computer goes down but does not come back up. If you do not have physical access to the Terminal Services Server, you are unable to bring the server back up for users until you can reboot it. The /POWERDOWN switch takes the Terminal Services server all the way down to the powered-off state; without using this switch, you arrive at the screen telling you it is safe to power off the computer. If you use /POWERDOWN with /REBOOT, the computer reboots instead of ending up in a powered-down state.

The /SERVER switch allows you to run TSSHUTDN on another machine, but TSSHUTDN is installed only on machines that have installed Terminal Services Server; you will not find it installed on a machine running Windows 2000 Professional. You can use Terminal Services Client to run a session on a machine with Terminal Services Server and, from the command line of that session, use TSSHUTDN.

Note that only administrators can run TSSHUTDN.

—Robert Patton, MCDBA, MCSD, MCSE+I, MCP+I

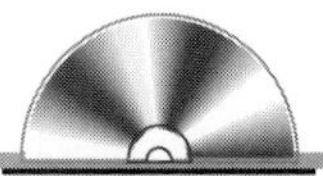

EXERCISE 15-4

Remote Control of a Terminal Services Session

1. From the Start menu, go to Programs | Terminal Services Client | Terminal Services Client.
2. Choose the server that you want to connect to, as shown in the following illustration, and choose screen resolution. You can type the name of the terminal server and then click Connect, or you can double-click a server name from the available servers list.

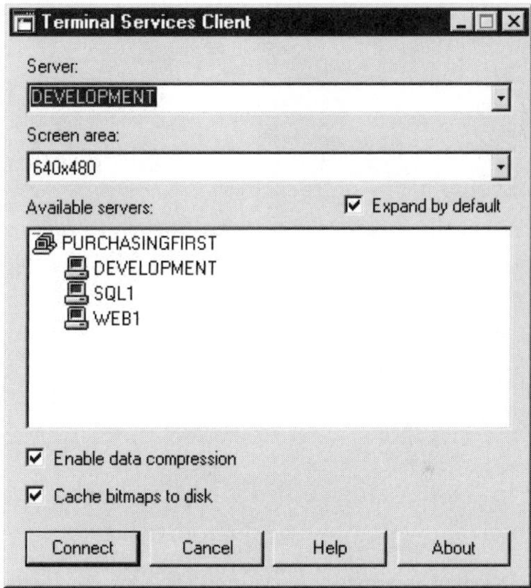

3. Provide your login and password in the Terminal Services window.
4. From the Start menu, go to Programs | Settings | Control Panel | Administrative Tools | Terminal Services Manager.
5. In Terminal Services Manager, as shown in the following illustration, right-click on the session on the server that you want to join.

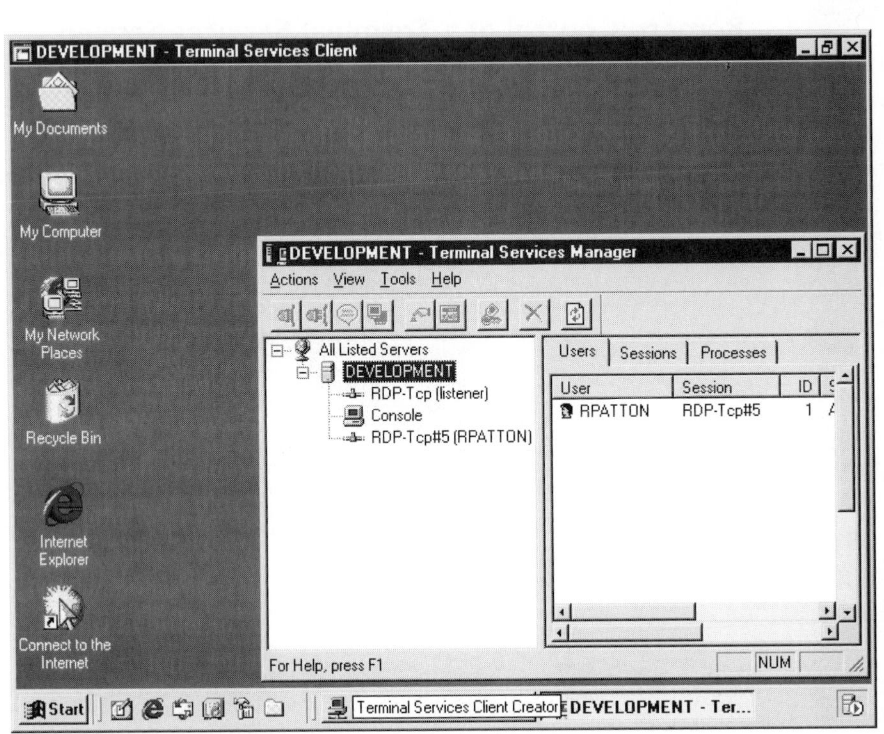

6. In the Remote Control dialog box, choose the keyboard combination that will allow you to end the joined session.
7. If you configured Terminal Services to allow the user to deny remote control, wait until they either accept or deny your attempt. Otherwise join the session.
8. Use your keyboard connection to exit the session.
9. Choose the Remote Control Menu option.
10. From the Start menu in the Terminal Services client window, go to Log Off. It is important that you log off your Terminal Services session; *clicking the control box on the Terminal Services window will not close your session.*
11. Close Terminal Services Client.

Establishing Policies for Terminal Services

You can determine feature selection or deselection at run time based on settings about the user in the registry. In Windows 2000 Server, you can use the Group Policy MMC snap-in to configure which features are available for which users; these policies can also be configured for only their terminal server sessions.

It is much easier to maintain user preferences and privileges through groups, so create Terminal Services-specific user groups. Likewise, using Terminal Services-specific profiles allows you to prevent waste of server resources by resource-intensive screen savers and background images. By assigning a specific profile to users, as shown in the Terminal Services Profile tab in Figure 15-4, you can conserve the resources of the server.

In order to set up a Terminal Services user account, the user must have an account either on the server or in a domain on the network. Terminal Services user accounts can be set up for a specific server using Local Users and Groups or for the domain using Active Directory Users and Computers. The Terminal Services user

FIGURE 15-4

Establishing the Terminal Services profile for a user

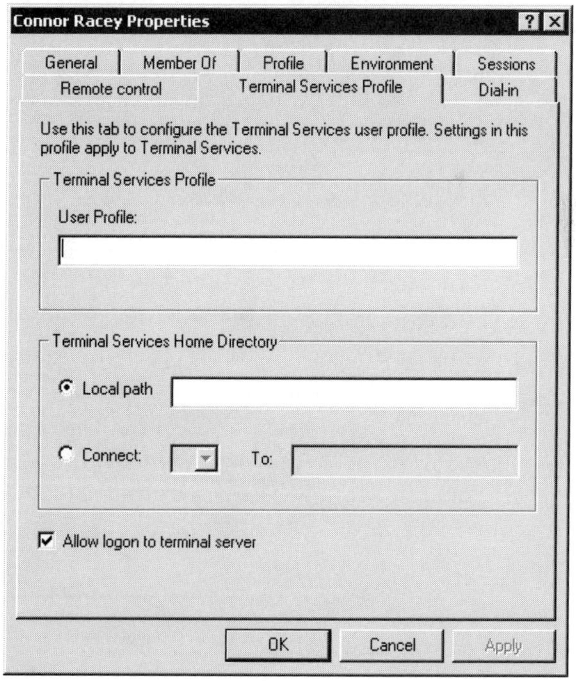

accounts contain additional information about the user, including where to retrieve desktop settings in varying circumstances.

Terminal Services Environment vs. Local Environment Settings

The Terminal Services environment can be very different from the local environment settings that a user sets up. You can configure new network and printer connections for a user to access during his or her session. You can restrict the applications that a user can access from the Start menu, and you can limit the user to a single application.

The Environment tab, shown in Figure 15-5, contains settings for creating the environment of a user connected to Terminal Services. If you specify a starting application, it automatically opens every time the user connects to a terminal server, and it is the only application that the user will be able to access through Terminal Services. In addition, if the user closes the application, the connection to the terminal server closes.

FIGURE 15-5

Establishing the environment for a Terminal Services user

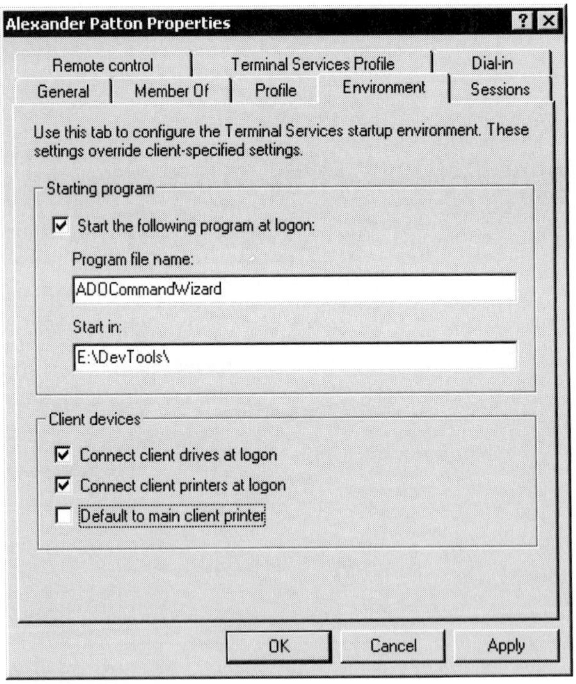

CERTIFICATION OBJECTIVE 15.04

Understanding Internet Information Services

Internet Information Services has been updated for Windows 2000 to perform better, be easier to manage, and be more reliable. IIS 5.0 interacts with clients using the HTTP and FTP protocols. One of the most important improvements in Windows 2000 Server is that multiple Web sites and FTP sites can be hosted on one PC without multihoming. Now, by choosing a different IP address, a different port, or a different host header name for a Web site, you can make a second Web site run on the same computer. In addition to making IIS easier to use, Microsoft emphasized making it easier to install. In Windows 2000, IIS can be installed using the Windows Components wizard. There is no need to get the Option Pack in order to add IIS to a Windows 2000 Server.

EXERCISE 15-5

Installing Internet Information Services

1. Log in to the Windows 2000 Server as an administrator.
2. From the Start menu, go to Settings | Control Panel and choose Add/Remove Programs.
3. Choose the Add/Remove Windows Components, and the Windows Components wizard appears.
4. Select Internet Information Services, as shown in the following illustration, and then click Next.

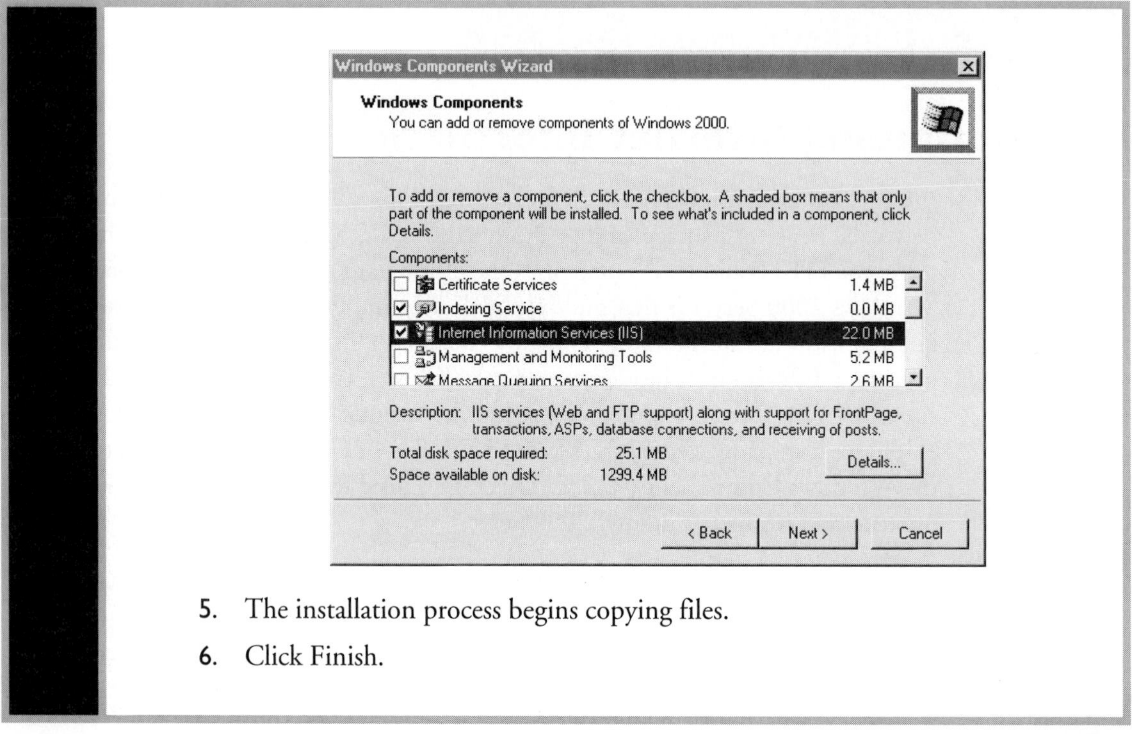

5. The installation process begins copying files.
6. Click Finish.

After you complete your IIS installation, a number of applications are available to you inside the Administrative Tools menu:

- Server Extensions Administrator
- Internet Information Services MMC snap-in

exam Watch ***The Internet Information Services MMC snap-in was formerly known as the Internet Services Manager.***

Monitoring, Configuring, and Troubleshooting Access to Web Sites

In addition to Server Extensions Administrator and the Internet Information Services MMC snap-in, "good old" Performance Monitor (called System Performance Monitor under Windows 2000) is still an excellent tool to monitor a Web site. With Performance, you can closely monitor the CPU, RAM, and disk usage of the server. In addition, System Performance Monitor has many specific counters, as shown in Figure 15-6, for Web Service, Internet Information Service Global, and Active Server Pages that will allow you to tap into almost any metric you need to monitor relating to your server's performance.

Analyzing the data provided by the System Performance Moniotr application, you should be able to tune your existing Web site thoroughly with the power of the Server Extensions Administrator and Internet Information Services MMC snap-in. A new option to audit Web server performance has been added to IIS 5. This option is called *process accounting*. You can turn it on for a Web site with the IIS MMC snap-in by clicking the extended log file format on the Extended Properties tab. With process accounting, you can record the information about how a Web site uses its CPU. This information is very useful when you are trying to isolate a single process that might need to be optimized.

Windows 2000 is a much more scriptable operating system than its predecessor; in its \Scripts directory, Microsoft provides scripts for many common management tasks for IIS. In a push for greater reliability in Windows 2000, Microsoft has built *reliable restart* into its services, allowing the automatic restart of its services in case of failure once, twice, or an unlimited number of times. In addition to being able to restart the service in event of a failure, you can also configure the system to run a file

FIGURE 15-6

Choosing counters in the System Performance Monitor to monitor a Web server

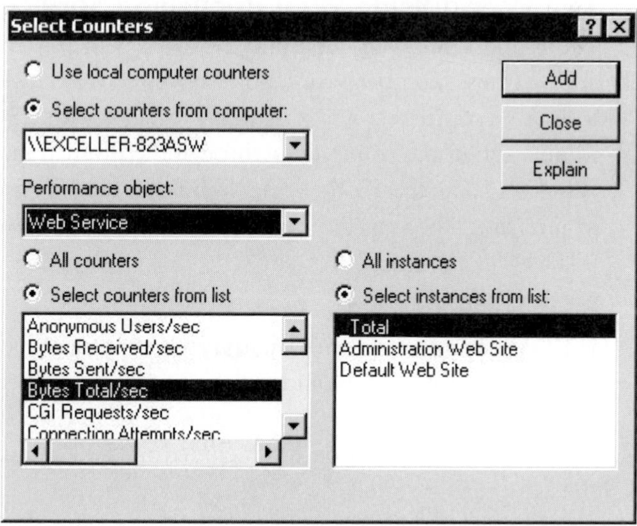

or reboot the server. The services associated with IIS can be set to automatically restart in the event of failure in order to provide the greatest possible uptime.

Accessing Files and Folders via Web Services

Windows 2000 implements a *distributed file system (Dfs)* that allows files residing in multiple network locations to reside in a single namespace. From an outside view, it is not even apparent that the files are residing in different computers, because they appear to be in one place on the network. IIS can use the Dfs available in Windows 2000.

Administration Tools

IIS can be administered using the IIS MMC snap-in or an HTML interface. The HTML interface offers much of the functionality of the snap-in, but not everything. The HTML interface was intended for remote use. However, with Terminal Services, you can use IIS MMC snap-in effectively from a remote location.

The Server Extensions Manager allows you to configure a number of parameters, including the number of expected hits for your Web site, how mail should be sent, cache sizes, and security settings for authoring. The Server Extensions Manager is available by itself in the Administrative Tools program group, but it is also incorporated within the IIS MMC snap-in.

The World Wide Web Publishing Service

The World Wide Web Publishing Service is perhaps the most important component of IIS because most people use IIS as a Web server. The World Wide Web Publishing Service is a service that is automatically installed with IIS 5.0 that provides Web administration and connectivity through the IIS snap-in. Like other services in Windows 2000, the World Wide Web Publishing Service in IIS 5.0 can be configured to automatically restart the service in case of failure, as shown in Figure 15-7.

FTP Services

HTTP is synonymous with the Internet because of its use in Web browsers, but FTP is still an important and widely used protocol to transfer files efficiently on the Internet. IIS continues to include an FTP service, which it has improved. In IIS in Windows 2000, Microsoft has included the FTP Restart protocol. To clients that

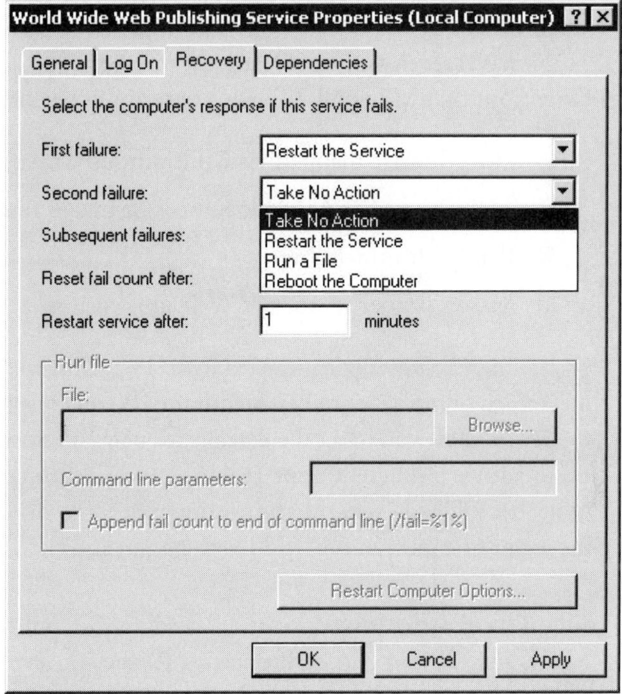

FIGURE 15-7 The World Wide Web Publishing Service Recovery tab

support it, this protocol provides the ability to continue, from the point of interruption, a download that has been interrupted.

TCP/IP is the protocol that FTP uses to transfer the information, whereas FTP is the protocol used on top of TCP/IP to execute and understand FTP. All the FTP servers can be administered from the Internet Service Manager.

Administrative Tasks

Many administrative tasks are needed to keep a Web server and its sites running optimally. You must ensure that each file and directory has the appropriate permissions. You need to set the proper cache sizes. The routine administrative tasks can be performed with the IIS MMC snap-in and the Windows 2000 Performance Monitor. Between the two, an administrator can tune a Web server for optimal performance.

Server-Level Administration

At the server level, you can set a great number of parameters for IIS and the Server Extensions that will apply to each site running on the server, such as:

- How files are mapped via Multipurpose Internet Mail Extensions (MIME)
- The server extensions (document or image and including cache sizes)
- Bandwidth throttling
- Master properties for the Web site

Bandwidth throttling is provided with IIS 5. This feature allows you to set a limit on how much of the network bandwidth the IIS can consume at a given time. The Master properties allow you to set the defaults for new and existing FTP and Web sites. If an existing value is different from a value you set in the master, you are asked whether you want that value to overwrite the existing value. To edit server properties, right-click on the server (the root) in the IIS MMC snap-in and choose Properties.

Site-Level Administration To edit a site, right-click on the site in the IIS MMC snap-in and choose Properties. At the site level, you can configure a great many things, including:

- The IP addresses, ports, and HTTP headers
- The type of logging that is done for the site
- Custom error messages
- Directory security
- Internet Server Application Programming Interface (ISAPI) filters and more
- Directory-level administration—at the directory, you can set many permissions, including:
  - Access to the directory (*Read* and *Write*)
  - Whether directory browsing is permitted

    - Execute permissions (*None, Scripts only, Scripts and Executables*)
    - To edit directory properties, right-click on the directory in the IIS MMC snap-in and choose Properties; anything you apply to a directory can also apply to all the subdirectories of the directory
- File-Level Administration—set the access for the file (anonymous, secured, etc.) if it requires Secure Sockets Layer (SSL); you can also set whether the file is marked for read, write, or logged; set the expiration of the file; or set any of the custom errors
- Access to the directory (*Read* and *Write*)
- Whether there is anonymous access
- Authenticated access (*Basic, Digested, Integrated*)

In order to have two sites on a single server, one of these three properties must be different from other sites on the server: IP addresses, ports, and host name headers. Two sites can share two of the properties, but as long as one is different, it responds to the outside world. Custom error messages allow you to set Web pages to respond to common predefined IIS errors. For instance, you could replace *Error 404* with a message that gives the user the impression that the error is handled better and is more consistent with the look and feel of your site.

To edit file properties, right-click the filename in the IIS MMC snap-in and choose Properties.

In order to aid the administration of security management in IIS, Microsoft has included some new wizards:

- Permission wizard
- Web Server Certificate wizard

The Permission wizard aids an administrator in creating and maintaining the *needed* permissions to the files and directories that should be restricted to some degree. The Web Server Certificate wizard helps with the installation, removal, and administration of certificates. This wizard makes it much easier to set up Web sites that use SSL to handle the transfer of secure information. Both are available from the IIS MMC snap-in.

Preventing Unauthorized Access to a Web Site A great deal of the HTML generated by IIS is dynamic and generated by Active Server Page (ASP) scripts. A common method for an intruder to gain unauthorized access to a Web site is by uploading scripts or an executable to the server and then having IIS execute them, giving the intruder the security privileges of the Internet Information Server. You can prevent that scenario by denying execute permissions to scripts and executables in directories where files are placed and denying write privileges to directories in which execute permissions to scripts and executables are allowed.

SCENARIO & SOLUTION

If you want a change to apply to all Web sites on a server, where should you set the property?	You should change the Master values for the Web service and, when prompted to overwrite existing value, respond "Yes."
If you set all files to be read only at the site level, can you override this setting at the file level?	Yes, you can overwrite it on a file-by-file basis, but all new files will follow whatever you set at the site level. If you want them to be different, you must edit either the file or the directory properties in which the file resides.
How do you set custom error messages in IIS 5?	On the Custom Error tab of the site, you can attach a specific file to respond in event of an error.

CERTIFICATION SUMMARY

The Microsoft Windows 2000 Server family has made great strides in unleashing the power of remote computing using client software. With either a Terminal Services client or a Web browser, clients with limited resources can do anything that powerful servers in remote locations can do.

Terminal Services for Windows 2000 greatly simplifies remote administration of back-office servers; because it is free and an integral component of Windows 2000, Terminal Services should become quite pervasive. Running Terminal Services for Windows 2000 as an application server has the potential to extend the capabilities of existing hardware, bringing the Windows 2000 interface to clients running other operating systems.

Internet Information Services provides powerful tools to provide and administer information over the Internet, building on the familiar tools of Windows 2000. Likewise, Windows 2000 has greatly simplified the management of IIS by consolidating it into a single MMC snap-in.

TWO-MINUTE DRILL

Understanding Terminal Services

- ❑ Terminal Services can be configured to run in either remote administration mode or in application server mode.
- ❑ Terminal Services Configuration allows you to change Terminal Services to run in remote administration mode or in application server mode.
- ❑ To use Terminal Services with the Microsoft Client software, you need to use TCP/IP and RDP.
- ❑ Third-party companies offer add-ons to Terminal Services that allow other network protocols and client operating systems.

Installing and Configuring Terminal Services

- ❑ Terminal Services client software can be installed over the network or with floppy disks.
- ❑ Terminal Services Client Creator creates installation disks for 16- and 32-bit Microsoft network clients.
- ❑ Microsoft recommends 128MB of RAM for Terminal Services in application server mode, plus 3.4MB of RAM for each data entry worker, 7.5MB for each knowledge worker, and 9MB of RAM for each structured task worker.
- ❑ Add applications using the Add/Remove Programs application in the Control Panel in order to ensure that the user can correctly access his or her configuration settings in the Registry and in .INI files.
- ❑ You can also add applications from the command line by running the CHANGE USER /INSTALL command.

Monitoring and Troubleshooting Terminal Services

- ❑ Terminal Services Manager is the primary tool to monitor and administer client sessions.
- ❑ Terminal Services Configuration allows you to create, modify, and delete sessions and to change high-level Terminal Services parameters.

- Through Terminal Services, you can use any standard network administration tool that is on the Terminal Services server, including Task Manager and the Performance application.
- You can join sessions to help users, sharing keystrokes, mouse movements, and the Windows 2000 GUI.

Understanding Internet Information Services

- The two primary communication protocols in Internet Information Services are HTTP and FTP.
- Windows 2000 Server allows multiple Web and FTP sites to be hosted on a single machine by giving the machine a unique IP, port, or host name header.
- Internet Information Services can be administered using the IIS MMC snap-in.
- Any property you set at one level of the IIS MMC snap-in can be inherited at a lower level. You are prompted as to whether you want those changes to apply.

MCSE

MICROSOFT CERTIFIED SYSTEMS ENGINEER

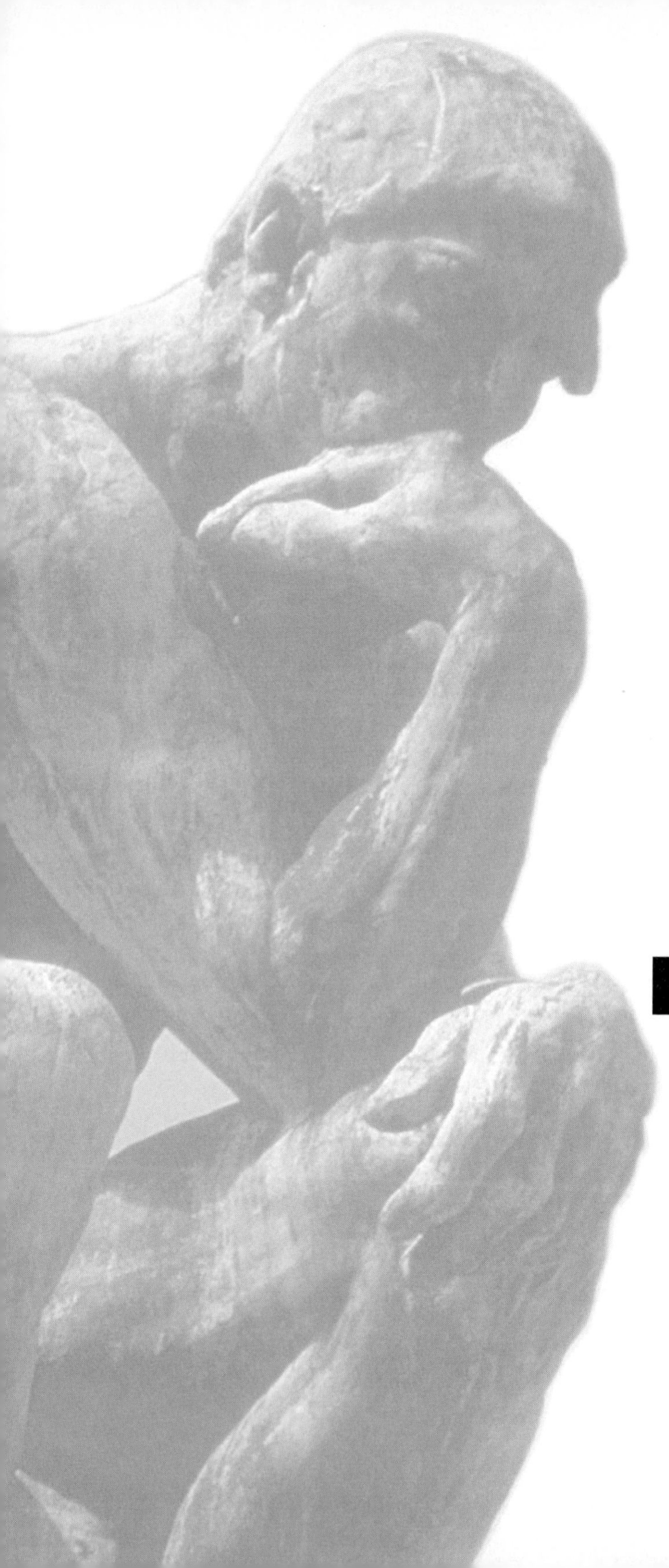

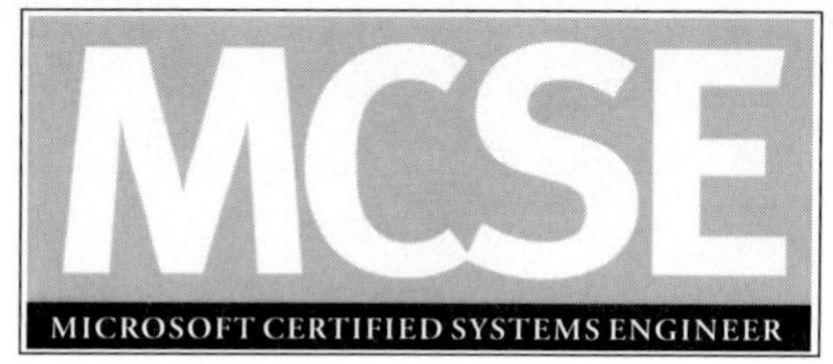

16

Securing Windows 2000 Resources with Encryption, Policies, and Profiles

CERTIFICATION OBJECTIVES

16.01 Encrypting Data on a Hard Disk by Using Encrypting File System (EFS)

16.02 Implementing, Configuring, Managing, and Troubleshooting Policies in a Windows 2000 Environment

16.03 Creating and Managing User Profiles

✓ Two-Minute Drill

This chapter details user security with encryption, policies, and profiles. Windows 2000 has a new Encrypting File System (EFS) that can be used to encrypt data either on a user's personal hard drive or on a file server. EFS is an extra level of protection for files susceptible to theft (for example, laptops). Each user has the capability to encrypt a document that they have access to as long as it is not a shared document. Once the document is encrypted, only the user who encrypted it (and the Recovery Agent) have the ability to decrypt it. Even though encryption is an additional level of security, it should not be used instead of NTFS permissions, because anyone with appropriate access to the encrypted data could delete it even though they cannot decrypt and view the file.

Policies are the next level of user security. Windows 2000 has group policies, which are a vastly improved version of Windows NT policies. The two types of group policies are user configurations and computer configurations. They are used to configure software settings, Windows settings, and administrative templates for specific users or computers. In addition, group policies can be used for software deployment, following Microsoft's software deployment life cycle definition. This previously required a separate product such as Microsoft's System Management Server (SMS). Group policies can be applied to a site, domain, or organizational unit, and a specific order of inheritance is followed when they are applied.

User profiles are an additional level of security. They are used to configure desktop settings for each user who logs on to a computer. This ensures that the next user to log on cannot see any changes that the previous user made. Windows 2000 user profiles are much more powerful than Windows NT 4 user profiles. Windows 2000 still has Local user profiles, Roaming user profiles, and Mandatory Roaming user profiles; however, they can now be used for several additional functions, such as bookmarks in the help system, My Network Places links, My Pictures, and printer connections.

CERTIFICATION OBJECTIVE 16.01

Encrypting Data on a Hard Disk by Using EFS

Microsoft's Encrypting File System (EFS) is used to encrypt Windows 2000 NTFS files and folders for added privacy beyond NTFS and share permissions. EFS is based on public key encryption, which encrypts each file with a randomly generated key that is separate from the user's public/private key pair. EFS is incorporated within the Windows 2000 NTFS file system. This makes it transparent to the user as it encrypts and decrypts in the background during normal read and write operations. When a user opens an encrypted file, EFS automatically locates the user's key from the system's key store to decrypt the file. EFS is very difficult to decipher, as it uses CryptoAPI architecture. CryptoAPI (CAPI) architecture is a collection of tasks that permit applications to digitally sign or encrypt data while providing security for the user's private key data. File encryption can be used only with information that is accessed by a single user, so EFS cannot be used with shared data. The user must also have sufficient NTFS permissions to the data in order to encrypt it.

To encrypt data, simply select the data that you would like to encrypt and check the Encrypt Contents to Secure Data check box on the folder properties advanced attribute dialog box. Figure 16-1 shows the Advanced Attributes dialog box with the encryption check box.

EFS uses two pairs of keys for the recovery policy:

- The user key pair, which is generated locally
- The recovery key pair that is issued by your Certificate Authority (CA)

FIGURE 16-1

Encrypting data within the Advanced Attributes dialog box

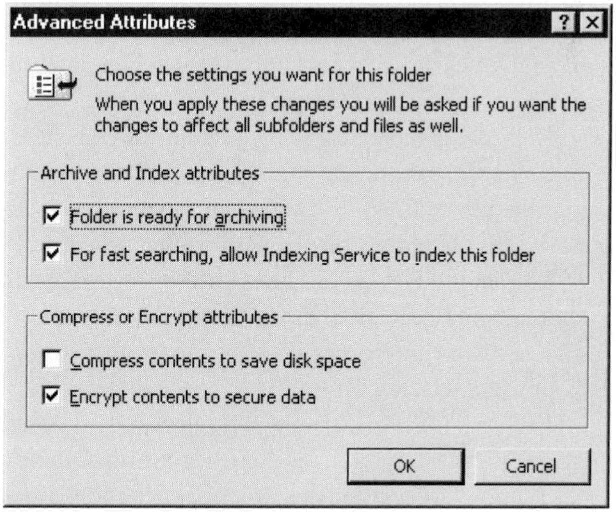

FROM THE CLASSROOM

Securing Your Encrypted Data

When you use file encryption, it is a good idea to have the users encrypt their My Documents directory. This way, the files that they create (or have previously created) will be encrypted automatically. It is also recommended that users encrypt all Temp directories. Thus, temporary files that are created when a user is modifying an encrypted document are also encrypted, which prevents unauthorized access to the data while it is in use. These two things will keep your encrypted data as secure as possible without a great deal of additional effort for the user.

—Holly Simard, MCSE, MCP+I, A+

A random key called a file encryption key (FEK) is used to encrypt each file and is then itself encrypted using the user's public key. At least two FEKs are created for every encrypted file. One FEK is created with the user's public key, and one is created with the public key of each recovery agent. There could be more than one recovery agent certificate used to encrypt each file, resulting in more than two FEKs. The user's public key can decrypt FEKs created with the public key.

EFS uses public key cryptography and requires certificate-based services in order to encrypt data. EFS uses CryptoAPI architecture, so it can store keys on secure devices such as Smart Cards.

Each key is generated using a randomly generated key (FEK) separate from the user's public/private key pair. EFS encrypts any temporary files while encrypting and gets the key certified from a CA automatically or self-signs it if there is no CA. EFS automatically renews certificates for users when they come due.

You should be very careful with private keys, as they can be a security risk. You should either generate them on a computer that is physically secure or export the key and certificate into a .pfx file protected with a strong password and store it on a floppy in a secure location.

EFS uses DESX (Data Encryption Standard-X) encryption technology. EFS also uses a 40-bit encryption level outside North America, and either a 56-bit or 128-bit encryption level within the United States and Canada. You cannot switch between encryption levels when you encrypt or decrypt at this time, although future service packs may allow you to do so.

When you see an "E" in the attributes column of Windows Explorer it means that the data is encrypted. Figure 16-2 illustrates Windows Explorer with the attributes column enabled. To view the "E" attribute, you may need to add the attributes column by going into View, Choose Columns and adding a check mark to the attribute check box. Alternatively, you can use the Cipher command to view encryption settings from the command line. Cipher will be discussed later in the chapter.

Encryption/decryption attributes are not exposed on individual files graphically because Microsoft is trying to encourage users to turn encryption on at the folder level, not on individual files. This is a better way to protect user data, as temporary files created in encrypted folders will be encrypted automatically. Table 16-1 describes the various encryption tasks that you may perform and the status of each file after you perform the task.

FIGURE 16-2

Viewing the "E" attribute

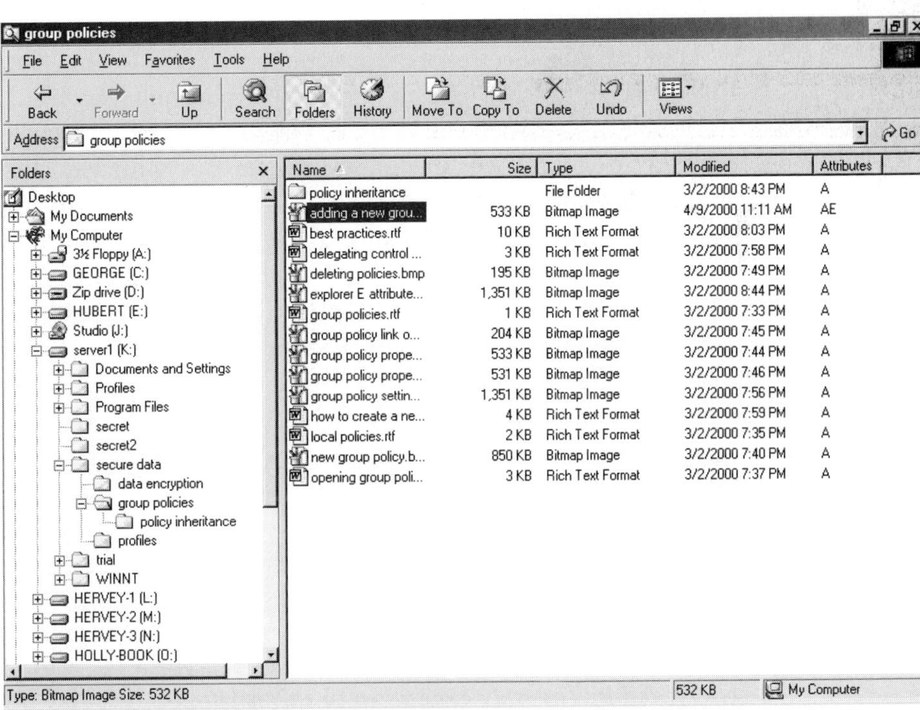

TABLE 16-1

Encryption Task and Resulting Status

Encryption Task	Status
Moving an encrypted file or folder to a non-Windows 2000 NTFS volume	Encryption is lost.
Copying an encrypted file or folder to a Windows 2000 NTFS volume	Encrypted.
Copying an encrypted file or folder to a non-Windows 2000 NTFS volume	Encryption is lost.
Moving or restoring encrypted files or folders to a different computer	Encrypted—if you use the Windows 2000 Backup tool, regardless of target volume. Otherwise, Encryption is lost. NOTE: You cannot open the file on the other computer unless it has your private key.

You can backup and copy encrypted files across systems, but they stay encrypted only if they are transferred to a NTFS version 5 system. Otherwise, the encrypted data is restored as plain text. File Encryption Keys (FEKs) cannot be exported across a network securely, so the remote copy will be encrypted with a new FEK.

As an integrated element of the operating system, Microsoft's Windows 2000 EFS is much better than other third-party encryption products, which require manual encryption and decryption on each use. This can cause security problems, as users may forget to encrypt their data after use, leaving the data vulnerable. These products also have potential leaks, as temporary paging files are left unencrypted during use. Third-party encryption utilities can also have weak security, as their encryption keys often use regular passwords that are easy to break. Most encryption products do not have the data recovery options provided by EFS. Only the user who encrypts the file and the recovery agent are capable of decrypting the document, because when a user encrypts a document, a private key is created that only the user has access to. The only other person who can decrypt the data is the administrator with the emergency recovery agent's private key. An administrator uses the recovery agent key only if a user's account has been deleted or the encryption key has been lost and the administrator requires access to the encrypted data. Once the recovery agent key is used to decrypt the data, the data cannot be reencrypted to the same state. Therefore, when users use EFS they will know for certain whether anyone else has decrypted and viewed their document.

exam Watch

Remember that the only person who can decrypt a file is the person who encrypted it. The only exception to this is when a recovery agent key is used.

The data recovery agent is defined by default the first time EFS is used on a domain or a stand-alone computer. The administrator group is defined as the recovery agent in a domain, and the local administrator account is defined as the recovery agent on a stand-alone computer.

EFS allows multiple recovery agents, which provides redundancy and flexibility with recovery procedures. EFS can also use scope-based enforcement of group policy to have different recovery agents for various parts of an organization. For example, the accounting staff may have a different recovery agent than the other staff for security reasons.

Users must obey the Encrypted Data Recovery Policy when they recover encrypted data. A default recovery policy is set up when Windows 2000 Server is installed on the first domain controller. This recovery policy designates the domain administrator as the recovery agent. Following that, a recovery policy is automatically set up when the administrator logs on to a system for the first time. This makes the administrator the recovery agent, as EFS enforces a recovery policy requirement.

You can define the following in the Encrypted Data Security Agents area of the Group Policy editor:

- No recovery policy, which allows the default local policy to be used
- Empty recovery policy, which turns EFS off
- Recovery policy with one or more X.509 v3 certificates belonging to recovery agents for that scope of administration. You can also add existing certificates or create new ones.

EFS requires that a data recovery policy be set up before EFS can be used. If a data recovery policy is set up and a user loses a private key, there are several ways to recover the encrypted file:

- The recovery agent restores the encrypted file on a secure computer with its private recovery keys. The agent decrypts it using the cipher command line and then returns the plain text file to the user.
- The recovery agent goes to the computer with the encrypted file, loads the recovery certificate and private key, and performs the recovery. It is not as safe as the first option, because the recovery agent's private key may remain on the user's computer.

Only the file's randomly generated encryption key, not the user's private key, is available when the recovery key is used. This ensures that no other private information is revealed to the recovery agent accidentally. Only the data that falls in the range of authority of a recovery agent is recoverable by the agent.

A user without the private key to a file who attempts to access it will receive an access denied message. EFS also cannot be used with data with the read-only attribute because you need to alter the file in order to encrypt it. You must have Write permission to encrypt any files that you own. You can also encrypt files that you don't own if you have Write permissions to them. This locks the owner of the files out, so as a file owner, you need to be especially careful to whom you give Write permissions. Administrators cannot encrypt system files, as these files are necessary for the system to boot. Windows 2000 ensures that this doesn't happen by failing any encryption attempts on system files. You also cannot encrypt the %systemroot% folder or any files or folders within it.

Encrypt Folders and Files

All that a user needs to do to encrypt data is to right-click the file or folder and choose Properties. Then click Advanced and add a check mark to the "Encrypt contents to secure data" check box. Once a user does this, a unique file encryption key is created that is used when the user wants to decrypt the data. To guarantee the utmost security, the file encryption key is encrypted as well.

Folders are not actually encrypted; they are simply marked to indicate that they contain encrypted files. The list of file names within a directory is also left unencrypted. Consequently, users with the correct permissions can see the names of your encrypted files even though they will not be able to decrypt and view them. If you choose to add an encrypted marking to a folder, you will be prompted to choose whether you would like to encrypt the files and subfolders that are already within the folder as well as the folder itself. Figure 16-3 shows the Confirm Attribute Changes dialog box asking if you would like to encrypt the files and subfolders within the folder that you chose to encrypt. If you opt to encrypt the files and subfolders within the folder, any data that you add to the encrypted folder subsequently will also be encrypted.

Data on remote file servers can be encrypted, although you should keep in mind that the data is not automatically encrypted as it travels over the network. To ensure the utmost security, you should implement protocol security (for example, SSL or IPSec) to encrypt the data as it crosses over the network. Users can encrypt files on a

FIGURE 16-3

The Confirm Attribute Changes dialog box

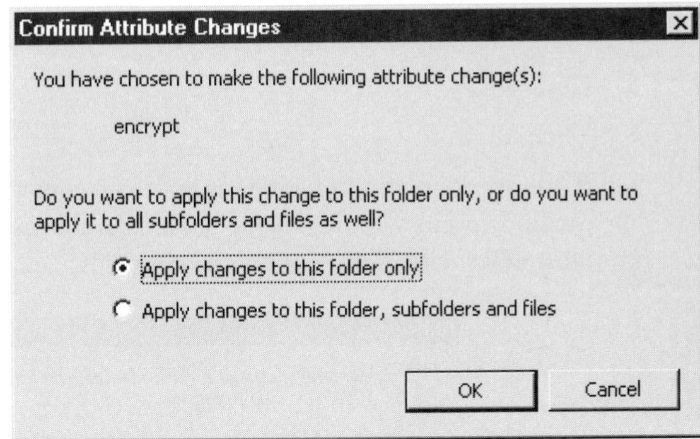

remote server only if the administrator has previously designated it as "trusted for delegation." Once the server is trusted for delegation, all users have the ability to encrypt their own documents that reside on the server. Once a file is encrypted, all reads and writes to the file are encrypted and decrypted transparent to the user. The only way a user can tell whether a file is encrypted is by checking the properties of the file. Data compression cannot be combined with encryption. They are mutually exclusive. If you rename a file or folder, it does not affect the encryption status, as it is the unique encryption key that defines the encryption status.

Exercise 16-1 shows you how to use EFS to encrypt a file or folder on an NTFS v5 partition.

EXERCISE 16-1

Using EFS to Encrypt Data

This exercise assumes that you are encrypting data on a partition that is formatted with NTFS v5.

1. Open Windows Explorer or My Computer and browse to the file or folder that you would like to encrypt.
2. Right-click the file or folder and choose Properties.
3. Click Advanced in the Properties dialog box.
4. Add a check mark to the "Encrypt contents to secure data" check box.

5. Click OK.
6. Click Apply.
7. If you are encrypting a file that is not in an encrypted folder, you will receive the Encryption Warning dialog box that is shown in the following illustration. Choose an option and click OK.

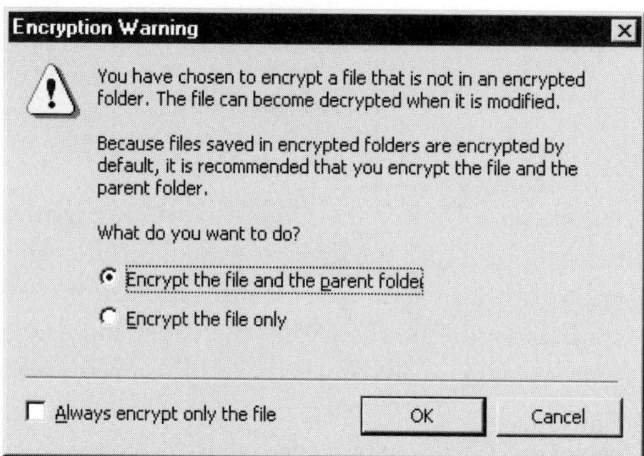

8. If you are encrypting a folder, you will receive a Confirm Attribute Changes dialog box, as seen in the following illustration. It asks whether you would like to apply changes to the files and subfolders within the folder. Choose an option and click OK.

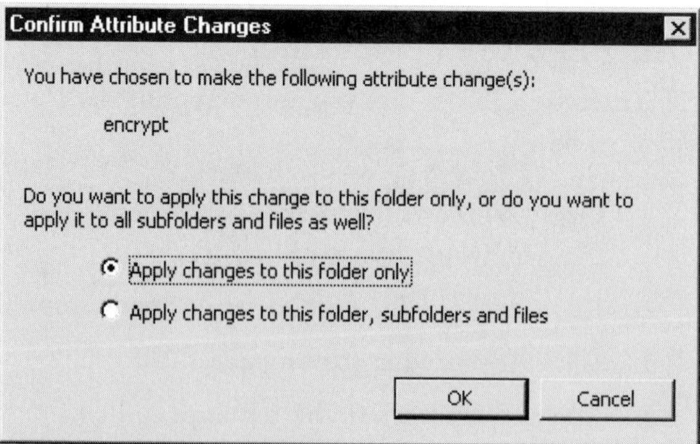

9. Click OK in the Properties dialog box.

Decrypt Folders and Files

Only the recovery agent and the person who initially encrypted it can decrypt a file or folder. To decrypt a file, you must first decrypt the file encryption key (FEK). To do this, the user's private key is matched up to the encrypted data's public key, which decrypts the file encryption key (FEK). Then the FEK can be used to decrypt the file. The only exception to this rule is when the emergency recovery agent's private key is used. This is used only if the person who encrypted the key is unavailable or if this person's account has been deleted and you must recover his or her encrypted information. Once the data is decrypted with the recovery agent's private key, only the original user can encrypt it back to the state it was in. The only time you need to decrypt data yourself is if you want to share encrypted data with other users. Encrypted data must be decrypted before other users can view it. To decrypt data, simply select the data that you would like to decrypt and remove the check mark from the encryption check box on the folder properties advanced attribute dialog box.

The Cipher Command

The cipher command is another way to encrypt and decrypt data. It can be used from the command line and has many switches so that you can define exactly what you want to have done. The Cipher.exe command syntax is simply CIPHER, followed by the switches that you would like to use, followed by the path and directory/file name. The most common switches are the /E switch, which encrypts the specified directories, and the /D switch, which decrypts the specified directories (for example, C:\>cipher /d "my documents"). You can use wildcards with the cipher command. For example, C:\>cipher /e /s *win* will encrypt all files and folders with "win" in the name and all files within them.

SCENARIO & SOLUTION	
What file system must be you use in order to use EFS?	Windows 2000 NTFS version 5
What does EFS use to encrypt files?	CryptoAPI architecture
What is an FEK?	The File Encryption Key
Other than the person who encrypted the file, who else can decrypt a file?	The data recovery agent

The cipher command line syntax is CIPHER [/E | /D] [/S[:dir]] [/A] [/I] [/F] [/Q] [H] [K] [pathname [...]]. It has the following parameters:

- **/E** Encrypts the specified directories. Directories will be marked so that files added afterward will be encrypted.
- **/D** Decrypts the specified directories. Directories will be marked so that files added afterward will not be encrypted.
- **/S** Performs the specified operation on directories in the given directory and all subdirectories. Default "dir" is the current directory.
- **/A** Operation for files as well as directories. The encrypted file could become decrypted when it is modified if the parent directory is not encrypted. It is recommended that you encrypt both the file and the parent directory.
- **/I** Continues performing the specified operation even after errors have occurred. By default, CIPHER stops when an error is encountered.
- **/F** Forces the encryption operation on all specified objects, even those that are already encrypted. Already encrypted objects are skipped by default.
- **/Q** Reports only the most essential information.
- **/H** Displays files with the hidden or system attributes. These files are omitted by default.
- **/K** Creates new file encryption key for the user running CIPHER. If this option is chosen, all the other options will be ignored.
- **pathname** Specifies a pattern, file, or directory.

If you use the Cipher command without parameters, it displays the encryption status of the present directory and any files it contains. Figure 16-4 shows an example of the Cipher command. You are required to put spaces between multiple parameters, and you may use multiple filenames and wildcards with the Cipher command.

FIGURE 16-4

The CIPHER command displaying the status of the folders on the E:\ drive

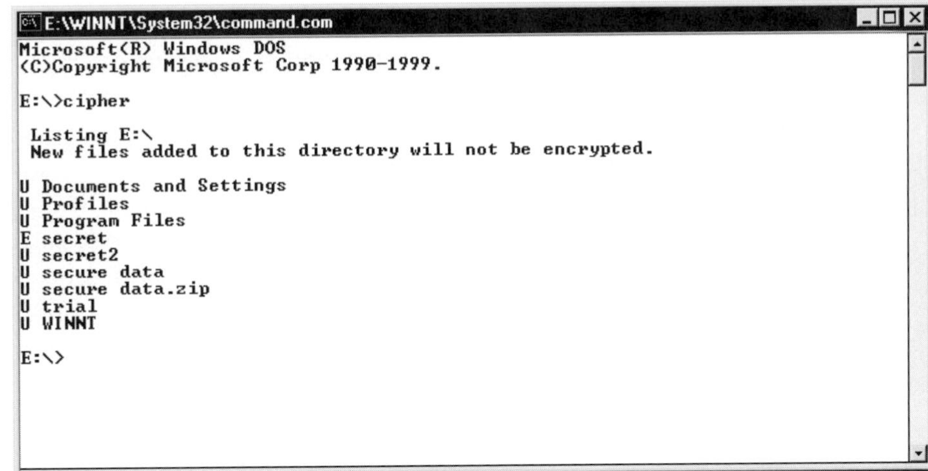
E:\WINNT\System32\command.com
Microsoft(R) Windows DOS
(C)Copyright Microsoft Corp 1990-1999.
E:\>cipher
Listing E:\
New files added to this directory will not be encrypted.
U Documents and Settings
U Profiles
U Program Files
E secret
U secret2
U secure data
U secure data.zip
U trial
U WINNT
E:\>

CERTIFICATION OBJECTIVE 16.02

Implementing, Configuring, Managing, and Troubleshooting Policies in a Windows 2000 Environment

Policies in Windows 2000 can be configured in many more ways than they could in Windows NT 4. There are local policies, system policies, and group policies that can be configured to allow you to manage your users more effectively.

Local Policy

A group policy stored locally on a Windows 2000 member server or a Windows 2000 Professional computer is called a local policy. The local policy can be used to set up the configuration settings for each computer and for each user. Local policies are stored in the \%systemroot%\system32\grouppolicy folder on the local computer. Local policies include the auditing policy, user rights and privilege assignment, and various security options. Figure 16-5 illustrates the Local Security Settings console.

Local policies are the least significant of the various policies, as objects associated with sites, domains, and organizational units can overwrite them. Figure 16-6 shows the Policy Setting dialog box where you can enable or disable policy settings. Local policies are more influential in nonnetworked environments, because then they will not be overwritten by other group policies. Remember that domain-level policies override local policy settings.

Local policies can be configured and analyzed using multiple options available from the security configuration and analysis tool set. If you import the local policy settings to a Group Policy Object (GPO) in Active Directory, they will have an effect on the local security settings of the computer accounts, which are associated with the GPOs.

FIGURE 16-5

Local Security Settings

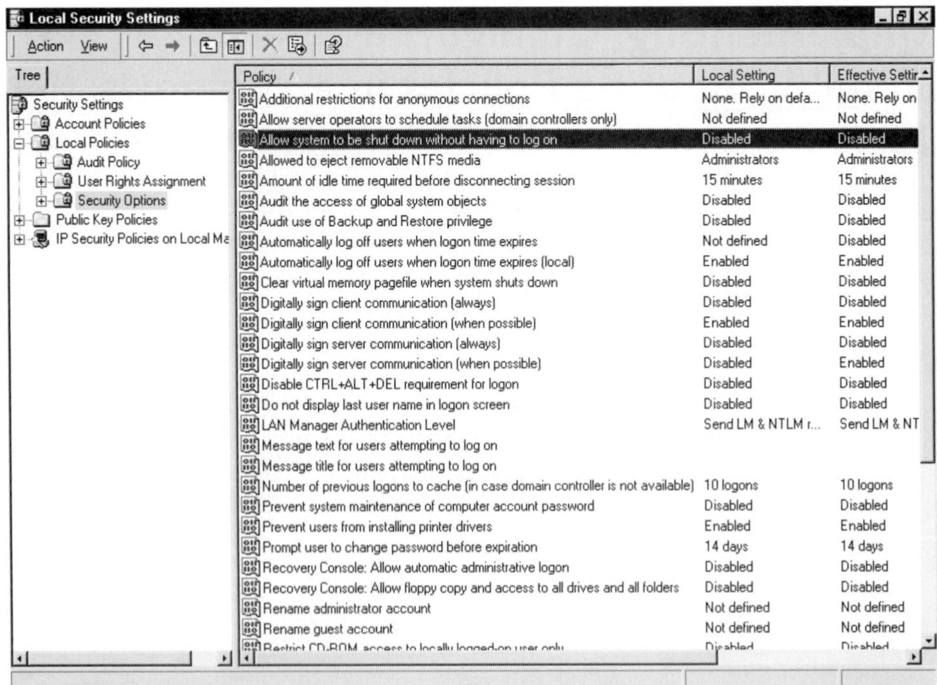

FIGURE 16-6

The Local Security Policy Setting dialog box

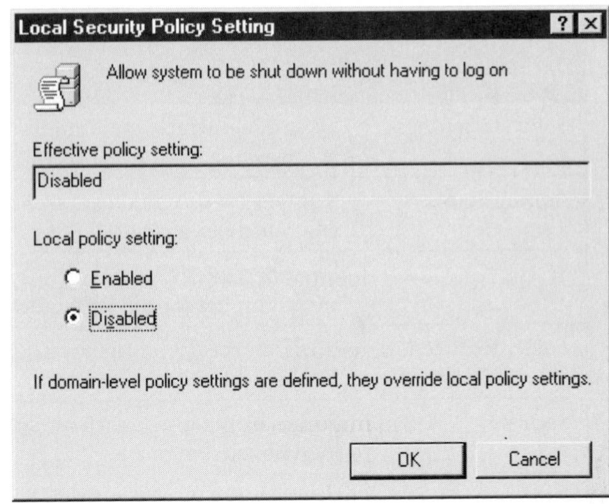

System Policy

System policies have been mostly replaced by group policies, which extend their functionality, although there are still a few situations in which system policies are valuable. The system policy editor is used to provide user and computer configuration settings in the Windows NT registry database. The system policy editor is still used for the management of Windows 9*x* and Windows NT server and workstations and stand-alone computers using Windows 2000. Windows 9*x* uses config.pol, and Windows NT Server and Workstation uses ntconfig.pol.

Group Policy

Group policies are settings that can be applied to Active Directory objects to control users' operating environments. Unlike local policies, group policies can be used to set policies across site(s), domains, or organizational units (OUs) within Active Directory. Group policies apply to users and computers within a certain container. Table 16-2 lists and describes the types of group policies.

Group policies define Microsoft certificate services, IP security, EFS, quality of service, user document management, user settings management, and software installation. You can also use group policies to set local disk quota limits. Only client computers that comprehend the Windows 2000 Active Directory (for example, Windows 2000 Professional) can utilize the Group Policy tool.

TABLE 16-2

Types of Group Policies

Type of Group Policy	Description
Software Settings	Determines which applications users have access to. Application assignment and Application publication.
Administrative Templates	Sets registry-based policies such as Disk quotas, offline files, and task scheduler options.
Scripts	Identifies batch files and scripts to be run at user logon or logoff and computer startup or shutdown.
Folder Redirection	Redirects special folders to network locations such as My Documents and My Pictures.
Security	Sets security settings such as file/folder access for account policies, local policies, public key policies, and IP security policies.
RIS	Controls Remote Installation Services options presented to the user, such as Automatic Setup options, Restart Setup option, and Custom Setup options.

To set a group policy for a selected Active Directory object, you must have a Windows 2000 domain controller installed with Read and Write permission access to the system volume (SysVol) and Modify right to the currently selected directory object. The SysVol folder is a shared directory that is automatically created and later replicated between domain controllers. Figure 16-7 shows the SysVol folder contents.

Group policies have an effect on all computers and users in a selected Active Directory container by default. You can filter the effects of a group policy based on user and computer security groups. You can also use security groups to set policies on users and computers within a site or organizational unit. In addition, you can use group policies to set policies on users and computers in a domain similar to Windows NT 4 with the System Policy Editor and poledit.exe. Group policies only pertain to users with at least Read permissions to that policy, so you can specify which groups are affected by a group policy by making sure that the groups that you want the policy applied to has the "Apply Group Policy" and read access to that Group Policy Object. Figure 16-8 shows the group policy's permissions.

The Group Policy container can be accessed via Active Directory Users and Computers, Active Directory Sites and Services, or the MMC if you have added the appropriate snap-ins. One object can have more than one group policy. For example, an object can have a user policy and a computer policy. Group policies are frequently used to enforce corporate policies. You can use them to do things such as

FIGURE 16-7

The SysVol folder

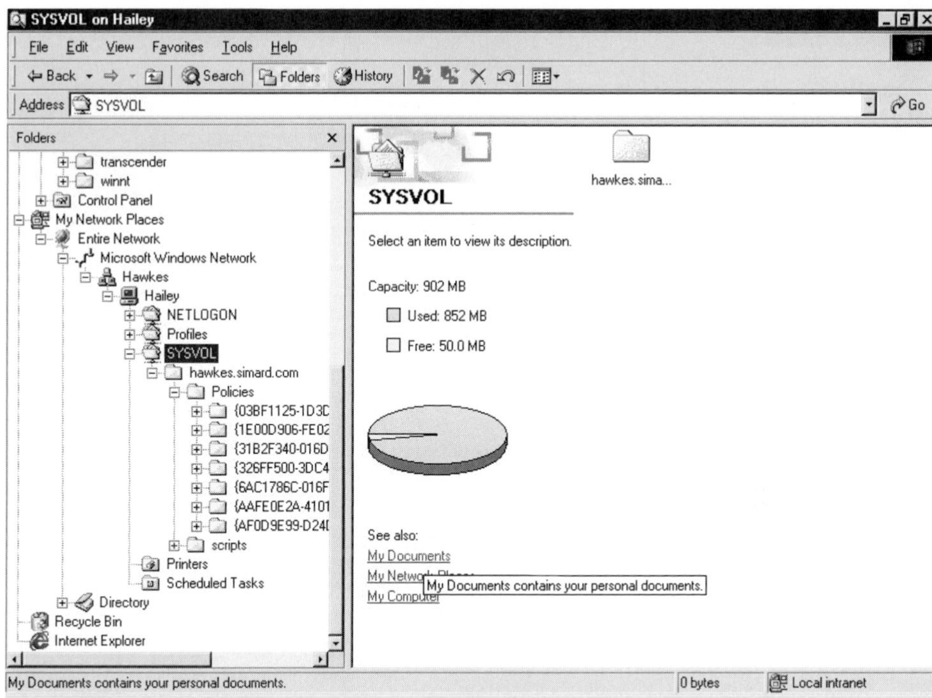

defining the applications available to a user or computer, determine whether the network is accessible, lock down computers, disseminate applications, file replication, and script processing. A special group policy administrator typically manages the group policies to remove some of the numerous administrative duties from the system administrator. The only exception to this is that administrators can unlock a user account that a group policy has locked out even if they are not the group policy administrators. You should take into account the effect that group policies have on user accounts and groups.

Group policies affect subjects no matter where they are. Group policies are inherited by child containers within a domain. For example, an OU is a parent container that can contain several OU child containers. Policies are applied sequentially in order of priority settings and they apply to authenticated users by default.

There are three main group policy management models:

- **Centralized model** This model consolidates administrative control of group policies. A single team of administrators is responsible for managing all GPOs

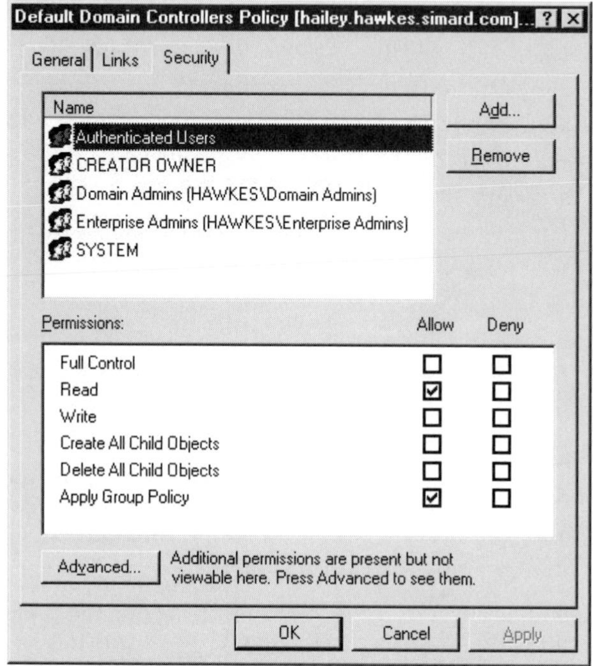

FIGURE 16-8 Group Policy Object Permissions

no matter where they are. This is usually applied by giving all the top-level OU administrators full control to all GPOs no matter where they are located. They give each second-level OU administrator Read permission only to each GPO. You can also decentralize other resources or keep all resources centralized, depending on the environment.

- **Decentralized model** This model is appropriate for companies that rely on delegated levels of administration. They decentralize the management of GPOs, which distributes the workload to a number of domains. To apply this model, simply give all OU administrators full control of their respective GPOs.
- **Task-Based model** This model is appropriate for companies in which administrative duties are functionally divided. This means that this model divides the management of GPOs by certain tasks. To apply this model, the administrators that handle security-related tasks will also be responsible for managing all policy objects that affect security. The second set of administrators that normally deploy the companies' business applications will be responsible for all the GPOs that affect installation and maintenance.

It is a good idea to limit the number of GPOs that affect any given computer or user, as the number of GPOs directly affects client performance. It can also become almost impossible to determine effective policy settings when many GPOs have been applied on top of each other. You should also use security groups to filter the effect of group policies. This reduces the number of GPOs that must be processed. User and computer portions of a GPO can also be disabled. You should disable the unused portions of GPOs, which speeds up user logons, as there are fewer policies for each logon to go through.

GPOs are inherited and cumulative. This means that they are processed hierarchically, starting with policies in the higher-level container in Active Directory. In addition, Group Policy naming conventions should reflect policy usage.

Group Policy Objects

After you create a group policy, it is stored in a Group Policy Object (GPO) and applied to the site, domain, or OU. GPOs are used to keep the group policy information; essentially, it is a collection of policies. You can apply single or multiple GPOs to each site, domain or OU. Group policies are not inherited across domains, and users must have Read permission for the GPO that you want to have applied to them. This way, you can filter the scope of GPOs by adjusting who has read access to each GPO.

You need to create one GPO before you can access the Group Policy Editor (GPE). Then you are required to open the GPE to make modifications to the group policy settings. You must also use the GPE to define the group policy settings for computer, user accounts, application and file deployment, security, scripts, and software. You can use the Active Directory Sites and Services Manager on a DC to edit a GPO for a site. Administrators with Read and Write permission to a GPO can make modifications to the group policy for that object and change who the group policy manager is.

You should limit how often group policies are updated, as updates require replication and the replication of group policies can take quite a long time. This is because the scope of a group policy may be huge. Think of it as regedit for the Active Directory. A single GPO may contain hundreds of settings. For security reasons, it is advantageous to limit the number of administrators who can edit GPOs. Also, don't bother making changes with profiles that group policies override, as it is simply redundant. By using GPOs, you can enforce and maintain the configuration settings, which can simplify computer management and lower the total cost of ownership (TCO). GPOs are a collection of settings that will affect a given user or computer. They are made up of a Group Policy Template (GPT) stored on SysVol and a Group Policy Container (GPC) stored in Active Directory.

Group Policy Containers

The Active Directory object Group Policy Containers (GPCs) store the information for the Folder Redirection snap-in and the Software Deployment snap-in. GPCs do not apply to local group policies. They contain component lists and status information, which indicate whether GPOs are enabled or disabled. They also contain version information, which ensures that the information is synchronized with the GPT information. GPCs also contain the class store in which GPO group policy extensions have settings.

Group Policy Templates

The subset of folders created on each domain controller that store GPO information for specific GPOs are called Group Policy Templates (GPTs). GPTs are stored in the SysVol (System Volume) folder, on the domain controller. GPTs store data for Software Policies, Scripts, Desktop File and Folder Management, Software Deployment, and Security settings. GPTs can be defined in computer or user configurations. Consequently, they take effect either when the computer starts or when the user logs on.

Gpt.ini files are kept in the root folder of each GPT. Gpt.ini files contain two entries. The first entry is Version=*x*, where the *x* is the GPO version number. The GPO version number starts at 0 when you create a GPO initially and then it automatically adds a 1 each time the GPO is modified. The second entry is Disabled=*y*, where *y* is either 1 or 0 and indicates whether the local GPO is disabled or enabled.

You use the System Policy Editor to add policy templates. To add a policy template, copy any .adm files to the folder containing .inf files (usually C:\winnt\inf). Then open the System Policy Editor by clicking Run from the Start menu. Type in **poledit.exe** and click OK. Figure 16-9 illustrates the System Policy Editor. Once you have the System Policy Editor open, click the Policy Template option on the Options menu. Then click Add and specify the policy template that you would like to use. Figure 16-10 shows the Policy Template Options dialog box, where you can add a new GPT. Finally, click OK.

You acquire policies from the Active Directory. To configure policies on a member server, you must use the Group Policy Editor, which is a snap-in to the MMC. It is launched from the property page of a site, domain, or OU.

FIGURE 16-9

The System Policy Editor

When you make a group policy, several folders are added to the SysVol folder share of the DC that you are connected to. The top folder in this structure is called the GUID (global unique identifier of the GPO). The other folders store the policy object's user and computer settings. They are stored in the SysVol share, so it can be replicated to all DCs in a domain.

FIGURE 16-10

Adding a policy template

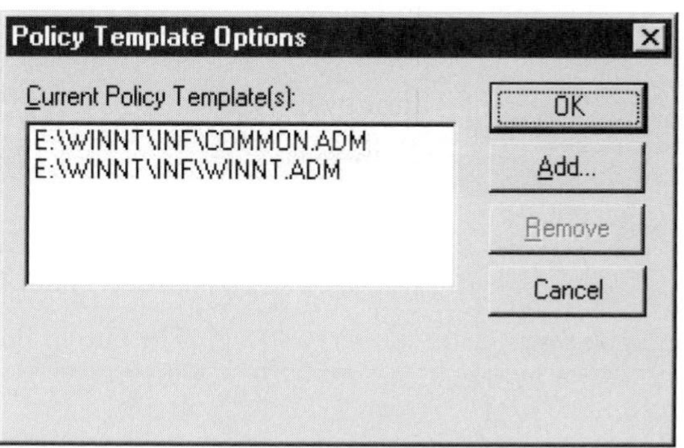

Applying Policies

To apply a group policy, simply open the group policy with either Active Directory Users and Computers or Active Directory Sites and Services. Then right-click the site, domain, or organizational unit in which you want to set a group policy and select Properties. Then select the Group Policy tab. Click New and choose Edit to define the settings. Figure 16-11 shows the group policy properties box. Group policies can also be managed in the Group Policy Management Console snap-in of the Microsoft Management Console. Use it as an interface to edit the registry. It is better to use administrative templates for group policies instead of administrative templates for system policies as in Windows NT 4. You can also delegate who controls each Group Policy. To do this, you need to first create and save Group Policy Management Consoles. Then you need to set Read and Write permissions for the appropriate administrators for each of the Group Policies.

Policy Inheritance

Group policies have an order of inheritance in which the policies are applied. Local policies are applied first, then group policies are applied to the site, then the domain, and finally the organizational unit (OU). Policies that are applied first are overwritten by policies applied later. Therefore, group policies applied to a site overwrite the local policies and so on. When there are multiple GPOs for a site, domain, or OU, the order in which they appear in the properties list applies. This policy inheritance order works well for small companies, but a more complex inheritance strategy may be essential for larger corporations.

Now that you have a better idea of policies, here are some possible scenario questions and their answers.

SCENARIO & SOLUTION	
Where are local policies stored?	On the local computer
What is a GPO?	Group Policy Object
Who manages group policies?	The Group Policy administrator

FIGURE 16-11

Adding a new Group Policy Object

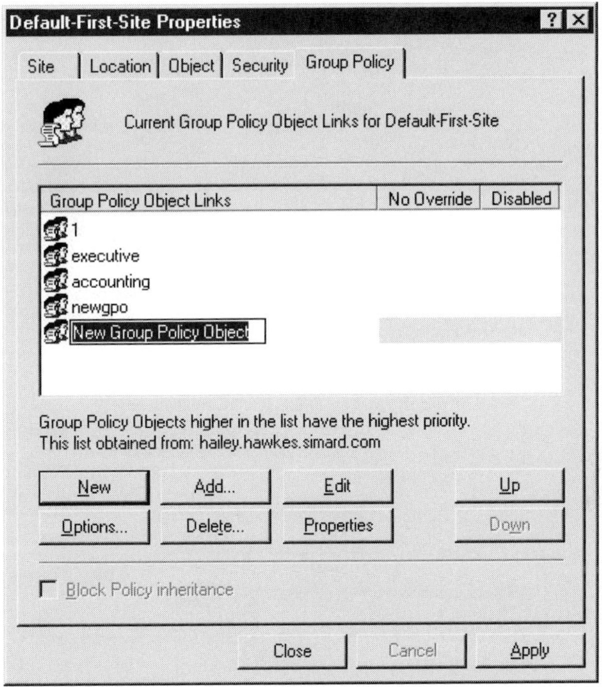

Further customization is accessible in the form of overriding inheritance and blocking inheritance. To block inheritance in a site, right-click the site, domain, or OU in the Users and Computers MMC. Then click on the Group Policy tab and add a check mark to the Block Policy inheritance check box. Figure 16-12 shows the domain controllers properties dialog box where you can add a Block Policy inheritance check mark. Blocking policy inheritance allows a child container to block policy inheritance from parent containers. The Block Policy inheritance setting only applies to sites, domains, and OUs, not on particular Group Policy Objects. This is a beneficial option to have when an OU requires unique settings. To override inheritance, simply click Options. Then add a check mark to the No Override check box in the Link Options dialog box, as shown in Figure 16-13. The No Override check box can be used to force a policy onto the child containers beneath it. Essentially, it is used to cancel any Block Policy Inheritance settings that may have been made. If there is a conflict, the No Override option wins over the block policy inheritance.

FIGURE 16-12

The Group Policy properties with the Block Policy inheritance check box

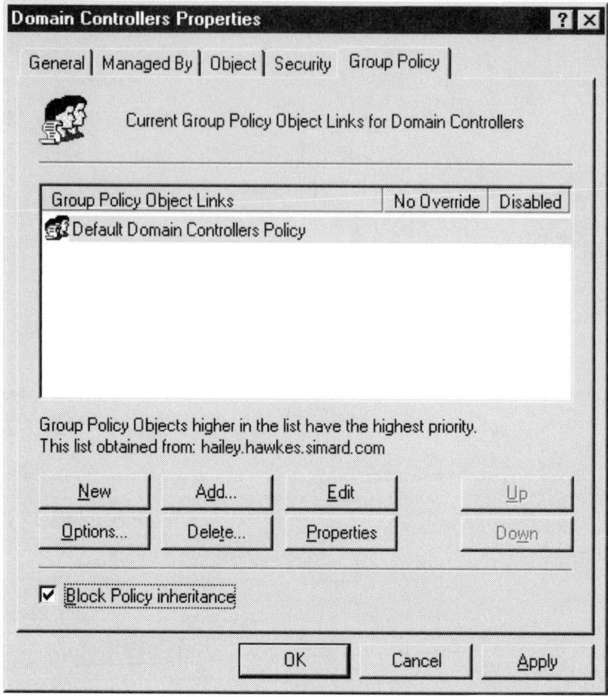

on the Job

It is a good idea to keep the number of group policies to the bare minimum necessary to get the job done. The more group policies you have, the longer it takes each user to log on. It can also get complicated to keep up with the administrative tasks involved with all the different policies. One way to decrease the number of group policies is to associate group policy objects through group membership instead of just by individual users.

FIGURE 16-13

The No Override check box. Use this to disable any override inheritance settings.

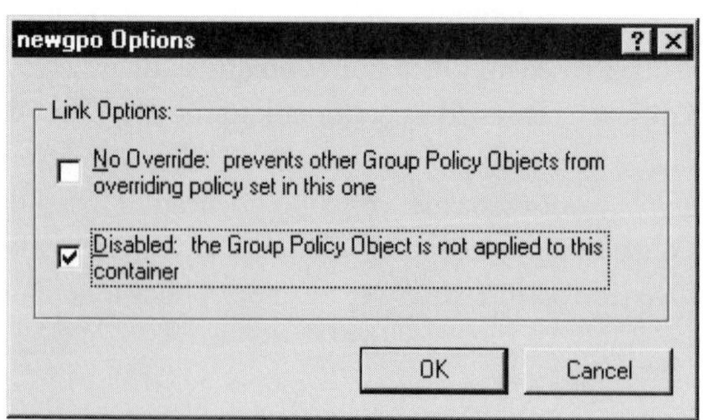

User vs. Computer Policies

There are two parent nodes at the root of the group policy snap-in:

- **User Configuration** User policies define all user-related policies that specify operating system behavior, desktop settings, application settings, security settings, assigned and published application options, user logon and logoff scripts, and folder redirection options. User policies are applied when users log on to a computer.
- **Computer Configuration** Computer policies define all computer-related policies that specify operating system behavior, desktop behavior, application settings, security settings, assigned application options, and computer startup and shutdown scripts. Computer policies are applied when a computer first starts up.

Both user and computer policies have Software settings, Windows settings, and Administrative Templates that can be configured. Figure 16-14 shows the User and Computer configurations.

FIGURE 16-14

User and Computer configurations

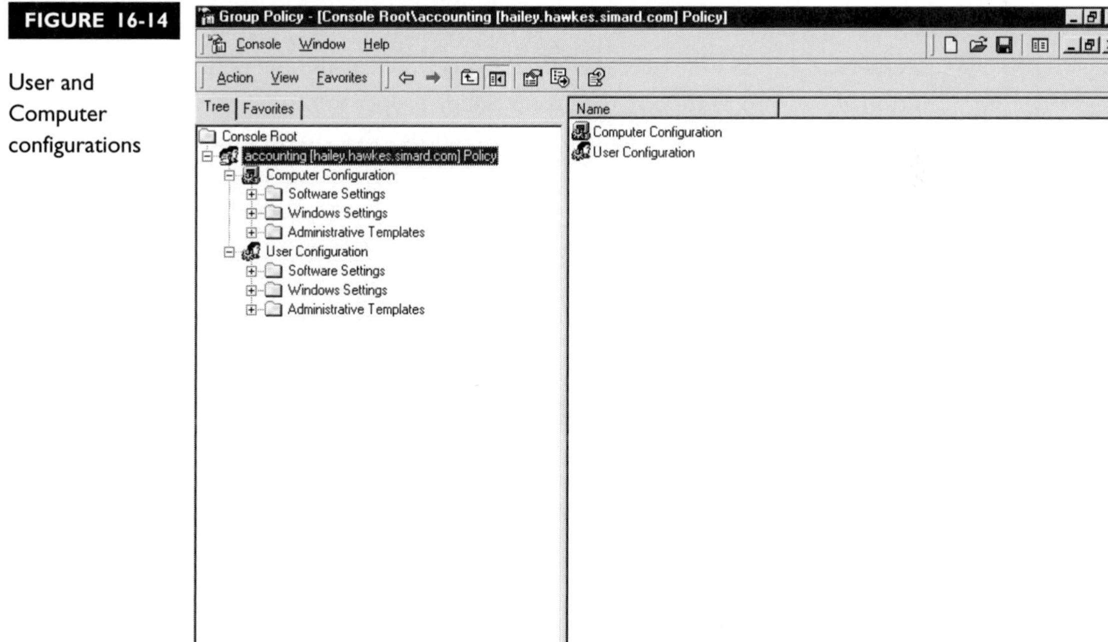

exam Watch

If there is a conflict between a user policy and a computer policy, the user policy setting overrides the computer policy.

Modifying Group Policy

There are two ways to modify group policies. You can select the site, domain, or organizational unit in Active Directory that you wish to modify and choose the group policy tab from the properties page. Alternatively, you can use the Group Policy Management snap-in. In the Group Policy tab, you can choose from several buttons. There is a New button that you can use to add and create a brand new policy. The Add button can be used to add a previously configured policy. The Edit button starts the Group Policy Object editor so that you can modify the policy object settings. The Options button is used to specify whether you want the object disabled for this container and whether you want to specify the No Override attribute, as shown in Figure 16-15. This prevents other Group Policy Objects from overriding that policy. You can use the Delete button to remove any of the group policies specified.

When you choose to delete a policy, you will be prompted to choose whether you simply want the policy removed from this object, or whether you would like to delete the policy entirely. Figure 16-16 shows the Delete dialog box. Be extremely careful that you do not select the latter if other objects use the policy. The Properties button allows you to modify the group policy properties. It has general, links, and security tabs, each with configuration settings that can be adjusted. Finally, there are Up and Down buttons that are used to determine the priority of each Group Policy Object. These only apply if you have multiple Group Policy Objects. The first policy in the list takes priority over the remaining policies.

Exercise 16-2 will show you how to modify a Group Policy Object.

FIGURE 16-15

Group Policy Options

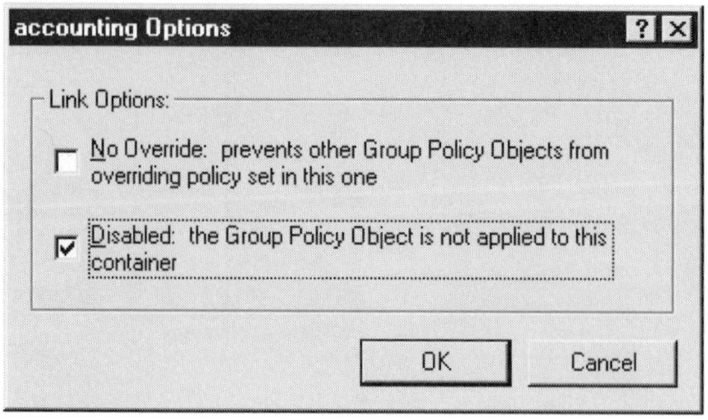

accounting Options

Link Options:

No Override: prevents other Group Policy Objects from overriding policy set in this one

Disabled: the Group Policy Object is not applied to this container

OK Cancel

FIGURE 16-16

Deleting a policy. Be careful when deciding whether to remove the GPO along with the link

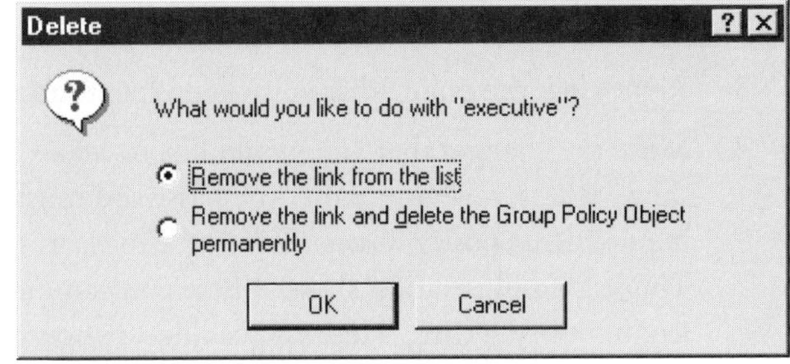

EXERCISE 16-2

Modifying a GPO

You can modify a GPO using MMC with a Group Policy snap-in on a Windows 2000 member server.

1. Open the MMC with a Group Policy snap-in.
2. Browse to the GPO that you would like to modify. In the following illustration, we have chosen to modify the Password Policy within Computer Configuration>Windows Settings>Security Settings>Account Policies.

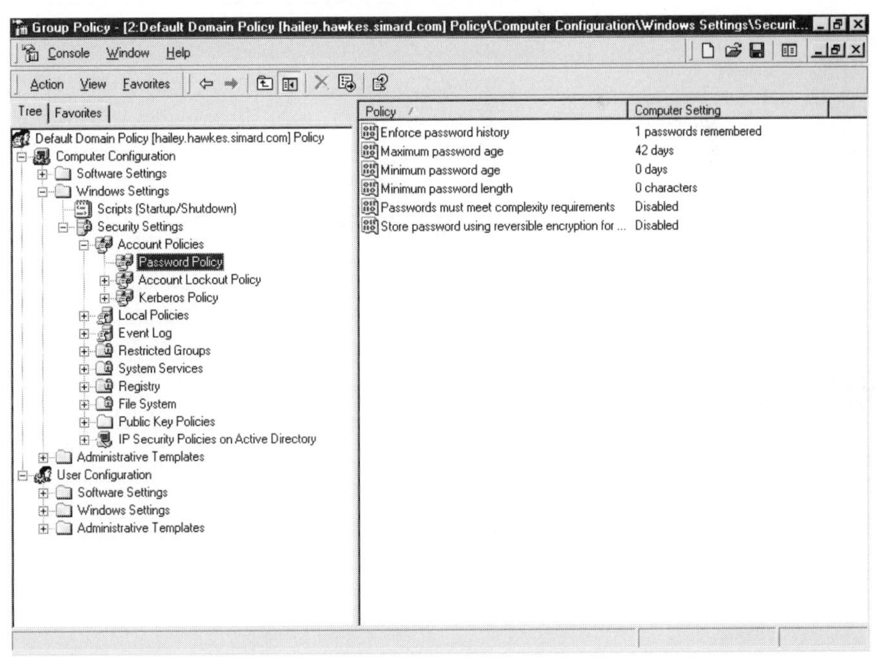

3. Right-click the policy that you would like to modify and choose Security.
4. Make the changes that you would like to make. The following illustration shows where you can modify the Password must meet complexity requirements policy setting. You can choose to enable or disable this setting. The second illustration shows where you can modify the Minimum password length policy setting. Here you can decide how many characters the password must be.

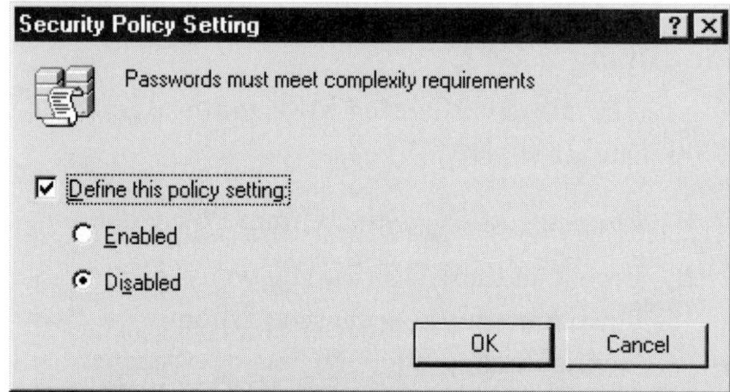

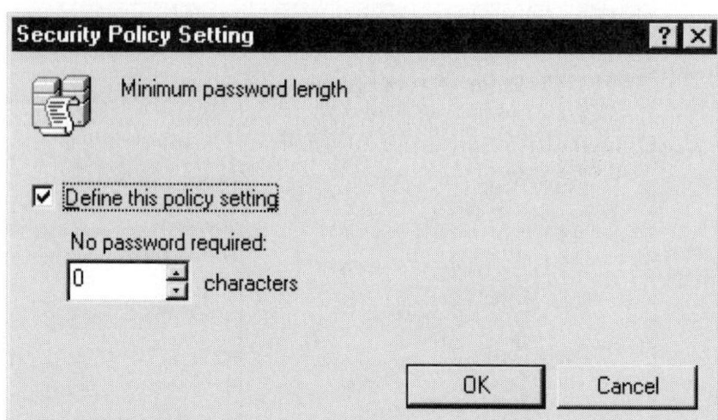

5. Once you make your changes, click OK to apply them.
6. Close the MMC and choose to save the settings.

Using Group Policy for Software Distribution

Group policies can be used for software distribution. There are two distinct types of software deployment:

- **Application assignments** Use to provide limited software distributions to a desktop. Once applications are installed, they cannot be deleted or modified without the user having the correct policy settings. Application assignments help to enforce standard desktop settings.
- **Application publications** Use to authorize a user or computer to install or uninstall software or software updates from a distribution list at their convenience. This allows the users to manage their hard drive space more efficiently, as they can add and remove programs as they require them.

Troubleshooting Local and Group Policies

Some common problems that you may come across include not being able to modify GPOs and GPOs that are not taking effect. There are several things that you should check when you troubleshoot policies. You should verify that authentication did not fail or that the user did not log on with cached information. You should make sure that the user belongs to a domain (unless it is a local policy problem). You should check to see whether the policy is being modified by someone else, check permissions, and check to see that the convergence time has passed (that the changes you have made have replicated). You could also be having problems because child-level GPOs are blocking policy inheritance or a GPO has been disabled. Last, you should confirm that your domain controllers are up to date and that there aren't any parent-level entries in the GPO taking precedence over your new GPO entries. The Group Policy and Active Directory troubleshooter can help walk you through some of these steps.

CERTIFICATION OBJECTIVE 16.03

Creating and Managing User Profiles

User profiles are collections of data and folders that are used to configure the desktop settings, applications settings, and personal data for each user. Thus when multiple users share a computer, each can have a unique desktop and connections when it logs on. This also provides consistency for each user. Desktop settings incorporate things like mapped network connections, files in My Documents, icons on the desktop, wallpaper, and Start menu items. As illustrated in Figure 16-17, profiles are defined on the Profile tab for each user's properties. This is where you assign a path to the user's profile.

There are three types of user profiles:

- **Local profiles** Local user profiles are kept on one local computer hard drive. When a user initially logs on to a computer, a local profile is created for them in the \%systemdrive%\Documents and Settings\<username> folder (for example, C:\Winnt\Documents and Settings\gsimard). When users log off the computer, the changes that they made while they were logged on will be saved to their local profile on that client computer. This way, subsequent logons to that computer will bring up their personal settings. When users log on to a different computer, they will not receive these settings, as they are local to the computer in which they made the changes. Therefore, each user that logs on to that computer receives individual desktop settings. Local profiles are ideal for users who only use one computer. For users that require access to multiple computers, the Roaming profile would be the better choice.
- **Nonmandatory Roaming profiles** Roaming user profiles are stored on the network file server and are the perfect solution for users who have access to multiple computers. This way their profile is accessible no matter where they log on in the domain. When users log on to a computer within their domain, their Roaming profile will be copied from the network server to the client computer and the settings will be applied to the computer while they are logged on. Subsequent logins will compare the Roaming profile files to the local profile files. The file server then copies only any files that have been

FIGURE 16-17

The user properties dialog box. This is where you enter the user profile path

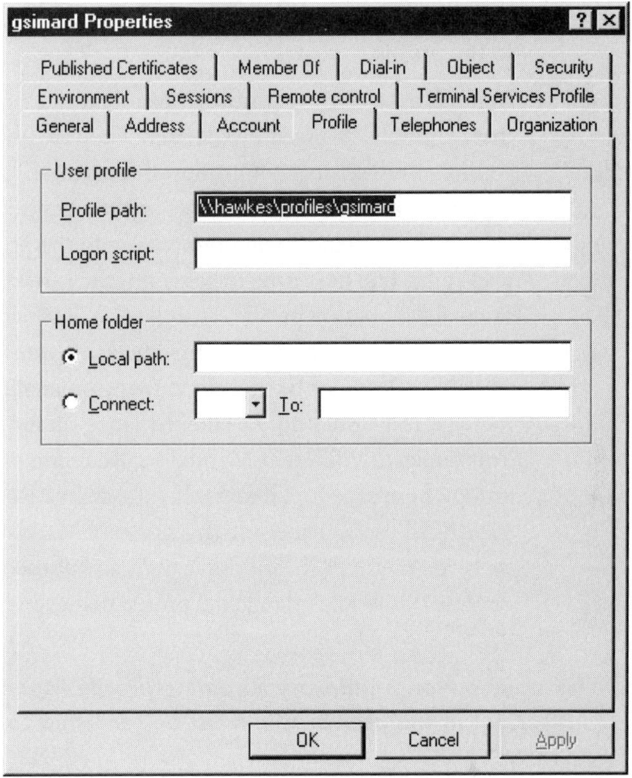

altered since the user last logged on locally, significantly decreasing the time required to logon. When the user logs off, any changes that the user made on the local computer will be copied back to the profile on the network file server. If a user attempts to log on to a computer with a Nonmandatory Roaming user profile and the profile is not available, the user can still log in. A user who has logged on to the particular computer previously receives a locally cached copy of the Roaming profile. Unfortunately, none of the changes that they make to the local Roaming profile will be saved if the file server is still unavailable when the user logs off. The changes will be saved back to the file server if it is back online by the time the user logs off.

If the user has never logged on to the computer before and the file server is unavailable, the computer gives the user a temporary profile created from the workstations default user profile. The temporary file is then stored in the \%systemroot%\Documents and Settings\Temp directory. As soon as the user logs off, the temp directory is deleted, and none of the changes are saved to the profile.

- **Mandatory Roaming profiles** Mandatory user profiles are Roaming profiles that cannot be changed by the user. They are usually created to define desktop configuration settings for groups of users in order to simplify administration and support. Users can make changes to their desktop settings while they are logged on, but these changes will not be saved to the profile, as Mandatory profiles are read-only. The next time they log on, their desktop will be set back to the original Mandatory profile settings. The downside to Mandatory user profiles is that a user who tried to log on when the Mandatory Roaming profile was not available would not be permitted to log on at all. The user would receive an error message and would not be allowed to log on until the profile could be loaded. You can have a different Mandatory Roaming profile for each user, for each group of users, or for all users. If you assign a Roaming profile to groups of users or all users, make sure that they are Mandatory. This is because more than one user uses it; you don't want any of them to make changes to it, because this would change the profile that everyone else receives.

exam Watch

To make a Nonmandatory Roaming profile Mandatory, a hidden file called ntuser.dat in the user profile must be renamed to ntuser.man.

on the Job

Mandatory Roaming user profiles are very handy to use from the help desk support perspective. The user support staff will be able to determine the causes of user problems more quickly, as they will see any changes to the profile immediately. They can also be used to lock down users' systems so that they are limited in the "damage" that they can do.

To switch between a Local profile and a Roaming profile on a particular computer, simply go into the System Properties for the computer and click the User Profiles tab. Figure 16-18 shows the User Profiles tab of System properties. Choose the user that you would like to change the profile type for and then click Change Type. Choose the profile type (Roaming or Local) that you would like the user to have and click OK twice to accept the changes you have made. Figure 16-19 shows the Change Profile Type dialog box.

FIGURE 16-18

The User Profiles tab of System Properties

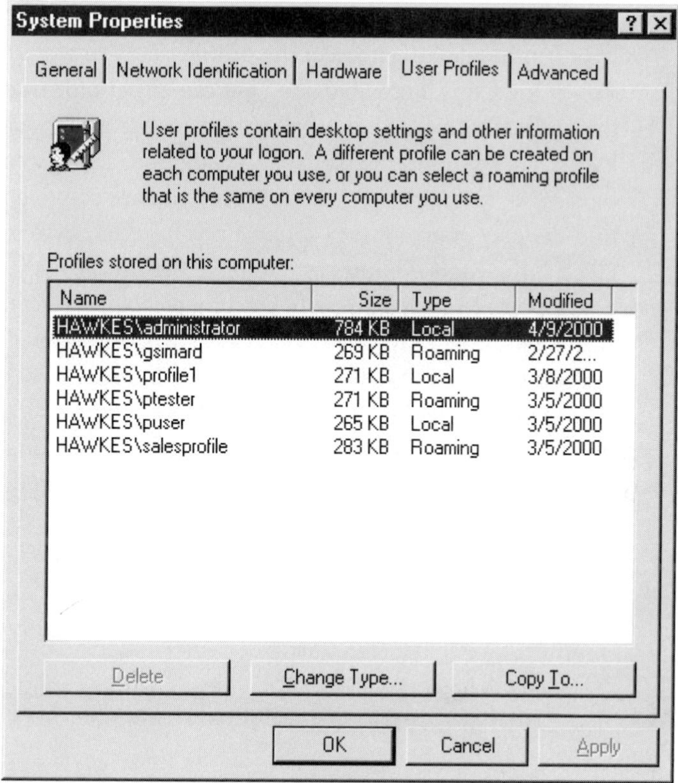

All new profiles are a copy of the default user profile. You can have them modified initially by an administrator or allow the users to log in and make changes

FIGURE 16-19

The Change Profile Type dialog box

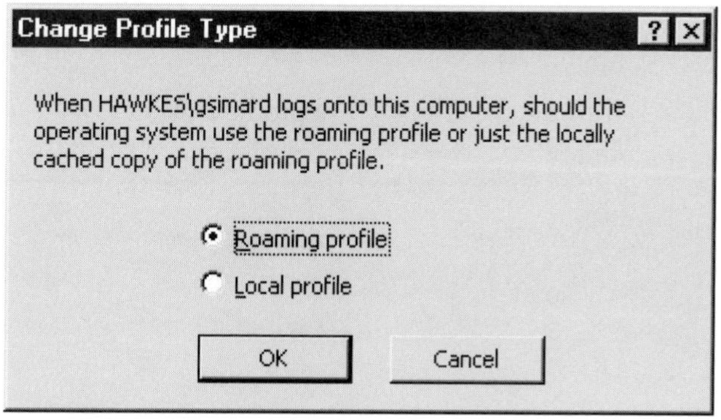

Change Profile Type

When HAWKES\gsimard logs onto this computer, should the operating system use the roaming profile or just the locally cached copy of the roaming profile.

- (•) Roaming profile
- ( ) Local profile

OK | Cancel

themselves. To copy a user profile, go into the System Properties and choose the User Profiles tab. Next select the profile that you would like to copy and click Copy To. In the Copy To dialog box, you can either type in or click Browse to look for the profile that you would like to copy to (for example, \\hawkes\profiles\gsimard). Figure 16-20 shows the Copy To dialog box. You also need to change the Permitted to use user to the person whose profile you are copying to. Simply click Change and find the user or group that you want to have access to the profile and click OK. Click OK two more times to complete the profile copy.

User profiles include the My Documents folder, which Windows 2000 automatically creates on the desktop where users can store their personal files. The My Documents folder is the default location for File Open and File Save As commands. Users can change their profiles by doing things such as adding an icon to the desktop, changing their screen saver, making a new network connection, or adding files to their My Document folder. These settings are then saved back to their profile on the server. The next time the user logs in, their profile changes are there.

You can create a customized Roaming user profile to give specialized profiles to users, depending on which department they are in. You can then add or remove any applications, shortcuts, and connections according to what each department

FIGURE 16-20

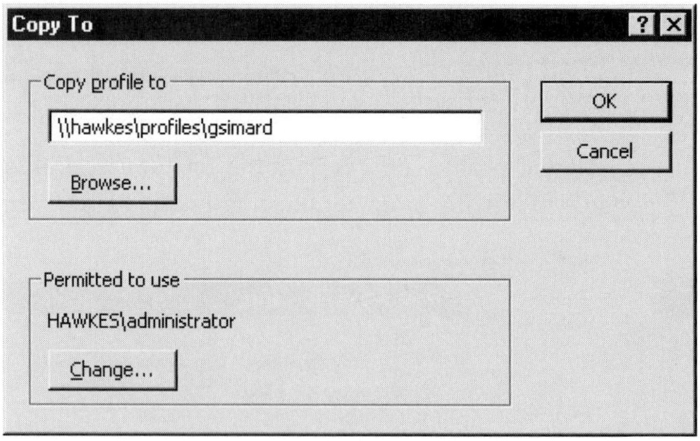

The Copy To dialog box. Be sure to give the appropriate permissions to the user to whom you are copying the profile

requires. Customized Roaming user profiles are also helpful for troubleshooting and for technical support. They make technical support easier, as the technical support staff would know what programs and exact shortcuts should be there, so they will notice any deviations immediately. To create a customized Roaming user profile, set up a desktop environment and connections for a user as a template. Once you have the template profile set up, you can copy the template profile to the user's Roaming profile location. Note: Windows 2000 does not support the use of encryption with Roaming user profiles.

exam Watch

When you use Roaming user profiles with Terminal Services clients, the profiles are not replicated to the server until the user logs off.

Exercise 16-3 demonstrates how to assign a customized Roaming profile to another user profile.

EXERCISE 16-3

CertCam 16-3

How to Create a Customized Roaming User Profile and Copy and Assign It to a User Profile

You can complete the following on any Windows 2000 member server.

1. Create an account called Profile1.
2. Log on with the Profile1 account.
3. Configure the desktop settings and network connections as you would like them to appear for the future users.
4. Log off the computer.
5. Log on as Administrator and click Start, Settings, Control Panel, and then choose the System icon.
6. Click on the User Profiles tab.

7. Select the Profile1 profile under Name and then click Copy To, as shown in the following illustration.

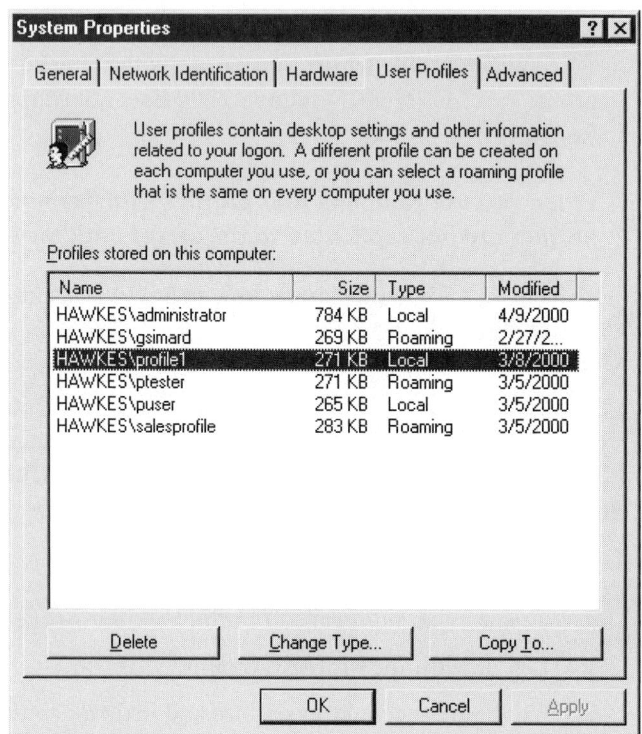

8. In the Copy To dialog box, you can either type in the profile path or click Browse to look for the profile that you would like to copy to. In the following illustration, we chose to copy the profile to E:\Profiles\gsimard and give permissions to HAWKES\gsimard.

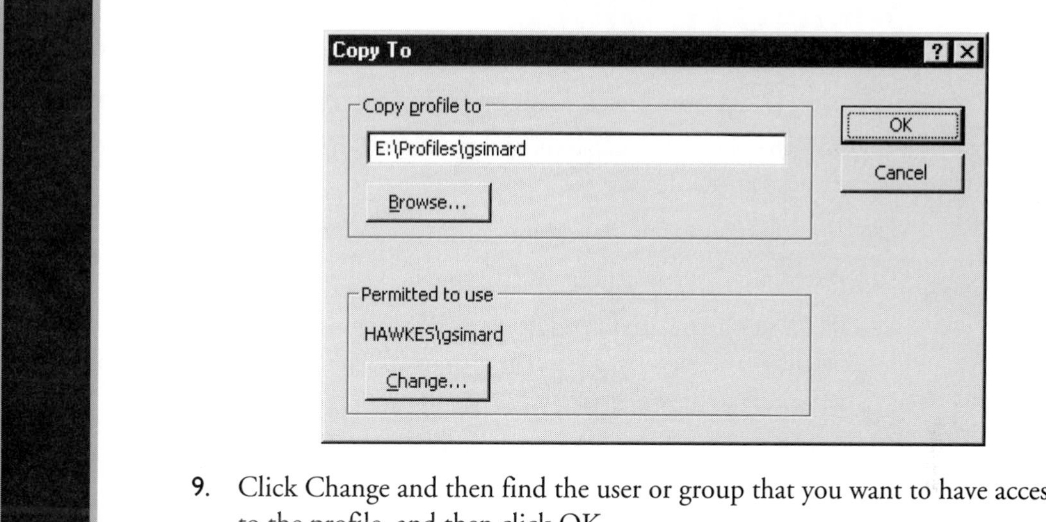

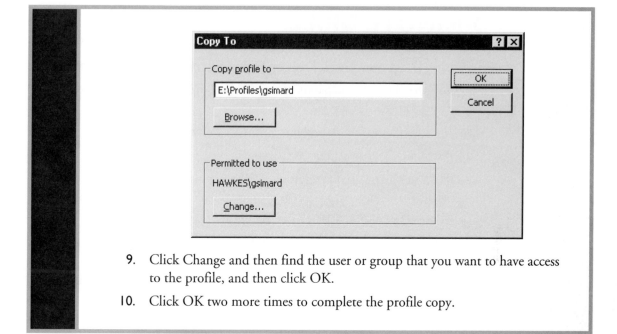

9. Click Change and then find the user or group that you want to have access to the profile, and then click OK.
10. Click OK two more times to complete the profile copy.

CERTIFICATION SUMMARY

The Windows 2000 Encrypting File System can be used to encrypt data on a hard drive. EFS is an extra level of security that can be used only on data that is accessed by a single user. Only the user who encrypted the data and the recovery agent have the ability to decrypt the data. Take into account that this can only be used once, as the emergency recovery agent cannot encrypt the data again apart from encrypting it with the recovery agent's own file encryption key.

Group policies are used to configure a user's computer settings such as the numerous software settings, windows settings, and administrative templates. Finally, user profiles are used to configure desktop settings for each user who logs on to a computer. There are Local user profiles, Roaming user profiles, and Mandatory user profiles which can perform things such as saving any user-specific program settings, user-definable settings for Windows Explorer, and all user-defined settings made in Control Panel. All of these items combined can increase the level of user security on your Windows 2000 network.

TWO-MINUTE DRILL

Encrypting Data on a Hard Disk by Using Encrypting File System (EFS)

- Only the person who encrypted the data and the holder of the recovery agent private key can decrypt the data.
- Data encryption and data compression are mutually exclusive.
- Shared files/folders cannot be encrypted.
- NTFS should be used in addition to EFS permissions because any user who has the permissions to access the encrypted data can delete it even without being able to read/decrypt it.
- Only Windows 2000 NTFS volumes support EFS.

Implementing, Configuring, Managing, and Troubleshooting Policies in a Windows 2000 Environment

- The two configuration types of group policies are user settings and computer settings.
- Group policies can be set for sites, domains, and organizational units (SDOU).
- Group Policy Objects (GPOs) are used to store configuration information.
- GPOs can be stored in Group Policy Templates (GPTs) or Group Policy Containers (GPCs).
- The group policy applied closest to the computer or user takes precedence over the group policies applied further toward the organizational unit.

Creating and Managing User Profiles

- Local user profiles are used to save any personal desktop settings made by a user on a particular computer and are stored locally on that computer.
- Roaming user profiles are used to save a user's settings to be used on any computer in the domain. These profiles are stored on a network file server.
- Mandatory profiles are read-only Roaming profiles.
- Default user profiles can be created as a basis for users' settings.
- Ntuser.dat in the user profile must be renamed to ntuser.man to make a Nonmandatory Roaming profile Mandatory.

17

Implementing a Windows 2000 Security Infrastructure

CERTIFICATION OBJECTIVES

17.01 Implementing, Configuring, Managing, and Troubleshooting Auditing

17.02 Implementing, Configuring, Managing, and Troubleshooting Local Accounts

17.03 Implementing, Configuring, Managing, and Troubleshooting Account Policy

17.04 Using the Security Configuration Toolset

✓ Two-Minute Drill

This chapter will look at one of the most talked-about elements in computing today: security. In order for your organization to protect its resources and data, it is essential that you understand the security components in Windows 2000 and how to implement them. This operating system greatly enhances your ability to provide your organization with protection against unauthorized access, both from within and from outside intrusion.

The key to a successful security system is careful planning. Windows 2000 provides several levels of defense that range from the way you set up local accounts, to account policies, to the use of the Security Configuration Toolset. Establishing standards that utilize the security options that Windows 2000 provides is not only a smart use of the technology, it's good business. This chapter will give you the information you need to make effective choices where the security of your organization is concerned.

CERTIFICATION OBJECTIVE 17.01

Implementing, Configuring, Managing, and Troubleshooting Auditing

With Windows 2000, administrators can deny, allow, or simply monitor access to specific objects in Active Directory or to specific files or folders. You can also track events like user logons, failed logon attempts, logoffs, and the use of special privileges that you may have granted. This type of security is called auditing. For Microsoft, auditing is defined as a process that tracks the activities of users by recording selected types of events in the security log of a server or workstation. The use of auditing is an effective security policy because it leaves behind a trail of breadcrumbs for an that administrator can mean the difference between finding or not finding a major security violation. Auditing not only detects unauthorized access to objects, it provides a log of that detection should an intruder be caught and prosecuted.

Configuring Auditing

Before Windows 2000 can audit access to files and folders, you must use the Group Policy snap-in to enable the Audit Object Access setting in the Audit Policy. If you do not, you will receive an error message when you set up auditing for files and folders, and no files or folders will be audited. To audit files and folders, you must be logged on as a member of the Administrators Group or have been granted Manage Auditing and Security Log rights in Group Policy. Note that you can set auditing only on files and folders that reside on an NTFS partition. Once Auditing is enabled in Group Policy and you have configured auditing for the desired events, view the security log in Event Viewer to review successful or failed attempts to access the audited files and folders. Exercise 17-1 details how to add the Group Policy snap-in and set up auditing files and folders.

EXERCISE 17-1

Adding the Group Policy Snap-in and Setting Up Auditing Files and Folders

1. Click Start, click Run, type **mmc /a,** and then click OK.
2. On the Console menu, click Add/Remove snap-in, and then click Add.
3. Under Add Standalone snap-in, click Group Policy, and then click Add.
4. In Select Group Policy Object, accept the default Group Policy Object of Local Computer, click Finish, click Close, and then click OK. If you were choosing to use a group policy that was the default domain policy, you would click the browse button and navigate to the location of that policy rather than using the local policy.
5. From Local Computer Policy, expand Computer Configuration, then Windows Settings, then Security Settings, then Local policies, and finally Audit Policy.
6. In the details pane, right-click Audit Object Access and then click Security.

The following illustration shows where to select Audit Policy in the Console 1 window.

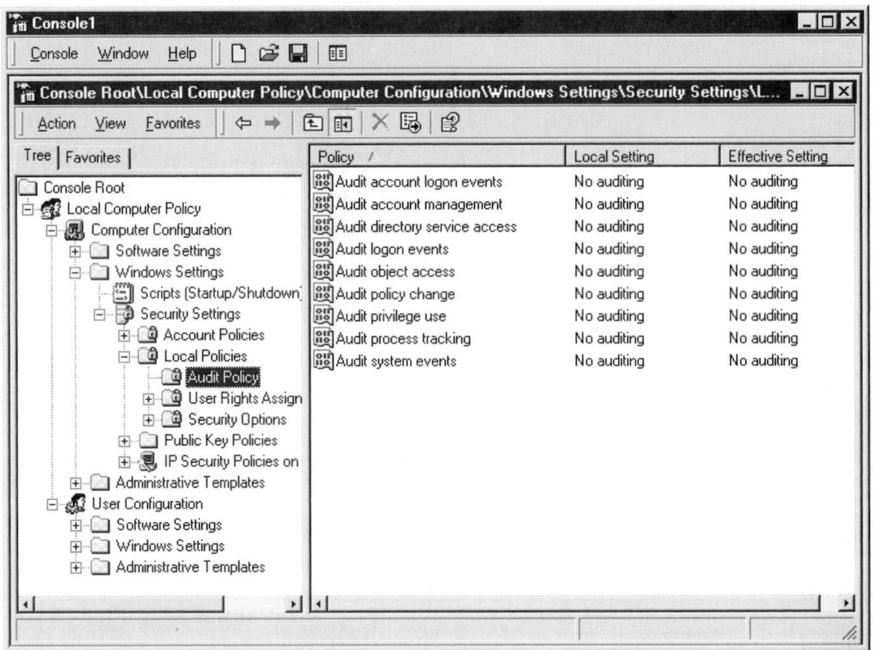

7. In Local Security Policy Setting, select both the Success and Failure check boxes and then click OK (see the following illustration).

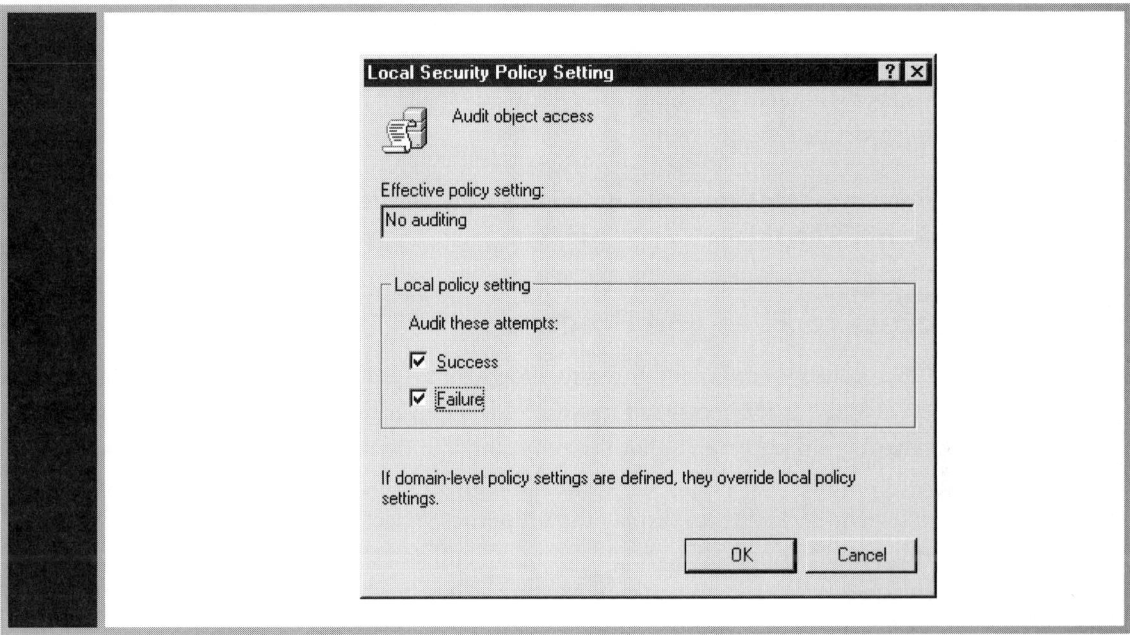

on the job

You have to use the Group Policy snap-in to enable the Audit Object Access setting in the object policy before you can audit files or folders.

Setting an Audit Policy

Now that you have configured the Group Policy snap-in to enable file and folder auditing, you should develop a policy that determines the security events to be reported, or what is called an audit policy. Windows 2000 can track a variety of events and you will need to decide which of those events will be most important for you to monitor. Auditing changes to group policy do not take effect immediately. User and computer group policy is refreshed periodically (every 90 minutes by default). It is also refreshed when users log on and when computers are started. You can also use the Secedit Command Line Tool with the /refresh policy switch to refresh policy settings manually. (Secedit is covered in more detail later in this chapter.) You will use your audit policy to select which events to audit, and those events will then be added as an entry in the computer's Security log. You will use the Event Viewer snap-in to view that Security log to track your audited events. You should keep in mind that the Security log is limited in size so you should select the events you choose to audit carefully. You should also decide how much disk space you are willing to give up for the Security log. The maximum size of your Security log is defined in the Event Viewer.

exam Watch

Remember that you can set auditing only on files and folders that reside on an NTFS partition.

Auditing Access to Files and Folders

Once your system is configured to allow you to audit, you can actually start tracking events such as the access of files and folders by various users and groups. This is a relatively simple process that is done using Windows Explorer. In order to audit a file or folder, you simply navigate to the file or folder through Windows Explorer and right-click on it to display the properties. Select the Security tab and click the Advanced button. Click the Auditing tab and add the user or group whose access to the object you wish to track. Now you can select which events you want to audit that relate to that user or group.

Auditing Access to Active Directory Objects

Using Windows 2000, administrators can monitor access to specific objects in Active Directory—for example, printers. You may be concerned that users are accessing printers outside work hours to print personal documents, or you may be concerned that users without privileges to a certain printer are attempting to use that printer. Using auditing, you could track the successful and failed attempts to use that printer. Using the Active Directory Users and Computers snap-in, you can monitor use of special privileges by users and groups as well as user logons, failed logon attempts, and logoffs. Each object has a set of security information attached to it. Part of this information specifies the groups or users that can access that object and the types of access that have been granted to those users or groups. In addition to the security information, objects also have auditing information. This information includes which users or groups to audit when accessing the object, the access events to be audited for each group or user, and success or failure in accessing each object. Auditing access to objects in Active Directory can be useful for looking at trends in the use of a particular object or tracking access to a certain object for security reasons. Before you can audit any objects in Active Directory, you must first enable auditing of the Directory Service Access Event. Exercise 17-2 details how to do that.

EXERCISE 17-2

Enabling Auditing of the Directory Service Access Event

1. Start the Active Directory Users and Computers snap-in (Start—Programs—Administrative Tools).
2. On the View menu, click Advanced Features.
3. Right-click on the Domain Controllers Container and choose Properties.
4. Click the Group Policy tab.
5. Click Default Domain Controller Policy, then click Edit. The following illustration shows the Default Domain Controllers Policy window.

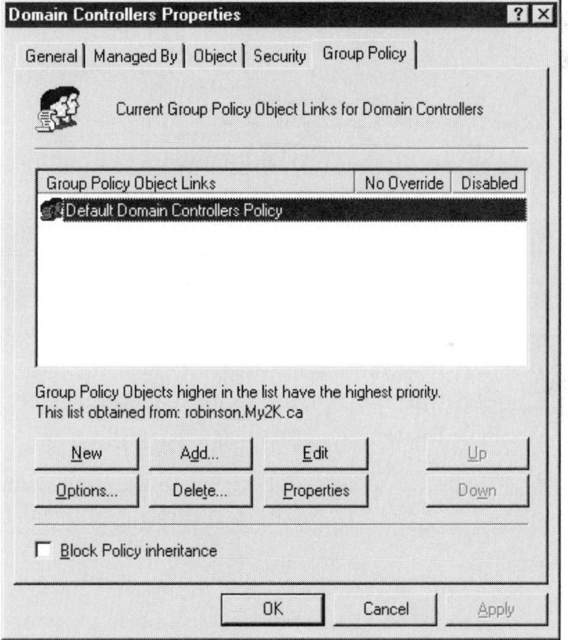

6. Double-click the following items to open them: Computer Configuration, Windows Settings, Security Settings, Local Policies, Audit Policy. The following illustration shows where to find the Audit Policy in the Group Policy Window.

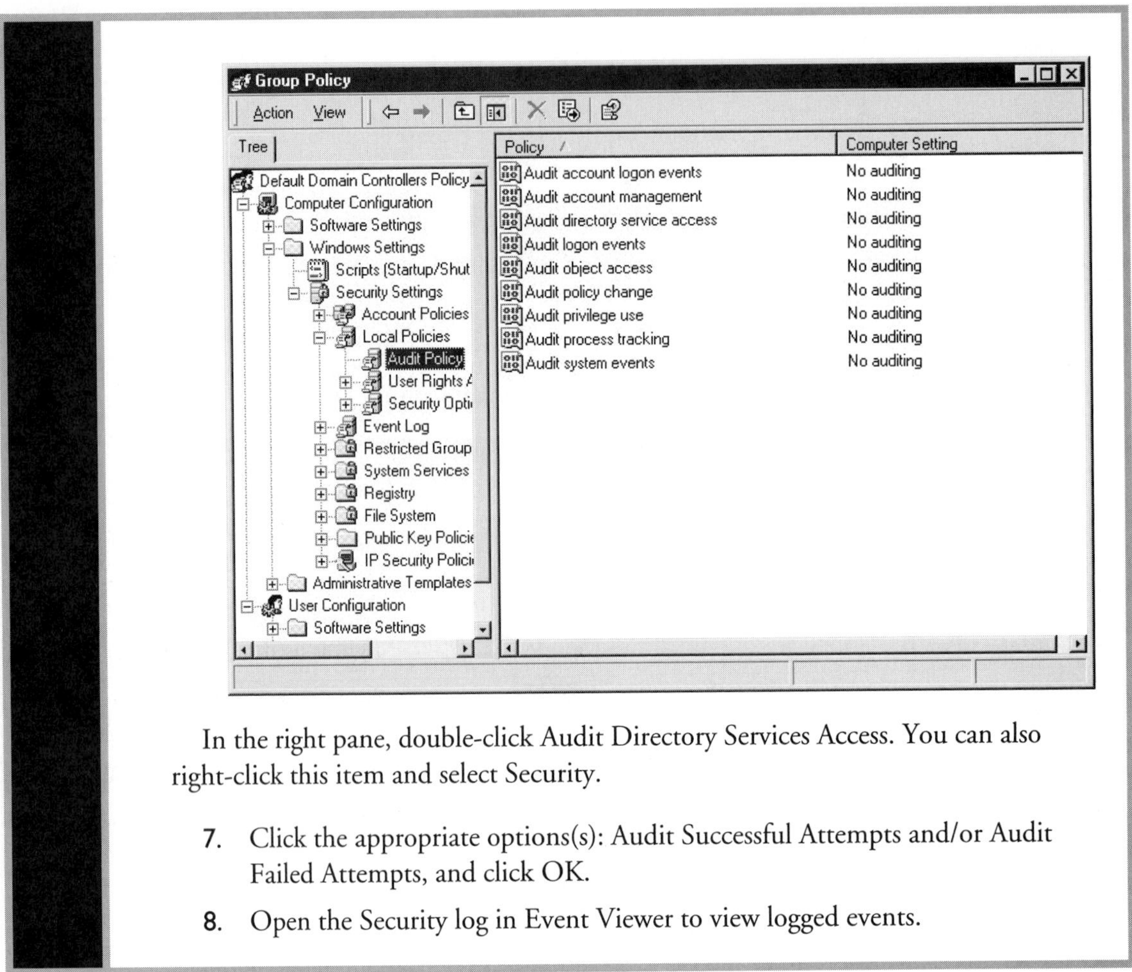

In the right pane, double-click Audit Directory Services Access. You can also right-click this item and select Security.

7. Click the appropriate options(s): Audit Successful Attempts and/or Audit Failed Attempts, and click OK.
8. Open the Security log in Event Viewer to view logged events.

The following scenarios and solutions are concerned with events you can record and audit in Windows 2000.

SCENARIO & SOLUTION	
How is Account Logon triggered?	It is triggered when a logon request is received by a domain controller.
How is Account Management triggered?	It is triggered when a user or group account is created or modified, or when a user password is changed or initially set.
How is Directory Service Access triggered?	It is triggered when an object in Active Directory level is accessed. (You would need to define this more at the level of the actual object.)
How is Logon Events triggered?	It is triggered when a user logs on or off a computer.
How is Object Access triggered?	It is triggered when a user accesses a file, folder, or printer. This differs from Directory Service Access. Directory Service Access is for specific Active Directory objects, while Object Access is for auditing users' access to files, folders, and printers.
What triggers Policy Change?	It is triggered when security options, user rights, or audit policies are altered.
What triggers Privilege Use?	It is triggered when a user right is used to perform an action.
What triggers Process Tracking?	It is triggered when an application performs an action that is purposefully being tracked by a programmer.
What triggers System Events?	It is triggered when an event occurs that affects security, or when a user restarts or shuts down a computer.

CERTIFICATION OBJECTIVE 17.02

Implementing, Configuring, Managing, and Troubleshooting Local Accounts

Users and groups are important because they allow the administrator the ability to limit the ability of users and groups to perform certain actions by assigning them rights and permissions. On Member Servers you can create and manage local users and groups using Computer Management Users and Groups. A local user or group is an account that can be granted permissions and rights from your computer. Local

Users and Groups is not available on Domain Controllers, as Active Directory is used to manage users and groups on Domain Controllers.

Creating and Managing User Accounts

Windows 2000 creates some users by default on a Member Server: the Administrator account and the Guest account (which is disabled by default). User Accounts that you create can have usernames that contain up to 20 uppercase or lowercase characters excluding the following: " / \ [ ] : ; | = + * ? < >. A username cannot consist solely of periods or spaces and cannot be the same as any other user or group name on the computer being administered. When creating a User Account, you will also need to assign the user a password, which the user will be prompted to change the first time he or she logs in to the system. Windows 2000 passwords can be up to 127 characters long; however, Windows 98 and Windows 95 support only 14 character passwords, so if you are working in a mixed environment, you will want to keep that in mind. Exercise 17-3 shows you how to add a new user.

EXERCISE 17-3

Adding a New User

1. Click Start, Programs, Administrative Tools, Computer Management. Open Local Users and Groups.
2. In the left pane, highlight the Users folder.
3. From the Action menu, select New User.
4. Give the user a username based on your organization's conventions. It is common to use the first initial and last name of the user. You should also give the user a description so that you and future administrators will be able to easily identify the user. You will also need to give the user a password. Note that the user will be prompted to change this password the first time he or she logs on. You may also disable the account at this screen if it is not needed immediately. The following illustration shows the New User window.

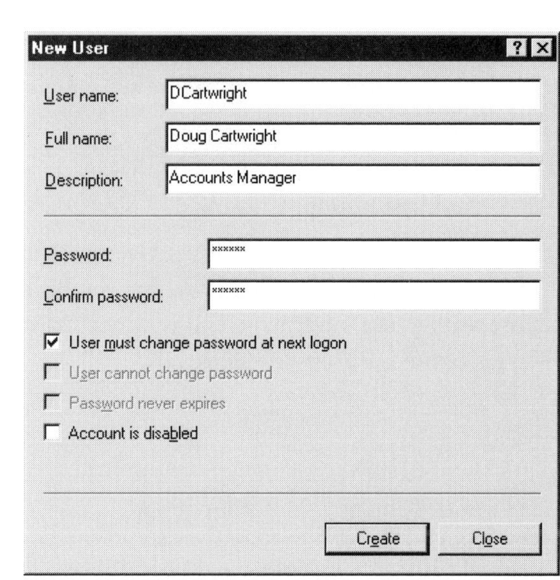

5. Click Create, then click Close. Note that in the following illustration, the new user appears in the list of users.

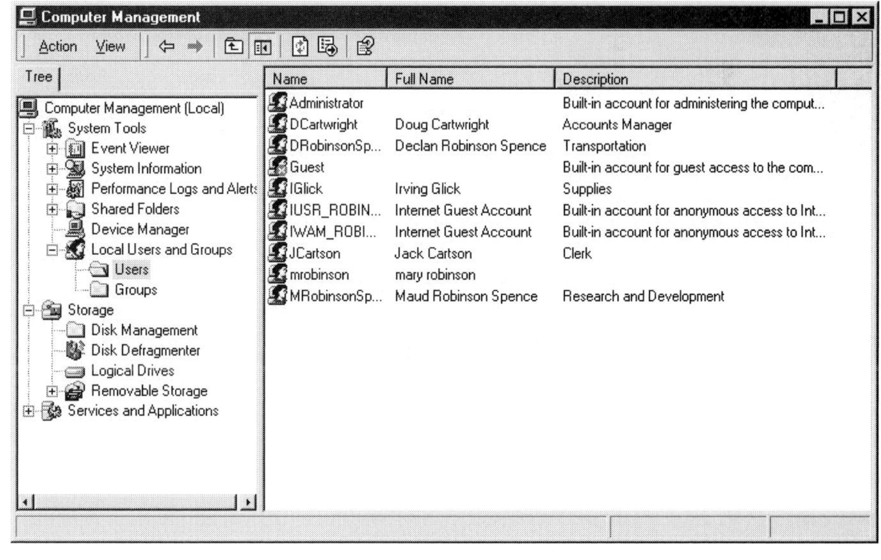

6. Now you can manage the new user account by double-clicking the new user in the right pane. Note that there are now four tabs associated with the properties of the user account.
7. Click the Member Of tab. Note that by default the user is only a member of the Users Group. Click Add.
8. From the top pane of the Select Groups Windows, highlight Backup Operators and click Add. Note that the Backup Operators group now appears in the lower pane and is associated with the computer on which it was created: Robinson. Click OK.

The Profile tab is used to map the user to the location of the profile, to give the user a login script, and to map the user to the home directory. In the Profile Path you would enter the location in which you want the user's profile to be stored. This profile can be stored locally or on another server. Figure 17-1 shows the Properties windows for the user.

FIGURE 17-1

The User Properties window

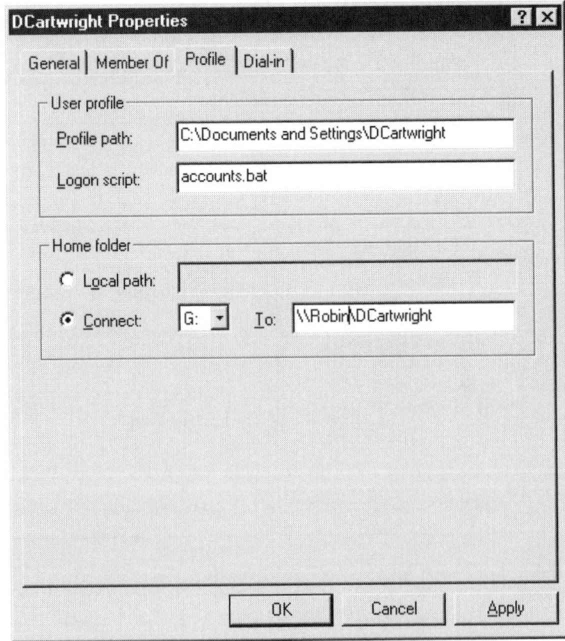

The Login Script will map the user to whatever network drives you choose as the administrator. This is written as a batch file using the Net Use command.

The user's home folder is generally a place where users are allowed to keep their own data. In many organizations, the only people with rights to this folder are the user and the administrator. If the folder is kept locally, use Local Path to enter its location. If the user's folder is kept on another server, connect it as a mapped drive using the \\servername\sharename convention.

The Dial-in tab is used to give the user permissions for a dial-in account to your network.

Creating Users on a Domain Controller is a very similar process to creating them on a Member Server except that the operations are performed in Start, Programs, Administrative Tools, and Active Directory Users and Computers.

Creating and Managing Computer Accounts

A computer account is an account that is created by an administrator and uniquely identifies the computer on the domain. The newly created account is used so that a computer may be brought into a Windows 2000 Domain.

exam Watch

In order to create a new computer account, you must be logged on as a member of the Domain Admins Group.

Exercise 17-4 shows you how to add a computer to your domain.

EXERCISE 17-4

Adding a Computer to the Domain

1. Log on as a member of the Domain Admins Group.
2. Open the Active Directory Users and Computers snap-in.
3. From the Action menu, choose New, then choose Computer. The New Object—Computer window will open.
4. From the New Object—Computer window, add the name of the new computer. The following illustration shows a computer named Scott being added to the domain.

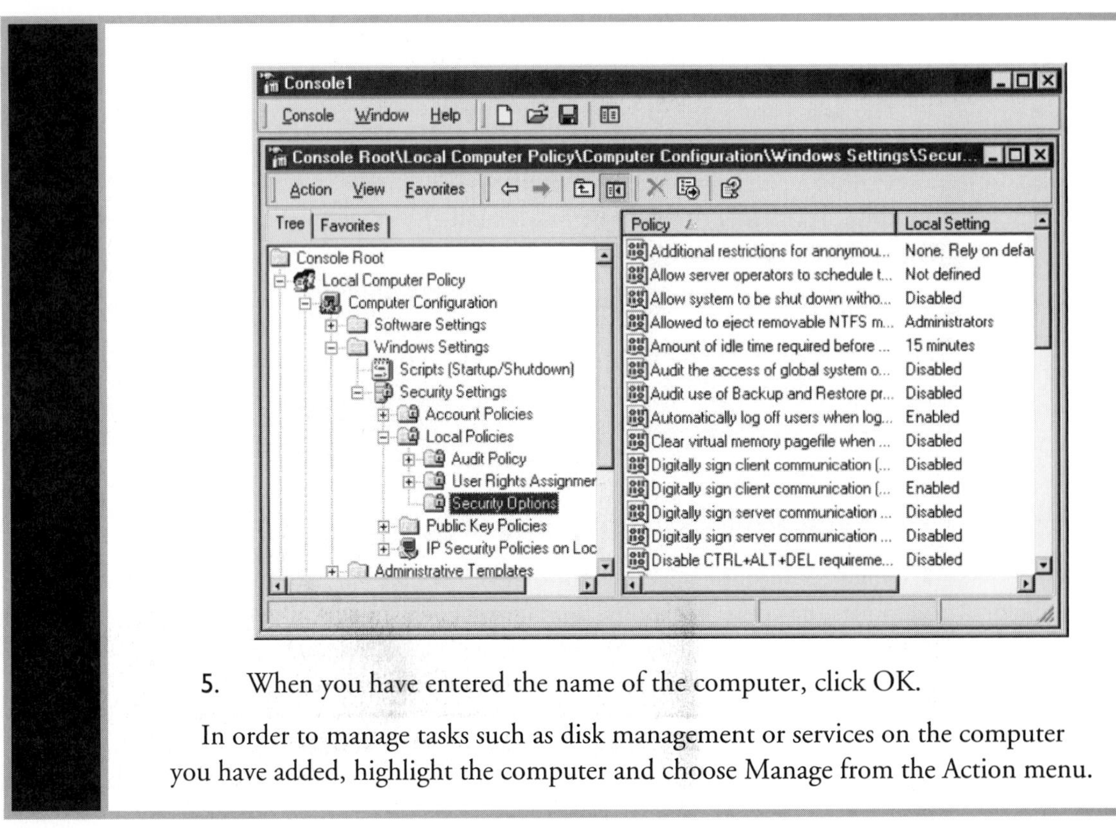

5. When you have entered the name of the computer, click OK.

In order to manage tasks such as disk management or services on the computer you have added, highlight the computer and choose Manage from the Action menu.

Creating and Managing Local Groups

On a Member Server, a local group is one that can be granted rights and permissions from its own computer and, if the computer participates in a domain, user accounts and global groups from its domain. Like local users, local groups are created in the Local Users and Groups portion of Computer Management in the Administrative Tools. By selecting Groups from the console tree, you can select New Group from the Action Menu. You will give the group a name and use the Add button to add members to your group. Figure 17-2 shows the members of the group Researchers.

A user who belongs to a group has all the rights and privileges assigned to that group. If a user is assigned to more than one group, then the user has all the rights and permissions granted to every group to which he or she belongs. If a user is a member of two groups, one of which has more restricted access to a particular file or folder, the user will have the least restrictive access provided by his or her group membership. (The exception is when any of the groups the user belongs to are specifically denied permission. The deny permission overrides all others.)

FIGURE 17-2

Group members

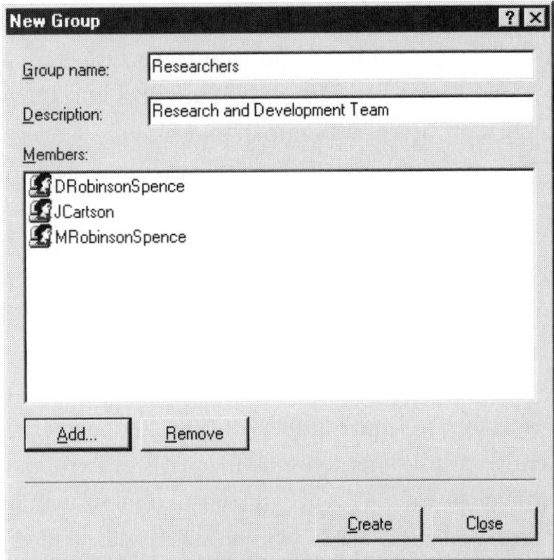

FROM THE CLASSROOM

User Rights

Administrators can assign specific rights to group accounts or to individual user accounts. These rights authorize users to perform specific actions such as logging on to a system interactively or backing up files and directories. User rights are different from permissions, because user rights apply to user accounts and permissions are attached to objects. User rights define capabilities at the local level. Although user rights can apply to individual user accounts, they are best administered on a group basis. This ensures that the user logging on automatically inherits the rights associated with that group. It also eases the amount of administration necessary. A new user who joins your organization and is part of the Personnel Department can be put in the group you have already created for that department and will automatically be able to access all the files and folders the rest of the users in the Personnel Department can access.

There are two types of user rights: privileges and logon rights. Privileges are activities like changing the system time, generating security audits, and shutting down the system. Logon rights are activities like logging on as a service and logging on locally to a machine.

—Mary Robinson, MCP

Windows 2000 provides several groups for you. By default, the following groups are placed in the built-in folders for Active Directory Users and Computers: Account Operators, Administrators, Backup Operators, Guests, Printer Operators, Replicator, Server Operators, and Users.

Security Groups

Windows 2000 allows you to organize users and other domain objects into groups for easy administration of access permissions. Defining your security groups is a major task for your distributed security plan.

The Windows 2000 Security Groups allow you to assign the same security permissions to large numbers of users in one operation. This ensures consistent security permissions across all members of a group. Using Security Groups to assign permissions means the access control on resources remains fairly static and easy to control and audit. Users who need access are added or removed from the appropriate security groups as needed, and the access control lists change infrequently.

Windows 2000 supports both Security Groups and Distribution Groups. The Security Groups can have security permissions associated with them and can also function as mailing lists. The Distribution Groups are used for mailing lists only; they have no security function.

There are three types of Security Groups: Domain Local, Global, and Universal.

Domain Local Groups are used for granting access rights to resources such as file systems or printers that are located on any computer in the domain where common access permissions are required. The advantage of Domain Local Groups being used to protect resources is that a member of the Domain Local Group can come from both inside the same domain and from outside as well.

Global Groups are used for combining users who share a common access profile based on job function or business role. Typically organizations use Global Groups for all groups in which membership is expected to change frequently. These groups can have as members only user accounts defined in the same domain as the Global Group.

Universal Groups are used in larger, multidomain organizations in which there is a need to grant access to similar groups of accounts defined in multiple domains. It is better to use Global Groups as members of Universal Groups to reduce overall replication traffic from changes to Universal Group membership. Users can be added and removed from the corresponding Global Groups with their account domains, and a small number of Global Groups are the direct members of the Universal Group. Universal Groups are used only in multiple domain trees or forests. A Windows 2000 domain must be in native mode to use Universal Groups.

CERTIFICATION OBJECTIVE 17.03

Implementing, Configuring, Managing, and Troubleshooting Account Policy

Another way of making your system more secure is to implement policies that protect your data from unauthorized access. An Account Policy encompasses several different means to accomplish a more secure organization. Account Policies are those enforced against the user accounts you have created for your users to gain access to data. There are three parts to an Account Policy: Password Policy, Account Lockout Policy, and Kerberos Policy.

Password Policy

A password policy regulates how your users must establish and manage their passwords. This includes password complexity requirements and how often passwords must change. There are several settings that can be used to implement a successful password policy. You can enforce password uniqueness so that users cannot simply switch back and forth between a few easy to remember passwords. This can be set to low, medium, or high security. With low security, the system remembers the user's last 1–8 passwords (it is your choice as administrator to decide how many); with medium, it remembers the last 9–16 passwords; with high, it remembers the last 17–24 passwords.

As in the last section, you must have added the Group Policy snap-in in order to manage account policies. (See Exercise 17-1.) Once you have the Group Policy snap-in installed, you can manage your account policies. Exercise 17-5 details how to make changes to your password policy.

EXERCISE 17-5

Changing Password Policies

1. From Start, Programs, Administrative Tools, select the Group Policy snap-in you have already added in Exercise 17-1.
2. Double-click on Computer Configuration, then Windows Settings, then Security Settings, then Account Policies, then Password Policy. The following illustration shows the Console window with the Security Settings.

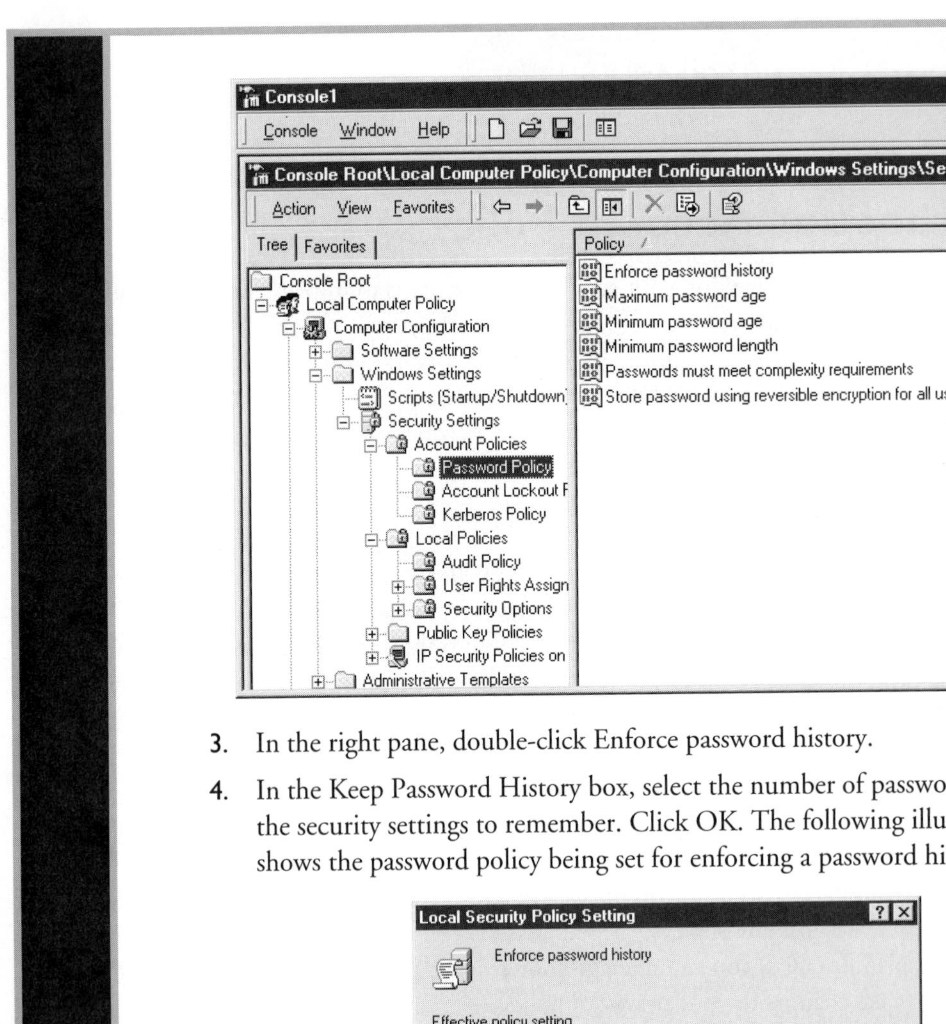

3. In the right pane, double-click Enforce password history.
4. In the Keep Password History box, select the number of passwords you wish the security settings to remember. Click OK. The following illustration shows the password policy being set for enforcing a password history.

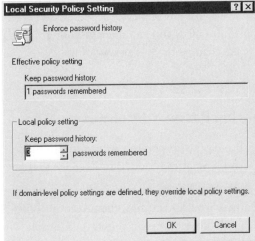

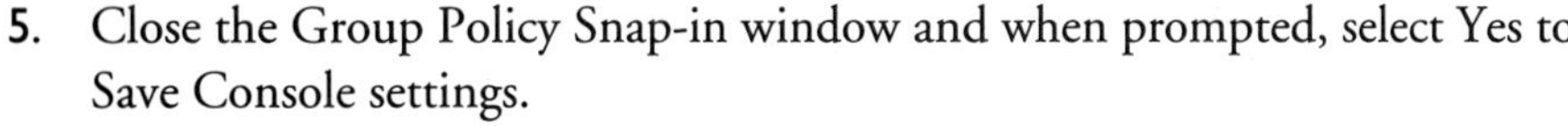

5. Close the Group Policy Snap-in window and when prompted, select Yes to Save Console settings.

Account Lockout Policy

The Account Lockout Policy dictates the behavior for locking and unlocking user accounts. This includes Account lockout threshold and how long to lock accounts. There are three configurable parameters: Account lockout threshold determines how many times users can attempt to log on before their accounts are locked. This can range from low (five attempts) to high (one or two attempts). The Account lockout duration parameter controls how long an account is locked after the Account lockout threshold parameter is triggered. The Reset account lockout counter after parameter is a counter for unsuccessful logon attempts which increments for x number of minutes before returning its value to zero. Account Lockout Policy is configured in the same place as the password policy: the Group Policy snap-in. This policy is very useful in the sense that someone who is trying to gain unauthorized access to your system may try logging on using a username and password they think might work. If the intruder tries three different passwords, for example, and you have configured your account lockout policy to lock users out after three unsuccessful login attempts, your intruder is now out of chances.

Kerberos V5 and Kerberos Policy

Using the Group Policy snap-in, you can also configure the Kerberos Policy. Kerberos V5 is the primary security protocol for authentication with the Windows 2000 domain. Kerberos is an industry-standard, platform-independent security protocol developed at the Massachusetts Institute of Technology (MIT). Kerberos network authentication enhances security because network servers and services need to know that the client requesting the access is actually a valid client and the client also knows that the servers it is connecting to are valid. The central component of Kerberos is the Key Distribution Center (KDC). The KDC runs on each Windows 2000 domain controller as a part of Active Directory, which stores passwords and other sensitive account information. The Kerberos V5 protocol verifies both the identity of the user and network services. The Kerberos V5 authentication method issues tickets for accessing network services. A ticket is a set of identification data for a security principal, issued by a domain controller for the purposes of user authentication. These tickets contain encrypted data, including an encrypted password that confirms the user's identity to the requested service. If a client wants to communicate with a server, the client sends the request to the KDC, and the KDC in turn issues a session key so that the client and server can authenticate with each other. The session key has a limited lifetime that is good for a single logon session. After the login session is terminated, the session key is no longer valid. The copy of the session key that the server receives is contained in a session ticket, which also contains information about the client. Now the client and the server can communicate.

Using Kerberos Policy, you can set rules for how the tickets are handled by the system. Kerberos Policy is set at the domain level and is stored within Active Directory and may be accessed on a server in the Group Policy snap-in. Only members of the Domain Admins Group have permission to change the policy. Kerberos Policy can define the following parameters: Maximum lifetime for user ticket renewal, Maximum lifetime for service ticket, Maximum tolerance for computer clock synchronization, and Maximum lifetime for user ticket. Enforce user logon restrictions is enabled by default and is used to validate every request for service tickets by making sure that the client has the correct user rights for logging on the requested server.

on the Job

The Enforce user logon restrictions portion of Kerberos Policy takes the server extra time to perform and can slow down your network. This is a setting that can be disabled, so if you are experiencing these problems, you may consider disabling this function.

The Maximum lifetime for service ticket parameter is set in minutes. A service ticket is the same thing as a session ticket. The setting for the lifetime of the service ticket cannot be more than the time specified in the Maximum User Ticket lifetime or less than ten minutes. It is advisable to make this setting the same as the Maximum User Ticket lifetime.

- The Maximum lifetime for user ticket parameter is set in hours. The default setting is ten hours.

The Maximum lifetime for user ticket renewal parameter is set in days. The default setting is seven days.

- The Maximum tolerance for computer clock synchronization parameter determines how much difference in the clocks is tolerated. This setting is in minutes, and five minutes is the default.

exam Watch

Policies may be set for the domain or for the local machine. Any time a local policy and a domain policy conflict, the domain policy will go into effect.

CERTIFICATION OBJECTIVE 17.04

Using the Security Configuration Toolset

The Security Configuration Toolset is a set of snap-ins for MMC that is designed to provide a central place for security-related tasks. With the Security Configuration Toolset, you will be able to use an integrated set of tools to configure and analyze security on one or more Windows 2000 machines in your network. It is intended to answer the need for a central security configuration tool. Most important, it provides a single place where the entire system's security can be viewed, analyzed, and adjusted, as necessary. The components of the Security Configuration Toolset are as follows:

- Security Configuration and Analysis snap-in
- Security Settings Extension to Group Policy
- Security Templates snap-in
- The command line tool, secedit.exe

Security Configuration and Analysis Snap-in

The Security Configuration and Analysis snap-in allows you to configure and analyze your system. By comparing what your system currently looks like in terms of security against a Security Template that you load into a personal database, the system's security setup is analyzed. The template contains the settings for how you want your system's security to be managed. If the analysis finds discrepancies between the template and the current state of your system, it will point out those discrepancies and make recommendations based on the template. Exercise 17-6 details how to set up the personal database and analyze your system's security.

EXERCISE 17-6

Setting Up the Personal Database and Analyzing System Security

1. First you need to set a working database. Open the MMC console into which you have loaded the Security Configuration and Analysis snap-in.
2. Right-click Security Configuration and Analysis under the Console Root and select Open Database.
3. If this is your first personal database, type in the name you want to give it and click Open.
4. You will be prompted to select a Security Template to import. For the purposes of this exercise we will use the basicsv file, as it is the default template for Windows 2000 servers that are not Domain Controllers. Double-click Basicsv. The following illustration shows the list of templates that are available by default.

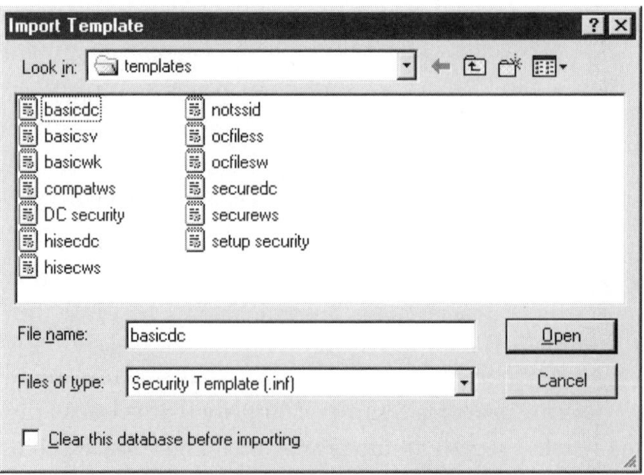

5. Now the system's security can be analyzed. Right-click Security Configuration and Analysis under Console Root and select Analyze Computer Now. Make a note of or change the location of the log file, as this is where you will view the results of the analysis. Click OK. The analysis will now run. The following illustration shows the analysis in progress.

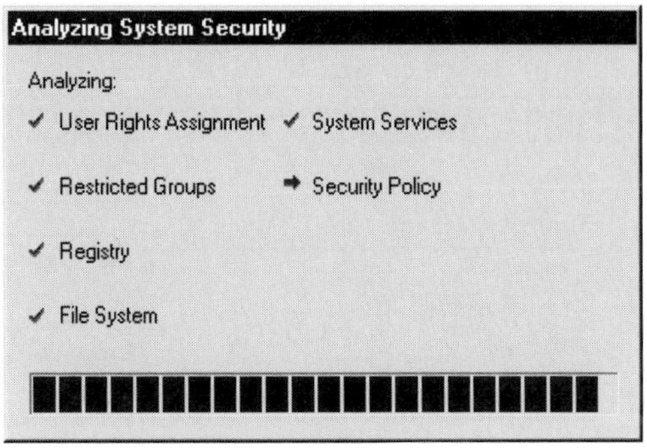

Analyzing System Security
Analyzing:
✓ User Rights Assignment ✓ System Services
✓ Restricted Groups ➔ Security Policy
✓ Registry
✓ File System

6. Go to the location of the log file and view the results.

Security Setting Extensions to Group Policy

The Security Configuration Toolset also includes an extension snap-in to the Group Policy Editor to configure local security policies as well as security policies for domains and organizational units. Local security policies only include the Account Policy and Local Policy. Exercise 17-7 details how to view your local security policy.

EXERCISE 17-7

Viewing Local Security Policy

1. Log on to your Windows 2000 Server computer as a user with administrative privileges.
2. Click Start, Programs, Administrative Tools, Console 1, which is the Group Policy snap-in you added earlier in this chapter.

3. Click the + next to Computer Configuration, then Windows Settings, then Security Settings, and then Local Policies to expand these folders.
4. Click the Security Options folder under Local Policies. The following illustration shows what your screen should look like.

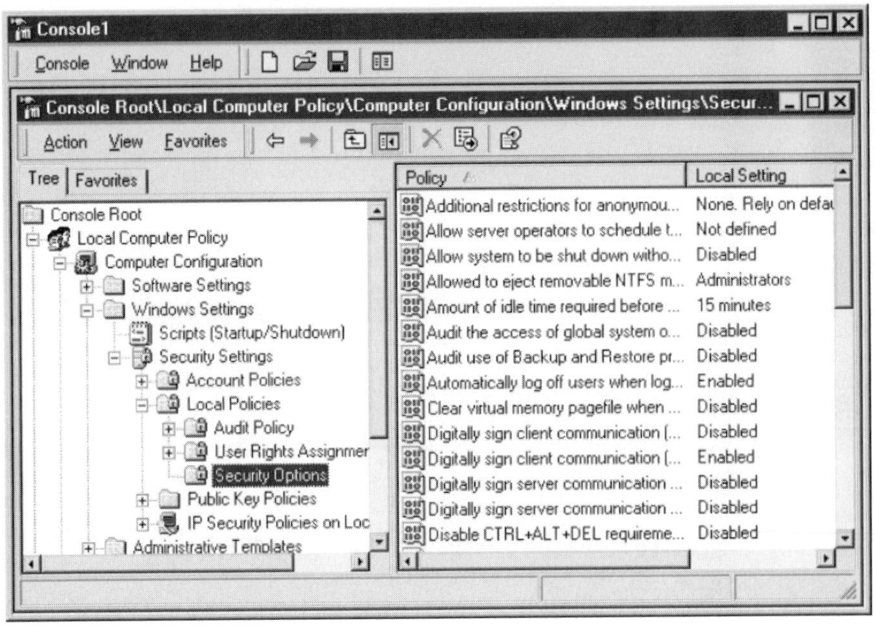

Templates

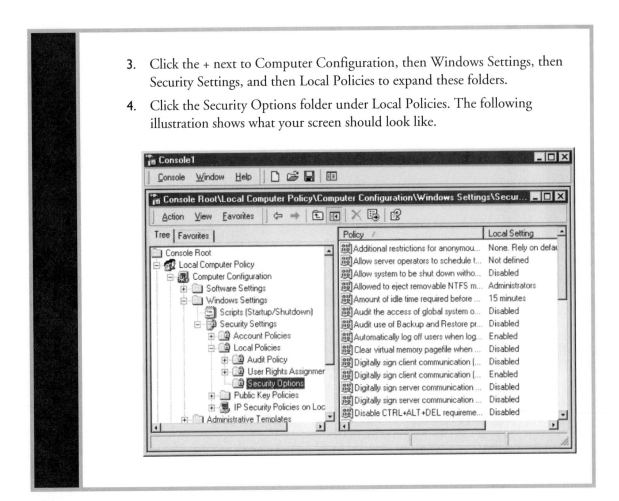

The Security Templates snap-in allows you to create a text based template file that can contain security settings for all of the security areas supported by the Security Configuration Toolset. You can then use these template files to configure or analyze system security using other tools.

Windows 2000 comes with several predefined Security Templates. These templates address several security scenarios. Security Templates come in two basic categories: Default and Incremental. The Default or Basic templates are applied by the operating system when a clean install has been performed. They are not applied if an upgrade installation has been done. The incremental templates should be applied after the Basic Security Templates have been applied. There are four types of incremental templates: Compatible, Secure, Highly Secure, and Dedicated Domain Controller.

The Compatible Template Security Level is used to alter the default permissions for the Users Group so that legacy applications can run properly.

The Secure template will increase the level of security for Account Policy, certain Registry keys, and Auditing. Permissions to file system objects are not affected with this configuration, but it removes all members from the Power Users group.

The Highly Secure templates add security to network communications. Legacy clients will not be able to communicate if this level is used.

The Dedicated Domain Controller template optimizes security for local users on domain controllers that do not run other server applications.

The secedit.exe Command Line Tool

The Secedit.exe Command Line tool offers much of the functionality of the Security Configuration and Analysis snap-in, only from the command line. Secedit.exe, when called from a batch file or from an automatic task scheduler, can be used to automatically create and apply templates and analyze system security. It can also be run dynamically from the command line. Secedit.exe allows the administrator to analyze system security, configure system security, refresh security settings, export security settings, and validate the syntax of a Security Template. There are many switches the administrator can use with secedit. Figure 17-3 shows the syntax used to refresh security settings for the local machine with the machine name Robinson.

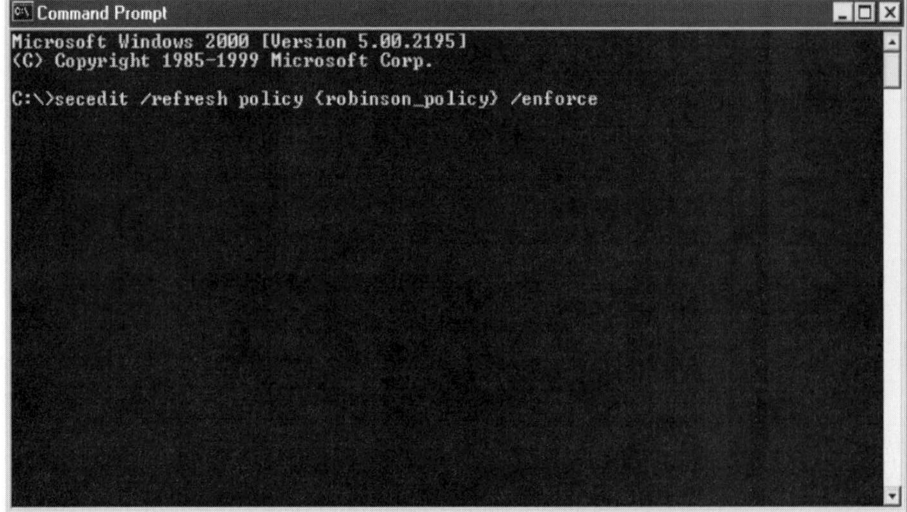

FIGURE 17-3 Using secedit.exe to refresh security settings

The following grid shows some of the secedit.exe switches and their uses.

SCENARIO & SOLUTION

Scenario	Solution
Initiate Security Analysis.	Use secedit /analyze. You would use this syntax with additional switches like /DB *filename* to inform secedit what database to apply the security analysis results to.
Apply a Template using the Configure Switch.	Use secedit /configure. You would also use switches like /CFG *filename* where filename is the location of the template that will be applied to the database.
Export the template stored in the database to an .inf file.	Use secedit /export with the switch /DB *filename*, for example, to inform secedit what database to extract the template from.

The secedit.exe command line tool will allow you to schedule regular security audits of local policies on the machines in any domain and organizational unit. By running scripts that call on the secedit.exe program, you can update each computer's personal database with the results of your security analysis. You can then later use the Security Configuration and Analysis snap-in to analyze the results of your automated analysis.

CERTIFICATION SUMMARY

Given the current buzz over newly created viruses, not to mention Denial of Service attacks on major organizations, having a handle on the security of your system is clearly a vital component of your Windows 2000 plan. In order to protect your data from unauthorized access, it is essential that you learn as much as possible about implementing effective security.

Using Auditing, you can track the activities of users in order to find security violations that need to be addressed. The log that is provided by event auditing will help you retrace the steps of an intruder so that you can close that security hole. You can audit access both to files and folders and to Active Directory objects.

With Local Accounts, you, as the administrator, can limit the ability of users and groups to perform certain actions and access certain objects. By creating accounts for users, groups, and computers, you can tighten your grip on what actually gets accessed in your system and uniquely identify these objects on your network.

Implementing policies such as Account, Password, and Kerberos Policies are excellent steps that you can take in developing a tight security system. Depending on how concerned you are about access to your data, you can impose a variety of policies that will help keep your system as secure as you want it to be.

The Security Configuration Toolset allows you ability to configure security for local machines, domains, or organizational units. Using the Security Configuration and Analysis snap-in you can apply a number of different security scenarios. With Templates, you can create files that contain security settings for export to other computers in your domain or used on the local machine. The secedit.exe Command Line Tool allows you much of the functionality of the Security Configuration Toolset, but from the command line so that you can schedule the application of Security Templates.

Defining an easy-to-use, effective security policy is a vital undertaking and shouldn't be taken lightly. Once you have this in place, however, you can feel safer knowing you have a thorough understanding of your potential vulnerabilities and that you have addressed them.

✓ TWO-MINUTE DRILL

Implementing, Configuring, Managing, and Troubleshooting Auditing

- ❑ Use the Group Policy snap-in to configure Auditing.
- ❑ Auditing can only be set on an NTFS partition.
- ❑ Use Windows Explorer to audit files and folders.
- ❑ Subfolders and files inherit auditing set on parent folders by default.

Implementing, Configuring, Managing, and Troubleshooting Local Accounts

- ❑ New Users are created in Computer Management, Users, and Groups.
- ❑ Users get all the rights and permissions granted to them by their group membership.

Implementing, Configuring, Managing, and Troubleshooting Account Policy

- ❑ Password Policy regulates how users establish and manage their passwords.
- ❑ Account Lockout Policy can be used to set how many times a user can try logging in with the incorrect login information and how long the account will stay locked once the lockout is enforced.
- ❑ Kerberos Policy is set for the domain level.
- ❑ Only members of the Domain Admins Group have permission to alter Kerberos Policy.
- ❑ The Security Configuration and Analysis snap-in uses a personal database to store computer-specific system Security Templates.
- ❑ Security Templates can be used to analyze your computer's current security settings and determine whether there are discrepancies between the template and your settings.
- ❑ Secedit.exe is a command line version of the Security Configuration Toolset and can by run dynamically or scheduled.

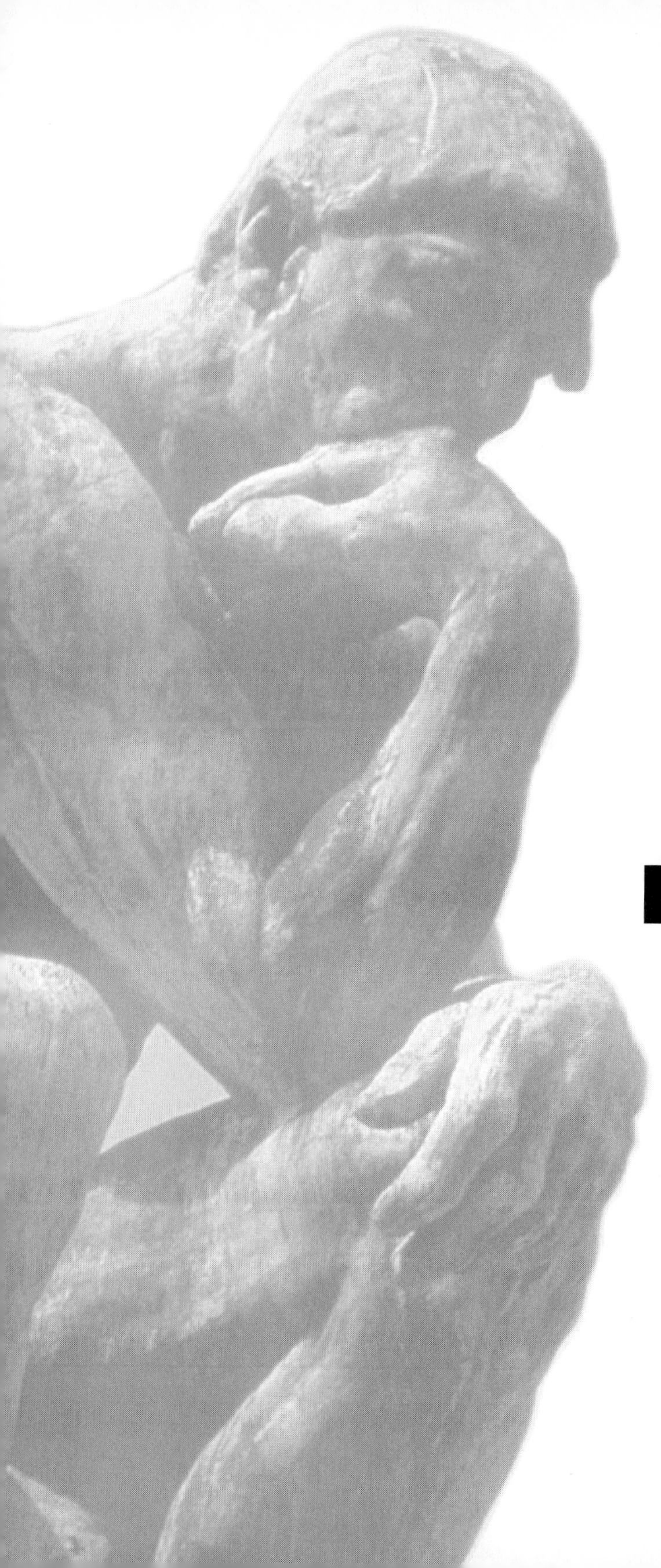

18

Windows 2000 Resource Protection and Disaster Recovery

CERTIFICATION OBJECTIVES

System availability and data safety are two of the primary concerns of any systems administrator. It is embarrassing for the administrator when for some reason the system does not start up or when urgently required data just vanishes. This chapter deals with methods used to fix system startup problems, as well as data backup and restore utilities included with Windows 2000 Server. The first part walks you through various advanced startup options in case of system boot-up failure and explains the recovery console and some important issues that arise with the recovery of system state data.

The second part details the Windows backup and restore utilities. You will learn how to configure these two wizards. We will also discuss the backup and restore procedures for Active Directory data, which is hosted by every Windows 2000 domain controller.

CERTIFICATION OBJECTIVE 18.01

Managing and Optimizing Availability of System State Data and User Data

In earlier versions of Windows NT, the Emergency Repair Disk was the only tool available for the system administrators to fix the system startup problems. The only safe startup mode was the VGA mode, which was helpful in overcoming potential display related problems. The administrator had to depend on third-party utilities to get access to the NTFS partitions. Windows 2000 has been built on strong foundations and comes loaded with numerous tools to ensure that the system downtime remains at a minimum.

The Recovery Console is a wonderful inclusion in the Windows 2000 family of operating systems. This utility not only gives access to all NTFS volumes on the system but can also re-create disk partitions. Another useful tool is the Task Scheduler, which was not available in graphical form in Windows NT 4.0. We will discuss these in detail later in this chapter.

Advanced Startup Options

If for some reason you are not able to start your system in a normal way, Windows 2000 Server gives you some advanced startup options. You can use these options to start the system and look for the problem that is preventing your system from starting. The advanced startup options are helpful for booting the machine in a basic mode and help in diagnosing and fixing the problem.

Pressing F8 from the initial boot menu accesses the advanced startup options. You have to be pretty quick in this action so that the wait time specified in the boot.ini file does not expire. In case the wait time is very low, you may press F8 during the initial startup phase. This will invoke the advanced boot options menu.

If you do not make any selection, the default operating system is started. In case you are not able to press F8 quickly, you still have a chance to do it during the initial startup phase of Windows 2000. The Windows startup screen is shown, and a small blue progress bar is shown saying that "Windows is starting up." Press F8 at this moment. The Advanced Boot Options menu has the following startup choices, which will be discussed in the following sections:

- Safe Mode
- Safe Mode with Networking
- Safe Mode with Command Prompt
- Enable Boot Logging
- Enable VGA Mode
- Last Known Good Configuration
- Directory Services Restore Mode (Windows 2000 domain controllers only)
- Debugging Mode
- Boot Normally

Use + and - to move the highlight to your choice.
Press ENTER to choose.

Safe Mode, Safe Mode with Networking, and Safe Mode with Command Prompt

The first three options give you the choice of starting the system in any of the safe modes. You may chose to start in simple Safe Mode, Safe Mode with Networking, or Safe Mode with command prompt. The choice depends on the problem you are facing with the system startup.

Safe Mode Safe Mode starts Windows 2000 using only some basic files and device drivers. These devices include monitor, keyboard, mouse, basic VGA video, CD-ROM, and mass storage devices. The system starts only those system services that are necessary to load the operating system. Networking is not started in this mode. The Windows background screen is black in this mode, and the screen resolution is 640 × 480 pixels with 16 colors (see Figure 18-1).

FIGURE 18-1 The Windows desktop in Safe Mode

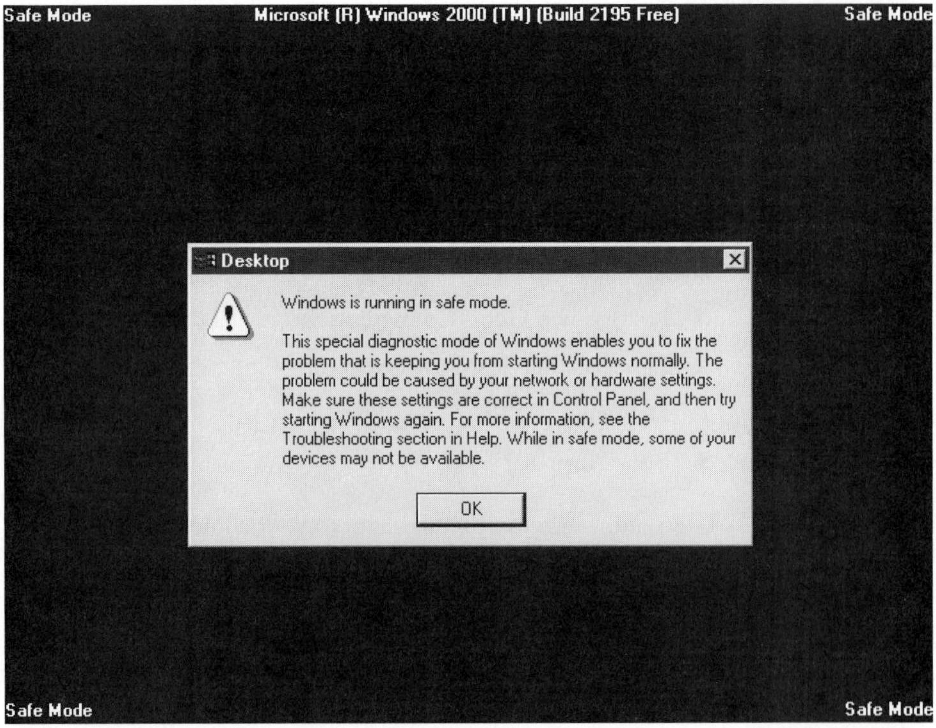

You may notice that a "Safe Mode" caption is displayed on all four corners of the screen. The dialog box tells you that this mode helps you in diagnosing and fixing any startup problems.

Safe Mode with Networking This mode is similar to the Safe Mode, but networking devices, drivers, and protocols are loaded. You may choose this mode when you are sure that the problem in the system is not due to any networking component.

Safe Mode with Command Prompt This option starts the operating system in a safe mode using some basic files only. The Windows 2000 command prompt is shown instead of the usual Windows desktop.

The choice of a safe startup mode largely depends on the type of startup problem you are facing. In case you are not sure about the cause of the problem, use the simple Safe Mode. If this mode works, try the Safe Mode with Networking. But if the simple Safe Mode is not able to start the system, you may have to use the emergency repair process.

Enable Boot Logging

This mode tries to start Windows 2000 in a normal way and writes the startup events to a log file. This log file collects the sequence of all installed devices and drivers as they are loaded by the system successfully. The drivers that fail to load are also listed in the log file. This mode works best when you want to know exactly what is preventing the system from starting. The log file is named ntbtlog.txt and is stored in the %SystemRoot% folder.

Enable VGA Mode

This mode starts Windows 2000 using the basic video driver. When you are sure that the startup problem is due to a bad video driver or improper display settings, you can use this mode. Video problems occur when you try to install a new video driver for your display adapter or when the installed video driver file becomes corrupted. The three safe modes discussed previously use this mode when trying to start up the system. This mode uses 16 colors and 640 × 480 screen resolution.

Last Known Good Configuration

This mode starts the system using the configuration that was saved in the registry during the last system shutdown. This startup option is useful when you have changed some configuration parameters and the system fails to boot. When this mode is used to start the system, all changes that were made after the last successful logon are lost. Use this option when you suspect that some incorrect configuration changes are causing the system startup failure. This mode does not help if any of the installed drivers have been corrupted or any driver files are deleted by mistake.

Directory Services Restore Mode

This startup mode is available on Windows 2000 Server domain controller computers only. This mode can be used to restore the SYSVOL directory and Active Directory on the domain controller.

Debugging Mode

This is the most advanced startup option of all. To use this option you will need to connect another computer to the problematic computer through a serial cable. With proper configuration, the debug information is sent to the second computer. The people associated with software development projects will most often use this mode.

Now that you have learned some of the advanced startup options for the Windows 2000 Server, let's consider some real-life questions:

SCENARIO & SOLUTION	
Your Windows 2000 computer is not starting up. How can you access the Advanced boot options?	Press the F8 function key when the initial operating systems menu is displayed.
What is the best option to start the system when some configuration changes are causing the system to fail at startup?	Start the system using the Last Known Good Configuration.
You deleted two directories by mistake. Can you use the Directory Services Restore Mode to get back these directories?	Sorry. The Directory Services Restore Mode is for restoring Active Directory and not for user data directories. In any case, it works only on domain controllers.
In what circumstances should you use the Safe Mode with Networking?	When you are sure that none of the networking components are preventing the system startup.

Recovery Console

The Recovery Console is a new command-line interpreter program feature in Windows 2000 that helps in system maintenance activities and resolving system problems. This program is separate from the Windows 2000 command prompt. The following tasks can be accomplished with the help of Recovery Console:

- Start a Windows 2000 computer that is having startup problems.
- Get limited access to local NTFS, FAT32, and FAT16 partitions and replace damaged files.
- Repair the Master Boot Record in case it is corrupted.
- Format partitions.
- Start and stop system services and drivers.

Using the Recovery Console is a secured process that allows only authorized users to access local system drives. You must have local administrative rights to start the Recovery Console on any Windows 2000 Server. The Recovery Console can either be started from the local hard disk or from the Windows 2000 CD-ROM. It requires approximately 7MB of free hard disk space.

Installing and Starting the Recovery Console

The Recovery Console can be started either from the Windows 2000 CD-ROM or from the local hard drive. In order to start the Recovery Console from the CD-ROM, the computer must be able to boot from the CD-ROM drive. Another way to start the Recovery Console is by using the Setup floppy disks. The recovery console can be installed from the Windows 2000 Server CD-ROM. Exercise 18-1 explains the steps necessary to install the Recovery Console on a computer that is running Windows 2000 Server.

The process given in this exercise assumes that you do not have mirrored drives in the computer where you are performing the installation. In order to install the Recovery Console on computers that have mirrored drives, the mirror set has to broken first. This can be reestablished after the Recovery Console is installed.

Starting the Recovery Console from Hard Disk When the Recovery Console is installed on a local hard disk, an option is added to the Startup menu. You may start the Recovery Console from this menu if the master boot record of

EXERCISE 18-1

Installing Recovery Console

1. Insert the Windows 2000 Server CD-ROM in your CD-ROM drive.
2. The dialog box appears, which prompts you to upgrade to Windows 2000 Server. Click No and close the window that appears.
3. From the Start menu click Start | Run. Type the following command: **d:\i386\winnt32.exe /cmdcons** where D is the letter of the CD-ROM drive.
4. A message is displayed on the screen, as shown in the following illustration.

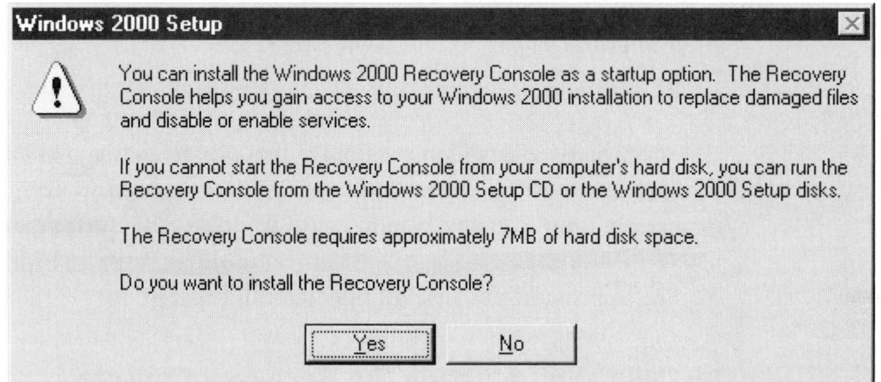

5. Click Yes to install the Recovery Console.

the computer is not corrupted. These steps are taken to start the Recovery Console from the boot menu:

1. Shut down and restart your computer.
2. Select Windows 2000 Recovery Console from the menu of operating systems.
3. The Recovery Console displays a command prompt. If you have more than one version of Windows installed, you are given an option to select a particular

system. Note that you can use the Recovery Console only to access installations of Windows 2000.

4. Select the operating system and press ENTER.
5. This starts the Recovery Console. You can now make the necessary changes in your system.

Starting the Recovery Console from Setup Media If you are not able to see the Startup menu, you have to use the setup floppy disk or the CD-ROM method. To use the Recovery Console, using either the Windows 2000 setup floppy disks or the CD-ROM, follow the steps given in Exercise 18-2.

Remember that use of Recovery Console requires the local administrative password. If you type an incorrect password three times or press ENTER, the Recovery Console quits and restarts the computer. Typing a correct password gives you access to the local drives. You may then start the necessary repair process.

In order to quit the Recovery Console at any time and restart the computer, type **exit** and press ENTER.

EXERCISE 18-2

CertCam 18-2

Starting Recovery Console from Setup Media

1. Start the computer with either the Window 2000 Setup floppy disks or the CD-ROM. Press ENTER when the Setup notification appears.
2. The Welcome to Setup screen appears. Press R to select Repair a Windows 2000 Installation.
3. Press C to use the Recovery Console.
4. You are prompted to select an installation in case you have more than one version of Windows 2000 running on the system. Select the installation to repair by pressing the number key corresponding to the displayed installations and press ENTER.
5. You are prompted to log on to this installation of Windows 2000 with the local administrator password. Type the password and press ENTER.

exam Watch

You must be the local administrator to use the Recovery Console. The Recovery Console will ask you for the administrator password when you start it. If you type an incorrect password three times, the Recovery Console quits and restarts the computer.

Recovery Console Commands

Once the Recovery Console has started, you can access the following directories on the NTFS drive:

- %SystemRoot%
- %Windir% and subfolders of this Windows 2000 installation (see exceptions below)
- %SystemRoot%\Cmdcons and subfolders

You also gain access to CD-ROM and floppy drives. The access to the floppy drive is limited because by default, you cannot copy files to the floppy disk. The floppy disk write access is disabled by default and has to be enabled using the **set** command. Once you are logged into a particular installation of Windows 2000, you cannot access other local installations without explicitly logging into another installation, using the **logon** command. Access is also restricted to other local folders, such as Program Files and the Documents and Settings folders.

You can use the **help** command to get a list of available commands in the Recovery Console. To get help on a particular command syntax and its usage, the /? switch can be used, which works with all commands. The Recovery Console keeps a history of previously used commands and can be accessed using the up and down arrow keys. This is similar to the Doskey function in MS-DOS. Most of the other Recovery Console commands are similar to MS-DOS commands.

A complete listing of the Recovery Console commands, their functions, and syntax is out of the scope of this book. For getting help on usage and syntax of any command, type the command name followed by the /? switch. One important command in the Recovery Console is **fixmbr,** which can be used to repair a bad master boot record.

In case you have even a little suspicion that some sort of virus is present in the master boot record, do not use the* fixmbr *command. The* fixmbr *command can damage the partition of your computer if the master boot record is infected by a virus. Microsoft recommends that you use the built-in AVBoot antivirus program to fix the master boot record. The AVBoot is located in the \Valueadd\3rdparty\Ca-antiv folder of the Windows 2000 Server CD-ROM.

The Recovery Console has some environment variables set by default. These can be viewed and changed using the **set** command. This command is a configuration command for the Recovery Console. The syntax for this command is: **set [variable = value]**. The **set** command supports the following environment variables:

- **AllowWildCards** This enables the use of wildcard for commands such as **copy**, **del**, and so on. By default, wildcards are not supported.
- **AllowAllPaths** This provides access to all files and directories on the computer.
- **AllowRemovableMedia** Allows copying of files and folders to removable media such as floppy disks and writeable compact disks.
- **NoCopyPrompt** Disables the prompt that appears when an existing file is overwritten.

The value of these variables can be either enable or disable. You will need to enable the full functionality of the **set** command from the Group Policy Snap-in of the Microsoft Management Console (MMC). Exercise 18-3 explains the necessary steps to enable full functionality of the **set** command.

Using Recovery Console to Start and Stop Services

When you have logged on to the system successfully using the Recovery Console, you may start, stop, or change the start type of any driver or system service. The **enable** and **disable** commands are used to perform these functions.

EXERCISE 18-3

Using Group Policy to Enable Set Command

1. Click Start | Run and type **mmc.** Press ENTER. This opens an empty Microsoft Management Console labeled as Console1.
2. From the Console menu, select Add/Remove Snap-in. The Add/Remove Snap-in window appears. Click Add.
3. Select Group Policy and click Add again, as shown in the following illustration.

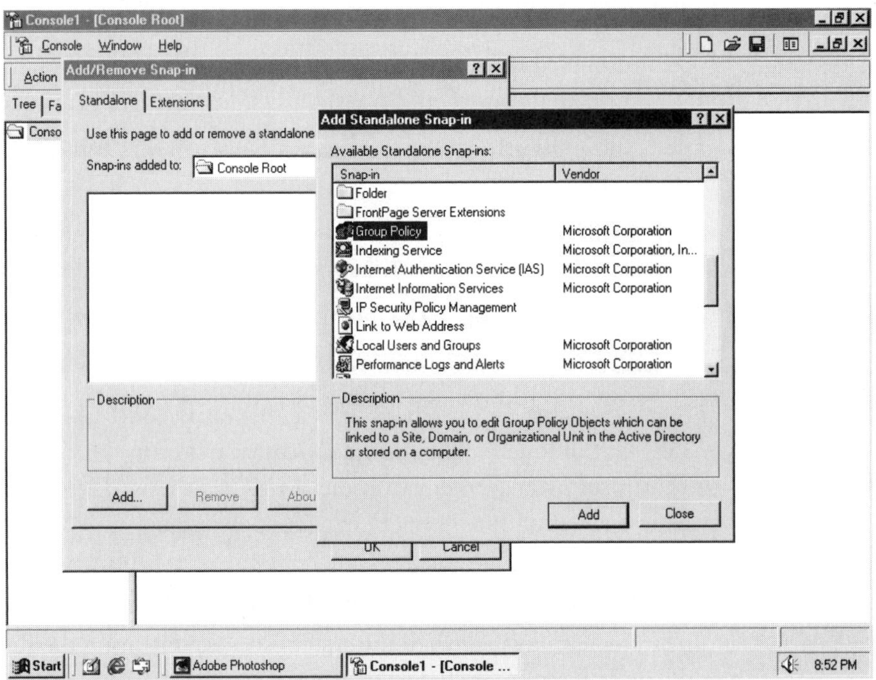

4. In the Select Group Policy Object, select Local Computer. Click Finish.
5. Click Close in the Add Standalone Snap-in window.

6. Click OK in the Add/Remove Snap-in Window.
7. Click the + sign before Local Computer Policy to expand it.
8. Click the + sign before each of the following to expand: Computer Configuration | Windows Settings | Security Settings | Local Policies.
9. Click Security Options. The Local Security Policy Settings appear on the right side of the console, as shown in the following illustration.

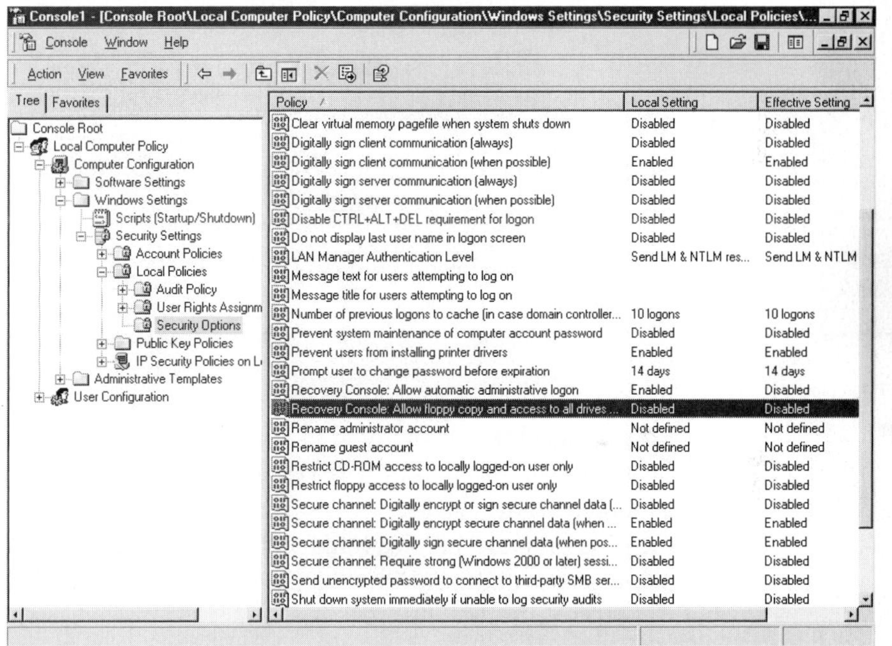

10. Double-click the policy Recovery Console: Allow floppy copy and allow access to all Files and all Folders.
11. This opens the Local Security Policy Setting window. Click the Enabled radio button. Click OK (see the next illustration).

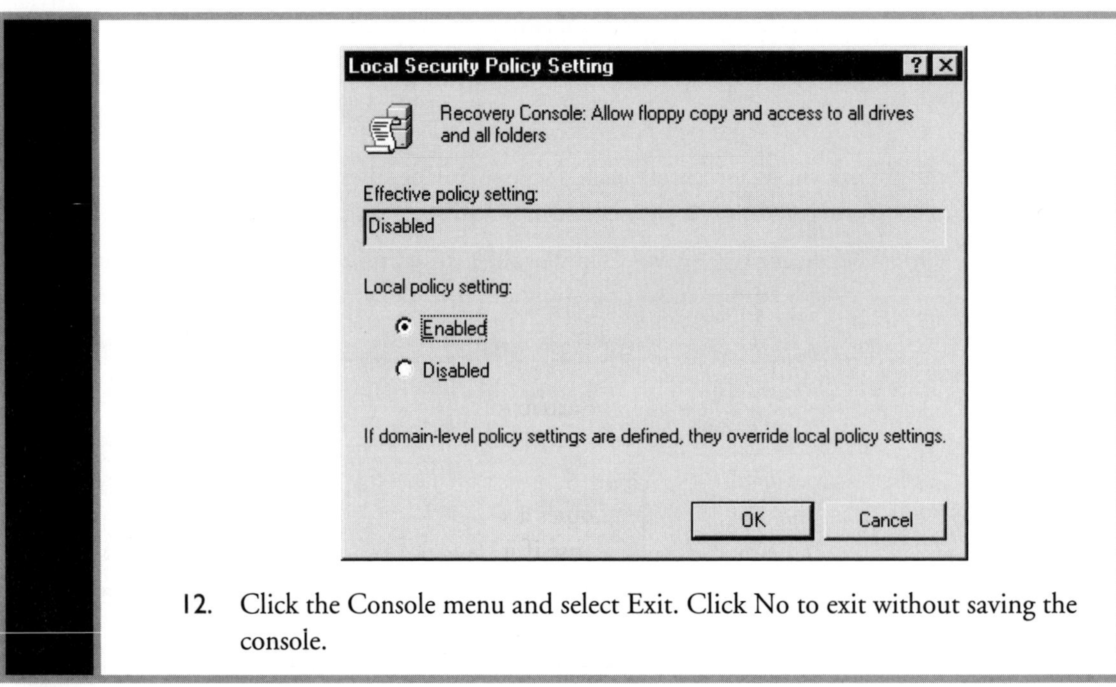

12. Click the Console menu and select Exit. Click No to exit without saving the console.

To Stop a Service If you need to disable a service on system startup, you can use the **disable** command from the Recovery Console prompt in the following syntax: **disable service_name.**

When you press ENTER, this command first displays the previously set startup type of the service or driver. After this the startup type is changed to disabled.

To Start a Service The **enable** command can be used to start a system service in the following syntax: **enable service_name [start_type].**

"start_type" specifies the startup type of the service. The valid values for this option are

- service_boot_start
- service_system_start
- service_auto_start
- service_demand_start

Another Recovery Console command that is helpful in starting and stopping services and drivers is the **listsvc** command. This command displays a list of available system services, drivers, and their startup type settings.

Using Recovery Console to Copy Files onto NTFS Drives

The Recovery Console can be used to replace corrupted files on FAT16, FAT32, and NTFS partitions of the installed disk drives. This is a useful tool for copying original files when system or driver files become corrupted or get deleted by mistake. The source of the original file may be a floppy disk, a CD-ROM, or any of the local disks or partitions. The following Recovery Console commands are helpful in file copy operations: **attrib –R |+R |-S |+S |-H |+H |-C |+C file_name.** This command is similar to the MS-DOS **attrib** command used to change the attributes of a single file.

Copy source [**destination**] copies a single file from the source to the destination. The destination is optional because if it is not specified, the file is copied to the current directory. When you use this command to copy any compressed files, these are uncompressed before copying.

del [**drive_name:**][**path**]**file_name** deletes a single file from the specified drive and path.

dir [**drive_name:**][**path**] gives a listing of all the files and subdirectories. This command displays even the system and hidden files.

Other useful commands that are similar to MS-DOS command are **cd/chdir, md/mkdir,** and **rd/rmdir,** which are used to change, make, and remove directories respectively.

After discussing various aspects of the Recovery Console usage, let's have a look at some real-life scenarios, on page 16.

Active Directory Data Considerations

Microsoft has tested Active Directory for over 40 million objects. Theoretically speaking, as the number of objects grows, the size of Active Directory grows and the performance of the domain controller should tend to slow down. Practically, this does not happen. Tests have shown that the performance remains consistent when the data size increases. The size of the Active Directory database does not affect the server performance.

SCENARIO & SOLUTION	
Can you use the Recovery Console if you have not installed it on your hard disk?	Yes. You can start the Recovery Console from either the Windows 2000 setup floppy disks or the setup CD-ROM.
The master boot record (MBR) of one of your servers has been infected with a virus. Is it possible to fix it using the Recovery Console?	No. The **fixmbr** command in the Recovery Console repairs only the boot code in the boot partition and cannot fix the MBR virus problems. Use an antivirus program to remove the MBR virus.
Can you copy some files to a floppy disk from the NTFS drive?	No and Yes. No, because by default the Recovery Console does not allow you to copy files to a floppy drive or removable media. Yes, because you can modify the Group Policy Settings to enable this option.
You are having system startup problems due to a faulty system service. Is there any way to stop this service so that it does not prevent the system from starting?	Yes. Use Recovery Console to change the system startup setting for the particular service. You must first know the exact service that is causing the problem.

When you build a server as a domain controller, make sure that you have enough disk space to hold the Active Directory database. The Active Directory database is stored in the NTDS.DIT file. This will ensure that as the number of objects in Active Directory grows with the passage of time, you don't have to rebuild the server again from scratch. This is particularly important when you have limited resources.

The availability of system data on a domain controller relies on availability of the Active Directory services. The following are some of the best practices:

- Keep at least twice the disk space estimated for the database. This takes care of future growth.
- Make a clear estimate of the database, allocating 3.6KB per user object or other security principle, 1.1KB per nonsecurity principle, and 75 bytes per Access Control entry per object.
- Allocate additional space for domain controllers that are also hosting Global Catalogs.

Active Directory File Structure

The Active Directory database is stored in a file named NTDS.DIT. In case you wish to perform the database sizing tests, you will need to find the size of the NTDS.DIT file. If you use Windows Explorer to check the size of NTDS.DIT file, you will notice that the size does not change even when multiple write operations are performed on the file. The reason for this is that on NTFS volumes, the size is determined when the file is opened and it is not refreshed until the file is closed.

The Active Directory database is opened when the domain controller computer starts up. It remains open while the computer is running. It is closed only when the computer is shut down. This means that using Windows Explorer or command prompt are not the correct ways to monitor the size of the NTDS.DIT database file.

The following two ways can be used to determine the size of the NTDS.DIT file:

- Restart the domain controller. This will close the file during shut down and reopen it during startup. This method is not always recommended. Use this when it is extremely necessary to monitor the database. The file size is shown in Figure 18-2.

FIGURE 18-2

Checking the size of the NTDS.DIT file

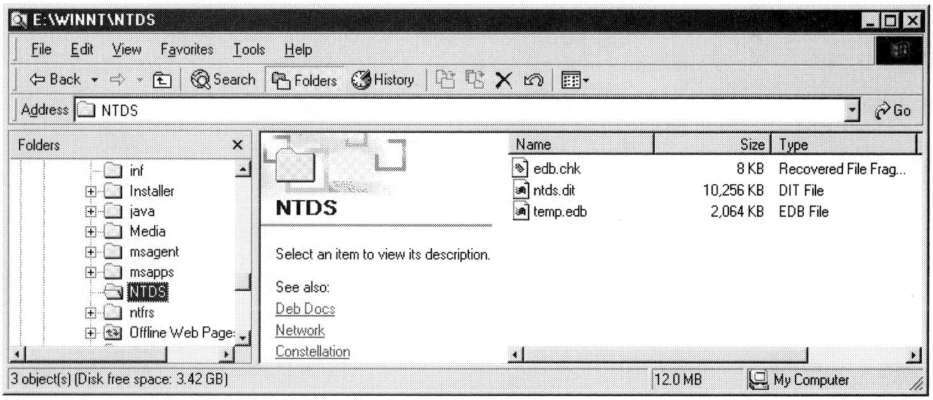

- Use Windows Explorer Properties on the partition that contains the NTDS.DIT file. This reports the correct size of used and free space on the partition. Make a note of the free space before and after the tests.

Placement of Log Files and System Files

Active Directory resides only on Windows 2000 Server domain controllers. The domain controllers in a network usually attract more network traffic than other servers. The larger the network, the busier is server. To achieve best performance from the server hosting Active Directory, it is recommended that the Active Directory data files are placed on a separate drive from the system root. If possible, also keep all the Active Directory log files separate from both the system and Active Directory data files. When you install Active Directory, you are given an option to select the location of the NTDS.DIT file and the log files (see Figure 18-3).

FIGURE 18-3

Selecting the location of Active Directory files

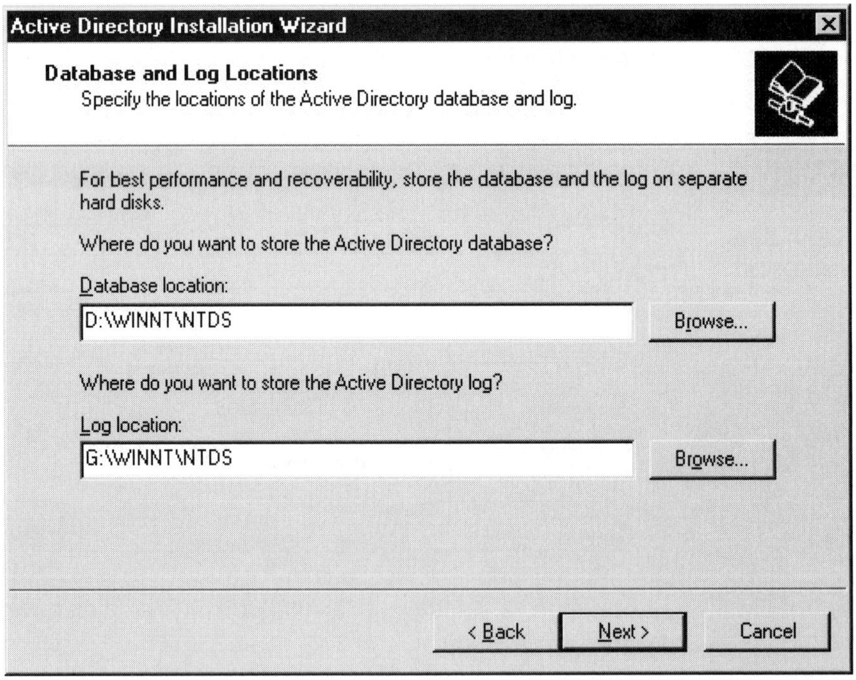

CERTIFICATION OBJECTIVE 18.02

Backing up and Recovering Systems and User Data

Data backup and restoration are important elements of the system recovery process in times of emergency. In spite of available tools for system recovery such as disk mirroring and implementing RAID 5, the data must to be backed up on regular basis for protection against disasters. The two types of data are systems data, which is necessary for the system to keep running, and the user data, which may contain the important files for the whole organization, covering nearly all kinds of data.

It is important to understand the importance of data backups. Backups are important not only in case of catastrophic system failure, but to also address less severe situations. Consider a user who deletes some important system files and causes the system to go down. Implementation of any type of RAID will not help in this case. You will definitely need a source from which you can recover the files. This is where data backup comes to the rescue of a system administrator.

Windows Backup

Windows Backup is a built-in Backup and Restore utility, which has many more features than the backup tool provided in Windows NT 4.0. It supports all five types of backup: Normal, Copy, Differential, Incremental, and Daily. Windows Backup allows you to perform the backup operation manually or you may schedule it to run at a later time in unattended mode. Included with the operating system, it is a tool that is flexible and easy to use.

Backup Strategies

Whether you use any third-party backup program or choose the built-in Windows Backup, there are some issues that you must consider. Before you can use any of the backup programs, you will need to do some planning. Some of the important planning issues for Windows Backup are discussed next.

What to Back Up? The first important issue is to determine what data needs to be backed up. This depends on the importance of data and the time it would take to re-create it if it were lost. For example, some organizations may have databases containing several years' worth of information.

Who Will Back Up? The next question to ask is who will be responsible for running the backup program and what rights and permissions will be required. This depends on the volume and location of data existing in an organization. If the data is spread on many workstations, the users can back up their own files. If the data is server-based, then it is better to have a dedicated operator to perform the backup jobs. In Windows 2000, the Administrators, Backup Operators, and Server Operators can backup and restore files on servers or workstations, irrespective of any NTFS permissions set on files and folders. In addition, any user who has Read, Read and Execute, Modify, or Full Control Permissions can perform backups. Every user is the creator/owner of his/her files by default and can perform backup of all such files.

How Often to Back Up? The answer to this question depends on how often the data changes. You have the choice of performing backups on a daily, weekly, or monthly basis. You may also have some other schedule.

When to Back Up? This also concerns the way you run the backup. There are two ways: attended mode and unattended mode. This depends on the availability of personnel, servers, and network bandwidth. It is always better to run backup jobs at night when there are few files open and the network traffic is also very low. Most backup programs allow you to schedule the backup jobs to be run at a later time.

What Media to Use? The data can be stored on tapes or other file systems. Tapes are inexpensive and are typically high-capacity but have a limited life. Data backed up to other file systems are stored in a single file containing all of the files and folders selected for backup. This file has a .bkf extension and can be stored on tape, Zip drives, writeable compact disks, optical disks, or another network server.

Once you have made a comprehensive plan, you are ready to use any backup program.

Using Windows Backup

The Windows Backup program contains four tools: the Backup Wizard, the Restore Wizard, the Job Scheduler, and the Emergency Repair Disk creation tool. The Windows Backup can be started in either of these ways:

- From the Start menu, select Programs | Accessories | System Tools | Backup.
- From the Start menu, click Run and type **ntbackup.exe.** Press ENTER.

Figure 18-4 shows the Windows 2000 Backup and Recovery Tools welcome screen.

The Windows Backup tool can be used to back up the data on any media: files, tapes, recordable compact disks, or Zip drives. The backed-up data can be restored at a later date using the Restore Wizard. These are some of the permissions and rights that are required for performing backup or restore operations on a Windows 2000 Server:

- Administrators, Backup Operators, and Server Operators have the Backup Files and Directories and Restore Files and Directories rights assigned to

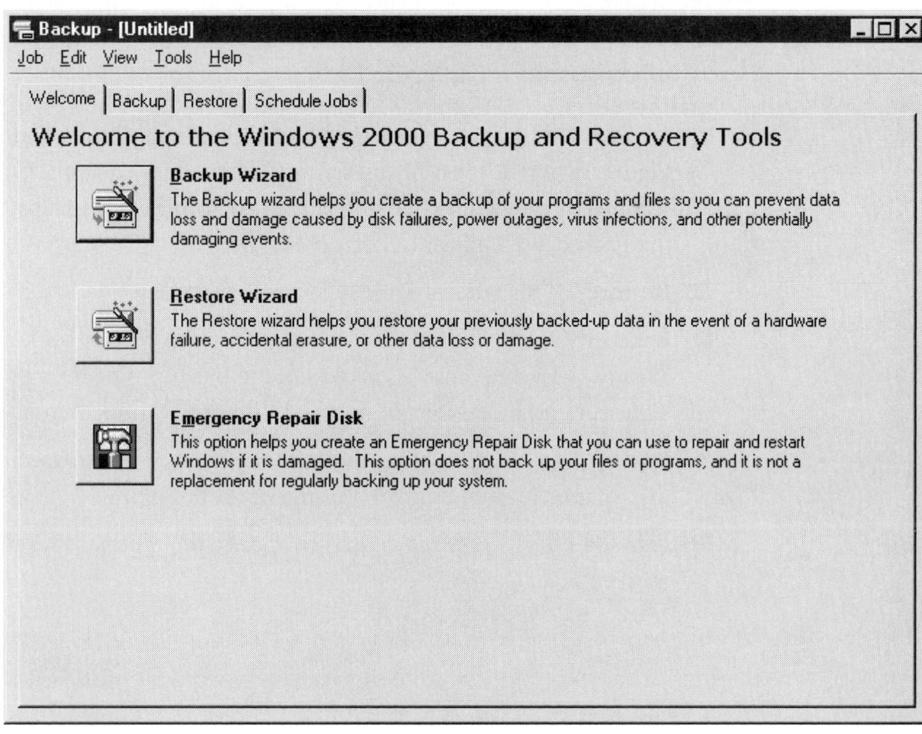

FIGURE 18-4 Windows Backup and Recovery Tools welcome screen

them by default. The persons in these groups can back up and restore all files and folders, regardless of the NTFS permissions.

- Any user can back up and restore files and directories for which he/she is the owner. Users can also back up files and directories for which they have Read, Read and Execute, Modify, or Full Control permissions.
- Write, Modify, or Full Control permissions are required for any user performing the restore operation.

exam Watch

From the exam point of view, it is important that you remember which of the user groups have the rights to perform backup and restore on Windows 2000 servers.

Backup Options

The Windows Backup program has some default settings for data backup and restore. You can modify any of these settings to suit your requirements. To view these settings click Options from the Tools menu. The General tab of the Options screen appears, as shown in Figure 18-5.

- **General** This is the opening tab of the options menu. You may notice from Figure 18-9 that most of the settings are made by default. One important setting is Verify data after the backup completes. This helps in verifying that the backed-up data is not corrupted.
- **Restore** This tab has some data restore settings.
- **Backup Type** This tab is used to specify the type of backup required. Windows Backup allows you to select a backup type for a particular job. The types include Normal, Copy, Differential, Incremental, and Daily.
- **Backup Log** The settings under this tab allow you to specify what information should be stored in the backup log files.
- **Exclude Files** This tab is used to specify the types of files that you do not want to be backed up.

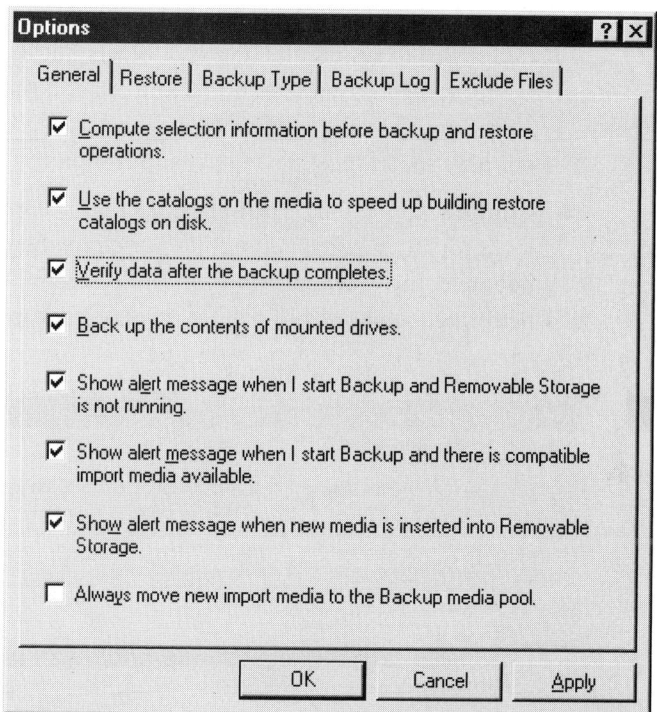

FIGURE 18-5 Windows Backup options screen

Backup Types

The requirement of backup jobs varies from one organization to the other. Some organizations prefer to perform a normal backup every day, while others may prefer only incremental backups on a daily basis and a full backup on the weekend. In addition, the availability of a particular server and network bandwidth also affect the choice of a backup type. Windows Backup supports five different types of backup: Normal, Copy, Differential, Incremental, and Daily. Figure 18-6 shows the backup screen where you can select the backup type.

- **Normal backup** This is the most common type and is also known as a full backup. The Normal backup operation backs up all files and folders that are selected irrespective of the archive attributes of the files. This provides the easiest way to restore the files and folders but is expensive in terms of the time it takes to complete the backup job and the storage space it consumes. The restore process from a Normal backup is less complex because you do not have to use multiple tape sets to completely restore data.

- **Copy backup** This type of backup simply copies the selected files. It neither looks for any markers set on files nor clears them. The Copy backup does not affect the other Incremental or Differential backup jobs and can be performed along with the other types of backup jobs.

FIGURE 18-6

Selecting backup type

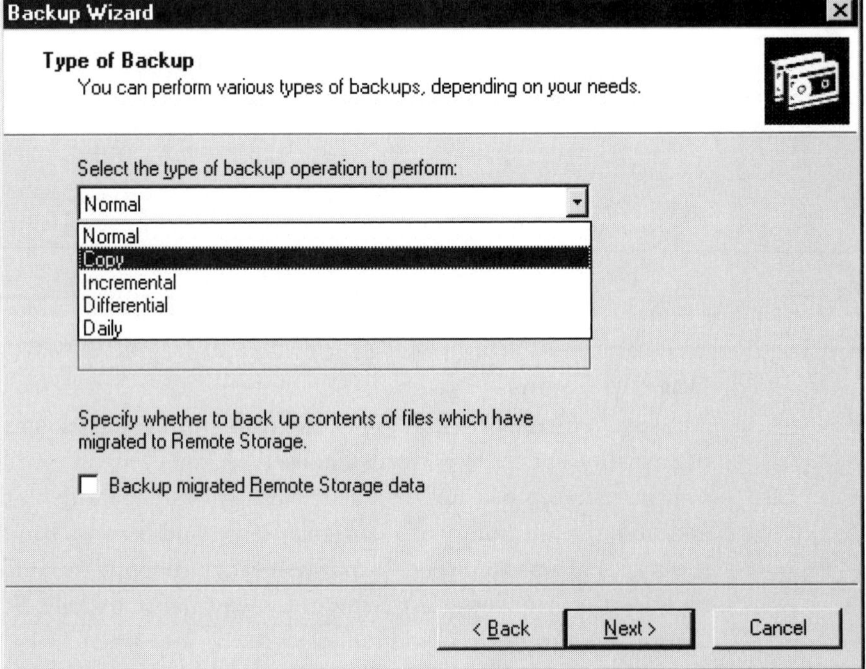

- **Differential backup** This backup process is relatively faster. The Differential backup checks and performs a backup of only those files that are marked. It does not clear the markers after the backup, which means that any consecutive differential backups will backup the marked files again. When you need to restore from a Differential backup you will need the most current full backup and the Differential backup performed after that.
- **Incremental backup** This backup process is similar to the Differential backup, but it clears the markers from the selected files after the process. Because it clears the markers, an incremental backup will not back up any files that have not changed since the last incremental backup. This type of backup is fast during the backup but is very slow while restoring the files. You will need the last full backup and all of the subsequent incremental backups to fully restore data. The positive side of this backup type is that it is fast and consumes very little media space.
- **Daily backup** This type of backup does not use any markers to back up selected files and folders. The files that have changed during the day are backed up every day at a specified time. This backup will not affect other backup schedules.

You may have noticed the term "marker" in the previous discussion. This is also known as Archive Bit, which is used to tell the backup program whether or not to back up a particular file.

Backup Logs

Windows Backup generates a backup log file for every backup job. These files are the best place to review the backup process in case some problem is encountered by the program. The backup log is a text file that records all the events during the backup process. The log files can be configured from the Backup Logs tab of the backup Options screen.

When you are restoring some files from a backup that was done using an incremental backup, you will need the last full backup and all the subsequent incremental backups. When you restore from a differential backup set, you need to restore the last full backup and only the last differential backup. Because of this, differential backups are typically quicker to restore.

Backup Files and Folders

Considering the importance of data backups, it is always better to plan things in advance. The backup operation requires you to consider all aspects of the job, which include speed, cost, availability of servers, network bandwidth, and data type. The local backups are not dependent on network bandwidth, but other factors such as the importance of data must be taken care of during planning.

First of all, you will need to select the files and folders you are planning to back up. The Windows Backup program cannot back up any files that are open or locked at the time of backup. If this is the case, you can send a notification to all the users to close any open files that are to be backed up. If the backup is to be performed during nonworking hours, this may not be required.

Using the Backup Wizard After you have decided on a particular backup type, the next step is to select the files and folders that you wish to back up. You can use the Windows Backup Wizard to proceed. (The Backup Wizard was shown in Figure 18-4.) When you start the Backup Wizard, the What to Back Up? screen gives these three options:

- Back up everything on my computer.
- Back up selected files, drives, or network data.
- Back up only the System State data.

You can make a choice and click Next to proceed. In Exercise 18-4, we have selected Back up selected files, drives, or network data. This is the option you may be frequently using because it is the most flexible one. You can also include the System State data on the local computer. Exercise 18-4 explains the steps you must take to perform a backup using this option.

EXERCISE 18-4

Backing Up Selected Files and Folders

1. Log on to the server as an administrator. Click Start | Run.
2. Type **ntbackup** in the dialog box. Click OK. This opens the welcome screen of the Windows 2000 Backup and Recovery Tools. Click the Backup Wizard tab.
3. The Backup selection window appears. You will notice another dialog box where you can select Backup selected files, drives, and network data, as shown in the following illustration. Click Next.

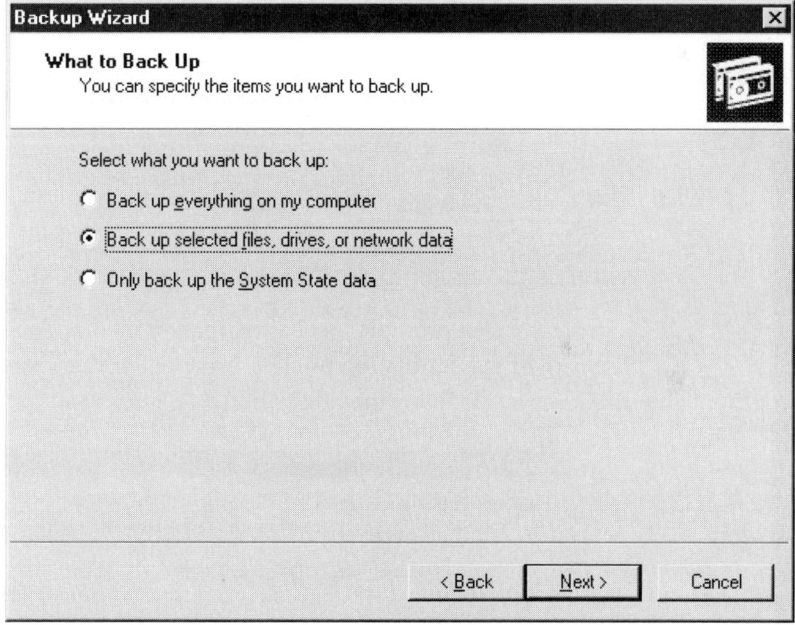

4. The Backup (Untitled) window appears next. Click My Computer to expand it. Select the files you wish to back up. Make sure you select the System State check box if you wish to include this (see the next illustration).

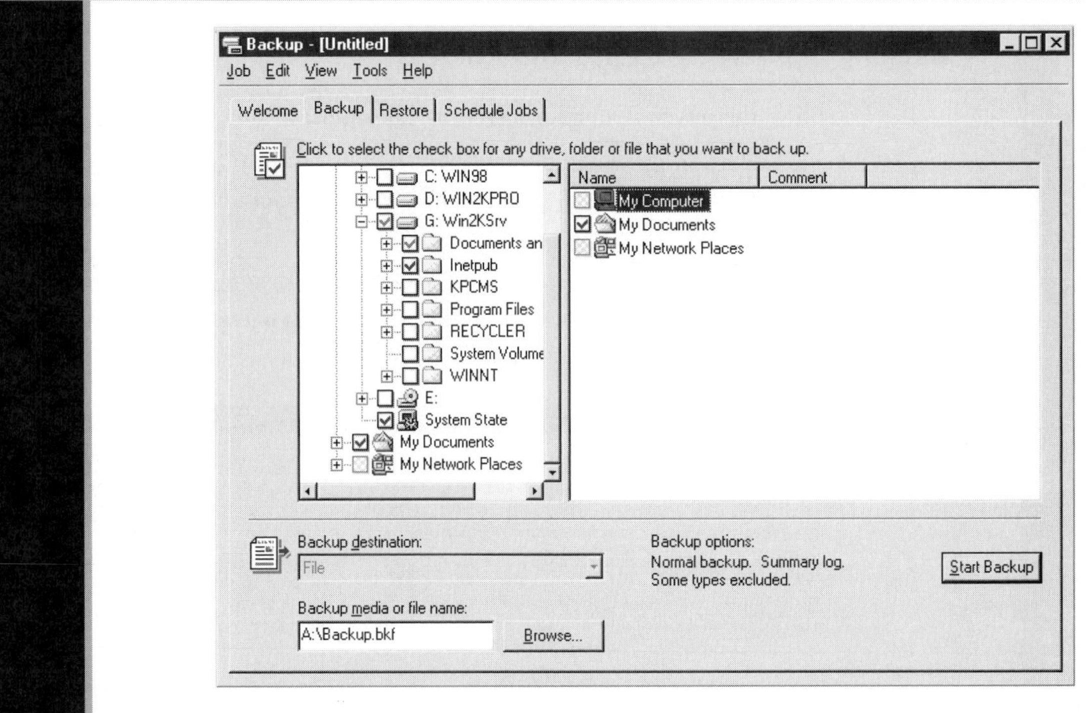

5. The next screen prompts for the destination media. You may either type in the path of the destination or click Browse. For this exercise, type **c:\testbk,** as shown in the following illustration.

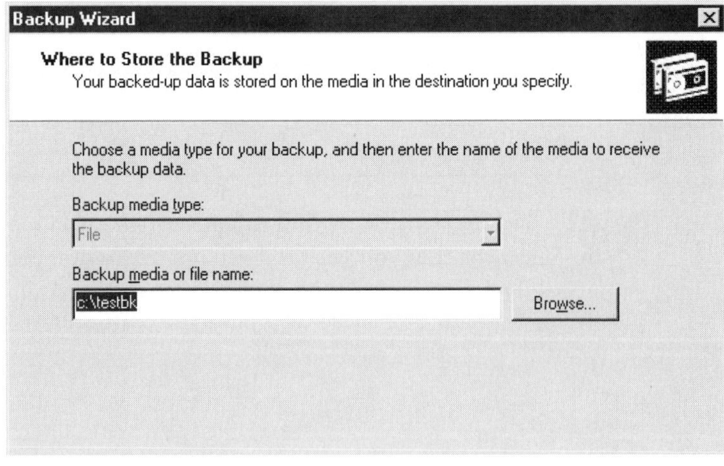

6. The next screen is the Completing the Backup Wizard, as shown in the following illustration.

7. Review the settings and click Finish to start the backup.

Advanced Backup Options You may have noticed an Advanced tab in the Completing the Backup Wizard screen. The advanced settings allow you to make these selections:

- **Type of Backup** Normal, Copy, Differential, Incremental, or Daily.
- **How to Backup** You can choose to verify the data after backup.
- **Media Options** You may choose to append data to the media or replace the old data already stored.
- **Backup Label** To specify a label.

After selecting any advanced settings, you are prompted to choose whether to back up now or later. If you select Backup Now, the backup starts. If you select

Backup Later, additional dialog boxes appear so that you can schedule the backup to start at a specified data and time.

Back Up and Restore System State Data

The System State data contains data that is essential in keeping Windows 2000 Server running. This data can be backed up on local computers only. It is not possible to backup System State data on remote computers. On a Windows 2000 Server, the System State data essentially contains

- System Registry database
- COM+ Class registration database
- System startup files

Depending on other services running on the server, the System State data may contain the following additional items:

- Certificate Services database if the server is a Certificate Server
- Active Directory services and the SYSVOL directory if the server is a domain controller
- Resource registry check points (Cluster database) if the server is running Cluster Services

When you select to back up or restore the System State data, all the components are automatically selected. It is not possible to perform a backup of the System State data by selecting individual components. You need to be an administrator or a member of the Backup Operators Group in order to back up or restore the System State data.

Schedule a Backup

Backup schedules are required when you want to run the backup in an unattended mode. The Windows Backup utility includes a backup scheduling program. This can be selected from the Schedule tab of the Backup program. It is best to perform backup on a busy server when there is comparatively a lesser load on the server and network traffic is also low.

To run the backup at a later time, you will first need to configure the Backup Wizard, as described in Exercise 18-4. Choose the option Later in the When to

Back Up dialog box. This activates the task scheduler. You will be prompted to select a user account and password that will be used to perform the backup job. After the username and password are conformed, you are prompted to select the date and time when you wish the backup to start (see Figure 18-7).

Type the name of the job. The Start date shows the current date and time as default start time. Click Set Schedule to specify a different date and time. When you finish entering the information, the job is put in the schedule and run later at the specified time.

FIGURE 18-7

Scheduling the backup time

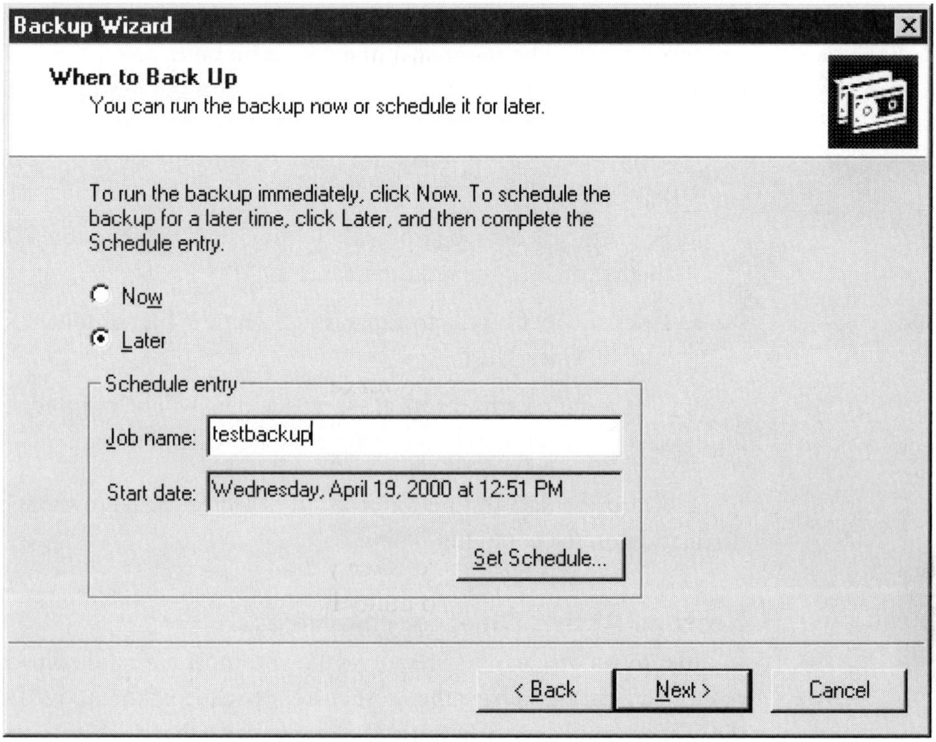

on the Job

When you are using a centralized backup server, it is always recommended that you run large backup jobs during the time when the network is having relatively little traffic—for example, during the nights when you have plenty of network bandwidth available. This will also ensure that the backup servers do not face extra load.

Restore Files and Folders

The backed-up data is useless unless you know how to restore it when the need arises. You may need to restore data in case of disaster or when some data becomes corrupted. When there is no need to run the data restore process, you must run trial restores to see whether everything works fine. This will make sure that the backup media is working properly and that the data will be available when it is required.

The Windows 2000 Backup program includes the Restore Wizard. This can be used to restore data from the backup archives. The first important thing is to decide what data needs to be restored. If the data is on tapes or Zip drives, you must keep these items handy. These steps explain how to run the Restore Wizard:

1. From the Windows Backup program select the Restore Wizard. The Restore window opens.
2. Select the media type from where the data is to be restored. Make sure the media contains the required data.
3. Click the media type to expand it. Select the files or folders you wish to restore. Click Next.
4. The default settings appear where the data will be restored. Check and verify that the location selected is appropriate. Click Next.

This starts the data restoration from the selected media to the specified destination on the computer.

Restore Active Directory Services

In order to restore Active Directory data, you must have domain administrative rights. You must also have the most current backup of the Active Directory data or the System State data. You must also decide beforehand whether the restore should be authoritative or nonauthoritative. The default method of Active Directory data restore is nonauthoritative. Authoritative Active Directory data restore ensures that the data is replicated to other domain controllers in the network. This requires you to run the Ntdsutil utility.

EXERCISE 18-5

Restoring Active Directory

1. Restart the computer and press the F8 key when the operating systems menu is displayed.
2. Select Restore Directory Services Mode.
3. Log on to the system as domain administrator.
4. From the Start menu click Run. Type in **ntbackup.exe** and press ENTER. The Windows Backup program starts.
5. Click Restore. This opens the Restore window.
6. Click the check box named System State. You may also select any other data that you wish to restore (see the following illustration).

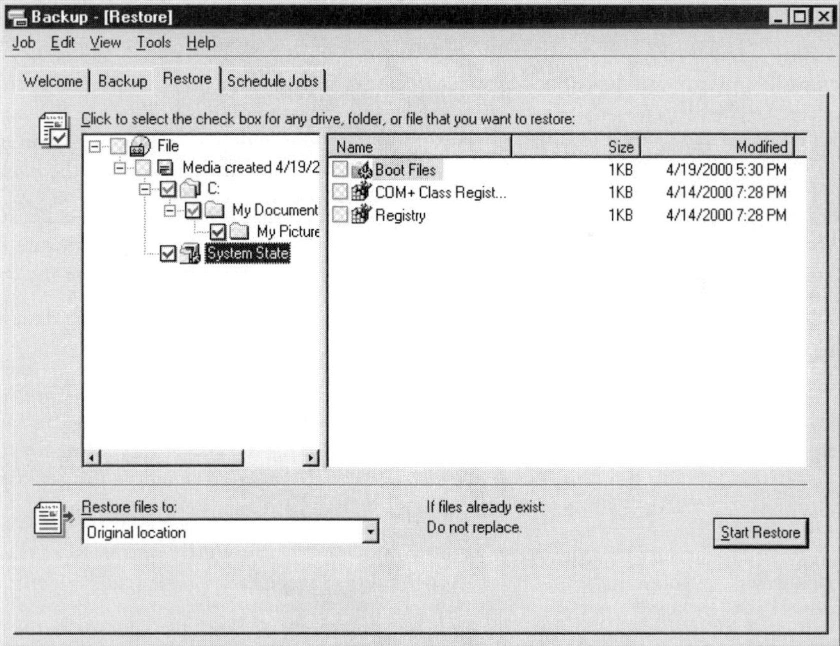

7. You will notice that the default mode of restore is Nonauthoritative. Select Authoritative Restore. Run the Ntdsutil utility.
8. This finishes the authoritative restore of Active Directory. Restart the computer and use the normal startup mode.

The Windows Backup Wizard can be used to restore the Active Directory data when the system is run in Restore Directory Services Mode. Since the Active Directory data is contained in the System State data, you will need to restore the System State data in order to restore it. Exercise 18-5 lists the steps needed to restore the Active Directory data.

exam Watch

The System State data contains the Active Directory database on domain controllers and can be backed up and restored on local computers only. You must have domain administrator rights to perform the restore.

The following table will help you find answers to some of the common scenarios that you may encounter on the job.

SCENARIO & SOLUTION	
Is it possible to run Windows Backup when nobody is present in the office?	Yes. You can schedule the backup job to run at any time you wish. When you configure the backup job you will get a dialog box that asks you to specify when you wish to start the backup.
You have only one domain controller. What kind of Active Directory restore do you need to perform, authoritative or nonauthoritative?	Nonauthoritative. This is because the Active Directory data is not replicated to any other domain controller. Be sure to use the most current backup.
You don't have much data to back up. What kind of backup should you perform?	If you do not have much data to back up, choose the Normal backup type.
When you run the Normal backup on a database server, it becomes very slow and the backup also takes very long to complete. What should you do?	This probably means that the server is experiencing excessive load during the backup and that the database size is very large. Switch to incremental backups or schedule the backup job for a time when the database is not in use.
How do you make sure that the data you are going to backup will be good?	Use the Verify option from the backup options screen.

FROM THE CLASSROOM

Planning Backup Policies

So, you finally have a backup tool that includes a graphical scheduling feature that ensures the backup will kick off at night while you are asleep. Excellent, but there are many factors that you should take care of while planning the backup policies, especially when you are responsible for a large company with gigabytes of data. Here are some important points:

1. Check the volume of data that needs backup. Use a dedicated backup server with the fastest tape devices available.
2. Decide on the backup type. In the case of large databases, do an incremental backup from Monday to Friday and a Normal (full) backup on Fridays.
3. Schedule the backup job when network traffic is low. A window between 10.00 P.M. and 4.00 A.M. is usually the best slot.
4. Prioritize the data based on importance. Start those jobs first that have incurred the most changes during the day.
5. Store the tapes off site, preferably out of town. Never keep the tapes in the same room where the servers are installed.
6. When you notice that the backup jobs are consuming a significant portion of your time, delegate your responsibilities. Two are always better than one.
7. Perform test restores to check that the backed-up data is in good condition and can be used in case of emergency situations. This will also ensure that the media works fine.
8. Document everything and keep a history of the changes.

One final word: You must perform backups at regular intervals, even if you will never need to do any restores. Don't worry about the media; it is reusable.

—Pawan K. Bhardwaj, MCSE, MCP+I, CCNA

CERTIFICATION SUMMARY

System availability and data safety are very important functions of a systems administrator. Windows 2000 comes with many tools that are helpful to keep the system downtime to a minimum. The Advanced Startup Options help in resolving system startup problems. The safe modes, Last Known Good Configuration, and the Enable VGA Mode are some of the advanced options available. The Directory Services Restore Mode is available on domain controllers to restore the Active Directory services. The Boot Logging Mode writes the startup events to a log file.

The Recovery Console is a new command-line tool in Windows 2000 that gives limited access to FAT and NTFS partitions on a hard disk. You can create, delete, or format partitions and fix the master boot record if it is corrupt. Being secure, it requires logon to the local system and does not allow you to copy files to any removable media by default. Any faulty services or drivers that are preventing the system from starting in the normal way can be stopped or restarted. The Recovery Console can be started from the setup media or from the hard disk if it is previously installed.

Windows 2000 comes with a built-in interactive backup and recovery utility. Five types of supported backup are: Normal, Copy, Differential, Incremental, and Daily. The graphical task scheduler allows you to run backup jobs at a specified time. Any user with Read, Read and Execute, Modify, or Full Control permissions can run a backup job. You must perform backups of system and user data on a regular basis and run test restores to check that the stored data is intact. Backups can be performed to file or tape. Most of the common backup media such as tape devices, Zip drives, and writeable compact disks are supported.

The System State data in a computer includes the Registry, system startup files, and COM+ class registration database. In addition, this data contains the Active Directory and the SYSVOL folder if the computer is a domain controller. The System State data cannot be backed up on remote computers through Windows Backup. The Active Directory restore can be done in Authoritative or Nonauthoritative Modes, and the person performing this restore must have domain administrator rights. The *ntdsutil* is run to update Active Directory data on other domain controllers when an Authoritative restore is done.

TWO-MINUTE DRILL

Managing and Optimizing Availability of System State Data and User Data

- The Advanced Startup Options are systems repair tools included with Windows 2000 for fixing system startup problems. You can access the Advanced Startup Options menu by pressing F8 when the initial operating systems menu is displayed.
- The three safe modes are Safe Mode, Safe Mode with Networking, and Safe Mode with Command Prompt. All safe modes use only the basic system files and a basic VGA driver for the display. The Safe Mode with Command Prompt starts the system in MS-DOS mode.
- The Last Known Good Configuration starts the system using the saved configuration values in the registry when the system was last shut down normally. The Directory Restore Mode is used on domain controllers to restore the Active Directory.
- The Recovery Console in Windows 2000 is a command line utility that can be started from either the setup floppy disks or the setup CD-ROM. It can also be started from the operating systems options menu if it is installed on the hard disk.
- You need to be a local administrator in order to start the Recovery Console. You can start and stop services, fix the MBR, work with partitions, and get limited access to the FAT and NTFS volumes on the hard drive. By default, you cannot copy files from hard disk to any removable media such as floppy disks.
- The **set** command is used in the Recovery Console to configure the environment variables for the console. You can also modify these settings using the Group Policy.
- The **enable** and **disable** commands are used to start and stop system services and drivers respectively. The **listsrv** command displays a list of available system services.
- The Active Directory data is stored in the NTDS.DIT file on the domain controller. It is not possible to check the size of this file on the fly. For best performance, it is recommended that the system files, the NTDS.DIT database and the log files be placed on separate hard drives.

Backing up and Recovering Systems and User Data

- The Windows Backup and recovery tools can be started by running NTBACKUP.EXE or from the Start menu by selecting Programs | Accessories | System Tools | Backup.
- You must back up your system and user data on a regular basis. Even if you will never need to restore, test restores should be done to check the integrity of data. You should have a concrete plan in place to perform backup jobs.
- Windows 2000 supports five types of backup: Normal, Copy, Differential, Incremental, and Daily. Normal and Copy do the full backup. The main difference between Differential and Incremental is that the latter clears the archive bits (markers).
- The General tab of the backup options allows you to verify the data after the backup job is over. The Exclude tab can be used to specify which files should not be included in the backup.
- Any user who has Read, Read and Execute, Modify, or Full Control permissions can run a backup job. If you want to delegate the backup responsibilities, you must make the person to whom you give this job a member of the Backup Operators Group.
- The Backup and Restore Wizards are easy to use tools for performing these jobs. You can run the backup job immediately or schedule it to run later at a specified time. Backups can be done to either file or tape.
- The System State data contains the system Registry, COM+ class registration database, and the startup files. On domain controllers the Active Directory data and the SYSVOL folder are also contained in the System State data.
- Active Directory can be restored in either Authoritative or Nonauthoritative Mode. You must be a domain administrator to restore Active Directory. When you run the Authoritative restore, you need to run the NTDSUTIL utility to update other domain controllers.

Part V

Configuring Windows 2000

CHAPTERS

19

Hardware and Device Driver Installation and Configuration

CERTIFICATION OBJECTIVES

19.01 Configuring Hardware Devices

19.02 Configuring Driver Signing Options

19.03 Updating Device Drivers

19.04 Troubleshooting Problems with Hardware

✓ Two-Minute Drill

Windows 2000 brings with it some exciting new features for configuring and troubleshooting hardware devices and drivers. The troubleshooting wizards will help walk users through most common hardware problems. Installation and configuration is made much easier with Plug and Play technology, and the risk of incompatible drivers is certainly lowered with digital signing.

In addition to numerous new features, Windows 2000 provides some familiar tools such as Device Manager and Hardware Profiles. Device Manager offers an organized interface for managing your hardware devices and drivers. Hardware Profiles helps manage different hardware configurations on a single machine.

The following sections of this chapter will take you on a journey through configuring, managing, and troubleshooting hardware devices and drivers.

CERTIFICATION OBJECTIVE 19.01

Configuring Hardware Devices

Windows 2000 has made it relatively easy to configure hardware devices. Plug and Play technology was available in Windows 95/98, but not in Windows NT 4.0. Windows 2000 marks the first operating system built on NT technology to support Plug and Play devices. When there is Plug and Play technology in place, there is generally little involved in configuring a hardware device. However, you must also be aware that there are some Non-Plug and Play devices that the operating system will not configure, leaving it up to you to install and configure the device properly on your own.

This section will discuss how to minimize problems before you begin, how to configure and troubleshoot Plug and Play and Non-Plug and Play devices, and how to properly utilize the Hardware Profiles.

Minimizing Hardware Problems Before They Begin

Although Windows 2000 Setup has built-in checks for hardware resources on your computer, you may want to take extra precautions to ensure a successful installation. Microsoft publishes a document called the Hardware Compatibility List (HCL). The HCL lists all devices that Microsoft deems compatible with their operating systems. You will find the most updated version of the HCL on the Web at www.microsoft.com/hcl/default.asp. The version that was released with Windows 2000 can also be found on the Windows 2000 CD-ROM in the Support folder in a file called HCL.TXT.

To determine whether or not you have the most current drivers for your hardware devices, check with the manufacturer of the device. For the most recent information on your device, check the manufacturer's Web site or give them a call.

In addition to verifying the drivers and devices for your computer configuration, it may be useful to take an inventory of them. Although Windows 2000 automatically takes an inventory of your hardware devices upon setup, taking your own inventory will also be helpful. Useful information would include IRQ (interrupt request) designations, COM (communications) port connections, I/O (input/output) addresses, DMA (Direct Memory Access), and drivers. Knowing what resources each device is using will help prevent resource conflicts.

Plug and Play and Non-Plug and Play Installations

Once you have physically installed your hardware device, it needs to be configured to work properly with your system. Configuring a hardware device requires two basic steps: 1) loading drivers and 2) configuring device properties and settings. If the installed hardware device is Plug and Play and the computer you are installing it on is an Advanced Configuration and Power Interface (ACPI) machine running in ACPI mode (most new computers on the market do), Windows 2000 will take care of the two basic configuration steps for you. On startup, Windows will perform an inventory of your system and detect any new hardware. Once it finds a new device, it will load the necessary drivers, configure the device, allocate resources, and update the system. Windows 2000 manages all the resources to ensure that each hardware device runs properly with other resources. This feature makes managing hardware very simple!

on the job

Windows 2000 Server may not immediately recognize some older Plug and Play devices. In such cases, you will be required to reboot before configuration is complete.

If the hardware device is Non-Plug and Play, you will need to load the drivers and configure the properties and settings for the device manually. You must be logged on as an Administrator or a member of the Administrators Group to manually configure a machine. Setup will differ for each Non-Plug and Play device based on the device and its manufacturer. Follow the instructions in the manual that came with the device. A word of caution: Microsoft does not generally recommend manually setting resource assignments. This is because the manually set resource assignments become fixed, giving Windows 2000 Server less flexibility when new Plug and Play devices are installed.

Troubleshooting Plug and Play Installations

Although Windows 2000 Server promotes the ability to install and configure Plug and Play devices with the greatest of ease, it is still possible that problems will arise once in a while. The most common problem in installing a Plug and Play device is a resource conflict. The conflict often stems from a previous Non-Plug and Play device installation. Because Non-Plug and Play devices are manually configured, there is a good chance that one of the resources it is using is actually preferred by the Plug and Play device you are trying to install, so you will likely be left to adjust the resource assignments manually. Again, Microsoft does not recommend manually changing resource settings. Try to avoid this if possible by checking your devices on Microsoft's HCL, taking an inventory of your hardware and resources, and diligently planning for new additions.

Adjusting Resource Assignments for a Non-Plug and Play Device

Only those with expert knowledge and experience in hardware should adjust resource assignments. Improper adjustments could cause your system to fail and become inaccessible, resulting in potential loss of data or extended periods of downtime. Windows 2000 Server will allow only Administrators or members of the Administrators Group to adjust resource settings.

Resource settings for a particular device are found in the Properties dialog of that device under the Resources tab. Figure 19-1 displays the Resources tab for COM Port 1.

Be sure to clear the box labeled "Use automatic settings." This will make the Change Settings button and Settings based on drop-down box available (otherwise they would be grayed out). Select the appropriate Hardware Profile to base your resource changes on. (Hardware Profiles are covered in the next section.) Select the resource type you are interested in changing, such as: DMA, IRQ, I/O Port, or Memory address. Click Change Setting and type in the new value.

FIGURE 19-1

Resources tab for COM Port 1

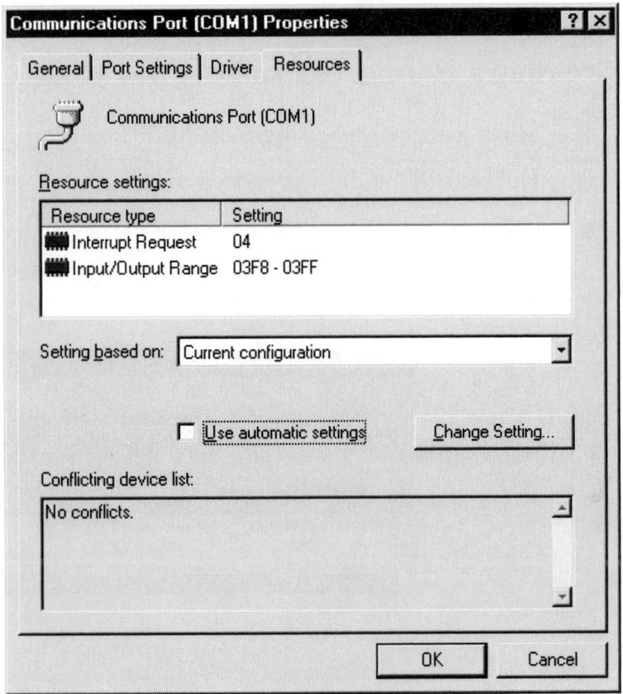

on the job ***It may seem as though this is a repeat of information, but it is very important to remember that only experts in hardware should attempt to adjust these settings!***

Using Hardware Profiles

A Hardware profile is a set of instructions that tells your computer how to boot the system properly, based on the setup of your hardware. Hardware profiles are most commonly used with laptops. This is because laptops are frequently used in at least two different settings; stand-alone and in a docking station on a network. For example, when the laptop is being used at a docking station, it requires the network adapter. However, when the laptop is used away from the network, it does not. The Hardware Profile dialog manages these configuration changes. If a profile is created for each situation, the user will automatically be presented these choices on Windows startup.

Exercise 19-1 illustrates how to create a hardware profile.

EXERCISE 19-1

Creating a Hardware Profile

1. Select Start menu/Settings/Control Panel.
2. Double-click on the System icon to bring up the System Properties dialog box.
3. Click the Hardware Profiles button located in the Hardware Profiles section of the System Properties dialog to bring up the Hardware Profiles dialog box, as shown in the following illustration.

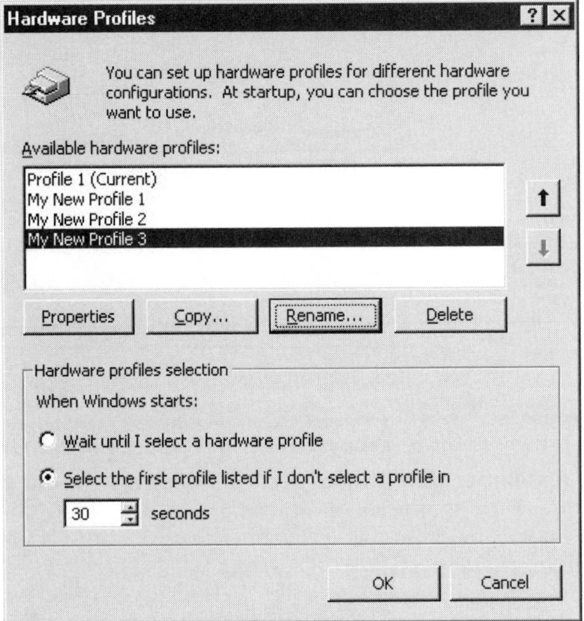

4. Highlight the current profile and click Copy.
5. Enter a name for your new profile. This is the name that will appear in the list of profile choices when the user boots up. Click OK.

6. Highlight your new profile from the list of Available Hardware Profiles and click Properties to bring up the Properties page for your profile (as shown in the following illustration).

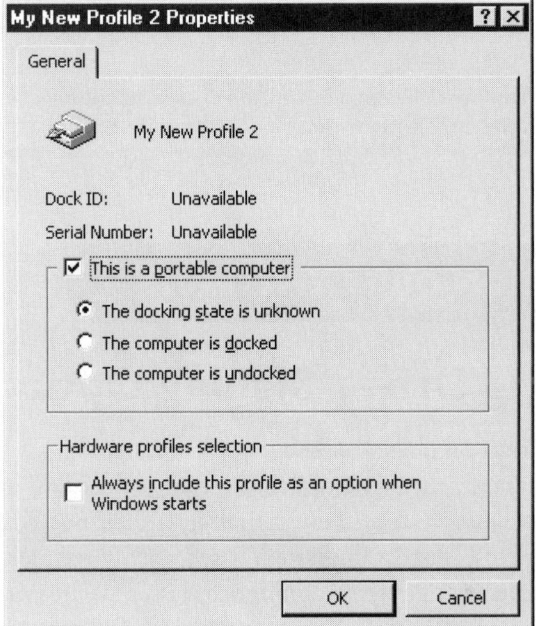

7. If you are creating a profile for a laptop computer, select the status "This is a portable computer." Mark the check box in the Hardware Profiles selection section if you always want this profile as an option. This would mean, for example, that if the profile is for a docked laptop and the laptop were booted away from the docking station, this profile would still show up as an option. Click OK to go back to the main Hardware Profiles dialog page.
8. Configure the Hardware Profiles Selection section to tell Windows 2000 Server what to do on startup.
9. Click OK to save your new profile and exit.

Now that you have learned about planning, configuring, and troubleshooting hardware devices, drivers, and profiles in Windows 2000 Server, here is a quick reference for possible scenario questions and the appropriate answers.

SCENARIO & SOLUTION	
You are not sure whether your new device is compatible with Windows 2000.	Check Microsoft's HCL to see whether your device is listed.
You need to manually adjust a resource for a new device.	Go to the Resources tab of the Properties dialog for the device.
You will be using Windows 2000 on a laptop at a docking station connected to a network and off site without a docking station.	Create hardware profiles for each of the two settings.

CERTIFICATION OBJECTIVE 19.02

Configuring Driver Signing Options

Driver Signing (also known as "code signing") is Microsoft's way of ensuring that only the highest-quality drivers are used. Windows 98 was the first Microsoft operating system to use digital signatures, but Windows 2000 marks the first Microsoft operating system based on NT technology to do this. By promoting driver signing for certain device classes, Microsoft intends to increase driver quality and decrease vendor costs in the area of support. Driver developers can submit their drivers to the Windows Hardware Quality Lab (WHQL) for testing with Windows 2000 products. Windows 2000 includes support for many different types of devices and their corresponding drivers, including keyboards, modems, mice, and network adapters. Windows 2000 Server also includes support for new devices, such as Smart Card Readers and USB devices.

Drivers that pass the WHQL testing are given a Microsoft digital signature certifying that the driver will not destabilize the user's system. The signature does not appear directly in the binary driver (.BIN) file. Instead, the signature appears in the catalog driver file (.CAT) that is created for each driver package. The information driver file (.INF) directs the operating system to the catalog file to read the digital signature.

FROM THE CLASSROOM

Exam Tips

For the exam it is important to remember that Microsoft will want to test you on new features of Windows 2000 Server. Make sure you understand the concepts surrounding Driver Signing Options, Windows 2000 Hardware Troubleshooter, and how Plug and Play affects the Windows 2000 Platform. In addition, Microsoft is bound to include some questions around the "tried and true" features that Windows 2000 has inherited from older NT technology. Be sure to familiarize yourself with the Device Manager MMC Snap-in and how Hardware Profiles work.

—Jocelyn Fowke

Setting Driver-Signing Options

Windows 2000 gives you three options for managing your certified drivers. These three options are:

- Ignore
- Warn
- Block

Ignore will install the driver files whether they are digitally signed or not. Warn will provide a message if you are about to install a driver that is not signed. The Warn message gives you the option of proceeding with the install or canceling at that point. Block will prohibit the installation of any driver that is not digitally signed. The default for Windows 2000 systems is Warn mode. Warn is provided as default so that users are not prevented from applying urgent driver updates before vendors are able to get them tested by WHQL.

Exercise 19-2 illustrates how to configure Driver Signing options as described above. It is important to remember that you must be logged on as the Administrator or a member of the Administrators Group in order to decrease the security of Driver Signing Options from Block to Warn or Warn to Ignore. All members of the group, however, have access to increase the security of Driver Signing Options from Ignore to Warn or Warn to Block.

EXERCISE 19-2

Configuring Driver Signing Options

1. Select Start menu/Settings/Control Panel.
2. Double-click on the System icon to bring up the System Properties dialog box.
3. Select the Hardware tab on the System Properties dialog.
4. Click the Driver Signing button located in the Device Manager section of the System Properties dialog to bring up the Driver Signing Options dialog box, as shown in the following illustration.

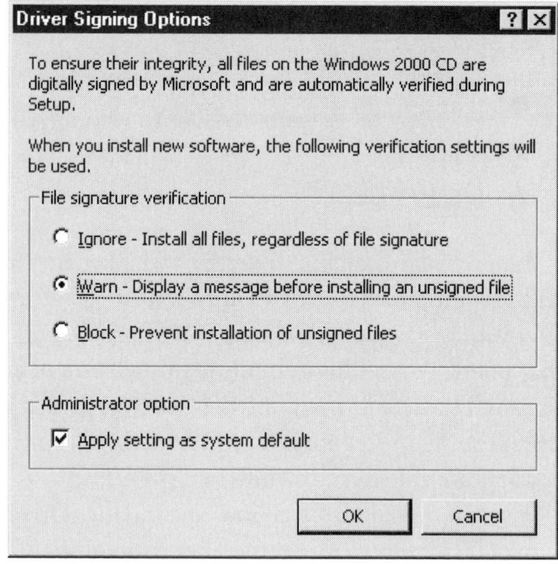

5. Pick one of the three options in the File signature verification section of the dialog.
6. If you want to apply the setting as system default then click in the Administrator option check box.
7. Click OK in the Driver Signing Options dialog box to apply your selection.
8. Click OK in the System Properties dialog to exit.

CERTIFICATION OBJECTIVE 19.03

Updating Device Drivers

There may come a time when you need to update a driver. For example, the company that developed your hardware may release an updated driver for a particular device, or an older machine on your network may be due for updated drivers. Sometimes devices need to be removed or disabled if they are no longer in use. This section will describe how you can manage, update, remove, or disable devices and their drivers.

Getting Familiar with Device Manager

The first step in managing your device is to locate the Device Manager. The Device Manager is an MMC snap-in included in the Computer Management console that is provided by Windows 2000 Server. The Computer Management console is pre-configured and saved in the Administrative Tools applet of the Control Panel. Although snap-ins is a new feature of Windows 2000 Server, you will already be familiar with the look and feel of Device Manager if you have used Windows NT 4.0. In the Device Manager, you can view and manage all the information about devices and their drivers such as connections, status of a device, and driver files.

Exercise 19-3 shows you how to open Device Manager.

EXERCISE 19-3

How to Open Device Manager

1. Select Start menu/Settings/Control Panel.
2. Double-click the System icon to bring up the System Properties dialog box.
3. Select the Hardware tab.
4. Click Device Manager to open the Device Manager and display what you see in the following illustration.

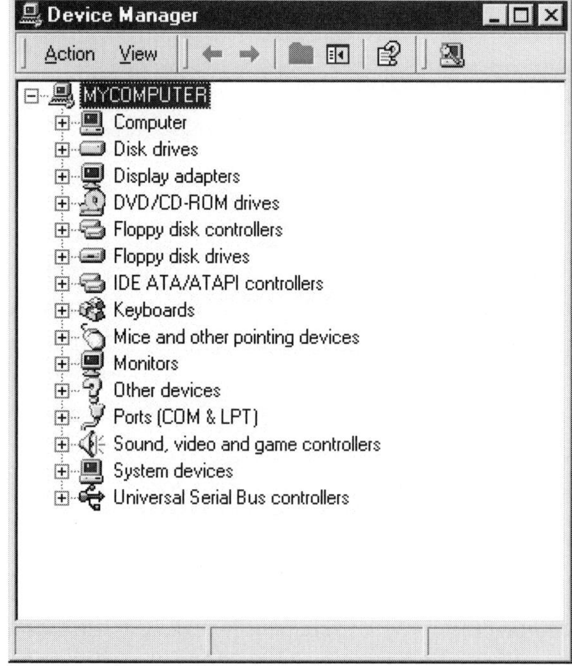

It is important to remember that you can also access Device Manager by right-clicking My Computer and selecting Properties. Once the Properties page pops up, select the Hardware tab and then the Device Manager button.

The Device Manager displays all the devices installed on your computer in one of four views. These views can be selected from the view menu, including:

- Devices by type
- Devices by connection
- Resources by type
- Resources by connection

Windows 2000 defaults to the "Devices by type" view.

You can also choose to show Hidden Devices from the View menu. Selecting Hidden Devices will add your Non-Plug and Play devices to the view. These are usually devices that have had drivers manually installed to the system. The Customize option from the View menu allows you to manage your menu and toolbar options.

Getting Details about a Device Driver

Details about a device driver that has been installed are found in the Properties dialog for each device. Exercise 19-4 shows you how to open the properties for a specific device.

EXERCISE 19-4

Opening Properties for a Device

1. From Device Manager, locate the device you want more information on. You may need to click a plus sign next to the device type in order to view the complete list of devices available.
2. Select the Device and click the Properties button on the toolbar. Another way to open the properties dialog is to right-click the device and select Properties from the pop-up menu. Alternatively, you can double-click the device in the list.

You are now in the Properties dialog for the device you selected. Note the various tabs including a combination of General, Drivers, Resources, and so on. The following illustration displays the Properties dialog for a hard disk drive.

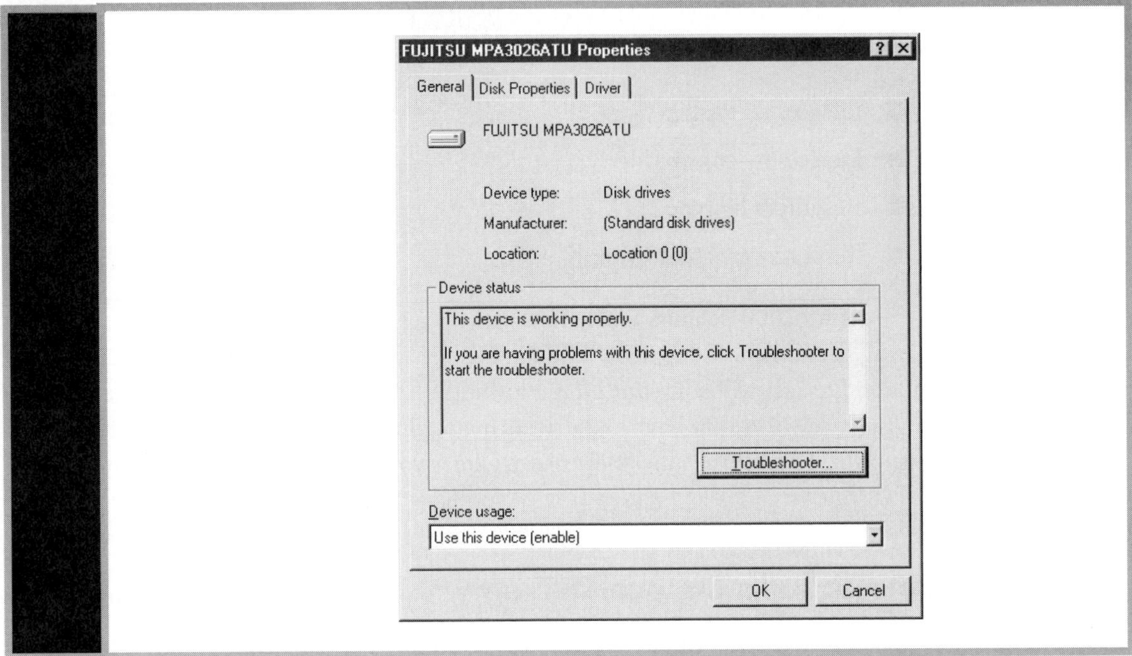

You will find various combinations of tabs in the Properties dialog, but driver-specific information is found in the Driver tab, where you will find general information about the driver such as Provider and Digital Signer. Three buttons are located at the bottom of the Driver tab:

- Driver Details
- Uninstall
- Update Driver

These buttons will be discussed more fully in the following two sections.

It is important to remember that Device Manager manages the local computer only and has read-only access to remote computers.

FIGURE 19-2

Driver tab for a CD-ROM drive

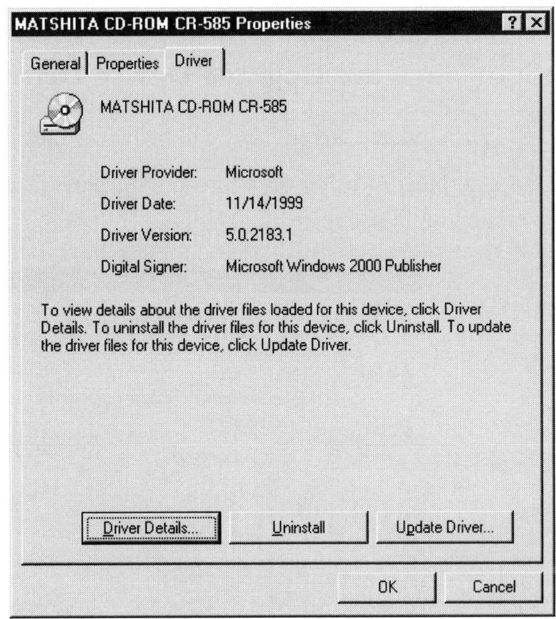

Device Driver Updating

A driver can be updated easily by clicking the Update Driver button, which is found on the Driver tab of the Property dialog for any given device. Figure 19-2 shows the Driver tab for a CD-ROM drive.

Clicking the Update Driver button will execute the Upgrade Device Driver Wizard. This wizard will walk you through the required steps for upgrading your driver. Be sure to have your new driver software ready, because the wizard will cue you when it is needed in your disk drive.

Exercise 19-5 walks you through the Upgrade Device Driver Wizard.

EXERCISE 19-5

Walk through the Upgrade Device Driver Wizard

1. Click Update Driver. This will bring up the Welcome screen.
2. Click Next to bring up a screen with detection options, as shown in the following illustration.

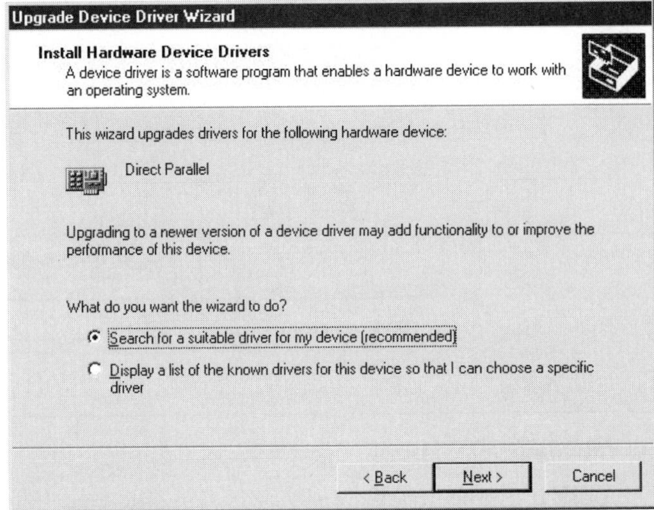

3. One option will allow Windows to detect the updated drivers and the other will allow you to manually pick the driver from a list. Microsoft recommends that you let the operating system do the detection. Select your choice and click Next.
4. The Locate Driver Files screen allows you to add additional search locations (floppy disk drive, CD-ROM drive) if you chose the first option in step 2. Select the options you wish to search and click Next.
5. Windows 2000 will now start searching for an updated driver. Once it has found the new driver it will display the path where it found the driver.
6. Click Next and then Finish to complete the Update.

Removing a Device

Most Plug and Play devices can be removed by simply disconnecting or removing the device from your system. Be sure to check your device manufacturer manual for special instructions such as turning off the computer before removing the device or rebooting after it is removed.

You can remove Non-Plug and Play devices by using one of these two tools:

1. **Device Manager** Clicking the Uninstall button on the Driver tab of the device you wish to remove (found on the device Properties page) will invoke a warning to confirm device removal. Click OK to immediately uninstall the device. Some devices may require a reboot after this step. Click Cancel to quit without uninstalling.
2. **Add/Remove Hardware Wizard** The Add/Remove Hardware Wizard is found by clicking Start menu/Settings/Control Panel and then double-clicking the Add/Remove Hardware applet. The wizard will walk you through the steps required to uninstall a device.

Exercise 19-6 takes you through the Add/Remove Hardware Wizard.

EXERCISE 19-6

Walk through the Add/Remove Hardware Wizard

1. Select Start menu/Settings/Control Panel and double-click on Add/Remove Hardware. This will bring up the Welcome screen. Click Next.
2. The Wizard will now ask you to choose a hardware task. Select Uninstall/Unplug a Device and click Next.
3. The Wizard will ask you to choose a removal task. Select Uninstall a Device and click Next.
4. Now the Wizard will display a list box of devices (see the following illustration). Select the device you want to uninstall and click Next. The check box on this screen provides the option to Show Hidden Device (Non-Plug and Play devices).

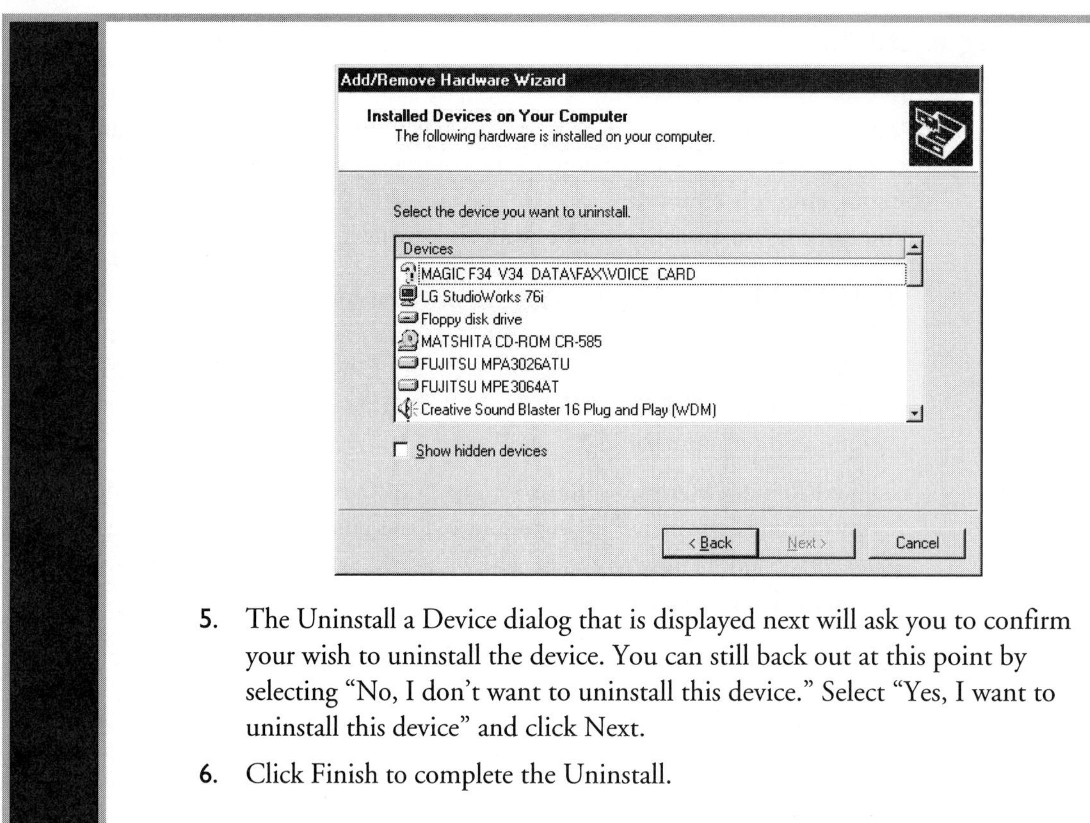

5. The Uninstall a Device dialog that is displayed next will ask you to confirm your wish to uninstall the device. You can still back out at this point by selecting "No, I don't want to uninstall this device." Select "Yes, I want to uninstall this device" and click Next.
6. Click Finish to complete the Uninstall.

Disabling a Device

Windows 2000 Server gives you the option to temporarily remove a device by disabling it. Disabling allows you to keep the device attached to the computer but prevents its drivers from loading on startup. Disabling a device is more or less asking the computer to temporarily ignore the device. In turn, when the device is required again in the future, enabling the device makes the driver available once again at startup. There are three ways to enable/disable your device:

1. Select your device from Device Manager and click on Disable/Enable from the Action menu.

2. Select your device from Device Manager, right-click, and select Disable/Enable from the pop-up menu.
3. From the Properties dialog for your device, select Do Not Use this device (disable)/Use this device(enable) from the Device usage drop-down box (see Exercise 19-4).

CERTIFICATION OBJECTIVE 19.04

Troubleshooting Problems with Hardware

No matter how well you plan your device configuration, problems are bound to arise, especially if you are working with a complex set of servers. If you have some experience in the IT industry, I am certain you have been exposed to troubleshooting at one time or another. It is important to remember that troubleshooting is not an exact science. It includes continuous forms of trial and error and, most important, patience! This section will take you through some common steps toward solving hardware problems.

SCENARIO & SOLUTION

You don't want to install any drivers that aren't digitally signed by Microsoft.	Set your Driver Signing Options to Block.
You're in Device Manager but can't see your Non-Plug and Play devices.	Select Hidden Devices from the View menu.
You want to remove your modem but plan on reinstalling it after a couple of weeks.	Disable the device instead of uninstalling it.

Identifying Problem Devices

If you suspect you have a problem with one of your devices, your first step should be to investigate and identify the problem device. Which device is not working properly? There are two tools to help you identify a device as a problem: Device Manager and System Information. Both of these tools are found in the System Tools section of the Computer Management console, seen in Figure 19-3.

As previously noted in this chapter, the Computer Management console is pre-configured and saved by Windows 2000 Server in Administrative Tools found in the Control Panel. As its name suggests, the Computer Management console is designed to help the user manage the computer by providing an easily accessible view of the system and all its pieces, including not only hardware but storage devices, services, and applications as well.

The fundamental difference between Device Manager and System Information tools is their access level to information. Device Manager includes more detailed information about devices, including resources and drivers. It also provides access to edit or change these items. The System Information tool provides a more general overview of the hardware components and allows you only to view general information about the hardware on your system, not to edit or change it.

FIGURE 19-3

Computer Management console

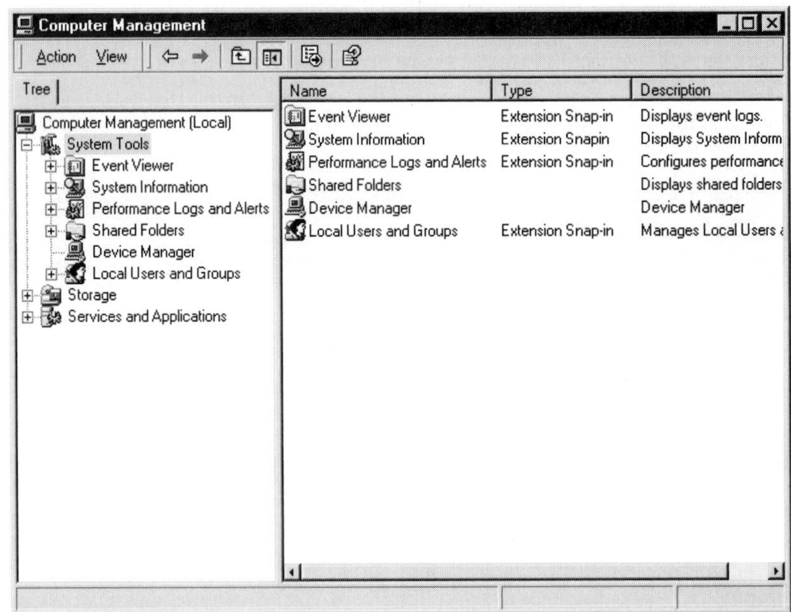

When a device has failed or it isn't working properly it will be marked with an exclamation mark in a yellow circle in Device Manager. Figure 19-4 shows us that a Lexmark printer isn't working properly. Whenever you see this symbol in Device Manager, you should take note, because it indicates that something isn't working properly.

To identify a problem device using System Information, open the Components folder and select the folder called Problem Devices. There you will find a list of all the current problem devices. Figure 19-5 shows a Lexmark printer as a problem device with error code 28.

exam Watch

The Computer Management Console, where System Tools is found, can also be accessed by selecting Start menu/Programs/Administrative Tools/Computer Management.

Checking the Status of a Device

When you have identified a device as a problem device, checking the status will provide you with the information you need about why the device isn't working and

FIGURE 19-4

Failed printer in Device Manager

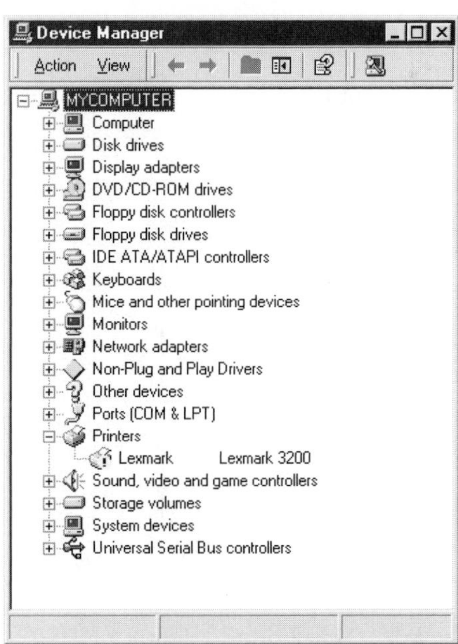

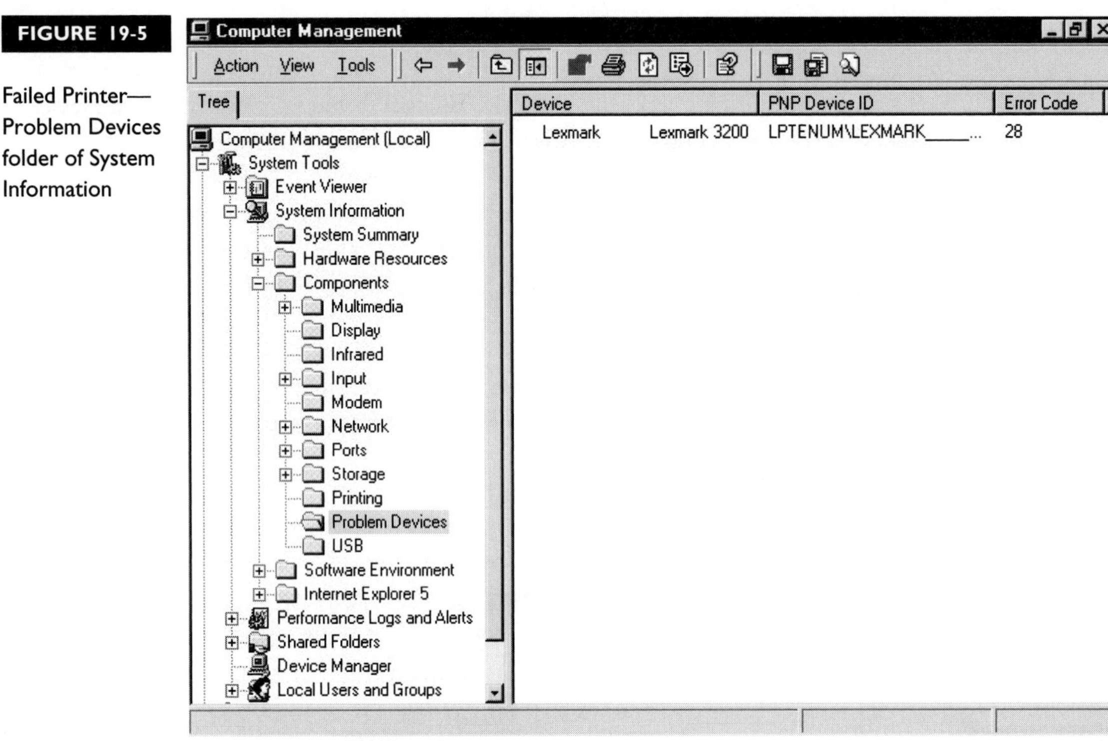

FIGURE 19-5 Failed Printer—Problem Devices folder of System Information

how to go about troubleshooting the problem. Exercise 19-7 shows you how to check the status of a printing device.

EXERCISE 19-7

Checking the Status of a Device

1. From Device Manager, locate the device you want more information on. You may need to click a plus sign next to the device type in order to view the complete list of devices available.
2. Select the Device and click the Properties button on the toolbar. You are now in the Properties dialog for the device you selected. By default, Windows 2000 brings you to the General tab of the Properties dialog (see the following illustration).

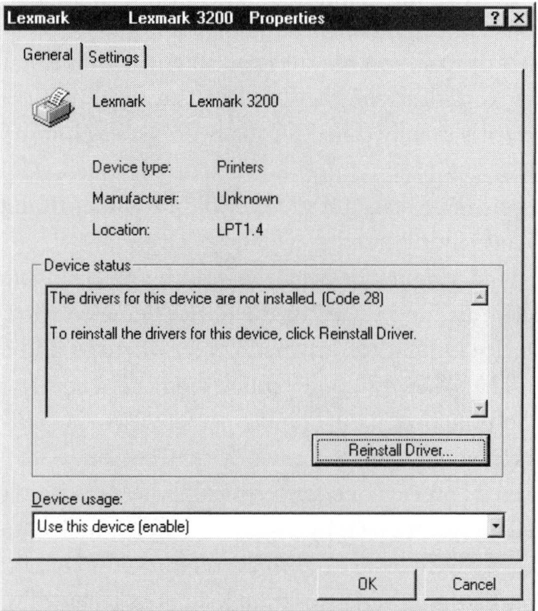

3. You will find the Device status section about halfway down the Properties dialog. The text provided in this section will indicate whether or not the device is working properly and may include information such as an Error code to help start the troubleshooting.

Troubleshooting a Device That Isn't Working Properly

When you have identified and checked the status of a problem device, you should have enough information to start troubleshooting the problem. There are many different possible error codes you might find in the Device status section but the solution to these codes can be summarized in four basic methods of troubleshooting:

1. Reinstall the device driver
2. Restart the computer
3. Update the device driver
4. Use the Windows 2000 Troubleshooter

If the solution requires you to reinstall or restart the system, it will generally state that very clearly in the Device status section of the General tab. Reinstalling a device driver is usually called for if the driver was improperly installed initially or if the driver has been removed. Restarting is usually required when the device installation required a restart but the user didn't bother to restart. Restart is also required if Windows is removing a faulty device.

Updating the device driver can fix problems such as incorrect configuration, the device failing to start, or the device being corrupt. See the section labeled Updating Device Drivers for instructions on where to find the Update Driver button.

The Windows 2000 Troubleshooter is a new feature included in NT technology. The Windows 2000 Troubleshooter wizard is a self-guided tool that uses a question-and-answer format that directs you to solutions for your hardware devices. Even if you are not clear on exactly where the problem is, the troubleshooter will help you narrow it down by asking some very general questions up front and then getting progressively more detailed as you move through the wizard.

There are a variety of troubleshooters included with Windows 2000 Server. The Hardware Troubleshooter covers devices such as cameras, CD-ROM drives, game controllers, hard disks, keyboards, mice, network adapters, and scanners. Other devices, such as display or video adapters, sound cards, and modems, have their own separate Troubleshooters.

To access the Windows 2000 Hardware Troubleshooter Wizard, go to the Properties dialog of the device you want to troubleshoot and click the Troubleshooter button on the General tab. You can also start the Troubleshooter by double-clicking the

Add/Remove Hardware Applet in Control Panel and selecting Add/Troubleshoot a device when asked to select a Hardware Task. Figure 19-6 displays the Hardware Troubleshooter.

When the installation or configuration of a device prevents your system from starting or continuing to run properly, there are a couple of options: Safe Mode and Last Known Good Configuration. Safe Mode allows you to start up the machine with minimal necessary services that would allow you to go in and fix the changes you made with the latest installation or configuration changes. Last Known Good Configuration restores your machine to the way it was last successfully booted. If you are lucky, that was just before you installed the device that is giving you trouble.

The Microsoft Web site is a wealth of knowledge in terms of troubleshooting problems. Go to www.microsoft.com and select Knowledge Base from the Support menu. This will bring you to a helpful search engine for information on Windows 2000 and other Microsoft products.

FIGURE 19-6

The Hardware Troubleshooter

CERTIFICATION SUMMARY

This chapter has walked you through the various features that support hardware devices and drivers in Windows 2000 Server. Configuration and troubleshooting hardware devices and drivers is made easy with old familiar tools like Device Manager and Hardware Profiles but also through features that are new to Windows 2000 Server such as Plug and Play, Digital Signing, and Hardware Troubleshooting wizards.

The addition of Plug and Play support on the Windows 2000 Server platform has made it much easier for hardware installation and configuration. However, Windows 2000 still provides the ability to manually adjust hardware settings in order to support Non-Plug and Play devices that still exist on the market. Whether you are installing Plug and Play or Non-Plug and Play devices and drivers, it still makes a lot of sense to plan ahead using the Microsoft HCL and to perform a personal inventory.

The new addition of Digital Signing functionality to Windows 2000 Server promotes increased quality of drivers while decreasing device conflicts. With the default setting of Warn, users are not prevented from applying hot fixes that haven't yet completed WHQL testing.

Device Manager has worked very well for previous Microsoft operating systems, so it continues to be featured in Windows 2000 Server. Management of hardware devices and drivers is centralized here for those with Administrators Group access rights. Although System Information gives a nice clear overview of hardware configuration for a given system, Device Manager is still the main focus for identifying problem devices. The addition of Hardware Troubleshooters keeps troubleshooting time to a minimum.

✓ TWO-MINUTE DRILL

Configuring Hardware Devices

- ❑ To ensure the successful installation and configuration of hardware devices and drivers, it is a good idea to take an inventory of your hardware devices and drivers and to check that your devices are listed on the HCL.
- ❑ Windows 2000 Server supports Plug and Play hardware. The server takes care of configuring hardware settings for those devices and their drivers.
- ❑ In case device conflicts arise, resource assignments can be adjusted manually using Device Manager; however, this is not recommended by Microsoft.
- ❑ Hardware Profiles are most often used for laptops that are used on and off the network and therefore require at least two different hardware configurations.

Configuring Driver Signing Options

- ❑ A Digital Signature is the "stamp" that Microsoft gives to device drivers that have passed the WHQL testing.
- ❑ Driver Signing Options can be set to Ignore, Warn, or Block, with Warn being the default setting.
- ❑ While any user can increase the security of Driver Signing Option from Ignore to Warn or Warn to Block, only Administrators or members of the Administrators Group can decrease the Driver Signing Option from Block to Warn or Warn to Ignore.

Updating Device Drivers

- ❑ The tool used to manage/update devices and drivers is Device Manager.
- ❑ The Drivers tab of the Properties dialog provides information about drivers and ways to change them.
- ❑ Windows 2000 Server provides a wizard for upgrading device drivers.
- ❑ Windows 2000 Server provides a wizard for adding and removing devices/drivers.

- Disabling a device allows you to temporarily remove a device from system startup, which makes it very easy to add again down the road.

Troubleshooting Problems with Hardware

- The System Information Extension snap-in provides a good overview of hardware, including Problem Devices.
- Checking the status of a device in Device Manager will indicate whether a device is working properly or not and usually provides error codes to aid in finding a solution.
- The Hardware Troubleshooter is a tool for solving hardware-related problems.

MCSE

MICROSOFT CERTIFIED SYSTEMS ENGINEER

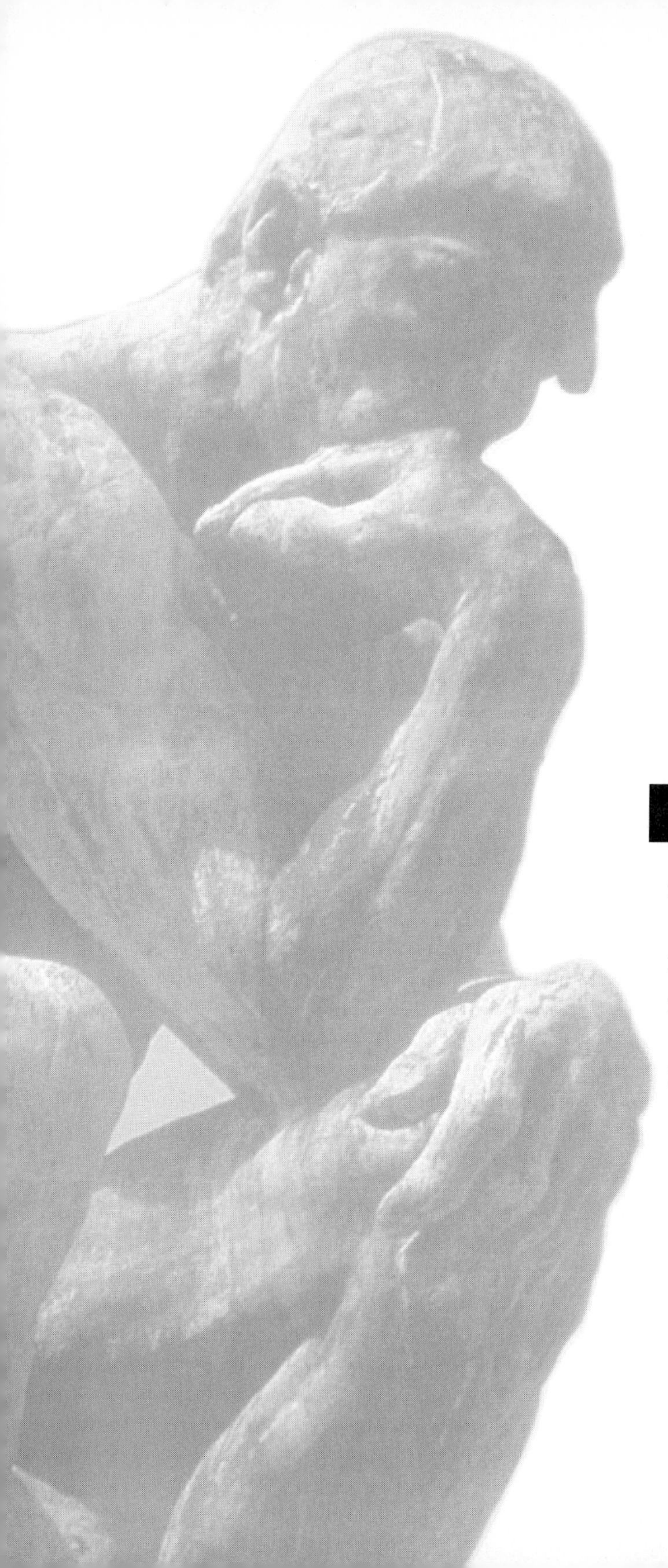

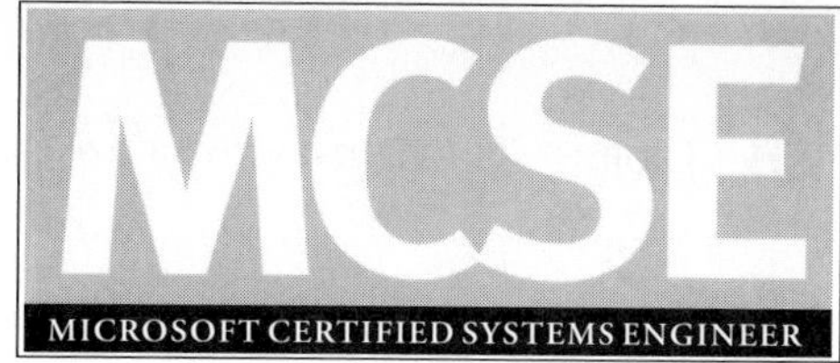

20

Managing Windows 2000 Data Storage

CERTIFICATION OBJECTIVES

20.01	Monitoring, Configuring, and Troubleshooting Disks and Volumes
20.02	Configuring Data Compression
20.03	Monitoring and Configuring Disk Quotas
20.04	Recovering from Disk Failures
✓	Two-Minute Drill

Proper management of storage media and timely recovery from disk failures are critical elements in the availability of a network's server. Windows 2000 Server, with its focus on less down time, includes support for dynamic disks and the new NTFS 5 file system. It also supports data compression and disk quota features that allow administrators to make the best use of available server storage space. This chapter describes the proper use of Windows 2000 Server's disk administration tools, as well as how to avoid, or recover from, disk failures.

CERTIFICATION OBJECTIVE 20.01

Monitoring, Configuring, and Troubleshooting Disks and Volumes

The performance and management of a server's storage media begins with the initial selection of an appropriate disk, volume, and file system configuration. The configuration you use will play a large role in the availability, security, and fault tolerance of the server.

To begin, Windows 2000 allows you to choose either a basic or dynamic disk configuration, depending on the server's resources and the desired level of availability. Windows 2000 supports a variety of fault tolerance methods, including striping, mirroring, and striping with parity. You can also select among a variety of file systems, including FAT 16, FAT 32, and NTFS 5. The file system you choose will determine the server's compatibility with older programs, and will affect the disk's security, space management, and recovery abilities.

Each of the disk, volume, and file system types are described here, as well as how to create or change storage configurations using the Windows 2000 Disk Manager utility.

Basic Storage

By default, Windows 2000 Server will configure storage devices as basic disks. Basic storage uses the traditional method of dividing physical disks into primary partitions and extended partitions with logical drives. Because this format can be recognized and accessed by DOS, Windows 9x, and Windows NT, it is a good choice to use when backward compatibility is an issue.

Partitioning Basic Disks

Before a basic disk can store information, it must first be partitioned, then formatted to use a particular file system. If only one partition is created, the disk appears as a single drive letter, usually C:. However, multiple partitions (divisions) can be created on a disk. Each partition can then be formatted with a different file system, and each will be assigned a different drive letter, just as if there were multiple hard disks in the computer. See Figure 20-1 for examples of single and multiple-partition disks. In a multipartition hard disk, each partition is assigned a different drive letter, and each can be formatted with a different file system.

Dividing a hard disk into partitions allows you to create a multiboot configuration with operating systems that use different file systems. It also allows you to logically separate types of data among drives without having to purchase and install extra physical disks.

Windows 2000 allows you to create, delete, or change the partition structures on basic disks, and it will recognize partition structures created by older operating systems, such as DOS, Windows 9x, and Windows NT. Most changes to the partition structure do not require a reboot to take effect.

A Windows 2000 basic disk can include up to four partitions on one physical hard disk, one of which may be an extended partition. The partition information of a disk is kept in a partition table, located on the first sector of the disk. If the first sector becomes corrupt, or otherwise unreadable, all data on the drive is effectively lost, since the partition information is inaccessible.

Primary Partitions Primary partitions are typically used to create bootable drives. Each primary partition represents one drive letter, up to a maximum of four on a single hard disk. One primary partition must be marked as active in order to boot the system, and most operating systems must place a few boot files on

FIGURE 20-1

A Windows 2000 basic disk can contain between one and four partitions (only one can be an extended partition)

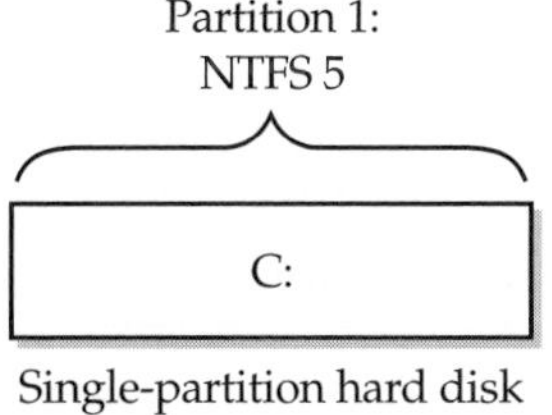

Single-partition hard disk

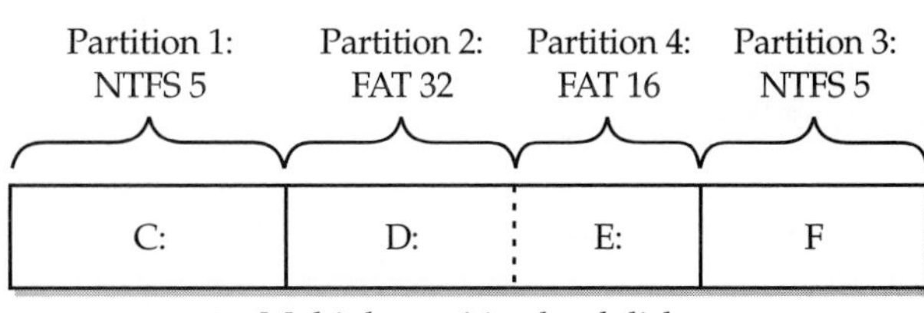

Multiple-partition hard disk

the primary active partition, although the operating system itself can usually be stored on a different partition.

Extended Partitions Although extended partitions can't be used to host operating systems, they can store other types of data, and provide an excellent way to create more drives above the four-partition limit. Here's how it works: Extended partitions do not represent one drive; rather, they can be subdivided into as many logical drives as there are letters in the alphabet. Therefore, one extended partition can contain several logical drives, each of which appears as a separate drive letter to the user. Figure 20-2 demonstrates the use of an extended partition to create extra drive letters.

Set Types on Basic Storage

Hard disk sets are groups of disks that work together to provide extra storage or fault tolerance. Basic disks support volume, stripe, and mirror sets and stripe sets with parity, all of which are described later. Each of these basic disk sets is supported by, but cannot be created within, Windows 2000. In other words, Windows 2000 will recognize basic disk sets that were created in older operating systems, but Windows 2000 does *not* allow you to create new ones. You must upgrade from basic to dynamic disk in order to create extra storage or fault tolerance sets.

Volume Set The term "volume" indicates a single drive letter. One physical hard disk can contain several volumes, one for each primary partition or logical drive. However, the opposite is also true. You can create a single volume that spans more than one physical disk. This is a good option when you require a volume that exceeds the capacity of a single physical disk. You can also create a volume set when you want to make use of leftover space on several disks by piecing them together as one volume. Refer again to Figure 20-1, which illustrates one disk with four volumes. Figure 20-3 demonstrates one volume spanning four disks.

FIGURE 20-2

An extended partition can contain multiple logical drives, each of which is assigned a separate drive letter

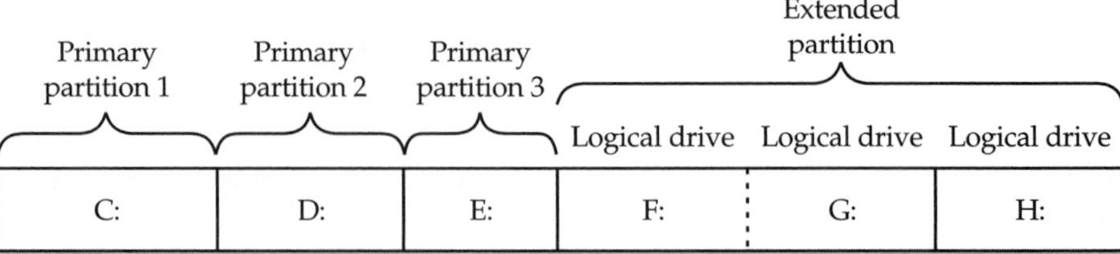

FIGURE 20-3

Drive E: represents a 5 GB volume set that spans four physical hard disks

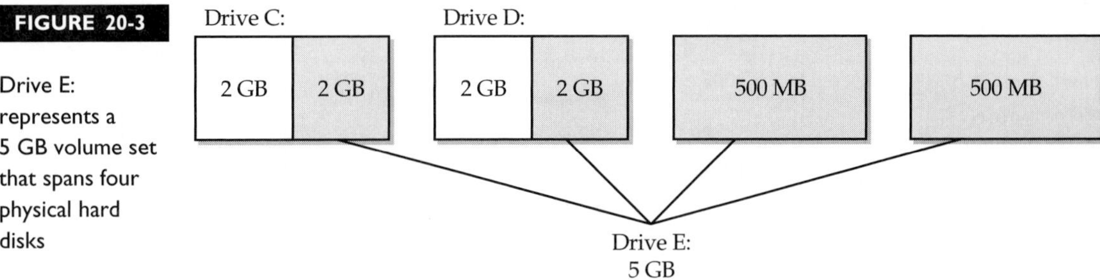

Mirror Set In a mirror set, all data on a selected partition or drive is automatically duplicated onto another physical disk. The main purpose of a mirror set is to provide fault tolerance in the event of missing or corrupt data. If one disk fails or contains corrupt files, the data is simply retrieved and rebuilt from the other disk.

A trade-off for this fault tolerance is decreased drive performance. In a mirror set, one disk controller is responsible for writing data to both disks, so these operations can take twice as long to perform. An alternative is to use disk duplexing, in which each disk uses its own disk controller to create duplicate data. The most common implementation of disk mirroring is RAID-1. RAID is an acronym for Redundant Array of Independent Disks. Mirror sets can be migrated to Windows 2000 from Windows NT Server.

Stripe Set The term "striping" refers to the interleaving of data across separate physical disks. Each file is broken into small blocks, and each block is evenly and alternately saved to the disks in the stripe set. In a two-disk stripe set, the first block of data is saved to the first disk, the second block is saved to the second disk, and the third block is saved to the first disk, and so on. The two disks are treated as a single drive, and are given a single drive letter. Figure 20-4 illustrates the concept of disk striping.

Disk striping provides increased storage capacity, and can increase the drive's performance, since data read/write tasks are evenly divided between the disks. It is important to note that disk striping alone does not provide fault tolerance, since each block of data is written only once. The most common implementation of this type of disk striping is RAID-0, or disk striping without parity. RAID is an acronym for Redundant Array of Independent Disks. Stripe sets can be migrated to Windows 2000 from Windows NT Workstation or Server.

FIGURE 20-4

Striped data is evenly interleaved across physical disks

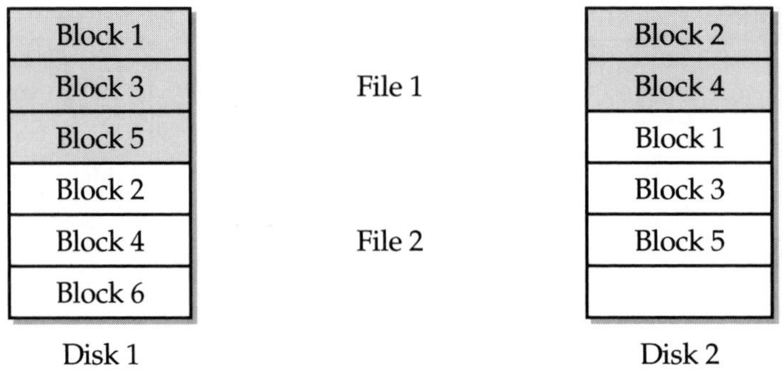

Disk striping does not provide fault tolerance.

Stripe Set with Parity A stripe set with parity requires at least three hard disks, and provides both increased storage capacity and fault tolerance. In a stripe set with parity, data is interleaved across three or more disks, and includes parity (error checking) information about the data. As long as only one disk in the set fails, the parity information can be used to reconstruct the lost data. If the parity information itself is lost, it can be reconstructed from the original data. Figure 20-5 illustrates the interleaving of data and parity information across disks.

The parity information is a calculated result of the data in the original data blocks. For example, suppose that the blocks of file 1 in Figure 20-5 contain the numbers 4 and 8, respectively. The parity calculation for this data is 12, since 4 + 8 = 12. If the first disk fails, the computer can use the parity information on the third disk

FIGURE 20-5

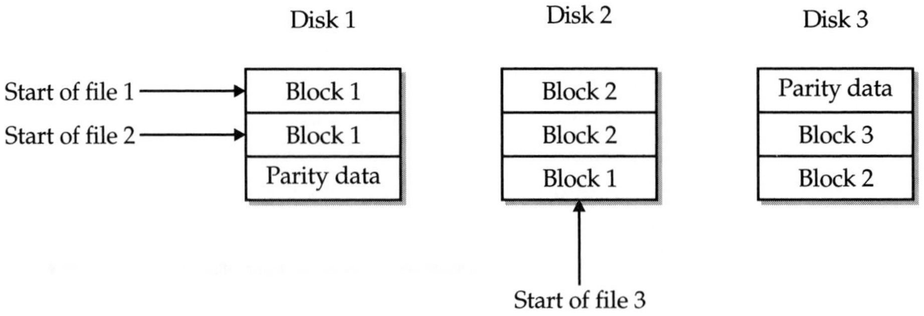

Data and parity information are interleaved among three or more disks in disk striping with parity

to reconstruct the data; n + 8 = 12, so the missing data from block 1 must be 4. Because the parity information is simply a calculation of the data existing on the first two drives, it can also be reconstructed in the event of a disk failure (4 + 8 = n; n equals 12).

Using a stripe set with parity increases available capacity, since the three (or more) disks are treated as a single drive. Also, drive performance is enhanced since read/write tasks are divided among the available disks. Finally, the largest benefit of using a stripe set with parity is the fault tolerance it provides.

A disadvantage to this type of disk structure is the obvious increased cost of having three or more disks, and the fact that the parity information takes up space that could otherwise be used for regular data storage. A common implementation of a stripe set with parity is RAID-5, which can be migrated into Windows 2000 from Windows NT Server.

Now that you are familiar with the basic storage set and partition types, you should be able to answer the following questions:

Set or Partition Type	How many disks?	Does it provide fault tolerance?	Other characteristics?
Primary or Extended Partition	One	No	One disk can contain many partitions and logical drives. Each is assigned a separate drive letter.
Volume Set	At least two	No	Increased capacity.
Mirror Set	Two	Yes	Provides a full backup of data. Write tasks can take much longer to perform.
Stripe Set	At least two	No	Read/write tasks are faster, increased capacity.
RAID-5 (Stripe Set with Parity)	At least three	Yes	Read/write tasks are faster, increased capacity.

Dynamic Storage

Windows 2000 supports a new storage type, called dynamic disk. This storage type is unique to Windows 2000 and cannot be used by other operating systems.

Furthermore, it is the preferred storage type of Windows 2000, so many disk management features in Windows 2000, such as implementing fault tolerance, can only be performed on a dynamic disk.

Dynamic disks introduce conceptual as well as technical changes from traditional basic disk structure. Partitions are now called volumes, and these can be created or changed without losing existing data on the disk. Recall that when using basic disks, you must first create primary partitions (up to a maximum of four), then extended partitions (a maximum of one) with logical drives. Dynamic disks allow you to simply create volume after volume, with no limit on the number or type that can exist on a single disk (you are limited only by the capacity of the disk itself).

Another important feature of dynamic disks is that information about volume number and type is stored in a disk management database on the last 1MB of the disk, rather than in the first cluster. In multidisk systems, this database is automatically replicated to all other dynamic disks in the system. That is, each disk's management database contains the volume information of all other disks, up to approximately 512 disks. If the database on any disk becomes lost or corrupt, the information is automatically restored by the other disks. Note that this replication can only occur within a single computer; disk management databases cannot be replicated between different computers.

Dynamic disks are not supported by laptops or removable media, such as Jaz or Zip drives. It is also important to note that although you can create a dynamic disk in a single-disk computer, there are few benefits in doing so, since the 1MB management database has nowhere to replicate.

exam Watch

Dynamic disks are not supported by removable media or laptops.

Volume Types on Dynamic Disks

Dynamic disks allow you to create a variety of configurations that can increase capacity, improve drive performance, and/or provide fault tolerance. The following sections describe the types of dynamic disk volumes and their relationship to basic volumes.

Simple Volume A simple volume is just that—it is a single volume that does not span more than one physical disk, and does not provide improved drive performance, extra capacity, or fault tolerance. One physical disk can contain a single, large simple volume, or several smaller ones. Each simple volume is assigned a simple drive letter, usually starting with C:; or the volume can be mounted to a folder using the new volume mount points feature of Windows 2000, removing limitations on number of volumes.

Spanned Volume When a dynamic volume includes the space on more than one physical hard drive, it is called a spanned volume. Spanned volumes can be used to increase drive capacity, or to make use of the leftover space on up to 32 existing disks. Like those in a basic storage volume set, the portions of a spanned volume are all linked together and share a single drive letter.

Mirrored Volume Like basic disks, dynamic disks can also be mirrored, and are called mirrored volumes. A continuous and automatic backup of all data in a mirrored volume is saved to a separate disk to provide fault tolerance in the event of a disk failure or corrupt file. Note that you cannot mirror a spanned or striped volume.

Striped Volume A striped volume is the dynamic storage equivalent of a basic stripe set, in which data is interleaved across more than one physical disk (up to 32 disks) to improve drive performance and increase drive capacity. Because each data block is written only once, striped volumes do not provide fault tolerance.

RAID-5 Volume A RAID-5 volume on a dynamic drive provides disk striping with parity, and is similar to a basic stripe set with parity. This disk configuration provides both increased storage capacity and fault tolerance. Data in a dynamic RAID-5 volume is interleaved across three or more disks (up to 32 disks), and parity information is included to rebuild lost data in the event of an individual disk failure. Like a spanned or striped volume, a RAID-5 volume cannot be mirrored.

SCENARIO & SOLUTION	
You don't need fault tolerance, and you have only one disk.	Create primary and/or extended partitions on a basic disk, simple volumes on a dynamic disk.
You want fault tolerance, but you have only two disks.	Create a mirror set or mirrored volume.
You have a large number of disks, and you want a fault tolerance method that won't slow down your computer.	Create a RAID-5 set or volume.
You want fault tolerance that will restore lost data without interfering with the use of the computer.	Create a mirror set or mirrored volume; when data is missing, it is retrieved off the backup disk, and users won't even know it's happening.
You don't need fault tolerance, but you want to improve read/write operations.	Create a stripe set or striped volume.

Upgrading Basic Storage to Dynamic Storage

By default, Windows 2000 configures all disks as basic. However, you can upgrade from basic to dynamic storage at any time by using the Windows 2000 Disk Management tool. All disks to be upgraded to dynamic must have at least 1MB of free space at the end. This space is for the disk management database.

Before planning a basic to dynamic upgrade, you must make sure the physical disk conforms to a few limitations. You cannot upgrade removable media to dynamic. You also cannot upgrade disks whose sectors are larger than 512 bytes. Finally, if you plan to upgrade a basic disk that contains volumes on other disks, all other disks in the set must also be upgraded from basic to dynamic. For example, mirror, volume, and stripe sets all rely on the use of more than one physical disk. For the upgrade to work, all disks involved in the set must be upgraded to dynamic. To upgrade a basic disk to a dynamic disk, follow the steps in Exercise 20-1.

EXERCISE 20-1

Upgrading a Basic Disk to Dynamic

1. Close any applications running from the disk to be upgraded.
2. Open the Computer Management console by right-clicking My Computer, then selecting Manage, or by selecting Start | Administrative Tools | Computer Management.
3. In the Computer Management screen, expand the Storage icon, then click Disk Management. A listing of all attached disks, as well as the type and status of each disk, will appear in the right pane. This screen is shown in the following illustration.

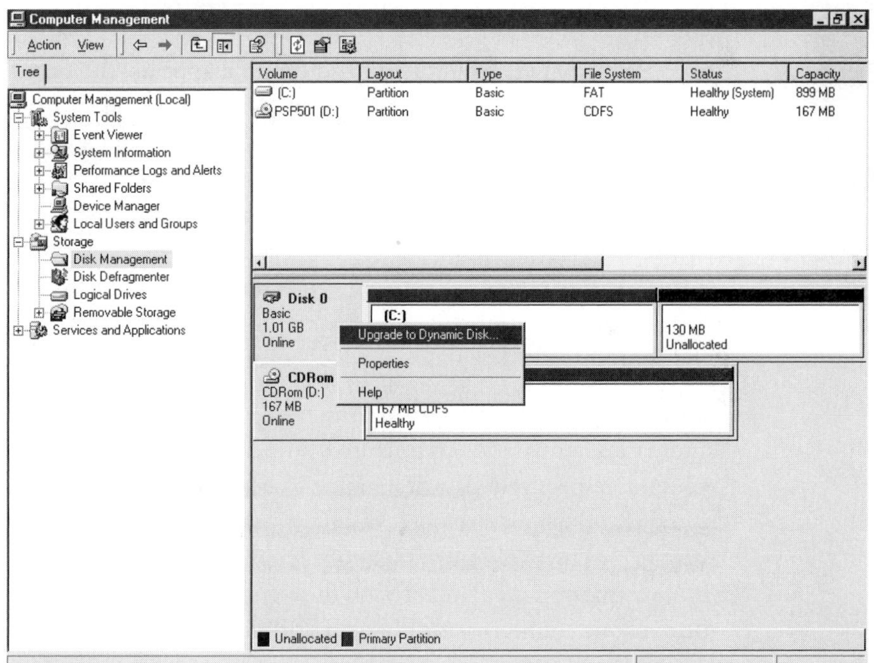

4. Right-click the basic disk you wish to upgrade, then select Upgrade to Dynamic Disk (the previous illustration). This will start the Upgrade Wizard.

5. In the next screen, shown in the following illustration, you will be prompted to select which disk (if there are more than one in the system) to upgrade. Place a check mark by each disk you wish to upgrade, then click OK.

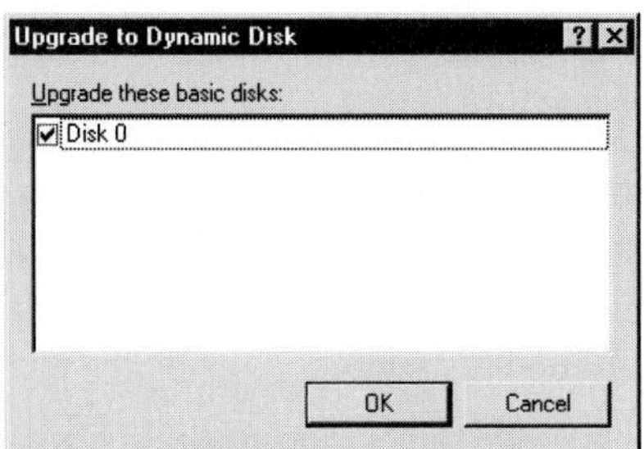

6. Select Upgrade from the next screen that appears, then confirm by choosing Yes. Choose Yes at the next prompt, informing you that filesystems on any of the chosen disks will be force dismounted. If you are upgrading a boot volume, you will be prompted to restart your computer. Otherwise, the changes will take effect immediately, without a reboot.

When a disk is upgraded from basic to dynamic, any existing basic partitions are converted to dynamic simple volumes. The new properties of the upgraded disks are shown in Figure 20-6. Any mirror, stripe, volume, and RAID-5 sets are automatically upgraded to mirrored, striped, spanned, and RAID-5 dynamic volumes, respectively. It is important to note here that you can upgrade a basic disk containing the boot partition, but only if that disk does not also include partitions that are part of a volume, stripe, mirror, or RAID-5 set.

Now that you are familiar with different disk types, you should be able to identify the dynamic counterparts of basic partitions and sets in Table 20-1.

Reverting to a Basic Disk Once a basic disk has been upgraded to dynamic, it is no longer accessible to older operating systems or in a dual-boot configuration. You may also find that some older or third-party disk utilities won't work. Fortunately, the upgrade from basic to dynamic is not one-way; you can revert to basic using the Revert to Basic Disk command in Computer Management.

FIGURE 20-6

The partitions on the basic disk have been converted to dynamic simple volumes

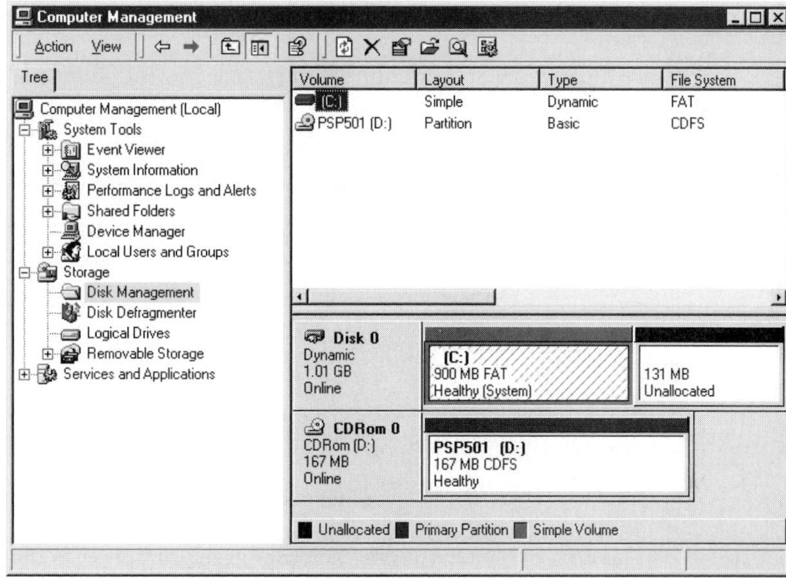

To use the Revert to Basic Disk command, however, you must first delete all dynamic volumes on the disk. This means you will lose all of the data on the disk, even data that was originally converted from basic to dynamic in the initial upgrade process. Reverting a dynamic disk back to basic is not a very involved process for the user. Simply right-click the disk you wish to revert, then select Revert to Basic Disk. The disk will be reverted with no further selection dialog boxes.

TABLE 20-1

Dynamic Counterparts of Basic Partitions

Basic Storage Term	Corresponding Dynamic Storage Term
Partition	Volume
Primary Partition / Logical Drive	Simple Volume
Volume Set	Spanned Volume
Mirror Set	Mirrored Volume
Stripe Set	Striped Volume
Stripe Set with Parity	RAID-5 Volume

File Systems

Once a partition, set, or volume is created, it must be formatted with a file system before it can store data. Windows 2000 Server supports a variety of file systems, including FAT16 and FAT32, as well as the newest file system, NTFS 5.

The file system you choose will depend on partition or volume size and the need for backward compatibility. The file system you use will affect the space efficiency and capabilities of the drive. Each time you create a new volume or partition, you are given the option to format it using any of the file systems described below.

FAT

The FAT file system allows the computer to use up to 4GB of disk space (DOS only supports 2GB), and is supported by DOS, Windows 3.x, Windows 9.x, and Windows NT. It is a 16-bit file system, so it is often referred to as FAT16, to distinguish it from the newer FAT32.

The FAT file system traditionally allows the computer to use up to 2GB of hard drive space (4GB in Windows 2000), and as the storage capacity increases, so does the cluster size. This means less efficient use of storage space since files cannot share clusters. For example, on a FAT16 2GB hard drive, each cluster is 32KB. If a 4KB file is saved, 28KB are wasted! However, the FAT16 file system has the advantage of being read and accessed by most popular operating systems, so you may decide to use it when backward compatibility is an issue.

FAT32

FAT32 was designed to eliminate the 4GB partition limitation and increase storage space efficiency. Introduced with Windows 95 OSR2, FAT32 can use up to 2TB (Terabyte) of space on a single drive, and keeps cluster sizes much smaller. A 32GB FAT32 drive has a cluster size of 16KB.

FAT32 is backward compatible with FAT16, so if you boot from a FAT32 drive, you will be able to access information on any FAT16 drives in the system. However, the reverse is not true. You cannot read a FAT32 drive if the computer is booted from a FAT16 drive. FAT32 is also not accessible by Windows NT or DOS without third-party utilities.

NTFS v5.0

The New Technology File System (NTFS) was first introduced with Windows NT. All versions of NTFS provide file and directory-level security, native file compression, the fault tolerance configurations described earlier, and support for large partitions or volumes. NTFS can support drives up to 2TB.

Windows 2000 improves on the NTFS file system with its new version, NTFS 5. Along with the features of NTFS 4, NTFS 5 also supports the Encrypting File System (EFS), sparse file support, and disk quotas. NTFS drives are not accessible by operating systems running from FAT16 or FAT32.

Converting to NTFS

When you install Windows 2000, all NTFS 4 drives are automatically upgraded to NTFS 5. You are also given the option to upgrade all FAT16 and FAT32 drives to NTFS. This conversion occurs without removing any data already existing on the drive.

If, however, you have chosen not to upgrade your FAT drives to NTFS during Setup, you can do so later using the NTFS conversion utility. Simply run CONVERT <driveletter> /FS:NTFS from a command prompt, and the selected partition or volume will be converted. Again, any data on the drive remains intact. An important note here is that the conversion utility only works one way; it will not convert NTFS drives to FAT16 or FAT32.

The Disk Management Tool

The Windows 2000 Disk Management Tool (introduced in Exercise 20-1) allows you to perform a large number of disk management tasks in an easy-to-use and intuitive interface. When you open the Disk Management Tool window, you will be presented with a screen similar to the one introduced in Figure 20-6.

The upper right-hand pane displays each partition or volume in the system, including information about the type of disk each resides on, and the file system, status, and capacity of each. Below that is information about each physical disk, and the partitions or volumes on each. This layout makes it easy to determine which volumes belong to which physical disks.

It is also easy to see whether one volume takes up more than one disk, or whether one disk has more than one volume. As you'll see in Exercise 20-2, for example, there are two basic disks. The first contains one primary partition and one extended partition with two logical drives. The remainder of the disk has unallocated space. The second disk is entirely occupied by a single primary partition.

Aside from displaying disk and volume information, the Disk Management Tool allows you to create, format, and delete partitions or volumes. Exercise 20-2 demonstrates how to create a simple volume on a dynamic disk in Disk Manager (these steps can also be used to create a simple or striped volume).

EXERCISE 20-2

Creating a Simple Volume with the Disk Management Tool

1. Open the Computer Management window by right-clicking My Computer, then selecting Manage.
2. Expand the Storage icon, then click Disk Management to see information about the disks and volumes within the system.
3. In the lower right-hand pane, right-click any unallocated space, then select Create Volume. The Create Volume Wizard will open.
4. In the Volume type section, select Simple, then click Next. You can also use this screen to select a spanned or striped volume. The screen shown in the following illustration will appear.

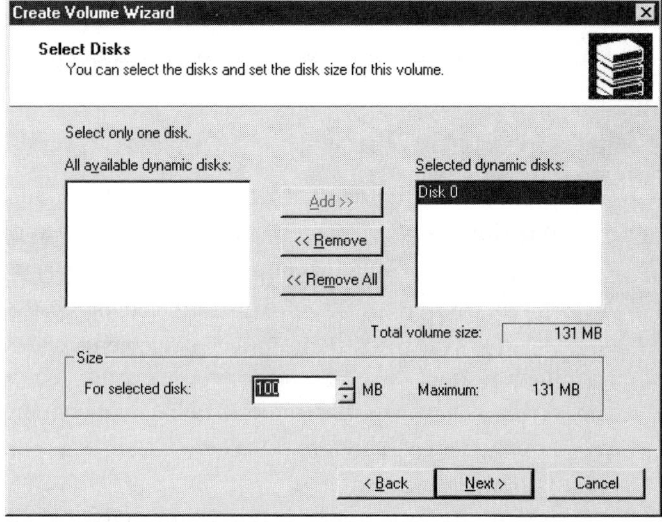

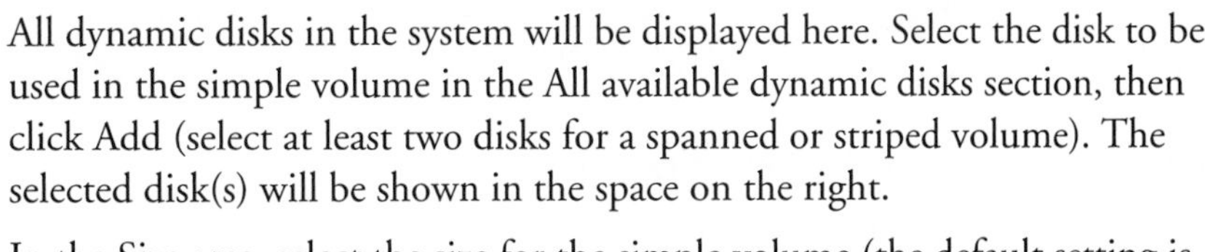

All dynamic disks in the system will be displayed here. Select the disk to be used in the simple volume in the All available dynamic disks section, then click Add (select at least two disks for a spanned or striped volume). The selected disk(s) will be shown in the space on the right.

5. In the Size area, select the size for the simple volume (the default setting is the combined available space on all of the selected disks). Click Next.
6. Assign a drive letter to the volume by selecting it from the drop-down list of available letters (only unused letters will be available here). Click Next.
7. Select to leave the volume unformatted, or choose to format it with NTFS, FAT, or FAT32. Click Next.
8. Following a confirmation dialog box, you will return to the Disk Management screen, and the simple volume will be created. The properties of the volume are displayed at the top right and its location on the disk is indicated in the disk section of the screen..

Aside from creating volumes, the Disk Management tool allows you to make changes to existing volumes. When you right-click a volume, you will be presented with a shortcut menu, with options to delete or reformat the volume, or change the drive letter. You can also use Disk Management to create fault tolerant volumes, described in more detail later in the chapter.

on the job

The Disk Management window is pretty intuitive and easy to use. However, if you get stumped, use the Windows 2000 Help system. It's written in easy-to-understand language, provides thorough help, and includes tons of information on disk management and recovery.

FROM THE CLASSROOM

Windows 2000 Disk Management

Windows 2000 Disk Management makes it so easy to make changes! But beware, many changes and upgrades are one-way only, so you must plan, plan, and plan some more before you make changes to the disk or volume structure.

For example, recall that a disk can be upgraded to dynamic only if there is 1MB free at the end of the disk. If you choose to install Windows 2000 on a single partition that takes up the entire hard disk, you will not be able to upgrade it to dynamic. Because it is the system partition, you will not be able to remove and re-create the partition without losing your Windows 2000 installation.

Another important point to remember is that the conversion of a disk to dynamic is essentially one-way. You can upgrade from basic to dynamic without losing any existing information, but you cannot revert back to basic in the same way. To do so, you must remove (delete) every volume on the dynamic disk (as well as any data on the volume), then revert it back to basic. The moral of the story is: Don't upgrade a basic disk (especially the one containing the system partition) unless you're absolutely sure you won't want to revert back to basic.

Finally, another one-way operation is the conversion of partitions or volumes to NTFS. This conversion does not remove any data from the volume, and enables you to use features like native compression, user quotas, and EFS. However, once a volume is converted to NTFS, it has to stay that way unless you remove the volume and re-create it (and lose all data on that volume).

—Amy Thomson, A+, MOUS Master

CERTIFICATION OBJECTIVE 20.02

Configuring Data Compression

The NTFS file system includes native data compression (no external compression utility is required). You can select to compress specific folders and files on an NTFS volume, or the entire volume itself. The steps for compressing an NTFS folder are outlined in Exercise 20-3.

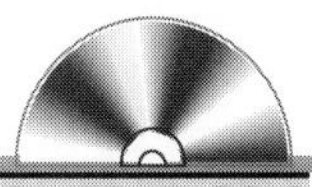

EXERCISE 20-3

Compressing an NTFS Folder

1. In My Computer or Windows Explorer, right-click the folder to be compressed. From the shortcut menu, select Properties, then click Advanced. The Advanced Attributes dialog box (the following illustration) will appear.

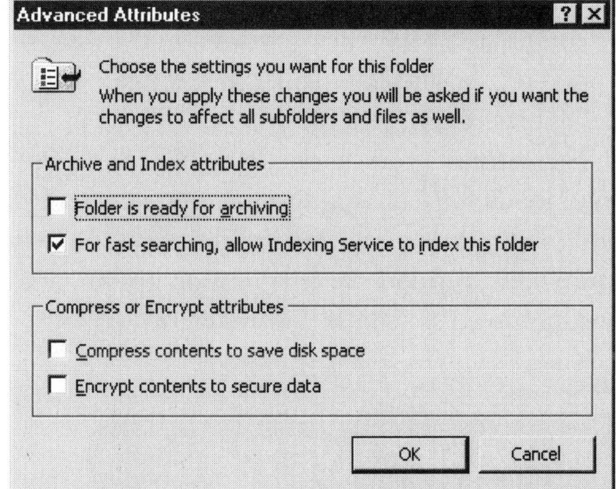

2. Select the option Compress contents to save disk space, then click OK.
3. In the Properties dialog box, choose either OK or Apply to accept your changes.
4. In the Confirm Attribute Changes dialog box (the following illustration), select to compress the current folder, or all files and subfolders within it. Click OK to complete the compression.

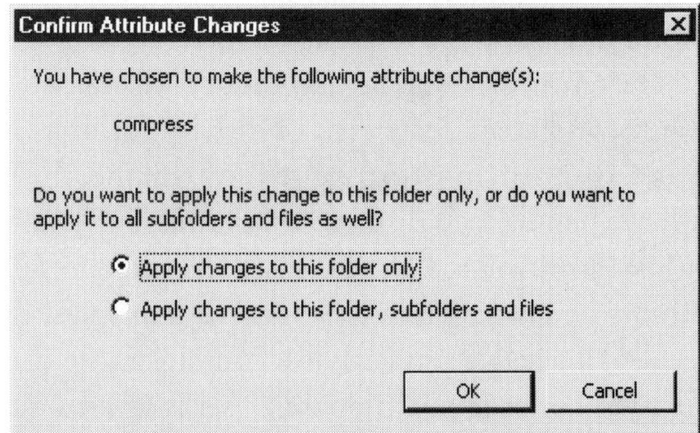

You can perform this type of compression only on volumes that have been formatted with NTFS. Any new file or subfolder that is added to the compressed folder will automatically be compressed as well.

You can compress any NTFS volume, including the system volume. You can also install Windows 2000 on a compressed volume, but only if it uses NTFS compression. While using NTFS native compression provides a quick method of increasing storage space, it can slow down disk read/write actions. All data must first be compressed before being written to the disk, or uncompressed in order to be read from the disk. Therefore, unless disk space is low, you may want to avoid compressing the system volume.

Furthermore, you cannot apply NTFS encryption to compressed files, folders, or volumes. Before encrypting a volume, folder, or file, you must first uncompress it. You can do this by returning to the properties windows for the compressed item. Once there, turn off the compression option, and the volume, folder, or file will be uncompressed as soon as you click OK.

CERTIFICATION OBJECTIVE 20.03

Monitoring and Configuring Disk Quotas

Windows 2000 allows administrators to assign drive space limits (quotas) to all users of a system or to individual users. Quotas can be set only on entire volumes, and not on individual files or folders. For example, if a user moves files from one folder to another on the same volume, their volume usage stays the same. If, however, a user copies files from one folder to another, their usage doubles.

The term "disk quotas" is a bit of a misnomer, since quotas are set per user, per volume and are independent of disk layout. If a volume spans more than one disk, as in a spanned, mirrored, or striped volume, the user's quota is applied to the entire volume, not to each disk in the volume. For example, suppose a user has a quota of 50MB on volume D:. The user is limited to 50MB, regardless of whether volume D: resides on one physical disk or spans three disks.

Also, if a single physical disk contains more than one volume, quotas can be set on each. For example, suppose a user is given a quota on each of volumes D:, E:, and F:, all of which reside on one physical disk. Usage of volume D: will not affect usage of volumes E: and F: or vice versa.

Disk quotas are set on volumes, not on physical hard disks.

Files are counted against a user's volume space every time the user saves, copies, or creates a file. Users are also "charged" for volume space whenever they take ownership of another user's file. If user 1 takes ownership of a 2MB file that was created by user 2, user 1's volume use increases by 2MB and user 2's volume use decreases by 2MB.

Setting, Assigning, and Configuring Disk Quotas

Administrators can set quotas either locally or on remote computers. Quotas can only be set on volumes formatted with the NTFS file system. Follow the steps in Exercise 20-4 to apply quotas for all users.

EXERCISE 20-4

Creating Quotas for All Users

1. In the My Computer or Disk Management window, right-click the volume on which you want to create the quota, then click Properties.
2. In the Properties dialog box, select the Quota tab.
3. Click the Enable quota management check box. The grayed-out options in the dialog box will become available for selection. Select to Deny disk space to users exceeding quota limit.

You can leave the Deny disk space option off if you simply want to keep a log of all users who exceed their quota. This may help you study users' work habits and determine appropriate quota levels before you actually limit their disk usage.

4. Click the Limit disk space to option and type in the limit you want to apply. Use the drop-down arrow to select KB, MB, GB, and so on. Repeat the process to set warning levels for users who are getting near their limit.

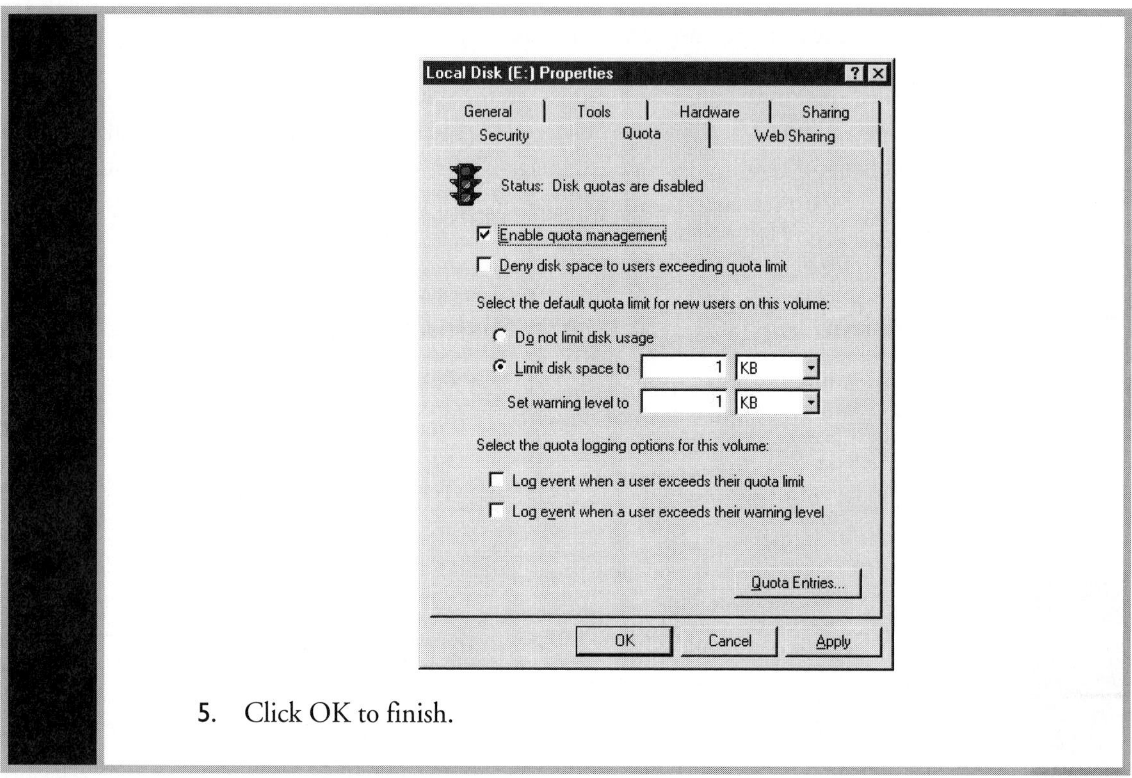

5. Click OK to finish.

Windows 2000 also lets you set different quotas for different users. To create a new quota entry, follow the steps in Exercise 20-5.

EXERCISE 20-5

Create New Quota Entries

1. In the Quota tab, click Quota Entries. A dialog box displaying all previously set quotas will open (the following illustration).

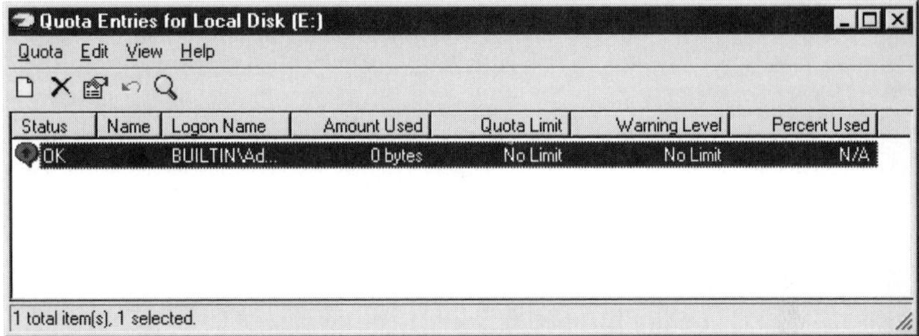

2. Select New Quota Entry from the Quota menu. A new dialog box will open, allowing you to select users (the following illustration).

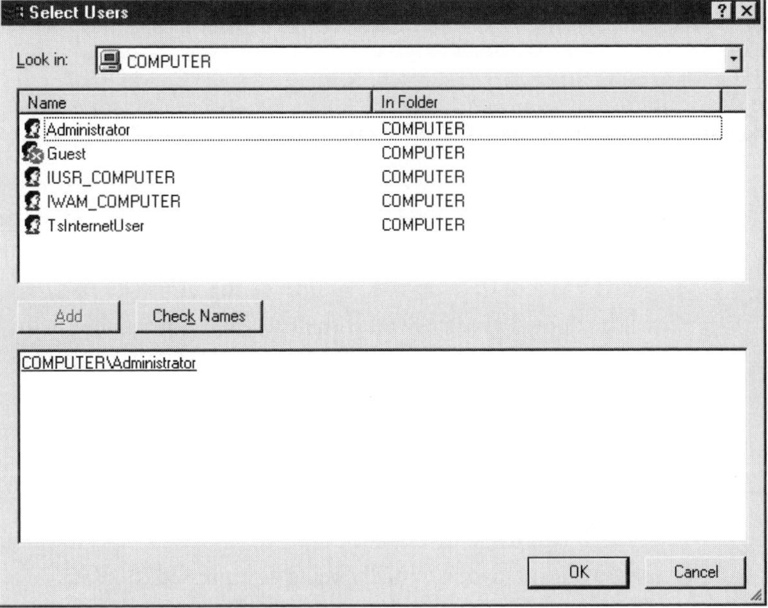

3. Select the user to whom you wish to apply the quota, then click Add. The dialog box shown in the following illustration will appear.

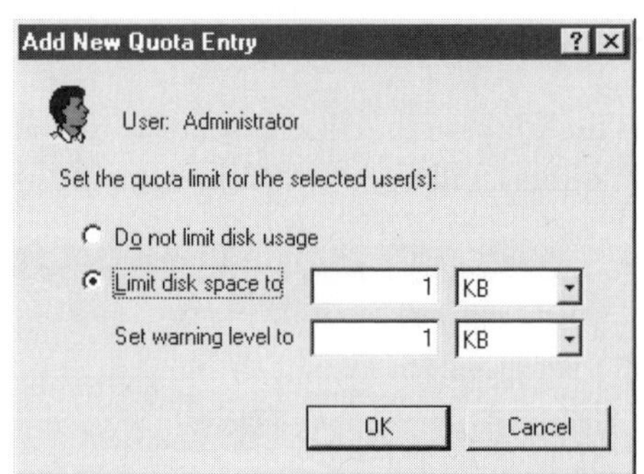

4. Click the Limit disk space to option, then enter the desired amount and unit. You can also set warning levels to users approaching the limit. When you are finished, click OK.

5. The Quota Entries dialog box will reappear, with the new quota in the list. Close the dialog box, then click OK to close the Properties dialog box and finish setting the quota.

Disk Quotas and Compression

Disk quotas are not affected by file, folder, or volume compression. That is, quotas are applied to the uncompressed size of files, whether they are compressed or not. For example, suppose a user has been assigned a quota of 10MB, and has already stored 9MB of data on the volume. If the user tries to save a 1.5MB file, the user will be denied access. Even if the user compresses the file to 1MB, he or she will still be denied access, since the uncompressed size of the file exceeds the user's quota.

Quotas can also be set on volumes that are compressed. When quotas are set, volume and file sizes are calculated in their uncompressed size. For example, suppose that a 2GB volume is compressed to 1.2GB. When you set the quotas on this volume, the total volume size will be reported as 2GB, not 1.2GB. If you divide the volume space equally between two users, each will be reported as having a 1GB quota limit, even though each user's volume space is actually being compressed to .6GB.

exam Watch

Quotas are set using the uncompressed size of files and folders.

CERTIFICATION OBJECTIVE 20.04

Recovering from Disk Failures

You have already been introduced to some methods for preventing loss of data from disk failures, such as using mirrored or RAID-5 volumes. Also, recall that all dynamic disks in a system keep the management database of all other disks in the system. These forms of data redundancy won't prevent disk failures from happening, but can be used to restore data on a failed or new disk when a disk failure does occur. This section describes the steps for creating fault tolerant volumes, and how to recover data from these volumes if they fail.

Implementing Fault-Tolerant Volumes

Like simple, spanned, and striped volumes, fault-tolerant volumes are created in the Disk Management window. Remember that Windows 2000 Server will recognize and use fault tolerant drives that were created on basic disks in Windows NT 4, but will not allow you to create new fault tolerant drives on basic disks. To create new fault tolerant drives, you must first upgrade each disk to dynamic.

Creating Mirrored Volumes

To create a mirrored volume, there must be two disks in the system. Use the same steps outlined in Exercise 20-2. When creating the mirrored volume, simply select the Mirrored Volume option in the Create Volume Wizard. Use this method to create a *new* mirrored volume from the unallocated space on two disks.

Creating a RAID-5 Volume

A RAID-5 volume requires at least three, and up to 32 disks. Use the steps outlined in Exercise 20-2, but select the RAID-5 option in the Create Volume Wizard. RAID-5 volumes can be created only from the unallocated space on three or more disks.

Recovering a Failed Mirrored Volume

In the case of a disk failure, Windows 2000 Server is able to give you some clues as to the cause of the problem. The Disk Management window includes status descriptions for each disk and volume in the system. These descriptions can be your key to pinpointing the disk at fault and the cause of the problem.

Working volumes with the status Healthy are behaving normally, and there are no known failures of the disk on which the volume resides. Working disks are given the status Online. A healthy volume on an online disk should experience no problems.

Offline or Missing Disks

If a mirrored volume resides on one or more nonfunctional disks, the faulty drive becomes an orphan, and is temporarily removed from the mirrored volume. This means the volume will no longer be fault tolerant. If the disk displays the status Offline, but Windows 2000 still recognizes the name of the disk, the disk is partially corrupted or intermittently accessible. You have to select a new area of free space that is the same size (or larger) as the members of the volume you are regenerating the data from the parity information on. Right-click the disk in the Disk Management window, then select Reactivate. The disk's status should return to Online, and the mirrored volume will automatically be regenerated.

However, some disk problems are more serious. If Windows 2000 cannot locate a disk, or if the disk is completely unreadable, the disk's status will be Offline and unnamed, or Missing. In this case, you must repair the physical disk, check the cables, then select to Reactivate the disk. If this solves the problem, the disk's status will return to Online and the mirrored volume will return to Healthy.

If the disk cannot be repaired, it must be replaced, and the mirrored volume must be re-created. To add a mirror to an existing volume, follow the steps in Exercise 20-6.

EXERCISE 20-6

Adding a Mirror to an Existing Volume

1. In the Disk Management window, right-click the volume you want to add the mirror to. From the shortcut menu that appears, select Add Mirror.
2. You will then be asked to select the disk to host the mirror. Select it from the available disks, then click Add Mirror.

Once the mirror is added, you will be returned to the Disk Management window, and the volume will display the status Regenerating until the mirror is established. The volume's status will then return to Healthy.

Online Disks (w/Errors)

When a disk is accessible, but contains underlying I/O errors, the disk's status will be Online (w/Errors). Simply reactivate the disk, and it should return to Online. The mirrored volume will automatically be regenerated and return to normal. However, keep a close eye on this disk, as the I/O errors may eventually lead to a total disk failure.

Reestablishing a Mirrored Volume

When an offline disk is reactivated, the mirrored volume should automatically return to Healthy. However, if it doesn't, you can use the Reactivate Volume command to fix the problem.

Not all mirrored volume failures occur because of underlying disk problems. If the volume itself is at fault, you can use Repair Volume to fix the problem. If the volume still doesn't return to Healthy, use the Resynchronize Mirror feature to synchronize the data on both disks in the volume.

If this doesn't work, as a last resort, you can remove part of the mirror, then add it again. To remove part of a mirror, right-click it, then select Remove Mirror. This part of the mirror will become unallocated space. You can then use Add Mirror to re-create the mirrored volume.

Recovering a Failed RAID-5 Volume

RAID-5 volume failures are a bit more serious than mirrored volume failures. RAID-5 volumes do not contain backup copies; rather, the data must be regenerated using the parity information on the remaining good disks. Fortunately, the recovery procedures for a RAID-5 volume are similar to those for a mirrored volume.

Offline or Missing Disks

An offline or missing disk must be returned to an online state before the RAID-5 volume can be accessed. Try reactivating the disk. If this doesn't work, repair the disk, then reactivate it. The volume's status should automatically change to Regenerating, then back to Healthy.

If the failed disk itself must be replaced, select Repair Volume. This feature will incorporate the new disk into the existing RAID-5 volume.

Online Disks (w/Errors)

When a RAID-5 volume resides on a disk with the status Online (w/Errors), the volume will be inaccessible. Reactivate the disk, and the RAID-5 volume should be automatically regenerated.

Regenerating a RAID-5 Volume

In some cases, a RAID-5 volume may not regenerate itself once a bad disk is brought back online. When this is the case, use the Reactivate Volume command.

If the volume itself is at fault, you can try to fix it using the Repair Volume command. If the volume is too badly damaged to be repaired, use the Regenerate Parity command.

For detailed information on working with fault tolerant disks, please visit www.shinder.net/Win2000/disks.

CERTIFICATION SUMMARY

Windows 2000 Server supports a large variety of disk configurations, including basic partitions and sets. Windows 2000 also introduces dynamic disks, with support for simple, spanned, and striped volumes. The new Disk Management tool allows you to easily upgrade from basic to dynamic disks, and to create or delete volumes without restarting the computer.

Also new to Windows 2000 is the NTFS 5 file system, which supports native file compression and user disk quota management. Files, folders, or even entire volumes can be easily compressed by enabling the compression option in the Properties window. Disk quotas can be set on NTFS volumes within the Quota tab in the Properties windows. A single quota can be set for all users who access a volume, or you may opt to set different quotas for different users.

Because a network's server is such a critical resource, fault tolerance methods can be configured to reduce data loss and server downtime. Windows 2000 Server allows you to create mirrored and RAID-5 volumes, each of which can be used to re-create or replace lost data. In the case of a disk or volume failure, the Disk Management tool provides easy troubleshooting tools to repair the disk or volume, and to recover the lost or damaged information.

✓ TWO-MINUTE DRILL

Monitoring, Configuring, and Troubleshooting Disks and Volumes

- ❑ Windows 2000 supports traditional basic disks and introduces the use of dynamic disks.
- ❑ Windows 2000 allows you to create basic partitions, and will recognize existing fault tolerant sets, but does not allow you to create new basic fault tolerant sets.
- ❑ Dynamic simple volumes reside on a single physical disk, and spanned volumes use space on more than one disk to create a single drive letter. Striped volumes interleave data evenly among two or more disks.
- ❑ A mirrored volume includes two identical copies of all information on two separate disks to provide fault tolerance, and a RAID-5 volume uses striping with additional parity information.
- ❑ Windows 2000 Server supports FAT16 and FAT32 file systems, and can convert them to NTFS 5 using the convert.exe utility.
- ❑ The Disk Management tool is the utility that allows you to create volumes, upgrade to dynamic disk, and configure fault tolerance.

Configuring Data Compression

- ❑ The NTFS 5 file system supports native data compression for files, folders, or entire volumes.
- ❑ Compression is enabled within the Properties dialog box.
- ❑ Compressed data cannot be encrypted.

Monitoring and Configuring Disk Quotas

- ❑ NTFS 5 supports disk quotas, which limit the amount of server disk space that can be used by the network's users.
- ❑ Disk quotas are created in the Quota tab within a volume's Properties dialog box.

- Quotas may be set that apply to all users, or you may select to set different quotas for different users.
- Quotas are based on the uncompressed size of files and folders.

Recovering from Disk Failures

- Mirrored and RAID-5 volumes are created with the Disk Management tool.
- Volume errors that stem from underlying disk problems will often fix themselves when the disk is reactivated or replaced.
- If the volume does not automatically repair itself, or if there is a problem with the volume itself, use the Reactivate Volume command.
- If reactivating the volume doesn't work, try the command Repair Volume, Regenerate Parity (for RAID-5 volumes), or Resynchronize (for mirrored volumes).

MCSE
MICROSOFT CERTIFIED SYSTEMS ENGINEER

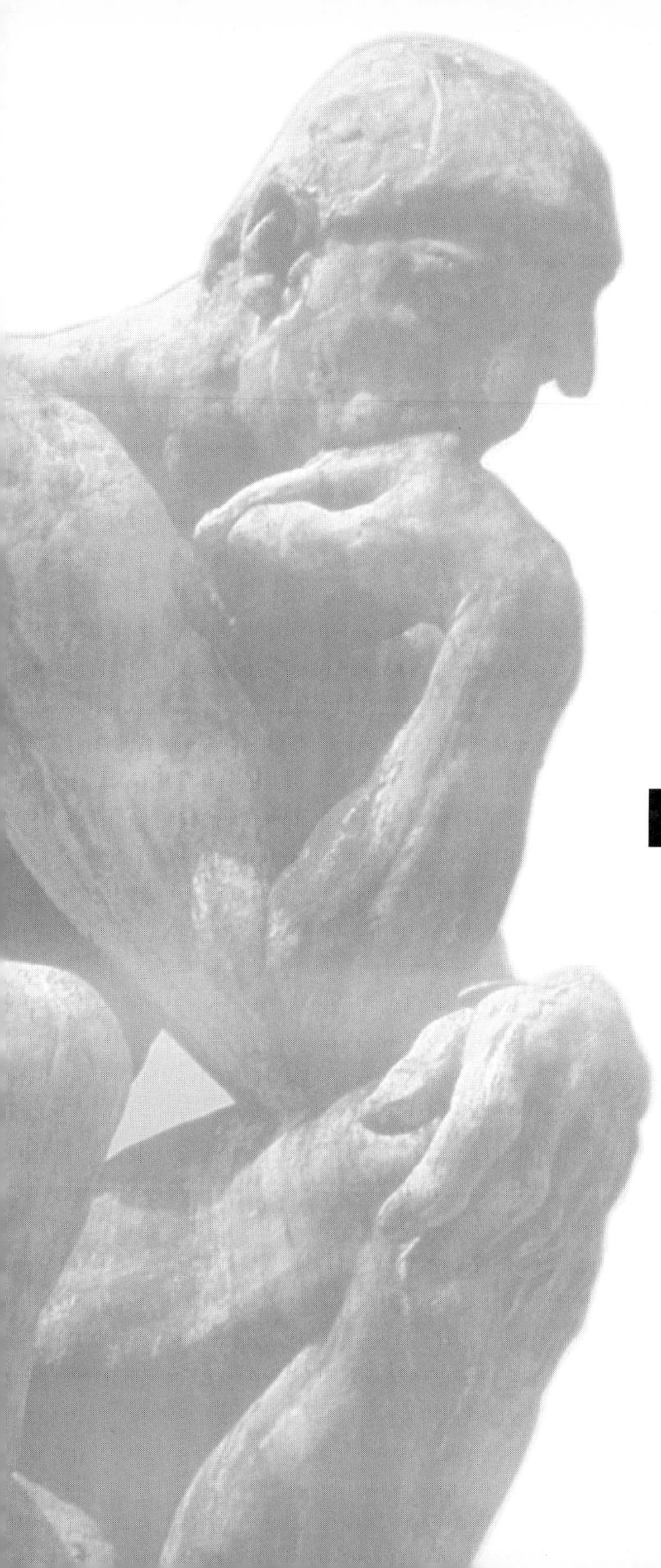

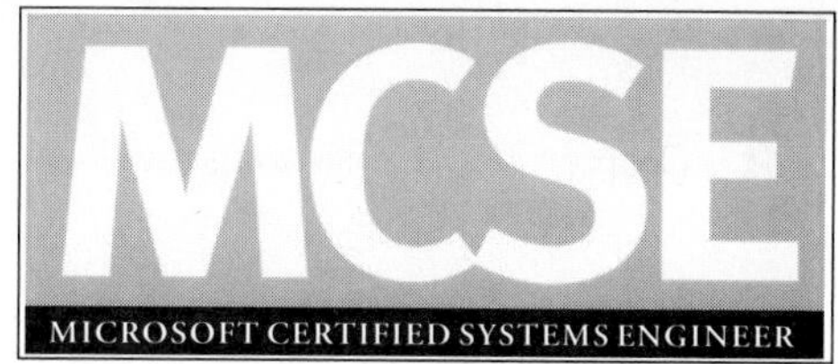

21

Configuring the Desktop Environment

CERTIFICATION OBJECTIVES

- 21.01 Configuring and Managing User Profiles
- 21.02 Configuring and Troubleshooting Desktop Settings
- 21.03 Configuring and Troubleshooting Accessibility Services
- ✓ Two-Minute Drill

In this chapter, we'll take a look at how you configure and manage the desktop environment. We'll follow the emphasis of Microsoft's exam, and focus on the configuration of the desktop environment—not at how a user configures his own desktop environment, but rather how an administrator sets up a desktop to allow multiple users to configure their own environments, and conversely, how an administrator can deny users configuration control.

In Windows 2000, this occurs largely through manipulation of user profiles and groups. We'll take a glance at group policy and local policy, and also examine Windows 2000 Professional's accessibility services.

CERTIFICATION OBJECTIVE 21.01

Configuring and Managing User Profiles

Let's say I share my computer with this guy named Steve. Steve does everything different from me—he likes to put his taskbar at the top of the screen instead of the bottom. He scatters his icons all over the screen, instead of leaving them in the neat little rows that I like to use. He likes to use Active Desktop to set up a bright, swirling pattern as his wallpaper, which gives me a headache.

Luckily, Steve and I are not forced to struggle over the computer's desktop. Windows 2000 Professional attaches a user profile to each individual account, storing configuration information on a per-user basis. No matter what Steve does to his desktop when he's using my computer, my desktop will always be neat, clean, and simple, as I like it (Figure 21-1).

A user profile consists of desktop settings, like whether or not Auto-Arrange is turned on, or what resolution the display is, or whether menus Scroll or Fade, as well as a desktop image. The user profile actually exists as a folder. If Windows 2000 Professional is installed in drive X:, then for each user, there will be a folder that exists as X:\Documents and Settings\ *Username*.

Inside this folder are folders representing your various settings—a Favorites folder, a Cookies folder, and a folder labeled Desktop. This folder contains almost all the things that are on your desktop—any files you move to your desktop, or any folders you create on your desktop. (Certain icons that appear on your desktop will

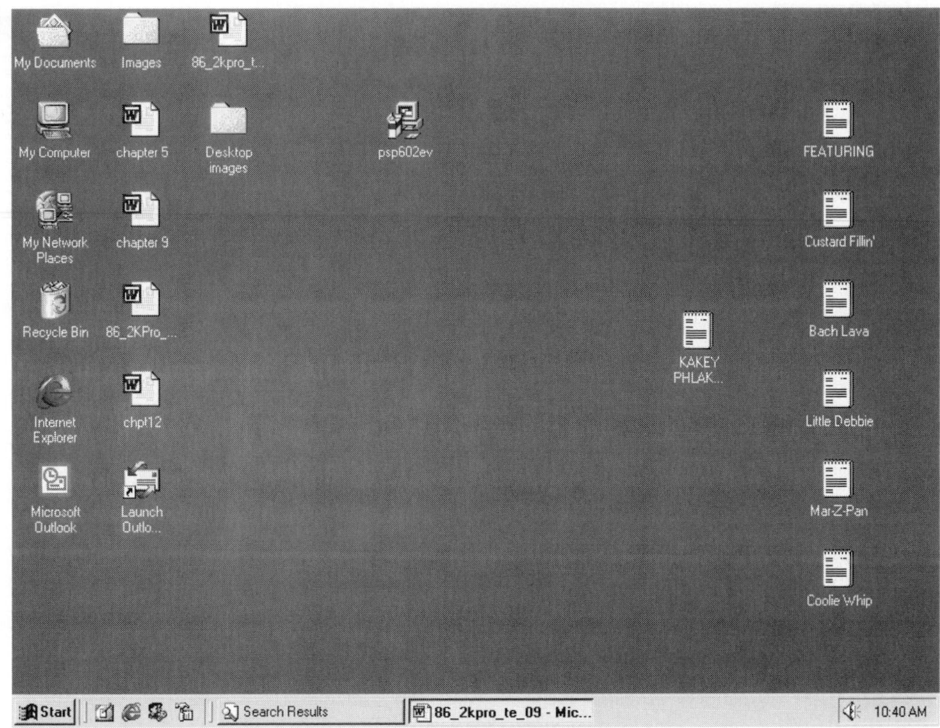

FIGURE 21-1 Here you can see how my desktop appears

not appear in this folder—Recycle Bin, Internet Explorer, and Outlook. Interestingly, shortcuts you place in the taskbar also do not show up.)

In Figure 21-2, you can see how all the files and folders that appear on the desktop are contained in the Desktop folder, within my *username* folder inside Documents and Settings.

exam Watch

The exception to the rule is the My Documents folder. The My Documents folder appears directly in the username folder, not in the username\Desktop folder. A hyperlink resides in the Desktop folder to the My Documents folder.

A new *Username* and *Username*\Desktop folder is created for each new user, and the *Username*\Desktop folder is populated with the standard set of shortcuts. Note that in the user account process, a new set of shortcut files are *created* and placed in the new desktop folder. That means that the Connect to the Internet icon on *my* desktop represents a different file from the Connect to the Internet icon on *Steve's* desktop (namely, the one on my desktop is the file X:\Documents and

FIGURE 21-2

Desktop folder

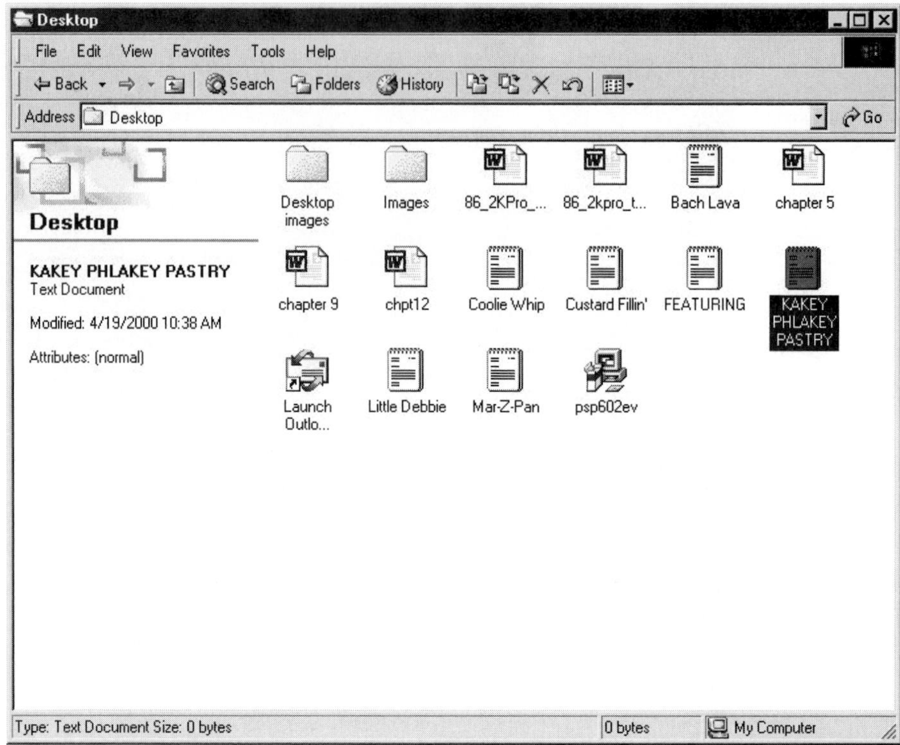

Settings\Chris Nguyen\Desktop\connect.lnk, and the one on his desktop is the file X:\Documents and Settings\Steve Smith\Desktop\connect.lnk). If Steve deletes or modifies his icon, that will do nothing to the Connect to the Internet icon on my desktop. (This does not apply to certain core icons, like My Computer and Recycle Bin, which don't exist as files in the Desktop folder.)

In Figure 21-3, you can see the C:\Documents and Settings\Chris Nguyen folder, attached to my profile. You'll notice that there's a Cookies folder, a Favorites folder, a Documents folder, and a My Documents folder.

The per-user nature of the Desktop also applies to Favorites from Explorer and the Start menu, which exist as *Username*\Favorites and *Username*\Start Menu, respectively.

FIGURE 21-3

The *username* folder

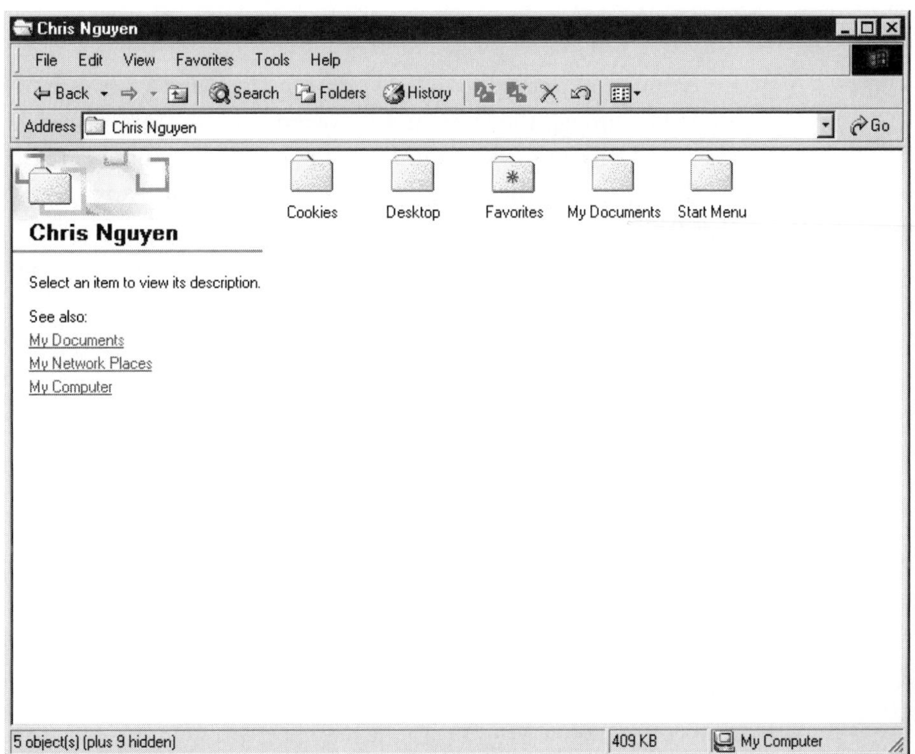

When you drag a file, like an executable, onto your desktop, it's important to drag it and Create a Shortcut instead of just selecting Move. Create a Shortcut will create a .lnk file in your desktop folder. If you actually Move the file, then the file will be shifted to your Username\Desktop folder, and thus be very hard to find for any other users who log on to your system and need to use that file. This is also why it's a bad habit to create or move a file that other people need access to; others will have a tough time finding it. If other people who use your computer need to find that file, create it somewhere else and make a shortcut to it on your desktop.

Adding a User Profile

Everything we're going to do will occur in Users and Passwords. This window is accessible through the Users and Passwords icon in Control Panel. To interact with Users and Passwords, you must be a member of the Administrators group.

The easiest way to add a new user is by running the Add User Wizard. Simply click Add from the Users and Passwords window.

The more powerful way to add and configure users is to use the Local Users Manager, a snap-in for the Microsoft Management Console. This is accessed simply by clicking the Advanced tab from the Users and Passwords window, then clicking Advanced, and opening up the Users folder. You have a lot more power from the Local Users Manager, so I'll show you how to do everything from here.

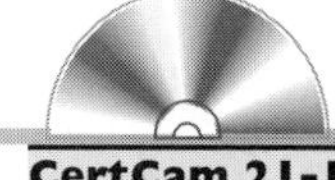

CertCam 21-1

EXERCISE 21-1

Adding a User Using Local Users Manager

Follow these steps to add a user using Local Users Manger.

1. Make sure you're logged on with Administrator status.
2. Open Control Panel | Users and Passwords. Click the Advanced tab, which will bring up the Advanced Users and Passwords screen, as shown in the following illustration. Then click Advanced. This will bring up the Local Users and Groups MMC snap-in. Open up the Users folder in the left-hand pane; this will bring up all local users in the right-hand pane.

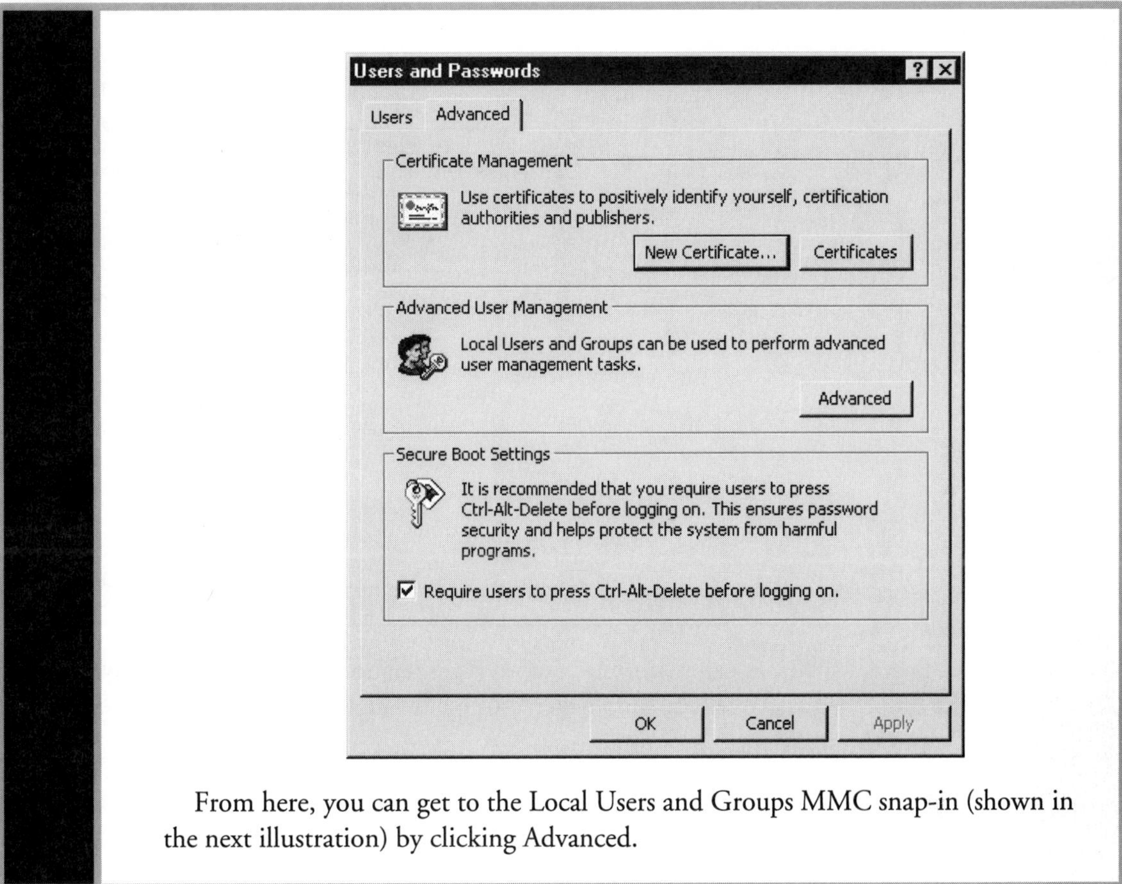

From here, you can get to the Local Users and Groups MMC snap-in (shown in the next illustration) by clicking Advanced.

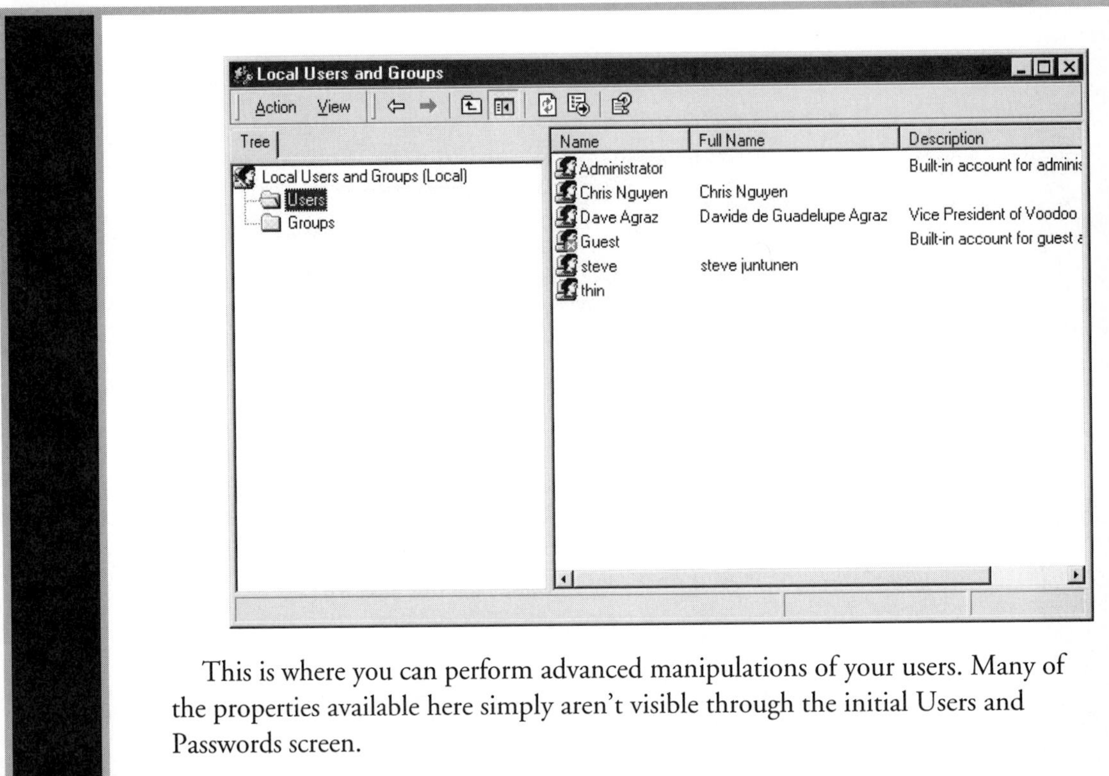

This is where you can perform advanced manipulations of your users. Many of the properties available here simply aren't visible through the initial Users and Passwords screen.

3. Right-click inside the right-hand pane, at an empty space; select New User… from the pull-down menu, as shown in the following illustration. This will start the New User wizard.

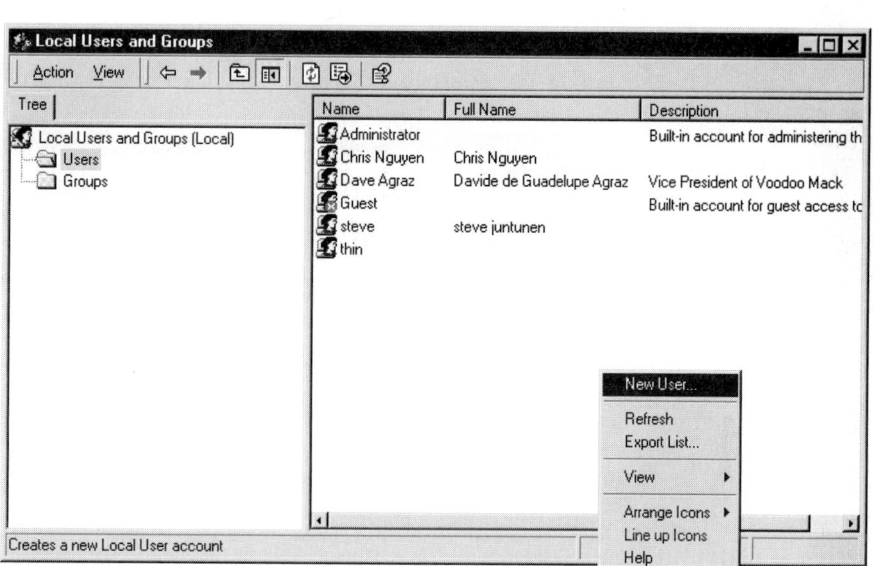

The fastest way to start the New User Wizard is by right-clicking somewhere within the right-hand pane, on an empty space. Make sure you don't right-click a name, which will bring up options concerning that particular user.

4. Fill in the information that the wizard requests, as shown in the following illustration. Be sure to specify if you want to force the user to change his or her password, allow the user to change his or her password, or specify that the user's password will never expire. The nice thing about the New User wizard as accessed from this advanced Local Users and Groups screen is that it doesn't automatically pop you back to the previous window; instead, you

get the same New User wizard screen again. This is handy for entering lots of new users. Click Close on an empty New User screen when you're done.

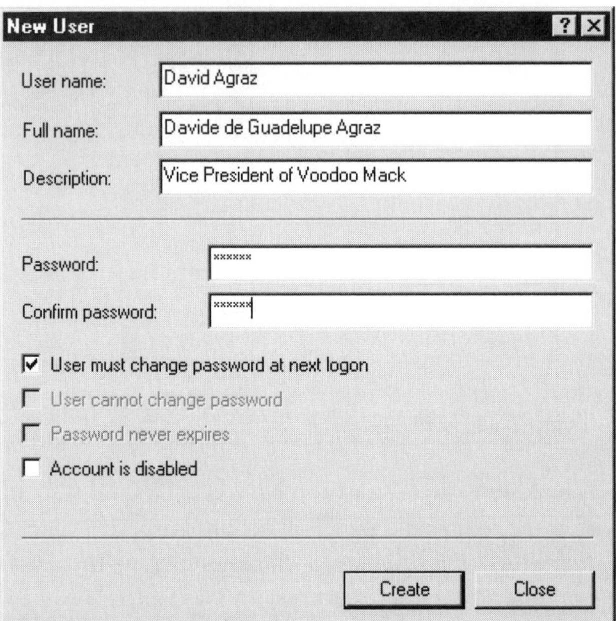

The wizard walks you through inputting all necessary information for a new user account. Click Create when you're done. Here, we're creating an account for Dave Agraz, our new Vice President of Voodoo Mack.

Password Options In Depth

One of the more important decisions you need to make when creating a new user is the option regarding passwords. You can choose from the following:

- **User Must Change Password at Next Logon** This forces the user to set his or her own password, changing the password from what the Administrator has set. When this option is selected, Windows shades out the User Cannot Change Password and Password Never Expires options.

- **User Cannot Change Password** This locks in the password that the Administrator has set. An Administrator can only change the password.
- **Password Never Expires** By default, Windows forces users to change their passwords every 42 days. This option removes the expiration process. This is useful for low-security environments, and for creating user accounts linked to particular applications or automated processes.
- **Account Disabled** This kills the account until the box is unchecked. The user cannot log on.
- **Account Locked Out** This option only appears if Group Policies have been set to allow lockouts, and a user has triggered a lockout. Lockouts are essentially automatic account disablements, triggered by some condition; typically, some failures to successfully log on, which can be indicative of an attempted security breach. An Administrator must manually uncheck the Account Locked Out box if, for example, the account's proper user has accidentally triggered the lockout process. If an Administrator wishes to manually lock out a user, he or she must use the Account Disabled function.

Configuring a User Profile

Most of the configurations you as an administrator will make will depend heavily on the security groups defined inside Active Directory at the server level.

The most elementary move to a user profile is adding that user to a group.

EXERCISE 21-2

Adding a User to a Group Using Local Users Manager

Let's walk through this exercise of adding a user to a group using Local Users Manager.

1. Now you need to specify advanced properties. Right-click the name of the new user from the Local Users and Groups screen; select Properties.
2. Now select the Member of tab. This brings up the group membership view, as shown in the following illustration.

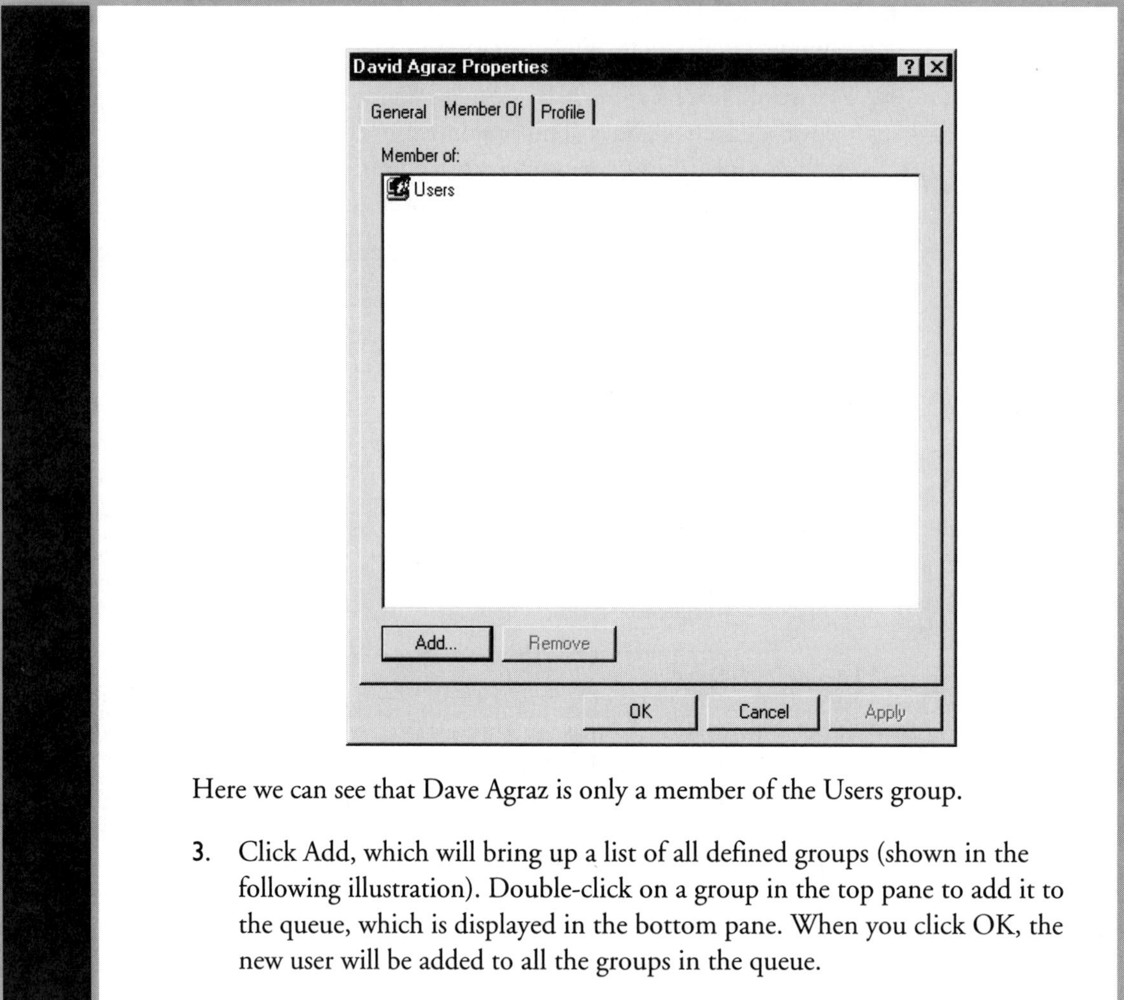

Here we can see that Dave Agraz is only a member of the Users group.

3. Click Add, which will bring up a list of all defined groups (shown in the following illustration). Double-click on a group in the top pane to add it to the queue, which is displayed in the bottom pane. When you click OK, the new user will be added to all the groups in the queue.

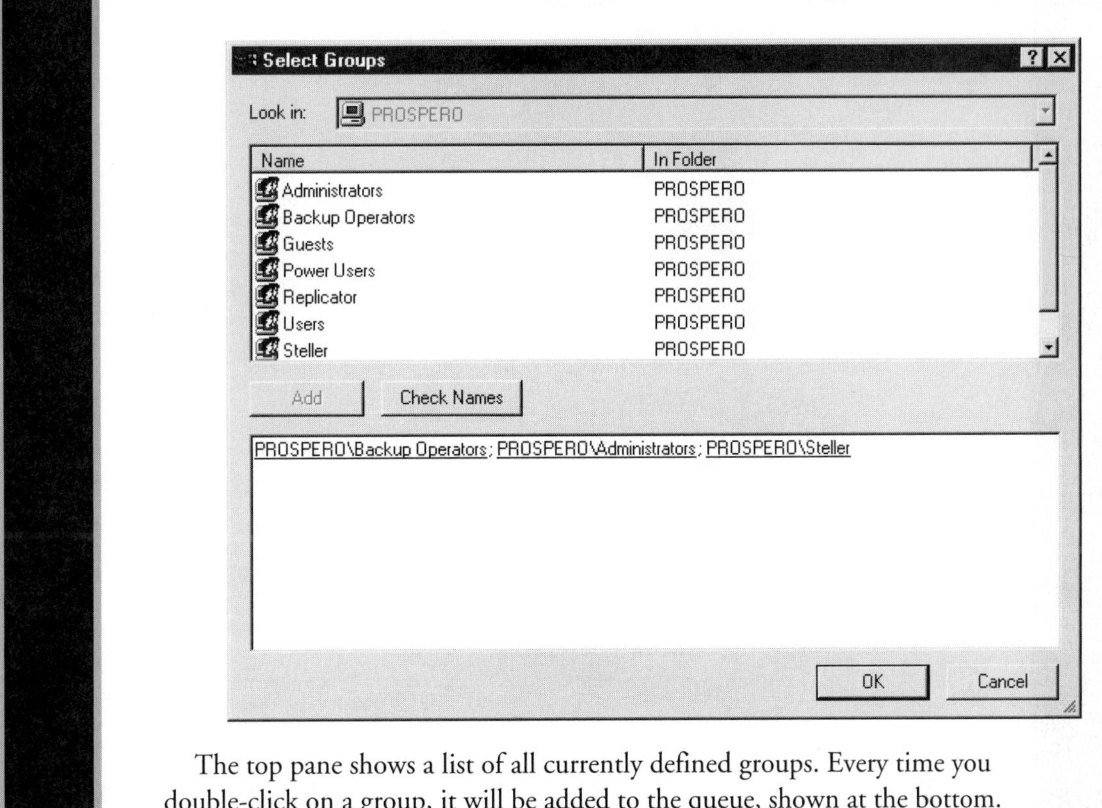

The top pane shows a list of all currently defined groups. Every time you double-click on a group, it will be added to the queue, shown at the bottom.

4. After you click on OK, you will return to the Group Membership view, where you'll see that the new user has been added to the groups that you selected, as you'll see in the following illustration.

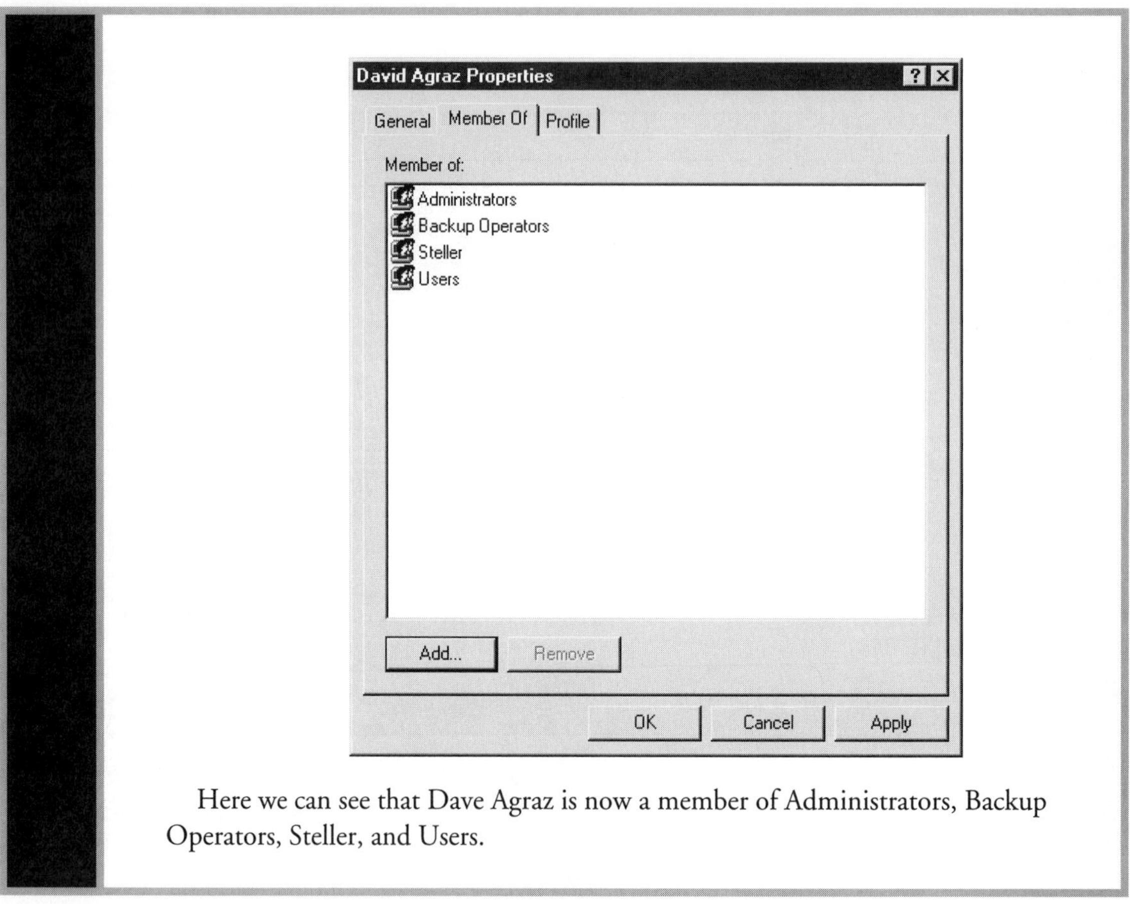

Here we can see that Dave Agraz is now a member of Administrators, Backup Operators, Steller, and Users.

EXERCISE 21-3

Removing a User from a Group

This exercise walks you through removing a user from a group.

1. From the Local Users and Groups menu, open up Users, and right-click a name. Select Properties, and click on the Member of… tab.
2. Select a group by single-left clicking the group. The group will appear highlighted, as in the following illustration. Click Remove, and the user will be removed from that group.

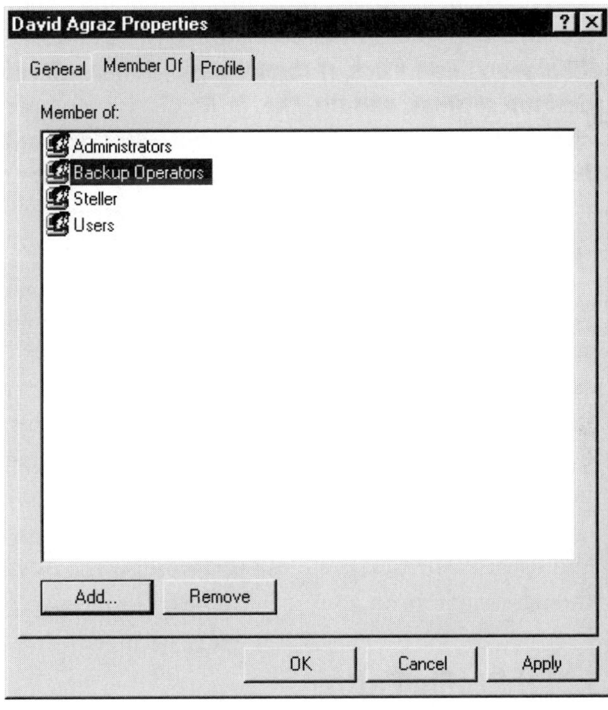

You can see that we've decided that it's unnecessary for Dave Agraz to be part of the Backup Operators Group. We've highlighted Backup Operators; we just need to click Remove.

Alternately, from the Users and Groups menu, you can open up Groups, and double-click a group. This will give you a list of members. You can highlight a member and click Remove.

exam Watch

Windows 2000 refers to an account via a security identification number (SID). This SID is connected to the user profile, the permissions, etc. The important thing to remember is that the username of an account is merely a property of that account; in other words, the "real name" of an account for Windows 2000 is the SID. That means you can change the username of the account and Windows 2000 won't lose track of things; the account will retain all group memberships, desktop settings, and the like. In fact, it is recommended that you immediately change the username on the Administrator account; that will make it much harder for unwanted visitors to gain Administrator access to your system.

Advanced User Profile Configuration

There are several very powerful account properties for user profile configuration. To access these tools, open a user's Properties, and click the Profile tab. From here, you can modify the profile path, set a logon script, or set a home folder.

All of the manipulations we'll be looking at in this Advanced User Profile Configuration section are not accessible from a Properties window called from the initial Users and Passwords screen. For any of the following tasks, you have to call up Users and Passwords, select the Advanced tab, click Advanced, right-click a user, and select Properties. We'll call this window the Advanced Properties window, even though it appears on your screen labeled Properties.

Local Profile Paths

In the Advanced Properties window, under the Profile tab, there's a fill-in box marked "Profile path:", as shown in Figure 21-4. This tells the operating system where to look for that important folder that stores everything associated with your user profile—the Favorites folder, the Cookies folder, the Desktop folder, and more. If this fill-in box is empty, then Windows defaults to:

[*system_drive*:]\Documents and Settings*Username*

FIGURE 21-4

Advanced Properties, Profile tab

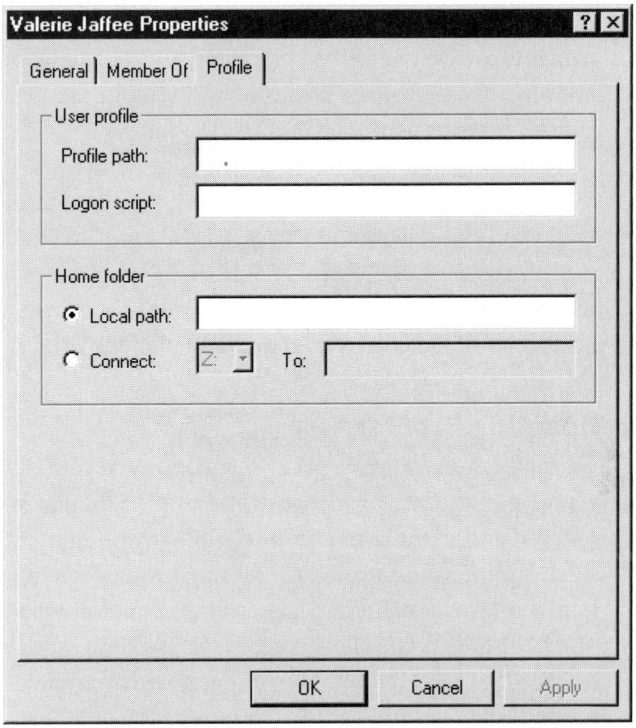

Here you can see the Profile tab in the Advanced Properties window. Remember that the Advanced Properties window is accessible by clicking Users and Passwords, Advanced tab, Advanced, and then from the Local Users and Groups right-clicking the desired user.

There are several reasons to change your profile path. You might want the profiles to be on a different disk drive, or in a different folder.

Manipulations for the profile path are very useful when a single user is running several accounts. For example, let's say that most of the time you log on as Jane Doe. But occasionally, you need to log on as Administrator, for whatever reason. By default settings, the Administrator account will have its own desktop and its own Favorites folder, rendering all the configurations that you've set under Jane Doe inaccessible.

You can fix this with the following modification. Let's say you leave the Jane Doe account set to its default profile path; that is, the "Profile path:" fill-in box is empty for the Jane Doe account. If your system drive is C:, the default profile path would be:

C:\Documents and Settings\Jane Doe.

Just open up the Administrator Properties menu, click on the Profile tab, and type this pathway into the box marked "Profile path:." Whenever you open up the Administrator account, Windows will look in the Jane Doe folder and give you the Jane Doe desktop and settings, and so forth.

This is much more effective than going in with Windows Explorer and simply copying the contents of the Jane Doe folder onto the Administrator folder. If you do that, you're simply making a *copy* of the Jane Doe desktop at a single point in time; after that point, any changes made to one account won't propagate to the other account. Whereas, when you set the profile path, you're working on *the very same* desktop, whether you log on as Jane Doe or as Administrator.

Roaming Profiles

The ability to set profile paths becomes much more valuable once you realize that you can set profiles for network addresses. This allows you to set a single profile on a server, and point your accounts on many different clients and servers to access a single profile. This creates a "roaming profile," giving you the same desktop and Explorer favorites and display settings no matter what computer you log on from.

The Profile path follows conventional naming conventions, starting with two backslashes, followed by the computer network name, backslash, folder share name, backslash, and profile name.

EXERCISE 21-4

Set Up a Roaming Profile

Follow these steps to set up a roaming profile in a workgroup.

1. Open Users and Passwords in the Control Panel.
2. Right-click on one of the users, then click on Properties.
3. Click on the Profile tab. In the Profile Path text box, type in the path to the user's local profile. Click Apply and then OK.
4. Go to each machine in the workgroup and create a user account with the same name and password as the one on your machine. Enter the same profile path you entered on your machine. Be sure that the path is entered as a UNC path.
5. Log on with the user account you created at one of the other machines in the workgroup. Your desktop should appear with the profile settings created on your machine.

6. Now, every time you create an account on a new desktop, immediately open up Users and Passwords, and open up the Properties on your account. Click the Profile tab.
7. Type into the "Profile path:" fill-in:

   \\servername\foldername\username.

FROM THE CLASSROOM

When to Use a Roaming Profile

Roaming profiles are incredibly useful for a number of reasons. Since your desktop environment data is stored at a network-accessible location, then wherever you go, you'll have the same desktop. If you consistently save your documents to a similarly network-accessible location like My Documents (if you leave the rest of the paths at their default while setting up a roaming profile, My Documents will be network accessible), you'll have your files at your fingertips, at the same place, wherever you may roam.

There are several downsides, however. This flexibility comes at the price of access speed. Every move you make on your desktop has to pass through the network. This may not be a problem for an enterprise with incredibly fast, clear internal pipes—sadly, this is rarely the case. If the local network is heavily congested, then you might get noticeable lag for doing simple things such as moving icons around on your desktop, let alone opening a file. Most of you are now familiar with working with a file over the network— remember, when you have a roaming profile, everything you do to your desktop environment is subject to the same advantages and disadvantages of using a network file. This is especially noticeable for those using slow connections. For example, those networking over a telephone line clearly shouldn't use roaming profiles.

More importantly, roaming profiles add to network traffic. If only a few administrators are set to have roaming profiles, this increased traffic is negligible. If, on the other hand, many or all employees have roaming profiles, then the network load is quite sizeable. Remember, every little change to the desktop will have to go over the network.

The lesson? Only give roaming profiles to those who genuinely need them. If a user

FROM THE CLASSROOM

spends 95% of his time at one workstation and 5% of his time roaming, and you create a roaming profile for him, remember that he'll still be adding to the network load and experiencing lag for the 95% of his time spent at his main workstation. Be judicious—each roaming profile puts a small but discernable, near-constant load on the network.

—*Chris Thi Nguyen*

Login Scripts

In the Advanced Properties window, Profiles tab, below the "Profile path:" fill-in is another fill-in window marked "Login script:." You can create a login script for a user, normally a batch file (.bat), OS/2 .cmd file, or an executable. Simply enter the pathway and login script name in the fill-in, and Windows will automatically execute this script whenever the user logs on.

Home Folder

Also in the Advanced Properties window, Profiles tab, is a small section labeled "Home folder."

By default, when you save a document for the first time, or do a Save As…, most applications will save the document to My Documents. When you set a home folder, this becomes the new default save location. This only applies to applications that make the call to Windows for the user's home folder (like all Microsoft's applications). Home folder settings will not affect applications that don't look up the user's home folder setting.

on the Job

You can usually tell which applications are making the call to the Home folder setting. Since the default Home folder setting is My Documents, most apps that default document saving to My Documents are making the call, and most apps that save to some other folder, like a folder within the app's program folder, aren't making the call.

You have two options under Home folder: entering something in the "Local path:" fill-in, or entering something in the "Connect:" fill in, as shown in Figure 21-5. Strangely enough, you can enter both local paths and network paths after the "Local path:" fill in. The "Connect:" fill-in performs an additional function: It will set the network path you provide it as the home folder, but also map a local drive onto that folder.

In Figure 21-5 we're doing two things simultaneously with one command: We're setting the folder Shared on the server Reliant as the home folder for user Jane Doe, and we're also mapping the drive T: on Jane DoeDoe's local computer to \\reliant\shared.

Setting up networked home folders can make life much easier for roaming users.

FIGURE 21-5

Home folder

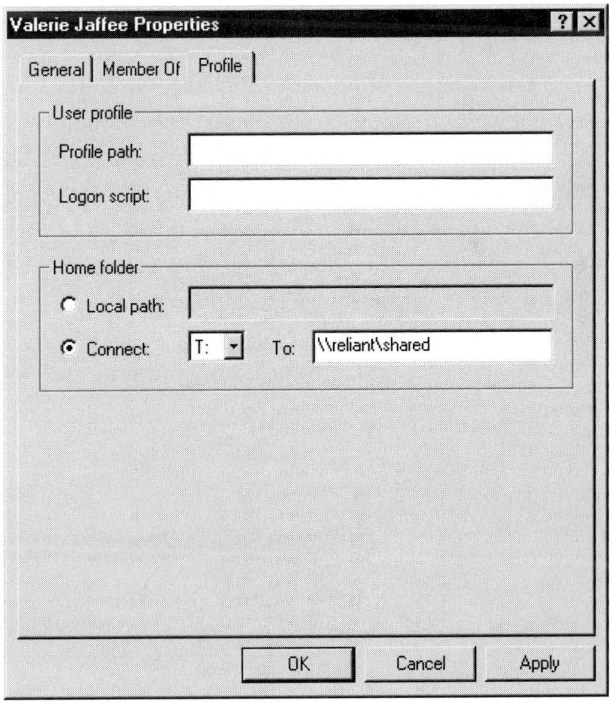

CERTIFICATION OBJECTIVE 21.02

Configuring and Troubleshooting Desktop Settings

In this section, we'll examine the meta-configuration of the desktop environment variables.

There are two forms of configuring the desktop environment. Regular configuration of the desktop involves things like rearranging the Start menu, putting icons in the Quick Start menu, and arranging icons on the desktop.

We'll assume you already know how to configure your *own* desktop environment. Instead, we'll focus on how you, as an administrator, can control how much control users have over their own desktop environments.

Getting to Group Policy

You can make all configurational changes from the Group Policy snap-in for the MMC. It's quite easy to access Group Policy from Windows 2000 Server; there are all kinds of links to Group Policy editors, especially from Active Directory. Group Policy is not as integrated into Windows 2000 Professional. All the policy-shaping power is there, but there's no icon for Group Policy in your Control Panel, or anywhere else. There are two ways to access this snap-in. First, you can run **gpedit.msc** from the Run menu, as in Figure 21-6. Or, you can create an icon for accessing the Group Policy snap-in and put it wherever you like.

Type **gpedit.msc** from the command line, and you'll bring up the Group Policy snap-in.

FIGURE 21-6

gpedit

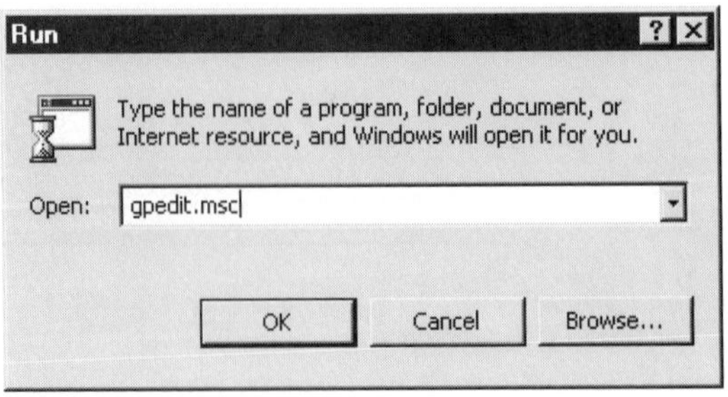

EXERCISE 21-5

Creating a Group Policy Icon

1. Select Run from the Start menu, and type **mmc /a**. You'll get the MMC Author mode, shown in the following illustration.

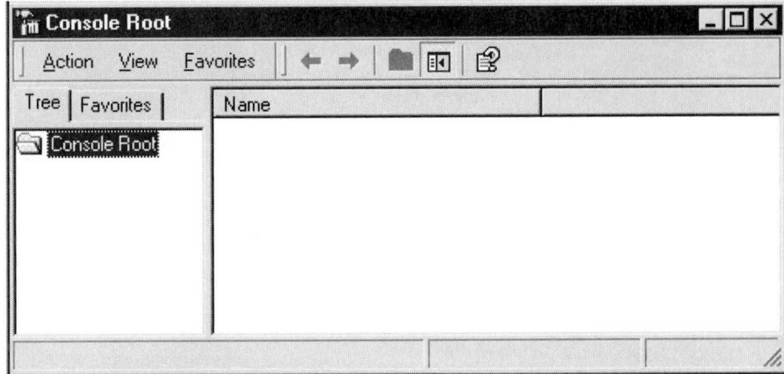

The MMC Author mode allows you to custom-create an MMC, populated with whichever snap-ins you want.

2. From here, select the Console menu and select Add/Remove Snap-in. This brings up the Add/Remove Snap-in window.
3. Click Add. This brings up a menu of snap-ins.
4. Find and double-click Group Policy. Leave the Group Policy Object set to Local Computer, and click Finish. Close the Add/Remove Snap-in window.
5. The Add/Remove Snap-in window should show Local Computer Policy, as in the following illustration, in the queue. Click OK and Windows will add everything in the queue to the snap-in.

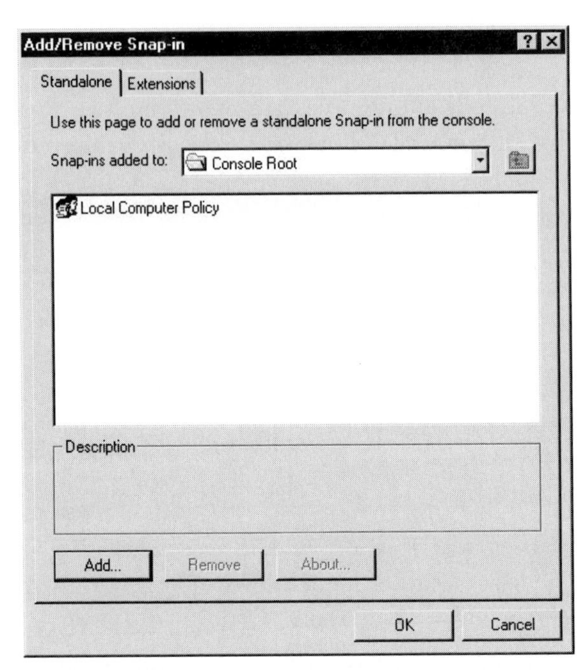

You can see in the following illustration that we've queued the Local Computer Policy snap-in for addition to the current MMC.

6. You'll see the newly configured MMC, with the Local Computer Policy snap-in added, as in the following illustration.

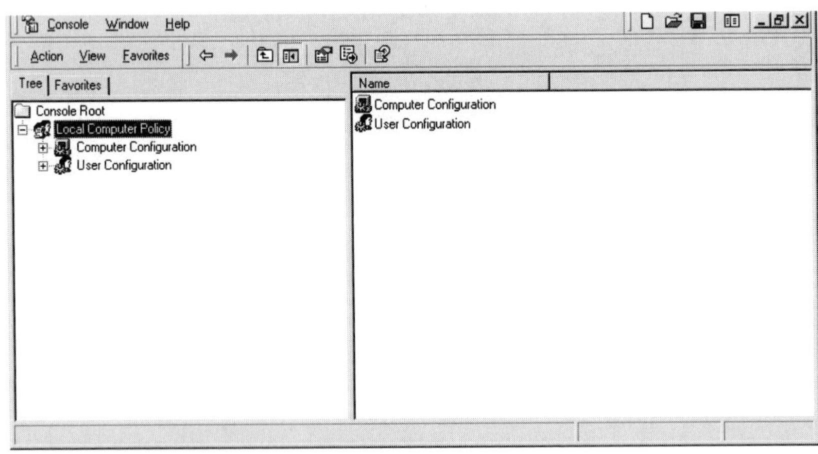

We've created an MMC with the Local Computer Policy. From here, you can access the Group Policy for your local computer.

Select the Console menu and select Save As. Choose a name and a location, and Windows 2000 will put the newly created MMC there.

Once you have access to the Local Computer Policy snap-in, either through a custom-created MMC or through the command-line call, you need to find the relevant templates.

Expand Local Computer Policy from the MMC. Expand User Configuration, and expand Administrative Templates. You'll see all the relevant sections in front of you, as in Figure 21-7.

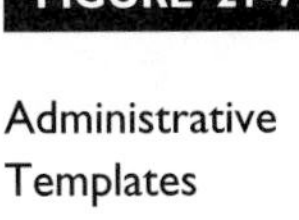

Group Policy is the general term for all policy setting. Local Computer Policy is the name for the console tree that controls Group Policy for the local computer; another way of referring to the Local Computer Policy snap-in is as the local Group Policy snap-in.

From your local Group Policy snap-in, you'll be able to access various attributes for the desktop environment.

FIGURE 21-7

Administrative Templates

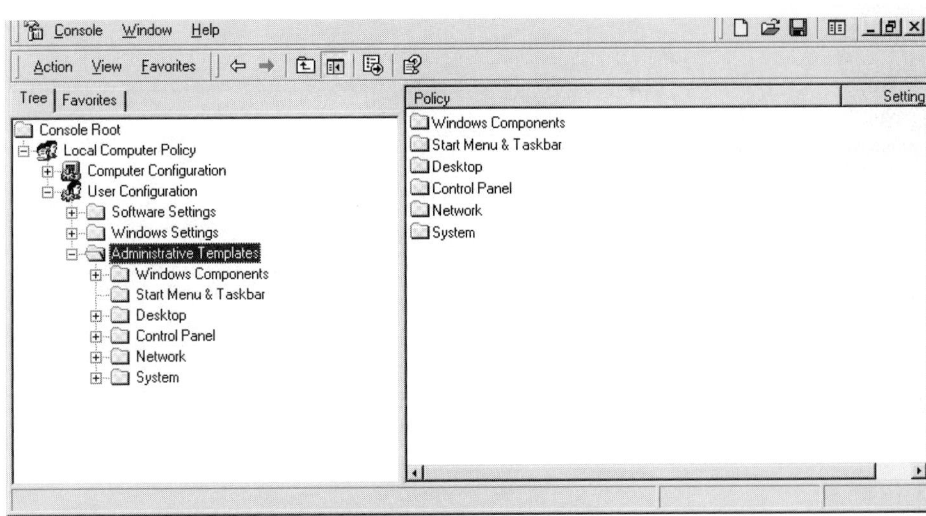

Setting Policy

From the Administrative Templates menu in the local Group Policy snap-in, click on Desktop. In the right pane, you'll see a long list of policies. By default, all these policies are turned off, as in Figure 21-8.

Once you select Desktop from Administrative Templates, you will see a variety of policies that you can configure in the right-hand pane.

By double-clicking on a policy, you'll bring up that policy's Properties window, as shown in Figure 21-9. The Policy tab lets you enable or disable a policy. Here you can set the policy to Not Configured, Enable, or Disable. The large empty pane in the middle of the Policy window is for configuration information. Since most policies are binary—you either can or can't do something—the configuration pane is empty. You only turn the policy on or off. Certain policies will ask you to set a number or a set of files; relevant buttons and directions will be contained in the configuration pane.

Here you can see the "Run only allowed Windows applications" Properties box, from Local Computer Policy | User Configuration | Administrative Templates |

FIGURE 21-8

Desktop Administrative Template

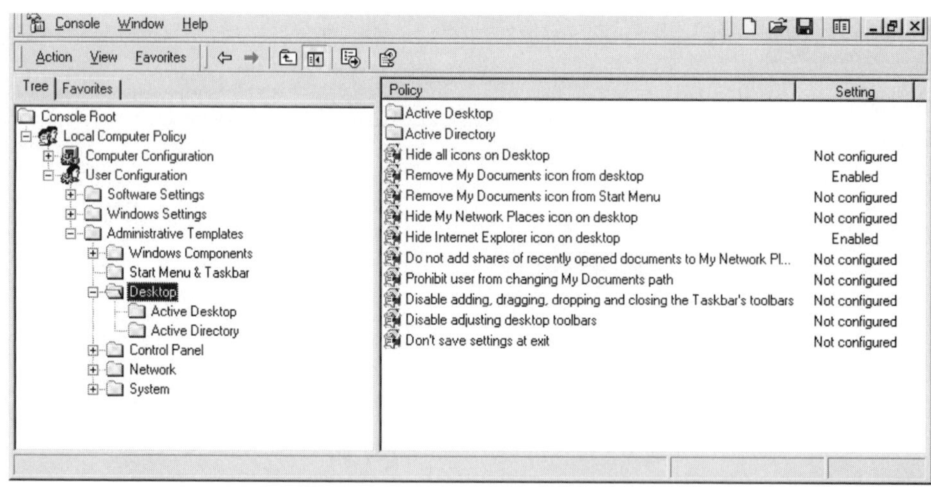

System. All Policy boxes look the same—Enabled, Disabled, and Not Configured boxes at the top, and a middle section that shows whatever particular configuration information is necessary for the policy in question.

The Explain tab in a policy's Properties window contains a description of what the policy does, as in Figure 21-10.

Here you can see the "Run only allowed Windows application" Properties, Explain tab box. This contains Microsoft's summary of this policy's effects.

FIGURE 21-9

Policy Properties

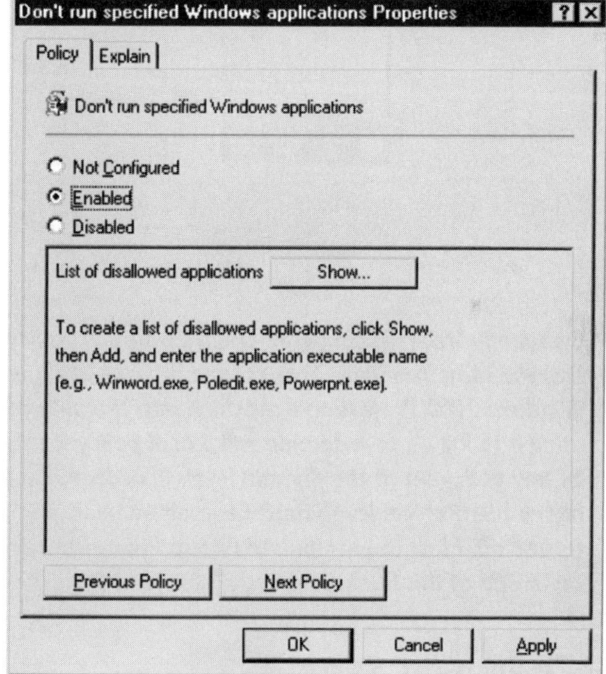

FIGURE 21-10

Policy Properties, Explain tab

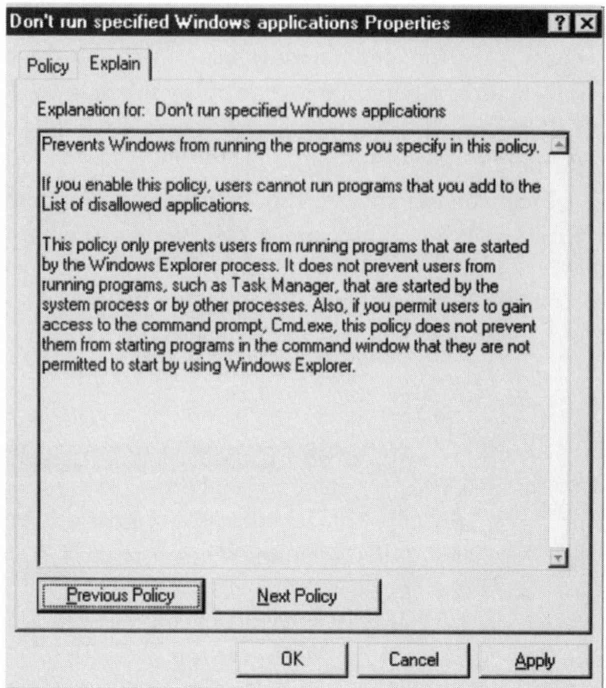

Don't run specified Windows applications Properties

Policy | Explain

Explanation for: Don't run specified Windows applications

Prevents Windows from running the programs you specify in this policy.

If you enable this policy, users cannot run programs that you add to the List of disallowed applications.

This policy only prevents users from running programs that are started by the Windows Explorer process. It does not prevent users from running programs, such as Task Manager, that are started by the system process or by other processes. Also, if you permit users to gain access to the command prompt, Cmd.exe, this policy does not prevent them from starting programs in the command window that they are not permitted to start by using Windows Explorer.

Previous Policy | Next Policy

OK | Cancel | Apply

Everybody trying to configure Local Computer Policy for a Professional machine runs into the same problem. They set the policy—and then nothing happens. Plugging a Windows 2000 Professional machine into the network will not cause the problem; using it to log on to a domain will. Local policy is the weakest policy; it is overridden by any policy set at the domain level. In order to set local policy, group policy at all higher hierarchical levels must be in agreement, not set to anything in particular, or turned off. How to manipulate Group Policy in Active Directory, of course, is beyond the scope of this book, and, luckily for you, of this test.

Desktop Environment Settings

There are many policies; we'll run through some important ones, but you should familiarize yourself with the full list.

Everything we're going to be doing to manipulate the desktop environment will be contained in Local Computer Policy | User Configuration | Administrative Templates in your Local Computer Policy MMC snap-in. The two main subfolders of Administrative Templates are the Start Menu & Taskbar folder, which contains policies governing the Start menu and the taskbar; and the Desktop folder, which contains all the policies for everything else on the desktop.

exam Watch

Remember, these are policy changes that apply across the board. If a user wants to kill personalized menus, he can do it from Control Panel, and it will only apply to his own profile. Use the policy settings described in the following sections when you want your changes to apply to anybody who will ever use the computer in question.

Start Menu & Taskbar Settings

Here are some of the more important policies that you can access from Local Computer Policy | User Configuration | Administrative Templates | Start Menu & Taskbar, as shown in Figure 21-11.

In the Local Computer Policy subfolder, you can manipulate policies regarding the Start menu and the taskbar.

- **Remove user's folders from Start Menu** The Start menu is divided into a user-specific section at the top, and the main section at the bottom. This policy, when activated, hides all folders (not files) in the top, user-specific section. This is useful when redirects are set in the system that replicate

FIGURE 21-11

Start Menu & Taskbar

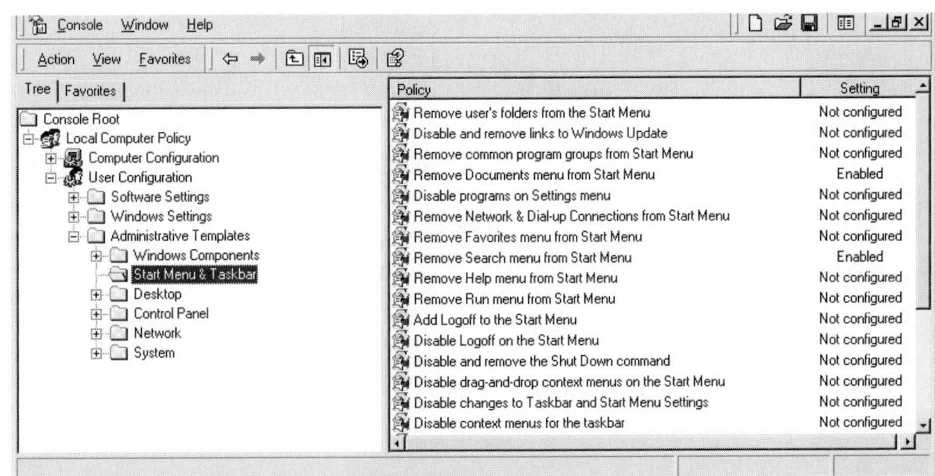

user-specific folders in the main section. This policy prevents the same folders from appearing twice.

- **Disable programs on Settings menu** This kills the programs in the Settings submenu of the Start menu. This includes Control Panel, Network & Dial up Connections, and Printers. Note that this does not affect the Taskbar & Start Menu Properties item from Settings, which has its own policy.

exam Watch

All the "disable something from the menu" items and the "remove icons from the desktop" policy items don't actually make it impossible for the user to access programs. They still start programs in alternate ways. For example, if you remove the My Documents icon from the desktop, users can still get to their My Documents by navigating Windows Explorer to the correct pathway. If you remove Networks and Dial-up Access from the Settings submenu, users can still right-click My Network and Dial-up Properties. And, of course, if users know how, they can run applications through the command-line interface.

- **Remove X from Start Menu** X can be Networks & Dial-up Connections, or the Favorites menu, or the Search menu, or the Help menu, or the Run menu. While it's hard to imagine why you'd want to disable Search or Help or Favorites (perhaps if you were setting up a kiosk for public use, where you wanted users to be able to run Internet Explorer but nothing else), disabling Run and Networks can be quite useful in securing and idiot-proofing a workstation.
- **Add Logoff to the Start Menu** This policy adds the item Logoff *username* to the Start menu, which makes life a little bit easier for users sharing computers. (It makes logging off slightly faster—the traditional process is to select Shut Down from the Start menu, and select Logoff from the pull-down.)
- **Disable and remove the Shut Down command** This policy removes Microsoft's shut-down command. It is useful if you need to use a different tool to shut down your computer, and want to prevent users from triggering the Microsoft shutdown.
- **Disable changes to Taskbar and Start Menu settings** This policy prevents users from accessing the Properties window for the Taskbar and Start Menu, either through the Settings submenu or by right-clicking the taskbar. It is useful for securing and/or idiot-proofing a computer.

Policies like "Disable changes to Taskbar and Start Menu Settings" are especially useful for computers like kiosks, which might have many people logging on under several different accounts, like different Guest accounts. These sorts of policies will keep mischief-makers from wreaking havoc with the settings.

- **Do not keep a history of recently opened documents** This policy kills the functionality of the Documents submenu in the Start menu which, by default, displays a list of all recently modified documents.
- **Disable personalized menus** This policy stops Windows from personalizing menus. When this policy is turned off, Windows will only display frequently called functions on its pull-down menus; the user must hit the expand button at the bottom of each pull-down to show every item.

Desktop Settings

In the Local Computer Policy | User Configuration | Administrative Templates | Desktop subfolder, you'll find many useful policies, as shown in Figure 21-12. Desktop has two subfolders: Active Directory and Active Desktop.

In the Desktop folder, you'll find many policies that allow you to fix or unfix elements of the desktop environment for all users.

FIGURE 21-12

Desktop policies

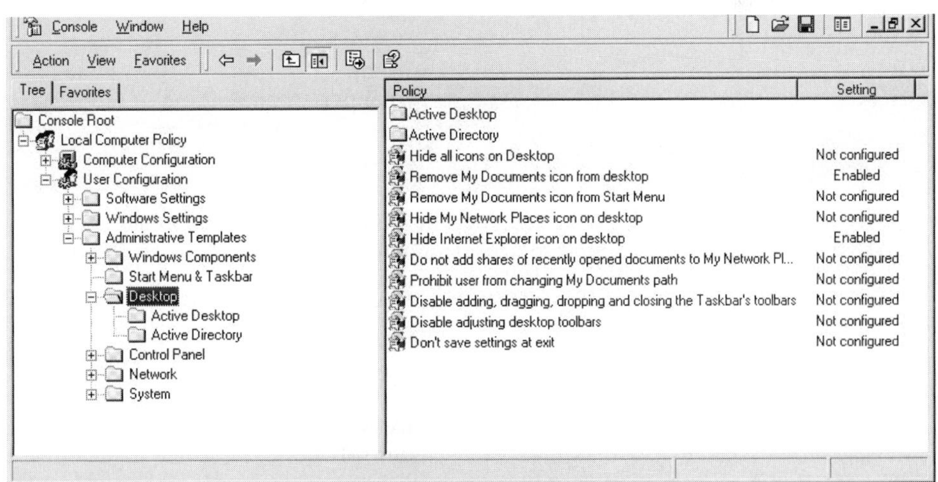

- **Hide all icons on Desktop** This policy kills everything—automatic shortcuts, user-defined shortcuts, documents. All of it. The user can still access things through Run, or the Start menu, or Windows Explorer.
- **Prohibit user from changing My Documents path** With this policy disabled, the user can change the pathway by right-clicking My Documents. This prevents the user from doing so, which is quite useful if you've set up multiple users to save to the same place, for cooperative purposes.
- **Disable adding, dragging, dropping, and closing the Taskbar's toolbars** This policy prevents the user from altering the presence or position of toolbars. The user may not add, dock, move, or close toolbars.
- **Disable adjusting desktop toolbars** This policy prevents the user from changing the length of adjustable toolbars.
- **Don't save settings on exit** When this policy is turned on, things such as which windows are open, and what size and position they're in, are not saved on shutdown or log off. "Settings" is not a super-general term here; even with this policy on, Windows will still remember things like movements of documents on to or off of the desktop.

There are also a bunch of options in the Active Desktop subfolder inside the Desktop folder. These are all pretty intuitive—you can enable, disable, or restrict Active Desktop. Let's run through a few policy scenarios.

SCENARIO & SOLUTION	
You are setting up a kiosk computer. You want the kiosk to look the same for everybody. How would you go about doing this?	Turn on all the "disable" changes and configurations policies.
You want to disallow changes to the toolbars on a computer. What do you need to do?	Turn on the policies *Disable dragging, dropping, and closing the Taskbar's toolbars* and *Disable adjusting desktop toolbars.*
You are setting up a kiosk computer. You want to force everybody who logs on as a Guest to have the same appearance, but allow others to log on with their roaming profiles and get their own configured desktop. What do you need to do to set this up?	Don't touch Local Computer Policy, User Configurations. These make universal changes. Make all your restrictions on the Guest profile.

CERTIFICATION OBJECTIVE 21.03

Configuring and Troubleshooting Accessibility Services

Windows 2000 Professional includes a bunch of accessibility options, designed for variously impaired users. A few of these features—mostly mobility/keyboard type accessibility services—are also useful for any user, in certain situations.

Most of the functionality is accessible from the Accessibility Options window, as shown in Figure 21-13, accessible through Control Panel.

Here you can see the Accessibility Options window, accessed from Control Panel, on the Keyboard tab. Virtually all accessibility options can be accessed through this window, except for the ones that are very particular applications—Magnifier, Narrator, and the On-Screen Keyboard.

Keyboard Options

You have a few simple options that can make a keyboard much easier to navigate. These are accessible through Accessibility Options, Keyboard tab.

- **StickyKeys** When turned on, StickyKeys makes the SHIFT, TAB, ALT, and CTRL keys act like toggle switches, like the CAPS LOCK key does. Instead of holding SHIFT down and pressing the "1" key to get the exclamation point, for example, you tap SHIFT to toggle SHIFT on, press the "1" key, and then tap SHIFT to toggle SHIFT off. StickyKeys is very useful for mobility impaired users or users lacking the use of some or many fingers. StickyKeys can also be quite useful for every user when using certain applications that demand many ALT or CTRL keys in rapid succession. StickyKeys can be set to turn off as soon as two keys are pressed simultaneously.
- **FilterKeys** When turned on, FilterKeys can filter out certain keystrokes. For those with shaky hands, for example, FilterKeys can filter out very rapidly pressed keystrokes, typical of accidentally double-pressing a key or accidentally pressing two keys at once. This is useful if you find your document full of things like "rthis iss the qway to ggo." FilterKeys is highly customizable.

- **ToggleKeys** When turned on, ToggleKeys will sound out notes whenever SHIFT, CTRL, ALT, or TAB is pressed. This is useful if you find yourself accidentally pressing one of these keys.

Also, under the General tab, you can find the following:

- **SerialKeys** When turned on, SerialKeys will let you use some alternative input device for keyboard input.

FIGURE 21-13

Accessibility Options

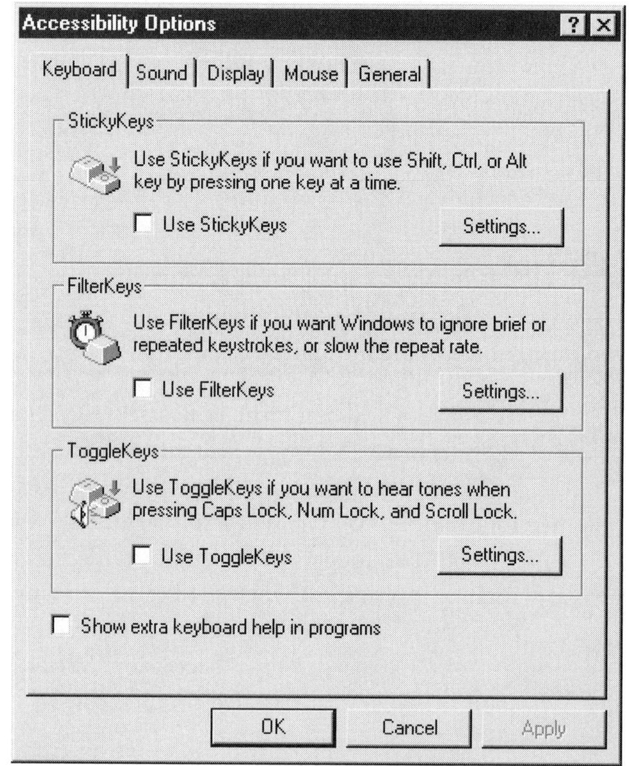

EXERCISE 21-6

Turning on StickyKeys

The following exercise demonstrates how to turn on StickyKeys.

1. Open Control Panel | Accessibility Options.
2. Check the "Use StickyKeys" box.
3. To configure StickyKeys, click Settings next to the "Use StickyKeys" box. This opens the StickyKeys Settings window, shown in the following illustration.

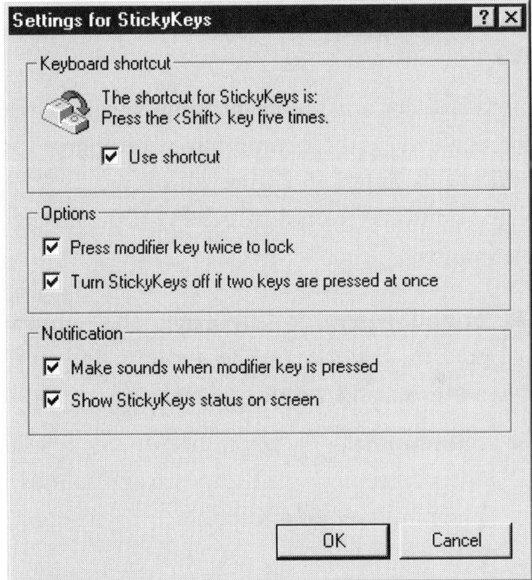

Every accessibility option has a different set of settings options. Here you have the options of activating the shortcut, automatically turning StickyKeys off when two keys are depressed simultaneously, and having a sound notification and an onscreen notification when StickyKeys turns on.

4. Check the "Use shortcut" box. This will allow you to turn on StickyKeys by pressing SHIFT five times.
5. Check the "Turn StickyKeys off when two keys are depressed simultaneously," which will automatically turn StickyKeys off when you don't need it.
6. Check both boxes under Notification. This will make Windows issue a sound when StickyKeys turns on, and leave an onscreen notice when StickyKeys is on.

Sound Options

Some useful options for the hearing-impaired, or for those who don't have or want sound enabled on their computer are available through Accessibility Options | Sound tab, as shown in Figure 21-14.

The Sound tab from Accessibility Options gives you access to SoundSentry and ShowSounds.

- **SoundSentry** When turned on, SoundSentry substitutes visual displays for sounds. SoundSentry lets you pick from various substitutes, like pop-up windows and words flashed in the caption bar.
- **ShowSounds** When turned on, ShowSounds tells caption-enabled programs to enter captioning mode. Speech and sounds will be captioned in whatever way the program is set up to caption.

Display Options

One useful option for the vision-impaired, or for those whose eyes get tired toward the end of the day, is changing the display. This is available through Accessibility Options | Display tab.

- **HighContrast** HighContrast makes things easier to see and read. Inside the HighContrast Settings box, accessible by clicking Settings, you can choose your HighContrast style. Simple versions include White on Black or Black

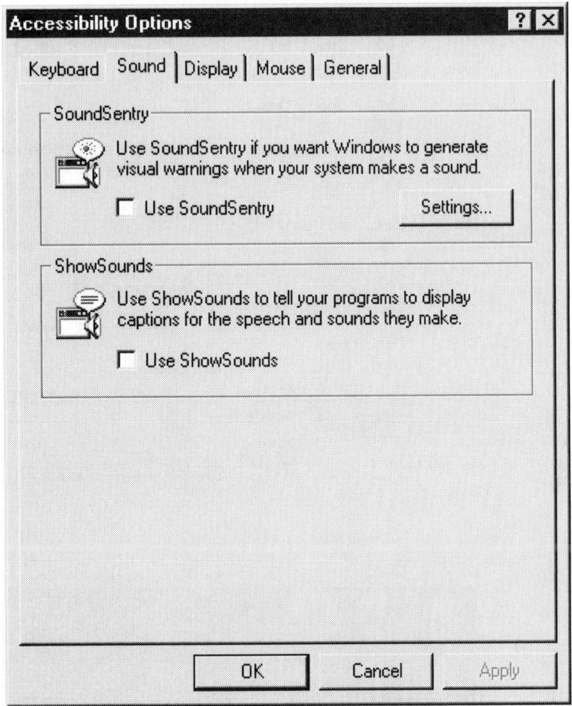

FIGURE 21-14 Accessibility Sound options

on White, each of which kills all the background color and makes fonts and icons much easier to see. Inside the Custom pull-down, you can choose lots of particular versions, like very large Black on White, as shown in Figure 21-15, or a simple high-contrast White on Black, as shown in Figure 21-16.

Another approach to allowing access to Windows for the vision-impaired is to use the Magnifier and Narrator utilities. To activate either Magnifier or Narrator, go to Start Menu | Programs | Accessories | Accessibility, and then choose the utility.

- **Magnifier** Magnifier opens a window that acts as a magnifying glass, magnifying whatever is around the mouse pointer, as shown in Figure 21-17. You can control the level of magnification. You can see that Magnifier pops a window onto the desktop, magnifying whatever is under the cursor.
- **Narrator** Narrator uses a speech synthesizer to turn whatever you type and whatever appears in the active window into speech.

FIGURE 21-15

One HighContrast option

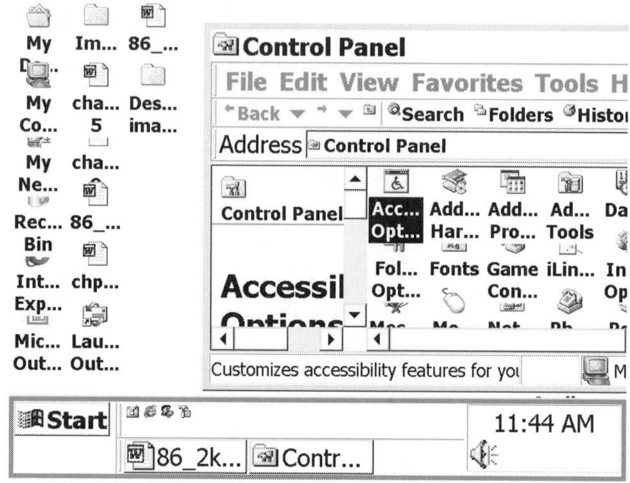

FIGURE 21-16

Another HighContrast option

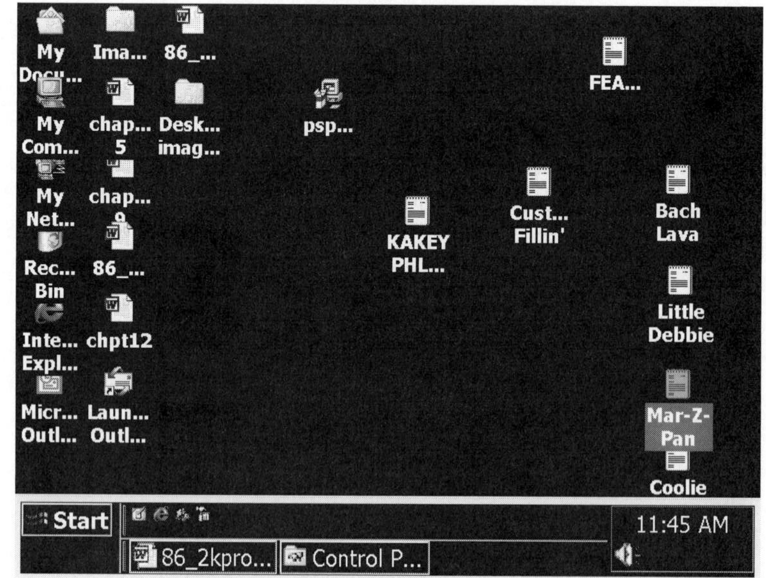

FIGURE 21-17

Magnifier

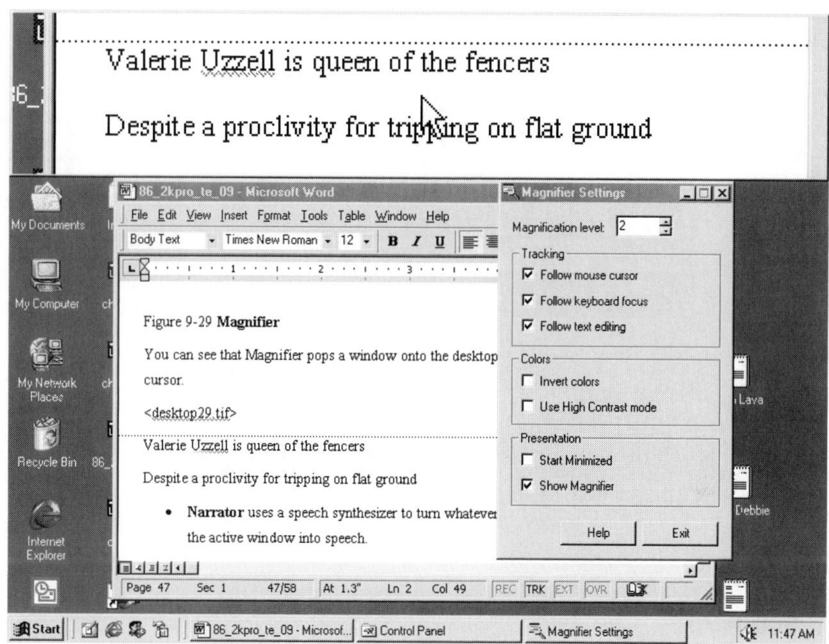

Mouse Options

There is one Mouse option, available through Accessibility Options | Mouse tab:

- **MouseKeys** MouseKeys allows you to substitute keyboard inputs for mouse handling. This is very useful for those able to type, but unable to grasp a mouse. Normally, MouseKeys allows you to use the numeric keypad to handle the mouse pointer, switching between traditional input and mouse-substitute input by depressing NUM LOCK.

On-Screen Keyboard

For those who are able to handle a mouse, but find it difficult or are unable to use a keyboard, Microsoft offers the On-Screen Keyboard, shown in Figure 21-18. This

FIGURE 21-18 On-Screen Keyboard

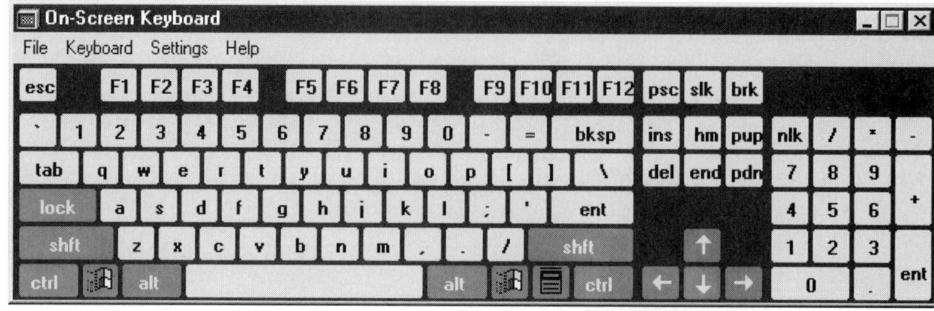

puts a graphic keyboard on your screen; you type by clicking buttons with your mouse pointer.

Turn on the On-Screen Keyboard from Start Menu | Programs | Accessories | Accessibility | On-Screen Keyboard.

Now that we've seen the accessibility options, we'll run some scenarios.

SCENARIO & SOLUTION

A user has shaking hands, and has trouble typing. He has trouble holding down keys, and accidentally hits keys repeatedly. How can you adjust his settings to accommodate for this condition?	Turn on FilterKeys, ToggleKeys, and StickyKeys. StickyKeys will relieve the user of having to hold down two keys at once, ToggleKeys will tell the user when he or she has accidentally pressed a critical key, and FilterKeys will filter out many accidentally pressed keys.
A user has trouble seeing words on the screen. What can you do to make it easier for him or her to read?	Play with different display settings. Perhaps changing to a HighContrast mode, especially a large HighContrast mode, will do. Perhaps the user will like using Magnifier. If he or she still cannot see, try using Narrator, which will perform text-to-speech translation.
A user is deaf, and cannot hear noises or speech. What function can you turn on to help the user?	Turn on SoundSentry and ShowSound, which will give visual cues instead of sounds, and trigger captioning in captioning-enabled programs.

CERTIFICATION SUMMARY

In this chapter, you learned how to configure the desktop environment. Windows 2000 Professional uses user profiles to allow different users to maintain their own distinct desktops on a single physical system. Each profile exists as a folder, by default at X:\Documents and Settings*username*. You can allow different accounts to access this profile, through manipulations of the Profile path entry, and allow one roaming account, through setting network paths in the Profile path entry.

We also covered basic Group Policy functionality. There are two ways to access the Group Policy Editor—**gpedit.msc** and **mmc /a** commands from the Run line. Group Policy lets you set some policies that apply to all users accessing the desktop, and other policies applied by group. Some of these policies allow you to restrict desktop modification, gain permissions, and more. Most policies are simply Enabled or Disabled, and some require a number or other variable to be entered. Group policies set at the local level—Local Computer Policy—are the very weakest, and can be overridden by Group Policy set at any higher level (the domain level, the OU level, etc.).

Finally, you learned about various accessibility services. Certain accessibility features increase visibility, filter bad keystrokes, turn regular keys into toggle keys, sound noises, or allow you to use the keyboard to enter mouse input, or vice versa. Other accessibility features include closed captioning and visual versions of warning noises.

TWO-MINUTE DRILL

Configuring and Managing User Profiles

- ❑ You must have Administrator status to manipulate Users and Passwords.
- ❑ Users and Passwords will let you Add and Remove users, change group membership, and manipulate the user profile and home folder.
- ❑ Group membership is the key to security; what a user can or cannot do depends almost entirely on what groups he is a member of.
- ❑ The default Profile folder for *username* exists at
  - ❑ [*system_drive*]:\Documents and Settings*username*
- ❑ To create a roaming profile, set all accounts to a profile on a server.
- ❑ Roaming profiles have profile paths that point to server folders.
- ❑ You can create a login script for a user, which will run whenever the user logs on.
- ❑ Your home folder is where many applications will save to by default.

Configuring and Troubleshooting Desktop Settings

- ❑ Local Computer Policy is a snap-in to Microsoft Management Console.
- ❑ The fastest way to access Group Policy is to type **gpedit.msc** at the Run prompt.
- ❑ You can set up a Local Computer Policy icon by typing **mmc /a** at the Run prompt, and then adding the Group Policy snap-in.
- ❑ Changes made inside Local Computer Policy/User Configuration are all local-computerwide; that is, they apply to all users who sit at that computer.
- ❑ Changes made to policy don't simply change the desktop environment, but set the principles by which users can change their own environments.
- ❑ Disabling icons and Start menu items through Local Computer Policy only removes the icons; the users can still access these items through Windows Explorer or the command line.

- ❑ You have tremendous control of the desktop environment, including features like the adjustability and presence of toolbars, the presence of logoff and many other Start menu items, and much more.
- ❑ Local Computer Policy is the weakest form of policy; it is overridden by policy set at any higher level, like in Active Directory at the server level.

Configuring and Troubleshooting Accessibility Services

- ❑ StickyKeys, FilterKeys, ToggleKeys, SerialKeys, MouseKeys, and On-Screen Keyboard can be very useful for mobility-impaired users, depending on the type of impairment.
- ❑ HighContrast, Magnifier, and Narrator are very useful for vision-impaired users.
- ❑ SoundSentry and ShowSounds are very useful for hearing-impaired users.
- ❑ All accessibility settings are configurable either through the Accessibility Options pane from Control Panel, or from the Accessibility menu inside Start menu | Programs | Accessories.

MCSE

MICROSOFT CERTIFIED SYSTEMS ENGINEER

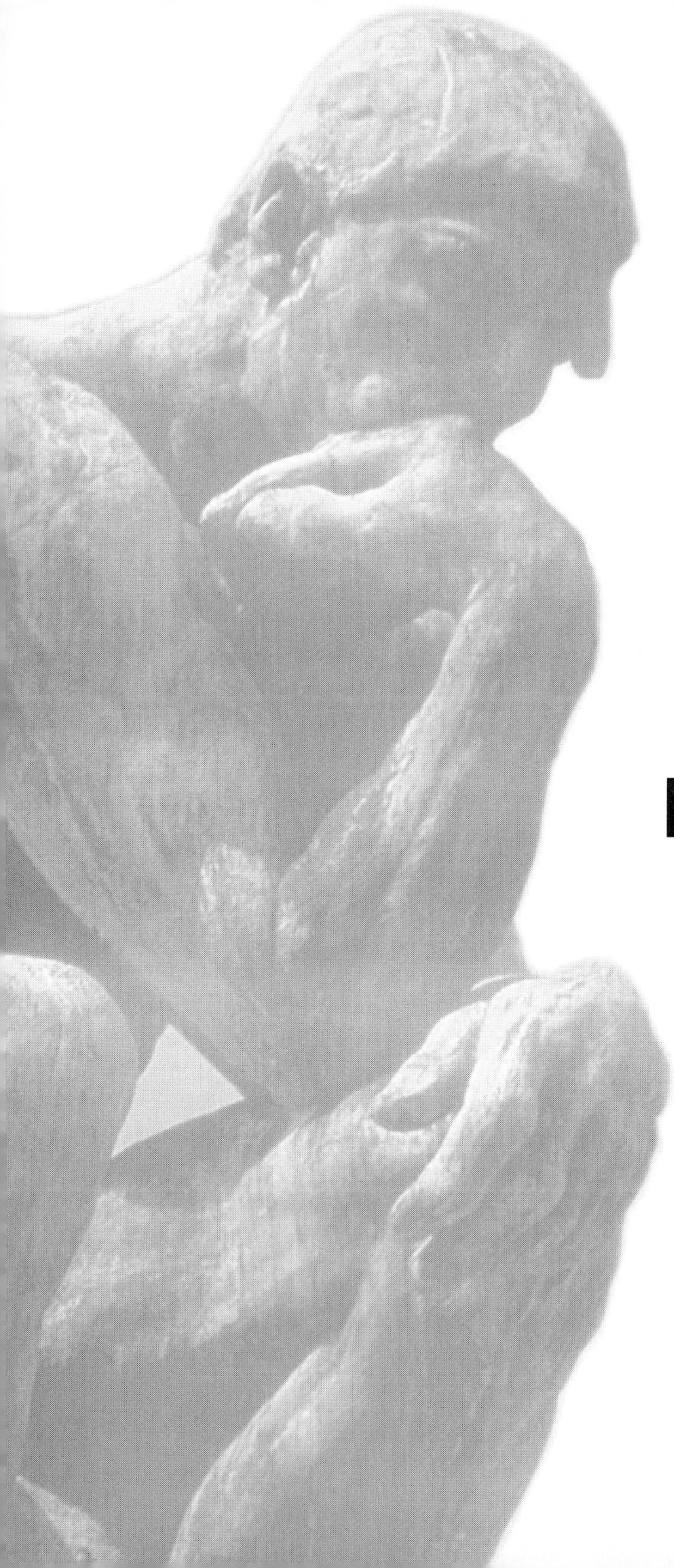

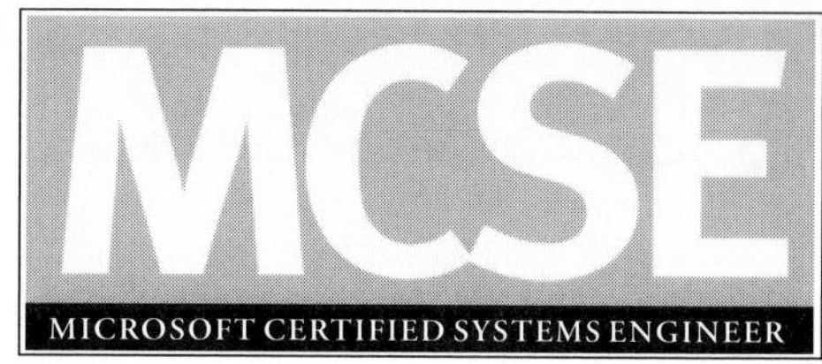

22

Optimizing Windows 2000

CERTIFICATION OBJECTIVES

22.01	Monitoring and Optimizing Usage of System Resources
22.02	Managing Processes
22.03	Optimizing Disk Performance
✓	Two-Minute Drill

Monitoring your system resources might seem like wasted effort sometimes, but it isn't. By continuously monitoring your system, you can create a baseline for it so you'll know when performance starts to degrade. Monitoring also allows you to fix problems before they devastate your system, by finding bottlenecks and fixing them before they cause significant harm. You can use System Monitor to help find bottlenecks.

In this chapter, we also talk about how to manage processes. We discuss starting and stopping processes and setting priorities. Then we see how to use the Disk Defragmenter to keep our hard disks running at optimal performance. Finally, we discuss performance logs and alerts.

CERTIFICATION OBJECTIVE 22.01

Monitoring and Optimizing Usage of System Resources

Part of keeping your Windows 2000 Server operating at peak performance is monitoring the performance of your server. In order to understand how your computer is operating, you need to establish a *baseline.* A baseline tells you how various aspects of the computer are running when the server is running at normal levels. By continuously monitoring the server, you can watch for performance degradation and solve any problems before they impact your network.

Using System Monitor

Part of administering your network includes monitoring the health of your servers. In order for your network to operate efficiently, you need to make sure your server's performance is good enough to handle the load the network places on them. By monitoring the performance of your server, you can see how the load placed on it affects your server's resources. You can monitor resource usage to see when upgrades are required. You can also create test environments to demonstrate the effects of changes to the network.

One of the tools to aid you in these monitoring activities is *System Monitor.* System Monitor replaces the Performance Monitor used in Windows NT. System Monitor allows you to collect information about your hardware's performance as well as network utilization. It also gives you the ability to view this data in many different ways. System Monitor is a snap-in to, and is installed automatically with Performance Console. *Performance Console* is a Microsoft Management Console (MMC), accessed through the Administrative Tools program group.

System Monitor can be used to measure various aspects of a computer's performance. It can be used on your own computer or other computers on the network. System Monitor can collect data for memory usage, processor utilization, network activity, and more. This data can be displayed as a graph, a histogram, or a report.

System Monitor can perform many tasks. It can collect real-time data, measuring various aspects of performance and allowing you to view this information or save it or print it for later viewing. System Monitor comprises three basic areas: the Graph area, the Legend, and the Value Bar. Figure 22-1 shows an example of System Monitor in the Performance Console. The example shows processor utilization.

FIGURE 22-1

System Monitor displaying processor utilization data

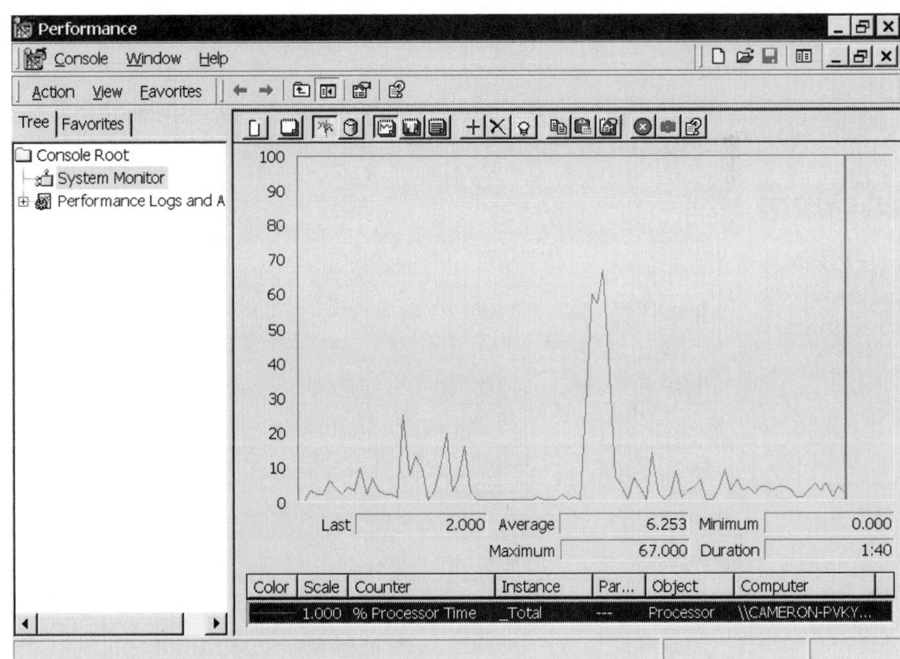

The type of data you can collect in System Monitor is extensive. There are two basic types of items on which you can collect data: objects and counters. An *object* is a component of the system, such as memory, a processor, or a hard disk. An object contains data measuring a component's tasks. As a component performs various tasks, the system collects performance data on those tasks. Generally, the object is named after the component it measures. *Counters* are the specific data of an object to be measured.

Objects can contain many different counters. Objects can also have multiple *instances*. If there are multiple objects in a computer, the objects are distinguished by instances. For example, in a computer that has multiple processors, you would use instances to differentiate between the objects for each processor. An example of a counter is the Available Bytes counter from the Memory object. See Table 22-1 for a listing of the most common objects and their functions.

The Graph Area

As mentioned earlier, the data that is collected by System Monitor can be viewed in several ways. You can view it as a chart, a histogram, or a report. By default, the Graph view is displayed when you open System Monitor. When you are creating baselines for your systems, you should create the baseline in the report format so that you can easily determine specific values.

Figure 22-1 showed an example of the graph display. When configuring a graph, you can choose settings for many attributes. Figure 22-2 shows the toolbar to

TABLE 22-1

System Monitor Objects and Their Function

Object	Function
Cache	Measure the disk cache usage.
Memory	Measure memory usage and/or performance of physical and virtual memory.
Objects	Measure miscellaneous data such as events, processes, and threads.
Paging file	Measure page file usage.
Physical disk	Measures hard disk utilization.
Process	Measure running processes.
Processor	Measure processor usage.
Server	Measure server performance.
System	Measure overall system performance.
Thread	Measure thread usage.

FIGURE 22-2

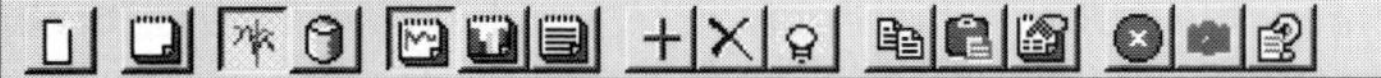

The System Monitor Graph toolbar

configure a graph. Table 22-2 contains a description of the buttons in the toolbar. The toolbar buttons are described as they appear from left to right.

The data that is collected by System Monitor can be updated automatically or on demand. To collect data on demand, stop the data collection by clicking the Freeze Display button on the toolbar; when you want to collect data, click the Update Data button on the toolbar. Each time you click the Update Data button, one sample of data is collected. The solid red vertical line in the graph shown in Figure 22-1 is called the *timer bar*. It moves across the graph as data is collected. The graph can display up to 100 samples at a time.

TABLE 22-2

System Monitor Toolbar Buttons

Button	Function
New Counter Set	Remove counters and collected data.
Clear Display	Remove all collected data.
View Current Activity	View live data.
View Log File Data	View data saved to a log file.
View Chart	View data in a chart.
View Histogram	View data in a histogram.
View Report	View data in a report.
Add	Add object counter(s).
Delete	Delete object counter(s).
Highlight	Highlight a counter.
Copy Properties	Copy counter data.
Paste Counter List	Paste counter data.
Properties	View System Monitor properties.
Freeze Display	Stop collecting data.
Update Data	Collect a sample of data.
Help	Help.

Some of the attributes that can be set for the graph include background color, font for text, and line style. You can also highlight a particular counter's data. To highlight a selected counter, either press CTRL-H or click the highlight button. When the data is highlighted, it is displayed in white.

The Value Bar

The *value bar* is positioned below the graph area. For a selected sample, it displays data such as the last sample value, the average of the counter samples, the maximum and minimum of the samples, and the duration of time the samples have been taken over. Figure 22-3 shows an example of the value bar.

The Legend

The *legend* displays information about the counters that are being measured. The legend is the set of columns at the bottom of System Monitor. The legend displays the following information:

- **Color** The color in which the counter is displayed.
- **Scale** The scale of the counter in the graph.
- **Counter** The counter being measured.
- **Instance** The instance of the object being measured.
- **Object** The object being measured.
- **Computer** The computer on which the counter is being measured.

You can select the counters in the legend. Notice in Figure 22-4 that the %Processor Time counter is selected. The value bar displays information about the selected counter. By clicking any of the columns, you can sort the list based on that column category.

FIGURE 22-3

The System Monitor value bar

Last	100.000	Average	51.871	Minimum	0.000
		Maximum	100.000	Duration	1:40

FIGURE 22-4

The System Monitor legend

Color	Scale	Counter	Instance	Par...	Object	Computer
———	1.000	% Processor Time	_Total	---	Processor	\\CAMERON-PVKY...
———	1.000	Pages/sec	---	---	Memory	\\CAMERON-PVKY...
———	0.0...	Avg. Disk Bytes/R...	_Total	---	PhysicalDisk	\\CAMERON-PVKY...
	1.000	Processes	---	---	Objects	\\CAMERON-PVKY...

Now that we have talked about System Monitor, let's do an exercise to see how we can use it.

EXERCISE 22-1

Using System Monitor

1. To start System Monitor from the Start menu, select Start | Programs | Administrative Tools | Performance. This choice brings up System Monitor in the Performance Console.
2. Now let's add some counters to measure. Click Add, or right-click the graph area and select Add Counters from the context menu.
3. The Add Counters dialog box appears. Select the "Use local computer counters" option button.
4. From the Performance object list, select Processor.
5. From the "Select counters from list" box, select %Processor Time. Your settings should look like the ones in the following illustration.

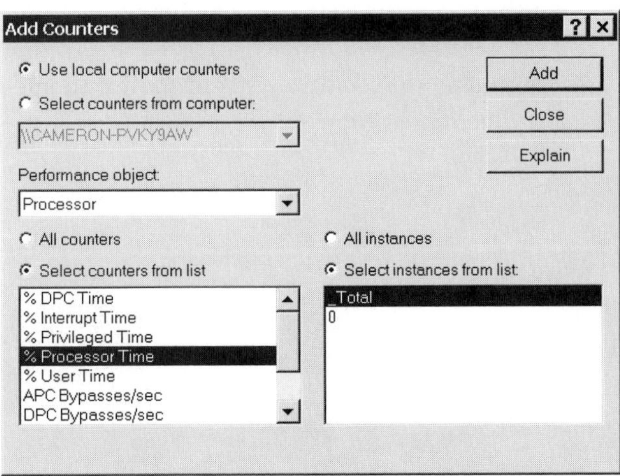

6. Click Add to add the counter.
7. Now let's add another counter. From the "Performance object" list, select Memory.
8. From the "Select counters from list" box, as shown in the following illustration, select Pages/sec and click Add. Click Close to exit the dialog box.

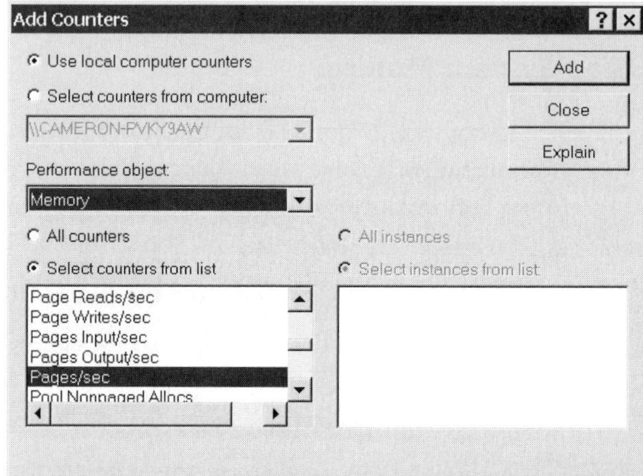

9. Notice the counters have been added to the Legend, and data is being displayed in the chart. Let's highlight the %Processor Time counter. In the Legend, select the %Processor Time counter and click the Highlight button on the toolbar. System Monitor should now show this counter highlighted in white.

10. Let's take a look at the histogram view. Click the View Histogram button. Your System Monitor should look similar to the following illustration.

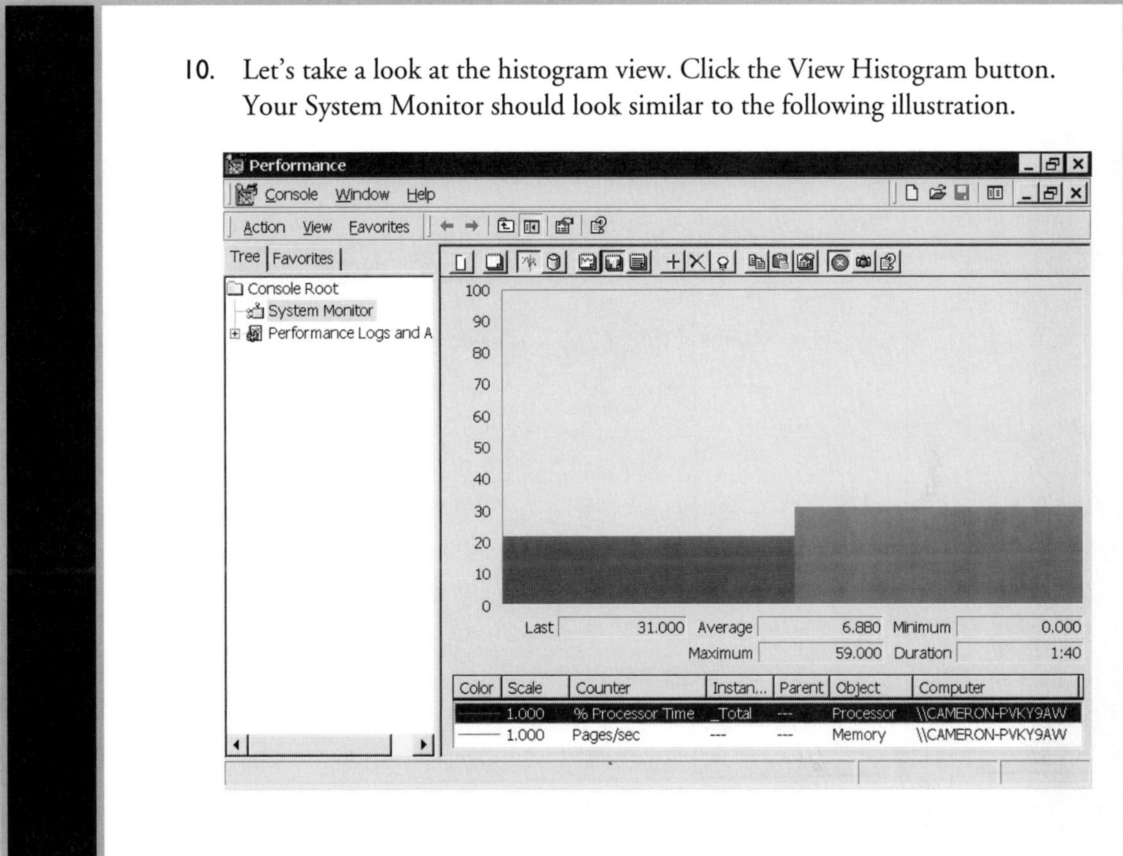

11. Now let's take a look at the report view. Click the View Report button. Your System Monitor should look similar to the following illustration.

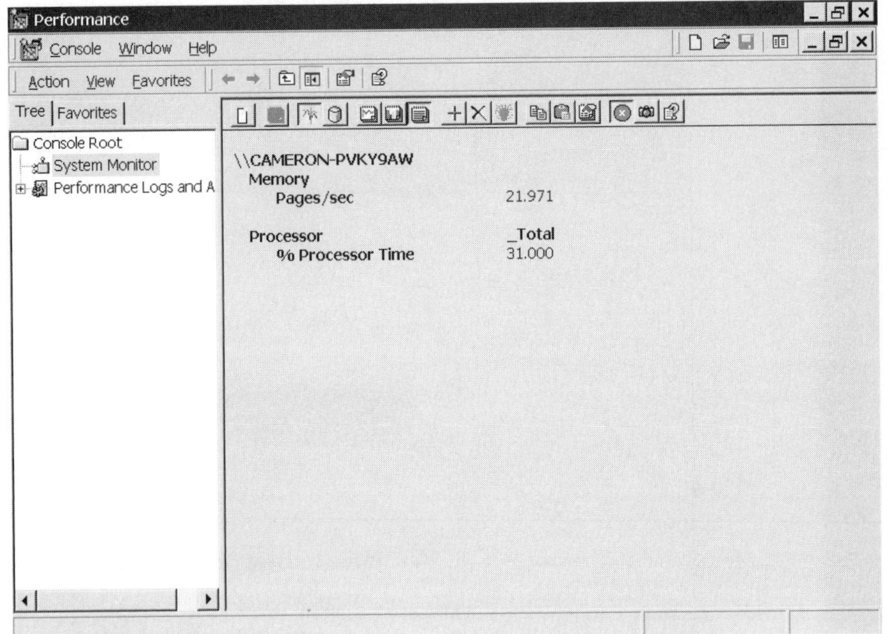

12. To close System Monitor, from the Console menu, select Exit.

Bottlenecks

Now that we have learned how to use System Monitor, what exactly do we use it for? One of the main reasons we use System Monitor is to find bottlenecks in our systems. A *bottleneck* is just what it sounds like: A bottle's neck restricts the flow from or into the bottle. A bottleneck in computer terms is a component of the system as a whole that restricts the system from operating at its peak. When a bottleneck occurs, the component that is blocking the system's functioning has a high rate of usage, and other components have a low rate of usage. In this section we discuss common computer system bottlenecks and how to find and fix them.

Identifying Bottlenecks in Processor, Memory, Disk Storage, or Network Performance

The most common causes of computer system bottlenecks are the processor, the memory, the hard disk, and the network. Let's look at how to measure for bottlenecks in these basic areas.

First, let's examine processor bottlenecks. If your applications perform large or many calculations, they can consume a great deal of processor time. If your processor cannot fulfill all these requests for processor time, it can become a bottleneck. With System Monitor, you can measure the Processor object's %Processor Time counter. When this counter reaches a sustained level of 80 percent, you need to fix the problem. This counter occasionally spikes to 100 percent, possibly when applications start or when certain operations are performed. Occasional spikes to 100 percent CPU utilization are not a cause for concern. If your processor is a bottleneck, however, you can either upgrade to a faster processor or add additional processors to the computer.

Memory issues are also prevalent bottlenecks. Arguably, memory is the most important component for system performance. Memory can be broken into two categories: physical memory and virtual memory. *Physical memory* is the actual random access memory (RAM) in the computer. When the physical memory becomes full, the operating system can also use space on the hard disk as *virtual memory*. When memory becomes full, rather than locking up the computer, the operating system stores unused data on the hard disk in a page file (in a process that is also called *paging* or *swap file*; it is known as paging because *pages* of memory are swapped at a time). Windows 2000 separates memory into 4KB pages to help prevent fragmentation. Data is swapped back and forth between the hard disk and physical memory as needed for running applications. If memory is needed that is in virtual memory, it is swapped back into physical memory.

Memory is a common cause of bottlenecks when your computer doesn't have enough memory for the applications and services that are running. When this is the case, too many pages of memory can be swapped from physical memory to the hard disk, slowing the system down. Swapping can get so frequent and cumbersome that you can hear your hard disk running constantly.

So, how do we know if memory is running low? The main counters to watch in System Monitor are the Memory object's Available Bytes and Pages/sec counters. The *Available Bytes counter* indicates the number of bytes of memory that are currently available for use by applications. When the available bytes of memory drop below 4MB (the size of the pages in which Windows 2000 stores memory), you should add more memory to the computer. The *Pages/sec counter* provides the number of pages that were either retrieved from disk or written to disk. When the Pages/sec counter reaches 20, you should look at your paging activity and consider adding more memory.

When a bottleneck occurs in memory, the most common solution is to add more memory. You can also create multiple swap files so that they are on different hard disks to increase performance. If possible, you can offload memory-intensive applications to other servers.

The hard disk can also be a bottleneck due to the many different operations it performs. For instance, when you boot your computer, the operating system is loaded from the hard disk. The operating system swaps between physical and virtual memory using the hard disk. Furthermore, applications are loaded from the hard disk, and many applications read and write data to the hard disk. Because the hard disk is such a workhorse, the rate at which the hard disk can read and write data can have a large impact on the performance of your computer.

You can use System Monitor to determine the performance of your hard disks, using the PhysicalDisk and the LogicalDisk objects. These objects measure the transfer of data to and from the hard disk. The *PhysicalDisk object* measures the transfer of data for the entire hard disk. The *LogicalDisk object* measures the transfer of data for a logical drive (e.g., C: or D:) or storage volumes. You can use the PhysicalDisk object to determine which hard disk is causing the bottleneck. Then, to narrow the cause of the bottleneck, you can use the LogicalDisk object to determine which, if any, partition is the specific cause of the bottleneck.

Enabling the disk objects can cause a drain on system performance because the counters interrupt the processor during disk operations. These objects should be enabled only when they are in use. By default, the PhysicalDisk object is enabled and the LogicalDisk object is disabled on Windows 2000 Server. You can enable and disable these objects using the DISKPERF command. The changes won't take effect until the computer is rebooted. The following is a list of the command-line switches available for DISKPERF:

- -Y Enables all the disk performance counters.
- -YD Enables the PhysicalDisk object performance counters.
- -YV Enables the LogicalDisk object performance counters.
- -N Disables all the disk performance counters.

- **-ND** Disables the PhysicalDisk object performance counters.
- **-NV** Disables the LogicalDisk object performance counters.
- **\\Computername** Allows you to set the counters for remote computers.

When measuring the performance of your hard disk, some of the commonly measured counters are %Disk Time, Current Disk Queue Length, Disk Reads/sec, and Disk Writes/sec. If the %Disk Time reaches 90 percent or higher, your hard disk may be a bottleneck. You should check the transfer rates that are specified by the hard disk's vendor to ensure that the rates are not higher than the specification. The disk queue length should not be more than the number of spindles (normally one spindle per disk) on the hard drive, plus 2. You should measure the disk queue length by the average.

If your hard disk becomes a bottleneck, there are several things you can do to alleviate the problem. You can upgrade the hard disk to a higher-speed disk or add disks on different disk controllers. You can create striped volume sets across different physical disks, which will allow multiple I/O operations to be executed simultaneously. Try to put some of the load on another server, if possible. If a program has heavy disk utilization, you can have that program use a hard disk that is not used by the operating system or other programs. See if the drives are fragmented, and defragment them as needed. You can also consider using Redundant Array of Inexpensive Disks (RAID).

exam watch

Increasing the size of the hard disk will not solve a performance bottleneck. It will help only if you are running out of disk space.

The performance of your network can be affected by your servers. To analyze your network, you should monitor the resources on the servers and overall network traffic. System Monitor also allows you to monitor network activities. When monitoring network performance of your server, you should monitor the services provided at each layer of the Open Systems Interconnection (OSI) model. OSI is a model that breaks networking tasks into layers. Each layer is responsible for a specific set of functions. Performance objects are available in System Monitor for analyzing network performance. See Table 22-3 for the performance objects at each layer of the OSI model.

If you suspect your server is a bottleneck on the network, start monitoring the objects at the lower layers first. One of the counters you should measure is the %Net Utilization of the Network Segment object. This counter shows you at what percentage your network capacity is operating. On Ethernet networks, the recommended

TABLE 22-3 Open Systems Interconnection Performance Objects for Monitoring Network Activities

OSI Layer	Performance Objects
Application, Presentation, Session	Browser, Server, Redirector, and Server Work Queues for NBT Connection.
Transport	TCP, UDP, NetBEUI for NetBIOS, and AppleTalk.
Network	Network Segment, IP, and NWLink IPX/SPX.
Data Link, Physical	Network Interface.

threshold is 30–40 percent. Once utilization reaches this range, you can start running into problems with collisions.

From the Server object, you should monitor the Bytes Total/sec counter. If the sum of this counter for all servers on the network is close to the maximum throughput of your network, you should consider segmenting your network. Network counters that are above or below normal could be caused by the servers' resources. You should also monitor a server's memory, processor(s), and hard disk(s).

You can do many things to increase network performance. For one thing, you can segment your network. For another, if you have any protocols that aren't used, you should remove the binding for the protocol or uninstall the protocol entirely. You can also place the most used protocol first in the binding list. If you have a network adapter that is not being used, remove the binding for the network adapter. If necessary, replace your network adapter with a higher-performance network adapter. For instance, if you have a 16-bit network adapter, replace it with a 32-bit network adapter.

SCENARIO & SOLUTION

Scenario	Solution
You have a server that you suspect is under-performing. What are the common resources that you should analyze?	When looking for bottlenecks on your server, monitor the processor, memory, hard disks, and network activity.
Which tools can be used to monitor your system resources?	System Monitor and Task Manager can be used to monitor your system resources.
How do you turn on your hard disk counters?	You use the DISKPERF command-line utility to enable the hard disk counters.

FROM THE CLASSROOM

Monitoring Your System for Bottlenecks

Students commonly ask, "Why bother with a baseline?" They claim that if a bottleneck occurs, it will be easy to spot. This is often true, but not always. Besides, it would be better to *prevent* the bottleneck. Creating a baseline takes some time, but the time is well worth it in the long run. You can use System Monitor to measure performance data to create the baseline against which you can compare your system's performance over time and be alerted when performance degradation occurs.

This chapter, and most classes that are taught, cannot cover everything that can be measured by System Monitor. Only the most important and common counters are discussed. The performance data that can be measured is quite extensive. You should start with these main counters to create your baseline and continue to monitor them over time. This allows you to see when performance is degrading.

At times, a bottleneck is not immediately apparent; in these cases, you need to add some counters to determine the bottleneck. To find out which ones to use, you can look in the *Windows 2000 Resource Kit* and on Microsoft TechNet for more detailed information on monitoring your system for bottlenecks.

One last thing to keep in mind is that you don't want to always measure every counter you can think of. When you are monitoring performance counters, it takes resources to measure them, and that can cause a drain on your system resources. It is best to use a main set of counters for your baseline and normal monitoring and use other counters when needed.

—Cameron Wakefield, MCSD, MCP

CERTIFICATION OBJECTIVE 22.02

Managing Processes

At times, you need to manage the processes that are running on your server. Sometimes a process stops responding, or it might not be getting enough CPU time. In this section, we talk about how to deal with these management tasks.

Setting and Configuring Priorities and Starting and Stopping Processes

As in Windows NT, Windows 2000 has a Task Manager. Task Manager can be used for a variety of tasks. It allows you to monitor applications, processes, and performance statistics. Task Manager can be started by pressing CTRL+ALT+DEL and selecting Task Manager, or pressing CTRL+SHIFT+ESC. You can also start Task Manager by right-clicking on the taskbar and selecting it from the context menu.

Task Manager has three tabs: Applications, Processes, and Performance, as shown in Figure 22-5. By default, the Task Manager Performance tab displays CPU and memory usage. It also displays the number of handles, threads, and processes that are running, as well as total KB for physical, kernel, and committed memory.

The Applications tab displays all the applications that are running. From this tab you can end an application, switch to an application, or start an application.

The Processes tab displays all the processes, services, and drivers that are running, as well as the process name, process ID (PID), percentage of CPU time being used, and

FIGURE 22-5

Windows Task Manager's Applications, Processes, and Performance tabs

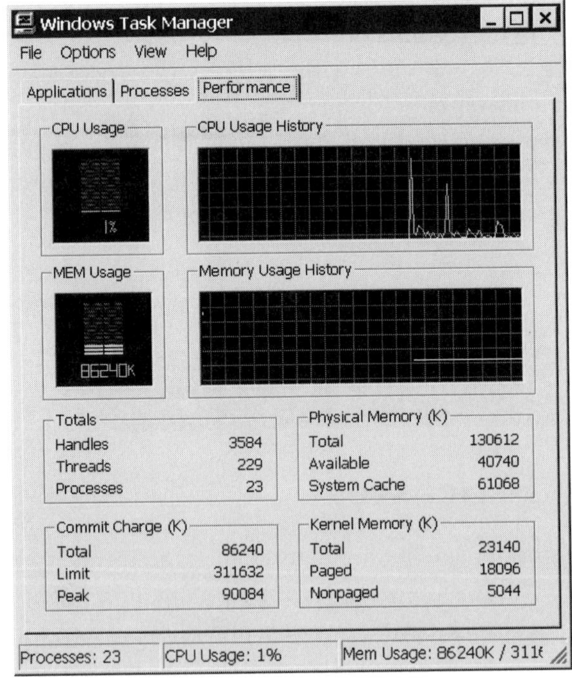

elapsed time using the CPU and memory. You can also select other columns to be displayed. See Figure 22-6 for the columns that can be displayed in the Processes tab.

From Task Manager, you can stop applications and processes from running using the Applications tab's End Task button. To stop an application, select the application you want to stop and click End Task.

You can also stop individual processes from running from the Processes tab. To stop a process, select the process and click the End Process button, or right-click the process and select End Process.

Yet another option, useful for applications that comprise multiple processes, is called *End Process Tree;* it stops all processes related to the process you want to stop. Furthermore, if you have multiple processors on your computer, you can assign a process to a processor or processors using the SET AFFINITY command, which is available only on multiple-processor computers. You should be careful using this command, because it limits the process to running only on those processors.

Exercise 22-2 gives you a chance to practice using Task Manager.

on the job

From Task Manager, you cannot stop processes that are critical to running Windows 2000.

FIGURE 22-6

The Task Manager Processes tab column options

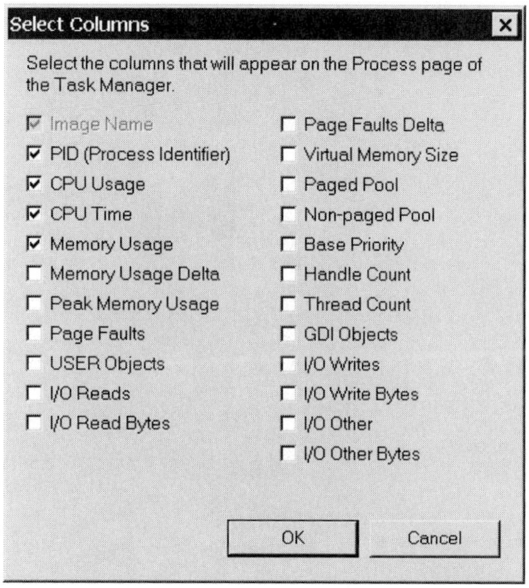

EXERCISE 22-2

Using Task Manager to Manage Processes

1. To start Task Manager, press CTRL+ALT+DEL. Then click the Task Manager button. (You can also press CTRL+SHIFT+ESC to bring up Task Manager.)
2. Go to the Applications tab to see the applications running on your computer. Let's start an application.
3. From the Start menu, select Run. Enter **winver** and click OK. Notice that the About Windows application is now running. Now let's stop it.
4. Select the About Windows application in the Task Manager Applications window and click the End Task button. Notice that the window no longer appears in the Applications tab.
5. Now let's end a process. Let's start the Winver program again. From the Start menu, select Run. Enter **winver** and click OK. Notice that the About Windows application is now running. Now let's stop it.
6. Select the WINVER.EXE process. Notice that it is using little or no CPU time. Also notice that it is using about 912KB of memory. While the process is selected, click the End Process button.
7. To close Task Manager, from the File menu, select Exit Task Manager.

Windows 2000 uses preemptive multitasking, whereby each process is given a slice of processor time. How much processor time a process receives depends on its *priority*. When processes are started, Windows 2000 assigns them levels of priority. There are 32 priorities, ranging from 0–31. Priority 31 is the highest. User applications and noncritical operating system functions use priority levels 0–15. Critical, real-time applications such as the operating system kernel use priority levels 16–31.

There are four base process priority levels: Real-time, High, Normal, and Idle. The priority levels between these are reserved for thread priority levels that are added to the processes' basic priority levels. A thread's priority is based on its base priority. A thread can be given one of the following priorities: Highest, Above Normal, Normal, Below Normal, and Lowest. A thread's overall priority is determined by adding the thread's priority to the process's base priority. Table 22-4 displays thread priorities by the four base process priority levels.

You can change the default priority level for a process from the command line or from Task Manager. To change a process's default priority from the command line, use the START command with one of these switches: /low, /normal, /high, or /realtime. When you use the priority switches, the threads have a default Normal priority. Therefore, the switches set the program's priority as follows: Real-time 24, High 13, Normal 8, Low 4.

TABLE 22-4 Thread and Process Priority Levels

Thread Priorities	Real Time	High	Normal	Idle
Highest	26	15	10	6
Above normal	25	14	9	5
Normal	24	13	8	4
Below normal	23	12	7	3
Lowest	22	11	6	2
Idle	16	1	1	1

In Exercise 22-3, you learn how to use the START command.

EXERCISE 22-3

Using the START Command to Set a Process's Priority

1. From the Start menu, select Programs | Accessories | Calculator.
2. Now let's see what the default priority is. To open Task Manager, press CTRL+SHIFT+ESC.
3. Go to the Processes tab and find the CALC.EXE process. Right-click it and select Set Priority. The default priority is Normal, as shown in the following illustration.

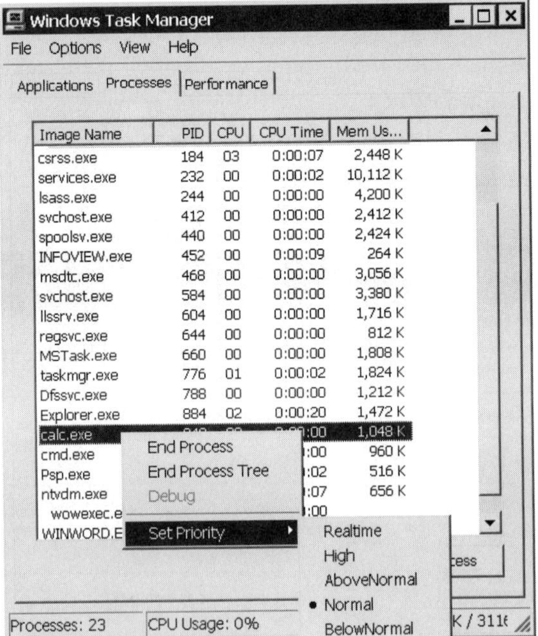

4. Close the Calculator program.
5. Now let's set the priority. From the Start menu, select Programs | Accessories | Command Prompt.

6. At the command prompt, enter **start /high calc** to start the Calculator program.
7. Now let's see what the priority level is. Go to the Processes tab of Task Manager and find the CALC.EXE process. Right-click it and select Set Priority. The priority is now set to High, as shown in the following illustration.

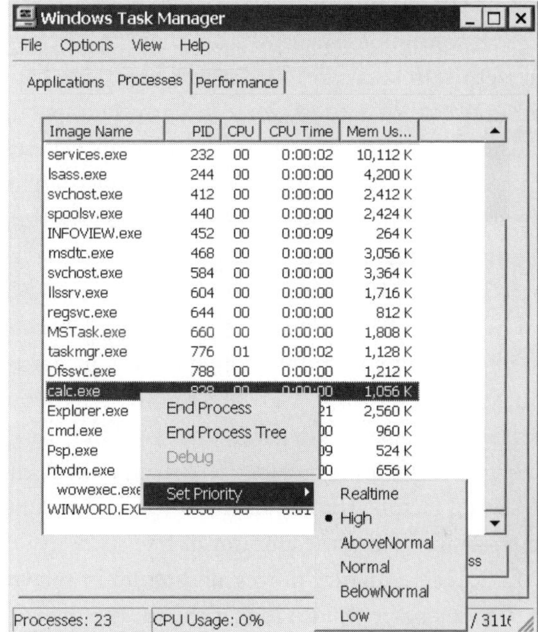

8. Close the Calculator program and close Task Manager.

CERTIFICATION OBJECTIVE 22.03

Optimizing Disk Performance

Hard disk performance can degrade over time due to fragmentation of files. A file is *fragmented* when it is not stored in physically contiguous spaces on the hard disk.

Fragmentation can happen as a file grows larger and the contiguous space near it is already in use by another file, so part of the file is stored elsewhere on the disk. When files become fragmented, additional reads and disk head movements are necessary to read or write the fragmented parts of the file. This, of course, means it takes longer to read from or write to a file.

Another result of fragmented existing files is that new files you create also become fragmented, because files are created in the first available free space and there is not enough contiguous space to store them in a defragmented condition. As you can guess, this process continues as files are created and deleted and as files are edited—and it just keeps getting worse, negatively impacting your system's performance.

The *Disk Defragmenter tool* can help alleviate this problem. Windows NT did not come with a defragmenter tool; the Defragmenter is new in Windows 2000. This tool can move and rearrange files so that they are stored in contiguous space on a hard disk. The task of finding fragmented files and moving them into contiguous space is called *defragmentation.*

Disk Defragmenter can analyze your volumes and make recommendations as to whether or not you should defragment your hard disk. Disk Defragmenter also gives you a graphical display showing you the fragmented files, contiguous files, system files, and free space. However, you wouldn't use this process lightly or without the Defragmenter's recommendation, because defragmentation can take hours, depending on several factors: the size of the volume, the number of files, the severity of the fragmentation, and the amount of free space available.

Disk Defragmenter moves all the files in the volume so that they are stored in contiguous space. It also moves the files to the front of the volume, which gives the added benefit of making the free space contiguous so that all newly created files can also be stored contiguously. Disk Defragmenter can defragment volumes formatted with FAT, FAT32, and NTFS. However, you can defragment system volumes only on the local computer. Furthermore, you can run only one instance of the Disk Defragmenter program at a time. You must have Administrator privileges to run Defragmenter.

Disk Defragmenter does not always completely defragment free space, which would have little benefit, anyway. It does move free space into just a few contiguous areas of the disk, which gives improved performance. Several factors prevent free space from being completely defragmented. For one thing, the paging file can become fragmented as it grows to meet the virtual memory requirements. The paging file is always opened exclusively by Windows 2000. This means that it cannot be defragmented using Disk Defragmenter, thus preventing free space from being completely defragmented.

Defragmenting the page file could improve the performance of your server. The only way to effectively defragment the page file is to move it to another volume. Microsoft also recommends placing the paging file on its own volume, if that's possible. Doing so prevents the paging file from becoming fragmented, and it can also increase performance if the volume that contains the paging file is low on free space. However, Microsoft also recommends leaving a small paging file on the boot partitions for recovery purposes.

On NTFS volumes, Windows 2000 reserves some free space for the *master file table (MFT).* The MFT stores the information needed by the operating system to retrieve files from the volume. Part of the MFT is stored at the beginning of the volume and cannot be moved. In addition, if the volume contains a large number of directories, it can prevent the free space from being defragmented.

The Disk Defragmenter has three main areas of display. The top area lists the volumes that can be defragmented. The middle area displays the fragmentation of the volume selected in the upper portion. The bottom portion displays the volume during and after defragmentation. The Disk Defragmenter is shown in Figure 22-7. The display shows fragmented files in red, contiguous files in blue, system files that cannot be moved by Disk Defragmenter in green, and free space in white. After running the Defragmenter, you can see the improvement in the fragmentation of the volume by comparing the Analysis display to the Defragmentation display.

When you analyze a volume, Disk Defragmenter generates a report. This report gives detailed information about your volume. The top of the report contains information such as volume information, volume fragmentation, file fragmentation statistics, page file fragmentation, and directory fragmentation statistics. The bottom of the report displays information on a file-by-file basis, showing the name of the file, its size, and the number of fragments. An analysis report is shown in Figure 22-8.

on the job

You should always analyze your volumes before defragmenting them. Analyzing your volumes will allow the system to see whether defragmentation is needed for the volume.

When should you run Disk Defragmenter? You should determine a working schedule to run the tool periodically. Note that the version that comes with Windows 2000 cannot be scheduled to run automatically; it has to be run manually.

FIGURE 22-7

The Disk Defragmenter tool

Disk Defragmenter

Action View

Volume	Session Status	File System	Capacity	Free Space	% Free Space
WINDOWS (...	Analyzed	FAT32	3,327 MB	1,334 MB	40 %
LOCAL (E:)		FAT32	1,424 MB	179 MB	12 %
LOCAL (F:)	Analyzed	FAT32	1,385 MB	903 MB	65 %
(D:)		FAT32	1,597 MB	496 MB	31 %
MISC (G:)		FAT32	2,505 MB	2,174 MB	86 %

FIGURE 22-8

A Disk Defragmenter analysis report

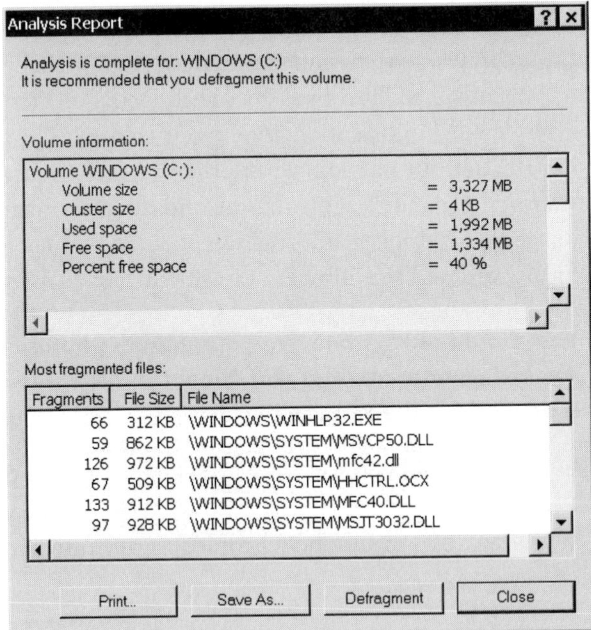

How often you run Defragmenter depends on how many file operations are generally performed on your computer.

You should run Defragmenter whenever you delete a large file or when a large number of files are created or deleted. Defragmentation is generally required on volumes on file servers more often than on workstations. For general use workstations, Microsoft recommends defragmenting volumes once a month. Furthermore, since running the Defragmenter uses file I/O resources, you should run it during low-volume times. Disk Defragmenter places an additional load on the server and can significantly degrade performance.

exam Watch

To run Disk Defragmenter, you must be logged in with an account that has Administrator privileges.

Exercise 22-4 shows you how to use Disk Defragmenter.

EXERCISE 22-4

CertCam 22-4

Using Disk Defragmenter

1. To start Disk Defragmenter, from the Start menu, select Programs | Accessories | System Tools | Disk Defragmenter.
2. When Disk Defragmenter starts, the Analysis and Defragmentation displays are blank. Let's see if volume C: needs defragmenting. Select volume C: and click the Analyze button. When analysis is complete, a message box appears, telling you whether or not defragmentation is needed. If defragmentation is needed, the message box will be similar to the one shown in the (first) following illustration. If defragmentation isn't needed, the message box will be similar to the one in the (second) following illustration.

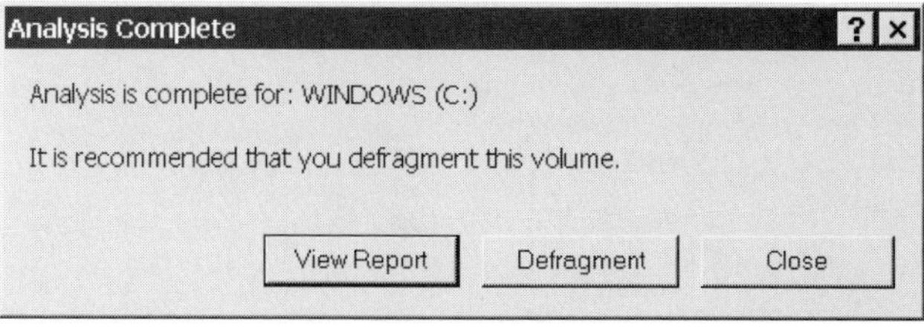

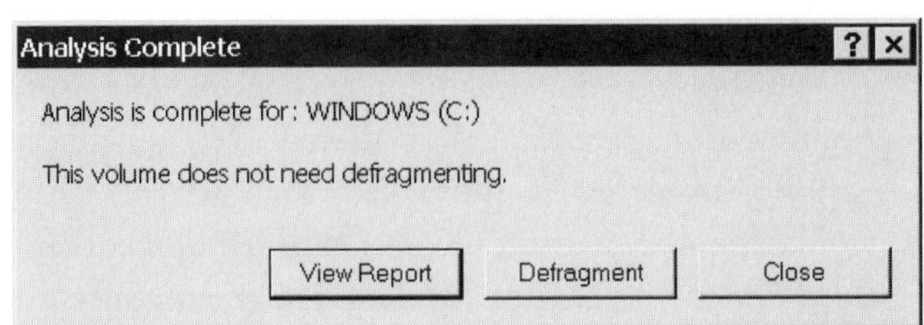

3. Click the View Report button.
4. Scroll through the top section to see the detailed information for your volume.
5. Click the Defragment button to start defragmenting the volume. As the defragmentation takes place, you should start seeing the red portion in the Analysis display become blue in the Defragmentation display. When the process is complete, a message box appears, as shown in the following illustration.

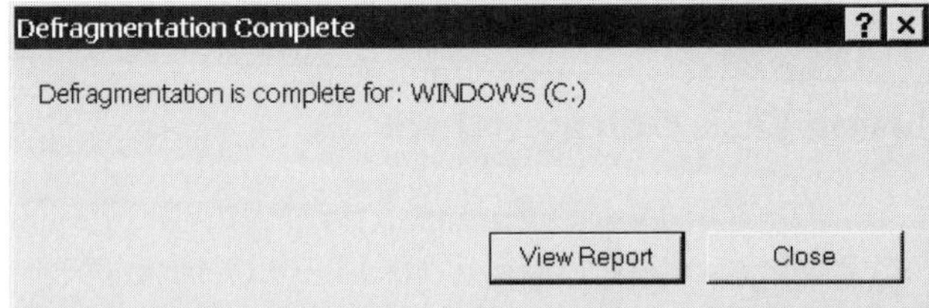

6. Your window should look similar to the next illustration. Notice that not all free space is consolidated and that the system files were not moved.

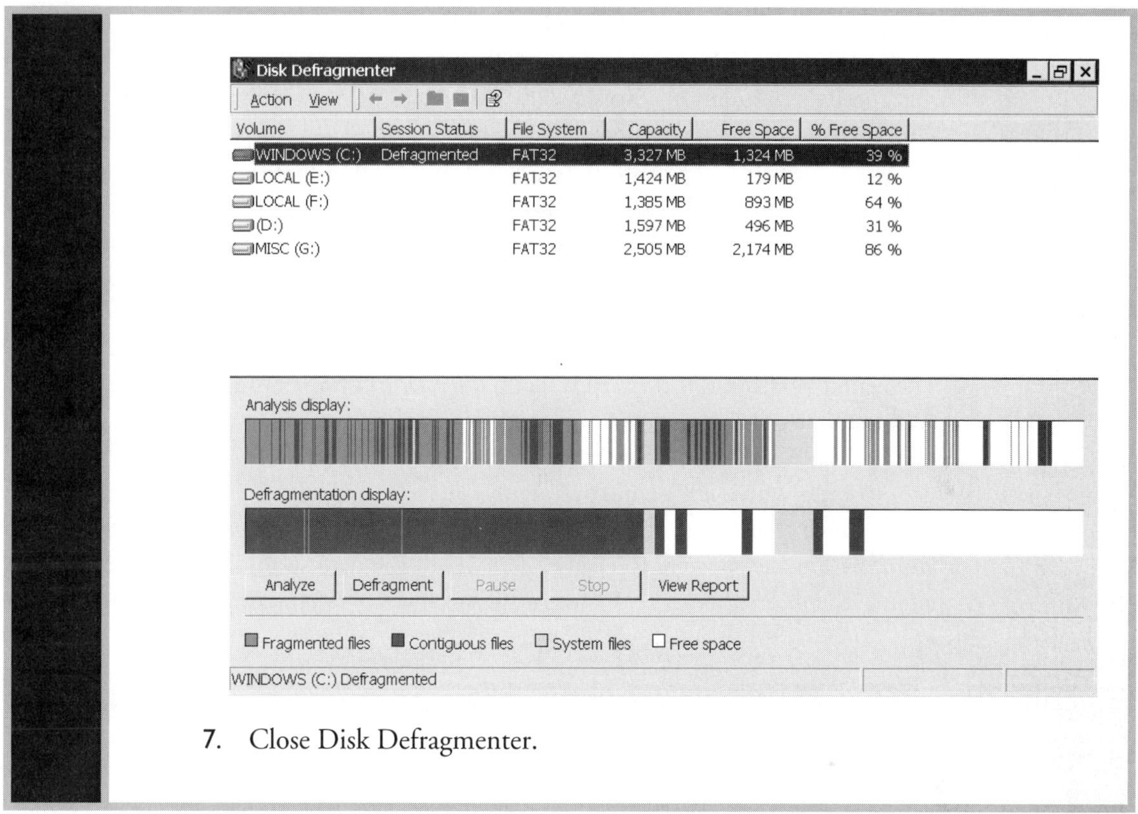

7. Close Disk Defragmenter.

Performance Logs and Alerts

Another useful item that is preconfigured with the Computer Management MMC is the Performance Logs and Alerts snap-in. It allows you to collect data from the local and remote computers to measure performance. This data can be logged and viewed in System Monitor, or it can be exported to Excel or a database. This flexibility allows you to use the tool of your choice to analyze this data and create reports.

You can set thresholds for specified counters, and if any of the thresholds set are reached, an alert can be sent to you via the Messenger service.

Performance logging has many features. The collected data is stored in a comma-delimited or tab-delimited format, which allows it to be exported to spreadsheet and database applications for a variety of tasks such as charting and reports. The data can also be viewed as it is collected. You can configure the logging by specifying start and stop times, the name of the log files, and the maximum size of the log. You can start and stop the logging of data manually or create a schedule for logging. You can even specify a program to automatically run when logging stops. You can also create trace logs. *Trace logs* track events that occur rather than measuring performance counters.

The Performance Logs and Alerts snap-in is shown in Figure 22-9.

You can use the Performance Logs and Alerts MMC snap-in to configure your logging and alerts. You can configure multiple alerts and logs to run simultaneously. If you want to configure performance counter logs, select Counter Logs in the tree on the left side of the Computer Management MMC, as shown in Figure 22-10. Counter Logs displays the name of the log. A sample log file called *System Overview* is provided by default. Counter Logs also displays a comment describing the log or alert, the type of log, and the name of the log file.

From the Action menu, you can create logs. When you create a log, the first thing you do is give it a name, preferably one that is intuitive. Then you can add performance counters to the log. These are the same counters we used in System Monitor. You also specify the interval at which the data should be collected. By default, the interval is set to 15 seconds. Next, you need to configure the log

FIGURE 22-9

The Performance Logs and Alerts snap-in's logs

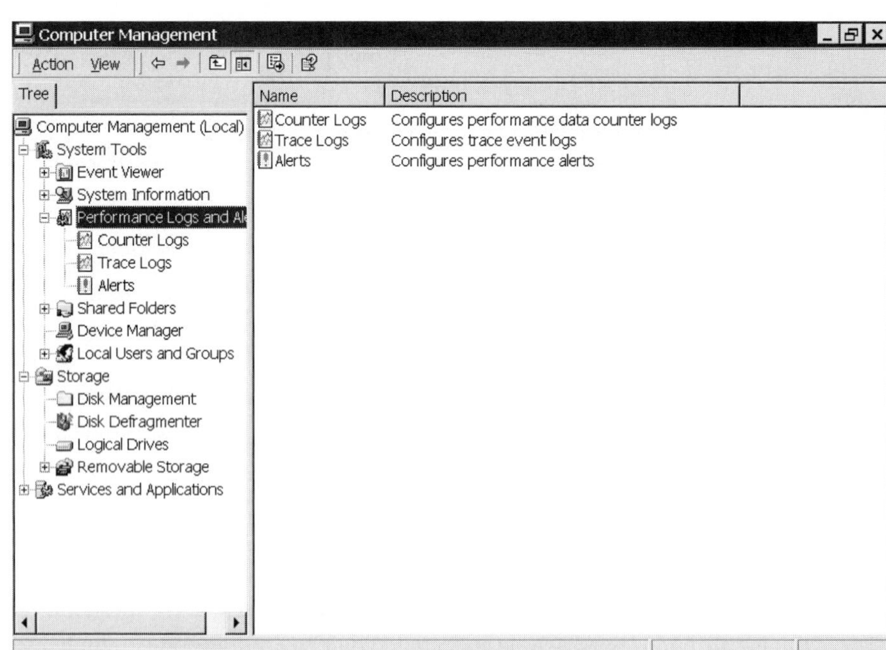

FIGURE 22-10

Viewing counter logs in Performance Logs and Alerts

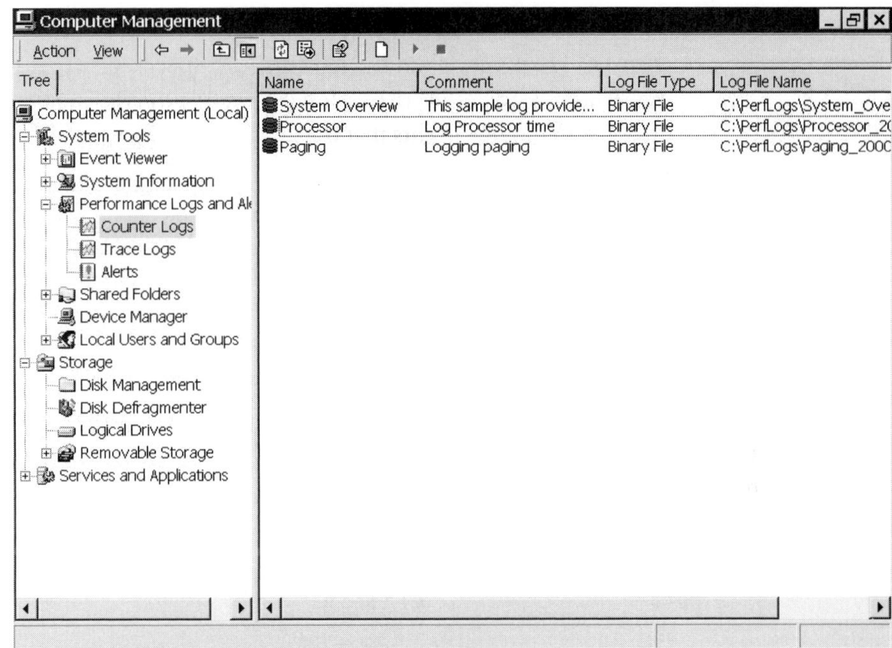

filename. The following list shows parameters you can use to specify the log filename:

- **Location** Specify the folder where the log file will be created.
- **Filename** Type in the base name for the log file. Do not type in the extension.
- **End filenames with** Allows you to specify the end of the filename, which is added to the specified filename. By default, this parameter uses a six-digit number. You can also choose from date and time options.
- **Start numbering at** When you choose the numbering scheme for the filename ending, you can specify where the automatic numbering starts.

After you have configured the log filename, you need to choose the type of log file to create. The log file type can be one of the following:

- **Binary** This is a counter log file that stores the data in a binary format. It has a .BLG extension.

- **Binary circular** This is a counter log file that stores the data in a binary format. However, when the log reaches a specified size, it starts overwriting the oldest data, rather than allowing the file to continue growing. It also has a .BLG extension.
- **Text-CSV** This is a counter log file in which the data is stored in a comma-delimited format, which is a common format that can be read by spreadsheet and database applications. It has a .CSV extension.
- **Text-TSV** This is a counter log file in which the data is stored in a tab-delimited format, which is a common format that can be read by spreadsheet and database applications. It has a .TSV extension.
- **Circular trace file** This is a trace log file. When the log reaches a specified size, it starts overwriting the oldest data, rather than allowing the file to continue growing. It has an .ETL extension.
- **Sequential trace file** This is a trace log file that saves data until it reaches the maximum size. When the maximum size is reached, it creates a new file. It also has an .ETL extension.

The next configuration option is the comment. The *comment* allows you to enter a description of the log file you are creating. Finally, you select the file size limit. You can either choose the maximum size for the log file allowed by the operating system or disk quotas, or you can specify a maximum size. For counter logs, you specify the size in kilobytes, with a maximum of 2 gigabytes for counter logs. For trace logs, you specify the size in megabytes. When you use the binary circular log type, you must specify the size of the log.

You can also schedule logging. To start the log file, you can elect to start it manually or specify a time and date for the process to begin. To stop the logging, you can elect to stop it manually, after a duration of time, at a specified time, or when the file reaches the specified size limit. When you select the duration or size to stop the logging, you can select the option to start a new log file when the current one is closed. You can also specify a program to be run when the log file is closed. A common use for this option is to copy the log file to a remote location for archiving.

Alerts

Alerts allow some action to be performed when a performance counter reaches a particular threshold. A common action is to log an event in the application event log. You can also send a network message to a specified computer. You can have the alert trigger a performance log to start logging when the alert occurs. Finally, you can configure an alert to start a program.

When you create an alert, some of the settings are similar to creating a log. The first thing you do is give the alert a name. As with logs, you should give an alert an intuitive name. Then you can enter a comment and choose the counter or counters for the alert. One difference between an alert and a log is that you have to set a threshold for the alert. You choose a value and whether you want the alert to occur when the value is over or under the threshold. Then you also specify the interval. The default for alerts is 5 seconds.

You have some options as to what happens when an alert occurs. You can write the alert to the application event log, send a network message to a specified computer, start a log, or run a program. You can also specify the command-line parameters for the program. You have the same basic options for scheduling alerts. You can specify the start and stop options. For continuous alert scanning, you can also have the alert start a new scan when it finishes. From the Performance Logs and Alerts console, you can start and stop alerts by right-clicking them and selecting Start or Stop from the context menu.

exam Watch

Make sure you know the settings for configuring logs and alerts, including sample rates, log file options, and scheduling options.

SCENARIO & SOLUTION

Scenario	Solution
When you ran the Disk Defragmenter, you noticed that the free space was still in several segments. Does this mean that your hard disk will still have a performance hit?	No, having the free space in several contiguous fragments will not have a noticeable performance hit. In fact, there is very little additional benefit from having all the free space in one contiguous space.
You created a new log file, and now your computer is running very slowly. How could this happen?	One common way this could occur is if the sample rate is set too low. For instance, setting it to less than 5 seconds can use a significant amount of resources. Try increasing the sample rate until the performance of your computer is at an acceptable level.
You don't want to continuously run logs, but you do want to know when your resources reach certain levels. How can you accomplish this?	You can use alerts. Alerts can be configured to automatically start logs and notify you when a threshold is reached.

CERTIFICATION SUMMARY

In this chapter, we discussed ways to monitor and optimize your server's resources. Creating a baseline is crucial to determining bottlenecks. A baseline allows you to easily determine which resource has become overburdened by comparing current resources to the baseline. You should monitor your server's resources continuously. This practice allows you to monitor for degradation of performance and fix it before it becomes a bottleneck. System Monitor can be used to measure the performance of your server and even other computers. Some of the common sources of bottlenecks include the processor, memory, hard disk, and network. You must use the DISKPERF utility to enable and disable the disk counters.

You can manage processes using Task Manager. You can stop or start processes and applications. This ability is useful when an application stops responding. If a process is not getting enough CPU time or if it is getting too much CPU time, you can also change the priority of the process using Task Manager. You can use the START command to set the priority of a process.

When a disk volume becomes fragmented, it can affect performance. New to Windows 2000 is the Disk Defragmenter, which you can use to defragment your volumes. When your volumes are defragmented, your system will exhibit better performance. You should run the Disk Defragmenter periodically to keep your hard disks running at peak performance.

You can use Performance Logs and Alerts to monitor performance without continuously logging data. You can create alerts with thresholds to notify you when your system meets a threshold, and you can have it start logging when an alert occurs. You can create logs for specific data and schedule them to save data as desired.

✓ TWO-MINUTE DRILL

Monitoring and Optimizing Usage of System Resources

- ❑ The MMC has a Performance snap-in that includes System Monitor and Performance Logs and Alerts.
- ❑ You can use System Monitor to analyze the health of your system.
- ❑ System Monitor can be used to collect data for memory usage, processor utilization, network activity, and more.
- ❑ System Monitor can display this data as a graph, a histogram, or a report.
- ❑ A bottleneck is a system component that restricts the system from operating at its peak.
- ❑ To properly resolve or, preferably, avoid problems, you need to monitor the processor, memory, hard disk, and the network for bottlenecks.
- ❑ Network bottlenecks are sometimes the result of running low on processor and memory resources.

Managing Processes

- ❑ You can use Task Manager to administer and configure processes.
- ❑ From Task Manager, you can start and stop processes and process trees, as well as set their priorities.
- ❑ You can assign a process to a processor or processors using the Set Affinity command.
- ❑ Process priorities range from 0–31, with 31 being the highest priority.
- ❑ There are four basic priority levels: Real-time, High, Normal, and Idle.
- ❑ You can set a process's priority from the command line using the START command.

Optimizing Disk Performance

- ❑ The performance of your hard disk can be degraded due to fragmentation.
- ❑ Fragmentation occurs when a file is not stored in contiguous space on a hard disk.
- ❑ The Disk Defragmenter can remove the fragmentation of your files.
- ❑ The paging file cannot be defragmented using Disk Defragmenter.
- ❑ To defragment a paging file, you would have to move it to another volume.

Part VI

Addressing and Name Resolution

CHAPTERS

MCSE
MICROSOFT CERTIFIED SYSTEMS ENGINEER

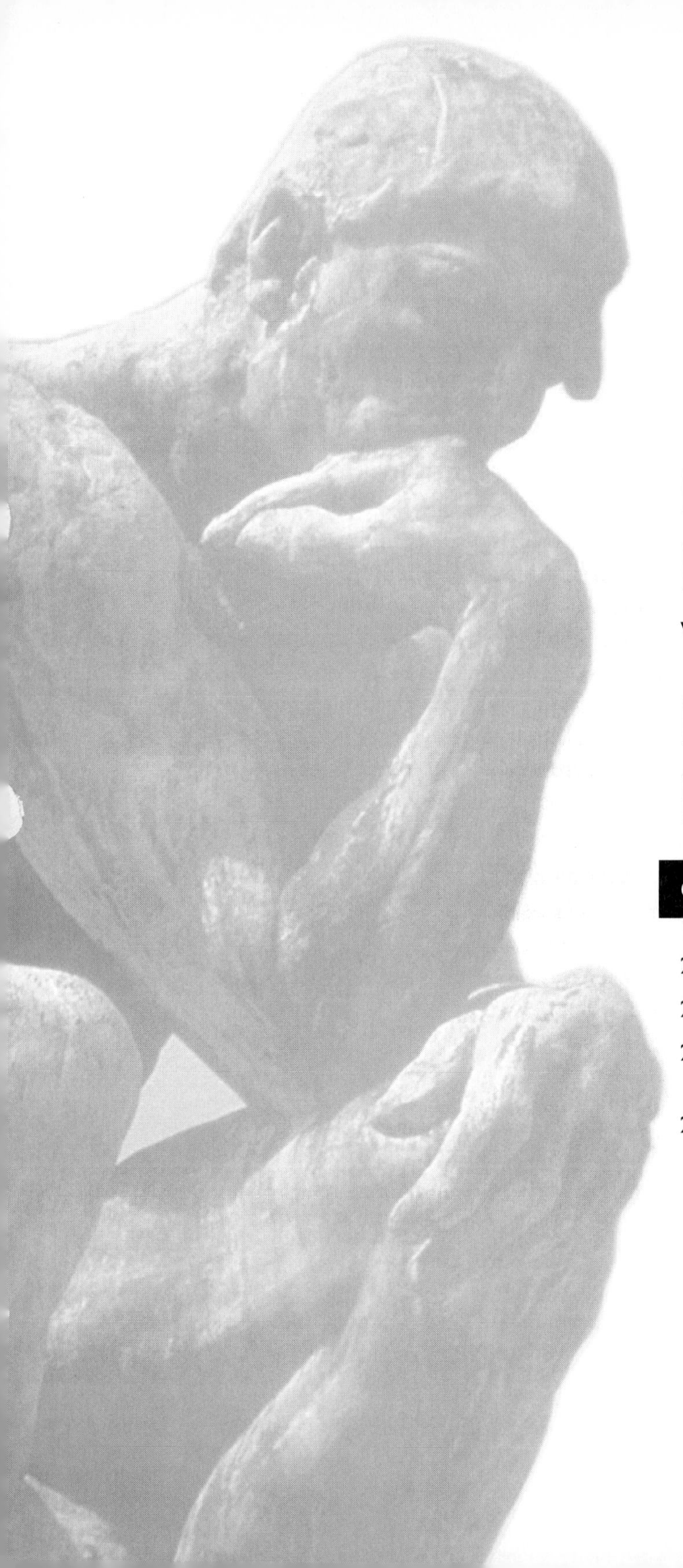

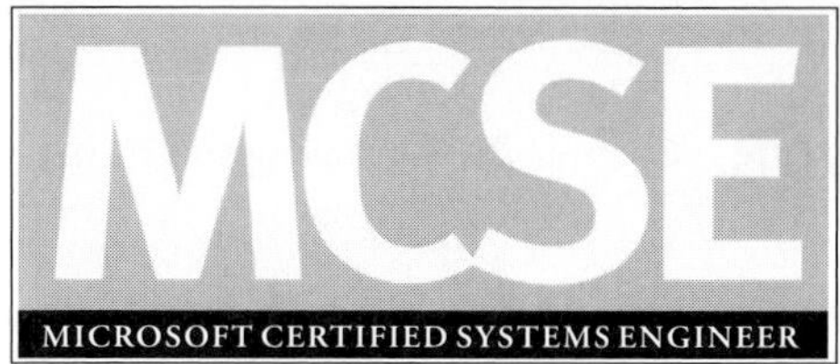

23

Installing and Managing Windows 2000 Networking Protocols

CERTIFICATION OBJECTIVES

23.01	Windows 2000 TCP/IP
23.02	IP Addressing
23.03	Installing, Configuring, Managing, and Monitoring TCP/IP
23.04	Installing and Configuring NWLink
✓	Two-Minute Drill

The Windows NT 4.0 certification track included an elective exam (taken by the vast majority of MCSE candidates) on the intricacies of the TCP/IP protocol suite and its implementation in various network environments. The new Windows 2000 track does not include an exam on this topic, which may lead some candidates to mistakenly believe that it is no longer necessary to study and understand TCP/IP. Nothing could be farther from the truth.

There is a good reason for the fact that there is no TCP/IP elective in the Windows 2000 MCSE track: a thorough knowledge and understanding of this set of protocols is no longer optional. TCP/IP is the foundation upon which Windows 2000 networking is built, and it is the default protocol stack installed with the operating system. The components of the suite and how to use them will be integral topics in the Windows 2000 core exams, as well as, of course, in the Accelerated exam.

TCP/IP is not peculiar to Microsoft networks. In fact, not so long ago, TCP/IP was regarded as a somewhat sluggish, difficult-to-configure protocol used primarily by university or government networks participating in an exotic wide area networking project called ARPAnet. Few private organizations used it for their local area networks (LANs) because it was considered too slow and complex.

There were other protocols available that seemed to offer many advantages over the TCP/IP suite. Microsoft and IBM workgroups could use NetBEUI, a fast and simple transport protocol that could be set up easily and quickly by someone without a great deal of expertise. Novell NetWare networks, prior to NetWare 5.0, required the IPX/SPX stack, which was routable and thus could be used with larger server-based networks. Few business networks had any need for a powerful but high-overhead set of protocols like TCP/IP.

That was before the explosive popularity of the global wide area network we call the Internet. Inexpensive and easy to implement instant worldwide connectivity changed the lives of many people—and it changed the nature of networking. The growth of the Internet, more than any other single phenomenon, was responsible for the popularity enjoyed by TCP/IP in networking today. TCP/IP is *the* protocol stack on which the Internet runs.

In this chapter, we will focus primarily on the TCP/IP protocol suite. We'll briefly discuss the history and evolution of TCP/IP, and the purposes of the various protocols included in the suite. We'll pay particular attention on how to configure and use TCP/IP in a Windows 2000 network, and we'll examine some common troubleshooting scenarios.

An important part of implementing and administering a TCP/IP-based network is working with IP addressing issues, and we will delve into this topic in some depth. We will include information on IP subnetting and supernetting, and talk about new developments on the TCP/IP front, such as Classless InterDomain Routing (CIDR) and IPv6, the future incarnation of the Internet Protocol.

Although TCP/IP is Microsoft's obvious protocol of choice for Windows 2000 local area networks, there are still many hybrid networks in existence, in which Windows 2000 machines must coexist with current and older versions of Novell NetWare. Microsoft provides support for NWLink, its own implementation of the IPX/SPX protocol stack that is necessary for connection to NetWare networks prior to version 5. We will look briefly at how to install and configure the NWLink protocol, and discuss the importance of binding orders when running multiple protocols on a Windows 2000 computer.

CERTIFICATION OBJECTIVE 23.01

Windows 2000 TCP/IP

The Transmission Control Protocol/Internet Protocol (TCP/IP) stack is often called the protocol of the Internet. It is also the protocol of choice for Windows 2000. The Windows 2000 implementation of TCP/IP is based on industry standards and designed to support networks of all sizes, up to the largest enterprise environments, as well as providing connectivity to the Internet.

Windows 2000 TCP/IP also includes a variety of built-in utilities used to configure, maintain, and troubleshoot the protocols, and to provide connectivity to many different types of systems, such as:

- Internet host computers
- Apple Macintosh systems
- IBM mainframe systems
- UNIX systems

- Open VMS systems
- Microsoft Windows NT and Windows 2000 computers
- Microsoft Windows 95 and 98 computers
- Microsoft Windows for Workgroups computers
- Microsoft LAN Manager networks
- Network-ready printers, such as HP JetDirect-equipped printers

Windows 2000 TCP/IP also includes utilities such as File Transfer Protocol (FTP) and Telnet. FTP is a character-based application protocol that allows you to connect to FTP servers and transfer files. Telnet is an application that allows you to log in to remote computers and issue commands as if you were sitting at the keyboard of the remote computer. There are many variations of FTP, Telnet, and other programs based on earlier Internet standards available on the Internet as freeware/shareware or for purchase from third-party vendors.

We will take a more detailed look at these utilities and how they are used later in this chapter.

Introduction to TCP/IP

Before we can understand the function of the TCP/IP protocols, we must first understand the role of protocols in computing and computer networking. A *protocol* is sometimes likened to a language that computers "speak" to communicate with one another, but a better analogy would be to think of the protocol as the syntax of a language. Protocols are sets of rules that specify the order and manner in which processes occur (in this case, the elements of the network communications process). A common protocol is necessary for two computers to "understand" one another.

Although TCP/IP is often referred to as "a" LAN protocol, in reality it is a set of protocols, also called a *protocol stack* or *protocol suite.* A *stack* consists of two or more protocols working together to accomplish a purpose (communication with another computer across a network). A *suite* is a more elaborate collection of communication protocols, utilities, tools, and applications. TCP and IP make up the stack, which handles the most important tasks of communication such as handling addressing and routing issues, error checking, and flow control. The suite includes a large number of additional protocols, used in various situations and for different purposes. Different vendors may include different tools and utilities in their implementations of the TCP/IP suite.

exam Watch

Some protocols that were developed specifically for the TCP/IP suite include Simple Mail Transfer Protocol (SMTP), Simple Network Management Protocol (SNMP), and File Transfer Protocol (FTP).

TCP/IP is known as an *open standard protocol.* In other words, it does not "belong" to any specific vendor, but is open to implementation by different companies. Thus we have not only Windows 2000 TCP/IP, but Novell's TCP/IP stack, UNIX stacks, TCP/IP stacks that are designed to run on Macintosh systems or mainframe computers, and so on. In order to maintain compatibility across these different operating systems and environments, all these vendors must adhere to certain standards.

TCP/IP Standards

Standards and specifications relating to various aspects of the TCP/IP suite are published as RFCs (Requests for Comments) on the Internet and serve as guidelines to promote standardization. The Windows 2000 implementation of Microsoft TCP/IP supports a large number of RFCs that define how the protocols work. These documents are used to describe Internet standards, and go through a formal approval process before being adopted.

Standards are also supported through the use of common networking models, such as the Open Systems Interconnection (OSI) model, developed by the International Organization for Standardization, and the DoD (Department of Defense) model, developed by the U.S. government in conjunction with the design of the TCP/IP protocols themselves during the creation of the ARPAnet. ARPAnet was a wide area network (WAN) of U.S. military installations and major educational institutions that was the predecessor to today's Internet.

Brief History of TCP/IP

In the 1960s, at the height of the cold war, the U.S. Department of Defense recognized that it would be valuable to establish electronic communications links between its major military installations, to ensure continued communication capabilities in the event of the mass destruction that would prevail if a nuclear war occurred. Major universities were already involved in their own networking projects. The DoD established the Advanced Research Projects Agency (ARPA), which funded research sites throughout the United States. In 1968, ARPA contracted with a company called BNN to build a network based on *packet-switching* technology.

The ARPAnet grew, as nodes (computers attached to the network) were added each year. Eventually the military network split off, calling itself MILNET. The remaining membership of the ARPAnet consisted primarily of an elite group of academics at major universities. However, in the late 1980s and early 1990s, the international network caught the eye of the business world. As commercial enterprises moved onto the network (which changed its name again during this period), access became less expensive and widely available to companies and individuals. The original ARPAnet thus evolved into today's global Internet. According to most estimates, by 1999 there were over 50 million host computers connected to the Internet. Figure 23-1 illustrates the growth of the Internet.

FIGURE 23-1

The Growth of the Internet over the years

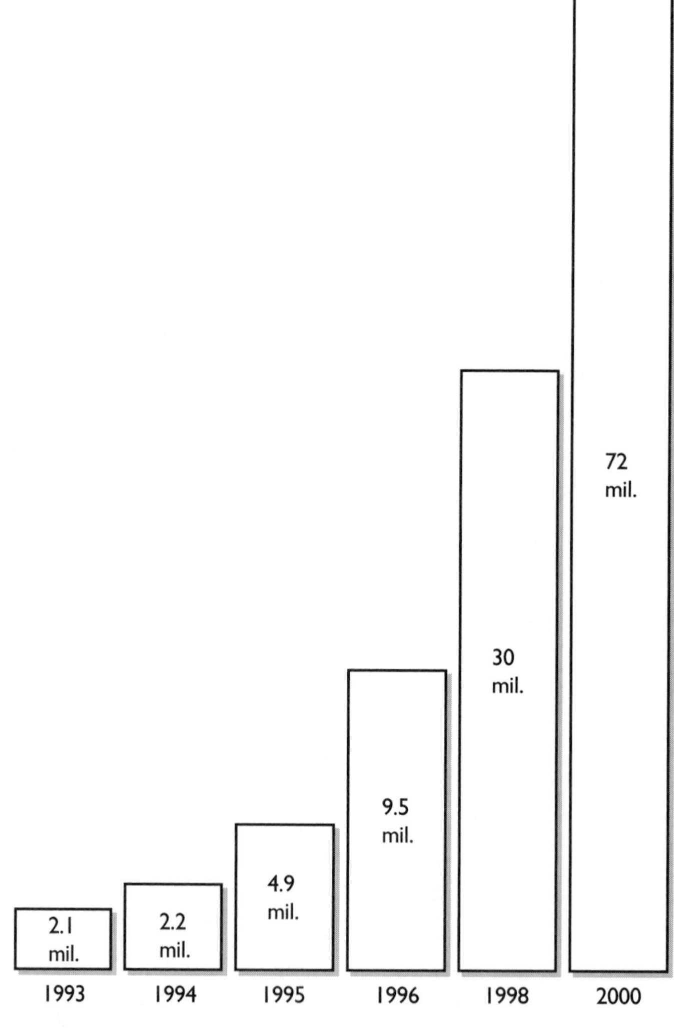

From its ARPAnet beginnings, the Internet has grown into a huge, worldwide network. ARPAnet originally used the Network Control Protocol (NCP), but in 1982 it converted to TCP/IP, also known as IPv4 (IP version 4). The DoD designed it for that purpose, and the focus was reliability, rather than speed. Despite later efforts to replace it with "better" protocols, such as the OSI suite, TCP/IP has endured. In addition to the Internet, the majority of medium to large networks today run on some implementation of the TCP/IP protocols.

Advantages and Disadvantages of TCP/IP vs. Other LAN Protocols

As noted, TCP/IP is relatively slow, it requires more overhead than most other LAN protocols, and it is also more difficult to configure and more complex to troubleshoot. Why, then, has it become so popular? Despite its shortcomings, the TCP/IP suite offers several advantages over other common LAN protocols such as IPX/SPX and NetBEUI.

The TCP/IP Advantages Reliability is TCP/IP's strong suit—the Department of Defense designed it that way. It is highly appropriate for mission-critical communications. But there are many other ways in which TCP/IP outdoes the competition and justifies the extra effort required to implement it:

- **Compatibility** TCP/IP could almost be considered the universal protocol. It is supported by most operating systems and platforms, and allows highly diverse systems—such as Macintosh workstations, UNIX servers, and Windows computers—to communicate with one another. Connection to the Internet *requires* the TCP/IP protocols.
- **Scalability** More than any other set of protocols in use, TCP/IP can scale from the smallest home network to the largest network of all: the Internet. Because of its unique addressing scheme, TCP/IP is especially suitable for large *internetworks* (networks that are interconnected with other networks).
- **Routability** Closely related to scalability is the protocol stack's capability of spanning subnets. Unlike unroutable protocols such as NetBEUI, its data packets can cross from one network, or *subnet,* to another by traveling through devices called *routers.* Internet communication often involves a journey through many different networks before the data reaches its destination.

Disadvantages of TCP/IP As already mentioned, compared to NetBEUI and NWLink (IPX/SPX), the TCP/IP protocols are slow. More resource overhead is required, and configuring the protocols correctly (IP address, subnet mask, default gateway) requires more knowledge and expertise. Most networking professionals feel that these are small prices to pay for TCP/IP's flexibility and power.

The TCP/IP Protocol Suite

TCP and IP make up the protocol "stack" that gets the messages to their destination, and ensures that they get there reliably. However, an entire suite of protocols has come to be associated with the name and included with most vendors' implementations.

Some of these are used to provide additional services, while others are useful primarily as information-gathering or troubleshooting tools. The different members of the suite work at different "layers" of the networking process. In order to understand this, let's take a look at the concept of layered networking models.

DOD TCP/IP and the OSI Networking Models

In the early days of computer networking, protocols were *proprietary*; that is, each vendor of networking products developed its own set of rules. This meant that computers using the same vendor's products would be able to communicate with each other, but not with computers that were using the networking product of a different vendor.

The solution to this problem was to develop protocols that are based on *open standards*. Organizations such as the International Organization for Standardization (also called the ISO, which derives from the Greek word for "equal") took on the responsibility of overseeing the definition and control of these standards, and publishing them so that they would be available to any vendor who wanted to create products that adhered to them. This is an advantage to consumers, because they are no longer forced to use the products of only one vendor. It can also benefit the vendors, in that its products are more widely compatible and can be used in networks that started out using a different vendor's products.

Graphical models were developed to represent these open standards. Models provide an easy-to-understand description of the networking architecture and serve as the framework for the standards. The ISO's Open Systems Interconnection (OSI) model has become a common reference point for discussion of network protocols and connection devices. Another widely used model is the DoD (Department of Defense) networking model, on which TCP/IP is based. Both of these are *layered* models that represent the communication process as a series of steps or levels. This layered approach provides a logical division of responsibility, where each layer handles prescribed functions.

The Open Systems Interconnection Model The OSI model consists of seven layers. The data is passed from one layer down to the next lower layer at the sending computer, until the Physical layer finally puts it out onto the network cable. At the receiving end, it travels back up in reverse order. Although the data travels down the layers on one side and up the layers on the other, the logical communication link is between each layer and its matching counterpart, as shown in Figure 23-2.

As the data is passed down through the layers, it is enclosed within a larger unit as each layer adds its own header information. When it reaches the receiving computer, the process occurs in reverse; the information is passed upward through each layer, and as it does so, the encapsulation information is stripped off one layer at a time. After processing, each layer removes the header information that was added by its corresponding layer on the sending side.

exam Watch

The process of enclosing data within a larger unit, with header information added by the protocol that is doing the enclosing, is called encapsulation.

FIGURE 23-2

Each of the seven layers of the OSI model communicates with its corresponding layer on the receiving side

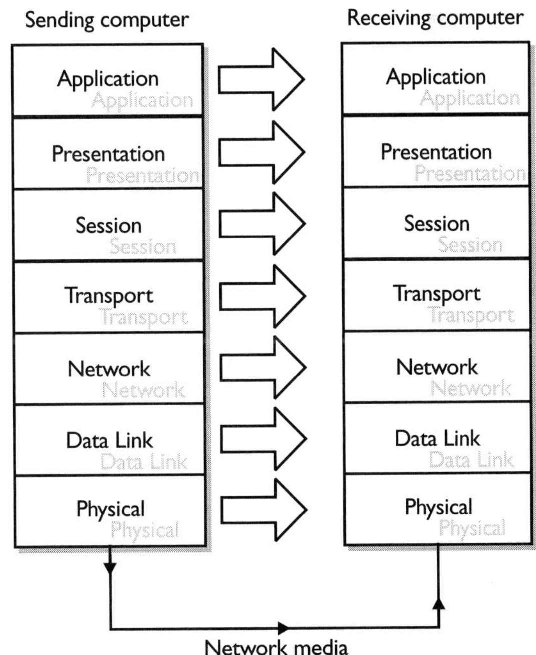

By the time the data is finally presented to the Application layer, which then passes it up to the user application at the receiving computer, the data is once again in the form it was in when it was sent by the user application at the sending machine. Figure 23-3 shows how the header information is added to the data as it moves down through the layers.

The layers of the OSI model (from the top down), and a brief summary of the functions of each, are as follows:

- **Application** This is the part of the networking component that interfaces with the user application.
- **Presentation** This layer handles issues such as compression and encryption.
- **Session** This layer is responsible for establishing a one-to-one connection, or session, between computers.
- **Transport** The protocols at this layer handle error checking, flow control, and acknowledgments.
- **Network** This layer is responsible for routing and logical addressing issues.
- **Data Link** This layer deals with the physical addressing and link establishment.
- **Physical** This layer interfaces with the hardware, and does not add headers to the data.

FIGURE 23-3 The protocols at each networking layer add header information that will be processed by the corresponding layer at the receiving computer

	Data	Link hdr						Application
	Data	Link hdr	Pres hdr					Presentation
	Data	Link hdr	Pres hdr	Ses hdr				Session
	Data	Link hdr	Pres hdr	Ses hdr	Transp hdr			Transport
	Data	Link hdr	Pres hdr	Ses hdr	Transp hdr	Net hdr		Network
Link trailer	Data	Link hdr	Pres hdr	Ses hdr	Transp hdr	Net hdr	Link hdr	Data Link

The Department of Defense Networking Model TCP/IP is often discussed in reference to the OSI networking model. However, the protocol suite was developed prior to development of the OSI model, and in conjunction with the DoD model. Therefore, the TCP/IP protocols do not map exactly to the seven OSI layers, but do map directly to the four layers of the DoD model.

Figure 23-4 shows how the OSI and DoD layers correlate.

Again beginning at the top and working our way down, the four DoD layers are as follows:

- **Application/Process** The Application layer of the DoD model corresponds to the top three layers of the OSI model, and handles the functions performed by the Application, Presentation, and Session layers. A number of the protocols included in the TCP/IP suite operate here, including File Transfer Protocol (FTP), Telnet, HyperText Transfer Protocol (HTTP), Simple Mail Transfer Protocol (SMTP), and others. Two Application Programming Interfaces (APIs) also reside here: NetBIOS and Winsock (Windows Sockets), which provide access to the transport protocols. Many *gateways* also operate in this layer. A gateway is software or a device that provides an interface to allow network communications between two disparate systems.

FIGURE 23-4

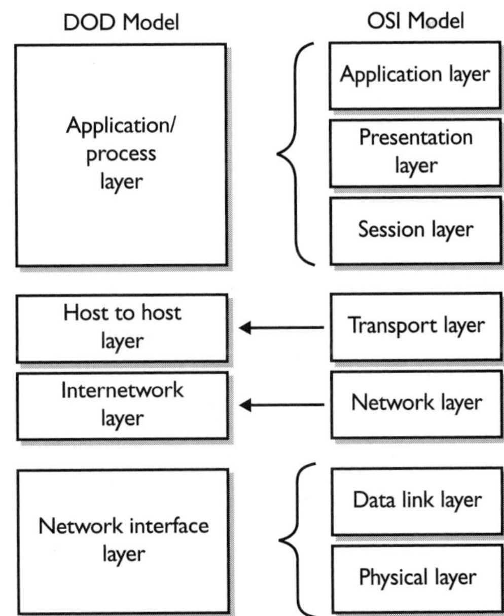

The four layers of the DoD (TCP/IP) model can be roughly mapped to the seven layers of the OSI model

- **Host to Host (Transport)** This layer is basically the same as the Transport layer in the OSI model. It is responsible for flow control, acknowledgments, sequencing (ordering) of packets, and establishment of end-to-end communications. TCP and the User Datagram Protocol (UDP) operate at this level.
- **Internetwork** This layer matches the Network layer in the OSI model. The Internet Protocol (IP) works here to route and deliver packets to the correct destination address. Other protocols that operate at this layer include the Address Resolution Protocol (ARP), Reverse Address Resolution Protocol (RARP), and the Internet Control Message Protocol (ICMP).
- **Network Interface** This bottom layer of the DoD model corresponds to both the Data Link and Physical layers of OSI. It provides the interface between the network architecture (Ethernet, Token Ring, AppleTalk, etc.) and the upper layers, as well as the physical (hardware) issues.

The most critical members of the TCP/IP suite are the Network and Transport layer protocols (or Internetwork and Host-to-Host): TCP/UDP and IP.

The Internetwork Layer Protocols

The protocols that operate at the Internet layer of the DoD model (Network layer of the OSI model) handle logical (IP) addressing issues and routing.

on the job

Routers work at the Internetwork layer. A router can be a dedicated device, or you can configure a Windows NT or Windows 2000 computer to route IP packets by installing multiple network interface cards and enabling IP forwarding. Routers are necessary for communication to take place between computers that are not on the same network (subnet).

IP routing involves discovering a pathway from the sending computer (or forwarding router) to the destination computer whose address is designated in the IP header.

The protocol most commonly associated with this layer is IP, the Internet Protocol (IPX, as part of the IPX/SPX stack, also operates at this layer, and Windows 2000 also supports IPX routing).

IP IP is a *connectionless* protocol; this means it must depend on TCP at the Transport layer above it to provide a connection if necessary.

Although IP does not establish a connection or acknowledgment receipt of messages, it is able to use number sequencing to break down and reassemble messages, and uses a checksum to perform error checking on the IP header.

ICMP and IGMP The Internet Control Message Protocol (ICMP) is a TCP/IP standard that allows hosts and routers that use IP communication to report errors and exchange limited control and status information. The PING utility (discussed later in this chapter) works by sending an ICMP echo request message and recording the response of echo replies.

The Internet Group Management Protocol is used for *multicasting,* which is a method of sending a message to multiple hosts but only addressing it to a single address. Members of a multicast group can be defined, and then when a message is sent to the group address, only those computers that belong to the group will receive it. IGMP is used to exchange membership status information between IP routers that support multicasting and members of multicast groups.

ARP and RARP The Address Resolution Protocol (ARP) is used to resolve IP (logical) addresses to Media Access Control (MAC) physical hardware addresses. ARP uses broadcasts to discover the hardware addresses, and stores the information in its *arp cache.*

RARP is the Reverse Address Resolution Protocol, which does the same thing in reverse; that is, it takes a physical address and resolves it to an IP address. The **arp –a** command can be used to view the current entries in the ARP cache. See Figure 23-5 for an illustration of this IP address to MAC address list.

The Transport Layer Protocols

Remember that the Transport layer's primary responsibility is reliability; it must verify that the data arrives complete and in good condition. It also must have a way to differentiate between the communications that may be coming to the same network address (the IP address) from—or to—different applications.

FIGURE 23-5

The current entries in the ARP cache, which matches IP addresses to MAC (hardware) addresses

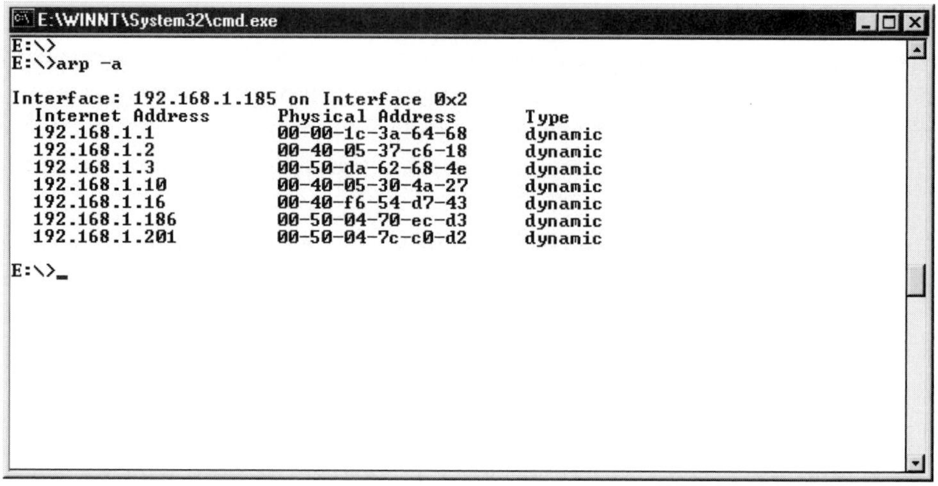

```
E:\WINNT\System32\cmd.exe
E:\>
E:\>arp -a

Interface: 192.168.1.185 on Interface 0x2
  Internet Address      Physical Address      Type
  192.168.1.1           00-00-1c-3a-64-68     dynamic
  192.168.1.2           00-40-05-37-c6-18     dynamic
  192.168.1.3           00-50-da-62-68-4e     dynamic
  192.168.1.10          00-40-05-30-4a-27     dynamic
  192.168.1.16          00-40-f6-54-d7-43     dynamic
  192.168.1.186         00-50-04-70-ec-d3     dynamic
  192.168.1.201         00-50-04-7c-c0-d2     dynamic

E:\>_
```

There are two protocols in the TCP/IP suite that operate at the Transport layer: the Transmission Control Protocol (TCP) and the User Datagram Protocol (UDP). TCP is called a *connection-oriented* protocol, and UDP is a *connectionless* protocol. A connection-oriented protocol such as TCP offers better error control, but its higher overhead means a loss of performance. A connectionless protocol like UDP, on the other hand, suffers in the reliability department but, because it doesn't have to bother with error-checking duties, is faster.

TCP TCP is based on *point-to-point communication* between two network hosts. This means a session is established before data transmission begins. This is done using a process called a *three-way handshake.* This is a way of synchronizing communications and establishing a virtual connection.

TCP processes data as a stream of bytes, which are divided into groups called *segments.* TCP bytes are grouped into segments that TCP then numbers and sequences for delivery. TCP sends *acknowledgments* when segments are received, to let the sending computer know that the data arrived. If data segments arrive out of sequence, TCP/IP can reassemble them in the correct order. If a segment fails to arrive, TCP lets the sending computer know so that segment can be sent again.

UDP UDP provides a service similar to that of TCP, but it does so in a different way. UDP is a connectionless protocol, which offers what is called *best-effort delivery*. This means that UDP does not guarantee delivery, nor does it verify sequencing. If a sending host needs reliable communication, it should use either TCP or a program that provides its own sequencing and acknowledgment services at the Application level.

Applications that need to send only a small amount of data at a time, or those that place a priority on speed of transmission rather than reliability, use UDP.

Ports and Sockets Thanks to the multitasking capabilities of Windows 2000 and other modern operating systems, you can use more than one network application simultaneously. For example, you can use your Web browser to access your company's homepage at the same time your e-mail software is downloading your e-mail. You probably know that TCP/IP uses an IP address to identify your computer on the network, and get the messages to the correct system, but how does it separate the response to your browser's request from your incoming mail when both arrive at the same IP address?

That's where ports come in. The two parts of an IP address that represent the network identification and the host (individual computer) identification are somewhat like a street name and an individual street number. In this analogy, the port number designates the specific apartment or suite within the building.

TCP and UDP, the Transport layer protocols, both use port numbers to ensure that the data intended for Apartment A doesn't get sent to Apartment B instead.

A *socket* is the combination of an IP address and a port number.

TCP Sliding Windows TCP is a reliable protocol, and as a result, in a TCP communication, every segment sent must be acknowledged. That way, if one segment doesn't arrive at its destination (and thus the receiving computer does not send back an acknowledgment for it), it will be sent again.

TCP has to have a way to control the "flow" of data transmission when multiple TCP connections have to share a busy link. Flow control is necessary so that the receiving computer doesn't get "overwhelmed" by a sending computer that deluges it with data faster than it can be processed, or alternately so that the receiver doesn't sit around waiting for the data to "trickle" in.

Flow control is the process of matching the outflow of data from the sending computer to the receiving computer's inflow. This is done by setting a limit on the number of packets that can be sent before acknowledgment is required, which signals the sender to slow down (or stop and wait) if data is "piling up" in the receiver's buffer. If the buffer overflows, data will be lost and must be retransmitted. Think of flow control as the effective management of the data flow between devices in a network so that the data can be handled at an efficient pace.

In the TCP communication process, those bytes of data that can be considered active are called the "window." These are the bytes that are ready to be sent, or they have been sent and are awaiting acknowledgment. As acknowledgments are received, the window "slides" past those bytes to send additional bytes. The *sliding window protocol* determines how much data is being transmitted based on actual bytes, rather than segments. See Figure 23-6 for an illustration of how the sliding window concept works.

Other Members of the Suite

There are several other protocols that belong to the TCP/IP suite. Many of these operate at the Application layer and are used for such tasks as transferring files,

FIGURE 23-6

TCP uses a "sliding window" for flow control

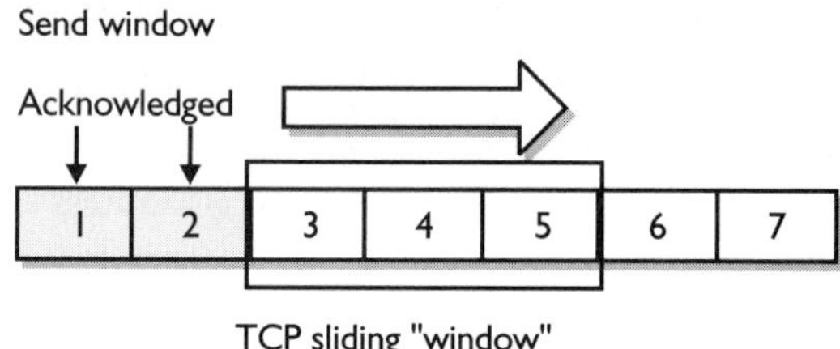

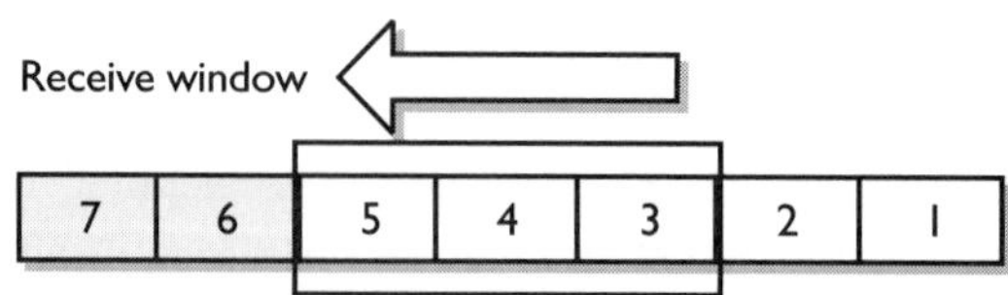

remote terminal emulation, messaging, and network management. Some of these protocols include:

- **File Transfer Protocol (FTP)** Used to download files from another computer, or to upload files to another computer.
- **Telnet** Used to connect to a remote computer and run programs or view files.
- **Simple Mail Transfer Protocol** Used for sending Internet mail (usually used in conjunction with the Post Office Protocol (POP), which is used to retrieve incoming mail from the mail server.)
- **Simple Network Management Protocol (SNMP)** Used to monitor and manage TCP/IP networks. SNMP has two components, the SNMP Agent and the SNMP Management System, which use SNMP messages sent using UDP to communicate host information, which is stored in a Management Information Base (MIB).

The following grid answers some common questions about the responsibilities of various layers of the networking models.

SCENARIO & SOLUTION	
At what networking layer do encryption and data compression take place?	The OSI Presentation layer DoD Application layer
Which networking layer is responsible for acknowledgment of receipts, flow control, and sequencing of packets?	The OSI Transport layer DoD Host-to-Host (Transport) layer
At what layer are hardware issues handled?	The OSI Physical layer DoD Network Interface layer
Which layer deals with routing and logical addressing?	The OSI Network layer DoD Internetwork layer

EXERCISE 23-1

Using the Windows 2000 FTP Client

To use the built-in FTP client in Windows 2000, perform the following steps:

1. Click the Run selection on the Start menu.
2. Type **cmd** in the Run box to invoke a command prompt.
3. At the command line, type **ftp**.
4. You should see a prompt displayed as **ftp>**.
5. At the prompt, type **open ftp.microsoft.com**.
6. You will be prompted for a username. Type **anonymous**.
7. You will receive a message that anonymous connections are allowed and be asked to give your e-mail address. Type in your e-mail address.
8. You will be welcomed to the Microsoft FTP site.
9. To get a list of files available for download, type **dir**. You will see a list like the one shown in the following illustration
10. You can use the GET command to specify a file to be downloaded, or the PUT command to specify a file to be uploaded. For a complete listing of FTP commands, type **help** at the FTP prompt.

```
Select E:\WINNT\System32\cmd.exe - ftp
E:\>
E:\>ftp
ftp> open ftp.microsoft.com
Connected to ftp.microsoft.com.
220 CPMSFTFTPA04 Microsoft FTP Service (Version 5.0).
User (ftp.microsoft.com:(none)): anonymous
331 Anonymous access allowed, send identity (e-mail name) as password.
Password:
230-This is FTP.MICROSOFT.COM. Please see the dirmap.txt file for more informati
on.
230 Anonymous user logged in.
ftp> dir
200 PORT command successful.
150 Opening ASCII mode data connection for /bin/ls.
dr-xr-xr-x   1 owner    group               0 Feb 25  0:17 bussys
dr-xr-xr-x   1 owner    group               0 Feb 25  0:59 deskapps
dr-xr-xr-x   1 owner    group               0 Feb 25  1:31 developr
-r-xr-xr-x   1 owner    group            7983 Jan 28  1999 dirmap.htm
-r-xr-xr-x   1 owner    group            4333 Jan 28  1999 dirmap.txt
-r-xr-xr-x   1 owner    group             710 Apr 12  1993 disclaim1.txt
-r-xr-xr-x   1 owner    group             712 Aug 25  1994 disclaimer.txt
-r-xr-xr-x   1 owner    group         1245110 Oct  7  1998 homemm.old
dr-xr-xr-x   1 owner    group               0 Feb 25  1:34 kbhelp
-r-xr-xr-x   1 owner    group        26147110 Apr 11  3:31 ls-lr.txt
-r-xr-xr-x   1 owner    group         5307699 Apr 11  3:31 ls-lr.z
-r-xr-xr-x   1 owner    group         2832441 Apr 11  3:31 ls-lr.zip
dr-xr-xr-x   1 owner    group               0 Apr  6  5:03 misc
dr-xr-xr-x   1 owner    group               0 Feb 25  3:55 peropsys
dr-xr-xr-x   1 owner    group               0 Feb 25  4:09 products
dr-xr-xr-x   1 owner    group               0 Mar 22 15:59 reskit
dr-xr-xr-x   1 owner    group               0 Feb 25  4:22 services
dr-xr-xr-x   1 owner    group               0 Feb 25  5:37 softlib
dr-xr-xr-x   1 owner    group               0 Feb 25  5:58 solutions
226 Transfer complete.
ftp: 1319 bytes received in 0.31Seconds 4.25Kbytes/sec.
ftp> _
```

CERTIFICATION OBJECTIVE 23.02

IP Addressing

The IP address is a *logical* address, assigned by the network administrator. It bears no *direct* relation to the network interface card's *physical* address (called the MAC address because it is used at the Media Access Control sublayer of the OSI's Data Link layer). The MAC address is hard-coded into a chip on the network card in the typical Ethernet network. The *Address Resolution Protocol* (ARP), which we will discuss later in this chapter, has the task of translating IP addresses to MAC addresses.

Locating IP Addressing Information

There are a couple of ways to find out what a computer's IP address is. TCP/IP configuration information is found in the Properties box for the protocol. Windows 2000 TCP/IP also includes a utility, IPCONFIG, which displays the computer's IP address and other TCP/IP configuration information.

How IP Addressing Works

In order to communicate over the network using the TCP/IP protocols, a computer must have an IP address that is unique on that network. A network administrator can manually assign the IP address, or it can be automatically assigned by an addressing service such as DHCP, APIPA (Automatic Private IP Addressing), or ICS (Internet Connection Sharing).

The IP address is usually represented as shown in the screenshots, in "dotted decimal" (also called "dotted quad") notation with four sections, called *octets*, separated by dots. This decimal notation is merely a "user friendly" way to express the binary number used by the computers to communicate. The *octets* are so named because each represents eight binary digits.

To identify which octet we're talking about, they are often referred to as the "W," "X," "Y," and "Z" as follows:

w.x.y.z

EXERCISE 23-2

Finding Your Computer's IP Addressing Information

To determine your computer's IP address and related information (subnet mask and default gateway), follow these steps:

Locating IP information via the TCP/IP Properties box.

1. Select Start | Settings | Network and Dial-up Connections.
2. In the Network and Dial-up Connections Folder, right-click on your local area connection and select Properties, as shown in the following illustration.

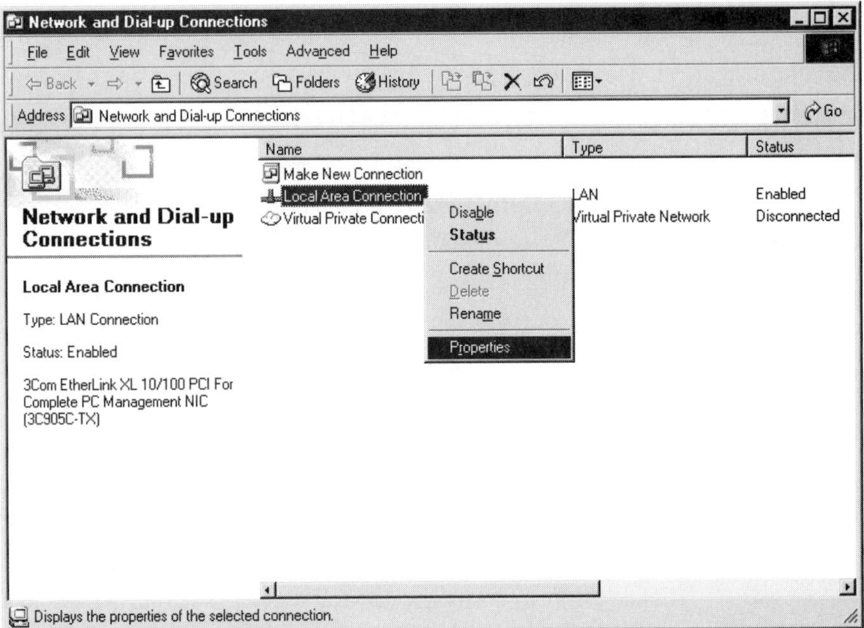

3. In the Properties dialog box, double-click on Internet Protocol (TCP/IP), or highlight it and click Properties.

4. You will see a dialog box displayed similar to the one shown in the following illustration.

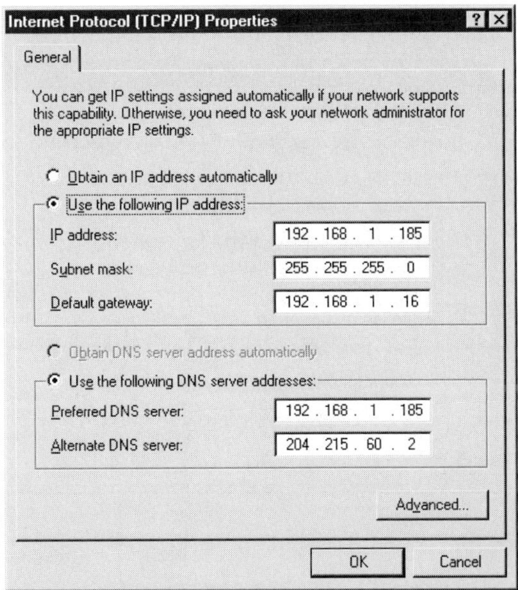

5. Note the assigned IP address, subnet mask, and default gateway information.

The IP address and subnet mask are always required for TCP/IP communication. The default gateway value is required to communicate on a routed network.

If the "Obtain an IP address automatically" radio button is selected, a DHCP (Dynamic Host Configuration Protocol) server on the network will assign the IP address and other TCP/IP configuration information. In that case, you will have to use the second method to determine the IP address being used by the computer.

Locating IP information via the IPCONFIG command.

The best way to determine IP addressing information is by using the TCP/IP command-line utility IPCONFIG. To do so, follow these steps:

6. Bring up a command window (select Start | Run and type **cmd**).

7. Type **ipconfig** at the prompt.
8. You will see information displayed similar to that shown in the following illustration.

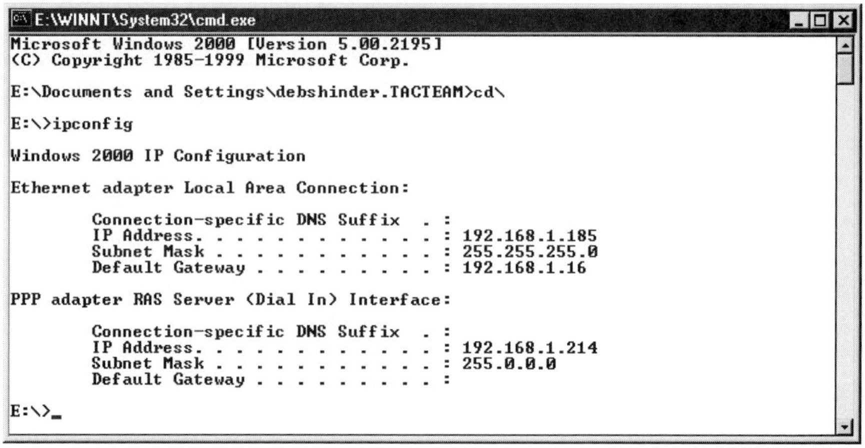

```
E:\WINNT\System32\cmd.exe
Microsoft Windows 2000 [Version 5.00.2195]
(C) Copyright 1985-1999 Microsoft Corp.

E:\Documents and Settings\debshinder.TACTEAM>cd\

E:\>ipconfig

Windows 2000 IP Configuration

Ethernet adapter Local Area Connection:

        Connection-specific DNS Suffix  . :
        IP Address. . . . . . . . . . . . : 192.168.1.185
        Subnet Mask . . . . . . . . . . . : 255.255.255.0
        Default Gateway . . . . . . . . . : 192.168.1.16

PPP adapter RAS Server (Dial In) Interface:

        Connection-specific DNS Suffix  . :
        IP Address. . . . . . . . . . . . : 192.168.1.214
        Subnet Mask . . . . . . . . . . . : 255.0.0.0
        Default Gateway . . . . . . . . . :

E:\>_
```

FROM THE CLASSROOM

The IP Address

IP addressing, used by the network protocols to deliver packets to the proper destination, is analogous to street addressing used by the postal service to deliver mail to the proper home or office. If you wish to send a letter to a specific location, you must indicate the street address on the envelope. Similarly, the computer's IP address is placed on the data packet's "envelope," in the form of header information. You also place a return address on the envelope so the post office will know where it originated in case it can't be delivered. The sending computer's address, called the source address, is likewise included in the header (there may be other information in addition to the source and destination address in some headers, just as you might have additional information or instructions, such as "Do not forward" or "Fragile—Do not bend" on the envelope you send through the postal system).

—*Debra Littlejohn Shinder, MCSE, MCP+I, MCT*

Ones and Zeros: Binary Addressing

Let's take a look at how IP addresses look in binary. This will help you to understand what the numbers really represent and how the computer uses them for communication.

For example: The IP address 192.168.1.185 *really* represents the following binary number: 11000000.10101000.00000001.10111001.

This number is made up of four groups of eight binary digits, the *octets* mentioned earlier. Binary uses only two digits—0 and 1—to represent all numerical values. Binary is a *base two* system, as opposed to decimal, which is a *base ten* system because it uses ten digits—0 through 9—to represent all numerical values.

How do you convert decimal to its binary equivalent? Well, you *could* just use the Windows calculator in scientific mode (choose "Scientific" from the View menu). Check the dec radio button and enter the number in decimal, then click on the bin radio button and Tada! As if by magic, you have the binary equivalent.

But you also need to know how to perform the calculation without the assistance of a calculator. It's really not as difficult as you may think.

Converting Decimal to Binary

Let's take a look at an octet:

11111111

We have eight binary digits, and each of them represents a decimal value, beginning with the rightmost digit and working our way back to the leftmost. The rightmost digits are sometimes referred to as the low order bits, and the leftmost as the high order bits.

Each bit that is "turned on" (that is, shows a 1 instead of a 0) represents the value of that bit as shown in Table 23-1.

You'll notice that the value increases by a power of 2 as you move from right to left. A bit that is turned "off" (represented by a 0) counts as 0. All we have to do then is add up the values of the bits that are "on."

TABLE 23-1 Values of Binary Digits in an Octet

1	1	1	1	1	1	1	1
128	64	32	16	8	4	2	1

If the octet we wish to convert is 10011011, we would add 1 + 2 + 8 + 16 +128 (the values of all the bits that are turned "on"), for a total of 155. So, 10011011 equals 155 in decimal notation.

The Components of an IP Address

What does this mean, then, in terms of the IP addresses we work with every day? Generally, when we configure TCP/IP properties, we enter IP addresses in *dotted decimal notation.* An IP address in its "pure" binary form consists of four octets (each octet being made up of eight binary digits), or 32 bits. The dotted decimal form shows the octets converted to their decimal equivalent with each octet separated by a dot. Thus, the address that the computer sees as 10011110 11101000 00011001 11111001 will be expressed as 158.232.25.249 (do the calculations as shown earlier or use the scientific calculator to make the conversion).

Network and Host ID This address is really made up of two parts, just as your street address contains both the *house number* and the *street name*; for example, 123 Main Street. Many houses share the "street name" portion of the address (everyone else on your street). There may also be other houses in your neighborhood that have the house number "123," but they will be on different streets. It's the combination of the house number and street name that makes up the unique identifier that describes to others which house is yours.

IP addresses work in a similar fashion. Part of the address is the *network ID,* which identifies the network (or subnet) on which the computer is located. All computers on the subnet share this part of the address. The second part of an IP address is called the *host ID,* and identifies the individual computer on that network or subnet. Combined, they create a unique address that differentiates this computer from all others on the internetwork.

The Role of the Subnet Mask How do we know *which* of the octets, or parts of the IP address, indicate the network ID, and which ones indicate the host ID? It would be easier if, for instance, the first octet always indicated the network, and the last three always indicated the host. Unfortunately, it's not that simple. However, we can determine what part of the IP address pertains to which by taking a look at our *subnet mask.*

The subnet mask is another 32-bit binary number, expressed in the same form as an IP address, but its purpose is to tell us (and more importantly, to tell the computers) which part of the IP address is *masked* (and thus represents the network ID). In the binary form of the subnet mask, the *masked bits* are those that are "on," or set to 1.

If the first eight bits from the left in the subnet mask (the first octet) are all ones, and the rest of the bits are zeros, that means the first octet represents the network ID and the remaining three octets represent the host ID. Let's convert that to decimal, since we usually see the subnet mask expressed in dotted decimal in the TCP/IP configuration.

11111111.00000000.00000000.00000000 =

255.0.0.0.

This generally means the first portion of the IP address identifies the network on which the computer "lives," and the last three parts identify the specific computer (host) on that network. In other words, if our IP address is 103.24.125.6 with a subnet mask of 255.0.0.0, the first octet (103) identifies the network, and the remaining three (24.125.6) identify the host computer on that network.

exam Watch

Certain addresses are used for special purposes. A host number of all 0s is used to identify the network, and a host number of all 255s is used as the broadcast address to send messages to all computers on that network.

There is one more thing we must factor in: the *address class* to which the IP address belongs.

Address Classes

In order for computers to communicate on a worldwide global internetwork like the Internet, which requires that each computer have a unique IP address, there must be some centralized authority in charge of assigning addresses and ensuring that none are duplicated. This has been handled by the Internet Assigned Numbers Authority (IANA) and the InterNIC, a company tasked with that responsibility. Traditionally, blocks of IP addresses have been assigned in "lumps" to organizations and Internet Service Providers (ISPs), depending on how many host addresses were needed for their networks.

These blocks of addresses came in three basic sizes: large, medium, and small. The networks for which these blocks of addresses were assigned were called Class A, B, and C networks.

Class A Addresses

Class A addresses are for the "large size" networks, those that have a tremendous number of computers, and thus a need for many host addresses. Class A addresses always begin with a 0 in the first octet (also called the W octet). This will be the first bit on the left. This leaves seven bits for the individual network ID, and 24 bits to identify the host computers. When we convert to decimal, we see that this means a Class A address will have a decimal value in the first octet of 127 or less.

Class A addresses, because they use only the first octet to identify the network, are limited in number. However, each Class A network can have a huge number of host computers, over 16 million. The Class A network numbers were all used up some time ago; they have been assigned to very large organizations such as IBM, MIT, and General Electric.

Class B Addresses

Class B networks are the "medium size" networks. Class B networks use the first two octets (the 16 leftmost bits) to identify the network, and the last two octets (or the 16 rightmost bits) to identify the host computers. This means there can be far more Class B networks than Class As (over 16,000), but each can have fewer hosts ("only" 65,535 each). Class B addresses always begin with a 10 for the two leftmost bits in the W octet, and the network is defined by the first two octets, which translates to decimal values of 128 through 191 for the first octet,16 bits identify the Network ID, and the remaining 16 bits identify the Host ID. Microsoft's network is an example of a Class B network.

Class C Addresses

The smallest size block of addresses designated by a class is the Class C network, each of which can have only 254 hosts. However, there can be over 2 million Class C networks. A Class C network always has 110 as its first three bits. This leaves 24 bits to identify the network, with only 8 bits to use for host IDs. A Class C network, in decimal notation, will have a first octet decimal value of 192 through 223.

on the job

Don't be confused if you read in some texts that the network ID in a Class B network is identified by 14 bits rather than 16, or in a Class C by 21 instead of 24. Technically this is correct—the first 2 bits define the address class, and the next 14 define the individual network. To simplify our understanding of addressing, these two are usually referred to together as the "network ID."

There are many, many class C networks. Most Internet Service Providers (ISPs) have been assigned Class C network numbers.

exam Watch

The address ranges 10.x.x.x, 172.16.x.x-172.31.x.x, and 192.168.x.x are reserved for use as private addresses. That is, these address ranges cannot be assigned by the Internet authorities to any network connected to the public Internet, but can be used as internal addresses that are not connected to the public network, without being required to be registered. Private addresses cannot send to or receive traffic from the Internet—at least, not directly. If a LAN is using private addresses, and the computers on the LAN need to communicate with Internet locations, the private addresses must be translated to a public address. NAT (Network Address Translation) software is used for this purpose, and Windows 2000 includes built-in NAT support.

Class D and E Addresses

We said there are *three* network sizes, so where do the Class D and E addresses fit in? These two classes are *not* assigned to networks, but are reserved and used for special purposes.

Class D addresses, whose four high order (leftmost) bits in the W octet are 1110, are used for *multicasting*. This is a method of sending a message to multiple computers simultaneously.

Class E addresses, with four high order bits of 1111, are reserved for experimental and testing purposes.

Default Subnet Masks

When an entire block of addresses from a specified class is assigned and used as one network (either a Class A, B, or C), the subnet mask is easy to determine and understand. Either the first, first two, or first three octets are "masked"; that is, all bits in those octets are 1s (turned "on"), indicating that those bits represent the network ID. The subnet masks used in these cases are called the *default subnet masks* for each address class. The default masks are as follows:

- **Class A** 255.0.0.0 (11111111.00000000.00000000.00000000)
- **Class B** 255.255.0.0. (11111111.11111111.00000000.00000000)
- **Class C** 255.255.255.0 (11111111.11111111.11111111.00000000)

Often, however, a block of addresses (such as the 254 addresses available in an assigned Class C network) needs to be split into two or more smaller networks. This is called *subnetting.* There are many reasons for subnetting a network, one of which is to cut down on broadcast traffic (broadcast messages go only to the computers on the same subnet) and make better use of network bandwidth.

It is also possible to do the opposite: combine two or more Class C networks together to create a larger network. This is referred to as *supernetting.*

on the Job

Remember that the default subnet masks indicate unsubnetted networks only when applied to the network class listed. This means the subnet mask of 255.255.0.0 when applied to a Class B network indicates an unsubnetted network. However, the same mask of 255.255.0.0, if applied to a Class A network, would be a subnetted network. The network class is always determined by the high order (leftmost) bits, as discussed earlier. A common mistake for new administrators is to assume that if the subnet mask is 255.255.255.0, for example, the network is a Class C network.

Subnetting and Supernetting

Both subnetting and supernetting are ways of modifying the IP address by "stealing" bits from one portion (network ID or host ID) to "give" to the other. To do this, you must use a *variable length subnet mask* (VLSM) to indicate which bits in the IP address pertain to the network ID and which to the host. Routers use the subnet mask to determine to which subnetwork a data packet should be sent.

exam Watch

Subnetting a network turns it into a routed network, as an IP router (either a dedicated device or a computer configured to function as a router) will be required for computers on one subnet to communicate with the computers on other subnets.

Subnetting Basics

If you are allocated an entire Class C network, remember that the default subnet mask is 255.255.255.0, or in binary, 11111111.11111111.11111111.00000000.

The eight bits on the right, represented as zeroes, are "yours." You can use all of them for host addresses, *or* you can "loan" some of them to the network ID, to divide your Class C network into two or more smaller networks.

To understand variable-length subnet masks, which indicate that the network is divided into subnets, you must work with the binary or you will probably end up hopelessly confused. Variable-length subnet masks are created by taking bits from the portion of the IP address normally used for the host ID and using it for the network (or subnet) ID. For instance, if you borrow four bits from the host portion of a class C network address, your subnet mask will look like this:

11111111 11111111 11111111 11110000

or, in decimal:

255 255 255 240

This technique allows us to divide our Class C network into 14 usable subnets with 14 hosts on each subnet, using the following formulae:

Number of subnets = 2^x *-2*, where x = the number of bits borrowed from the host ID.

Number of hosts = $2^x - 2$, where x = the number of unmasked host ID bits remaining.

Note that we subtract two from the number of subnets, because conventional IP subnetting rules say we can't have a subnet ID that is all 1s or all 0s. Thus we must "throw out" the first and last subnet IDs. We also subtract two from the number of hosts, because two host addresses are always reserved for use as the network ID and the broadcast address.

Determining the Number of Subnets The first step in creating a subnetted network is to decide how many subnets you want to define. Remember that the more bits you "steal" from the host ID portion of the address, the more subnets you can create—but this *reduces* the number of hosts you can have per subnet.

Table 23-2 illustrates how many new subnets can be created for each bit that you "steal" from the host ID. Use the formula 2^n-2 (where n is the number of bits that are available to be used for the host ID) to figure out the number of host addresses you will have. Remember that Class A addresses have 24 bits minus the number of bits used for the mask, Class B addresses have 16 bits minus the number used in the mask, and Class C addresses have 8 bits minus the number used in the mask.

Determining the Mask There are three basic steps involved in determining the appropriate subnet mask:

1. Determine the number of subnets you want.
2. Convert the number to binary. Notice how many bits were required.
3. Covert the number of bits required to decimal.

About Supernetting

Supernetting is a way of combining several small networks into a larger one. For example, a company may need a Class B network, but because those have all been assigned, it can't get one. However, Class C networks *are* available, so the company can be assigned multiple Class C networks with contiguous addresses. By "stealing" bits again, but in the opposite direction (sort of like taking from the poor and giving to the rich instead of vice versa), you can use some of the bits that originally represented the network ID to represent host IDs, reducing the number of networks but increasing the number of hosts available per network.

TABLE 23-2 Determining How Many Bits Are Needed for a Given Number of Subnets

Subnets	Bits needed	Mask
2	2	192
6	3	224
14	4	240
30	5	248
62	6	252
126	7	254
254	8	255

For instance, you can combine two Class C networks using a subnet mask of 255.255.254.0 to provide for 512 hosts on the network instead of the 254 to which a Class C network is traditionally limited. Or, we could combine 1024 Class C networks with a subnet mask of 255.252.0.0 and obtain 262,144 host addresses (although we probably wouldn't want to).

exam Watch

The addresses of the two Class C networks must be contiguous for this to work.

Supernetting is often used in conjunction with an IP addressing scheme called CIDR.

Classless Addressing: CIDR

The use of address classes is the traditional way of working with IP addressing and subnetting. A more recent development is called *Classless InterDomain Routing,* abbreviated as CIDR (and pronounced "cider").

One Internet resource describes CIDR as "subnetting on steroids." CIDR networks are referred to as "slash x" networks, with the "x" representing the number of bits assigned originally as the network ID (before subnetting). Think of this as the number of bits that don't "belong" to you.

With CIDR, the subnet mask actually becomes part of the routing tables. CIDR allows us to break networks into subnets and combine networks into supernets.

A traditional Class C network, you'll recall, contained 8 bits in the IP address that you could use as you wished for host IDs or subnetting, leaving 24 bits that were not under your control. Using CIDR, this would be designated as a "slash 24" network. Thus, a CIDR IP address would look like this: 192.168.1.27/24. Using the same formula, a traditional unsubnetted Class A network would be a /8, and a traditional unsubnetted Class B would be designated as /16. Of course, subnetted networks that would use variable length subnet masks are also designated in the same way. See Table 23-3 for the correlation of the subnet masks to the "slash x" designations.

TABLE 23-3 CIDR Network Designations as They Correlate to Subnet Masks

"Slash x" Designation	Subnet Mask
/8	255.0.0.0
/12	255.240.0.0
/16	255.255.0.0
/20	255.255.240.0
/21	255.255.248.0
/22	255.255.252.0
/23	255.255.254.0
/24	255.255.255.0
/25	255.255.255.128
/26	255.255.255.192
/27	255.255.255.224
/28	255.255.255.248
/29	255.255.255.252
/30	255.255.255.254

CERTIFICATION OBJECTIVE 23.03

Installing, Configuring, Managing, and Monitoring TCP/IP

In order to put all this theory into practice, you must first install (if you haven't already) and configure the TCP/IP protocol on your Windows 2000 computer. Network protocols are installed via the Network and Dial-up Connections window (this is different from NT 4.0, where you could right-click on Network Neighborhood and bring up the Properties sheet to install new protocols). In this case, you will select your local area connection, right-click, and choose Properties.

Installing TCP/IP in Windows 2000

The Properties sheet will list the networking protocols and components that are already installed, and will allow you to install, uninstall, and configure the properties of your networking components (Figure 23-7).

FIGURE 23-7

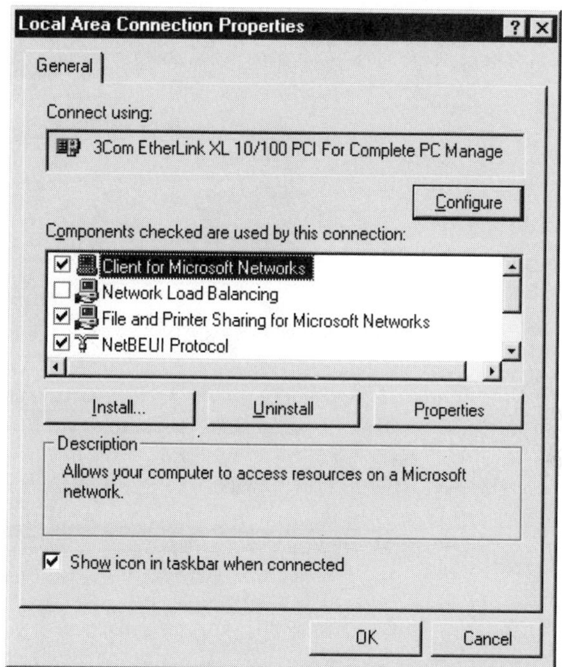

The Properties sheet for the Local Area connection

In the following exercise, we will walk through the steps of installing and configuring TCP/IP on a Windows 2000 computer. Note that you must be logged on with administrative privileges to install TCP/IP or other network protocols.

EXERCISE 23-3

CertCam 23-3

Installing TCP/IP in Windows 2000

1. Select Start | Settings | Network and Dial-up Connections.
2. In the window displaying the contents of the Network and Dial-up Connections folder, right-click on your local area connection and choose Properties.
3. Click Install, and you will see a dialog box as shown in the following illustration.

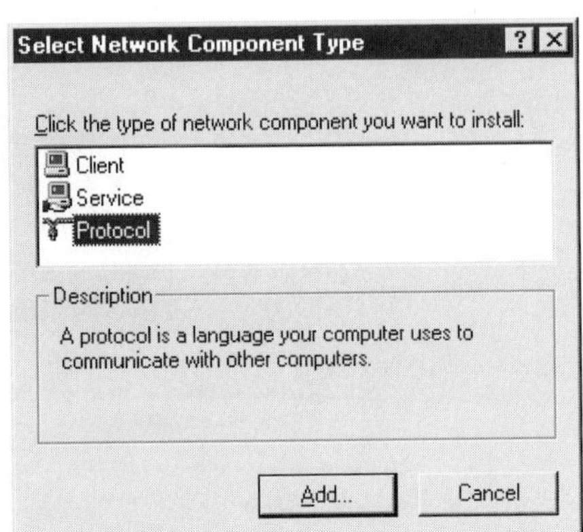

4. A list of available protocols will be shown, as in the following illustration.

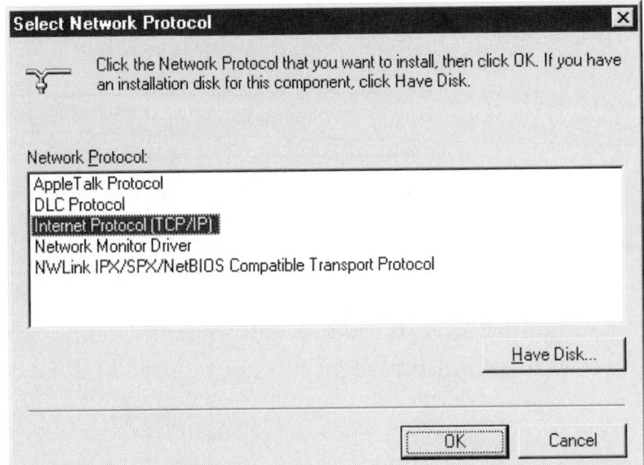

5. Select Internet Protocol (TCP/IP).
6. Click OK. You may be prompted for the Windows 2000 installation CD. The protocol will be installed and can now be configured.

Configuring TCP/IP in Windows 2000

Once TCP/IP has been installed, you must enter the proper configuration information before the computer can communicate on the network using the TCP/IP protocols. The following exercise will walk you through the process.

exam Watch

The default gateway address must be on the same subnet as the computer's IP address.

EXERCISE 23-4

Configuring TCP/IP

Return to the Properties sheet for the local area connection and select Internet Protocol (TCP/IP), then double-click or click Properties.

1. If your network has a DHCP server that will be used to obtain an IP address for this computer, select the "Obtain an IP address automatically" radio button. The DHCP server will provide both the IP address and other configuration information, such as the subnet mask and default gateway. If the network does not have a DHCP server, or you will not use the DHCP server to obtain an address automatically, skip to Step 4.
2. Select "Obtain DNS server address automatically" if the DHCP server will provide this information. Otherwise, select "Use the following DNS server address" and enter a preferred DNS server and, if available, an alternate DNS server to perform host-name-to-IP-address resolution.
3. Click OK and skip the remaining steps.
4. If you will not use DHCP to assign an address, select the "Use the following IP address" radio button, then complete the remaining steps.

   You will then see the TCP/IP Properties dialog box, as shown in the following illustration.

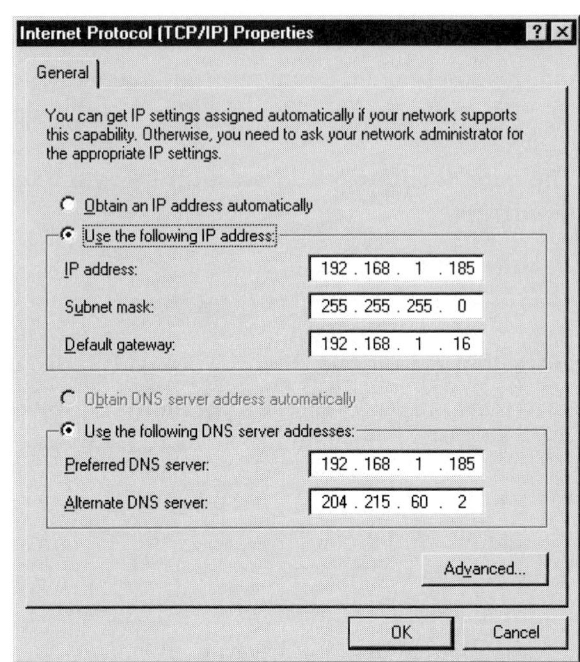

5. In the IP address field, enter a valid IP address for the subnet on which this computer is located. Remember that the network ID must be the same as other computers on the subnet, and the host ID must be unique to the subnet.
6. Enter the correct subnet mask, based on the address class and whether and how the network is subnetted.
7. If the network is routed (contains more than one subnet), enter a *default gateway* address. The default gateway is the address of the router (or computer functioning as a router) to which messages are sent when they are addressed to a destination that is on a different subnet.
8. Enter a preferred and (optionally) alternate DNS server. Click OK.

Advanced TCP/IP Properties

Windows 2000 will allow you to more finely tune your TCP/IP settings. When you click Advanced in the Properties box, you will see the tabbed Advanced TCP/IP Settings Properties sheet shown in Figure 23-8.

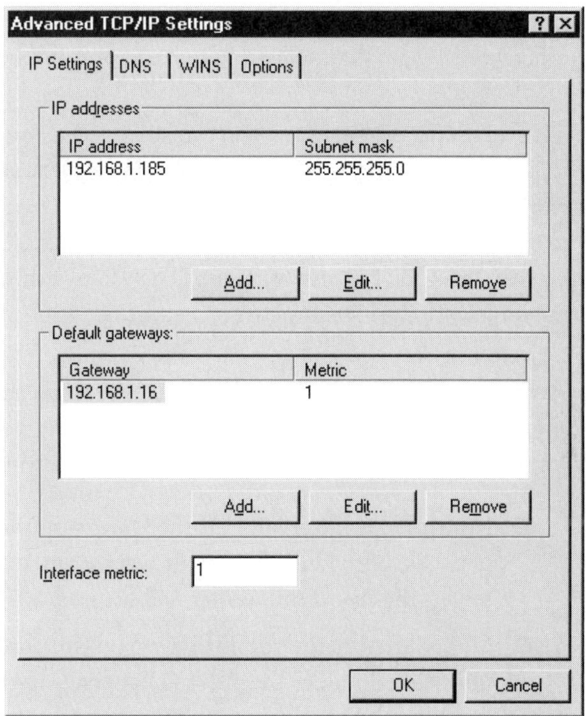

FIGURE 23-8

The Advanced TCP/IP Settings property sheet

The Advanced Settings allow you to further configure the IP settings, DNS, WINS, and other options.

IP Settings Under Advanced IP Settings, you can configure the computer to use more than one IP address or default gateway. Note that you can add, remove, or edit the properties of both in this dialog box.

Assigning Multiple IP Addresses You can use multiple IP addresses in various situations, such as public addresses used for the Internet and private addresses used for an internal network, or for multiple logical IP networks on the same physical network segment.

Assigning Multiple Default Gateways Windows 2000 supports a feature called *dead gateway detection*, which is used to detect routers that have gone down. If multiple default gateways are configured, a failing TCP connection will update the IP routing table with the next default gateway in the list. Although you can assign multiple gateways, the second (or subsequent) gateway(s) will be used *only* if the first fails. In other words, more than one default gateway cannot be active simultaneously.

The Interface Metric You can specify a custom metric for the connection by typing a value in this field (the default value is 1). A *metric* is the cost of using a particular route from one destination to another. Generally this will be the number of *hops* to the IP destination. Anything on the local subnet is one hop, and every time a router is crossed, this adds 1 to the *hop count*. The value of this is that it lets Windows 2000 select the route with the lowest metric if there are multiple routes to the same destination.

Advanced DNS Settings The DNS tab on the Advanced Settings sheet is shown in Figure 23-9.

You can configure the following Advanced settings for DNS:

- **Multiple DNS servers** If there are multiple DNS servers configured on the network, and TCP/IP doesn't receive any response from the current DNS server, the next DNS server will be used.
- **Unqualified name resolution** You can configure TCP/IP to resolve unqualified names by either (1) appending the primary and connection-specific DNS suffixes to the unqualified name for DNS queries, or (2) appending a series of configured DNS suffixes to the unqualified name for DNS queries.
- **Connection-specific DNS suffixes** Each connection in the Network and Dial-up Connections can be set up to have its own DNS suffix, along with the primary DNS suffix that is configured for the computer on the Network Identification tab in the System applet (in Control Panel).
- **DNS dynamic update behavior** If you have DNS servers that support DNS dynamic update (DDNS), you can enable the DNS dynamic update of the domain name and IP addresses for the computer. Windows 2000 DNS servers support dynamic update.

FIGURE 23-9

You can fine-tune DNS settings with the Advanced Settings property sheet

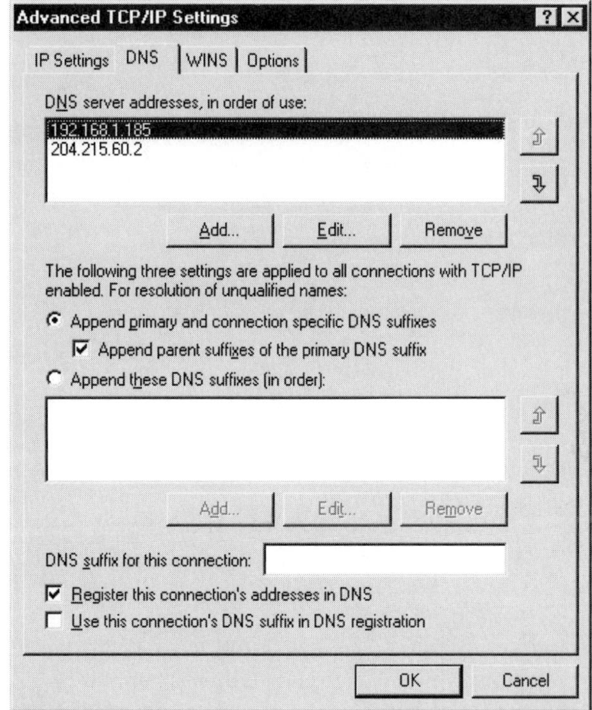

Advanced WINS Settings You can also make advanced settings to WINS, using the WINS tab shown in Figure 23-10.

Some settings that can be configured include:

- **Multiple WINS servers.** If you have multiple WINS on the network, and TCP/IP fails to receive any response from the current WINS server, the next WINS server in the list will be tried.
- **Enabling and disabling the use of the Lmhosts file.** You can use this selection to enable or disable the Lmhosts file. If it is enabled, TCP/IP will use the Lmhosts file found in the *systemroot*\System32\Drivers\Etc folder during the process of NetBIOS name resolution. The Lmhosts file is enabled by default.

FIGURE 23-10

The WINS Advanced properties tab allows you to fine-tune your WINS settings

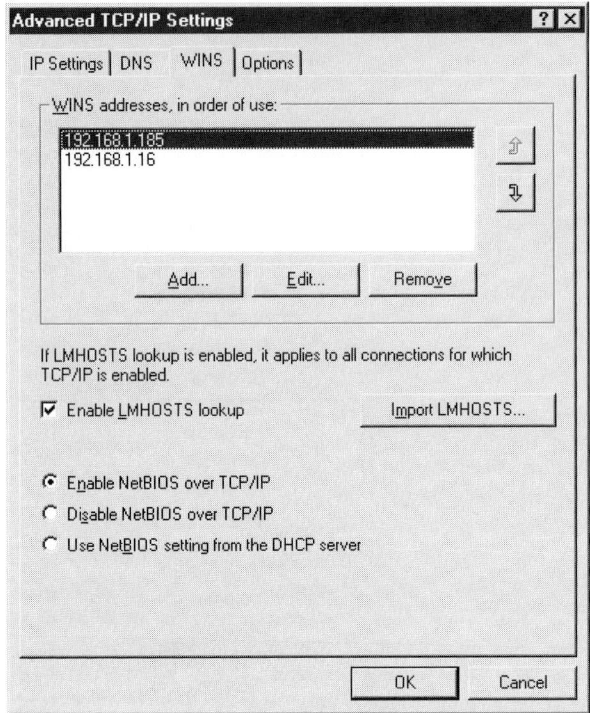

- **Enabling and disabling the use of NetBIOS over TCP/IP.** You can enable or disable the use of NetBIOS over TCP/IP here. When it is disabled, NetBIOS programs cannot run over TCP/IP, which means you may not be able to connect to computers that are running downlevel operating systems such as Windows 95 or NT. NetBIOS over TCP/IP should be disabled only if all computers on your network have been upgraded to Windows 2000 and your network is not using NetBIOS-based applications.

Other Advanced Options The last tab in the Advanced TCP/IP Settings sheet is the Options tab, shown in Figure 23-11.

The two available options allow you to do the following:

- **Enable Internet Protocol security (IPSec)** You can provide for secure end-to-end communication of IP-based traffic on a private network or the Internet by enabling IPSec (it is disabled by default). When IPSec is enabled, you can also specify an IPSec security policy.

- **Enable TCP/IP filtering** This option allows you to enable filtering of TCP/IP packets. If TCP/IP filtering is enabled, you can specify what types of TCP/IP traffic are processed.

Although the help file indicates that the settings apply to all adapters, the filtering is specific for the adapter for which you are adjusting the filters. TCP/IP filtering specifies the types of incoming traffic destined for this adapter and passed up to the TCP/IP protocol for processing.

To configure TCP/IP filtering, select this check box and specify the types of allowed TCP/IP traffic for all adapters on this computer in terms of IP protocols, TCP ports, and UDP ports. The protocols are determined by the protocol number. You can determine protocol numbers by looking at the contents of RFC 1700.

Configuring TCP/IP filtering can get a little tricky, because when you first enable it, all traffic is filtered out. You add filters for protocols and ports that will want to allow traffic to pass through. If you run into problems with network communications after enabling the filters, you should first disable TCP/IP filtering

FIGURE 23-11

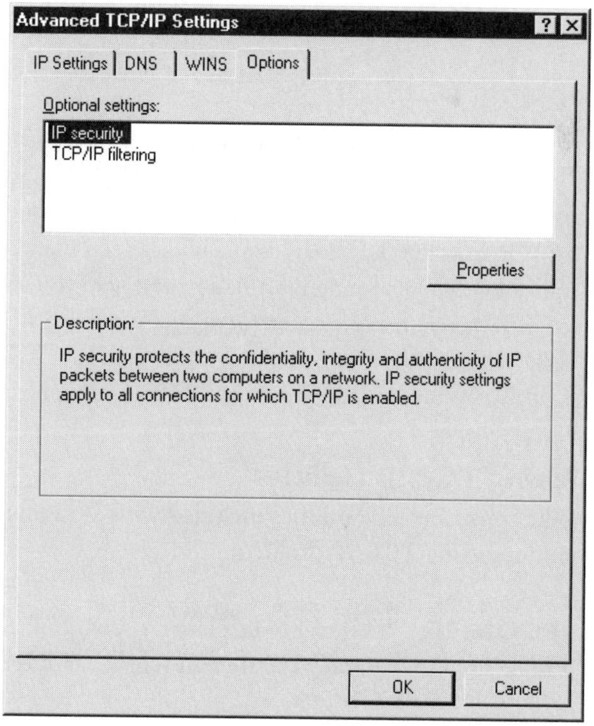

The Options tab allows you to configure IPSec and TCP/IP filtering

and see if that fixes the problem. If so, there is a protocol or port that you must add in order to resume normal network functioning.

TCP/IP Best Practices

Microsoft recommends the following best practices when setting up a TCP/IP-based Windows 2000 network:

- If your local network will be connected to the Internet, either obtain registered public IP addresses for all computers that will access the Internet and use an IP router to send traffic to the public network, or establish the Internet connection using one computer, install *Network Address Translation* (NAT) on that computer, assign private (nonregistered) IP addresses to the other computers on the internal network, and let NAT translate the private addresses to the public address to provide access to the Internet for all the computers on the LAN.
- If you assign private addresses, use the address ranges in each class that are designated as reserved for that purpose by IANA.

Troubleshooting TCP/IP

TCP/IP is a powerful, flexible, and reliable protocol suite. Generally it works well, but because it is so complex, there are many ways in which it can be misconfigured or, for other reasons, fail to provide network communications.

Windows 2000 TCP/IP comes with several useful utilities that can provide you with valuable troubleshooting information and help you to diagnose the problem when your TCP/IP network experiences connectivity problems. These include the command-line utilities IPCONFIG, PING/PATHPING, TRACERT, and NETSTAT/NBTSTAT, as well as Windows 2000's protocol analysis tool, Network Monitor.

Using TCP/IP Utilities

The command-line utilities included with Windows 2000 are useful in identifying and resolving TCP/IP problems.

IPCONFIG This utility displays current TCP/IP configuration values, and can be used to manually release and renew (with the /release and /renew switches, respectively) a TCP/IP configuration lease assigned by a DHCP server. It can also be used to reset DNS name registrations with the /registerdns switch. Typing **IPCONFIG** provides basic configuration information: IP address, subnet mask, and default gateway. Typing **IPCONFIG /ALL** provides more detailed information, as shown in Figure 23-12.

As you can see, the /all switch provides much more information, including the host name, DNS suffix, node type being used, whether IP routing and WINS proxy are enabled, as well as the MAC (physical) address of the network card and the addresses of assigned DNS and WINS servers.

PING and PATHPING The PING command is used to verify whether TCP/IP is configured correctly and to test connectivity to other host systems. It is often used as the first step in diagnosing network problems. Microsoft recommends that PING be used in the following order to isolate a connectivity problem on the TCP/IP network:

1. First, ping the loopback address (127.0.0.1) to verify that TCP/IP is installed and configured correctly on the local computer.
2. Next, try pinging the IP address of the local computer itself to verify that it was added to the network correctly.

FIGURE 23-12 Using the /all switch with the IPCONFIG command provides more detailed information

```
E:\WINNT\System32\cmd.exe
E:\>
E:\>ipconfig /all

Windows 2000 IP Configuration

        Host Name . . . . . . . . . . . . : CONSTELLATION
        Primary DNS Suffix  . . . . . . . : tacteam.net
        Node Type . . . . . . . . . . . . : Hybrid
        IP Routing Enabled. . . . . . . . : Yes
        WINS Proxy Enabled. . . . . . . . : No
        DNS Suffix Search List. . . . . . : tacteam.net

Ethernet adapter Local Area Connection:

        Connection-specific DNS Suffix  . :
        Description . . . . . . . . . . . : 3Com EtherLink XL 10/100 PCI For Com
plete PC Management NIC (3C905C-TX)
        Physical Address. . . . . . . . . : 00-50-DA-0D-F5-2D
        DHCP Enabled. . . . . . . . . . . : No
        IP Address. . . . . . . . . . . . : 192.168.1.185
        Subnet Mask . . . . . . . . . . . : 255.255.255.0
        Default Gateway . . . . . . . . . : 192.168.1.16
        DNS Servers . . . . . . . . . . . : 192.168.1.185
                                            204.215.60.2
        Primary WINS Server . . . . . . . : 192.168.1.185
        Secondary WINS Server . . . . . . : 192.168.1.16

E:\>_
```

3. Then ping the IP address of the default gateway (sometimes called the "near side of the router") to verify that the default gateway is functioning and that you can communicate with a local host on the local network.
4. Finally, ping the IP address of a remote host (called the "far side of the router") to verify that packets are being forwarded and you can communicate through the router.

If the TCP/IP connection is working, PING will return a response, as shown in Figure 23-13.

PATHPING was not available in Windows NT, but is provided in Windows 2000 to allow you to trace the route a packet takes to a destination and display information on packet losses for each router in the path as well as the links between routers. You can also use PATHPING to troubleshoot *Quality of Service* (QoS) connectivity. PATHPING combines features of both the PING and the TRACERT commands, and includes additional information that neither of those tools provides.

TRACERT TRACERT traces the network route taken by an IP datagram to its destination. It does this by sending Internet Control Message Protocol (ICMP) echo packets with varying Time-To-Live (TTL) values to the destination address. Each router along the path must decrease the TTL on a packet by at least 1 before forwarding it, so the TTL is basically a hop count. When the TTL on a packet reaches 0, the router is supposed to send back an *ICMP Time Exceeded* message to the source system. TRACERT determines the route by sending the first echo packet with a TTL of 1 and then incrementing the TTL by 1 on each additional transmission until a response is received or the maximum TTL count occurs. Examining the ICMP Time Exceeded messages sent back by intermediate routers allows the route to be determined.

The results of a TRACERT command are shown in Figure 23-14.

NETSTAT and NBTSTAT NETSTAT displays protocol statistics and information on current TCP/IP connections. There are several options available for the NETSTAT command, as listed in the following grid.

NBTSTAT is used to check the state of current NetBIOS over TCP/IP connections (also called NetBT connections). It can also update the NetBIOS Remote Name Cache and determine the registered names and scope IDs.

FIGURE 23-13

PING returns a response indicating TCP/IP connectivity is good

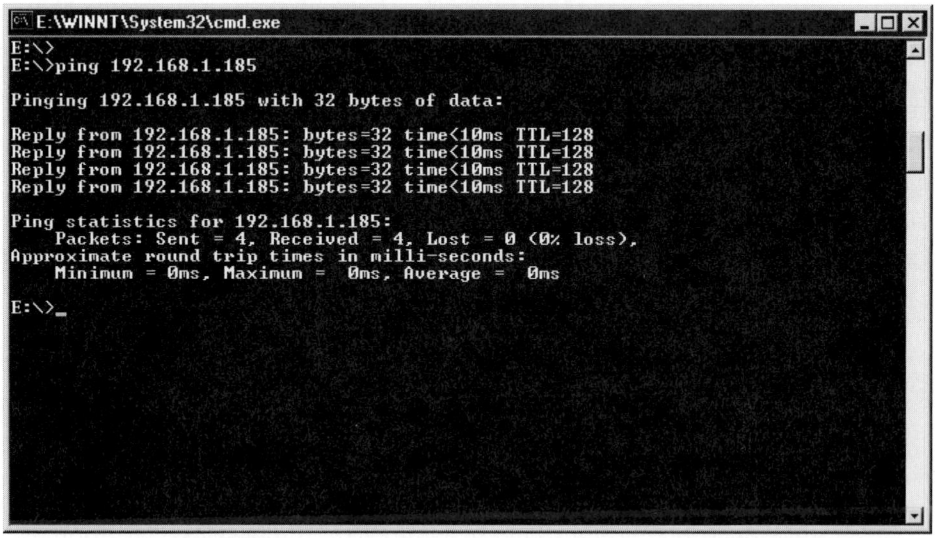

```
E:\WINNT\System32\cmd.exe
E:\>
E:\>ping 192.168.1.185

Pinging 192.168.1.185 with 32 bytes of data:

Reply from 192.168.1.185: bytes=32 time<10ms TTL=128
Reply from 192.168.1.185: bytes=32 time<10ms TTL=128
Reply from 192.168.1.185: bytes=32 time<10ms TTL=128
Reply from 192.168.1.185: bytes=32 time<10ms TTL=128

Ping statistics for 192.168.1.185:
    Packets: Sent = 4, Received = 4, Lost = 0 (0% loss),
Approximate round trip times in milli-seconds:
    Minimum = 0ms, Maximum =  0ms, Average =  0ms

E:\>_
```

NBTSTAT can be used to troubleshoot NetBIOS name resolution problems, and like NETSTAT, includes a number of options:

- **-n** Used to display names that were registered locally by programs and services.

FIGURE 23-14

TRACERT returns information about each router passed through to reach the destination address

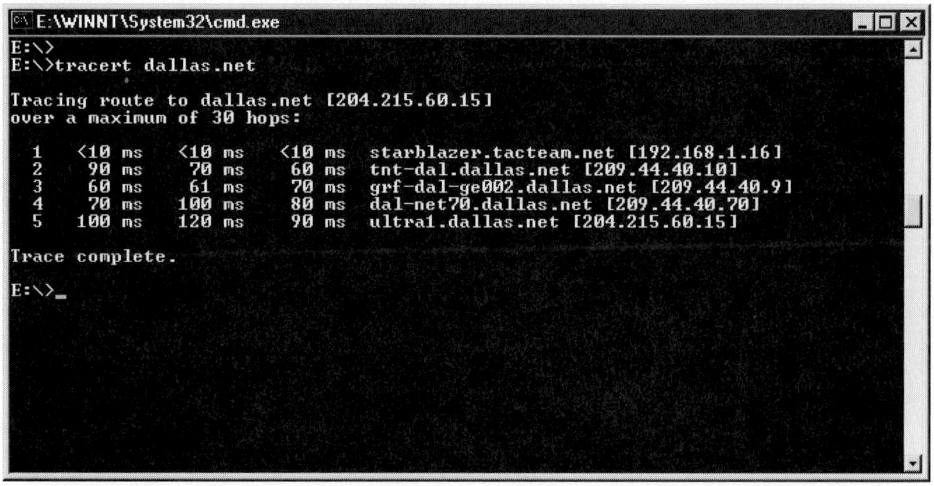

```
E:\WINNT\System32\cmd.exe
E:\>
E:\>tracert dallas.net

Tracing route to dallas.net [204.215.60.15]
over a maximum of 30 hops:

  1   <10 ms   <10 ms   <10 ms  starblazer.tacteam.net [192.168.1.16]
  2    90 ms    70 ms    60 ms  tnt-dal.dallas.net [209.44.40.10]
  3    60 ms    61 ms    70 ms  grf-dal-ge002.dallas.net [209.44.40.9]
  4    70 ms   100 ms    80 ms  dal-net70.dallas.net [209.44.40.70]
  5   100 ms   120 ms    90 ms  ultra1.dallas.net [204.215.60.15]

Trace complete.

E:\>_
```

- -c Used to display the NetBIOS Remote Name Cache (a mapping of names to addresses for other computers).
- -R Used to purge the name cache and reload it (from the LMHOSTS file).
- -RR Used to release the NetBIOS names registered with the WINS server, then renew their registrations with the server.
- -a Used in conjunction with a computer name (in the format *nbtstat –a <computername>)* to return the NetBIOS name table for the computer named, as well as the MAC address of the network adapter.
- -s Used to list current NetBIOS sessions and the status of each, with statistical information, as shown in Figure 23-15.

NETDIAG The Resource Kit for Windows 2000 Professional includes the NETDIAG utility. This is a command-line diagnostic tool that helps isolate networking and connectivity problems. It does this by performing a series of tests designed to determine the state of the network client software, and ascertain whether it is functional. This tool does not require that parameters or switches be specified, which means support personnel and network administrators can focus on analyzing the output, rather than training users on how to use the tool.

SCENARIO & SOLUTION	
What does the –a option in NETSTAT do?	Causes all connections and listening ports to be displayed (server connections are not normally shown).
What is the –e option used for?	To display Ethernet statistics.
What is the purpose of the –n option?	Used to display addresses and port numbers in numerical form instead of by name.
How is the –s option used?	To display statistics on a per-protocol basis (type netstat –p <protocol type>).
Why would you use the –r option?	To display the routing table.

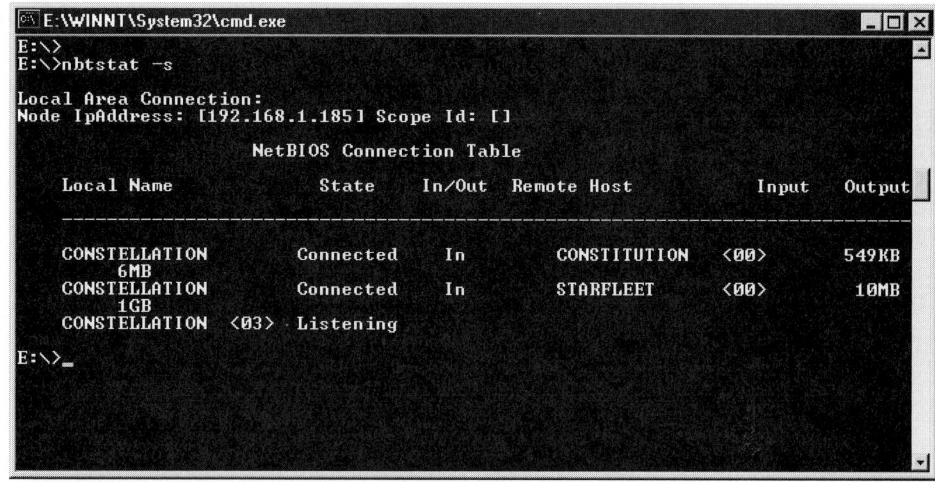

FIGURE 23-15 The nbtstat –s command lists current NetBIOS sessions, status, and statistics

Managing and Monitoring Network Traffic

Because TCP/IP is such a widely used set of protocols, there are numerous hardware and software tools available for monitoring and managing traffic on a TCP/IP network. You can practice preventative maintenance, establish baselines, or troubleshoot existing problems. One of the most popular types of tools is called a *protocol analyzer.* This is usually a software program that allows you to copy the individual packets and analyze their structure. The process of copying frames for review and analysis is called *capturing.*

Windows 2000 Server includes a "lite" version of the protocol monitor that comes with Systems Management Server (SMS), Network Monitor. This tool can be used to capture and display the frames or packets that a Windows 2000 Server receives from a LAN. You can use Network Monitor to detect and troubleshoot many networking problems.

Installing the Windows 2000 Network Monitor

The Network Monitor tool can be installed on Windows 2000 Server from the Add/Remove Programs applet in Control Panel. Open the applet and click on Add/Remove Windows Components, select Management and Monitoring Tools, and then click Details. Select the Network Monitor check box. You may be prompted to insert your Windows 2000 installation CD.

After installation is complete, the Network Monitor will appear in the Administrative Tools submenu of the Programs menu.

Using the Windows 2000 Network Monitor

The version of Network Monitor included in Windows 2000 has some limitations. It cannot run in what is referred to as *promiscuous mode.* This is a state in which the network card can listen to all the traffic on the network, not just that which is sent from or received by the computer running the Network Monitor software. The more sophisticated version of Network Monitor that comes with SMS is capable of promiscuous mode. Even so, there is a great deal of information that can be collected with Windows 2000's Network Monitor utility. Figure 23-16 shows the Network Monitor interface, with information from a capture.

As you can see, there is a great deal of statistical information available, including such useful values as the percentage of network utilization during the capture, the number of frames and bytes transferred, as well as how many frames were dropped.

After you have captured the data, you can view it by selecting Display Captured Data from the Capture menu. You will then see detailed information for each frame (packet), as shown in Figure 23-17.

Network Monitor Best Practices

Microsoft recommends that you run Network Monitor at off-peak (low-usage) times or only for short periods of time, in order to decrease the detrimental impact on system performance that can be caused by Network Monitor.

You can filter the data captured, as well as the data displayed. A *capture filter* works somewhat like a database query; you can use it to specify the types of network information you want to monitor. For example, you can capture packets based on the protocol or based on the addresses of two computers whose interactions you wish to monitor. When a capture filter is applied, all packets are examined and compared to the filter's parameters; those that do not fulfill the filter requirements are dropped. This can be a processor-intensive activity during periods of moderate or high network utilization when the network card is placed in promiscuous mode.

Display filters work on data that has already been captured. They do not affect the contents of the Network Monitor capture buffer. You can use a display filter to determine which frames you want to display. The frames can be filtered by source or destination address, protocols used to send it, or the properties and values it contains.

You can also use *capture triggers* to specify a set of conditions that will cause ("trigger") an event to occur in a Network Monitor capture filter. Triggers allow

FIGURE 23-16

The Windows 2000 Network Monitor interface

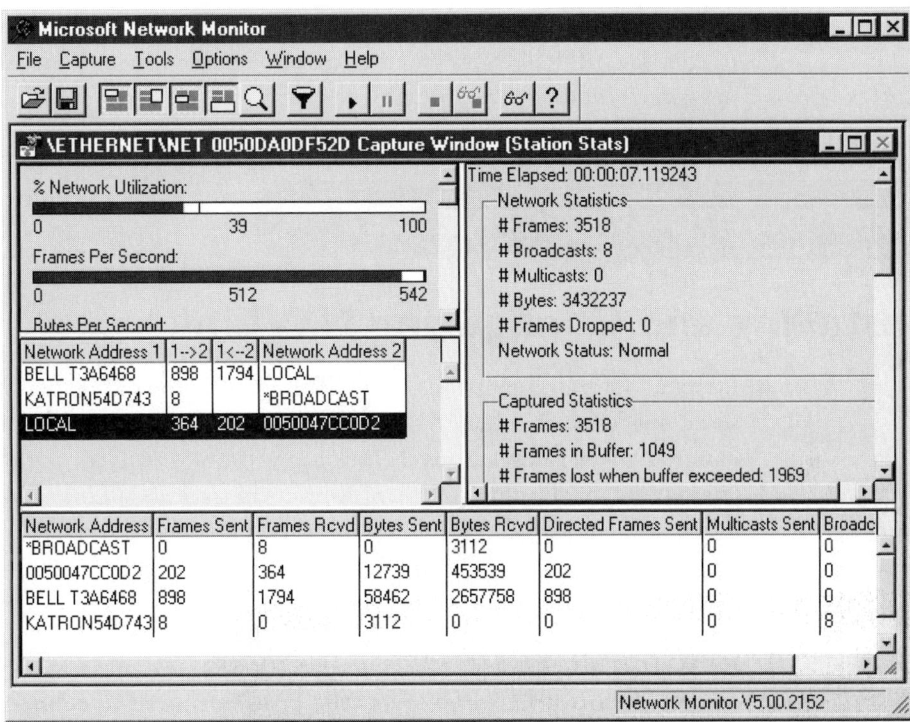

FIGURE 23-17

Capture detail summary displays information about each data frame

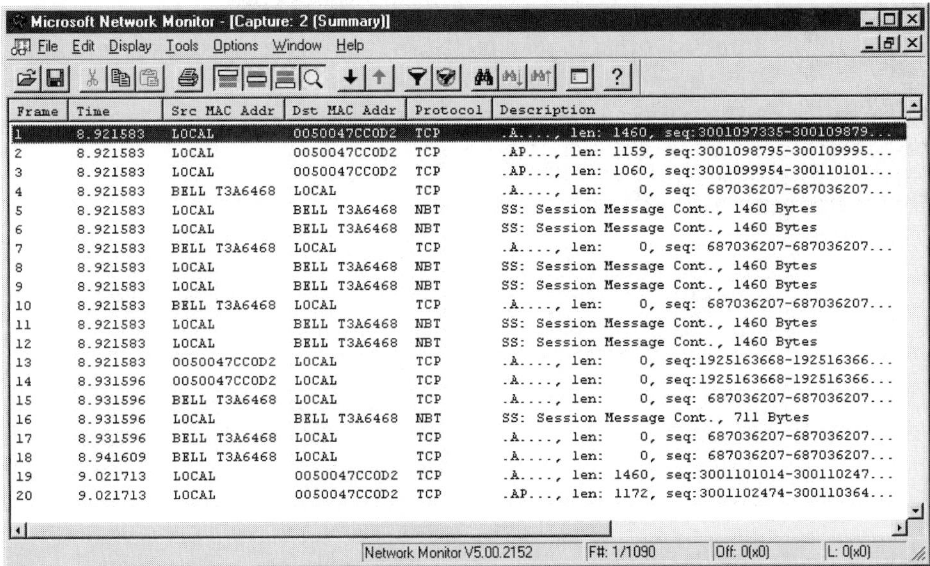

Network Monitor to respond to events on your network. For example, you can set triggers so that if Network Monitor detects a particular set of circumstances on the network, it will start an executable file.

CERTIFICATION OBJECTIVE 23.07

Installing and Configuring NWLink

Despite Microsoft's emphasis on TCP/IP for Windows 2000 networks, there are situations in which other LAN protocols are required or desirable. For instance, connectivity to NetWare servers (prior to version 5) requires that the connecting computer(s) be running an IPX/SPX protocol stack. NWLink is Microsoft's implementation of IPX/SPX (the Internetwork Packet Exchange/Sequenced Packet Exchange protocols). You can install NWLink on Windows 2000 machines to allow them to access NetWare servers.

on the job

Be aware that although NWLink and IPX/SPX are often thought of in Microsoft networking circles as "the protocols used to connect to NetWare networks," you can also use these protocols to connect Windows machines to one another. Because NWLink is faster and easier to configure than TCP/IP and routable (unlike NetBEUI), it can be an appropriate LAN protocol choice for a small or medium network that is not connected to the Internet, even if there are no NetWare servers anywhere in sight.

Installing the NWLink Protocol

NWLink is installed in the same way as TCP/IP, through the Network and Dial-up Connections properties box. Note that you must be logged on with administrative privileges to install NWLink or other network protocols.

When you install the NWLink protocols, they will be installed to all your network connections. However, you can change this. After the installation is completed, i f you do not want to use NWLink on a particular connection, you can right-click that connection, click Properties and uncheck the NWLink IPX/SPX/NetBIOS Compatible Transport Protocol check box on either the General or Networking tab.

Configuring NWLink

There is less configuration information required to set up NWLink than is necessary for TCP/IP, but there are still a few pieces of information you will need to have on hand. The configuration box asks you for a network number; if you are uncertain of this number, the default value of 00000000 will usually work.

Another setting that can be configured is the *frame type*. You can use automatic frame type detection, however. In most cases, this is preferred.

You can use the IPXROUTE CONFIG command to get information about the internal network number being used by the routers on the network, as well as the frame type being used by the servers.

In order for Windows 2000 clients to access a NetWare server directly, you will also need to install *Client Services for NetWare* (CSNW) on the client computer(s). The users must also have valid user accounts on the NetWare server to log on.

Windows 2000 machines that are clients to a Windows 2000 Server can also access the NetWare server through the Windows 2000 Server, without having extra client software installed, if you install *Gateway Services for NetWare* (GSNW) on the Windows 2000 Server and configure the NetWare server to allow access through a special gateway account. To accomplish this, you must create a group on the NetWare server called NTGATEWAY and create a NetWare user account in that group. On the Windows 2000 Server, you must then enable the gateway service and enter the name of the

EXERCISE 23-5

Installing and Configuring NWLink in Windows 2000

To install NWLink on your Windows 2000 computer, follow these steps:

1. Select Start | Settings | Network and Dial-up Connections.
2. Right-click on the icon for the local area connection and click Properties.
3. On the General tab, click Install.
4. In the Select Network Component Type dialog box, click Protocol, and then click Add.
5. In the Select Network Protocol dialog box, click NWLink IPX/SPX/NetBIOS Compatible Transport Protocol and then click OK.

To configure NWLink, follow these steps:

1. In the Local Area Connection properties box, select NWLink IPX/SPX NetBIOS Compatible Transport Protocol and click Properties. You will see the General properties sheet displayed, as shown in the following illustration.

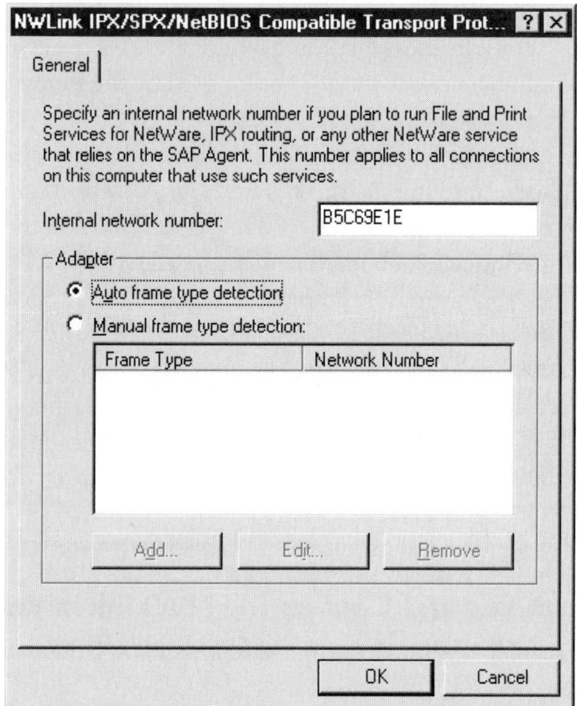

2. Enter the internal network number used on your network, or use the default of 00000000.
3. Select "Auto frame type detection" unless there is a compelling reason for manual frame type specification (this may be necessary if you have servers using different frame types on the same network).

4. If you choose "Manual frame type detection," you will need to specify a network number and select from the supported frame types shown in the following illustration.

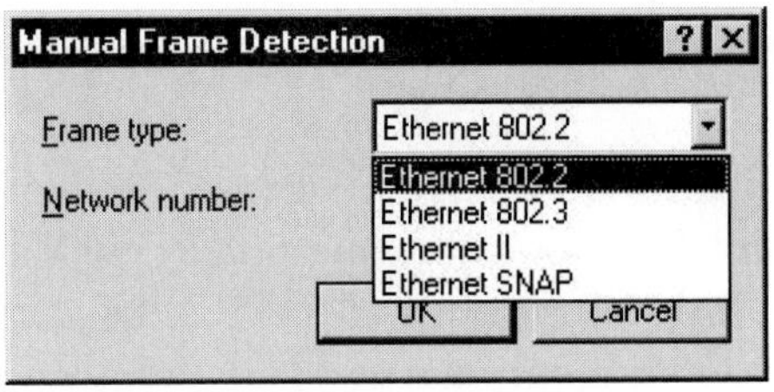

gateway group and the password for the gateway account. All Windows 2000 clients can now connect to the NetWare server through this same account. Note, however, that all will be using the same user account for access, and thus will all have the same permissions. If you wish for a user to have different permissions, that user must have a valid individual user account on the NetWare server through which he or she can access the server's resources and client software installed on the client machine.

Protocol Binding Order

Network protocols are bound to network services installed on a particular client or server. Multiple protocols can be bound to multiple network services. For example, you can bind NetBEUI, TCP/IP, and NWLink to the Microsoft network client.

When a client attempts to establish a session with a server, it will request to use the protocol on the top of its binding order for the particular service. If the service is the Microsoft Network Client, then the protocol binding order for that list is processed. Just as was the case you learned with Windows NT 4.0, the client determines the preferred protocol.

For example, the Microsoft network client service on the client has NetBEUI and TCP/IP installed, with NetBEUI on the top of the binding order. The destination server also has NetBEUI and TCP/IP installed, but has TCP/IP on top of the binding order. Since the caller determines the binding order, they will negotiate using TCP/IP first, because that is on top of the client's binding order.

exam Watch

To change the binding order you must open the Network and Dial-up Connections folder first. After opening the folder, click on the Advanced menu and click Advanced Settings. On the Adapters and Bindings tab, you will be able to use the up and down arrows to change the binding order.

CERTIFICATION SUMMARY

This chapter has covered a wide scope of topics pertaining to the networking protocols used for communication by the Windows 2000 operating systems, particularly the members of the TCP/IP protocol suite. In fact, we started the chapter with an introduction to the Windows 2000 implementation of TCP/IP and a brief history of the protocols, discussed the advantages and disadvantages of TCP/IP and where it fits into the popular networking models, the Open Systems Interconnection (OSI) model and the Department of Defense (DoD) model.

TCP/IP is the protocol stack of the global Internet, so we discussed the growth of the Internet and how TCP/IP played a part in that growth. We talked about IP addressing, including subnetting and supernetting, and we walked through an exercise on how to install and configure the TCP/IP protocols in Windows 2000.

Then we briefly discussed troubleshooting TCP/IP connectivity problems, and some of the tools and utilities that are either included in Windows 2000 or are available elsewhere to make troubleshooting easier. We examined the Network Monitor protocol analysis tool that Windows 2000 includes, and learned how to install it and how to use it to capture packets on the network.

Finally, we turned our attention to another popular protocol stack, IPX/SPX, which is used in many NetWare networks and is implemented in Windows 2000 as NWLink. We completed an exercise in installing and configuring NWLink, and we discussed the services—Client Services for NetWare and Gateway Services for NetWare—that are used, along with the NWLink protocols, to allow Windows 2000 machines to connect to and access the resources of NetWare servers.

TWO-MINUTE DRILL

Windows 2000 TCP/IP

- ❑ TCP/IP is the default network transport protocol in Windows 2000, and is required for connectivity to the Internet.
- ❑ The TCP/IP protocol suite is relatively slow and difficult to configure, but has the advantages over NWLink and NetBEUI of a flexible, scalable addressing scheme, compatibility with many platforms and operating systems, and routability.
- ❑ The TCP/IP suite consists of many different protocols that operate at different layers of the networking model, including IP, ICMP and IGMP, ARP/RARP, TCP, UDP, FTP, Telnet, SMTP, SNMP, and others.

IP Addressing

- ❑ IP addresses are 32-bit binary numbers (often expressed as their dotted decimal equivalent), in which one portion represents the network ID and the other portion represents the host ID.
- ❑ The subnet mask is a 32-bit binary number used to indicate which bits in the IP address represent the network and which represent the host.
- ❑ IP networks were traditionally divided into three classes: Class A for large networks, Class B for medium-sized networks, and Class C for small networks.

Installing, Configuring, Managing, and Monitoring TCP/IP

- ❑ Utilities included with TCP/IP that are useful for troubleshooting include IPCONFIG, PING and PATHPING, TRACERT, NETSTAT and NBTSTAT, and a resource kit utility called NETDIAG.
- ❑ Network Monitor is a software protocol analyzer included with Windows 2000 Server that allows you to capture and analyze packets sent to or from the Windows 2000 machine on which the software is installed.

- ❑ Windows 2000 supports assigning multiple IP addresses, multiple gateways, and setting the interface metric under Advanced TCP/IP settings.
- ❑ Disabling of NetBIOS over TCP/IP (NetBT) is done via the Advanced WINS configuration options, and should only be done if your network does not have any non-Windows 2000 machines and does not use NetBIOS applications.
- ❑ TCP/IP filtering allows you to specify what types of TCP/IP traffic are processed.

Installing and Configuring NWLink

- ❑ NWLink is Microsoft's implementation of the IPX/SPX protocol stack used by Novell for its NetWare networks. It can be installed, along with NetWare client or gateway software, to provide access by Windows 2000 machines to a NetWare server, or it can be used as the LAN protocol for Microsoft networks that don't need to connect to the Internet.
- ❑ Connectivity to NetWare servers (prior to version 5) requires that the connecting computer(s) be running an IPX/SPX protocol stack.
- ❑ Configuration settings for NWLink include the internal and external network numbers and the frame type.
- ❑ The protocol binding order on the client machine determines which LAN protocol will be used for the connection if multiple protocols are installed and configured.

24

Installing and Managing the DHCP Server

CERTIFICATION OBJECTIVES

24.01	Overview of DHCP
24.02	DHCP Server Configuration
24.03	DHCP Relay Agents in a Routed Environment
24.04	Integrating DHCP with DDNS
24.05	Integrating DHCP with RRAS
24.06	Integrating DHCP with Active Directory
24.07	DHCP and APIPA
24.08	Monitoring and Troubleshooting DHCP
✓	Two-Minute Drill

All common network protocols assign each computer a unique identifier. In the case of IPX, this number is assigned automatically by the workstation in a way that is guaranteed to make the number unique: NetBEUI uses a 16-byte NetBIOS name. The TCP/IP protocol uses an IP address. In its original implementation, TCP/IP was designed to connect a relatively small number of servers together. The designers of DHCP did not portend that hundreds or thousands of computers in a single network would require IP address assignment.

To solve the problem of managing the hundreds or thousands of IP addresses an organization might have, DCHP was developed to provide a way to dynamically assign IP addresses to computers when they connect to the LAN.

Having a DHCP server on your network makes it easier for users who use laptops to connect to various office and home networks. In addition to assigning basic IP addressing information such as an IP address and a subnet mask, the DHCP server gives out other TCP/IP configuration information to the client. This additional information includes the IP address of the default gateway, Domain Name System (DNS) server, and the client's DNS domain name.

The Windows 2000 DHCP server is integrated with the Windows 2000 DNS server. This new feature allows a Windows 2000 DHCP server to communicate IP addressing and host name information to a Windows 2000 Dynamic DNS (DDNS) server. The Windows 2000 DHCP server can now provide dynamically the host name and IP address mapping information directly to the DDNS server. As application standards move toward using the WinSock interface, and away from NetBIOS, it is critical in large corporate networks to locate clients by host name and IP address.

CERTIFICATION OBJECTIVE 24.01

Overview of DHCP

Dynamic Host Configuration Protocol provides IP addressing information for DHCP clients. To obtain IP addressing information, the client must obtain a *lease* from a

DHCP server. In this section, we will examine the process of DHCP client lease assignment and the conversations that take place between a DHCP client and server.

DHCP Leases

When a DHCP server assigns IP addressing information to a DHCP client, the DHCP client does not own that IP address. The DHCP server continues to own the IP address, and the client has merely leased that information. Think of an IP address as a plot of land. When the DHCP server assigns the IP address to the DHCP client, it is renting out some land on the network. The DHCP client rents a parcel of land out on the network, but if its lease is not renewed, it won't be able to live on the network anymore.

In order to obtain a lease, a DHCP server and client participate in a conversation that includes four steps: Discover, Offer, Request, and Acknowledgement. Let's look at this process in more detail.

The DHCP Lease Process

The DHCP client and server participate in a dialog that consists of four primary interchanges:

- DHCPDISCOVER
- DHCPOFFER
- DHCPREQUEST
- DHCPACKNOWLEDGEMENT

The result of this dialog is the assignment of an IP address and additional TCP/IP parameters.

Discover

When the DHCP client initializes, it broadcasts a DHCPDISCOVER message to the local segment. The destination IP address is the limited broadcast address, 255.255.255.255. The destination hardware address is FFFFFFFFFFFF, which is the hardware broadcast address. All DHCP servers on the segment respond to the

DHCPDISCOVER message. The DCHP client does not have an IP address yet, so it includes with the DHCPDISCOVER message its Media Access Control (MAC) address (identified as the *ciaddr* field in a packet analysis). Other information in the DHCPDISCOVER message includes:

- The client's host name
- A "parameter request list" that includes DHCP option codes the client supports
- A message ID that identifies this particular request, and will be included in each of the messages the DHCP client and server send to each other
- The "hardware type" of the client's network interface card, such as 10-Mb Ethernet

Offer

All DHCP servers that receive the DHCPDISCOVER message respond by offering an IP address from their *pool* of available IP addresses. This offer is made in the form of a DHCPOFFER message. The DHCP client will accept the IP address from the first server that it receives a DHCP offer from.

The DHCPOFFER message is a broadcast message like the DISCOVER message. In order for the correct client to receive the information, the destination MAC address is included in the *ciaddr* field. Other information in the DHCPOFFER message includes:

- DHCP server IP address
- The offered IP address
- The offered subnet mask
- DHCP option information: Windows Internet Name Service (WINS) and DNS servers, default gateway
- Lease interval
- First and second lease renewal intervals (Renewal [T1] and Rebinding [T2] Time Values)

The DHCPOFFER message contains the basic IP addressing information the client computer will use when the TCP/IP stack is initialized. This basic information includes the client's IP address and subnet mask.

Request

The client responds to the offer by issuing a DHCPREQUEST broadcast message. Some questions may come to mind at this point: "Why use a broadcast message? Doesn't the client now have an IP address?" Recall that all DHCP servers respond to the initial DCHPDISCOVER message. The purpose of the DHCPREQUEST broadcast is to inform other DHCP servers that their offers have been rejected. The rejected DHCP servers then return the IP addresses they offered back to their pools of available IP addresses.

The DCHPREQUEST message is a confirmation of the information sent to the client in the DHCPOFFER message. The DHCPREQUEST message includes:

- The client's hardware address
- The DHCP server's IP address
- The client's requested IP address
- The client's host name

ACK/NACK

Finally, the DHCP server responds to the DHCPREQUEST message with a DHCPACK broadcast message. The reason this message is broadcast is that the client doesn't "officially" obtain its IP address until it is acknowledged. Again, the client's MAC address is included in order to identify the proper destination of this message.

The DHCPACK message contains similar information to that included with the DHCPOFFER message, and acts as a confirmation of the DHCPREQUEST message. At this point, the client has leased the IP address and can use it for network communication. The address is marked as "leased" by the DHCP server and will not be leased to any other client during the active lease period. It is also during the ACK phase that DHCP options are delivered to the client.

Lease Renewal

A lease is an agreement to let someone use something for a defined length of time. The DHCP client leases IP addressing information from the DHCP server. The DHCP client does not own this information, and does not get to keep it forever.

Because the DHCP server owns this information, it allows the DHCP server to maintain a dynamic pool of IP addresses. The lease process prevents computers no longer on the network from retaining IP addresses that other computers might use.

The length of the lease is defined at the DHCP server. The default lease period on a Windows 2000 DHCP server is eight days. This can be changed depending on the needs of the network administrator and his or her specific network requirements.

A DHCP client must renew its lease. The DHCPOFFER and DHCKACK messages include the amount of time a client is allowed to keep its IP address, which is its lease period. Also included are the times when the client is required to *renew* its lease. The DHCPOFFER message includes not only the lease period, but also a *Renewal Time Interval (T1)* and the *Rebinding Time Value (T2).*

Renewal and Rebinding Intervals

The Renewal Time Value represents 50% of the lease period. If the lease period is eight days, then the Renewal Time Value (T1) is four days. At T1, the DHCP client will attempt to renew its IP address by broadcasting a DHCPREQUEST message containing its current IP address. If the DHCP server that granted the IP address is available, it will renew the IP address for the period specified in the renewed lease. If the DHCP server is not available, the client will continue to use its lease, since it still has 50% of the lease period remaining.

The Rebinding Time Value represents 87.5% of the lease period. If the lease period is eight days, then the rebinding interval is 168 hours. The client will attempt to rebind its IP address at this time only if it was not able to renew its lease at the Renewal Time (T1). The client broadcasts a DHCPREQUEST message. If the server that granted the IP address does not respond, the client will enter the *Rebinding State* and begin the DHCPDISCOVER process, attempting to renew its IP address with any DHCP server. If it cannot renew its IP address, it will try to receive a new one from any responding DHCP server. If unsuccessful, TCP/IP services are shut down on that computer.

EXERCISE 24-1

The DHCP Lease Process

In this exercise, you are to answer some questions about how the DHCP lease process works.

1. What are the four steps in the DHCP lease process?
2. At what point does the DHCP client first attempt to renew its DHCP lease?
3. What are the advantages of using DHCP rather than manually assigning static IP addresses?

Answer

1. The four steps in the DHCP lease process are DISCOVER, OFFER, REQUEST, and ACKNOWLEDGEMENT. One way to remember this process is to think of "Aunt DORA."
2. The DHCP client first tries to renew its IP address at 50% of its lease interval, which is also known as T1. If the DHCP server that assigned its lease is online, and if the IP address is still available, then the DHCP client will keep its current IP address. If the server is not available, the client will continue to use its current IP address and attempt to renew the IP address lease later. At 87.5% of the lease period, the client attempts to renew its lease with any DHCP server (T2). If the DHCP server that assigned the original lease is online, and the IP address is still available, then it will renew the lease.
   If the IP address is not available, or the server is offline, then the DHCP client will start all over with the DHCPDISCOVER message.
3. Some advantages of using DHCP over manually assigned IP addresses include decreasing risk of human error when entering IP addressing information on multiple clients, centralizing the management and tracking of IP addresses, and eliminating the need to visit each client workstation or server to assign the manual IP address.

EXERCISE 24-2

Installing the DHCP Server Service

In this exercise, you will install the DHCP server service on a Windows 2000 Advanced Server machine. This exercise will work fine on a Windows 2000 Server machine as well, but you cannot install the DHCP server service on a Windows 2000 Professional computer. Do not perform this exercise on a live, production network without the permission of your network administrator. Improper installation of a DHCP server can lead to network errors and communication disruptions.

1. Log on as Administrator.
2. Open Control Panel, and then double-click on Add/Remove Programs. You should see something similar to what appears in the following illustration.

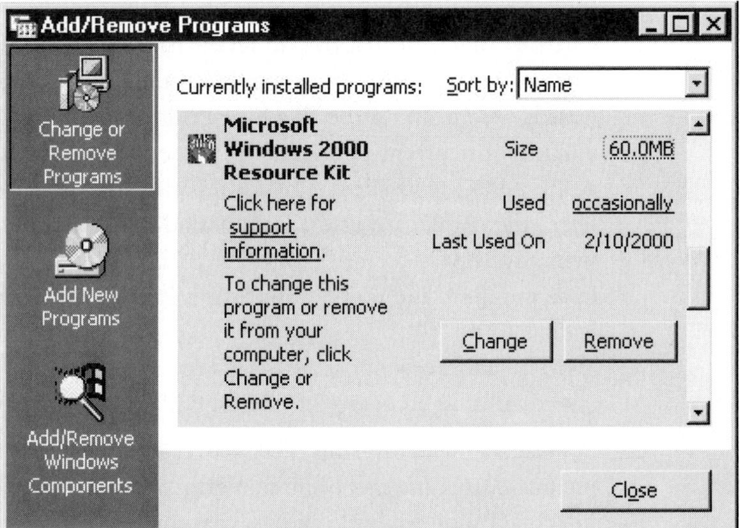

3. Click Add/Remove Windows Components in the left pane of the dialog box.
4. Scroll down the list of Components until you find Networking Services. If there is a check mark in the check box to the left of Networking Services,

leave it there; if there is not, place a check in the box. Then, click Details. You should see what appears in the following illustration.

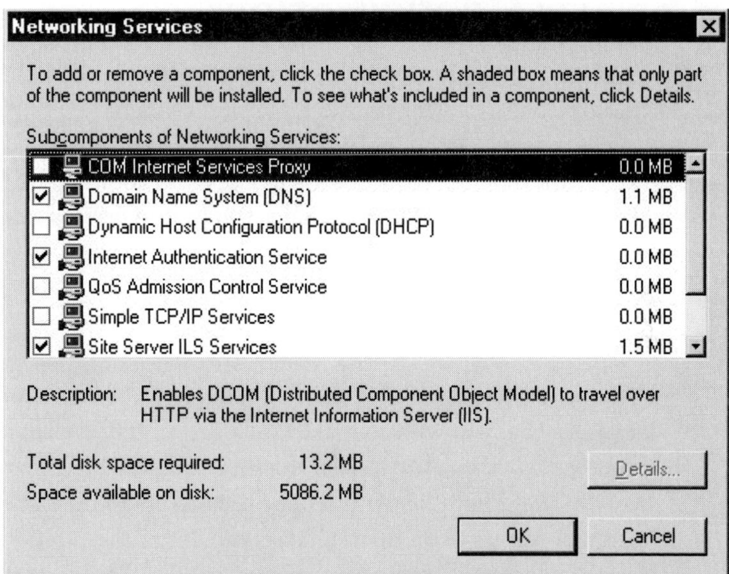

5. Place a check mark in the check box for Dynamic Host Configuration Protocol. Then, click OK.
6. You are returned to the Windows Components dialog box. Click Next.
7. The Configuring Components dialog box appears while the DHCP server service installs. You can monitor the progress of the installation by observing the progress bar.
8. When the installation finishes, you see the Completing the Windows Components Wizard dialog box. Click Finish.

You have successfully installed the DHCP server service. There is still some work to do, but before you continue, let's talk about one DHCP server configuration and specifically, the creation and configuration of DHCP scopes.

CERTIFICATION OBJECTIVE 24.02

DHCP Server Configuration

Your major configuration task when implementing a DHCP solution for your organization is knowing how to set up and configure DHCP *scopes.* Scopes are the *containers* for the "sack" of IP addresses the server has to hand out. In this section, we'll explore the different types of DHCP scopes. In addition, we'll cover Bootstrap Protocol (BOOTP) and BOOTP tables, since you just might find some questions on those on your exam.

DHCP Scopes

A scope is a collection or pool of IP addresses. A single scope includes all the IP addresses that you wish to make available to DHCP clients on a single subnet. *Only one scope can be created for each subnet.* A single DHCP server can manage several scopes. The DHCP server does not need to be on the same subnet as the DHCP clients that it services. Remote hosts can access the DHCP server via Request For Comments (RFC) -compliant routers or DHCP relay agents.

Each scope must contain at least the following elements:

- Scope name
- Start and end IP address
- Lease duration
- Subnet mask

You should create the scope so that it includes all the IP addresses of your network or subnetwork ID. If you have clients with static IP addresses, such as WINS server, DNS server, or other DHCP servers, you can configure a range of excluded IP addresses. The excluded IP addresses are removed from the scope and are not available for distribution.

Creating a new scope in Windows 2000 is a much easier task because it is wizard driven. Most configuration options are included in the wizard, which helps you define and configure the scope.

DHCP Options

A DHCP server must be configured to supply a minimum amount of information, which includes the IP address and the subnet mask. Configuration details such as the IP address of the WINS server, DNS server, and default gateway can be included in a client lease. However, you don't have to include these values; they are *optional.* These optional configuration details are referred to as *DHCP options.*

There are several types of DHCP options, including:

- Server options
- Scope options
- Client options
- Vendor class or user class options

There are a large number of options available in the Windows 2000 DHCP server. However, Microsoft client operating systems support a small number of these options. Of the standard set of DHCP options, Microsoft clients support:

- **003 Router** The IP address of the default gateway.
- **006 DNS** The IP address of the DNS server.
- **015 Domain Name** The DNS domain name the client should use.
- **044 WINS/NBNS Servers** The IP address of the WINS server.
- **046 WINS/NBT Node Type** The NetBIOS node type.
- **047 NetBIOS Scope ID** The NetBIOS scope ID.

Each of these options is configured at the DHCP server. Let's look at the different option types and see how to configure options at each level.

Remember, they are called DHCP options because their use is optional. You do not need to assign any options if you choose not to. However, you will find that using the appropriate DHCP options will make your life as an administrator a lot easier.

Server Options

Server options apply to all scopes configured on a single DHCP server. Server options were known as *global options* on the Windows NT 4.0 DHCP Server. For example, you have three scopes on your DHCP server that assign IP addresses for the following subnets:

192.168.1.0
192.168.2.0
192.168.3.0

Now you want all the DHCP clients from each of those subnets to receive the same WINS server address. You can do this by creating a WINS server option that includes the IP address of the WINS server. Clients receiving their lease from any of these scopes will be given the same WINS server address.

Figure 24-1 shows the WINS configuration option on the DHCP server.

FIGURE 24-1

The WINS Server Options dialog box

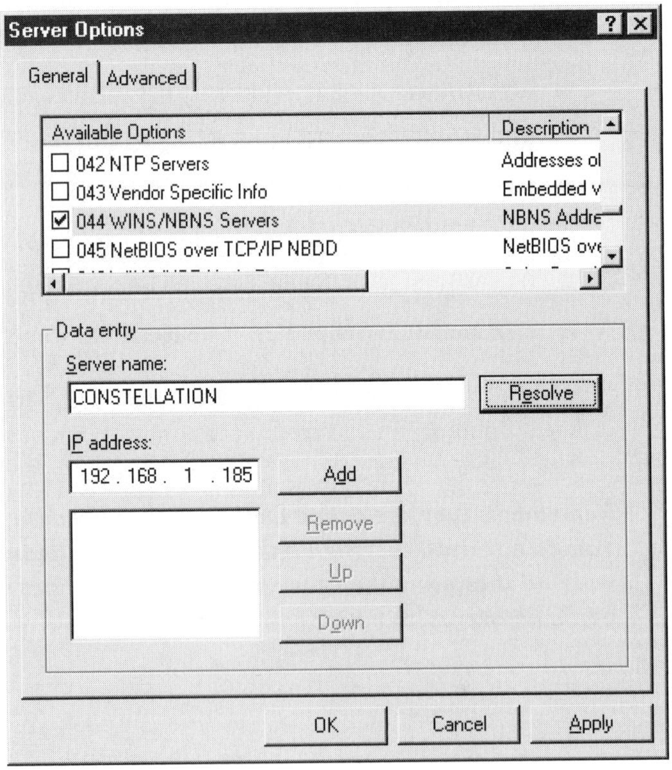

Scope Options

Scope options allow you to specify DHCP options that apply to a single scope. A good example of when you want to set scope options is when you want to automatically configure the IP address of the default gateway for the DHCP clients. Each subnet must have a different default gateway, since the default gateway must be local to each subnet. It wouldn't make much sense to assign the same default gateway to all the scopes. Therefore, you configure a scope option for the default gateway for each scope that has a different default gateway.

Figure 24-2 shows the Scope Options configuration dialog box, where you would configure the IP address of the DNS server for a particular scope.

Client Options

In order to assign client options, you must first create a *reserved client.* A reserved client is a DHCP client that you configure to always receive the same IP address.

FIGURE 24-2

The DNS Scope Options dialog box

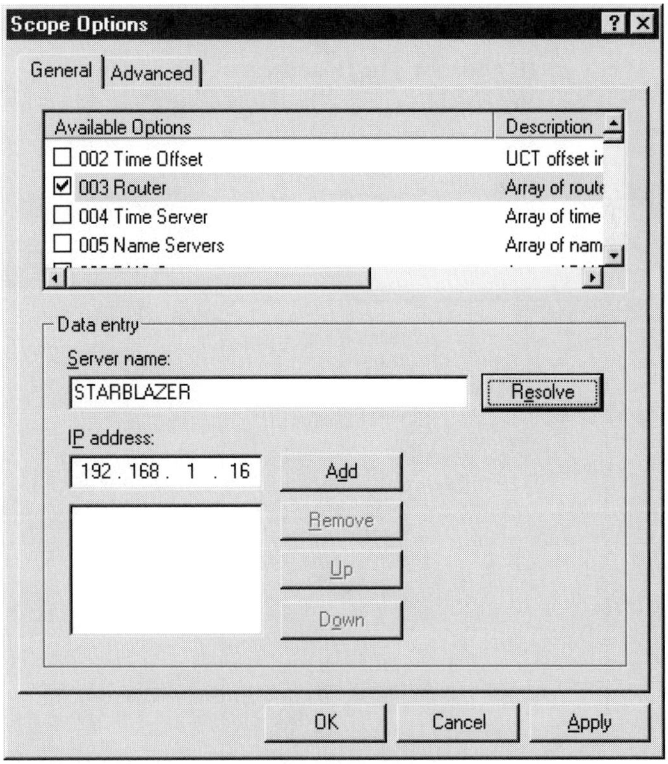

Creating reserved clients allows you to assign functionally *static* IP addresses to computers that require these, such as WINS and DNS servers. DHCP servers also require a static IP address. However, the DHCP server itself cannot be a DHCP client, so creating a client reservation for them would be a waste of IP addresses. Client reservations allow you to centrally manage virtually the entirety of your IP addresses space, with the exception being your DHCP servers.

To create a client reservation, perform the following steps:

1. Open the DHCP management console.
2. In the left pane, expand the server name, and then expand the scope object. You will need to already have a scope in place to do this. Click on the Reservations folder.
3. Right-click on the Reservations folder, and select New Reservation. You should see the New Reservation dialog box as it appears in Figure 24-3.
4. In the New Reservation dialog box, enter the following information:

   Reservation name: The host name of the computer.
   IP address: The IP address of the computer.
   MAC address: The Media Access Control address (do not include dashes).

FIGURE 24-3

Creating a client reservation

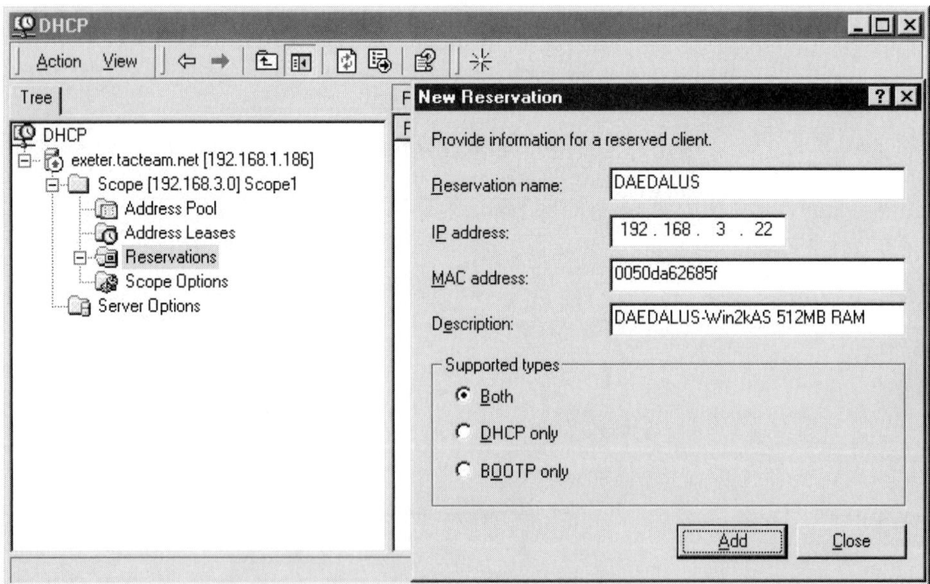

Description: An optional field to describe the reserved client.
Supported types: Indicate whether this reservation is for a DHCP client, a BOOTP client, or either one.

5. Click Add to complete the operation, then click Close.

A reserved client's IP address must be one that is part of an existing scope. You do not need to create an exclusion for the IP address that has been given to the reserved client. Many administrators feel that they need to do this in order to prevent other computers from taking the reserved client's IP address. However, as you can see in Figure 24-4, once you create the client reservation, the IP address is automatically removed from the pool and assigned to the reserved client. In this example, the reserved client is offline and has not yet received its new IP address via the client reservation.

Client options can be now be configured. To create client options:

1. Open the DHCP management console.
2. In the left pane, expand the server name, expand the Scope folder, and then expand the Reservations folder. You need to have a scope in place to do this. Right-click on the name of the client reservation for which you want to configure options, and then click Configure Options.
3. Configure options in the Reservation Options dialog box, as shown in Figure 24-5.

FIGURE 24-4 The reserved client's IP address is removed from the pool of available IP addresses

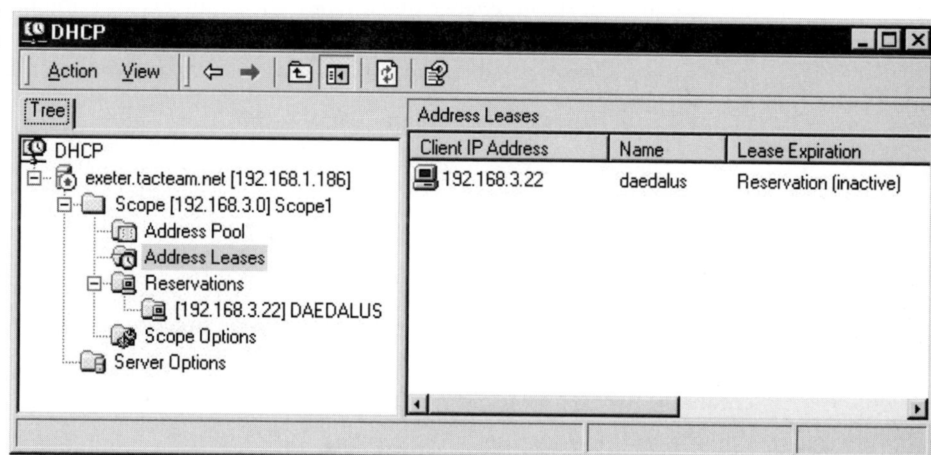

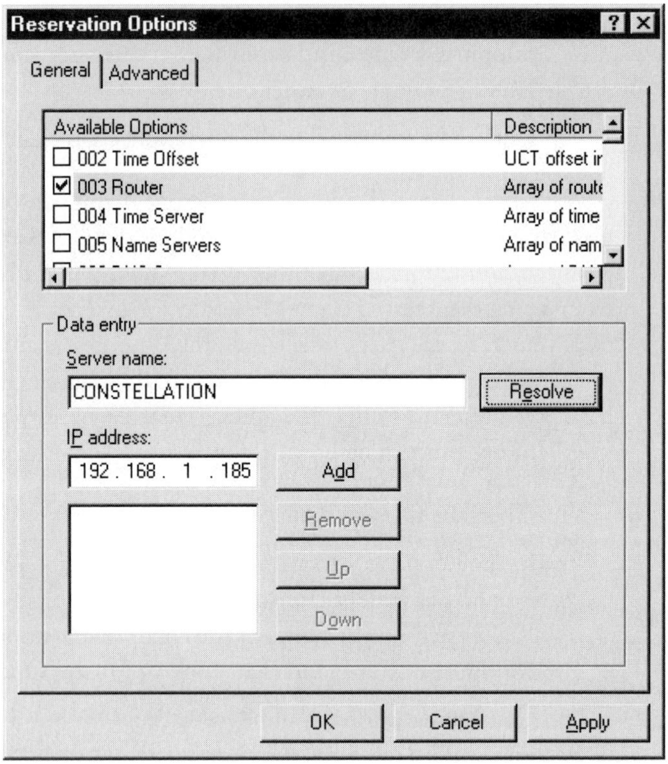

FIGURE 24-5

The Reservation Options dialog box

DHCP Options Order of Precedence

There is an order of precedence that applies when conflicts arise among DHCP options:

1. Locally configured options (the DHCP client has been manually configured)
2. Vendor/user class options
3. Client options
4. Scope options
5. Server options

The higher the options on the list, the higher "precedence" they have. For example, if there is a conflict between a scope option and a server option, the conflict is resolved in the scope option's favor.

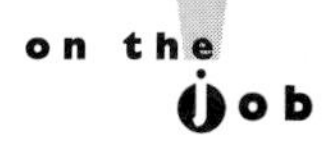

There is another set of DHCP options that you can define at the DHCP server. These are the *predefined options.* ***You create predefined options when you want default option settings for the new scopes you create.***

Vendor-Specific Options

RFCs 2131 and 2132 define DHCP *vendor class options*, which allow hardware and software vendors to add their own options to the DHCP server. These options are additions to the list of standard DHCP options included with the Windows 2000 DHCP Server.

If a manufacturer wants custom DHCP options sent to the DHCP client, the DHCP client can be configured to request these options during the lease assignment process. The vendor's customized set of options is installed on the DHCP server itself, so that it can respond to the DHCP clients' request. The DHCP server will recognize the vendor's class identifiers sent by the DHCP client and forward the vendor-configured options to the client.

The vendor options must be installed and configured on the DHCP server. Microsoft has included vendor class options for Windows 2000 and Windows 98 clients, as well as a generic Microsoft operating system vendor class. The latter is used to deliver DHCP options to any Microsoft operating system that includes "MSFT" as a client identifier during the client initialization. You can see these options in Figure 24-6.

Microsoft vendor-specific options include:

- **Disable NetBIOS over TCP/IP (NetBT)** Allows an option to be sent to the client to disable NetBT.
- **Release DHCP lease on shutdown** Informs the client to release its lease at shut down. You might use this with laptop computers that move on and off the network frequently. This will free up IP addresses in the scope.
- **Default router metric base** Sets the default base metric for the DHCP client. This value is used to calculate the fastest and least-expensive routes.
- **Proxy Autodiscovery** Used only by clients that have Internet Explorer 5.0 or higher. This option informs the client of the location of the Internet Explorer 5.0 automatic configuration file.

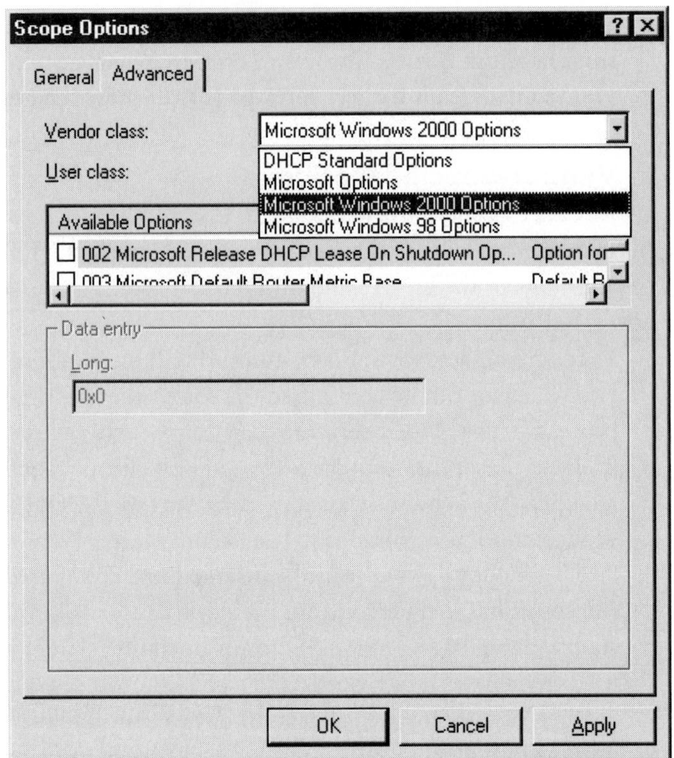

FIGURE 24-6 Vendor class options included with the Windows 2000 DHCP Server

The administrator cannot create vendor class options; the hardware or software vendor provides them. The administrator can implement these options when the software or hardware manufacturer makes them available.

User Class Options

User classes allow DHCP clients to identify their *class membership* to a DHCP server. The server can return to the client a specific set of options relevant to the *class*. The process is the same as how vendor class options are requested by the client and sent by the DHCP server.

You define the user classes at the DHCP server. User classes allow you as the administrator to customize a set of class options that fit your specific needs. For example, you could classify a group of computers that should use a specific WINS server and default gateway as "Portable." Then you create a Portable user class on the DHCP server and you configure the laptop computers to identify themselves as members of the Portable class.

Microsoft has included some built-in classes that are available "out of the box." These include user classes with special options for BOOTP and remote access clients, as shown in Figure 24-7.

on the job

Scope options override server options, client options override scope options, and user class options override all other options, except those manually configured on the DHCP client. For example, if we have a machine with a client reservation, this machine's reserved client options will override any other options that might be set for the server or for the scope. However, if the reserved client identifies itself as a member of a certain user class, the user class options will override any reserved client options that are in conflict.

FIGURE 24-7

User classes available "out `of the box" on Windows 2000

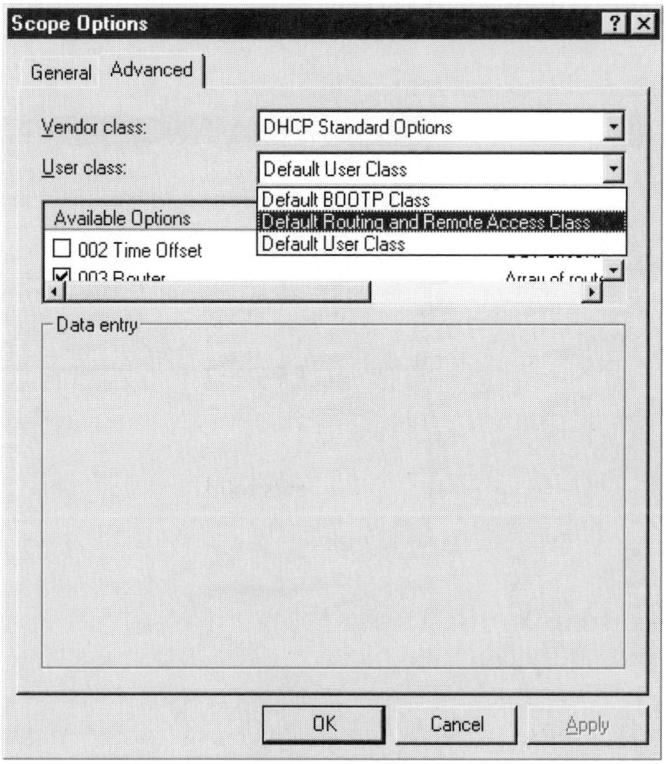

To create a new user class:

1. In the DHCP management console, right-click on the server name, and then click on Define User Classes.
2. The DHCP User Classes dialog box appears. Click Add. You should now see the New Class dialog box, as shown in Figure 24-8.
3. Enter the Display name of the class, and a Description. To enter the user class ID in ASCII, click on the right side of the lowest text box under ASCII and type in the class ID. This is the class ID you will use with the ipconfig command on the clients to configure them to send their class membership to the DHCP server.
4. Click OK, and then click Close to close the DHCP User Classes dialog box.
5. Right-click on Server Options and click Configure Options. Click on the Advanced tab, and then click the down arrow for the "User class" drop-down list box, as shown in Figure 24-9. Select Portable.

FIGURE 24-8

Creating a new user class

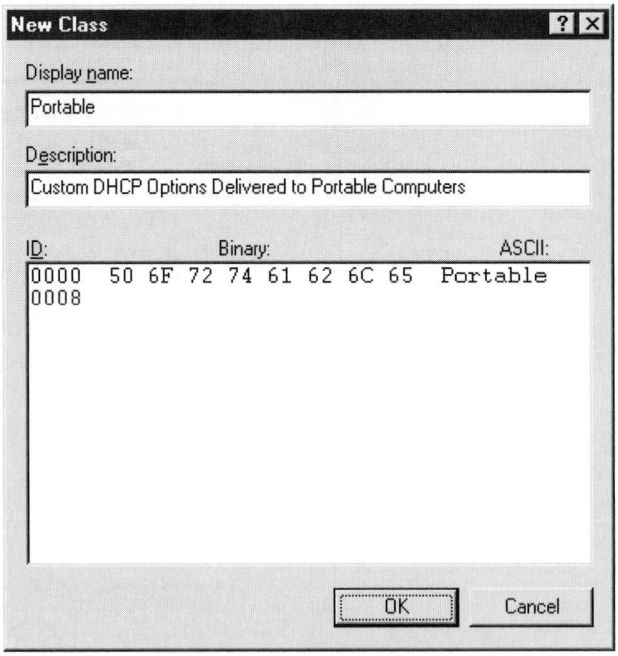

6. After selecting the Portable user class, you will see a list of DHCP options you can set for the class. Note that this is just a list of the standard DHCP options. The difference is that members of the Portable class will have different values for the options that you select. Figure 24-10 shows an example of this.
7. Click Apply, then OK, and you're set.

At the client machine, type in the following command to have the client identify itself as a member of the class:

ipconfig /setclassid adapter [classidtoset]

In the preceding example, the new class ID was Portable. As the clients, we would open a command prompt and type:

ipconfig /setclassid 3Com portable

FIGURE 24-9

Selecting the Portable user class from the Advanced tab in the Server Options dialog box

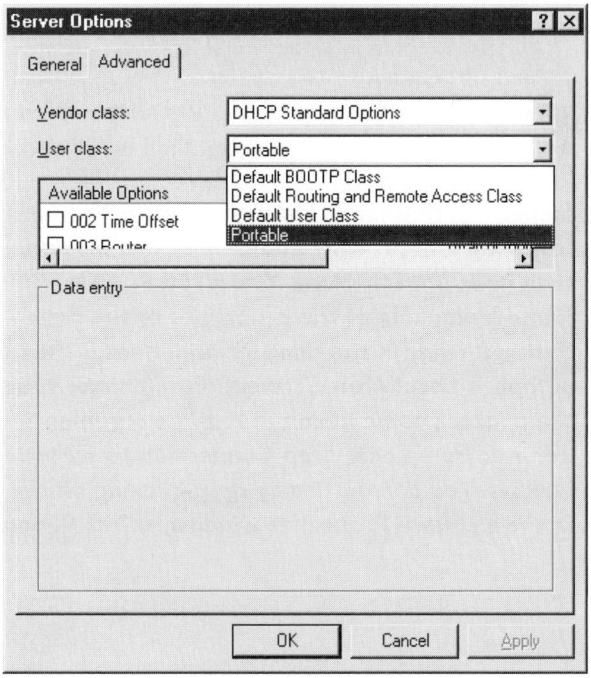

FIGURE 24-10

The Portable user class options

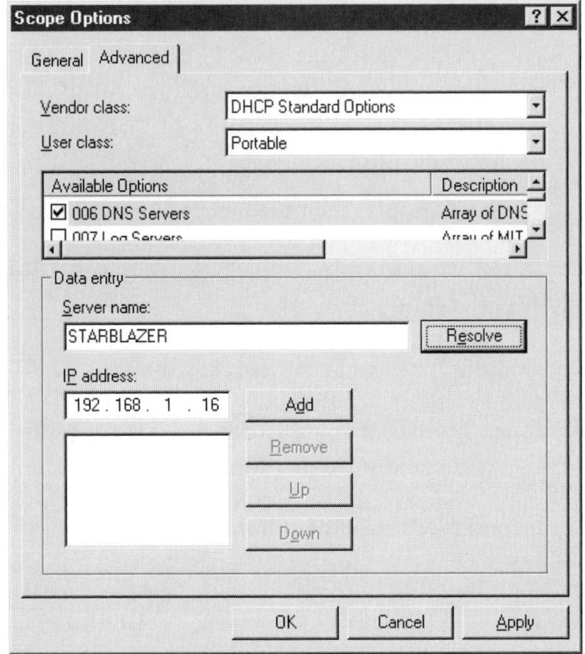

User options allow us a greater level of granularity in the assignment of DHCP options. This improved granularity gives the administrator greater control over the TCP/IP parameters configured on the DHCP clients in his network.

on the Job

Something that might drive you nuts is the "adapter" argument of the setclassid switch. One would think this would be the name of the NIC itself, such as 3Com EtherLink XL 10/100 PCI TX NIC (3C905B-TX), which can be found by looking at the properties of the network card. However, the name that you enter in the adapter argument is the name of the interface, which by default is Local Area Connection. To make your life easier when working with the adapter name in command-line arguments, change the name of the adapter from Local Area Connection to something simpler like 3Com or LinkSys. You can do this by right-clicking on the Local Area Connection icon in the Network Properties window, select Rename, and type in the new name.

BOOTP Tables

BOOTP is the predecessor to DHCP. It was originally designed to provide IP address configuration to diskless workstations, which not only received IP addressing information from a BOOTP server, but also received information regarding where to download its operating system image. DHCP was developed to improve on the host configuration services offered by BOOTP, and address some of the problems encountered in using it.

exam Watch

BOOTP specifications are defined in RFC 951.

Similarities between DHCP and BOOTP

Because DHCP is based on BOOTP, they are alike in many ways. For instance, the request and reply messages they use are basically the same, using one 576-byte User Datagram Protocol (UDP) datagram for each message. The headers are almost the same as well, although there is a slight difference in the final message header field that carries optional data: It is called the *vendor-specific area* in BOOTP, whereas DHCP calls it the *options field*. The size of the field differs, too; the vendor-specific area is only 64 octets, while the DHCP options field can hold as much as 312 bytes of information. This allows DHCP to provide many more options than can be provided via the BOOTP protocol.

Another thing the two protocols have in common is the use of the same UDP ports for communication between server and client. UDP 67 is used for receiving client messages, and UDP 68 is used to accept replies from a server.

Because of these similarities, relay agents generally don't distinguish between BOOTP and DHCP packets, treating them both the same.

Differences between DHCP and BOOTP

Despite the similarities noted in the preceding section, there are some important differences between the two host configuration protocols. The IP address allocation methods are not alike—BOOTP normally allocates one IP address per client, which it permanently reserves in its database on the BOOTP server. DHCP, as its name implies, leases addresses dynamically, assigning an address to the client from a pool of available addresses and only temporarily reserving it in the server's database.

Many of the differences between BOOTP and DHCP stem from the difference in intended purpose. Unlike BOOTP, DHCP was originally designed to configure addressing information for computers with hard drives from which they could boot, especially laptops and other computers that are moved frequently.

For this reason, BOOTP uses a two-phase configuration process in which client computers first contact a BOOTP server for address assignment, and then contact a TFTP (Trivial File Transfer Protocol) server to transfer their boot image files to boot the operating system. DHCP clients, which are capable of booting from their own hard drives, use a one-phase configuration process: The client negotiates a leased IP address from the DHCP server, which contains any other needed TCP/IP configuration details (such as subnet mask, default gateway, DNS and WINS server addresses).

Another difference is that BOOTP clients must restart in order to renew the configuration with the server. DHCP clients, however, can automatically renew their leases with the DHCP servers at preset intervals. It is valuable for a Windows 2000 administrator to be aware of the characteristics of BOOTP, since it is the foundation upon which automatic host configuration was founded.

exam Watch

BOOTP clients can have the IP addressing information assigned statically, via client reservations, or dynamically, via a scope configured to support BOOTP requests. However, if the client receives its information from a dynamic pool, it will not be able to download the boot image file.

Superscopes

Microsoft recommends the use of *superscopes* when you have more than one DHCP server on a subnet. A superscope is a Windows 2000 DHCP feature that lets you use more than one scope for a subnet. The superscope contains multiple "child" scopes, grouped together under one name and manageable as one entity. The situations in which superscopes should be used include:

- When many DHCP clients are added to a network so that it has more than were originally planned for.
- When the IP addresses on a network must be renumbered.

- When two (or more) DHCP servers are on the same subnet for fault tolerance purposes.

Using superscopes gives the administrator the flexibility to support DHCP clients in *multinet* configurations. A multinet is a network configuration in which multiple logical networks reside on the same physical segment. The administrator is able to activate the individual scope ranges of IP addresses used on the network, and provide leases from multiple scopes to the DHCP clients on the same physical network.

Superscopes are valuable in situations where the available DHCP addresses have almost been used up, and additional computers need to join the same segment. Using a superscope will allow you to extend the address space for the network segment. In this situation, you can create a superscope with two child scopes: the original scope of addresses that is almost depleted, and a new scope for the additional computers that need to join the network.

To create a new superscope you must have at least two scopes already in place. After creating the two scopes, perform the following steps:

1. Right click on the DHCP server name in the left pane of the DHCP management console and click on New Superscope.
2. That starts the New Superscope Wizard; click Next to move past the welcome screen. Type in the name of the superscope in the Name text box and click Next.
3. In the Select Scopes dialog box, select two or more scopes from the list that will be members of the superscope. Figure 24-11 shows what this looks like. (Note that you have to hold down CTRL while you click on multiple entries.)
4. Click Next to move to the last page of the wizard. The final page displays the name of the superscope and the member scopes you included in the superscope. If everything looks good, click Finish.
5. Now when you look at the DHCP management console, you see the individual scopes represented as objects within the Superscope container, as shown in Figure 24-12.

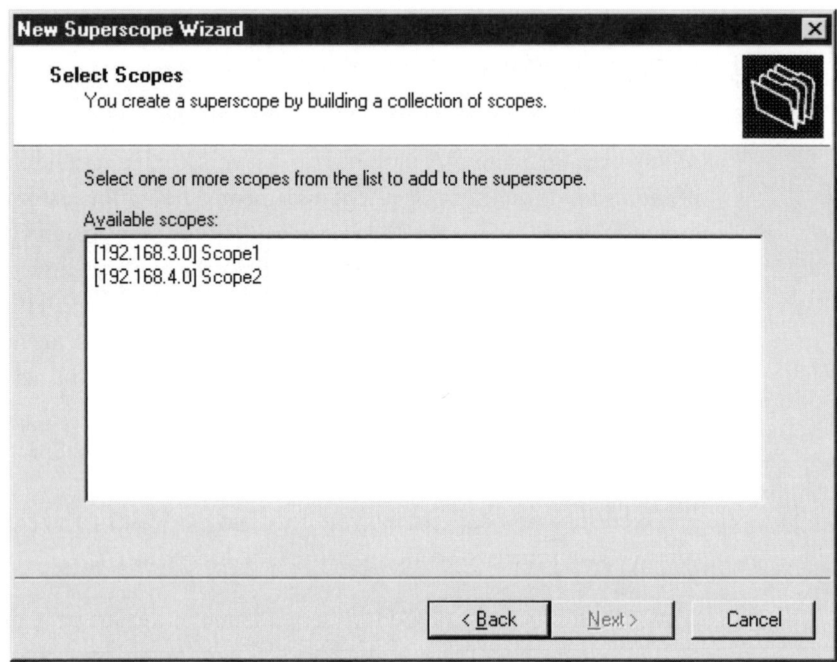

FIGURE 24-11 The Select Scopes dialog box

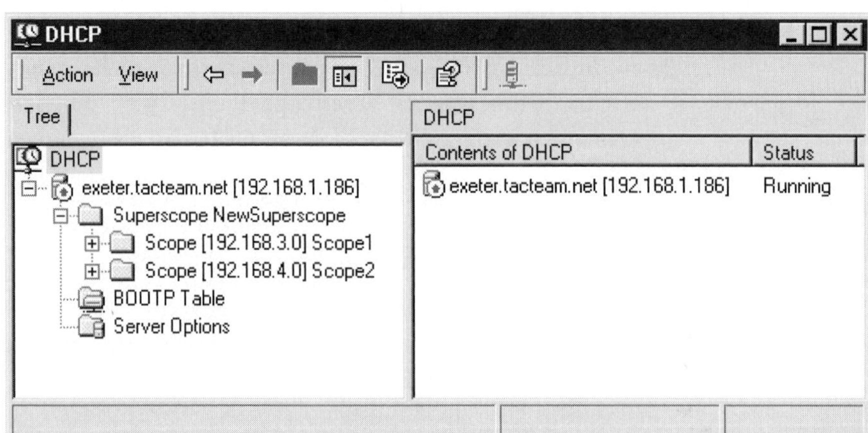

FIGURE 24-12 Member's scope objects inside a Superscope container object

SCENARIO & SOLUTION

Do you have to create scope options?	No. You do not have to create or use any of the DHCP options if you don't want to; or, you can use just server options. However, you will probably want to create at least the default gateway option for each scope, since each subnet needs to use a different default gateway, and you don't want to have to manually configure the gateway address on all the DHCP client computers.
What computers should you create client reservations for?	You can create client reservations for all computers that need to have the same IP over time. Examples include WINS servers and DNS servers. The reason these machines need the same IP address is that the client configuration for these services uses IP addresses rather than NetBIOS or host names. Client reservations are a good way for you to almost completely centralize the management of your IP address space. The only machines that typically can't be DHCP clients are the DHCP servers themselves.
You have tried to create a vendor class on your Windows 2000 DHCP Server, but you can't find where to do this. Is there something wrong with your DHCP server?	You cannot create your own vendor classes; you must obtain custom vendor class options from the product vendors that wish to create their own vendor class options on the Windows 2000 DHCP Server.

EXERCISE 24-3

Creating a New Scope

In this exercise, you will configure a scope on the DHCP server. Remember, a single DHCP server can host multiple scopes. We will configure a single scope using the Windows 2000 Scope Wizard.

1. Log on as Administrator.
2. Select Start | Programs | Administrative Tools. Click on DHCP to start the DHCP management console.
3. Expand all nodes in the left pane. Right now, the console doesn't look too exciting. All you should see is the name of your DHCP server and the Server Options node in the left pane, and some instructions on how to configure the DHCP server (see the next illustration).

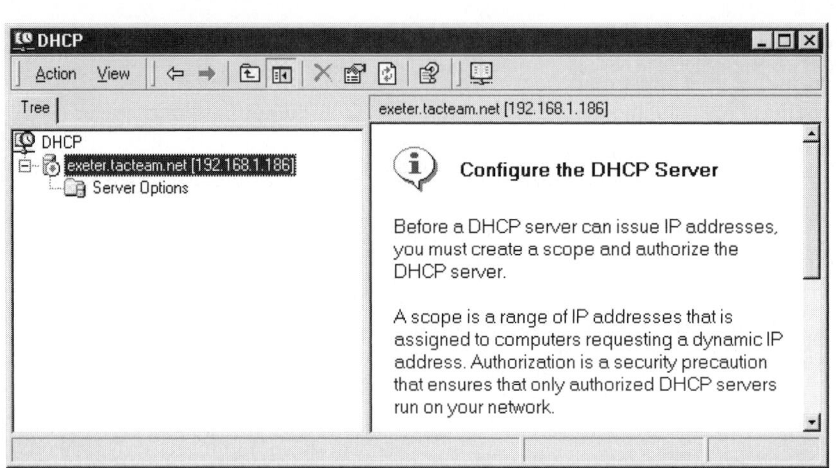

4. Right-click on your DHCP server's name and click New Scope. This begins the New Scope Wizard. Click Next.
5. In the Name box, give the Scope the name NewScope1. In the description box, type **First Scope**. Click Next.
6. In the IP Address Range dialog box, type **192.168.3.1** for the Start IP address and **192.168.3.254** for the End IP address. Note that the Length and the Subnet mask text boxes are filled in for you automatically, as shown in the following illustration. Click Next.

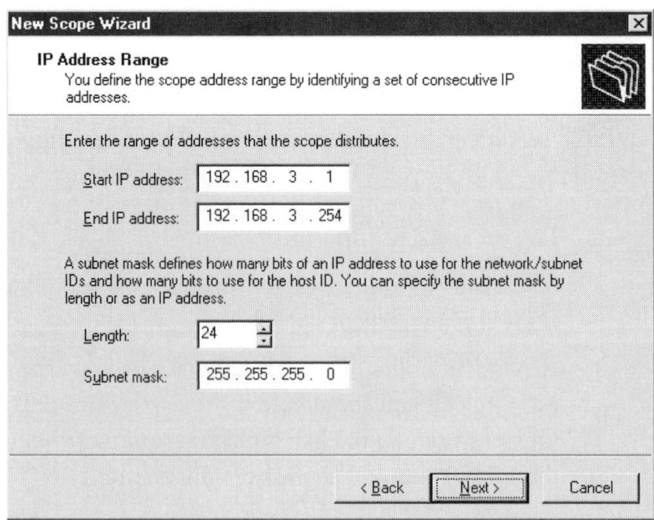

7. In the Add Exclusions dialog box, type **192.168.3.1** for the Start IP address and **192.168.1.10** for the End IP address. Then click Add. Your screen should look like the following illustration. Click Next.

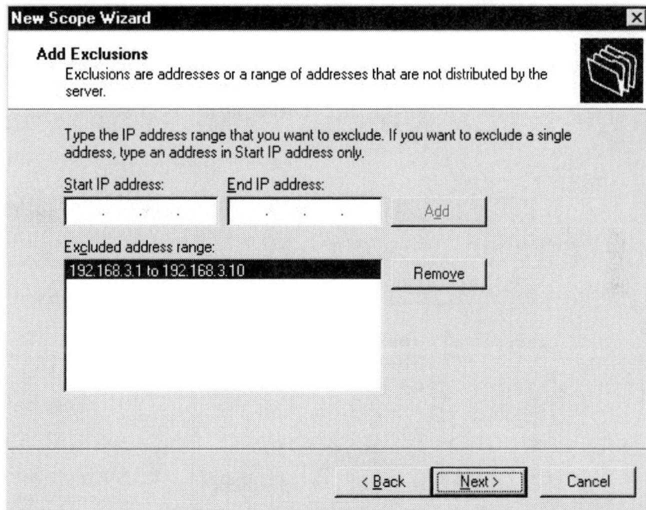

8. For the Lease Duration, accept the default lease period of eight days and click Next. In the Configure DHCP Options dialog box, select "No, I will configure these options later," then click Next.
9. The Completing the New Scope Wizard dialog box appears. Click Finish to complete the definition of your new scope.

Now that you've defined your scope, let's configure some options.

EXERCISE 24-4

Configuring Options

In this exercise, you will configure scope options for the scope you just created. You will configure a scope option for the DNS server IP address. Do not perform this exercise on a live, production network without the permission of your network administrator.

1. Log on as Administrator if you have not done so already.
2. Expand all nodes in the left pane. You should see what appears in the following illustration.

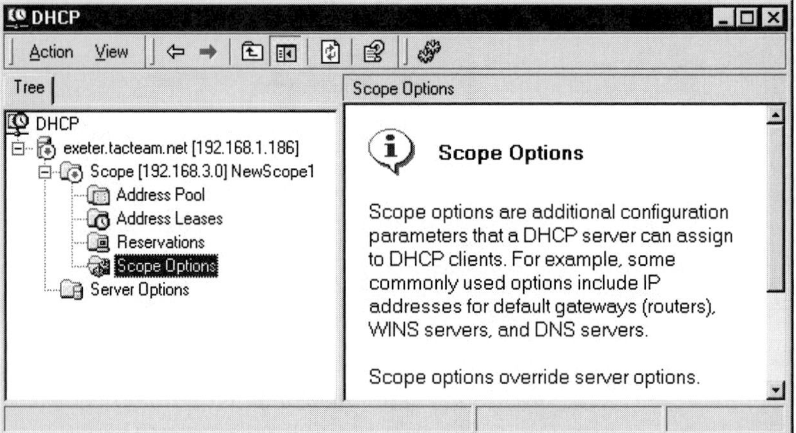

3. Right-click on Scope Options, and click on Configure Options.
4. On the General tab, scroll down the list of options until you find DNS Servers. Place a check mark in the check box next to DNS Servers. Type in

he name of one of your DNS servers and then click Resolve. Your screen should look like the following illustration. Click Add, then click Apply, and then OK.

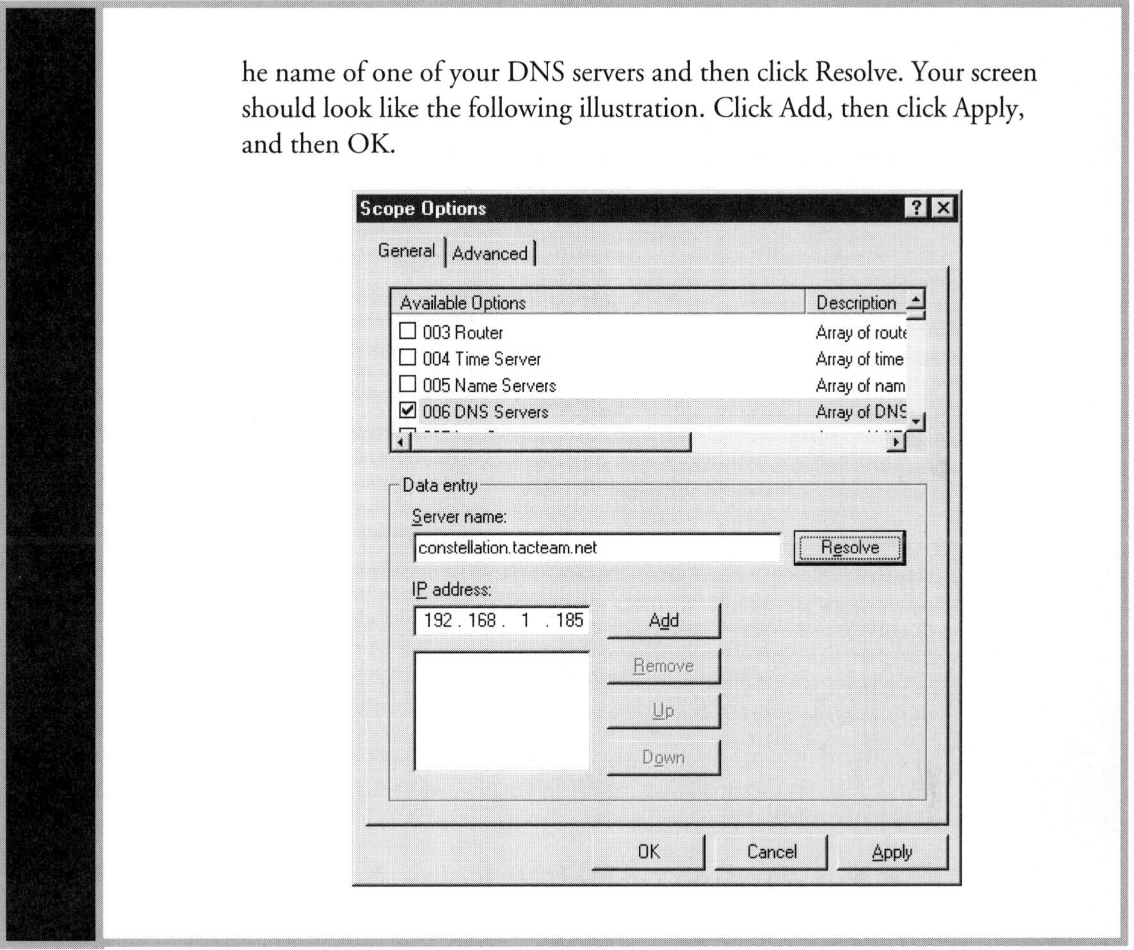

You have successfully configured a scope option that will deliver the DNS server IP address to the DHCP clients that receive IP addresses on the subnet represented by that scope.

CERTIFICATION OBJECTIVE 24.03

DHCP Relay Agents in a Routed Environment

Deploying DHCP in a single segment network is easy. Since all DHCP messages are broadcast messages, all the computers on the segment can listen and respond to these broadcasts. A single scope on a solitary DHCP server is all that is required.

The complexity of the DHCP server placement problem increases with the number of segments on the network. This is because the DHCP broadcast messages do not by default cross the routers. One solution is to put a DHCP server on each segment. This obviates the need for broadcast messages to traverse routers. This solution can be cost prohibitive and labor intensive if there are a large number of subnets. This also defeats your primary goal of centralizing management of IP addressing for your organization.

A better option is to use fewer DHCP servers and place these machines in central locations. To solve the problem of DHCP broadcast management, routers can be configured to pass DHCP/BOOTP messages selectively. This is referred to as *BOOTP Relay.*

If you cannot change the router configuration to accommodate BOOTP Relay, then placing a *DHCP relay agent* on each segment allows DHCP clients and servers to communicate. The relay agent communicates with a DHCP server and acts as a proxy for DHCP broadcast messages that need to be routed to remote segments.

Using BOOTP Forwarding or DHCP Relay Agents

Routers that conform to RFC 2132 can be configured to pass DHCP/BOOTP broadcast messages. These broadcast packets pass through UDP Port 67, which is the DHCP server port number for receive DHCP client messages. This is known as BOOTP Relay. Most modern routers support BOOTP Relay; if your router does not, contact the router manufacturer for a software or firmware upgrade.

If you cannot upgrade routers to support BOOTP Relay, you can configure a Windows NT 4.0 or Windows 2000 server to become a DCHP relay agent. The DHCP relay agent will listen for DHCP broadcast messages and forward these to a DHCP server on a remote subnet. The relay agent itself does not depend on broadcasts when forwarding these messages because it is configured with the IP address of the DHCP server, and therefore can send directed datagrams to the DHCP server. When the remote DHCP server receives the messages from the DHCP relay agent, it forwards replies to the DHCP relay agent, which broadcasts the reply on its local subnet.

The following are the details of this exchange when an RFC-compliant router acts as a relay agent via BOOTP Relay:

1. The DHCP client broadcasts a DHCPDISCOVER message.
2. The DHCP relay agent intercepts the message. In the message header there is a field for the gateway IP address. If the field is 0.0.0.0, the relay agent inserts its own IP address.
3. The DHCP relay agent forwards the DHCPDISCOVER message to the remote DHCP server.
4. When the DHCPDISCOVER message arrives at the DHCP server, the service examines the gateway IP address (*giaddr*). The server determines whether it has a scope for the network ID specified in the giaddr.
5. The DHCP server prepares a lease for the client and issues a DHCPOFFER message directly to the address included in the giaddr.
6. Since the client does not yet have an IP address, the local router interface broadcasts the DHCPOFFER to the subnet.
7. The same processes take place for the DHCPREQUEST and DHCPACK messages.

A similar series of events takes place when a Windows computer is used as a DHCP relay agent.

Configuring the DHCP Relay Agent

The Routing and Remote Access Service (RRAS) must be installed prior to configuring the DHCP relay agent. After installing RRAS, open the Routing and Remote Access console, expand the server name, expand the IP routing node, then click on the DHCP Relay Agent node. In the right pane, you will see a list of Interfaces listening for DHCP broadcasts. Figure 24-13 shows how the Routing and Remote Access console should appear to you at this point.

FROM THE CLASSROOM

DHCP Relay Agents vs. BOOTP Forwarders

Remember that a DHCP relay agent and a BOOTP forwarder are two different entities. I have found in the classroom that students often confuse these two, and think they are just two terms for the same thing. They are not! A DHCP relay agent is typically, on a Windows 2000 network, a computer that is configured to intercept DHCP messages and forward them to a specific DHCP server.

BOOTP forwarding is done at the router. The router can be a multihomed Windows 2000 machine configured as a router, or a dedicated hardware router. When BOOTP forwarding is enabled, DHCP broadcast messages are passed through the router interface to the next network. In order for BOOTP forwarding to work correctly, all router interface between the source of the DHCP broadcast and the destination must have BOOTP forwarding enabled.

—Thomas W. Shinder, M.D., MCSE, MCP+I, MCT

FIGURE 24-13

DHCP Relay Agent node in the Routing and Remote Access console

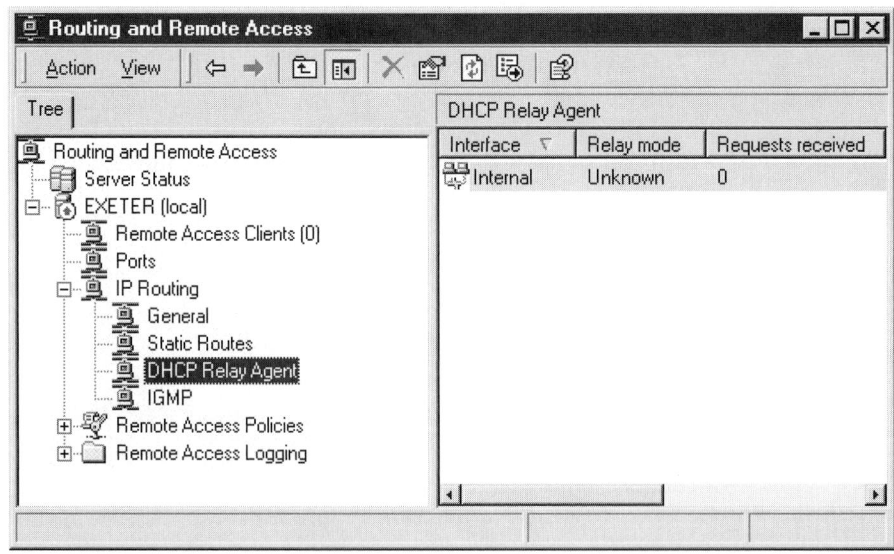

Right-click on the DHCP Relay Agent node in the left pane and click on Properties. You should see what appears in Figure 24-14. This is where you enter the IP address of the DHCP server that the relay agent will forward the DHCP broadcast message to.

Double-click on the interface of choice. You will see the Internal Properties dialog box as shown in Figure 24-15.

Put a check mark in the "Relay DHCP packets" box to enable DHCP relay for the selected interface. The "Hop- count threshold" allows you to configure the number of networks a DCHP broadcast message can pass through before being silently discarded. This prevents DHCP messages from looping endlessly throughout the network. The maximum setting is 16.

The "Boot threshold" defines the number of seconds the relay agent waits before forwarding DHCP messages. This option is useful if you are using a combination of local and remote DHCP servers, as in the case of fault tolerant setups. The relay

FIGURE 24-14

The DHCP Relay Agent Properties box

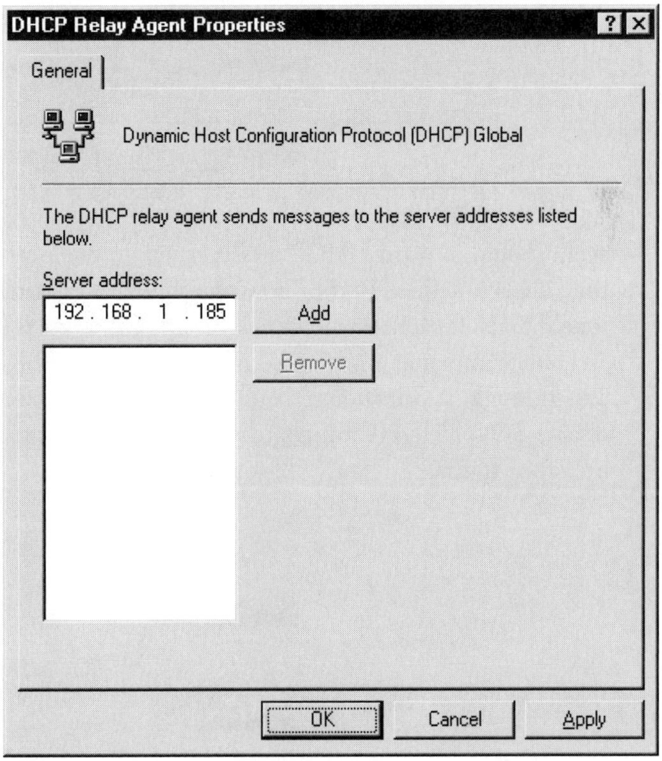

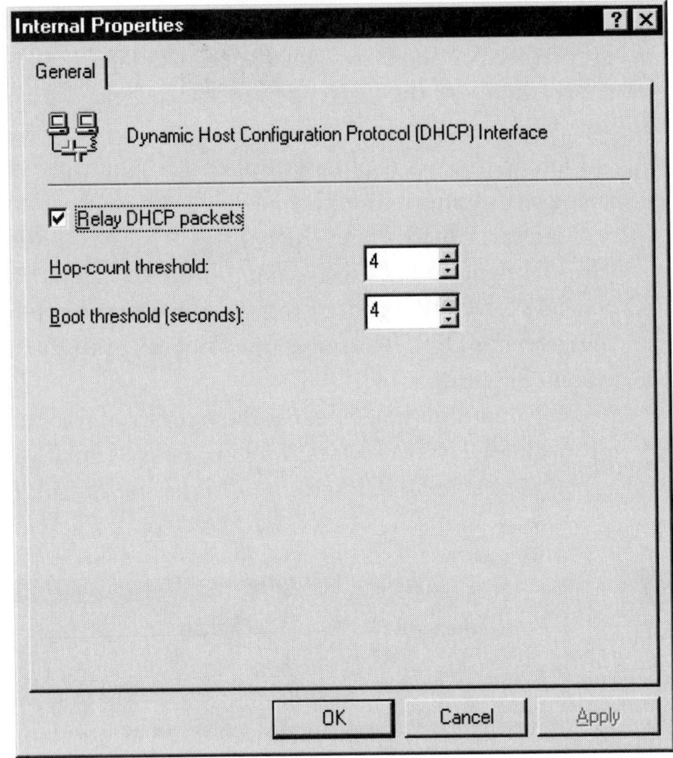

FIGURE 24-15

The DHCP Relay Agent Internal Interface Properties sheet

agent should forward DHCP messages only if the local server fails to respond in the time interval defined in the "Boot threshold." This setting helps prevent a "flood" of routed DHCP packets when the local DHCP server is busy.

Do not implement both a DHCP relay agent and RFC-compliant router pass-through. If you choose the DHCP relay option, reconnoiter your network and disable BOOTP/DHCP forwarding on your routers to minimize pass-through broadcast traffic.

SCENARIO & SOLUTION

Does the DHCP relay agent rebroadcast the messages sent by the DHCP clients?	No. When the DHCP relay agent intercepts the DHCP broadcast messages, it sends a directed datagram to a DHCP server whose IP address has been entered into the DHCP relay agent.
How does the DHCP server know what scope to use when it receives a request from a DHCP relay agent?	When the DHCP relay agent forwards the request to a DHCP server, it includes its IP address and subnet mask, from which the DHCP server can access the network ID and select the appropriate scope.
Does Microsoft use DHCP relay agents or BOOTP forwarding at their campus in Redmond?	In an article entitled "Windows 2000 Infrastructure Services Design and Deployment: DNS and DHCP Deployment within Microsoft," it appears that they use primarily BOOTP Relay rather than DHCP. You can search for this article on your TechNet CD-ROM, or at: www.microsoft.com/technet.

EXERCISE 24-5

Configuring a DHCP Relay Agent

In this exercise, you will configure a DHCP relay agent to forward DHCP broadcast messages to a remote DHCP server. In order to complete this exercise, you must have already installed and configured the Routing and Remote Access Service on you computer. Do not perform this exercise on a live, production network without the permission of your network administrator.

1. Log on as Administrator.
2. From the Administrator Tools menu, open the Routing and Remote Access management console.
3. Expand all nodes in the left pane. Locate the DHCP Relay Agent node, which is a subobject of the IP Routing node. Right-click on the DHCP Relay Agent node and click Properties.
4. In the DHCP Relay Agent Properties dialog box, type in an IP address for a DHCP server that is located on a remote subnet in the "Server address" text box and click Add. Click Apply, and then OK.

All DHCP broadcast messages on the segment will now be forwarded to a remote DHCP server with a directed datagram.

CERTIFICATION OBJECTIVE 24.04

Integrating DHCP with DDNS

The Windows 2000 DHCP server has a number of improvements over the DHCP server found in Windows NT 4.0. The most significant is the Windows 2000 DHCP server's ability to deliver host name and IP addressing information to a Windows 2000 Dynamic DNS (DDNS) server.

After the Windows 2000 DHCP server assigns the DHCP client an IP address, the Windows 2000 DHCP server can interact with a Windows 2000 Dynamic DNS server in one of three ways:

- It will update the DNS server by providing information to create a Host (A) record and PTR (Pointer) record on the DNS at the client's request.
- The DHCP server will update both the Host (A) record and the Pointer (PTR) record regardless of the client request.
- The DHCP server will never register information about the DHCP client. However, the client itself may directly update its information with the DDNS server.

These configuration options are made at the DHCP server, as shown in Figure 24-16.

The Windows 2000 DHCP server supports the Client FQDN Option (Option Code 81), which allows the DHCP client to send its FQDN to the DHCP server. Only Windows 2000 clients support Option Code 81. The Windows 2000 DHCP client and server interact in the following way:

1. The Windows 2000 DHCP client and server participate in the DORA process for lease assignment. After officially obtaining a lease, the Windows 2000 client registers its own Host (A) record with the Dynamic DNS server.

2. The DHCP server registers the client's Pointer (PTR) record with the DDNS server.
3. Client and server configuration can be manipulated to allow the DHCP server to update both Host (A) and Pointer (PTR) records. If desired, the DHCP server and DCHP client can be configured so that no dynamic update of client information reaches the DDNS server.

To prevent the client from registering directly with the DDNS server, you must alter the default settings. Figure 24-17 shows the Advanced TCP/IP settings dialog box on a DNS client. If you remove the check mark from the "Register this connection's addresses in DNS," it will not attempt to update the DNS directly.

FIGURE 24-16

Configuring DNS updates from the DHCP server

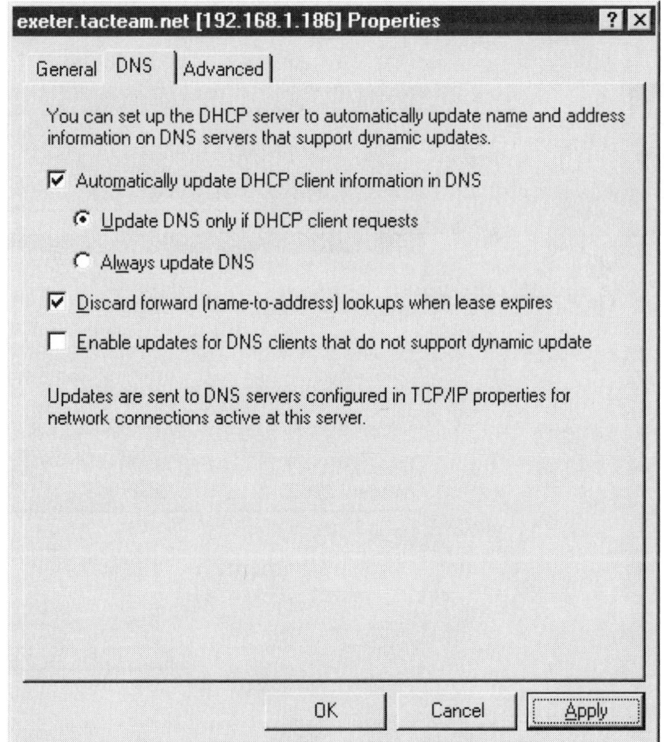

The "Use this connection's DNS suffix in DNS registration" option refers to entries made in the textbox for the "DNS suffix for this connection." Each network connection can be customized to provide its own DNS domain suffix. If you remove the check mark from both of these, it will prevent the client from registering directly with the Dynamic DNS server.

Integrating Downlevel DHCP Clients and Dynamic DNS

Downlevel clients are not able to communicate directly with a DDNS server. In this case, the Windows 2000 DHCP Server can act as a "proxy" and forwards both Host (A) and Pointer (PTR) information on its behalf to the DDNS server. To enable support for these downlevel clients, place a check mark in the "Enable updates for DNS clients that do not support dynamic update" check box in the DHCP server's Properties dialog box.

FIGURE 24-17

Advanced TCP/IP Settings dialog box and the DNS tab

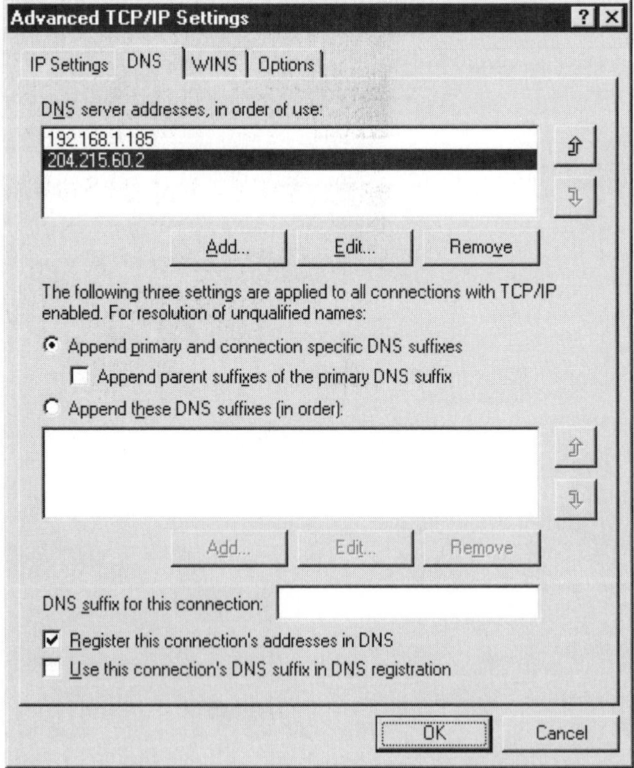

Windows 2000 computers configured with static IP information will update their own Host (A) and Pointer (PTR) records with the DDNS server. If you change the name or IP address of a Windows 2000 client with manually configured IP addressing information, you can force an update to that client's entry in the DDNS server by issuing the command:

ipconfig /registerdns

Downlevel clients with static IP addresses are not able to communicate directly with the DDNS server. DDNS entries for these clients must be manually reconfigured at the DDNS server.

exam Watch

Downlevel clients such as Windows NT 4.0 computers cannot communicate with a Windows 2000 DNS server. To dynamically update downlevel client information on a DDNS server, you must use a Windows 2000 DHCP server to assign the downlevel clients IP addressing information.

EXERCISE 24-6

Enabling a DHCP Server to Update Downlevel DHCP Client Information

In this exercise, you will enable the DHCP server to update both the Host (A) and Pointer (PTR) records on the DDNS server on the behalf of downlevel clients. Do not perform this exercise on a live, production network without the permission of your network administrator.

1. Log on as Administrator.
2. Open the DHCP management console from the Administrative Tools menu. Expand all nodes in the left pane. Right-click on the DHCP server name and click Properties.
3. In the DHCP server's Properties dialog box, place a check mark in the check box for "Enable updates for DNS clients that do not support dynamic update." Click Apply, and then OK.

The DHCP server is now able to update Host (A) and Pointer (PTR) record information for the downlevel clients.

CERTIFICATION OBJECTIVE 24.05

Integrating DHCP with RRAS

The Routing and Remote Access Service (RRAS) is able to obtain IP addresses to assign to RAS clients. The RRAS server acts as a *proxy* between the RRAS client and the DHCP server. The way the RRAS server uses the DHCP server to distribute IP addresses differs from how LAN clients receive DHCP IP address information.

If the RRAS server is configured to use DHCP to assign IP addresses, it will obtain a group of IP addresses from the DHCP server. This block is obtained when RRAS services initialize. RRAS *clients* do not directly interact with the DHCP server. However, they can obtain option information via DHCPINFORM packets that are forwarded by a DHCP relay agent installed on the RRAS server they have dialed in to. The number of IP addresses retrieved is equal to the number of RAS ports configured to receive calls on the RRAS server plus one. The RRAS server itself uses the additional IP address.

When the RRAS server obtains its group of IP addresses, any option information sent from the DHCP server to the RRAS server is ignored. Typical DHCP option parameters such as WINS and DNS IP addresses are obtained from the specific RRAS connection. Each RRAS connection can be independently configured. However, if a DHCP relay agent is installed on the RRAS server, the RAS clients will be able to obtain option information.

There is no effective lease period for the RRAS client; the lease immediately expires after the connection is terminated. You can perform an `ipconfig` on the client machine to see if the RRAS server has assigned DHCP configuration parameters.

EXERCISE 24-7

Configuring RRAS to Use DHCP to Assign IP Addresses

In this exercise, you will configure an RRAS server to use DHCP to assign IP addressing information to RAS clients. In order to do this exercise, you must have RRAS installed and configured. Do not perform this exercise on a live, production network without the permission of your network administrator.

1. Log on as Administrator.
2. From the Administrative Tools menu, click on Routing and Remote Access.
3. Expand all nodes in the left pane. Right-click on the RRAS server name in the left pane, and click on Properties. You should see what appears in the following illustration.

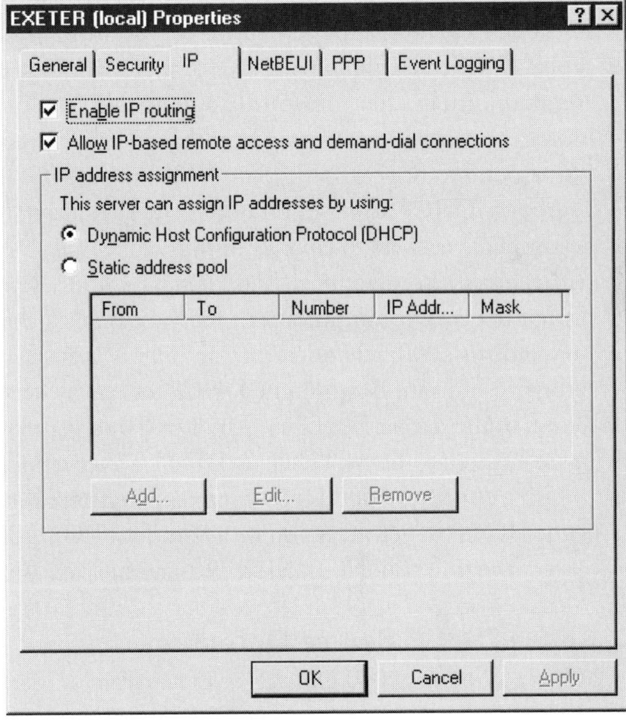

4. Select the option for Dynamic Host Configuration Protocol (DHCP) under "This server can assign IP addresses by using." Click Apply, and then OK.

CERTIFICATION OBJECTIVE 24.06

Integrating DHCP with Active Directory

The Windows 2000 DHCP Server is tightly integrated with the Windows 2000 Domain Security infrastructure. By integrating with the Active Directory, the Windows 2000 DCHP server can prevent errors in network communication by shutting down DHCP servers that have not been approved by the network administrator. The process of approving these DHCP servers is called *authorizing*.

Authorizing DHCP Servers

As a network administrator, you probably have had the experience of having someone "test" a new DHCP server on your live, production network. And, you probably suffered from having to figure out what the problem was with network communications after someone had done this. The problem is that DHCP messages are broadcast messages, and any DHCP server that hears the broadcast can respond to the DHCPDISCOVER message from a DHCP client.

A *rogue* DHCP server (a DHCP server that has not been approved by the IT department) is likely to contain invalid scopes and DHCP options. Rogue DHCP servers can assign inaccurate IP addressing information to DHCP clients, which may disrupt network communications for these hapless clients.

Windows 2000 networks running only Windows 2000 DHCP servers can recognize and shut down rogue DHCP servers by keeping a list of *authorized* DHCP servers in the Active Directory. Any DHCP server that starts up and is not included in the authorized list will have its DHCP server service shut down automatically.

Only Windows 2000 DHCP servers can detect rogue DHCP servers, and the rogue DHCP server must also be a Windows 2000 computer. Rogue NT DHCP server detection will fail to detect an unauthorized Windows NT DHCP server.

Rogue DHCP Server Detection

When a Windows 2000 DHCP server initializes, it broadcasts a DHCPINFORM message to the local segment. The DHCPINFORM message contains vendor-specific option codes that can be interpreted by Microsoft Windows 2000 DHCP servers. These option types allow the Windows 2000 DHCP server to obtain information about the network from other Windows 2000 DHCP servers on the segment.

The DHCPINFORM message submits queries to other Windows 2000 DHCP servers, and when a Windows 2000 DHCP server on the segment receives this message, it responds to a DHCPINFORM query. This query asks for information about the Enterprise root name and location. The queried Windows 2000 DHCP server responds by sending back a DHCPACK that includes Directory Services Enterprise Root information.

If the new DHCP server receives information about an existing Directory Services Enterprise Root, it will query the Active Directory, which maintains a list of authorized DHCP servers. If the machine's IP address is on the list, it will successfully initialize DHCP server services. If not, DHCP server services will not initialize.

The new DHCP server will start DHCP Server Services if:

- There are other DHCP servers on the segment that are authorized DHCP servers and the new DHCP server is listed in the Active Directory's list of authorized DHCP servers.
- The new DHCP server is the *only* DHCP server on the segment (If the new DHCP does not receive a response to the DHCPINFORM message query, the new DHCP server cannot be made aware of existing Directory Services Enterprise Roots).
- The new DHCP server is on a segment with other Windows 2000 DHCP Servers that are workgroup members, or all other DHCP servers on the segments are downlevel systems (such as Windows NT 4.0 DHCP servers).

In the second and third instances, the new DHCP server is unable to contact another DHCP server that has information about a Directory Services Enterprise Root. The "lone" DHCP server will continue to send a DHCPINFORM message every five minutes. If the new DHCP server later receives a DHCPACK from a DHCP server that contains information about the Enterprise Root, the new DHCP server will look to see if it is authorized in the Active Directory, and if not, will disable its DHCP server services.

EXERCISE 24-8

Authorizing a DHCP Server in the Active Directory

In this exercise, you will authorize a DHCP server in the Active Directory. Do not perform this exercise on a live, production network without the permission of your network administrator.

1. Log on as Administrator.
2. Open the DHCP management console from the Administrative Tools menu.
3. Right-click on the DHCP server's name in the left pane, and click Authorize, as shown in the following illustration.

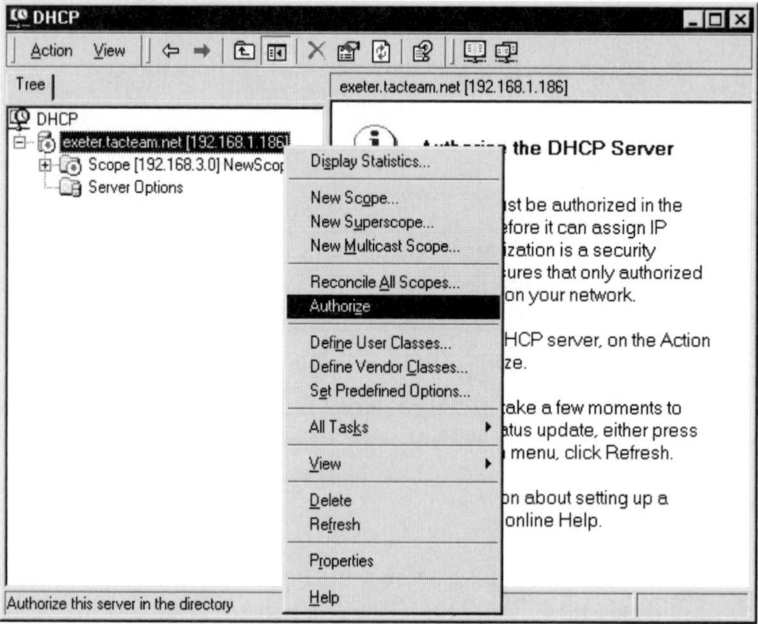

The DHCP server is now authorized. Because the DHCP Server is authorized, the DHCP server service will not be shut down as a rogue DHCP server.

CERTIFICATION OBJECTIVE 24.07

DHCP and APIPA

Automatic Private IP Addressing, or *APIPA*, allows Windows 2000 computers configured as DHCP clients to assign their own IP addresses. This technology is available on Windows 98 clients and has been ported to Windows 2000. APIPA allows a Windows 2000 DHCP client unable to contact a DHCP server to assign itself an IP address.

There are two situations where APIPA is useful. The first scenario occurs when the machine has not previously bound an IP address. In this case:

1. The Windows 2000 computer configured as a DHCP Client starts up. A DHCPDISCOVER message is broadcast to the segment. If the machine does not receive a reply, it starts to autoconfigure its IP address.
2. The machine will select, at random, an IP address from the APIPA reserved Class B network ID 169.254.0.0 with the default Class B subnet mask of 255.255.0.0.
3. A *gratuitous ARP* message is broadcast for this randomly selected IP address. If no machine responds to the ARP request, the machine will bind the new IP address to the network adapter configured as a DHCP client.
4. If another machine on the segment responds to the ARP request, the self-configuring computer will choose another IP address and issue another ARP request. It will continue this process for up to 10 addresses. If the machine cannot configure an IP address after 10 attempts, it will stop and disable TCP/IP.

If a DHCP client who has an active lease starts up and cannot contact a DHCP server, the process is a little different.

1. When the DHCP client with a valid lease starts up, it issues a DHCPREQUEST broadcast to renew the lease.
2. If the client does not receive a DHCPACK from the DHCP server, it will start to PING the IP address of the default gateway configured in its lease.

3. If the default gateway responds, the machine "assumes" there must be a problem with the DHCP server itself. The DHCP client attempts to renew its lease at 50% and 87.5% of the lease period.
4. If the default gateway fails to respond to the PING, the machine assumes it has been moved. In this case, the DHCP Client abandons its lease, and autoconfigures itself as described above.

In both cases, the DHCP client issues a DHCPDISCOVER message every five minutes, attempting to contact a DHCP server. If the client receives a DHCPOFFER message at any time, it will bind a valid IP address from the DHCP server sending the offer.

Windows 2000 DHCP computers communicate with Network Driver Interface Specification (NDIS) 5.0 compliant network interface card drivers to obtain information about network connection status. This *media sense* capability allows the operating system to detect whether the computer has been disconnected from the network. If the operating system senses the computer has been removed from a network and plugged into another, it will begin the lease renewal and Autoconfiguration process.

EXERCISE 24-9

Disabling Automatic Private IP Addressing

In this exercise, you will disable APIPA on your computer. Do not perform this exercise in a live, production networking environment without the permission of your network administrator.

1. Log on as Administrator.
2. Open the Registry editor. You can do this by clicking Start | Run. In the text box for the Run command, type **regedt32** and press ENTER.
3. Maximize the Hkey Local Machine window. Expand CurrentControlSet, then expand Services, then expand TCP/IP, then expand Interfaces, and then click on the node that matches the name of your adapter.
4. Click the Edit menu and then click Add Value.

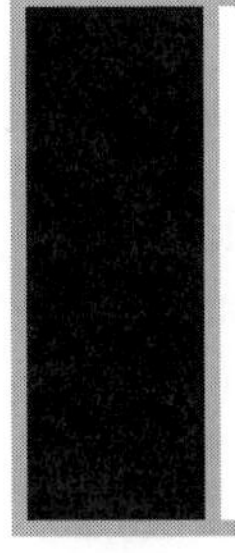

5. In the Value Name text box, type **IPAutoconfigurationEnabled** and make the Data Type REG_DWORD. Then click OK.
6. In the DWORD Editor dialog box, set the value to 0 and click OK.
7. The new value should show in the right pane. Close the Registry Editor.

Keep in mind that APIPA is only useful on single-segment networks where all machines are using APIPA. Otherwise, the self-configuring machines will assign themselves to a network ID that's unlikely to be in use on your network.

CERTIFICATION OBJECTIVE 24.08

Monitoring and Troubleshooting DHCP

The Windows 2000 DHCP server is a self-tuning service for the most part. However, there are times when the server will not function properly, and you will need to troubleshoot problems with your DHCP server. In this section, we'll explore three tools provided with the Windows 2000 DHCP server: The Event Viewer, System Monitor, and DCHP Logging.

Using Event Viewer

The DHCP server will report significant errors to the Windows 2000 Event Viewer. Whenever you have problems related to the DHCP server, you should look at the Event Viewer first to assess what the problem might be. Typically, the DHCP server service will report an error code to the Event Viewer. The Windows 2000 Support Tools, which are on the Windows 2000 CD-ROM, include a help file that contains a large number of these error codes. Be sure to install these support tools and look up cryptic error codes when you encounter them.

Using System Monitor

The Windows 2000 System Monitor takes over for the Windows NT 4.0 Performance Monitor. The System Monitor allows you to monitor many different aspects of your Windows 2000 Server installation. The Windows 2000 System Monitor contains a large number of counters that allow you to track all types of messages a DHCP server sends and receives, how much processor time is devoted to the DHCP server service, and the volume of packets that are dropped by the DHCP server due to a heavily taxed server.

Table 24-1 includes a sample of the more important counters that you should be familiar with when monitoring and troubleshooting your DHCP server.

TABLE 24-1 System Monitor DHCP-Related Counters

Counter	Description
Packets Received/sec	The average number of DHCP messages received by the server. After performing a baseline, if you see an unusually large number, you should investigate the reasons for the excessive DHCP traffic.
Packets Expired/sec	If DHCP message packets are held in the DHCP server's queue for an excessive period of time, the server will expire these packets and drop them. After base lining, if you find a large number of packets are being expired, you should troubleshoot the problem with the server's slow response time to DHCP messages.
Nacks/sec	This is the average number of negative acknowledgments received per second. If this value is high, it's likely that many machines are moving from segment to segment, or there is a configuration problem with the client or server. Common reasons for this sort of behavior include deactivated scopes and a large number of laptops moving on and off the network.
Declines/sec	A DHCP client issues a gratuitous ARP message when it receives an IP address from a DHCP server. If the DHCP client discovers that the IP address is already in use, it will send a DHCPDECLINE message to the DHCP server and reject the offered IP address. If this happens frequently, enable conflict detection on the DHCP server for troubleshooting purposes while you're investigating the problem. Do not leave conflict detection enabled for extended periods of time.

Using Logs

Windows 2000 has auditing to allow the administrator to monitor the DHCP server. However, auditing introduces another problem: logging. Since Windows 2000 now has disk quotas, it is much easier for the logs to fill the available disk space. Windows 2000 reduces the problems by introducing *registry keys* to change the logging settings for the DHCP's audit log. To edit the values, edit the key: HKEY_LOCAL_MACHINE\SYSTEM\CurrentControlSet\Services\DHCPServer\Parameters. The values for the registry key parameters are:

```
DhcpLogFilePath
DhcpLogMinSpaceOnDisk
DhcpLogDiskSpaceCheckInterval
DhcpLogFileMaxSize
```

The DhcpLogFilePath key, which is of data type REG_SZ, lets the user specify the full path to the log file. The DhcpLogMinSpaceOnDisk, which is of data type REG_DWORD, allows the administrator to specify the amount of disk space left before the audit logging is stopped. The DhcpLogDiskSpaceCheckInterval, which is of data type REG_DWORD, is the number of times the log is written before the free space is checked. DhcpLogFileMaxSize, which is of data type REG_DWORD, is the maximum size of the log file in megabytes. The default is 7 megabytes.

EXERCISE 24-10

Enabling DHCP Server Logging

In this exercise, you will enable detailed logging on your DHCP server. Do not perform this exercise on a live, production DHCP server or network without the permission of your network administrator.

1. Log on as Administrator.
2. From the Start menu, go to the Administrative Tools and then click DHCP.
3. Right-click on the name of your DHCP server, and click Properties.
4. On the General tab in the Properties dialog box, place a check mark in the "Enable DHCP audit logging" check box.
5. Click OK and close the DHCP management console.

CERTIFICATION SUMMARY

The DHCP server service is designed to make the management and assignment of IP addresses easier for the network administrator. You can centrally manage all the IP addressing information for even the largest of organizations by employing just a handful of DHCP servers.

DHCP clients do not usually keep IP addresses indefinitely. Instead, IP addressing information is "leased" to DHCP clients. There are four steps to the lease process: DHCPDISCOVER, DHCPOFFER, DHCPREQUEST, and DHCPACK. All DHCP messages are broadcasts.

A client must have a valid lease to retain an IP address, and will not be able to continue network activity if is does not retain a valid lease.

Remember that broadcast messages do not traverse routers. DHCP messages can be communicated across routers if you configure a router to pass through BOOTP/DHCP messages via UDP Port 67 (BOOTP Relay), or if you implement a DHCP relay agent. A DHCP relay agent intercepts multicast DHCP messages and forwards them as unicast messages to a DHCP server.

The pool of available IP addresses is called a *scope.* Only one scope is allowed per logical subnet. Scopes typically include all the available IP addresses for a specific network ID. Clients that require static IP addresses can be excluded from the scope. Excluded addresses will not be allocated to DHCP clients.

The DHCP server can deliver additional IP addressing information in the form of *DHCP options.* A large number of DHCP options are available, but Microsoft network clients support only a small number of DHCP options.

DHCP options can be configured at several levels, including server options, scope options, client options, and vendor class/user class options. Server options apply to all scopes configured on a single server. Scope options apply only to a single scope. Scope options override server options.

A DHCP server can deliver the same IP address to a machine each time it renews a lease, if a client is designated as *reserved.* A reserved client is a computer whose MAC address and IP address have been configured at the DHCP server.

A reserved client can be configured with its own DHCP options, and reserved client options override scope options.

Vendor class options are introduced for the first time in the Windows 2000 DHCP Server.

The DHCP client can identify itself as a member of the Vendor's class, and the DHCP server will send class members a custom set of options.

The DHCP administrator configures user class options, which are delivered to machines identifying themselves as a member of a particular user class. For example, a user class named "laptops" could be created. All laptops would be configured to send their class ID to the DHCP server, and DHCP options configured for the "laptops" user class are then sent to these machines. Vendor and user class options override all other DHCP options.

DHCP clients unable to contact a DHCP server can autoconfigure their IP address. APIPA (Automatic Private IP Addressing) allows DHCP clients to self-assign an IP address from the 169.254.0.0 Class B network ID.

Autoconfiguration prevents TCP/IP from shutting down when a DHCP server cannot be contacted.

Routing and Remote Access Service (RRAS) can use DHCP to assign IP addresses to RRAS clients. The RRAS server obtains a block of IP addresses from a DHCP server during initialization. The RRAS server retains only the IP address itself and all options information is discarded. Then the RRAS server assigns WINS and DNS settings to the RRAS client based on connection-specific configuration on the RRAS server. This information does not come from the DHCP server. An RRAS client lease lasts for the duration of the connection.

The Windows 2000 DHCP server also supports dynamic assignment of IP addresses to BOOTP clients, and client reservations can be configured for BOOTP clients as well. The name of a TFTP server and the location of the Boot Image are configured in the DHCP server Boot Table.

A single physical network containing multiple logical subnetworks is called a *multinet.* A *superscope* must be configured to support multinet configurations. To create a superscope, you need to first create individual scopes. Then you use the Superscope wizard to join the individual scopes into a single administrative unit.

TWO-MINUTE DRILL

Overview of DHCP

- ❑ The DHCP server centrally manages and assigns IP addresses for an organization, which simplifies the life of the network administrator.
- ❑ A DHCP server leases addresses. DHCP clients do not keep their IP addressing information indefinitely.
- ❑ You can remember the lease process by thinking of DORA: DISCOVER, OFFER, REQUEST, ACKNOWLEDGEMENT.
- ❑ DHCP broadcast messages can be conveyed without forwarding broadcasts to remote DHCP servers by using DHCP relay agents that intercept the broadcasts and forward the broadcast request as a unicast message to a remote DHCP server.

DHCP Server Configuration

- ❑ DHCP servers store groups of IP addresses to hand out to DHCP clients in *scopes*. Each scope represents a different subnet, and only a single subnet can be included in a scope.
- ❑ In addition to assigning an IP address and subnet mask, the DHCP can provide other information such as WINS server, DNS server, and default gateway addresses. These are configured as DHCP options.
- ❑ The Windows 2000 DHCP server includes server options, scope options, client options, reserved client options, and vendor/user class options. Know what these options represent and their order of precedence.
- ❑ BOOTP is used to assign IP addressing information to diskless workstations such as Net PCs and other "dumb" client machines.

DHCP Relay Agents in a Routed Environment

- ❑ Use a DHCP relay agent on segments that do not have a DHCP server located on them. The DHCP relay agent will intercept DHCP messages from DHCP clients and forward those messages to a DHCP server on remote subnets.

- ❑ If you choose not to use a DHCP relay agent, you can configure your routers to provide *BOOTP forwarding*. When enabled, BOOTP forwarding allows DHCP messages to pass through the router. Be mindful of the hop count for DHCP messages when using BOOTP forwarding to allow DHCP clients to access remote DHCP servers.

Integrating DHCP with DDNS

- ❑ The Windows 2000 DHCP server is able to convey information to a Windows 2000 Dynamic DNS server. By default, Windows 2000 DHCP clients update their own Host (A) record, and the DHCP server updates its Pointer (PTR) record.
- ❑ The Windows 2000 DHCP server can act as a proxy for downlevel DHCP clients that are unable to communicate directly with Dynamic DNS servers. In this case, the DHCP server will update both the Host (A) record and the Pointer (PTR) record on the behalf of the downlevel client.

Integrating DHCP with RRAS

- ❑ The Windows 2000 RRAS server obtains blocks of IP addresses from a DHCP server when the RRAS server has been configured to assign IP addresses via DHCP. Any option information associated with the IP addresses it obtains is ignored.
- ❑ The RRAS client never communicates directly with the DHCP server. It receives its IP address and option-related information directly from the RRAS server. RRAS clients drop their lease when they shut down.

Integrating DHCP with Active Directory

- ❑ Windows 2000 DHCP server is able to detect rogue DHCP servers. Rogue DCHP servers are those that are not authorized for use in the Active Directory. Rogue DHCP server detection is performed with the help of DHCPINFORM messages.
- ❑ Rogue server detection only works when all operating systems are Active Directory aware. Therefore, if you introduce a Windows NT 4.0 DCHP server into the network, it will not be detected as a rogue DHCP server,

because the Windows NT 4.0 DHCP server does not register itself with the Active Directory.

DHCP and APIPA

- DHCP clients can self-configure their IP addressing information using Automatic Private IP Addressing (APIPA). If the DHCP client is not able to contact a DHCP server, it will self assign an IP address in the Class B network ID of 168.254.0.0.
- You can disable APIPA by editing the Registry. It is often a good idea to disable APIPA on certain machines, such as servers, on your network.

MCSE

MICROSOFT CERTIFIED SYSTEMS ENGINEER

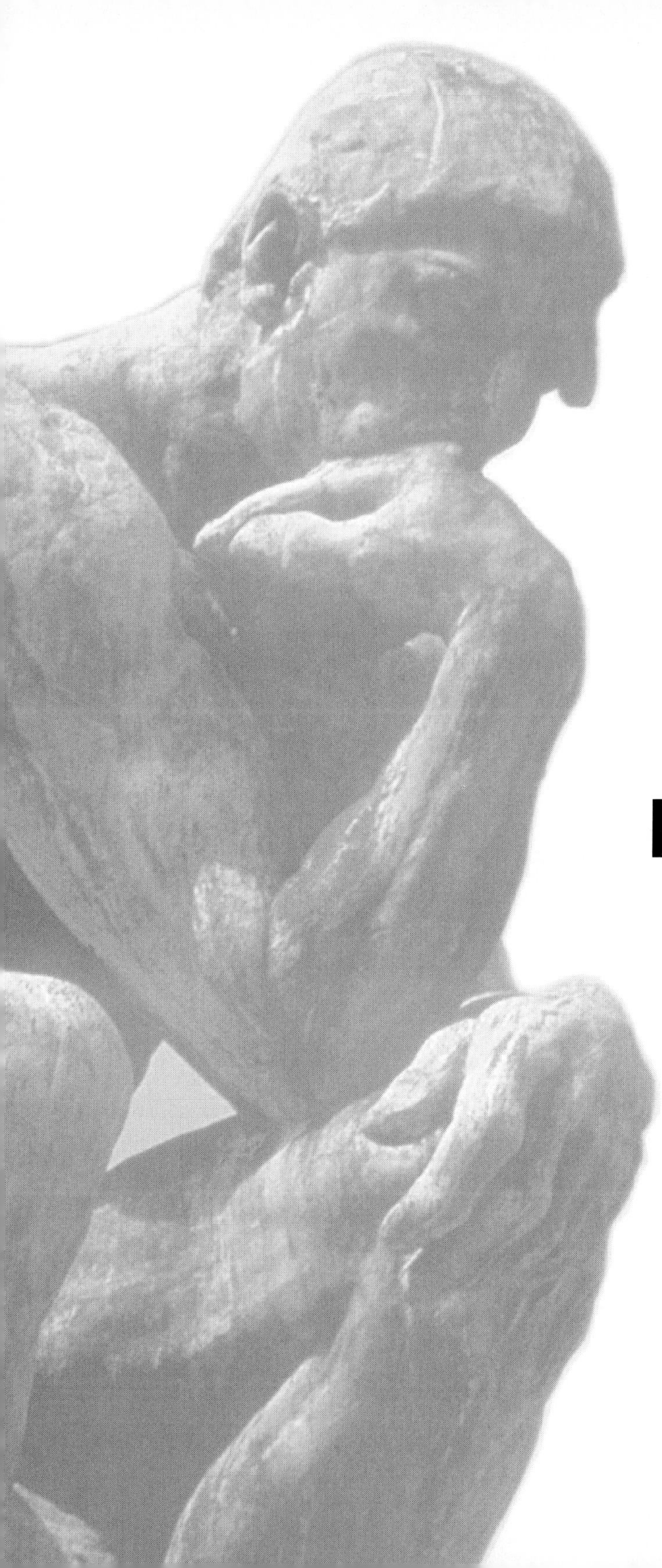

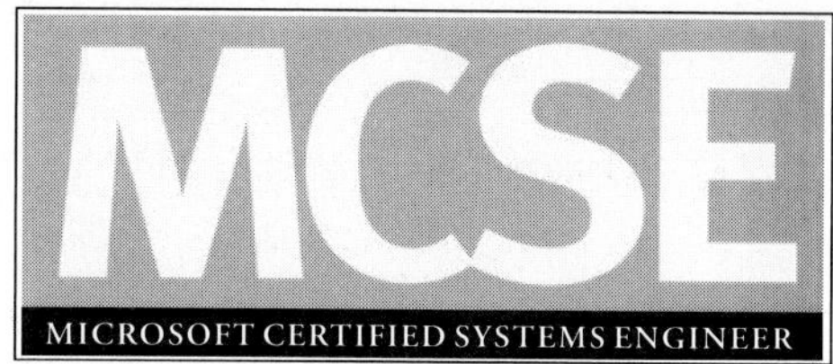

25

Installing and Managing the Windows 2000 WINS Server

CERTIFICATION OBJECTIVES

25.01 Introduction to NetBIOS Name Resolution

25.02 Planning and Implementing a WINS Solution

25.03 Interoperability Issues

25.04 Monitoring and Troubleshooting WINS

✓ Two-Minute Drill

In this chapter, we'll focus on a service familiar to those who have been working with any Microsoft network operating system: The Windows Internet Name Service, or WINS. WINS solves the very important problem of resolving NetBIOS names for remote hosts on Microsoft networks. Without WINS, you would need to use methods such as LMHOSTS files in order to resolve the names of remote NetBIOS hosts.

Microsoft's goal is to eliminate NetBIOS from Microsoft networks. However, the history of Microsoft networking is the history of NetBIOS. Because of the intimate ties between NetBIOS and Microsoft networking and Microsoft networked applications, a large cadre of legacy applications exists that depend on the NetBIOS interface. Therefore, in spite of the long-term goal of eliminating WINS, it's likely that NetBIOS name resolution will be an important problem for the network administrator in the foreseeable future.

In the chapter, we will look at the mechanics of NetBIOS name resolution, how to plan and implement a WINS networking solution, some important interoperability issues, and finally, how to monitor and troubleshoot your WINS implementation.

CERTIFICATION OBJECTIVE 25.01

Introduction to NetBIOS Name Resolution

All Microsoft networks prior to Windows 2000 were NetBIOS networks. NetBIOS was developed for IBM by a company name Sytek in 1983 in order to support small local area networks (LANs). It was initially a broadcast-based, monolith transport protocol for workgroups. Microsoft's implementation of the NetBIOS transport protocol is the NetBIOS Extend User Interface, or NetBEUI. NetBEUI was the workhorse of Microsoft networks during the early growth of the Microsoft networking model. In fact, Microsoft had intended NetBEUI to become even more robust, and even routable. They were working on a networking protocol dubbed "JetBEUI" that would have been a routable implementation of NetBEUI.

However, everything changed with the ascendance of the Internet. In 1995, Microsoft recognized the future of network computing as intimately tied in with the Internet. The protocol of the Internet was, and is, TCP/IP. Therefore, the decision was made to abandon NetBEUI as the standard Microsoft protocol, and replace it with TCP/IP.

However, the changeover from NetBIOS networking to TCP/IP-based networking would not be easy or seamless. NetBIOS protocols use the NetBIOS name of the destination host as the endpoint of communication. TCP/IP is unaware of NetBIOS names. TCP/IP uses IP addresses and port numbers as the endpoints of communication. The vast majority of programs written for Microsoft networks were written to the NetBIOS programming interface. A mechanism had to be put into place that would solve this problem.

NetBIOS over TCP/IP

To understand the solution to the problem, you need to understand a little more about what the problem is with programs written specifically for NetBIOS-based networks.

When programs are designed, they are written with a particular protocol in mind. NetBIOS programs were written for NetBIOS based networks; in other words, all Microsoft networks prior to Windows 2000. These programs are able to access the network protocols via the NetBIOS session layer interface. NetBIOS programs establish sessions with other computers via their NetBIOS names by broadcasting the destination computer's name over the segment, and waiting for the destination computer to respond with its Media Access Control (MAC) address.

The challenge was to get NetBIOS-based programs to work over TCP/IP-based networks. Since TCP/IP uses destination IP addresses and port numbers as the endpoint of communication, a NetBIOS *session layer interface* was added. This NetBIOS session layer interface is known as NetBIOS over TCP/IP, or NetBT.

NetBT is one of two session layer interfaces programs can use to access the networking protocols. The other is the *Windows Sockets interface*, or *Winsock.* Programs written expressly for TCP/IP-based networks access the TCP/IP protocol stack via the Winsock interface.

The main job for NetBT is to resolve NetBIOS names to IP addresses. In this way, we can get programs that are unaware of IP addresses to work with a protocol that is unaware of NetBIOS names. Once the destination computer's NetBIOS name is matched up, or *resolved* to an IP address, the request can be passed from the Application layer to the lower layers of the protocol stack.

Names and Naming Conventions

NetBIOS names are 16-byte names. You can configure the first 15 bytes with legal NetBIOS name characters, and the 16th byte is reserved for a service identifier. The NetBIOS convention is that all characters are treated as uppercase regardless of how you type them in various dialog boxes. Legal characters in NetBIOS names include A–Z, 0–9, #, $, !, -, _, @, %, (,), [,]. However, some of these *exotic* nonalphanumeric characters have other meanings in the Microsoft NetBIOS implementation, so you need to be careful in your use of these characters.

No two computers on a NetBIOS-based network can have the same NetBIOS name. This has caused many administrators to pull their hair out because in large networks of 40,000 computers or more, the challenge of coming up with a meaningful, yet different name for each computer required a certain level of creativity.

The NetBIOS namespace is a *flat* namespace. It is flat because the single NetBIOS name represents the only *partition* of the namespace. It's as if everyone in the world was required to have a different first name. What a challenge it would be to find a meaningful name for every person in the world if that were the case!

Service Identifiers A computer running the TCP/IP NetBIOS interface actually has several NetBIOS names. Each name is used by a service to "advertise" that the service is running on that particular computer. It's like putting a sign on the door saying "these people live here." For example, if a Windows 2000 machine is running both the Server service and the Workstation (Microsoft *Redirector*) service, it will register two NetBIOS names, one for each of the services running. This is a way for the NetBIOS applications to let other machines know that they are running and available.

You can see a list of the registered NetBIOS names for your computer by using the nbtstat utility from the command line. Open a command prompt and type: **nbtstat –n**.

You'll see something similar to what appears in Figure 25-1.

The key concept to appreciate is that computers running NetBIOS services don't typically have a NetBIOS name; they have *NetBIOS Names.*

FIGURE 25-1

Registered NetBIOS names for a computer named Constellation

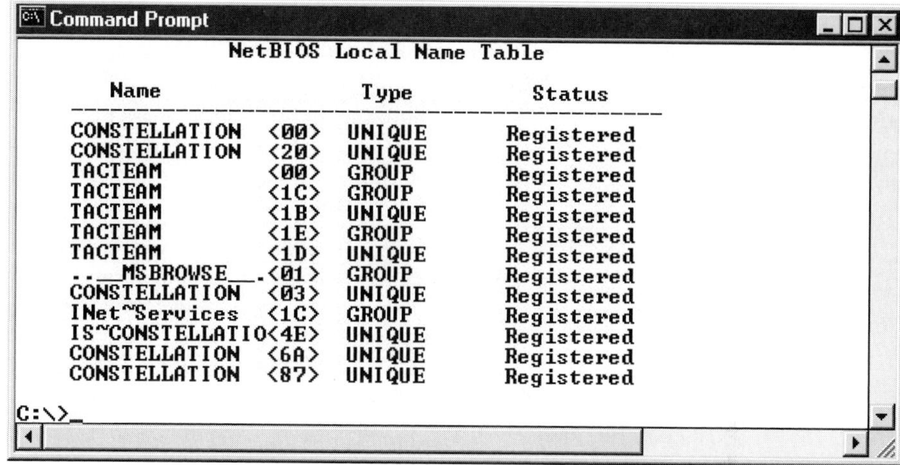

Command Prompt
NetBIOS Local Name Table
Name Type Status
CONSTELLATION <00> UNIQUE Registered
CONSTELLATION <20> UNIQUE Registered
TACTEAM <00> GROUP Registered
TACTEAM <1C> GROUP Registered
TACTEAM <1B> UNIQUE Registered
TACTEAM <1E> GROUP Registered
TACTEAM <1D> UNIQUE Registered
..__MSBROWSE__.<01> GROUP Registered
CONSTELLATION <03> UNIQUE Registered
INet~Services <1C> GROUP Registered
IS~CONSTELLATIO<4E> UNIQUE Registered
CONSTELLATION <6A> UNIQUE Registered
CONSTELLATION <87> UNIQUE Registered
C:\>_

Table 25-1 lists the common NetBIOS name service identifiers.

TABLE 25-1

Common NetBIOS Name Suffixes

Suffix	Description
<USERNAME><03>	Used to register the name of the user currently logged on in the WINS database so that the messenger service can locate users via their NetBIOS names.
<COMPUTER><00>	Used by the Microsoft Redirector to indicate that the computer is running the Microsoft Networking Client Service. This is the computer name registered by the Workstation Service.
<COMPUTER><03>	Used as the computer name that is registered for the Messenger Service on a computer that is a WINS client.
<COMPUTER><20>	Used as the name that is registered for a computer running the Server service on a Windows 2000 computer that is a WINS client.
<COMPUTER><Be>	Used as the *unique name* that is registered when the Network Monitor agent is started on the computer.Unique means that the name used is not a *group* name.
<COMPUTER><Bf>	Used as the *group* name that is registered when the Network Monitor agent is started on the computer. If this name is not 15 characters in length, it is padded with plus (+) symbols.
<COMPUTER><1f>	Used as the unique name that is registered for network dynamic data exchange (NetDDE) when the NetDDE service is started on the computer.

TABLE 25-1 Common NetBIOS Name Suffixes *(continued)*

<01><02>MS BROWSE<02><01>	Used by master browsers to periodically announce their domain on a local subnet. This master browser announcement contains the domain name and the name of the master browser server for the domain. In addition, master browsers receive the domain announcements sent to this name and maintain them in their internal browse list along with the announcer's computer name.
<DOMAIN><00>	Used by workstations and servers to process server announcements to support Microsoft LAN Manager. Computers running the Server service including Windows 95, Windows NT, and Windows 2000 do not broadcast this name unless the LMAnnounce option is enabled in the computer running the Server service.
<DOMAIN><1b>	Used to identify the *domain master browser* name, which is a unique name that only the primary domain controller (PDC) or PDC Emulator can add. WINS assumes that the computer that registers a domain name with the <1b>character is the PDC.
<DOMAIN><1c>	Used for the internet group name, which all the domain controllers register. The internet group name is a dynamic list of up to 25 computers that have registered the name. This is the name used to find a Windows NT domain controller for pass-through authentication.
<DOMAIN><1d>	Used to identify a segment master browser (*not a domain master browser*). The master browser adds this name as a unique NetBIOS name when it starts. Computers running the Server service announce their presence to this name so that master browsers can build their browse list.
<DOMAIN><1e>	Used for all domain-wide announcements by browser servers in a Windows 2000-based server domain. This name is added by all browsers and potential browsers in the workgroup or domain. All browser election packets are sent to this name.

Resolving NetBIOS Names to IP Addresses

In order for NetBIOS applications to communicate with each other on TCP/IP-based networks, the destination NetBIOS name must be matched up, or *resolved*, to an IP address. This is known as *NetBIOS name resolution.*

There are multiple ways to resolve a NetBIOS name to an IP address. This is because resolving a NetBIOS name to an IP address is critical to communications on most Microsoft networks. The NetBIOS-specific methods of resolving a NetBIOS name to an IP address are:

- NetBIOS Name Servers (WINS)
- Broadcasts
- LMHOSTS file

Let's look at each of these methods and see how they work, and how they *don't* work, on your TCP/IP network.

Broadcasts

NetBT can use broadcasts to resolve a NetBIOS name to an IP address. Broadcasts are of limited utility, because the destination host must be on the same segment in order for NetBIOS name resolution to be successful via broadcast. Routers do not, and should not, forward NetBIOS broadcast messages. If routers were configured to pass NetBIOS messages via UDP Ports 137 (NetBIOS Name Service) and 138 (NetBIOS Data Service), the network could become flooded with NetBIOS name registration and query traffic.

When the broadcast is issued, a request is sent for the IP address of a given NetBIOS name. When the IP address is returned, another broadcast takes place in the form of an ARP (Address Resolution Protocol) request. The ARP request broadcasts a query onto the segment requesting resolution of the IP address to a hardware (Media Access Control, or MAC) address. After the MAC address is obtained, a session can be established.

exam Watch

NetBIOS is not the only protocol that issues broadcasts for resolution purposes. Network architectures such as Ethernet are broadcast dependent, because logical addresses must be resolved to hardware addresses. This is in contrast to Asynchronous Transfer Mode (ATM) networks, where a MARS (Media Access Resolution Service) server is used to resolve logical addresses to hardware addresses.

LMHOSTS

An LMHOSTS file is a plain-text file that contains NetBIOS names to IP address mappings. LMHOSTS can be useful as a backup method of resolving names of especially important computers when other methods fail.

An example LMHOSTS file for our small office network appears in Figure 25-2.

The LMHOSTS file looks somewhat like the HOSTS file, the major difference being that the LMHOSTS file resolves NetBIOS names, and the HOSTS file resolves host names. Another significant difference between LMHOSTS and HOSTS is that the LMHOSTS file supports a number of *tags* that enhance its utility.

A list of the supported LMHOSTS tags appears in Table 25-2.

Some of things to note about the LMHOSTS file:

- The file is parsed (read and processed) from top to bottom.
- Parsing stops after the first successful match (unless the #MH tag is used).
- The *NetBIOS Names* are not case sensitive.
- The *tags* are case sensitive.
- The LMHOSTS file does not have a file extension.

FIGURE 25-2

A sample LMHOSTS file

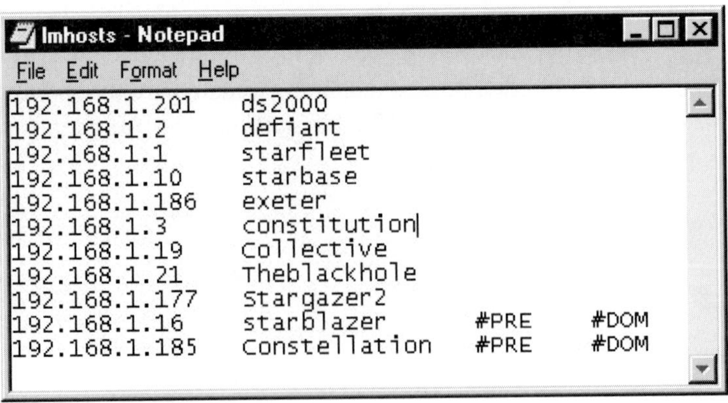

TABLE 25-2

Commonly Used LMHOSTS File Tags

#BEGIN_ALTERNATE	Used to group multiple #INCLUDE statements. Any single successful #INCLUDE statement in a group causes the group to succeed. The included groups will not be searched until a successful name resolution is accomplished. Rather, the success of an included group is determined by whether or not access to the file is successful.
#END_ALTERNATE	Used to mark the end of a group of #INCLUDE statements.
#DOM:<*domain*>	Determines that the NetBIOS name mapping is for a domain controller. This keyword affects how the Browser and Logon services behave in routed TCP/IP environments. Since domain controllers are important for many domain-related functions, it is often preferred to preload a #DOM entry; the #PRE keyword must appear first in the entry.
#INCLUDE <*file name*>	An *included* lmhosts file is located on a remote server that has a shared directory with a file that can provide NetBIOS name to IP address mappings. Specifying a Universal Naming Convention (UNC) <file name> allows you to use a centralized LMHOSTS file on a server. If the server on which <file name> exists is outside of the local broadcast subnet, you must add a mapping in the LMHOSTS file for that server above the #BEGIN_ALTERNATE statement.
#MH	Multihomed machines have multiple IP addresses. Typically, a search for a NetBIOS name to IP address mapping will stop with the first successful match. However, if you append the #MH tag to the entry, the search will continue to find subsequent entries for the same NetBIOS name in the LMHOSTS file. The maximum number of addresses that can be assigned to a unique name is 25.
#PRE	Part of the NetBIOS name to IP address mapping entry that causes that entry to be preloaded into the NetBIOS remote name cache. By default, entries are not preloaded into the name cache, but are parsed only after WINS and name query broadcasts fail to resolve a name. *The #PRE keyword must be appended to entries that also appear in #INCLUDE statements; otherwise, the entry in the #INCLUDE statement is ignored.* Therefore, be sure when you create the mapping for the server that has the included LMHOSTS file that you put the #PRE tag on it.

Because the file is parsed from top to bottom, you should put the entries with the #PRE tags on the bottom of the list. This is because those entries have already been evaluated when the NetBIOS remote name cache has been evaluated at the beginning of the NetBIOS name resolution sequence.

on the job

The tags in the LMHOSTS file are case sensitive and should be entered in uppercase.

EXERCISE 25-1

Creating an LMHOSTS File

In this exercise, you will create an LMHOSTS file for your network. Do not perform this exercise on a live, production environment without your network administrator's permission.

1. Identify three computers on your network by NetBIOS name and IP address. If possible, find one that is a domain controller.
2. Open Notepad from the Start menu.
3. Type in the names of the three computers and their IP addresses in Notepad. Separate the computer name from the IP address with a TAB. Make the domain controller the last entry in the list, and use both the #DOM: and the #PRE tags for the domain controller. Be sure to press ENTER after completing the last line. Your LMHOSTS file should look something like the following illustration.

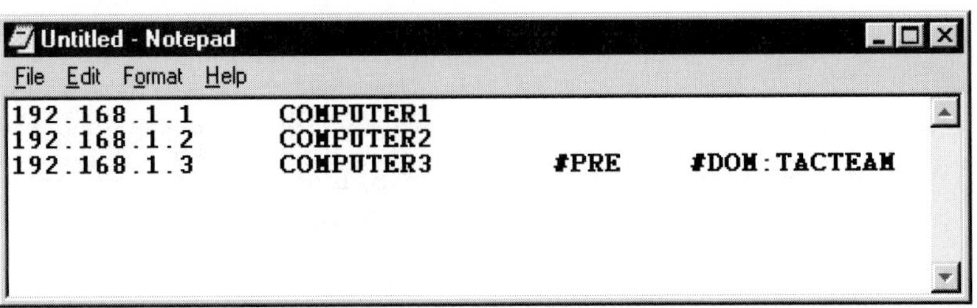

4. Save the file in the %systemroot%\system32\drivers\etc directory on your hard disk. Click the File menu and then the Save command. Save the file as "LMHOSTS" with the quotation marks, as seen in the following illustration.

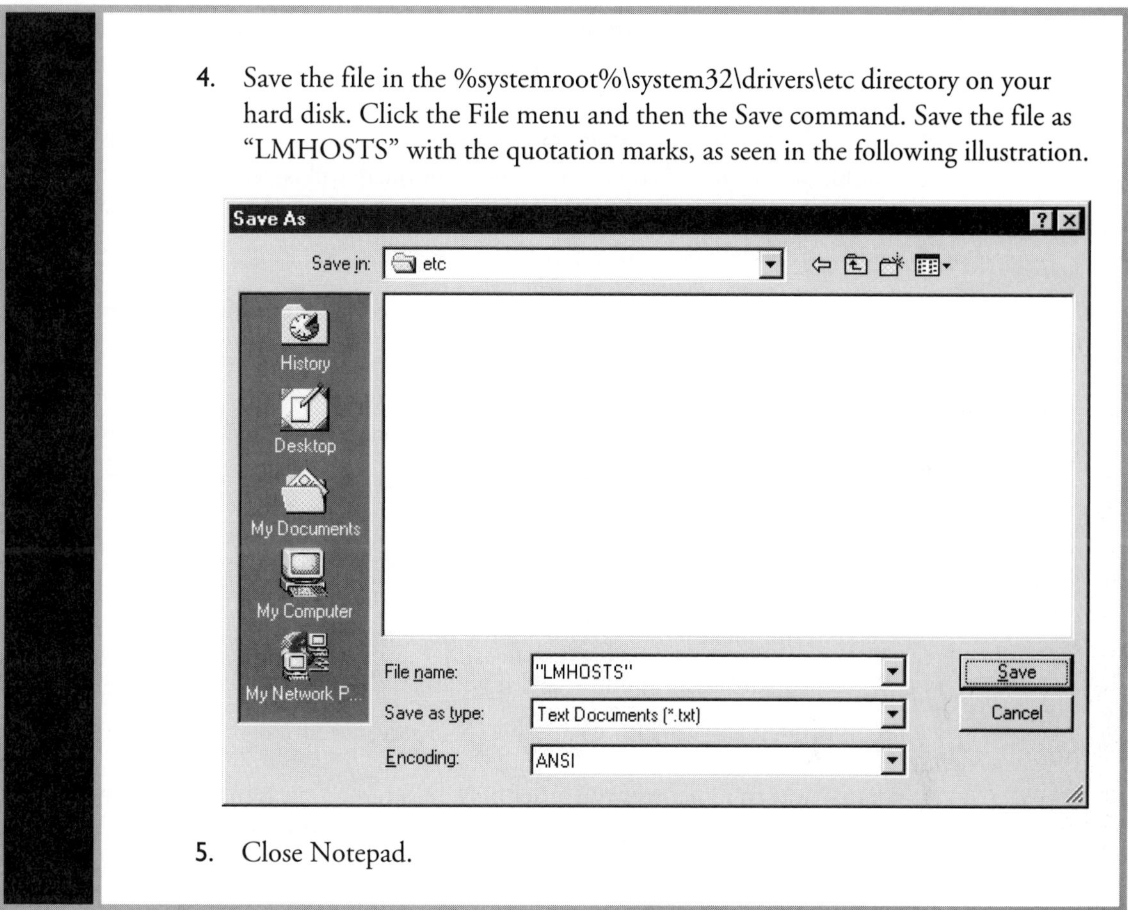

5. Close Notepad.

NetBIOS Name Server

A NetBIOS Name Server (NBNS) is a machine that runs server software dedicated to resolving NetBIOS names to IP addresses. The NBNS contains a database file that can accept dynamic NetBIOS name registrations and answer queries for NetBIOS name resolution.

The most popular and only widely used NetBIOS Name Server is the Microsoft Windows Internet Name Server, or WINS. We will talk more about WINS as we move through the chapter.

The Order of NetBIOS Name Resolution and Node Types

When an application using the NetBIOS API issues a name query on a WINS-enabled client, the first thing the operating system does is evaluate the name. If it is longer than 15 characters, or if it is hierarchical (contains "dots" or periods, such as constellation.tacteam.net), the query will be sent to DNS.

If neither of the preceding conditions apply, name resolution will proceed in the follow sequence:

1. The NetBIOS remote name cache is checked to determine if the name has been recently resolved.
2. If the name is not found there, it will contact the WINS server(s) whose address(es) have been entered in the WINS client's TCP/IP properties.
3. If the WINS server cannot resolve the name, it will issue a broadcast to the other computers on its subnet.
4. If this doesn't work, and the TCP/IP properties are configured to use LMHOSTS lookup, it will check the LMHOSTS file in the <systemroot>\system32\Drivers\Etc directory.
5. If the name is not found there, it will next check the HOSTS file.
6. Finally, it will attempt to query a DNS server.

An easy way to remember the order of WINS resolution is by memorizing the sentence "Can We Buy Large Hard Drives." The first letter of each word—C, W, B, L, H, D—stands for the resolution methods: Cache, WINS, Broadcast, LMHOSTS, Hosts, DNS.

This is the sequence when the Windows 2000 machine is configured as an H-node client. When NetBIOS machines are configured as other node types, the name resolution sequence is slightly altered.

NetBIOS clients must be configured with a *node type* that defines how they process NetBIOS queries. The NetBIOS node type will determine which services are invoked, and in what order. The NetBIOS node types include:

- b-node
- p-node

- m-node
- h-node

Let's look at each node type in a little more detail, and examine the circumstances in which each node might find its best use.

B-Node A *b-node* (broadcast node) client uses broadcasts instead of a WINS server. A Windows NetBIOS client computer without a configured WINS server is a b-node client. The NetBIOS name resolution order for the b-node client is:

1. NetBIOS remote name cache
2. Broadcast
3. LMHOSTS
4. HOSTS
5. DNS server

P-Node A *p-node* (peer node) WINS client uses a WINS server and does not issue broadcasts. When a WINS client is configured as a p-node WINS client, it will *not* broadcast to resolve a NetBIOS name to an IP address. The advantage of configuring WINS clients as p-nodes is that there is no possibility of NetBIOS broadcast traffic using up valuable network bandwidth. On the other hand, if the p-node client is not able to access a WINS server, it will have to use alternate methods to resolve the NetBIOS name to an IP address, even if the destination host is local. This can lead to strange things, like the p-node client accessing a remote DNS server to resolve the IP address of a host on the local segment.

The NetBIOS name resolution order for the p-node client is:

1. NetBIOS remote name cache
2. WINS server
3. LMHOSTS
4. HOSTS
5. DNS server

M-Node *M-node* (mixed node) WINS clients use both broadcasts *and* WINS servers to resolve NetBIOS names to IP addresses. The mixed-node client preferentially uses broadcasts before querying a WINS server.

Consider this example. You have a company with three sites. The main site is located in Dallas, and has 1200 computers. The company also maintains two satellite offices, one in Houston and another in Amarillo, which have 20 computers each. The satellite offices require very little network services support from the main office, and most sessions take place among the machines located within the remote sites. The only WINS server is in Dallas.

In this situation, you would be better off to configure the computers in the satellite offices as m-node clients, since these computers are all located on the same segment, and broadcasts will easily resolve the NetBIOS names to IP addresses. This will prevent the machines from having to query a remote WINS server for local addresses. If the client needs to resolve names for machines on remote segments, they can still query the remote WINS server.

The NetBIOS name resolution order for the m-node client is:

1. NetBIOS remote name cache
2. Broadcast
3. WINS server
4. LMHOSTS
5. HOSTS
6. DNS server

H-Node H-node (hybrid node) WINS clients are similar to M-node, but use WINS NetBIOS name resolution first, before initiating a NetBIOS broadcast message.

exam Watch

The node type can be changed manually by editing the Registry, or can be automatically assigned when using a DHCP server. The NetBIOS node type setting is stored in the registry at:

HKLM\System\CurrentControlSet\Services\NetBT\Parameters

The Entry is named *NodeType* and is of type REG_DWORD. The possible values are:

B-node = 0×1

P-node = 0×2

M-node = 0×4

H-node = 0×8

Hybrid node clients are best suited for a multiple segment LAN/WAN environment, where destination NetBIOS clients and resources are located on remote segments.

The NetBIOS name resolution order for the h-node client is:

1. NetBIOS remote name cache
2. WINS server
3. Broadcast
4. LMHOSTS
5. HOSTS
6. DNS server

WINS Network Components

In order to resolve NetBIOS names using WINS, you need to architect the components of your WINS network. A *WINS network* is the collection of WINS servers on your network that will service the NetBIOS name query requests they receive from network clients.

WINS Servers

At the heart of your WINS network are the WINS servers. The WINS server maintains a database of NetBIOS names to IP address mappings. A single WINS server and a backup WINS server can easily accommodate up to 10,000 computers. One issue many Windows NT 4.0 networks faced was that of deploying too many WINS servers. This is because when you increase the number of WINS servers, you also increase the probability that you will have lags in the WINS database consistency. No matter how large the organization, you should limit yourself to less than 20 WINS servers total. If you believe you require more, Microsoft strongly recommends that you consult the Microsoft Consulting Services division.

While the WINS servers are the heart of your WINS network, there are other components that you need to set up: WINS clients, and possibly WINS Proxies.

WINS Clients

A WINS client is any computer that can register with and query a WINS server. The Microsoft operating systems that can act as WINS clients include:

- Windows 2000
- Windows NT Server
- Windows NT Workstation
- Windows 98
- Windows 95
- Windows for Workgroups
- LAN Manager 2.*x*

In addition to these Microsoft operating systems, non-Microsoft client operating systems can be WINS enabled, although this is rarely seen in actual practice.

WINS clients are configured with at least one IP address for a WINS server. Figure 25-3 shows the Windows 2000 Advanced TCP/IP Settings properties dialog box where WINS client configuration is accomplished.

The Windows NT 4.0 WINS client configuration allowed you to enter a Primary and Secondary WINS server. The WINS client would initially try to register its NetBIOS names with the Primary WINS server, and if that machine were not available, it would attempt to register with the Secondary WINS server. The same applied to the NetBIOS name query process. The Windows 2000 WINS client allows you to enter up to 12 Secondary WINS servers. This allows an extra measure of fault tolerance for your WINS client NetBIOS name resolution requirements.

WINS Proxy Agents

WINS Proxies are similar to DHCP Relay Agents. A WINS Proxy intercepts NetBIOS name resolution requests for b-node clients that cannot be configured as WINS clients. The most common example of the non-WINS client you might encounter is the UNIX computer that is running a NetBIOS Service and requires NetBIOS name resolution for remote NetBIOS hosts.

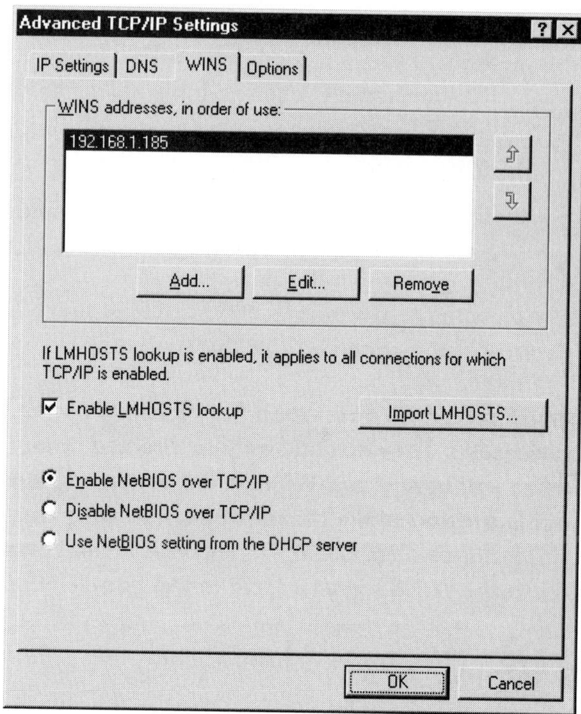

FIGURE 25-3

WINS client configuration dialog box

When a non-WINS client needs to resolve a NetBIOS name of a remote host, it issues a *NetBIOS Name Query Request.* If there is a WINS Proxy on the local subnet, it intercepts the request. After intercepting the request, the WINS Proxy does the following:

1. Checks its own NetBIOS Remote Name Cache for an entry for the destination NetBIOS host. If the name and IP address mapping are contained in the cache, this information is returned to the requesting machine.
2. If the name of the destination computer is not in the WINS Proxy's NetBIOS Remote Name Cache, it will query a WINS server via a directed datagram. The original query is placed in a *resolving state* until the WINS server responds. This is done so that the WINS Proxy does not send another query for the same NetBIOS name if another machine issues a NetBIOS Name Resolution Request for the same NetBIOS name while the WINS Proxy is waiting for the WINS server's response.

3. The WINS server replies with either a positive or negative response to the WINS Proxy's request. The WINS Proxy places the result in its NetBIOS Remote Name Cache and forwards the answer to the requesting host. The WINS Proxy will keep the name resolution in its cache for a default period of 10 minutes.
4. The requesting host, armed with the IP address of the remote host, establishes a session with the destination NetBIOS host.

To configure a Windows 2000 machine as a WINS Proxy, you must edit the Registry. There is no GUI for this procedure.

WINS servers do not respond to NetBIOS Name Resolution Query Request broadcasts. They respond only to directed datagrams. This becomes an issue when you have a non-WINS client on the same segment as a WINS server. Some administrators make the mistake of thinking they do not need a WINS Proxy in this instance since the WINS Server is local. You do need a WINS Proxy, even when the WINS server is local to the non-WINS client.

How WINS Works

The WINS server is a client/server application. Think of the WINS server as a database server, since it contains a database of NetBIOS names to IP address mappings. The WINS client and server participate in four basic activities: *name registration, name renewal, name release,* and *name resolution.*

Name Registration

When a WINS client starts up, it tries to register its NetBIOS names with its Primary WINS server. If the Primary WINS server does not respond after the first attempt, it will try two more times, 500ms apart. If the first WINS server fails to respond after a total of three connection attempts, the WINS client proceeds down its list and attempts to register with its Secondary WINS servers until it is successful. If none of the Secondary WINS servers respond, it begins again at the top of the list with the Primary WINS server.

on the job

In Windows NT 4.0, there was a specific text box that said "Primary WINS Server." The Windows 2000 WINS client does not contain a dedicated text box for the Primary WINS server. The Primary is the WINS server located at the top of the list.

The WINS server checks to see if the name already exists in the WINS database. If it does not, then the WINS client receives a *Positive Name Registration Response.* If it does exist in the WINS database, the WINS server sends the WINS client a *Wait for Acknowledgement (WACK)* message. Then it sends up to three challenges, 500ms apart, to the computer with the IP address of the requesting WINS client. If it receives no response, the WINS client receives a *Positive Name Registration Response.* If the WINS server does receive a response from the owner of the WINS database record, the WINS client attempting to register the same name receives a *Negative Name Registration Response.*

Note that if the WINS client tries to register a name and IP address that are the same as one already contained in the WINS database (i.e., its own name and IP address), the registration request becomes a *NetBIOS Name Renewal.*

Renewal

When the WINS server sends the WINS client a Positive NetBIOS Name Registration Response, it also sends with that a *Renewal Interval* or *TTL (Time-to-Live)* for the name it just registered. The WINS client must renew its name periodically to keep its name *Active* in the WINS database.

When a WINS client renews its name, its sends a *Name Refresh Request* to its Primary WINS server. This request is sent at one-half of the renewal interval. If the Primary WINS server does not respond, it will try at 10-minute intervals for up to an hour, then move on to its Secondary WINS servers. If the Secondaries do not respond, it goes back to the Primary WINS server and starts the whole process over again. Once the name is refreshed, it may receive a *new* renewal interval.

exam watch

WINS clients typically receive the same renewal interval after the name refreshes. However, under certain circumstances the renewal interval may change, such as when the WINS administrator makes changes to the renewal interval or when *Burst Handling Mode* ***is in effect.***

Release

When a WINS client shuts down "gracefully" (the operating system didn't crash and wasn't powered off before shutting down), it will send a *NetBIOS Name Release* message to its Primary WINS server. If the name and IP address of the WINS client sending the release message is the same as that contained in the WINS database, then the entry is marked as released in the WINS database and becomes *inactive.*

If the IP address is different from the WINS client that is seeking a release, the release request is ignored.

After the record is marked as inactive, it stays that way for the period known as the *extinction interval.* During this period, if another computer wants to register the name, no challenge will be issued. After the extinction interval has passed, the record is marked *extinct* and is *tombstoned.* The record remains tombstoned for a period called the *extinction timeout.* After the expiration of the extinction timeout period, the record is deleted, or *scavenged,* from the WINS database.

We'll talk more about tombstoning later in this chapter.

Resolution

A WINS client will go through the following process to resolve a NetBIOS name to an IP address:

1. After a request is sent to the TCP/IP protocol stack from the NetBIOS application, it will first check its *NetBIOS Remote Name Cache.*
2. If the mapping is not in the NetBIOS Remote Name Cache, the WINS client will send a *Name Query Request* directly to its Primary WINS server. If the WINS server does not respond, it will query two more times, for a total of three attempts. If the Primary WINS server fails to respond, then the Secondary WINS servers will be contacted.
3. When a WINS server is contacted, it will respond with either a *Positive Name Query Response* or a *Negative Name Query Response,* depending on whether the server did or did not have a mapping for the requested NetBIOS name.
4. If a Negative Name Query Response is received, the WINS client will issue up to three NetBIOS Name Query Request broadcasts to the local segment, 750ms apart. If this fails, the client may use other methods of NetBIOS name resolution.

EXERCISE 25-2

Installing the WINS Server Service

In this exercise, you will install the WINS Server service onto either a Windows 2000 Server or Windows 2000 Advanced Server computer, whichever you have available. Do not perform this exercise on a live, production network without the permission of your network administrator.

1. Log on as Administrator.
2. Open the Control Panel and double-click on Add/Remove Programs.
3. In the Add/Remove Program dialog box, click Add/Remove Windows Components in the left side of the dialog box.
4. In the Windows Components Wizard dialog box, scroll through the list and double-click on Networking Services. Place a check mark in the check box next to Windows Internet Name Service (WINS) as it appears in the following illustration. Then click OK.

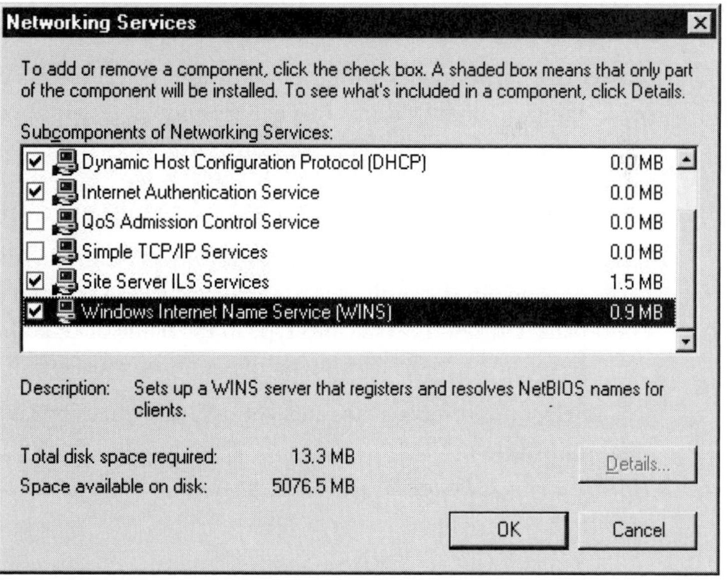

5. Click Next. The wizard will display a progress bar indicating how far the installation has completed. If asked for the CD-ROM, point the wizard to the correct location of the Windows 2000 installation files.
6. When the files have completed copying, the Completing the Windows Components Wizard dialog box appears. Click Finish to complete the installation.

Note that you do not need to restart the computer after installing the WINS server service.

EXERCISE 25-3

Configuring Intervals on the WINS Server

In this exercise, you will configure the various intervals related to WINS database record aging. Do not perform this exercise on a live, production network without the permission of your network administrator.

1. Open the WINS console from the Administrative Tools menu.
2. Right-click on the name of your WINS server in the left pane. (If your server does not appear in the left pane, right-click on where it says WINS in the left pane, click Add Server, and type in the name or IP address of your WINS server.) After right-clicking on the name of your WINS server, click Properties.
3. Select the Intervals tab, and you will see what appears in the following illustration.

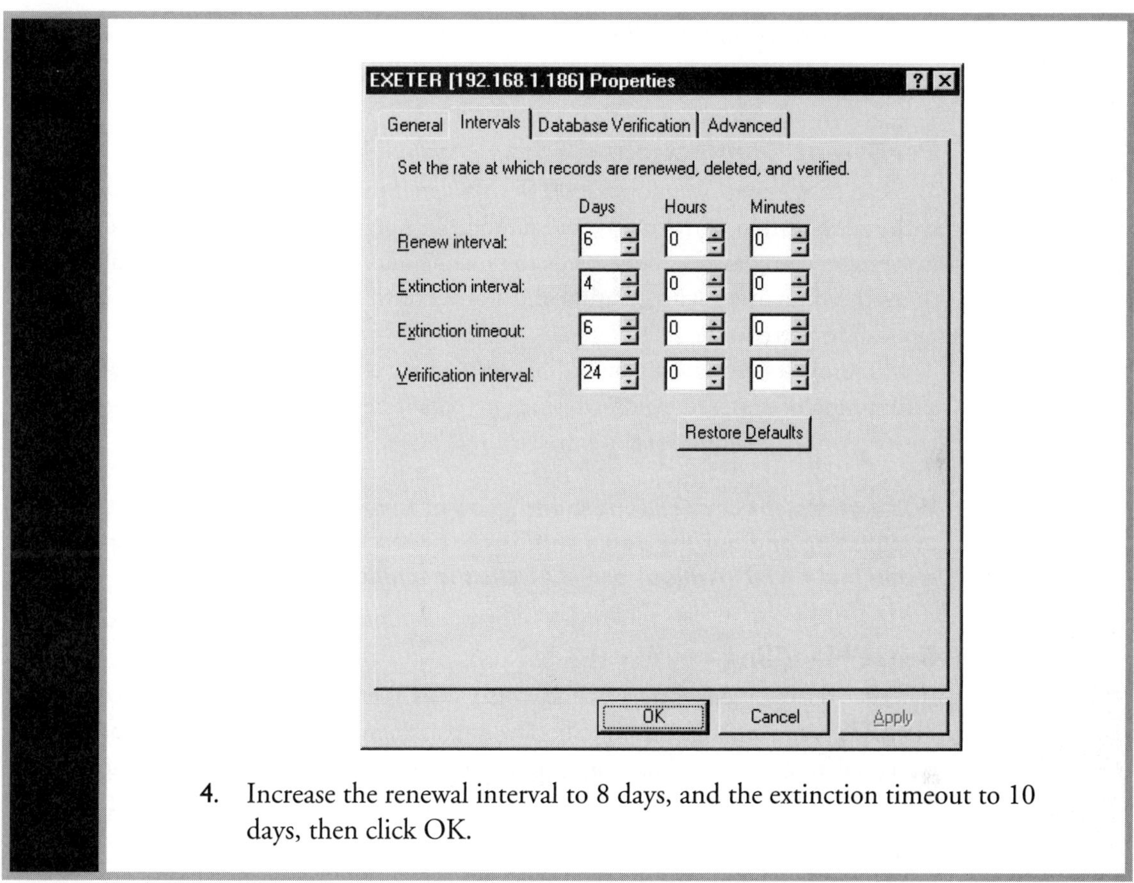

4. Increase the renewal interval to 8 days, and the extinction timeout to 10 days, then click OK.

New and Improved Windows 2000 WINS Server Features

Although Microsoft's long-term goal is to phase out NetBIOS from Microsoft networks, the WINS server will continue to hold an important place on Windows 2000 networks. The history of Microsoft networking is imbued with NetBIOS, and it will be many years before all important network applications move completely over to the Winsock interface.

Three new or improved features you will find of particular utility are *persistent connections*, *burst handling*, and *manual tombstoning*.

Persistent Connections

You can configure a Windows 2000 WINS server to maintain a *persistent connection* with its replication partners. By maintaining an open channel, the session setup process between partners only needs to be done once. This reduces the amount of overhead incurred with creating and tearing down sessions between WINS replication partners.

Microsoft states that this should have a positive effect on server performance with a minimum of network overhead, since no data is being transferred over the open connection the majority of the time.

on the Job

While persistent connections sound good in theory, the overall impact of establishing and tearing down sessions between WINS Replication Partners is nominal on K7 (Athlon) or P-III class machines.

Burst Handling

In a large organization, there are times when WINS servers can be overwhelmed with NetBIOS name registration requests. The typical example is when a systemwide power outage takes place, and all machines come online simultaneously and attempt to register their NetBIOS names. Normally, the WINS server can cache a certain number of requests, after which it begins to drop NetBIOS Name Registration Requests.

Windows NT 4.0 WINS server with Service Pack 3 and above supports high-volume WINS registration requests through a process called *burst handling*. Windows 2000 WINS servers also support WINS server *burst mode* responses.

The number of simultaneous requests may be so great that the efficiency and accuracy of name registration may suffer. In this scenario, the WINS server will switch into *burst mode*. When the WINS server is in burst mode, any name registration requests received over a predefined number receive immediate acknowledgement. However, the WINS server does not check the NetBIOS against the WINS database; it does not issue a challenge against duplicate names, and it does not write an entry to the WINS database.

exam Watch

Remember that once burst mode takes effect, no entries are recorded into the WINS database for those machines that are offered the short TTLs.

The default queue size is 500. When the number of pending registration requests exceeds 500, the WINS server switches into burst mode, immediately acknowledges the WINS client's request for NetBIOS name registration, and sends with the acknowledgement a shortened renewal interval or Time-to-Live (TTL). For the first 100 registrations over 500, the clients are given a name renewal period of 5 minutes. For the next 100 pending name registrations, the WINS clients receive a name renewal interval of 10 minutes. This pattern of incrementing the name renewal period by 5 minutes per 100 pending requests continues until the TTL reaches 50 minutes (1000 pending registrations). Then the process starts all over with the WINS server sending the next 100 pending registration requests a TTL of 5 minutes. The maximum number of queued responses is 25,000. After that point, the WINS server starts dropping the requests without providing an acknowledgement or TTL.

Burst handling allows the WINS server to accommodate WINS clients' attempts at name registration at times when the WINS server is too busy to write to the database.

on the job

Remember that burst handling is not new to Windows 2000, and is available on your Windows NT 4.0 WINS servers after they have been upgraded to Service Pack 3 or above.

Tombstoning Records

To understand tombstoning, you need to understand the WINS record life cycle. When a WINS client registers its NetBIOS names with a WINS server, a WINS database record is created for that WINS client. This record stays *active* in the WINS database for a period of time determined by the *renewal interval.* While the record is active, the WINS server will defend it by issuing challenges when another machine attempts to register the same NetBIOS name to a different IP address. The WINS client must update its record with the WINS server before the renewal interval expires. The expired record is then marked as *inactive.* The main difference between an active and an inactive WINS database record is that no challenge is issued when another computer tries to register the name.

An inactive record remains in the WINS database for a period known as the *extinction interval.* After remaining in the inactive state for the period defined by the extinction interval, the record is marked as *extinct.* Another term for an extinct record is *tombstoned.* The record remains in the tombstoned state for a period defined by the *extinction timeout,* after which it is removed, or *scavenged,* by the WINS server that owns it.

If a WINS server has a copy of a replicated tombstoned record owned by another WINS server, it checks with the owner WINS server after the expiration of the *verification interval* to see if the record still exists. If the record is no longer at the owner WINS server, it is scavenged from the non-owner WINS servers.

The Value of Tombstoning Imagine that we have three WINS servers in our WINS network: WINS-A, WINS-B, and WINS-C. WINS-B is the hub of the WINS network, and WINS-A and WINS-C are spokes (Figure 25-4). WINS-A receives a NetBIOS name registration for a computer named BLOBALOCITY. After registering

FIGURE 25-4 The example WINS network

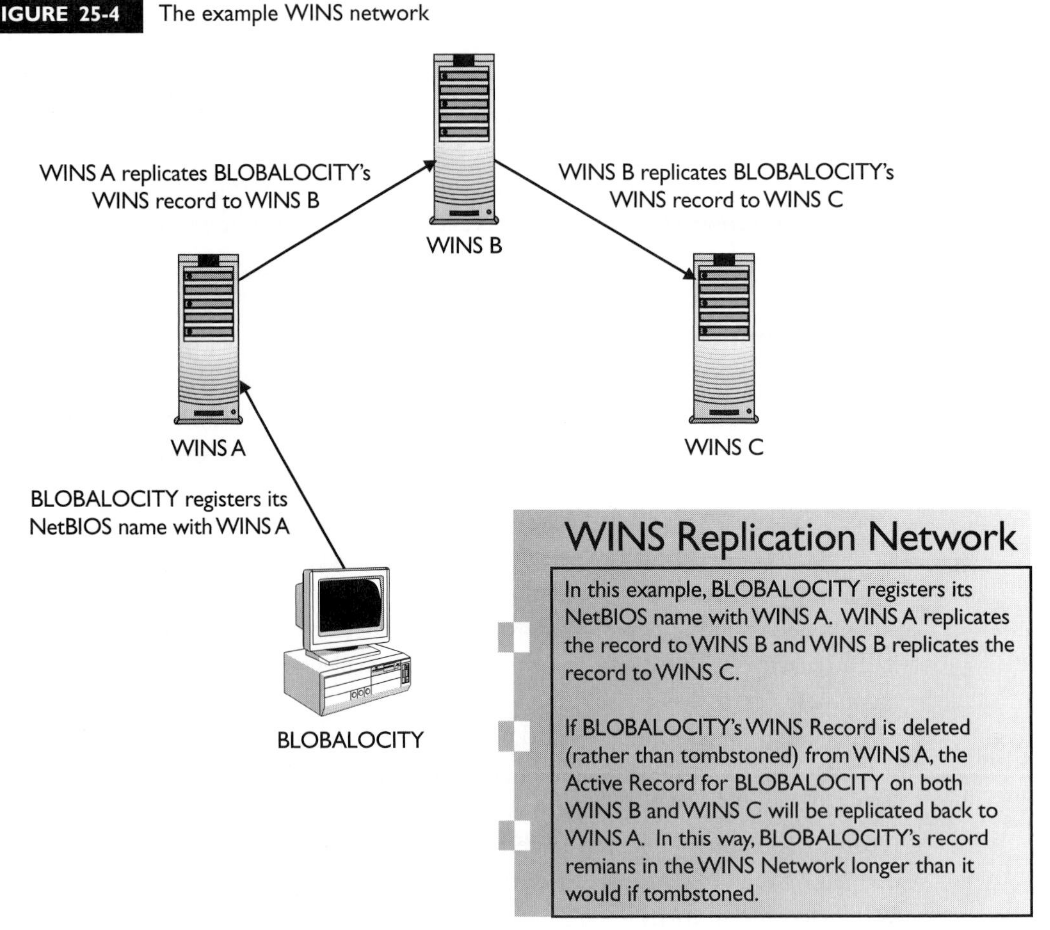
WINS A replicates BLOBALOCITY's WINS record to WINS B
WINS B replicates BLOBALOCITY's WINS record to WINS C
WINS B
WINS A
WINS C
BLOBALOCITY registers its NetBIOS name with WINS A
BLOBALOCITY
WINS Replication Network
In this example, BLOBALOCITY registers its NetBIOS name with WINS A. WINS A replicates the record to WINS B and WINS B replicates the record to WINS C.
If BLOBALOCITY's WINS Record is deleted (rather than tombstoned) from WINS A, the Active Record for BLOBALOCITY on both WINS B and WINS C will be replicated back to WINS A. In this way, BLOBALOCITY's record remians in the WINS Network longer than it would if tombstoned.

its NetBIOS name, we decide that we're going to take BLOBALOCITY off the network. Meanwhile, BLOBALOCITY's record is replicated to WINS-B, and WINS-B replicates the record to WINS-C.

To increase the speed and responsiveness of WINS registrations and queries, you want to keep the WINS database lean and mean. You open your WINS management console and delete the record for BLOBALOCITY. You figure the fact that the record was deleted will be replicated over to the other WINS servers, and you can bid adieu to BLOBALOCITY from your WINS network.

When WINS-A next replicates with WINS-B, it doesn't replicate BLOBALOCITY's WINS record—it can't, since the record was deleted. What happens when WINS-B replicates with WINS-A? Since WINS-B still has BLOBALOCITY's record in its database, it replicates it back to WINS-A. Now BLOBALOCITY has risen from the dead and its record reappears, marked active, in the WINS-A database.

Eventually, BLOBALOCITY's record will exceed its renewal interval, then its extinction interval, then its extinction timeout, and finally will be deleted. But, if you just delete records, the entire process will take longer than it should, and the stale WINS database records will have a negative impact on WINS server performance.

Manual Tombstoning The Windows 2000 WINS console allows you to manually tombstone WINS database records, rather than delete them outright. When a record is tombstoned, its tombstoned status is replicated with it. When you tombstone a record, it doesn't "magically" reappear as an active record. The tombstoned record is removed from the owner WINS database after completion of the extinction timeout, and will be removed from replication partners WINS databases after expiration of the verification interval.

To tombstone a WINS record, open the WINS management console and click on Active Registrations. Right-click on Active Registrations and select Find by Owner. On the Owners tab, select the option button for "All owners," and click Find Now. Right-click on one of the records in the right pane and select Delete. You will see a dialog box as shown in Figure 25-5.

exam Watch

Manual tombstoning of WINS database records is not entirely new with Windows 2000. In Windows NT 4.0, you could use the command-line utility winscl.exe to manually tombstone records, but it was a cumbersome solution for a simple problem. The Windows 2000 GUI makes a simple task simple to execute.

FIGURE 25-5

The Delete Record dialog box

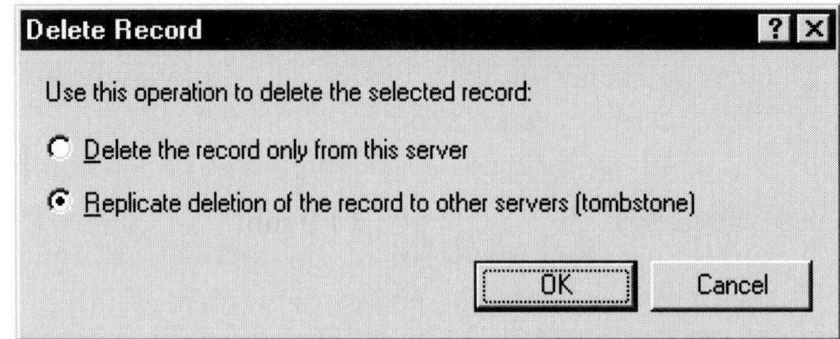

WINS Replication

You should deploy multiple WINS servers for fault tolerance and efficient NetBIOS name resolution. To maintain consistency among all WINS servers on a network, there must be a way for all the WINS servers to share what they "know" with each other. This method of sharing information is known as *WINS replication.*

WINS clients normally register their NetBIOS names with their Primary WINS server, and if the Primary WINS server is not reachable, the WINS client registers with one of its Secondary WINS server. In large internetworks, multiple WINS servers handle the name registration requests of WINS clients near them. Those same WINS servers also answer NetBIOS name queries for these same WINS clients.

A problem arises as WINS clients register their names with different WINS servers. Imagine we have the following setup:

WINS server IP address:

192.168.1.2

WINS clients from subnets:

192.168.1.0

192.168.2.0

Register with and query this WINS server

WINS server IP address:

192.168.3.2

WINS clients from subnets:

192.168.3.0

192.168.4.0

Register with and query this WINS server

When clients on the 192.168.1.0 subnet need to resolve a NetBIOS name for a client on subnet 192.168.2.0, they can query the WINS server at 192.168.1.2, and a mapping for that client is located in the WINS database. If a client on the 192.168.3.0 subnet needs to resolve a NetBIOS name for a client on the 192.168.4.0 subnet, it can do so successfully because a mapping for clients on both the 192.168.3.0 and 192.168.4.0 subnets are at the WINS server 192.168.3.2. However, what happens when a client on the 192.168.1.0 subnet needs to resolve a NetBIOS name of a client on the 192.168.4.0 subnet?

The client on the 192.168.1.0 subnet issues a NetBIOS Name Query Request to its Preferred WINS server at 192.168.1.2. However, no clients on the 192.168.4.0 registered their NetBIOS names with this WINS server; therefore, no mapping exists for computers on that segment. To solve this problem, we configure the WINS servers to be replication partners.

WINS Replication Partners

Replication partners share their information. This makes it possible for any WINS client to query any WINS server and successfully resolve a NetBIOS name, regardless of what WINS server originally received the NetBIOS name registration.

WINS servers are configured as replication partners in two ways: *pull* and *push.* The pull partner receives WINS database information based on a configured replication interval. A push partner sends database information based on how many changes have taken place in the WINS database.

Pull Partners A WINS server is notified by its pull partner when it's *time* to request the changes to the WINS database since the last time it received replicated information. This determination is made based on WINS database version IDs. If the PULL partner's WINS database has a version ID higher than the one last *pulled* by the pull partner, it will request the changes. If the pull partner's database version is the same or smaller (an unlikely event, but possible), then records are not replicated from the pull partner.

Push Partners Push replication causes the push partner to send changes based on *the number of* changes made in the WINS database. After the minimum number of changes have been made, the push partner sends a pull notification to the WINS server to request the changes. Windows 2000 WINS Servers are able to maintain persistent connections, which allow push partners to push changes as soon as they take place.

Automatic Partner Discovery You can configure your WINS servers to find other WINS servers on the network and create a replication partnership with them automatically. When you enable *Automatic Partner Discovery,* WINS servers use the multicast address 224.0.1.24 to discover or find other WINS servers.

How many of your WINS servers can be found through Autodiscovery depends on how the routers on your network have been configured. If routers do not support Internet Group Management Protocol (IGMP) (multicasting), WINS servers only find other WINS servers on the same segment. WINS servers that set up partner arrangements via Autodiscovery will become push/pull partners with a replication pull interval of two hours. Microsoft documentation does not state what push trigger number is, however. Automatic partner discovery can be configured on the Advanced tab of the WINS server's Properties dialog box.

Push and Pull Partner Recommendations Microsoft recommends that replication partners be configured as both push and pull partners. This reduces the chance of inconsistencies or lags in the WINS database. A notable exception to this policy is when WINS servers are separated by slow WAN connections. In this circumstance, it may be more efficient to configure the WINS servers on both sides to be PULL partners. These pull partners are configured to exchange WINS database information during times of reduced network utilization, and therefore not impact normal network communications to such a large extent.

exam Watch

The definition of a slow versus fast link is a moving target in the fast-paced world of network hardware. However, many authorities consider a connection supporting 512 kbps or higher as being fast. However, in the Microsoft documentation, *fast* ***seems to be a relative term based on how fast the site links are. You'll have to use good judgment when you encounter these questions.***

Disabling NetBT

Windows 2000 allows you to disable NetBIOS (NetBT) on any network interface installed on the computer. You should be very careful about disabling NetBIOS on the computers on your network. The great majority of network applications designed to work on Microsoft networks were written for, and dependent on, the NetBIOS interface. There are some specialized situations when you definitely would want to disable NetBIOS. These include computers in specialized or secured roles for your network, such as an edge Proxy server or bastion host in a firewall environment. In these environments, you improve security by disabling NetBT.

The following are considerations for disabling NetBT on computers running Windows 2000:

- The Browser service was no longer functioning on the computer with NetBIOS disabled. The computer will not act as a browser, nor will it issue announcements of its server status to the Master Browser on its segment.
- You will no longer be able to use certain core Windows 2000 networking utilities, such as net send and the Alerter service.
- If the computer must be a WINS client, it will need to have NetBIOS enabled. The only reason why you would want the machine to be a WINS client is that it runs either NetBIOS server or client services.
- If you want to install the WINS server on a Windows 2000 server family computer, you must have NetBIOS enabled, even if the server will not be used for any other NetBIOS functions.

The classic example of when it's a good time to disable NetBIOS is on the external public interface on a Proxy server. By disabling NetBT on only the Internet connection, the multihomed computer continues to function as either a WINS server or client for the internal network, and WINS clients are still serviced for connections made by using other physical network adapters installed on the computer.

There are a couple of ways you can disable NetBIOS on your Windows 2000 machine: You can go to the WINS tab in the Advanced TCP/IP Settings, or you can use the Microsoft vendor-specific options at a DHCP server. Figure 25-6 shows the WINS tab.

FIGURE 25-6

Disabling NetBIOS via the WINS tab on the Advanced TCP/IP Settings properties dialog box

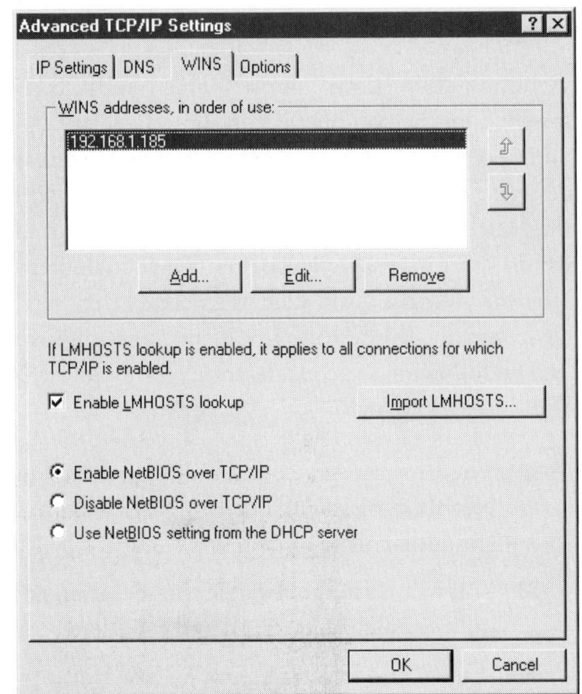

CERTIFICATION OBJECTIVE 25.02

Planning and Implementing a WINS Solution

When you are ready to implement a WINS solution for the NetBIOS environment, make sure that you have planned where you want to place the WINS servers, and how the WINS servers will be configured to support your WINS networking plan. In this section, we will focus on the installation and configuration of the WINS server. In the *Designing a Windows 2000 Networking Infrastructure Study Guide*, we'll go over the more complex issues regarding how to design a reliable, fault-tolerant WINS network.

Installing and Configuring the WINS Server and Client

The first thing you need to do is install the WINS Server service on a Windows 2000 server family computer. You cannot install the WINS service on a Windows 2000 Professional machine. The only other requirement for the WINS server is that you configure the machine with a static IP address. It requires a static IP address because WINS clients are configured with the IP addresses for their Primary and Secondary WINS servers. There is no provision for you to enter a NetBIOS name on the WINS clients.

Configuring Replication

Prior to configuring replication, you need to have your WINS network planned. You'll need to know the IP addresses of the WINS servers on the network, and you must plan what WINS servers will be partners, and the types of partnerships they will have. After the planning is completed, you can get to the task of using the WINS management console to configure the replication parameters.

Using Static Mappings

You may run into the situation where you need to resolve the NetBIOS name of a remote host that is *not* a WINS client. Non-WINS clients do not register their names automatically in the WINS database. If you try to query the WINS server for these computers, you will get a Negative NetBIOS Name Query Response.

You can get around this problem by using *static* mappings. A static mapping is a nondynamic entry in the WINS database. You must enter the static mapping information *manually* into the WINS database. This is similar to traditional DNS databases, such as those in Windows NT 4.0, where you had to manually add the host record information yourself. Static mappings are not normally overwritten by dynamic name registrations unless the *migrate on* option is enabled.

exam Watch

The migrate on setting is best used when you have a number of non-WINS clients that you plan to subsequently upgrade to WINS clients. However, not all of your static entries will be overwritten by dynamic registrations. One example is the [1Ch] entry for a domain controller.

The UNIX Scenario The classic scenario involves a WINS client that needs to contact a UNIX server running a NetBIOS application. In order for the WINS client to establish a NetBIOS session with the UNIX server, its NetBIOS name must be resolved. The Windows client is located on a remote subnet and does not have a mapping for the UNIX host in its LMHOSTS file. The solution to this problem is to create a static mapping for the UNIX machine in the WINS database. The WINS client is then able to locate a mapping for the UNIX host and resolve its NetBIOS name to an IP address.

The only information required is the NetBIOS name, an optional scope ID, the type of mapping, and the IP address of statically mapped host. Table 25-3 defines the types of WINS mappings.

TABLE 25-3 Types of WINS Static Mappings

Type	Explanation
Unique	Configure a Unique mapping when a single IP address defines the host computer. Three NetBIOS names arise when you configure a Unique static mapping. A NetBIOS name associating the host name for the workstation service (redirector), messenger service, and server service are created. For example, NOSTROMO will have three entries in the WINS database: NOSTROMO[00h], NOSTROMO[03h], and NOSTROMO [20h].
Group	If the computer is a member of a workgroup, you can configure a Group entry for the machine. The IP address of the host is not included and Group name resolution is performed via local subnet broadcasts only. This is known as a "Normal Group."
Domain Name	A Domain Name entry creates a [1Ch] mapping in the WINS database. This mapping points to domain controllers in Windows NT environments. A WINS client queries the WINS database for [1Ch] entries for a machine to authenticate a logon.
Internet Group	Configure an Internet Group when you want to create Administrative Groups of shared resources that appear as members of the group when browsing for resources. Examples include grouping file servers and print servers into such Administrative Groups. The Group identifies itself by the shared group name with the [20h] service identifier.
Multihomed	Use the Multihomed mapping to configure multiple IP address for a single NetBIOS host computer. A computer may have multiple adapters or multiple IP addresses bound to a single adapter.

EXERCISE 25-4

Creating a Static Mapping

In this exercise, you will learn how to create a static mapping for a NetBIOS client in the WINS server. Do not perform this exercise on a live, production network without the permission of your network administrator.

1. Log on as Administrator.
2. Open the WINS management console.
3. Expand all nodes in the left pane and click on New Static Mapping. You should see what appears in the following illustration.

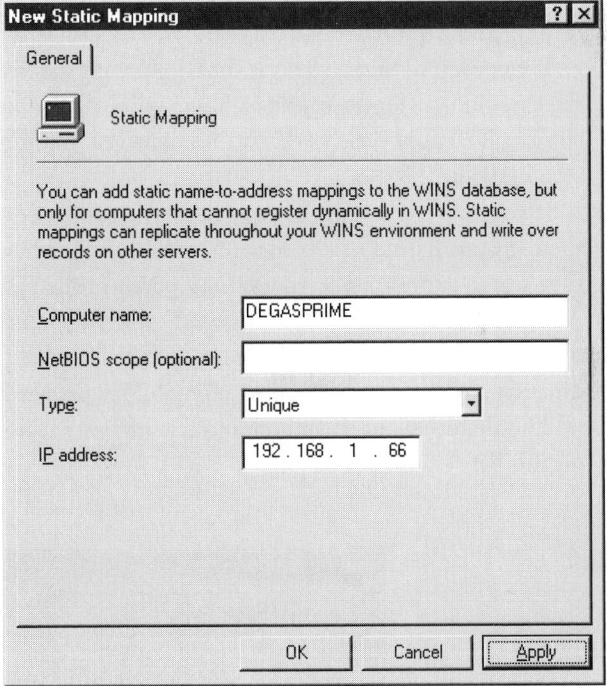

4. Type in the name of a non-WINS client in the "Computer name" text box. Type in the IP address in the text boxes provided. It will be unusual to have a scope ID, but you can enter one here as well. Individual computers will have the unique type of Static Record.
5. Click Apply, and then click OK. Close the WINS management console.

Managing the WINS Database

For the most part, the WINS database is self-tuning. However, there is a small handful of administrative tasks to ensure that your WINS server is working at tip-top efficiency and reliability. The Windows 2000 WINS server provides the new and improved WINS management console that makes these administrative tasks easier than ever.

Finding and Viewing WINS Records

If you've ever worked on a large enterprise network using Microsoft networking technologies, you know how unwieldy your WINS databases can get. In the past, if you wanted to find a record or a group of records in the WINS database, you had to sift through the list manually. Windows 2000 WINS servers have enhanced record finding and filtering (Figure 25-7).

If you want to find all servers that begin with the letter "S," all you need to do is type the letter in the "Find names beginning with" dialog box in the WINS management console. The right pane in the WINS manager will display the results of the query, as seen in Figure 25-8.

If you want to see all the records in the database, you can type an asterisk (*) in the text box instead of a computer name string. The asterisk is the only wildcard type search supported by the WINS search mechanism.

You can also specify a search based on the owners of the WINS records. The owner is the WINS server that received the name registration from the WINS client directly, and not via replication. Figure 25-9 shows the Find by Owner dialog box.

The IP address of the server and the highest version ID number is also included on this list.

FIGURE 25-7

The Find by Name dialog box

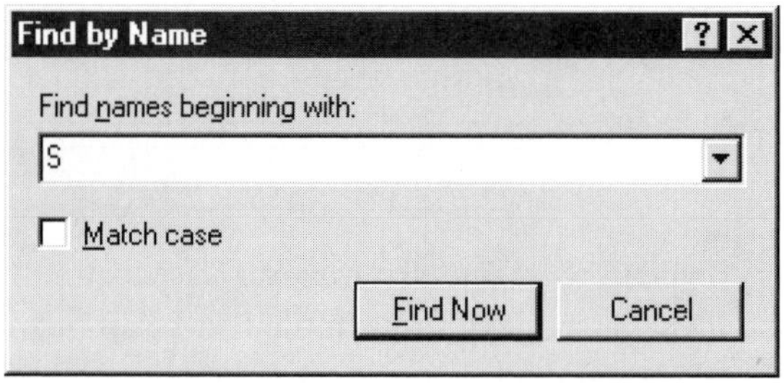

FIGURE 25-8

Results of the Find by Name query

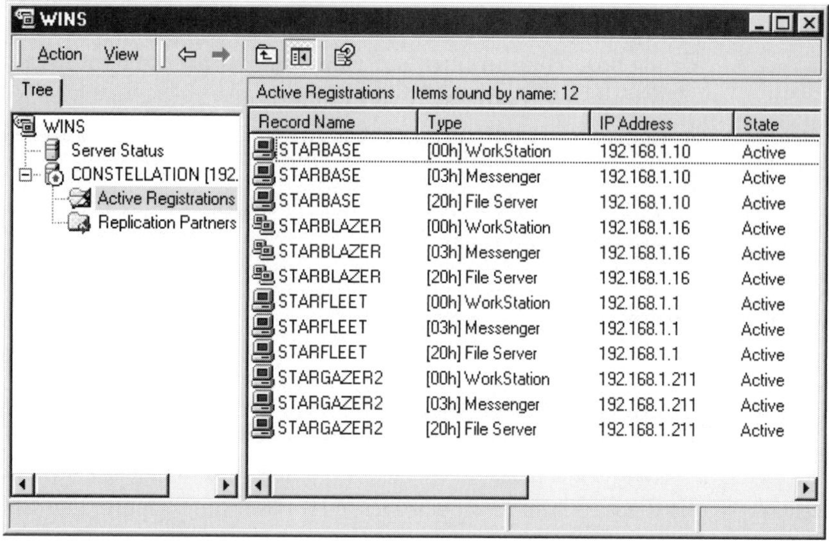

FIGURE 25-9

The Find by Owner dialog box

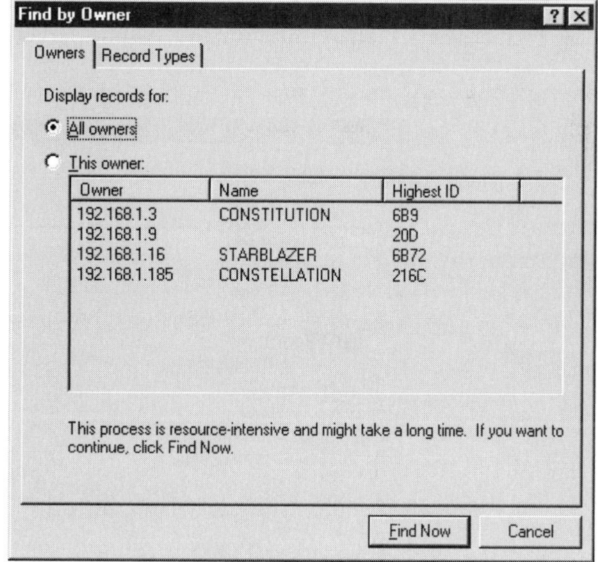

Figure 25-10 shows the contents of the Record Types tab in the Find by Owner dialog box. You can filter and view records that have specific NetBIOS service identifiers. For example, if you wanted to find all domain controllers registered in the WINS database, you could limit your search for only entries with the [1Ch] service identifier.

The find and filter features make life a lot easier for the administrator in a large enterprise environment.

Compacting the Database

The Windows 2000 WINS database uses the performance-enhanced Extensible Storage Engine, which is an updated version of the storage engine that serves both Microsoft Exchange 5.5 and Windows 2000 Active Directory.

One of the great advantages of the new WINS database structure is that there is no hard-coded limit to the number of entries it can support. The size of the WINS database grows as entries are added via NetBIOS name registrations. As entries populate the database and are removed, the amount of space taken by the scavenged entries is not immediately returned.

Like most databases, it should be compacted periodically in order to maintain optimal efficiency. In Windows 2000, WINS server database compaction occurs as

FIGURE 25-10

Selecting records by service identifier

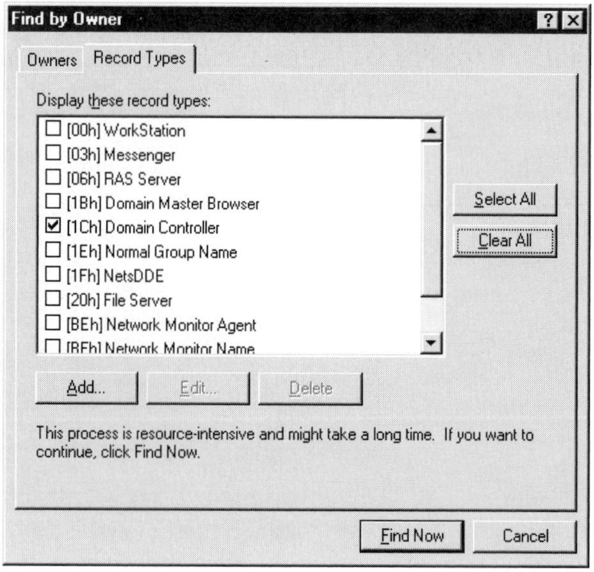

an automatic background process during idle time; this is known as *online compaction.*

However, online compaction is not 100% efficient, and the database will continue to grow in size, albeit at a slower pace. To regain lost space, you will need to perform an *offline compaction* occasionally. Offline compaction requires you to take the WINS server service offline (you do not need to shut down the computer, just stop the WINS server service).

The WINS database files are stored in the directory

```
%SystemRoot%\System32\Wins
```

Table 25-4 explains what the various WINS database files are and what they do.

Checking for Consistency

You can verify whether a WINS server contains correct entries in its database by performing a consistency check on the WINS database. When a WINS server verifies its database, it compares all of its entries against entries on other WINS servers that are replication partners of the WINS server you are checking. All records pulled from the other WINS servers are compared to records in the local database.

If the record in the local database is identical to the record pulled from the WINS server that owns the record, the timestamp on the local record is updated.

TABLE 25-4 WINS Database Files and Their Functions

File	What It Does
J50.log and J50*xxxxx*.log	A log of all transactions done with the database. This file is used by WINS to recover data in the event of a server or service crash.
J50.chk	The J50.chk file is used when the WINS database starts up to determine whether the last shutdown was clean and all databases are consistent. If the last shutdown was "dirty," this file will determine what log file to use to make the proper updates.
Wins.mdb	The WINS server database file that contains NetBIOS names to IP address mappings.
Winstmp.mdb	A temp file created by the WINS service. The database uses it as a swap file during index maintenance operations. It might remain in the directory %*SystemRoot*%\System32\Wins after a crash.

If the record that is pulled from the owner database has a higher version ID than the record in the local database, the pulled record is added to the local database, and the original local record is marked for deletion (tombstoned).

Depending on your replication topology, consistency checking can be a processor- and network-intensive task. It's best to wait for periods of low network utilization before undertaking a consistency check. You perform the WINS database consistency check by right-clicking on the name of the WINS server in the left pane of the WINS management console, and clicking on the Verify Database Consistency command.

Backing Up and Restoring the Database

The Windows 2000 WINS Server automatically backs up the WINS database to a folder of your choice every three hours. However, before this automated backup schedule begins, you must configure a directory to store the WINS database backup files. To configure WINS backup directory, open the WINS console, right-click on the name of your WINS server in the left pane, and click Properties. You will see the dialog box that appears in Figure 25-11.

exam Watch

You might think it's a good idea to create a mapped network drive and save the WINS database backups on that drive. Unfortunately, this won't work. WINS will not save backup copies of the WINS database to a remote location. Make a note to include your WINS backup folder in your routine backup schedules.

Backing Up the WINS Registry Settings If you've spent a good amount of time configuring your WINS server, you should take some time to back up the WINS server's Registry settings. These Registry settings are saved at:

```
HKLM\System\CurrentControlSet\Service\WINS
```

To save these settings, open the Registry using Regedt32. Then, click the Registry menu and click Save Key. Back up the saved key to a safe place. When you need to rebuild the WINS server, open the Registry editor on the new machine, click the Registry menu, and click Restore. This will copy the saved key into the new Registry.

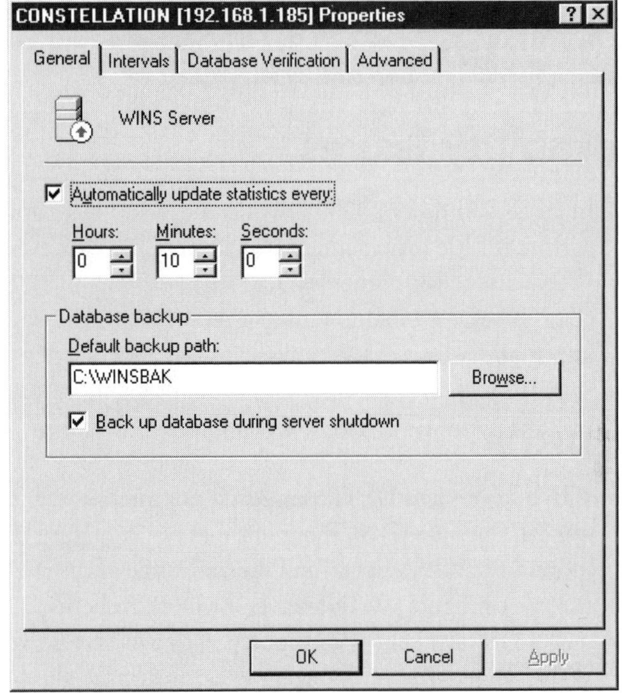

FIGURE 25-11 The WINS server Properties dialog box where the WINS backup directory is configured

Restoring the WINS Database To restore the WINS database from the local backup:

1. Stop the WINS service. You can stop the WINS Server service by going to a command prompt and typing **net stop WINS,** or right-click on the WINS server name in the left pane of the WINS management console, trace to All Tasks, and then trace over and click Stop.
2. After stopping the WINS Server service, the Restore Database command appears. Click on the Restore Database.
3. The Browse for Folder dialog box appears. Select the directory housing the WINS database backup files, and click OK.

The database is restored, and the WINS Server service is restarted automatically.

CERTIFICATION OBJECTIVE 25.03

Interoperability Issues

In an all Windows 2000 network, the Windows 2000 WINS server works flawlessly with very little management from your end. However, if you plan to integrate the WINS server with other services such as Dynamic Host Configuration Protocol (DHCP) and Domain Name System (DNS), you should be aware of some important issues.

WINS and DHCP

WINS servers and DHCP servers do not interact with one another directly. However, you can configure DHCP options that can configure the WINS client with the IP address of a WINS server, and the node type of the WINS client. Of course, you can also not configure a WINS server for DHCP clients.

If a DHCP client is configured with a WINS server, it will register with that WINS server after receiving an IP address from the DHCP server. Name registration is done via the normal mechanisms that were discussed earlier in this chapter.

WINS and DNS

All previous Microsoft operating systems are NetBIOS dependent for their networking infrastructure components. If you run a heterogeneous network that includes not only Windows 2000 computers, but also Win9*x* and Win3.*x* computers, you will need to enable NetBIOS name resolution mechanisms for those clients. Windows 2000 is not NetBIOS dependent, and the preferential method of name resolution for Windows 2000 computers is via DNS. What we need is a way for the Windows 2000 computers to use DNS and still be able to resolve the NetBIOS names of the downlevel clients that have registered with a WINS server.

The Windows 2000 DNS server can be configured to query a WINS server for names that it cannot locate via DNS. Windows 2000 (and any other) DNS Client can gain access to information in a WINS database without having to query a WINS server directly. The client communicates only with the DNS server, and the DNS server will act as a "proxy" for the DNS client in querying the WINS database.

In Windows 2000, you can configure the interoperability between WINS and DNS to enable non-WINS clients to resolve NetBIOS names by querying a DNS server. For example, if a non-WINS enabled client needs to access NetBIOS resources on another computer on the network, it can use its DNS server to resolve the name to an IP address. The DNS server then queries a WINS server, and the name is resolved and returned to the client.

How the Windows 2000 DNS Server Queries the WINS Server

When a DNS client issues a request for a NetBIOS resource to be resolved by a DNS server, the following sequence of events takes place:

1. The DNS client service on the DNS client formulates a DNS query. For example, the query is sent for a computer named FILESERVER. The query is fully qualified by appending the domain name to the NetBIOS name, and a query for FILESERVER.tacteam.net is issued to the DNS server.
2. The DNS server attempts to resolve the host name to an IP address using normal DNS mechanisms, which may include iteration.
3. If the DNS server is not able to resolve the host name to an IP address, and the DNS server is configured to query a WINS server, it will strip off the characters to the left of the leftmost period (dot) in the FQDN and issue a NetBIOS Name Query Request to the WINS server using those characters.
4. The WINS server resolves the name and replies with the IP address to the DNS server. The DNS server returns this information to the DNS client.

Interoperability with Downlevel DNS Servers When you enable WINS lookup on a Windows 2000 DNS Server, it creates resource records on the DNS server that are not compatible with downlevel DNS servers, such as the Windows NT 4.0 and UNIX-based implementations for DNS. If you plan to make downlevel DNS server authoritative for any zone on which you have enabled WINS lookups, you need to be sure that the "Do not replicate this record" check box is checked to prevent problems with zone transfer. You configure this option in the Properties of the zone on your DNS server, as shown in Figure 25-12.

Any zone can be enabled to perform WINS lookups. However, there are a number of reasons why it is a good idea to disable WINS lookups on all populated

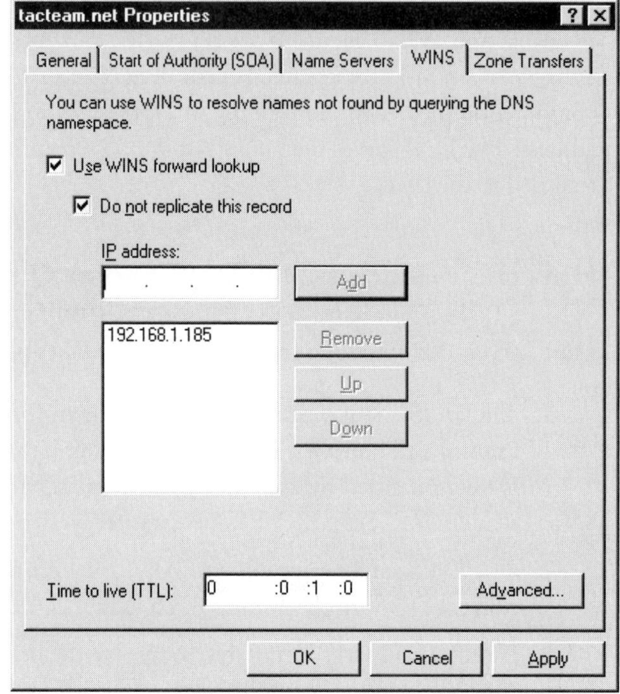

FIGURE 25-12 Configuring a Windows 2000 zone to not replicate the WINS forward lookup information to downlevel DNS servers

zones (zones that have resource records in them) and create an empty WINS lookup enabled zone.

First, you would create a DNS zone without host records and enable it for WINS lookup. For example, assign the name wins.tacteam.net to the DNS zone. Then for each DNS client computer, on the DNS tab of the Advanced TCP/IP properties dialog box, add the wins.tacteam.net zone that you created to the "Append these DNS suffixes (in order)" text box.

This configuration allows for WINS lookup, and allows downlevel DNS servers to be authoritative for the domain tacteam.net.

CERTIFICATION OBJECTIVE 25.04

Monitoring and Troubleshooting WINS

When troubleshooting your WINS environment, you need to first consider where the problem lies. Is the problem due to errors on the WINS client or the WINS server? In this section, we'll see what sorts of problems you'll run into for common WINS-related troubleshooting issues.

Troubleshooting WINS Client-Related Problems

Problems with WINS clients are most likely to show up as failed NetBIOS name resolution requests. The following sections include some questions to ask if you are having WINS client-related problems.

Is the WINS Client Configured Correctly?

The WINS client may have the wrong IP address configured for its Primary and Secondary WINS servers. If the machine is a DHCP client, it could be that someone has manually reset the WINS server IP addresses. If a number of computers are DHCP clients and they all have problems with NetBIOS name resolution, the problem probably lies with a misconfiguration of the WINS DHCP option. Check the DHCP server to correct this situation.

Is There an Interruption in Connectivity between the WINS Client and Server?

It could be that the WINS client cannot contact the WINS server because of loss of connectivity. PING the WINS server addresses configured on the WINS client. If you don't get a response, then the problems are not with WINS or NetBIOS resolution, but with the network client or network.

Does the WINS Client Have Secondary WINS Servers Configured?

WINS clients should always have at least one Secondary WINS server configured in case the Primary server becomes disabled. However, you must be aware that you can significantly slow the NetBIOS name resolution process if you enter too many WINS servers. Although the Windows 2000 WINS client can be configured with up to 12 Secondary WINS servers, this might not be a good thing.

Using multiple Secondaries is a double-edged sword that can cause delays in receiving an error message regarding a failed query. If you configure 12 Secondaries for a NetBIOS name that does not exist, each Secondary must be queried in order to conclude that the name does not indeed exist, and get the error message returned.

Has NetBIOS Been Disabled?

If NetBIOS (NetBT) has been disabled on the WINS client's network adapter, it will not be able to participate in NetBIOS-dependent communications. Check to see if the user has disabled NetBIOS during an episode of "experimenting." If multiple users have the same problem, check to see if the DHCP server has been configured to deliver the Windows 2000 vendor option that disables NetBIOS on DHCP client machines.

Troubleshooting WINS Server-Related Issues

WINS server-related problems usually show up as widespread problems with NetBIOS name resolution. This is in contrast to problems you see with WINS client issues where usually a single computer or segment is having problems with name resolution.

Some questions to ask when troubleshooting WINS server-related problems are discussed in the following sections.

Is There a Problem with the WINS Database?

The WINS database can become corrupt if the system is shut down improperly or during impending disk failures. Check the Event Log to see if there have been errors reported regarding problems with the WINS database.

You can enable detailed event logging that will be reported to the Event Log by right-clicking on the name of the WINS server in the left pane of the WINS management console and clicking Properties. You will see what appears in Figure 25-13.

Is There a Static Mapping for the Name?

Static mappings can be a difficult problem to troubleshoot if you have inherited a network from another administrator that used static mappings, and then you subsequently upgraded non-WINS client to WINS-enabled systems. The upgraded systems will not automatically overwrite the static mappings. To correct this situation, enable *Migrate On* at the WINS servers.

Did the WINS Server Service Start?

A Windows 2000 server with inadequate memory resources and a large number of services installed can easily experience "hangs" of some of the services during the boot-up process. Always check in both the Services applet and in the WINS

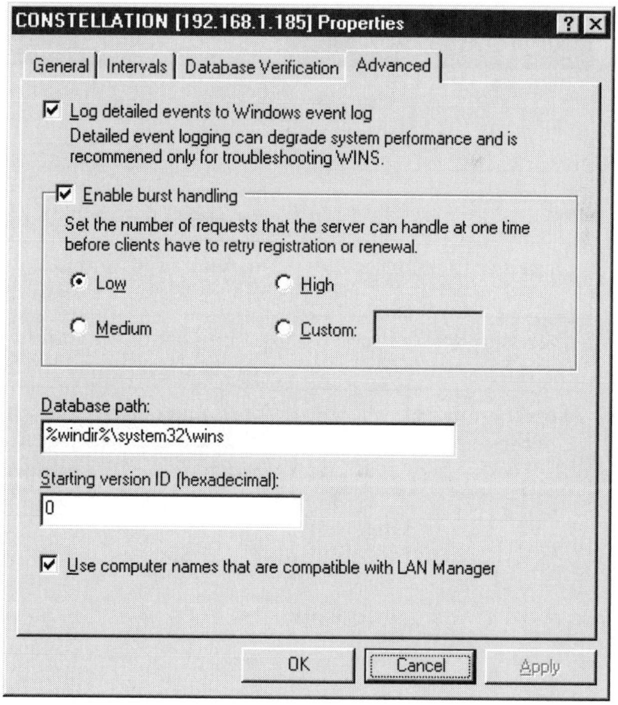

FIGURE 25-13 Enabling detailed event logging in the WINS server Properties dialog box

CONSTELLATION [192.168.1.185] Properties

General | Intervals | Database Verification | Advanced

Log detailed events to Windows event log
Detailed event logging can degrade system performance and is recommened only for troubleshooting WINS.

Enable burst handling
Set the number of requests that the server can handle at one time before clients have to retry registration or renewal.

Low | High
Medium | Custom:

Database path:
%windir%\system32\wins

Starting version ID (hexadecimal):
0

Use computer names that are compatible with LAN Manager

OK | Cancel | Apply

console to see if the WINS server service has started properly. The Event View may provide additional information regarding the nature of the failure.

Are the Network Traffic Problems on the WINS Server's Interfaces?

If the WINS server's adapter is located on a network segment that has its bandwidth saturated, queries may time out and cause a failure in NetBIOS name resolution. You may need to run a protocol analyzer such as Network Monitor on that segment to assess the percentage of network utilization.

System Monitor

When you install the WINS server service on your Windows 2000 Server computer, a number of counters are added to the System Monitor. Table 25-5 shows a list of those counters.

TABLE 25-5 Counters Added to the System Monitor After Installing the WINS Server Service

Counter	Description
Queries/sec	The number of queries per second received by the WINS server. A number that far exceeds baseline may represents a possible excessive load on the WINS server.
Releases/sec	The number of NetBIOS Name Release Requests receive per second by the WINS server.
Successful Queries/sec	The number of NetBIOS Name Query Request successfully resolved by the WINS server.
Successful Releases/sec	The number of successfully NetBIOS Name Releases performed per second by the WINS server.
Total Number of Conflicts/sec	The number of NetBIOS name conflicts detected by the WINS server per second. Conflicts of both unique and group numbers are included in the calculation.

TABLE 25-5 Counters Added to the System Monitor After Installing the WINS Server Service *(continued)*

Counter	Description
Total Number of Registrations/sec	The Total number of NetBIOS Name Registration Requests processed per second. This includes both unique and group NetBIOS names.
Total Number of Renewals/sec	The number of NetBIOS Name Renewal Requests processed by the WINS server per second. This includes both unique and Group names.
Unique Conflicts/sec	The number of conflicts in unique NetBIOS names processed by the WINS server per second. Only conflicts in unique NetBIOS names are detected.
Unique Registrations/sec	The number of unique NetBIOS names registered with the WINS server per second.
Unique Renewals/sec	The number of unique NetBIOS names registered per second.

EXERCISE 25-5

Configuring WINS Server Startup Behavior

In this exercise, you will learn how to configure the WINS Server service startup behavior. Do not perform this exercise on a live, production network without the permission of your network administrator.

1. Log on as Administrator.
2. Open the Services applet from the Administrative Tools menu.
3. Scroll down the list of services until you find Windows Internet Name Service (WINS), and then double-click on it.

4. You should see what appears in the following illustration. Click Stop. You will see the progress bar indicating that the service is being stopped. Click Start to restart the service. Ensure that the Startup type is Automatic.

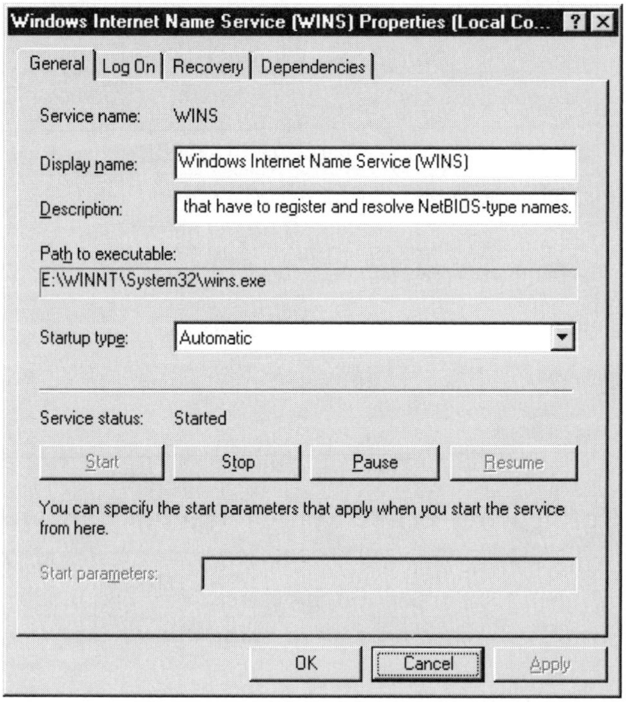

Windows Internet Name Service (WINS) Properties (Local Co...

General | Log On | Recovery | Dependencies

Service name: WINS

Display name: Windows Internet Name Service (WINS)

Description: that have to register and resolve NetBIOS-type names.

Path to executable:
E:\WINNT\System32\wins.exe

Startup type: Automatic

Service status: Started

Start | Stop | Pause | Resume

You can specify the start parameters that apply when you start the service from here.

Start parameters:

OK | Cancel | Apply

5. Click on the Recovery tab. You should see what appears in the following illustration.

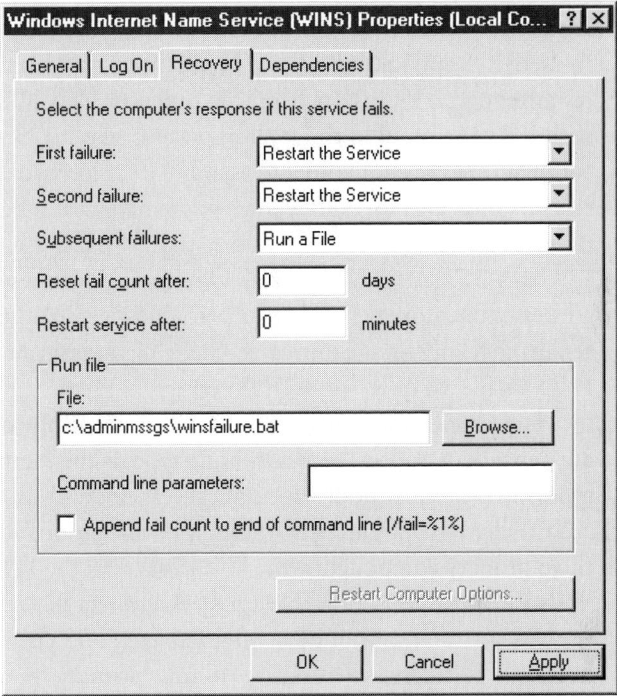

6. For the "First failure" and the "Second failure," select Restart the Service. For "Subsequent failure," select the Run a File option. You can create a simple batch file to inform you that the service didn't start using the net send command. Or, you can configure more complex command parameters to send a pager message or Simple Mail Transfer Protocol (SMTP) e-mail message.
7. Click Apply and then OK. Close the Services console.

CERTIFICATION SUMMARY

The Microsoft Windows 2000 WINS server provides NetBIOS name resolution for NetBIOS hosts on both Windows 2000 and other Microsoft network clients that require NetBIOS name resolution.

NetBIOS applications use the NetBIOS session layer interface to access network resources over a TCP/IP network. In order for NetBIOS applications to create a session with a destination host, the application must use the NetBIOS name of the destination computer. However, in order to establish a session over a TCP/IP network, that name must be translated to an IP address so the request can be passed down the TCP/IP protocol stack.

NetBIOS hosts can use a variety of methods to resolve NetBIOS names to IP addresses, including checking its NetBIOS Remote Name Cache, querying a WINS server, checking local broadcasts, checking a local LMHOSTS file, checking a local HOSTS file, or querying a DNS server.

The methods the NetBIOS host will use, and the order in which it will use them, are dependent on the NetBIOS node type of the NetBIOS host. The basic node types are b-node, p-node, m-node, and h-node.

In order to configure a working WINS solution, you must install and configure three primary components: the WINS servers, the WINS clients, and if required, a WINS Proxy Agent. A WINS Proxy Agent can be used to provide WINS services to machines that cannot be configured as WINS clients.

The WINS server participates in four primary interactions with WINS clients: NetBIOS name resolution, NetBIOS name registration, NetBIOS name renewal, and NetBIOS name release. When WINS client machines start up, they register their names with their configured WINS servers. The WINS client must renew its name with the WINS server periodically in order to keep its name *active* in the WINS database. A WINS client will release its name in the WINS database when it no longer needs it.

WINS clients also query a WINS server to resolve NetBIOS names to IP addresses. The WINS server is essentially a database server and accepts these queries for NetBIOS name resolution.

The Windows 2000 version of WINS includes some new and improved components: the ability to maintain persistent connections between replication partners, burst handling, and easy manual tombstoning of WINS database records.

All WINS servers on your network should have the same entries in their WINS databases so that they are able to resolve the NetBIOS names to IP addresses for all the NetBIOS servers on the network. In order to ensure that the WINS database is distributed correctly, you must configure WINS servers to be replication partners of one another.

WINS servers can be either *push* or *pull* replication partners. The push partner forwards the changes made in its WINS database based on how many changes have taken place. The pull partner is configured to send a pull request to its pull partner based on an interval of time. Once the interval is expired, the pull request is sent, and the pull partner's WINS database changes are sent.

Activities that you carry out when managing the WINS server include compacting the database when it becomes too large, adding static entries for non-WINS clients, backing up the database, and checking for consistency of WINS database entries.

The Windows 2000 WINS server can interoperate with the DHCP service and the Windows 2000 DNS server. The Windows 2000 DNS server can be configured to query a WINS server for name resolution.

The Windows 2000 WINS server is reliable and mostly self-tuning. However, there may be times when you must troubleshoot and monitor the WINS server. The majority of problems with WINS server issues are related to connectivity between the WINS client and WINS server. You can use the System Monitor to monitor the health and performance of your WINS server.

TWO-MINUTE DRILL

Introduction to NetBIOS Resolution

- NetBIOS applications are written to interact with the networking protocols via the NetBIOS interface. The Microsoft implementation of the NetBIOS interface for TCP/IP is called NetBIOS over TCP/IP, or NetBT.
- NetBIOS applications use the NetBIOS name as the endpoint of communication. TCP/IP uses IP addresses and port numbers. NetBIOS names must be translated to IP addresses via a process called NetBIOS Name Resolution.
- Windows 2000 can use several methods to resolve NetBIOS names, including the NetBIOS Remote Name Cache, WINS servers, Broadcasts, LMHOSTS files, HOSTS files, and DNS servers.

Planning and Implementing a WINS Solution

- The WINS database is kept consistent throughout a WINS network via WINS database replication.
- WINS replication partners can be push partners, pull partners, or both. A push partner sends a pull notification message to its push partner after a defined number of changes have been made to the WINS database. A pull partner sends a pull request to its pull partner after a specified period of time has elapsed. WINS replication partners can be configured as both push and pull partners.
- WINS servers can find each other via a process of *Autodiscovery*. Autodiscovery is accomplished via multicast messages to the multicast address 224.0.1.24. Autoconfigured WINS replication partners are configured as push and pull partners. The pull interval is two hours.

Interoperability Issues

- A DNS server can query a WINS server for NetBIOS name resolution if the DNS server does not contain an entry for the sought-after host name.

- WINS servers and DHCP servers do not communicate directly with each other. DHCP options can be used to assign WINS server IP addresses to DHCP clients, and the NetBIOS node type can also be set via DHCP options.
- Downlevel DNS servers such as UNIX BIND DNS servers, do not support WINS Lookup. If you are using BIND Secondaries, you should disable replication of WINS lookup information.

Monitoring and Troubleshooting WINS

- You can use the Windows 2000 System Monitor to assess WINS server performance and monitor WINS server usage statistics.
- When troubleshooting WINS-related problems, try to assess whether the problem lies with the client or with the server.

MCSE

MICROSOFT CERTIFIED SYSTEMS ENGINEER

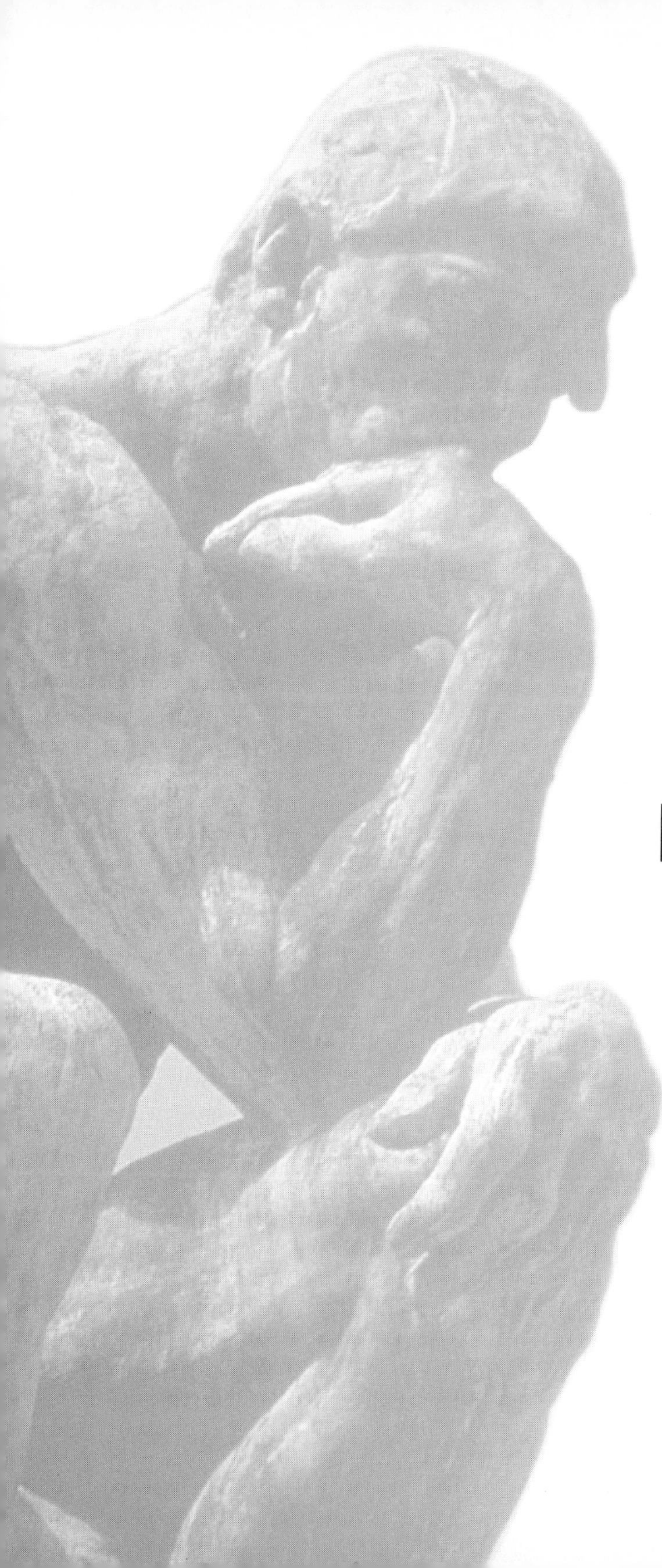

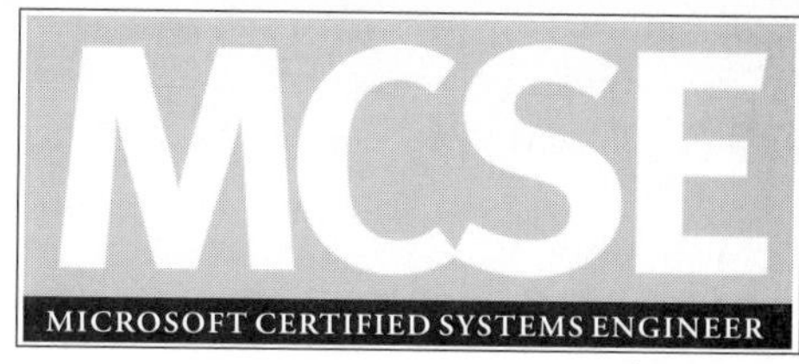

26

Installing and Managing the Windows 2000 DNS Server

CERTIFICATION OBJECTIVES

26.01	The Domain Name System: Introductory Concepts and Procedures
26.02	How Host Names Are Resolved
26.03	Windows 2000 DNS Server Roles
26.04	Integrating Windows 2000 Server with Active Directory
26.05	Integrating Windows 2000 Server with DHCP
26.06	Managing the Windows 2000 DNS Server
26.07	Monitoring and Troubleshooting DNS
✓	Two-Minute Drill

The Domain Name System (DNS) provides a solution to the problem of host naming and host name resolution for WinSock applications. In this chapter, we'll look at a variety of concepts, such as DNS server roles and how the Windows 2000 DNS Server integrates with the Active Directory and the Windows 2000 DHCP Server. Then we'll looks at the nuts and bolts of managing the actual zones and the Server itself via the DNS Management Console. Finally, you'll learn how to use some of the tools available that allow you to monitor and troubleshoot your Windows 2000 DNS installation.

CERTIFICATION OBJECTIVE 26.01

The Domain Name System: Introductory Concepts and Procedures

In order to understand some of the key concepts of DNS, it is helpful to contrast DNS with another commonly used naming system on Microsoft Networks, the NetBIOS naming scheme. Prior to Windows 2000, all Microsoft networks used NetBIOS as their primary naming scheme and method of identifying machines and services on the network. NetBIOS was initially designed as a monolithic transport protocol for IBM by Sytek in 1983. Since then, the NetBIOS command set has been integrated as a Session layer interface for other protocols, including its most common implementation: NetBEUI (NetBIOS Extended User Interface).

NetBIOS was designed for small, single-segment LANs. NetBIOS protocols are *broadcast based.* NetBIOS clients can find other network clients by using NetBIOS broadcast messages to identify the destination computer's hardware address, also called the Media Access Control (MAC). Once the hardware address is known, a session can be established with the destination computer (Figure 26-1).

While the broadcast method worked well for small departmental LANs that occupied a single segment, this method of identifying other computers on Ethernet (broadcast-based) networks became problematic for several reasons:

- As the number of computers on a network segment increased, so did the volume of broadcast traffic.

- NetBIOS-based protocols (NetBEUI) have no mechanism that allows them to include routing information. Routing instructions were not included in the NetBIOS frame specification.
- Even if a mechanism is employed to allow NetBIOS messages to be routed (such as overlaying NetBIOS over another, routable protocol), routers do not, by default, forward NetBIOS broadcasts. Forwarding broadcast traffic across segments significantly increases the amount of network volume and would have a profound negative effect on overall network performance.

The broadcast nature of NetBIOS is the first of two factors that limit its usefulness on enterprise internetworks. The second major problem with the NetBIOS naming scheme is that it is *flat.*

FIGURE 26-1

A NetBIOS broadcast to resolve a NetBIOS name to a MAC address

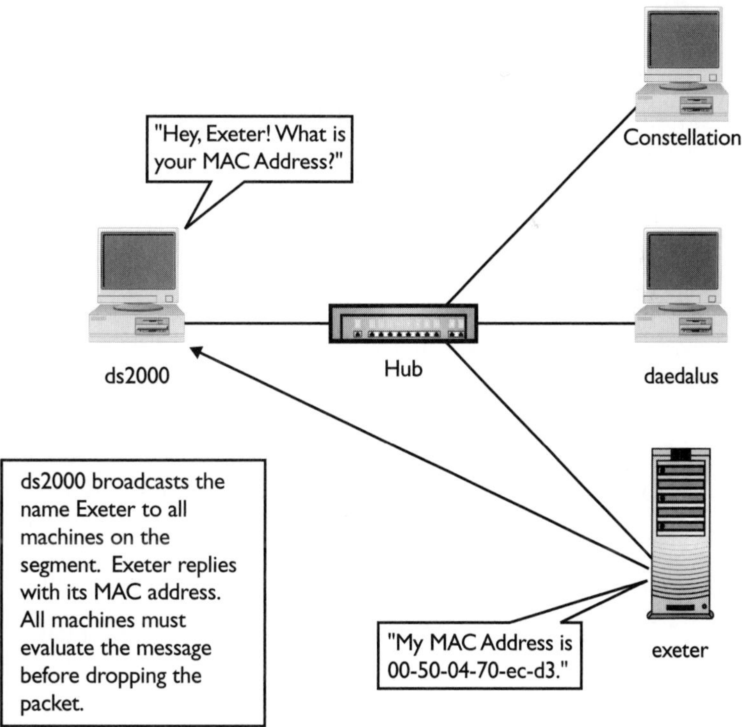

The Flat NetBIOS Namespace

To understand the limitations of a flat naming scheme, imagine that everyone in the world had just a first name, and this was the only way people were identified. Now imagine that you run a government agency, such as the Department of Motor Vehicles. Each person in your state gets a driver's license. How many Georges are there? How many Carols? How many Debbies? How many Harrys? When an officer stops you and checks your license, he calls in with "I've got George here, do you have any priors on him?" Which George? Yes, one of the Georges out there has a warrant, but the officer has no idea if he has the right George sitting in front of him. So, he arrests you and lets the courts sort it out later.

One solution to the problem of multiple Georges is to require that everyone in the world have a different first name. In this way, when the officer calls up for a warrant search for "George," he will know that if there is a warrant out for George, then he just got his man!

How would you coordinate the naming of everyone in the world (or at least in your country or state) so that everyone's name was different? And what would happen if some people didn't want to comply and decided that they wanted to name their child with a name that had already been used?

It would be virtually impossible to coordinate the naming of individuals so that everyone had the same name. And, even if you were to implement such as system, some people would defy it and name their child with a name that was the same as one already in use. This would cause confusion in the naming structure for the people or the world; the possibility would exist that a communication meant for one individual would be directed to the other person with the same name.

This is an example of the limitation of a flat namespace. The NetBIOS namespace is a flat namespace. This means that every computer on the network must have a different name. If two computers on a NetBIOS network have the same name, messages could be mistakenly forwarded to a computer that was not the intended destination.

The NetBIOS and WinSock Interfaces

DNS solves these problems because it does not use a flat naming structure. It uses a *hierarchical* naming system, much like our system of using First Name, Middle Name, and Last Name to aid in naming and identifying each other. Before we go into the details of the DNS namespace, we should discuss how applications access the network protocols and, specifically, how they interact with the TCP/IP protocol.

Network-enabled applications for Microsoft operating systems interact with the TCP/IP protocol stack via one of two Session layer interfaces: The *Windows Sockets (WinSock)* interface, or the *NetBIOS interface.*

These interfaces solve a key problem in name resolution on TCP/IP-based networks. Programs written to the NetBIOS interface treat the destination computer name as the "endpoint" for communications. NetBIOS applications only care about the name of the destination computer in order to establish a session with that machine. However, the TCP/IP protocol stack, including the Transmission Control Protocol and the Internet Protocol, has no awareness of NetBIOS computer names, and really doesn't care about them at all.

NetBIOS over TCP/IP or NetBT

In order to resolve this situation, NetBIOS applications interface with the TCP/IP protocol stack via the NetBIOS interface, which is implemented as *NetBIOS over TCP/IP*, or *NetBT*. When a request for a network resource is passed from a NetBIOS application down to the Application layer of the TCP/IP protocol stack, it interfaces with NetBT. It is at this point that the NetBIOS name is translated, or *resolved*, to an IP address. Once the NetBIOS name of the destination computer is resolved to a NetBIOS name, the request can be passed down the TCP/IP protocol stack. Figure 26-2 shows you how the process works.

The Windows Sockets (WinSock) Interface

Programs that were specifically written for TCP/IP-based networks use the WinSock interface. These programs, however, do not require a name for the destination computer in order to establish a session with it. All they require is a destination IP address in order to connect with the destination host.

While your computer may have little problem with the voluminous numbers of IP addresses out there for the servers we connect to, humans have a different opinion about remembering long lists of numbers. Think about the servers that you frequent on a regular basis: microsoft.com, zdnet.com, cnet.com, syngress.com, shinder.net, and a host of others. Do you know the IP addresses of those Web servers to which you connect regularly? Do you care to know all those IP addresses? Are you already unhappy that you have to remember 10-digit phone numbers and therefore bought a Windows CE Pocket PC in order to handle the added complexity?

All but the most "alpha" of geeks find remembering computer names much easier than remembering numbers. So, while WinSock applications do not require a

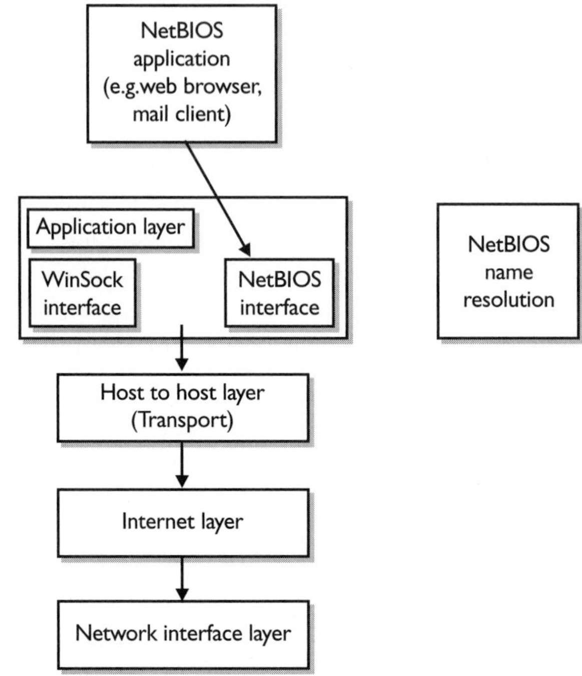

FIGURE 26-2

A NetBIOS communication moving down the protocol stack

computer or host name to establish a session with a destination computer, they can employ a mechanism to do so. This is the process of *host name resolution.*

The Bottom Line on the Difference between NetBIOS and WinSock

Remember, NetBIOS-based programs must have the NetBIOS name translated or resolved to an IP address before a session can be established with a destination computer, while WinSock programs can use host names rather than IP addresses, but this is not required. Host names represent a convenience only.

This is an important distinction because until Windows 2000, all the core networking components of Windows operating systems were NetBIOS based. That is why so much time has been devoted to the subject of NetBIOS name resolution in the past. Windows 2000 does not depend on NetBIOS names for the vast majority of its networking subsystems, and uses DNS host names instead. We will see the implications of these changes as we move through this chapter.

The DNS Namespace

As you learned earlier, the DNS namespace is hierarchical rather than flat. Because of its hierarchical nature, you can have multiple computers with the same name on the same network and not have problems with misdirected messages. This is in contrast to the NetBIOS flat naming scheme, where you cannot have two computers on the same network with the same name.

The DNS namespace has at its top the *root domain.* The root domain is often represented either as a dot (".") or an empty space (" "). While the latter usage is technically correct, you won't get any questions wrong on the test if you use a dot instead.

Just under the root domain are the *top-level* domain names. Examples of the top-level domain names include .com, .net, .org, and .edu. Organizations that seek to have an Internet presence will obtain a domain name that is a member of one of the top-level domain names.

Each top-level domain is intended for a specific type of organization (although for the most part, it is a voluntary action to seek a top-level domain that represents your company best). For example, a commercial, profit-seeking entity would fit with the .com domain, an educational institution with the .edu domain, and a United States Federal Government institution with the .gov domain. Table 26-1 includes a list of some of the top-level domain names and their intended memberships.

TABLE 26-1 Top-Level Domain Names

Top-Level Domain Name	Description	Examples
.com	The .com domain is meant for commercial, profit-making organizations. If your company is a for-profit entity, it would seek membership in the .com domain.	microsoft.com syngress.com osborne.com
.edu	The .edu domain is reserved for educational institutions. In the past, all educational institutions could gain membership to the .edu domain, but now only colleges and universities are allowed in the .edu domain.	mit.edu dcccd.edu berkeley.edu cornell.edu
.gov	United States Federal Government agencies are assigned membership to .gov domains.	whitehouse.gov irs.gov faa.gov

TABLE 26-1

Top-Level Domain Names *(continued)*

Top-Level Domain Name	Description	Examples
.int	International organizations are assigned to the .int domain.	nato.int
.mil	Various Branches of the United States Military establishment are assigned to the .mil domain.	ddn.mil navy.mil
.net	The .net domain was originally designed to include members that were part of the networking infrastructure on the Internet. However, competition for popular .com names has led to a wide variety of organizations belonging to the .net domain.	nsf.net dallas.net shinder.net tacteam.net
.org	Only nonprofit organizations belong to the org domain.	ama.org ana.org

For an organization to have a place in the domain namespace that is separate and distinct from all other organizations, they must obtain a *second-level* domain name. It is the second-level domain name that distinguishes your organization from all others on the Internet. Examples of second-level domains are microsoft.com, osborne.com, and syngress.com.

A graphical view of the DNS hierarchy appears in Figure 26-3.

Note that at each level of the domain name hierarchy, all names must be different. For example, there cannot be two .com domains, there cannot be two .org domains, and there cannot be two microsoft.com domains. However, names can be repeated as long as they are not located at the same level in the hierarchy. This explains how we can have an untold number of servers on the Internet with the name "www."

The root, top-level, and second-level domains are the only centrally managed aspects of DNS. In order to register your second-level domain, you must contact a domain registrar. In the past, the only organization that had the authority to register second-level domain names in the United States was Network Solutions Incorporated (or NSI, which you can find at www.nsi.com). However, NSI's monopoly over the domain registration business is no longer extant, and now a number of different organizations have the authority to register your second-level domain names.

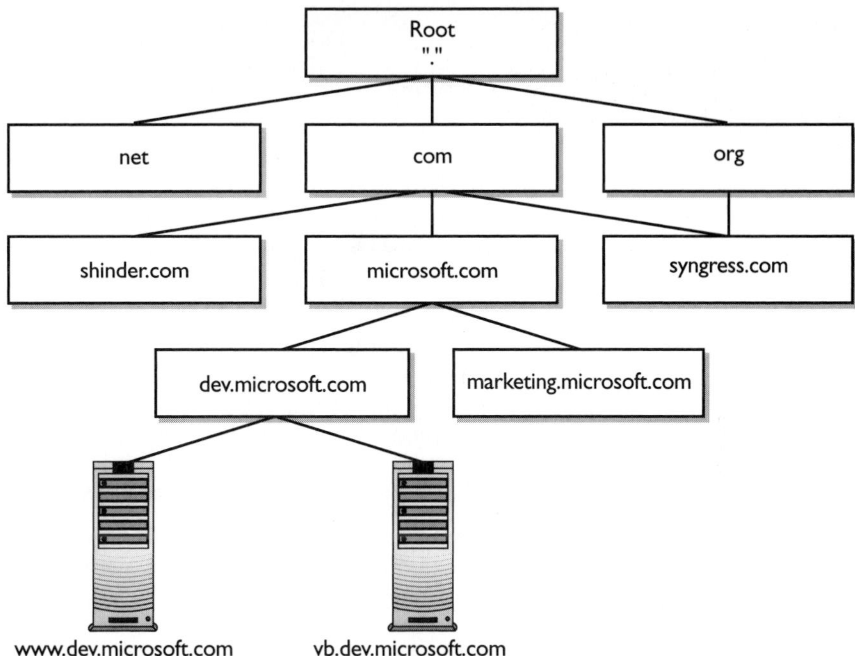

FIGURE 26-3 The Domain Name System (DNS)

You, as the DNS administrator for your organization, are responsible for all domains underneath your second-level domain name. You can partition your organization's namespace under the second-level domain however you want. You will also be responsible for maintaining at least two DNS servers that are *authoritative* for your second-level domain if you will be making resources available to Internet users. *Authoritative* means that your DNS servers have the authority to answer questions about host name resolutions for your domain. It will be your responsibility to maintain the accuracy of the information about the resources contained in your organization. This information will be stored on your authoritative DNS servers.

Domain and Host Name Specifications

Every computer participating in the DNS namespace is a member of a domain. In order to understand the usefulness of the hierarchical nature of the DNS namespace, you should understand what a fully qualified domain name (FQDN) is and how they are used.

SCENARIO & SOLUTION	
How much does it cost to register a domain name?	In the past, the cost structure for registering a domain name was simple. However, there are a large number of domain registrars from which to choose. If you choose to register your domain name with Network Solutions, Inc., you should expect to spend $70.00 for your initial registration, which is good for two years. After that, you must renew your registration.
Are you limited to the number of domain names that you can register?	At present, there is no limit on the number of domains you can register at once. However, there are some moves to control the number of domains that can be registered to a single individual at the same time in order to prevent "domain squatting." Domain squatting is the practice of registering a domain name in the hope that some company will buy it from you for a large sum of cash. This practice is very much frowned upon.
How long do you get to keep your domain name?	If you register with NSI, your initial registration is typically good for two years. They have recently made available a program where you can register you domain name for up to 10 years. Check www.nsi.com for details on registration.
What happens if you let your domain name registration expire?	If you allow your domain name registration to expire, it will become available to anyone who wishes to use it. In addition, your DNS server addresses will be dropped from the zone database and users will no longer be able to contact your public servers using FQDNs. In addition, a competitor or domain squatter may purchase your domain name if you let the registration expire. It is very important that you keep track of your domain name expiration dates for this reason.

Fully Qualified Domain Names, or FQDNs

An FQDN represents a particular machine's location in the DNS namespace. By using the FQDN, you are able to pinpoint the machine's location in the domain namespace. A FQDN is the combination of a machine's *host* name, which is the computer name of the machine, and its domain membership name. For example, if you are running a company called widgets, you may have obtained the second-level domain name widgets.com. If you run a Web server for widgets.com, you probably will want to name it "www" so that users will be able to locate it easily at www.widgets.com.

The FQDN contains two elements: a *label* that includes a domain or host name, and periods ("dots"). Each label is separated by a dot. Each label can contain up to 63 *bytes*. Note that we specify the length of a label by the number of bytes it uses, rather than the number of characters. This is because the Windows 2000 DNS server supports *UTF-8* characters. Unlike the 8-bit (1 byte) ASCII characters that you usually work with, a single UTF-8 character can consume more than 8 bits per character. The entire FQDN must be less than or equal to 255 bytes.

Think of the FQDN as an address. For example, consider the addresses 123 Main Street, Dallas, TX, and 123 Hitt Street, Dallas, TX. The street and city name would be comparable to the domain name, and the house number would be similar to the host name. Note that we are able to have two homes with the same house address (123) because these homes are located on different streets. In the same fashion, we are able to have machines with the same host names on the Internet, because they "live" in different domains.

Recently, the 63-byte limitation has been increased to over 200 bytes by the domain registrars. However, you must be careful when using domain or host names that exceed the 63-byte limit, because WinSock applications are often hard-coded not to accept more than that number of bytes per label in the FQDN.

Legal and UTF-8 Characters Standard DNS servers support the label naming conventions as prescribed in Request For Comments (RFC) 952 and 1123. These naming conventions state that legal characters for domain names include the following:

- A–Z
- a–z
- 0–9
- The dash (-)

Note that the underscore is *not* supported. This is important for you to remember, because many NetBIOS naming schemes unfortunately included the underscore character for the naming of machines on Microsoft networks prior to Windows 2000. If you choose to upgrade computers to Windows 2000 that have established NetBIOS names, Windows 2000 will replace the underscore character with a dash.

The Windows 2000 DNS server supports an expanded character set that you can use when creating host and domain names. The *UTF-8* (UTF stands for *Unicode Character Set Transformation Format*) is a "superset" of the US-ASCII character set, and is a "translation" of the *UCS-2 (Universal Character Set-2)* character set. The UTF-8 character set supports the characters used in virtually all known human languages. This makes the Windows 2000 DNS server a truly universal DNS solution. RFC 2044 includes the specifications for supporting the UTF-8 character set for DNS servers.

If you do plan to implement the extended UTF-8 character set, you must be careful that you only employ Windows 2000 or other DNS servers that support UTF-8 naming. If a Windows 2000 server has zones that include resource records with UTF-8 names and it tries a zone transfer with a downlevel DNS server that does not support this character set, the zone transfer will most likely fail. Also, be aware that many WinSock applications do not recognize these characters and will not be able to access hosts or domains that include the UTF-8 character set.

SCENARIO & SOLUTION	
You have heard that a fully qualified domain name must include a "dot" at the end. However, you never have to type this dot in order to access machines via their host name. Why is that?	They are right. A fully qualified domain name must include the trailing period. If it does not, then it is considered an unqualified domain name. However, most user applications (sometimes referred to as *user agents)* will automatically place the period for you when you enter the FQDN in the address line.
Do you have to name your Web server "www"? Do you have to name your ftp server "ftp" and your mail server "mail"?	You do not have to use www, ftp, or mail for your servers that deliver those services. Those host names are used conventionally to help denote the service provided on a particular server. However, you can use any host name you like, even when they are providing network services such as ftp, Web, and mail services.
What do you mean by "bytes" in a label? You thought that people used characters to figure out how long a label could be.	Since RFC 2181 allows any binary character string to be used for FQDN labels, it is better to think about the size of the label rather than the number of characters. This is especially the case when you are using the UTF-8 character set, where some characters will require more than 8 bits (1 byte).
How do you know if your WinSock application will support UTF-8 characters and labels longer than 63 bytes?	Compatibility is always an issue when upgrading to a new operating system. In order to know if your WinSock application will support the extended character set, you can contact the developer, or better yet, test your application yourself to see if they are compatible.

Planning Domain Names for an Organization

Before implementing a DNS naming scheme for your organization, you need to consider the following:

1. Is your organization using DNS now for intranet communication?
2. Does your organization have an Internet presence?
3. Does your organization already have a registered domain name?
4. Does your organization use the same domain name for internal and Internet resources?
5. Does you organization use different domain names for intranet and Internet resources?

If your organization plans to have an Internet presence, and plans to be connected to the Internet, you need to consider whether you want to use the same domain name both internally and externally, or if you want to use different domain names for your internal resources and your Internet resources.

Using the Same Domain Name for Both Intranet and Internet Resources

Using the same domain name for both your internal corporate resources and your Internet resources seems attractive at first—all machines are members of the same domain, and users don't have to remember different domain names based on whether a resource is internal or external.

However, there are some problems with this arrangement. In order to protect your DNS zone data from intruders, you must not keep any information about your internal resources on a DNS server that is accessible from the Internet. Therefore, you are going to need to maintain two different DNS zone databases for the single domain (we will discuss zones in a little bit). One of the zones will track your internal resources, and one of the zones will be responsible for resources that are accessible from the Internet. This means extra administrative effort on your part and can seriously cut into your "watercooler" time.

Implementing the Same Domain Name for Internal and External Resources Another thing you must do when implementing the same domain name for internal and external resources is to mirror the external resources internally. For example, imagine that tacteam.net used the same domain name for its intranet- and Internet-located resources. We have Web servers for our intranet that employees use to access personnel information and other corporate inside information. We also have Web servers that we want to use to make information available to users who want information about us on the Internet.

We want to use the same host name for these servers in order to reduce the number of help desk calls from users who believe every Web server must be called "www." The problem is that when we use the same domain name for both the internal and external resources, the request for www.tacteam.net will resolve to a single computer, which we want to have available to Internet users.

However, since we do not want Internet users to be able to access the confidential corporate information, it would be unwise to place that information on an external Web server. But we still want our internal users to have access to the information that is located on the external Web server.

The solution is to mirror the Internet resources internally, and create a separate DNS zone database that is used for internal users. When a user issues a query for www.tacteam.net from within the intranet, it will be resolved from the internal DNS server that contains the internal zone database file. When an Internet user tries to access www.tacteam.net, it will send its DNS query to the Internet DNS server, which will reply with the IP address of the external DNS server. Figure 26-4 shows how this arrangement works.

Using the same domain name for your internal and external resources is the option you are usually presented with when working with a company that already has an established Internet presence and has been using DNS for internal resources for some time. It's also a decision that is often made by someone other than you; therefore, you are presented with the situation and it's your job to implement it.

Using Different Domain Names for Intranet and Internet Resources

If your company is connected, or planning to connect, to the Internet you can choose to use different domain names for the internal and external resources maintained by the company. This makes life a lot easier because you don't have to worry about keeping

FIGURE 26-4 Mirroring external resources internally

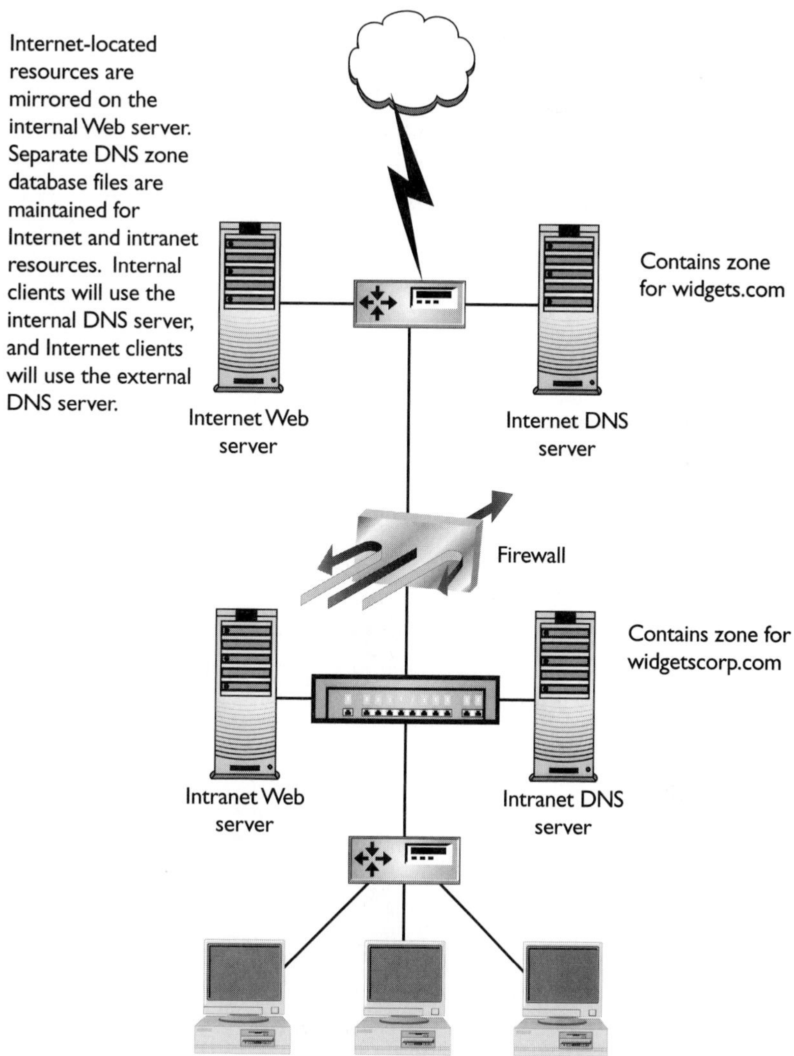
Internet-located resources are mirrored on the internal Web server. Separate DNS zone database files are maintained for Internet and intranet resources. Internal clients will use the internal DNS server, and Internet clients will use the external DNS server.
Contains zone for widgets.com
Internet Web server
Internet DNS server
Firewall
Contains zone for widgetscorp.com
Intranet Web server
Intranet DNS server

different zone databases for the same domain name as you would have to do when you are using the same domain name for internal and external resources.

When you use different domain names, you pick an easy-to-remember, intuitive name for your external domain. If your company's name was Widget's Inc., then you would want a name like widgets.com. For your internal resources you should pick a related name, such as widgetscorp.com. Now, when users want to connect to internal resources they use the widgetscorp.com domain servers, and when they want to connect to external resources they use the widgets.com domain servers. Figure 26-5 demonstrates this easier-to-manage arrangement.

Since your internal domain is not accessible from the Internet, there will be no delegation record of your internal domain name on any Internet servers. This means there is no requirement to register your internal domain name.

FIGURE 26-5

Maintaining intranet and Internet resources using different domain names

Using different domain names simplifies DNS zone management. While separate zone files are maintained for internal and external resources, they are for different domains and therefore easier to identify.
Contains zone for widgets.com
Internet Web server
Internet DNS server
Firewall
Contains zone for widgetscorp.com
Intranet Web server
Intranet DNS server

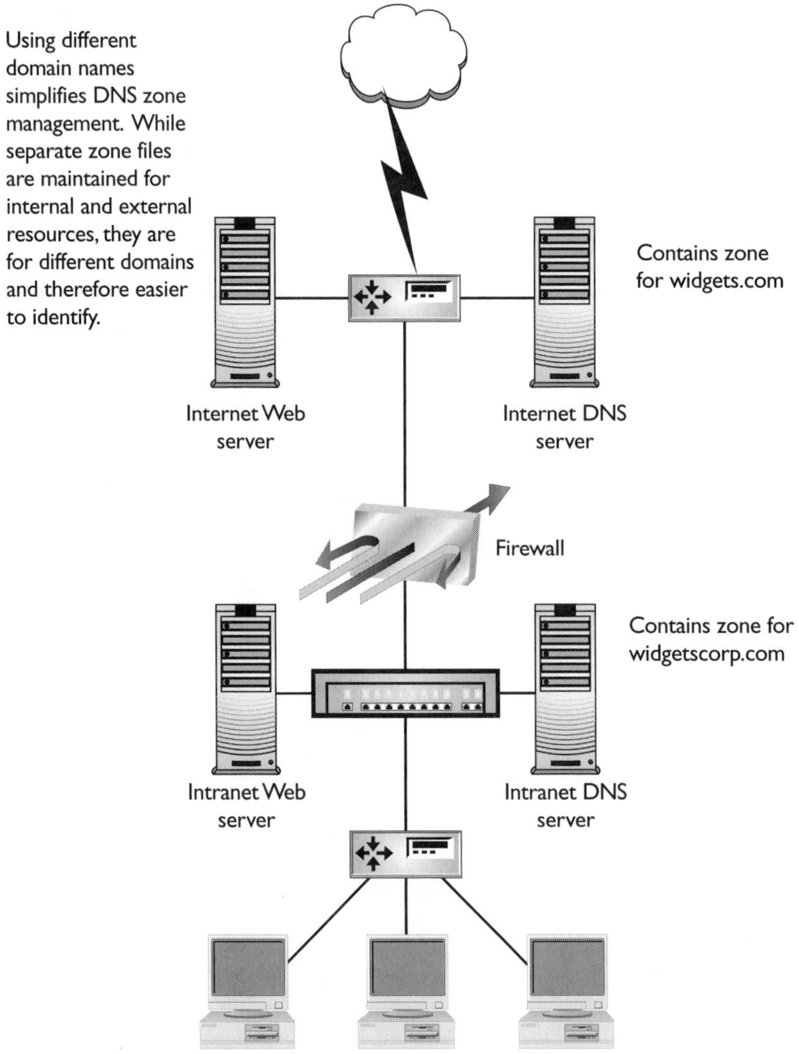

However, you might want to register your internal domain name in order to avoid confusion. For example, imagine the boss, who isn't very computer literate, goes to a big meeting where a major account is at stake. He wants to impress the other people at the meeting with the fancy Web site you have put together for you internal domain. He fires up the browser in the meeting room and types in the URL for *your internal* domain's Web server. When the browser connects, lo and behold, it's your major competitor's Web site! This sad situation can be avoided if you spend a few dollars and get your internal domain registered with an Internet domain registrar.

Naming Your Subdomains

Remember that only the root, top-level, and second-level domains are managed centrally for Internet accessible domains. The DNS administrator of the organization manages any domains below the second-level domains.

Therefore, you have to consider the naming scheme you want to use for your subdomains. There are two approaches you can take when naming your subdomains:

- Names based on geographical location
- Names based on business unit

Examples of subdomain names based on business unit include sales.stuff.com, marketing.stuff.com, or hr.stuff.com. Each of these subdomains would contain the resources of the Sales, Marketing, and Human Resources divisions, respectively.

Naming Domains Based on Business Units

There are some problems with naming your domains based on business units. Since business, political, and sociological influences can bear heavily on the existence and names of business units, you might find yourself in a pinch when these units change their names. For example, in the past, the business unit that was responsible for managing employees was called "personnel." However, as people have become more commoditized, the name changed to "Human Resources" (I suppose this helps to differentiate them from the physical plant). If this trend continues, it's likely that today's "Human Resources" will turn into tomorrow's "Organic Assets." When that change comes around, you would have to change the entire domain name and reassign all the resources belonging to that domain, which is neither a pleasant nor easy task.

Naming Domains Based on Geography

A better alternative is to use geographical considerations when naming your subdomains. This is because geography is less likely to change than business units. If you want to make your life as easy as possible, you should keep your geographical designations as general as possible.

For example, use the subdomain names west.stuff.com, east.stuff.com, north.stuff.com, south.stuff.com, europe.stuff.com, and the like. This is in contrast to using losangeles.stuff.com, boston.stuff.com, fargo.stuff.com, and dallas.stuff.com. A location might change from Dallas to Houston, but you would not need to change the domain name, since the organization's employees would consider both Dallas and Houston "south."

Since Windows 2000 now uses DNS domain names rather than NetBIOS names for its Domain Security model, you might still have need for more granular control over resources based on business units. Since this is likely to be the case, you can create organizational units (OUs) within the appropriate domain that you can use to fine-tune permissions and other parameters using a Group Policy applied to that OU.

Root Name Servers

Something you'll need to understand for the Microsoft exams is what a *root* name server is and why we care. We've already covered the idea of the Internet root name servers, which represent the top of the Internet DNS hierarchy. Your organization will also have a root name server, which is the DNS server that has authority for your second-level domain.

The concept of the root name server for your organization is important, because a root name server for your Windows 2000 domain must be in place before you can install Active Directory. If you don't have a root name server in place when you install the Active Directory, you can install one during the Active Directory installation process. The root name server is authoritative for your second-level domains, and may contain *delegations* for your subdomains. A delegation is a way of informing DNS clients which DNS server or servers are authoritative for your subdomains. We will talk more about delegating authority for your subdomains later in the chapter.

Zones of Authority

The domain namespace is a conceptual entity; you can't reach out and grab something in the domain namespace. The DNS is just a structure you use to categorize and track the machines by host name on a network. In order to make the DNS something that we can work with, you must have a way of storing the information in the DNS. The actual information about domains and what they contain is stored in a file called a *zone database* file. These are physical files that are stored on the DNS server in a folder on the DNS server's hard disk. The location of these zone files on disk is:

%systemroot%\system32\dns

In this section we will focus on *standard* zones. This is to differentiate them from *Active Directory integrated* zones. We will cover Active Directory integrated zones later in the chapter.

There are two types of zones we need to create:

- Forward lookup zones
- Reverse lookup zones

We'll focus on forward lookup zones first, and then discuss the utility and requirements of reverse lookup zones.

Forward Lookup Zones

Forward lookup zones are used to provide a mechanism to resolve host names to IP addresses for DNS clients. A forward lookup zone will contain what are known as *resource records.* These resource records contain the actual information about the resources available in the zone.

The Difference between Zones and Domains It is important to realize that zones are not the same as domains. A zone can contain records for multiple domains, as long as those domains are *contiguous.*

For example, let's look at the microsoft.com domain. Microsoft will likely have subdomains to track its resources at various locations. Suppose Microsoft has a West coast domain and an East coast domain that go by the names of west.microsoft.com and east.microsoft.com. Microsoft also owns the msn.com domain, and msn.com might have a subdomain called mail.microsoft.com.

Figure 26-6 depicts both domains in the domain namespace.

Notice in the figure that the microsoft.com domains are contiguous with each other, in that they all "touch" microsoft.com. The msn.com and the mail.msn.com

FIGURE 26-6

Contiguous and noncontiguous domains

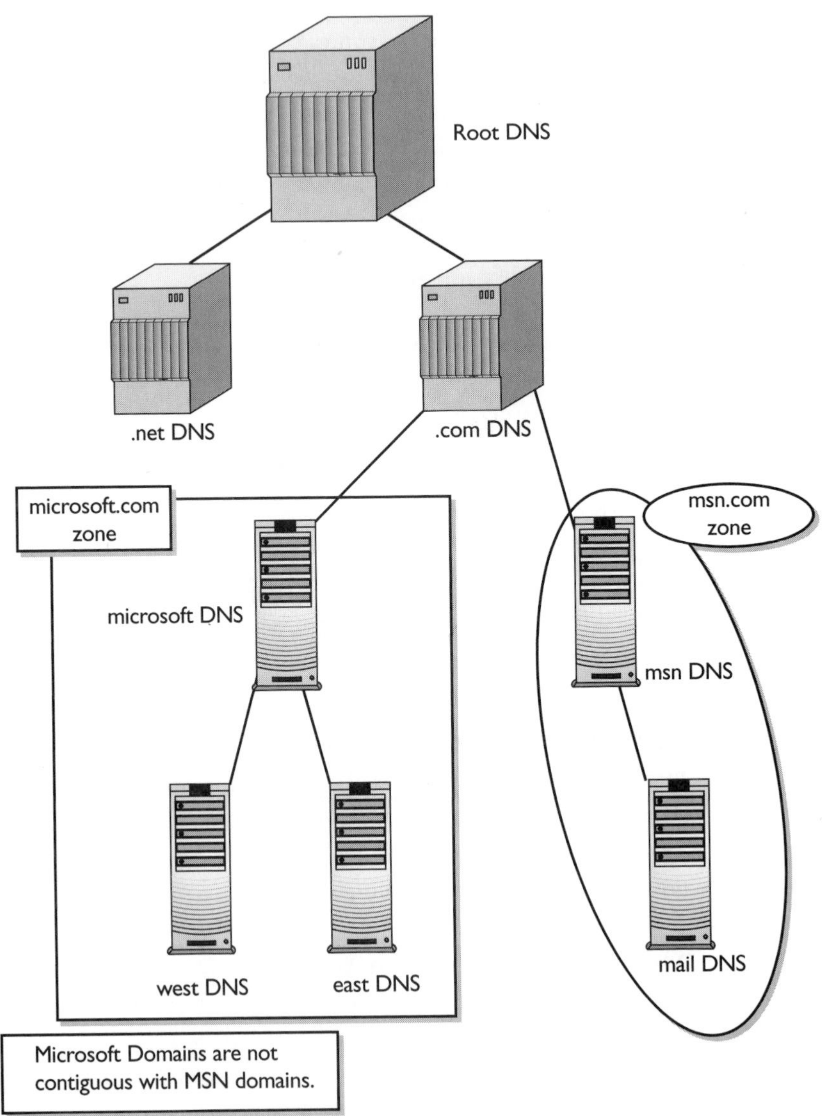

domains are contiguous because they "touch" each other as well. However, the microsoft.com and the msn.com domains do *not* touch each other. Therefore, the msn.com domains and the microsoft.com domains cannot be members of the same zone because they are not contiguous.

Zones Allow for Delegation of Responsibility for Maintaining Zone Resources Zones also provide a method to delegate responsibility for maintaining the zone database. For example, suppose we have a company called TACteam, Inc. The company uses the domain name tacteam.net. TACteam has offices in San Francisco, Dallas, and Boston. The main office is in Dallas, where there are several experienced administrators who can manage the DNS database for the Dallas resources. The San Francisco office also has several experienced administrators onsite who can reliably manage the zone database for their local resources.

The Boston location has mainly sales, marketing, and development staff, and while they are very good at what they do, they are not experienced DNS administrators. Therefore, we would be very wary of assigning responsibility to anyone in Boston for maintaining the DNS zone database for the Boston location.

The Dallas site's resources will be contained in the tacteam.net domain. The San Francisco resources will be maintained in the west.tacteam.net domain, and the Boston resources will be stored in the east.tacteam.net domain. However, we will create only two *zones* to manage these three domains: a tacteam.net zone that will be responsible for both the tacteam.net and the east.tacteam.net resources, and the west.tacteam.net zone that will store the San Francisco resources. Figure 26-7 shows how we would set this up.

How do we name these zones? The zone for the west.tacteam.net domain will be called the west.tacteam.net zone. The zone file that stores information for both the tacteam.net and the east.tacteam.net domains will be called the tacteam.net zone. Zones get their names from the "root" or highest-level domain contained in that zone.

When a DNS query for a resource for the west.tacteam.net domain arrives at the tacteam.net DNS server, the tacteam.net DNS server will not contain a zone file that can answer DNS queries. However, the tacteam.net DNS server will contain a *delegation* that will point to the west.tacteam.net DNS server so the query can be directed to the correct server for resolution.

Reverse Lookup Zones

While forward lookup zones allow DNS clients to resolve a host name to an IP address, a reverse lookup zone allows the DNS client to do the opposite: resolve an IP address to a host name.

For example, you know the IP address of the destination computer, such as 192.168.1.3, but you want to know the host name assigned to that computer. In order to accomplish the task, the DNS client would use the reverse lookup zone for the Network ID in the request.

FIGURE 26-7

The tacteam.net and the west.tacteam.net zone configurations

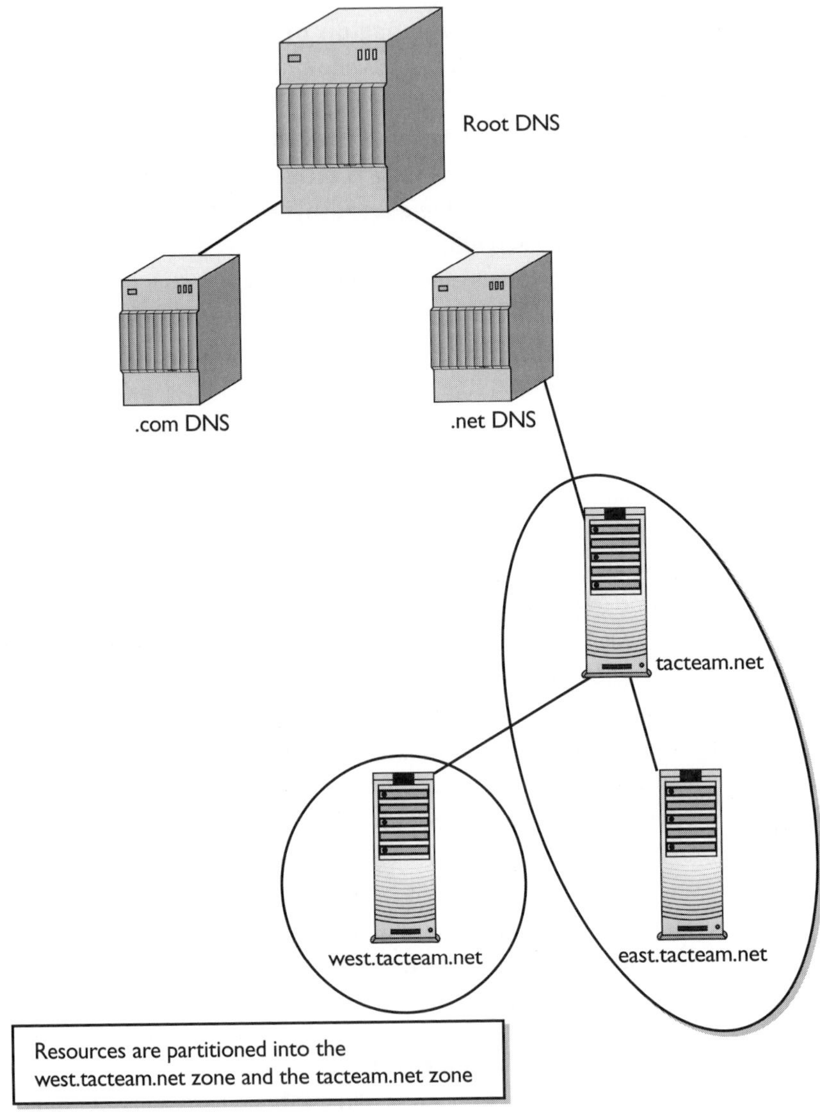

Reverse lookups are not something that can easily be accomplished using forward lookup zones. Think of forward lookup zones as something similar to a phone book. A phone book is indexed using people's last names. If you want to find a phone number quickly, you just go to the letter of the alphabet for his or her last name, and then go down the alphabetical list until you find the name. The phone number is right next to the person's name. What if we already knew the phone number, and wanted to find out whose name goes with that phone number? Since the phone book is indexed using names, our only alternative would be to look at *every* phone number in the book. If we start at the beginning, we can hope to be lucky and find that it's one in the front of the book.

This clearly isn't a very efficient method to search the IP address "namespace." At one time, "inverse lookups" were used to trawl the IP address space, but these were very limited because they searched forward lookup zones in a manner similar to what we talked about, searching the "phone book" from the beginning. As we have seen, this is very time consuming and inefficient.

The in-addr.arpa Domain To solve the problem, a new domain called the *in-addr.arpa* domain was created. The in-addr.arpa domain indexes host names based on Network IDs and makes reverse lookups much more efficient and speedy.

You can create reverse lookup zones easily using the Windows 2000 DNS Management Console. Just right-click on your computer name in the console, and select New Zone. That will start up the New Zone wizard that walks you through the process of creating new zones, either forward or reverse lookup. The wizard will ask what type of zone you want to create, and you will select Reverse Lookup Zone rather than Forward Lookup Zone. The wizard will ask for the Network ID and automatically create a zone database file based on your answers.

The construction of the reverse lookup zone database file can be found in the DNS folder, which is a subfolder of the system32 folder in the system root directory. The name of the file is the network ID in reverse with the .dns file extension appended to it. For example, if you created a reverse lookup zone for 192.168.1.0, the name of the reverse lookup zone would be 1.168.192.in-addr.arpa.dns. This is because queries are examined and executed from right to left, just as they are with forward lookup zones.

Reverse lookup zones are especially helpful if your organization is using inventory or security software that depends on reverse lookups to identify the host names of the IP addresses they discover.

EXERCISE 26-1

Installing the Windows 2000 DNS Server

In this exercise, you will install the Windows 2000 DNS server. You can actually install the Windows 2000 DNS server during operating system installation, or after the operating system has been installed.

If you intend to install the Windows 2000 Active Directory, you will be required to install the DNS server at that time if there are no other Windows 2000 domain controllers online for that domain. In this exercise, we will install the Windows 2000 DNS Service on a member server running Windows 2000 Advanced server.

Warning: Do not install a Windows 2000 DNS server on a live, production network unless you first contact your network administrator and confirm that this will not create problems with your existing network infrastructure.

1. Log on as Administrator to the Windows 2000 Advanced server.
2. Open the Control Panel and open the Add/Remove Programs applet. You should see something similar to what appears in the following illustration.

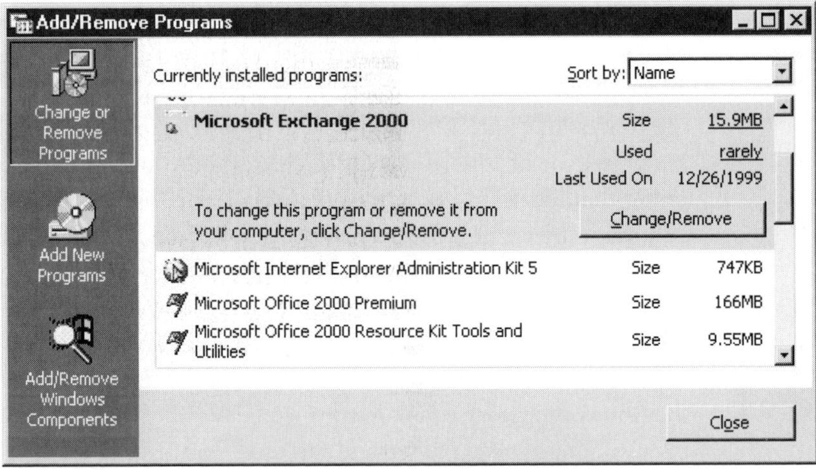

3. Click Add/Remove Windows Components on the left side of the Add/Remove Programs dialog box. You will see what appears in the following illustration.

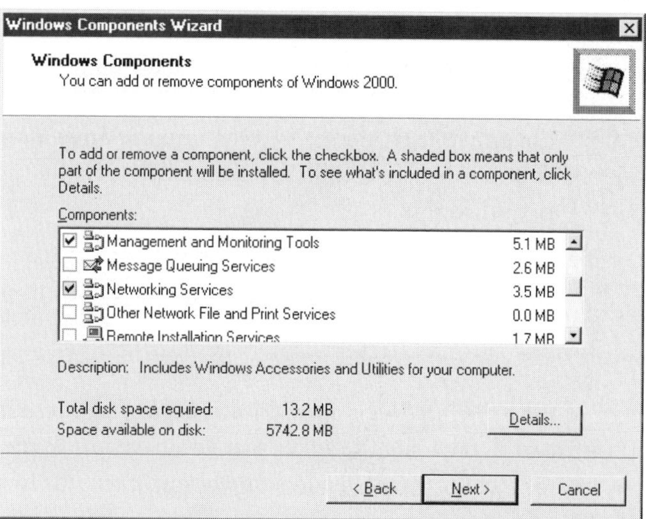

4. Scroll down the list of Components in the Windows Components Wizard dialog box and find Networking Services. Click once on Networking Services so that the option is highlighted, but do not click on the check box. Next, click Details. You will see what appears in the following illustration.

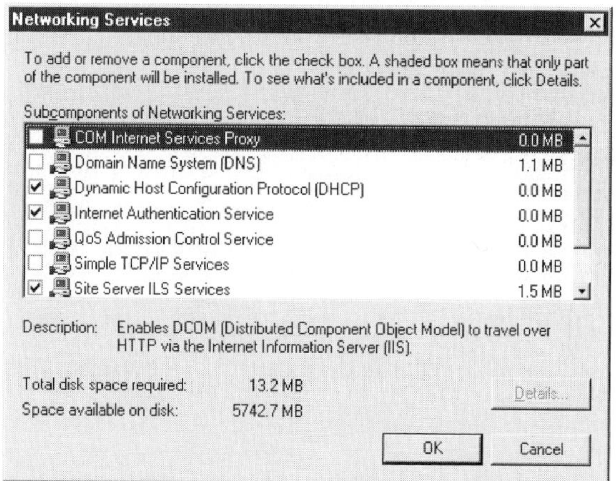

5. In the Networking Services dialog box, place a check mark in the Domain Name System (DNS) check box. Then click OK.
6. You are returned to the Windows Components Wizard dialog box. Click Next.
7. You may encounter the Insert Disk dialog box, which asks you to insert the Windows 2000 Advanced Server CD-ROM into your CD-ROM drive. You can either insert the CD-ROM into the drive, or click OK and point the wizard to a network share point. Click OK after pointing the wizard in the right direction.
8. When the wizard completes, you will see the Completing the Windows Components Wizard dialog box. Click Finish to complete the installation.

In the next section, you will learn more about resource records. Resource records are used to populate the zones that you have just created. At the end of the resource records section, you will add some resource records to these zones.

Resource Records

We have established at this point that the DNS server is actually a database server. Like all databases, it contains a file where the data is stored, which in this case is the zone database file. The database itself must be filled with data in the form of a record. If you are familiar with database design, then you know that a record is typically represented as a single row in a table. In order for us to add new rows or records to our DNS zone database file, we add *resource records.*

The resource record contains data about the resources contained in the domain. The resource record that you'll use most is the A, or Host Address, record. This record contains the host name to IP address mappings that most DNS clients will ask for when seeking to resolve a host name to an IP address.

The zone database can also contain information other than just simple host name to IP address mappings. Table 26-2 provides a list of some of the more commonly used resource records that are used to populate the DNS zone database files.

TABLE 26-2 Important Resource Record Types

Resource Record Type	Name	Description
SOA	Start of Authority	The SOA identifies which DNS server is authoritative for the data within a domain. The first record in any zone file is the SOA.
NS	Name Server	An NS record lists the DNS servers that can return authoritative answers for the domain. This includes the Primary DNS server for the zone, and any other DNS servers to which you delegate authority for the zone. The NS record is also used to direct DNS client requests to other DNS servers when the server is not authoritative for a zone. For example, when you issue a query for the microsoft.com domain, the .com domain DNS server is not authoritative for the microsoft.com domain. However, an NS record is contained on the .com DNS server that can return a referral answer to the requesting client, which will direct it to the microsoft.com DNS server.
A	Address (or Host)	The Address record contains the host name to IP address mapping for the particular host. The majority of the records in the zone will be A address records.
SRV	Service	The SRV record provides information about available services on a particular host. This is similar to the "service identifier" (the hidden 16th character) in NetBIOS environments. If a particular host is looking for a server to authenticate against, it will check for a SRV record to find an authenticating host. SRV records are particularly important in Windows 2000 domains. Since the DNS server is now the primary domain locator for Windows 2000 clients, the appropriate SRV records must be contained on the DNS server to inform Windows 2000 clients of the location of a Windows 2000 domain controller that can authenticate a log on request.

TABLE 26-2 Important Resource Record Types *(continued)*

Resource Record Type	Name	Description
CNAME	Canonical Name	This is an alias for a computer with an existing A record. For example, if you have a computer called "bigserver" that is going to be your Web server, you could create a CNAME for it, such as "www." It is important to note that you must have an A record for the host that you intend to create the alias for, since the CNAME record requests that you include the host name of the computer for which you wish to create the alias.
MX	Mail Exchanger	Identifies the preferred mail servers on the network. If you have several mail servers, an order of precedence will be run. Note that the MX record has similar requirements to the CNAME record. You must have an existing A record for the machine that you wish to create a MX record for.
HINFO	Host Information	HINFO records provide information about the DNS server itself. Information about the CPU and operating system on the host can be included in the HINFO record. This information is used by application protocols such as FTP that can use special procedures when communicating between computers of the same CPU and OS type. (RFC 1035)
PTR	Pointer	The Pointer record is created to allow for reverse lookups. Reverse lookups are valuable when doing security analysis and checking authenticity of source domains for e-mail.

When we add a specific host to a domain, we add an A record. If we have a mail server, we would add that server's name and IP address with an MX record. A single computer can have multiple records of different types. For example, your Web server's host name on the Internet would most likely be named "www." However, internally you may want to refer to it by another name, such as "bigserver." You would enter an A record for "bigserver" and then create a CNAME record for "www." Both records would map to the same IP address.

In order to populate your reverse lookup zones, you use the Pointer (PTR) records. A Pointer record contains the IP address to host name mappings required to answer reverse lookup requests.

Zone Delegation

Zone delegation provides a way for you to distribute responsibility for zone database management, and provides a measure of load balancing for DNS servers. When you create a delegation for a zone, you are "passing the buck" to another DNS server to answer DNS queries for a particular zone. Zones can be delegated to Secondary DNS Servers or Primaries.

In the earlier example, we talked about tacteam.net and how we distributed responsibility for its domains into two zones: the west.tacteam.net zone and the tacteam.net zone. Recall that the west.tacteam.net zone included the resource records for machines located in San Francisco, and the tacteam.net zone contained resource records for machines located in both Dallas and Boston.

You might be wondering at this point, "What DNS server actually answers the queries for these zones?" What we would like to do is have a machine located in San Francisco answer queries for the west.tacteam.net zone, and have machines in Dallas answer queries for the tacteam.net zone. In this way, the machines in Dallas don't have to answer all the queries for the entire tacteam.net domain and its subdomains.

Creating Delegations

The way we accomplish the goal is to create a delegation on a DNS server that is authoritative for the tacteam.net zone. You can create a delegation by making an NS record for the DNS server that is authoritative for the tacteam.net zone. In the present example, this delegation would point DNS clients to a DNS server in San Francisco that is authoritative for the west.tacteam.net zone.

You can create delegations for any domain for which a particular server is authoritative. For example, imagine for a moment that you are the DNS administrator for the .com domain. You do not want to be responsible for maintaining the zone database files for all the subdomains of the .com domain because that would be a monumental task. It would also put quite a bit of stress on your DNS servers. In order to distribute the responsibility for maintaining all the subdomains of the .com domain, you create *delegations* for each of those subdomains.

You would create a delegation, which includes an NS Record, for microsoft.com, syngress.com, osborne.com, and all the other .coms out there. When a DNS query is received by the .com DNS servers for one of these domains, the delegation record (NS resource record) will point the DNS client to the correct IP address of the DNS server authoritative for the zone.

In the example of tacteam.net, the .net DNS server will include a delegation record for the tacteam.net server, and the tacteam.net server will contain a delegation for the west.tacteam.net DNS server in San Francisco. The DNS server in San Francisco, which contains the resource records for the west.tacteam.net zone, will then be able to answer the DNS query authoritatively.

Glue Records

In Windows NT 4.0 when you created an NS record, the only information you had to include was the FQDN of the machine to be included in the referral. This lead to problems because in order to resolve the name of the machine noted in the delegation record, you had to have a Host (A) Address record to allow for the forward lookup.

This Host (A) Address record is referred to as a *glue record.* It's called a glue record because it associates the host name in the NS record with an IP address of the machine noted in the NS record. It glues together the name server's host name and IP address in this way.

Whenever you split your domains into subdomains, you must include on all parent domains delegation information, which will include NS records for authoritative servers and their corresponding glue records. This could be thought of as a *lame delegation.* Technically, a lame delegation occurs when the NS record points to a server that does not contain a zone database file relevant to the zone being referred to.

The Windows 2000 DNS server includes a *Delegation Wizard.* The Delegation Wizard will walk you through the process of creating delegations for your domains and subdomains. This takes a lot of the guesswork out of the process of creating NS records and delegations. In fact, if you try to manually add an NS record via the "Add New Record" command in the DNS console, you will find that you are not provided that option. In order to add an NS record, you will *have to* use the Delegation Wizard. You still may need to add your glue records manually.

Zone Transfer

In order to provide a measure of fault tolerance for the DNS zone database, the DNS was designed to have at least *two* DNS servers responsible for answering queries for each zone. As you will learn more about later, Standard zones support Primary and Secondary DNS zone types. A *Standard Primary zone* is the only read/write copy of the zone database file. A *Standard Secondary zone* is a read-only copy of the zone database file. The Primary and Secondary zones are contained on Primary and Secondary DNS servers for those zones. In order to copy the Primary zone file to the Secondary DNS server, a process of *zone transfer* is used.

Methods of Zone Transfer

The zone transfer process can be considered a "pull" operation. This is because the Secondary DNS server initiates the zone transfer process. The Secondary DNS server will initiate a zone transfer when:

- A Primary DNS server sends a "notify" message to the Secondary DNS server informing it that there has been a change to the zone database.
- The Secondary DNS server boots up.
- The Secondary DNS server's *Refresh Interval* has expired.

These are depicted in Figure 26-8.

The Secondary DNS server initiates the actual zone transfer. When the Secondary sends a "pull" request to the Primary DNS server, the first record the Primary DNS server sends is the *Start of Authority (SOA)* record. The SOA record is always the first record created on a DNS server authoritative for any particular zone.

The SOA record contains information about the *Refresh Interval.* The Secondary waits the amount of time specified by the Refresh Interval before asking for another update to its zone database file. The Refresh Interval determines how often the Primary DNS server for the zone updates the zone database on the Secondary.

When you create a new zone, it has a *serial number* of 1. Each time a change is made to the zone database on the Primary DNS server, the serial number is incremented by 1. Each time the Primary updates the Secondary's zone file, the

FIGURE 26-8

Zone transfer methods

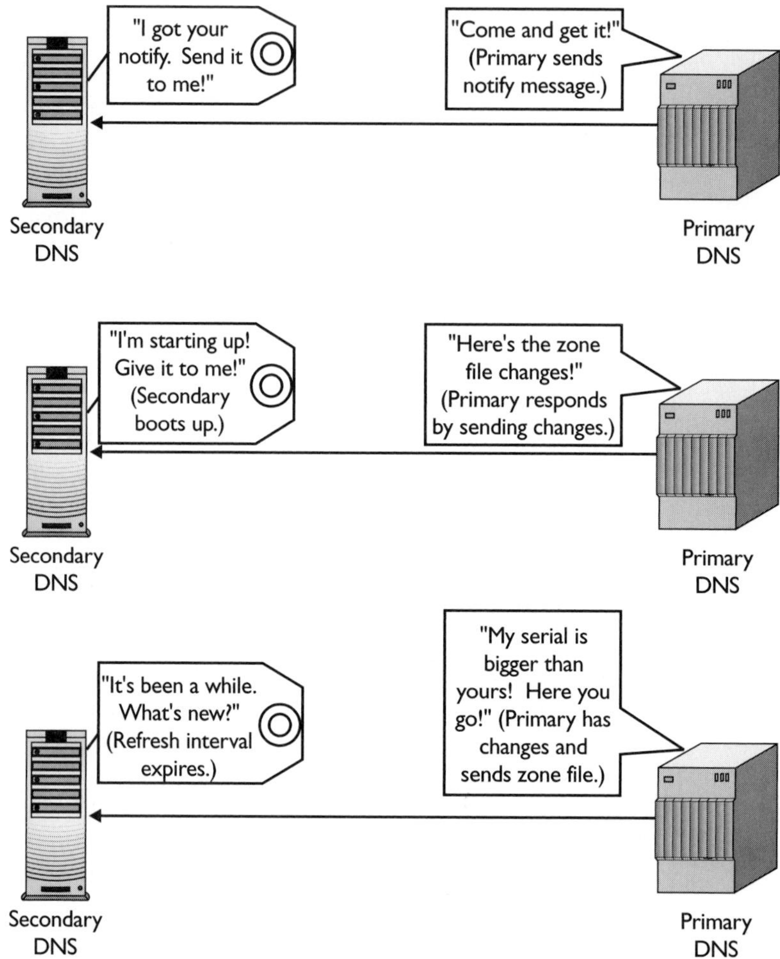

Secondary's zone serial number is updated to match the serial number of the Primary's zone database as of the time of the zone transfer.

The serial number is included in the SOA Record sent by the Primary DNS server when the Secondary initiates the zone transfer. The Secondary examines the serial number in the SOA record and compares it to the serial number of its own zone file. If the Primary DNS server's serial number is larger, the Secondary sends one of two types of queries that begin the zone transfer process.

Types of Zone Transfer

Windows 2000 DNS server supports two types of zone transfer, depending on what type of query request is sent to it from the Secondary DNS server:

- Entire Zone Transfer (AXFR)
- Incremental Zone Transfer (IXFR)

AXFR Queries Secondary DNS servers that only support the AXFR query type will receive a copy of the *entire* zone database file during the zone transfer process. The Windows NT 4.0 DNS server is only capable of asking for a copy of the zone database file via an AXFR request, and therefore always receives the entire zone database, regardless of how many changes have been made to the database since the last time it queried the Primary DNS server for changes in the DNS zone database file.

IXFR Queries Windows 2000 Secondary servers are able to include in their requests information about the serial number of the zone database they currently own. These servers are able to issue IXFR queries, which allow for *incremental* zone transfers. During an incremental zone transfer, only records that have changed since the last zone transfer are sent to the Secondary DNS server. Sending only the records that have been changed saves bandwidth during the zone transfer process.

Windows 2000 DNS Servers Can Respond to Both IXFR and AXFR Requests

A Windows 2000 DNS server is able to respond to both AXFR and IXFR queries. In addition, a Windows 2000 DNS server that is acting as a Secondary can send both AXFR and IXFR queries. This allows the Windows 2000 DNS server to be flexible in networks that have a mix of Windows 2000 and downlevel DNS servers.

There are times when the Primary will send the *entire* zone database in spite of receiving an IXFR request. These circumstances include:

- The sum of the changes is larger than the entire zone.
- The age of the Secondary's zone database exceeds the number of changes tracked in the Primary's change log.
- The DNS server doesn't know what to do with an IXFR request.

In the first situation, it would make no sense to send the changes if the number of changes exceeds the number of records in the entire zone database file. To do so would waste bandwidth needlessly. The second situation is comparable to the change log that is kept by Windows NT 4.0 domain controllers that is used to determine which records in the Security Accounts Manager (SAM) database need to be sent to the backup domain controllers (BDCs). If the Secondary has a zone with a serial number out of range of those being tracked in the Primary's change log, then the entire zone file will be sent to ensure the integrity of zones on the Secondary. The third situation is seen when a Windows 2000 Secondary sends an IXFR to a downlevel Primary, such as a Windows NT 4.0 DNS server. In this case, the Windows NT 4.0 Primary will send the entire zone database file.

exam Watch

Be sure you know which DNS servers support which types of zone transfers. Remember that a Windows 2000 DNS server can respond to either AXFR or IXFR queries from downlevel servers such as the Windows NT 4.0 DNS server.

Masters, Secondaries, and Slaves

Understanding the relationships between servers transferring zone databases and what to call them can get confusing. It's important here to make some critical distinctions.

The server that is transferring the zone file to another server is called the *Master* server. The server receiving the zone files can be called either a *Slave* server or a *Secondary* server. It is preferred to refer to the machine receiving the zone file as a secondary, because the term *Slave DNS server* has another meaning that refers to an inability to perform recursion for DNS clients.

Another thing to know is that a Primary DNS server can also act as a Secondary for another zone. For example, dns.shinder.net is the Primary DNS server for the shinder.net zone. There is a Secondary for the shinder.net zone named dns1.shinder.net. We can make dns1.shinder.net a Secondary for the shinder.net zone. We have another DNS server that is the Primary for the tacteam.net zone named dns.tacteam.net. We want it to be a Secondary for the shinder.net zone. When dns1.shinder.net transfers the zone database for the shinder.net zone to dns.tacteam.net, dns1.shinder.net then becomes the Master for the zone transfer (Figure 26-9).

The Retry Interval

There are going to be times when the Primary is not available when the Secondary sends its pull request. To deal with this inevitable situation, the Start of Authority

FIGURE 26-9 How Secondaries can become Masters

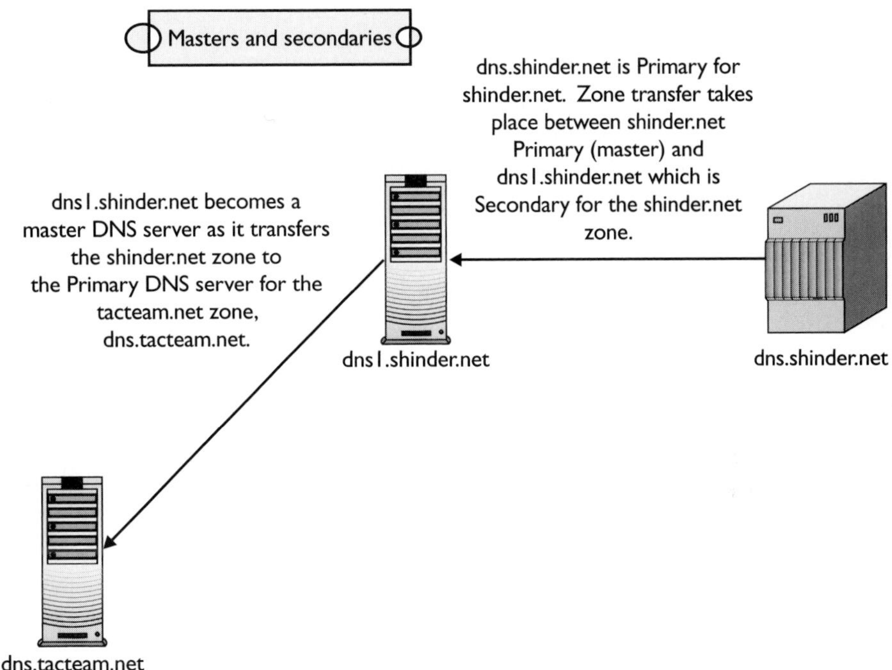
Masters and secondaries
dns.shinder.net is Primary for shinder.net. Zone transfer takes place between shinder.net Primary (master) and dns1.shinder.net which is Secondary for the shinder.net zone.
dns1.shinder.net becomes a master DNS server as it transfers the shinder.net zone to the Primary DNS server for the tacteam.net zone, dns.tacteam.net.
dns1.shinder.net
dns.shinder.net
dns.tacteam.net

(SOA) record includes information about a *Retry Interval*. The Retry Interval defines the period of time the Secondary should wait until sending another pull request message. The Secondary will continue to retry the zone transfer until it is successful in contacting the Primary for its zone.

When setting the Retry Interval, remember to make it shorter than the Refresh Interval. Otherwise, there's no sense in even setting a Retry Interval, since it will retry anyhow during the new Refresh.

Compatibility of DNS Server Versions

If you are running a mixed DNS environment that includes both Windows 2000 and downlevel DNS servers (Berkeley Internet Name Domain [BIND] and Windows NT 4.0), then there are some issues you will need to address to minimize problems you might encounter.

Incremental Zone Transfers Some downlevel DNS servers do not support incremental zone transfer. They cannot issue an IXFR query to the Master server.

Downlevel DNS servers only issue AXFR queries. However, as mentioned earlier, the Windows 2000 DNS server is able to respond to downlevel clients' AXFR requests. The major issue you will need to deal with here is that of bandwidth consumption. If you have planned your DNS replication topology around the benefits of incremental zone transfers, you may want to make some changes to your DNS server network if you have Secondaries that do not support IXFR.

Fast Transfers The Windows 2000 DNS server supports a method of zone transfer that allows multiple records to be included in a single message. This compressed form of zone file transfer is referred to as a *fast transfer*. Not all DNS servers support the fast transfer mode, although most of the popular ones do. One popular DNS server that does not support fast transfers is BIND versions before 4.9.4. Subsequent versions of BIND do support the fast transfer mode. If you do maintain BIND versions lower than 4.9.4, you can use the Advanced Options in the DNS server to indicate you have BIND Secondaries, and this disabled the fast transfer mode. (Note: It is recommended that if you are using BIND that you upgrade to BIND version 8.2.2 patchlevel 5 for security reasons.)

WINS and WINS-R Records Windows 2000 and Windows NT 4.0 DNS server support WINS and WINS-R records. These resource records allow a DNS server to perform forward and reverse lookups by referring to a WINS server. Since WINS is a Microsoft Proprietary technology, other DNS implementations do not support the WINS and WINS-R resource records. This may cause problems when transferring a zone from a Windows 2000 Primary to a third-party Secondary. If you have DNS servers that do not support Windows Internet Name System (WINS) and Windows Internet Name System-Reverse (WINS-R) records, you can prevent these records from being transferred by selecting the check box for "do not replicate this record" in the WINS and WINS-R tabs in the appropriate forward and reverse lookup zones.

Third-Party Transfers to Windows 2000 DNS Servers If you have third-party DNS servers that act as Primaries for Secondary Windows 2000 DNS servers, you may run into a situation where the third-party products supports resource record types that are not supported by Windows 2000 DNS servers. When the Windows 2000 machine receives record types that it does not support, it will drop the record and continue with the zone transfer process.

Table 26-3 sums up the compatibility issues you may run into when running in a mixed DNS server environment.

Be sure to check out this table when implementing a Windows 2000 DNS server in a mixed environment. This is especially important if you are introducing Windows 2000 DNS into an established DNS environment where UNIX DNS servers are already deployed. It is extremely important that you work closely with the UNIX DNS administrators during all phases of your Windows 2000 DNS deployment.

TABLE 26-3 Comparison of Support Features Among Popular DNS Servers

Feature	Windows 2000	Windows NT 4.0	BIND 8.2	BIND 8.1.2	BIND 4.9.7
SRV records	Yes	Yes (with SP4)	Yes	Yes	Yes
Dynamic Update	Yes	No	Yes	Yes	No
Secure Dynamic Update (GSS-TSIG)	Yes	No	No	No	No
WINS/WINS-R	Yes	Yes	No	No	No
Fast Transfer	Yes	Yes	Yes	Yes	Yes
IXFR	Yes	No	Yes	No	No
UTF-8	Yes	No	No	No	No

CERTIFICATION OBJECTIVE 26.02

How Host Names Are Resolved

WinSock applications require the IP address of the destination host to establish a session. However, most people find numbers difficult to remember, so most users prefer to use host names to access resources. The process of matching up an IP address to a known host name is called *host name resolution.*

The DNS client must have some method of formulating a question that the DNS server can understand before it can send an answer. *Resolver* software on the DNS client formulates and issues query statements sent to the DNS server. Resolver software can be included in the WinSock application, or in the case of Windows 2000, it can be a component of the operating system. The Windows 2000 operating system has a system-wide caching resolver. Examples of WinSock programs that make use of resolver software include:

- Web browsers (such as Microsoft Internet Explorer)
- FTP clients (such as the command-line FTP program found in Windows 2000)
- Telnet clients
- DNS servers

exam Watch

Any program or service that issues DNS queries uses resolver software. The resolver can be included within the application itself, or it may take advantage of a system-wide resolver, such as that included with Windows 2000.

The Order of Host Name Resolution

No, this is not a secret religious order, it is the order of methods the DNS client service uses in an attempt to resolve a host name to an IP address. You may remember learning this in your Windows NT 4.0 studies when you learned the Host Name Resolution Sequence: Large Hard Drives? Can We Buy Legally? (localhost, HOSTS, DNS, NetBIOS Remote Name Cache, WINS, Broadcast, LMHOSTS). Things have changed a little since Windows NT 4.0.

The Windows 2000 resolver now caches the contents of the HOSTS file on system startup. You will remember the HOSTS file as a static text file that stores host name to IP address mappings. When an entry is entered into the HOSTS file and the file is saved, the entries will be immediately placed into the local computer's DNS cache. This saves some time since the HOSTS text file itself does not have to be loaded and searched each time access to those entries is required.

When the resolver receives a request for an entry that is longer than 15 bytes, or if it contains a period, it will be sent through the host name resolution sequence. If the request does not meet either of these specifications, it will be sent through the NetBIOS name resolution sequence.

Once the request begins the host name resolution sequence, the first step is to check whether the destination is the local host. If not, the local DNS client will check its own DNS cache. Note that at this point it does *not* check the HOSTS file, as was the case with Windows NT 4.0, because the contents of the HOSTS file have been loaded into cache. If the destination host's IP address is not in the local DNS cache, the query will be sent to the DNS client's Preferred DNS server. If the DNS server cannot resolve the query, the host name portion of the fully qualified domain name (FQDN) will be processed through the NetBIOS name resolution sequence.

So, when remembering the host name resolution sequence for Windows 2000, think of L C D C W B L (Liquid Crystal Displays? Can We Buy Legally?, or think of a better one yourself).

The Windows 2000 Caching Resolver

We have touched on the local client's DNS cache in the preceding section. You should know that Windows 2000 includes a system-wide *caching resolver.* This caching resolver is responsible for formulating and issuing queries on behalf of the DNS client for host name resolution. The caching resolver is implemented as part of the *DNS Client Service.*

The caching resolver is able to cache both positive and negative responses. When a positive response is cached, the time-to-live (TTL) on the record returned to the client is respected by the DNS client receiving the DNS response. For example, if you resolve *www.shinder.net* to 209.217.17.13, the response from the DNS server resolving the request will include a TTL for that record.

The caching resolver not only caches queries that have been answered positively, but also caches negative results as well. When a DNS query fails, this failed result is placed in cache for five minutes, by default. If the machines issues a DNS query for the same object within five minutes, no query will be sent, and a failure message will

FIGURE 26-10

A negatively cached DNS query

```
C:\>ipconfig /displaydns

Windows 2000 IP Configuration

   localhost.
   ------------------------------------------------------
     Record Name . . . . . : localhost
     Record Type . . . . . : 1
     Time To Live  . . . . : 31502561
     Data Length . . . . . : 4
     Section . . . . . . . : Answer
     A (Host) Record . . . :
                             127.0.0.1


   1.0.0.127.in-addr.arpa.
   ------------------------------------------------------
     Record Name . . . . . : 1.0.0.127.in-addr.arpa
     Record Type . . . . . : 12
     Time To Live  . . . . : 31502561
     Data Length . . . . . : 4
     Section . . . . . . . : Answer
     PTR Record  . . . . . :
                             localhost


   www.not-there.microsoft.com.
   ------------------------------------------------------
          Negative cache entry for name error
```

be retrieved from cache. This can significantly reduce the overall DNS query traffic on a large network. Figure 26-10 shows an example of a negatively cached DNS query result.

Recursive Queries

When you type an FQDN in the address bar of a Web browser, the resolver formulates a DNS query and sends the query to the client's Preferred DNS server. The DNS client most often will send a *recursive query.* When a recursive query is sent to the client's Preferred DNS server, the server *must* respond to the query either positively or negatively. A positive response returns the IP address; a negative response returns a "host not found" or similar error. A recursive query is one that requires a definitive response, either affirmative or negative. A *Referral* response from the DNS server is not an option.

If you were asked "Who was the 17th president of the United States?," how might you go about answering this question? You could give the correct answer (a positive response), or admit that you don't know (a negative response). This type of query where you only have two options is an example of a recursive query. When you were in the process of figuring out the answer, you were performing recursion (i.e., coming up with a definitive answer).

Iterative Queries

Is there any other approach you can use to answer the question? Yes! You could say, "Hold on, I'm going to find out and get some help with this recursion." Then you would ask other people, who might *refer* you to other people who *might* know the answer. You have this option if I were to issue to you an *iterative* query.

Iterative queries allow the DNS server responding to the request to make a best-effort attempt at resolving the DNS query. If the DNS server receiving an iterative query is not authoritative for the domain included in the query, it can return a *Referral* response. The Referral contains the IP address of another DNS server that may be able to service the query. The Referral is based on information contained in delegations (NS records) on the DNS server being queried.

The DNS client sends a recursive query to its Preferred DNS server. If the Preferred DNS server is not authoritative for the host domain in the query, it will issue a series of iterative queries to other DNS servers. Each queried DNS server can respond with a Referral to another DNS server that brings the query closer to resolution. Figure 26-11 displays an iterative query in progress.

Passing the Buck

When the DNS client sends a recursive query to its Preferred DNS server, it asks for recursion. Think of this as a way for the DNS client to "pass the buck" and get someone else to do the actual work of resolving the DNS query. It becomes the DNS server's responsibility to find the answer. There are several advantages in having the DNS client issue recursive requests rather than having each DNS client perform its own recursion:

- There is much less network traffic when a DNS server performs recursion rather than having each client perform its own.
- The DNS server maintains a cache of host names and domains that it has recently resolved. All machines using a particular DNS server benefit from having access to this centralized cache.
- There are security risks to having machines access external DNS servers. You can strategically place your DNS servers so that no external DNS server ever requires access to a DNS server located on the internal network.

So, while "passing the buck" might sound like a bad thing at first, a lot of good comes out of having the DNS client issue recursive requests to its Preferred DNS servers.

FIGURE 26-11

Using iterative queries to resolve a host name

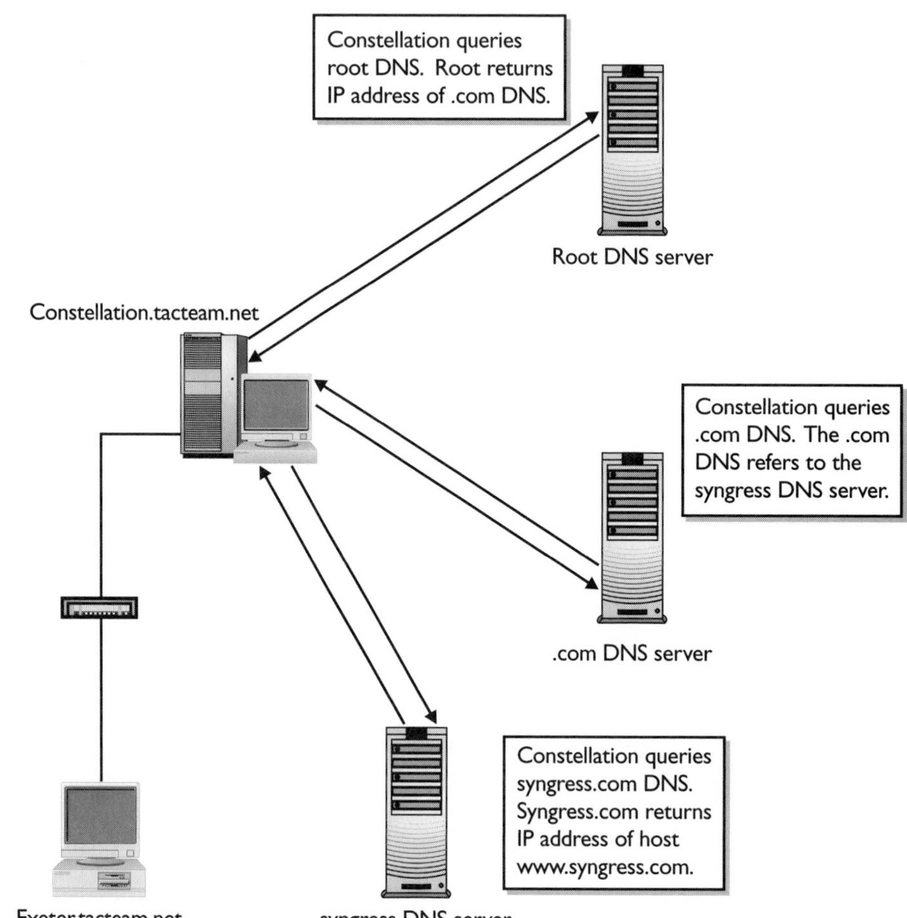
Constellation queries root DNS. Root returns IP address of .com DNS.
Root DNS server
Constellation.tacteam.net
Constellation queries .com DNS. The .com DNS refers to the syngress DNS server.
.com DNS server
Constellation queries syngress.com DNS. Syngress.com returns IP address of host www.syngress.com.
Exeter.tacteam.net
syngress DNS server

Looking Up an Address from a Name

The following represents the sequence of events during the host name resolution process using both recursive and iterative queries. In this example, we want to connect to a Web server named Exeter at tacteam.net. (Note that in this example, the query is for an FQDN and *not* an *unqualified* request.)

Type **exeter.tacteam.net** in the address bar of the Web browser and press ENTER. After pressing ENTER, the resolver formulates a recursive DNS query and sends it to the client's Preferred DNS server.

The Preferred DNS server will check to see if it is authoritative for the zone in the query. The server will also check its cache to see if it has recently resolved the same host name and to see if it has the IP address of a DNS server authoritative for the zone included in the query. If the required information is not in its cache, and if the DNS server is not authoritative for the queried domain, it will send an iterative query to an Internet Root Name server. At this point, the Preferred DNS server becomes a DNS client itself and uses its own caching resolver to formulate the iterative DNS queries. The Preferred DNS server starts the iterative query process in order to complete recursion. Once recursion is complete, a definitive answer can be returned to the client.

The Root Name server is not authoritative for tacteam.net. However, the Internet Root DNS server is authoritative for all top-level domains and contains delegations for all of them. This includes the .net domain. The Root server sends the IP address of a DNS server authoritative for the .net domain to the Preferred DNS server.

The Preferred DNS server connects to a DNS server authoritative for the .net domain. The .net domain DNS server is not authoritative for the tacteam.net domain. However, the .net DNS server does contain a delegation record that points to the DNS server authoritative for the tacteam.net domain. The .net domain DNS server returns to the Preferred DNS server the IP address for the DNS server authoritative for the tacteam.net domain.

At this point, the Preferred DNS server queries the DNS server authoritative for the tacteam.net domain. The tacteam.net DNS server checks its zone files for a Host (A) resource record for Exeter. Exeter is located in the tacteam.net domain, and there is an Address record for it in the zone database. The tacteam.net DNS server responds to the Preferred DNS server with the IP address of host computer Exeter.

The Preferred DNS server has completed recursion. It responds to the client with a recursive response and sends the IP address of exeter.tacteam.net. You can now establish a session to the destination host because the IP address is known. If the tacteam.net DNS server did not have a Host (A) resource record for Exeter, the Preferred server would have replied negatively to the query.

In this example, both the DNS client and the Preferred server acted as resolvers in the process. The example is depicted in Figure 26-12.

FIGURE 26-12

Performing both recursive and iterative queries

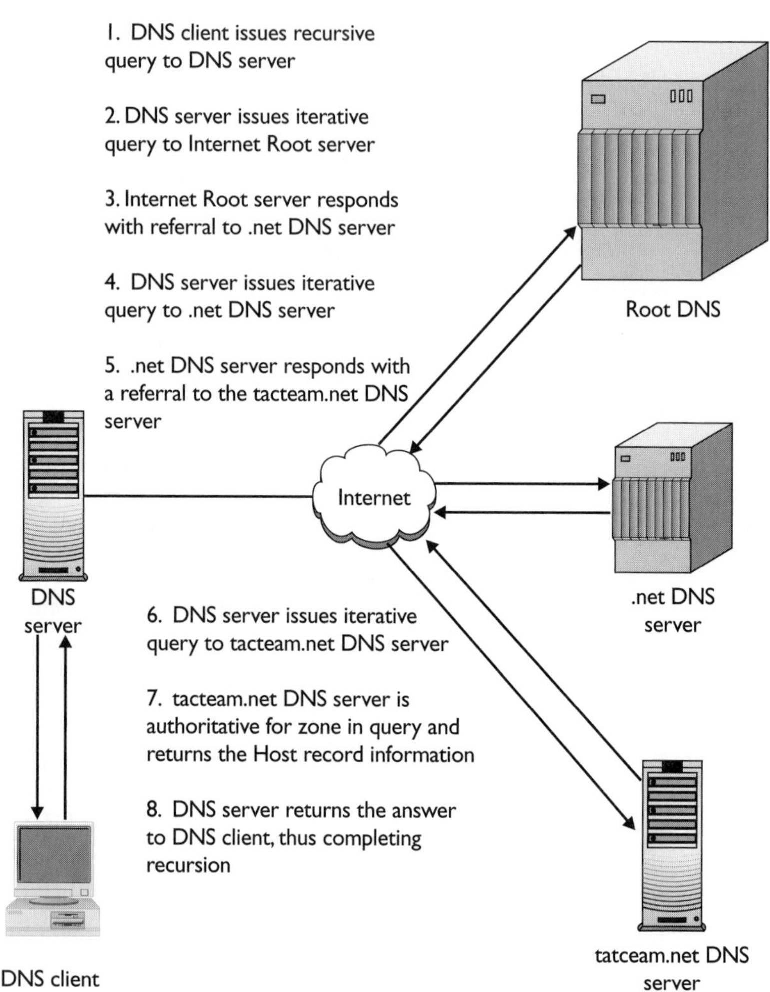

1. DNS client issues recursive query to DNS server
2. DNS server issues iterative query to Internet Root server
3. Internet Root server responds with referral to .net DNS server
4. DNS server issues iterative query to .net DNS server
5. .net DNS server responds with a referral to the tacteam.net DNS server
Root DNS
DNS server
Internet
.net DNS server
6. DNS server issues iterative query to tacteam.net DNS server
7. tacteam.net DNS server is authoritative for zone in query and returns the Host record information
8. DNS server returns the answer to DNS client, thus completing recursion
DNS client
tatceam.net DNS server

EXERCISE 26-2

Performing a Forward Lookup

In this exercise, you will perform a forward lookup by querying a forward lookup zone. In order to complete this exercise, you will need to be connected to the Internet via a modem or a network connection that allows nslookup queries to pass through any existing firewalls.

1. Log on as Administrator.
2. Open the Command Prompt from the Accessories menu.
3. At the Command Prompt, type: **nslookup www.tacteam.net** (be sure to include the trailing period).
4. You should see what appears in the following illustration. Note that you will see our Internet IP address 198.41.0.9 rather than our intranet IP address.

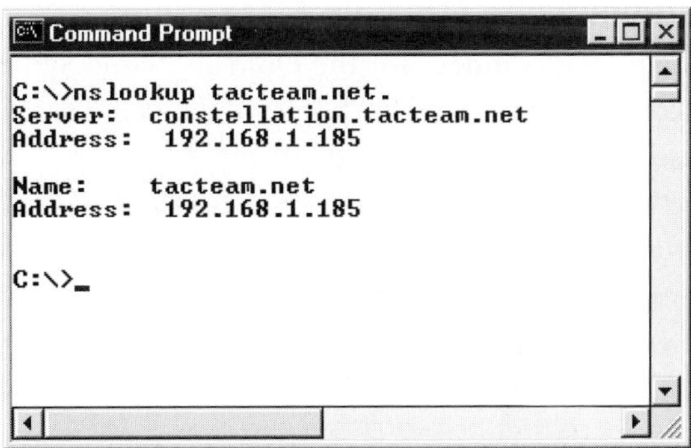

Looking Up a Name from an Address

We have examined how a host name is resolved to an IP address. Occasionally, we need to do the opposite: resolve a known IP address to a host name. IP address to host name resolution can aid in investigating suspicious activity. Many security analysis programs use IP address to host name resolution. The process of resolving a known IP address to a host name is called a *reverse lookup*, in contrast to the forward lookup where a host name is resolved to an IP address. Reverse lookups query *reverse lookup zones.*

As you saw earlier, a HOSTS file can be used to map host names to IP addresses. It is simple to search the HOSTS file to find an IP address to host name mapping. However, this becomes much more complex when dealing with a worldwide distributed database.

Indexing the Domain Databases

The primary "index" for the Domain Name System is the domain name. The DNS is comparable to a phone book, which is indexed by last names. Forward lookups are based on a similar indexing scheme. Locating a domain name using the IP address as the value would require an exhaustive search of the entire DNS. This would be like trying to find the person associated with a particular phone number by using a conventional phone book. Reverse lookups could be accomplished this way, but performance would be so dismal, they would be of no use.

The in-addr.arpa Domain

The answer lies in creating *another* domain that uses Network IDs as the index value. Then we can search this domain in the same way we searched the forward lookup zones. This is the *in-addr.arpa* domain.

Each node in the in-addr.arpa domain is named after numbers found in the w, x, y, and z octets of the Network ID. Each level (or branch) in the in-addr.arpa domain can contain 256 (0–255) domains corresponding to the possible values for each octet. The leaf objects in the in-addr.arpa domain are the actual resource records (PTR records) that contain the IP address to host name mapping.

The in-addr.arpa zone file notation mimics the forward lookup zone construction. For example, if tacteam.net has a Network ID of 21.18.189.0, the in-addr.arpa subdomain is 189.18.21.in-addr.arpa. This maps to the domain name tacteam.net. Just as forward lookup zones go from specific to general when moving from left to right, so do the reverse lookup zones.

This arrangement allows Network ID based domains to be hierarchical in the same fashion as the forward lookup zones. The Network IDs themselves are assigned by central authorities in the same way that root, top-level, and second-level domain spaces are centrally managed. Like subdomains within the second-level domain, you can subdivide or subnet your Network ID any way you like.

We can delegate authority for a reverse lookup zone in the same way as is done for the forward lookup zones. For example, the 126.in-addr.arpa domain contains reverse mappings for all hosts and subdomains whose IP addresses start with 126. The administrator of network 126 can delegate authority for the 256 subdomains of the 126.in-addr.arpa domain. The American Registry for Internet Numbers is the central authority that manages the delegations for the in-addr.arpa domain. You can find more information about them at www.arin.net.

The iterative and recursive query process works the same when performing reverse lookups as it does when performing forward lookups.

CERTIFICATION OBJECTIVE 26.03

Windows 2000 DNS Server Roles

A Windows 2000 DNS server can take on a variety of different roles. We will focus on Standard DNS zones in this section. Zone databases can be integrated with the Active Directory. When the zone database is integrated with the Active Directory, some of the concepts discussed in this section may not apply. We'll talk more about Active Directory integrated zones later in this chapter.

A Windows 2000 DNS server may take the role of:

- Primary DNS server
- Secondary DNS server
- DNS Forwarder
- Caching-only server
- DNS slave server
- Dynamic update server

Each role determines how the zone database is handled on the server and/or how DNS client queries are evaluated. First, let's examine the different DNS server roles.

Primary DNS Server

A Primary DNS server contains the only copy of the zone database that can be changed. A Primary DNS server is *authoritative* for the domain or domains contained in its zone files. Primary DNS servers are authoritative because they can respond directly to DNS queries. Primary DNS servers share characteristics with all DNS servers, including:

- Zone database information is stored in the %systemroot%>\system32\dns directory.
- The ability to boot from either the registry or a boot file.
- The ability to cache resolved queries.
- A cache.dns file (or "*root hints*" file) that contains host name to IP address mappings for the Internet DNS Root servers.

All zone files are stored in the %systemroot%\system32\dns directory. Zone file names are based on the name of the zone and are appended with the ".dns" file extension. For example, the tacteam.net zone file is named tacteam.net.dns.

Configuring the DNS Server via the Boot File and DNS Management Console

A Windows 2000 DNS server's configuration information is stored in the Registry. Server configuration is done via the DNS Management console. This is the default and preferred setting.

You may choose to administer the DNS server configuration via a file called BOOT. UNIX Administrators are accustomed to manipulating DNS server behavior by manipulating the BOOT file.

You can choose to boot from:

- The Registry
- The **BOOT** file
- Active Directory and the Registry

These configuration choices can be made in the Advanced tab for the DNS server you are administrating.

Microsoft recommends that you use either the BOOT file or the DNS Management Console exclusively, and not switch between the two. This is because errors may occur when editing the BOOT file directory that the DNS console may not be able to handle efficiently. Choose one or the other and stick with it.

DNS Server Caching

All DNS servers cache resolved queries. When a DNS server issues an iterative query to another DNS server, the results are placed in the requesting server's cache. Cached information is stored in system memory and is not written to disk. Because the cached DNS is stored solely in RAM, the information is lost after a server reboot. Therefore, DNS servers are most effective when reboots are avoided.

The cache.dns file (also known as the Root Hints file) will typically contain host name and IP address mappings for the Root Internet DNS servers. If a DNS server receives a recursive query for a domain for which it is not authoritative, it must complete recursion by issuing iterative queries. The iterative query process may begin with the Root DNS servers if the target domain in the DNS query is not contained in the DNS server's cache. The cache.dns file is located in the same directory as the zone files.

The Internet Root server mappings change periodically. You can download the current Internet Root server mappings from:

ftp://ftp.rs.internic.net/domain/root.zone.gz

DNS Servers Can Be Authoritative for Multiple Domains

A DNS server can be authoritative for multiple domains. For example, the tacteam.net.dns zone file can contain entries authoritative for tacteam.net and dev.tactem.net. Since it is authoritative for these domains, it does not need to issue iterative queries to other DNS servers in order to resolve the request.

As we learned earlier, a Primary DNS server can also be a Secondary DNS server. A Primary DNS server that receives zone transfers from another Primary server acts in the role of Secondary. Any DNS server can contain either or both Primary or Secondary zone files. The only difference between the two is that the Primary zone file is read/write, while the Secondary zone file is read-only.

This leads us to the next subject: How do we provide fault tolerance for zone database files? And how can we gain a measure of load balancing for our DNS servers? A corporation is highly dependent on reliable host name resolution in order to access both intranet and Internet servers. In order to provide for fault tolerance, we configure Secondary DNS servers.

on the job

You will find that various administrators, enterprise architects, and writers use the terms Primary and Secondary DNS servers. The server software is the same for both. What makes a machine a Primary or Secondary DNS server is the type of zone files it contains. This explains why a machine can be both a Primary and Secondary DNS server: because it contains both Primary and Secondary DNS zone files.

Secondary DNS Servers

The Domain Name System was designed to include at least two DNS servers authoritative for each zone. Secondary DNS servers are authoritative for the zones they contain. Secondary DNS servers provide the following functions:

- **Fault tolerance** If the Primary DNS server is somehow disabled, the Secondary can answer requests for the zone.
- **Load balancing** By distributing the query load, the Primary server is not as impacted by large volumes of query traffic.
- **Bandwidth conservation** Secondary servers can be placed in remote locations, which reduces the need to traverse a WAN for name resolution.

Zone Fault Tolerance

Like Primary servers, Secondary DNS servers contain zone database files. The copy is received via zone transfer. A Primary DNS server for the zone acts as a *Master server* and copies the zone file to the Secondary during a zone transfer. Secondary DNS servers can answer DNS client queries; therefore, they are also authoritative for the zones they contain. DNS clients are configured with the IP addresses of Preferred and Alternate DNS servers for fault tolerance. Name resolution services can continue without interruption by querying the Secondary server if the Primary should become disabled.

Zone Load Balancing and Bandwidth Preservation

Load balancing allows you to distribute the DNS query load among multiple DNS servers. A single DNS server could be overwhelmed by name query traffic if all client computers were to access a single Primary server simultaneously. Clients on different segments can be configured to query local Secondary servers. This disperses the query load among Primary and Secondary DNS servers for a zone.

Fault tolerance, load balancing, and bandwidth preservation provide cogent reasons to implement Secondary DNS servers. If you plan to maintain your own DNS servers on the Internet, the Domain Registrar will require you to have at least one Primary and one Secondary DNS server for your second-level domain.

Caching-Only Servers

All DNS servers cache results of queries they have resolved. The *caching-only* DNS server does not contain zone information or a zone file. The caching-only server builds its database of host name and domain mappings over time from successful DNS queries it has resolved for DNS clients.

All DNS servers have a cache.dns file that contains the IP addresses of all Internet Root servers. The Windows 2000 cache.dns file is also referred to as the *root hints* file. You can view the contents of the Root Hints file via the DNS server properties dialog box, as seen in Figure 26-13. The caching-only server uses this list to begin building its cache. It adds to the cache as it issues iterative queries when responding to client requests.

Caching-only servers are valuable because:

- They do not generate zone transfer traffic.
- They can be placed on the far side of a slow WAN link and provide name resolution services for remote offices that do not require a high level of host name resolution support.
- They can be configured as secure DNS forwarders.

Satellite locations are often connected to the main office via slow WAN links. These locations benefit from caching-only servers for a couple of reasons, which follow.

- There is no zone transfer traffic. For large corporate intranets with small remote branches, eliminating zone transfer traffic can be very beneficial, since these offices often have a slow link to the corporate headquarters.
- DNS queries do not have to traverse the WAN after an adequate cache is built from successfully resolved queries.

These caching-only servers do not require expert administration. A satellite office is unlikely to have trained DNS administrative staff onsite. This saves the cost of having an experienced DNS administrator visit the site.

on the job

There is no risk of an intruder obtaining zone information from a caching-only server. Therefore, caching-only servers make excellent candidates for forwarders.

FIGURE 26-13

The Root Hints tab in the DNS server Properties dialog box

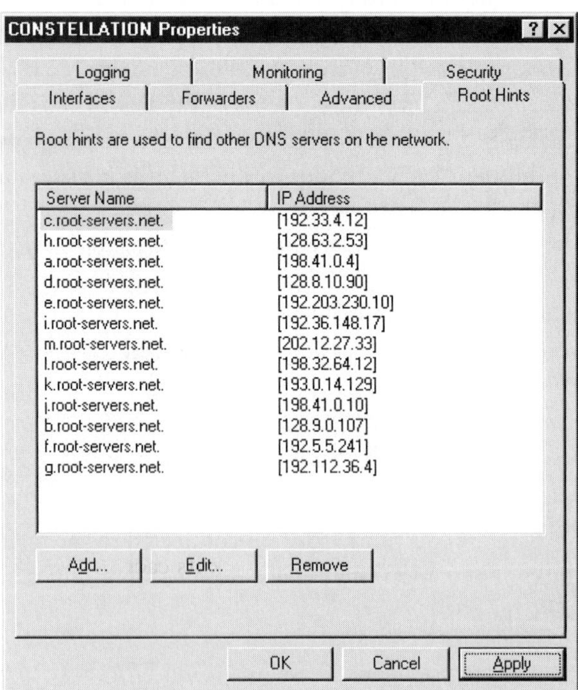

DNS Forwarders and Slave Servers

A DNS forwarder is a DNS server that accepts recursive queries from another DNS server. Caching-only servers make good forwarders. A forwarder can be used to protect internal zone files from Internet access.

For example, a DNS client sends a recursive query to its Preferred DNS server. The request is for a host in a domain for which the Preferred server is not authoritative.

The Preferred server must resolve the host name for the client or return a "host not found" or similar error. You can configure the DNS client's Preferred DNS server to *forward* all queries for which it is not authoritative. This DNS server issues a recursive query to another DNS server called a *forwarder*.

Forwarding and Forwarder Servers

Some of the terms used in the forwarding process require clarification. In our example, the client's Preferred server is "forwarding" the request to the "forwarder." The client's Preferred server is the *forwarding* DNS server. The DNS server receiving the forwarding server's query is the *forwarder*. Therefore, the process of forwarding a DNS query involves both a *forwarding* DNS server and a *forwarder* DNS server.

exam Watch

Be careful not to be fooled on the exam by the terms* forwarder *and* forwarding *DNS server. You might be tricked by the question using one or the other term in the wrong context in order to trip you up.

Host Name Lookup Using Forwarders The forwarder begins to resolve the host name in the query. It can do this by retrieving the information from its cache, from a zone file, or by issuing a series of iterative queries. If successful, it will answer the recursive query affirmatively and return the IP address to the forwarding server. The forwarding server completes its recursion by returning this IP address to the DNS client that initiated the query (Figure 26-14).

If the forwarder cannot resolve the host name to an IP address, it will return to the forwarding DNS server a "host not found" error. If this happens, the Preferred DNS server (the forwarding server) will attempt to resolve the host name itself. The forwarding server will check its cache, zone files, or perform iterative queries to resolve the host name. If unsuccessful, a "host not found" or similar error is finally returned to the client.

You may not want the forwarding DNS server to issue iterative queries to servers located on the Internet. This may be true when the forwarding server is an internal

DNS server. Internal DNS servers that issue iterative queries for Internet host name resolution are easy targets for hackers.

You can configure the forwarding server to not resolve host names when the forwarder fails to return a valid IP address. When the forwarding computer is configured in this fashion, it is referred to as a *slave* server. The slave server accepts responses from the forwarder and relays them to the client without attempting host name resolution itself, which it would do if the forwarder were not able to answer the query.

FIGURE 26-14

The forwarder completing recursion for the forwarding server

Bottom: The forwarding server completing recursion via its own iterative queries

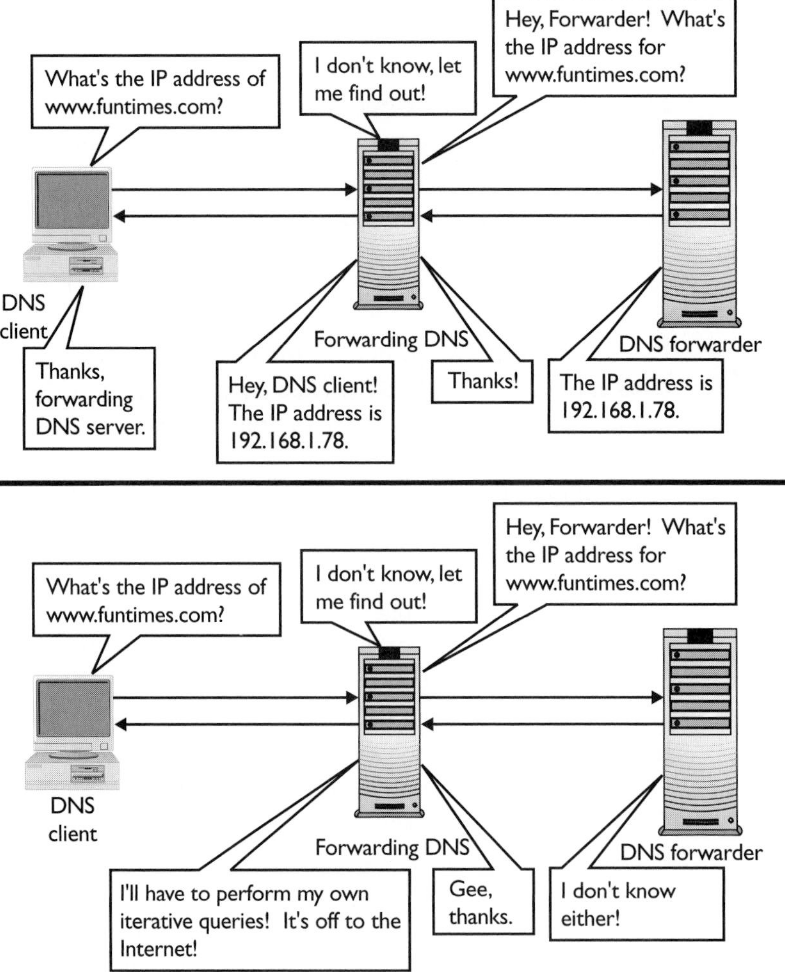

Forwarders and Firewalls The *slave server/caching-only forwarder* combination is very helpful in protecting your intranet zone data from Internet intruders. We can use this combination to prevent users on the other side of a firewall from having access to information on our Internal DNS server.

For example, at tacteam.net we have an internal DNS server we use to resolve DNS requests for resources inside of our corporate environment. As long as the requests are only for hosts in our internal network, DNS requests represent no security risk. However, what happens when users on the internal network need to access resources on the Internet?

Let's say a user wants to connect to www.funtimes.com. When the recursive request hits our internal DNS server (which is authoritative for only tacteam.net), what does the server do? It begins to issue iterative queries to other DNS servers on the Internet in order to resolve the Internet host name. In the process, Internet DNS servers must send their responses directly to our internal DNS machine through the firewall. This exposes our internal DNS server, its zone data, and the nature of our requests to users on the Internet. How can we avoid this potentially dangerous situation?

The Solution

We can place a caching-only forwarder on the outside of a firewall and configure our internal DNS server to be a slave server. Now, when one of our clients issues a name resolution request for an Internet host to our internal DNS server, the internal server will forward the request to the forwarder on the outside of the firewall. The forwarder will attempt to resolve the host name to an IP address. If successful, it will return the IP address to our internal DNS server, which will in turn return the IP address to the client that issued the request. If the forwarder is unsuccessful, it will report that to our internal server, which will report to the client that the host was not found. Our internal slave server will *not* attempt to resolve the host name itself. The slave then returns what the forward told it to the DNS client, and the query fails.

At no time does an Internet DNS server attempt to send a response directly to our internal server when we use the slave server/caching-only forwarder combination. In this way, our internal zone records are safe. Figure 26-15 illustrates this setup.

Dynamic DNS Servers (DDNS)

If there is one characteristic that defines the difference between the Windows 2000 DNS server and previous versions of Microsoft DNS servers, it is the Windows

FIGURE 26-15 Forwarders and slaves

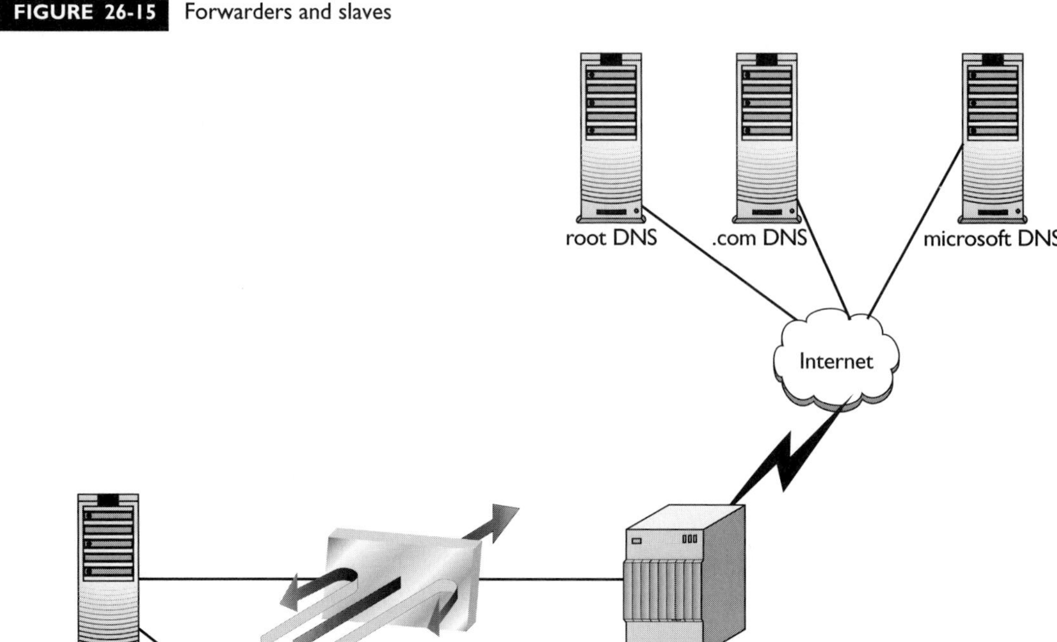

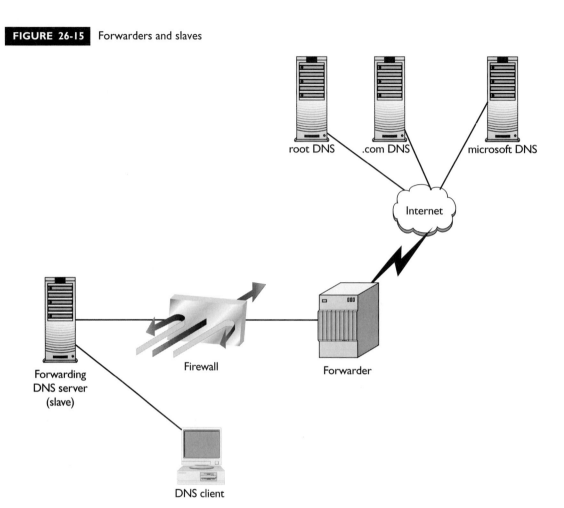

2000 DNS server's ability to dynamically update the information contained in its zone databases.

This behavior is very much like what you have seen with WINS servers. A WINS server allows NetBIOS nodes on the network to update their NetBIOS name and IP address mappings dynamically. This was a real advantage on earlier versions of Microsoft networks, since all of them had been NetBIOS based.

Windows 2000 is free of the shackles of NetBIOS (for the most part) and uses the DNS scheme for computer and domain naming. While there are many advantages to using the DNS rather than NetBIOS, there is a major problem: Zone database files were originally designed to be *static* databases. If any update is needed to be done to the zone contents, it would have to be done manually by the DNS administrator.

Manual administration of the zone databases on a large DNS-based network, such as an enterprise Windows 2000 network, would be a huge and difficult task. The task would be even more onerous when Dynamic Host Configuration Protocol (DHCP) is used extensively, and when DHCP assigns varying IP addresses to shared network resources. The Dynamic DNS Update Protocol eliminates this major hurdle to widespread implementation of DNS on Windows networks.

The DNS Update Protocol

The Windows 2000 DNS server supports the Dynamic DNS update protocol as described in RFC 2136. Windows 2000 DNS clients actually use the *DHCP client service* to update a Dynamic DNS server with their host name and IP address information. All Windows 2000 computers, regardless if they are a DHCP client or not, have the DHCP client service installed and running in order to provide them with the capability of updating a Dynamic DNS server.

If a DNS client is going to update its information dynamically, it must be updated on a Primary DNS server, regardless of whether you have employed Active Directory integrated or Standard zone types. The update is initially sent to the DNS client's Preferred DNS server. If the Preferred DNS server is a Secondary, then the client will query the Secondary for the Start Of Authority (SOA) record for the zone. The SOA record contains the name of the Primary DNS server for the zone.

When the Windows 2000 client obtains the name of a Primary server for the zone, it will attempt to update its Host (A) and Pointer (PTR) records, depending on how you have configured dynamic updates to occur. A Windows 2000 machine with a static IP address always updates both its A and PTR records itself.

A Windows 2000 *DHCP client* updates its own A record, and the DHCP server updates the PTR record (by default, although you can alter this behavior). A downlevel client cannot directly update its information directly with a Dynamic DNS server, but can use a Windows 2000 DHCP server as a "proxy" to update its information.

Remote Access Service (RAS) Clients and Dynamic Update RAS clients will always register their own information directly with the DNS server and never interact with a DHCP server. The RAS client registers both its A and PTR records itself. If an orderly disconnection of the RAS client occurs, it will remove its own records from the DNS before signing off. If a "disorderly" disconnection occurs, the RAS client's records will not be removed from the zone database. This can cause "stale" or outdated and inaccurate resource records to exist in the zone database.

Name Collisions

When a machine tries to update its name in the zone database, and finds that its name is already there with a different IP address, it has experienced a *name collision.* The default behavior of the DNS client is to overwrite the existing record with its own information.

This can be a bit of a problem, because it has the potential of being a security risk. There are two ways you can prevent the default update behavior from taking place:

- **Disable the client's ability to overwrite the existing record.** You can change the default setting so that instead of replacing the IP address, the client backs out of the registration process and logs the error in Event Viewer. To do so, add the **DisableReplaceAddressesInConflicts** entry with a value of 1 (DWORD) to the following registry subkey:

  ```
  HKEY_LOCAL_MACHINE\SYSTEM\CurrentControlSet\Services\
  Tcpip\Parameters
  ```

  The entry can be 1 or 0, which specify one of the following:

  1. If the name that the client is trying to create already exists, the client does not try to overwrite it.

  0. If the name that the client is trying to create already exists, the client tries to overwrite it. This is the default value.

- **Enable secure dynamic updates.** Secure updates can only be done with Active Directory integrated zones.

Name collisions can also take place in Active Directory integrated zones when two administrators enter differing information into the zone. When this situation occurs, the most recent record added will be considered the valid record, and will overwrite the older entry during replication. Prior to replication, there will be inaccurate data provided to some of the DNS clients. Microsoft has termed this temporary disparity "loose consistency." Therefore, the DNS database can be considered *loosely consistent.*

CERTIFICATION OBJECTIVE 26.04

Integrating Windows 2000 DNS Server with Active Directory

Windows 2000 allows DNS integration with the Active Directory. There are significant advantages to integrating Windows 2000 zones with the Active Directory, including:

- Active Directory integrated zones use the Active Directory replication engine, thus obviating the need to create separate DNS and Active Directory replication topologies.
- Per property (rather than the entire record) zone transfers are available when the zone is Active Directory integrated.
- All Active Directory integrated DNS zones are Primary zones (multimaster). This offers a greater degree of fault tolerance when DNS clients need to dynamically update their records on a Dynamic DNS server.
- Secure dynamic updates of the DNS zone database prevent rogue machines from taking over a mapping that belongs to another machine.

DNS is required for Windows 2000 domains. Windows 2000 domain controllers are located via DNS queries. The Netlogon service searches for a logon server via DNS. Prior to Windows 2000, WINS servers provided a similar function. However, Windows 2000 is no longer dependent on NetBIOS. Core network functionality is mediated through the WinSock interface and not the NetBIOS interface.

When Active Directory is installed on a domain controller, it will seek out a DNS server authoritative for the domain. If it cannot find an authoritative DNS server, or if the authoritative DNS server does not support Dynamic updates and SRV resource records, the installer will require you to create a DNS server on that machine. Active Directory domain names are DNS domain names.

Secure Dynamic Updates

Active Directory integrated zones can be protected from updates by invalid or rogue hosts. This can be accomplished by using *secure dynamic updates.* When secure updates are enabled on the Active Directory integrated zone, machines that register records in the zone become the owners of those records. Access controls are placed on the records to prevent other machines from overwriting them.

Mechanisms of Dynamic Updates

The mechanism by which this is accomplished is via the *Generic Security Service Application Programming Interface (GSS-API),* which is defined in RFC 2078. Other methods of secure update, such as *System Security Extensions* (RFC 2535) and *Secure Domain Name System Dynamic Update* (RFC 2137), are not supported in Windows 2000.

Security tokens are passed back and forth between the DNS client and secure DNS server. This token-passing process continues until the client and server settle on a security context in which information can be securely transferred between client and server.

The Windows 2000 implementation of the GSS-API uses Kerberos as the security method for establishing a secure connection. The GSS-API is defined in a way that allows other security providers to establish a secure context (such as smart cards and certificate-based authentication), but these haven't yet been implemented.

Two types of resource records are used to establish the secure context:

- **TKEY** The TKEY resource record is used to transfer security tokens between the DNS client and server. It allows for the establishment of the shared *secret key* that will be used with the TSIG resource record.
- **TSIG** The TSIG resource record is used to send and verify messages that have been signed with a hash algorithm.

Negotiating a Secure Context When a DNS client attempts to complete a secure update, it begins with a TKEY negotiation that will establish the shared secret. This will determine the security mechanism used during the actual data exchange. Keys are exchanged at this point.

The DNS client then sends its update request to the DNS server. This request is signed with the TSIG resource record, and the server acknowledges that it has received the signed request. The DNS server then attempts to update the Active Directory on behalf of the client.

Secure dynamic updates prevent machines from pirating the name of `another legitimate machine on the network. You can configure security on resource records or entire domains via the Active Directory Users and Computers interface. Figure 26-16 shows the secure dynamic update negotiation in progress.

DnsUpdateProxy

With secure DNS zone updates, only the "owner" of the record can update a resource record. This improves overall security, but it can cause some problems you might have to deal with. For example, you can use a DHCP server to assign IP addresses to Windows 2000 clients. The default behavior for Windows 2000 DNS clients that are also DHCP

FIGURE 26-16 Negotiating a secure context for dynamic updates

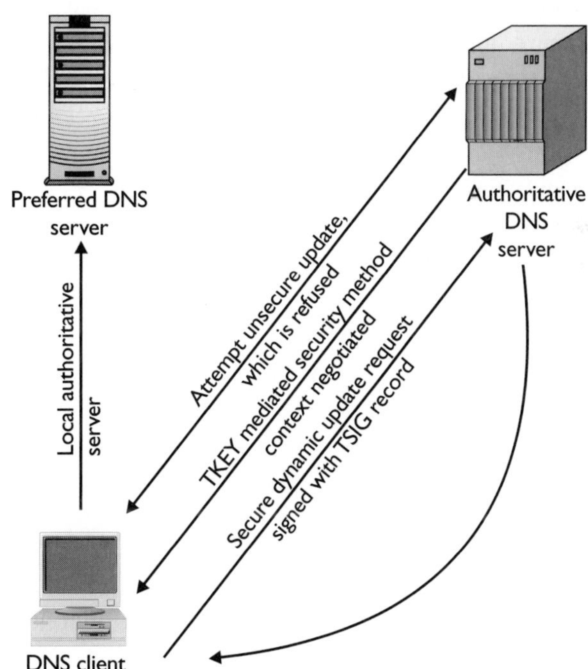

clients is to update their own addresses record and to allow the DHCP server to update the Pointer PTR record. The DNS client therefore "owns" the Host (A) record, and the DHCP server "owns" the PTR record. Access controls are placed on these records so that no other machine can update or "touch" them.

The Problem Suppose your DHCP server crashes. You have a backup DHCP server, so you might not worry about it too much. However, when the backup DHCP server tries to update the PTR record for the DNS client, it won't be able to—it doesn't own that pointer record and therefore has no access to it.

Another problematic situation is when you are working with downlevel clients. Suppose you have a Windows NT 4.0 computer that is a DHCP client for a Windows 2000 DHCP server. The Windows 2000 DHCP server has been acting as a "proxy" for the downlevel client and has been registering the client's Host (A) record and Pointer (PTR) record for it.

What happens after you upgrade the Windows NT 4.0 computer to Windows 2000? The Windows 2000 DNS client will try to update its own DNS Host (A) record information if it continues to be a DHCP client. Unfortunately, when the upgraded client tries to do so, the update will fail because the DHCP server that originally registered its Host (A) and Pointer (PTR) records owns them, and access controls prevent any other computer from accessing and changing those records. Figure 26-17 illustrates these interactions.

The Solution The solution to these problems is to place DHCP servers in a special group known as the *DnsUpdateProxy* group. When a DHCP server that is a member of the DnsUpdateProxy group creates an entry for a machine in DNS, no access controls are attached to the record.

For example, let's say a DHCP server creates a Host (A) and a Pointer (PTR) record for a machine by the name of *daedalus.tacteam.net.* Normally, the DHCP server would become the owner and restrict access to this record, but if the DHCP server is a member of the DnsUpdateProxy group, no one will be registered as the owner of the resource record and no access controls are placed on it.

The DnsUpdateProxy solution does create a complication: We've just eliminated the security in secure dynamic updates for DHCP clients (at least for the PTR records for Windows 2000 DHCP clients)! Any machine can be brought online and

FIGURE 26-17

Problems when DHCP servers go offline and downlevel clients are upgraded

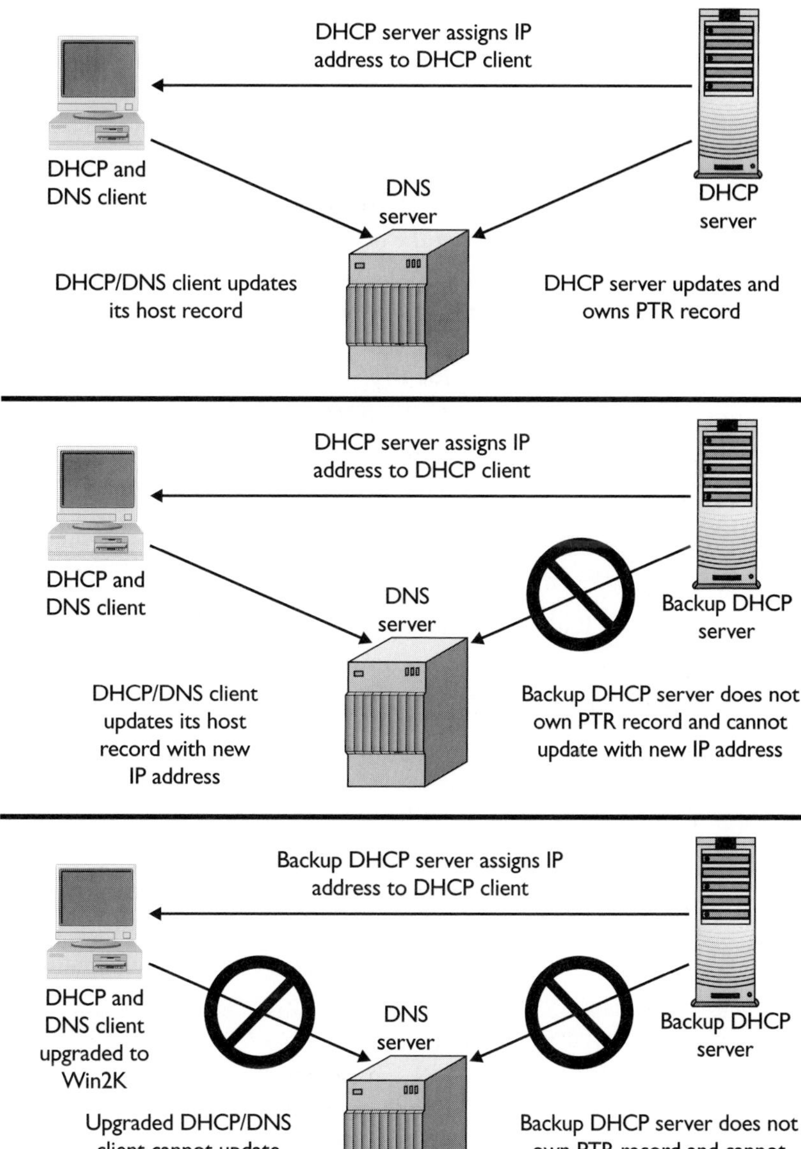

claim the name of a machine that has been legitimately registered by a DHCP server. Consider this the trade-off between convenience and security.

Domain Controllers in the DnsUpdateProxy Group The most significant issue relating to membership in the DnsUpdateProxy group is that of domain controllers that run the DHCP server service. If the DHCP server is on a domain controller, it will register the domain controller's information in a nonsecure context. This allows any machine to register itself as the domain controller in question. This represents a significant security hole.

on the job

Microsoft recommends that you not implement DHCP servers on domain controllers because of the potentially adverse security consequences.

EXERCISE 26-3

Adding a DHCP Server to the DnsUpdateProxy Group

In this exercise, you will add a DHCP server to the DnsUpdateProxy group. Be sure that the DHCP server is not located on an active, production network, and is not presently being used to assign IP addresses. Placing a DHCP into the DnsUpdateProxy can represent a security breach.

1. Log on as Administrator at a domain controller.
2. Open the Active Directory Users and Computers console from the Administrative Tools menu.
3. When the Active Directory Users and Computers console is open, expand the domain name and open the Computers node in the left pane. Your screen should appear similar to the following illustration.

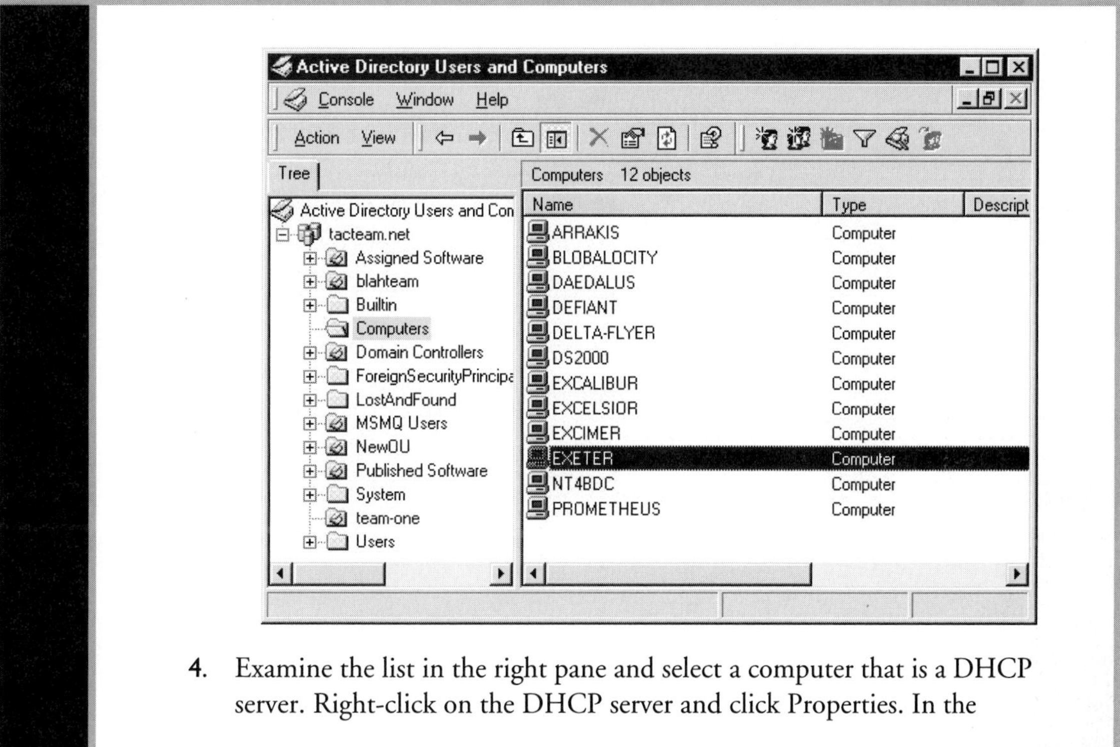

4. Examine the list in the right pane and select a computer that is a DHCP server. Right-click on the DHCP server and click Properties. In the

Properties dialog box, click on the Member of tab. You should see what appears in the following illustration.

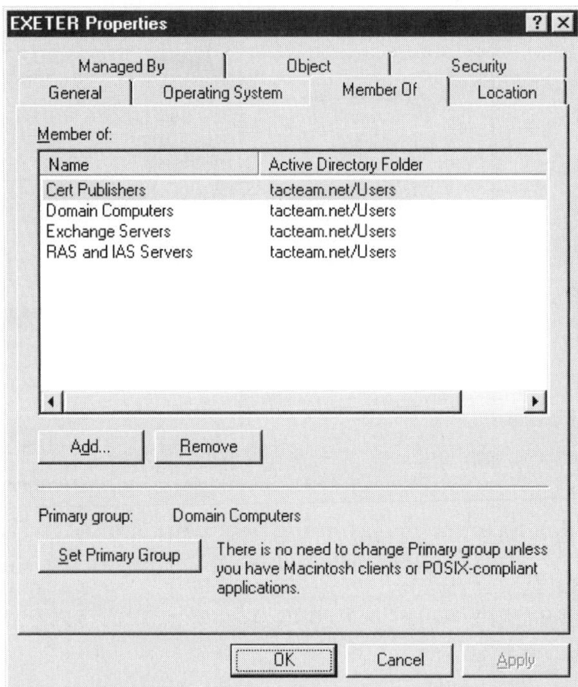

5. Click Add. You will see the Select Groups dialog box. Scroll down the list until you find DnsUpdateProxy. Select it and then click Add. That will add the computer to the DnsUpdateProxy group. Click OK.
6. You are returned to the <Computer> Properties box. Click Apply and then OK. The machine has been successfully added to the group.

Be aware at this point that no security will be applied to any records added by this DHCP server. However, no changes have been made to existing records.

Active Directory Integrated Zone Replication

In a Standard zone environment, the DNS Primary contains the only read/write copy of the zone database. Zone transfer takes place when the Refresh interval has expired. Secondary DNS servers send a pull request to a Master DNS server to receive the zone database. The Secondary DNS server contains a read-only copy of the zone database. Standard zones have a single point of failure for both manual and dynamic zone updates. If the Primary server for the zone is disabled, zone updates and zone transfers are halted.

The Active Directory integrated zone does not have a single point of failure because all Active Directory integrated zones are Primary. The Active Directory allows for *multimaster* replication using the Active Directory replication engine. DNS zone information is stored in the Active Directory and each authoritative server contains a read/write copy of the zone database. A single "downed" Primary will not prevent zone transfers and zone updates.

SRV Records in Windows 2000 DNS

Active Directory domain controllers (DC) must be registered in the DNS. Domain controller entries in the DNS include special SRV resource records that contain information about their DC status. The Netlogon service on domain controllers automatically registers these SRV resource records via dynamic DNS update.

SRV Records Replace the "Hidden" 16th Character (to some extent)

These *SRV* (Service) resource records provide a function similar to the service identifier used in the NetBIOS name. For WINS clients, the client could query the WINS database for the service desired by examining the 16th character service identifiers recorded in the WINS database. Windows 2000 domain controllers are able to dynamically update SRV resource records on a Dynamic DNS server and provide information about available services. Examples of such services include Lightweight Directory Access Protocol (LDAP), FTP, and WWW (although all these service identifiers are not implemented at the present time). Domain clients must find a SRV resource record for a domain controller in the DNS database in order to authenticate logon. There is an SRV resource record for Kerberos information. This allows Kerberos clients to locate the Key Distribution server in their domain.

Manually Adding SRV Resource Records

There may be times when you will have to manually add SRV resource records for domain controllers. An unfortunate example is the administrator who inadvertently deletes these records via the DNS console. It is important to restore these records on a timely basis, since domain clients are dependent on these records for domain activity.

To view the SRV resource records created by a domain controller, open and view the *netlogon.dns* file. The Active Directory Installation Wizard created this file during setup. It can be found in:

%systemroot%\System32\Config\Netlogon.dns

Each record contains the complete Active Directory path. Be sure when creating a new SRV resource record for a domain controller that the record is placed in the appropriate container object in the Active Directory as indicated by the path defined in the netlogon.dns file.

CERTIFICATION OBJECTIVE 26.05

Integrating Windows 2000 DNS Server with DHCP

The Windows 2000 DHCP server can deliver host name and IP addressing information to a Windows 2000 DNS server. This added functionality allows even downlevel clients to take advantage of the services available via a Dynamic DNS server.

The Windows 2000 DHCP server interacts with a Windows 2000 DNS server in one of three ways after assigning a DHCP client an IP address:

- It will update the DNS server by providing information to create a Host (A) resource record and PTR (Pointer) record depending on the DNS client request.
- The DHCP server will update both the Address and the Pointer Record regardless of the client request.

The DHCP server will never register information about the DHCP client. However, the client itself may contact the Dynamic DNS server directly with this information.

The DCHP/DNS interaction varies with the client operating system receiving the IP addressing information from a DHCP server. The interplay between the Windows 2000 client and Windows 2000 DHCP server encompasses the following:

- The Windows 2000 client broadcasts a DHCPREQUEST message and receives an IP address. The Windows 2000 client registers its own Address record with the Dynamic DNS server after obtaining a lease. The DHCP server registers the client's PTR record with the DNS server. This is the default behavior for a Windows 2000 client and Windows 2000 DHCP server.
- Client and server parameters can be manipulated to allow the DHCP server to update both Address and PTR records. If desired, the DHCP server and DCHP client can be configured so that no dynamic updates are made to the DNS server via DHCP.

In a pure Windows 2000 environment, the Windows 2000 DNS client has several options in terms of how its information is registered in the DNS. Downlevel clients are not able to directly update their own records on the DNS server. However, the DHCP server can act as "proxy" and will forward both Host (A) and PTR information to the DNS server for downlevel clients. Figure 26-18 shows these interactions.

FIGURE 26-18

Windows 2000 DHCP client/server interaction with the DNS server

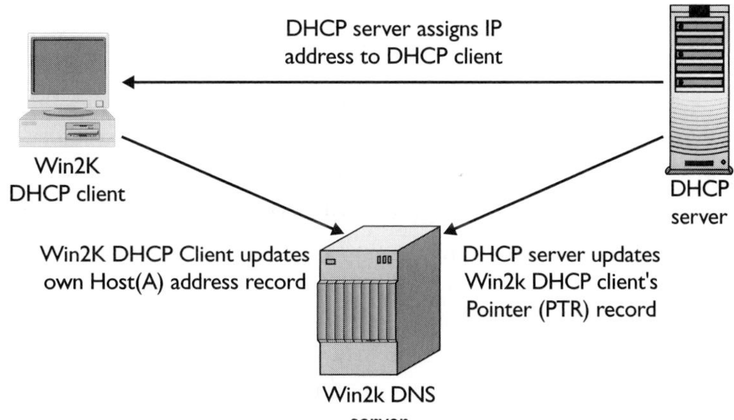
DHCP server assigns IP
address to DHCP client
Win2K
DHCP client
DHCP
server
Win2K DHCP Client updates
own Host(A) address record
DHCP server updates
Win2k DHCP client's
Pointer (PTR) record
Win2k DNS
server

Windows 2000 computers configured with *static* IP addresses update their own Host (A) and Pointer (PTR) records with the DNS server. If you change the name or IP address of a Windows 2000 client with a static IP address, you can manually update the client's entry in the DNS server by issuing the command:

ipconfig /registerdns

The /registerdns switch refreshes all DHCP leases and re-registers DNS names at the DNS server.

Downlevel clients with static IP addresses are not able to communicate directly with the DNS server. You must manually add the Host (A) and Pointer (PTR) records for these clients.

exam Watch

If you want the DHCP server to act as a "proxy" for downlevel clients that cannot update their own information with the Windows 2000 DNS server, you must be sure to use only Windows 2000 DHCP Servers on your network.

CERTIFICATION OBJECTIVE 26.06

Managing the Windows 2000 DNS Server

Managing the Windows 2000 DNS Server involves a thorough understanding of the DNS console and the dialog boxes and options available to you, the DNS administrator. In this section, we will uncover some of the mysteries of the configuration parameters of the Windows 2000 DNS Server.

Configuring Server Properties

When configuring the Windows 2000 DNS Server properties, you are making decisions about how the entire system, including all zones, functions for that DNS installation. To access the DNS server properties, open the DNS console and right-click on the name of the server you wish to configure. You should see what appears in Figure 26-19. The first tab you are presented is the Interfaces tabbed properties sheet (henceforth known as "tab").

FIGURE 26-19

The Interfaces tab on the DNS server's Properties dialog box

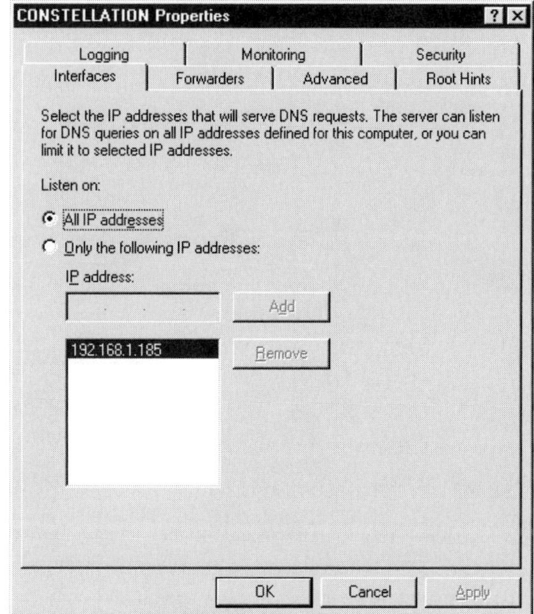

The DNS Server Properties Interfaces Tab

If you are running a multihomed DNS server, you may wish to exclude an interface from answering DNS queries. Perhaps the server is used for other purposes, such as a file server. You may have added a second network interface card that you use exclusively for high-speed backups on a separate segment. You would not want other network traffic on the interface you use for the backups. In this case, you would select the "Only the following IP addresses" option and add the IP address of the interface that you want to answer the queries in the text box.

The DNS Server Properties Forwarders Tab

Click on the Forwarders tab and you will see what appears in Figure 26-20.

If you choose to use a forwarder, you would place a check mark in the "Enable forwarders" check box. Then enter the IP address of the forwarder in the text box under **"IP address:"**. If you wish to make the machine a slave server that does not perform recursion, place a check mark in the "Do not use recursion" check box.

FIGURE 26-20

The Forwarders tab

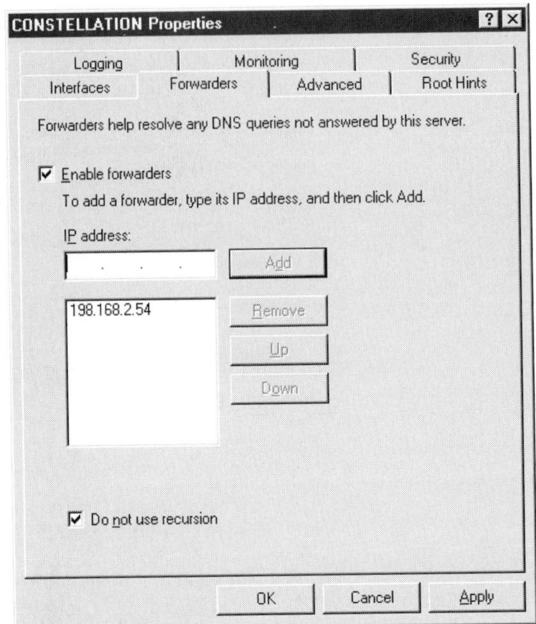

The DNS Server Properties Advanced Tab

Click the Advanced tab and you will see what appears in Figure 26-21.

There are some pretty obscure entries on the Advanced tab, so pay close attention. Hey, didn't we see the "Disable recursion" option somewhere else? Yes, and if you place a check mark in the box located on the Advanced tab, it will have the same effect. Think of it as getting another chance in life.

The "BIND secondaries" option is selected if you have BIND secondaries that do not support the *fast transfer* we spoke about earlier. Versions of BIND prior to 4.9.4 do not support the fast transfer, so if you have any of these, you should put a check mark in the "BIND secondaries" check box.

If you want the zone database file to load only if there are no faulty records in it, select the "Fail on load if bad zone data." If you don't select this option, the zone database will load and the error will be noted in the DNS log. Data will be determined as bad or not, depending on the options you selected in the "**Name checking:**" drop-down list box.

The "Enable round robin" option determines whether the DNS server rotates and reorders a list of multiple Host (A) records if a queried host name is for a number of

FIGURE 26-21

The Advanced tab

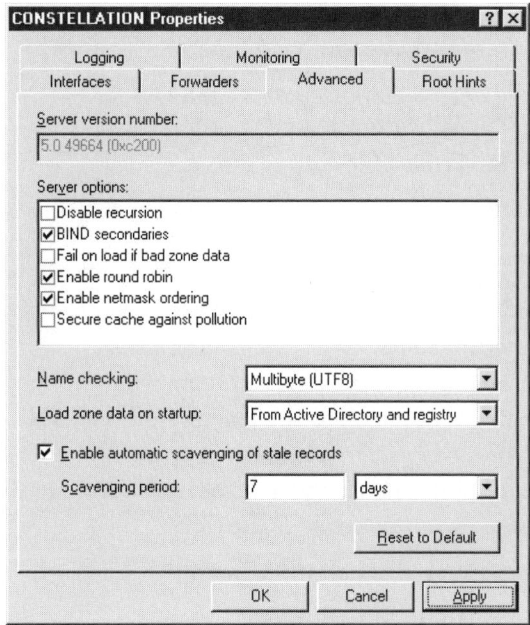

computers each configured with multiple different IP addresses but the same host name. *Round robin* is useful for load balancing and commonly used for Web and Proxy servers.

If a machine sends a DNS query for another machine that is multihomed, you probably want to connect to the interface that is located on your own subnet, if there is one. When you enable "Enable netmask ordering," this is exactly what you get.

Sometimes a DNS server sending back a referral will include "extra" information. For example, if the DNS server begins an iterative query process for stuff.microsoft.com, it may get additional referrals for msn.com. This is enabled by default because it allows the cache to learn about the namespace in a more timely fashion. However, this is considered *pollution* of the DNS cache. You can disable cache pollution by selecting the option "Secure cache against pollution."

The "Name Checking" drop-down list box is used to determine which names are valid and which are not. The choices are:

- Strict RFC (ANSI)
- Non RFC (ANSI)
- Multibyte (UTF8)
- All Names

The "Load zone data on startup" drop-down list box allows you to choose to load the zone information from:

- The Registry
- From a file
- From the Active Directory and Registry

The Windows 2000 DNS server defaults to booting from the Active Directory and the Registry. This accommodates both Active Directory integrated and Standard zones.

Scavenging is the process of removing stale entries from the zone. The default setting is not to allow scavenging from the DNS database. Scavenging can be set on a per-server or per-zone basis. The details of the scavenging process are beyond the scope of this book, and are covered in detail in the *Designing a Windows 2000 Network Infrastructure Study Guide.*

The Root Hints Tab

Click on the Root Hints tab and you will see what appears in Figure 26-22.

The Root Hints tab displays servers that can be used to answer authoritatively for servers that are authoritative for *non-root* zones. For example, a non-root zone could be a subzone of the microsoft.com zone, such as sales.microsoft.com. The DNS servers authoritative for the sales.microsoft.com zone use the root hints in the process of performing iterative queries. It gives them a "leg up" in the process of learning about the DNS namespace.

For example, suppose a DNS server DAEDALUS has a zone called west.tacteam.net. In the process of answering a query for a higher-level domain, such as the tacteam.net domain, DAEDALUS needs some assistance to locate an authoritative server for this domain, which in this case is CONSTELLATION.

In order for DAEDALUS to find CONSTELLATION, or any other servers that are authoritative for the tacteam.net domain, it needs to be able to send a DNS query to the Root servers for the DNS namespace (with tacteam.net being the root in this example). The Root servers can then refer DAEDALUS to the authoritative servers for the .com domain. The servers for the .net domain can, in turn, offer referral to CONSTELLATION or other servers that are authoritative for the tacteam.net domain.

FIGURE 26-22

The DNS server Properties Root Hints tab

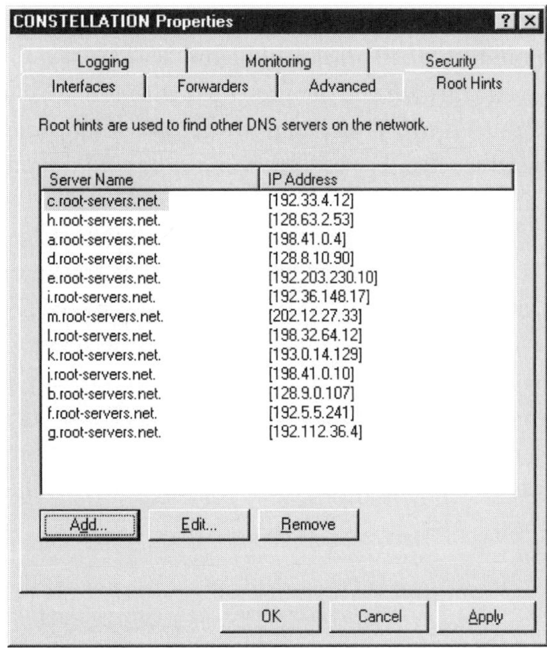

How to Use the Root Hints Tab In order to use the Root Hints properly, you need to make a few assessments:

- Will you be using DNS to resolve internal host names?
- Will you be using DNS to resolve external host names?
- Is the server used as a Root server?

Resolving Internet Host Names If the DNS server will be resolving names for Internet hosts, you must have the names and IP addresses of the Internet Root servers. The cache.dns file, which is included with your DNS server installation, provides the names and addresses of the Internet Root servers. This file is stored in the %systemroot%\system32\dns folder.

Configuring Zone Properties

Once the server is configured, you will need to configure the zones you have created on the server. Each zone you create can be configured separately. Right-click on the zone of choice and then click the Properties command on the context menu. You should see what appears in Figure 26-23.

The first tab you are presented with is the General tab. If you are making chances to the server and you do not want any additional connections to it while you are working, click Pause. This will not disconnect any existing connections to the DNS server.

You can change the *type* of zone by clicking Change. Your choices are Primary, Secondary, and Active Directory integrated. Note that you cannot choose "Active Directory integrated" unless you are running the DNS server on a domain controller.

In the "Allow dynamic updates?" drop-down list box you can choose among Yes, No, or "Only secure updates." The latter is only available on DNS servers running on domain controllers and the zone is Active Directory integrated.

Aging is used to control the scavenging properties for the zone. We go over scavenging in detail in the *Designing a Windows 2000 Network Infrastructure Study Guide.*

FIGURE 26-23

The Zone Properties dialog box General tab

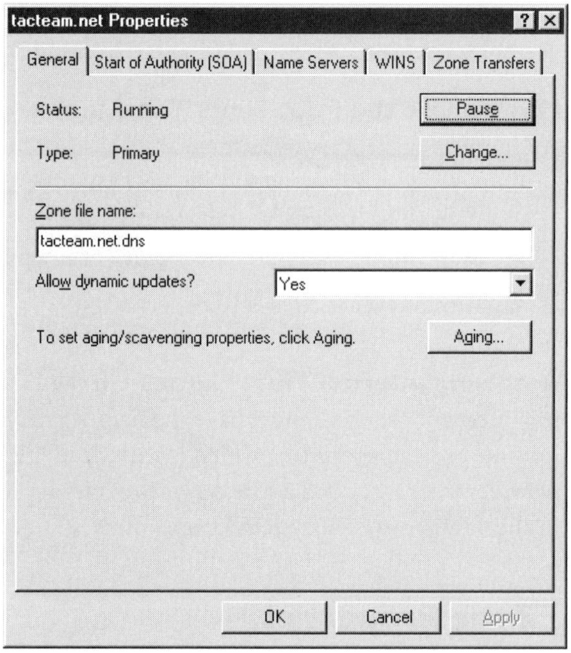

The Start of Authority (SOA) Tab

Click on the Start of Authority (SOA) tab and you will see what appears in Figure 26-24.

The "Serial number" text box tells you what the current serial number is for the zone. If for some reason you want to increment the serial number, you can click Increment.

You might want to manually increment the serial number in order to force all Secondaries to download the zone database.

The "Primary server" text box contains the name of the DNS server that is Primary for the zone. If you want to change the name, you can type it in or click Browse and locate it via the GUI. The "Responsible person" is typically the DNS administrator who manages the zone. This is the e-mail address of that person, and the username and domain name are separated by a period rather than an @ sign.

"Refresh interval:" determines how often the Secondary will call a Primary to check for zone updates. "Retry interval:" is the amount of time a Secondary will

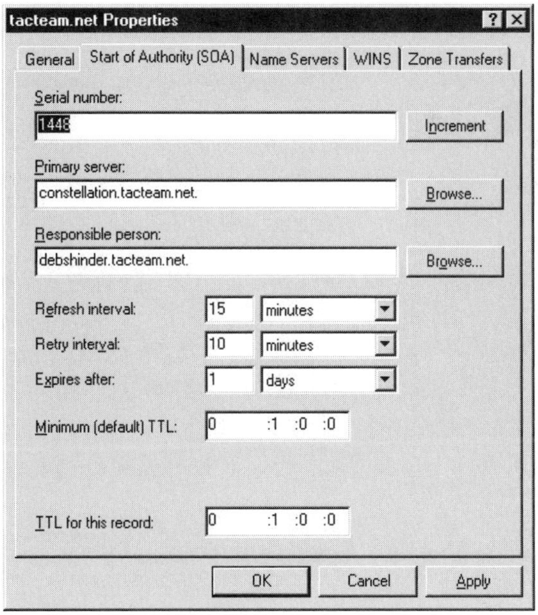

FIGURE 26-24

The Start of Authority tab on the Zone Properties dialog box wait after an unsuccessful refresh attempt. Be sure to make the refresh interval longer than the retry interval!

The "Expires after:" interval determines how long the Secondary can go without being about to update its zone data from a Primary before considering its zone data invalid. For example, if the Primary went down 25 hours ago and the expiration interval for the zone is 24 hours, the Secondary will no longer answer queries for the zone. This is because after the expiration interval has passed, the Secondary assumes that the zone data is no longer valid, and will not hand out potentially invalid DNS replies.

"**Minimum (default) TTL:**" determines the time-to-live for all records in the zone. Note that this is the *default* TTL for all records; you can assign TTLs more granularly by giving individual records their own TTL. "TTL for this record:" allows you just this sort of granular control over the TTL. However, since the SOA record is a resource record in its own right, you have the opportunity to change its TTL here.

The Name Servers Tab

Click on the Name Servers tab and you will see what appears in Figure 26-25.

The Name Servers tab allows you to manually add and remove the names of servers that are authoritative for the zone. This includes the Primary and all

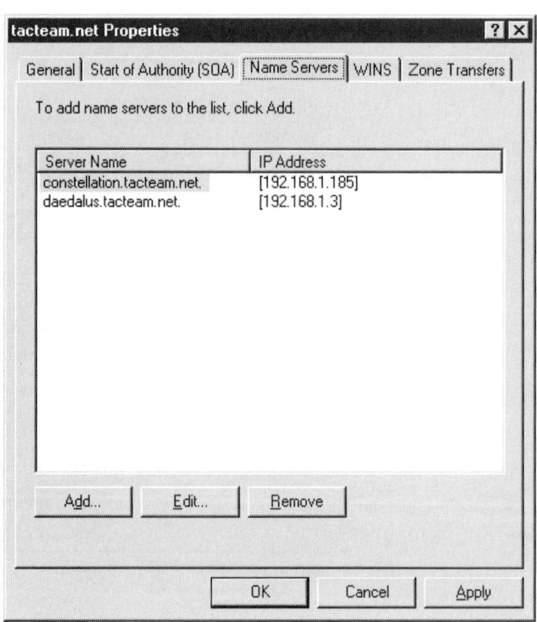

FIGURE 26-25 The Name Servers tab on the Zone Properties dialog box

Secondaries in Standard DNS zones. These machines all require NS resource records. If you find that a server with an NS record does not enter itself onto this list, you must enter it manually. Also, if you manually enter a server onto this list, you will need an NS record for that server, including in the zone.

The WINS Tab

Click on the WINS tab. You will see what appears in Figure 26-26.

The Windows 2000 DNS server can query a WINS server before finally giving up on a query. The WINS server is not queried until the DNS server confirms that it does not record for the host in any of its zones, and the results of iterative queries have failed.

You enabled WINS forward lookups by placing a check mark in the "Use WINS forward lookup" check box. Check the "Do not replicate this record" check box if you have downlevel DNS servers that are not Windows NT 4.0 or Windows 2000 DNS servers. Add the IP address of the WINS server you want the DNS server to query in the "IP address:" text box, and then click Add. You can also adjust the TTL on WINS lookups in the "Time to live (TTL):" text box.

FIGURE 26-26

The WINS tab on the Zone Properties dialog box

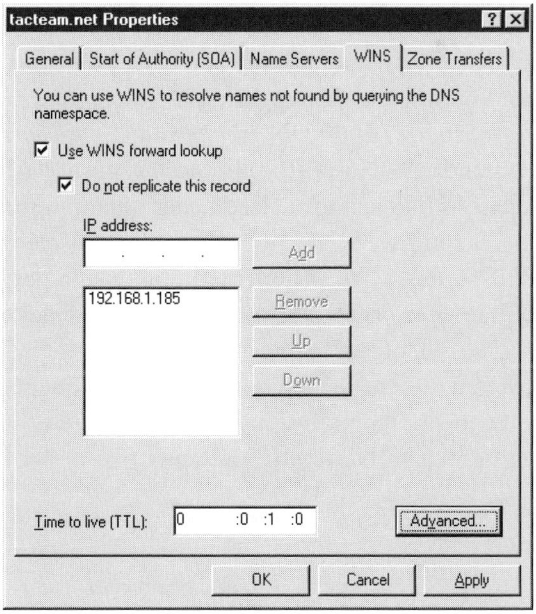

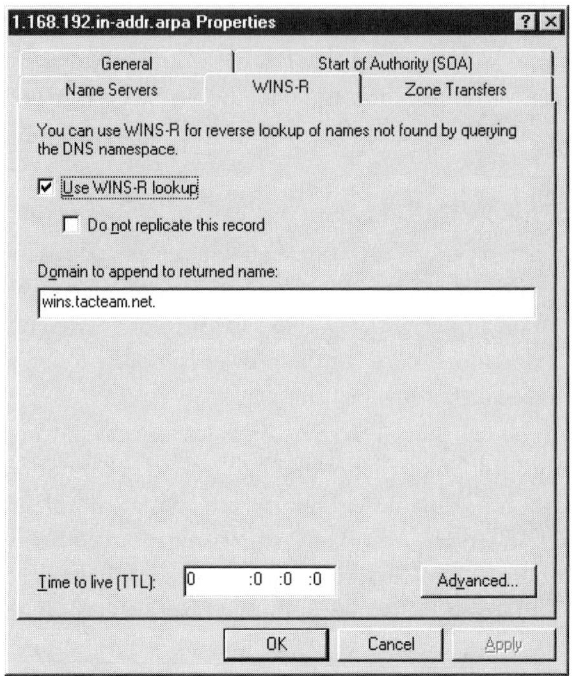

FIGURE 26-27 The WINS-R tab in the Reverse Lookup Zone's Properties dialog box

The WINS tab looks a little different for reverse lookup zones. Right-click on one of your reverse lookup zones and click Properties, and then click on the WINS-R tab. You will see what appeared in Figure 26-27.

A Windows 2000 DNS server can also query a WINS server for reverse lookups if the standard DNS-centric approach is unsuccessful. To enable the server to perform reverse WINS lookups, place a check mark in the "Use WINS-R lookup:" check box. If you have Secondaries that are not Windows 2000 or Windows NT 4.0 DNS servers, place a check mark in the "Do not replicate this record" check box to prevent errors in zone transfer with those downlevel DNS servers.

In the "Domain to append to returned name:" text box, place the domain name that you want appended to reverse WINS queries. This is important since security and network monitoring/inventory software will use this domain name when performing WINS reverse lookups.

Microsoft recommends that you enable only a single zone to answer forward WINS lookups and to designate that zone in the WINS-R record. This prevents confusion related to the domain location of clients that were located via WINS queries.

Configuring Windows 2000 DNS Clients

You can configure your DNS clients in two ways:

- Manually
- Via Dynamic Host Configuration Protocol (DHCP)

The easier and less error-prone approach is to let the DHCP server hand out the relevant IP addressing information. We will take a look at both approaches in this section.

Manually Configuring DNS Client Settings

You must be sitting at the local machine to perform manual configuration. Right-click on the My Network Places icon on the desktop and select Properties, then double-click on Local Area Connection and then click Properties.

This brings up the Local Area Connection Properties dialog box. Scroll down the list of network components, find the Internet Protocol (TCP/IP) option, and click Properties. Then click Advanced on the General tab. This brings you to the Advanced TCP/IP Settings dialog box. Click on the DNS tab and you will see what appears in Figure 26-28.

You can add more DNS servers to your DNS server search list in the "DNS server addresses, in order of use" area. Click Add to add more DNS servers. If the top entry is not available, the second entry will be contacted and will be moved to the top of the search list. The search order can be changed by using the up and down arrow buttons on the right side of the DNS servers list.

The configuration options for how to handle unqualified DNS queries are underneath the region where additional servers are added. The option "Append

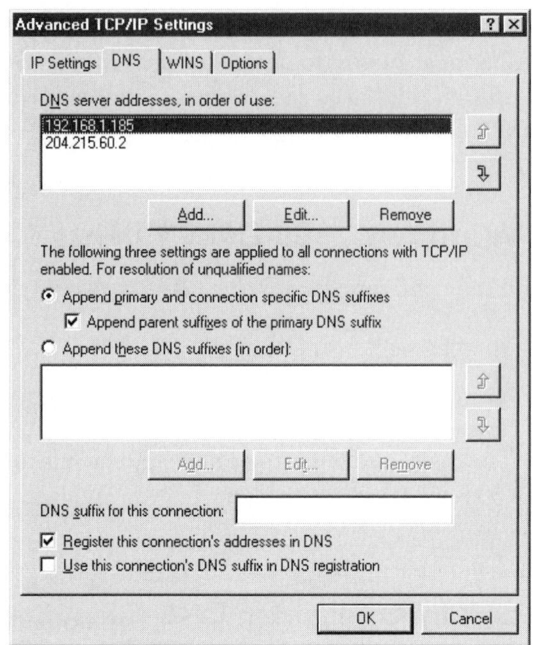

FIGURE 26-28

The DNS tab in the Advanced TCP/IP Setting Properties dialog box

primary and connection specific DNS suffixes" refers to what DNS *suffixes* should be included in a request to a DNS server if an *unqualified* DNS query is issued to the DNS server.

Issuing an Unqualified Request If you were to type *http://constellation* in the address bar of your Web browser, for example, you would be issuing an unqualified request. This is because no domain name is included in the request, just a host name. A DNS server must receive an FQDN in order to process a DNS query. The *Primary suffix* is the computer's domain membership included in the Network Identification tab of the System Properties dialog box, as seen in Figure 26-29.

The "Append parent suffixes of the primary DNS suffix" option specifies whether resolution for unqualified names issued by the computer includes the parent suffixes of the primary DNS suffix up to the second-level domain. This is sometimes referred to *devolution* of the DNS query.

For example, your primary DNS suffix is dev.west.tacteam.net. You type **ping xyz** at a Windows 2000 command prompt. The first FQDN sent in the DNS

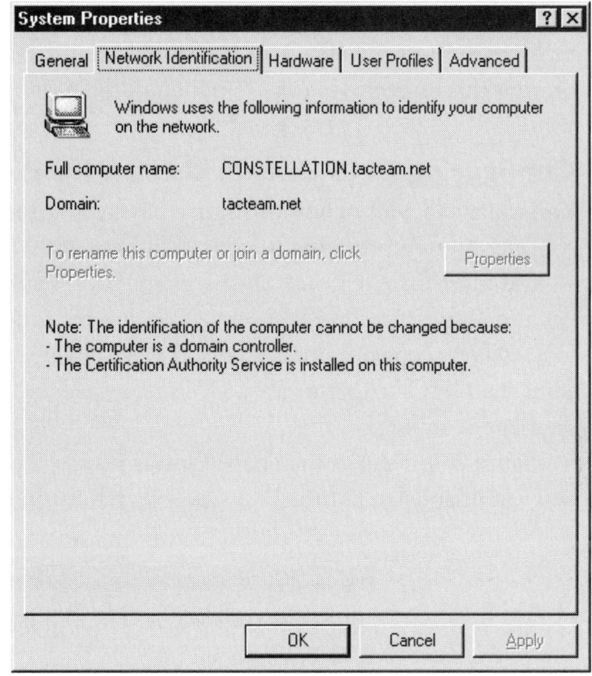

FIGURE 26-29 The System Properties dialog box

query will be xyz.dev.west.tacteam.net. If this fails, Windows 2000 will query for xyz.west.tacteam.net, and if that fails, it will query for xyz.tacteam.net. Devolution will not extend past the second-level domain name.

If you choose "Append these DNS suffixes (in order)," you can configure a customized set of domain names to append to DNS queries. Click Add to add DNS suffixes to the list. One situation where you might wish to add your own DNS suffixes to the list is when you are deploying special *WINS referral* zones. When and how you configure these special zones is discussed in the *Designing a Windows 2000 Network Infrastructure Study Guide.*

The Windows 2000 DNS client by default registers its own Host (A) address records with the Primary DNS server for its zone. The "Register this connection's addresses in DNS" is selected by default. The domain name for this registration is defined in the System Properties dialog box. If you uncheck this box and the DNS client is also a DHCP client, the DHCP server will register both the Host (A) and Pointer (PTR) records for the host on the Dynamic DNS server.

Connection-specific domain name registrations can be made as well. By default, each connection-specific DNS suffix is also registered with the DNS server. You can prevent this by removing the check mark from that option.

Configuring DNS Clients Using DHCP

You can avoid a lot of administrative hassle by using a DHCP server to assign DNS configuration information to your Windows 2000 DHCP clients.

You must first create a scope on the DHCP server. After creating the scope, you need to define the 006 DNS Servers option for the scope. When configuring your DNS server scope option, consider the placement of your DNS server. Ideally, you want the DHCP client to use a DNS server closest to it, and preferably on its own segment or subnet.

Figure 26-30 shows the Scope Options dialog box on a DHCP server. Note that you can include an entire DNS server search list in the 006 DNS Servers option.

FIGURE 26-30

The Scope Options dialog box

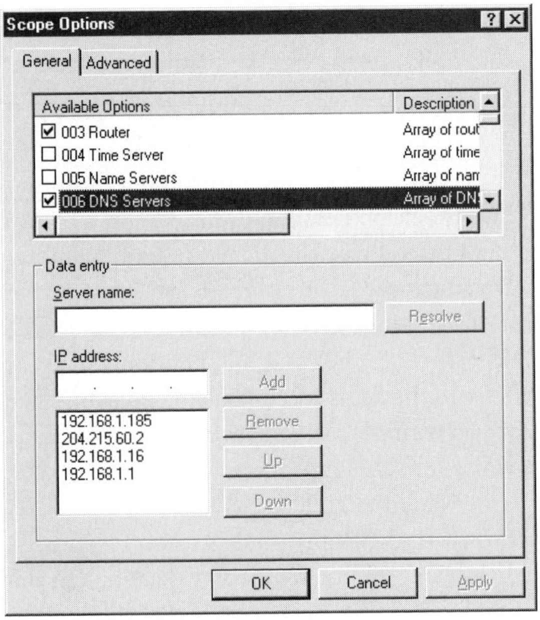

SCENARIO & SOLUTION	
What is this "WINS Referral Zone"? Is it something you need?	A WINS Referral Zone is usually a forward lookup zone that has no resource records in it. After creating the WINS Referral Zone, you disable WINS Referral for all other zones. After you have done this, any queries that are resolved via WINS are returned with the FQDN that contains the NetBIOS name returned from the WINS server with the WINS Referral Zone's domain name appended to it. In this way, it is easy to identify what queries have been resolved via WINS lookups.
What happens when you use Windows NT 4.0 DHCP servers for your Windows 2000 clients?	The Windows NT 4.0 DHCP server cannot update the Dynamic DNS server. If you require the DHCP server to update the DDNS server, then you must use the Windows 2000 DHCP server.
How often do you need to update the cache.dns file?	Not very often. The current implementation of the cache.dns file is circa 1997. Those Internet Root servers don't change much.

CERTIFICATION OBJECTIVE 26.07

Monitoring and Troubleshooting DNS

In this section, we will cover some important tools and techniques that you can use to monitor and troubleshoot your DNS configuration. The Windows 2000 DNS server service works very well, once you have it configured correctly. However, there will be times when things go awry, and you must be ready for those circumstances.

IPCONFIG

If you are a seasoned Windows NT 4.0 professional, you know all about the ipconfig command. However, you should know that ipconfig has been improved in

Windows 2000. Ipconfig includes new switches that increase its usefulness beyond a great tool for getting IP addressing information about your machines.

The Windows 2000 ipconfig utility includes three new switches that help in DNS management:

- **ipconfig /flushdns** The flushdns switch allows you to clear the local machine's DNS cache. When you make zone changes or machine IP address configuration changes and then do an nslookup, you may receive information that doesn't reflect the changes you thought you made. This is because the information is being retrieved from cache rather than from the DNS server itself. Use the flushdns switch to clear the cache, and then repeat the nslookup you were doing before.
- **ipconfig /displaydns** The displaydns switch prints out the local DNS cache. This is particularly helpful to use after you have completed the flushdns command, to confirm that the cache is indeed empty. The displaydns switch allows you to see the entries in the host file loaded into the cache.
- **ipconfig /registerdns** The /registerdns switch will renew a DHCP client's lease and re-register the DNS client's address information with a DNS server. This is sometimes helpful in "reminding" the DNS server of the DNS clients' addressing information.

The ipconfig utility that was so helpful in Windows NT 4.0 has become even more so in Windows 2000. Use it early and often!

NSLOOKUP

Nslookup is a command-line utility that allows you to test and query your DNS server's zone databases. Nslookup works in two modes: *interactive mode* and *command mode.* Command mode is used when you only want to do a single query. For example, if you type the command:

```
nslookup exeter.tacteam.net.
```

you'll get the following output:

```
Server:  constellation.tacteam.net
Address:  192.168.1.185
```

```
Name:     exeter.tacteam.net
Address:  192.168.1.186
```

Notice that we are returned to the command prompt when the lookup is completed. If you plan on doing a number of nslookup queries, you should use interactive mode. To enter interactive mode, just type **nslookup** at the command prompt. Your output should look like this:

```
C:\>nslookup
Default Server:  constellation.tacteam.net
Address:  192.168.1.185
>
```

Observe that you are not returned to the command prompt, but to the nslookup command's *interactive prompt*. Once you enter interactive mode, you can use the "set" commands to determine the nature of your queries. Some of the "set" commands are listed in Table 26-4. When you're ready to leave interactive mode and return to the command prompt, just type **exit** at the interactive mode command prompt.

TABLE 26-4 Selected "set" Commands that are used in Interactive Mode

Command	Description
all	Prints out a list of current options and server parameters
[no]debug	Prints out detailed information from the lookup
[no]d2	Prints out "exhaustive" debugging information
[no]defname	Appends a specific domain name to each query
[no]recurse	Ask for recursion for the query
[no]search	Uses the domain suffix search list
[no]vc	Always use a virtual circuit
domain=NAME	Allows you to set a default domain name for the lookup
root=NAME	Defines the name of the Root server to use for lookup
retry=X	Defines the number of retries for the lookup
timeout=X	Defines the timeout for the lookup
type=X	Defines the Query Type. For example: ANY,CNAME,MX,NS,PTR,SOA,SRV

The d2 option gives you the most information about the query you're performing. If you want the benefits of debug mode while still in command mode, you can issue nslookup using –ds switch. For example, type the command:

```
nslookup -ds www.microsoft.com.
```

You get detailed information about the query with the –ds switch.

exam Watch

When you do an nslookup, be aware that the most likely reason that you might receive a "non-authoritative" answer to a query is because your DNS server is answering from cache.

You should become well versed in the use of the nslookup command. It is an extremely useful and powerful tool for troubleshooting your DNS server.

EXERCISE 26-4

Using the Nslookup Utility

In order to complete this exercise, you must be connected to the Internet via a dial-up connection or via your network. If a firewall is implemented on your network, it must support passing nslookup queries.

1. Log on as Administrator if you have not already done so.
2. Open a command prompt.
3. At the command prompt, type: **nslookup.** Then press ENTER.
4. Note that the command prompt changes its appearance to that of the nslookup interactive prompt. At the interactive prompt, type: **set debug.** Then press ENTER.
5. Note that the command prompt doesn't change its appearance. That's OK, since it doesn't give you any feedback after you set one of the nslookup options. At the interactive command prompt, type: **www.syngress.com.** Then press ENTER.
6. Note the detailed information you receive. Here's a question: What is the "actual" name of the server for www.syngress.com? Check the Web site for the answer!

Using the System Monitor

When you install the Windows 2000 DNS server, it will place a large number of DNS-related counters into the System Monitor application. Many new counters have been added to the Windows 2000 DNS Object counter list. Table 26-5 lists these counters and their functions.

TABLE 26-5 DNS Performance Counters

Counter	Description
AXFR Request Received	Total full zone transfer requests received by the Master DNS server
AXFR Request Sent	Total full zone transfer requests sent by the Secondary DNS server
AXFR Response Received	Total full zone transfer responses received by the Secondary DNS server
AXFR Success Received	Total successful full zone transfers received by the Secondary DNS server
AXFR Success Sent	Total successful full zone transfers of the Master DNS server
Caching Memory	Total amount of caching memory used by the DNS server
Database Node Memory	Total database node memory used by the DNS server
Dynamic Update NoOperation	Total number No-operation/empty dynamic update requests received by the DNS server
Dynamic Update NoOperation/sec	Rate at which No-operation/empty dynamic update requests are received by the DNS server
Dynamic Update Queued	Total dynamic updates that are queued by the DNS server
Dynamic Update Received	Total dynamic update requests that are received by the DNS server
Dynamic Update Received/sec	Rate at which dynamic update requests are received by the DNS server
Dynamic Update Rejected	Total dynamic updates rejected by the DNS server
Dynamic Update TimeOuts	Total dynamic update timeouts of the DNS server
Dynamic Update Written to Database	Total dynamic updates written to the database by the DNS server

TABLE 26-5 DNS Performance Counters *(continued)*

Dynamic Update Written to Database/sec	Rate at which dynamic updates are written to the database by the DNS server
IXFR Request Received	Total incremental zone transfer requests received by the Master DNS server
IXFR Request Sent	Total incremental zone transfer requests sent by the Secondary DNS server
IXFR Response Received	Total incremental zone transfer responses received by the Secondary DNS server
IXFR Success Received	Total successful incremental zone transfers received by the Secondary DNS server
IXFR Success Sent	Total successful incremental zone transfers of the Master DNS server
IXFR TCP Success Received	Total successful TCP incremental zone transfers received by the Secondary DNS server
IXFR UDP Success Received	Total successful UDP incremental zone transfers received by the Secondary DNS server
Nbstat Memory	Total Nbstat memory used by the DNS server
Notify Received	Total notifies received by the Secondary DNS server
Notify Sent	Total notifies sent by the Master DNS server
Record Flow Memory	Total record flow memory used by the DNS server
Recursive Queries	Total recursive queries received by the DNS server
Recursive Queries/sec	Rate recursive queries are received by the DNS server
Recursive Query Failure	Total of recursive query failures
Recursive Query Failure/sec	Rate of recursive query failures
Recursive Send TimeOuts	Total of recursive query sending timeouts
Recursive TimeOut/sec	Rate recursive query sending timeouts
Secure Update Failure	Total secure update failures of the DNS server
Secure Update Received	Total secure update requests received by the DNS server
Secure Update Received/sec	Rate at which secure update requests are received by the DNS server
TCP Message Memory	Total TCP message memory used by the DNS server
TCP Query Received	Total TCP queries received by the DNS server

TABLE 26-5 DNS Performance Counters *(continued)*

TCP Query Received/sec	Rate TCP queries are received by the DNS server
TCP Response Sent	Total TCP responses sent by the DNS server
TCP Response Sent/sec	Rate TCP responses are sent by the DNS server
Total Query Received	Total queries received by the DNS server
Total Query Received/sec	Rate queries are received by the DNS server
Total Response Sent	Total responses sent by the DNS server
Total Response Sent/sec	Rate responses are sent by the DNS server
UDP Message Memory	Total UDP message memory used by the DNS server
UDP Query Received	Total UDP queries received by the DNS server
UDP Query Received/sec	Rate UDP queries are received by the DNS server
UDP Response Sent	Total UDP responses sent by the DNS server
UDP Response Sent/sec	Rate UDP responses are sent by the DNS server
WINS Lookup Received	Total WINS lookup requests received by the DNS server
WINS Lookup Received/sec	Rate WINS lookup requests are received by the DNS server
WINS Response Sent	Total WINS lookup responses sent by the DNS server
WINS Response Sent/sec	Rate WINS lookup responses are sent by the server
WINS Reverse Lookup Received	Total WINS reverse lookup requests received by the DNS server
WINS Reverse Lookup Received/sec	Rate WINS reverse lookup requests are received by the DNS server
WINS Reverse Response Sent	Total WINS reverse lookup responses sent by the DNS server
WINS Reverse Response Sent/sec	Rate WINS reverse lookup responses are sent by the server
Zone Transfer Failure	Total failed zone transfers of the Master DNS server
Zone Transfer Request Received	Total zone transfer requests received by the Master DNS server
Zone Transfer SOA Request Sent	Total zone transfer Start of Authority (SOA) requests sent by the Secondary DNS server
Zone Transfer Success	Total successful zone transfers of the Master DNS server

The system monitor allows you to draw a fine bead on the activities of your DNS installation. There is a counter that will aid you in troubleshooting and baselining just about any situation you might run into.

Using Event Viewer

The Windows 2000 Event Viewer has a dedicated log for DNS-specific information. The Event Viewer can provide you information on when zone transfers have taken place, if there was a problem with a zone transfer, when changes have taken place within the zone, or even report that an excessive number of changes have occurred to the zone for a specific period of time.

Since the Event Viewer is easy to access and doesn't require configuration changes on your part, it is often wise to start there and see if it supplies any clues to any type of DNS-related problem you might have.

on the Job

Often, the Event Viewer will return cryptic error message numbers. The Windows 2000 Server Resource Kit has a help file that you can install on your computer that has very large and useful list of event codes and what they mean.

Using Trace Logs

The Windows 2000 DNS server allows you to enable trace logging via the GUI if you require extremely detailed information about the DNS server's activities. The information gathered in the trace is saved to a text file on the local hard disk. A trace log can track all queries received and answered by the DNS server.

To enable trace logging, right-click on the server name in the DNS Management Console and click Properties. Click on the Logging tab, and you will see a dialog box similar to that in Figure 26-31.

exam Watch

Trace logging can be a very processor- and disk-intensive procedure, so be judicious in your use of this feature.

The logs are stored in a plain text file located at:

```
%system_root%\system32\dns\dns.log
```

FIGURE 26-31

Configuring trace logging for the DNS server

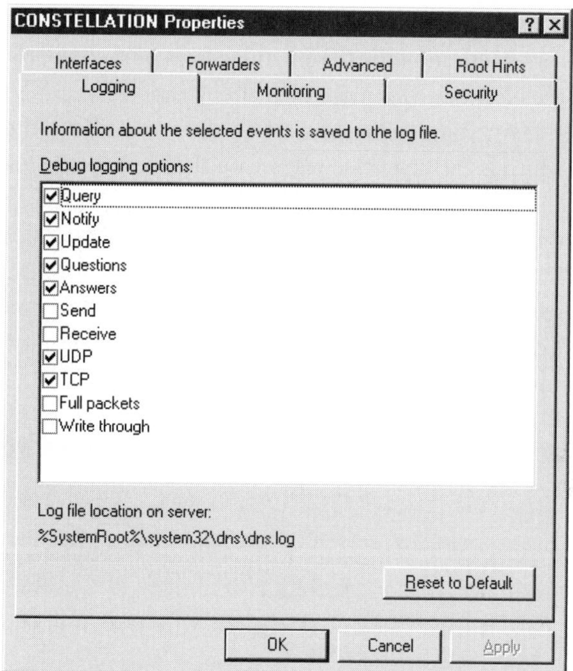

Note that problems with trace logging observed in beta versions of the Windows 2000 DNS server appear to continue with the final release version. You may find trace logging unreliable when attempting to perform traces on your own servers.

Network Monitor

The Network Monitor included "in the box" of the Windows 2000 server products allows you to analyze packets coming to and leaving the server running the Network Monitor application.

exam Watch

If you want a "full-fledged" version of Network Monitor that allows you to listen to all traffic on the segment, you can purchase Microsoft Systems Management Server 2.0.

Network Monitor will allow you to identify problems with network communications, including the details of the DNS query frames. Figure 26-32 displays the Network Monitor screen after a capture of DNS frames has been done.

Something to focus on when analyzing a DNS message is the message identifier, which is the first value you see on the Description line. For example, look at frames 376 and 377. Each of those has at the beginning of the description line "0x174E," which is the query identifier. You can use this number to track related queries and responses.

If there is a packet of particular interest—for example, a failure message is returned by the server—you can select the frame in the top pane and then click the Edit menu and then Copy. Open Notepad or another text editor and paste the contents of the frame into the application.

FIGURE 26-32

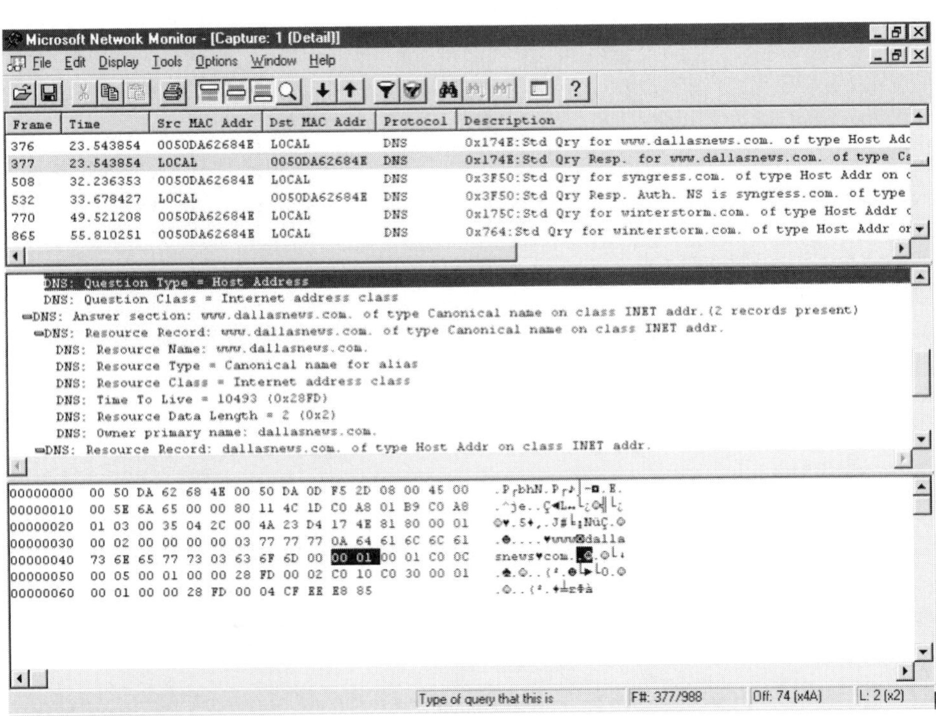

Capture of DNS packets in Microsoft Network Monitor

The Monitoring Tab

After you have completed your installation and configuration of the DNS server, you can perform a "quick check" to see if the server can successfully perform simple and iterative queries. A simple query would be one for which the server is authoritative, and an iterative query would be generated if a DNS request was received for which the server was not authoritative.

You can have the DNS server perform these queries for you automatically by right-clicking on the name of the server, selecting Properties, and clicking on the Monitoring tab. There you will be able to perform two different tests.

- **A simple query against the DNS server.** A query will be sent to the local server for resolution of a name on a zone for which the server is authoritative. The server is not asked to perform recursion for this simple query.
- **A recursive query to other DNS servers.** When you ask the server to perform a recursive query, it will act as a DNS client to other DNS servers in the process of performing recursion. This query will ask for the NS record information for the root of the Internet Domain Name Space. This requires that the cache.dns file is up to date and accurate.

You can also have the server perform these tests automatically, and the results of the automated testing will appear in the Test Results box. When configuring automated testing, you must choose an interval between tests. Each test will consume a small degree of network and processor resources.

on the job

If you have problems with your test failing using the tests in the Monitoring tab, try opening the Computer Management Console and using the DNS console from there. Often your queries will pass there when they have failed in the "official" DNS console. This is an "undocumented feature" included with Windows 2000 and should be repaired with the first service pack.

CERTIFICATION SUMMARY

The Domain Name System (DNS) provides for a more robust method of naming network resource than the NetBIOS naming scheme. NetBIOS uses a flat name space, and no two machines on a network can use the same NetBIOS name. The DNS allows for a hierarchical namespace where machines can use the same name as long as they live in different levels of the hierarchy.

The DNS uses fully qualified domain names (FQDNs) to identify hosts on the network. An FQDN is a combination of a host name and that host's domain name. Requests for network resources via an FQDN are passed through the WinSock interface, while requests for NetBIOS resources are passed through the NetBIOS interface.

NetBIOS applications use the NetBIOS name as the endpoint of communication. TCP/IP uses the destination IP address and Port number (socket) as the endpoint of communication. In order to allow NetBIOS applications to work on a TCP/IP network, a method must be available to resolve NetBIOS names to IP addresses. This is the primary function of NetBT or NetBIOS over TCP/IP.

WinSock applications do not require a host name to connect to a network resource. All that is required is an IP address. However, host names are easier to remember than IP addresses; therefore, a method must be in place to resolve host names to IP addresses. DNS servers provide this function.

When planning domain names for your organization, it is better to use geographical naming schemes rather than business unit-based naming schemes. The geographical approach tends to be more stable and makes the DNS administrator's life easier.

A DNS zone represents the physical component of the DNS. A DNS zone file contains information about domains and network resources contained within the domain. Remember that a single zone can contain multiple contiguous domains, and that a single DNS server can support multiple zones.

The two basic zone types are forward lookup zones and reverse lookup zones. A forward lookup zone resolves host names to IP addresses, and a reverse lookup zone resolves IP addresses to host names. Reverse lookup zones are not required, but are recommended. Reverse lookup zones use a special domain referred to as *in-addr.arpa.*

The zone file is a database file. The type of record added to the zone database is referred to as a resource record. These resource records populate the zone database and provide information about the resources contained within each zone and domain within the zone.

The DNS is a distributed database. You can take advantage of the distributed nature of the DNS by delegating responsibility among various servers for answering questions for a zone or group of zones. This is known as zone delegation. Secondary DNS servers are used to answer queries for a zone in order to take some of the load off a Primary DNS server.

Standard zones consist of single Primary and multiple Secondary DNS servers. The Primary DNS server contains the only read/write copy of the zone database file, while Secondaries contain read-only copies of the file. The Secondaries provide for both load balancing and fault tolerance for the zone.

Copies of the zone database file are placed on the Secondaries via zone transfer. When a zone is transferred from a Primary to a Secondary, either an AXFR or IXFR query initiates the process. Downlevel DNS servers such as the Windows NT 4.0 server can only issue AXFR queries. When the AXFR query is used, the entire zone is transferred. Windows 2000 DNS servers support the IXFR query, which causes only the changed elements of the zone to be transferred.

Windows 2000 DNS servers are RFC compliant. However, in a mixed DNS environment, not all DNS servers will support the same DNS options. Be sure in any mixed DNS environment that you check zone transfer compatibility among different DNS Server implementations.

We also covered more advanced concepts of how DNS and the Windows 2000 DNS server function. We started with how host names are resolved and learned about the new Windows 2000 caching resolver. You saw how the host name resolution order has changed with Windows 2000, and that the entries in the HOSTS file are immediately copied into the DNS client's local DNS cache.

Different types of queries were covered next. DNS clients and DNS servers issue the two main types of queries, recursive and iterative, in the process of resolving a host name. A recursive query must be answered definitively, either with a positive or a negative response. An iterative query allows responses that include a referral to another DNS server that may aid in resolving the query.

There are two types of "lookups," the forward lookup and the reverse lookup. A forward lookup seeks to resolve a host name to an IP address, and a reverse lookup resolves an IP address to a host name.

We then covered the different DNS servers' roles, which include Primary DNS server, Secondary DNS server, caching-only server, forwarding and forwarder DNS servers, and dynamic update DNS servers.

A Primary DNS server contains a read/write copy of the zone database and is authoritative for the zones it contains. A Secondary DNS server contains a read-only copy of the zone database and receives its copy from a Primary DNS server. Caching-only DNS servers do not contain any zone data, and are able to answer queries based on iterative queries and an ever-growing cache that builds over time, as queries are successfully resolved.

A forwarding DNS server sends recursive requests to a DNS forwarder. This allows the forwarding DNS server to offload some of the responsibility for resolving queries. A slave DNS server is a forwarding server that has the ability to perform recursion by issuing its own iterative queries disabled.

A Dynamic DNS server is able to receive dynamic updates from either or both DNS clients and/or a DHCP server. Only Windows 2000 DNS clients and Windows 2000 DHCP servers are able to update the DNS via the GSS Dynamic Update protocol.

The Windows 2000 DNS server can integrate its zones with the Active Directory on a zone-by-zone basis. There are advantages to integrating zones with the Active Directory, including the advantage of not having to create a separate Active Directory and DNS replication topology, using the Active Directory replication scheme, and the multimaster nature of the Active Directory, which helps avoid problems with dynamic updates and zone transfers when a single DNS server becomes unavailable.

Managing the DNS server includes configuring both the server as a whole and the zones it contains. When configuring the server, you must make decisions about what "root hints" you will use, whether or not you will use forwarders, and what interfaces will participate in answering DNS queries. There are also several Advanced options that you can configure for the server.

Zone configuration involves reviewing and adjusting the Start of Authority (SOA) record, defining additional Secondary Name servers for the zone, and configuring zone update behavior.

There are several monitoring and troubleshooting tools available for the Windows 2000 DNS server, including ipconfig and its new switches, nslookup utility, the Event Viewer's DNS log, and trace logging. The Network Monitor allows you to view DNS traffic moving to and from the machine running the Network Monitor program.

TWO MINUTE DRILL

The Domain Name System: Introductory Concepts and Procedures

- The NetBIOS namespace is flat.
- The DNS namespace is hierarchical.
- NetBIOS applications use the NetBIOS Session layer interface, while WinSock applications use the WinSock interface.
- An unqualified domain name does not contain the entire domain path.
- It is best to name your subdomains based on geographical consideration rather than business units, because geography is more stable.
- A forward lookup zone resolves host names to IP addresses.
- A reverse lookup zone resolves IP addresses to host names and uses the special in-addr.arpa domain to store its resource records.
- Zone transfer is the process of transferring the zone database file from one DNS server to another. Standard zones transfer the zone file from Master servers to Secondary servers.
- Zone transfers can be either complete or incremental. Downlevel DNS servers such as Windows NT 4.0 support only complete zones transfers, while the Windows 2000 DNS server supports both incremental and complete zone transfers.

How Host Names Are Resolved

- Host name resolution resolves DNS names to IP addresses. This is in contrast to NetBIOS name resolution, which resolves NetBIOS names to IP addresses.
- The order of host name resolution is localhost, DNS client cache, DNS, NetBIOS Remote Name cache, WINS, Broadcast, LMHOSTS.
- A Windows 2000 DHCP server can be configured to update records on a forward lookup when a host name is resolved to an IP address.
- A reverse lookup is when an IP address is resolved to a host name.

Windows 2000 DNS Server Roles

- A Primary DNS server contains a read/write copy of the zone database file.
- A Windows 2000 DNS server can be configured via a BOOT file or via the Registry and Active Directory.
- All Windows 2000 DNS server types cache the results of successful and unsuccessful queries.
- A forwarding DNS server is a DNS server that forwards queries to a DNS forwarder.
- When there is a name collision, the more recent record is considered the valid record.
- RAS clients release their Host (A) and Pointer (PTR) records after they gracefully sign off.

Integrating Windows 2000 with Active Directory

- Zones can be integrated with the Active Directory on a zone-by-zone basis.
- When you place a machine in the DnsUpdateProxy group, no security is placed on that record, and the next machine to "touch" the record becomes the owner of that record. DHCP servers can be placed in the DnsUpdateProxy group to avoid complications regarding access controls on secured DNS records.
- Domain controllers register SRV resource records with DNS servers. A DNS server that supports SRV resource records must be available in order to create a new Windows 2000 domain.

Integrating Windows 2000 Server with DHCP

- A Windows 2000 DHCP server can act as a proxy for downlevel DNS clients that cannot interact with a DNS server. The Windows 2000 DHCP server will update both the Host (A) and Pointer (PTR) record on behalf of the downlevel client.

Managing the Windows 2000 DNS Server

- The Windows 2000 DNS server can be managed via the DNS console.
- The DNS server properties are managed separately from the zone properties.
- The DNS client can be configured manually or via DHCP.
- DNS clients support multiple DNS servers. The one on the top of the list is referred to as the Preferred DNS server, and the others are called the Alternate DNS servers.

Monitoring and Troubleshooting DNS

- The ipconfig utility has added functionality, including the /flushdns, /displaydns, and /registerdns switches.
- System Monitor provides a larger number of counters than the Windows NT 4.0 version of Performance Monitor.
- The Event Viewer contains a new log named the DNS Log, which is dedicated to logging DNS specific errors.

Part VII

Internetworking Windows 2000

CHAPTERS

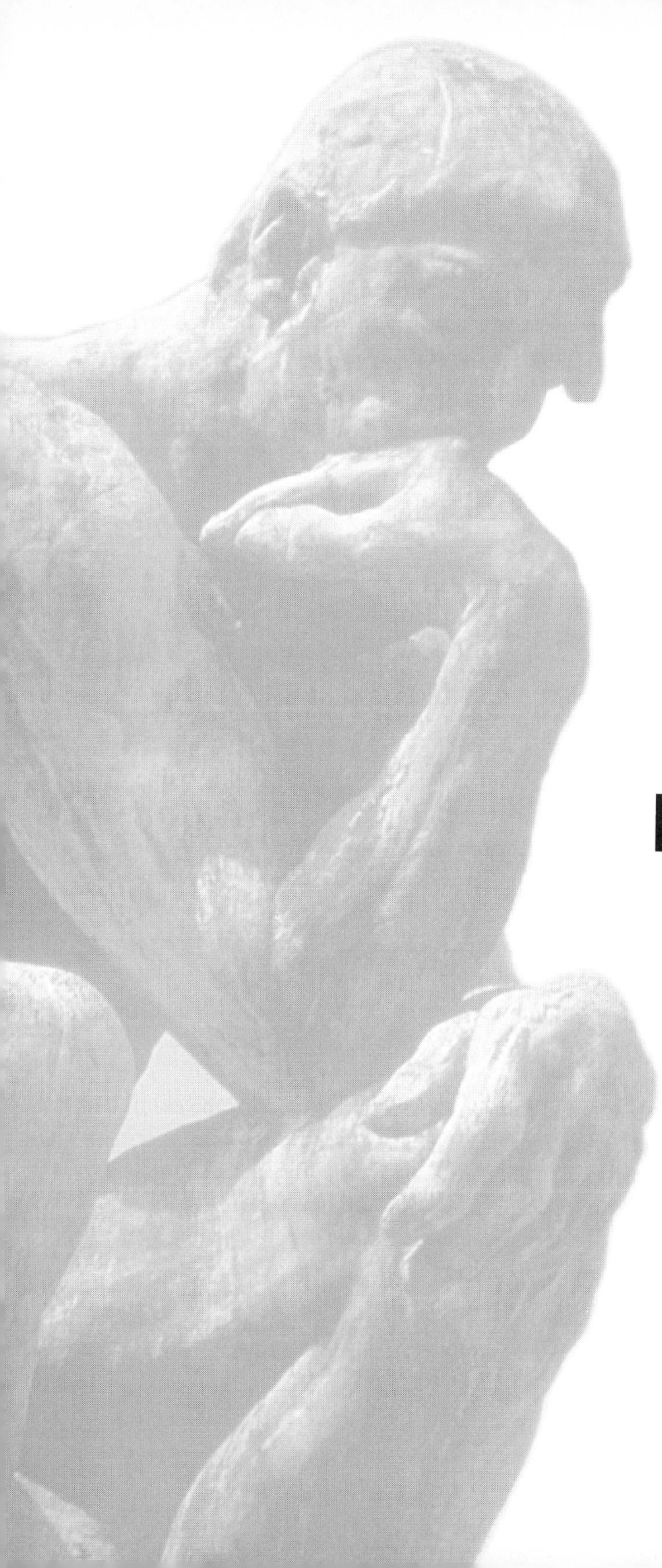

27

Planning and Configuring Windows 2000 Remote Access

CERTIFICATION OBJECTIVES

This chapter discusses some of the elements that make up the Windows 2000 Routing and Remote Access Service, but in particular it concentrates on Remote Access with dial-up or dedicated connections. It covers essential information you will need to know in the exam, as well as practical considerations for a live environment.

CERTIFICATION OBJECTIVE 27.01

Introduction

It is not difficult to set up the Windows 2000 Routing and Remote Access Service to provide users with remote access to your corporate network. In fact, it is very easy with the Windows 2000 new and integrated administration tool, the Routing and Remote Access snap-in. However, it does not follow that it is easy to set it up correctly and securely for a particular environment.

Being connected over public networks means that a remote access server is a high security risk and potentially one the most vulnerable gateways into your company's resources and confidential information. If it is your responsibility to set up and configure remote access, a thorough understanding of the underlying concepts will help you make informed choices of how best to configure it to meet the needs of your company without unnecessarily compromising security. You will also be better equipped to troubleshoot any problems if you can break down and analyze each component that makes up this complex service.

Finally, a thorough understanding of this service will be required for the exam "Implementing and Administering a Windows 2000 Network Infrastructure"—either directly with questions specifically on such favorite topics as VPNs and dial-up, or indirectly with questions on security, permissions, and routing.

This chapter details the various building blocks that make up the Routing and Remote Access Service to help you make some informed choices for configuring, managing, monitoring, and troubleshooting a Windows 2000 remote access server.

CERTIFICATION OBJECTIVE 27.02

Overview: Windows 2000 Routing and Remote Access Service

Remote access (RAS) was first introduced with NT3.51 Service Pack 2 to offer an inexpensive solution for remote users to access local resources via a dial-up connection. This was carried over into Windows NT 4.0 and then significantly changed when Microsoft released the Routing and Remote Access Server (RRAS) with considerable improvements to replace the previous version with a single integrated service that provided both remote access and multiprotocol routing.

The Routing and Remote Access Service for Windows 2000 server continues its line of evolution with the following new features:

- Internet Group Management Protocol (IGMP) support and support for multicast boundaries
- Network Address Translation with addressing/name resolution components that simplify Internet connections for a Small Office/Home Office (SOHO)
- Integrated AppleTalk routing
- Layer 2 Tunneling Protocol (L2TP) over IP Security (IPSec) support for router-to-router VPN connections
- Improved administration and management tools with a Routing and Remote Access MMC snap-in and a command-line utility called *Netsh* (the latter also allows scripting for automated configuration)
- Improved support for RADIUS

The following are components of the Routing and Remote Access Service:

- Multiprotocol router—routing IP, IPX, AppleTalk
- Demand-dial router
- Routing IP and IPX over on-demand or persistent WAN links (e.g., telephone lines, ISDN, or over VPN connections with PPTP or L2TP/IPSec)

- Remote Access Server—providing remote access connectivity to remote dial-up or VPN clients using a range of LAN protocols including IP, IPX, AppleTalk, and NetBEUI

Note that some of the components such as NAT, IPSec, routing, IGMP, and multicasting are covered in other chapters in this book.

What Is Remote Access?

A Windows 2000 server running the Routing and Remote Access Service enables a computer to be a remote access server that accepts connections from users who are physically separated from the corporate network but connect to it when needed over a WAN. This connection has traditionally used standard dial-up technologies such as analog telephone lines with modems.

Depending on your remote access requirements and corporate security policies, successfully connected and authenticated remote users can then either:

- Access resources on that server but not beyond the server
- Access resources on both that server and on other machines that have a connection with the server, so that remote users can access all resources on the corporate network as if they were locally connected

Remote Access vs. Remote Control

Many people get confused with the difference between remote access (such as RRAS supports) and remote control (such as Terminal Service supports or third-party applications such as PCAnywhere).

Although both involve connecting two computers usually over a WAN, the two are fundamentally different.

Remote access is when a workstation connects to a remote network so that remote resources can be transparently accessed. All applications are still run on the workstation—the only processing done on the remote access server involves the connection process (e.g., routing, authentication, encryption) rather than running any applications for the remote client.

Remote control is when a workstation shares (controls) a remote machine's resources (screen, keyboard, mouse, processor) over a remote link. This means that the remote machine can run applications for the client workstation because the CPU is shared. In this case, the workstation effectively becomes a dumb terminal, because it is not running applications itself but using the CPU on the remote machine.

Remote Access Connections

Similar to the new RRAS service in Windows NT 4.0, the Windows 2000 Routing and Remote Access Service provides two remote access connection methods for remote users:

- Dial-up networking
- Virtual private networking

Dial-Up Networking

Remote users make a nonpermanent dial-up connection using telecommunications services (e.g., analog telephone line with modem, ISDN, or X25) that connect similarly to a physical port on the remote access server. This is a direct physical connection between the client and the server. For added security, you can encrypt the data sent over this connection, but because the connection is point-to-point, this is not usually deemed necessary.

Typically, a mobile user will dial up with a modem and connect to a remote access server with a bank of dedicated modems listening for incoming calls.

Virtual Private Networking

Remote users make use of an IP internetwork to tunnel their remote access connection, making a virtual private network between them and the Remote Access Server (acting as a VPN Server). In contrast to dial-up networking, virtual private networking is a logical and indirect connection between remote user and connecting server. It is not necessary to encrypt the data sent over this connection, but usually considered advisable if connecting over a public internetwork. Typically, a remote user will connect to the Internet via an ISP, and from there initiate a virtual private network call to the VPN server that is also connected to the Internet.

Remote Access Clients

The following clients can connect to a Windows 2000 server running Routing and Remote Access Service:

- Windows 2000
- Windows NT 3.5
- Windows NT 4.0

- Windows 9*x*
- Windows for Workgroups
- MS-DOS
- Microsoft LAN Manager remote access clients

Additionally, almost any third-party client using the Point-to-Point Protocol (PPP) can connect, which includes UNIX and Apple Macintosh clients.

Remote Access Administration

There are two main utilities you use for Remote Access administration:

- The GUI Routing and Remote Access snap-in
- The Net Shell command line

The Routing and Remote Access Snap-In

The Routing and Remote Access snap-in allows you to perform a variety of administration tasks, including:

- Enabling/disabling routing and remote access
- Managing routing interfaces
- Configuring ports
- Controlling security
- Controlling remote access permissions
- Assigning network addresses
- Configuring remote access policies

This utility is available from the Administrative Tools folder, and is the primary management utility for configuring your company computers running Windows 2000 Server with Routing and Remote Access Service.

Additionally, you will need to configure the Dial-In tab on a user's account properties. If you are unsure how to do this, refer to Table 27-1.

The Dial-in options are shown in Figure 27-1. Refer to Table 27-2 for an explanation of these user properties.

TABLE 27-1

How to Configure the Dial-in Tab

Server Type	Where to Specify Dial-In Permissions
Stand-alone server	Specify the dial-in permissions and other related properties on the Dial-in tab of the user account properties in the Local Users and Groups snap-in.
Active Directory based server	Specify the dial-in permissions and other related properties on the Dial-in tab of the user account properties in the Active Directory Users and Computers snap-in.

FIGURE 27-1

Dial-in tab on the User Properties sheet

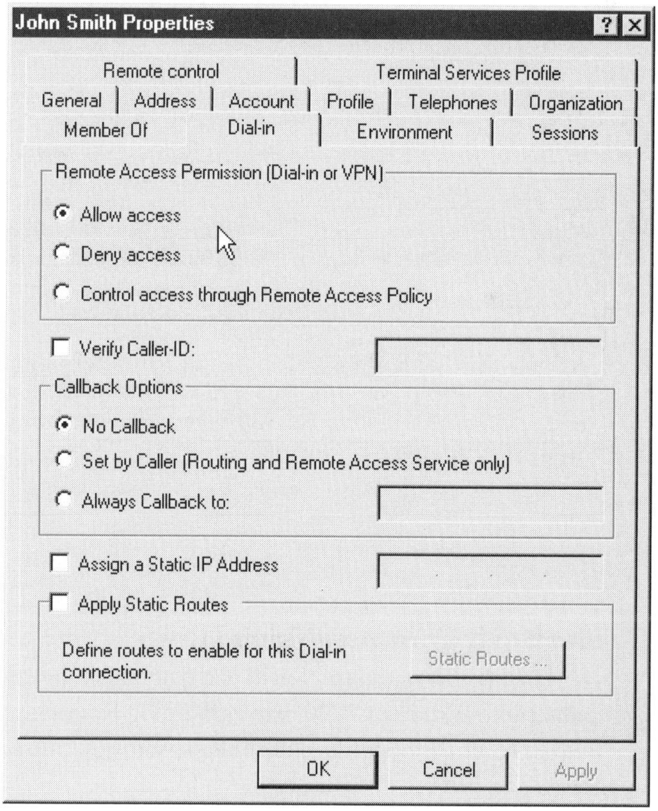

TABLE 27-2 Dial-in Properties on User Account

User Account Properties - Dial-in Options	Explanation
Remote Access Permission (Dial-in or VPN)	This is used to verify whether remote access is allowed. An explanation of these three options is in "Assigning Remote Access Permissions" later in this chapter.
Verify Caller ID	This is used to verify the caller by the hardware being used rather than username/password; if used, you must specify the Caller ID here. See the section "Caller ID" under "Remote Access Security."
Callback Options	Callback is when the remote user dials in and requests the server to call back, so the connection cost of the remote access session is charged to the server's line and not the user.
No Callback	This option doesn't allow the user to request being called back.
Set by Caller	This option doesn't automatically call back the user; however, if the user requests to be called back, it will do so.
Always Callback to	This is "Secure Callback" and is covered in more detail in the section "Secure Callback" under "Remote Access Security." If used, you must specify the number to be used here.
Assign a Static IP Address	This is used if you want to assign a static IP address to this user rather than using DHCP or allowing them to choose their own IP address.
Apply Static Routes	Use this if the user needs to access resources beyond the server, and automatic routes do not exist.

Net Shell Command-Line Utility

Net Shell (abbreviated to **Netsh**) is a command-line and scripting tool for both local and remote Windows 2000 servers running Routing and Remote Access. It can be used in conjunction with remote access settings, but is also for routing, DHCP Relay, and NAT.

It is automatically installed in *%systemroot%\system32* when Windows 2000 is installed, and when executed will run taking commands in either Online or Offline mode until you exit the shell.

- **Online mode** Commands are executed immediately.
- **Offline mode** Commands are accumulated and executed as a batch only when the special command "commit" is issued (you can discard accumulated commands with the "flush" command).

One example of using this utility is for doing a quick backup of your Routing and Remote Access server. To do so, type: **Netsh dump >*filename*.txt.**

This dumps your current RRAS configuration to the named text file (which you can view with any text editor). To restore this configuration, ensure you have a default RRAS server enabled, and then type: **Netsh exec <*filename*.txt>.**

Other useful Netsh commands for remote access include **ras show client** to display currently connected remote access clients, **ras show activeservers** to display all Windows 2000 servers running RRAS on your network, and **ras show authtype**, which displays the permitted authentication types. Refer to the Windows Help for more information on Netsh and other available commands.

CERTIFICATION OBJECTIVE 27.03

Installing and Configuring the Remote Access Service

This section will cover typical hardware environments, and how to enable and configure remote access service on a Windows 2000 server.

Hardware Requirements

First of all, ensure your Windows 2000 uses hardware that complies with the Windows 2000 Hardware Compatibility List (HCL), and bear in mind that additional processing power will be required—particularly if you intend to use data encryption.

Dial-Up Hardware and WAN Infrastructure

The physical or logical connection between the Routing and Remote Access server and the remote access client uses dial-up equipment (e.g., modem or ISDN) and the telecommunications infrastructure that may be one of the following:

- Public Switched Telephone Network (PSTN)
- Digital Links and V90
- Integrated Services Digital Network (ISDN)
- X25
- Asynchronous Transfer Mode (ATM) over Asymmetric Digital Subscriber Line (ADSL)

Public Switched Telephone Network (PSTN) Also known as POTS (Plain Old Telephone Service), this is the analog telephone system originally designed to transfer human voice. The dial-up equipment consists of an analog modem at the client and at the server. The maximum bit rate is low.

Digital Links and V.90 Instead of the Routing and Remote Access server having to convert analog signals to digital and vice versa (which is what a standard modem does), a connection through a digital switch based on a T-Carrier or ISDN will greatly improve the bit rate throughput because of the reduction in quantization noise. This presupposes that no other conversion is carried out before reaching the remote modem. Although this setup can only eliminate noise on one side of the connection, it does greatly improve the throughput from server to client.

The remote access client must be using a V90 modem, and the RRAS server must be using a V90 digital switch, using a digital link to connect to the PSTN (e.g., T-Carrier or ISDN).

Integrated Services Digital Network This offers a fully digital connection more suited for data transmissions by using an ISDN adapter on both sides of the connection (remote access client and Routing and Remote Access server).

ISDN offers multiple channels, which means that two or more data channels can be combined for greater throughput—this is called *multilink*.

Typically, remote access users will use Basic Rate ISDN (BRI) with two 64-Kbps channels, and large organizations that require a high throughput will use Primary Rate ISDN (PRI) with 23 64-Kbps channels.

X25 X25 uses an international standard for sending data across public packet-switching networks.

The Windows 2000 Routing and Remote Access server will only support direct connections to X25 networks by using an X25 smart card.

ATM over ADSL ADSL offers a new technology aimed at small businesses and residential customers. It offers a higher throughput than PSTN and ISDN connections, but the bit rate is higher downstream than upstream—typically 384 Kbps when going out and 384 Kbps–1.544 Mbps when coming in (this usually suits Internet traffic usage where users download a much higher percentage of data than they upload).

ADSL equipment can appear to a Windows 2000 server as one of two interfaces: Ethernet or dial-up. When seen as an Ethernet interface, the ASDL behaves in the same way as a standard network adapter connected to the Internet. When seen as a dial-up interface, ADSL provides the physical connection for ATM traffic.

Other, Slower Connections Slower connections are also possible via direct connection over:

- RS-232C null modem cable
- Parallel port
- Infrared port

Enabling the Routing and Remote Access Service

This is one service that you don't install as you would normally with Add/Remove Programs in Control Panel. Instead, it is automatically installed in Windows 2000, but in a disabled state. However, before you enable it, ensure that all interfaces and protocols you want to use for the Routing and Remote Access Service are installed, configured, and working correctly. This may include dial-up equipment and Internet interfaces.

EXERCISE 27-1

Enabling the Routing and Remote Access Service

1. Ensure you are logged on with Administrator privileges, and choose Routing and Remote Access from Start | Programs | Administrative Tools.

   If Routing and Remote Access hasn't been previously enabled on this server, it will show your local server status as disabled with a red cross, as shown in the following illustration.

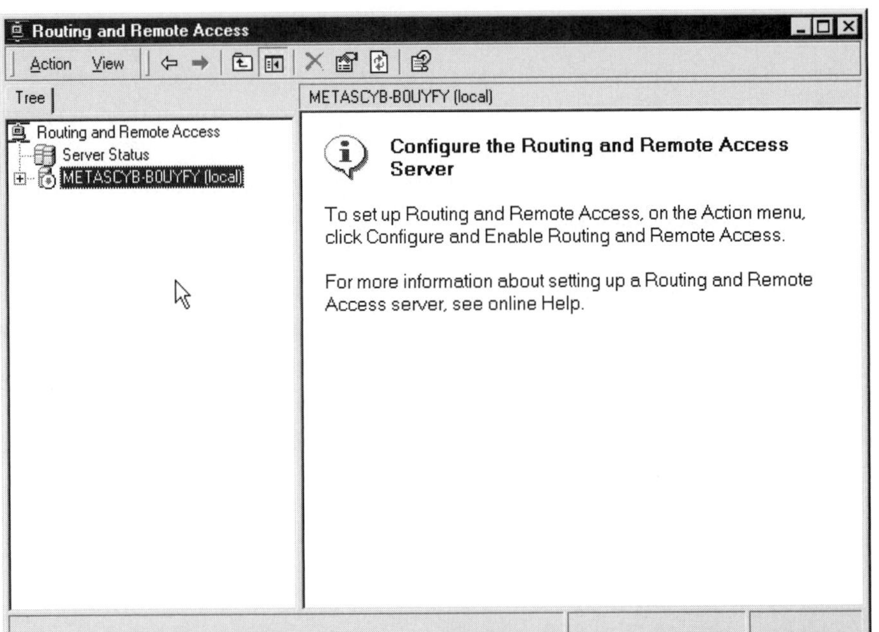

2. Right-click on your server and from the shortcut menu, select Configure and Enable Routing and Remote Access. This starts the Routing and Remote Access Server Setup Wizard. Click Next.
3. You will have a choice of common configurations to choose from as in the following illustration.

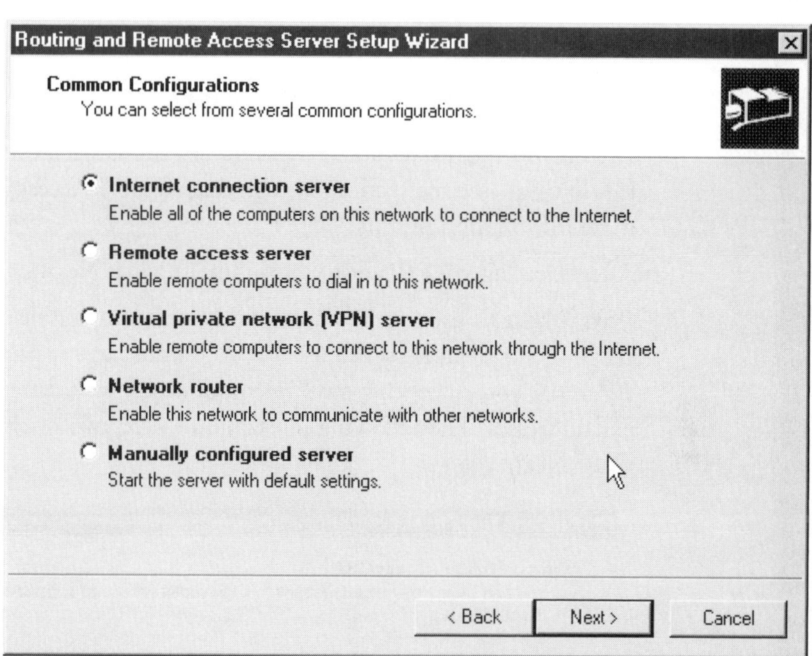

For more details on these choices, see Table 27-3, but for now, select "Remote access server" and click Next.

4. You will be asked to verify that the protocols you want to use are already installed with a list of installed protocols displayed. If you select the option to install other protocols and click Next, the wizard will inform you that it cannot continue until the protocols you need are installed. You will be given a choice to Finish (so you can install the protocols you need and then call up the Routing and Remote Access Server Setup Wizard again) or Back.
5. When you select "Yes, all of the required protocols are on this list" and click Next, you will be prompted for the Network Selection you want to use. If your server is multihomed, this is particularly important. You will see a list of all network adapters with their description and assigned IP address—select the one you want to use on your internal network. Click Next.

6. You will then be asked about IP Address Assignment, whether to use DHCP or define a static pool of addresses. The recommended setting is "Automatically" if you have a DHCP server on the same subnet as your remote access server. Even if you don't have a DHCP server on the same subnet, you can still use this setting—see the section "Integrating Remote Access and DHCP" for more information on this.

   After selecting your IP address assignment, click Next.

7. If you chose to use a static pool of addresses, you will be asked to specify a range (pool) of addresses to use. If you do not have enough free contiguous addresses, you can specify multiple pools, each with different start and end addresses. The following illustration shows two pools of IP addresses. Click Next.

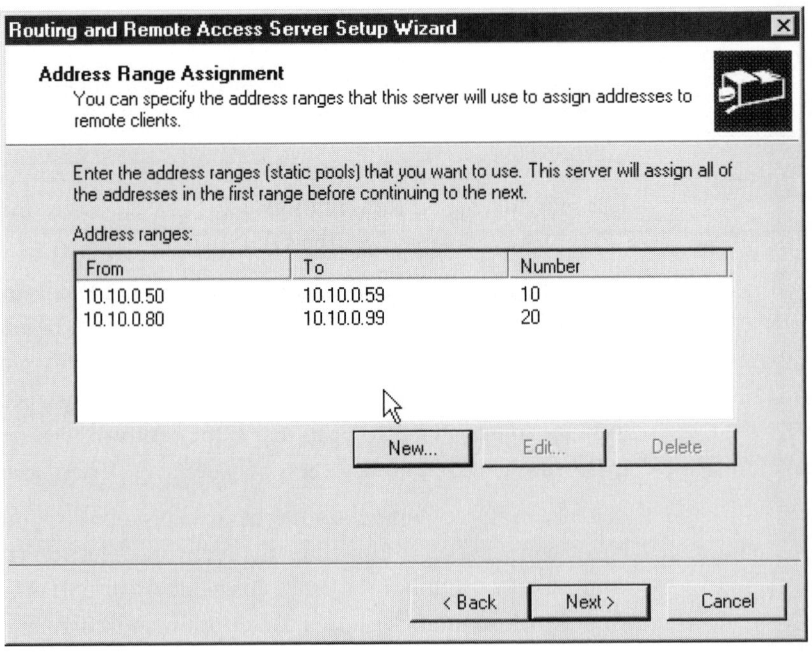

8. The next dialog asks whether you want to use Windows authentication or RADIUS. Choosing RADIUS configures RRAS to be a RADIUS client, which means it doesn't authenticate remote access clients itself, but passes authentication requests to another server that holds such authentication information.

   If you do select the RADIUS option, you will then be prompted to specify details of the RADIUS server/s and the password (shared secret) to connect to it. When you click OK, your RRAS server will attempt to connect to the RADIUS server with the credentials provided to verify that it can communicate with it. If the RADIUS server cannot be located, setup cannot continue.

   The default setting is "No, I don't want to set up this server to use RADIUS now." Select this and click Next.

9. The final screen tells you that you have successfully completed the setup configuration, and prompts you to click Finish if you want to automatically load Help.

   Note that at this time, if you have selected to use automatic TCP/IP address assignment and the server cannot find a DHCP server on its subnet, you will be reminded to configure the DHCP Relay Agent.

10. When this wizard closes you will be returned to the Routing and Remote Access snap-in, where your local server should now show a green up arrow assigned to it, indicating that the service is enabled and started.

11. If you wish to stop or pause the service, right-click on the server, and from the shortcut menu select All Tasks, and then either Stop or Pause. To revert to an enabled state again, choose Start or Resume from the same shortcut menu.

Table 27-3 lists the installation options in the Routing and Remote Access Server Setup Wizard.

TABLE 27-3 The Installation Options in the Routing and Remote Access Server Setup Wizard

Common Configurations	Description
Internet connection server	This offers two ways of sharing a single Internet connection with other computers on your network. Internet Connection Sharing (ICS) is the simplest setup, and selecting this will to prompt you to use the Network and Dial-up Connections folder to configure an Internet connection, which is then shared. Network Address Translation (NAT) is another way to provide Internet access to other computers on your network. NAT requires more configuration, but has greater flexibility. It is installed as a routing protocol within RRAS.
Remote access server	This is what we will be configuring, and the typical scenario is a dial-up modem or bank of modems attached to the server that allow remote clients to dial in and then access local resources.
Virtual private network (VPN) server	We will also be configuring a VPN server, and the typical scenario is a multihomed server with one adapter connected to the Internet and the other connected to your company network. Remote clients dial up to the Internet and then tunnel a second connection over the first to connect securely to the server.
Network router	This allows the server to route packets to other routers when required, which could be over a persistent link or on demand. Multicasting and unicast boundaries are also supported.
Manually configured server	This simply loads the Routing and Remote Access snap-in so you can manually configure the options you need without being prompted by the Setup wizard.

CERTIFICATION OBJECTIVE 27.04

Configuring the Remote Access Server

There are several configuration options you should check and change if necessary before allowing remote access clients to connect to this server, including:

- Allowing remote access
- Settings for authentication and auditing
- IP address assignment

EXERCISE 27-2

Configuring the Remote Access Server

1. If not already open, load the Routing and Remote Access Service snap-in from the Administrative Tools folder.
2. Right-click your remote access server in the left pane and select Properties. This will display the dialog box shown in the following illustration.

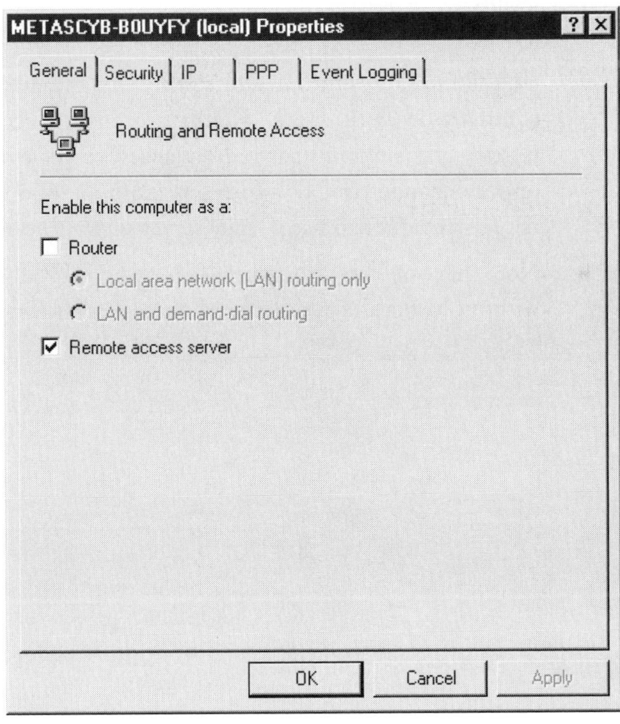

3. Under the General tab, you will find the most important setting that enables Routing and Remote Access to accept remote connections. Ensure the check box "Remote access server" is selected.
4. Under the Security tab, you will find properties for authentication and accounting. Unless you are using a RADIUS server, select Windows Authentication and Windows Accounting.

   Authentication Methods allows you to choose the authentication protocols you want the server to use. If a remote access client cannot match one of your chosen authentication protocols, they will not successfully connect.

   For more details on each of these authentication protocols, see "Secure Authentication" under the "Remote Access Security" section later in this chapter.
   The default setting is MS-CHAP and MS-CHAP v2.
5. The IP tab shows the current settings for the internal connection to your company network. Here you can stop remote access clients from connecting to resources beyond your remote access server with the **"Enable IP routing"** option, change your IP address assignment, and specify an alternative network adapter to use if your server is multihomed.

   Note that you can switch between using DHCP and a static IP address pool without losing the address pool details, as shown in the following illustration.

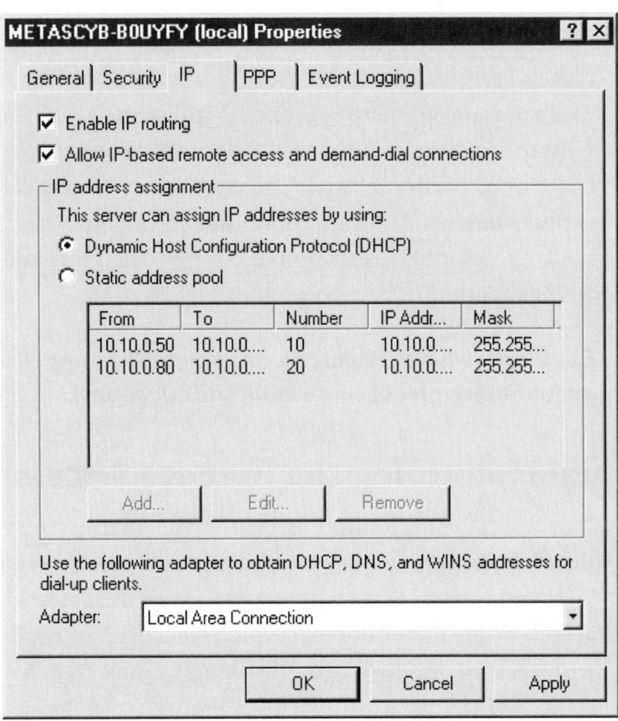

6. The PPP tab allows you to compression. See the section "Connections using PPP Multilink and BAP" later in this chapter for more details on these options.
7. The Event Logging tab allows you to specify the level of information that the remote access server automatically sends to the Event Log. The default is errors and warnings. For more information about logging, see the section "Event Logging" under "Managing and Monitoring Remote Access" later in the chapter.

   You can also set PPP logging in this dialog box. For more information, see the section "PPP Tracing" under "Managing and Monitoring Remote Access" later in the chapter.
8. When you have finished looking at or changing the server's properties, Click OK.

Testing Connectivity to the Remote Access Server

To test a connection to the Remote Access server, ensure that your test user has dial-in permissions (check the "Allow access" option under the Dial-in tab of the user's account properties as shown in Figure 27-1), and attempt to connect to your remote access server using a standard PPP connection.

As listed previously, your choice of remote access clients is varied but the following xercise takes you through configuring a remote access connection for a Windows 2000 Professional user who is dialing in from his modem to the remote access server's modem.

Each user who connects to an incoming connection must have a valid user account (e.g., local or domain user account).

Managing and Monitoring the Remote Access Server

The Routing and Remote Access Service snap-in provides most of the dynamic information you will need to manage and monitor remote access connections.

If you expand Ports, you should see all the external ports available to the remote access server. For example, if you have a bank of modems, these should be displayed with their name, device (modem), and status. When a connection comes in, the status will change from Inactive to Active, and if you right-click on it to obtain Status information, you will be able to see information such as the line speed, bytes in and out, errors such as CRC failures, and network registration (e.g., assigned IP address). You can reset a port from this status dialog box.

If your remote access server is connected to the Internet, you will also see VPN ports listed as WAN Miniports—the default being 5 using PPTP and 5 using L2TP. See the section "Virtual Private Networking" for more information on configuring VPNs.

Remote Access Clients will indicate a number in brackets, which is the number of currently connected users. Expand Remote Access Clients to view details of who is connected, with details of their username, the duration of the call, and the number of ports allocated (the latter is applicable only when using multilink—see the section "Connections using PPP Multilink and BAP" later in this chapter for more information). When a user is connected, you can send him or her a message by right-clicking on the session and selecting Send Message. Similarly, you can choose to send a message to all currently connected remote clients.

The Event Log will record certain events to help provide a history of what happened on your remote access server; for example, who connected and when, and what IP address they were assigned. You can change the level of information written to the Event Log, but this not advisable unless you are experiencing technical difficulties and require detailed information for analysis. See the section "Managing and Monitoring Remote Access" for more information on logging and recording events.

CERTIFICATION OBJECTIVE 27.05

Assigning Remote Access Permissions

In Windows NT 3.51 and Windows NT 4.0, remote access was granted to domain users based solely on whether the user's account had dial-in permission—configured in User Manager or the Remote Access Administration utility.

In Windows 2000, remote access authorization can still be determined by the dial-in properties for the user account. For a stand-alone server, you specify the dial-in permission and other related properties on the Dial-in tab of the user account properties in the Local Users and Groups snap-in. For an Active Directory based server, you specify these dial-in options on the Dial-in tab of the user account properties in the Active Directory Users and Computers snap-in as we saw previously in Figure 27-1.

For those of you familiar with configuring dial-in properties in Windows NT 4.0, you will probably notice a new option for dial-in permission that's new to Windows 2000. It's rather an unusual one, because it's only available when running in a native mode domain: Control access through Remote Access Policy. Irrespective of whether your Windows 2000 Server running Routing and Remote Access Service is in a mixed or native domain, the Remote Access Permission setting here is very important when it comes to assigning remote access permissions.

Remote Policies

New to Windows 2000, Routing and Remote Access uses remote access policies to allow greater flexibility in configuring and managing remote access.

A remote access policy not only allows you to manage who has remote access permission and under what circumstances (e.g., only on certain days and times), but also allows you to impose conditions and connection settings for your remote users. For example, you can set the maximum session time allowed, require certain authentication, require encryption, and so forth. If the remote user does not meet these conditions and constraints, the connection is refused or disconnected.

If you use multiple remote access policies, you could have different sets of conditions for different remote access clients, and/or you could have different requirements for the same remote user based on certain factors (for example, if connecting over the Internet rather than your modem pool, impose higher security restrictions such as a strong authentication protocol and encryption).

The Default Remote Access Policy

When you first enable Routing and Remote Access Service, you will see a single built-in policy: "Allow access if dial-in permission is enabled." This is referred to as "The Default Policy." You would have seen this when you finished enabling the Routing and Remote Access Service. If it is not displayed in the right pane, expand the Remote Access Policies in the console tree. The details pane lists this policy, and if you right-click it and choose Properties, you will see as in Figure 27-2 that this policy consists of a single condition that must be met before a remote access client can connect.

FIGURE 27-2

Settings in the Default Policy

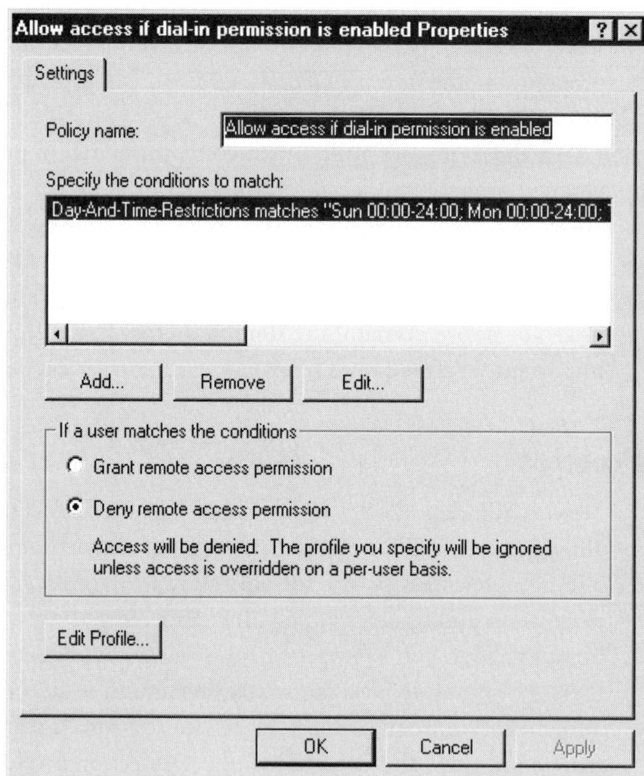

If you click Edit, you will see it allows you to specify the times of day, as shown in Figure 27-3.

Because the only condition is Any Day, Any Time, this effectively makes this policy transparent (not effective), but you could restrict your condition to certain days and times (for example, designated office working hours).

However, on the Settings dialog box there is another section labeled "If a user matches the conditions" with two choices:

- Grant remote access permission
- Deny remote access permission (the default)

Therefore, the default condition of this policy is Any Day, Any Time, but Deny remote access permission. You might deduce that this Default Policy would deny anybody connecting to the Remote Access server; however, the Deny permission can be overwritten by the Dial-in properties on a user's account. If a user's account explicitly grants dial-in permission (rather than "Deny access" or "Control access through Remote Access Policy" as shown in Figure 27-1), with the Default Policy in place, a user can (when authorized and authenticated) connect to this server any day or any time.

Therefore, the final remote access permission consists of four elements:

- The conditions of the remote access policy or policies
- The remote access permission for the policy ("If a user matches the conditions")

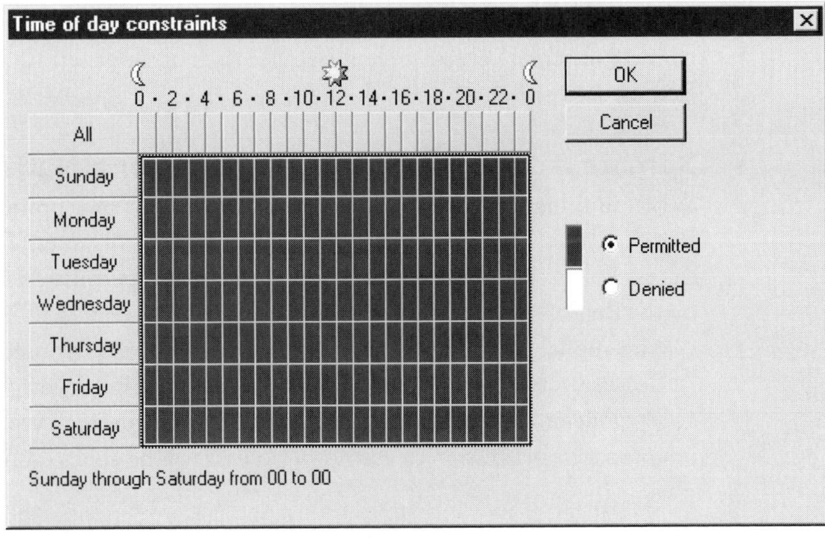

FIGURE 27-3 Time of day constraints within the Default Policy

- The policy's profile (additional settings such as permitted media and required authentication)
- The Dial-in Remote Access Permission on the user's account

The Administrative Models for Remote Access Policy

The four elements that control who has remote access permissions work together, and how you choose to configure them will depend on factors such as whether your network is a mixed or native mode domain, the numbers of users you have, and the degree of control you require when configuring remote access. Microsoft recommends that you choose one of the following three Administrative Models when designing and implementing your Remote Access Policies:

- Access by User
- Access by Policy in a Windows 2000 mixed-mode domain
- Access by Policy in a Windows 2000 native-mode domain

Remote Access Permission by User

This is simplest to administer for a small number of users.

As in Windows NT 4.0, remote access permission is granted on individual user accounts. As we have seen in Windows 2000, this is from the Remote Access Permission on the Dial-in tab of the Properties window for the user account.

Even with the Remote Access Default Policy in place (of "Deny remote access permission"), the individual users with Dial-in permission will have permission to connect to remote access servers, because their account setting will override the Remote Access Policy.

Remote Access Permission by Policy for a Native-Mode Domain

When running in native mode, user accounts have a new option available under the Remote Access Permission in the Dial-in tab: Control Access Through Remote Access Policy. When this is selected, remote access permission is solely determined by the Remote Access Policy or policies.

This model is easier to administer for a large number of users.

Because you have no individual user account settings overriding any remote access policies, you must change or create a new Remote Access Policy that gives remote access permission to users—or no user will be able to connect to your Remote

Access Server. The simplest way to do this would be to edit the Default Profile such that the "Deny remote access permission" is changed to "Grant remote access permission." However, this would mean that all users would have remote access permission at all times; for security reasons, you would probably want to restrict this to either certain users/groups or to other conditions.

If you prefer a more secure policy design and do not want to grant remote access permission to everybody, it is better to grant or deny access by group membership. Group membership is granted with the Windows-Group attribute, which will be explained in more detail later.

Decide whether you want to explicitly grant permission only if users belong to a selected group (and implicitly reject access if users don't belong to your selected groups), or whether you want to explicitly deny permission if users belong to a selected group (and implicitly accept users if they don't belong to your selected groups). You will then need to delete or edit the Default Policy and have a new policy (or policies) to reflect your choice.

If you want to grant access by group membership:

1. Create a new policy called something similar to "Allow Access If Member of Selected Groups."
2. Add the Windows-Groups attribute to the policy, and then select the group or groups to be granted access. On the policy itself, select the "Grant remote access permission" option.

If you want to deny access by group membership:

1. Create a new policy called something similar to "Deny Access If Member of Selected Groups."
2. Add the Windows-Group attribute to the policy, and then select the group or groups to be denied access.
3. On the policy itself, select the "Deny remote access permission" option.

Remote Access Permission by Policy for a Mixed-Mode Domain

In this model, you cannot enable the "Control access through Remote Access Policy" option in the user account properties under the Dial-in tab. Instead, the Remote Access Permission can be set to either "Allow access" or "Deny access."

Set this option to "Allow access" for all users, and then delete or modify the Default Policy to control who has remote access permission. If you don't delete or change the Default Policy, all users will be granted permission (because the profile overrides the "Deny remote access permission" in the policy).

As described in the native mode model, you can create policies that explicitly or implicitly grant or deny access by group membership.

However, if you decide to explicitly deny access by membership, you cannot as before use the "Deny remote access permission" in the policy, because each user profile has "Allow access," which will override the policy.

One alternative is to add a condition to your profile that is impossible to match; for example, specify that the user has to be calling in to the server with an invalid telephone number. To do this, edit the profile, and on the Dial-In Constraints tab, select Restrict Dial-In To This Number Only and specify a number that isn't valid for your remote access server.

Remote Access Policy Conditions

The Default Policy has only the one condition: the Day-And-Time-Restriction. We mentioned earlier that you could add another condition by adding an attribute called Windows-Group, which allowed us to explicitly grant or deny access permission based on group membership. Remember that with Windows 2000, you can have both nested groups and universal groups.

Table 27-4 lists the Remote Access Policy conditions.

TABLE 27-4 Remote Access Policy Conditions

Condition Attribute	Explanation
Called-Station-ID	The telephone number of the remote access server. Note that the telephone line, hardware, and hardware drivers must all support passing the station-ID.
Calling-Station-ID	The telephone number used by the remote user. Note that the telephone line, remote server, and all connecting hardware must support passing the caller ID; if not, the connection will be denied.
Client-Friendly Name	Only applicable if the RRAS server is acting as a RADIUS client.
Client-IP-Address	Only applicable if the RRAS server is acting as a RADIUS client.

TABLE 27-4 Remote Access Policy Conditions *(continued)*

Condition Attribute	Explanation
Client-Vendor	Only applicable if the RRAS server is acting as a RADIUS client.
Day-And-Time-Restriction	Days and times that are valid for connections; note the time taken from the RRAS server.
Framed-Protocol	Only applicable if the RRAS server is acting as a RADIUS client.
NAS-Identifier	Only applicable if the RRAS server is acting as a RADIUS client.
NAS-IP-Address	Only applicable if the RRAS server is acting as a RADIUS client.
NAS-Port-Type	The type of media used by the caller; for example, analog telephone lines (asynch), ISDN, virtual private networks (virtual).
Service-Type	Only applicable if the RRAS server is acting as a RADIUS client.
Tunnel-Type	Tunneling protocols to be used (PPTP and L2TP).
Windows-Groups	Domain groups (can be nested or universal) of which the remote user is a member. Note local groups not supported.

NAS is an abbreviation for "Network Access Server," and is a generic term for a server offering remote access services. ISPs will use this generic term, while Microsoft's two specific products that deliver these services are the "Routing and Remote Access Service" (often abbreviated as RRAS) and the "Internet Authentication Service" (abbreviated as IAS).

Remote Access Policy Profiles

The policy's profile is a further set of conditions that apply after a connection is authorized. The profile applies irrespective of whether access permission has been granted by user or policy.

Click Edit Profile on the policy's Properties sheet to view/edit the Profile. You will see the six tabbed options as shown in Figure 27-4.

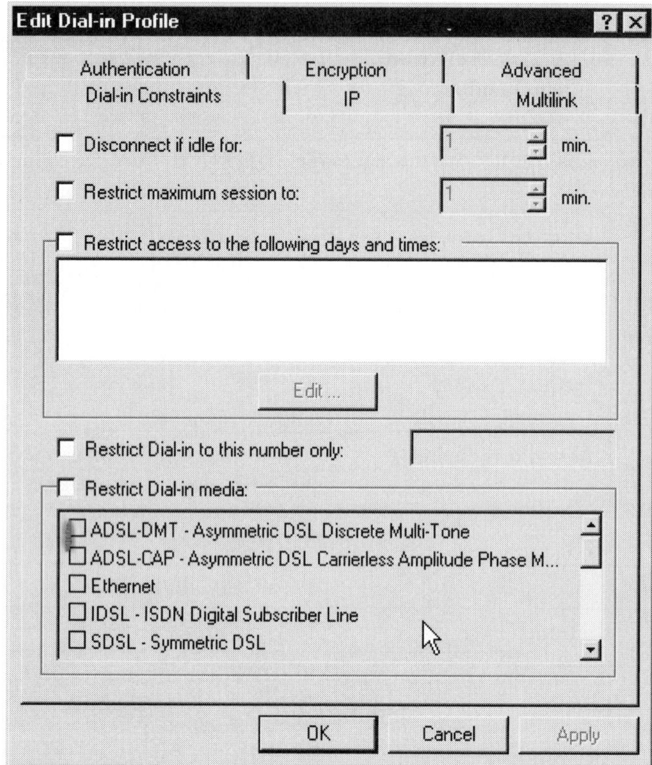

FIGURE 27-4

Remote Access Policy's Profile options

Policy Profile Options under Dial-In Constraints

This tab has the following options where you can define with a high degree of control these dial-in conditions:

- **Restrict access to the following days and times** By default, this is not set, but allows you to specify when a connection will be allowed. Connection attempts outside permitted times will be denied, although currently connected sessions will not be disconnected.
- **Restrict Dial-In to this number only** By default, this is not specified, but allows you to set a specific number that the remote user must call for a connection to be allowed.
- **Restrict Dial-In media** By default, this is not specified, but allows you to restrict exactly which medium the remote access user should use (e.g., ISDN, T1). If the medium being used is not the one specified when this option is set, the connection will be rejected.

Policy Profile Options under IP Address Policies

This tab has the following options where you can define a high degree of control over the IP options for a connecting remote user:

- **IP address assignment policy** By default, the remote access server supplies an IP address for the remote access clients when they connect. However, this option allows you to explicitly specify whether the server must specify an address, or whether the remote access user can request to use its own choice of IP address.
- **IP packet filters** By default, no packet filtering is enabled, but for security purposes, you could specify parameters such as inbound and outbound protocols, IP addresses, ports, etc. You can set these on an exception basis—either all traffic except the packets specified in the filters, or no traffic except the packets specified in the filters.
- **Disconnect if idle for** By default, this is not set, but allows you to set a period of time after which you can disconnect the remote user if the link has been idle.
- **Restrict maximum session to** By default, this is not set, but allows you to specify the maximum time a remote user can be connected at any one time.

Policy Profile Options under Multilink

This allows you to enable multilink and the Bandwidth Allocation Protocol (BAP) if the remote access server has these enabled. Multilink allows you to combine multiple physical connections into a single logical connection to increase the available bandwidth for a single connection.

Because multilink cannot automatically adapt to changing bandwidth requirements, you should also enable BAP so that the multilinks can be automatically added, dropped, and managed as needed.

For more information on multilink and BAP, see the section "Connections using PPP Multilink and BAP" later in this chapter.

- **Multilink Settings** This takes the default setting from the server itself, but here it allows you to disable multilink, or to set the maximum number of ports that a connection can use.
- **Bandwidth Allocation Protocol Settings** This allows a multilink connection to be reduced automatically if the throughput on the link falls below a specified capacity for a specific time.

Policy Profile Options under Authentication

You can specify the authentication methods allowed for the connection. The authentication protocols specified here must also be enabled on the server. For more information on authentication protocols, see "Authentication Protocols" in the "Remote Access Security" section.

Policy Profile Options under Encryption

This tab has the following options, where you can specify a high degree of control over the encryption required for remote access users:

- **No Encryption** This allows nonencrypted data over the connection, which may be preferable if the need for performance is higher than security.
- **Basic** This is for dial-up and PPTP connections and uses Microsoft Point-to-Point Encryption (MPPE) with a 40-bit key, and for L2TP over IPSec connections, uses a 56-bit Data Encryption Standard (DES) encryption.
- **Strong** This is for dial-up and PPTP connections, and uses MPPE with a 56-bit key and for L2TP over IPSec connections, uses a 56-bit DES encryption.

Policy Profile Options under Advanced

These are not relevant to Routing and Remote Access, but are for RADIUS attributes that are sent to the RADIUS client by the IAS server.

EXERCISE 27-3

CertCam 27-3

Modifying the Default Remote Access Policy

Remember that we looked at the Default Policy, which was effectively any day, any time. This exercise takes you through modifying this by adding a further condition that is to only accept Domain Users to make the condition more restrictive.

1. Expand the Remote Access Policies to display the Default Policy in the details pane. Right-click on it and select Properties.
2. Click Add and you will see that you can add conditions mentioned in Table 27-4, as shown in the following illustration.

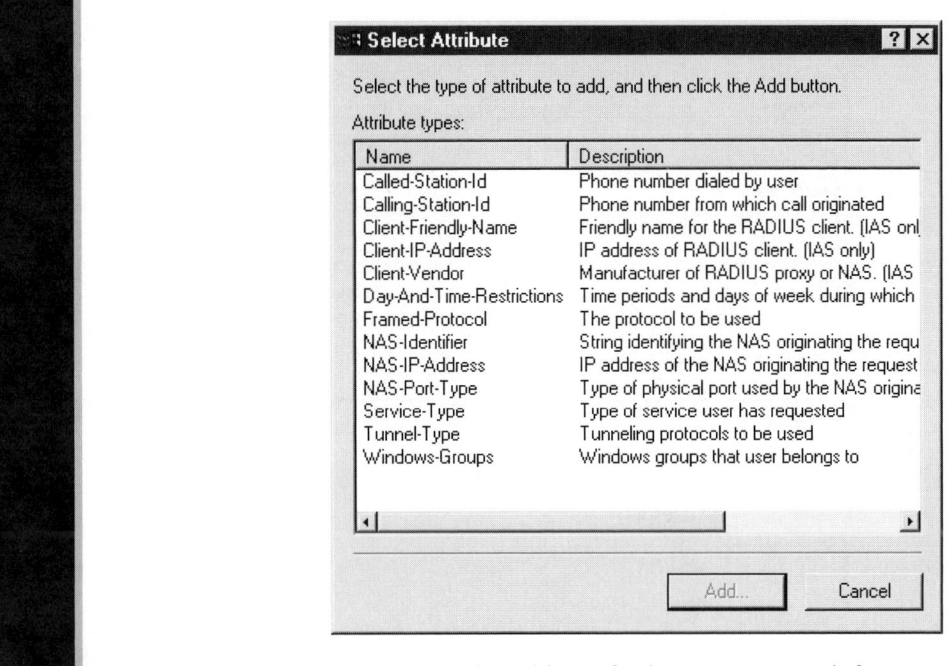

3. Each attribute when selected has a further prompt to ask for more information relevant to the attribute you have selected. For example, we need to select the Windows-Groups, so select it and click Add. You will now see a list of all groups already in the condition, and you can add or remove them.
4. Since we have no existing groups defined, click Add to see a list of available groups. Select Domain Users and then click OK. After adding the group to the policy, it should look similar to the following illustration.

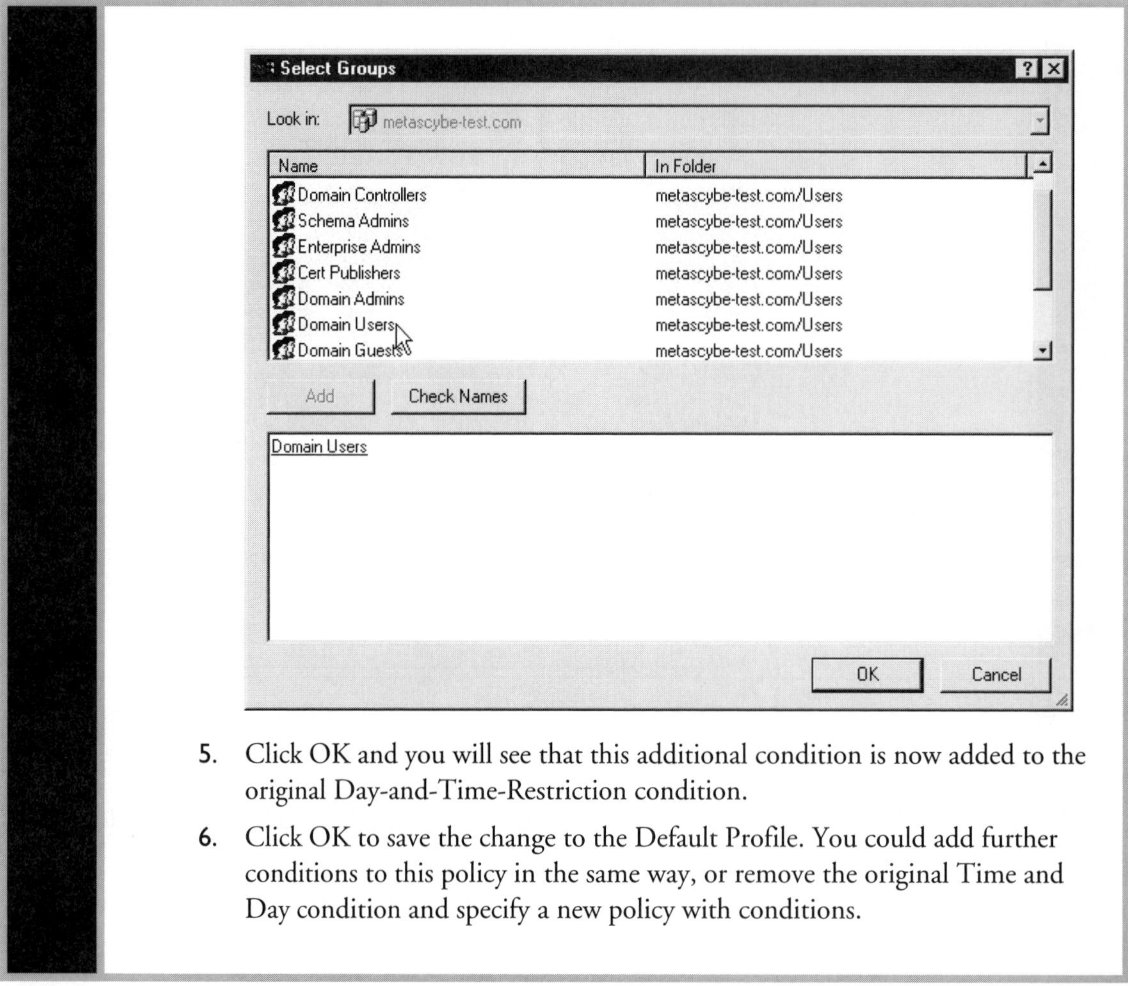

5. Click OK and you will see that this additional condition is now added to the original Day-and-Time-Restriction condition.
6. Click OK to save the change to the Default Profile. You could add further conditions to this policy in the same way, or remove the original Time and Day condition and specify a new policy with conditions.

Determining Access Permissions—Putting It All Together

We have looked at the various elements that determine whether a remote access connection is allowed or denied, but how do you put them all together? For a quick check list, refer to the following:

- **Windows 2000 allows remote access when:**
    - It matches the conditions of a Remote Access Policy.

- It is allowed by the combination of the remote access permission on the user account and the remote access permission of the matching Remote Access Policy.
- It meets the connection constraints of the matching Remote Access Policy profile and the dial-up properties of the user account.

- **Windows 2000 denies remote access when:**
  - It matches the conditions of a Remote Access Policy, but is not allowed by the combination of the remote access permission of the user account and the remote access permission of the policy.
  - It matches the conditions of a Remote Access Policy, but does not meet the connection constraints of the matching Remote Access Policy profile or the dial-up properties of the user account.
  - It does not match the conditions of any Remote Access Policy.

Troubleshooting Remote Access Connections

The following lists some basic checks and common problems/resolutions you should bear in mind if you are having problems connecting your remote access clients through the Windows 2000 Routing and Remote Access server.

- Verify that the Routing and Remote Access Service is running on the remote access server.
- Verify that remote access is enabled on the remote server.
- Verify that the dial-up ports on the remote access server are configured to allow inbound remote access connections.
- Verify that dial-in properties of the user account, together with remote access policies and profiles, permit dial-in access.
- Verify that settings in the Remote Access Policy profile do not conflict with properties of the remote access server; for example, check settings for multilink, BAP, authentication.
- Verify that any dial-up equipment being used is working correctly.
- Verify that you have free dial-up ports to accept new connections on the remote access server.

- Verify the user's specified credentials are correct (username, password).
- Verify connectivity from the remote access server to other resources on your network.
- Verify that the LAN protocols used by remote clients are either enabled for routing or remote access.
- For a remote access server that is a member of a Windows 2000 native-mode domain, verify that the remote access server has joined the domain.
- If the Routing and Remote Access server was manually added to the RAS and IAS servers security group, bear in mind this addition will not take effect immediately because of the way Active Directory caches directory service information. Your safest bet in this scenario is to reboot the remote access server.
- Verify that the remote client and server have at least one LAN protocol in common.
- If the remote client's protocol is TCP/IP and the access server is configured with a static address pool, verify that there are free addresses available.
- If the remote client's protocol is TCP/IP and the remote access server is configured for DHCP, ensure that a DHCP server is reachable from the server.
- If the remote client's protocol is IPX and tries to use its own IPX node number, verify the server's configuration allows this.
- If the remote client's protocol is IPX and the remote access server allocates an IPX node number, ensure this number is not being used elsewhere on your network.
- If the remote client's protocol is IPX and they cannot create file or printer shares, NetBIOS over IPX broadcast forwarding must be enabled on the LAN adapter connected to your company network.
- If the remote access server shares a modem with the Windows 2000 Fax service, ensure the modem supports adaptive answer. If not, you must disable fax on the modem when you need to accept remote client connections.
- Make use of the tools (tracing and logging facilities) mentioned later in this chapter to help diagnose the problem.

CERTIFICATION OBJECTIVE 27.06

Virtual Private Networking

This section provides an overview of virtual private networks (VPNs), describing the various components and how they work together, and outlines some of the key technologies that permit private networking over public internetworks.

VPN Overview

A virtual private network (VPN) is an extension of a corporate network that uses encapsulated, encrypted, and authenticated links across shared or public networks.

In practice, this means that remote users can connect to a corporate server over a standard Internet connection. Instead of directly connecting to the remote access server, they first connect to the Internet (or other public or shared network), via their local ISP, for example. Then using the first connection, they make another connection to the remote access server. This second connection is "tunneling" over the first, and the actual data packets sent are said to be "encapsulated."

The second connection from client to server creates a virtual network that is private to the client and server, despite the first connection being over a public network. VPNs actually use the in-place routing infrastructure of the Internet, but to remote users, it will seem as if they have a dedicated (private) link.

Why connect in this way, rather than simply connecting directly? Cost. A long distance call from client to server will cost much more than if the client connects via the Internet, because they only pay the cost of a local call to their local ISP.

Note that both sides (client and server) must be connected to the Internet, and the server's connection must be dedicated.

The Internet, by definition being an open and public network, is not a secure medium on which to securely transfer data. However, when that data is encrypted, it then becomes secure.

In addition to remote users connecting to the corporate network, the same technology can be used to connect branch offices, with either dedicated lines or dial-up.

It is even possible to use the same technology within the corporate network itself where privacy is the main benefit of having a virtual network within the main network. The use of IPSec would normally be more appropriate here, but IPSec is not available to downlevel clients such as Win9*x* and Windows NT4.0. In a mixed environment, a VPN within the corporate network may be a viable solution to securely transferring data.

Encapsulation and Encryption

To emulate a point-to-point link, data is encapsulated with a header that provides routing information that allows it to travel across the shared or public internetwork, and reach its final destination. This provides the virtual network. To achieve this securely, the data within the packets must also be encrypted. This provides the virtual private network.

exam Watch

Although it is possible to create a virtual network with a tunnel and not encrypt the data, this is not by definition a virtual private network. With VPNs, encapsulation and encryption always go together.

Components of Windows 2000 VPN

These consist of:

- A VPN server
- A VPN client
- A VPN connection using tunneling protocols

VPN Server

This is the Windows 2000 Server running Routing and Remote Access, with one connection to the Internet and a separate connection to your corporate network. Typically, the connection to the Internet will be over a dedicated line (e.g., T1, Fractional T1, or Frame Relay).

The server must be configured to support VPN connections as either remote access, or as a router-to-router connection.

Because the WAN adapter appears as a network adapter, you must configure this external interface with the IP address and subnet mask supplied by your ISP (or assigned for your domain), and configure the default gateway as being the IP address of the router that connects to the Internet.

When you enable Routing and Remote Access with Internet connectivity, it automatically creates VPN ports (10 in all).

VPN Client

This computer initiates the VPN connection to the VPN server. For remote access, this will be a user calling up remote access software. However, this connection could also be an automatic router-to-router call.

Many clients can initiate a VPN call, including:

- Windows NT 4.0
- Windows 2000
- Windows 9*x*
- Any third-party dial-up clients that support the tunneling protocols in Windows 2000

Additionally, both Windows 2000 Servers and Windows NT 4.0 Servers can create router-to-router VPN connections.

LAN Protocols

Although the initial connection to the Internet has to be TCP/IP (because this is the common protocol of the Internet), the client can use either TCP/IP or other network protocols within the tunnel. Remember that for a client to access a resource, there must be at least one protocol in common; therefore, if your internal network runs IPX rather than TCP/IP, the client should use IPX as the protocol to be tunneled over the VPN.

The choice of which LAN protocol should be used is no different from the same choice when configuring a direct point-to-point connection to a remote access server. And similarly to remote access, you must correctly configure onward routes if remote clients need to access resources on the network rather than just on the Routing and Remote Access server.

Tunneling Protocols

Windows 2000 supports two tunneling protocols: Point to Point Tunneling Protocol (PPTP) and Layer 2 Tunneling Protocol (L2TP).

Both sides of the connection must agree to the creation of a tunnel and be aware that it exists so it can be monitored and maintained (e.g., keep-alive messages if no data is being transferred). However, it does not guarantee reliable data delivery.

PPTP uses TCP with a modified Generic Routing Encapsulation (GRE) protocol, and L2TP uses UDP.

PPTP The Point-to-Point Tunneling Protocol is an extension of PPP that allows the encapsulation of PPP frames into IP datagrams for transmission over an IP internetwork.

PPTP uses a TCP connection for tunnel maintenance, and uses modified GRE encapsulated PPP frames for tunneled data. The data can be encrypted and compressed.

PPTP tunnels must be authenticated by using the same authentication methods as PPP. However, to compress and encrypt (with MPPE) the tunneled data, you must use either MSCHAP or EAP-TLS. Remember that the encryption is only from remote client to VPN server, which may not be the final resource destination if the remote access server allows remote routing. This is another way of saying PPTP does not support end-to-end security.

If you need end-to-end security, your choices include either using L2TP with IPSec as an alternative tunneling protocol, or using PPTP to the VPN server and then employing IPSec from the VPN server to the remote resource machine.

L2TP Layer 2 Tunneling Protocol is a combination of PPTP and Layer 2 Forwarding.

In theory, L2TP encapsulates PPP frames to be sent over any one of the following networks:

- IP
- X25
- Frame Relay
- ATM

In practice, however, Windows 2000 only supports L2TP over IP, and in this scenario it is suitable to be used as a tunneling protocol over the Internet.

L2TP uses UDP and a series of L2TP messages for maintaining the tunnel. L2TP also uses UDP to send L2TP-encapsulated PPP frames as the tunneled data. The data can be encrypted and compressed.

Windows 2000 supports IPSec instead of PPP encryption for L2TP; however, it is possible for third-party implementations to use PPP encryption with L2TP.

L2TP is very similar to PPTP in that an L2TP must be supported on both sides of the connection, and standard PPP authentication is still required. However, where L2TP differs from PPTP is that although it supports (inherits) PPP data compression, PPP encryption is not supported due to lack of security. This is why you must encrypt the data with IPSec.

WAN Options and Internet Support

There may be reasons why you want all your remote connections to be over a VPN but don't want your remote users to initiate it; for example, you don't want the support overhead of the additional dial-up configuration at the client end, and/or the client computer does not have the required tunneling protocol installed.

Access Concentrators and Network Access Servers In this scenario, it is possible to still obtain your VPN connection by using another computer or network device to create the tunnel on the client's behalf. This intermediary device is referred to as an "access concentrator." The access concentrator must have the appropriate tunneling protocol installed (matches the tunneling protocol on your VPN server) and be capable of establishing the tunnel for remote clients when they initiate a connection to connect to your VPN server.

An ISP, for example, may offer a company the service of running a tunneling-enabled Network Access Server (NAS) so that specifically identified remote users can connect to this ISP with a standard PPP connection. The access concentrator on the NAS automatically creates the tunnel for them into the company network VPN server. Because the connecting user does not choose to connect over a tunnel, this configuration is called *compulsory tunneling*.

An extension of this is *realm-based tunneling*, where the access concentrator makes decisions on the tunnel's final destination (VPN server) based on additional group information about the user (referred to as the *realm*). For example, one user called JohnB@domain1.com is always directed to one VPN server that serves the realm domain1.com, and another user called JackD@domain2.com is always directed to a different VPN server that serves the realm domain2.com. Realm compulsory tunnels that work in this way are "static," because a set of rules predetermines the route for each realm and cannot accommodate any flexibility at connection time.

An elaboration on this is when you have *dynamic compulsory tunnels* where a connection is dynamically assessed and the tunnel directed accordingly. For example, based on certain criteria, the same user may be directed to different VPN servers depending on what time of day the connection is made. Or, realms can be further divided into usernames, departments, the telephone number being used, and so forth. In this way, dynamic compulsory tunnels offer the highest degree of flexibility and granularity. An additional advantage for the owner of the Network Access Server is that it can simultaneously support both tunneling and nontunneling connections.

Each concentrator can store its own database for this filtering process; however, for large-scale solutions it would be better to host this information on a centrally maintained server and reference it when needed. RADIUS provides this type of solution.

exam Watch

***A transit internetwork* refers to the shared or public internetwork used by the encapsulated data. Although the transit internetwork can be either the public Internet or a private IP-based network, in Windows 2000 scenarios it invariably refers to the Internet.**

Security

Security is an important aspect of a VPN, because you are potentially offering your corporate resources to the open Internet.

In addition to deciding upon which authentication and encryption methods you will employ, you should also filter for only PPTP and/or L2TP packets (as appropriate) on the VPN server and/or your company firewall or router that connects to the Internet.

For more information on configuring packet filters, see the section "Configuring Firewalls with VPNs."

Security When Using PPTP PPTP offers user authentication and encryption in the same way that a PPP connection can—inheriting Microsoft Point-to-Point Encryption (MPPE) when used with MSCHAP (both versions) or EAP-TLS. MPPE can use 40-bit, 56-bit, or 128-bit encryption keys, and by default, the highest key strength supported by both client and server is negotiated during the connection establishment. If the server is configured to require a higher key strength than the client can support, the connection attempt fails. Note that 40-bit encryption provides backward compatibility for clients that aren't running Windows 2000.

One other added security change to PPTP over a standard PPP connection is that the encryption key is changed for every packet sent.

Security When Using L2TP over IPSec L2TP over IPSec offers user authentication, mutual computer authentication, encryption, data authentication, and data integrity.

- Authentication of the VPN client occurs at both the computer and then the user.
- Mutual computer authentication is performed when an IPSec Encapsulating Security Payload security association is established through the exchange of computer certificates. IPSec security association is established with an agreed encryption algorithm, hash algorithm, and encryption keys.

You must have computer certificates on both the VPN server and client before being able to use L2TP over IPSec connections. Computer certificates can be automatically obtained by configuring an auto-enrollment Windows 2000 Group Policy, or manually using the Certificates snap-in.

User authentication is performed with the usual PPP user authentication protocols such as EAP, MSCHAP, CHAP, SAP, and PAP (see "Authentication Protocols" in the "Remote Access Security" section later in this chapter for more information on these authentication protocols). Any authentication protocol can be used, but for stronger security with mutual authentication, use MS-CHAPv2 or EAP-TLS.

You can also authenticate the endpoints of an L2TP tunnel (L2TP tunnel authentication), although this isn't configured on Windows 2000 by default.

Encryption is determined by the IPSec Security Authority, and available encryption algorithms include:

- DES with a 56-bit key
- Triple DES (3DES)—three 56-bit keys designed for high-security environments

Data authentication and integrity is provided with one of the following:

- The hash message authentication code (HMAC) Message Digest 5 (MD5)—128-bit hash
- The hash message authentication code Secure Hash Algorithm (HMAC SHA-1)—160-bit hash

Installing and Configuring the VPN Server

You must have a permanent and dedicated link to the Internet to support a VPN. This dedicated connection is typically a second network adapter that connects to an Internet router. In this configuration, the Routing and Remote Access Service will automatically assign VPN ports that appear as WAN Miniports under Ports in the main console tree.

The default configuration is five ports that support PPTP and five ports that support L2TP. To enable or disable these for inbound traffic, right-click Ports and then select Properties from the shortcut menu. This will display the Devices dialog box similar to the one shown in Figure 27-5.

For each tunneling protocol (e.g., PPTP) you can configure whether to allow remote access, specify the telephone number being used (if any), and change the number of simultaneously supported ports for that particular device.

Note that as with any security setting in Windows 2000, the strongest setting will be tried first, and only if that fails will it try to negotiate down to the next strongest level. For VPN connections, this means that if a Windows 2000 Professional attempts to connect to the VPN server, the client's default Server Type of "Automatic" will try a L2TP/IPSec connection first, and then a PPTP connection if the first fails. This behavior may explain unexpected connection patterns for the VPN ports you have configured.

FIGURE 27-5

Device Ports Properties dialog box

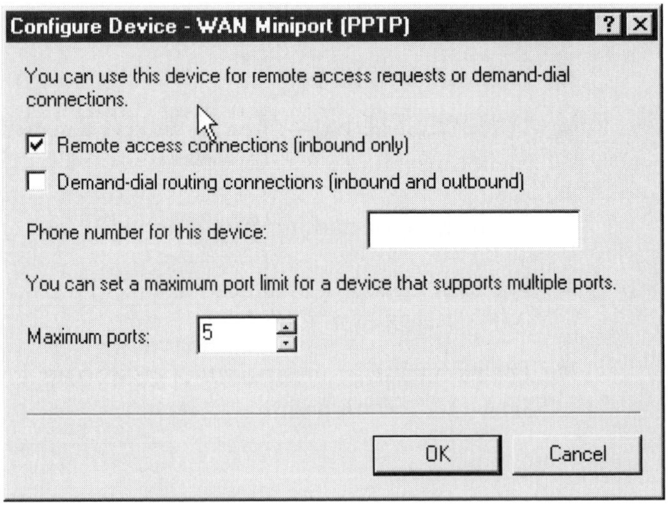

exam Watch

By default, both PPTP and L2TP ports are enabled on a VPN server. If you want the VPN server to accept one of these tunneling protocols only, set the number of ports on the unwanted protocol to zero. You cannot as you might expect, simply delete either of these ports. Alternatively, you could disable the remote access permission on the port.

If you are using L2TP over IPSec, you must ensure the IPSec policies are in place for the remote access server. Table 27-5 shows where to configure these IPSec settings.

Configuring Firewalls with VPNs

How to correctly configure a firewall when using a VPN is a very commonly asked question, and this is information you need to know irrespective of whether you pass on this information to somebody else who manages the firewall, or you manage it yourself. There's no point in having a perfectly configured VPN if the firewall won't let connections through!

Although you can have the scenario where the VPN server is attached to the Internet and the firewall is between the VPN server and the intranet, the more typical firewall setup is such that the firewall is attached to the Internet, and the VPN server is between the firewall and the intranet. In this way, the VPN server is another Internet resource on the *demilitarized zone* (DMZ), perhaps sharing it with Web servers, proxy servers, ftp servers, and so forth.

In addition to any standard filters designed for protecting your other DMZ resources, for your VPN server you must configure the firewall with input and output filters on its Internet interface to allow the relevant tunneling protocols and data to pass from the Internet to the VPN server.

TABLE 27-5 Where to Set IPSec Settings for Your VPN Server

Role of VPN Server	How to Create IPSec Policies
If the VPN server is a stand-alone server or a member of a Windows NT 4.0 domain.	Configure local machine IPSec policy.
If the VPN server is a member of a Windows 2000 domain.	Local IPSec policies are overwritten by assigned domain IPSec policies. To create an IPSec policy that only applies to the VPN server, create an organizational unit in the Active Directory, put the VPN server computer account in this OU, and then use the Group Policy to create and assign IPSec policies for the VPN server's OU.

The information in this section can also be applied if you decide to use packet filtering on the Routing and Remote Access server itself.

Packet Filters for PPTP

Configure the following input filters to drop all packets except those that meet the criteria listed.

Input Filter	Explanation
Destination IP address of the VPN server's Internet interface and TCP destination port 1723.	This allows PPTP tunnel maintenance traffic from PPTP client to PPTP server.
Destination IP address of the VPN server's Internet interface and TCP destination port 1723.	This allows PPTP tunnel maintenance traffic from PPTP client to PPTP server.
Destination IP address of the VPN server's Internet interface and IP Protocol ID 47.	This allows PPTP tunneled data from the PPTP client to PPTP server.
Destination IP address of the VPN server's Internet interface and TCP (established) source port 1723.	This is required only if VPN server is acting as a VPN client (i.e., calling router) in a router-to-router VPN connection.

Configure the following output filters to drop all packets *except* those that meet the criteria listed.

Output Filter	Explanation
Source IP address of the VPN server's Internet interface and TCP source port 1723.	This allows PPTP tunnel maintenance traffic from VPN server to VPN client.
Source IP address of the VPN server's Internet interface and IP Protocol ID 47.	This allows PPTP tunneled data from VPN server to VPN client.
Source IP address of the VPN server's Internet interface and TCP (established) destination port 1723.	This filter is only required if the VPN server is acting as a VPN client (i.e., calling router) in a router-to-router VPN connection.

Packet Filters for L2PT over IPSec

Configure the following input filters to drop all packets *except* those that meet the criteria listed.

Input Filter	Explanation
Destination IP address of VPN server's Internet interface and UDP destination port 500.	This allows Internet Key Exchange (IKE) traffic through to the VPN server.
Destination IP address of VPN server's Internet interface and IP Protocol ID 50.	This allows IPSec Encapsulating Security Payload traffic from VPN client to VPN server.

Configure the following output filters to drop all packets *except* those that meet the criteria listed.

Output Filter	Explanation
Source address of the VPN server's Internet interface and UDP source port 500.	This allows Internet Key Exchange traffic from the VPN server.
Source IP address of the VPN server's Internet interface and IP Protocol ID 50.	This allows IPSec Encapsulating Security Payload traffic from VPN server to VPN client.

There are no filters required for L2TP traffic at UDP port 1701; at the firewall, all L2TP traffic (including tunnel maintenance and tunneled data) is encrypted as part of the IPSec Encapsulating Security Payload.

Testing Connectivity to the VPN Server

You will need to configure a VPN client to connect to your VPN server, and although many remote access clients support this (e.g., Windows NT 4.0, Windows 98), we will look at how to configure a VPN client on Windows 2000 Professional.

The underlying concept remains the same for other clients. You must first have a valid Internet connection that is dialed first and connected, and then dial a second connection that specifies the VPN server's address (e.g., IP address or DNS name) as the destination rather than specifying a telephone number.

When you dial the VPN server, you will be asked to log on, and once authenticated, your remote access permissions will be assessed. If all goes well and you pass the security checks, you will be connected to your internal network and should be able to access resources just as if you were locally connected (albeit more slowly).

Note that if you want to use L2TP with IPSec (rather than PPTP), you must use Windows 2000 Professional as your VPN client—this tunneling protocol is not supported on other Microsoft platforms.

EXERCISE 27-4

Configuring a VPN Remote Access Client on Windows 2000 Professional

If you haven't already configured a dial-up connection to the Internet, you will need to do this first. Select Dial-up to the Internet to load the Internet Connection Wizard, which will walk you through setting up your Internet connection. When you have completed this step, test the connection to ensure you can connect to the Internet without problems. You are then ready to configure your VPN connection.

1. Under Network and Dial-up Connection, select Make New Connection.
2. This loads the Network Connection Wizard. Select the option "Connect to a private network through the Internet," and click Next.
3. You will then be prompted whether you want the required Internet connection to be automatically dialed before trying the VPN connection (recommended). If you choose to automatically dial up to the Internet first, select the Internet connection you need from the drop-down list box. Click Next.
4. You will then be prompted for the destination address of the VPN server, as shown in the following illustration. You can enter this in any valid Internet format, which may be IP address, DNS name, or host name.

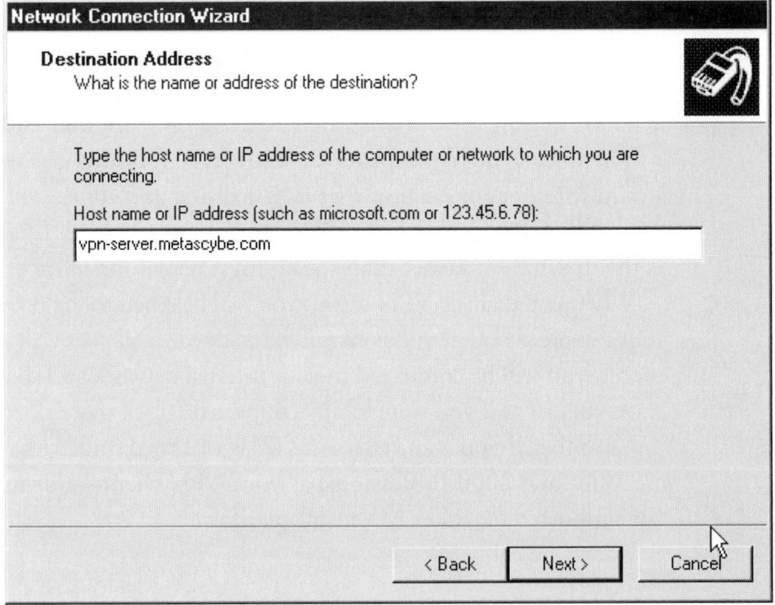

If in doubt, specify the IP address to eliminate any name resolution problems. Click Next.

5. You will next be prompted whether you want exclusive access to this connection, or share it with others. Note that even if sharing, it will only be shared when you are logged on. Select "Only for myself," and click Next.
6. You will then be prompted to specify a name to identify this connection. The default is Virtual Private Connection, which you can either accept or edit as you wish.
7. If you want to automatically create a shortcut for this connection on your desktop, click the "Add a shortcut to my desktop" check box at the bottom of the dialog box.
8. Click Finish and you will be prompted whether to connect your chosen Internet connection now, with a check box to say whether you want this reminder displayed again. Click Yes, which will prompt you to dial your Internet connection, and once connected, prompt you to dial your VPN connection.

Troubleshooting VPNs

The VPN problems you encounter will probably fall into one of these categories:

- Connection attempt fails when it should be accepted
- Connection attempt is accepted when it should fail
- Unable to access resources beyond the VPN server
- Unable to establish a tunnel

Check through the previous Routing and Remote Access server troubleshooting list to eliminate any standard remote access problems. The following are specific to VPN problems:

- If you are not using packet filtering on the VPN server and/or your firewall allows through a ping command from the Internet, try pinging the VPN server from the client to test basic connectivity. If this works, ping by the same host name specified in the client's VPN connection destination if an IP address isn't being used (this ensures correct name to IP resolution).
- Verify that PPTP and/or L2TP ports are enabled for inbound remote access.
- Verify that free PPTP and/or L2TP ports are available; increase if necessary.

- Verify that the VPN client's tunneling protocol is supported by the VPN server, and vice versa.
- If using L2TP over IPSec, verify that computer certificates are installed on both the VPN server and the VPN client.
- If using PPTP, verify that GRE isn't being filtered out by your ISP.
- Verify there are no TCP/IP filters on the profile properties of the Remote Access Policy being used by the VPN connection that block required packets.
- Verify there are no IP packet filters that block required packets from the server, the Internet connected adapter, or within remote access policies.
- Verify firewall configuration is not blocking required packets.
- Verify the VPN connection configuration on the remote access client. If identifying the VPN server by DNS name, change this to the actual IP address.
- Check to see whether the remote access client has a policy that excludes tunneling.
- Verify that the Winsock Proxy client is not currently running on the VPN client (which will forward all IP traffic to the proxy server rather than the VPN server).
- To improve the performance of VPN connections, look to improve the processor and memory on *both* sides of the connection (i.e., server and client) that is required to support the additional encapsulation and encryption.

CERTIFICATION OBJECTIVE 27.07

Connections Using PPP Multilink and BAP

Windows 2000 remote access supports the following when aggregating multiple physical links into a single logical link:

- PPP Multilink Protocol (MP)
- Bandwidth Allocation Protocol (BAP)
- Bandwidth Allocation Control Protocol (BACP)

These protocols are explained in Table 27-6.

Multilink PPP and BAP are enabled on the remote access server through the PPP tab on the Properties sheet of the remote access server in the Routing and Remote Access snap-in. Settings for multilink and BAP can also be configured from the Multilink tab on the Properties sheet of a Remote Access Policy profile. However, you must have multilink and BAP enabled on the server before you can fine-tune these settings in the remote policy profile.

exam watch

Multilink supports multiple devices but not multiple servers—you cannot span multilinked devices over more than one Routing and Remote Access server.

PPP Multilink Protocol

This protocol is used to combine multiple physical links into a single logical link to increase throughput. The most common use of multilink is the aggregation of the two B-channels of an ISDN Basic Rate Interface connection.

MP fragments, sequences, and reorders alternating packets sent across multiple physical connections, the resulting bandwidth becoming the sum of the combined links. Although MP can be done for any ISDN adapter, MP must be supported on both sides of the connection.

On the Windows 2000 Routing and Remote Access Service, you can enable multilink as one of the server's properties, and you can also enable it in a policy's profile.

TABLE 27-6

MP, BAP, and BACP

Protocol	Explanation
MP	MP allows multiple physical links to appear as a single local link over which data can be sent and received at a higher throughput than if going over a single physical link.
BAP	BAP is a PPP control protocol that is used to dynamically add or remove additional links to an MP connection.
BACP	BACP polices multiple peers using MP; for example, electing a favored peer when more than one PPP peer requests to add or remove a connection at the same time.

BAP

Although MP allows multiple physical links to be combined, there is no automatic way of adapting to changing conditions; for example, adding additional links when greater throughput is required, or closing links that are no longer required.

This extra facility is provided by the Bandwidth Allocation Protocol (BAP) and the Bandwidth Allocation Control Protocol (BACP).

An example of this working is when an MP- and BAP-enabled remote client and remote access server create an MP connection that is only a single physical link because they are not sending much data. However, should the throughput increase, at a configured level, the remote client could issue a *BAP Call Request* to add an additional link (e.g., additional ISDN channel, or modem). The remote access server responds with a *BAP Call Response* that contains the information needed to access one of its available ports (e.g., telephone number).

When the throughput then drops again, either side could send a BAP Link Drop Query Request so that the additional link that is no longer needed is dropped and becomes available again (e.g., for another connecting client).

on the job

Adding or dropping telephone lines may not work successfully with generic modem drivers that don't correctly provide send/receive status information—causing BAP to use false throughput values. The result of this can be unexpected and expensive dial-up costs! Monitor line activity, and if you suspect this to be a problem, try to obtain the latest modem drivers, or disable BAP.

To set the telephone number of a port that is sent in the BAP Call Response message:

1. Use the Routing and Remote Access snap-in to obtain properties on the Ports object.
2. Select the port you want to configure and click Configure.
3. Type in the telephone number in the "Phone number of this device" text box.

Bandwidth Allocation Control Protocol (BACP)

The sole job of this protocol is to elect a favored peer when necessary. If both peers of an MP- and BAP-enabled connection send a BAP Call Request or BAP Link Drop Query Request message at the same time, only one request can succeed, and it is the responsibility of this protocol to elect which peer wins.

EXERCISE 27-5

Configuring Multilink Support on Your Remote Access Server

Your Routing and Remote Access server has a multiport serial adapter that supports 16 modems for a small group of homeworkers. Some of these users have requested to use multilink to improve the speed of their connection, but you are keen to restrict this to just two modems per user to ensure that enough free ports are available for other users.

You therefore configure your Routing and Remote Access server to enable multilink, but you also set up a Remote Access Policy for these homeworkers that restricts them to only two links.

1. If you haven't already done so, load up the Routing and Remote Access snap-in, select your server, right-click and select Properties.
2. On the PPP tab, ensure that all options are selected. Click OK.
3. Click on Remote Access Policies and right-click to select New Remote Access Policy.
4. Enter as the Policy Friendly Name: "Restrict Homeworkers to 2 modems only" and click OK.
5. On the Conditions dialog box, click Add, select Windows-Group, and click Add.
6. Select the user group that contains your homeworkers (for this exercise, if you don't have any additional groups set up, you could select the Domain Users group). Click Add and click OK.
7. Click OK again and you will see your one condition displayed. Click Next to continue.
8. On the Permissions dialog box, select to "Grant remote access permission" and click Next.
9. Before you click Finish, click Edit Profile. It is in the profile where you can fine-tune your settings that include multilink settings.
10. Select the Multilink tab and under the Multilink Settings instead of the default "Default to server settings," select "Allow Multilink," and underneath the Limit Maximum Ports will automatically default to 2, which is the setting we require.

11. Click OK to close the Profile dialog box, and then click Finish to complete this Remote Access Policy.

You have now successfully enabled multilink on your remote access server, but are restricting all users in this group to just two ports.

CERTIFICATION OBJECTIVE 27.08

Integrating Remote Access and DHCP

Although you have a choice of whether to use a static address pool defined on the Routing and Remote Access server or use DHCP, Microsoft recommends using DHCP where possible. This means that IP address assignment is centrally configured and maintained, and therefore less prone to errors such as duplicate addresses. However, there are some considerations to be taken into account when using DHCP with remote access, which are discussed in the following sections.

Obtaining DHCP Addresses via RRAS

When the Routing and Remote Access Service first starts and it is configured to automatically assign IP addresses, it looks to obtain from a DHCP server a pool of 10 addresses. These addresses are stored in the remote access server's Registry to allocate as needed to remote access clients when they connect. The remote access server manages these IP leases, noting from which DHCP server they were assigned and their lease time so it can renew them appropriately. Note that the lease is actually between the DHCP server and the RAS server, rather than the DHCP server and the remote access client.

When remote access clients disconnect from the RAS server, their IP address is returned to the RAS server rather than to the DHCP server. This means that other connecting remote clients can reuse their IP addresses. However, if there are no more free addresses, a further block of 10 addresses is obtained from a DHCP server. When the Routing and Remote Access Service is stopped, all addresses obtained by the remote access server are released. You cannot release them manually on the server—for example, issuing an ipconfig /release all command.

If you know the number of simultaneous addresses your RAS server will need (for example, you know on average you will have 20 simultaneous RAS connections), you can change the number of "pre-booked" addresses so that an adequate number is initially cached on startup of the RRAS service. To change this number of addresses, modify the following Registry key and change the default value of 10 to the number you require:

```
HKEY_LOCAL_MACHINE\SYSTEM\CurrentControlSet\Services\RemoteAccess\
Parameters\IP\InitialAddressPoolSize
```

Obtaining DHCP Options via RRAS

The IP address is not the only DHCP setting that can be passed to DHCP clients. Once the IP address has been offered and accepted, DHCP clients send a DHCPInform message to the DHCP server to obtain any DHCP configured options, such as WINS servers, DNS servers, Class options, and the domain name. However, when a remote access client has been allocated an address by the RAS server through DHCP, and sends its DHCPInform message to the RAS server, the RAS server discards this message and does not pass it on to the originating DHCP server.

This means that remote access clients by default will not obtain any DHCP scope options. Instead, the RAS server allocates to the remote access workstation its own default gateway address, and its own WINS and DNS server addresses (if configured). In most cases, this will ensure successful network connectivity for the remote access clients beyond the RAS server. It also allows workstations to automatically receive appropriate configurations depending on whether they are connecting directly on the local area network or remotely by the RAS server.

However, if the RAS server is configured to use the DHCP Relay Agent on the internal interface, DHCPInform messages will be passed to the DHCP server, and in this way remote workstations can receive DHCP scope options (such as a WINS and DNS address) from the DHCP server. This applies even if you are using static addresses.

The settings from the DHCP server override (replace) settings inherited from the RAS server (such as WINS server, DNS server). This is particularly useful for configuring the domain name, which cannot be inherited from the RAS server, and if you specifically want remote access clients to obtain other configured DHCP options.

If you want your remote access clients to receive DHCP scope options, use the DHCP Relay Agent on the RAS server.

Location of the DHCP Server

The DHCP server may be the same server that's hosting the Routing and Remote Access Service; however, in all but a very small network environment, this is unlikely.

If there is a DHCP server on the same subnet as the Routing and Remote Access server, the RAS server will be able to obtain IP addresses directly for remote clients because both servers are on the same subnetwork. If there is no DHCP server on the same subnet as the Routing and Remote Access server, the DHCP Relay Agent must be running on the Routing and Remote Access server so that it can forward requests to the DHCP server in order to obtain the IP addresses it needs for remote access clients.

Automatic Private IP Addresses—APIPA

If the Routing and Remote Access server is configured to automatically assign IP addresses for remote access clients, but no DHCP server can be found when the Routing and Remote Access Service starts, the server will still be able to assign IP addresses through the Windows 2000 support of Automatic Private IP Addresses, or APIPA.

The private address range is 169.254.0.1–169.254.255.254.

The remote access server will randomly choose an address from this range for connecting remote access clients, so the lack of a DHCP server will not prevent remote connections. However, this use of APIPA is only practical with remote access when all your internal computers are also using APIPA (including the remote access server itself) and there are no routers on the internal network. This setup is very unusual and not recommended except for the smallest of networks.

Multihomed Servers

If remote access clients are being connected but cannot access resources on the internal network, check the allocated IP address of the connecting remote access client (under Remote Access Clients in the Routing and Remote Access snap-in) to see if they are using a 169.254.xxx.xxx address instead of the one you were expecting had a DHCP server been available.

If a DHCP server is available and your remote access server is multihomed, check the adapter selected for DHCP requests. When multiple network adapters exist on a server running Routing and Remote Access, it will by default randomly choose an adapter for sending out DHCP requests. Obviously, it may select an adapter that has no link to a DHCP server, in which case you will have to manually change the selected adapter (Routing and Remote Access snap-in | <server-name> | Properties | IP tab | Adapter dropdown box).

If DHCP has been enabled to assign IP addresses to remote clients, but no DHCP server could be located, by default this will be recorded in the Event Log displaying which private address was used in the absence of a DHCP server (see Exercise 27-6).

Typically, in this scenario users will not be aware that they do not have their expected IP address because they will be successfully connected. However, they will not be able to access resources beyond the server and will receive a "The network path was not found" error message.

Off-Subnet Addressing and On-Subnet Addressing

Another consideration occurs when the DHCP server allocates an IP address that is on a different subnet to the remote access server itself; this is called *off-subnet addressing*. When the allocated addresses are on the same subnet as the remote access server, this is called *on-subnet addressing* and is by far the more common setup.

Why might you want to use off-sub addressing? Well, you might decide that all your remote users, although transparently connected to your network as if they were locally connected, should be differentiated logically with a different subnet address. In this case, the remote access server is acting as a router between the remote access workstations and your company resources.

When a remote access user obtains a different subnet address to the RAS server, the RAS server automatically adds a new route for the remote access client to its routing table so it can forward packets to and from the remote access users and the company network

Additionally, if the RAS server has installed an IP routing protocol, this new route will be automatically advertised to neighboring routers on the company network so they too will add the network path of the remote access users to their routing tables. This ensures that traffic can flow between the remote access workstations and resources on the company network.

However, if the RAS server does not have an IP routing protocol installed, other routers and other computers will not know about the new network route, and packets destined for the remote access users from any computer other than the RAS server will have no automatic path back to them. If this is the case, static routes should be added that define a path back to the remote access clients via the RAS server. If you do not add static routes in this situation, the connection between the remote access client and company resource (beyond the RAS server) will fail. You may decide to turn this into a security advantage by only adding static routes on certain computers to ensure that only these resources can be accessed remotely.

EXERCISE 27-6

Demonstrating APIPA

This exercise steps through showing APIPA in action so that remote access clients can still connect. However, it does require you to stop the DHCP server to simulate a network or DHCP problem.

1. Ensure that your remote access server is set to allocate IP addresses automatically to remote access clients (within the Routing and Remote Access snap-in, this is specified under your server, Properties, and then the IP tab), and your server has a static address. Ensure that a DHCP server is not available. How you make the DHCP server unavailable depends on your setup. See Table 27-7 for various solutions.

TABLE 27-7 How to Make the DHCP Server Unavailable

DHCP Setup	How to Stop the Routing and Remote Access Server from Obtaining IP Addresses from a DHCP Server
If the DHCP service is running on the same server as the remote access server.	Stop the service (Start | Programs | Administrative Tools | DHCP Manager), then select your server in the left pane, right-click, select All Tasks, then either Stop or Pause.
If the DHCP server is on another subnet and you are using the DHCP Relay Agent to locate it.	Stop this service under IP Routing, DHCP Relay Agent. Right-click and select All Tasks | Stop.
If the DHCP server is on the same subnet and you are able to temporarily pause or stop the DHCP service.	Pause or stop the DHCP service.
If you cannot stop the DHCP service (because it's servicing live clients), but your RRAS server is a stand-alone server.	Change your internal IP address to be a different network address, which will mean that the DHCP broadcast will now fail.

2. Before you connect a remote access client, stop and restart the Windows 2000 Routing and Remote Access Service. Then connect the workstation to the Remote Access Server (refer to Exercise 27-3 if necessary). Expand

Remote Access Clients in the Routing and Remote Access snap-in, and double-click on the connected user to view the connected IP address. Similar to the following illustration, the IP address should now be in the APIPA address range.

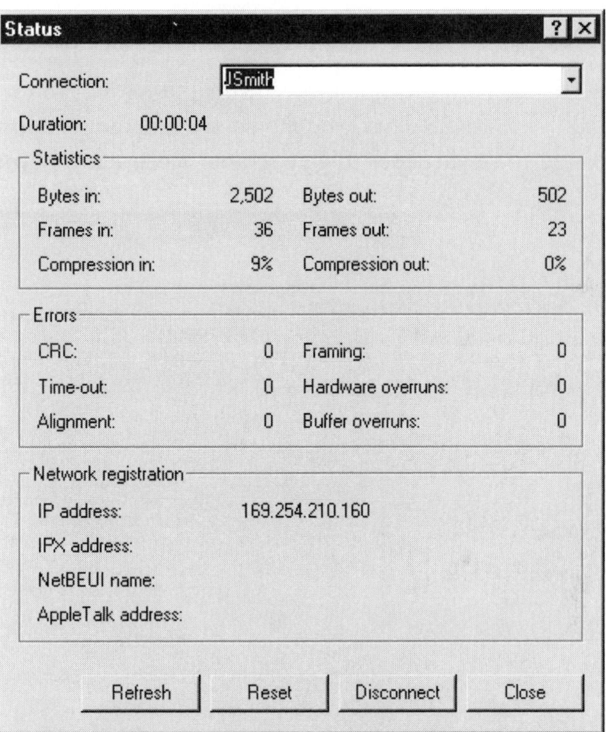

3. The user has connected successfully, but are remote resources available beyond the server? Try connecting a mapped drive on your internal network to a share that would normally be accessible. You should see the "The network path was not found" error message similar to the one shown in the following illustration.

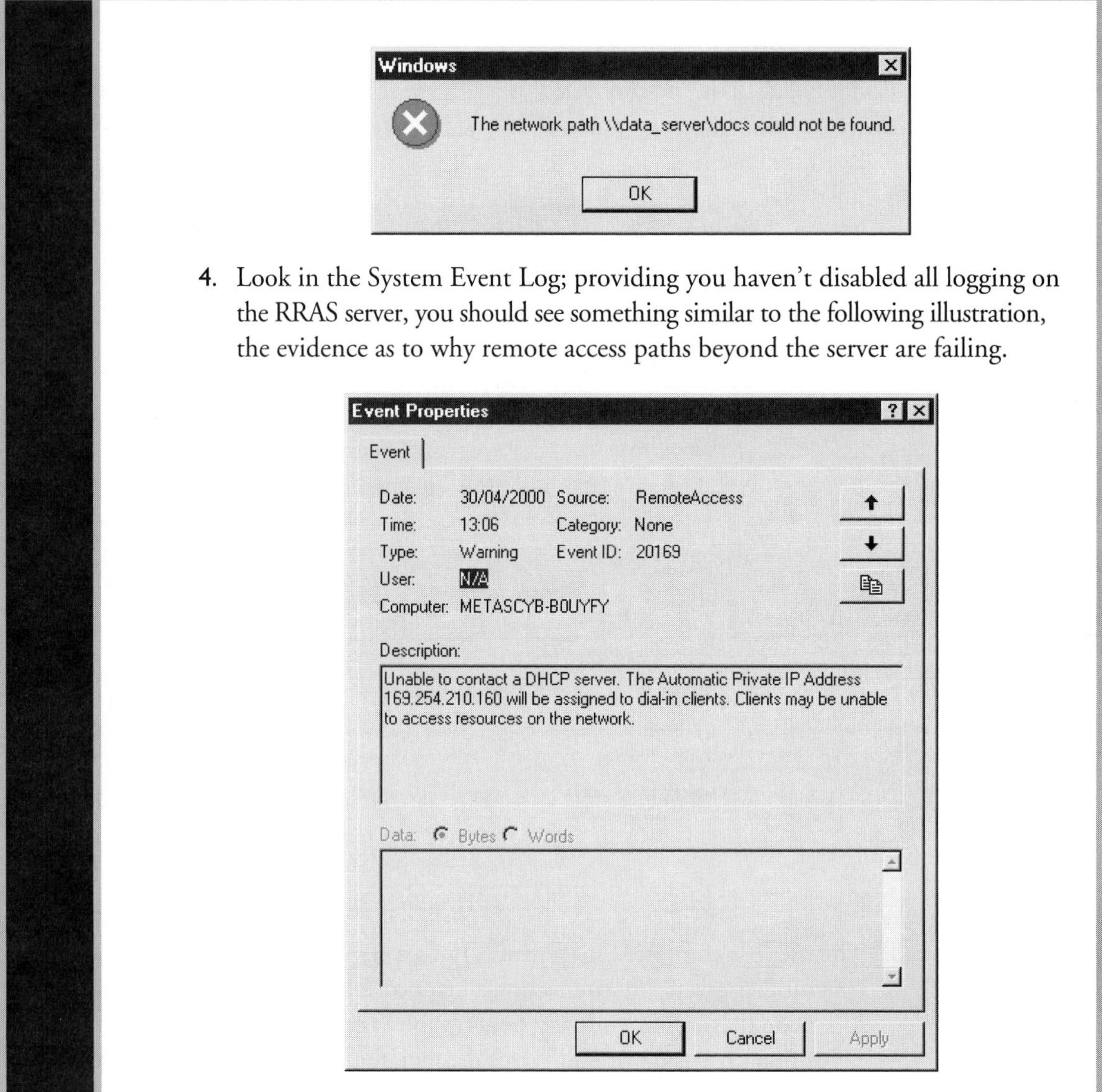

4. Look in the System Event Log; providing you haven't disabled all logging on the RRAS server, you should see something similar to the following illustration, the evidence as to why remote access paths beyond the server are failing.

You will see in the System log multiple errors as the RAS server tries to obtain its initial pool of addresses. As the network administrator, you would now know you had to resolve a DHCP problem rather than have to check other possible causes (e.g., modem problems, remote access permission, authentication issues, etc.)

Once you have completed this exercise, don't forget to restart your DHCP service and stop/restart the Windows 2000 Routing and Remote Access Service!

CERTIFICATION OBJECTIVE 27.09

Managing and Monitoring Remote Access

Once you decide on your remote access strategies and configure your remote connections accordingly, you will still need to manage and monitor this service to ensure that it offers and delivers a reliable and secure service.

Additional Routing and Remote Access Administration Tools

In addition to the Routing and Remote Access Service snap-in, and the command-line utility Netsh, the following tools are available to help support various RRAS administrative tasks:

- Event Logging
- Authentication and Account Logging
- Network Monitor
- PPP Logging
- Tracing
- SNMP MIB Support
- API Support for third-party components and utilities

Event Logging

Four levels of logging can be set for recording RRAS information to the Event Log. These can be seen on the Properties sheet of the remote access server's Event Logging tab.

- Log errors only
- Log errors and warnings
- Log the maximum amount of information
- Disable event logging

The DHCP error we saw earlier was one of the "Log errors and warnings" entries that will be recorded. Other events relate to the general functionality of the remote access server (for example, which user connected at what line speed, what IP addresses were allocated, and were there any security or authentication messages).

Obviously, the more detailed the logging, the more resources your computer must devote to this job, which may be at the expense of the Routing and Remote Access service itself.

Authentication and Accounting Logging

The remote access server can log authentication and accounting information in local logging files that are separate from events written to the Event Log.

This sort of logging is very helpful for troubleshooting Remote Access Policy problems, because for each authentication attempt, it logs the name of the Remote Access Policy that either accepts or rejects the connection.

If the remote access server is configured for Windows 2000 authentication and accounting, the authentication and accounting information is stored locally by default in:

%SystemRoot%\System32\LogFiles

If the remote access server is configured for RADIUS authentication and accounting, and this RADIUS server is a Windows 2000 server running IAS, the same log path and file will be used, but on the IAS computer instead.

The default format of this file is IAS 1.0, which is a comma-delimited file displaying various attributes about each connection. However, the alternative *Database compatible file format* is often the more useful setting since it not only supports the use of ODBC-compliant tools so that the raw data when imported into a database can be easily interpreted and analyzed, but unlike the IAS-format log it saves the data in a standard structure that is compatible with other Network Access Servers. In a multivendor environment, this setting would be more appropriate.

Set authentication and accounting logging (and an alternative path for the log file if preferred) from the server's Remote Access Logging properties from the Routing and Remote Access snap-in. To do this, expand Remote Access Logging in the left pane, right-click Local File in the details pane, and select Properties. This reveals two tabs, one for Settings (where you specify what you want to log) and another for Local File (where you specify the log format and path, and how often you want to save log information).

Network Monitor

This allows you to capture the PPP traffic (connection establishment and PPP-encapsulated user data) sent between the remote client and the remote access server. Note that Network Monitor does not interpret the compressed or encrypted portions of remote access traffic, but it can be useful in determining the following:

- What is happening during the PPP connection establishment process
- Whether data is being encrypted
- Whether data is being compressed

Although you cannot read the contents of encrypted/compressed packets, you can identify them by their protocol ID, which is 0x3D.

Network Monitor captures can be saved and sent to Microsoft support for analysis.

PPP Tracing

PPP tracing was available in Windows NT 4.0 and is useful to help track down connecting problems, because it specifically logs detailed information on the PPP connection establishment process. It does not log any user data once the connection is established.

It is set by selecting Enable Point-to-Point Protocol (PPP) Logging from the Event Logging tab on the properties of the remote access server in the Routing and Remote Access snap-in.

Information is saved to a file called *Ppp.log* in the *%Systemroot%*\tracing folder and includes the programming calls and actual packet contents of PPP packets for PPP control protocols.

Tracing

Tracing can be used to help diagnose complex network problems, such as recording internal component variables, function calls, and interactions. Additionally, separate routing and remote access components can be independently enabled to log tracing information to files, and you can even enable/disable these without disruption to a live router.

Bear in mind not only will tracing put additional load on your computer's resources, but this level of information is aimed at network specialists rather than general network administrators.

Tracing can only be enabled by setting to 1 each component (e.g., RIP2) under the following Registry key:

HKEY_LOCAL_MACHINE\SOFTWARE\Microsoft\Tracing\<component>

By default, all tracing files are saved to *%systemroot%*\Tracing and are named after the component they are tracing. However, you can specify an alternative path under the same key as above.

The default level of tracing is set to maximum, but this can also be changed for each component by setting the value of the FileTracingMask under the same key as above—ranging from 0 to FFFF0000.

The default maximum trace file size is 64 K, but this can be changed for each component by setting the value of the MaxFileSize under the same key as above (64 K is represented as 10000).

SNMP MIB Support

Windows 2000 with Routing and Remote Access supports Simple Network Management Protocol (SNMP) agent functionality with support for Internet MIB II.

Network Management Stations such as the popular HP OpenView can compile the MIB to manage IP Network layer events relating to Windows 2000 remote access router functions—providing the remote access server itself has the SNMP agent installed and running.

API Support for Third-Party Components and Utilities

Routing and Remote Access has fully published API sets for unicast, multicast routing protocol, and administration support, which means that third-party developers can write their own routing protocols, interfaces, and management tools that directly interface with the Routing and Remote Access architecture.

EXERCISE 27-7

Setting Up a Log File for Database Analysis

You have been asked to set up and provide monthly log files of remote connections from your Windows 2000 Routing and Remote Access server so that the Accounting Department can import them into Microsoft Access. The logged data can then be easily sorted and presented to indicate which users and departments are using the remote access services—and charge by department accordingly.

Your one Routing and Remote Access server is configured to use Windows as both the Authentication and Accounting Provider.

1. Load up the Routing and Remote Access snap-in and expand the Remote Access Logging.
2. Right-click on the Local File in the right pane and select Properties.
3. On the Settings tab, ensure the first option, "Account logging requests," is selected, but no others.
4. Click on the Local File and select "Database compatible file format," rather than the default of IAS Format.
5. Because you have been asked for monthly logs, select the "New log time period" of Monthly—you will see the log file name displayed below change to Inyymm.log to indicate which year and month the log will refer to.
6. Finally, because you don't want the logging to be in competition with the server's system files, you know that specifying the log path to go to an alternative partition would be preferable to keeping to the default of *%systemroot%*\System32\LogFiles. If you can use a different partition (or even machine) to store the log files, enter it in the Log file directory field.
7. Click OK. If you changed the file path, this will be reflected in the Description field against the Local File in the right pane.

Your monthly accounting log files are now set up.

CERTIFICATION OBJECTIVE 27.10

Remote Access Security

In addition to the dial-in permission and remote access policies, Windows 2000 Routing and Remote Access offers a wide range of security features, including:

- Secure authentication (of both user and server)
- Data encryption
- Packet filtering
- Secure callback
- Caller ID
- Remote access account lockout

Which security options you choose to implement will depend on the level of security required, which must be decided within the considerations of administration overheads (e.g., setting, monitoring, maintaining, and troubleshooting failed valid connections).

Secure Authentication

Part of establishing a PPP connection is authenticating the remote access client. Both sides must agree on a single, specific authentication protocol.

A secure authentication provides protection from:

- Replay attacks
- Client impersonation
- Server impersonation

Table 27-8 lists the authentication risks.

Secure user authentication occurs through the encrypted exchange of user credentials using PPP with an authentication protocol. Windows 2000 Routing and Remote Access offers two different security Authentication Providers:

TABLE 27-8

Authentication Risks

Authentication Risk	Explanation
Replay attack	This is when somebody captures the packets of a successful connection attempt and then later replays the same packets in an attempt to obtain an authenticated connection.
Client impersonation	This is when somebody takes over an existing authenticated connection by obtaining connection parameters from a successfully authenticated client, disconnecting the client, and then taking control of the original connection.
Server impersonation	This is when a bogus server appears to be a valid server so that it can capture credentials of a remote user trying to connect so it can use these to the valid server.

- Windows authentication
- RADIUS authentication

This is configured under the Routing and Remote Access server Properties, Security tab; the default setting is for Windows authentication.

Windows Authentication

User credentials sent by users attempting remote access connections are authenticated using normal Windows authentication mechanisms.

RADIUS Authentication

User credentials and connection request parameters are sent as a series of RADIUS request messages to a RADIUS server, which might be another Windows 2000 server running the Internet Authentication Service (IAS). In this mode, the Windows 2000 RRAS server is acting as a RADIUS client.

The RADIUS server authenticates the remote access client against its authentication database, and it can also inform the RRAS server of other connection parameters for the particular user, such as the maximum time it can be connected, and how it assigns IP addresses.

RADIUS can use its own database for authenticating users, or it can use a database on another server running an ODBC interface, or even on a Windows 2000 PC.

Authentication Protocols

Both authentication providers allow you to specify which authentication protocols you require the remote access clients to use. Click Authentication Methods on the same Security tab to view and edit the authentication protocols.

If the connecting remote access client cannot perform a secure authentication with your selected authentication protocol/s, the connection will be denied.

To the other extreme, you can have an open Routing and Remote Access server without any authentication by selecting the last option to allow unauthenticated access. Although this is obviously not a secure configuration, there may be appropriate reasons for selecting unauthenticated PPP connections:

- When using Automatic Number Identification/Calling Line Identification (ANI/CLI) authentication, where the authentication is based on the telephone number of the remote user rather than on a username/password basis.
- When using guest authentication, and the Guest account is being used as the identity of the remote user.

PAP (Password Authentication Protocol)

The Password Authentication Protocol is the least secure of the authentication protocols provided using a simple, plain-text authentication. It offers no protection against replay attacks, client impersonation, or server impersonation. However, it is offered in Windows 2000 Routing and Remote Access for downward compatibility for older clients and non-Microsoft clients that cannot support a stronger authentication protocol.

Allow PAP authentication only with caution and good reason!

SPAP

The Shiva Password Authentication Protocol is a reversible encryption mechanism used by Shiva remote access servers. Although a remote access client might use SPAP to authenticate on a Windows 2000 Routing and Remote Access server, this protocol is more likely to be used by clients who need to connect to a Shiva remote access client.

This protocol is more secure than PAP, but less secure than the other protocols, and offers no protection against server impersonation. It is unlikely you would need it on a server running Windows 2000 Routing and Remote Access Service.

CHAP

The Challenge Handshake Authentication Protocol is a challenge-response authentication protocol that uses the industry-standard Message Digest 5 (MD5) one-way encryption scheme to hash the response to a challenge issued by the remote access server.

This protocol is more secure than PAP and SPAP because the password is never actually transferred, so it cannot be captured. It protects against replay attacks by using an arbitrary challenge string for each authentication, but offers no protection against server impersonation. It is useful for non-Microsoft clients but should not be needed if your remote access clients are running any version of Windows.

MS-CHAP

This is Microsoft's version of the Challenge Handshake Authentication Protocol, and offers the same features as CHAP with some additional advantages. It is supported on all versions of Windows, and as such, makes a suitable default authentication protocol. However, where you have the choice, you should instead use the later version, MS-CHAPv2, which is a more secure protocol that protects against server impersonation.

If mutual authentication (where both sides can verify they are who they say they are) is important to your security policies, then you should ensure that Microsoft clients have the latest MS-CHAPv2 and disable MS-CHAP on the server.

MS-CHAPv2

This later version of the Challenge Handshake Authentication Protocol provides stronger security for remote access connections because of the following additions:

- LAN Manager encoding of responses/password changes is no longer supported.
- Mutual authentication occurs, which eliminates both client and server impersonation.
- Separate cryptographic keys are generated for transmitted and received data.

Cryptographic keys are based on user's password and the arbitrary challenge string, so even when the user reconnects with same password, a different cryptographic key will be used.

on the Job

MS-CHAPv2 is supported on Windows 2000 without modification. It is supported on Service Pack 4 or later for NT 4.0, on Service Pack 1 or later for Windows 98, and in Windows Dial-up Networking 1.3 Performance & Security Upgrade for Windows 95 for PPTP connections. However, it is not supported for PPP connections.

EAP

The Extensible Authentication Protocol is an extension to PPP that allows for arbitrary authentication mechanisms to be used to validate a PPP connection. Its design is such that it allows authentication plug-in modules at both the client and server. One example is using security token cards ("smart cards"), where the remote access server queries the client for a name, PIN, and card token value. Another example is using biometrics; for example, a retina scan or finger print match to uniquely identify an individual.

Once the connection authentication phase is reached, the client negotiates which EAP authentication it wants to use, which is known as the EAP type. Once the EAP type is agreed upon, the server can issue multiple authentication requests to the client (as in the client name, then PIN, then card token value).

EAP offers the highest flexibility in authentication uniqueness and variations, even offering the ability for third-party vendors to supply their own EAP type library (which would need to be installed on both the server and client).

exam Watch

Of all Microsoft platforms, Windows 2000 is the only one to support EAP, and it is required for smart cards.

EAP-MD5 This is the CHAP authentication used with EAP.

EAP-TLS This is the Transport Layer Security protocol, based on Secure Sockets Layer (SSL), that allows applications to communicate securely. It offers the following:

- Client and two-way authentication using encryption
- Negotiation of the specific encryption algorithm
- Secured exchange of encryption keys used for encrypting messages
- Message integrity and user authentication using a message authentication code

The mutual authentication is done by the exchange and verification of certificates—the connecting client sends a user certificate, and the server sends a machine certificate.

EAP-RADIUS

EAP-RADIUS passes EAP messages from the remote access server to the RADIUS server for authentication. In this way, the remote access server simply passes through the EAP messages from the client to the destination RADIUS server and does not process them. Because the remote access server is not processing the EAP messages, it does not need to have the EAP type installed, which is certainly an advantage if using multiple remote access servers.

In a typical use of EAP-RADIUS, the remote access server is configured to use EAP, and to use RADIUS as the authentication provider rather than Windows 2000. Then when a remote client attempts to connect and sends its EAP message, the remote access server will pass on to the RADIUS server any EAP messages until the connection is successfully authenticated or denied.

Data Encryption

Just as you can configure the Routing and Remote Access server to require that a certain authentication occurs, so the server can require that remote access clients encrypt data sent between them and the server. If the connecting remote access client cannot encrypt as required, the connection will be denied.

Note that data encryption over PPP does not ensure end-to-end encryption if the remote access client is connecting *beyond* the RRAS server. If this is required, IPSec should be used and configured to encrypt data that can be used with or without L2TP.

If you don't use IPSec, data encryption can still be used between the remote client and remote access server. However, data encryption can only be supported when one of the following authentication protocols is also being used:

- EAP-TLS
- MS-CHAP
- MS-CHAP v2

All Microsoft's 32-bit remote access clients support the Microsoft Point-to-Point Encryption Protocol (MPPE) for encrypting data. This uses the Rivest-Shamir-Adleman (RSA) RC4 stream cipher, and 40-bit, 56-bit, or 128-bit secret keys (the higher the key number, the stronger the security). These MPPE keys are generated during the authentication process.

Although encryption can be set by the client (and is set by default on a Windows 2000 Professional VPN connection), you can only set encryption for all data on a Routing and Remote Access server within a remote access policy. Select Edit Profile, and then under the Encryption tab are options for No Encryption, Basic, or Strong.

Packet Filtering

Usually, packet filtering for a device that communicates with the outside world would be configured at a firewall. However, you can configure these on the server itself, and there may be good reasons why you may want to do this in addition to the firewall's settings (for example, use packet filtering on certain users with no fixed source address).

There are actually three places where you can employ packet filtering on a Windows 2000 Server running Routing and Remote Access Service, and each allows you to specify the filtering with a higher degree of control. These levels are at the server (all adapters), at a particular adapter (e.g., adapter connected to the Internet), and for individual policies.

If you decide to use packet filtering, don't forget to check all three places and ensure that you haven't blocked valid packets at a higher level that are needed at a lower level. For example, there's no point in configuring a Remote Access Policy to allow only packets through for PPTP if packet filtering at the Internet adapter has been set to block PPTP packets!

Packet Filtering at the Server

This is rather well-hidden under the properties of the TCP/IP protocol, General | Advanced Options | TCP/IP filtering with the option Enable TCP/IP Filtering (all adapters) where you can specify TCP and UDP ports and Protocol IDs. You cannot specify source and destination addresses here. This dialog box is very similar to the one in Windows NT 4.0, but the important difference is that these settings apply to *all adapters* in the computer.

Packet Filtering on Individual Adapters

This is specified within the Routing and Remote Access snap-in. Select IP Routing | General, and then right-click on the interface you want to use (e.g., your Internet connected adapter) and select Properties. From there, select the buttons for Input Filters and Output Filters, supplying in each the source/destination address, protocol, and ports to filter. This setting applies to all packets on that interface.

Packet Filtering on Individual Remote Access Policies

Finally, you can specify packet filtering in the Profile of a remote access policy, under the IP tab. You will see under IP packet filters two buttons: From client and To client. These are the equivalent to the Input and Output filters. Select one button and then click Add to define source and destination addresses, protocols, and ports. Figure 27-6 shows an example of an Input filter that blocks any packets coming in to the server (from any client) except those suitable for the VPN. You can then add the Windows-Group condition to this profile so that these filters would only apply to a specific group of users.

Refer to the section "Configuring Firewalls with VPNs" for more information on the settings you should know for secure connections. For other connections, decide what services you need to allow or block, and with reference to a list of well-known ports and protocol IDs, build these into your packet filtering. Don't forget to reboot and test after any changes to ensure you are not blocking valid connections.

FIGURE 27-6

Example Input filters within a Remote Access Policy

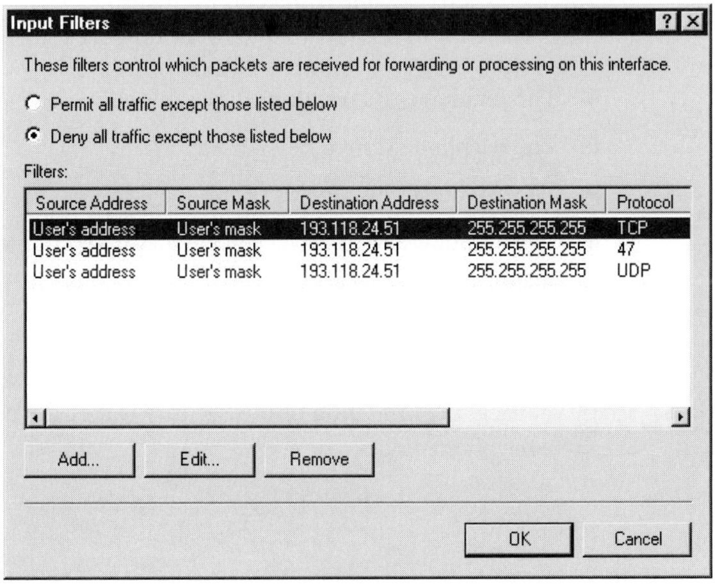

Input Filters

These filters control which packets are received for forwarding or processing on this interface.

Permit all traffic except those listed below

Deny all traffic except those listed below

Filters:

Source Address	Source Mask	Destination Address	Destination Mask	Protocol
User's address	User's mask	193.118.24.51	255.255.255.255	TCP
User's address	User's mask	193.118.24.51	255.255.255.255	47
User's address	User's mask	193.118.24.51	255.255.255.255	UDP

Add... Edit... Remove

OK Cancel

Secure Callback

This occurs when the remote access server calls back the remote client after a successful authentication, and is used particularly when the connection charge should be the responsibility of the server rather than the client. Either the client can specify the number that should be called back (greatest flexibility so they can dial in from anywhere), or this feature can be restricted for security to only call back on a specific number (secure callback).

Callback uses the *Callback Control Protocol (CBCP)* immediately after authentication.

Before remote clients can be called back, the dial-in properties of their accounts must be enabled for callback, and the number to be called back must be specified by either the client (if allowed) or the server.

You cannot use this facility with VPN solutions.

Caller ID

Caller ID can also be used to verify that the incoming connection is from a specified telephone number; again, it is configured in the dial-in properties of the user account.

If the Caller ID number of the incoming connection for the user does not match the specified Caller ID, the connection is denied.

Caller ID requires that the following all support Caller ID:

- The remote user's telephone line
- The telephone system being used
- The remote access server's telephone line
- The Windows 2000 driver for the dial-up equipment (modem, ATM adapter, etc.)

If any link in this path fails to pass on the Caller ID, it will not get through and an account configured for Caller ID will not be able to connect. Note that as with secure callback, the limitation of this security is that the user is restricted to using the same telephone line.

Remote Access Account Lockout

Remote Access Account lockout is *not* related to the "Account locked out" setting in the properties of a user's account (specified under the Account tab) and has nothing to do with the administration of account lockout policies in Windows 2000 group policies. Instead, it relates *only* to remote access and specifies how many times a remote access authentication is allowed to fail against a valid user account before denying the user remote access (not allowing them to try another password).

The RAS specific account lockout is particularly relevant for VPN servers that are connected to the Internet and will help combat a *dictionary attack*, which is when a malicious user attempts to gain access by "cracking" a password by automatically trying a list of words or commonly used phrases. By enabling the remote access account lockout feature, such an attack will be thwarted after a specified number of failed attempts.

However, remember that this setting has no compassion for genuine users who have forgotten their password and in desperation retry every password they have ever used, so set the threshold number of attempts with care or you might be spending your time constantly resetting lockouts!

Setting RAS Account Lockout

You cannot set the remote access lockout setting with the usual Routing and Remote Access administrative tools; it must be set directly in the Registry of the computer that provides the authentication. In most cases, this will be on the Routing and Remote Access server itself, but if you are using RADIUS authentication to a Windows 2000 server running the Internet Authentication Service (IAS), you will need to edit the Registry on the IAS computer.

There are two settings:

- **MaxDenials**, which is the number of failed attempts permitted before the account is locked out.
- **ResetTime (Mins)** for an automatic release after a specified period of time.

Set the MaxDenials to enable remote account lockout:

```
HKEY_LOCAL_MACHINE\SYSTEM\CurrentControlSet\Services\RemoteAccess\
Parameters\AccountLockout
```

This should be set to 1 or greater (the default is 0, which disables this setting).

Change the automatic reset (if required), by setting the ResetTime (Mins) under:

```
HKEY_LOCAL_MACHINE\SYSTEM\CurrentControlSet\Services\RemoteAccess\
Parameters\
AccountLockout
```

This should be set in hours (but in hex values; for example, the default of b40 is 48 hours).

If you cannot wait for the automatic reset, you can *manually unlock* a locked account by deleting the Registry subkey that corresponds to the user's account name under:

```
HKEY_LOCAL_MACHINE\SYSTEM\CurrentControlSet\Services\RemoteAccess\
Parameters\
AccountLockout\<domain_name:user_name>
```

EXERCISE 27-8

Enabling and Configuring Suitable Authentication Protocols for Different Types of Users

You have two different types of users who need remote access:

1. Traveling salespeople who have been issued Windows 2000 laptops with smart cards who need to dial in over the Internet.
2. Occasional homeworkers running Windows 98 (with SP1) and dialing in with V90 modems.

You have been asked to configure security to accommodate remote access for both types of users at the same time, so you decide to configure the following:

- VPN connections with L2TP/IPSec for the salespeople, accepting only EAP-TLS authentication
- Modem connections with PPP for the homeworkers, accepting only MS-CHAP v2 authentication

This exercise involves creating two new remote access policies, and because this has been covered in previous exercises, it assumes you know what they are and how to create them.

1. Ensure these users have dial-in permission, either directly from their user account (with Allow access) or by using Control access through Remote Access Policy.

2. If you haven't already done so, load the Routing and Remote Access snap-in, select your server, and right-click on it to select Properties.
3. Ensure that Remote Access Server is selected under the General tab and then select the Security tab.
4. Ensure that the Authentication Provider is set to Windows Authentication and then click Authentication Methods.
5. Click the Extensible Authentication Protocol box and then click EAP Methods.
6. Under the EAP Methods listed, select Smart Card or other Certificate, and click OK to return to the Authentication Methods dialog box.
7. Ensure the Microsoft encrypted authentication version 2 (MS-CHAP v2) is selected. Deselect the option called Microsoft encrypted authentication (MS-CHAP).
8. Ensure no other option on this dialog box is selected and click OK.
9. Click OK again to finish configuring your server properties.

The server is now configured to support these authentication protocols, but by default, either will be accepted—and you do not want the salespeople to be able to authenticate with the less-secure protocol. Therefore, you need to set up two remote access policies, one for salespeople that only allows EAP authentication, and another for homeworkers that allows MS-CHAP-v2 (strictly speaking, the second policy isn't needed, because if the stronger authentication protocol fails, a weaker one will then be tried, and if supported on the server, the connection will succeed).

10. Right click on Remote Access Policies and then Add New Policy—call it "Restrict to Salespeople with smart cards over VPN."
11. Add the following conditions:
    Windows-Group The group that contains the Salespeople
    Tunnel-Type Layer 2 Tunneling Protocol (L2TP)
12. Edit the profile, and on the Authentication tab, select the Extensible Authentication Protocol, and underneath ensure that Smart Card or other Certificate is selected and configured. Deselect any other authentication protocol on this dialog box. Finish the policy with a Grant permission.
13. Repeat the Add New Policy and this time call it "Homeworkers with MS-CHAP v2."

14. Add the following condition:
    Windows-Group The group that contains the Homeworkers
15. Edit the profile, and on the Authentication tab, deselect Microsoft Encrypted Authentication (MS-CHAP), and make sure the only protocol selected is Microsoft Encrypted Authentication version 2 (MS-CHAP-2). Finish the policy with a Grant permission.

That's it; your server now allows both authentication protocols, but you have implemented different security restrictions appropriate to different groups of users without the risk of negotiating down to a less-secure connection.

Troubleshooting Remote Access Security

The following provides some common problems/resolutions when experiencing authentication problems with remote access connections.

- If connections using callback and/or Caller ID fail, verify that these are enabled and configured correctly on the dial-in properties of the user account. In addition, verify the Link Control Protocol (LCP) Extensions are enabled on the PPP tab on the properties of the remote access server.
- If Caller ID is failing, verify that all communication hardware supports this feature.
- There are actually three places where you can specify packet filters on the remote access computer; make sure none of these are blocking valid packets.
- Unless you allow unauthenticated access, ensure both the remote access client and the remote access server are enabled to use at least one common authentication protocol.
- If either the client or server requires encryption, ensure that both have a common encryption method.
- For connections using MS-CHAP, verify that the user's password is not longer than 14 characters (this restriction does not apply to MS-CHAP v2). If it is, either change the password so it is less than 14 characters, or use a different authentication protocol.

- Verify that the user's account has not been disabled or locked out on the properties of the user account. For example, if the password has expired, the remote client must use MSCHAP or MSCHAPv2 to be able to change an expired password during a remote access connection attempt.
- Check the Registry to see if the remote account lockout is enabled, and if so, reset the user account in the Registry.
- Verify that the correct authentication provider is configured on the remote access server, and if using RADIUS authentication, verify communication between the two computers (network and password authentication).
- If using L2TP over IPSec, temporarily disable the encryption to eliminate the IPSec authentication and negotiation process—don't forget to reset this after your tests!

CERTIFICATION OBJECTIVE 27.11

Remote Access Best Practices and Tips

The following lists our recommended best practices and tips for running a successful and secure remote access server.

- Disable any protocols and services not being used on the Routing and Remote Access server, for security reasons and to ensure the best performance from your server. For this reason, a dedicated member server is preferable to running Routing and Remote Access on a domain controller, and it is a more secure solution.
- There is no reason why you can't run a Routing and Remote Access Service on a Windows 2000 server in an otherwise completely Windows NT 4.0 domain—you can immediately benefit from the added granular control of remote access permission with remote policies. However, bear in mind that Windows 2000 itself does require a higher specification of computer than if you were running the equivalent service on a Windows NT 4.0 member server.

- Particularly when being used as a VPN server, baseline your server with the Performance Monitor utility and ensure the processor is not unduly stressed. If necessary, upgrade or rethink your remote access strategies (e.g., use multiple remote access servers). The overhead of encryption comes at a price! Bear in mind that the new tunneling protocol L2TP over IPSec requires greater processing than PPTP.
- Use DHCP when DHCP servers are installed on your network—centrally configured and maintained IP addresses are less prone to configuration errors than statically configured addresses.
- To help avoid routing problems when the LAN protocol being used is TCP/IP, ensure that remote access clients and the remote access server are on the same subnet.
- Similarly, use automatic IPX network IDs for remote access clients wishing to use IPX as their LAN protocol, and use the same network ID as the one your remote access server is using.
- Use strong authentication with long passwords that are a mixture of letters and numbers, and not a common name or word that can be found in dictionaries.
- If you are using EAP-TLS as your authentication protocol, Microsoft recommends using smart cards rather than Registry-based certificates.
- If all your remote access clients will be running Windows 2000 Professional, disable MS-CHAP on your remote access server to ensure a stronger and mutual authentication. Consider also using IPSec for all remote connections. For Microsoft remote access clients that are Windows NT 4.0 or Windows 9*x*, obtain the latest MS-CHAP v2 from Microsoft.
- Avoid unnecessarily complicated remote access policies—plan in advance how to construct the simplest set of conditions and settings with the minimal number of policies. In particular, avoid configuring remote policies such that more than one policy applies to the same user.
- Remote access policies are tried in order, so typically you would want to place more specific policies before more general policies.
- If remote access is important to your company, consider putting in place contingencies so that you can ensure minimal downtime. For example, if using a VPN, install and preconfigure a point-to-point connection as well

(e.g., a modem), which by default is not enabled for incoming remote access. Then if there are problems with the VPN (e.g., ISP problems), you can enable the modem connection so that remote users can still connect (albeit at a slower throughput).

- If throughput performance is a high priority, and especially if you want to transfer voice and video over your remote connections, a dedicated high-speed private line is a better choice than a VPN.
- If you have a large number of remote access clients, consider using Connection Manager and the Connection Manager Administration Kit to provide a custom dialer with preconfigured connections to your remote access server/s. This ensures a consistent client configuration and will reap rewards from fewer support calls!
- If you have multiple remote access servers, consider configuring them as RADIUS clients connecting to a Windows 2000 server running the Internet Authentication Service. This will provide and support central configuration for remote access policies, accounting, and logging, rather than having to specify these individually for each server. An additional benefit of this solution is that the Windows 2000 with IAS will allow a Windows NT 4.0 Server running Routing and Remote Access Services to take advantage of remote access policies.
- Remember, Routing and Remote Access Services should not only provide remote access to users who require this facility, but also provide protection from outside attack. If in doubt, use stronger security configuration rather than weaker—users will always tell you when something isn't working, but you won't be aware of security holes or potential breaches until it's too late!
- The Routing and Remote Access Service is more complex in Windows 2000 than in previous versions. When you have decided upon the configuration you want and have thoroughly tested it, document the settings (particularly the policies)—not just what the settings are, but why they are configured as they are. If you ever need to troubleshoot problems, or review/configure settings in the future, this document could be a lifesaver!

CERTIFICATION SUMMARY

This chapter introduced you to some of the new services, components, and interfaces that make up the Windows 2000 Routing and Remote Access Services. Remote Access is a vital resource for many companies, but it goes hand-in-hand with the need for security and managing such connections.

Windows 2000 is able to take advantage of new technologies and hardware, while the Routing and Remote Access Service allows you to take advantage of secure connections that can be configured with a high degree of flexibility.

We examined some of the basic components that make up the Windows 2000 Routing and Remote Access Service, looked at both dial-up and virtual private networking, and detailed the main configurations required on the server. Assigning remote access permission is more complicated that it was in Windows NT 4.0, and particularly with the new Remote Access Policies, each connection and permission can be fined-tuned to a high degree.

We outlined various utilities and tools that can be used to help monitor and troubleshoot remote connections. And because security is very important for a server with connections to a public network, we also looked at the various security options and configurations available to help secure your server. Finally, we offered a list of best practices and tips for running a trouble-free and secure remote access server.

TWO-MINUTE DRILL

Overview: Windows 2000 Routing and Remote Access Service

- Routing and Remote Access Service (RRAS) in Windows 2000 builds on previous versions, with new features offering IGMP and support for multicasting, Network Address Translation (NAT), integrated AppleTalk routing, L2TP over IPSec, improved administration tools, and better support for RADIUS.
- Remote access allows users who are physically separated from the company network to access company resources on either just the RRAS server itself, or on the whole network.

Installing and Configuring the Remote Access Service

- A variety of new hardware are supported, including ATM over ADSL, digital links with V90 modems and X25 smart cards, in addition to the traditional modem. Check your choice of communication hardware against the Hardware Compatibility List before installing it.
- RRAS is automatically installed; you must enable it rather than use the normal Add/Remove Programs procedure.

Configuring the Remote Access Server

- Dynamic information about currently connected remote access clients can be obtained by expanding Remote Access Clients in the MMC—you will see information such as their assigned network address, username, etc.
- VPN ports are referred to as WAN Miniports; the default is five PPTP ports and five L2TP ports.

Assigning Remote Access Permissions

- Remote Access Policies are new to Windows 2000 and allow you to centrally control remote access and also more finely control connection restrictions and settings.

- The three Administrative models for Remote Access Policy are "Access by User," "Access by policy in mixed-mode," and "Access by policy in native-mode." Choose the one most appropriate for your environment and requirements.

Virtual Private Networking

- A VPN connection uses encapsulated, encrypted, and authenticated links across a shared or public network.
- A VPN offers a low-cost solution, because it only incurs local charges to the user's ISP, rather than long distance charges from user to server.

Connections using PPP Multilink and BAP

- Multilink is when you combine multiple physical links into a single logical link for greater throughput. It needs to be supported at both ends of the connection—enable multilink for the server and you can fine-tune settings with remote access policies.
- Multilink now supports the Bandwidth Allocation Protocol (BAP), which dynamically adds or removes links in a multilink connection.

Integrating Remote Access and DHCP

- DHCP is recommended over static address pools for assigning IP addresses to remote clients.
- When configured for DHCP, the RRAS server precaches a pool of addresses from a DHCP when the service first starts, and the RRAS server then manages these leases—assigning IP addresses to remote access clients when they connect.
- When using DHCP with RRAS, only the IP address is passed from the DHCP server to the remote access clients; other configured options on the DHCP are discarded by the RRAS server. Remote access clients inherit other IP configuration options such as those for DNS and/or WINS from the RRAS server.

Managing and Monitoring Remote Access

- ❑ Additional tools that help you manage, monitor, and troubleshoot remote access include the Event Log, authentication and account logging, Network Monitor, PPP logging, tracing, SNMP, and third-party utilities that use the RRAS APIs.

Remote Access Security

- ❑ Security features in RRAS include authentication, data encryption, packet filtering, secure callback, caller ID, and remote access account lockout.
- ❑ The two security providers supported for remote access are Windows and RADIUS. With Windows authentication, Windows 2000 security verifies the authentication, the dial-up properties of the user account, and any locally stored remote access policies. With RADIUS authentication, the credentials of the connection attempt will be passed to a specified RADIUS server for authentication and authorization, and if accepted, it will pass this confirmation back to the RRAS server.

Remote Access Best Practices and Tips

- ❑ Disable any unused services and protocols on the RRAS server—it's better to have a dedicated member server running RRAS rather than a domain controller.
- ❑ Use strong security rather than weak.
- ❑ Document how your RRAS server is configured.

28

Planning and Configuring IP Routing

CERTIFICATION OBJECTIVES

- 28.01 Overview of Windows 2000 IP Routing
- 28.02 Enabling and Configuring Windows 2000 as an IP Software Router
- 28.03 Implementing Routing Protocols
- 28.04 RIP for IP
- 28.05 OSPF
- 28.06 Demand-Dial Routing
- 28.07 Troubleshooting IP Routing Problems
- ✓ Two-Minute Drill

Although Windows 2000 supports routing for TCP/IP, IPX, and AppleTalk, this chapter concentrates on the routing capabilities and features that comprise the Windows 2000 IP Router. Specifically, this includes support for the following components:

- Internet Group Management Protocol (IGMP)
- Internet Control Message Protocol (ICMP) Router Discovery
- Routing Information Protocol (RIP) and Open Shortest Path First (OSFP) routing protocols
- Demand-dial routing

Additionally, Routing and Remote Access Service (RRAS) supports the Dynamic Host Configuration Protocol (DHCP) Relay Agent and Network Address Translation (NAT).

At the end of this chapter, you should have a much better understanding of how to install, configure, manage, monitor, and troubleshoot Windows 2000 as an IP router.

CERTIFICATION OBJECTIVE 28.01

Overview of Windows 2000 IP Routing

The Internet Protocol, or IP, is today's common network protocol that communicates over many different interconnected networks. The different networks can be within the same building and using the same media (e.g., Ethernet), or they can be worldwide using many different mediums such as Fiber Distributed Data Interface (FDDI), Frame Relay, Integrated Services Digital Network (ISDN), cable modems, analog modems, and others. Obviously, the Internet falls into the latter category, and in its simplest conceptual form, "The Internet" is merely a mesh of interconnected networks all using the same protocol suite and joined by multiple routers.

IP can span multiple networks precisely because it supports routing. Routing is the process of forwarding packets from one computer (*source host*) on one network to another computer (*destination host*) on another network. There are many different kinds of routers you can use with different routing protocols, but essentially they are all doing the same job: making decisions about forwarding traffic they receive from one network to another.

What Is a Router?

When the word *router* is used, typically people think of a physical box that is dedicated to just routing. Cisco, Bay Networks, and Cabletron Systems, for example, are just a few of the best known vendors offering this kind of technology. So, how does this equate with Windows 2000 server acting as a router? Windows 2000 server offers a routing component tightly integrated into its operating system and network services so that it can take advantage of other Windows 2000 features (e.g., a shared Graphical User Interface [GUI], security policies, authorization, etc.). It offers the flexibility to run additional or complementing services; for example, Remote Access is tightly integrated with the routing component.

Characteristics of a Software Routing Service

The routing service is one of many services running on the computer, and is dependent on the underlying operating system (e.g., Windows 2000).

The benefits of using Windows 2000 server with the routing service include:

- Tight integration with Windows 2000 features and benefits
- Built-in monitor and keyboard with standard Windows 2000 GUI for ease of use and a reduced learning curve
- Flexibility of running other applications/services on the same computer
- Potentially cheaper than a separate hardware box
- Same vendor environment as other workstations/servers

Characteristics of a Hardware Router

Hardware routers are usually configured across the network with a Telnet session or from a dial-in port on the router, so they are less "user friendly" and typically employ their own vendor-specific language for configuration. However, because they are exclusively aimed to route packets, they do offer a higher degree of control and configuration; for example, employing multiple protocols and advanced routing features. And, because their sole job is routing, they make more efficient use of their processing resources.

The benefits of using a hardware router include:

- Faster, more efficient throughput
- Offers and supports a greater number of protocols and configurations

Some hybrid routers attempt to offer the best of both worlds with the basic routing functionality handled by hardware, and system configuration and routing table management done by software. ExponeNT switches from Berkeley Networks are an example of this, where the software component actually runs on Windows NT.

Routed vs. Nonrouted Networks

If we define a routed network as being one or more networks joined together by a common protocol and a router, what is a nonrouted network? A nonrouted network is one or more networks that can be physically joined together, but have no means of communicating with each other over the network layer. This may be for a number of reasons, including:

- They do not have a common protocol (e.g., one is running TCP/IP and the other IPX).
- The protocol in use is not routable (e.g., NetBEUI or Data Link Control [DLC]).
- There is no router to forward the packets.
- The router is not configured to forward packets.

Having nonrouted networks may be desirable in certain circumstances if, for example, you don't need or want to pass packets from one network to another (for security or bandwidth reasons). Additionally, if there is no need for computers on different networks to communicate, why employ the administrative burden of installing, configuring, and monitoring a router?

However, just because one network is not routed to another doesn't preclude the passage of traffic from one network to another. This could still be accomplished higher up than the network layer; for example, with a gateway at the session layer, converting one protocol into another (e.g. IPX to IP). Another example is using a proxy server at the application layer, where one computer connected to two networks proxies traffic between the two networks. Additionally, you may prefer to use NAT rather than direct routing.

exam Watch

It's not just routers that allow packets to pass from one network to another; this can also be accomplished by gateways, proxy servers, and so forth.

Routing Fundamentals

We have already said that routing is the process of forwarding packets from one computer on one network to another computer on another network. This section looks at how IP achieves this.

Static vs. Dynamic Routing

Routers make decisions of where to forward packets they receive based on the routes (paths) they know. These routes can be *static*, *dynamic*, or a mixture of both.

Static routes are paths manually specified by an administrator and do not change until they are similarly manually changed by the administrator. Dynamic routes are paths that are "learned" and updated automatically by using routing protocols designed to automate the process of forwarding packets between networks.

Dynamic routing reduces administrative overhead, since the paths are learned automatically and they are resilient to changing circumstances because they are periodically updated automatically. However, such benefits invariably come at the price of efficiency and bandwidth. As a result of the automatic updates, routers have to "talk" to other routers at specified times, which can introduce problems of reduced bandwidth, an increase in processing on the router itself, a drop in routing efficiency since large routing tables are amassed, potential security risks, and other limitations and problems (discussed later).

Static routing has a greater administrative overhead because it relies on an administrator manually entering the paths, which is an error-prone and time-consuming process. It is also vulnerable to being out of date (non fault tolerant) when changes occur on the network (e.g., someone changes an IP address or a router is suddenly unavailable). Although it lends itself to a more efficient and tightly secured system with minimal loss of bandwidth, the administrative overhead for static routing is prohibitive for anything but a small network.

exam watch

Dynamic routing results in additional overhead on the routers and the network; however, one of its greatest benefits is that the routers can automatically sense and recover from internetwork faults.

The Default Gateway

Historically, the terms *gateway* and *router* have been used interchangeably in the IP world. Personally, I always prefer the term *router* because, technically speaking, a gateway is higher up the seven-layer Open Systems Interconnect (OSI) model than a router, which is why it can convert one protocol to another. However, a gateway can also "convert" an IP packet into another IP packet, and one reason why you might want to do this is to pass IP packets from one network to another, which is exactly what routing is doing!

Microsoft has always used *gateway* to mean *router* within the context of IP address assignment—this is not changed in Windows 2000. If you want to route packets from your computer to a different network, and you do not have an existing route defined, the assigned default gateway can be used for all nonlocal traffic for which there is no specific route.

exam Watch

A TCP/IP computer sends nonlocal traffic to its default gateway when there is no specific route defined for it.

Default Gateway Issues If packets destined for a different network are sent but delivery fails, there are many potential reasons for the failure, but a good starting point is to check the routing table on the sending workstation and the default gateway assignment. See if a specific route exists for that network, and if not, verify that a default gateway has been assigned. The default gateway is often assigned with the IP address; for example, this could be a DHCP setting.

Assuming there is no specific route on the workstation for the destination network, and you have verified that a default gateway is assigned, ensure that it is reachable by pinging that address. If it fails when neighboring local addresses ping successfully, you should check that the IP address of the default gateway is correct, that the router is up, and that you have the correct IP address and subnet mask assigned.

on the Job

Pay particular attention to the subnet address—remember that it's the combination of the IP address and the subnet mask that is used by the TCP/IP workstation to determine whether the packet it has to send is local or remote.

Additionally, because Microsoft's TCP/IP implementation only has a single-route table, you can only ever have *one* current default gateway per machine. Although you can configure multiple default gateways, the second gateway will only be used if the first gateway is unavailable (this is called "Dead Gateway Detection" and depends on a certain algorithm employed by the protocol). Microsoft advises that you only configure one default gateway per machine to avoid confusion. This holds true even for multihomed computers where it might appear to be a valid option to configure a default gateway on each adapter—a common misconception.

exam Watch

Each Microsoft Windows computer can only have one active default gateway. If you specify multiple gateways, the first choice will always be used unless the computer detects that it has become unavailable. Only then will it try the next default gateway defined.

Routing Interfaces

A routing interface is an entry point into a router in the form of an IP address; typically, this equates to a network card. However, because routing occurs at the network layer and not the physical layer, a routing interface depends on a logical IP address rather than a physical interface, although it is unusual to have more than one IP address assigned to one physical interface on a router.

For example, if you had two network adapters in your Windows 2000 server with routing enabled, but one of these had two IP addresses assigned to it, you would have three routing interfaces, not two.

Routing Tables

Each router uses a list of known routes (static or dynamic routes, or a mixture of the two) that it amalgamates into one or more routing tables. When it receives a packet to forward, it consults its routing table to see which interface should be used to forward the packet. There may be more than one possible route, in which case the better path will also be evaluated to see which one should be used.

Having a routing table does not define a router, however. Each Microsoft client running the Microsoft TCP/IP protocol will also have its own routing table, even though it might only have one network card and is not configured with a routing service or routing protocols. This routing table on IP workstations similarly instructs the protocol on which interface to direct packets; for example, a client workstation will have entries in its routing table for its own loopback address (127.0.0.1), its own subnet address, and its default gateway.

Host Routing vs. Router Routing When a workstation has traffic to send and consults its local routing table, the workstation is performing *host routing,* because it still has routing decisions to make and forwards packets according to its routing table. In comparison, a "real" router performs *router routing* when it receives a packet to be forwarded between routers (when the destination network is not directly attached to the router), or between a router and the destination workstation (when the destination network is directly attached). This distinction in defining these two kinds of routing is very subtle, but important.

Even a host router has the ability to dynamically update its host routing table; for example, the *Internet Control Message Protocol (ICMP) Redirect* message sent from an IP router can inform workstations of a better route to a destination host. If the TCP/IP workstation supports ICMP Redirect (which Windows 2000 does), this better route will be added to the routing table. Another example is being able to automatically find a default gateway if one wasn't configured with its TCP/IP address assignment (discussed later in this chapter).

EXERCISE 28-1

Viewing a Routing Table on a Windows TCP/IP Computer

This exercise demonstrates how every Microsoft TCP/IP computer (workstation or server) has its own routing table, even when it only has a single adapter and no default gateway assigned.

1. Find a Microsoft TCP/IP workstation that has a single adapter installed and no default gateway assigned (if it has a default gateway statically assigned, temporarily remove it for the purposes of this exercise).
2. To view the routing table on a Microsoft TCP/IP workstation, load the command prompt (Start | Run | Command on a Win9x machine; Start | Run | Cmd on a Windows NT 4.0 or Windows 2000 machine).
3. Type **route print**.

4. This should display the TCP/IP routing table similar to the following illustration, which is from a Windows 2000 Professional system.

```
D:\winnt\system32\cmd.exe
Microsoft Windows 2000 [Version 5.00.2195]
(C) Copyright 1985-1999 Microsoft Corp.

D:\winnt\system32>route print
===========================================================================
Interface List
0x1 ........................... MS TCP Loopback interface
0x2 ...00 a0 24 d0 5b 5b ...... ELNK3 Ethernet Adapter
===========================================================================
===========================================================================
Active Routes:
Network Destination        Netmask          Gateway       Interface  Metric
         10.0.0.0        255.0.0.0        10.0.0.15       10.0.0.15       1
        10.0.0.15  255.255.255.255        127.0.0.1       127.0.0.1       1
   10.255.255.255  255.255.255.255        10.0.0.15       10.0.0.15       1
        127.0.0.0        255.0.0.0        127.0.0.1       127.0.0.1       1
        224.0.0.0        224.0.0.0        10.0.0.15       10.0.0.15       1
  255.255.255.255  255.255.255.255        10.0.0.15       10.0.0.15       1
===========================================================================
Persistent Routes:
  None

D:\winnt\system32>_
```

5. Even though this computer only has one IP address on one adapter with no default gateway assigned, it still has multiple entries automatically added to its routing table. We will define the routing entry fields in more detail later, but you should be able to see entries defining routes for your IP address and subnet mask, the loopback address, the broadcast address to your subnet, an address for multicasting, and a broadcast address to all hosts.

If you have access to a Microsoft multihomed computer (more than one adapter installed and configured with TCP/IP) that is routing between its adapters (e.g., Microsoft NT 4.0 server with two or more adapters and IP Forwarding enabled), type the **route print** command on it (without changing any TCP/IP parameters!) and compare the routing table. It will be longer because twice the number of adapters that can pass packets to each other will result in at least twice as big a routing table; however, it will still have the same format with the same sort of routing entries.

Single-Route Router vs. Multiple-Route Router An important difference between a hardware router (such as Cisco routers) and Microsoft's software routing component is that Windows 2000 server, when acting as a router, only ever has one single routing table, irrespective of how many routing interfaces it has. This means that when a call comes in to the single-route router, only one routing table is used to determine the best way to direct the packet.

In comparison, a multiple-route router (most hardware routers) can usually be configured such that each interface maintains its own routing table. This obviously requires more processing, which is why hardware routers are dedicated to this sole job and can provide a faster and more efficient throughput of traffic.

Routing Table Structure Routing table information usually contains the following routing information fields:

- Destination Address (and subnet mask)
- Gateway (or sometimes termed *forwarding address*)
- Interface
- Metric
- Lifetime

It is important to understand what these fields are for both managing and troubleshooting routing tables and for manually assigning routes (Table 28-1).

TABLE 28-1 Routing Table Attributes and Explanations

Routing Table Attribute	Explanation
Destination Address (and subnet mask)	This contains the IP network address (or name that resolves to an address) for a network route or an internetwork address for a host route.
Gateway (forwarding address)	This identifies where the packet should be forwarded (e.g., the IP address of the interface). This can be blank if the host is on the same network as one of the router interfaces.
Interface	This is the network interface to be used when forwarding packets to the destination address. It can be expressed as an IP address, as a port number, or a logical name that refers back to an IP address.

TABLE 28-1 Routing Table Attributes and Explanations *(continued)*

Routing Table Attribute	Explanation
Metric	This indicates the cost (preference) of a route, which is applicable if multiple routes exist to the same destination network. The route with the lowest metric is used. Different routing protocols use different metrics; for example, RIP uses *hops*. To reduce delays when making routing decisions, Windows 2000 never stores multiple routes when they are learned; typically, only the lowest-cost route is retained, so this value is used to determine which route should be stored in the routing table.
Lifetime	This is the "shelf-life" of a route—how long it is considered valid. Static routes automatically have an infinite lifetime, but dynamic routes have a finite lifetime and must be refreshed before the lifetime expires in order to be retained in the routing table. The timing out of dynamic routes provides fault tolerance because it allows routers to reconfigure themselves and adapt to changing circumstances such as a downed link or router. This value is typically not visible in routing tables, but is an important attribute of a routing entry.

CERTIFICATION OBJECTIVE 28.02

Enabling and Configuring Windows 2000 as an IP Software Router

This is a service on Windows 2000 server that needs to be enabled rather than installed, and when it is initially enabled, it will invoke the Routing and Remote Access Service Setup Wizard. You may also remember that one of the wizard configuration options was for a Network Router, which you could select and let the wizard guide you through the rest of the setup.

If you haven't already configured RRAS for remote access, you can use the wizard to guide you through the setup of enabling routing. Or, if you are willing to forego your original RRAS configuration, you can disable RRAS and reenable it to invoke the setup wizard again.

However, if you have already set up and configured RRAS (e.g., for remote access) and now want to add support for routing, you will need to manually enable the Routing option as one of the server Properties.

on the Job

Don't forget that if your server is going to route, by definition it must have two or more interfaces—so install and configure these before enabling routing!

Do You Need to Install Routing Protocols?

Enabling routing makes a change in the Registry to automatically forward packets between your computer's interfaces.

If this router is the only router on your network that joins all segments (two or more), and workstations are configured with one of the server's IP addresses as their default gateway (the one that is on their subnet), packets destined for another network will now be delivered by the RRAS router. There is no need to install routing protocols to achieve this.

You would only need to either define static routes or install a routing protocol if you have multiple routers in your network. This is because your router would need to know to which router it should forward packets in order to achieve successful packet delivery when it receives packets for a network that is not directly attached.

exam Watch

You do not need to install routing protocols to be able to route packets from one interface on your router to another interface.

Static Routes

Defining static routes is an alternative, or can be used as complementing dynamic routes. They are not mutually exclusive.

You can add a static route to Windows 2000 server running the Routing and Remote Access Service in three ways.

- Route add command
- Netsh utility
- RRAS snap-in

Which one you decide to use will depend on your personal preferences and which is more appropriate for what you want to achieve.

Technically, you can also add static routes through an account used with demand-dial routing. Demand-dial routing is discussed later in this chapter.

Route Add Command

On Microsoft's host routers and router routers, you can use the command **route add.**
For example:

```
route add 192.10.11.0 mask 255.255.255.0 192.10.10.1 metric 1
```

This adds a route for the network 192.10.11.0 with the subnet mask of 255.255.255.0. When a packet needs to be sent to this network, it should be directed from the router's interface with the IP address of 192.10.10.1, which is one router away.

Use the **route print** command to review your routing table to confirm the successful addition of your static route.

If you are used to defining static routes in this way, you may find it more convenient to simply add a new static route in this fashion—particularly when the need is ad-hoc.

Netsh Utility

To add a new static route, you would use the command **netsh routing ip add persistentroute.**
For example:

```
netsh routing ip add persistentroute dest=192.10.11.0 mask 255.255.255.0
name="Internet Connection"
"
```

Use the netsh command **netsh routing ip show persisentroute** to confirm the successful addition of the static routes

Using netsh is very useful if you have a list of static routes you need to define, and for quickly adding routes onto a remote RRAS server.

The RRAS Snap-In

Using the RRAS snap-in is the easiest way to add a static route, and the new graphical user interface makes this process much less error prone. Navigate to your server, IP Routing, and right-click on Static Routes to select New Static Route.

This will display a dialog box similar to Figure 28-1 in which to enter your route details.

When you have finished and clicked OK, confirm the successful addition of your static route by right-clicking on Static Routes again, this time selecting Show IP Routing Table.

Defining static routes with RRAS is easier and less error prone than command-line alternatives. However, it can become a little tedious and time-consuming if you have multiple routes to add. Using a batch file of commands instead would be quicker, and this batch file could also be reused (e.g., for backup or modified slightly for similar routers).

Configuring the Router for IGMP

Once you have enabled the Windows 2000 RRAS service, it can support other services in addition to routing data packets from one network to another. One of these is the IGMP router and IGMP proxy. Multicasting is being used increasingly on TCP/IP networks and is an intrinsic component of the Windows 2000 router.

Multicasting vs. Broadcasting vs. Unicasting

Unicasting is sending a packet directly to a single TCP/IP client—it's a one-to-one relationship. *Broadcasting* is the opposite of unicasting, where multiple packets go to all TCP/IP clients. It can do this by using a broadcast address of 255.255.255.255—

FIGURE 28-1

Defining a static route with the Routing and Remote Access snap-in

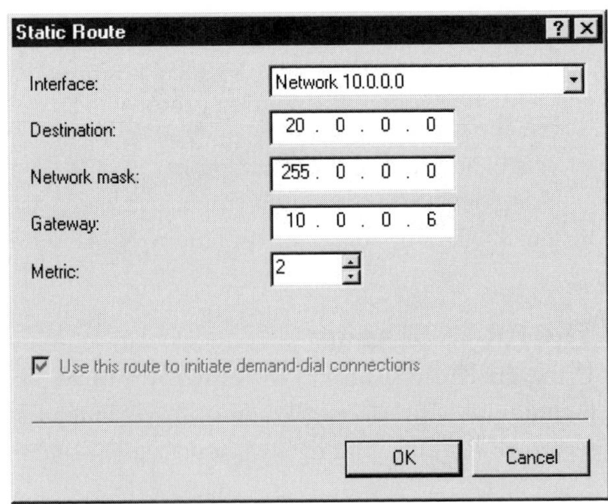

all computers receive this and have to process the packets even if the information in the packet means nothing to them, so it puts an unnecessary drain on each computer resource. Also, because broadcasts are sent out without checking to see if they were received (they can't because they don't know which computers should receive it), they are frequently sent many times in quick succession, which can flood a network. Broadcasts are one reason why networks are segmented—because broadcasts typically cannot pass through routers.

Halfway between both of these, *multicasting* is sending a single packet to multiple hosts but with a specific IP address. The IP address used is not a host address (which unicasting uses), but a reserved one from the Class D address range (224.0.0.0 to 239.255.255.255). Using a specific address means that packets can be acknowledged (if required), and they can span multiple networks via routers.

Multicast Members

If a TCP/IP host supports multicasting, it can register itself with a specific multicast address that lets the server that sends out the multicasts know that it wants to receive its multicast traffic. It then becomes a member of that multicast group and receives data sent to that group until it leaves the group.

A Windows 2000 router uses multicasting with its routing protocols (RIPv2 and OSPF); for example, 224.0.0.9 is used with a RIPv2 router, and 224.0.0.5 and 244.0.0.6 are used with OSPF routers. In these cases, the Internet Group Multicast members are the Windows 2000 servers.

Multicasting Across Networks

When multicasting is used with the Windows 2000 routing protocols, there is no need to install the IGMP routing protocol, because multicasts will go directly from one interface on one router to another interface on another router on the same segment. In other words, the multicast packets are able to be delivered and received directly, rather than having to be routed.

The IGMP routing facility needs to be installed when a direct connection between an IGMP host and IGMP server is not possible, because one or more routers are in the complete route. If a client on your TCP/IP network registers with a multicast group that is on the Internet, at least one router (yours) will be in the path between IGMP host member and IGMP server. In this case, multicast packets need to be routed from the network the client is on, and then forwarded to the Internet network the server is on.

A typical example of IGMP Internet services that workstations might want to use is Internet real-time streaming audio and video. However, because of the problem of having to route multicasting traffic, not all routers on the Internet can support multicasting—only a portion of the Internet known as the MBONE (multicast backbone) currently supports multicasting. Therefore, for TCP/IP clients on your networks to be able to use multicast services on the Internet, ensure their packets are routed through your router that is enabled for IGMP routing, and ensure the server is attached to the MBONE.

If your server is not directly connected to a multicast network, you can delete the IGMP interface from your RRAS server.

Enabling IGMP

Support for IGMP is enabled by installing the IGMP router and IGMP proxy services as if they were a protocol (if not already installed), and then adding to it two or more interfaces. You must add one interface that is directly connected to the multicast network; typically, this would be your Internet connection. Your other interfaces would typically be local area connections.

You then configure IGMP properties for these interfaces. The interface that is directly connected to the multicast network should be configured for IGMP *proxy mode.* Other interfaces not directly connected to the multicast network (e.g., any local area network connections) should be configured for *router mode.*

Figure 28-2 displays a typical configuration for IGMP.

FIGURE 28-2 A typical configuration for IGMP

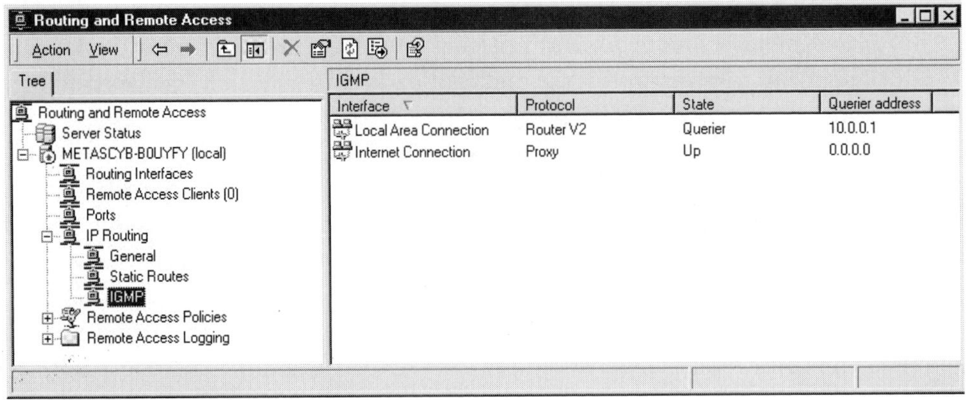

exam Watch

To offer the benefits of Multicasting Groups on the Internet to clients on your intranet: Ensure your router is connected to the MBONE on the Internet, enable IGMP on the router, add IGMP in Proxy mode on the Internet interface, and add IGMP in router mode on your local area connection interface/s.

Configuring the Router for ICMP Router Discovery

Another service the Windows 2000 server offers is the Internet Control Message Protocol (ICMP) Router Discovery. This means that it can automatically assign a default gateway to workstations if they don't already have one to ensure that nonlocal traffic from workstations can be routed.

What's the purpose of this if you can define the default gateway as part of the IP address? First, it is less prone to administrative error—the IP address of the default gateway is automatically sent out, so there's no need to type in any IP addresses. Second, by virtue of the fact that the router is sending out packets informing workstations about its router service, it offers service reliability that a statically assigned default gateway cannot offer. It also offers fault tolerance, because a TCP/IP workstation using this method to obtain a default gateway can automatically detect when its router is down, and therefore automatically switch to a new (available) router. In short, it ensures that TCP/IP clients can always automatically find an available router on their subnet for their nonlocal traffic.

Components of the ICMP Router Discovery Service

ICMP Router Discovery has two components:

- Router Advertisements (sent out by the router to advertise its availability)
- Router Solicitations (sent out by TCP/IP workstations to request router availability)

Router Advertisements When the Windows 2000 RRAS IP router is configured for ICMP Router Discovery Advertisement, it will periodically send out an ICMP Router Advertisement to the all-hosts multicast address of 224.0.0.1.

This message will also contain an *Advertisement Lifetime* and a *Preference Level*. The Advertisement Lifetime refers to the length of time between advertisements so hosts know that if this time is exceeded without a new advertisement, the route is no longer valid (the default is 30 minutes). The preference level is used when there are multiple routers also offering themselves as default gateways—workstations select the router with the highest preference level.

If a TCP/IP workstation has registered with this multicast address (i.e., it supports ICMP Router Discovery), it will receive the ICMP Router Discovery Advertisement from the router. If the workstation already has a default gateway statically assigned, the advertisement will be ignored. However, if it doesn't already have a default gateway assigned, it can update its routing table with the advertised default route and use it to send nonlocal traffic when there is no specific route (see Table 28-2).

Router Solicitations When a TCP/IP host supports the ICMP multicast and it requires a default gateway (either because one has not been assigned, or because its previously discovered default gateway is down), it doesn't need to wait until the next router advertisement before it can benefit from the advertised Default Gateway service. Instead, it sends out a Router Solicitation ICMP message to the all-routers IP multicast address of 224.0.0.2.

Routers that have been configured for Router Advertisement will immediately respond, and the TCP/IP workstation can then choose the router with the highest preference level as its default gateway.

TABLE 28-2 ICMP Router Discovery Settings—Values and Explanations

Router Discovery Settings	Description and Default Values
Level of Preference	The preference level for this router to be the default gateway if multiple routers are all sending similar advertisements. The highest preference level router is chosen as the default gateway. The default value is 0.
Advertisement Lifetime (minutes)	The time after which a workstation will consider this router to be unavailable. In other words, if this value expires before sending another advertisement, the workstation will remove this router as its default gateway. The default value is 7 minutes.
Advertisement interval minimum time (minutes)	The minimum time between advertisements. The default is 7 minutes.
Advertisement interval maximum time (minutes)	The maximum time between advertisements. Advertisements are sent at a random interval between the minimum and maximum times. The default is 10 minutes.

CERTIFICATION OBJECTIVE 28.03

Implementing Routing Protocols

If you want to use dynamic routing protocols to automatically build a routing table for networks that are not directly attached, you must install the routing protocols you want to use and then define on which interface/s they should be used. You can configure global settings for the routing protocol, and set routing options individually for each added interface.

Installing Dynamic Routing Protocols

The two dynamic routing protocols you can install with Windows 2000 RRAS are RIP and OSPF. For RIP, the default configurations may suffice for the majority of situations, which is why RIP is such an easy routing protocol to use. However, OSPF is more complicated and must be configured correctly before your router will function correctly with this protocol.

The steps you perform for adding any protocol with RRAS are the same: Add the protocol and then add to the protocol the interface/s you want to use with the protocol. Unlike Windows NT 4.0, there is no automatic binding of protocols to adapters.

Once the protocol has been added, you can configure global options for the protocol and configure protocol options that only apply to the selected adapter. When the configuration is complete, you should then be able to exchange routing information with other routers on the network to automatically construct a local dynamic routing table. Similarly, neighboring routers will update their routing tables to include your router.

Silent RIP for IP

Silent RIP for IP is when an IP router (using the RIP routing protocol) dynamically updates its own routing table with information obtained from other RIP routers without sending out its own routing information. In this case, the routing "exchange" between the Silent RIP router and other routers is not complete because the information is one-way only—listening for routing information but not reciprocating. You can use Silent RIP on a workstation too, but this requires modifying the Registry. On a Windows 2000 RRAS router, Silent RIP is configured as one of the RIP interface properties.

Adding Interfaces to the Routing Protocols

The next step is to add the interfaces you want to use with your dynamic routing protocol/s (binding the protocol to the interface).

You must add at least two interfaces to the routing protocol, but if you have more than two interfaces in your router, you do not need to add all of them to the dynamic routing protocol. For example, you may be running RIP on interfaces 1 and 2, and OSPF on interfaces 3 and 4. Adding only specific interfaces to your routing protocols prevents unnecessary routing traffic that produces wasteful overhead on the network, router, and other routers.

The "Internal" routing interface that you might see displayed in the RRAS snap-in details pane appears automatically to represent all Remote Access Service devices. All RAS clients are part of this interface—do not delete it!

Dynamic Routing Issues

As we have seen, two dynamic routing protocols are supported in Windows:

- Routing Internet Protocol (RIP) Versions 1 and 2—a distance vector routing protocol
- Open Shortest Path First (OSPF)—a link state routing protocol

Although dynamic routing protocols put additional overhead onto the router and the network, one of their most valuable assets is that they can sense and recover from internetwork problems such as a downed link or downed router. How quickly it can recover is determined by the type of fault, how it is sensed, and how the updated information is propagated throughout the internetwork.

Convergence

When all the routers on the internetwork have the correct routing information in their routing tables, the internetwork is said to have *converged.* When convergence is achieved, the internetwork is in a stable state, and all routing occurs along optimal paths.

When a link or router fails, the internetwork must reconfigure itself to reflect the new topology, and to achieve this, routing tables must be updated. Until the internetwork has converged again, routing will be vulnerable to loops and black holes. The time it takes for the internetwork to reconverge is known as the *convergence time*, and the optimal aim is for the shortest convergence time with minimum traffic.

exam watch

Convergence time *refers to the time it takes for all routing tables to be updated.*

The main difference between distance vector and link state routing protocols centers on these issues:

- What routing information is exchanged
- How the information is exchanged
- How quickly the internetwork can recover from an internetwork fault such as a downed router

Distance Vector vs. Link State Routing Protocols

Distance vector-based routing protocols periodically send out their known routes from their routing table, and update their routing table after receiving similar information from other routers. By "listening" to other routers, it can be determined where routers are on the network in relation to each other, so that a "hop count" can be determined. This exchange of information is unsynchronized and unacknowledged.

Link state-based routing protocols exchange link state advertisements using directed (multicast) traffic. These link state advertisements include the router's network ID (a logical number) and are sent to neighboring routers upon startup and when changes in the internetwork topology are sensed. Link state routers build a database of link state advertisements, and use this to calculate the routing table. Routing information exchanged is synchronized and acknowledged.

Features of Distance Vector Routing The advantages of a distance vector-based routing protocol are that it's simple to configure and understand in concept. This results in low administrative overhead when used in a suitable environment.

The disadvantages of a distance vector-based routing protocol include the following:

- In a large network, it produces large and unwieldy routing tables, which take time to process on the router and are difficult for an administrator to understand when troubleshooting is required.
- High bandwidth requirements, since routing information is sent out periodically even after convergence.
- Does not scale, producing large routing tables, and a single route has a limitation of 15 routers.
- High convergence time, which leaves the internetwork vulnerable to routing problems.

Features of Link State Routing Link state routing was designed specifically to overcome some of the shortcomings of the older distance vector routing protocol, which was never designed for today's wide-scale enterprise internetworks.

The advantages of a link state-based routing protocol include the following:

- Smaller routing tables which means they are quicker to process.
- Lower bandwidth requirements because routing information is not exchanged unnecessarily, and traffic is directed rather than sent out indiscriminately.
- Ability to scale to very large networks.
- Lower convergence time.

The disadvantages of a link state-based routing protocol include the following:

- Complex in design and configuration from an administrator's point of view, and therefore prone to human error.
- Potentially resource intensive on large networks.

Even with this short introduction to distance vector-based and link state routing protocols, you should now have a good idea of which is best suited for a particular requirement.

SCENARIO & SOLUTION	
Which would be a better choice on your network, a distance vector-based routing protocol or a link state routing protocol?	Distance vector or link state routing protocol.
You have a small network with just four routers.	Distance vector is well suited for small networks.
You want the simplest to configure.	Distance vector is simple to configure and understand.
Routing reliability is more important than ease of configuring.	Link state offers a more reliable routing service, since route advertisement is directed and acknowledged.
You have a large network to manage, and require a low convergence time with minimal bandwidth loss.	Link state is more efficient in updating its routing tables, it doesn't flood the network with broadcasts, and only sends information when necessary.

Common Problems with Dynamic Routing

Before we look at RIP and OSPF, it would be helpful to identify common problems and issues that arise when using dynamic routing protocols. Once we are aware of known issues and shortcomings, you will be better able to judge which is the better routing protocol to use for your network, and how best to configure it to minimize these potential problems.

Common problems with dynamic routing include:

- Rogue routers
- Routing loops
- Count to infinity
- Black holes
- Overheads of large and complex routing tables
- High network bandwidth and broadcast flooding
- Slow convergence

Rogue Routers

If routing announcements are unacknowledged, there is no way of knowing whether other routers received the information, or if a rogue router sent conflicting information, such as a route redirect, to divert traffic from a legitimate destination.

Authentication of routing information is one way to verify that such information is legitimate, and some routing protocols now allow you to assign a password that must be authenticated on the receiving router before updates are allowed. Alternatively, you could define exactly which routers you recognized as valid, and discard routing information from any others (however, because this is configured with IP addresses, this is still vulnerable to IP spoofing where a rogue router can send out packets with a different source IP address to its own).

Routing Loops

During routing, packets are forwarded on the optimal path as reflected in the current routing table. Providing the routing table contains only correct and current entries, and everything works fine—until the information becomes out of date. This could lead to a routing loop where the packet is directed according to the routing information, but ends up being routed back to itself rather than its desired destination. This is the perpetual "Go to" statement with all its inherent dangers, and can be very difficult to detect without network tools (e.g., network capture or tracert utility), except for high processing on routers and a slow delivery (if at all).

The Time-to-Live value (TTL) helps to prevent infinite looping because each router that handles a data packet decreases the TTL by 1, and when it reaches 0, the packet is discarded and the router sends a *Time Exceeded* message back to the sending host.

Count to Infinity

Distance vector-based routing protocols are vulnerable to this problem because of the way they send out routing announcements. It is possible for routing tables to become out of date, and routes become advertised with an increasing hop count (the count to infinity). This is one reason why the RIP maximum hop count is set to 15 to prevent an ever-increasing hop count. When a hop count reaches 16, the destination will be considered unreachable; therefore, the route will be timed out.

Black Holes

Because RIP is a distance vector-based routing protocol that uses unacknowledged delivery, data can often be lost without trace. One router could realize that its neighboring router was unavailable and send out information to broadcast this, but if the information is never received, other routers can continue to send data to the downed router in the mistaken belief it is still available. This is a "black hole" because there is nowhere for the packets to go, but the sending system hasn't realized this. Link state routing protocols that use directed and acknowledged announcements are not vulnerable to this problem.

Another example of a black hole is a *Path Maximum Transmit Unit* black hole when a router discards packets that must be fragmented, but fails to send a message to the sending system to fragment further packets. Similarly, if a host system cannot process all the packets it is receiving and fails to send out a Source Quench message to the sending system for a respite, the packets it cannot handle will be silently discarded.

Overhead of Large and Complex Routing Tables

Because vector-based routing protocols store a complete list of all the networks and all the possible ways to reach each network, the amassed routing tables in a large internetwork can become very large, which takes time to process, results in more information being exchanged, and becomes more difficult to troubleshoot.

This is one reason why some routers (which includes Windows 2000) only store a single route (typically the one with the lowest metric) for any network. However, it results in an incomplete routing table of the internetwork if all routes are not listed.

Link state-based protocols do not have this problem, as they have smaller routing tables that provide only pertinent information that is relevant to their position on the internetwork.

High Network Bandwidth and Broadcast Flooding

Distance vector-based routing protocols that announce their routes typically every 30 seconds can take up a high proportion of network bandwidth, and if using broadcasts, these messages are received by every computer on the network, which necessitates processing irrespective of whether they are also routers or even TCP/IP computers.

When available network bandwidth is low (e.g., WAN links), a high proportion of the limited bandwidth has to be given over to these periodic messages even if all routing tables are converged—leaving little bandwidth for anything else. The bigger the network, the bigger the routing tables, and the more information that has to be announced. This is certainly one reason why distance vector routing protocols do not scale well.

Using multicasts instead of broadcasts helps to alleviate this problem, and additionally, link state-based routing protocols only send out routing information when there are changes.

Slow Convergence

When a router or link fails, it can take a while for this information to be reflected in all the routing tables on the internetwork. It can take several minutes for the changes and adjustments to be propagated throughout all of the remaining routers.

RIP is particularly vulnerable to this, and it is exacerbated by the use of unacknowledged broadcasts that do not guarantee that the new routing information has been received by neighboring routers. However, you can often modify the announcement algorithms to help reduce convergence time.

Because link state routing protocols have smaller and more efficient routing tables, their convergence time is less on all but very large-scale internetworks.

Options employed to help reduce convergence time include:

- Split horizon
- Split horizon with poison reverse
- Triggered updates

Split Horizon Split horizon prevents routers from advertising networks in the direction from which those networks were learned, so the only information sent in routing announcements are for those networks that are beyond the neighboring router in the opposite direction. This also helps to eliminate count-to-infinity and routing loops.

Split Horizon with Poison Reverse This announces all networks, but all networks learned in a given direction are announced with a hop count of 16 (network unreachable). This works well in a multi-path internetwork by helping to eliminate count-to-infinity and routing loops.

Triggered Updates This option allows a router to announce changes in a route's metric almost immediately, rather than waiting for the next periodic announcement. For example, if a route is unreachable, the metric will change to 16 in RIP, and it is better for other routers to know about this unavailable route as soon as possible.

Triggered updates usually have a trigger time interval so the network is not flooded with similar announcements from multiple routers.

Triggered updates help to reduce the convergence time, but require additional bandwidth.

Combining Different Routing Protocols on the Same Router

Bearing in mind that a software router only has one routing table, a Windows 2000 router with both routing protocols installed may have to decide which route is preferable (and therefore stored) if it learns of two different routes by both protocols to the same destination. Normally, if a single protocol reported multiple routes to the same network, only the one with the lowest metric would be stored. However, RIP and OSPF use different metrics—which one should be chosen as the preferred route?

The answer lies in choosing the route from the *preferred source*, irrespective of the metric in the route. For example, a Windows 2000 RRAS configured for both RIP and OSPF adds both types of routes to its Route Table Manager (RTM) IP routing table. If OSPF is configured as the preferred source, and the router learns of two different routes to the same network (one from RIP with a metric of 2, and one from OSPF with a metric of 4), the OSPF route will be retained, and the RIP route discarded.

exam Watch

When two different routes from the same routing protocol are learned that provide paths to the same destination, the metric is used to determine which is the preferred route. When two routes from different routing protocols are learned that provide paths to the same destination, the metric is ignored, and the route that comes from the preferred source is retained.

Setting Preference Levels on the Router

Preference levels for route sources can be viewed and configured on the Preference Levels tab as in IP Routing | General Properties (Figure 28-3). You can also set a specific preference level for a static route with the netsh command: **routing ip add rtmroute.**

FIGURE 28-3

Preference levels for route sources

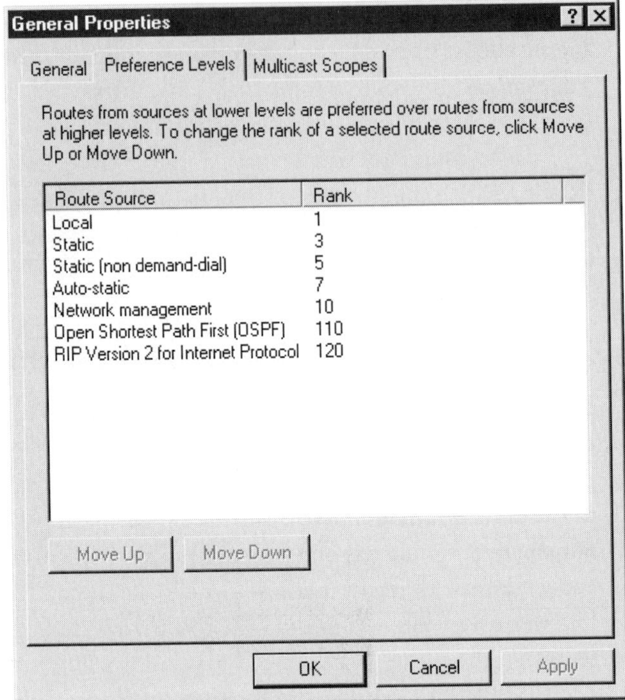

Common Routing Terminology Used with Large Internetworks

These terms are used normally only in conjunction with large internetworks, and you will see them being used in OSPF contexts; however, they are not restricted to just OSPF.

AS—Autonomous System

A group of routers and networks under the same administration using a common routing protocol is referred to as an Autonomous System (AS). There is no single definition or restriction of what constitutes an AS; it could be a SOHO network, a large company spanning many buildings, and an ISP that is responsible for many Internet accounts and routes.

IGP—Interior Gateway Protocols

Routing protocols used within the AS are referred to as *Interior Gateway Protocols* (IGP), with both RIP and OSPF being examples of IGPs. Routers that handle these protocols are known as *interior gateways*, and they handle *intra-AS routing*.

EGP—Exterior Gateway Protocols

When a routing protocol is being used to exchange routing information from one AS to another AS, it is referred to as an *Exterior Gateway Protocol* (EGP), with the Exterior Gateway Protocol (EGP) and Border Gateway Protocol (BGP) being examples of EGPs. Routers that handle these protocols are known as *exterior gateways*, and they handle *inter-AS routing*.

An important distinction is that while all interior gateways must use the same Interior Gateway Protocol within an AS, Exterior Gateway Protocols within an AS are independent from the Interior Gateway Protocols within the same AS. This means that exterior gateways can exchange routes between ASs that use different Interior Gateway Protocols. For example, if one AS uses RIP, and another AS uses OSPF, the two networks can communicate and direct packets through the other network (AS) through their exterior gateways.

Windows 2000 RRAS router does not provide Exterior Gateway Protocols; however, it does support an Application Programming Interface (API) for independent vendors to write and provide their own Exterior Gateway Protocol to be used with the RRAS router.

CERTIFICATION OBJECTIVE 28.04

RIP for IP

Windows 2000 supports both RIPv1 and RIPv2, both of which use a distance vector algorithm.

The first version of RIP (Routing Internet Protocol) was originally designed in 1988 for use in a simple local area network environment. In its day, it met its requirements very well, but in today's larger and more complex internetworks, the early version of RIP has many limitations.

RIPv2 seeks to address many of these shortcomings, and for many companies and networks now offers a more practical dynamic routing protocol that is easier to understand and manage than link state routing protocols.

Furthermore, compatibility is possible in a mixed RIP version environment. Routers that support only RIPv1 can still read and process RIPv2 packets by extracting the RIPv1 information and discarding the newer RIPv2 additional information. In addition, a RIPv2 router can send RIPv1 packets to a RIPv1 router so that redundant information is not sent—for security, this option is configurable.

on the job

Be careful when reading information on RIP; it may have been written before RIPv2 was available, and as such, be relevant only to RIPv1. For example, it may assert RIP shortcomings that apply only to RIPv1 but are now addressed with RIPv2. This also applies to answering questions on the exam that might seem to assume that you have to use OSPF rather than RIP in order to support more modern features of today's internetworks.

RIPv1

As a simple distance vector-based routing protocol, RIPv1 is very easy to configure—often as simple as enabling a single option. However, it does have the following shortcomings:

- Broadcast rather than multicast announcements
- Subnet mask not announced with the route
- No protection from rogue routers

Broadcast vs. Multicast Announcements Broadcast announcements are not suitable for today's networks, because they indiscriminately put a high processing overhead on all network cards. Even if a network card is not a RIP router, it still has to process these packets.

A multicast announcement would be more efficient so that only network cards with a registered interest in RIP announcements would have to process these packets; however, RIPv1 doesn't support multicast announcements.

One advantage of broadcast announcements is when using Silent RIP; this allows a TCP/IP host to listen and act on advertised routes without having to participate. It is possible to use Silent RIP with multicasts, but not all implementations may support it.

Subnet Mask Not Announced with the Route RIPv1 was designed for class-based IP networks where the default subnet mask would always be used; therefore, there was no need to include it in routing announcements. The scarcity of IP addresses today has brought about the evolution of more complex subnet masks, where nondefault masks are used to subdivide a network, and subnetting/supernetting and variable-length subnet masks are now commonly employed.

Because RIPv1 doesn't include the subnet mask with routing announcements, routers have to try to determine the network ID based on a limited set of information.

As a result, a default subnet mask may be incorrectly assumed, and a supernetted route might be interpreted as a single network rather than a range of networks.

No Protection from Rogue Routers There is no protection against a rogue RIP router announcing false or inaccurate routes, since RIPv1 announcements have no authentication mechanism.

RIPv2

The next (and current) version of RIP has the following advantages over its predecessor:

- Multicast option rather than broadcast announcements
- Subnet mask announced
- Authentication
- Route tag

Multicast Option Rather than Broadcast Announcements RIP announcements can be sent to the IP multicast address of 224.0.0.9, which means that network cards that do not wish to share RIP routing information do not have to process unnecessary packets.

However, if you are using Silent RIP, this will need to be modified to use the multicast announcement—if it is supported.

For downward compatibility, broadcast announcements can still be used.

Subnet Mask Announced Because the subnet mask is included in the routing announcements, subnetted, supernetted, and variable-length subnet masks are now fully supported.

Authentication You can now authenticate incoming RIP announcements with a predefined password. The password can be clear text or encrypted. However, Windows 2000 currently supports only clear-text passwords, which means that they are vulnerable to a network capture exposing them.

Route Tag A route tag is additional administrative information you can include with announcements on specific routes. It was designed for environments that used multiple routing protocols (e.g., RIP and another distance vector-based routing protocol such as HELLO) so that RIP-based routes could be identified from non-RIP-based routes.

on the job

Configure and use RIPv2 with greater care when it will be used with RIPv1 routers. They must have a common announcement mechanism, which means using broadcast announcements rather than multicasts, and incoming packets should be set for RIPv1 and RIPv2. Remember that while RIPv2 can support subnetted, supernetted, and variable-length subnet masks, RIPv1 may incorrectly interpret these. In particular, you should exclusively use RIPv2 if you are using variable-length subnet masks and disjointed subnets.

Windows 2000 as a RIP Router

Windows 2000 server when configured as a router with the RIP routing protocol supports the following:

- Convergence options for split horizon, poison reverse, and triggered updates
- The ability to modify the announcement interval (default is 30 seconds)
- The ability to modify the routing table entry timeout (default is 3 minutes)
- The ability to support Silent RIP
- Peer filtering, which is the ability to accept or reject RIP announcements from specific routers (by IP address)
- Route filtering, which is the ability to accept or reject RIP announcements of specific networks or specific routers
- RIP neighbors, which is the ability to send unicast RIP announcements to specific routers that could not normally accept multicast announcements (e.g., routers over Frame Relay)
- The ability to announce or accept default routes or host routes

You should now have a better understanding of when RIP can meet your routing requirements, or when your requirements are such that you should use the more complex link state routing protocol, OSPF.

SCENARIO & SOLUTION

Can you use RIP as your routing protocol if...	Choice of Routing Protocol: RIP or OSPF
You want to use multicasts rather than broadcast announcements?	RIPv2 allows you to do this, but remember it can't be used with RIPv1 routers because they must have a common announcement. The other consideration is if you have Silent RIP hosts on your network; ensure they can also support the multicast announcements.
You want protection from rogue routers?	RIPv2 allows you do this, although Windows 2000 only supports clear-text passwords, which are not as secure as an encrypted password exchange. However, OSPF in Windows 2000 also currently does not support encrypted passwords. Cisco routers support Message Digest 5 (MD5) with OSPF, which may be a better choice if this is important to you.Remember, you can also specify peer and route filtering to exactly define from which routers you will accept announcements.
You want to use a variable-length subnet mask (VLSM)?	RIPv2 supports this, but again, remember not to use this more modern IP facility in conjunction with RIPv1 routers.
You want to use routes that are greater than 15 hops?	For all its improvements, RIPv2 still can't handle this! Because of potential problems inherent with distance vector-based routing protocols (such as count to infinity and looping holes), it is debatable whether this value should be allowed to increase.OSPF is your only option here; it supports up to 255 routers.
You want to be able to fine-tune and optimize convergence time?	RIP allows you to do this with options for split horizon, poison reverse, and triggered updates. However, inevitably in a large internetwork, a state link routing protocol such as OSPF will have a faster convergence time.
You want to decrease the network traffic by sending fewer announcements?	This is tricky! Technically, you can decrease the network traffic by sending fewer announcements with RIP, because you can specify the periodic announcement time to be a high value. However, the higher the value, the greater the risk of being out of date. Similarly, you can disable triggered updates. Also, remember that within each announcement all the routes are announced even if there are no changes, so bandwidth is being used unnecessarily. If what you really want to do is have a lower and more efficient bandwidth utilization by only sending announcements when there are changes, and within each announcement send the minimum amount of information required to update routes, then OSPF would be the better routing protocol.

EXERCISE 28-2

Changing RIP Interface Properties to Support RIPv2 Exclusively and with Authentication

You want the benefit of a routing protocol that supports VLSMs (Variable Length Subnet Masks), uses multicast instead of broadcast, and offers protection against rogue routers. You don't want the administrative overhead of configuring OSPF, so you update all your routers with RIPv2. On your Windows 2000 RRAS router with RIP installed and added to the interfaces you want to use, you now need to make configuration changes to support your requirements.

1. If not already loaded, load the RRAS snap-in located under Start | Programs | Administrative Tools | Routing and Remote Access.
2. Navigate to RIP under your server, right-click on the interface you want to configure and select Properties.
3. Under the General tab, change the "Outgoing packet protocol" to "RIP version 2 multicast."
4. On the same tab, change the "Incoming packet protocol" to "RIP version 2 only."
5. On the same tab, select the "Activate authentication" box and type in the Password box the password you are going to use for all your routers.

6. Your configuration changes should look similar to the following illustration.

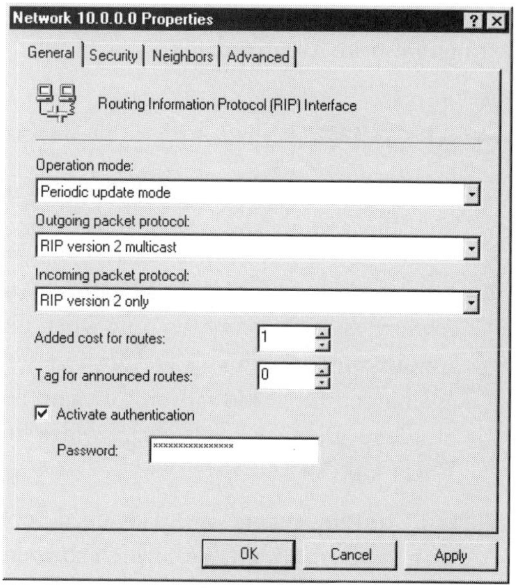

Network 10.0.0.0 Properties

General | Security | Neighbors | Advanced

Routing Information Protocol (RIP) Interface

Operation mode: Periodic update mode

Outgoing packet protocol: RIP version 2 multicast

Incoming packet protocol: RIP version 2 only

Added cost for routes: 1

Tag for announced routes: 0

☑ Activate authentication

Password: xxxxxxxxxxxxxxxx

OK | Cancel | Apply

7. Click OK and repeat this for any other interfaces on which you have added RIP.

CERTIFICATION OBJECTIVE 28.05

OSPF

Open Shortest Path First is a link state routing protocol designed for use in large-scale internetworks, and seeks to redress some of the shortcomings associated with traditional distance vector-based routing protocols.

For many of us, OSPF is a new and unfamiliar routing protocol. It is outside the scope of this chapter to give a complete and detailed description on every aspect of OSPF, but it does aim to provide the basic understanding and provide a framework of concepts and terminology to get you started. Without this, the OSPF configuration options themselves will make little sense, let alone understanding the consequences of setting their values.

Unless you have access to many routers in a large internetwork to try out OSPF in a test environment, it is difficult to see in action all that OSPF offers. Therefore, a good grounding in the basic terminology and concepts is essential to help provide you with understanding and information about this protocol that you may not be able to gleam from experience.

Characteristics of OSPF

We have already stated some of the benefits of using a link state routing protocol such as OSPF over a distance vector routing protocol such as RIP. These include:

- Efficient use of network bandwidth, by using directed (multicasts) and acknowledged information only when necessary rather than periodic announcements. This also results in faster convergence times and more reliable routing information (for example, eliminating the count to infinity problem). Because it is less bandwidth hungry, it can be used over slower WAN links.
- Only routing changes are exchanged between neighboring routers rather than whole routing tables, which considerably speeds up the routing announcements and updates.
- Routing tables are smaller and therefore more efficient, because only routes immediately adjacent are stored in the routing table rather than a complete list of every available route. This makes computing the best route much quicker and less error prone. OSPF calculated routes are always loop-free.
- It scales well for large networks, accommodating more than 15 routers (up to 255).
- Like RIPv2, it supports authenticated communication between routers as protection against rogue routers. Windows 2000 only currently supports a clear-text password rather than a more secure, encrypted password mechanism.

However, for all these benefits in comparison with RIP, OSPF is a more CPU-intensive protocol. For all the improvements you gain from using a link state routing protocol, on large networks it will become prone to routing and update delays unless the network is divided into smaller and therefore more manageable sections. When divided, obviously these sections must have a defined set of rules and mechanisms for communicating both within themselves and with each other. This is when the configuration gets complex!

OSPF Terminology and Concepts

If your previous experience of routing was limited to only RIP, you may find it difficult to separate the familiar RIP-specific terms from general routing concepts. For example, you may be used to equating a routing metric with a *hop*, and think of the two as interchangeable. However, a hop is a distance vector's implementation of a routing metric; there are no hops with a link state routing protocol, because the routing implementation works differently with a link-state implementation.

This is when it is important to understand the underlying concept before you learn a specific implementation of it. If you are familiar with RIP terminology, you may find the new OSPF terms difficult to grasp, and the plethora of new acronyms don't help! It is always difficult to "unlearn" something, redefine a familiar term with a new term, and remember that it might work differently in another implementation.

Where RIP and OSPF have different terms for an equivalent function, Table 28-3 may help.

The following sections discuss some of the terminology you will encounter when configuring OSPF, and describe how the components work and fit together.

Advertisements within an Area

The divided and manageable network sections are referred to as OSPF *areas.* Each area has a *boundary* that sets the limit on where routing announcements can go (called *Link State Advertisements,* or *LSAs* in OSPF terms). When routing announcements are sent, this is called *flooding.*

TABLE 28-3 RIP and OSPF Terms for Equivalent Functions

RIP Term	OSPF Equivalent Term
Routing Announcement	Link State Advertisements (LSAs)
Routing Table	Link State Database (LSD)
Hop	Cost
Default Gateway	Default Route

The Link State Database

All routers within a boundary contain the same routing table (called *Link State Database,* or *LSDB*) that reflects the topology of only that area. The route metric (called the *cost*) is a unitless number that indicates the preference level of that route. Entries for the routing table are calculated to determine the least-cost path to each network in the internetwork—the *Shortest Path First (SPF) Tree.*

Using multiple areas reduces the size of the routing table within each area, which therefore reduces the time and processing required for routing decisions and maintenance. Additionally, when an AS is subdivided into contiguous areas, routes within areas can be *summarized* to further minimize route table entries.

The Default Route

Each area can be configured with a *default route* (which is used when a direct route is not known) that summarizes all routes outside the AS or outside the area. This contrasts with RIP, which can only summarize subnets in a given network ID.

Identifying Areas and Routers

An ID number uniquely identifies areas in the AS, and similarly, each router is assigned a unique ID number. Although this ID number uses the same format as an IP address (32-bit dotted decimal number), it is important to remember that these IDs are not IP addresses but logical "names." However, the ID does borrow from some of the concepts used in IP address assignment in that it represents a hierarchical structure that can reflect its position to its neighbors (e.g., area 0.0.0.1 is next to area 0.0.0.2, etc.).

Although there is no direct relationship between OSPF IDs and IP addresses, it is a common industry convention to use the largest or smallest IP address assigned to the router as the Router ID, and this convention obviously closely relates the two.

The Backbone

An OSPF network must have at least one area. If an OSPF network contains more than one area, it must have a *backbone* area with the ID of 0.0.0.0. The backbone is the center, the hub of all the other areas, and is the common point of reference. All areas must report their routing information to the backbone, so the backbone can distribute this information to other ASs.

A general rule of thumb for routing efficiency in OSPF networks is to divide a network into areas when it has more than 40 routers.

Different Types of Networks

The type of network being used determines OSPF message format. When you configure an interface on an OSPF router, you must define what type of network it is going to talk to. The choices are:

- Broadcast
- Point-to-Point
- Non-Broadcast Multiple Access

Broadcast Network Architectures This represents a network that can support a hardware broadcast where a single packet sent by the router is received by all routers on the network; however, an OSPF IP multicast message will be sent rather than a broadcast. Examples of broadcast networks include:

- Ethernet
- Token Ring
- FDDI

OSPF sends multicasts and not broadcasts over a Broadcast network. Do not assume that OSPF will send broadcasts just because a Broadcast network type is being used. OSPF never sends broadcasts, only multicasts or unicasts.

Point-to-Point Networks This represents a network that can be connected by two routers only. An OSPF IP multicast message will be sent over this media. Examples of Point-to-Point networks include:

- Leased-line WAN links (e.g., Digital Data System [DDS])
- T1, T3, or fractional T1-Carrier links

Nonbroadcast Multiple Access (NBMA) This represents a network that can connect more than two routers, but cannot support hardware broadcasts. In this particular case, because multicasts cannot be used, OSPF must be configured to use unicast to the specific IP addresses of the routers on the NBMA network. Examples of NBMA networks include:

- X.25
- Frame Relay
- Asynchronous Transfer Mode (ATM)

Different Types of Routing Communication

A router that sits in between areas—on the border of two or more areas—is called an *Area Border Router* (ABR), and is responsible for exchanging routing information from one area to another.

Because each area must communicate with the area's backbone, this is done either *directly* (if an area border router joins the area with the backbone) or *indirectly* with multiple border routers. When areas do not directly join to the backbone, they use *intermediate areas* and their border routers to exchange their routing information. In OSPF terms, the intermediate area is called a *transit area.*

Because these indirect connections have a virtual rather than physical link between the area and the backbone, a *virtual interface* set up in Windows 2000 RRAS is required.

Different Types of Routers

There are three classifications of OSPF routers:

- Area Border Router (ABR)
- Internal Router (IR)
- AS Border Router (ASBR)

Area Border Router (ABR) The *Area Border Router* as previously described has its interfaces in different areas and handles inter-area communication. To reduce the amount of information sent, the ABR sends only the summarized routing information (route summary) instead of individual routes.

Internal Router (IR) An *Internal Router* (IR), as its name suggests, is a router that sits in its area, and only in its area, and handles intra-area routing.

AS Border Router (ASBR) An *AS Border Router* (ASBR) is a router that connects different ASs. When the ASBR exchanges routing information with an external network, the routing information received from outside the AS is referred to as *external routes.*

How Routers Exchange Information—Forming Adjacencies with Neighbors When an OSPF router initializes, it sends out a periodic OSPF *Hello* packet that contains router configuration information, such as the router's Router ID and the list of neighboring routers that it knows about as a result of receiving similar Hello packets.

When incoming Hello packets are received, the router determines the specific router or routers with which it should communicate. This relationship is called an *Adjacency,* and should lead to the synchronization of the Link State Database (LSDB). Should adjacencies fail to establish, the internetwork will not converge successfully.

After the adjacency has been formed, each neighboring router sends periodic Hello packets according to the *Hello interval* (which defaults to 10 seconds) as confirmation that they are still there with active links. The absence of an expected Hello packet (expected within the assigned *dead interval,* which defaults to 40 seconds) signals a downed router, and the Link State Database is changed accordingly. Both of these options are found under the Advanced tab of an OSPF's interface Properties.

When these Hello packets are sent by unicast rather than multicast (such as on a nonbroadcast network), the poll interval is much longer to accommodate the different network—120 seconds by default.

Electing Routers as "Designated Routers" or "Backup Designated Routers" To minimize the amount of routing information exchanged when routers are powered on, OSPF elects a *Designated Router* (DR) on every segment except on Point-to-Point segments. All other routers in the same segment establish an adjacency with the designated router, which leads to the exchange of routing information that synchronizes the link state database with the DR. The routing information exchanged between the DR and other routers uses *multicasting* in a broadcast network, but *unicasting* in a nonbroadcast network.

on the Job

If you are comfortable with how Master Browsers and Backup Browsers are elected on Windows NT 4.0 networks, the following section will feel very familiar!

How does the election work? Each interface in a router has a priority that can range from 0 (lowest) to 255 (highest). The default priority is 1. These priorities, which are sent out in Hello packets, are used to elect the DR—the router with the highest priority becomes the DR.

If two or more routers have the same priority, the router with the highest router ID will become the DR.

You can "fix" the election by assigning a 0 priority to routers you don't want to become a DR (they won't participate in the election) and assign a 255 priority to the router you do want to become a DR.

For fault tolerance, a Backup Designated Router (BDR) is similarly elected so that should the DR fail, the BDR quickly and automatically becomes the DR, and a new election is held for a new BDR.

exam Watch

You must ensure that at least one router on your OSPF network (broadcast or NBMA) has a router priority configured to be 1 or greater. If all routers have this set to 0, a DR will not be elected, the Link State Database cannot be synchronized, and no transit traffic (traffic across that network) can be passed.

The Router Priority is set under the OSPF's interface's Properties | General tab, as shown in Figure 28-4.

FIGURE 28-4

Router priority setting that determines whether this router will become a Designated Router or a Backup Designated Router

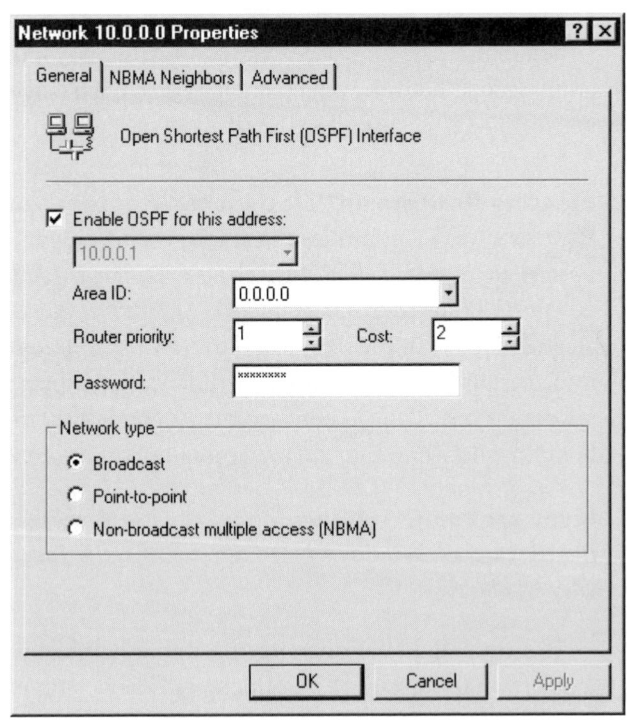

Reducing Routing Information

OSPF goals include reducing the routing information to be processed, which results in greater efficiency, and ensures the integrity of routing information. To help achieve these, two other facilities can be used:

- External Route Filters
- Stub Areas

External Route Filters By default, OSPF routers acting as ASBRs import and advertise all external routes that may not be desirable from a security perspective. You may prefer to filter out external routes to protect the AS from incorrect or malicious routing information. Additionally, you may simply want to restrict the external routing information that is imported into the AS, if it is not required.

You can filter external routes on the ASBR by the external route source, or by the individual route. You can configure the ASBR to accept or ignore the routes of specified external sources; for example, certain routing protocols (e.g., RIP) or other sources (e.g., static routes or Simple Network Management Protocol [SNMP]).

On an ASBR router, external filters are configured as an OSPF global property on the External Routing tab, as shown in Figure 28-5. Note that you cannot configure external filters if the router is not an ASBR—this wouldn't make sense. The other two routers have no direct contact with routes outside the AS, and therefore no need to specify external filters.

Stub Areas You can import external routes into an OSPF AS with an AS Border Router, but to stop external routes from flooding into an area, you can use what is called a *stub area.*

A stub area applies the default route 0.0.0.0 to keep the topology database size small. In OSPF, you can assume that any destination that you can't reach through a designated route is reachable through the default route.

To implement a stub area, one or more of the stub area's Area Border Routers must advertise the default route 0.0.0.0 to the stub area, and the route summary.

However, a limitation of using stub areas is that you cannot use them on the backbone, and you cannot configure stub areas through virtual links.

A stub area accepts the default route and route summary, but no external routes. An extension to this is a *totally stubby area* (also known as a *stub area without a summary*), where the default route is accepted, but neither route summary nor external routes are accepted.

FIGURE 28-5

Configuring External Routing filters to protect the AS from incorrect or malicious routing information

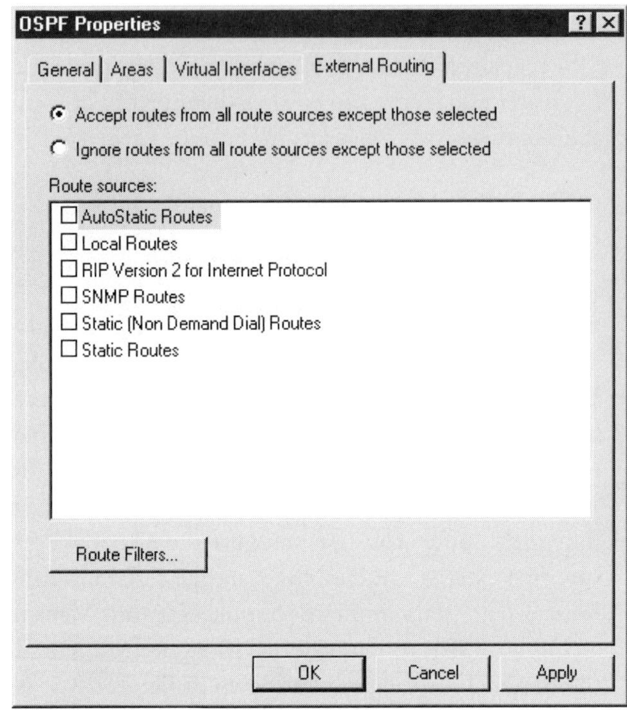

EXERCISE 28-3

Configuring Your Router with Area Information

Your RRAS router has been configured with OSPF to be an Interior Router (IR) that will be going into a stub area with the area ID of 0.0.0.5. You need to define and configure your router accordingly.

1. If not already loaded, load the RRAS snap-in located under Start | Programs | Administrative Tools | Routing and Remote Access.
2. Ensure your server is selected in the left pane, and if you see OSPF listed, right-click on it and select Properties. If OSPF is not listed, double-click on IP Routing, which should then expand to show OSPF.
3. Under the General tab, ensure you have configured your Router ID correctly, and that the "Enable Autonomous system boundary router" is not set.
4. Click on the Areas tab and then click Add.

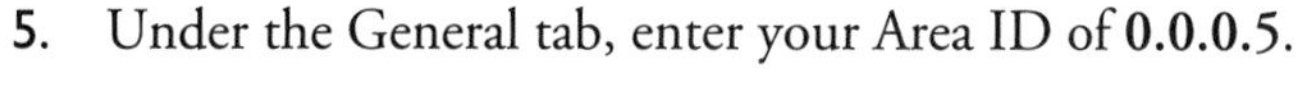

5. Under the General tab, enter your Area ID of **0.0.0.5**.
6. Still under the General tab, select the "Stub area" check box. Your dialog box should look similar to the following illustration.

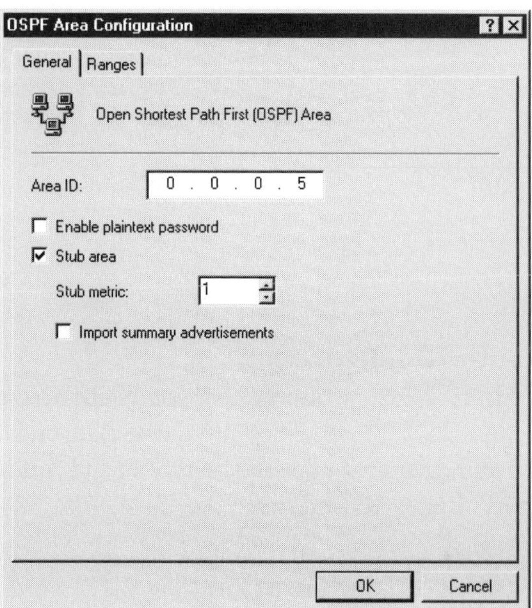

7. Click OK.

OSPF Configuration Requirements

We have discussed the various types of OSPF routers that can be used, and the OSPF options. The actual configuration options that will be applicable will depend first and foremost on what kind of OSPF router you are configuring within the overall structure of the OSPF network. Because an OSPF router is highly dependent on the whole topology of its internetwork, you cannot arbitrarily change routing options and still expect routing to work!

TABLE 28-4

Check List for OSPF Router Configuration

Type of OSPF Router	Options to Configure
IR	If in a stub area, enable this option.
ABR	Configure route summary (the network range) for each area this router belongs to. If in an ordinary stub area and not on a virtual link, enable the stub area option and enable the "Import summary advertisements" but disable the "Import summary advertisements" if the area is a totally stubby area. If on a virtual link, you'll need to set up the ABR's virtual interface by linking it to the other end via a transit area.
ASBR	Configure the external routes you will accept, and which protocols will be used (e.g., RIP or static routing).

Router Configuration

Table 28-4 lists the options that you might need to configure, depending on the role of your OSPF router. They all assume that you have successfully installed OSPF, added the required interfaces to OSPF, and configured OSPF on the router with its correct Router ID and Area IDs.

Interface Configuration

When you have configured the router, verify the OSPF configuration for each interface, which includes the following:

- Areas
- Priority for DR election
- Cost based on bandwidth
- Password for authentication (must be same as other routers in the area, and is case sensitive)
- Network type (if NBMA, must define NBMA neighboring routes)
- Values for Hello Interval, Dead Interval, and Poll Interval should be the same as other routers in the area

CERTIFICATION OBJECTIVE 28.06

Demand-Dial Routing

When you are routing packets over a local area network or a permanent wide area network, these connections have interfaces that are always available; consequently, their interface status is always active or connected. Any packets forwarded over these types of connections do not require additional physical or logical connections to be established.

In comparison, a dial-on-demand connection does not have this permanent connection. The connection is only made when required; for example, when the dial-on-demand interface is asked to forward packets over its interface. Before the packet can be forwarded, an extra connection needs to be made (for example, a modem dialing out on an analog telephone line), which is established with an additional PPP link.

When the dial-up is completed, packets can be forwarded as if it were any other routed connection. Using the same technique on a router to forward packets on a dial-on-demand interface is referred to as *demand-dial routing*.

The PPP link is established over either a physical medium or a tunnel medium. Physical mediums include analog telephone lines and ISDN. Tunnel mediums include the two tunneling protocols: PPTP (Point-to-Point-Tunneling Protocol) and L2TP (Layer 2 Tunneling Protocol).

Demand-dial routing can be used to connect your router to the Internet, connect together branch offices, or to implement router-to-router virtual private network (VPN) connections.

What Is Demand-Dial Routing?

Dial-on-demand connections are normally used when a permanent connection is not available, so demand-dial routing is used to connect your router to the required host or router when there is no permanent connection to do this. They can be used as a backup to a permanent connection, or if no permanent connection is possible.

Because dial-up connections are usually charged on a time basis, a demand-dial connection is an efficient method of only paying for a connection when you have data to transfer. An idle timeout value allows the connection to automatically terminate when there is no more data to transfer.

exam Watch

Demand-dial connections have the benefit of offering cost-efficient dial-up WAN links when they are configured with an idle timeout, because you only pay for the connection when there is data to transfer.

Alternatively, demand-dial routing interfaces may be used as a security precaution so that a routed connection is only made when there is data to transfer, and you are controlling the open link. Alternatively, a dial-up connection may be your only choice to connect to your destination network.

Although it is more common for a demand-dial connection to fit into the category above, there are, in fact, two types of demand-dial connections:

- On-demand
- Persistent

There are also two different ways to control and configure the demand-dial connection:

- Two-way initiated
- One-way initiated

On-Demand Demand-Dial Connections

The more common use of a demand-dial connection is to create the connection when there is data to send over the interface, and terminate it when the transfer of data is complete (the link is idle). This is an on-demand demand-dial connection.

exam Watch

On-demand connections only establish a connection when traffic is forwarded, and the connection is terminated after a configured amount of idle time.

You can configure the idle timeout on either the calling router or the answering router.

Persistent Demand-Dial Connections

There is also the scenario in which you actually want a permanent connection, but do not have the infrastructure of a permanent connection (e.g., fractional T1, etc.) to support this; therefore, a dial-up connection is your only option. If the efficiency of the connection were more important than the cost of being permanently connected (for example, you had a flat-rate leased line, or your line incurs only a local charge), you would probably find a persistent demand-dial connection more beneficial.

What's the benefit of having a persistent demand-dial connection? The benefit is in efficiency and speed of connection when needed. It takes time to establish the PPP link (this is called the *connection establishment delay*), which can be anything from just a couple of seconds to more than 20 seconds. The actual delay will depend on many factors, including the type of connection; for example, a modem connection over an analog telephone line will take much longer than an ISDN connection.

This connection establishment delay could impact on the applications that are being used over a demand-dial routed connection, because an application could time out before the connection is established and therefore fail to connect.

Another factor in favor of using a persistent demand-dial connection may be cost. It may actually be cheaper to keep the same connection active than frequently establishing new connections.

Unlike the idle timeout option, which can be configured on either the calling router or the answering router, persistent demand-dial connections must be configured on both sides of the connection—on the calling router and the answering router.

exam Watch

Persistent demand-dial connections must be configured on both the calling router and the answering router.

Two-Way Initiated Demand-Dial Connections

A two-way initiated demand-dial connection is where routers can both initiate a connection when needed, and also respond to the same router calling it—over the same demand-dial interface. In other words, in a two-way initiated connection, both routers can be a calling router, or an answering router on the same interface. Use two-way initiated connections when traffic from either router can create the demand-dial connection. This offers the greatest flexibility, but also requires the greatest configuration, since not only do both routers need to be configured, but also they have to be configured similarly to ensure their configurations match.

One-Way Initiated Demand-Dial Connections

A one-way initiated connection restricts one router to being the calling router and the other to being an answering router. In many ways, this is the easiest of configurations because there is less to configure. It also offers a more secure routing environment from the perspective of the calling router, because it has complete control over when a connection is made.

exam Watch

A two-way initiated connection offers the greatest flexibility, but requires more configuration. A one-way initiated connection offers tighter control for the calling router (and therefore can be more secure), with less configuration required.

Connection Authentication

For calling routers, you must specify credentials with which to call out (which match a valid account on the answering router), and for answering routers, you must have an account that will be used to authenticate a calling router with their calling credentials.

On the answering router, the account used to authenticate the calling router must be configured with a username that matches the name of the demand-dial interface to which it corresponds. This account must also have dial-in permission and a password that never expires.

exam Watch

If the calling router supplies credentials with a username that doesn't correspond to the name of a demand-dial interface on the answering router, the calling router will be identified as a remote access user rather than a router.

When your routers will be performing two-way demand-dial routing, the usernames and demand-dial interface names must correspond on both routers. For example, a corporate router in London that wants a demand-dial routing connection to the branch office in Brighton might call its demand-dial interface *Brighton Remote Router* (an arbitrary name, but it identifies to where it's connecting), and creates an account called *Brighton Remote Router* to authenticate incoming connections. It sets the calling credentials (username) on this demand-dial interface to be London Remote Router. To match this, the branch office in Brighton would create its demand-dial interface calling it London Remote Router, and create an account called London Remote Router to authenticate incoming connections. It sets the calling credentials (username) on this demand-dial interface to be called Brighton Remote Router. This is summarized in Table 28-5.

TABLE 28-5

Demand-dial Interfaces, Routers, and Usernames

Router	Demand-Dial Interface Name and Username on Account that Will Authenticate Incoming Connections	Username Set on the Demand-Dial Interface Credentials
Corporate office router in London	Brighton Remote Router	London Remote Router
Branch office router in Brighton	London Remote Router	Brighton Remote Router

Security on Incoming Connections

Because the demand-dial connection uses PPP, the authentication and security features for incoming connections are the same as would be used for remote access connections. These security features include:

- Remote access permission
- Authentication
- Encryption
- Callback
- Caller ID
- Remote access account lockout

Remote Access Permission The calling router must specify credentials for a valid user account that the answering router can authenticate (e.g., local security database, domain security database, or Remote Authentication Dial-In User Service [RADIUS] server). This account must have remote access permission in one of two ways:

- Explicitly in the dial-in account
- Implicitly through "Control access through Remote Access policy" with a matching remote access policy set to "Grant remote access"

Authentication The calling router can be authenticated at the user level and the computer level.

The computer level is used when certificates are used with Internet Protocol Security (IPSec) (e.g., L2TP/IPSec tunneling connection) and Extensible Authentication Protocol-Transport Layer Security (EAP-TLS).

Differentiation between Remote Access Clients and Routers

Remote access connects a single user to a network, whereas demand-dial routing connects together networks. However, they both have many components in common, which is why the Routing and Remote Access service so tightly integrates the two. Common components include:

- The PPP connection to negotiate and authenticate the connection
- The use of physical (e.g., modem) or logical (e.g., VPN) ports
- Use of dial-in permission
- Security (including authentication protocols and encryption)
- Use of remote access policies
- Use of authentication providers (either Windows or RADIUS)
- Use of PPP features such as Multilink, Bandwidth Allocation Protocol (BAP), and Microsoft Point-to-Point compression (MPPC)
- Logging, auditing, and tracing

Enabling Demand-Dial Routing

When you first enabled RRAS, one option was to select routing, and then you were asked whether you wanted to use just LAN routing or demand-dial routing. Choosing the demand-dial option will automatically configure the router for demand-dial routing, in addition to LAN routing, and invoke the Demand Dial Interface Wizard to guide you through configuring a demand-dial interface.

Alternatively, you can manually enable demand-dial routing, and then manually add a new demand-dial interface, which will invoke the Demand Dial Interface Wizard.

The steps needed to enable demand-dial routing include:

- Enabling the router for demand-dial routing in addition to LAN routing
- Enabling one or more ports for demand-dial routing
- Adding one or more demand-dial interfaces

If you want to add another demand-dial interface, repeat this procedure. For example, if your router supported VPN connections, you may want to use some VPN demand-dial interfaces in addition to your modem demand-dial interface.

EXERCISE 28-4

Enabling Demand-Dial Routing

This exercise takes you through the steps involved in adding a physical demand-dial interface to be both a calling and answering router.

1. If not already loaded, load the RRAS snap-in located under Start | Programs | Administrative Tools | Routing and Remote Access.
2. Right-click on your server in the left pane to select Properties. It's here that you select whether to support routing and remote access.
3. Ensure the Router option is selected, and underneath ensure you select "LAN and demand-dial routing." You must have the LAN and demand-dial routing selected in order to support demand-dial routing. Until this option is selected, you cannot add demand-dial interfaces.
4. Click OK. You will be prompted to stop and restart the router. Click OK and wait for the RRAS service to stop, restart, and initialize.
5. We need to ensure you have at least one port that can be used for demand-dial routing. To do this, right-click on Ports in the RRAS left pane and select Properties. This displays a list of available ports (e.g., modem/s, WAN miniports (for VPNs), and Direct Parallel). If you have no modem, for the sake of this exercise you can use the Direct Parallel port. Click on the port you want to enable for demand-dial routing (e.g., your modem), click Configure, and ensure it has selected the option "Demand-dial routing connections (inbound and outbound)," similar to the following illustration. Click OK.

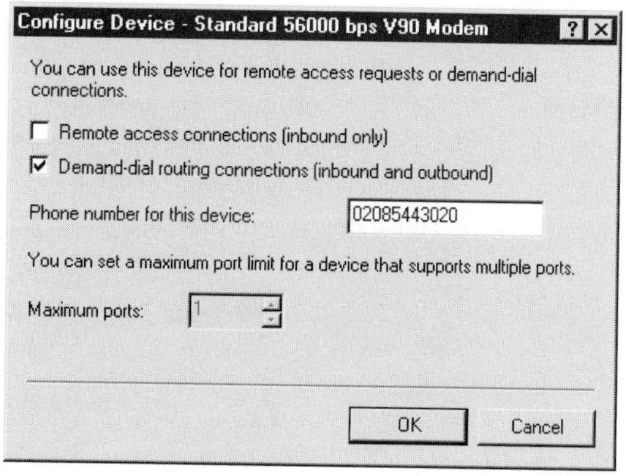

Configure Device - Standard 56000 bps V90 Modem

You can use this device for remote access requests or demand-dial connections.

☐ Remote access connections (inbound only)

☑ Demand-dial routing connections (inbound and outbound)

Phone number for this device: 02085443020

You can set a maximum port limit for a device that supports multiple ports.

Maximum ports: 1

OK Cancel

6. When you have finished enabling the ports you want to use with demand-dial routing, click OK.
7. Click Routing Interfaces | Properties | New Demand-Dial Interface to invoke the Demand Dial Interface Wizard. Click Next on the initial Welcome page.
8. You will then be prompted to enter a name to identify this demand-dial interface. Accept the default name of Remote Router and click Next.
9. You will then be asked to specify the telephone number of the router you will be calling (if you selected a parallel connection, this page does not appear). Type in the calling number and click Next.
10. The next page asks which connection type you want. Select "Connect using a modem, ISDN adapter, or other physical device" and click Next.
11. You will then be asked to select a device from the list of ports enabled for demand-dial routing. Select a modem if you have one configured for demand-dial routing, or if you have no modem and previously enabled the Direct Parallel port, select this. Click Next.
12. The next page is *important*—the Protocols and Security page. Ensure you select "Route IP packets on this interface" and the "Add a user account so a remote router can dial in," as shown in the following illustration. Click Next.

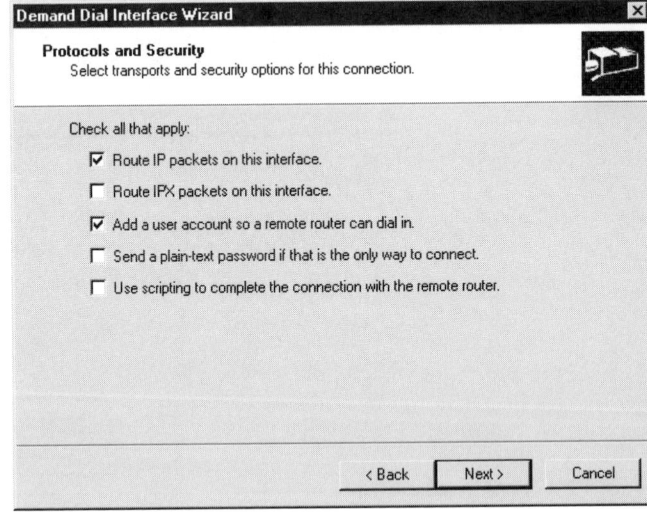

13. You will then be asked to specify Dial In Credentials that will be used to authenticate the router calling in to you. You will notice that the username has automatically been set to the same name as you chose for the demand-dial interface name. Specify a password, confirm it, and click Next.
14. You will be asked to supply the Dial Out Credentials, which need to match a valid account on the answering router. The following illustration shows this page with example credentials. When you have specified these, click Next.

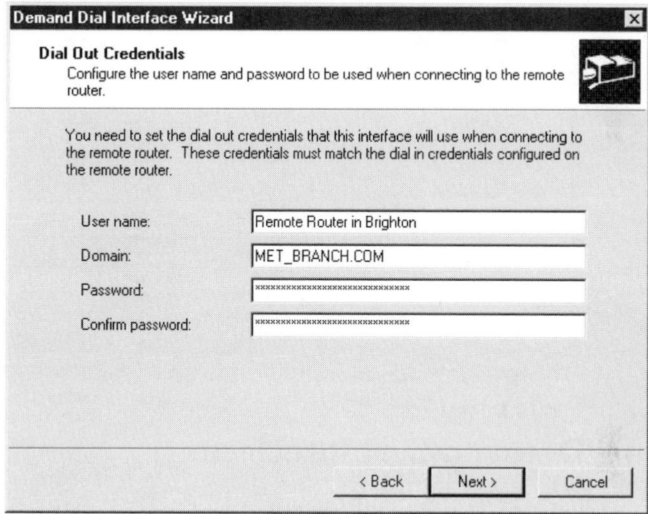

15. Next, you are told that your demand-dial interface will be installed and enabled, and that you can configure it by selecting it in the RRAS snap-in, right-clicking on it and selecting Properties. Click Finish.

16. Your demand-dial interface should now be added and listed in the RRAS details pane with the Type of *Demand-dial,* the status of *Enabled,* and the Connection Status of *Disconnected,* similar to the following illustration.

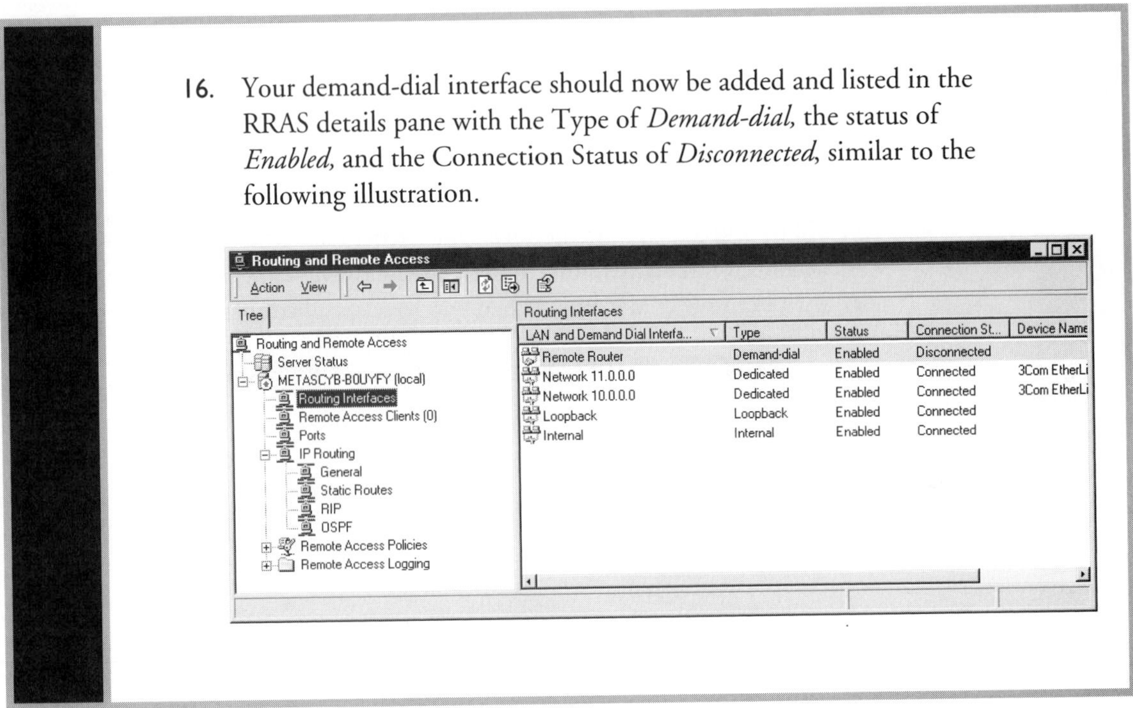

Configuring Demand-Dial Interfaces

Once you have added a demand-dial interface, select it and right-click. You will see the options that are available in Figure 28-6.

Set Credentials

This allows you view and edit the calling credentials of User name, Domain, and Password.

Connect and Disconnect

These options allow you to manually control the connection rather than, for example, relying on routing to initiate the connection, or the idle timeout to expire. The Connect option is particularly useful for allowing you to manually test the basic connection and authentication.

FIGURE 28-6 Options available on a demand-dial interface

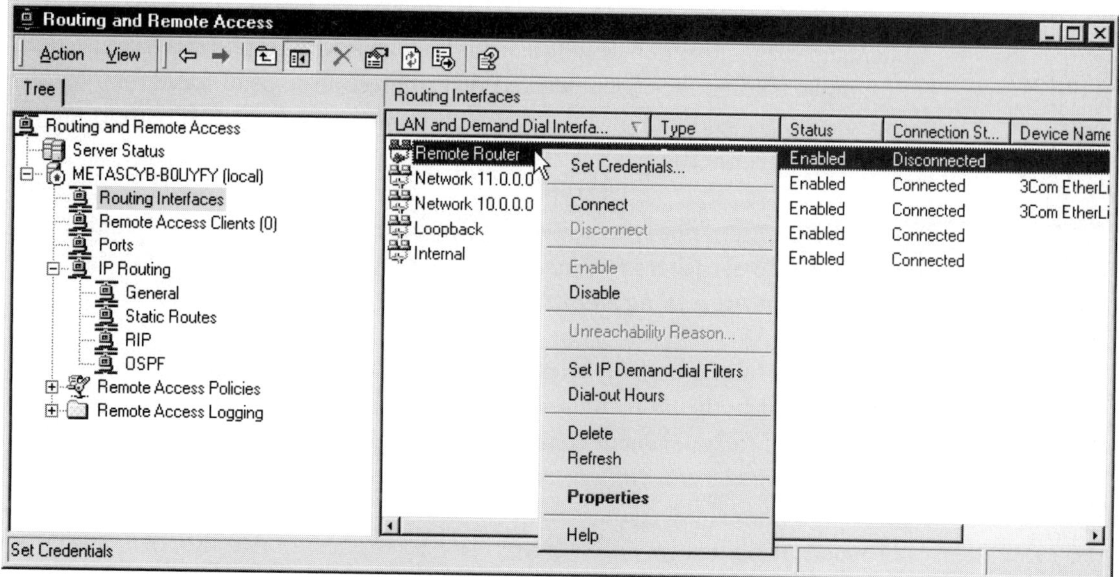

Enable and Disable

This enables or disables the demand-dial interface and, for example, could be configured but disabled for security reasons until needed (e.g., permanent connection unavailable).

Unrachable Reason

This displays the last failure-to-connect error message and is useful in troubleshooting or monitoring demand-dial routing. When you manually connect the demand-dial interface and it fails to connect, you will see displayed in a dialog box the reason why the connection failed (e.g., no reply). However, when the connection is being raised automatically on demand but fails to complete the connection, this option will show the last unreachable reason recorded. Note it doesn't keep a history, just the last unreachable reason.

Potential unreachable reasons include:

- No port was available for the demand-dial interface (e.g., all in use).
- The RRAS service was paused.
- The demand-dial interface was disabled.
- Dial-out hours have prevented the connection.

Set IP Demand-Dial Filters

Demand-dial filters are used to specify what types of TCP/IP traffic either initiate the demand-dial connection or ignore it for the purposes of creating the connection. For example, if you only want a demand-dial connection to be initiated for Web traffic, set the demand-dial filters so that only traffic to TCP destination port 80 can initiate the connection.

exam Watch

Demand-dial filters apply to outward connections (calling), not inbound (answering). To set filters for answering connections, use remote policies on the account used to authenticate the demand-dial interface.

Demand-dial filters are only relevant for a demand-dial interface that is in a disconnected state; therefore, they will be ignored if the interface remains connected or if configured for a persistent connection. The RRAS *Dynamic Interface Manager* is responsible for checking the interface's configured demand dial filters before trying to initiate a connection.

Demand-dial filters are different from IP packet filters in that they define what traffic initiates a demand-dial connection. IP packet filters define what traffic is allowed in and out of the demand-dial interface once it is connected.

Because IP packet filters are applied after the connection is initiated, it is recommended that if you have configured IP output packet filters that prevent the flow of TCP/IP traffic on the demand-dial interface, then configure the same filters as demand-dial filters. This means that the demand-dial connection is never established for traffic that is discarded by the IP packet filters for the demand-dial interface.

exam Watch

Demand-dial filters are different from IP packet filters in that they define what traffic initiates a demand-dial connection. IP packet filters define what traffic is allowed in and out of the demand-dial interface once it is connected.

Dial-Out Hours

Dial-out hours are used to specify when the demand-dial connection can be made. Similarly, the Times of Day and Week restriction in a Remote Access policy condition (it uses the same dialog box) allows you to specify the time of day and day of the week that a demand-dial connection is either allowed or denied for outbound connections.

Dial-out hours only apply to outward connections (calling), not inbound (answering). To set time/day restrictions for answering connections, use remote policies on the account used to authenticate the demand-dial interface.

As with the demand-dial filters, dial-out hours only apply to demand-dial interfaces that are in a disconnected state. The RRAS Dynamic Interface Manager is responsible for checking the interface's configured dial-out hours before trying to initiate a connection.

As with the similar remote access policy condition, by default all times on all days are permitted, and a connection is not automatically disconnected when it crosses the boundary from a time allowed to a time denied. The specified times denied only apply to new connections. Similar to the day and time restriction in remote access policies, the day and time taken is from the router.

Demand-Dial Interface Properties

The four property tabs are General, Options, Security, and Networking.

Important demand-dial interface properties include:

- The actual device being used (e.g., modem and specification), and connection details (e.g., telephone number) under the General tab
- Connection type of Demand-dial (with idle timeout value defaulting to 5 minutes) or Persistent connection under the Options tab
- User callback option under Callback in the Options tab
- Require data encryption (disconnect if none) under the Security tab
- Advanced (custom settings) under the Security tab, Settings allows you to specify exactly which authentication protocols to use (e.g., only EAP or Microsoft Challenge Handshake Authentication Protocol [MS-CHAP] for mutual authentication)
- Device callback option under Settings in the Networking tab
- Run Script under the Networking tab

Using Remote Access Policies with Demand-Dial Routing

As with Remote Access, remote access policies can be used to define and control to a high degree certain conditions and settings for the account used to authenticate an answering demand-dial interface. For example, this could include only allowing a connection at restricted times, permitting only tunneled connections, enforcing strong authentication and encryption, etc.

A common implementation of remote access policies for demand-dial routing is to change the dial-in permission to control through remote policies and put all *remote router accounts* into a group. Create a policy that allows connections for the Windows-Group condition set to your remote router group, and then set all common conditions and profile settings you want to use with all demand-dial routers.

Routing over Demand-Dial Interfaces

Once you have your demand-dial interface/s configured such that your router connects over them to the answering router and is authenticated, and (if necessary) the other router can connect and authenticate with your router, you are ready to think about routing again!

How you update the routing table when using demand-dial routers depends on whether your demand-dial connection is on demand or persistent:

- If your demand-dial connection is *on-demand*, use static routing.
- If your demand-dial connection is *persistent*, use dynamic routing with routing protocols.

Static routing should be used for on-demand connections, because the periodic advertising from routing protocols can cause the connection to be permanently up if the advertising interval is less than the idle timeout.

Routing protocols can be used over persistent connections, because the periodic advertisement is not a problem if the link is always up.

Defining Static Routes for Demand-Dial Interfaces

Add your static route for a demand-dial interface as described previously—Routing | Static Routes | New | Static Route. The important difference between defining static routes for a demand-dial interface and a standard interface is that you must specify in the Interface drop-down box that you are using a demand-dial interface. You will notice that this blanks the Gateway option because it is not relevant for a PPP connection, and you can control whether this route will initiate the demand-dial connection with the option: "Use this route to initiate demand-dial connections."

Another option for defining static routes with demand-dial routing is to specify static routes on the dial-in properties of the user account that is used to authenticate the incoming connection. When the calling router connects and is authenticated, these static routes will be amalgamated into the routing table on the answering router. If the remote network has multiple segments, the remote router should be configured for dynamic routing protocols so it can update neighboring routers with the new routes.

Auto-Static Updates An alternative to manually defining each static route if using RIP is the use of auto-static updates. When this command is initiated, it requests all known routers or services from the connecting router and adds them to its own routing table.

An auto-static update is a one-time, one-way exchange of routing information. After the routes are sent, the two routers do not periodically advertise, even if the connection remained in a connected state. The default settings for RIP already support auto-static updates—the actual options are "Auto-static update mode" and "RIP version 2 multicast" for outbound packets.

If you want to use auto-static updates with RIP, add the demand-dial interface to RIP and ensure these settings are set correctly. To perform an auto-static update, in the RRAS snap-in, double-click IP Routing | General, then select your demand-dial interface, right-click and select Update Routes.

You can also schedule auto-static updates by using a netsh script to perform the auto-static update (connect, update, disconnect), and then schedule this script to be run as one of the Windows 2000 Scheduled Tasks.

on the job

When an auto-static update is performed, any existing auto-static routes for the interface are deleted before the update is requested from the other router. If there is no response from the other router, the deleted routes cannot be updated or replaced, which could obviously cause routing problems.

Using Routing Protocols over a Demand-Dial Interface

If necessary, add the routing protocol and then add the demand-dial interface to the protocol, as we did for standard interfaces.

Table 28-6 lists some configuration options that should be changed such that they are more sympathetic to a dial-up connection.

TABLE 28-6 Configuring Routing Protocols for a Persistent Demand-Dial Connection

Routing Protocol	Configuration Changes for a Persistent Demand-Dial Connection
RIP	Set the operation mode for RIP to Periodic update mode, and enable triggered updates.
OSPF	On the Advanced properties of an OSPF interface, you may want to increase the values of the transit delay, the retransmit interval, the hello interval, and the dead interval.

CERTIFICATION OBJECTIVE 28.07

Troubleshooting IP Routing Problems

Troubleshooting IP routing is one of the most complex and challenging areas of managing TCP/IP networks. This is partly because, as we have seen, there is a lot of conceptual information to understand even before we start looking into actual implementations and configuration issues. This section cannot possibly try to cover everything you will need to troubleshoot IP routing problems, and there is no "blueprint" that guarantees success. However, it will try to highlight key areas and help identify where and how you should concentrate your resources.

When Is Routing Troubleshooting Required?

So, when would you need to troubleshoot IP routing? Remember our earlier definition of routing:

Routing is the process of forwarding packets from one computer (source host) on one network to another computer (destination host) on another network, either directly if the destination host is on a network directly attached to the router, or indirectly via another router if the destination host is not on a network directly attached to the router.

First of all, if possible, ensure that you really do have a routing problem and not a hardware problem (e.g., cabling fault or adapter not working), that TCP/IP is correctly installed and configured on each end system (source computer and destination computer), and that you don't have a name resolution problem (check Domain Name System [DNS] and/or Windows Internet Naming Service [WINS] functionality). All of these problems could result in a source computer failing to connect to a destination computer—but they are not routing problems. Routing problems are when IP packets fail to be correctly forwarded to their destination.

In its simplest form, you would need to troubleshoot IP routing when routing wasn't working or wasn't working well. Therefore, this usually falls into one of three categories:

- Packets sent from the source computer do not arrive at the destination computer (a total routing failure).
- Packets sent from the source computer only arrive at the destination computer sometimes (intermittent routing failure).
- Packets sent from the source computer often take a long time to arrive at the destination computer (routing efficiency problem).

These three conditions seem so simple a view of what the problem is, yet you as a network administrator know that any one and all three could be a result of many different problems. Such problems could be anything from incorrect routing tables, incorrect or inappropriate router configurations, or even signs of vulnerability to the limitations of your network capability and routing strategy. Adding to these network administration problems of trying to work out how to route between networks, why something isn't performing well or is producing errors, or even how to use the tools provided, and you could be very busy doing nothing but troubleshooting all the time!

Obstacles to Troubleshooting IP Routing

One of the taxing issues that makes IP routing difficult to troubleshoot is that it is not a single tangible service, it is a truly distributed service with many components (e.g., different hardware, different mediums, and even handled by multiple ASs), and it's constantly changing. Remember that routing tables can dynamically change even when no dynamic routing protocols are being used, and you usually have no control over when new computers and routers enter or leave the network, which means you have a constantly changing network map. So, where do you even start looking?

Of course, it always helps if the network in question is well documented, and certainly networking diagrams that identify IP networks and addresses, major servers and routers will assist in grasping the basic topology of your network. It would also help if every router were thoroughly documented with all the configuration options and why their values are so configured. However, such documentation rarely exists, and even when it does, this static information is immediately vulnerable to being out of date, inaccurate, and incomplete, simply because networks do have the capability to dynamically evolve and change very quickly. So don't rely on network documentation, but by all means use it as a "first base" and look to substantiate it with your own proof of how routing appears to be working (or not!).

Different Troubleshooting Approaches

So, where do you go next if you have no such documentation, can't find it, or the problem is too urgent for you to wade through reams of network diagrams? In my experience, I think there are actually four main typical approaches to troubleshooting IP routing problems, which divide into methodical and spontaneous.

Random Panic Mode

The first spontaneous approach is not a recommended course of action but happens far too often. Someone with little understanding of how routing works rushes about randomly checking and changing things in the desperate hope that it'll all suddenly start working. My advice to this approach is: Don't go there! The odds are against you that you'll resolve the problem, and it's much more likely you will inadvertently cause more problems (even if you are not immediately aware of them).

You are much more likely to effectively resolve problems by having a good understanding of the concepts of how routing works, in addition to understanding how it is implemented in your environment. This will allow you to deduct through logic and understanding the area/s on which to concentrate when things go wrong. This is why this chapter has contained more theoretical than practical information in explaining the basic concepts—networks are very different, and once you understand the principles, you can then transfer the concepts to your specific implementation.

Methodically Checking Forward

The methodical approach is where someone verifies all the components until he or she finds the problem, by starting at the beginning and working forward to find the problem. So, if the source computer fails to send a packet to the destination computer on another network, the forward approach would be to check that everything was working and configured correctly on the source computer before even beginning to look at the source network, the first router, and so on.

This approach allows you to logically verify each stage of the path from source to destination until you find your failure. Conceptually, this is an easy method to follow, and more suitable if you don't have control over all the resources involved in the complete path. For example, if you have control over the source network resources, but another department (or even AS) is responsible for remote networks resources, it makes more sense to check the areas over which you have control—if only to eliminate them.

Methodically Checking Backward

This is the inverse of the previous method—verifying the destination host first, and then working backward to the source computer in order to find the break in the route link. This could be a quicker approach, particularly if other workstations on the same segment don't all have basic routing problems, which may seem to suggest it's more likely to be a remote rather than local problem. However, it is slightly more complicated to "think backwards," and you may not have control over the remote resources, which means delays in requesting additional help.

Intuition Based on Knowledge and Experience

The fourth approach is harder to precisely define; it's when someone who has a good knowledge of routing and can count on practical experience appears to bypass the methodical approaches. Instead, he or she instinctively focuses on exactly where the problem is and how to resolve it, without having to logically and methodically eliminate other possible causes. This is true networking expertise and rarely comes to novices.

When this approach works (and it won't always), it saves a lot of time and frustration. However, be aware that it does take a certain amount of knowledge and experience to be able to successfully use this approach—there's a fine line between this and the first method! If the methodical approach does not appeal to you, try this, but always remember to think about the consequences of what you're doing, and be prepared to go back to a more methodical elimination approach if it isn't working.

TCP/IP Tools and Utilities

There are many different tools and utilities that you can use to help support and diagnose TCP/IP problems. For example, *ping* and *tracert* are two of the most commonly employed tools used to help troubleshoot routing problems. There are other TCP/IP troubleshooting utilities that can also be used (e.g., *netdiag*, *netstat*, etc.) that are not covered in this section, because they are general TCP/IP troubleshooting utilities rather than ones that are most useful for specifically troubleshooting IP routing problems.

However, as with any tool, remember that they are only a tool to help you diagnose and resolve routing problems; you still have to understand when it is appropriate to use them, how to use them, and how to interpret their results. You will rarely use just one by itself, but a combination. Tools are no substitute for understanding the basic concepts and logically deducing what the problem actually is.

The following are common TCP/IP tools Microsoft provides with Windows 2000 and, with the exception of Network Monitor, can all run from the command line (which means that typing the main command followed by /help will display the correct syntax and possible parameters):

- ARP -a
- Route Print
- Ping
- Tracert
- PathPing (new in Windows 2000)
- Network Monitor or similar network capture utility

Note this list isn't extensive and doesn't include third-party products (for example, remember that the RRAS snap-in provides APIs) or SNMP (which can be used to monitor and manage routers and their routing tables).

ARP -a

The Address Resolution Protocol is responsible for resolving IP addresses (logical addresses) to MAC addresses (physical addresses). Beneath the IP routing layer, a frame carrying the IP packet has to know to which MAC address it should go. If the incorrect MAC address is used, the routed IP packet will also fail.

It's unusual for an incorrect MAC address to be returned, but it is worth checking; for example, it could be incorrectly defined in an ARP table, or two computers could have the same IP address assigned (Microsoft automatically detects duplicate IP addresses, but older systems may not).

You can only directly check the IP address to MAC address when the two systems are on the same segment. When you ping a remote address, because it gets routed, you will see instead the MAC address of the first router. If the address is still remote to the router, the router will find the MAC address of the next router until the host is on the same segment, and only then will the final MAC address be discovered.

Therefore, checking the ARP cache for IP to MAC address is in practice limited to verifying the MAC address of a host on the same segment or the MAC address of the first router.

To view the local ARP cache, type **ARP –a**. To ensure that the IP address to MAC address is in the cache, ping the destination address first.

Route Print

We have already looked at this command, which can be used in addition to the RRAS snap-in equivalent as we saw in the section *Managing and Monitoring Routing Protocols*. Use it to view the current routing table on host computers as well as Windows 2000 routers, and don't forget that routing tables are dynamic—the output from a computer's routing table today may not be the same tomorrow, or even a few minutes later!

If you want to aim for a totally static routing table configuration, ensure no dial-up connections are made, no routing protocols are installed, and consider blocking ICMP traffic that could dynamically change the routing table. Such traffic might be ICMP type 9 and 10 (for Router Advertisement and Solicitation), and type 5 (code 1) for Redirection. However, beware of blocking all ICMP traffic—the useful *Ping, Tracert* and *PathPing* utilities will no longer work!

Ping

This is every network administrator's simple and reliable friend. By sending ICMP Echo Requests to a destination address (e.g., ping 10.10.0.5), it verifies that TCP/IP is correctly installed on the source computer, and when a positive reply is returned, it confirms that the destination computer is available (a route was found to it).

It is one of the quickest and easiest troubleshooting tests you can do, and the results it yields is helped greatly if you have prior knowledge of the network topology. Ping addresses on your local subnet first, then the destination address. If a remote ping fails, try pinging another remote address—perhaps one on the same remote subnet as the previous address that failed to respond (which, if successful, may indicate a host problem rather than a routing problem to the remote network), or one that is the other side of your first router.

If any of these fail, you have a break in the routing path. The next thing to check could be the current routing table on the source computer if you were troubleshooting forward, or you could try pinging another remote address if you were troubleshooting backwards.

Figure 28-7 shows the results of pinging two different addresses over the Internet. The first one responds successfully, and the second fails to respond.

Even though both addresses are on the Internet, I have some prior knowledge of the network topology, which helps me to narrow down the possible problem. I know the first address is a Web server in my country (the UK), and the second is a Web server in a different country (the U.S.). Working backward, I could try to ping an alternative IP address for the Web server (if multiple addresses are assigned, repeatedly ping the DNS name to see if round robin is being used, and if so, ping one of these alternative addresses). If an alternative IP address for the Web server is successful, I could deduce that either a different route is being used (use tracert to check), or the original destination host is down.

FIGURE 28-7 A successful ping and an unsuccessful ping to different IP addresses

```
H:\WINNT\System32\cmd.exe

C:\>ping 212.58.224.32

Pinging 212.58.224.32 with 32 bytes of data:

Reply from 212.58.224.32: bytes=32 time=30ms TTL=246
Reply from 212.58.224.32: bytes=32 time=20ms TTL=246
Reply from 212.58.224.32: bytes=32 time=20ms TTL=246
Reply from 212.58.224.32: bytes=32 time=20ms TTL=246

Ping statistics for 212.58.224.32:
    Packets: Sent = 4, Received = 4, Lost = 0 (0% loss),
Approximate round trip times in milli-seconds:
    Minimum = 20ms, Maximum =  30ms, Average =  22ms

C:\>ping 207.46.131.30

Pinging 207.46.131.30 with 32 bytes of data:

Request timed out.
Request timed out.
Request timed out.
Request timed out.

Ping statistics for 207.46.131.30:
    Packets: Sent = 4, Received = 0, Lost = 4 (100% loss),
Approximate round trip times in milli-seconds:
    Minimum = 0ms, Maximum =  0ms, Average =  0ms

C:\>
```

Another way to use ping with working backward is to see if other addresses in the U.S. failed to respond to a ping, which would verify routing between the two countries.

Tracert

Tracert can be used to determine which routers are used in a complete source to destination path, and also shows where the packet stops on the network if routing fails. The routing might fail because the last router didn't have a correct forwarding route, its forwarding address didn't respond (e.g., downed router), or because the Time-to-Live value (TTL) had expired (e.g., a bad link).

Because each router is reported in the route trace, this utility will indicate routing loops when the same router address is displayed more than once in the complete path, which indicates a router configuration problem (e.g., too slow a convergence time, or static routes incorrectly configured).

Note, however, that some routers will silently drop packets when the TTL value is expired rather than reporting that the value has expired; as such, these routers will be invisible to Tracert.

PathPing

PathPing is new to Windows 2000 and combines features from both Ping and Tracert by sending packets to each router in the source to a destination route, and then computing results based on the information returned from each discovered router.

It helps to indicate the degree of packet loss at each link of the route, which allows you to identify which routers or links might be causing problems in the way of packet loss and delays.

Network Monitor or Similar Network Capture Utility

Capturing the actual packets from the source computer to the destination is often the only way to determine exactly what happened on the network. However, it does have its limitations in troubleshooting routing problems. First of all, because routing is usually dynamic, there are no guarantees that the captured route is typical or will be repeated in the future—it shows a historic snapshot rather than "this is what will happen" information. The only exception to this is when employing "source routing," which is when the source system (through specific programming) defines the exact destination route rather than just specifying the source address and relying on routers to dynamically determine a path. Source routing is traffic intensive and slow in comparison to dynamic routing, but sometimes used in debugging or network testing when the route needs to be predetermined.

Analyzing the captured data is more complex when it spans multiple segments, and in fact is often difficult to effectively capture when you don't know in advance which segments it will traverse. You may not be able to capture it if it includes networks outside your AS (e.g., Internet links).

However, its biggest drawback is it doesn't explain *why* a certain route was chosen (just that it was).

Verifying Each Component

Routing consists of many components, and troubleshooting routing is easier if the overall process and service can be broken down into individual components that can be verified as individual connecting links in the overall chain. In general, it is a good idea to verify basic components and configurations before honing in on specific configurations. Having said that, if you are getting a specific error message that appears to be referring to a specific configuration, it would make sense to check that first. However, when you have so many links in the chain, it is possible that a specific component failure could be a result of something else in the chain rather than the component itself.

The following lists some of the components that should be verified:

- TCP/IP configuration on hosts (e.g., source workstations)
- Routing tables
- Router configuration
- Dynamic routing protocol configuration

TCP/IP Configuration

Starting with the basics, ensure that TCP/IP is loaded and running on the source and destination computers. If the computer is a Windows 2000 or Windows NT 4.0 computer, type **ipconfig /all** to view all TCP/IP configurations, which include IP address, subnet mask, and assigned default gateway. Verify that these are correct and you can ping your default gateway. Also verify your DNS and WINS server assignment (if any)—always remember to separate routing problems from name resolution problems (e.g., wrong DNS server assigned).

Routing Tables

Remember that routing tables are dynamic, even for hosts that aren't using dynamic routing protocols. Always check the routing tables on hosts and routers to see if a specific route exists for a destination host or network. If no specific route exists, check and verify the current default gateway. The default gateway can change; for example, if using ICMP Router Discovery, or when using remote access.

Use the **route print** command to verify the routing table entries. Additionally, on a Windows 2000 server you can use the netsh command and Show IP Routing Table option in the RRAS snap-in.

When adding static routes, remember that you will probably need to specify one or more corresponding routes back on the connecting hosts/routers. Also ensure that when specifying the gateway to use, you specify an interface on your logical subnet. If you are specifying a route for a host rather than a network, either do not specify the destination subnet mask, or specify 255.255.255.255 to indicate that this is a host address and not a network address.

Verifying dynamic routes in the routing table will be more difficult simply because there could be so many of them (particularly if using RIP), and they are more difficult to verify.

Router Configuration

First, ensure that the Windows 2000 server is correctly enabled for routing, which allows it to forward packets between its interfaces. If you intend to use demand-dial routing, ensure you have configured your port/s, dial-up adapter/s, and account information appropriately.

If you are not using dynamic routing protocols, and you have at least one other router in your network, you will need to have a mechanism for forwarding packets to the correct interface:

- Static routes defined
- Silent RIP enabled
- Dynamic routing protocols installed and added to two or more interfaces

Also check to see whether you have enabled and configured correctly any other services you need to offer, which may include:

- IGMP support

- ICMP Router Discovery
- Packet filtering

Dynamic Routing Protocol Configuration

Verify the configuration of both the protocol settings that apply globally, and protocol settings on individual interfaces.

RIP Following are some common problems and issues associated with RIP configuration. In particular, pay attention to compatibility issues if you are using a mixture of RIPv1 and RIPv2 on your network.

- Remember that the limitation of RIP is that it supports a maximum of 15 routers—if your network exceeds this number, it cannot support RIP. Whenever RIP identifies more than 15 hops between source and destination host, the path will fail with a "Destination Unreachable" routing error. Sometimes hop counts are artificially changed so that slow links are allocated a higher hop number—remember, the total number of hops must not exceed 15!
- For efficiency problems such as slow convergence times, check the RIP convergence options.
- On networks with RIPv1 routers, verify that RIPv2 is configured for broadcast announcements rather than using multicasts, and verify that incoming announcements are set to RIPv1 and RIPv2.
- If you are using RIPv2 configured for multicasts, ensure Silent RIP hosts are correctly updating their routing tables. If they are not, it could be because the routers cannot support RIP2. See if you can upgrade them, or consider configuring the routers for broadcast announcements instead of multicasts.
- If you have routers on your network that use RIPv1, ensure you are not using VLSMs, disjointed subnets, or supernetting.
- If you are using RIPv2 with authentication, ensure all routers are configured similarly, all with authentication and all using the same (case-sensitive) password.
- If you are using peer filtering, verify you have the correct IP addresses for the neighboring peer RIP routers.
- If you are using RIP route filtering, verify that the ranges of network IDs for your internetwork are included (rather than being excluded).

- If you are using RIP neighbors, verify you have specified the correct IP addresses for unicast RIP announcements.
- Verify IP packet filtering is not preventing the receiving (through input filters) or sending (through output filters) of RIP announcements on the router interfaces enabled for RIP. Similarly, verify that TCP/IP filtering on the router interfaces is not preventing the receiving of RIP traffic. RIP traffic uses User Datagram Protocol (UDP) port 520.
- If you are using demand-dial routing with auto-static updates, ensure the demand-dial interface is configured to use RIPv2 multicast announcements. Broadcasts will not work in this environment because the two systems are on different subnets.
- If you want to propagate host and/or default routes between routers, configure this nondefault setting in the Advanced tab on the RIP interface Properties.

OSPF Because of the differences between how RIP and OSPF work, configuration issues with this protocol are very different. It is important to configure each router for its assigned role and ensure that it forms adjacencies with its neighbors—a failure to do so will result in incomplete routing tables.

The following configurations must be the same on neighboring routers:

- Authentication set on or off, and when it is being used, all routers must use the same (case-sensitive) password
- The Hello interval (default 10secs)
- The Dead interval (recommendation is four times the Hello interval)
- Area ID
- The stub setting

To test adjacencies, use *tracert* to report the path between one router and its neighbor—there should be a direct path.

Also bear in mind the following:

- The Router ID of two neighboring routers must not match.
- Ensure you have correctly assigned multicast addresses for NBNA networks.

- There must be a Designated Router per area (the State column on the relevant OSPF interface will display "Designated Router," and for resilience you should also have a Backup Designated Router assigned). If you do not have a DR, check the Router Priority Level of your routers—one or more should be higher than 0.
- Ensure all ABRs are either physically or logically (via virtual link) connected to the backbone.

If your AS fails to route with other ASs (e.g., routes using other protocols such as RIP), check the configuration of the external routes on the ASBRs to ensure they aren't blocking these packets. ASBRs are responsible for learning and then propagating external routes, which then become integrated with the OSPF routing table, except in stub areas. If you want to increase routing efficiency when routing to other ASs, do not use stub areas so that a shortest path will have a lower cost (but at the expense of larger routing tables which results in a higher convergence time). However, if your priority is to increase routing efficiency when routing just within the AS, use stub areas to prevent external routes flooding each area—traffic to external routes will still succeed via the ASBR, but will have a higher cost.

CERTIFICATION SUMMARY

We covered a lot of material in this chapter because IP routing is such a large and complex subject! Before explaining how to install and configure Windows 2000 as an IP router, we looked at some basic definitions and concepts of what routing is, how it works, and some of the problems associated with it. This basic level of understanding is fundamental to understanding how specific implementations work and the configuration choices you have.

We then covered installing and configuring Windows 2000 as an IP router, including such components as multicasting and support for IGMP, ICMP Router Discovery, and defining static routes. We looked in some detail at installing and configuring the two routing protocols Windows 2000 supports: RIP and OSPF. You should now have a better understanding not just of how each of these routing protocols works, but the advantages and disadvantages of both, so you can make a better-informed choice of which to use. Although RIP will undoubtedly remain a more popular choice for many companies, we spent more time discussing and explaining OSPF because it is a more complex routing protocol, and for many of us requires learning new terminology and new concepts before being able to understand the configuration options.

Demand-dial routing was covered next for nonpermanent links, and we saw how tightly this integrated with remote access, including components such as security and authentication, and remote access policies.

The RRAS snap-in offers a nice GUI to pull together all of the features and services the Remote Access and Routing server offers. From here you can view, monitor, log, and configure the various services and protocols installed.

Finally, we looked at some troubleshooting methods with suggestions of how to narrow down and identify problems, and things to watch out for.

TWO-MINUTE DRILL

Introduction

- ❑ The Routing and Remote Access Service offers a complex and tightly integrated suite of services, including acting as a router for IPX, AppleTalk, and IP.
- ❑ Additionally, it offers Remote Access, DHCP Relay Agent, Network Address Translation, ICMP Router Discovery, and IGMP support.

Overview of Windows 2000 IP Routing

- ❑ Routing is the process of forwarding packets from one computer (source host) on one network to another computer (destination host) on another network, either directly if the destination host is on a network directly attached to the router, or indirectly via another router if the destination host is not on a network directly attached to the router.
- ❑ Windows 2000 offers a software routing service rather than a hardware router, which has advantages of tight integration with other Windows 2000 features and benefits, ease of use with a GUI, flexibility of running in conjunction with other applications/services, and is potentially cheaper than a hardware router.
- ❑ A hardware router is generally faster and more efficient at routing because it is dedicated to this function. Additionally, a hardware router usually supports a greater number of protocols and advanced routing configuration options.

Enabling and Configuring Windows 2000 as an IP Software Router

- ❑ Enabling the Router option in the RRAS snap-in automatically allows packets to pass between each of its interfaces.
- ❑ You do not need to install routing protocols to be able to route packets from one interface on your router to another interface.
- ❑ You can add static routes with the Route Add command, Netsh utility, and RRAS snap-in.

Implementing Routing Protocols

- ❑ To use dynamic routing protocols, you first add them via RRAS, and then add to them the interfaces you want to use.
- ❑ Two dynamic routing protocols offered by Windows 2000 are RIP (a distance vector-based routing protocol) and OSPF (a link state-based routing protocol).
- ❑ Convergence time is very important in dynamic routing, and refers to the time it takes for all routing tables to be updated so that all network routes are known and valid. It is desirable that this is done quickly and with the minimum amount of information.

RIP for IP

- ❑ RIP for IP supports both RIPv1 and RIPv2. RIPv1 can only work with broadcasts, has no protection from rogue routers, and does not announce the subnet mask. RIPv2 can use multicasts as well as broadcasts, offers authentication as protection against rogue routers, supports a route tag, and does announce the subnet mask (which means nondefault masks such as VLSMs are supported).
- ❑ You can configure a Windows 2000 router for RIPv1 compatibility if you have other RIPv1 routers on your network.
- ❑ RIPv2 supports many of the newer and more desirable features found in OSPF, but with lower administrative costs. This makes it a suitable choice in all but very large networks (it can still only support paths of up to 15 routers).
- ❑ Windows 2000 with RIP offers the ability to modify the following: convergence options, announcement intervals, and the routing table entry timeout. It supports the following: silent RIP, peer filtering, route filtering, RIP neighbors, and announce or accept default routes or host routes.

OSPF

- ❑ Benefits of using this routing protocol include the following: more efficient use of network bandwidth, uses only multicasts with acknowledgments, lower convergence times, smaller routing tables, routing information is only announced when there are changes rather than periodically, scales well (up to 255 routers), and offers protection against rogue routers with authentication.

- ❑ OSPF's terminology includes areas, boundaries, Link State Advertisements (LSAs), flooding, Link State Database (LSDB), cost, and default route.
- ❑ Areas and routers are uniquely identified by logical names that have the same format as IP addresses—32-bit dotted decimal number.
- ❑ An OSPF network must have at least one area; if more than one area, it must have a backbone area with ID 0.0.0.0 that all other areas report to.

Demand-Dialing Routing

- ❑ A dial-on demand routing connection does not have a permanent connection—the connection is only made when required (for example, when the dial-on-demand interface is asked to forward packets over its interface).
- ❑ All connections use PPP over either a physical medium (e.g., modem or ISDN) or tunnel medium (e.g., PPTP or L2TP).

Troubleshooting IP Routing Problems

- ❑ Before troubleshooting an IP routing problem, ensure it is a routing problem and not a problem with hardware, basic TCP/IP configuration, or name resolution.
- ❑ Troubleshooting IP routing problems is difficult and complex because routing is a distributed and dynamic service.
- ❑ One of the most reliable and recommended approaches to troubleshooting routing is to methodically check forward from the source computer to the final destination computer until you find the break in the complete route.
- ❑ Don't dive into changing routing options without an understanding of how routing works and appreciating the potential consequences of your changes.
- ❑ Troubleshooting tools include ARP –a to check the MAC to IP address, route print to check the current routing table, ping to check reachability of a host, tracert to check the route a packet travels, pathping to both trace the route taken and compute response times on each link, and Network monitor to capture the traffic.
- ❑ Verify the following: TCP/IP configuration on hosts, routing tables, router configuration, and dynamic routing protocol configuration.

MCSE
MICROSOFT CERTIFIED SYSTEMS ENGINEER

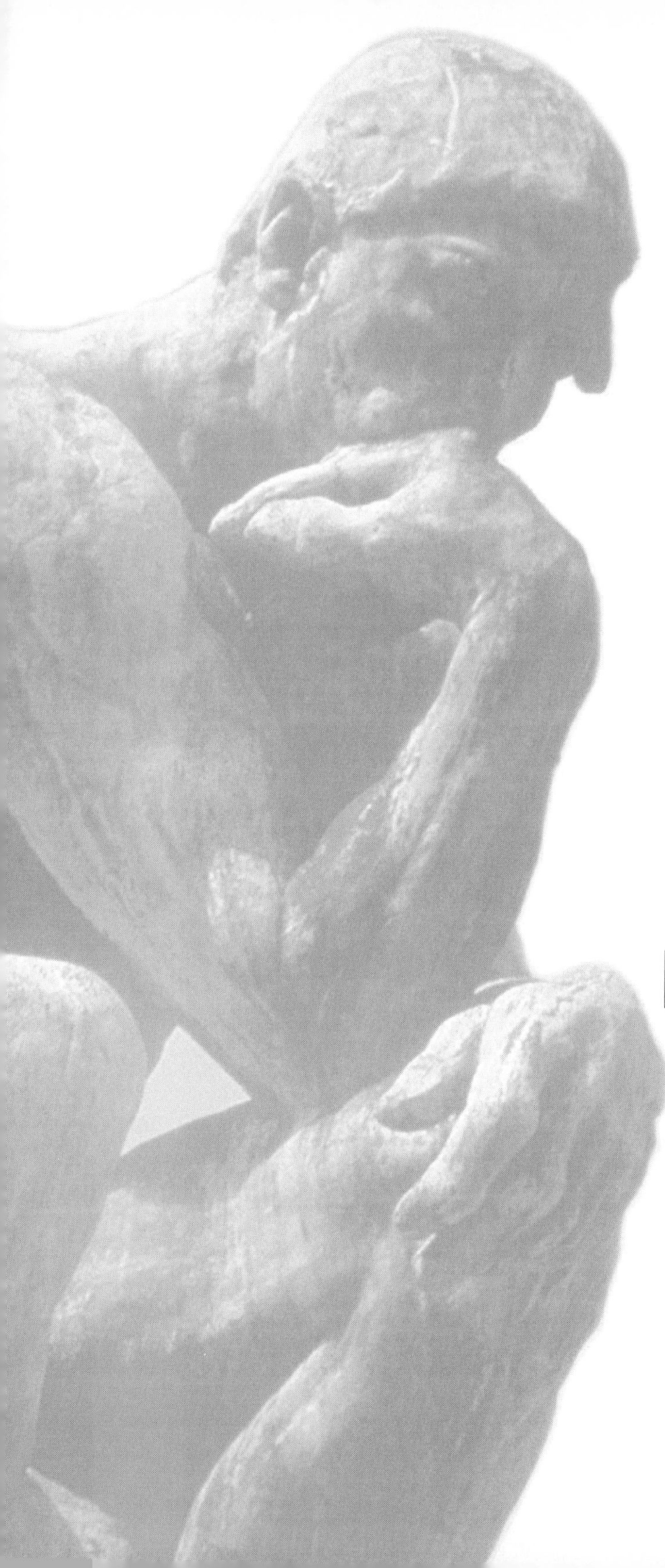

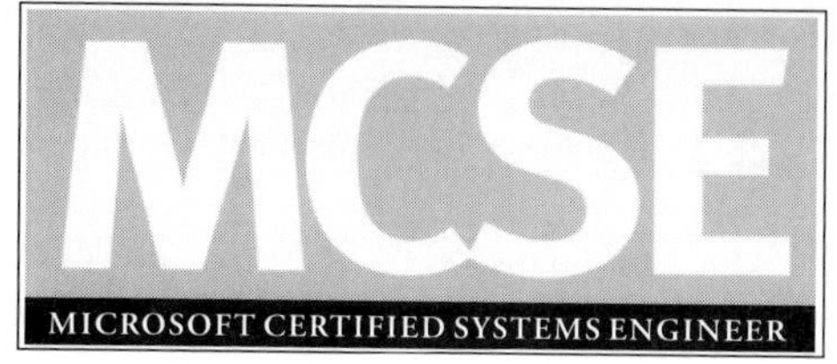

29

Installing, Configuring, and Troubleshooting Windows 2000 NAT

CERTIFICATION OBJECTIVES

29.01	Overview of ICS and NAT
29.02	Internet Connection Sharing
29.03	Network Address Translation
29.04	Troubleshooting ICS and NAT
✓	Two-Minute Drill

Many of the new features in Windows 2000 are aimed at the large enterprise environment, so it comes as rather a surprise to see new features specifically aimed at the smallest of networks. However, Windows 2000 is very Internet oriented, and this does relate directly with network address translation (NAT), which is the topic of this chapter.

NAT is a very useful new feature in Windows 2000 from which many people can immediately benefit. As such, it has received a lot of media attention and is being heralded as one of the Windows 2000 benefits. Also, since address translation was not available in Windows NT 4.0 (only in Windows 98 Second Edition), you can be sure it will be covered in the Microsoft exams. Unless you had Windows 98 Second Edition, the previous choices for connecting a Microsoft network to the Internet were to use a directly routed connection, Proxy Server, or a third-party product—so you can see how NAT fills a critical gap in Microsoft networking services. Networking services are the core of Windows 2000, and as such, NAT claims an important role.

This chapter describes in detail exactly what is Network Address Translation is, how it works, how to configure it in Windows 2000, when to use it, and its limitations.

CERTIFICATION OBJECTIVE 29.01

Overview of ICS and NAT

Windows 2000 Internet Connection Sharing (ICS) and the Network Address Translation (NAT) protocol both offer a relatively simple and inexpensive way for small networks to benefit from an Internet network connection. As such, you will see the abbreviations ICS and NAT in close proximity to another acronym: SOHO, which stands for *Small Office/Home Office* and is the environment perceived as the most likely to benefit from this simple method of connecting to the Internet.

A user on a SOHO network frequently needs to use more than one computer, and also needs to be able to share resources from one computer to another, such as files, applications, and printers.

However, despite these typical characteristics that define SOHO, bear in mind this is only a theoretical definition. In reality the clear textbook definitions can blur into less distinct categories. For example, SOHO may include workstations with multiple protocols, servers for DHCP, WINS, and DNS. And, it may have more than one segment. Additionally, although ICS and NAT are envisaged as being suited to SOHO, it may also have a place in the corporate network. So be prepared to be flexible in your perceptions of how and when these services could be deployed. They could even be mixed; for example, a small branch office could be defined as a SOHO network that connects via the Internet to your corporate network. Using VPNs in a SOHO environment will be covered in a later section.

When you connect a workstation on a private network to the Internet, your connection will be either *routed* or *translated.* The theory of connecting together two private networks still holds for when you want to connect your private network to the public Internet. However, in this scenario, you have the administrative overhead of more carefully managing and configuring network traffic and security, because you don't want to expose your internal networks and resources to unlawful access or unwanted traffic.

A translated connection transparently transfers packets between one network (such as your internal company network) and another (such as an external network like the Internet). One computer connected to both networks converts packets from your internal network (with private addresses) to packets to the Internet (with public addresses), and vice versa. The benefit of this is that internal addresses are completely hidden from the Internet, because all traffic appears to come from the one computer. This is the opposite of a routed connection, where the source and destination IP addresses remain the same irrespective of how many hops (routers) the packets have to traverse before reaching their final destination. With a translated connection, the source and destination addresses of the computers on the internal network are converted into the address of the one computer running the translation service—which is how the IP addresses of computers remain "hidden."

Why Share an Internet Connection?

As outlined earlier, security is one of the automatic advantages of having a translated connection—and both ICS and NAT use translation rather than routing. A translated connection is easier to secure than a routed connection, because hosts on the Internet will not know the true identity of your workstations (which, for example, will significantly reduce the risk of Denial of Service attacks).

Simplicity is another reason to share an Internet connection—it is easier to set up, configure, and share one single Internet connection than correctly set up and configure multiple connections for each computer on your network that needs Internet access. You can allow multiple computers on your network to have Internet access without adding additional client software or reconfiguring them.

Cost is another factor when considering whether to share an Internet connection. It is obviously cheaper to have just one Internet connection with its single associated hardware and ISP costs and share it among multiple computers than have an Internet connection on each computer. Also, the administrative overheads of managing and configuring just one connection rather than multiple connections will be lower.

However, some limitations of a translated connection determine whether ICS and/or the NAT protocol are suitable. These limitations will be discussed later.

exam Watch

Benefits of ICS and NAT include low cost and low administrative overhead.

What's the Difference between ICS and NAT?

Internet Connection Sharing and NAT both work by offering to workstations on small networks:

- Address translation
- Address assignment
- Name resolution

So what's the difference between ICS and NAT?

Although similar in purpose, the NAT protocol offers more functions and greater flexibility than ICS—ICS is a cut-down, simplified version of NAT. This doesn't necessarily denigrate the status of ICS because in the simplest environments, ICS may be a better choice over NAT. As a network administrator, it is your responsibility to know the differences between them, and what each offers before making an informed choice as to which is better to implement.

Features of ICS

First, protocols are distinguished by how and where you configure them. ICS is a feature of the Network and Dial-Up Connections, while NAT is presented as a routing protocol to be added and configured through the Routing and Remote Access Service snap-in.

ICS in Windows 2000 offers the simplest Internet connection service, and can be configured on either a computer running Windows 2000 Professional or on a Windows 2000 Server. The ICS computer must have two network connections—one to your internal network with a private address, and the other to the Internet, which will use a publicly assigned IP address. Typically, the connection to the Internet would be a dial-up modem or ISDN adapter, but you could also use a dedicated connection such as cable modem, DSL, or even a fractional T1 line. Your ISP could statically assign your public IP address to you, or it could be dynamically assigned when you connect.

To configure ICS on Windows 2000 Professional/Server, use the Make New Connection Wizard to create your Internet connection, selecting the "Dial-up to the network" option and specifying the adapter to use with a number to connect to the Internet (e.g., as supplied by your ISP). ICS is then enabled when you select the option "Enable Internet Connection Sharing for this connection" in the Internet Connection Sharing dialog box. If you have already configured your Internet connection, this option is under the connection's Properties | Sharing tab.

This option will configure automatic IP address assignment for the workstations on the private network so that all workstations on the private network use the same (private) network address, and it automatically assigns the IP address of 192.168.0.1 to the internally connected adapter.

ICS is suitable for a single segmented private network with up to 254 workstations, where all workstations are configured to automatically receive an IP address. It allows you to share one public IP address among these workstations, providing there are no other servers on the same segment offering DNS or DHCP services. In such a configuration it automatically resolves Internet DNS names, but it doesn't offer WINS resolution for your internal workstations. The only configuration is for defining static mappings (discussed later). There may be some applications and services that will not translate correctly (this will be discussed later), which may limit what applications you can use through an ICS connection.

exam watch

To configure Internet connection sharing, you must be a member of the Administrators group.

NAT Features

NAT can only be run on a Windows 2000 Server through the Routing and Remote Access snap-in as a routing protocol. You'll need to add at least two interfaces to the new NAT component (minimum of one connected to the Internet and one connected to your private network), but you can use multiple adapters, which allows you to use multiple subnets on your private network. The Internet-connected interface would typically be a dedicated connection such as a fractional T1 line, DSL, or cable modem, but you can also use it with a demand-dial adapter/modem.

NAT configuration options include settings for dynamic mappings, static mappings, address assignment, and name resolution (all discussed later). These options include allowing your internal clients to automatically receive IP addresses from this server or from a standard DHCP server (or use static addresses), and whether you want the NAT server to resolve DNS names for connecting clients. As with ICS, there may be some applications and services that will not translate correctly (this will be discussed later), which may limit what applications you can use through a NAT connection.

Multiple Public Addresses on the NAT Server An importance difference with NAT is that you can use more than one public IP address on the server, which provides scalability since your internal workstations can be mapped to a pool of public Internet addresses to take advantage of better throughput and availability. Or, you can more finely control access by assigning certain services or machines to specific Internet IP addresses—this being one way of offering secure reverse proxying where a machine on your internal network is dedicated to offering example, an Internet Web server without revealing its real (private) address. Similarly, you can use special port mappings where, for example, the default http port 80 is advertised for your company Web server but the Web server on your private network is actually hosting this service on port 1234.

exam Watch

You cannot use more than one Internet IP address with ICS—only NAT allows you to do this with either multiple Internet adapters and/or Internet address pools.

What's the Difference between an Address Translation Service and a Proxy Server Service?

"Microsoft and third-party vendors offer both NAT and Proxy server solutions for connecting private networks to the Internet. In either case, there are two interfaces as described above. Proxy servers also use a form of address translation to convert private addresses to a single public address. However, proxy translation may not

SCENARIO & SOLUTION

Which Should You Use If...	ICS or NAT
You want the easiest solution to set up and configure?	ICS is the easiest solution to set up and configure; it's simply a check box as one of your Dial-up connection properties. NAT is more complicated to set up and configure because it offers a more flexible service.
You want to use Windows 2000 Professional rather than Windows 2000 Server?	ICS can be set up on either Windows 2000 Professional or Windows 2000 Server, but NAT can only be set up on a Windows 2000 Server with Routing and Remote Access Service enabled.
You want to take advantage of a pool of public Internet addresses for better availability, or reserve an Internet address just for an Internet Web server on your private network?	Only NAT allows you to have more than one Internet address on your single connection.
You want to host Internet services on your internal workstations with a fractional T1 line?	Both ICS and NAT allow you do this.
You want your workstations to get IP addresses and other DHCP options from a standard DHCP server rather than from the computer hosting the Internet connection?	Only NAT allows you to do this.
You want a choice over how DNS names are resolved?	Only NAT gives you this choice.
You want to configure settings for static mappings?	Both ICS and NAT allow you do this.
You want to configure settings for dynamic mappings?	Only NAT gives you this choice.

comply with RFC 1631 (NAT specifications), and proxies provide additional features such as sophisticated filtering and web caching."

The "easy" and theoretical answer to this is that Microsoft's Proxy Server is aimed at large and complex corporate networks, NAT at the medium-small sized networks, and ICS at the smallest and simplest of networks. However, it's more useful to know why these generalizations apply by looking into what services they offer and their limitations.

Application Layer vs. Network Layer

For a start, a proxy server works at the Session or Application layer, and NAT at the Network layer. While this may seem to be a theoretical difference only, in practice this means that additional software and/or reconfiguration is needed on the client workstations in order to use the proxy server's services. For example, in a Microsoft Proxy Server environment, a workstation running Windows 2000 Professional on a private network that wants to connect a telnet session to an Internet host must have the Winsock Proxy Client software installed.

Additionally, because the conversion is processed higher up the stack, additional processing is needed at the workstation and/or the server. Microsoft's Proxy Server actually offers three services: Web Proxy, Winsock Proxy, and Socks Proxy. Together, these three services offer just about any and every Internet application and service a workstation could need (including IPX clients and non-Microsoft workstations such as UNIX and Macintoshes).

For Web and File Transfer Protocol (FTP), Internet Explorer 5 can be automatically configured to use proxy servers. However, for other connections such as Telnet, Network News Transfer Protocol (NNTP), Post Office Protocol 3 (POP3), Network File System (NFS), and Internet Relay Chat (IRC), and for IPX clients, you will have to install and configure the Winsock Proxy Client software. Paradoxically, for larger organizations the additional overhead of configuring the client workstations could be less important than it might be for smaller networks, because larger organizations are usually more adept at deploying workstation configurations (e.g., use of SMS and/or specialist deployment teams).

Administrative Overhead

For the additional overhead in configuring a more complex service, as well as additional computer resources required, a proxy server may be a more expensive solution for a SOHO environment. In a larger network, Microsoft's Proxy Server offers better security and greater flexibility than ICS or NAT. For example, you can define which services can be used by users and groups, ban access to specified domains and IP addresses, and set up alerts on packet filtering. IP address assignment is not a component of Microsoft's Proxy Server, which allows greater flexibility for configuring workstations on different subnets—which is obviously more suited to enterprise environments.

Also, Microsoft's Proxy Server supports Windows clients that don't use TCP/IP (workstations running IPX can use the proxy server to access Internet Web servers). Proxy servers can also centrally cache Web pages to make better use of Internet bandwidth, and when you have multiple proxy servers, they can be grouped together in an array to offer better throughput and availability.

In short, although NAT and proxy servers appear to do the same job, they differ in how they technically achieve this, the flexibility they offer, and the ease of configuration. If ICS or NAT cannot meet your requirements, it is possible that the better choice is to use a proxy server irrespective of the size of your network.

Using VPNs in a SOHO Environment

There are benefits to using a Virtual Private Network (VPN) connection to securely connect over the Internet to your corporate network. Normally, VPN users would have to dial up to their ISP first and then initiate the VPN connection. Using ICS or NAT in Windows 2000 means each SOHO workstation could create its own VPN connection, but use the shared Internet connection for the underlying connection. This would allow each user to securely connect to a corporate network without the need for additional modems/adapters or individual ISP accounts for his or her own IP address.

As with any VPN connection, each user must have a valid user account to authenticate him or her on the VPN server, which could be a local account on the VPN server, an account in the Active Directory, or a Remote Authentication Dial-In User Service (RADIUS) account.

The only limitation of tunneling with NAT is that the tunneling protocol used would have to be Point-to-Point Tunneling Protocol (PPTP) rather than Layer 2 Tunneling Protocol/Internet Protocol Security (L2TP/IPSec) (because IPSec is one of the protocols that NAT cannot translate). If you are running Windows 2000 Professional, the default setting for a VPN connection is to try L2TP/IPSec first and then PPTP. To decrease your initial VPN connection time, change the Properties of your VPN connection so the Server Type is set to PPTP.

How Address Translation Works

Network address translation works by translating a private address to a public address, and vice versa. For example, if a workstation on your private network had the IP address of 10.0.0.2 and it wanted to connect to a Web site on the Internet with an address of 207.46.131.137 (one of Microsoft's addresses), it would send its packet to the Internet via the computer offering the Internet connection. This computer would have one connection to the private network (e.g., address 10.0.0.1) and one connection to the Internet (e.g., dial-up modem with assigned IP address of 162.1.2.3). The translation would keep the destination address of 207.46.131.137, but would change the source address to 162.1.2.3. When the reply came back from the Web site (for example, the data for its homepage), it would send this packet to 162.1.2.3, but the translation service would know that this maps to the original IP address of 10.0.0.2 and would send it to that computer with its 10.0.0.1 interface.

These are the basics of how the translation service works, but for full Internet services to function, it works in conjunction with other components such as address assignment and name resolution. Therefore, the three elements of a network address translation service are:

- Translation
- Addressing assignment
- Name resolution

Translation

We have already discussed how one address is translated into another. The NAT component translates packets that contain IP addresses, Transmission Control Protocol (TCP) port, and User Datagram Protocol (UDP) port information in the IP, TCP, and UDP headers. If the application contains any of these in the *application header* instead of the *IP header*, NAT is unable to directly translate these packets. In other words, for NAT to directly translate packets between a private network and a public network, the following must be true:

- Packets have an IP address in the IP header.

And one of the following:

- Packets have TCP port numbers in the TCP header.

Or

- Packets have UDP port numbers in the UDP header.

Some protocols do not fulfill these requirements. For example, PPTP packets cannot be directly translated because PPTP doesn't use a TCP or UDP header—PPTP uses a Generic Routing Encapsulation (GRE) header and, in fact, the tunnel ID in the GRE header identifies the data. Similarly, FTP stores the IP addresses in the FTP header in the port command rather than in the IP header.

NAT Editors However, these protocols and some others that do not directly translate will work through Windows 2000 ICS and NAT because of the addition of *NAT editors*. Both ICS and the NAT routing protocol include built-in NAT editors for FTP, Internet Control Message Protocol (ICMP) (e.g., ping packets), and PPTP (for VPN support), so these can be used with address translation. Examples of protocols that do not directly translate and for which there are no NAT editors include IPSec and Kerberos. This means you cannot use IPSec or Kerberos authentication through ICS/NAT, which is one of the major limitations of these services.

Additionally, Windows 2000 NAT includes proxy software for the following protocols:

- H.323 (for voice and video)
- DirectPlay (for multiplayer gaming)
- Lightweight Directory Access Protocol (LDAP)-based Internet Locator Service (ILS) registration
- Remote Procedure Call (RPC)

This means that for those protocols, the computer running ICS or the NAT routing protocol will send out these protocols directly to the Internet from its public address on behalf of the client workstation, rather than translating them.

on the job

When you install NAT, you will see errors in the Event Log (IDs 33001 and 34001) that relate to DirectPlay Proxy. This is a known event error and will appear even if you select to disable NAT event logging. DirectPlay will only support one client at a time on your private network when using ICS/NAT.

Addressing Assignment

The addressing component refers to how client workstations obtain an IP address and other related configurations, including the subnet mask, default gateway, and IP address of a DNS/WINS server. This configuration is important because it defines how these clients communicate with each other, the computer offering the shared Internet services, and ultimately with Internet resources.

When the computer offering the shared Internet service assigns IP addresses, it acts as a simplified DHCP server. This works well in a small network, since computers running Windows 2000, Windows NT, and Windows 9*x* configured with TCP/IP have a default configuration to be a DHCP client.

The DHCP Allocator For ICS, you have no choice over this component. When you enable ICS, you automatically invoke what is referred to as the *DHCP* *allocator*. A DHCP allocator is a simplified DHCP service without the database or configurable options. Invoking the DHCP allocator means that the computer will automatically assign IP addresses to other workstations on the same subnet using a private address range, and it will assign the default gateway and the DNS server to be the same IP address as the computer running ICS. Note there is no WINS server allocation.

When using the NAT routing protocol, you have a choice of whether to use the built-in DHCP allocator. If you don't use the DHCP allocator, you can instead use a standard DHCP server that has been installed on your network, or use static addresses. If you are using the DHCP allocator, you can define what address range you want to use, and exclude addresses that are already in use on your private network. It would be a wise precaution to add the server's static IP address as one of the reserved addresses, whether on this server if running the DHCP allocator, and/or on other DHCP servers.

If you choose to use the DHCP allocator on the NAT server, it will assign clients an IP address in the range specified (you can choose the range) and exclude addresses you have defined. It will also assign the default gateway, and the DNS server to be the same IP address as the internal interface on the NAT server. Additionally, if the NAT server is configured with a WINS server on the internal interface, requests for NetBIOS name resolution from clients will be sent to that WINS server.

If you already have a DHCP server on your network, you should use that rather than using the NAT DHCP allocator—you can't run the two together on the same subnet. In fact, using a standard DHCP server allows greater flexibility because you can more precisely define and configure IP address assignment to include DHCP Class options and the choice of which DNS/WINS server to use.

exam Watch

The DHCP allocator component in ICS and NAT acts as a simplified DHCP server. It is not the same as running a full DHCP Server, and you cannot disable the DHCP allocator in ICS.

When you are using the DHCP allocator, it will use the predefined settings listed in Table 29-1.

Host Name Resolution

When using the DHCP allocator, both ICS and NAT assign to clients the DNS server as being the IP address of the internal interface on the computer offering the Internet connection. This allows both local and remote DNS names to be resolved.

TABLE 29-1 DHCP Allocator's Predefined DHCP Options that Cannot Be Changed

DHCP Option Number	Description	Option Value
1	Subnet mask	255.255.255.0
3	Default gateway	IP address of private interface
6	DNS server (providing name resolution is set in NAT)	IP address of private interface
58	Renewal time	5 minutes
59	Rebinding time	5 days
51	IP address lease time	7 days
15	DNS domain	Primary domain name of computer

For Internet name resolution, this means that *DNS proxying* will be used to resolve Internet names to IP addresses.

For example, workstation A on your private network wants to connect to a Web server www.microsoft.com. Before a connection can be made, it needs to resolve the name to an IP address—so it uses its DNS server to find the answer. The DNS server in this case is the IP address of the computer offering the Internet connection, so when the DNS request for www.microsoft.com comes in, it queries its own DNS server specified on the Internet interface (e.g., your ISP's DNS server), and when the response comes back, it passes this back to workstation A.

You can disable DNS resolution for clients on the NAT server, but you can't disable this for ICS.

Another solution would be to use your own local DNS server, which would resolve local names and then forward unresolved names to the Internet. This is only possible with NAT rather than ICS because you can specify not to use IP name resolution and also disable the DHCP allocator. Instead, workstations could use a local DHCP server that assigns to clients a local DNS server rather than the IP address of the NAT server.

NetBIOS Name Resolution

Resolving NetBIOS names works slightly differently. There is no WINS server assignment with ICS, which means that if clients wanted to connect to shares on each other in the form of \\computer_name\share, this would be resolved by broadcast. On a single segment and small network this NetBIOS name resolution should not be a problem, but you may prefer to use an LMHOSTS file to keep such broadcasts to a minimum.

NAT as WINS Proxy With NAT configured to use the DHCP allocator, the NAT server acts as a *WINS proxy* in much the same way as the DNS proxying works, except that requests would go to the server's local WINS server rather than out to the Internet. When a NetBIOS name needs to be resolved to an IP address, the NAT server will query the WINS server on behalf of the private workstations and return the IP address to name resolution. However, it doesn't register the clients in the WINS database or check for duplicate names.

In practice, this means that if workstation A wanted to connect to workstation B in the form of a share name, and both received their IP address assignment from the NAT server, the name could be resolved. However, if you had another workstation that didn't receive its IP address assignment from the NAT server so it was configured to use the WINS server directly, the name resolution by WINS would fail, and the resolution would only succeed if a broadcast was successful (not possible if on a different subnet) or if an LMHOSTS file was in place.

You can see how in all but the simplest of network configurations, using a full DHCP server rather than the built-in DHCP allocator on the NAT server allows you to assign specific DNS and WINS servers to your workstations, which in turn offers greater flexibility in name resolution.

Dynamic vs. Static Mapping

So far, in our discussion of how address translation works, we have mainly concentrated on outbound connections from a private network to the Internet. We have seen how a mapping occurs where a private address is dynamically translated into a public address. It's dynamic because the ICS computer or NAT server handles the translation automatically, keeping track of which addresses/ports are mapped in a mapping table that it periodically refreshes. If these mappings are not refreshed by users reusing the connection, the mappings are removed from the table after a set time. For TCP connections, this time period is 24 hours; for UDP connections, this time period is 1 minute. You can change these default timeouts in NAT, but you cannot change them in ICS.

Now that you understand how name resolution works with ICS and NAT, you should be able to select which is an appropriate solution depending on your name resolution requirements.

SCENARIO & SOLUTION

Should you use ICS or NAT if...	Answer
You have just a few workstations on your single segment network with no other servers?	Both ICS and NAT would work in this situation, but ICS would the simplest to configure.
You already have a DHCP server on your network?	NAT, because you can disable the DHCP allocator, and with the full DHCP server assign specific DNS/WINS servers—you can't do this with ICS.
You want to resolve DNS names?	Both ICS and NAT allow you do this, but only NAT allows you to disable this option.
You want to resolve local NetBIOS names?	Both ICS and NAT allow you to resolve local NetBIOS names, but NAT allows greater flexibility. ICS does not assign a WINS server to clients, so names have to be resolved by broadcast or preconfigured LMHOSTS files. In NAT, the DHCP allocator invokes WINS proxying. However, you may prefer to disable the DHCP allocator, and through a standard DHCP server assign a local WINS server to clients so they can directly register with the WINS server.

Dynamic Mappings

For dynamic mappings, the default setting is to translate not just the address, but also the source port. So, for example, your client workstation initiates a TCP/IP connection with a source port of 1024, but after translation this goes out as port 5001. This is necessary when you have more private addresses than public addresses, in order to ensure the same source port is not used again.

For example, client workstation A initiates a TCP/IP connection with source port 1024 and so does workstation B—the translation of the source port in addition to the address would be necessary; otherwise, the ICS/NAT computer would attempt to use duplicate source ports, which is not allowed. Source ports must be unique to the computer sending out the connection request. There is no problem sending out the same destination port from the same computer, and by default, the destination port number is not translated.

Static Mappings

If you wanted to define in advance how the addresses and/or ports should be mapped rather than letting the ICS/NAT computer make this decision, you would have to define *a static mapping*. The most common reason for defining a static mapping is if you wanted to host an Internet resource on one of your client workstations, because the ICS/NAT computer would need to know where to direct the incoming connection.

At the simplest level, you could define a static mapping so that the public IP address Internet users call of 162.1.2.3 with TCP port 80 should map to your internal IP address of 192.168.0.2, port 80. However, you may also want to change the internal port number for added security, or if the Web server may be hosting different sites based on different port numbers.

If you have multiple Internet addresses, it would be wise to reserve one for an incoming connection service such as your company Web server or FTP server, and use the others for dynamic outbound sessions. You can do this with NAT because it allows you to use more than one Internet address, but with ICS you can only use one Internet address. However, ICS does allow you to define static mappings for both incoming and outbound connections.

In ICS, static mappings are configured with the Application Settings button in the Sharing tab. In NAT, outbound static mappings are part of the NAT global properties, and inbound static mappings are part of the Internet interface properties. Later sections will cover how to configure these for both services.

exam Watch

Static mapping is a requirement if you want to host Internet services on your private network.

Mappings for Outbound Internet Traffic

When ICS or NAT receives connection requests for the Internet from the private network, it assesses whether a mapping already exists. This could be either a static mapping you have defined, or a dynamic mapping that is still in memory (the mapping table). If a mapping already exists, that is used. If a mapping does not already exist, a new dynamic mapping is created in one of the following ways:

- If NAT is being used with multiple Internet addresses, and one of these is free, it maps the private address of the originating workstation to its own public address, and passes through the source port number unchanged.

When the last Internet address is available, it behaves as if it only had one Internet address.

- If NAT is being used with only one Internet address, or if ICS is being used, it maps the private address of the originating workstation to its public address, AND it maps the original source port number (e.g., 1024) to a new source port number (e.g., 5000).

After the mapping is complete, it will look to see if a NAT editor is needed, and modify the packet as necessary before sending it out onto the Internet.

Mappings for Inbound Internet Traffic

When ICS or NAT receives connection requests from the Internet (which will happen, for example, if you are hosting your own FTP server on the private network for Internet users), it assesses whether a mapping exists for the destination address and port number. If a mapping exists, it will redirect the connection accordingly to the workstation on the private network (IP address or workstation name and port number). If a mapping does not exist, the connection request is discarded.

Additionally, after the mapping is complete, it will look to see if a NAT editor is needed, and modify the packet as necessary before sending it to the workstation on the private network.

exam Watch

NAT automatically offers security against malicious Internet connections, because dynamic mappings are only used for outbound connections; static mappings have to exist for inbound connections.

Private vs. Public IP Addresses

The connection protocol of the Internet is IP, and for computers to communicate with each other over the Internet, they need a valid IP address that has been allocated by the Internet Network Information Center (InterNIC). These addresses are known as public addresses, and typically an ISP will have a limited range of public addresses available for customers who want Internet access. A small business or home office will usually be granted one or more such public addresses, and the scarcity of these addresses is one reason why Internet connection sharing is so attractive.

Private Address Ranges

Because there is a very real limit on the number of available public addresses, the InterNIC provided an address reuse scheme by reserving certain network IDs for private networks.

- 10.0.0.0-10.255.255.255 with the subnet mask 255.0.0.0
- 172.16.0.0-172.31.255.255 with the subnet mask 255.240.0.0
- 192.168.0.0-192.168.255.255 with the subnet mask 255.255.0.0

Private addresses cannot receive traffic directly from Internet locations. This has several implications for a network that requires an Internet connection. The first is that you must convert a private address to a public address before you can connect to the Internet. This is because routers on the Internet will not route addresses from the private address range. The second is that if private addressing is being used, this offers immediate security for your workstations, because traffic can only pass from the Internet to your network via a network translation service or a routed service. This will be on designated points on your network (e.g., your NAT server) rather than having to configure and maintain each workstation's connection integrity.

IP Addressing Issues on the Internal Network It is highly recommended that you use private addresses on your network even if you initially have no plans to connect to the Internet, because changing your IP address scheme if you later decide to connect to the Internet is not a quick or easy conversion once connectivity patterns have been established.

If you continue to use IP addresses that are valid public addresses but haven't been allocated to you by the InterNIC or an ISP, you will probably be using the same addresses as another organization on the Internet. This is called *illegal* or *overlapping IP addressing.* Not only do you run the higher risk of unwanted Internet traffic coming into your private network, but you will also not be able to connect to the legal IP network, because connections that should be remote will appear as local and never leave your company network.

Private addresses are assumed when using Internet sharing. With ICS, you have no choice over the internal addresses—they will be in the 192.168.x.x range. With NAT, you do have the choice of which IP address range to use, both when configuring the DHCP allocator on the NAT server itself and when using a full DHCP server. However, it is strongly recommended you keep to the practice of using addresses from the private address range.

EXERCISE 29-1

Walkthrough of Address Translation in Action

This exercise is a theoretical run-through of what happens when address translation is being used for both the source address and source port, either when using ICS or NAT.

1. Workstation A is a SOHO workstation with a single network adapter, configured to automatically receive TCP/IP address assignment, and as such, receives the following:
   IP address: 192.168.0.2
   Subnet mask: 255.255.255.0
   Default gateway: 192.168.0.1
   DNS server: 192.168.0.1
2. Workstation B is another SOHO workstation, but also has a connection to the Internet that is shared. As such, it has two interfaces:
   SOHO interface (for private network)
   IP address: 192.168.0.1
   Subnet mask: 255.255.255.0
   Internet interface (for public network—these values assigned by an ISP)
   IP address: 130.100.1.2
   Subnet mask: 255.255.0.0
   Default gateway: 130.100.100.222 (ISP's router)
   DNS server: 200.100.100.243 (ISP's DNS server)
3. When workstation A running Internet Explorer tries to connect to the Web site www.microsoft.com, it first needs to resolve this DNS name to IP address. It sends out the DNS query to its DNS server, which is the computer running the Internet sharing connection. This machine sees the DNS query, and on behalf of the client, it queries its own DNS server (on the Internet). When the reply comes back that www.microsoft.com resolves to the IP address 207.46.130.45, it passes this information back to workstation A.
4. Workstation A knows that address 207.46.130.45 is not on its local subnet, so it sends the http request via its default gateway. The default gateway is the internal IP address of the computer hosting the Internet sharing.

5. Workstation B receives the packet and passes it to the Internet via its Internet connected interface (IP address 130.100.1.2), but before it sends it out, it changes the source address from 192.168.0.2 to 130.100.1.2. It also changes the source port number from 1026 to 5001. As far as the host on the Internet is concerned, the call is initiated by the machine with address 130.100.1.2 and source port 5001—and has no knowledge of workstation A with address 192.168.0.2, source port 1026.
6. When the reply comes back from the Internet host, it sets the destination address to be 130.100.1.2 and destination port to be 5001. When the computer running the Internet sharing receives the packet, it looks in its translation mapping table, finds that this packet is really destined for workstation A, and changes the destination address from 130.100.1.2 to 192.168.0.2, and changes the destination port from 5001 to 1026.
7. Further exchange of packets between workstation A and the Microsoft Web site continue in this manner, with the mapping table directing packets until workstation A no longer needs to communicate with this Internet host. The mapping remains in the mapping table for the default timeout period of 24 hours, and then is discarded. After this time, any new connection from workstation A to the same host would have to set up a new dynamic mapping.

CERTIFICATION OBJECTIVE 29.02

Internet Connection Sharing

Now that we have looked at how Internet connection sharing works in theory, let's look at how to put this into practice for a machine running ICS.

Creating and Sharing a Dial-Up Connection

You must already have installed and configured the hardware to connect your computer to the Internet (e.g., modem or ISDN adapter), and have a network connection specified to the Internet that uses this interface (for example, specify your ISP's details).

Then sharing this connection is simply a matter of selecting its Properties, then the Sharing tab, and selecting the check box "Enable Internet connection sharing for this connection." If your Internet connection is dial-up rather than dedicated, you will also need to check the option "Enable on-demand dialing."

At this point, if you only require dynamic mappings so SOHO workstations can connect to Internet resources, your job is finished for configuring ICS. However, there may be two circumstances in which you need to specify static mappings, which you do with the Settings button on the same Sharing dialog box. This displays two tabs, one for Applications and one for Services.

Application-Specific Mappings

The Applications tab allows you to specify static mappings for outbound connections. You would not normally need to do this, but it may be required if the application requires particular port numbers (rather than letting ICS dynamically choose a number) and/or additional associated connections. For example, some firewalls are configured to allow through only a certain range of source port numbers, so if you were connecting over the Internet with this restriction, you would have to configure a static mapping to ensure the connection went out with the source port number that was required. Another example would be when using multiuser applications over the Internet (e.g., games) that require one or more additional inbound connections.

Service-Specific Mappings

The Services tab allows you specify static mappings for inbound connections; for example, if you want to offer Internet services (e.g., a Web server, FTP server, mail or NNTP server) on your SOHO workstations for other Internet users. Because these connections will be initiated by other people on the Internet rather than users on your internal network, the computer running ICS will need to know the workstation details to which it should map the connection.

The Services tab displays a list of well-known Internet services, such as FTP Server, POP3, and SMTP. For those not listed, click Add to specify your own reference name to identify the service (e.g., "company Web server"), the port number the remote client will be calling (e.g., TCP port 80 for Web services), and then identify to which workstation it should be mapped. Then when a connection comes in from the Internet, ICS will look up its static mapping and direct the call to the correct workstation on the internal network.

FROM THE CLASSROOM

Identifying the Workstation

How can you know what IP address the workstation will have if it's using DHCP? In theory, you may immediately think that these two are mutually exclusive— if a workstation is using DHCP, you cannot guarantee what IP address it will have, and therefore, it is better to specify the workstation name, which remains constant. However, if you are running a full-time service, the SOHO workstation will remain up and running and therefore be able to renew its initially obtained IP address (viewed with ipconfig or winipcfg). Despite this, you may prefer to identify the workstation by its constant host name.

—Carol Bailey, MCSE+I

exam Watch

You must have a dedicated Internet connection to offer incoming Internet services (such as FTP servers or Web servers) to Internet users

EXERCISE 29-2

Enabling Internet Connection Sharing for Dynamic Mapping

1. Ensure you are logged on with Administrative privileges and click on Start | Settings | Network and Dial-up Connections.
2. Right-click the Internet connection you want to share (e.g., your dial-up to your ISP) and select Properties | Sharing. Select the check box "Enable Internet connection sharing for this connection."
3. If your Internet connection uses a dial-up connection rather than a dedicated link, also select the check box "Enable on-demand dialing."
4. When you click OK you will see the dialog box shown in the following illustration, warning you that your internal IP address will be changed for one supported by ICS.

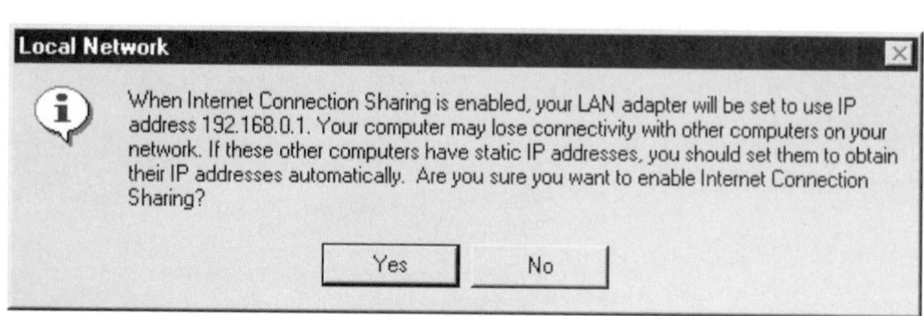
Local Network

When Internet Connection Sharing is enabled, your LAN adapter will be set to use IP address 192.168.0.1. Your computer may lose connectivity with other computers on your network. If these other computers have static IP addresses, you should set them to obtain their IP addresses automatically. Are you sure you want to enable Internet Connection Sharing?

Yes No

5. Click Yes.
6. That's it! Ensure you have no other DHCP servers on your network, and reboot your SOHO client workstations with DHCP configuration enabled so that they receive their new automatic IP address assignment from the ICS computer.

EXERCISE 29-3

CertCam 29-3

Enabling Internet Connection Sharing for a Static Mapping

The most likely time you will want to do this is if you want to host an Internet resource (e.g., Web server) on your private network. Ensure you have a dedicated link to the Internet and have completed the previous exercise. The workstation on your private network that will be hosting the Web server is called WRKST1-WEB, and uses the default TCP port of 80. To configure access to this Web server from the Internet, complete the following:

1. On the Sharing tab, click Settings and select the Services tab.
2. In the "Name of service," type in a name for your reference, such as Company Web Server.
3. In the "Service port number," type in **80** and keep the default selection of TCP rather than UDP.
4. Under the "Name or address of server computer on the private network," type in **WRKST1-WEB.**

Your dialog box should look similar to the following illustration.

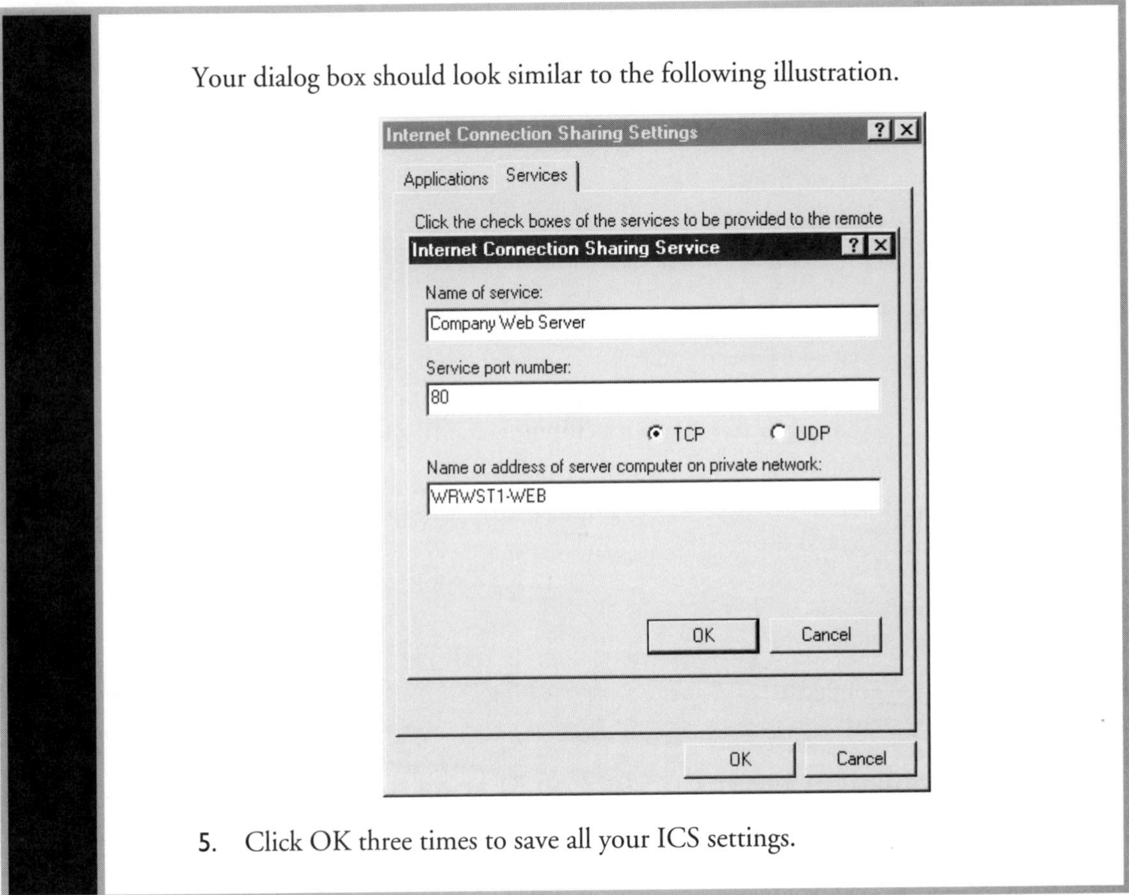

5. Click OK three times to save all your ICS settings.

Configuring Connection Sharing on the Clients

You will need to configure Internet Explorer on the client workstations to use Internet sharing, which means a local area connection rather than a direct Internet connection. Additionally, Internet Connection Sharing is *not* using a proxy server or automatically detecting settings, so options for these should be cleared.

The first time Internet Explorer is started on a particular machine, you will need to complete the following steps for Internet Explorer 5 on a Windows 2000 Professional computer.

1. Start | Programs | Internet Explorer.
2. When prompted, select "I want to set up my Internet connection manually, or I want to connect through a local area network (LAN)," and click Next.

3. Clear the option "Automatic discovery of proxy server [recommended]"—NAT was not available when IE5 was released! Then click Next.
4. You will then be prompted to configure mail options; either supply these if known, or click No (you can supply them later). Then click Finish.

If you have already set up Internet Explorer for a direct Internet connection and need to reconfigure it to use your Internet Connection Sharing service, you will need to complete the following steps for Internet Explorer 5 on a Windows 2000 Professional:

1. Start | Programs | Internet Explorer.
2. From Tools | Internet Options | Connections, click "Never dial a connection," and then click LAN Settings.
3. In the Local Area Network (LAN) Settings dialog box, ensure that all three check boxes are cleared. These are "Automatically detect settings," "Use automatic configuration script," and "Use a proxy server."
4. Click OK and Apply.

If you have already set up Internet Explorer for a Proxy Server connection, you will need to deselect these settings in the Local Area Network (LAN) Settings dialog box as described earlier in order to use your Internet Connection Sharing service.

Note that these instructions also apply to workstations if connecting via NAT.

Limitations of ICS

As stated previously, ICS has some limitations in comparison with the NAT routing protocol when it comes to sharing an Internet connection. If these limitations are relevant to your network and/or requirements, you should consider using NAT instead if that fulfills your requirements.

- ICS cannot disable the DHCP allocator service, so the full range of DHCP options are not available to SOHO clients, such as your choice of local DNS and/or WINS server.
- ICS is restricted to using just one Internet address, so you cannot make use of better throughput and availability, cannot disable dynamic port mappings, and cannot reserve a single Internet address for an inbound connection (e.g., Web server).

- ICS cannot be used on a network already using network services such as DHCP, DHCP Relay, domain controllers, routers, etc.
- You cannot scale ICS by running it on two computers within the same segment. You can do this with NAT if you disable the DHCP allocator, which also provides some (not automatic) backup should one computer/connection fail.
- You cannot mix static and dynamic IP addresses on the client workstations.
- You cannot exclude addresses from the DHCP allocator.
- ICS can only work in a single segmented network.
- There is no WINS proxying with ICS, so either use broadcast to resolve NetBIOS names or configure and implement an LMHOSTS file for each workstation.
- You cannot as easily monitor ICS. There is no desktop utility or command to see what addresses have been allocated, what DNS names have been resolved, and what mappings are in memory. The System Event Log is the only indication of what ICS is doing, and the information passed to this is limited.

CERTIFICATION OBJECTIVE 29.03

Network Address Translation

You may prefer to use Windows 2000 Server and install a NAT routing protocol to overcome some of ICS' limitations. However, NAT does require more configuration, which will be covered in the following sections.

Enabling RRAS with NAT on the Server

The Routing and Remote Access Service snap-in utility is available under Start | Programs | Administrative Tools | Routing and Remote Access. This is a service on Windows 2000 Server that needs to be enabled rather than installed, and when it is initially enabled it will invoke the Routing and Remote Access Service Setup Wizard. You may also remember that one of the wizard configuration options was to enable NAT, which when selected will ask whether you wanted to use ICS or NAT.

If you haven't already configured RRAS for remote access and/or routing, you can use the wizard to guide you through setting up NAT. Or, if you are willing to forego your original RRAS configuration, you can disable RRAS and reenable it to invoke the Setup Wizard again.

If you have already set up and configured RRAS (e.g., for remote access) and now want to add support for NAT, you will need to ensure that your RRAS server supports routing, and then add NAT as a routing protocol. The next step is to add the NAT protocol to the interfaces you want to use, and review and, if necessary, configure properties to ensure you have the best setup for your workstations.

The NAT server uses ICMP Router Solicitation and DHCP Discover packets to detect if there are competing DHCP servers or routers on your network. If it gets a positive response, it will attempt to shut down or disable its own services. Ensure these are not running before installing the NAT protocol.

Ensuring RRAS is Configured for Routing

You may not have to complete this step if your server is already configured for routing. If it isn't or you want to, check this, select your server under the Routing and Remote Access Service snap-in, and select Properties. Here you can select whether to support routing and remote access. You must have the Router option selected in order for NAT to work. If you also want to offer remote access on the same server, be sure that the "Remote access server" check box is also selected, as shown in Figure 29-1.

Installing the NAT Protocol

If the Routing and Remote Access snap-in is already opened with the RRAS service enabled, but no NAT support, you need to add NAT as if it were a routing protocol.

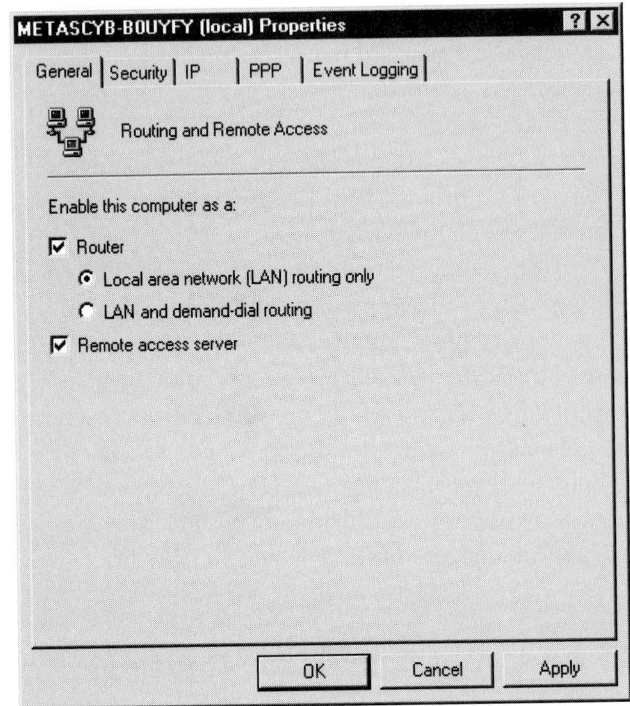

FIGURE 29-1 This RRAS server is configured to allow routing (for NAT) and remote access

EXERCISE 29-4

Installing the NAT Protocol

1. Double-click your server from the left console pane to expand its contents, until you see IP Routing.
2. Right-click on Routing and select General.
3. Select New Routing Protocol and you will see a list of routing protocols for selection, similar to the following illustration.

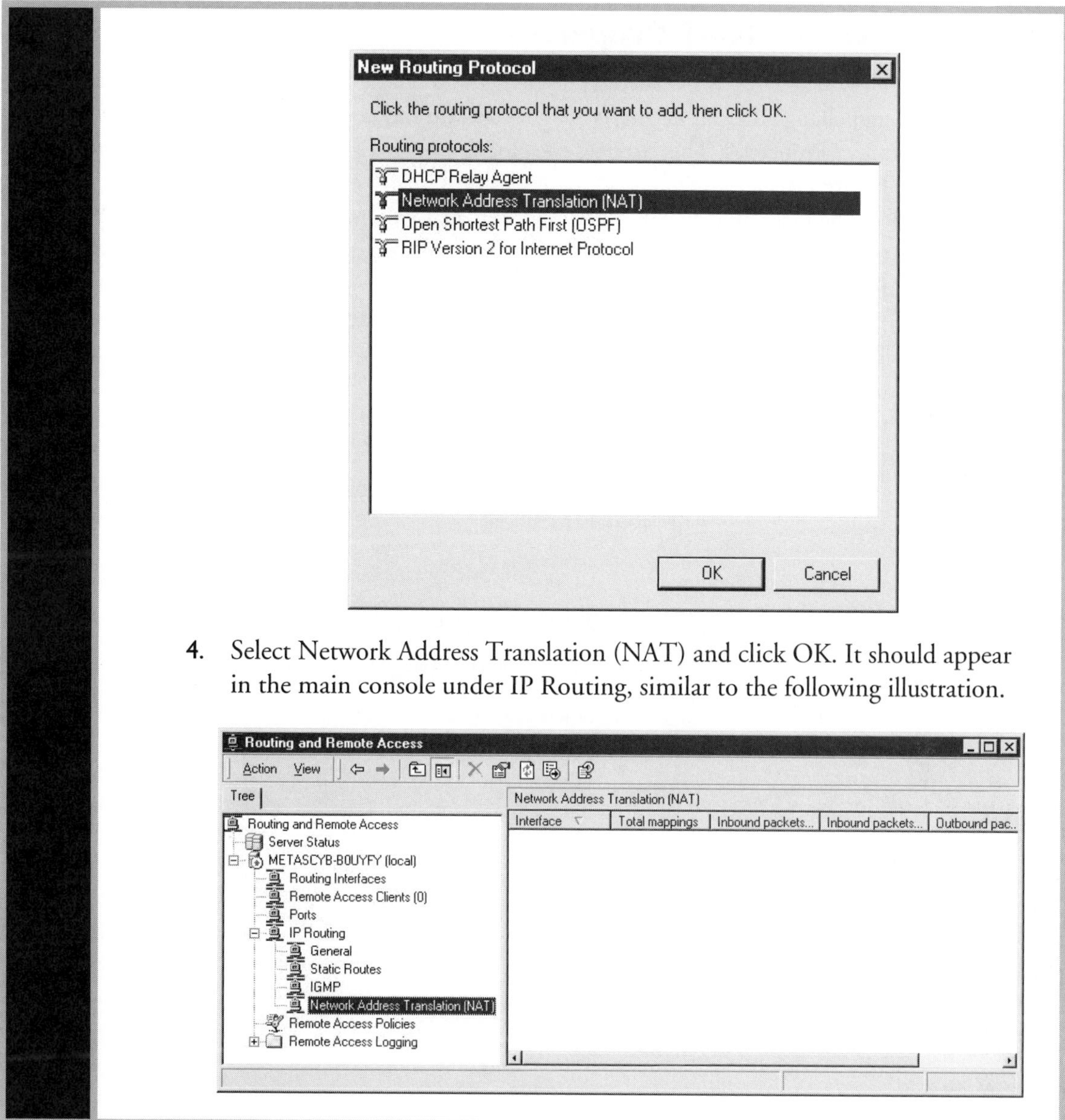

4. Select Network Address Translation (NAT) and click OK. It should appear in the main console under IP Routing, similar to the following illustration.

Configuring Global NAT Properties

Now that NAT is installed, you will need to review its default global properties and change them if necessary. Right-click on the new NAT routing protocol and select Properties. This displays the global properties with four tabs, as shown in Figure 29-2.

The first tab, General, is fairly self-explanatory, and is similar to other components under the RRAS snap-in, which provides various levels of logging in the System Event Log.

The Translation tab deals with both dynamic and static mappings. "Remove TCP mapping after (minutes)" and "Remove UDP mapping after (minutes)" govern how long a dynamic mapping remains in memory. The defaults should suffice for most applications (the 1440 minutes for TCP is 24 hours). Clicking Applications on the same tab allows you to create static mappings for outbound connections similar to the Applications tab option in ICS, allowing you to statically map both IP addresses and ports if needed.

FIGURE 29-2

Global Properties for the NAT routing protocol

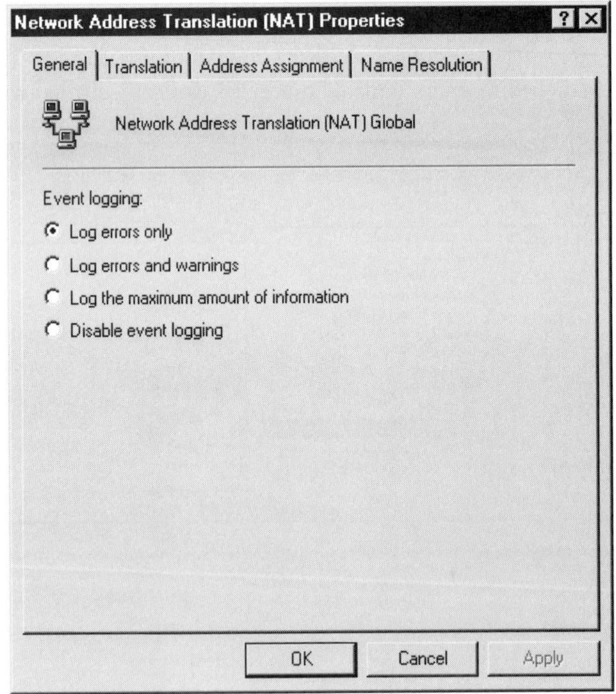

The Address Assignment tab allows you to specify whether the DHCP allocator should be used (this is the "Automatically assign IP addresses by using DHCP" check box), and allows you to specify the private address range that should be used for connecting workstations. If you are using a static address on your internal interface, an appropriate range will be suggested from this setting. Otherwise, the default of 192.168.0.0 with subnet mask of 255.255.255.0 is suggested, but unlike ICS, you can actually change this here. You can also exclude addresses from this range by clicking Exclude. If you want to use a standard DHCP server to take advantage of a different WINS server or some of the advanced DHCP options you get with Windows 2000 DHCP server, uncheck "Automatically assign IP addresses by using DHCP."

exam watch

"Automatically assign IP addresses by using DHCP" refers to the DHCP allocator, a cut-down version of the Windows 2000 DHCP service. If this is unchecked and you do not have a standard DHCP server on your network, NAT will not work.

If you change the default address range, don't forget to also change the IP address of the private interface. It is recommended that you change it to be the first IP address in the configured range, and then exclude this (by clicking Exclude).

The Name Resolution tab allows you to specify whether the NAT server should resolve DNS names to IP addresses for connecting clients. If your Internet DNS server is available only over a dial-up connection, you can additionally specify here which dial-up connection to use. Note that this tab has nothing to do with NetBIOS name resolution.

Configuring NAT Interface Properties

Now that NAT is installed and configured, you need to tell it which interfaces to use and configure their properties.

Adding the Interfaces to NAT

It's not enough to just install NAT, you must tell it which interfaces to use—it won't automatically use NAT on all interfaces as you might expect.

You must add at least two interfaces (for example, one adapter on your private network and another on your Internet modem/adapter). To add interfaces to NAT, select the NAT routing protocol you have just added, right-click and select Add. You will be able to select your interface connections from the next dialog box.

When you have selected your interface, you will immediately be presented with its General Properties options. For your internal connection, select the "Private interface connected to private network" option. For your external connection, select the "Public interface connected to the Internet" and also the check box for "Translate TCP/UDP headers (recommended)."

When you configure your Internet interface as your Public interface connected to the Internet, you will then see two more Properties tabs: Address Pool and Special Ports.

Configuring IP Address Ranges

The Address Pool tab is where you specify multiple public addresses if these have been allocated by your ISP and you wish to use more than one public IP address on this one server. Click Add to specify your start and end range, or if your address range is a power of 2, you can define your range with one address and a subnet mask.

You can also reserve specific IP addresses with the **Reservations** button, which may be applicable if, for example, you want to keep one address separate for an Internet service you want to host on one of the workstations.

Configuring Interface Special Ports

The Special Ports tab allows you to specify static mappings for inbound connections. It corresponds to the Services tab in ICS where you can specify ports and addresses to which packets should be sent when they come in to the server from the Internet—to either the server's Internet address or to one of the reserved addresses in the 8address pool.

Monitoring NAT

When NAT is installed and configured, it should now look similar to Figure 29-3, which shows one internal adapter for the private interface and one external adapter for the Internet connection.

As you can see, you can monitor the NAT service from the Routing and Remote Access Service snap-in by viewing statistics for each NAT interface. The details pane on the right has columns for the number of mappings, inbound/outbound packets

FIGURE 29-3

NAT installed and configured for two interfaces, and working

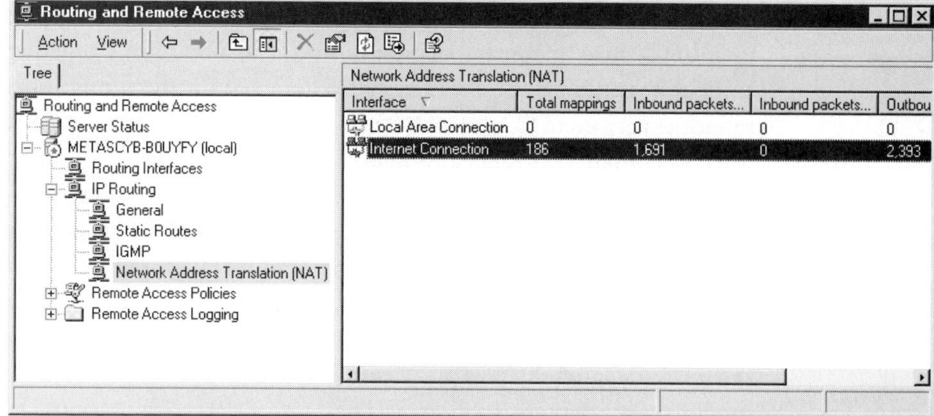

translated or rejected, and so forth, and when NAT is being used, you will see mappings dynamically updated here.

Additionally, the current mappings table can be viewed for each interface—select your Internet interface, then right click on **Show Mappings** to see exactly what protocols, ports, and addresses are mapped in memory.

If you right-click on the **Network Address Translation** (NAT), you can select **Show DHCP Allocator Information** and **Show DNS Proxy Information** to display statistics on these components. Another way to see the DHCP Allocator Information would be to use Netsh with the following command: **routing ip autodhcp show global.**

CERTIFICATION OBJECTIVE 29.04

Troubleshooting ICS and NAT

This chapter has included troubleshooting information by describing how these services work and what their configuration options are. If you have problems when using ICS and NAT, rather than blindly running through a list of possible problems and solutions, think about how these services work so you can better define what is going wrong and at what stage.

First check that you're not asking ICS and NAT to do something that is outside their limitations. For example, you can't run ICS and NAT together on the same computer, and since these services were designed for the simplest networks you cannot expect them to run correctly if in competition with other network services (such as domain controllers, routers, DHCP servers, etc).

Both of these services will only work with the TCP/IP protocol—so be sure it is installed and, particularly for ICS, ensure that a DHCP client component is also installed (this will be automatic for later Windows computers such as Windows 9x, Windows NT, and Windows 2000).

As with any networking service, ensure that basic connectivity is not the problem (for example, ping the computer running ICS or NAT from a workstation, which should check adapters, cabling, and basic TCP/IP configuration). Ensure that your connection to the Internet is functioning correctly (try running an Internet application on the computer running ICS or NAT first, before trying to share that connection).

Common Troubleshooting Issues

When you have verified that the settings are correct and then checked your configuration of ICS or NAT, some other common problems and situations may occur, as discussed in the following sections.

Address Assignment

These relate to connectivity issues—between the client workstation and the ICS/NAT computer, and the ICS/NAT computer and the Internet resource.

- For ICS, ensure that the Enable Internet Connection Sharing option is set under the Sharing tab. For NAT, ensure that the server supports routing, and the NAT routing protocol is installed with at least one internal interface (for your private network connection) and one external interface (for your Internet connection) added to the NAT protocol.
- The default private address range can be changed for NAT, but not for ICS. If you change this, ensure that the private addresses assigned to the clients are in the same network address range as the IP address on the private network interface on the NAT computer. If they are not, your connections will fail.

- Verify that clients have received the correct TCP/IP configuration by typing on the client computers **ipconfig /all** (or **winipcfg** for Win9*x*). The default TCP/IP address assignment will be an address in the 192.168.x.x range (although you can change this with NAT). Additionally, verify that the Default Gateway IP address corresponds to the IP address on the internal interface of the ICS/NAT computer.
- If clients do not receive correct IP address settings, and you have no standard DHCP server on your network, ensure that for NAT you have "Automatically assign IP addresses by using DHCP" set as a global NAT option. There is no equivalent setting for ICS because you cannot disable this in ICS.
- If you have changed the addressing information on the NAT server so it is not using the default of 192.168.x.x, but you are using the DHCP allocator ("Automatically assign IP addresses by using DHCP"), verify that you are using instead one of the other private address ranges (10.0.0.0 with a subnet mask of 255.0.0.0, or 172.16.0.0 with a subnet mask of 255.240.0.0).
- If you have a standard DHCP server on your network and you wish to use this rather than the DHCP allocator with NAT, uncheck "Automatically assign IP addresses by using DHCP," and ensure that your DHCP server is available and configured correctly to offer clients an IP address in the same network range as the internal network adapter on the NAT server. Also ensure that other DHCP options are set correctly; for example, setting your local WINS server if you have one, and the IP address of your local DNS server if it is configured to forward to the Internet.
- Verify that you have entered the correct IP address, subnet mask, default gateway, and DNS server on the Internet interface—these would normally be supplied by your ISP. If you have been given more than one public IP address to use with NAT (you cannot use more than one with ICS), ensure that you have entered these correctly in the Address Pool tab of the NAT Internet Interface properties. If you enter an invalid public address for outbound connections, you will not be able to use that address, and the translation will fail because the connection will fail. If you enter an invalid public address for inbound connections (e.g., you are hosting a Web server for Internet access on one of your client workstations), your Web server will be inaccessible to other people on the Internet.

Network Address Translation

This applies to how applications work through a translated connection.

- If you have specific programs that do not seem to work correctly through ICS or NAT, but standard programs (e.g., Web access) that are okay, check whether this program can be translated. If the program runs from the computer with the direct connection to the Internet, but not from a workstation on the private network, chances are the application uses packets that may not be translatable. However, before giving up on it, check with the vendor about how their application works in a translated environment, because it may just need a certain static mapping defined to work correctly (multiuser Internet games fall into this category).
- For incoming connections (e.g., if you want to host your own Web server on the Internet), ensure that you have a permanent connection to the Internet, your ICS or NAT computer is not turned off, you have defined a correct static mapping for the internal workstation, and the workstation is left switched on with the service running.
- Unless you specifically need a one-to-one mapping of source ports (only possible with NAT if you have multiple public IP addresses), verify that the "Translate TCP/UDP headers (recommended)" check box on the General tab of the properties of the public interface is selected.

Internet Name Resolution

This applies to how "friendly" Internet names are resolved to IP addresses; for example, if a client workstation can connect by an IP address (e.g., http://207.46.130.45), but not through the DNS name (e.g., http://www.microsoft.com).

- Verify that DNS name resolution is enabled; for ICS, this should be automatic. Use ipconfig (or winipcfg on Win9*x* computers) to view the assigned DNS server—it should correspond to the same IP address as the internal interface on the NAT server or ICS computer. If you want to use your own DNS server, you must assign this with a standard DHCP server and disable the name resolution on the NAT server. Also ensure that your DNS server can forward to the Internet for nonlocal names.

Other Configuration Issues

This applies to general configuration issues for applications, the NAT computer, and the network.

- Ensure that client applications (e.g., Internet Explorer) are configured correctly for ICS or NAT, rather than directly connecting to the Internet or via a proxy server.
- On the NAT server, check the status of both interfaces in the RRAS snap-in. Under IP Routing | General, the two interfaces should show their correct IP address and that they are Operational.
- Check that packet filtering on the interface, server, or a firewall/router isn't blocking valid packets. You can easily check whether packet filtering has been enabled on your NAT interfaces by checking under the Filters column under the relevant interface in RRAS under IP Routing | General | <interface connection>.

Miscellaneous

Finally, this applies to help in identifying or eliminating problems.

- Check the System Event Log for any errors or warnings (for example, if it detects any configuration errors or conflicting services). If problems still persist with NAT, try setting logging to the maximum, stop and restart RRAS, and then check the System Event Log again (set maximum logging under NAT properties, General tab).
- Use Network Monitor or an equivalent to capture and analyze the packets as they travel from the workstation to the ICS/NAT computer, and from the ICS/NAT computer to the Internet (if possible). Now that you have a good understanding of how ICS and NAT work, you should be able to verify the packets, or identify where the problems lie.

If such a conflict occurs with ICS, you do not get any errors in the System Event Log—ICS simply won't work.

EXERCISE 29-5

Detecting a Conflicting DHCP Server

How would you know if there was a conflicting DHCP server on your network? Suppose your NAT server had been running fine for about a month, and suddenly you came in one day to discover that some people couldn't access the Internet from their workstations. The reason for this is that someone installed a DHCP server without your knowledge and it is allocating a different network address—which means that workstations will get new IP address assignments from the DHCP server rather than your NAT server. Because the new address range is different from the one on your NAT server, the new leases when obtained will result in workstations being unable to access your NAT server, and hence be unable to access the Internet.

If you can, simulate this by installing a DHCP server on your network, and configure it to use a different address range (if it has the same address range, NAT will continue to work). This exercise explains some of the troubleshooting steps you might go through in a similar situation.

1. Ensure that your NAT server is up and functional—connect one of your workstations to the Internet to verify the NAT connection.
2. Install a DHCP server that assigns a different range of IP addresses to your NAT server's range, and activate the scope.
3. Stop and restart the RRAS service on the NAT server.
4. On one of your workstation clients, release and renew your IP address (e.g., ipconfig /release and then ipconfig/renew).
5. Try to connect your browser to the Internet with Internet Explorer. You should receive a "The page cannot be displayed" message if your connection fails.
6. Check that the NAT server is running and available—the interfaces both say they are operational, so you know it's not an interface failure problem (e.g., modem not functioning).
7. Check that you can access the Internet resource from the NAT server directly, so you know it's not a basic Internet connectivity problem (e.g., ISP link down or Internet resource not available).

8. Check the System Event Log on the NAT server; you should see an entry similar to the one shown in the following illustration that explains the problem. The DHCP allocator (on IP address 10.10.0.1) was disabled in favor of a standard DHCP server with address 192.168.0.1.

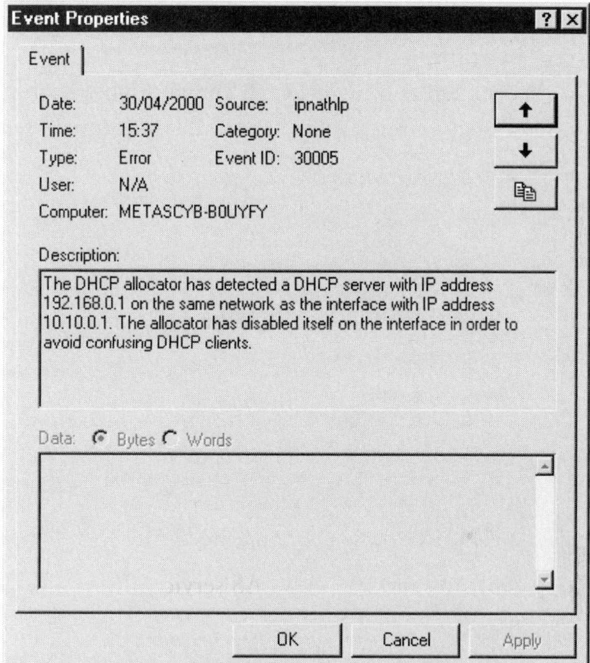

9. You confirm this is the problem on the workstation by viewing the IP address details (e.g., by typing **ipconfig /all**). Your choice now is to either stop the DHCP server if it is not needed, or use the same address range so workstations can connect to the NAT server.

CERTIFICATION SUMMARY

To provide a good understanding of network address translation, this chapter has detailed how it works, with both its benefits and limitations. In Windows 2000, Microsoft offers network address translation in two different forms: ICS and NAT.

Which one you use (if at all) will depend on your requirements. Both have advantages as well as limitations, and it is better to understand thoroughly how they both work rather than make assumptions. You may instinctively feel that ICS should only be used when a server is not available and NAT is always the better choice, but that may not always be the case. To make such assumptions may cost you in the exam when you are asked how each technically works, since they both share many components in common—it is dangerous to dismiss ICS as the "poor relation!"

We looked at how to install and configure both ICS and NAT, and finally offered suggestions on how to troubleshoot these services, should you have problems.

✓ TWO-MINUTE DRILL

Overview of ICS and NAT

- ❑ Network Address Translation is aimed at small, not large networks.
- ❑ Network Address Translation was not available in Windows NT 4.0.
- ❑ The introduction of Network Address Translation has been perceived and pushed as one of the immediate benefits to be gained from using Windows 2000.
- ❑ Internet Connection Sharing and Network Address Translation are two Windows 2000 services that offer an easy-to-configure and simple Internet connection typically suited to a SOHO environment.
- ❑ A SOHO (Small Office or Home Office) network is typically a single-segment network with a few peer-to-peer workstations running TCP/IP, where just one computer has an Internet connection with demand dial-up or a dedicated link.
- ❑ Connections to the Internet are either routed or translated; a translated connection hides the IP addresses on the private network from the Internet.
- ❑ Translated connections are easier to set up and secure in comparison to routed connections; as such, they have low administrative overheads.
- ❑ ICS is less flexible in configuration than NAT, but can be run on Windows 2000 Professional as well as Windows 2000 Server.
- ❑ ICS is configured through Dial-up Network Connections on the Sharing tab; NAT is configured as a routing protocol in the RRAS snap-in.
- ❑ Not all applications are suitable for translation; some will only work with the addition of NAT editors and proxying.
- ❑ Although Microsoft's Proxy Server is usually aimed at medium-sized to large networks, it may be a better choice than ICS/NAT in certain circumstances; for example, it offers better security, central caching facilities, and Internet connectivity for IPX clients.
- ❑ Address translation has the following components: translation, addressing assignment, and name resolution.

- ❑ Automatic address assignment is handled by the DHCP allocator, which is a simplified version of a standard DHCP server.
- ❑ Address translation uses either dynamic or static mappings—you must have a static mapping for incoming connections such as Web hosting, and you must have a dedicated Internet connection.
- ❑ Private addresses cannot directly send or receive packets to or from the Internet, which is why you need a routed or translated connection for Internet access. InterNIC reserved three ranges of addresses for private networks to cater for Class A, B, and C networks; ICS and NAT default to the Class C range of 192.168.0.0.

Internet Connection Sharing

- ❑ Configuration could be as simple as a check box in the Sharing tab: "Enable Internet sharing for this connection."
- ❑ You cannot disable the DHCP allocator, and the private address range will be 192.168.0.0 with a subnet mask of 255.255.255.0.
- ❑ Static mappings are set by clicking Applications on the Sharing tab—specify outbound static mappings with the Applications tab, and inbound static mappings with the Services tab.
- ❑ Although using a dial-up modem is the more common setup with ICS, there is no reason why you cannot use a faster, dedicated connection to the Internet.

Network Address Translation

- ❑ With RRAS configured for routing, you install NAT as a routing protocol with the RRAS snap-in.
- ❑ You have to add at least two interfaces to the NAT protocol: one that is connected to the Internet, and the other that is connected to the private network.
- ❑ Global NAT properties include Event logging levels, defining address assignments, outbound mappings, and DNS name resolution.
- ❑ Inbound static mappings are defined on the external (Internet) interface properties with the Special Ports tab.

Troubleshooting ICS and NAT

- ❑ Verify basic network connectivity from client to computer running ICS or NAT.
- ❑ Verify that the application works directly from the computer hosting ICS or NAT—that should verify your Internet connection configuration details and hardware.
- ❑ Verify that the application supports a translation connection; check with the vendor if in doubt, or in case it needs static mappings to work correctly.
- ❑ Break down the various elements that make up the ICS/NAT service so that you can identify which element is causing the problem. This will enable you to more effectively concentrate on your troubleshooting efforts.
- ❑ Verify that NAT is not in competition with other network services, such as a standard DHCP server, DHCP Relay, or routers. Check the System Event Log for automatic detection.

Part VIII

Windows 2000 Networking Security

CHAPTERS

30

Configuring and Troubleshooting IPSec

CERTIFICATION OBJECTIVES

30.01 Overview of IP Security

30.02 Enabling and Configuring IPSec

30.03 Managing, Monitoring, and Troubleshooting IPSec

✓ Two-Minute Drill

For those who are responsible for the integrity of millions of bytes of data that travel over our networks, much of it sensitive information, security is a real and growing concern. We are inclined to agree with E. R. Stettinius who said, *"happiness has many roots, but none more important than security."*

Computer security is a term that encompasses many different issues, and in designing their new operating system, Microsoft has attempted to cover as many of the bases as possible. Improved authentication technologies, using Kerberos, certificates, Secure Sockets Layer (SSL), and—for compatibility with previous Microsoft operating systems—NTLM, provide for positive confirmation of the user's identity at logon. The new Encrypting File System (EFS) provides the means to encode data stored on disk so that it is not readable to unauthorized users.

But what about the safety of that data as it travels over the network? That's where IP Security (IPSec) comes in. Most network traffic today uses the TCP/IP protocol stack, including that which is sent over the Internet. IPSec allows you to encode data at the Network layer of the popular OSI network communications model to protect it from malicious or accidental access by persons for whom it was not destined.

In this chapter, we will look at what IPSec is, how it works, how it is enabled and configured in Windows 2000, and methods for managing, monitoring, and troubleshooting IP Security on your network.

CERTIFICATION OBJECTIVE 30.01

Overview of IP Security

IP Security, as its name implies, operates at the same layer as the Internet Protocol (IP), and this allows for a high level of protection with little overhead, and with no requirement to change your existing applications.

This is important because, unlike other security methods that operate at higher layers —for example, Secure Sockets Layer (SSL)—IPSec can provide security to applications that do not have to be aware of its existence (SSL works only with application programs that were designed to use SSL). And, unlike security methods that operate at lower layers of the OSI model, such as link layer encryption, IPSec is able to protect data from host to host, even when routed across the Internet or another internetwork. IPSec protects not only the IP protocol, but also those protocols that operate at higher levels in the TCP/IP protocol suite, such as Transmission Control Protocol (TCP), User Datagram Protocol (UDP), and Internet Control Message Protocol (ICMP).

IPSecis a set of protocols that were developed to provide for highly reliable, standardized, cryptographic-based security for data communications over IPv4 and IPv6 (sometimes referred to as IPng).

Elements of IP Security include:

- The Authentication Header (AH) and Encapsulating Security Payload (ESP) protocols, sometimes referred to as "traffic security" protocols
- Cryptographic key management protocols
- Security Policy Database (SPD), which defines the security services
- Security Associations (SA), which are relationships between two or more systems that define how the systems will use the security services

IPSec supports two security association modes: tunnel mode and transport mode. A primary use of the IP Security protocol is to provide more protection for virtual private network (VPN) connections. IPSec works in conjunction with the Layer Two Tunneling Protocol (L2TP)—which is included with Windows 2000 along with the more traditional Point-to-Point Tunneling Protocol (PPTP)—to accomplish this.

IPSec can be used to provide security to workgroups, client/server LANs, and remote access connections.

FROM THE CLASSROOM

Understanding IPSec

You are probably familiar with the way the TCP/IP protocols, as members of a protocol suite, work together to provide network communications. It may help you to understand IPSec if you realize that it, too, is made up of a suite of protocols that work together to provide security for IP communications. Components of IP Security include AH (Authentication Header), ESP (Encapsulating Security Payload), IKE (Internet Key Exchange), ISAKMP (Internet Security Association and Key Management Protocol), Oakley, and transforms (which define the algorithm, key sizes and how they are derived, and the transformation process used to secure the data). A true understanding of IPSec requires that you understand how all these protocols interact with one another and with the other protocols in the TCP/IP suite.

—Debra Littlejohn Shinder, MCSE, MCP+I, MCT

IPSec Terminology

One of the biggest barriers to understanding IPSec and some of the other security features built into Windows 2000 is the avalanche of new terms and unfamiliar acronyms with which you will be bombarded when you start to study in this area.

Before we discuss encryption, IPSec standards, and how it is implemented in Windows 2000, we will attempt to untangle some of this bewildering jungle of words and abbreviations you may not have previously encountered, even as an experienced NT administrator.

Glance through the following list of quick definitions and familiarize yourself with the terminology before you tackle the rest of the chapter.

- **Algorithm** A procedure or formula used to solve a problem.
- **Asymmetric algorithm** A cryptographic algorithm that utilizes a different key for encrypting data from the one used to decrypt the data. Also see *symmetric algorithm.*
- **Authentication** The validation of the identity claimed by an end user or a device.
- **Certificate** A message that contains the digital signature of a trusted third party, called a *certificate authority,* which ensures that a specific public key belongs to a specific user or device.
- **Certificate Authority** A third-party entity that is trusted to sign digital certificates verifying the identity of others.
- **Cipher** The process that turns readable text data into *ciphertext,* which is encrypted data that must be *deciphered* before it is readable.
- **Cryptography** The science of encrypting and decrypting data. The science (and art) of breaking cryptographic code is called *cryptanalysis.*
- **Diffie-Hellman key exchange** Provides a method for two parties to construct a *shared secret* (key) that is known only to the two of them, even though they are communicating via an insecure channel.
- **Digital signature** A string of bits that is added to a message (an encrypted hash), which provides for data integrity and authentication.
- **ESP (Encapsulating Security Payload)** A header used by IPSec when encrypting the contents of a packet.

- **Hash function** A mathematical calculation that produces a fixed-length string of bits, which cannot be reverse-engineered to produce the original.
- **ISAKMP (Internet Security Association and Key Management Protocol)** An IPSec protocol required as part of the IPSec implementation, which provides a framework for Internet key management.
- **MAC (Message Authentication Code)** A cryptographically generated fixed-length code associated with a message in order to ensure the authenticity of the message (a digital signature is a *public key MAC).*
- **Private key** A digital code used to decrypt data, which is kept secret and works in conjunction with a published *public key.*
- **Public key** A digital code used to encrypt or decrypt data, which is published and made available to the public, used in conjunction with a secret *private key.*
- **Public Key Infrastructure (PKI)** A key and certificate management system that is trusted.
- **Secret key** Also called a *shared secret,* a digital code shared between two parties and used for both encrypting and decrypting data.
- **Symmetric algorithm** A cryptographic algorithm that uses the same key to both encrypt and decrypt, also called a *secret key* algorithm. See *asymmetric algorithm.*

on the job

IPSec should be implemented as one part of an overall security policy. Never rely on just one line of defense to protect your network, and remember that IP Security offers protection of data only in very specific circumstances—when it is transmitted over the network using the Internet Protocol. Other considerations in designing a strong network security plan include password security, encryption of data on the hard disk—which can be done using EFS in Windows 2000—and physical security of servers, workstations, cable/media, and connectivity devices.

Basics of Encryption

IPSec uses *encryption algorithms* to protect data. What is encryption, and how did modern encryption technologies develop? It might be useful to take a brief look at the history of cryptography and various encryption methods of the past and present.

A (Very) Brief History of Cryptography

The science of cryptography is an old one; some sources estimate that it goes back at least 4000 years, to the cryptic hieroglyphics used to decorate the tombs of ancient Egyptian rulers and ancient Chinese ideographs. It is perhaps human nature to want to keep secrets—what child hasn't yearned for some form of the infamous secret decoder ring, or an "invisible ink" that can only be seen by the intended recipient, or experimented with speaking "pig latin" so the uninitiated could not (at least in theory) understand him? And for better or worse, the innate desire to uncover the secrets of others also seems to be inborn.

The Origins of Encryption In early cultures, most information was imparted through the spoken word, in a face-to-face transaction. You had to be on the lookout for eavesdroppers, but you could be fairly sure to whom you were speaking. However, as societies developed sophisticated means of communication, more and more information was transferred by nonverbal methods. Written communications were more vulnerable to interception by unauthorized third parties, so ways had to be devised to disguise the meaning of confidential messages.

The first encryption methods were crude and, although often effective at protecting written communications from the prying eyes of casual observers, could be "cracked" relatively easily by knowledgeable—or merely persistent—persons.

Simple Encoding Methods One of the simplest "codes," usually discovered and delighted in by elementary school children, involves transposing letters of the alphabet and/or replacing letters with numbers. Under the former method, for instance, each letter of the alphabet would be "moved forward" by five letters, so that an "f" in the encoded message, for instance, represented an "a" in the real message. It's easy to construct a "key" to decipher this simple form of encryption, as seen in Table 30-1.

TABLE 30-1 A Simple Form of Encryption

a	b	c	d	e	f	g	h	i	j	k	l	m	n	o	p	q	r	s	t	u	v	w	x	y	z
f	g	h	i	j	k	l	m	n	o	p	q	r	s	t	u	v	w	x	y	z	a	b	c	d	e

This simple key makes it easy to create a message that says:

gzd utyfytjs

which makes no sense to someone who doesn't have the "key." To another who is working from the same table, however, it's obvious that I'm saying:

buy potatoes

The latter method is just as simple—a number is assigned to each letter of the alphabet; for example, we could start numbering with "a" as "8." In this case, our "buy potatoes" message would be encoded as 9-28-32 23-22-27-8-27-22-12-26. Again, without the key, it's meaningless, and with the key, it's a simple matter of substitution.

Added Complexity Increases Security The problem with these "secret codes" is obvious: Someone who has enough patience can eventually hit on the correct substitution process (or *algorithm*), and if our low-tech hacker ever got his or her hot little hands on a decrypted message, the entire key would be readily reconstructed, and all future communications that used it could be deciphered.

This led to the creation of more complex encryption methods. For instance, in order to decode a numerical message, you might follow this procedure:

1. Subtract 7 from the encoded number.
2. Go to the page of the Bible represented by the result.
3. Add 3 to the original number.
4. Count the words on the page and go to the one represented by the result in step 3.
5. The last letter in that word represents the character in the actual message that corresponds to the original number.

The key (literally) is knowing the precise steps of the formula. So long as this is kept secret and known only to the sender and the recipient, there would be a certain amount of security provided by this encoding method. Of course, it is important that both parties' versions of the Bible match exactly; even if both use the King James version, the method falls apart if the pages are not printed precisely alike.

Modern Encryption Methods

All of the early encryption methods described so far can be referred to as *secret key* technologies. The same key (substitution formula or set of steps) is used to encrypt and then decrypt the information. When the same key is used to both encrypt and decrypt the data, it is referred to as a *symmetric key* encryption method.

Secret Key Encryption Secret key encryption methods are still used today. The widely used Data Encryption Standard (DES) uses secret key algorithms. Standard DES operates on 64-bit blocks of data, and uses a series of complex steps (even more complex than our Bible-assisted method) to transform the original input bits to encoded output bits.

In secret key encryption, the key is called a *shared secret* because two (or more) people know the key. The problem with *this* comes in if you want to send encoded messages to more than one person. If you used one of the keys discussed earlier to send secret messages to Jim, and then you wish to encode a message to send to Jack, you'll probably need to come up with a different key. If you use the same one you know and are used to, Jim will be able to read the messages that pass between you and Jack, *and* Jack will be able to read all the past and future messages sent to Jim. Having to remember and use all these different keys could become a real pain.

Enter a new type of encryption technology: *asymmetric encryption.* This is popularly used in *public key encryption.*

Public Key Encryption Doesn't *sound* very secure, does it? If the key is public, won't any and everyone be able to decrypt your data? Certainly "secret key technology" sounds much more secure than "public key technology." However, this is one of those instances where names can be deceiving. Actually public key, or *asymmetric* encryption methods, are more secure than secret key methods. This is because public key technologies actually involve the use of not one, but *two* keys. The "public" key is only half of the equation. A better term for public key encryption would be "public/private key encryption."

Three methods of Public Key Encryption are as follows:

- **Confidential Data Exchange** Think of the method used to secure safety deposit boxes at banks. When you rent a box, you have a key to it—but your key alone won't unlock it. The bank officer also has a key, but again, that key by itself isn't of much value. When *both* keys are used, however, the authorized person can access the box. Likewise, with public key encryption technologies, it takes two keys to tango. One is the public key, which is made available to all those who want to send you an encrypted message. They can all use that public key to encrypt their messages, but they *can't* use it to decrypt them—only your private key, which you keep secret, can do that. This is called a *confidential data exchange.*

- **Authenticated Data Exchange** The only problem with the preceding scenario is that there is no assurance that the person who used your public key to encrypt and send you a message is really whomever he or she claims to be. How can we ensure that?

  Well, let's look at using the public and private keys in a slightly different way: What if the sender encrypted the message using his or her *private* key, and then you decrypted it using his or her public key? What would this accomplish? We get the same confidentiality of the data as with the first method, but since presumably only the sender has the private key, we can be confident of his identity. Now we have an *authenticated data exchange.*
- **Double the Protection** If we want the benefits of both methods, we can combine them and double the protection. That is, the sender would encrypt the message with the recipient's public key, then sign it again with the sender's private key.

exam Watch

A property of a security system that ensures the identity of the sender and prevents that sender from later being able to deny having sent the message is called nonrepudiation.

Key Generation Of course, the mechanisms that are used to generate these keys are much more complex than our five-step process discussed earlier.

One method that is used to create secret session keys that allow the communicating parties to share a secret key known only to them is called the *Diffie-Hellman algorithm.*

Public/private *key pairs* are generated by complicated algorithms such as the RSA algorithm (named after its creators, Ron Rivest, Adi Shamir, and Leonard Adelman).

on the Job

Best practice is for the private key to be generated by the person identified by the key, and for it to never leave the possession of that person. Public keys should be distributed by trusted third parties (certificate authorities) to ensure that they belong to the claimed user if authentication—rather than just confidentiality—is required.

Data Encryption Standard (DES) The most commonly used encryption algorithm used with IPSec is the Data Encryption Standard (DES) algorithm. DES is the current U.S. government standard for encryption. The DES algorithm is an example of a symmetric encryption algorithm. A symmetric encryption algorithm has each side of the communication employ the same "secret key" for encryption and decryption. This is in contrast to a public key infrastructure, where two different keys are used. The public key approach is referred to as "asymmetric" encryption.

DES works on 64-bit "blocks" of data. The DES algorithm converts 64 input bits from the original data into 64 encrypted output bits. While DES starts with 64-bit keys, only 56 bits are actually used in the encryption process. The remaining 8 bits are used for parity.

A stronger version of DES is also available for use in Windows 2000 IPSec. This is called 3DES, or *Triple DES.* Triple DES processes each block three times, which increases the degree of complexity over that found in DES.

Cipher Block Chaining (CBC) Because the blocks of data are encrypted in 64-bit chunks, there must be a way to "chain" these blocks together. The chaining algorithm will define how the combination of the unencrypted text, the secret key, and the encrypted text (also known as *ciphertext*) will be combined to send to the destination host.

DES can be combined with Cipher Block Chaining (CBC) to prevent identical messages from looking the same. This DES-CBC algorithm will make each ciphertext message appear different by using a different "initialization vector" (IV). The IV is a random block of encrypted data that begins each chain. In this fashion, we are able to make each message's ciphertext appear different, even if we were to send the exact same message a hundred times.

IPSec Standards

In the past decade, communications over the Internet and other large networks that use the TCP/IP protocols has increased exponentially. As more data flows across these public and corporate networks, it has become more important to devise methods of providing security for information that is intended to remain private.

IPSec is actually a collection of open standards, developed by the Internet Engineering Task Force (IETF), for providing secure communications over IP networks. The IETF is a huge international community of network designers, operators, vendors, and researchers, which was established by the Internet Architecture Board (IAB) and is organized into *working groups* devoted to various Internet-related topics.

The IPSec working group issues RFCs (Requests for Comments), which are documents that propose and establish standards for protocol implementation. A collection of their working papers on IPSec can be found at:

www.ietf.org/ids.by.wg/ipsec.html

RFCs

Numerous RFCs have been published addressing various aspects of IP Security. All published RFCs can be accessed via the Web site of the RFC Editor, who is funded by the Internet Society (ISOC) and is responsible for their official publication. The following grid defines some of the more important IPSec-related RFCs.

SCENARIO & SOLUTION	
Where can you find the IP Security Document Roadmap?	RFC 2411
Where can you find standards relating to the IP Authentication Header (AH)?	RFC 2402
Where can you find information about the Encapsulating Security Payload (ESP)?	RFC 2496
Where can you find an RFC relating to the Internet Security Association and Key Management Protocol (ISAKMP)?	RFC 2407
Which RFC addresses the Internet Key Exchange (IKE)?	RFC 2409

IPSec Resources

The IETF produces the IPSec Working Group news on the Web, accessible at www.cs.arizona.edu/xkernel/www/ipsec/ipsec.html.

For general discussions about IP Security, you can also join the IPSec mailing list. To subscribe, send e-mail to ipsec-request@lists.tislabs.com. Or check the IPSec archives at ftp://ftp.tis.com/pub/lists/ipsec or ftp.ans.net/pub/archive/ipsec.

IPSec Architecture

IPSec defines a network security architecture that allows secure networking for the enterprise, allowing you to secure packets at the network layer. By performing its services at the network layer, IPSec secures information in a manner that is transparent to the user and to the protocols that lie above the transport layer. IPSec provides "Layer 3" protection.

The IPSec security architecture provides an "end to end" security model. This means that only the "endpoints" of a communication need to be IPSec aware. In other words, computers and devices that serve as intermediaries of message transfer do not need to be IPSec enabled. This allows the administrator of a Windows 2000 network to implement IPSec for end-to-end security over diverse network infrastructures, including the Internet. Network devices that are in between the sending and receiving computers, such as bridges, switches, and routers, can be oblivious to IPSec.

This end-to-end capability can be extended to different communication scenarios, including:

- Client to client
- Gateway to gateway (also called "tunneling")

Transport vs. Tunnel Mode

IPSec can operate in two different modes, depending upon the scope of the secure communication. These are known as *transport mode* and *tunnel mode.*

Transport Mode When IPSec is used to protect communications between two clients (for example, two computers on the same LAN), the machines can utilize

IPSec in what is known as *transport mode*. In this example, the endpoints of the secure communication are the source machine and the destination host.

exam Watch

In transport mode, both clients must use TCP/IP as their network protocol.

Tunnel Mode The second communication mode is a gateway-to-gateway solution. IPSec protects information that travels through a transit network (such as the Internet). Packets are protected as they leave the exit gateway, and then decrypted or authenticated at the destination network's gateway.

When gateways represent the endpoints of the secure communication, IPSec is operating in *tunnel mode*. A tunnel is created between the gateways, and client-to-client communications are encapsulated in the tunnel protocol headers.

Tunnels can be created using IPSec as the tunneling protocol, or you can combine IPSec with L2TP (Layer Two Tunneling Protocol) to establish a virtual private network (VPN) connection. In this case, it is L2TP rather than IPSec that creates the tunnel.

exam Watch

In tunnel mode, the host and destination computers do not employ IPSec, and can use any LAN protocol supported by IPSec (IPX/SPX, AppleTalk, NetBEUI, TCP/IP).

IPSec Protocols

The IPSec protocols used by Windows 2000 to provide security for IP packets consist of the following:

- Authentication Header (AH)
- Encapsulating Security Payload (ESP)

We will examine each of these protocols and how they work.

AH

The Authentication Header ensures data integrity and authentication. The AH does not encrypt data, and therefore provides no confidentiality, but does protect the data from modification. When the AH protocol is applied in transport mode, the Authentication Header is inserted between the original IP header and the TCP or UDP header, as depicted in Figure 30-1.

FIGURE 30-1

Datagram after the application of AH in transport mode

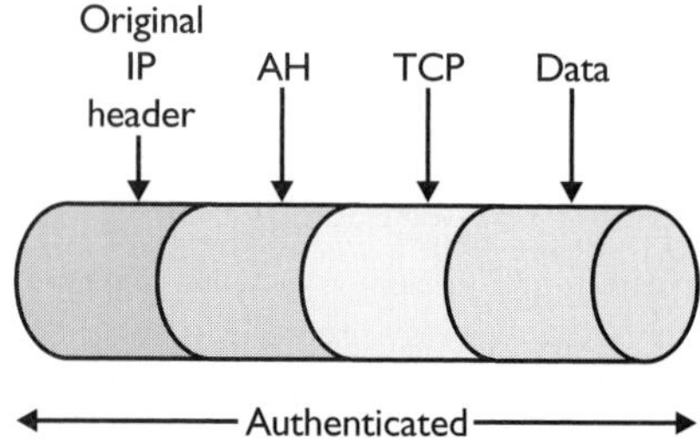

Note that the entire datagram is authenticated using AH.

The Authentication Header signs the entire packet, using HMAC (Hash-based Message Authentication Code) algorithms. This ensures that the source and destination addresses in the IP header, as well as the data, cannot be changed without invalidating the packet.

exam Watch

Microsoft refers to AH as a "medium security method," and recommends it when your network requires standard—but not high—levels of security.

ESP

The Encapsulating Security Payload (ESP) protocol, like AH, provides authentication, integrity, and anti-replay to an IP datagram—but it does more; it also provides *confidentiality*. Note that, although authentication services are available with ESP, the original IP header (prior to application of the ESP header) is not authenticated by ESP.

FIGURE 30-2

The ESP header in transport mode, used in conjunction with AH

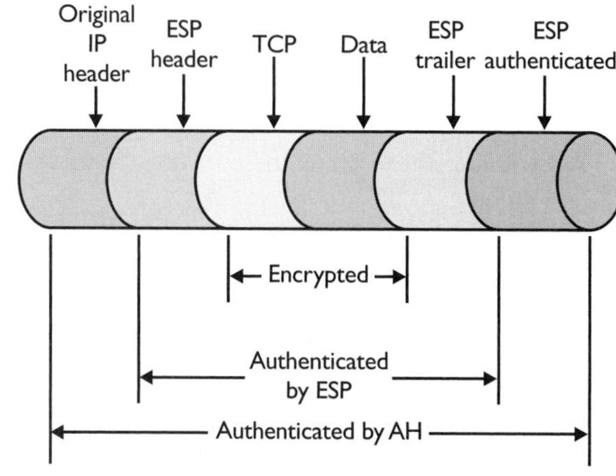

The ESP header, in transport mode, is placed between the original header and the TCP header, as seen in Figure 30-2.

As you can see, only the TCP header, data, and ESP trailer are encrypted. Unlike AH, ESP normally does not sign the entire packet (the exception is in tunneling mode). This means there is no protection provided for the IP header.

If authentication of the original IP header is required, you can combine and use AH and ESP together, as you saw in Figure 30-2.

Microsoft recommends that ESP be used in high security environments, where encryption of the data is required. To use ESP and AH together, to provide security for both the data and the IP header (and the addressing information it contains), you must create a *custom security method* in Windows 2000's security method configuration.

See the section on enabling and configuring IPSec later in this chapter for information on how to select AH, ESP, or a combination (customized) as your security method.

Security Negotiation

Security negotiation ensures that the authentication and encryption methods used by the sending and receiving computers are the same. If they are not, reliable communication cannot take place. To provide for compatibility between the security systems being used, there must be protocols in place to negotiate the security methods. IPSec uses ISAKMP and IKE (discussed later in this chapter) to define the way in which *security associations* are negotiated. Let's look at what security associations are, and how they work.

Security Associations

Security Associations (SAs) define IPSec secured links. One of the tasks of IPSec is to establish a Security Association between the two computers desiring to communicate with one another securely. This could include:

- Communications between remote nodes and the network
- Communications between two networks
- Communications between two computers on a local area network (LAN)

Each Security Association is defined for one unidirectional flow of data, most commonly from one single point to another. Whatever traffic flows over a specific SA will be treated the same.

The two communicating computers must agree on the method for exchanging and protecting information before secure communications can take place. Here is how that works:

1. The computer that is initiating the communication will transmit an *offer list* to the receiving computer, which contains a list of potential levels of security.
2. The receiving computer can accept the offer, or reject it. If the latter, it transmits a message back to the sender that notifies the sender that no offer was accepted.

Security Association Types One of two types of Security Associations can be established:

- A *soft SA* is established if the active security policies are set to permit unsecured communications with computers that are not IPSec-capable.
- A *hard SA* is established if the active policies are compatible. A hard SA is a secured security association.

Number of Security Associations A separate SA is established for outgoing and incoming messages, necessitating at least two security associations for each IPSec connection. In addition, a single SA can be applied to either AH or ESP, but not both. If both are used, then two more security associations are created.

Security Parameters Index A Security Parameters Index (SPI) tracks each SA. The SPI uniquely identifies each SA as separate and distinct from any other IPSec connections current on a particular machine. The index itself is derived from the destination host's IP address and a randomly assigned number. When a computer communicates with another computer via IPSec, it checks its database for an applicable SA. It then applies the appropriate algorithms, protocols, and keys, and inserts the SPI into the IPSec header.

Key Exchange

The first phase of security negotiation is *key exchange*. IPSec standards support either manual or automated key exchange, but large-scale implementations necessitate automated key exchange.

Automated Key Management uses a combination of the Internet Security Association Key Management Protocol and the Oakley Protocol (ISAKMP/Oakley). This combination of protocols is often referred to collectively as the Internet Key Exchange (IKE). The IKE is responsible for exchange of "key material" (groups of numbers that will form the basis of new key), session keys, SA negotiation, and authentication of peers participating in an IPSec interaction. During this exchange, the Oakley protocol protects the identities of the negotiating parties.

There are two phases involved in the key exchange:

- Establishment of the ISAKMP SA
- Establishment of the IPSec SA

Establishing the ISAKMP Security Association The steps involved in establishing the ISAKMP SA are:

1. The computers establish a common encryption algorithm (either DES or 3DES).
2. A common hash algorithm is agreed upon—either Message Digest 5 (MD5) or Secure Hashing Algorithm (SHA1).
3. An authentication method is established. (Depending on policy, this can be Kerberos, public-key encryption, or prearranged shared secret).
4. A Diffie-Hellman group is agreed upon in order to allow the Oakley protocol to manage the key exchange process.

Establishing the IPSec Security Association In the second phase of key exchange, Security Associations are negotiated for security protocols (AH, ESP, or both).

After a secure channel has been established by the creation of the ISAKMP SA, the IPSec SA(s) will be established. The process is similar, except that a separate IPSec SA is created for each protocol (AH or ESP) and for each direction of traffic (inbound and outbound). Each IPSec SA must establish the following:

- Encryption algorithm
- Hash algorithm
- Authentication method

Each IPSec SA uses a different shared key than that negotiated during the ISAKMP SA. Depending on how policy is configured, the IPSec SA works by repeating the Diffie-Hellman exchange, or by reusing "key material" derived from the original ISAKMP SA. All data transferred between the two computers will take place in the context of the IPSec SA.

Data Protection

IPSec uses authentication to ensure that data is not changed, and encryption to protect the confidentiality of the data. The Windows 2000 implementation of IPSec can use DES (Data Encryption Standard), or it can use a strong encryption algorithm such as 3DES, which provides a higher level of security than DES because it uses a longer key.

The High Encryption Pack needs to be installed to use 3DES, and if the computer does not have the High Encryption Pack installed and receives a policy with 3DES settings, it will revert to DES.

DES Standard DES is 64-bit encryption. The key used by the algorithm is 64 bits long, and 56 bits are selected randomly, while 8 bits are for parity. (There is also a 40-bit version of DES, but it basically exists only to comply with U.S. export regulations).

3DES This stronger version of DES can be supported by IPSec policies, but the Windows 2000 High Encryption Pack (HEP) must be installed. The HEP provides for 128-bit encryption, and affects not only IPSec, but file encryption on the disk, NDIS connections, SSL, and Terminal services. The High Encryption Pack can be downloaded from the Microsoft Web site (before installing, note that there is no provision for uninstalling the HEP).

Use, and especially export, of strong encryption is subject to federal regulations. For more information, see the Department of Commerce Commercial Encryption Export Controls Web site at

www.bxa.doc.gov/encryption

How IPSec Works

Let's look now at some of the important components of IP Security and how it actually works. In this section, we'll discuss IPSec authentication, the IPSec driver, the IPSec filter list, and the ISAKMP service in Windows 2000.

IPSec Authentication

Authentication methods are the means used by IPSec to define the way in which identities are verified. In order for two computers to communicate securely using IPSec, they must have at least one authentication method in common. A computer can have multiple authentication methods, and configuring multiple methods will increase the chances that, in attempting communication with another computer, there will be a common method. We will explore how IPSec rules affect authentication methods a little later in this chapter.

The authentication methods that can be used by IPSec include:

- Kerberos v5
- Public Key certificates
- Preshared keys

We will briefly discuss the characteristics of each.

Kerberos v5 Version 5 of the Kerberos security protocol is the default authentication method in Windows 2000. Client computers that belong to a trusted domain can use the Kerberos authentication method, which is based on a *shared secret,* as long as they are running the Kerberos v5 protocol. They do not have to be Windows 2000 machines to use this method.

Public Key Certificates A second authentication method involves the use of public key certificates in conjunction with a trusted certificate authority (CA). An advantage of this method is that it can be used with computers that are not running the Kerberos v5 protocol. Public key certificates are appropriately used for remote access communications or those that go across the public Internet.

A viable public key infrastructure includes the following three elements:

- Secret private keys
- Freely available public keys
- A trusted third party to confirm the authenticity of the public key

The trusted third party is required to digitally sign each party's public key. This is to prevent people from providing a public key that they "claim" is theirs, but is in fact not; it is the public key of the person they are impersonating.

Preshared Keys The third option is to use a *preshared key,* which is a secret key that was agreed upon previously by the two users conducting the transaction. This method, like the public key certificate, has the advantage of working with computers that are not running Kerberos v5. The disadvantage is that IPSec must be configured, on both sides, to use the specified preshared key. However, this simple method is also appropriate for non-Windows 2000 computers, and works well in cases where only authentication protection is required.

The process for authenticating using a preshared key is as follows:

- The sending computer can hash a piece of data (a challenge) using the shared key and forward this to the destination computer.
- The destination computer will receive the challenge, perform a hash using the same secret key, and send this back.
- If the hashed results are identical, both computers share the same secret and are thus authenticated.

The ISAKMP Service

ISAKMP is used in conjunction with session key establishment protocols like Oakley, which is a leading *key management* method. The ISAKMP service is responsible for managing the exchange of the cryptographic keys used in IPSec communications, and Oakley generates and manages the authenticated keys used to secure the information.

ISAKMP centralizes the management of security associations, which in turn reduces connection time.

IPSec Driver

The IPSec driver, along with the other IPSec components, is incorporated into the Windows 2000 TCP/IP protocol. If the driver becomes corrupted, it can be reinstalled by removing and reinstalling TCP/IP. The IPSec driver is the component that first checks the *IP filter list* in the policy that is active, and notifies the ISAKMP service to begin security negotiations.

exam Watch

To force the restart of the IPSec driver, you can restart the* IPSec Policy Agent*, using the Services console in the Administrative Tools menu.

IPSec Packet Handling

Let's look now at how IPSec handles data at the packet level. A typical IPSec transaction involves the following steps:

1. The IPSec driver receives the filter list.
2. The driver inspects each packet (both inbound and outbound traffic) and compares it to the filter list.
3. The driver applies the filter to any matching packets.
4. The packet is allowed through (received or sent) if the filter action allows transmission. The packet is discarded if the filter action blocks transmission.

The security association (SA) that has been negotiated is used to process the incoming and outgoing packets. If there are multiple SAs configured, the SPI (Security Parameters Index) is used to determine which SA goes with the packet.

IPSec Filter Lists

IPSec uses *IP filter lists,* each of which contains one or more filters. An IP filter defines IP addresses and types of IP traffic. The administrator can specify the source or destination address, and/or the traffic type to be filtered. Each IP packet will be checked against the filter list.

IP Filters *Inbound filters* are, as the name suggests, applied to incoming IP packets, while *outbound filters* are applied to IP packets being sent out onto the network. The filter list triggers a security negotiation when a match is made to the source or destination address or the type of IP traffic.

Filter Settings Filter settings include the following:

- **Source/destination address** This is the IP address of the sending and receiving computer. It can be one IP address or a group of addresses, a subnet, a network, or multiple networks.
- **Protocol** This is the protocol being used to transfer the packet. The default is TCP/IP and all related protocols in the TCP/IP suite.

- **Source/destination port for TCP or UDP** The default setting is all ports, but the administrator can configure this setting to specify only a particular port(s).

In the section "Enabling and Configuring IPSec" later in this chapter, you will learn how to configure IP filter settings in Windows 2000.

IPSec and SNMP

The Simple Network Management Protocol (SNMP) is a protocol included in most implementations of the TCP/IP suite, which is used to monitor and manage networks and network devices. When the SNMP service is running and IPSec is used, SNMP messages will be blocked unless you configure a rule in your current active IPSec policy to prevent this.

In order to do this, the IP filter list needs to specify the source and destination addresses of the SNMP management systems and agents for the UDP protocol on ports 161 and 162 (inbound and outbound). Two filters will have to be configured to accomplish this, one for each port. *Filter action* should be configured to permit the traffic that matches the filter list. In this way, the SNMP packets will be allowed through.

IPSec and L2TP

One of the new features in Windows 2000 is the ability to establish a secure virtual private network (VPN) connection using L2TP (the Layer Two Tunneling Protocol) in combination with IPSec for improved security. Windows NT 4.0 supported only the Point-to-Point Tunneling Protocol (PPTP) for virtual private networking.

exam Watch

Windows 2000 supports both L2TP and PPTP for VPN connections, but IPSec can be used only with L2TP.

A secure VPN is created by using L2TP to establish the tunnel through which the data is transferred, and IPSec to provide security to that data.

When to Use L2TP

Instances in which you might use the L2TP/IPSec combination (referred to as *L2TP over IPSec)* include:

- Providing a secure link between remote clients and a corporate network (End to End security).

- Providing a secure connection for company's offices located at multiple sites (Secure tunneling).

The configuration properties sheet for L2TP is used, instead of IPSec policies, to configure IP security over the VPN connection. This creates a *virtual private network* within the public network. L2TP determines authentication, and the IP filters and filter lists are set, dynamically, during the time the connection is active.

You can provide *end-to-end encryption* for the data in this way. That is, the data is encrypted from the remote client to the destination host. This differs from the *link encryption* provided by Microsoft Point-to-Point Encryption (MPPE), used by PPTP in establishing VPNs.

exam Watch

In order to use L2TP over IPSec, both the Layer Two Tunneling Protocol and IPSec must be supported by both the VPN client and the VPN server.

How L2TP Security Works

L2TP over IPSec provides data security by using both encryption and *encapsulation.* Encapsulation refers to the enclosing of one thing inside another. In this context, we're talking about putting one data structure within another structure so that the first data structure is hidden temporarily. An encapsulated packet or frame of data is recognized according to the outer headers.

This concept is the basis for the term *tunneling,* which refers to the process of hiding the original packet inside a new packet. The *tunnel* is the path through which the encapsulated packets travel across the network.

Two-Tiered Encapsulation Packets are encapsulated twice, first by L2TP and then by IPSec, so that we end up with "encapsulation inside encapsulation."

- **L2TP encapsulation** First the PPP frame (the IP datagram, or an IPX datagram or NetBEUI frame) is encapsulated, or wrapped, inside an L2TP header. A UDP header is also added.
- **IPSec encapsulation** The L2TP packet created by the preceding process is then wrapped by an IPSec ESP header and trailer, an IPSec authentication trailer, and finally an IP header.

Encryption IPSec encrypts the L2TP message. This is done using keys that have been created during the IPSec authentication process. Although you can establish an L2TP connection that is not encrypted (and therefore does not use IPSec), this is not recommended if you are transmitting over the public Internet. The PPP frame would then be sent in plain text and the data would not be secure.

The following scenarios and solutions grid answers some questions about the encryption levels that can be configured when using IPSec with L2TP for VPN connections.

The L2TP settings are configured through Network and Dial-up Connections on the VPN client. For the VPN server, and for gateway-to-gateway connections, the configuration is done via the RRAS console.

SCENARIO & SOLUTION	
If you configure L2TP for "no encryption," does this mean IPSec will not be used?	No. The "no encryption" security level still uses IPSec to negotiate AH, which authenticates the IP header. AH can ensure authentication and integrity.
What happens if you set L2TP for "optional encryption?" What determines whether encryption is used for a particular communication?	When L2TP is configured for "optional encryption," the security level used by IPSec will depend on the request or requirements of the other computer with which you are communicating.
What is the effect of configuring L2TP's security level as "required encryption?"	Secured communication will be required; the computer will not allow unsecured communication.

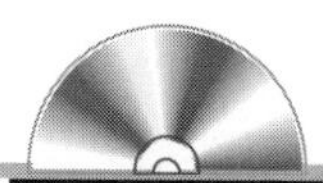

EXERCISE 30-1

Setting the Encryption Level on a VPN Client

To set the security level for a VPN client, perform the following steps:

1. From the Start | Settings | Network and Dial-up Connections folder, select the VPN connection that you wish to configure, as shown in the following illustration.

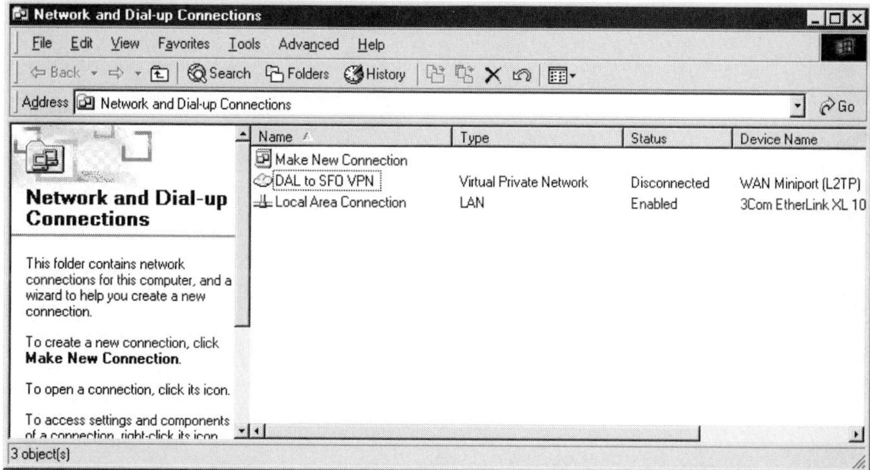

2. Right-click on the selected VPN connection name and choose Properties from the context menu.
3. On the Properties sheet, select the Security tab, as shown in the following illustration.

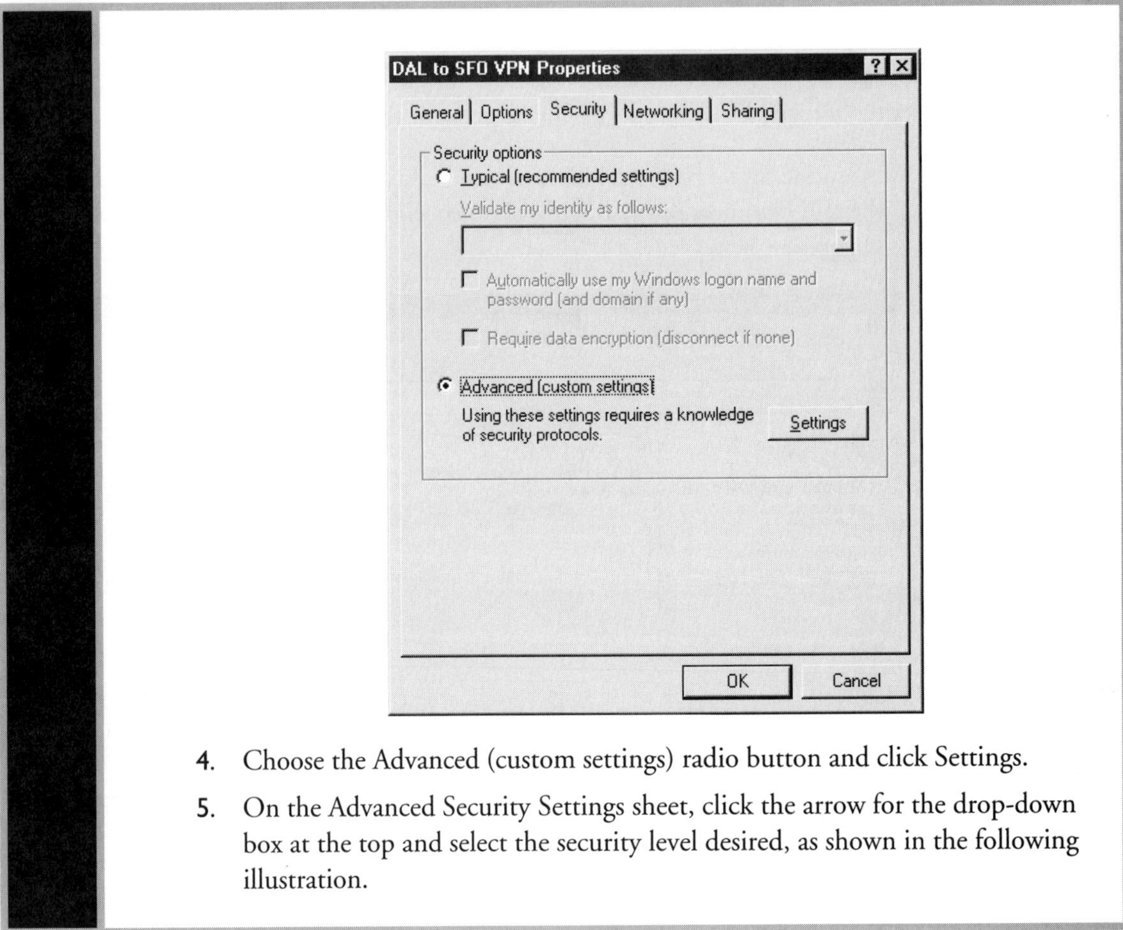

4. Choose the Advanced (custom settings) radio button and click Settings.
5. On the Advanced Security Settings sheet, click the arrow for the drop-down box at the top and select the security level desired, as shown in the following illustration.

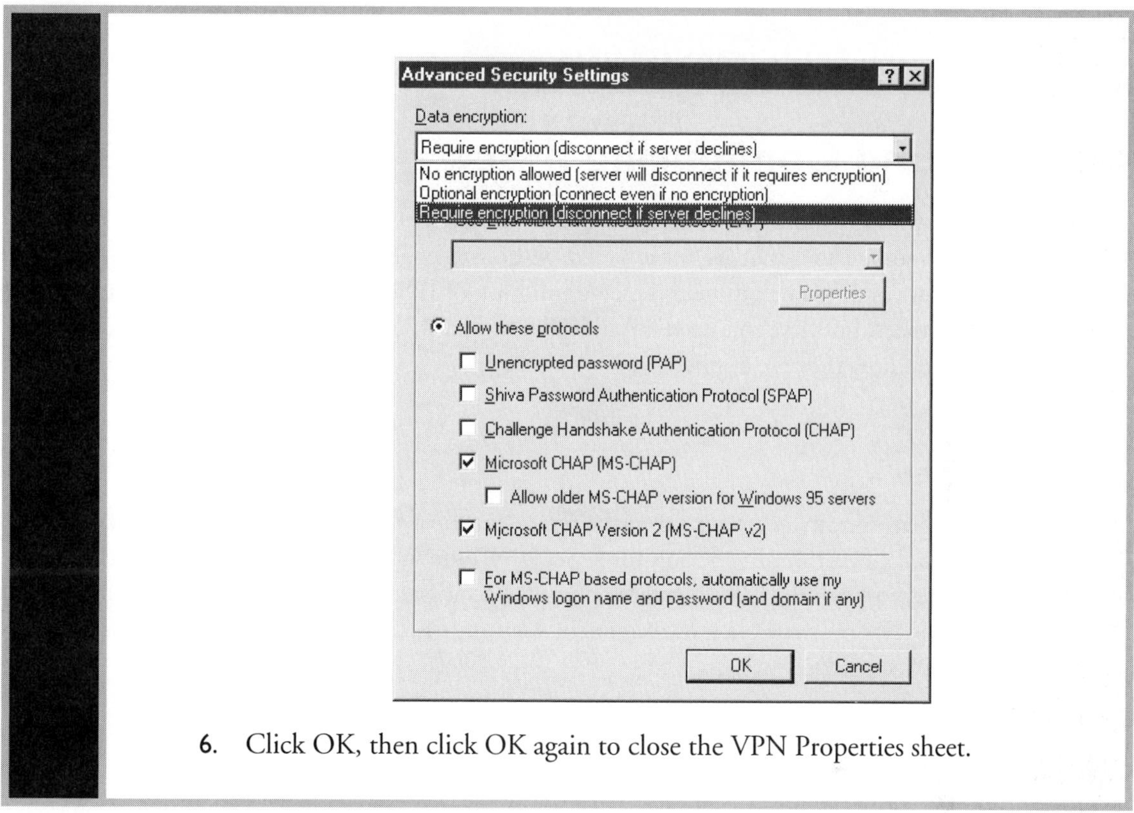

6. Click OK, then click OK again to close the VPN Properties sheet.

CERTIFICATION OBJECTIVE 30.02

Enabling and Configuring IPSec

Now that you know something about the concepts behind IP Security, let's turn to some issues that are more practical: how to enable and configure IPSec for your network. We will discuss the configuration of IPSec for both transport and tunnel modes, but first you need an understanding of IPSec policies, how they are created, and how they are applied.

IPSec Policies

Microsoft, in an attempt to make management of IP Security easier, has implemented *policy-based* administration for IPSec in Windows 2000. In other words, you, as a network administrator, create policies to configure IPSec. Windows 2000 provides the IP Security Policy Management snap-in, which is used to define and manage IPSec policies.

Factors to Consider

Developing a security plan begins with the awareness that security represents a balance. Complete security means no one has access to anything. All assets would be protected at the cost of no one being able to use them; this is not a very practical solution. On the other end of the continuum is total "openness," where no security controls are placed on any of the network's assets or resources. No one will have any problem accessing the information or resources needed, but the downside is that your information has essentially become public domain.

To implement an effective security policy, you will have to balance accessibility with security. The more secure the resource, the more difficult it will be to access, even for those who are allowed access. The easier the access, the more chance that an unauthorized person will be able to view, use, change, or delete the data.

Prior to implementing them on the network, you should design, create, and test the IPSec policies to determine which policies are truly necessary. Microsoft recommends that during the testing of your deployment scenarios, you should run normal workloads on applications to gain realistic feedback. Also note that during the initial tests, if you want to view the packet contents with Network Monitor or a sniffer, you should use the Medium security method level (or a custom security method set to AH), because using High or ESP will prevent you from being able to view the packets.

Evaluating Security Needs

Some of the things you will want to assess in developing the plan upon which your policies will be based include:

- The type of information typically sent over the network. How sensitive is it? Does it include trade secrets, confidential financial data, sensitive client records, and the like?
- Where is the sensitive information stored, and how will it be routed through the network?
- What is your vulnerability to network attacks? Do you have an always-on Internet connection? Do you have a remote access server to which outside users can dial in? Do you have a Web server or FTP server open to the public?

Your security plan should focus on the basic issues illustrated by the following grid.

SCENARIO & SOLUTION	
What network traffic should be secured?	Determine whether you need to secure the traffic between all computers or only some of them. Also, decide if security is needed for only some protocols and ports, or all of them.
What levels of security are needed?	Determine whether you need only data authentication and integrity, or whether you want to ensure confidentiality of the data.
Which connections should be secured?	Decide whether you need security only on remote access connections, or also on the internal network.
What about interoperability issues?	Determine whether the encryption settings selected will work with all computers that need access.

Evaluating Potential Security Threats

Part of developing your security plan involves evaluating the potential threats to which your network may be exposed. Many administrators envision the black-hat "hacker" as the most dangerous enemy of the network's information store, but this may not be entirely true. Depending on the nature of the data and the physical infrastructure of your network, more likely dangers may include:

- The "power user" who is interested in what he can "do" over the network.
- The casual user who stumbles upon information that was not secured properly.
- The authorized user who accesses a document or file that has poorly designed access control, leading to a misinformation situation that can create havoc in the corporation.
- The disgruntled employee seeking revenge from a former employer.
- The greed driven individual who sells his legitimate access controls to others for a profit.
- Competing companies that hire agents to carry out corporate espionage in order to access your proprietary secrets.

on the Job

Although many companies go to great lengths to "harden" the network against outside intrusion, it is a fact of life that most risk emanates from within the company. While it is important to shore up portals to the Internet and other external networks, the security analyst's major concerns should usually be directed toward security breeches from *within*___—both malicious and accidental.___

Designing and Implementing IP Security Policies

In Windows 2000, IPSec configuration and deployment is intimately intertwined with the Active Directory and Group Policy. You must create a policy in order to deploy IPSec in your organization.

exam Watch

A policy can be applied to a forest, a tree, a domain, an organizational unit, or to a single computer.

Within the Group Policy, we can choose from built-in policies or create custom policies to meet our specialized needs. We configure these policies by creating an MMC and then using the appropriate MMC plug in.

EXERCISE 30-2

Creating a Custom IPSec MMC

1. Create a new console by starting the Run command and typing **mmc**.
2. Click OK to open up an empty console.
3. Click the Console menu and then click Add/Remove snap-in, as shown in the following illustration.

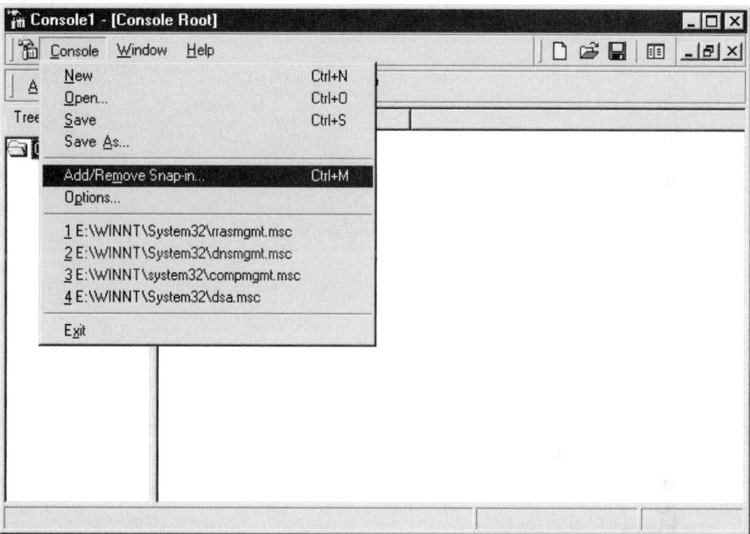

4. Click Add, select Computer Management, as shown in the following illustration, and click Add.

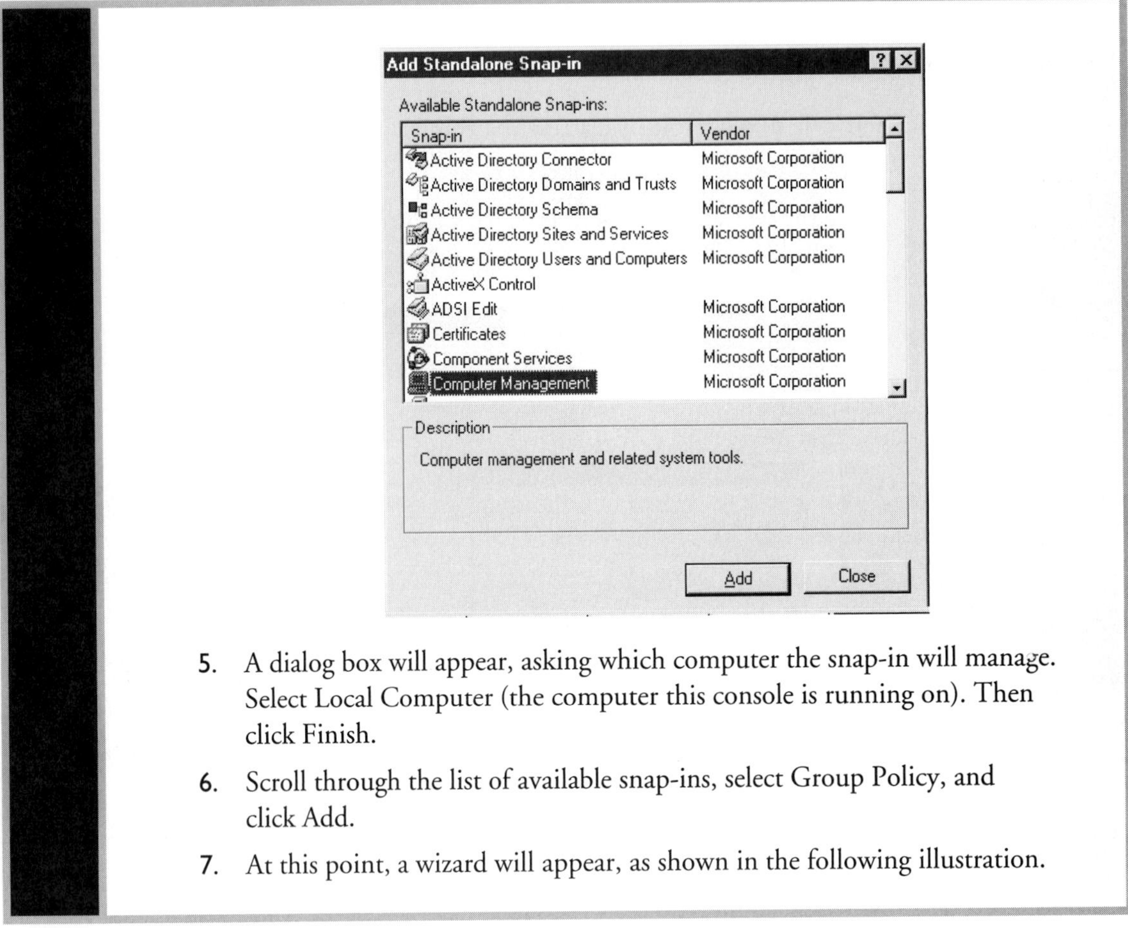

5. A dialog box will appear, asking which computer the snap-in will manage. Select Local Computer (the computer this console is running on). Then click Finish.
6. Scroll through the list of available snap-ins, select Group Policy, and click Add.
7. At this point, a wizard will appear, as shown in the following illustration.

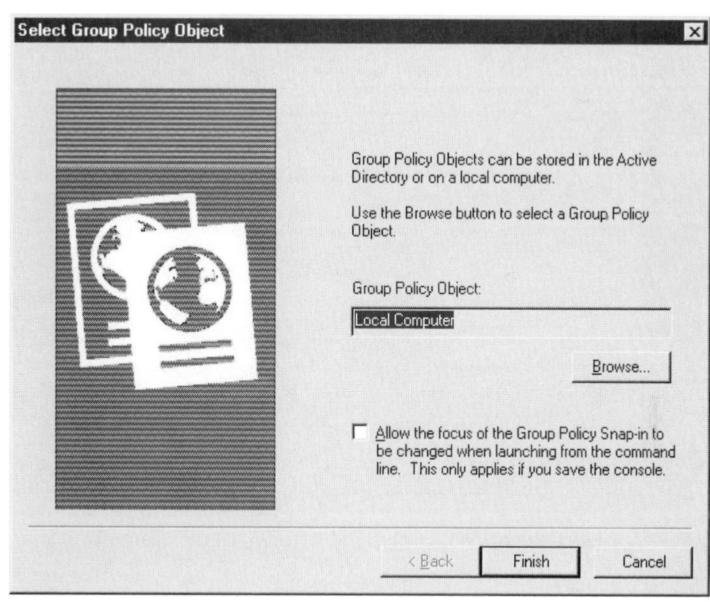

8. The wizard will query you on what group policy object you want to manage. In this case, confirm that it says Local Computer in the text box and click Finish. If you want to define a policy for another group policy object, you would click Browse and select from the list.
9. Scroll through the list of snap-ins one more time, this time looking for Certificates. Select Certificates and click Add. A dialog box will appear, as shown in the following illustration.

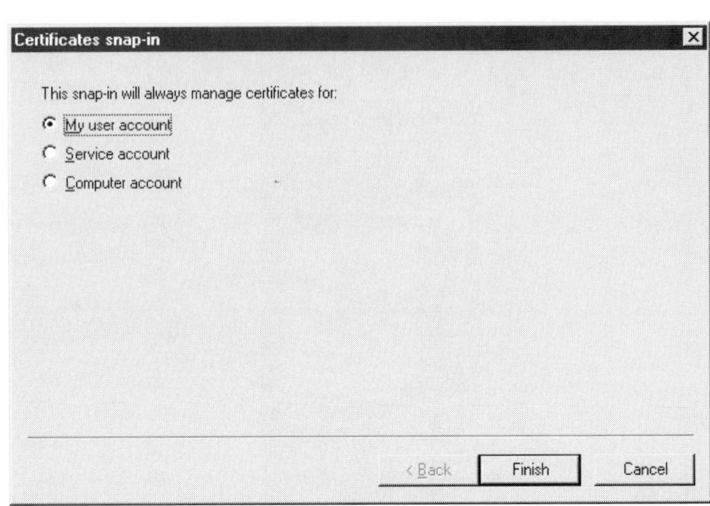

10. Select the appropriate radio button, depending upon what account you want the snap-in to always manage. In this case, select Computer Account and click Next.
11. Select Local Computer for the computer that you want the snap-in to manage. Then click Finish.
12. Click OK to close the Add/Remove Snap-ins dialog box. You now have a custom MMC that can be used to manage IPSec policies, which should look something like the one shown in the following illustration.

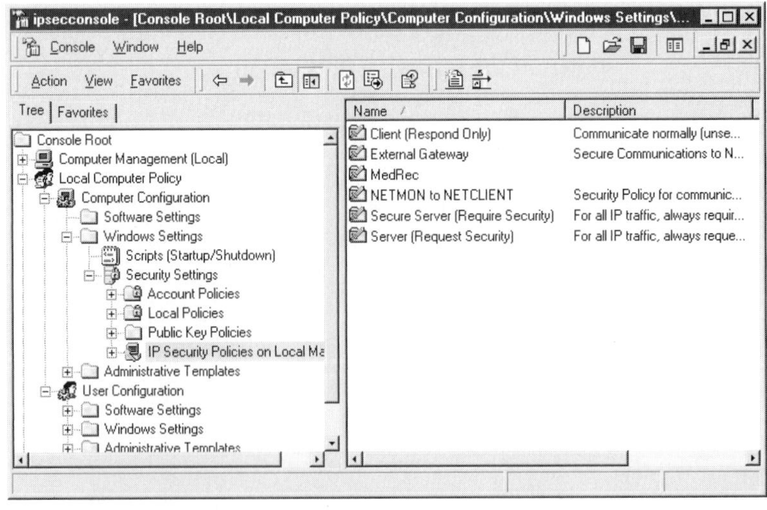

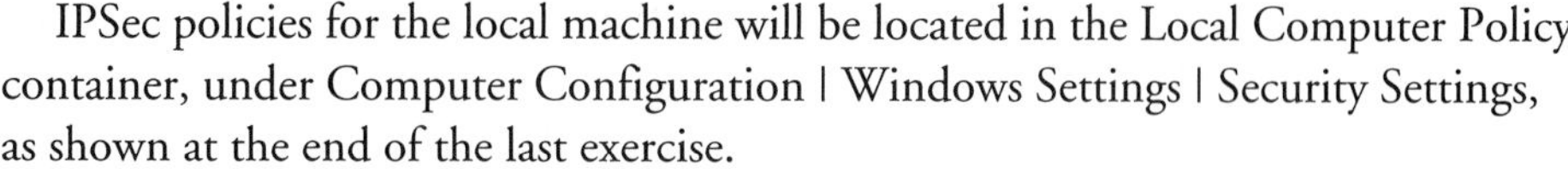

IPSec policies for the local machine will be located in the Local Computer Policy container, under Computer Configuration | Windows Settings | Security Settings, as shown at the end of the last exercise.

For this exercise, we have chosen to manage IPSec policy for this single machine. This might be appropriate if you were configuring IPSec policy for a file or application server. To manage policy for an entire domain or organizational unit, you would select the appropriate policy when selecting the Group Policy snap-in configuration.

IPSec Policy Properties

Because IPSec policies are implemented via Group Policy, we have a great deal of flexibility in how they are implemented. We can choose from three built-in IPSec Policies, or create our own custom policies. Let's first examine the built-in policies.

The Built-In IPSec Policies

The three built-in IPSec policies are as follows:

- **The Client (Respond Only) policy** Used when you require secure IPSec connections when another computer requests them. For example, you are using a machine as a workstation that wants to connect to a file server that requires IPSec security. The workstation with the built-in Client policy enabled will negotiate an IPSec security association. However, this client will never *require* IPSec security; it will only use IPSec to secure communications when requested to do so by another computer.
- **The Server (Request Security) policy** Used when you want to request IPSec security for all connections. This might be used for a file server that must serve both IPSec-aware (Windows 2000) clients and non-IPSec aware clients (such as Windows 9*x* and NT). If a connection is established with an IPSec-aware computer, the session will be secure. Unsecured sessions will be established with non-IPSec aware computers, and soft security associations will be established. This allows greater flexibility during the transition from mixed mode Windows networks to native mode Windows 2000 networks.
- **The Secure Server (Require Security) policy** Used when all communications with a particular server *must* be secured. Examples include file servers with

high impact information, and security gateways at either end of an L2TP/IPSec tunnel. The server with the Secure Server policy will always request a secure channel. Connections will be denied to computers that are not able to respond to the request.

exam Watch

You must have appropriate administrator rights to Group Policy, or be a member of the local system Administrators group in order to define IPSec policies.

Creating Custom Policies

You will often need to define your own custom policies. To add or edit IPSec policies, follow these steps:

1. In IP Security Policy Management, choose whether to define a new policy or edit a current one. If you wish to create a new policy, click on the IP Security Policies folder in the console tree, then click Create IP Security Policy in the Action menu, as shown in Figure 30-3. This will invoke the IP Security Policy wizard. Complete the instructions in the wizard until the Properties dialog box for your new policy appears.
2. If you wish to edit an existing policy, just right-click the policy and then click Properties. You will see the dialog box displayed in Figure 30-4.

FIGURE 30-3

Creating a new IP security policy

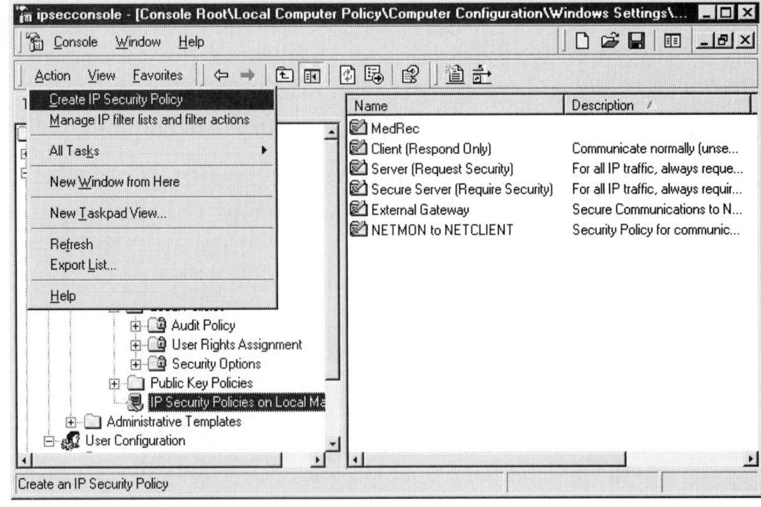

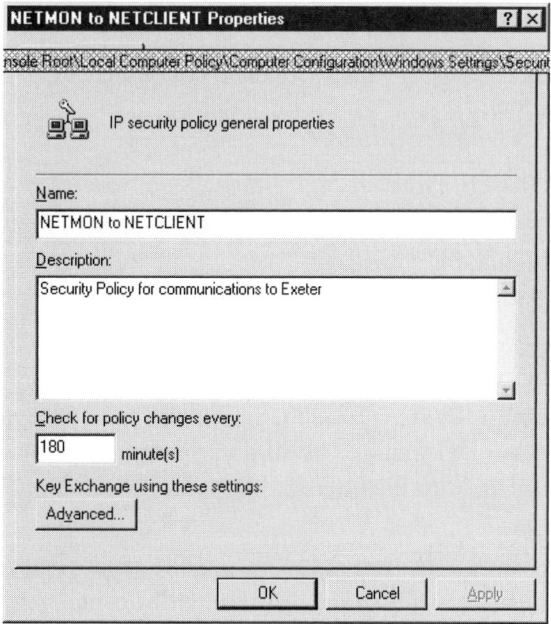

FIGURE 30-4 The Properties dialog box for an existing security policy

3. Click the General tab, then in the Name field, enter a unique name.
4. In the Description field, type a description of the security policy, such as which groups or domains it affects.
5. If this computer is part of a domain, type a value in "Check for policy changes every" *number* minute(s) to specify how often the policy agent will check Group Policy for updates.
6. Click Advanced if you have special requirements for the security on the key exchange.
7. Click the Rules tab and create any necessary rules for the policy.

New policies may not be displayed immediately in the console tree. If you do not see the new policy, right-click on IP Security Policies in the Description folder, then select Refresh from the context menu.

You cannot delete the built-in policies, but you can edit them. However, it is recommended that you leave the built-in policies as they are, and create new policies for custom requirements.

Configuring IPSec Policy Components

An IPSec policy has three main components:

- IP Filter rules
- IP Filter lists
- IP Filter actions

Let's look at each of those in more detail.

Configuring Filter Rules

Filter rules are created to specify how and when communication is to be secured. Each rule contains a list of filters and a collection of security actions. When a match is made with the filter list, the specified actions will occur.

How Rules Are Applied Rules are applied to computers that match criteria specified in a filter list. An IP filter list contains source and destination IP addresses. These can be individual host IP addresses or network IDs. When a communication is identified as a participant included in an IP filter list, a particular filter action will be applied that is specific for that connection.

How to Add or Edit Rules To add or edit filter rules, perform the following steps:

1. Right-click the policy you want to modify in the IP Security Policy Management console.
2. Click Properties and select the Rules tab.
3. You can either use the Security Rule wizard, or you can add or edit the rule manually. If you wish to use the Security Rule wizard to add a rule, check the Use Add Wizard check box, as shown in Figure 30-5.
4. Click Next and then follow the instructions in the wizard.
5. If you wish to add or edit a rule manually, clear the Use Add Wizard check box. Click Add or Edit. Continue to the next step.
6. Define the IP Filter List, Filter Action, Connection Type, Authentication Methods, and Tunnel Setting properties.

FIGURE 30-5

The Rules tab on the IP Security Policy Properties sheet

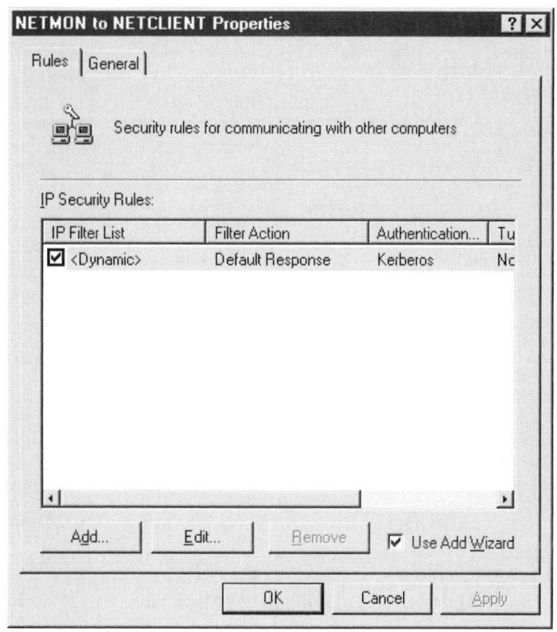

exam Watch

New rules are automatically applied to the policy being edited or created. The Default Response rule is automatically added in each new IPSec policy that you create. If you do not want this rule to be part of your policy, you will need to deactivate it, as predefined rules are not removable.

Configuring Filters and Filter Lists

Filters are the most important part of IPSec policy, because if you fail to specify the proper filters (in either the client or the server policies), the connection may not be secured. This is also true if the IP addresses change before the policy's filters are updated.

Filter Lists The IP filter list is a collection of filters.

exam Watch

Filters are applied in the order of most-specific filters first. Filters are not applied in the order in which they appear in the list. All of the filters used in tunnel rules are matched first, before any end-to-end transport filters are matched.

How to Add or Edit Filters To add or edit filters in Windows 2000 IPSec, perform the following steps:

1. Right-click the policy you want to modify in the IPSec Security Management console.
2. Click Properties.
3. Click the rule that holds the filter list you want to modify.
4. Click Edit.
5. To add a filter, select the IP Filter List tab, as shown in Figure 30-6, and click Add.
6. To reconfigure an existing filter list, click the IP filter and then click Edit.
7. In the IP filter list, you can use the IP Filter wizard to create a filter. Just check the Use Add Wizard check box and follow the instructions of the wizard. (You can also create a filter manually, by clearing the Use Add Wizard check box and clicking Add, or reconfigure an existing filter by clearing the check box and clicking Edit).
8. Select the Addressing tab, as shown in Figure 30-7.

FIGURE 30-6

Selecting the IP Filter List tab

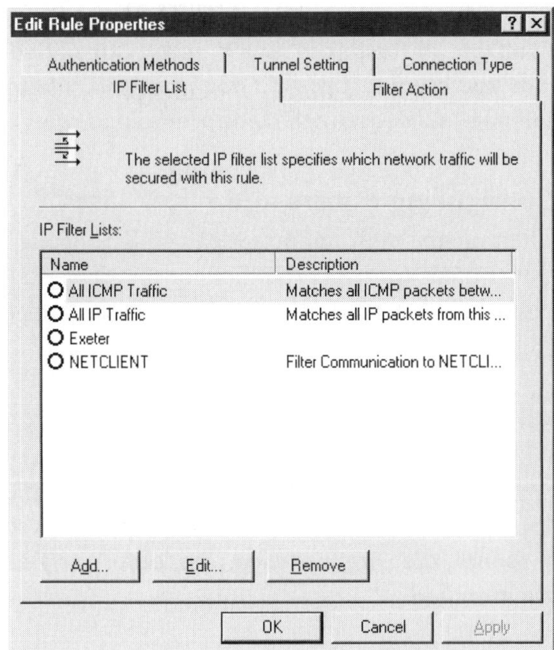

FIGURE 30-7

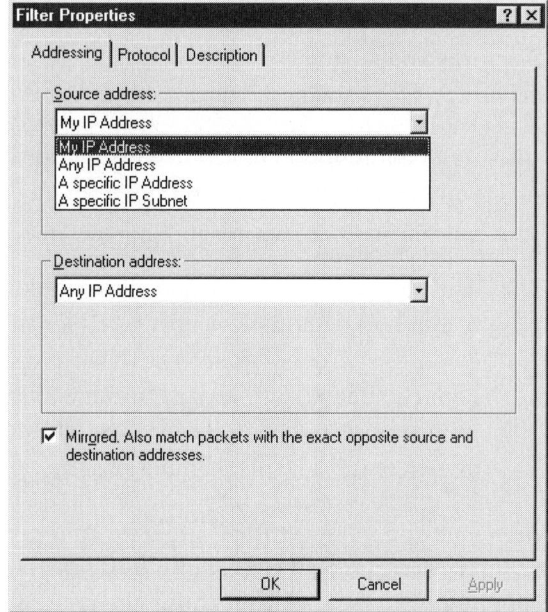

Specifying the source address from which packets are to be secured

9. Select the Source address. Choose from the following options:
   - **My IP Address** Secures packets from all IP addresses on the computer for which the filter is configured.
   - **Any IP Address** Secures packets from all computers.
   - **A Specific IP Address** Secures packets from the IP address you type into the IP Address field.
   - **A Specific IP subnet** Secures packets from the subnet you designate in the Subnet Mask field.
10. Click the Destination address and repeat step 5 for the destination address.
11. Select the desired setting under Mirrored from the following options:
    - Check the Mirrored check box to create a filter for end-to-end security (to secure packets from the source to the destination computer).
    - Clear the Mirrored check box to create a filter for an IPSec tunnel (you must also create two rules, one inbound and one outbound, with different filter lists).
12. In the Description field, type a description for this filter (such as what hosts and traffic types are applicable).

Filter Actions

Filter actions define the type of security and the methods in which security is established. The primary methods are: Permit, Block, and Negotiate security.

- The Permit option blocks negotiation for IP security. This is appropriate if you never want to secure traffic to which this rule applies.
- The Block action blocks all traffic from computers specified in the IP filter list.
- The Negotiate security action allows the computer to use a list of security methods to determine security levels for the communication. The list is in descending order of preference. If the Negotiate security action is selected, both computers must be able to come to an agreement regarding the security parameters included in the list. The entries are processed sequentially in order of preference. The first common security method is enacted.

on the job

When you add a new static IP address to a protected host, you should modify the policy filters on all clients and hosts that make security requests to the protected host. Be sure that those clients updated their policies before you add the new address. Look at the policy being used on the protected host. If the filters there specify static IP addresses for local connections, you should edit and save the new filter list to include the new static IP address after adding the new IP address to the interface.

Configuring IPSec Authentication Methods

You can define the authentication method(s) to be used by IPSec, and set the order of preference, by following these steps:

1. Right-click on the policy in the IPSec Policy Management console and select Properties, as shown in Figure 30-8.
2. On the Properties sheet, select the rule you wish to edit, as shown in Figure 30-9, and click Edit.
3. Now select the Authentication Methods tab, as shown in Figure 30-10.
4. You can add or remove authentication methods, edit the properties of the existing methods, and move a method up or down in the preference order using this dialog box.

FIGURE 30-8

Selecting the IPSec policy to be modified

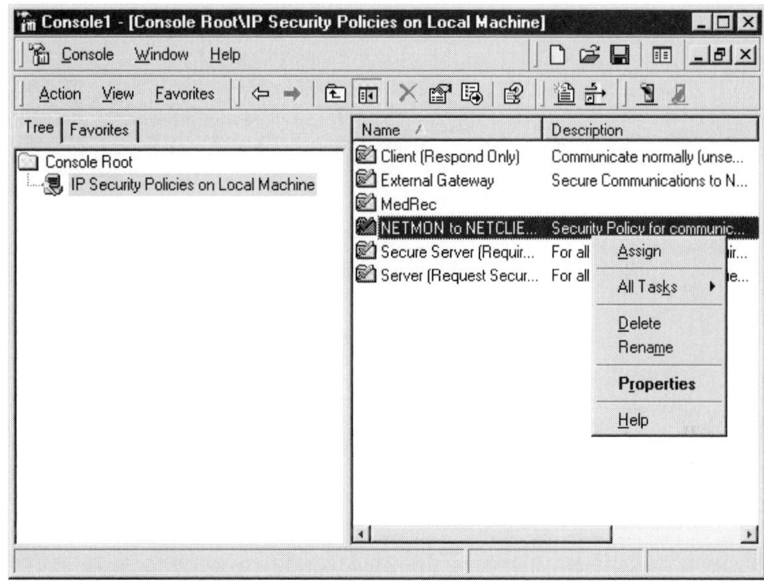

FIGURE 30-9

Selecting the IPSec rule to be edited

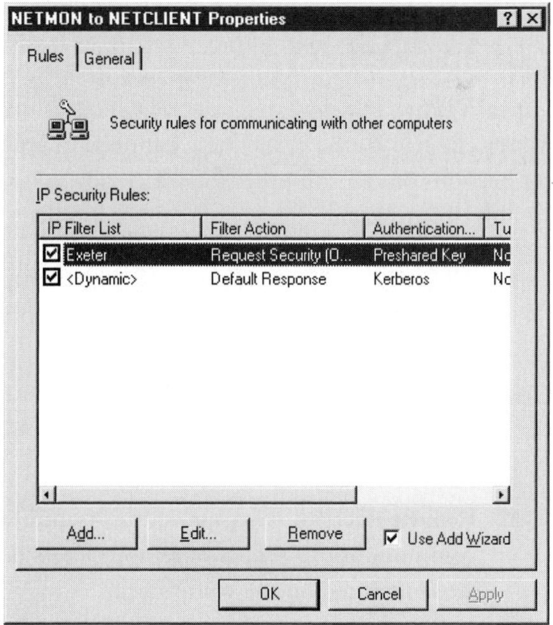

FIGURE 30-10

The Authentication Methods tab

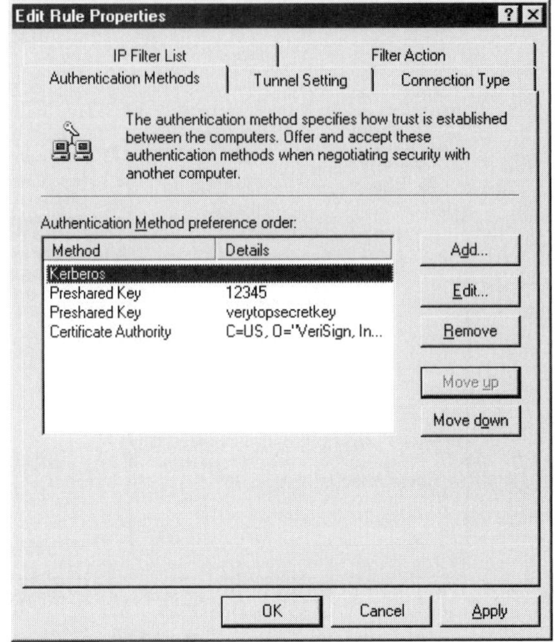

Configuring Connection Types

For each IPSec rule, you must define which connection types on your computer will be affected by the rule. These connection types apply to all network and dial-up connections on the computer for which you are configuring the IPSec policy. There are three connection type settings:

- **All Network Connections** If you select this option, the rule will apply to communications sent over any of the network connections that are configured on the computer.
- **Local Area Network (LAN)** If you select this option, the rule will only apply to communications sent over the LAN connection(s) that are configured on the computer.
- **Remote Access** If you select this option, the rule will only apply to communications sent over remote access or dial-up connections that are configured on the computer.

To specify IPSec connection types for an IPSec rule, perform the following steps:

1. In the IP Security Policy Management console, right-click on the policy you want to edit.
2. Click Properties.
3. Click the rule to which you want to make changes.
4. Click Edit.
5. On the Connection Type tab, select the type of network connections to which this rule will apply, according to the three options discussed earlier (Figure 30-11).

Each rule can have one connection type specified. The rule will be applied only to connections of the type specified.

FIGURE 30-11

Selecting the network connection type

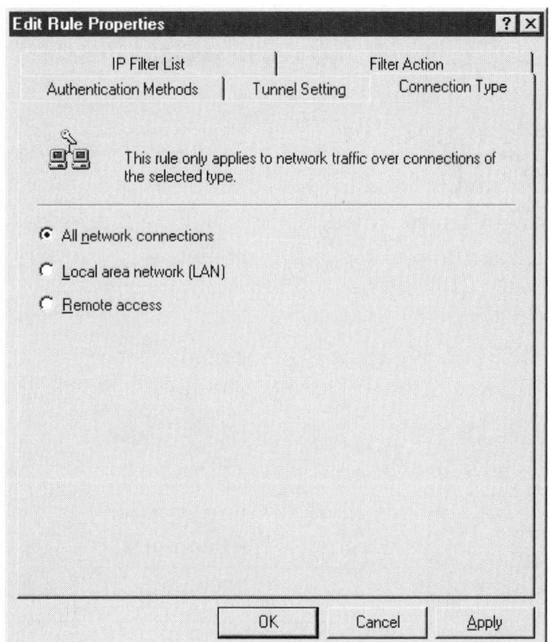

Configuring IPSec Tunneling

As mentioned earlier, an IPSec tunnel requires two separate IPSec rules to define the endpoints. This is done via the Tunnel Setting tab on the Edit Rules Properties sheet, as shown in Figure 30-12.

A second rule must be created to specify the other endpoint of the tunnel.

Configuring Advanced Settings

Key Exchange settings are specified by clicking Advanced on the General tab of the IPSec policy Properties sheet, as shown in Figure 30-13.

When you click Advanced, you will see the Key Exchange Settings dialog box shown in Figure 30-14.

FIGURE 30-12

Configuring IPSec tunneling

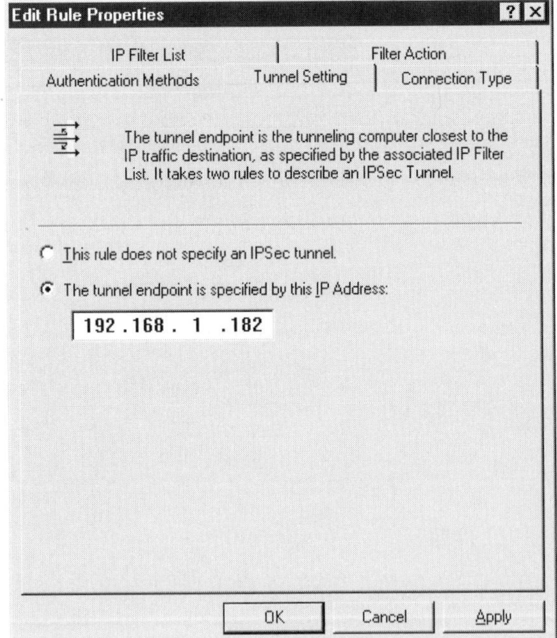

FIGURE 30-13

To specify Key Exchange settings, click Advanced

NETMON to NETCLIENT Properties
Rules
General
IP security policy general properties
Name:
NETMON to NETCLIENT
Description:
Security Policy for communications to Exeter
Check for policy changes every:
180
minute(s)
Key Exchange using these settings:
Advanced...
OK
Cancel
Apply

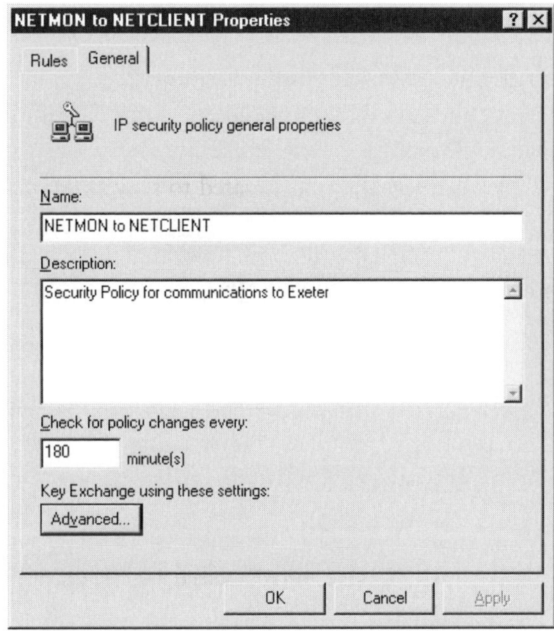

This is where you control the security of the Internet Key Exchange (IKE) process and configure the security methods that are used to protect identities during the Key Exchange process. Methods that may be selected include 3DES and DES for encryption, and SHA1 and MD5 for integrity, as shown in Figure 30-15.

FIGURE 30-14

The Key Exchange Settings dialog box

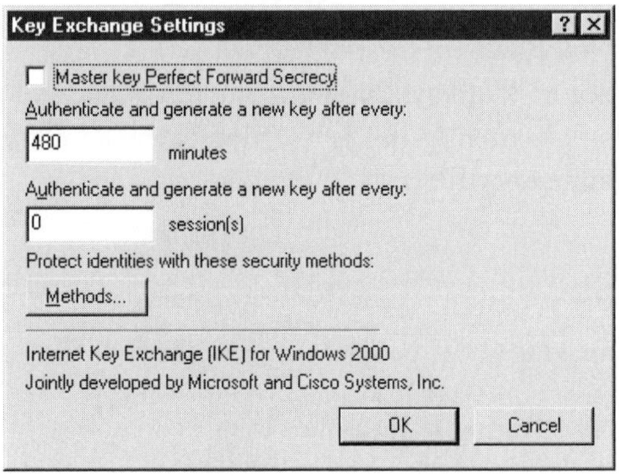

Key Exchange Settings
Master key Perfect Forward Secrecy
Authenticate and generate a new key after every:
480
minutes
Authenticate and generate a new key after every:
0
session(s)
Protect identities with these security methods:
Methods...
Internet Key Exchange (IKE) for Windows 2000
Jointly developed by Microsoft and Cisco Systems, Inc.
OK
Cancel

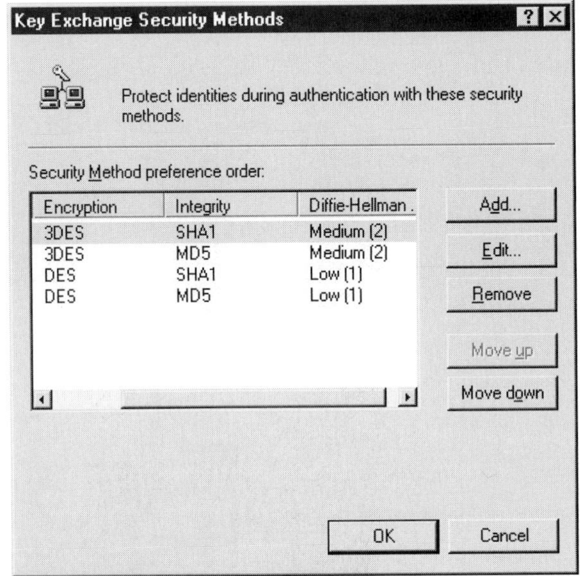

FIGURE 30-15

The available Key Exchange Security Methods

CERTIFICATION OBJECTIVE 30.03

Managing, Monitoring, and Troubleshooting IPSec

As you no doubt have discerned, IP Security is a complex feature, and working with IPSec in Windows 2000, despite the wizards and management tools provided, is no simple matter. In this last section, we will look at how to manage, monitor, and troubleshoot IPSec.

Managing IPSec

Managing IPSec policies involves the following activities:

- Testing IPSec policy integrity
- Restoring predefined IPSec policies
- Exporting IPSec policies

- Importing IPSec policies
- Refreshing the list of IPSec policies
- Deleting IPSec policies
- Renaming IPSec policies

Let's look at each of these a little more closely.

Testing Policy Integrity

Microsoft has made it easy to check the integrity of IPSec policies in Windows 2000. Just follow these steps:

1. In the IP Security Policy Management console, click on the folder labeled IP Security Policies on Local Machine.
2. Click Action, or right-click on the folder.
3. Select All Tasks, as shown in Figure 30-16.
4. Click Check Policy Integrity.

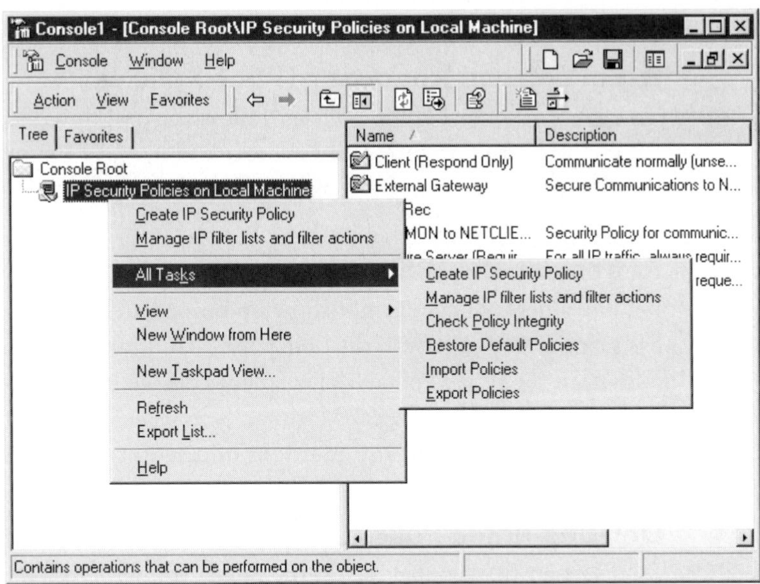

FIGURE 30-16 Many policy management tasks are accomplished from the All Tasks menu

The Policy Integrity Check provides verification that the changes that have been made to policy settings have been properly propagated by Group Policy to the computer accounts in the GPO.

This same context menu will be used for most of the common policy management tasks.

Restoring Predefined IPSec Policies

There may be times when you wish to restore the predefined default policies (Client, Server, and Secure Server, as noted earlier) to replace custom policies you may have created. To return to the defaults, follow these steps:

1. In the IP Security Policy Management console, click on the folder labeled IP Security Policies on Local Machine.
2. Click Action, or right-click on the folder.
3. Select All Tasks.
4. Click Restore Default Policies.
5. Click Yes in response to the "Are you sure?" dialog box, and the predefined policies will be restored.

Exporting and Importing IPSec Policies

To export or import IPSec policies, follow the first three steps in the preceding section, then from the All Tasks context menu, select Export Policies or Import Policies, as the case may be. Type in the path and name of the file.

Refreshing the IPSec Policy List

Because a new policy may not show up immediately after you create it, Microsoft has made it easy to refresh the policy list—all it takes is a couple of clicks of the mouse. In the IPSec Policy Management console, right-click on the folder labeled IP Security Policies on Local Machine. Select Refresh from the context menu. The list will be updated, and any additions or deletions you have made will be reflected.

Deleting IPSec Policies

To delete an IPSec policy, select the policy you wish to remove in the IPSec Policy Management console, right-click on it, and choose Delete. Remember that you may have to refresh the policy list, as discussed previously, to see the effect of the change.

Renaming IPSec Policies

Renaming an IPSec policy is similar to renaming a file in the Windows Explorer. Just right-click the policy name in the IPSec Policy Management console, select Rename in the context menu, and type in the new name. Press ENTER to apply the change and refresh the list, if necessary, to display the new name.

Using IPSec Monitor

Windows 2000 includes a monitoring tool, the IPSec Monitor, which allows you to view the active security associations both on local and remote computers.

EXERCISE 30-3

Accessing the IPSec Monitor

To use the Monitor, perform the following steps:

1. Click Start.
2. Select the Run command.
3. Type **ipsecmon <computername>** in the Run box. You will see the IPSec Monitor, as shown in the following illustration.

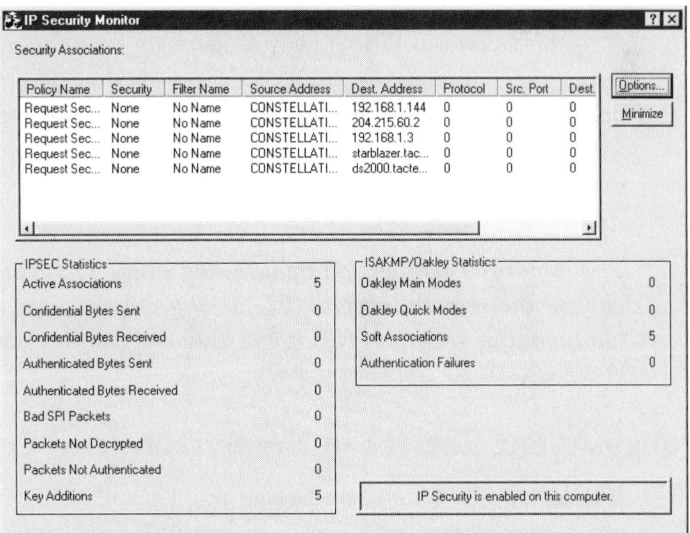

If you type the command without designating a computer name, the Monitor will default to the local machine.

The Components of the IPSec Monitor

When you run the Monitor, you should see an entry for each security association that is currently active. The policy name, security level, filter name, and the source and destination address will be shown. If tunneling mode is used, the endpoint of the tunnel will be shown. The Monitor also displays statistical information such as:

- The number of active security associations
- The types of security associations that are active
- The number of keys generated
- The number of confidential (ESP) and authenticated (ESP and AH) bytes sent and received

Using the IPSec Monitor

You can use the IPSec Monitor to perform the following:

- Verify that your communications have been secured successfully
- Track patterns of authentication failures or security association failures
- Aid in performance tuning

You can confirm IPSec policy assignments with the monitor. The message in the lower-right corner of the display tells you whether IPSec is enabled on the computer being monitored. If no policies have been assigned, IPSec is not enabled. If policies have been assigned, but no security associations are active with another computer, there will be nothing listed in the SA list.

exam Watch

The monitor's display will be updated every 15 seconds by default. You can change the refresh interval, by clicking Options and typing in a new setting, in number of seconds. This is the only option that can be configured.

IPSec Policy Agent Entries in the System and Security Logs

Windows 2000 starts event logging automatically whenever the operating system is booted. The System and Security logs in Event Viewer can be used in troubleshooting IPSec.

The System Log

The System log is used in troubleshooting the Policy Agent. IPSec-related messages you might encounter in the System log include:

- **Event (Informational) 279** This event is logged for informational purposes and does not indicate a problem. It tells you if an IPSec policy is in effect, and if so, whether it is a local or domain policy. If a change has been made to the policy, the message "updating IPSec policy" will be displayed.
- **Event (Error) 284** This is an error message, which indicates a problem. In this case, it means the policy agent was not able to access the Active Directory.

The Security Log

Messages pertaining to ISAKMP/Oakley appear in the Security log. An example would be the establishment of a security association in conjunction with a successful logon.

Common Troubleshooting Scenarios

Following are a few common troubleshooting scenarios related to IPSec, and suggestions for resolving them.

IPSec Communications Are Not Working as Expected

If communications that should be secured with IPSec do not appear to be secured, you should first verify that IPSec is enabled. You can do this with the IPSec Monitor as described earlier. Ensure that a policy is assigned.

You should also check to be sure that the network connection between the two computers is working properly. Network problems could appear to be IPSec communication failures. Determine whether you can PING. If you are using the Server or Secure Server policies, the ICMP packet sent when you PING will match the IP Filter List in these policies, and IPSec will attempt to apply security to the PING. Note that this may take longer than it usually takes to respond to the PING command.

If the computer with which you are trying to communicate is not capable of using IPSec, you may get a "timed out" response. You can exempt ICMP packets in all of your IPSec policies to avoid this. To do this, you must create a rule (you can use the Security Rule wizard), select the All ICMP traffic filter list, and choose Permit as the filter action.

You can use PING in combination with the IPSec Monitor. When a PING command is successful, the Monitor should display a security association.

No Security Associations Indicated in IPSec Monitor

Soft security associations may be preventing hard SAs from occurring. You may need to restart the IPSec Policy Agent. To do so, right-click the IPSec Policy Agent in the Services console (accessed from the Administrative Tools menu), and click Restart, as shown in Figure 30-17.

An alternate method of restarting the service is to double-click on the service name, click Stop and then Start.

Security Negotiations Fail

Negotiations may fail if the IPSec policy settings on the two communicating computers are not compatible. If the Security log in Event Viewer shows failed attempts at Oakley negotiation, perform the following steps to find the source of the policy incompatibility:

1. Check the *authentication* methods on both computers and ensure they are compatible.

FIGURE 30-17

Restarting the IPSec Policy Agent

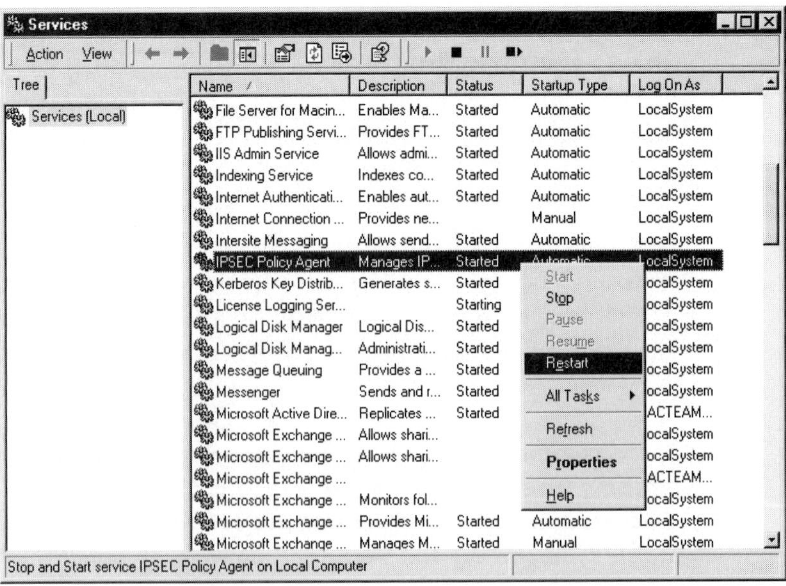

2. Check the *security* method(s) specified on both. There must be at least one common security method.
3. If *tunneling* mode is being used, make certain that the tunnel endpoint settings are correct.

Accidental Deletion of the IPSec Files

IPSec requires the IPSec driver and policy agent files, as well as the files for ISAKMP/Oakley. If any of the components of IPSec are deleted, or the files become corrupted, you can reinstall the IPSec files by removing and reinstalling the TCP/IP protocols.

The following scenarios and solutions grid answers some common questions in regard to troubleshooting IPSec.

SCENARIO & SOLUTION	
After you enabled IPSec, things seemed to slow down. Is this normal, and what can you do about it?	When you enable IPSec, you will find that IP traffic and packet size increase. Additionally, the computer's processor will be taxed more. This can cause a slowdown in performance. You should evaluate whether you need the level of security provided by IPSec and if not, disable it or choose a lower level of encryption.
Your two computers cannot communicate with one another with IPSec enabled. They are able to communicate when you stop the IPSec policy agent. What should you do?	You should first consult the Security log and address any error messages. Be sure an SA is established, using IPSec Monitor. Ensure that policies are assigned to both computers, and that they are compatible. Restart IPSec Monitor to apply any changes.
The Security log shows failed attempts at Oakley negotiation. What should you do?	This indicates a policy mismatch. Check the following for compatibility: 1) authentication methods, and 2) security methods. If IPSec is used in tunneling mode, check the settings on the tunnel endpoints.

CERTIFICATION SUMMARY

In this chapter, we discussed both the concepts and practical implementation of the IP Security protocol, IPSec, in Windows 2000. We began with an overview of IP Security—what it is, why it's needed, and how it works. We discussed the components of security: authentication, integrity, and confidentiality, and you learned how IPSec provides each. We provided some background information about the history and development of cryptography and encryption methods of the past and present.

You became acquainted with the two IPSec protocols: Authentication Header (AH) and the Encapsulating Security Payload (ESP). You learned that AH provides authentication for the entire packet, but does not encrypt data for confidentiality, while ESP does encrypt the data, but ordinarily does not protect the IP header.

We discussed the two modes in which IPSec can operate: transport mode and tunnel mode. We also examined how IPSec works in conjunction with L2TP to provide end-to-end security over a virtual private networking connection that is transmitted through the public Internet.

You learned how to configure IPSec, and how to use the IPSec Monitor and the System and Security event logs to aid in the troubleshooting process. Finally, we looked at some common troubleshooting scenarios, and suggestions for how to resolve them.

IP Security is an important topic—both on the Microsoft Implementing and Administering a Windows 2000 Network Infrastructure exam, and (more and more so every day) in the day-to-day world of a professional network administrator.

TWO-MINUTE DRILL

Overview of IP Security

- ❑ IPSec operates at the network layer of the OSI model, and provides protection to data that travels across the network, without a requirement to make changes to your applications.
- ❑ The elements of IPSec include the Authentication Header (AH) and Encapsulating Security Payload (ESP) protocols, cryptographic key management protocols, the Security Policy Database (SPD), and Security Associations (SAs).
- ❑ AH provides authentication and signs the entire packet, while ESP provides encryption but does not, in transport mode, protect the IP header. The two can be used in combination.
- ❑ Key Exchange is the first phase of security negotiation. This involves the use of the Internet Security Association Key Management Protocol (ISAKMP) and the Oakley protocol, collectively referred to as the Internet Key Exchange (IKE).
- ❑ IPSec will block SNMP messages unless you configure a rule to prevent it.
- ❑ IPSec is used in conjunction with the Layer Two Tunneling Protocol (L2TP) to provide a secure link over a virtual private network connection.

Enabling and Configuring IPSec

- ❑ Windows 2000 provides policy-based administration of IP Security, accomplished via the IP Security Management console.
- ❑ Before you can create and implement security policies, you must develop an overall security plan by assessing the organization's security needs and evaluating potential security threats.
- ❑ There are three built-in (predefined) IPSec policies: Client (Respond Only), Server (Request Security), and Secure Server (Require Security). You can also create custom policies.

Managing, Monitoring, and Troubleshooting IPSec

- Managing IPSec policies involves testing policy integrity, restoring predefined policies, exporting and importing policies, refreshing the list of IPSec policies, and deleting and renaming policies. These tasks can be accomplished via the IP Security Policy Management console.
- The IPSec Monitor can be used to verify that communications have been secured successfully, to track patterns of authentication failures of security association failures, and to aid in performance tuning.
- The Windows 2000 Event Viewer can be used to view IPSec-related messages via the System log and the Security log.

31

Installing and Configuring Certificate Services

CERTIFICATION OBJECTIVES

31.01 Overview of Certificate Services

31.02 Management and Administration of Certificates

31.03 Creating and Issuing Certificates in Windows 2000

31.04 Certificate-Based Authentication

31.05 Encrypting File System (EFS) Recovery Keys

31.06 Troubleshooting Certificates

✓ Two-Minute Drill

Windows 2000 incorporates more industry-standard (as well as industrial-strength) security features to protect data. Microsoft has included Public Key Infrastructure (PKI) based technology in the form of Certificate Services to ensure that critical data remains secure.

Originally, certificates and public key encryption was an Internet-based phenomenon. Encryption keys were exchanged between Web servers and clients via certificates or cookies, and used to verify the identity of each party and authenticate transactions carried out between them.

Microsoft Certificate Servers generate X.509 certificates that are used by clients and other servers to establish their identity and the identity of the issuing server. Certificates are commonly used on Web sites to accurately verify the identities of individuals accessing the site and to secure data passed between the Web browser and the Web server.

In this chapter, we look at Windows 2000 Certificate Services, and how certificate-based authentication and the Encrypting File System (EFS) are used to further extend security past the limits of the NTFS file permissions used in Windows NT.

CERTIFICATION OBJECTIVE 31.01

Overview of Certificate Services

To gain a good understanding of Certificate Services, we need to look at the underlying technology that drives it: Public Key Infrastructure, or PKI.

Public Key Infrastructure is one of the cryptography methods developed to protect data exchanged between computer systems. PKI was developed to overcome the limitations of network size on client and server authentication processes. PKI uses cryptography algorithms, the most widely used of which is the Rivest-Shamir-Adleman (RSA) algorithm, to scramble and unscramble data. The system uses a pair of keys, a public encryption key and a private encryption key, to perform cryptographic functions on data. Each key can be used to encrypt or decrypt data passed between two systems. For example, if the public key is used to encrypt some data, then the corresponding private key can be used to decrypt the data, and vice versa.

The public encryption key is freely distributed by the system that owns it, while the private key is kept securely on the system and never distributed. The reason public key encryption works is because even though the keys are created in pairs, unlike encryption keys used in other cryptography systems, they are distinctly different from each other. Public encryption keys are digitally signed by the issuer of the public key to guarantee authenticity. This digital signature is essential when the owner of the private key intends to send encrypted data to another computer that possesses the public key. The computer verifies the identity of the sender by using the public key to check the digital signature. Digital signatures are unique to each system, so there is no mistaking who the owner of the certificate is. PKI basically works using the following method, as shown in Figure 31-1:

1. System A contacts System B, requesting a secure connection.
2. System B gives its public encryption key to System A.
3. System A uses System B's public encryption key to encrypt the data it wishes to exchange with System B and submits the encrypted data.
4. System B receives the data, verifies the signature on the public encryption key, and uses its private encryption key to decrypt the data. If System B needs to pass any data back to System A, it also uses the private encryption key to encrypt that data.

Windows 2000 Certificate Services is Microsoft's implementation of PKI technology. Certificate Services were introduced with Microsoft Internet Information Server 4.0 in the Windows NT Option Pack as a component of Internet Information Server. Microsoft has taken the original intention of Public Key Infrastructure a step further, by incorporating Certificate Services as another level of security and authentication on private networks as well as on the Internet.

Certificates along with the Encrypting File System (EFS) help further secure data by applying a public encryption key to it, rendering it undecipherable to anyone without the corresponding private encryption key.

Encryption keys are created in pairs: a private encryption key that stays protected on the server, and a public key that is freely distributed by the server to clients

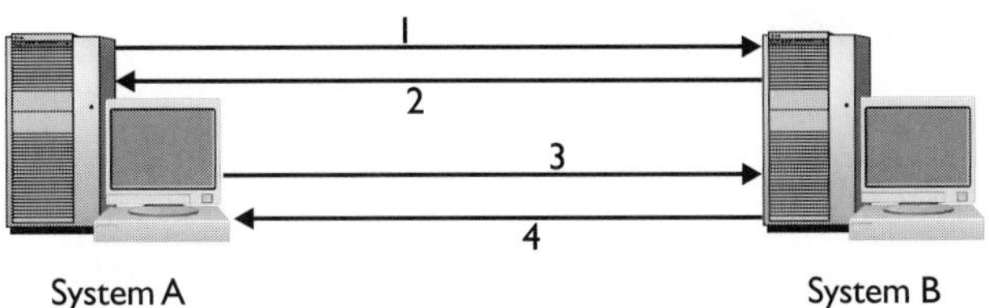

FIGURE 31-1 Two systems exchanging secure data via PKI

requesting a connection to the server. The client uses the public encryption key issued to it by the server to encrypt data it intends to send to the server. The server then uses its corresponding private encryption key to decrypt the data received.

Certificates are typically either created by a well-known Certificate Authority company such as VeriSign, or are created by a certificate server owned and operated by the company running the Web site. Certificate Services servers allow systems to exchange information securely both on the Internet and within private networks. Certificate Services employs a hierarchical structure (Figure 31-2) with the main server, called the Certification Authority, or CA, as the root of the hierarchy. A CA is a trusted server responsible for generating, issuing, and signing certificates. The original server certificates stay on the CA, but the public key certificates are issued to subordinate certificate servers that rely on the root CA. These subordinate certificate servers, in turn, issue public key user certificates to clients that request secure communications.

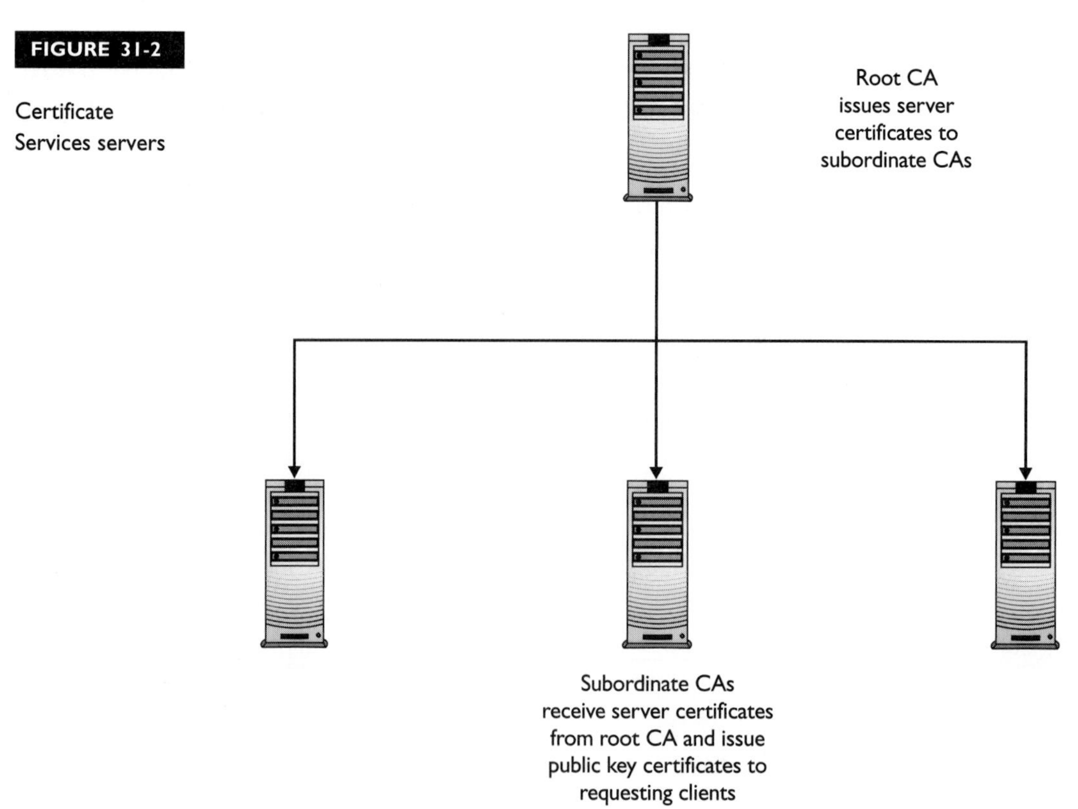
Root CA
issues server
certificates to
subordinate CAs
Subordinate CAs
receive server certificates
from root CA and issue
public key certificates to
requesting clients

FIGURE 31-2

Certificate Services servers

on the Job

You cannot change the name of the server that you install Certificate Server on. You will find that the option is unavailable. If you wish to change the name of the sever, you will need to remove certificate services.

EXERCISE 31-1

Installing Certificate Services

1. Click Start | Settings | Control Panel.
2. Double-click Add/ Remove Programs.
3. Click Add/Remove Windows Components.
4. Select Certificate Services, as shown in the following illustration.

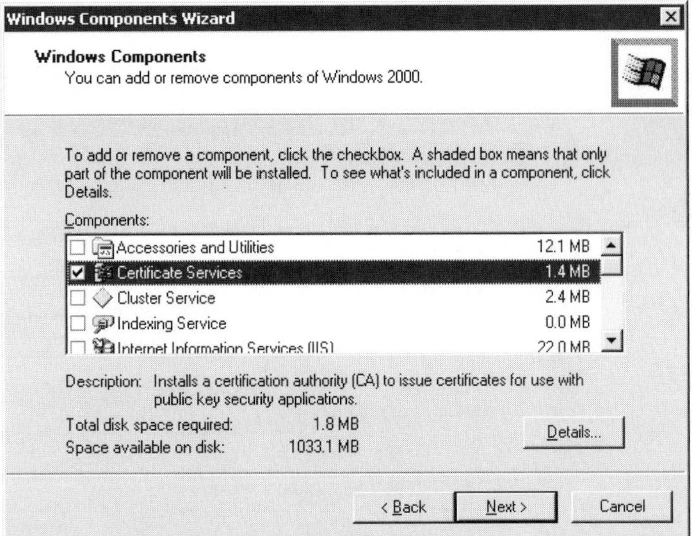

5. Select the type of server you wish to install, and click Next. For our purposes, a Stand-alone root CA will do, as shown in the following illustration.

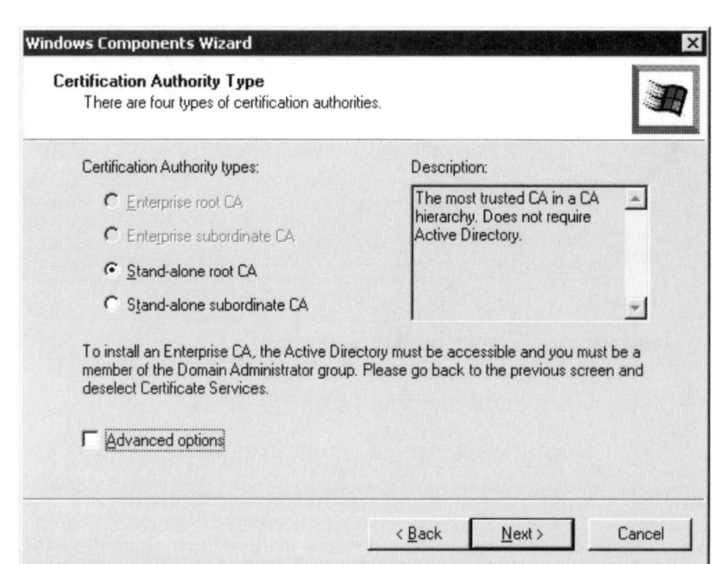

6. Enter your information in the next window, shown in the following illustration, and click Next.

Windows Components Wizard

CA Identifying Information

Enter information to identify this CA

CA name:

Organization:

Organizational unit:

City:

State or province: Country/region: US

E-mail:

CA description:

Valid for: 2 Years Expires: 6/1/2002 3:59 PM

< Back Next > Cancel

7. Click Next at the following screens to accept the defaults (see the following illustration). The Certificate Services is installed.

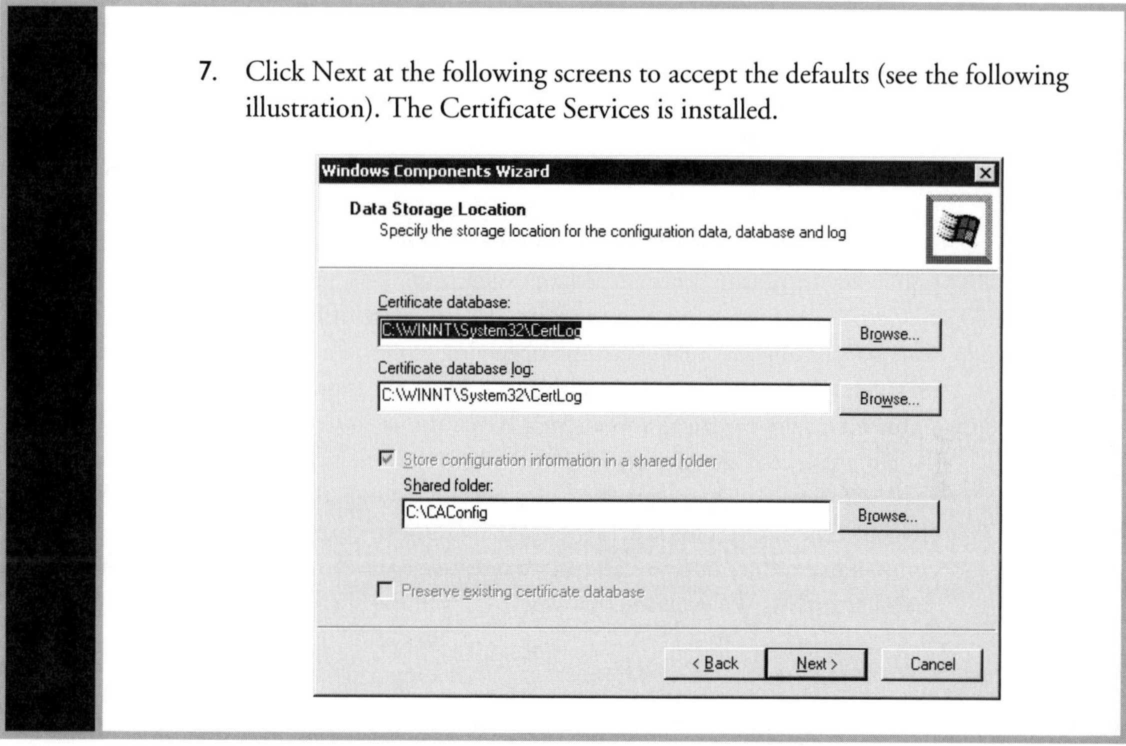

What Is a Public Key Certificate?

A Public Key Certificate is a security token that is passed between two computer systems that allows data exchanged between the two to be encrypted. A public encryption key included in the public key certificate is responsible for encoding the data. As mentioned before, only the corresponding private encryption key can decrypt the encrypted data exchanged between the client and the server. Certificates can be either single use (e.g., secure e-mail [Secure/Multipurpose Internet Mial Extensions (S/MIME)] only) or multiuse (e.g., secure e-mail [S/MIME], Encrypting File System, and client authentication). So, we can easily see that the certificates can be applied in various scenarios.

Uses of Certificates

A public key certificate exchanged between a client and a server identifies the server to the client as the correct entity with which to communicate. Public key certificates are popular on e-commerce Web sites or secure sites that offer file downloads. Users need to know that they can trust the site with which they exchange data. For example, as a result of the high security provided by certificates, it is common practice now for people to do their banking over the Internet—even in cases where the bank doesn't even have a physical premises. Users with accounts at the bank can trust that their financial transactions and data will remain secure even though they are accessing them over the public Internet, because the CA at the bank issued a public key certificate bearing the bank's identity.

Certificates are a good way to verify identity without having to do any time-consuming, manual checking, or having to create a user account for each user that contacts a site. Some popular e-mail applications like MS Outlook and Lotus Notes use certificates to encrypt e-mail, thus ensuring that only the intended recipient can read the message. Apart from Web security, using certificates is also an excellent way to authenticate users and protect data via the Encrypting File System (EFS) on the LAN. This is evident via the advent of corporate extranets, where companies conduct business and share sensitive data with each other and with their customers. We examine this aspect later in the chapter.

Information Contained in Certificates

Certificates usually contain the following information, as shown in Figure 31-3.

- The public or private encryption key value.
- The name and digital signature of the certificate bearer, which may be either a user or a service.
- The length of time the certificate is valid.
- The identity of the Certificate Authority.

The public and private encryption key values are used in the encryption/decryption process. The name and digital signature serve as proof of identity for the client. Certificates have life spans, after which they cannot be used to encrypt or decrypt data and need to be reissued. The receiving computer uses the length of time information to note how long it can use the certificate. The identity of the CA verifies that the issuing CA is valid and trusted.

FIGURE 31-3

Information contained in a certificate

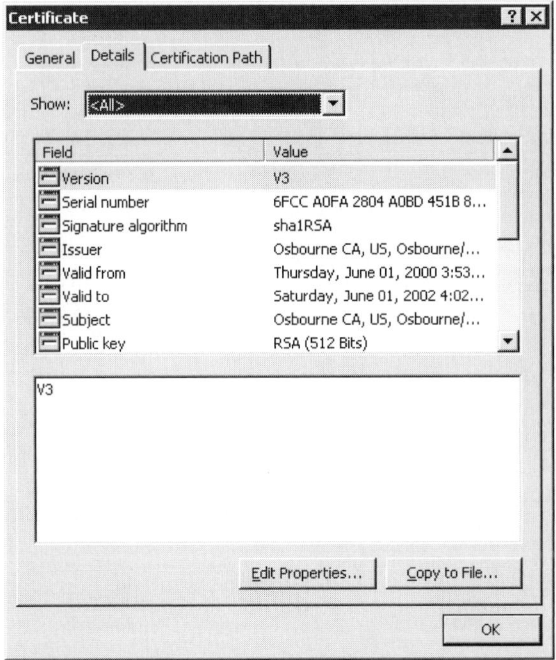

The Certification Hierarchy

Certificate hierarchies pretty much resemble Domain Name System (DNS) hierarchies in that they are structured in a top-down fashion (Figure 31-4). This hierarchical structure results in a flexible infrastructure that is scalable and easy to administer. The certification hierarchy is one of the characteristics of PKI that makes it such an effective security model. The certification path is also another feature of the hierarchy that makes management easier. A certificate's certification path is what is used to verify the authenticity and validity of a certificate. The path tracks the certifiers of a certificate back to the original root CA that issued the certificate in the first place. As mentioned previously, this is usually a well-known, respected CA company.

Certification Authorities

A Certification Authority (CA) is a trusted server responsible for generating, issuing, and signing certificates. The CA handles all certificate requests. There are two main types of Certification Authority in a certification hierarchy: the root CA and the subordinate CA, as shown in Figure 31-4.

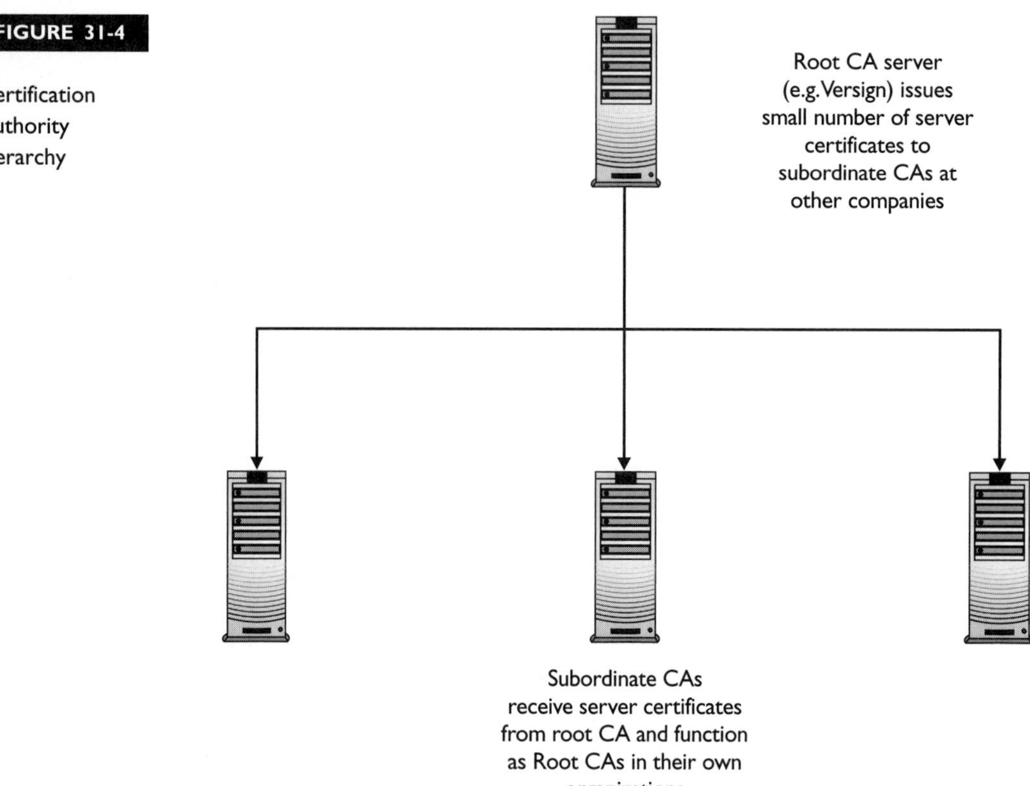
Root CA server
(e.g.Versign) issues
small number of server
certificates to
subordinate CAs at
other companies
Subordinate CAs
receive server certificates
from root CA and function
as Root CAs in their own
organizations

FIGURE 31-4 Certification Authority hierarchy

Root Authorities

A Root Authority is the supreme CA. Root CAs are responsible for issuing certificates to subordinate CAs. Much like root DNS Servers only know a small number of other DNS servers, root CAs only sign a small number of certificates. These certificates are issued to subordinate CAs, as shown in Figure 31-4.

Subordinate Certification Authorities

Subordinate Certification Authorities are servers that rely on the root CA. These subordinate certificate servers receive certificates from root CAs and, in turn, issue public key certificates to clients that request secure communications.

During installation of Certificate Services, the administrator can select the level of CA to create. Subordinate CAs receive signed server certificates from the root CA, which they use to service clients. In a Windows 2000 domain, CAs come in two flavors: Enterprise CAs and Stand-alone CAs. Enterprise CAs require and use the Active Directory. Stand-alone CAs do not require the Active Directory, but will use it if the CA is installed on a domain controller.

Certificate hierarchies should typically mimic the domain administration hierarchy. This guarantees their security and availability, and makes management simpler. A Subordinate CA can exist in the same Windows 2000 domain, as its root CA, in a child domain, or even in a domain in a separate Windows 2000 forest. Management of subordinate CAs can be delegated to the local administrators where the server resides.

Certificate management in the hierarchy is affected through group policies. The policies are basically a set of rules for issuing, verifying, and signing certificates. The policies differ depending on whether the CA enforcing the policy is an Enterprise root CA or a Stand-alone root CA. Enterprise CAs rely on Active Directory and the Windows 2000 security model to recognize and authenticate certificates, whereas Stand-alone CAs rely on direct administrator action to verify client requests.

Well-known, commercial CA organizations possess root CA servers that issue certificates to subordinate CAs in other companies (for a fee, of course!). These subordinate CAs function as root CAs in their own organization and issue certificates to clients requesting secure communication and authentication.

The Certificate Store

The Certificate Store is a database created during the installation of a CA. If Certificate Services is installed on an Enterprise root CA, the store resides in the Active Directory. If it is installed on a Stand-alone root CA, the store resides on the server itself. The certificate store is a repository for supporting or verifying certificates issued by that particular CA. A single certificate store can support up to 250,000 certificates.

Now that we've covered the basics of Certificate Services, here are some possible scenario questions and their answers.

SCENARIO & SOLUTION

You are installing a root Enterprise Certification Authority…	**Your domain should be running Active Directory.**
How do you know that your certificate is authentic?	The Digital Signature on the certificate proves the identity of the issuer.
Can you use Certificate Services to secure your mail?	Yes, certificates can be used to secure mail as well as data.
Can users on your Web site access your private encryption key?	No, private encryption keys are kept secret.

CERTIFICATION OBJECTIVE 31.02

Management and Administration of Certificates

As you no doubt already know, the Microsoft Management Console (MMC) is used to manage and administer many configurable services in Windows 2000. These services are accessed via snap-ins, modules that contain the objects that control settings for the services.

Using the Certificates MMC

Certificate management and administration is done via the Certificates or Certificate Authority Management MMC snap-in. Certification Authority management is done in the same snap-in, but administrator privilege is required.

EXERCISE 31-2

Using the MMC Certification/Certification Authority Snap-In

1. Start the Microsoft Management Console, by clicking Start | Run, and typing **mmc** in the Open: field.
2. In the MMC, click Console, and select Add/Remove Snap-in.
3. In the Add/Remove Snap-in window, click Add, as shown in the following illustration.

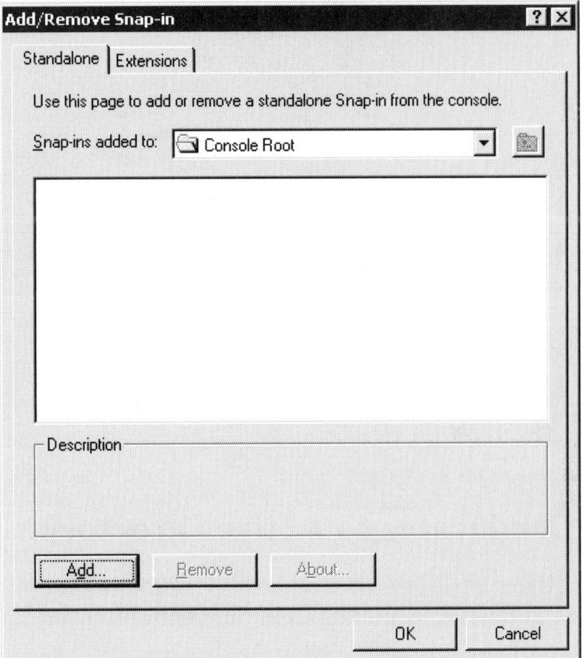

4. Select Certificates or Certification Authority from the Add Standalone Snap-in list, as shown in the following illustration.

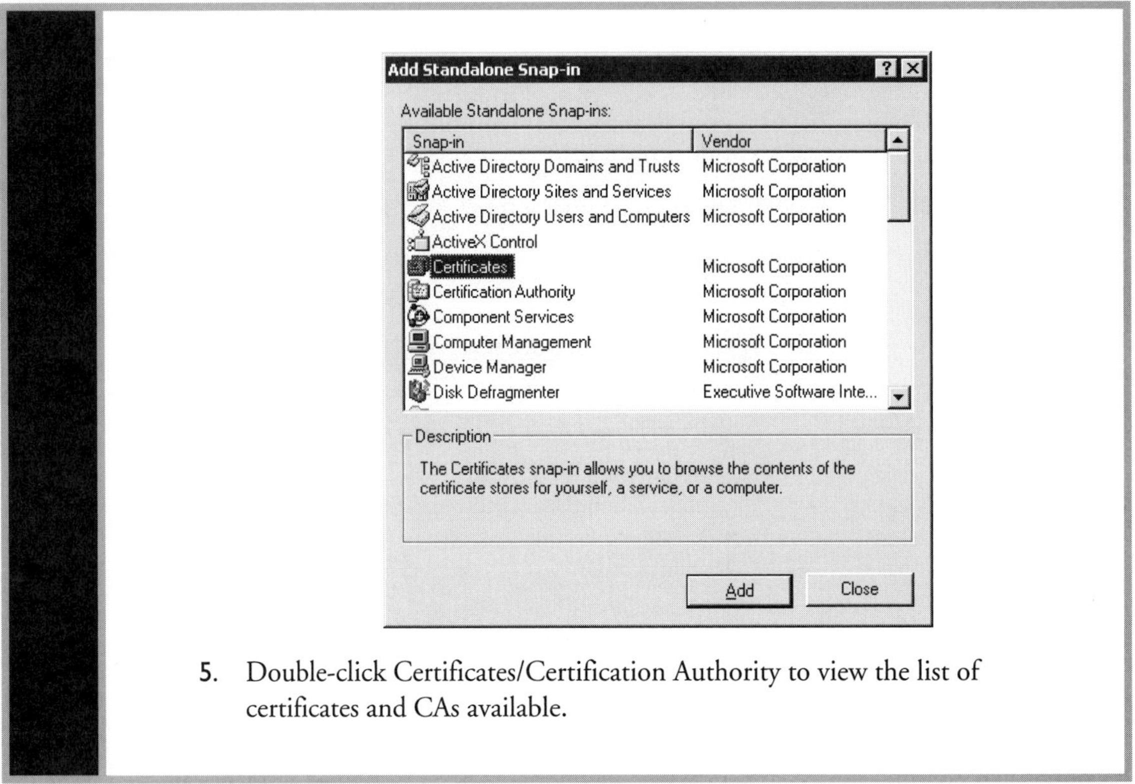

5. Double-click Certificates/Certification Authority to view the list of certificates and CAs available.

Publishing Certificates to Active Directory

When Certificate Services are installed on an Enterprise CA, certificate information is automatically published in different objects in Active Directory. The following information is published in Active Directory:

- **User Certificates** Used for data exchange applications; e.g., Encrypting File System.
- **CA Certificates** Used for building certification paths to trusted root CAs.
- **Certificate Revocation Lists** (CRL) Used to facilitate checking of certificate validity status.

Active Directory has three directories for specific types of data, only two of which are pertinent to this topic. The Domain Data directory contains all of the objects in the Active Directory for one particular domain. User certificates are published in the User object in the Domain Data directory. CA certificates are published on a "CertificationAuthority" object, and CRLs (Certificate Revocation Lists) are published in CRLDistrbutionPoint object in the Configuration Data directory.

Certificates from a Stand-alone CA can also be published in Active Directory, but this must be done by an administrator.

A common security practice at root CA sites is to take the server running Certificate Services off the network and physically store the server in a vault to prevent tampering.

Certificate Formats

Windows 2000 Certificate Services supports four standard certificate formats.

Personal Information Exchange

The Personal Information Exchange format, also known as the Public Key Cryptography Standards #12 (PKCS #12) format, is an industry standard format that facilitates backup and restoration of a certificate and its private key. This vendor-independent certificate format enables certificates and their corresponding private keys to be transferred from one computer to another, or from a computer to removable media. Personal Information Exchange format is the only format used by Windows 2000 when exporting certificates and private keys because it avoids exposing the keys to unintended parties. Certain conditions must exist for the format to be used:

- The Cryptographic Service Provider (CSP) must recognize the certificate and keys as exportable.
- The certificate is for EFS or EFS recovery.
- The certificate is requested via the Advanced Certificate Request certification authority Web page with the "Mark keys as exportable" check box checked.

Cryptographic Message Syntax Standard

Better known as PKCS #7, this format enables the transfer of a certificate and all other certificates in its certification path either from one computer to another, or from a computer to removable media. PKCS #7 files use the .p7b file extension.

DER Encoded Binary X.509

This is the format used for non-Windows 2000 certification authorities. Since the Internet is still dominated by non-Windows servers, it is supported for interoperability.

Base64 Encoded X.509

This format is also used by non-Windows certificate servers, and therefore supports interoperability. Base64 Encoded X.509 certificate files also use the .cer file extension.

Importing and Exporting Certificates

The usefulness of certificates is again seen in the ability to pass certificates between organizations. Certificates can be imported from other sources, be it a CA external to your organization or simply another computer. Certificates can also be exported from your organization to another, or simply to media as with a PKCS #12 certificate. The Certificates/Certification Authority MMC snap-in is used to import and export PKCS #12, PKCS #7, and DER encoded binary X.509 certificate files.

When a certificate is imported, it is copied from a certificate file that uses one of the standard certificate storage formats introduced earlier to a certificate store for a user or computer account. Certificates may be imported in order to:

- Install a certificate that was sent in a file by another user, computer, or CA.
- Restore a damaged or lost certificate that was previously backed up.
- Install a certificate and its associated private key from a computer that the certificate holder was previously using.

Certificates are exported by copying the certificate from its certificate store to a file that uses one of the standard certificate storage formats. Certificates may be exported in order to:

- Back up a certificate.
- Back up a certificate and its associated private key.
- Copy a certificate so it can be used on another computer.
- Remove a certificate and its private key from the current certificate holder for installation on another computer.

You will only be able to export to a Personal Information Exchange PKCS#12 file if you want to export the private key.

CERTIFICATION OBJECTIVE 31.03

Creating and Issuing Certificates in Windows 2000

Every client of a CA receives its own public key certificate. The next section discusses the process of creating and issuing these certificates to clients. This process is also referred to as X.509 certificate enrollment.

Generating Encryption Keys and Certificate Requests

PKI standards dictate the process for generating encryption keys and certificate requests. PKI allows the use of multiple methods of requesting and receiving certificates, some of which are Web-based enrollment, and policy-based auto-enrollment. Web-based enrollment is commonly seen when a user visits a site and requests a certificate, whereas policy-based auto-enrollment can be configured to occur when a user logs on to a Windows 2000 domain. In Windows 2000, this process is handled by Microsoft's X.509 certificate enrollment control.

The enrollment control either identifies or generates the user's key, builds the certificate request, and signs it. The certificate request is generated as a standard PKCS #10 certificate request and is submitted to the issuing certificate server. The PKCS #10 certificate request is comprised of:

- A version value
- The subject name and subject public key

- The signature algorithm and the digital signature of the requesting user
- Additional optional attributes

The Certificate Services server processes the requests and returns PKCS # 7 X.509 certificates to the client.

CryptoAPI

CryptoAPI is a software component that allows management of cryptographic functionality to be added to certificates. During certificate generation, CryptoAPI introduces cryptographic hardware or software modules called Cryptographic Service Providers (CSP) to the private key.

The CSP

A Cryptographic Service Provider, or CSP, is a hardware or software module used to perform a variety of cryptographic operations. CSPs are responsible for creating and destroying keys, as well as using the keys to perform a variety of cryptographic functions within the certificate.

Microsoft uses a base CSP that employs the RSA cryptographic algorithms; however, additional CSPs are available from third-party vendors like smart-card manufacturers. Traditionally, hardware-based CSPs are used because they offer better performance and significantly reduce the risk of tampering. Each CSP uses a different implementation of the CryptoAPI.

Processing Certificate Requests

Once a certificate request is submitted to the certificate server, the request is processed and a certificate is returned to the requesting client. Let's look at this as a step-by-step process, as shown in Figure 31-5.

Request Reception

A client sends a certificate request to the server via an intermediary application, sometimes known as an Entry Module. The application interprets the request, formats it into a PKCS #10 type request, and submits it to the Certificate Services engine.

The Certificate Services engine queues the request and passes it to the Policy Module, which queries the request properties to determine if the request is authorized. The module also adds any extra information asked for in the request to the certificate.

FIGURE 31-5 How certificate requests are processed

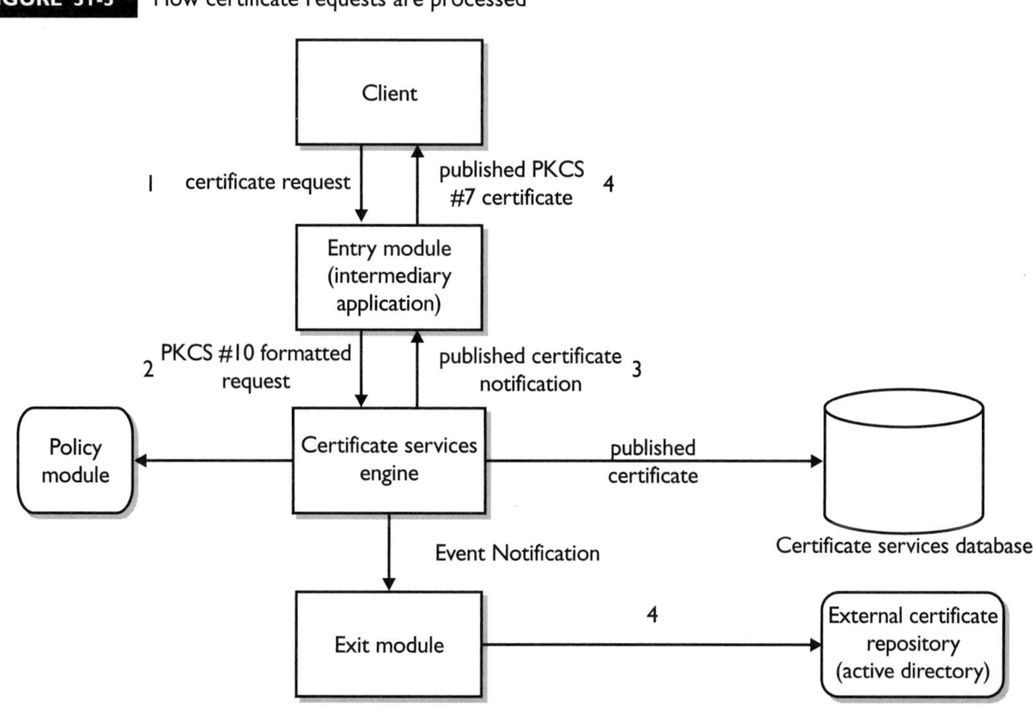

Request Approval

If the request is approved, the Certificate Services engine takes the request and builds a complete certificate. The engine also logs the certificate creation. If the request is denied, the log will also record the revoked request.

Certificate Formation

The Certificate Services engine stores completed certificates in the Certificate Services database and notifies the Entry Module of the status of the request. The Entry Module retrieves the certificate from the Server engine and passes it back to the requesting client.

Certificate Publication

The Services engine also notifies an Exit Module that publishes the certificate to an external repository such as the Active Directory.

EXERCISE 31-3

Requesting a Certificate via the Web-Based Request Form

Because we installed a Stand-alone root CA, we will have to request a certificate using the Web-based enrollment form.

1. Launch Internet Explorer.
2. Type in the URL for the Web-based certificate request form (http://servername/Certsrv).
3. Select "Request a certificate," as shown in the following illustration, and click Next.

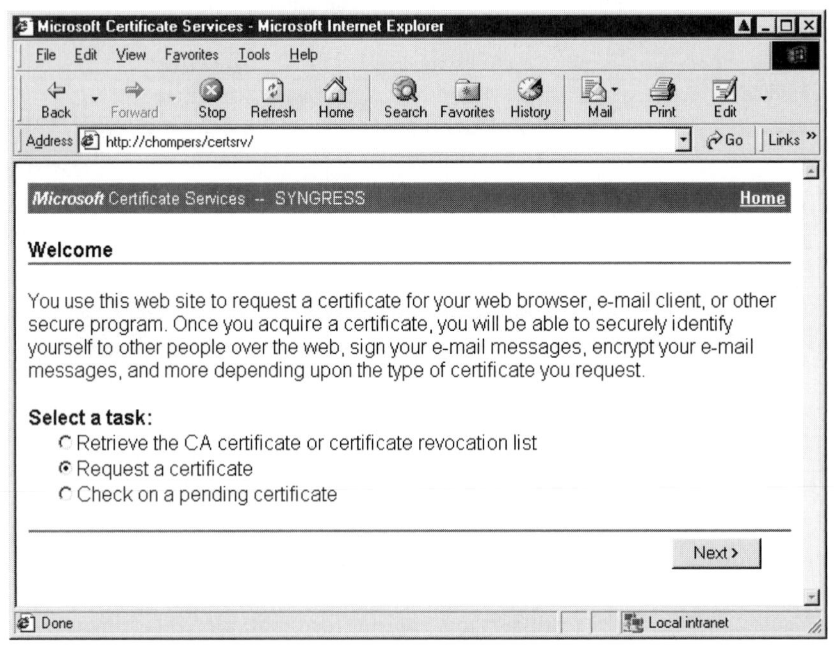

4. Select Web Browser Certificate type, as shown in the following illustration, and click Next.

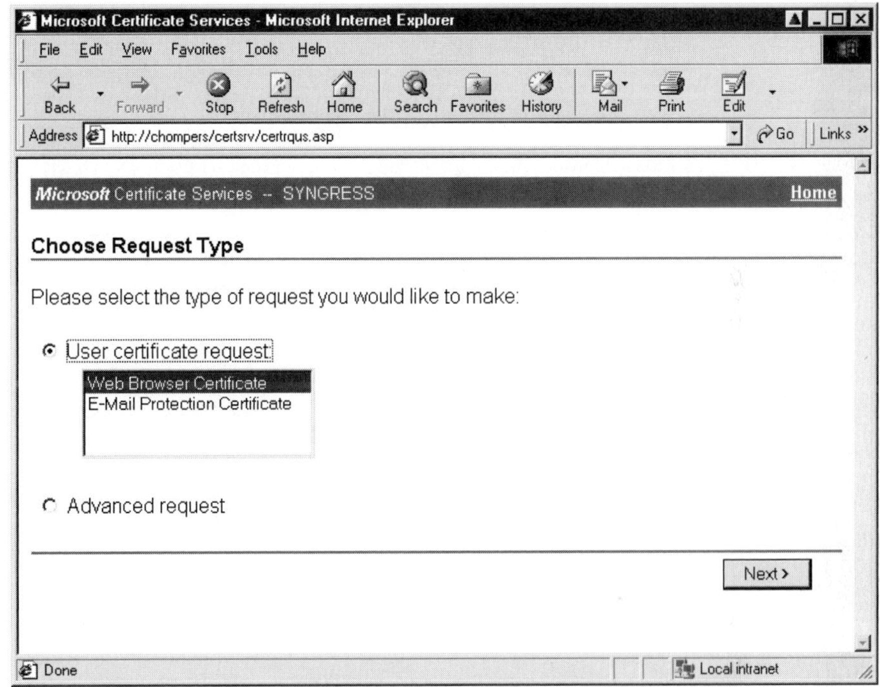

5. Enter your personal information in the fields shown in the following illustration, and click Submit. Clicking More Options allows you to pick from a list of Cryptographic Service Providers.

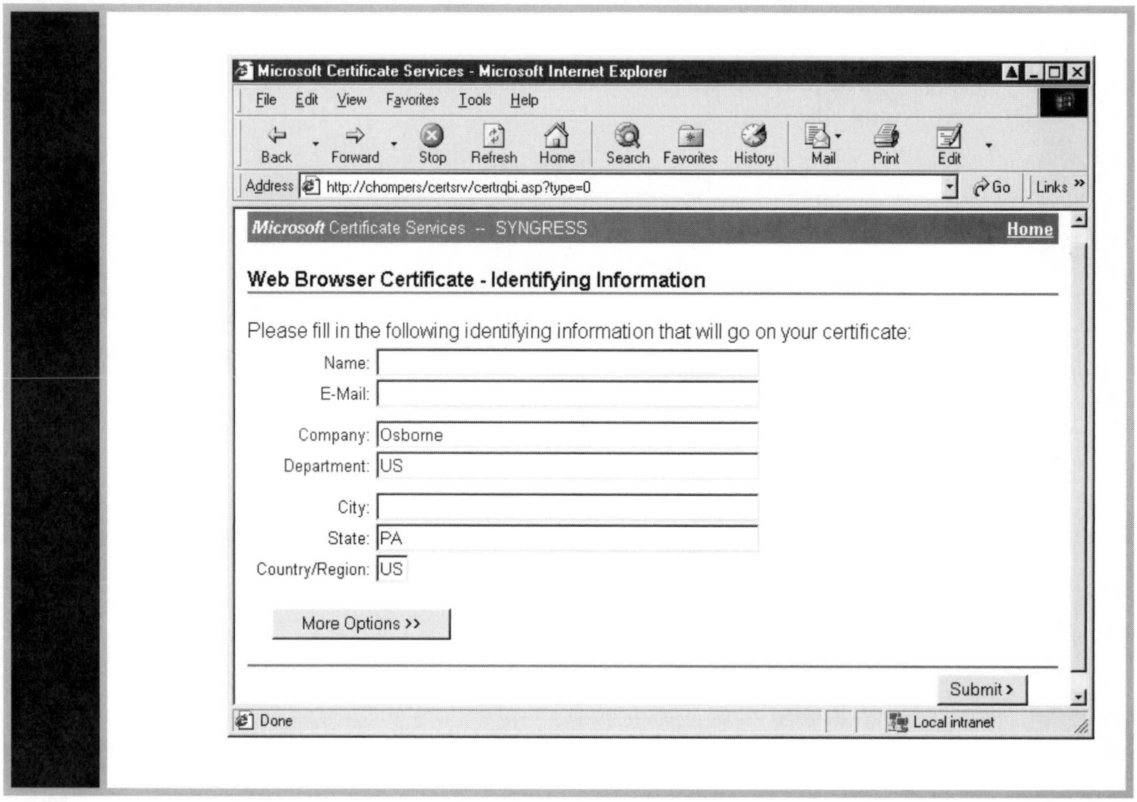

Revoking Certificates

Certificates or certificate requests can be revoked either automatically by using a Certificate Revocation List (CRL), or manually by an administrator.

Internet Information Services for Windows 2000 supports real-time Certificate Revocation List checking. A Certificate Revocation List is a list of certificates that are denied access to a Web server or Web site. CRLs are built using the Certificate Authority MMC snap-in. Real-time CRL checking allows the Web server to enforce access control on the fly. An administrator can also manually revoke certificates.

exam Watch

Revoked certificates can be re-signed and reissued by a Domain Administrator.

EXERCISE 31-4

Revoking a Certificate

1. Select the Issued Certificates folder in the Certification Authority snap-in.
2. Right-click the certificate to be revoked.
3. Click All Tasks.
4. Select Revoke Certificate.
5. Select the reason for revocation from the drop-down box (see the following illustration).

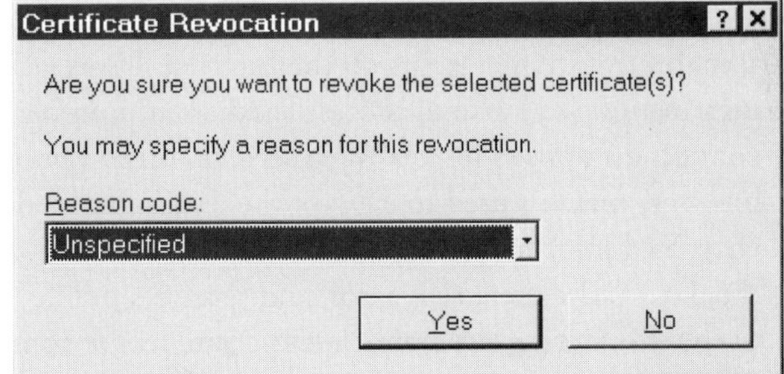

6. Click OK.

CERTIFICATION OBJECTIVE 31.04

Certificate-Based Authentication

Certificate-based authentication occurs in two ways:

- **User domain authentication** When a user in a Windows 2000 domain requests a certificate, Active Directory identifies the user to the CA, which in turn uses the user's security context to generate certificates with the correct user rights.

- **Computer auto-enrollment** Here, domain authentication is used to identify the computer account in the Windows 2000 domain. Group policies define the certificate the computer is eligible to receive. If the computer does not have a certificate corresponding to each of its eligible templates, the computer automatically enrolls with an Enterprise CA to receive the missing certificate.

External Users

Users who are not part of a Windows 2000 domain are handled differently. This scenario commonly occurs on the Internet. Users visit a Web site, supply personal information (e.g., name, address, credit card number), and request a secure connection to the site. The Web server returns a public key certificate to the client browser, which is used to encrypt the data submitted to the site by the browser. The encrypted information is passed to the server where the private key is used to decrypt the data. Once users visit a site, and receive a public key certificate, they can return to the site and use the certificate to create secure connections over and over again until the certificate expires.

Mapping a Certificate to a User Account

Mapping certificates to user accounts provides a way to seamlessly authenticate users and grant access to resources both on and off the Internet. Two types of certificate mapping are used, one-to-one mapping and many-to-many mapping. Let's look at these types of mapping more closely.

User Principal Name Mapping

This is a special kind of one-to-one mapping only available through the Active Directory. An Enterprise CA inserts an entry called a User Principal Name (UPN) into each of its certificates. UPNs are unique to each user's account within a Windows 2000 domain, and they are of the format *user@domain.* The UPN is used to locate the user account in Active Directory, and that account is logged on. This only occurs if the following conditions are met:

- The mapped certificate contains a UPN.
- The Windows 2000 domain is in the hierarchy of the Active Directory.
- The CA that issued the certificate is trusted to insert UPNs into the certificate.

If all of these conditions are not met, the user account can't be retrieved, and the Active Directory is searched for a mapping set by an administrator.

One-to-One Certificate Mapping

This type of mapping simply involves mapping a single user certificate to a single Windows 2000 user account. Certificates may be issued from your own Enterprise CA or from a trusted CA. These certificates are then manually mapped to their respective user accounts.

Many-to-One Certificate Mapping

This involves mapping many certificates to a single user account. This is particularly convenient when organizations need to share specific information with each other. An administrator must install the root CA certificates of all the desired CAs as trusted root CAs in his or her enterprise. The administrator can then set a rule that maps all certificates installed by the trusted CAs to a single Windows 2000 account. Users using these mapped certificates possess access rights defined by the rights set on the mapped account.

EXERCISE 31-5

Mapping a Certificate to a User Account

Certificate mapping is done via the Internet Services Manager on an IIS server. We will now attempt to map a certificate to a user account.

1. Click Start | Programs | Administrative Tools | Internet Services Manager, as shown in the following illustration.

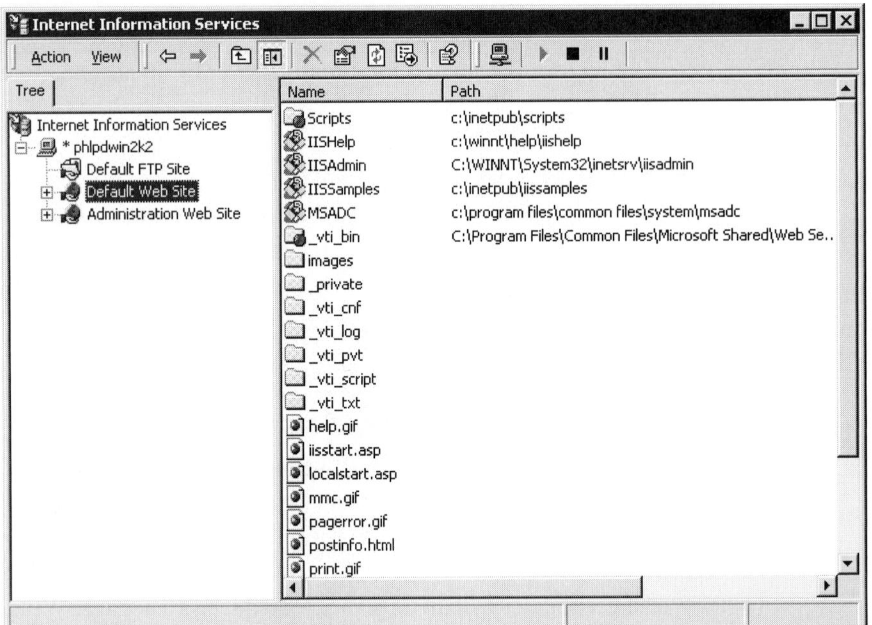

2. Expand the computer name folder. Right-click the Default Web Site folder, and click Properties on the submenu.

3. Click the Directory Security tab on the Default Web Site Properties dialog box, as shown in the following illustration.

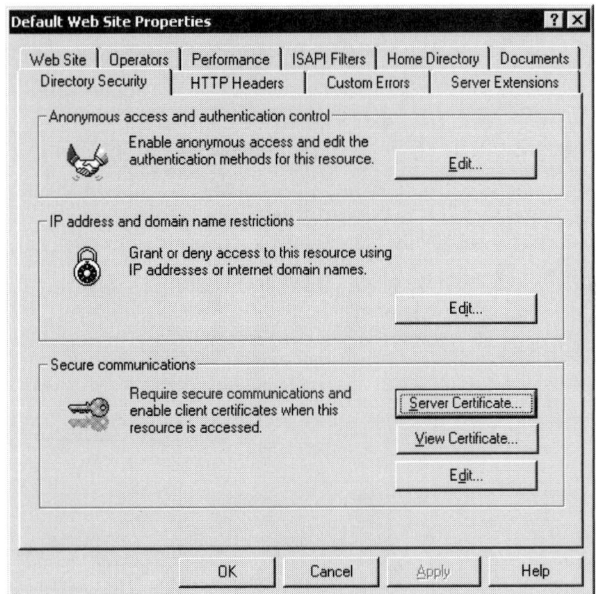

4. Click Edit in the "Secure communications" section. A Server Certificate must be installed in order for the Edit button not to be ghosted.

5. In the Secure Communications dialog box, verify that the "Enable client certificate mapping" option is selected, and click Edit, as shown in the following illustration.

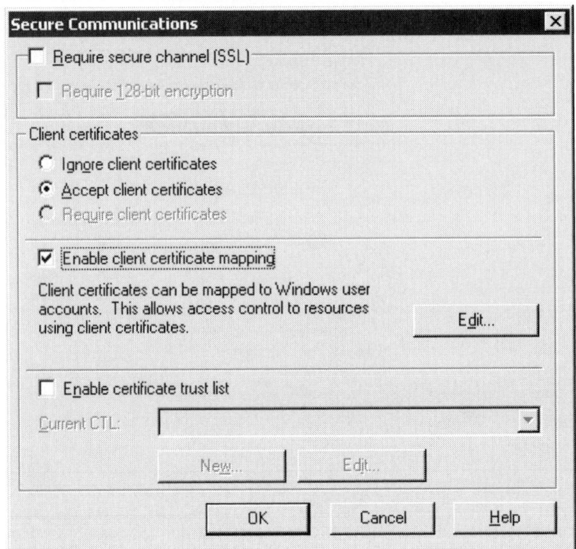

6. On the Account Mappings page, click the 1-to-1 tab, and click Add, as shown in the following illustration.

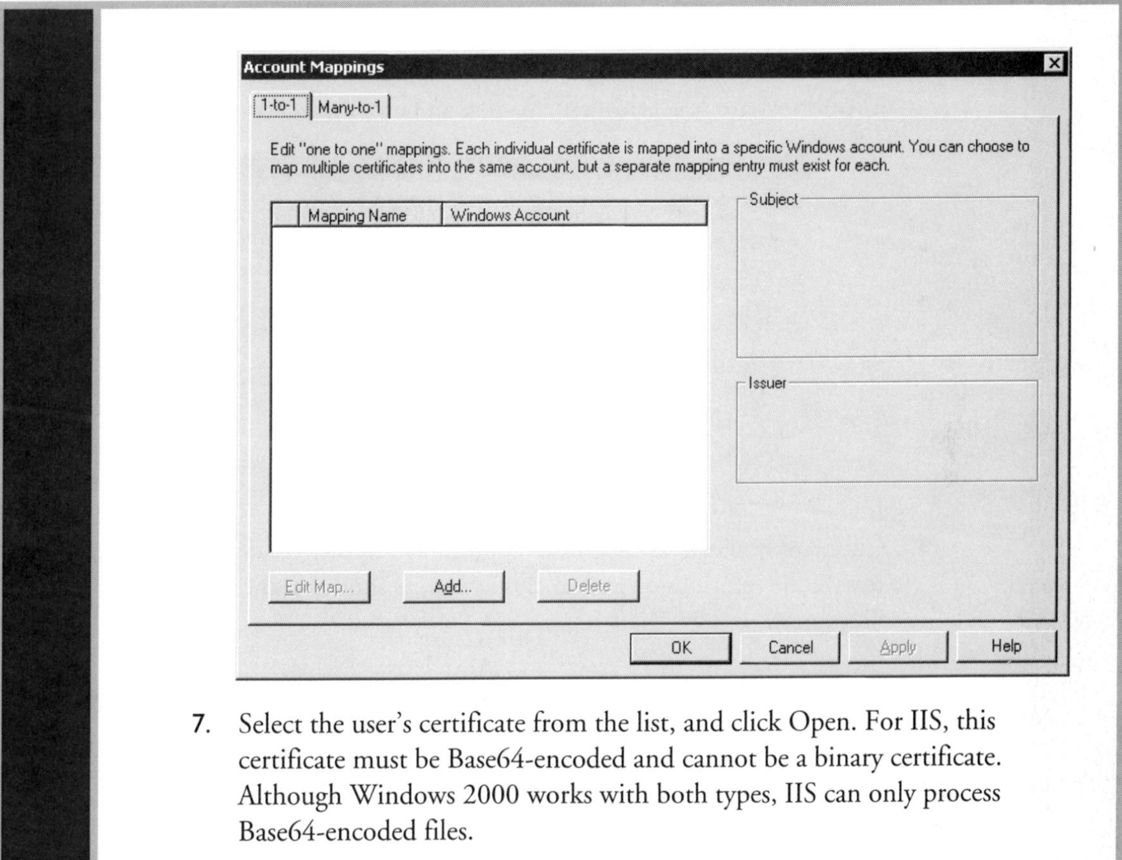

7. Select the user's certificate from the list, and click Open. For IIS, this certificate must be Base64-encoded and cannot be a binary certificate. Although Windows 2000 works with both types, IIS can only process Base64-encoded files.

8. The Map to Account dialog opens, as shown in the following illustration. Click Browse to select the desired account. Enter the password, and click OK.

Map to Account
Enable this mapping
Account mapping
When this certificate is presented by a web client and authenticated, the user can automatically be logged in as a specific Windows user.
Map Name: My Mapping
Account: EXE\EXEsuser
Browse...
Password: *********
OK
Cancel
Help

9. Click Apply and/or click OK, as appropriate, in the remaining dialog boxes to save the information and to close them, as shown in the following illustration.

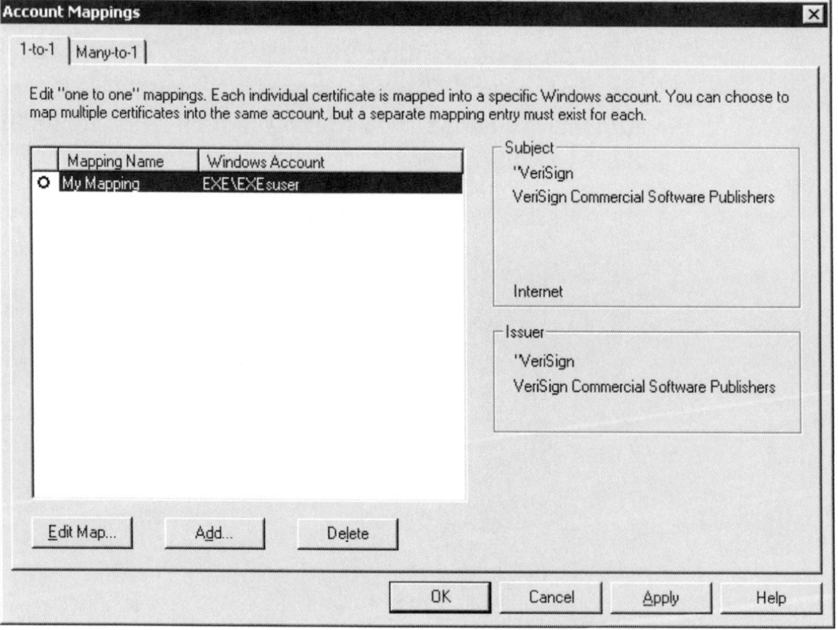

SCENARIO & SOLUTION	
You want to give each user his or her own certificate…	Use one-to-one mapping.
You are using Active Directory…	Use UPN mapping.

CERTIFICATION OBJECTIVE 31.05

Encrypting File System (EFS) Recovery Keys

Encrypting File System (EFS) uses PKI-based security to encrypt and decrypt data on a computer. Combining the data in them with their public encryption key value contained in their public key certificate encrypts files. Only the private encryption key of the user who encrypted it can decrypt the data. This way, no one can access this data except the user who encrypted it and the Recovery Agent. The Recovery Agent is the Domain Administrator by default.

When the "Encrypt contents" check box is selected in a file's properties, Windows 2000 creates a private encryption key for the file that it uses to encode the data contained within the file. A public encryption key is then created to protect the private encryption key. This is commonly referred to as *lock-box security.* A further step is taken to create a spare private encryption key that is capable of decrypting the data, and map that key to a trusted account (e.g., the Domain Administrator). This is the EFS recovery key. All the EFS recovery keys in a domain are mapped to the Domain Administrator account.

exam watch

Administrators can designate backup EFS Recovery Agents to decrypt data if the default agents have been removed.

EXERCISE 31-6

Removing the EFS Recovery Key

Removing the EFS recovery key allows an administrator to have even more control over the access of sensitive data. Removing the key prevents anyone, even someone with the administrator password, from accessing the data unless he or she has the recovery key. This exercise walks you through removing and securing the recovery key. You must be logged on with the local Administrator account to perform this exercise.

1. Click Start | Settings | Control Panel, and double-click Administrative Tools.
2. Double-click Local Security Policy. The Security Policy console appears, as shown in the following illustration.

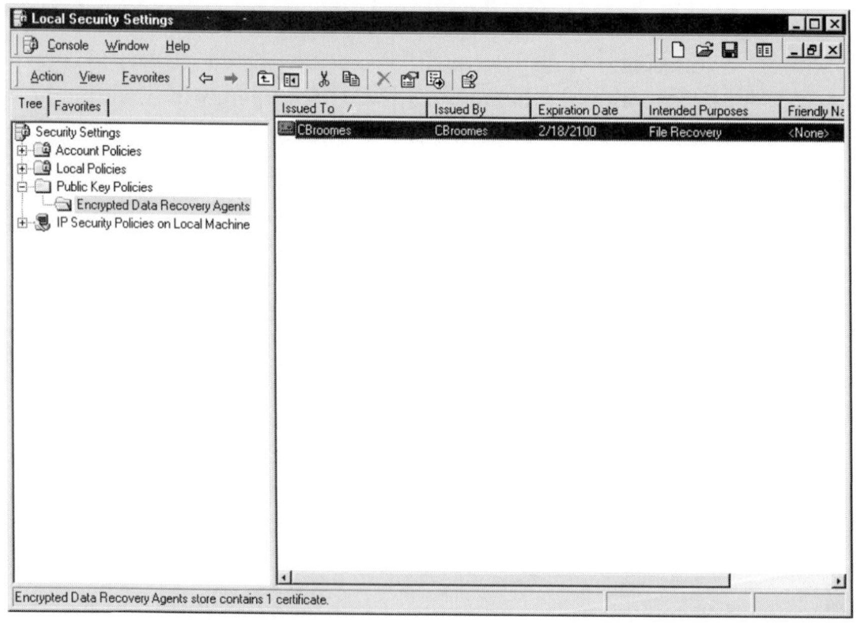

3. Click the Public Key Policies folder and then the Encrypted Data Recovery Agents folder to display all the recovery keys (see the previous illustration).
4. Right-click each Agent, select All Tasks, and then select Export. The Certificate Export Wizard launches. Follow the instructions for exporting certificates to floppy. After you have exported all the recovery keys, move on to Step 5.
5. Right-click the file recovery agent and select Delete to remove the recovery keys (see the following illustration).

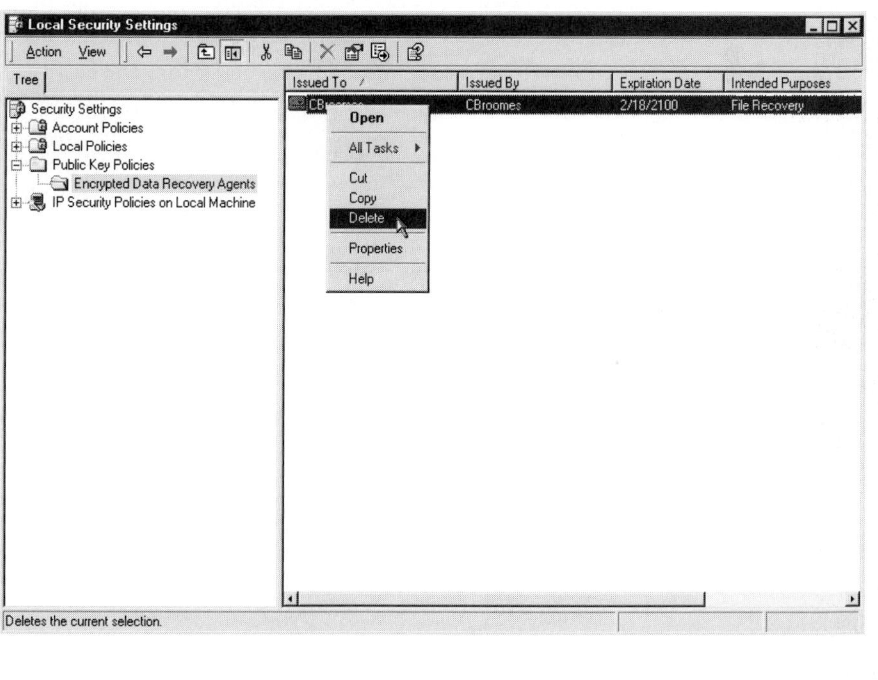

CERTIFICATION OBJECTIVE 31.06

Troubleshooting Certificates

Nonfunctional certificates may come about as a result of a number of factors. Troubleshooting and resolving problems with certificates requires understanding how certificates are requested, created, and issued, as well as familiarity with the contents of certificates. Some common sources of problems with certificates include:

- **Data corruption** This usually manifests itself as an invalid password or account error message. Troubleshooting this entails checking the password on the referenced account, and ensuring that the certificate content is properly formatted.
- **Invalid request format** The certificate request may have been incorrectly processed as a result of an invalid request format. This may have resulted in an inappropriate certificate being created and issued to a client. This may be resolved by checking the purpose of the certificate in the certificate properties and recreating the certificate request with the correct format.
- **Incorrect certificate mapping** In this case, the certificate is mapped to the wrong user or computer account. This is resolved by revoking the original certificate from the incorrect account, importing it, and mapping it to the correct account.

Apart from the scenarios just mentioned, regular performance monitoring on your certificate servers is essential to ensure their proper function.

EXERCISE 31-7

Troubleshooting a Certificate

The following exercise involves using what we just learned about troubleshooting certificates to solve a problem with a certificate.

You set up a secure intranet site for Human Resources so that the staff can access employee information via a Web browser. You sent an e-mail to the HR staff instructing them to request a certificate for access to this site via a certificate request Web page. One of the staff members calls and says that he gets a "page not available" error message when he tries to access the site. You and other employees in HR can access the site. You suspect that it is a problem with his certificate. Now let's troubleshoot it.

1. Click Start | Run, and type **mmc**.
2. Load the Certificates console, and then go to the Personal folder.
3. Select the Certificates folder to view the problem certificate. Look at the Intended Purpose field to see what the certificate is used for. In this case, the Intended purpose is Secure Email (see the following illustration), not Web browser as it should be.

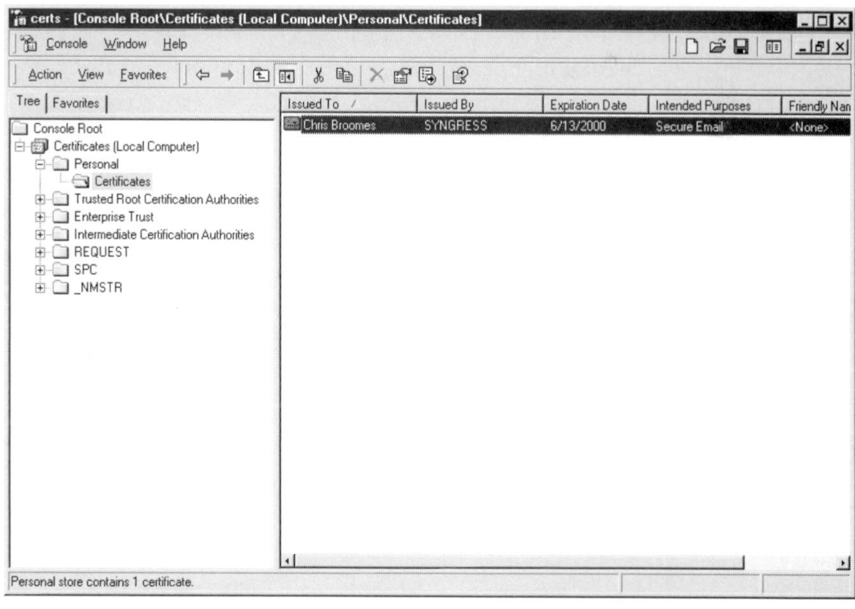

CERTIFICATION SUMMARY

In this chapter, we discussed Windows 2000 Certificate Services. We talked about Public Key Infrastructure and outlined how it works. We learned how to install and configure a root Certification Authority server and how to manage certificates. We looked at the elements that make up a certificate, and we saw how a certificate is created. We've talked about the hierarchical structure of Certification Authorities (CA), and about distributing certificates between enterprises.

Some of the applications of certificates and Certificate Services were covered, as well as some possible problems that may occur, and how to troubleshoot and resolve them.

✓ TWO-MINUTE DRILL

Introduction

- ❑ Certificate Services is built on Public Key Infrastructure standards.
- ❑ Certificate Services uses standard X.509 certificates.

Overview of Certificate Services

- ❑ Certification Authorities exist in a hierarchical structure.
- ❑ Public Key Certificates may be single or multiuse certificates.
- ❑ A single Certificate Store can support up to 250,000 certificates.

Management and Administration of Certificates

- ❑ Certificate Management is performed in the Certificates/Certification Authority MMC snap-in.
- ❑ If the CA is a domain controller, its certificates are published in Active Directory.
- ❑ Windows 2000 supports four standard certificate formats.

Creating and Issuing Certificates in Windows 2000

- ❑ Windows 2000 Certificate Services generate PKCS #10 certificate requests.
- ❑ Cryptographic Service Providers are hardware or software devices used to perform encryption tasks on certificates.
- ❑ Certificates can be manually revoked or revoked via a Certificate Revocation List.

Certificate-Based Authentication

- ❑ There are two main types of certificate-based authentication: one-to-one mapping and many-to-one mapping.
- ❑ A User Principal Name (UPN) is a user identifier used by Active Directory to locate a user account.

Encrypting File System (EFS) Recovery Keys

- ❑ Encrypting File System creates a private encryption key to encode data.
- ❑ The default Recovery Agent used to recover encrypted files is the Domain Administrator account.

Troubleshooting Certificates

- ❑ Common certificate problems involve data corruption, incorrect mapping, or server performance issues.

MCSE

MICROSOFT CERTIFIED SYSTEMS ENGINEER

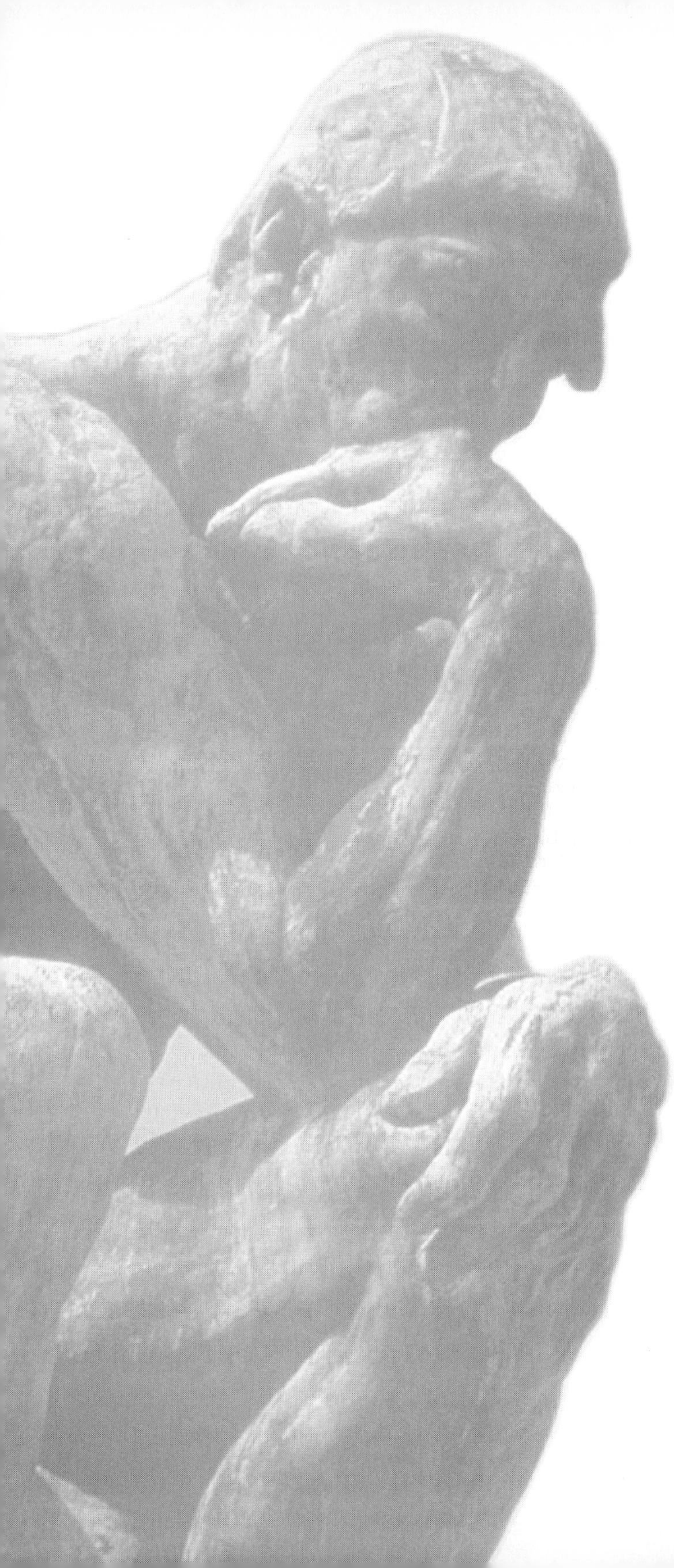

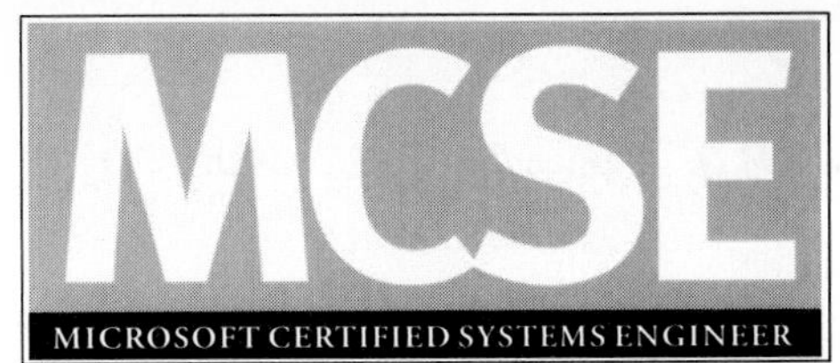

A

About the CD

This CD-ROM contains the CertTrainer software. CertTrainer comes complete with ExamSim, Skill Assessment tests, CertCam movie clips, the e-book (electronic version of the book), Lab Questions & Answers, and Self Test Questions. CertTrainer is easy to install on any Windows 98/NT/2000 computer and must be installed to access these features. You may, however, browse the e-book directly from the CD without installation.

Installing CertTrainer

If your computer CD-ROM drive is configured to autorun, the CD-ROM will automatically start up upon inserting the disk. From the opening screen you may either browse the e-book or install CertTrainer by pressing the *Install Now* button. This will begin the installation process and create a program group named "CertTrainer." To run CertTrainer use START | PROGRAMS | CERTTRAINER.

System Requirements

CertTrainer requires Windows 98 or higher and Internet Explorer 5.0 or above and 600 MB of hard disk space for full installation.

CertTrainer

CertTrainer provides a complete review of each exam objective, organized by chapter. You should read each objective summary and make certain that you understand it before proceeding to the SkillAssessor. If you still need more practice on the concepts of any objective, use the "In Depth" button to link to the corresponding section from the Study Guide or use the CertCam button to view a short .AVI clip illustrating various exercises from within the chapter.

Once you have completed the review(s) and feel comfortable with the material, launch the SkillAssessor quiz to test your grasp of each objective. Once you complete the quiz, you will be presented with your score for that chapter.

ExamSim

As its name implies, ExamSim provides you with a simulation of the actual exam. The number of questions, the type of questions, and the time allowed are intended to be an accurate representation of the exam environment. You will see the following illustration when you are ready to begin ExamSim:

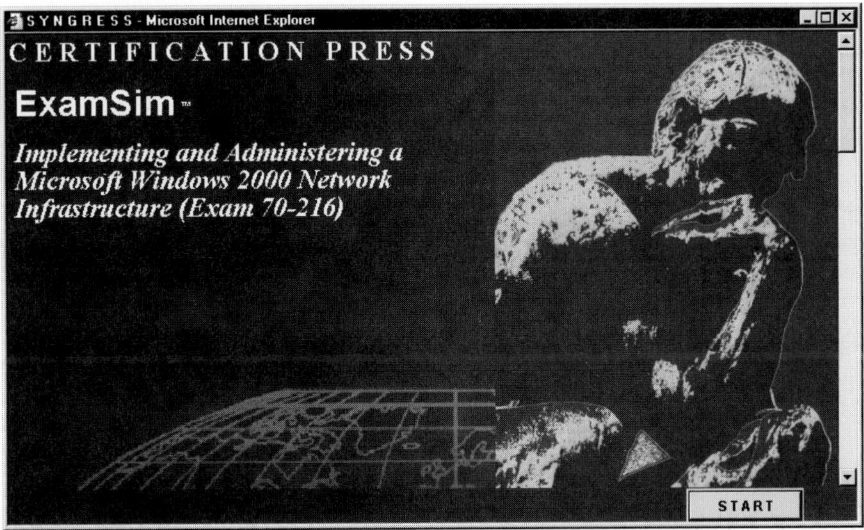

When you launch ExamSim, a digital clock display will appear in the upper left-hand corner of your screen. The clock will continue to count down to zero unless you choose to end the exam before the time expires.

There are three types of questions on the exam:

- **Multiple Choice** These questions have a single correct answer that you indicate by selecting the appropriate check box.
- **Multiple-Multiple Choice** These questions require more than one correct answer. Indicate each correct answer by selecting the appropriate check boxes.
- Simulations These questions simulate actual Windows 2000 menus and dialog boxes. After reading the question, you are required to select the appropriate settings to most accurately meet the objectives for that question.

Saving Scores as Cookies

Your ExamSim score is stored as a browser cookie. If you've configured your browser to accept cookies, your score will be stored in a file named *History*. If your browser is not configured to accept cookies, you cannot permanently save your scores. If you delete this History cookie, the scores will be deleted permanently.

E-Book

The entire contents of the Study Guide are provided in HTML form, as shown in the following illustration. Although the files are optimized for Internet Explorer, they can also be viewed with other browsers including Netscape.

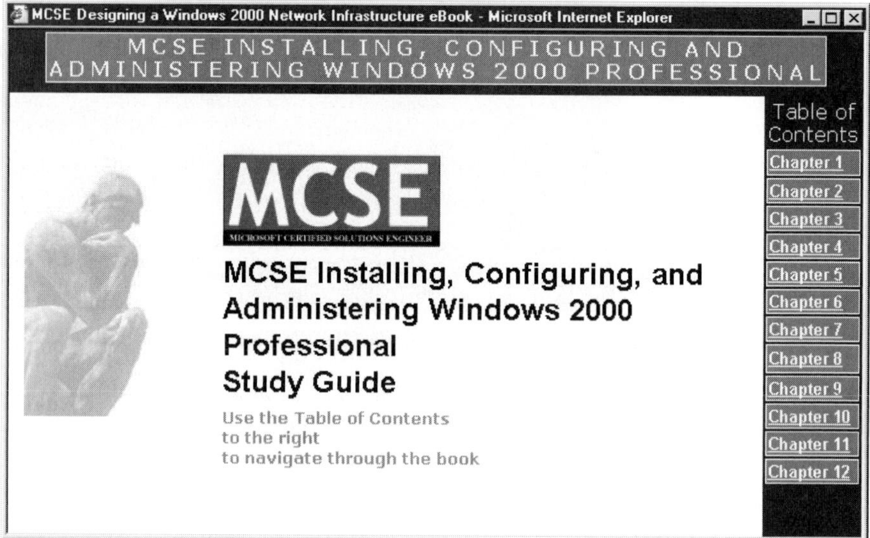

CertCam

CertCam .AVI clips provide detailed examples of key certification objectives. These clips walk you step-by-step through various system configurations and are narrated by Thomas Shinder, M.D., MCSE, MCT. You can access the clips directly from the CertCam table of contents (shown in the following illustration) or through the CertTrainer objectives.

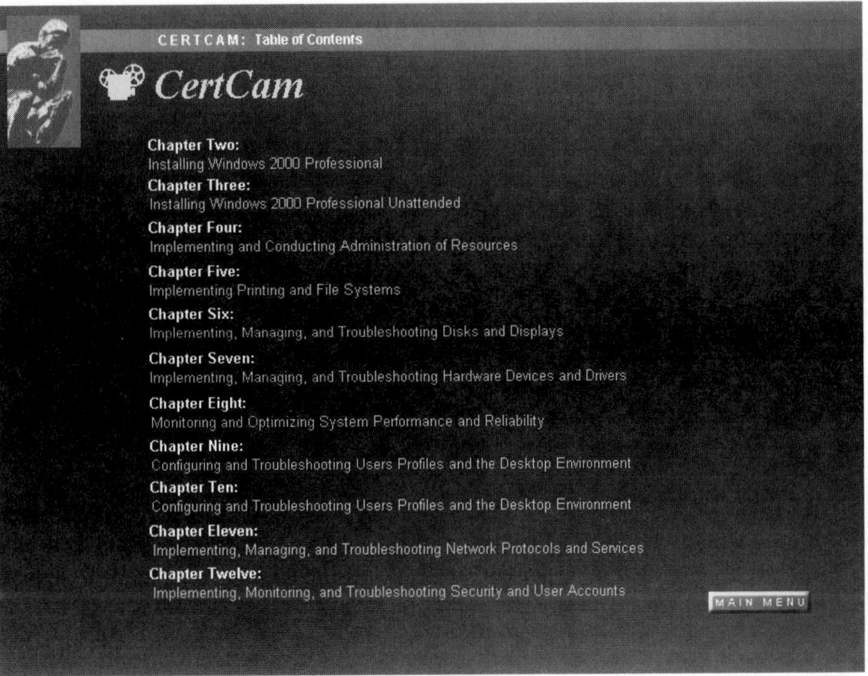

The CertCam .AVI clips are recorded and produced using TechSmith's Camtasia Producer. Since .AVI clips can be very large, ExamSim uses TechSmith's special AVI Codec to compress the clips. The file named **tsccvid.dll** is copied to your Windows\ System folder when you install CertTrainer. If the .AVI clip runs with audio but no video, you may need to re-install the file from the CD-ROM. Browse to the "bin" folder, and run TSCC.EXE.

Lab Questions & Answers

The Lab Questions & Answers offer a unique and challenging question format that requires the reader to understand multiple chapter concepts to answer correctly. These questions are more complex and more comprehensive than the other questions, as they test your ability to take all the knowledge you have gained from reading the chapter and apply it to complicated, real-world situations. These questions are aimed to be more difficult than what you will find on the exam. If you can answer these questions, you have proven that you know the subject!

Self Test

The Self Test offers questions similar to those found on the certification exams in printable HTML format. The answers to these questions, as well as explanations of the answers, can be found reviewed from the CD or printed.

Help

A help file is provided through a help button on the main CertTrainer screen in the lower right hand corner.

Upgrading

A button is provided on the main ExamSim screen for upgrades. This button will take you to www.syngress.com where you can download any available upgrades.

INDEX

A

B

D

E

F

G

H

I

J

K

L

M

N

O

P

R

S

T

U

X

Z

LICENSE AGREEMENT

THIS PRODUCT (THE "PRODUCT") CONTAINS PROPRIETARY SOFTWARE, DATA AND INFORMATION (INCLUDING DOCUMENTATION) OWNED BY THE McGRAW-HILL COMPANIES, INC. ("McGRAW-HILL") AND ITS LICENSORS. YOUR RIGHT TO USE THE PRODUCT IS GOVERNED BY THE TERMS AND CONDITIONS OF THIS AGREEMENT.

LICENSE: Throughout this License Agreement, "you" shall mean either the individual or the entity whose agent opens this package. You are granted a non-exclusive and non-transferable license to use the Product subject to the following terms:

(i) If you have licensed a single user version of the Product, the Product may only be used on a single computer (i.e., a single CPU). If you licensed and paid the fee applicable to a local area network or wide area network version of the Product, you are subject to the terms of the following subparagraph (ii).

(ii) If you have licensed a local area network version, you may use the Product on unlimited workstations located in one single building selected by you that is served by such local area network. If you have licensed a wide area network version, you may use the Product on unlimited workstations located in multiple buildings on the same site selected by you that is served by such wide area network; provided, however, that any building will not be considered located in the same site if it is more than five (5) miles away from any building included in such site. In addition, you may only use a local area or wide area network version of the Product on one single server. If you wish to use the Product on more than one server, you must obtain written authorization from McGraw-Hill and pay additional fees.

(iii) You may make one copy of the Product for back-up purposes only and you must maintain an accurate record as to the location of the back-up at all times.

COPYRIGHT; RESTRICTIONS ON USE AND TRANSFER: All rights (including copyright) in and to the Product are owned by McGraw-Hill and its licensors. You are the owner of the enclosed disc on which the Product is recorded. You may not use, copy, decompile, disassemble, reverse engineer, modify, reproduce, create derivative works, transmit, distribute, sublicense, store in a database or retrieval system of any kind, rent or transfer the Product, or any portion thereof, in any form or by any means (including electronically or otherwise) except as expressly provided for in this License Agreement. You must reproduce the copyright notices, trademark notices, legends and logos of McGraw-Hill and its licensors that appear on the Product on the back-up copy of the Product which you are permitted to make hereunder. All rights in the Product not expressly granted herein are reserved by McGraw-Hill and its licensors.

TERM: This License Agreement is effective until terminated. It will terminate if you fail to comply with any term or condition of this License Agreement. Upon termination, you are obligated to return to McGraw-Hill the Product together with all copies thereof and to purge all copies of the Product included in any and all servers and computer facilities.

DISCLAIMER OF WARRANTY: THE PRODUCT AND THE BACK-UP COPY OF THE PRODUCT ARE LICENSED "AS IS." McGRAW-HILL, ITS LICENSORS AND THE AUTHORS MAKE NO WARRANTIES, EXPRESS OR IMPLIED, AS TO RESULTS TO BE OBTAINED BY ANY PERSON OR ENTITY FROM USE OF THE PRODUCT AND/OR ANY INFORMATION OR DATA INCLUDED THEREIN. McGRAW-HILL, ITS LICENSORS, AND THE AUTHORS MAKE NO GUARANTEE THAT YOU WILL PASS ANY CERTIFICATION EXAM BY USING THIS PRODUCT. McGRAW-HILL, ITS LICENSORS AND THE AUTHORS MAKE NO EXPRESS OR IMPLIED WARRANTIES OF MERCHANTABILITY OR FITNESS FOR A PARTICULAR PURPOSE OR USE WITH RESPECT TO THE PRODUCT. NEITHER McGRAW-HILL, ANY OF ITS LICENSORS, NOR THE AUTHORS WARRANT THAT THE FUNCTIONS CONTAINED IN THE PRODUCT WILL MEET YOUR REQUIREMENTS OR THAT THE OPERATION OF THE PRODUCT WILL BE UNINTERRUPTED OR ERROR FREE. YOU ASSUME THE ENTIRE RISK WITH RESPECT TO THE QUALITY AND PERFORMANCE OF THE PRODUCT.

LIMITED WARRANTY FOR DISC: To the original licensee only, McGraw-Hill warrants that the enclosed disc on which the Product is recorded is free from defects in materials and workmanship under normal use and service for a period of ninety (90) days from the date of purchase. In the event of a defect in the disc covered by the foregoing warranty, McGraw-Hill will replace the disc.

LIMITATION OF LIABILITY: NEITHER McGRAW-HILL, ITS LICENSORS NOR THE AUTHORS SHALL BE LIABLE FOR ANY INDIRECT, SPECIAL OR CONSEQUENTIAL DAMAGES, SUCH AS BUT NOT LIMITED TO, LOSS OF ANTICIPATED PROFITS OR BENEFITS, RESULTING FROM THE USE OR INABILITY TO USE THE PRODUCT EVEN IF ANY OF THEM HAS BEEN ADVISED OF THE POSSIBILITY OF SUCH DAMAGES. THIS LIMITATION OF LIABILITY SHALL APPLY TO ANY CLAIM OR CAUSE WHATSOEVER WHETHER SUCH CLAIM OR CAUSE ARISES IN CONTRACT, TORT, OR OTHERWISE. Some states do not allow the exclusion or limitation of indirect, special or consequential damages, so the above limitation may not apply to you.

U.S. GOVERNMENT RESTRICTED RIGHTS: Any software included in the Product is provided with restricted rights subject to subparagraphs (c), (1) and (2) of the Commercial Computer Software-Restricted Rights clause at 48 C.F.R. 52.227-19. The terms of this Agreement applicable to the use of the data in the Product are those under which the data are generally made available to the general public by McGraw-Hill. Except as provided herein, no reproduction, use, or disclosure rights are granted with respect to the data included in the Product and no right to modify or create derivative works from any such data is hereby granted.

GENERAL: This License Agreement constitutes the entire agreement between the parties relating to the Product. The terms of any Purchase Order shall have no effect on the terms of this License Agreement. Failure of McGraw-Hill to insist at any time on strict compliance with this License Agreement shall not constitute a waiver of any rights under this License Agreement. This License Agreement shall be construed and governed in accordance with the laws of the State of New York. If any provision of this License Agreement is held to be contrary to law, that provision will be enforced to the maximum extent permissible and the remaining provisions will remain in full force and effect.